BERNARD SHAW

MICHAEL HOLROYD

PIMLICO

Published by Pimlico 2011

2 4 6 8 10 9 7 5 3 1

Bernard Shaw by Michael Holroyd was originally published in four volumes.
Volume 1 *The Search for Love 1856–1898*, Volume 2 *The Pursuit of Power 1898–1918*,
Volume 3 *The Lure of Fantasy 1918–1950*, Volume 4 (Epilogue) *The Last Laugh* by
Chatto & Windus © Michael Holroyd 1988, 1989, 1991, 1992, and reprinted by
Penguin Books Ltd in 1990, 1991, 1992, 1993. This present edition is a substantial
abridgement, with revisions, of the complete work by the author

Copyright © Michael Holroyd 1997

First published in Great Britain in 1997 by
Chatto & Windus

First published in Great Britain in paperback in 1998 by
Vintage

Pimlico
Random House, 20 Vauxhall Bridge Road,
London SW1V 2SA

www.vintage-books.co.uk

Addresses for companies within The Random House Group Limited can be found at:
www.randomhouse.co.uk/offices.htm

The Random House Group Limited Reg. No. 954009

A CIP catalogue record for this book is available from the British Library

ISBN 9781845951856

The Random House Group Limited supports The Forest Stewardship Council (FSC®), the
leading international forest certification organisation. Our books carrying the FSC label are
printed on FSC® certified paper. FSC is the only forest certification scheme endorsed by
the leading environmental organisations, including Greenpeace. Our paper procurement
policy can be found at www.randomhouse.co.uk/environment

Printed and bound in Great Britain by Clays Ltd, St Ives PLC

CONTENTS

CONTENTS

LIST OF ILLUSTRATIONS

ACKNOWLEDGEMENTS

The many people and institutions that helped me to prepare the original four volumes of my Shaw biography are comprehensively listed in those volumes, and I take this opportunity to renew my thanks to them all. I have continued reading *The Annual of Bernard Shaw Studies* in the United States and *The Shavian* in Britain, as well as new publications about G.B.S. and his contemporaries, and to keep an eye out for Shaw manuscript material coming up at auction, so as to make necessary adjustments to my text in this abridgement. I owe special thanks to Sarah Johnson who transcribed my increasingly illegible marginalia on to immaculate discs; to my editor Alison Samuel who has continued walking in my steps and issuing corrections when I put a foot wrong; and to Howard Davies who queried anything queryable in this revised narrative.

MICHAEL HOLROYD
Porlock Weir, December 1996

ILLUSTRATIONS

1, 3 Courtesy of the British Library, London. 2 Courtesy of Archibald Henderson, *Man of the Century*, Appleton, Century, Crofts, New York, 1956. 5, 24 Courtesy of the Dan H. Laurence Collection, University of Guelph Library, Guelph, Ontario. 6, 12 Courtesy of Dan H. Laurence, *Bernard Shaw: Collected Letters*, Vol. 1, Max Reinhardt Ltd, London, 1965. 7, 10, 13 Courtesy of the National Portrait Gallery, London. 8 Courtesy of the National Trust, 9 Courtesy of the Fales Library, New York University Library, New York. 11 Courtesy of John Kelly (ed.), *Yeats Letters*, Vol. 1, Oxford University Press, 1986. 14 Courtesy of the Burgunder Collection, Cornell University Library, New York. 15, 18, 26 Hulton Getty (Picture Library), London. 16 Courtesy of Mary Shenfield, *Bernard Shaw: A Pictorial Biography*, Thames & Hudson, London, 1962. 17 Courtesy of the Trustees of the Victoria & Albert Museum, London. 19 Courtesy of the Sir Barry Jackson Trust, Birmingham. 20 Courtesy of Allan Chappelow, *Shaw the Villager and Human Being*, Charles Skilton, London, 1961. 21 Pictorial Parade Inc. 22 Courtesy of Allan Chappelow, *Shaw 'The Chucker-Out'*, George Allen & Unwin, London, 1969. 23 Courtesy of *Smithsonian* Magazine, Washington DC. 25 Courtesy of London of School of Economics and Political Science, British Library of Political and Economic Science, and the Society of Authors, London. Front endpaper Courtesy of Mander & Mitchenson Theatre Collection, Beckenham. Back endpaper Photo by Vandamm.

PREFACE

In the late 1960s the Shaw Estate decided to commission a new biography of G.B.S. Previous biographies had been 'partial', usually written by friends of Shaw, and the time had come for 'an assessment of the man in his period'. Shaw's executor, the Public Trustee, had recently relinquished his control of the publication and production arrangements for Shaw's works and set up an independent Committee of Management composed of nominees from the Estate's three residuary legatees (the British Museum and Royal Academy of Dramatic Art in London, and the National Gallery of Ireland in Dublin). Its first chairman, Sir John Wolfenden, director and principal librarian of the British Museum, took advice as to who should write Shaw's life from an eminent biographer and incunabulist at the museum, and my name came up. So the Society of Authors (which acted as agent for the Shaw Estate) was asked to sound me out.

I was then thirty-four, had published a biography of Lytton Strachey the previous year and already agreed to write a biography of Augustus John. But this invitation surprised me. I was more accustomed to appeals from people wanting me *not* to write about their friends and members of their family. Perhaps, it occurred to me, I was becoming respectable. The feeling was not altogether comfortable. In fact, I was terrified. To my eyes G.B.S. appeared as a gigantic phenomenon with whom I felt little intimacy. At the same time he presented a challenge I really ought to accept. Nevertheless I hesitated. I had heard that Shaw used to write ten letters every day of his adult life and that correspondents kept his letters. I knew he had composed over fifty plays, that his collected works extended over almost forty volumes (and were well exceeded by his uncollected writings), and that there were libraries of books about his work and huge deposits of unpublished papers around the world. I suspected that with his shorthand and his secretaries G.B.S. could actually write in a day more words than I could read in a day. Since he lived into his mid-nineties, writing vigorously almost to the end, this was an alarming speculation. I therefore prevaricated, replying that while I would in principle be delighted to write Shaw's Life, I could not in practice begin until I had finished *Augustus John*.

To my surprise the Society of Authors was undeterred by this delay. I did not begin my research until early in 1975 when I went to Dublin. I lived in Rathmines, strategically placed between a convent and a barracks, and a mile or so from Shaw's birthplace in Synge Street. Intermittently

I worked at the National Library of Ireland (to which Shaw had donated the manuscripts of his novels) and I visited Dalkey where he had passed his happiest hours while growing up. I also met a number of writers – John O'Donovan, Monk Gibbon, Vivian Mercier, Arland Ussher, Terence de Vere White – who encouraged me. Yet, however hard I try, I cannot account for my time in Ireland very coherently. The atmosphere was thick with goodwill. There was almost no one who, even when they had no information at all, would not be prepared to volunteer something over a jar or two. People I had never heard of came to advise me that they knew nothing, and then stayed on awhile. Many wrote letters to the same effect: some hopefully in verse; others more prosaically enclosing business cards. And everyone pressed in on me so warmly that I was moved to reply with such politeness that my replies elicited answers to which I felt bound to respond. One lady (whom I had never met) eventually enquired whether we had ever had an affair, the crucial part of which had escaped her. I was swimming in the wake of the great Shaw legend, swimming and almost drowning.

The writing of my book, which took me all over the world, must have tested the patience of the Shaw Estate to its utmost. But the extra time I was obliged to spend with Shaw helped to give me that sense of intimacy I had found lacking at the beginning of my research and which I believe is an essential ingredient for the writing of biography. Between Shaw's work and his life, I found, moved an unexpected current of passion which I sought to navigate. I felt eventually as if I were breaking a Shavian code, the alpha and omega of his dramatic style (so assertive yet so reticent), and was picking up subtle themes that, to gain an immediate public, he orchestrated for trumpet and big drum.

Many people had come to think of the legendary G.B.S. as having only ink in his veins. I began to dismantle this literary superman and replace him with a more recognizable if still uncommon human being. I wanted to demythologize him without reducing him. Behind the public phenomenon was hidden a private individual, intermittently glimpsed, who gave G.B.S. his concealed humanity. He covered up his vulnerability with dazzling panache; I have tried to uncover it and show the need he had while alive for such brilliant covering. He became the saint of the lonely and a fugleman for those who were out of step with their times. He gave them a heartening message. For every disadvantage, in Shavian terms, becomes a potential asset in disguise. The art of life therefore is the art of heroic paradox.

The paradox continues into our own times. G.B.S. is in his element by virtue of still being heroically out of step. I had already noticed, with respect to my previous biographies, how quickly a prevailing mood could change and how unpredictable these changes sometimes were. In the 1960s I had been assailed by a good deal of homophobic mail after my *Lytton Strachey* was published; but when a rewritten version of that book came out twenty-five years later I received no hate mail at all. On the other hand Augustus John, generally seen in the mid-1970s as an adventurous heterosexual character who might have emerged from the pages of Fielding's *Tom Jones*, attracted much greater puritan censoriousness twenty years later, mostly from men who, though responding to the rise of feminism, put me in mind of Dr Johnson's attack on *Tom Jones*.

By the end of the 1980s most people expected there would soon be a Labour Government in Britain. But the country did not embrace change as the United States appeared to be trying to do by turning from the Republicans to the Democrats. Instead it was preparing to dig in against the rest of Europe over what was to be a radically retrogressive period. We returned to past battlefields. Many of the political campaigns in which Shaw took part, and which had been manifestly won, were being fought out again a hundred years later, and with opposite results. The break-up of the Soviet Union, the 'end of communism' and of 'history', the spread of privatization across the world and the rise of nationalism, the fear in Britain of the very word 'socialist' (as frightening as 'liberal' in the United States) were to make Shaw's beliefs deeply unfashionable. While Oscar Wilde's once-faded aestheticism was being revitalized and revived by modernists, Shaw's persistent progressiveness had become dated. Yet being thoroughly out of fashion, wilfully marching in an alternative direction, was a Shavian speciality – and perhaps a useful one. Many pages which I wrote as a contribution to social history now appear to me, as I reread them, to have gained a peculiar relevance to our contemporary politics.

'Trust your genius rather than your industry,' Shaw advised his biographer St John Ervine. In preparing this abridgement, which was planned and contracted for over ten years ago, I have done away with all signs of industry by following the example of Leon Edel's abridged Life of Henry James and eliminating reference notes. I have also trusted to my instinct while reducing ninety-four years of Shaw's hectic life, and more than fifteen years of my own work, into a form that a general reader can get through in a matter of weeks or days. I have weeded out errors I detected in earlier versions, and occasionally added a passage founded on recent Shaw scholarship. What I have aimed at is something equivalent in biographical narrative to the 'revolver shooting' of Shaw's own dramatic dialogue where 'every line has a bullet in it and comes with an explosion'. Undoubtedly this technique reveals a rather different G.B.S. from the one conveyed by my original armada of volumes. It is for readers rather than myself to say what the difference is. All I can say is that it emerges from this synthesis, rather than being premeditated or imposed.

When infiltrating the work of his biographers with concealed autobiography, Shaw sacrificed something of his own life so that these 'partial' biographies might act as endorsements to his political ideas. Treating the Gospels as early examples of biography, he noted in the Preface to *Androcles and the Lion* how St Matthew ('like most biographers') tended to 'identify the opinions and prejudices of his hero with his own', while St John used biography as a record of the 'fulfilment of ancient Jewish prophecies'. Since Shaw's death, biographical technique has grown more ingenious and the range of subject matter has expanded so that biography embraces most human experience, insofar as it is recoverable, and accepts it as fit for publication. So far as I am aware, I do not specifically identify my opinions with Shaw's, nor have I used his life to record the fulfilment or non-fulfilment of socialist predictions. My deepest involvement is with biography itself and its never-ending love-affair with human nature, and my aim has been to come a little nearer a biographical ideal described by Hugh Kingsmill as 'the complete sympathy of complete detachment'.

ONE

FERMENTING GENEALOGY

Eternal is the fact that the human creature born in Ireland and brought
up in its air is Irish.
'Ireland Eternal and External', *New Statesman* (30 October 1948)

Bernard Shaw died on 2 November 1950. For almost a decade interviewers
had been recording his emphatic farewells. All were rehearsing for the
time when G.B.S. could no longer have the last word, and when it arrived
actors appeared nostalgically on new-fangled television sets; writers spoke
without interruption on the wireless; statesmen round the world uttered
their prepared addresses in newspapers.

The critic Eric Bentley bought several of these papers, but 'what I was
reading made me sick', he wrote. ' . . . Such mourning for Shaw was a
mockery of Shaw . . . Grasping the first occasion when Shaw was powerless
to come back at them, the bourgeoisie brayed and Broadway dimmed its
lights.' To Bentley's mind it was the final acceptance of Shaw at the
expense of all Shaw stood for.

Shaw had asked that his ashes should be mixed inseparably with those
of his wife, which had been kept at Golders Green Crematorium, and
then scattered in their garden. In the Dáil a proposal was made to
convey them back to Ireland and place them beside Swift's at St Patrick's
Cathedral in Dublin. For having lived his first twenty years in Ireland,
Shaw felt 'a foreigner in every other country'. But it was only outside
Ireland that he was recognized as Irish. As the Taoiseach John Costello
said, 'Bernard Shaw never forgot his Irish birth.' Yet he had set out in
his writings to give himself a new birth: a re-creation. He claimed to be
as indigenous as the half-American Winston Churchill or a half-Spaniard
such as Éamon de Valera, both excellent examples of cross-breeding. 'I
am a typical Irishman; my family come from Yorkshire,' he assured G. K.
Chesterton who, typically English, confirmed that 'scarcely anyone but a
typical Irishman could have made the remark'.

*

The Shaws made no secret of being aristocrats. No Shaw could form a
social acquaintance with a Roman Catholic or tradesman. They lifted up

their powerful Wellingtonian noses and spoke of themselves, however querulously, in a collective spirit (as people mentioning the Bourbons or Habsburgs) using the third person: 'the Shaws'.

The family had come from Scotland, then moved to England. In 1689 Captain William Shaw slipped from Hampshire into Ireland to fight in the Battle of the Boyne. He was rewarded with a large grant of land in Kilkenny. There, as landed gentry, the Shaws hunted, shot and fished.

Most successful was Robert Shaw, who entered the Irish Parliament, founded the Royal Bank and in 1821 was made a baronet. His cousin Bernard (grandfather of G.B.S.) also seemed set for success. On 1 April 1802, aged thirty, he married the daughter of a clergyman, Frances Carr, who over the next twenty-three years gave birth to fifteen children. As High Sheriff of Kilkenny, Bernard spent much of his time in the country and neglected his Dublin business, with the result that his partner absconded with his money. Bernard woke up to find himself penniless, collapsed, and died in his sleep. His widow had to apply for help to Sir Robert. The banker-baronet was a wealthy man. 'Unlike the typical Shaw, he was plumpish and had the appearance somewhat of a truculent bear disturbed out of a doze.' He was hopelessly in love with Frances who, though disdaining his offers of marriage, accepted rent free 'a quaint cottage, with Gothically pointed windows' at Terenure. From here she launched her sons and daughters on the world 'in an unshaken and unshakeable consciousness of their own aristocracy'.

Like most large families, these Shaws were not exclusively teetotallers. We see them through the eyes of G.B.S. Of his four aunts, Cecilia (Aunt Sis), the eldest, was a temperate maiden lady. She had been pronounced dead when a child and placed in a coffin; but, climbing out, lived on into her nineties, 'a big, rather imposing woman, with the family pride written all over her'. Aunt Frances, a gently nurtured lady, drank secretly over many years before, submitting to it openly, she passed away. Charlotte Jane ('Aunt Shah') married an irreproachable man connected with a cemetery. Aunt Emily, exceeding in nothing but snuff, married a scholastic clergyman, William George Carroll, who, but for his temper (it was said), would have been a bishop.

'I know as much about drink as anybody outside a hospital of inebriates,' G.B.S. later wrote. His knowledge had come largely from his father and some uncles. Two of his uncles were unknown to him, having emigrated to the Antipodes and 'like Mr Micawber, made history there'. A third, Robert, was blinded in his youth and 'never had an opportunity of drinking'. Uncle Henry was the rich man of the family, able to afford two wives and fifteen children. But he invested his money in a collapsing coal mine and before his death became mentally unstable.

The other three brothers, including Shaw's father, were alcoholics. Uncle Barney (William Bernard) and Uncle Fred (Richard Frederick) both died in the family mental retreat, Dr Eustace's in the north of Dublin. The youngest, Uncle Fred, didn't drink until he married a girl named Waters. His drinking bouts then grew excessive but he gave up alcohol altogether once his wife left him to live in London. He was reputed to be ungenerous (he worked in the Valuation Office) and, in retirement, 'harmlessly dotty'.

Uncle Barney was an inordinate smoker as well as a drunkard. He lived a largely fuddled life until he was past fifty. Then, relinquishing alcohol and tobacco simultaneously, he passed the next ten years of his life as a teetotaller, playing an obsolete wind instrument called an ophicleide. Towards the end of this period, renouncing the ophicleide, he married a lady of great piety, and fell completely silent. He was carried off to the family asylum where, 'impatient for heaven', he discovered an absolutely original method of committing suicide. It was irresistibly amusing and no human being had yet thought of it, involving as it did an empty carpet bag. However, in the act of placing this bag on his head, Uncle Barney jammed the mechanism of his heart in a paroxysm of laughter – which the merest recollection of his suicidal technique never failed to provoke among the Shaws – and the result was that he died a second before he succeeded in killing himself. The coroner's court described his death as being 'from natural causes'.

'Drink is the biggest skeleton in the family cupboard,' G.B.S. told one of his cousins. But he did not leave this skeleton in its cupboard. He had a choice of making the Shaw drunkenness into 'either a family tragedy or a family joke', and he chose the joke. So, in the bookshop window of his works, we may see a cabaret of Shavian aunts and uncles with a chorus of inebriate cousins, and at the centre, a wonderfully hopeless chap, second cousin to a baronet, George Carr Shaw, G.B.S.'s father.

2

AN IRISH MARRIAGE

Fortunately I have a heart of stone: else my relations would have broken it long ago.

Shaw to Rachel Mahaffy (6 June 1939)

The story of George Carr Shaw's life was simple. He would tell you it had evolved as the retribution for an injury he had once done a cat. He had found this cat, brought it home with him, fed it. But next day he had let his dog chase it and kill it. In his imagination this cat now had its revenge, seeing to it that he would have neither luck nor money. He was unsuccessful because of this cat; unskilled, unsober, and unserious too.

Between the ages of twenty-three and thirty he had been a clerk at a Dublin ironworks, but in 1845 he lost this job. By means of family influence he landed up with a perfectly superfluous post at the Four Courts, a job without duties or responsibilities. Unfortunately, it was one of the first of such positions to be abolished in the legal reforms of the early 1850s, for which 'outrage' George Shaw received a pension of £44 a year. There were opportunities in Dublin for a wholesale corn-merchant (retail trade was impossible for a Shaw). But George Shaw needed capital. Until now he had walked by himself, a gentleman who was no gentleman, and all places were alike to him. He was in his thirty-eighth year and had recently come in contact with a twenty-one-year-old girl, Lucinda Eliza-beth Gurly, called 'Bessie'. She was short, thin-lipped, with the jaw of a prize-fighter and a head like a football; but she had an attractive inheri-tance. George Carr Shaw felt drawn to her. 'It was at this moment,' G.B.S. records, 'that some devil, perhaps commissioned by the Life Force to bring me into the world, prompted my father to propose marriage to Miss Bessie Gurly.'

*

The master-spirit among Bessie's forebears had been her maternal grand-father, a country gentleman of imposing presence whose origin was so obscure that he was understood to have had no legal parents. But he lived *en grand seigneur* on his property of over two thousand acres in Kilkenny and at a place called Whitechurch to the south of Dublin. Each week he would drive in to a little pawnshop in Winetavern Street, one of the poorest quarters of the city. The name on the door was Cullen, an employee, under cover of whose identity John Whitcroft made his money.

The squire-pawnbroker wanted respectability by blood. On 29 December 1829 his daughter Lucinda married a ginger-whiskered squire from Carlow named Walter Bagnall Gurly, who was then living nearby at Rathfarnham. 'He was a wiry, tight, smallish handknit open-air man,' G.B.S. remembered, able to make his own boats and to ride the most ungovernable horses; an ingenious carpenter, dead shot, indefatigable fisherman: in short, 'able to do anything except manage his affairs, keep his estate from slipping through his fingers'.

In ten years of marriage they had one daughter and a son. Then, on 14 January 1839, Mrs Gurly died. Bessie was nine. She was placed under the care of her great-aunt, Ellen Whitcroft, a terrible hump-backed lady. This spidery creature taught her how to dress correctly, to sit motionless and straight; how to breathe, pronounce French, convey orders to servants. She was schooled in harmony and counterpoint, playing the piano 'with various coins of the realm on the backs of my hands, also with my hair which I wore in two long plaits down my back, tied to the back of my chair, also with a square of pasteboard hung on my neck by a string pretty much as pictures are hung . . . in order to prevent me looking at my hands'.

By a programme of constraints and browbeatings, she was 'educated up to the highest standard of Irish "carriage ladies" '. She never said anything coarse, loved flowers more than human beings and walked through the streets seeing nobody. Her aunt intended a great destiny for her – something that because of her deformity she had never achieved herself: marriage into the nobility. With these superior expectations, Bessie was floated into Dublin Society where she encountered the sinking George Carr Shaw.

Secretly Bessie detested her aunt and everything that, masquerading as education and religion, had made her childhood miserable. It was now that George Carr Shaw drifted forward to make his bid for Aunt Ellen's property by proposing marriage to her niece.

He was not a romantic figure. Almost twice her age, he had a weak mouth, one squinting eye and a number of epileptic ways. 'If any unpleasant reflection occurred to him, he, if in a room, rubbed his hands rapidly together and ground his teeth. If in a street, he took a short run.' He was an unconvivial man, with little interest in women. Drink and money were his world.

But Bessie, who had fallen out with her father, overlooked the squinting eyes, the grinding teeth, and took stock only of George Carr Shaw's social position and the prospects such a proposal offered of a better life. Yet this was to be a marriage of two blind people, each treating the other as guide dog. 'Money in marriage is the first and, frequently, the only passion,' wrote St John Ervine of nineteenth-century Irish marriages. G.B.S.'s parents married for money and were to live impecuniously ever after.

Aunt Ellen had tolerated George Carr Shaw as Bessie's chaperon because of his well-connected harmlessness. To be with Shaw was an alibi for almost anything; never before had he been known to take an initiative. So now Aunt Ellen declared the marriage impossible. Then, when none of her objections prevailed, she revealed that Shaw was a known drunkard – in any event it was notorious in the family. Bessie knew how to deal with this. She went round to Shaw and asked him; and he confessed that all his life he had been a bigoted teetotaller. But he did not tell her that he was a teetotaller who drank.

So the marriage went ahead. Aunt Ellen had one more card to play: she disinherited her niece. This was undeniably a serious blow to Shaw. Needing money to take advantage of a business opportunity from his brother Henry, he sold his pension for £500 and used this capital to buy a partnership in a corn-merchant business with his brother's ex-partner, George Clibborn. It was a start – to be supported after his marriage by his wife's own money and whatever could be regained of Aunt Ellen's inheritance. It could have been worse.

This was a good summer for Walter Bagnall Gurly. On 25 May 1852 he married his second wife who, two months before, had given birth to their first daughter; and twenty-three days later, at the same church, St Peter's in Aungier Street, he attended the wedding of his daughter and George Carr Shaw. As a wedding gift, Aunt Ellen had sent the couple a bundle of IOUs signed by Gurly – which he seized and burnt. Better still was the marriage settlement he had insisted on their signing a few hours before the ceremony. Bessie's personal assets were listed as 'one thousand two hundred and fifty-six pounds Nine shillings and two pence Government three and a quarter per cent Stock'. All this, together with income to be derived from her father's first marriage settlement and from the will of her pawnbroker grandfather, was transferred by deed to two trustees. The effect of this was to ensure that the inheritance would remain Gurly-money, never the Shaw-money it would otherwise have become. So George Carr Shaw had gained a wife and lost a fortune.

When they drove off after the wedding, George Carr Shaw turned to kiss his bride. She felt so disgusted that she was still protesting more than thirty years later. 'The rebuff must have opened his eyes a little too late,' their son judged, 'to her want of any really mately feeling for him.'

3

DEVIL OF A CHILDHOOD

William Morris used to say that it is very difficult to judge who are the best people to take charge of children, but it is certain that the parents are the very worst.

Shaw to Nancy Astor (21 August 1943)

They had chosen Liverpool for their honeymoon, and here their first child was conceived. It was nearly the end of their marriage. Years later,

Mrs Shaw told her son that, opening her husband's wardrobe, she had 'found it full of empty bottles'. The truth had tumbled out. 'I leave you to imagine,' wrote G.B.S., 'the hell into which my mother descended when she found out what shabby-genteel poverty with a drunken husband is like.'

They returned to Dublin and moved into 'an awful little kennel with "primitive sanitary arrangements"', 3 Upper Synge Street – a road of eleven small squat houses which runs round the corner from Harrington Street. Here their three children were born: Lucinda Frances, called Lucy, on 26 March 1853, Elinor Agnes, nicknamed 'Yuppy', two years later; and, on 26 July 1856, their son George Bernard, 'fifty years too soon', he calculated.

It was a difficult delivery, a vaginal breech birth that was carried out at Upper Synge Street by Dr John Ringland, Master of the Combe Lying-In Hospital, who had been called in by Bessie's general practitioner.

In his nursery days he was called Bob; by the time he had grown into his holland tunic and knickerbockers he had become 'Sonny'; it was not until he was reborn the child of his own writings in England that he developed the plumage of 'G.B.S.'

We first see Bob at the age of one. 'The young beggar is getting quite outrageous,' his father writes proudly to Bessie who was staying with her family. 'I left him this morning roaring and tearing like a bull.' He could eat his hat, vomit up currants, annoy his teeth and make a jigsaw of unread newspapers. But his chief accomplishment was to go off on marvellous walking expeditions from Papa to Nurse (who was threatening a breakdown) and back again. From his bed he plunged head-first onto the floor; and from the kitchen table he cascaded through a pane of glass without 'even a *pane* in his head'.

Once domesticated, this bull of a boy soon became the sedate Sonny. The most affectionate sound in Synge Street was his father's jokes. From their talks, Sonny was let in on the secret of how his father had saved the life of Uncle Robert – 'and, to tell you the truth, I was never so sorry for anything in my life afterwards'. It became a game between them, almost an intimacy, that the son should provoke his father to such exhibitions.

In a letter to his wife, George Carr Shaw had written of 'a Mill which Clibborn & I are thinking of taking at Dolphin's Barn . . . Wont it be great fun and grandeur to find yourself when you come back the wife of a dusty Miller, so be prepared to have the very life ground out of you . . .' Bessie was not amused: he never did anything positive. 'You are out for once in your life,' he told her. 'We *have* taken the Mill.'

Dolphin's Barn Mill was on the country side of the canal. Sonny, who sometimes walked there with his father and sisters before breakfast, used to play under the waterwheel by the millpond and in the big field adjoining the building. 'The field had one tree in it, at the foot of which I buried our dead dog. It was quite wild. I never saw a human soul in it.' On the front of Rutland Avenue was a Clibborn & Shaw warehouse, one corner of which had been made into a shop where corn, wheat, flour and locust beans were surreptitiously retailed to the villagers. But they did not prosper. Once, when the firm was almost ruined by the bankruptcy of a debtor, Clibborn wept openly in their office, while Shaw retreated to a corner of the warehouse and cried with laughter at the colossal mischief of it all.

It was this sense of mischief that Sonny loved, and that G.B.S. believed he inherited. But planted in so many of Papa's comedies were seeds of disaster. When pretending to fling his son into the canal, he almost succeeded: and a suspicion began to crawl into Sonny's mind. He went to his mother and whispered his awful discovery, 'Mama: I think Papa's drunk.' 'When is he ever anything else?' Bessie retorted with disgust.

*

Though he transferred the responsibility for his desolate childhood to his father, the central character in this scene had been his mother. Bessie was a grievously disappointed woman. She believed, and persuaded her son to believe, that 'everybody had disappointed her, or betrayed her, or tyrannized over her'. From this time onwards Sonny began to see his father through his mother's eyes, as a man to imitate, but in reverse. It suited George Carr Shaw's temperament to play along. When he caught Sonny pretending to smoke a toy pipe, he entreated him with dreadful earnestness never to follow his example. In this special Shavian sense, George Carr Shaw became a model father.

Of his mother, G.B.S. once admitted, 'I knew very little about her.' This was partly because she did not concern herself with him. Her own childhood had been made miserable by bullying, but Bessie never bullied; she made her son miserable by neglect. 'She was simply not a wife or mother at all.' Needing her attention, he found with dismay that he could do nothing to interest her. In her eyes he was an inferior little male animal tainted with all the potential weaknesses of her husband.

In his books and letters, G.B.S. places his mother on a carpet of filial loyalty, and he invites every potential biographer to pull it from beneath her feet. His American biographer, Archibald Henderson, scrupulously overlooking this invitation, received in red ink a brusque rebuff: 'This sympathy with the mother is utterly false. Damn your American sentimentality!'

In a rare moment of emotion, G.B.S. wrote to Ellen Terry of his 'devil of a childhood, Ellen, rich only in dreams, frightful & loveless in realities'. But looking directly at such bleakness was too painful. Usually he put on the spectacles of paradox. This paradox became his 'criticism of life', the technique by which he turned lack of love inside out and, attracting from the world some of the attention he had been denied by his mother, conjured optimism out of deprivation.

The fact that neither of his parents cared for him was, he perceived, of enormous advantage. What else could have taught him the value of self-sufficiency? He was spared, too, by their unconcealed disappointment in each other, from lingering illusions about the family. It was remarkable how these paradoxical privileges began to multiply once he became skilled at the game. From his observations he soon deduced the wonderful impersonality of sex, and the kindness and good sense of distancing yourself from people you loved.

'The fact that I am still alive at $78\frac{1}{2}$ I probably owe largely to her [Bessie's] complete neglect of me during infancy,' G.B.S. confided to Marie Stopes. ' . . . It used to be a common saying among Dublin doctors in my youth that most women killed their first child by their maternal care . . . motherhood is not every woman's vocation.' G.B.S. believed that his mother preferred her daughters, in particular the red-haired Yuppy, who wilted under her slight attentions. As a child she developed a goitre; only the fortunate absence of medical aid enabled nature to perform a cure. Then at the age of twenty-one, assisted by a sanatorium of doctors, she died of tuberculosis. It could be no accident either that Lucy, Bessie's second favourite, was to die next following a long period of anorexic ill-health, seven years after her mother's death. She 'suffered far more by the process than I did,' G.B.S. wrote of their upbringing, 'for she . . . was not immune, as I and my mother were, from conventional vanities'.

There was no feuding at Synge Street. The house was small, but so far as possible they treated one another like furniture. 'As children,' G.B.S. explained, 'we had to find our own way in a household where there was no hate nor love.' Sonny's own way led him to the conclusion that nature had intended an element of antipathy as a defence against incest. Happily his family had been well dosed with this preventative.

G.B.S. believed that he had inherited from his parents qualities that they had found incompatible but which, in expiation, he must reconcile within himself. Only by marrying opposites, through paradox or a dialectical process of synthesis, did he feel that he could fulfil his moral obligation to optimism and a better future. In place of the warring of envy and class, he was to substitute a Hegelian policy of inclusiveness. But to include everything in his sights he was obliged to fly his balloon of words into a stratosphere of hypothesis where, in all its thin remoteness, his vision became complete.

He writes of a strangeness 'which made me all my life a sojourner on this planet rather than a native of it ... I was at home only in the realm of my imagination, and at my ease only with the mighty dead.' It is this voice from the living dead that, despite the marvellous cadence, chilled his audience. In the lost childhood of Sonny the philosophy of G.B.S. was conceived. 'What else can I do?' he had asked. He strove to bring the world into harmony with his lonely nature, but the world reacted subconsciously to what was suppressed as well as to what he proclaimed. He could see everything but touch little. For what he had done was replace the first loveless reality with a dream. 'I very seldom dream of my mother,' he told Gilbert Murray;

'but when I do, she is my wife as well as my mother. When this first occurred to me (well on in my life), what surprised me when I awoke was that the notion of incest had not entered into the dream: I had taken it as a matter of course that the maternal function included the wifely one; and so did she. What is more, the sexual relation acquired all the innocence of the filial one, and the filial one all the completeness of the sexual one ... if circumstances tricked me into marrying my mother before I knew she was my mother, I should be fonder of her than I could ever be of a mother who was not my wife, or a wife who was not my mother.'

Only in his imagination was such completeness possible.

Most of the time Sonny and his sisters were abandoned to the servants – 'and *such* servants, Good God!' The exception was 'my excellent Nurse Williams' who left while Sonny was still very young. But what could you expect on £8 a year? 'I had my meals in the kitchen,' G.B.S. recalled, 'mostly of stewed beef, which I loathed, badly cooked potatoes, sound or diseased as the case might be, and much too much tea out of brown delft teapots left to "draw" on the hob until it was pure tannin. Sugar I stole ... I hated the servants and liked my mother because, on one or two rare and delightful occasions when she buttered my bread for me, she buttered it thickly instead of merely wiping a knife on it ... I could idolize her to the utmost pitch of my imagination and had no sordid or disillusioning contacts with her. It was a privilege to be taken for a walk or a visit with her ...'

Occasionally Bessie would take him to see Aunt Ellen, hoping that the old lady would feel sufficiently attracted to leave him her property. Sonny seemed mesmerized by this strange little hump-backed lady with her pretty face and magical deformity. One Sunday morning Papa announced that she was dead, and Sonny ran off to the solitude of the garden to cry, terrified that his grief would last for ever. When he 'discovered that it lasted only an hour,' wrote G.B.S., 'and then passed completely away', he had his first taste of realism.

Shaw was unable to tolerate feelings of sadness. 'People who cry and grieve never remember,' he wrote. 'I never grieve and never forget.' Sadness was a poison to his system and before absorption it had to be converted into something else. His attitude to death was the most extreme example of this manufacture of cheerfulness. Papa, he saw, 'found something in a funeral, or even in a death, which tickled his sense of humor.

' . . . the sorest bereavement does not cause men to forget wholly that time is money. Hence, though we used to proceed slowly and sadly enough through the streets or terraces at the early stages of our progress, when we got into the open a change came over the spirit in which the coachmen drove. Encouraging words were addressed to the horses; whips were flicked; a jerk all along the line warned us to slip our arms through the broad elbow-straps of the mourning-coaches, which were balanced on longitudinal poles by enormous and totally unelastic springs; and then the funeral began in earnest. Many a clinking run have I had through that bit of country at the heels of some deceased uncle who had himself many a time enjoyed the same sport. But in the immediate neighbourhood of the cemetery the houses recommenced; and at that point our grief returned upon us with overwhelming force: we were able barely to crawl along to the great iron gates where a demoniacal black pony was waiting with a sort of primitive gun-carriage and a pall to convey our burden up the avenue to the mortuary chapel, looking as if he might be expected at every step to snort fire, spread a pair of gigantic bat's wings, and vanish, coffin and all, in thunder and brimstone.'

In this way, Sonny began to laugh pain out of existence. Detachment from the fear of death was a step towards Shavian invulnerability in life. His death-anxiety was transferred into a fear of poverty (which, with a little courage and thought, we could eliminate), and any sediment of apprehension absorbed into a hygienic campaign against earth burial. Freed from escapist fables of personal immortality, death became an intensely democratic process. We began to die when more people wished us dead than wished us alive. Many a colleague, on the death of a wife, son or mother, was to find himself in receipt of Shaw's feeling congratulations. 'Rejoice in his memory; and be radiant,' he instructed Edith Lyttelton after the death of her husband. ' . . . Dying is a troublesome business: there is pain to be suffered, and it wrings one's heart; but death is a splendid thing – a warfare accomplished, a beginning all over again, a triumph. You can always see that in their faces.'

4

THE MAGICIAN APPEARS

I am an Irishman without a birth certificate.
Shaw to Denis Johnston (1 April 1938)

Sometime after her marriage Bessie was raised up into a new world of 'imagination, idealization, the charm of music, the charm of lovely seas' by a mysterious intruder, called Lee, one of the originals of George du Maurier's Svengali. He was a 'mesmeric conductor and daringly original teacher of singing,' G.B.S. records. It was the extraordinary effect he produced on Bessie that impressed her son. Sonny watched him closely.

There was something gypsy-like about his appearance. His face 'was framed with pirate-black whiskers' and he wore his luxuriant black hair long. He had a deformed foot and limped with peculiar elegance. But it was the confidence with which he asserted his heterodox opinions that Sonny noticed more than anything else. He noticed too the way his mother listened, the way she came alive under Lee's spell.

Sonny did not like Lee, but he could not help admiring him. He was, it seems, about six years old when his mother introduced this stranger into Synge Street. But, 'as his notion of play was to decorate my face with moustaches and whiskers in burnt cork in spite of the most furious resistance I could put up, our encounter was not a success; and the defensive attitude in which it left me lasted, though without the least bitterness, until the decay of his energies and the growth of mine put us on more than equal terms'.

G.B.S. never knew when Lee and his mother met. Lee claimed to have been born in Kilrush, County Clare, the natural son of Colonel Crofton Moore Vandeleur, MP. When he was a boy he had fallen down a flight of stairs. His wound was badly dressed, and though he wore his lameness 'as if it were a quality instead of a defect', he was left with a lifelong animosity towards orthodox medical science. He had never been to school and had 'nothing good to say of any academic institution'. Instead he provided himself with the title 'Professor of Music' and went on to pioneer a revolutionary discipline of voice training which he called 'the

Method'. He was more than a singing teacher: he was a philosopher of voice. Music, he would tell Sonny, was his religion.

But there were some facts of Lee's career that Sonny never heard. He had been born in 1830, the elder of two sons of Robert Lee, coalman, and his wife Eliza. At the age of eight he was living at 4 Caroline Row in Dublin and attending the Christian Brothers' O'Connell School nearby. In the school records his name is given as George Lee, and his brother's as William. This was a Catholic school, and it was here he took violin lessons and instruction in singing. On 9 January 1843, Robert Lee died. By 1851, the family was living at 2 Portobello Place. Less than two years later they had moved to 16 Harrington Street. Between 1851 and 1853 the family must have found some money – possibly from Colonel Vandeleur on the coming of age of George and William. The rateable value of 2 Portobello Place had been £5 10s., that of 16 Harrington Street was £34. It was in 1852 also that Lee founded his Amateur Musical Society, taking some sort of professional rooms for a year or two at 11 Harrington Street on the opposite side of the road. From nowhere in the published writings or letters of G.B.S. can it be inferred that Lee started his musical society and set up as singing teacher within a few months of Bessie's marriage to George Carr Shaw; nor is it clear that 2 Portobello Place was about two hundred yards from the Shaws in Synge Street, that 16 Harrington Street was some one hundred and twenty-five paces distant, and that two houses only separate Sonny's future birthplace from Lee's professional chambers.

Sonny sometimes speculated as to whether he might have been Lee's natural son; and G.B.S. was aware of other people's speculations. 'About G.B.S.'s parentage,' wrote Beatrice Webb in her diary for 12 May 1911. 'The photograph published in the Henderson Biography makes it quite clear to me that he was the child of G. J. V. Lee – that vain, witty and distinguished musical genius who lived with them. The expression on Lee's face is quite amazingly like G.B.S. when I first knew him.'

That Shaw may have had an unconscious wish to be the son of the remarkable George Lee and not of the miserable George Carr Shaw is possible. His campaign to demonstrate that he was George Carr Shaw's son was conducted primarily in defence of his mother. He was to model himself on Lee because of the extraordinary effect Lee had produced on Bessie and, in a number of three-cornered relationships, he was to play out the presumed asexuality of their liaison by refusing to compromise his own chastity. The themes of consanguinity and illegitimacy recur obsessively in his plays, but it is the emotional independence of the woman that is stressed. Eliza's parting from Professor Higgins in *Pygmalion* to marry Freddy Eynsford-Hill is Shaw's restatement of Bessie's economic attachment to Lee who is seen as a means to her self-sufficiency. In logic,

Sonny should have been Lee's son. But as Shaw demonstrated in his most deliberately pleasant play, *You Never Can Tell*, remarkable children were frequently born to incompatible parents.

But G.B.S. had to be certain. So he obliterated the ambiguous Christian name he shared with George Lee and George Shaw, using only the initial G. 'Professionally I drop the George,' he told an editor. 'Personally I dislike it.' 'Don't George me,' he would growl at people who made this mistake. He would remain George only to his family.

By finding a use for the knowledge of harmony and counterpoint hammered into her in her youth, Lee gave Bessie 'a Cause and a Creed to live for'. She became the chorus leader and general factotum of his musical society.

Lee's life had changed in those years. On 6 March 1860 his mother died, and two years later, on 7 May 1862, his brother William also died, aged twenty-seven, and was buried near Robert and Eliza Lee in the Roman Catholic Glasnevin Cemetery. His death brought Lee 'to the verge of suicide'. Since life outside music seemed to offer little to either Lee or Bessie, they became wedded to 'the Method'.

In his Preface to *London Music* G.B.S. touches on a peculiar aspect of this story. 'Lee soon found his way into our house, first by giving my mother lessons there, and then by using our drawing-room for rehearsals.' He presents Lee as a man apart, 'too excessively unlike us, too completely a phenomenon, to rouse any primitive feelings in us'. Because he was a cripple 'marriage and gallantry were tacitly ruled out of his possibilities, by himself, I fancy, as much as by other people. There was simply no room in his life for anything of the sort.' What little we know about Lee contradicts this view of the man. His Byronic limp was a focus of romantic interest; at least two women in his musical society, and possibly Sonny's sister Yuppy, fell in love with him. Later in life he made advances to Lucy Shaw and ended his days running a sort of night-club in London where he carried on an affair with his housekeeper. G.B.S. does not conceal this. But he presents it as a late-flowering sentimentalism that bloomed when, having been seduced by the capitalist atmosphere of 'overfed, monied London', he proved unfaithful to 'the Method' and had been dropped by Bessie.

To disinfect the relationship from all sexual implication, he built Bessie into 'one of those women who could act as matron of a cavalry barracks from eighteen to forty and emerge without a stain on her character'. 'To the closest observation' she was 'so sexless' that it was a wonder how she could have conceived three children. He could only guess that George Carr Shaw, when drunk, had forced himself on her and that to this operation he owed his existence. 'I was just something that had happened to them,' he bleakly concluded. Such a beginning, which explained his mother's neglect, was preferable to having the Lee–Bessie association 'unpleasantly misunderstood'. George Carr Shaw 'was Papa in the fullest sense always,' he wrote, 'and the dynamic Lee got none of the affection Papa inspired'. His arguments reflect the urgent need Shaw felt to make his case, in the light of what was to happen next between Lee and his mother.

5

MÉNAGE À TROIS

We must reform society before we can reform ourselves ... personal righteousness is impossible in an unrighteous environment.

Shaw to H. G. Wells (17 May 1917)

Two experiences, both visual, dominate Sonny's early years. The first was his sight of the Dublin slums. 'I saw it and smelt it and loathed it.' His nurse would take him to the squalid tenements of her friends, or lead him off to a public house and (it is suggested) add to her £8 a year by picking up soldiers at the barracks. Shaw's lifelong hatred of poverty was born of these lonely days of slumming.

On being asked, at the age of seventy-five, to name the happiest hour of his life, Shaw was to answer: 'When my mother told me we were going to live on Dalkey Hill.' In 1864, two years after his brother's death, Lee moved from Harrington Street to 1 Hatch Street. He proposed a new arrangement: to lease a cottage on Dalkey Hill, nine miles south of Dublin, and to share it with the Shaws. Torca Cottage, into which they all moved in 1866, had four reasonably-sized rooms, a back room for Sonny, and a kitchen and pantry into which they squeezed the servant's bed. The front garden overlooked Killiney Bay, and the back garden Dublin Bay.

'I owe more than I can express to the natural beauty of that enchanting situation commanding the two great bays between Howth and Bray Head,' Shaw remembered towards the end of his life, 'and its canopied skies such as I have never seen elsewhere in the world.' In the miserable Synge Street house, opposite a big field blotted out by hoardings and behind 'the bare dark walls, much too high ... too high to be climbed over', Sonny had felt a prisoner. At Torca he became 'a prince in a world of my own imagination'. His playground was Killiney Hill, a wonderland of goat-paths and gorse slopes down which he would run to the sandy shore and into the sea. But the beauty of Dalkey, taking him out 'of this time and this world', delayed his development. 'With a little more courage & a little more energy I could have done much more; and I lacked these because in my boyhood I lived on my imagination instead of on my work.'

The work of G.B.S. was a product not so much of his happy memories of Dalkey but of his visits to the Dublin slums which, 'with their shocking vital statistics and the perpetual gabble of its inhabitants', reflected the unhappiness Sonny seldom escaped. 'An Irishman has two eyes,' Shaw told G. K. Chesterton. One was for poetry, the other for reality. As Sonny grew into an adult the Dalkey eye closed. This is why, at his most serious, G.B.S. always seems to be winking.

After a year at Dalkey, Lee and the Shaws agreed to extend the *ménage à trois* to Hatch Street, while they continued to occupy Torca Cottage for summer holidays. 'The arrangement was economical,' G.B.S. explained, 'for we could not afford to live in a fashionable house, and Lee could not afford to give lessons in an unfashionable one.' Lee paid the rent for all of them – the rateable value being £35 – in addition to the costs at Dalkey. The amalgamation gave the Shaws a well-appointed three-storeyed house. 'Being a corner house it had no garden,' Shaw remembered; 'but it had two areas and a leads. It had eight rooms besides the spacious basement and pantry accommodation as against five in Synge St.' The hall door was in one street and the windows (with one exception) were in another. The exception, a window over the hall door and near the roof, was Sonny's bedroom where, his friend Edward McNulty remembered, 'there was barely room for anything but his bed'.

Like his mother Sonny was dazzled by Lee and adopted many of his startling ideas – sleeping with the windows open, eating brown bread instead of white and parading his disdain for doctors, lawyers, academics, clergymen. Lee filled the house with music and banished family prayers. In the Synge Street days, George Carr Shaw, as sole head of the household, had sent his children to Sunday School where genteel Protestants aged five to twelve, well-soaped and best-dressed, mouthed religious texts and were rewarded with inscribed cards. After this they would be marched to the Molyneux Church in Upper Leeson Street to fidget interminably round the altar rails. 'To sit motionless and speechless in your best suit in a dark stuffy church on a morning that is fine outside the building, with your young limbs aching with unnatural quiet . . . is enough to lead any sensitive youth to resolve that when he grows up and can do as he likes, the first use he will make of his liberty will be to stay away from church.'

Such respectable habits had been largely ridiculed by Bessie's dissolute brother Walter Gurly, a ship's surgeon who visited them between transatlantic voyages. 'He was a most exhilarating person,' G.B.S. remembered, '. . . always in high spirits, and full of a humor that was barbarous in its blasphemous indecency, but Shakespearian in the elaboration and fantasy of its literary expression . . . He was full of the Bible, which became in his hands a masterpiece of comic literature; and he quoted the sayings of Jesus as models of facetious repartee.'

G.B.S. uses the entertaining figure of Uncle Walter as a comet, shimmering across the skies, to distract our attention from a more significant feature in the religious firmament of the Shaws. There was nothing in Walter Gurly's irreverent jokes that quarrelled with the tradition of Protestant gentry. Irish Protestantism, Shaw explains, 'was not then a religion: it was a side in political faction, a class prejudice, a conviction that Roman Catholics are socially inferior persons who will go to hell when they die and leave Heaven in the exclusive possession of Protestant ladies and gentlemen'.

It is evident from what he wrote that G.B.S. knew that Lee was a Catholic. But he prevaricated. To Stephen Winsten he proclaimed that 'music was the only religion he [Lee] ever professed'; to Frank Harris he wrote: 'The Method was my mother's religion. It was the bond between her and Lee. A bond of sex could not have lasted a year'; to Demetrius O'Bolger he revealed that Lee was 'sceptical' about religion, and added, 'the religion of our house was the religion of singing the right way'. By such means he directed his biographers where he wanted. For although he claimed to be 'in intense reaction against the Shaw snobbery', his own snob-tragedy was to be G.B.S.'s disappointment with Sonny for having felt ashamed among his school friends at sharing a house with someone no Shaw should rightly know.

The only person for whom there seemed no special advantages at Hatch Street was George Carr Shaw. He became 'full of self-reproaches and humiliations when he was not full of secret jokes, and was either biting his moustache and whispering deep-drawn Damns, or shaking with paroxysms of laughter'. In a private note, written for a medical friend in 1879, Shaw described the pattern of his father's drinking:

'In society he drank porter, champagne, whisky, anything he could get, sometimes swallowing stout enough to make him sick . . . Although he was never sober, he was seldom utterly drunk. He made efforts to reform himself, and on one occasion succeeded in abstaining for sixteen months; but these efforts always ended in a relapse. On one or two occasions he disappeared for a few days and returned with his watch broken, clothes damaged and every symptom of uncontrolled excess; but ordinarily he came home in the evening fuddled, eat [*sic*] his dinner, had a nap, and then kept going out for drams until he went to bed. He never drank or kept drink in the house . . . I have seen him when drunk, seize a small article on the mantelpiece and dash it upon the hearthstone, or kick a newspaper into the air; but though he was very irritable, he never used the slightest violence to any person . . . his timidity probably made forbearance habitual to him.'

After his father was dead, G.B.S. eliminated much of this sordidness by giving to his published descriptions of it a hilarious Shavian gloss.

'A boy who has seen "the governor", with an imperfectly wrapped-up goose under one arm and a ham in the same condition under the other (both purchased under heaven knows what delusion of festivity), butting at the garden wall of our Dalkey Cottage in the belief that he was pushing open the gate, and transforming his tall hat to a concertina in the process, and who, instead of being overwhelmed with shame and anxiety at the spectacle, has been so disabled by merriment (uproariously shared by the maternal uncle) that he has hardly been able to rush to the rescue of the hat and pilot its wearer to safety, is clearly not a boy who will make tragedies of trifles instead of making trifles of tragedies.'

After two or three years at Hatch Street, George Carr Shaw was felled on the doorstep by a fit. Shortly afterwards he became so rigid a teetotaller that those who knew him found it 'difficult to realize what he formerly was'.

In a letter to a prospective biographer, G.B.S. wrote: 'You ask whether my father liked Lee. He certainly did not, and would not have tolerated the arrangement if he could have afforded a decent house without it, or if he could have asserted himself against my mother, who probably never consulted him in the matter. There was never any quarrelling in the house: my mother went her own way, which happened to be the musical way of Lee, just as Lee went his; and my father could only look on helplessly.'

It was this impotence that appears to have driven George Carr Shaw to greater drinking excesses. 'When his children had grown too big for him to play with, and the suspense as to whether he would come home drunk or sober never ceased,' G.B.S. told a cousin, 'he got practically no comfortable society from them. His relatives did not want to see him; and my mother did not want to see his relatives: she was interested only in people who could sing, and they were mostly Catholics, not proper company for the Protestant caste of Shaw.'

Before his marriage, and during its early years, George Carr Shaw had been on visiting terms with his smart Protestant relatives. By the 1860s their doors were shut to him and his family. 'My immediate family and the Shaw clan,' G.B.S. recalled, '... were barely on speaking terms when we met which we did only accidentally, never intentionally.' Social conditions, which had helped to drive his father to drink, would also one day pervert Lee, and both men disappointed his mother. So Society became the dragon against which the fabulous G.B.S. would lead his campaign of lifelong knight-errantry.

6

THE SHAME OF EDUCATION

If I had not returned to the house, I don't think they would, any of them, have missed me.

Preface to *London Music* (1937)

At Synge Street Sonny and his sisters had been provided with a day governess. Caroline Hill was an impoverished gentlewoman who puzzled the children by her attempts to teach them the alphabet and mathematical tables. She would punish her pupils when their laughter grew too out-rageous by 'little strokes with her fingers that would not have discomposed a fly'.

At the beginning of the summer term of 1865, when he was almost ten, Sonny was sent to his first school, the Wesleyan Connexional, less than half a mile away at 79 St Stephen's Green. He hated this school. 'I have not a good word to say for it,' he wrote. '... A more futile boy prison could not be imagined. I was a day-boy: what a boarder's life was like I shudder to conjecture.' The chief reason for his dislike of school appears to have been that it took him further away from his mother. This, he came to believe, had been its real purpose – that of 'preventing my being a nuisance to my mother at home for at least half the day'.

The Wesleyan Connexional School occupied an old private house next door to the mansion of Sir Benjamin Lee Guinness. Its big schoolroom stood at the end of a yard at the rear where the stables had been and which by the 1860s served as a playground. It was the cheapest of those Dublin schools patronized by Protestants. The sanitation was primitive and the lessons meagre. 'In the large classes,' Shaw recalled, 'the utmost examination possible in the lessons meant one question for each boy in alphabetical order, or at most two. If you could answer the questions or do the sums, or construe the few lines that fell to your lot, you passed unscathed: if not, or if you talked in class or misbehaved, you were marked in your judgement book for caning by the headmaster.'

The headmaster when Sonny first went there was Robert Cook, a young Methodist minister who would prepare boys for flogging with spasms of weeping. He was eventually succeeded by a man named Parker who conducted his classes with a ferocious cane in hand.

'When Parker appeared armed with a long lithe chestnut colored oriental cane, which had evidently cost much more than a penny, and slashed our hand with it mercilessly, he established an unprecedented terrorism. He was young (really too young), darkly handsome: apparently a perfect Murdstone. But he soon found that he was carrying his youthful terroristic logic too far ... he had what no schoolmaster should allow himself to indulge: a dislike of stupid boys as such.'

To his biographers, G.B.S. represented Sonny at school as 'rampant, voluble, impudent ... a most obstreperous player of rough games ... [who] avoided his school tasks ... and was soon given up as incorrigible'. That was how he had felt: it was not how he appeared to others. He was remembered as a quiet boy and on two occasions was awarded good conduct certificates. The other boys liked him for his comic stories about a character called Lobjort borrowed from *Household Words*, but otherwise his remote personality, designed to protect him from unhappiness at home, did not make him popular. His command of long words gave him an air of maturity that appealed more to adults than to children. He seemed unfitted for boy society. 'I think my treatment as an adult at home (like the Micawbers' treatment of David Copperfield) made school very difficult for me.'

The roll books at Wesley show that after only three months in 1865 he was taken away and did not return there until August 1867. After another three months he left again, then came back in February 1868 for nine months. During one or more of these intervals he attended a preparatory school at 23–24 Sandycove Road, Glasthule, near Dalkey.

'My parents,' Shaw wrote, ' ... acted as if ... I would come out as an educated gentleman if I wore the usual clothes, ate the usual food, and went to the same school or other every day.' But by the end of 1868 he had fallen so far behind that he was withdrawn altogether from the Wesleyan Connexional.

It was Lee, rather than Sonny's parents, who took the initiative. He had got to know the drawing-master at the Central Model Boys' School in Marlborough Street, Joseph Smeeth, who persuaded him that the teaching there was better than at any other of the cheaper genteel schools in Dublin. By the beginning of February 1869, Sonny was sent to Marlborough Street, where he remained a little over seven months. He was to focus on this school almost all the unhappiness of his boyhood. The Central Model Boys' School, he wrote, was 'undenominational and classless in theory but in fact Roman Catholic ... It was an enormous place, with huge unscaleable railings and gates on which for me might well have been inscribed "All hope abandon, ye who enter here"; for that the son of a Protestant merchant-gentleman and feudal downstart should pass those bars or associate in any way with its hosts of lower middle class Catholic children, sons of petty shopkeepers and tradesmen, was inconceivable from the Shaw point of view ... I lost caste outside it and became a boy with whom no Protestant young gentleman would speak or play.'

The enrolment books of the Central Model show that Sonny's form contained eight members of the Established Protestant Church, only five Roman Catholics and one 'Other Denomination'. Fathers' occupations included a hotel porter, two carpenters, a farmer, butcher, solicitor, brick-layer, shopkeeper, hatter, sergeant and gaol warder. It was, in fact as well as theoretically, what Shaw denied it to have been: a non-sectarian experimental school for persons of modest means. What Shaw did, many years afterwards, was to transfer to this place the 'shame and wounded snobbery' arising from his Catholic-infested home at Hatch Street.

When Sonny asked to be taken away from school, George Carr Shaw, relishing perhaps the defeat of Lee's programme, supported him. Sonny left the Central Model on 11 September 1869 and was transferred to the last of his boy prisons. The Dublin English Scientific and Commercial Day School was a large building with broad staircases and stately rooms on the corner of Aungier and Whitefriars Streets, sponsored by the Incorporated Society for Promoting English Protestant Schools in Ireland. Sonny remained here almost two years and became joint head boy. But his repugnance for all schools was implacable.

*

Sonny made one friend at the Dublin Commercial School. Matthew Edward McNulty, later to become a novelist, bank manager and play-wright, was 'a corpulent youth with curly black hair'. His first sight of Sonny, at the age of thirteen, was of 'a tallish, slender youngster with straw-colored hair, light greyish-blue eyes, a skin like that of a baby and lips like those of a beautiful girl. There was a faint smile over his face as he listened to his companions and looked around the strange class room ... We were, in fact, friends at first glance.'

McNulty was the only person with whom Sonny could share his dreams and ideas. When apart they entered into a tremendous correspondence, full of drawings and dramas.

Sonny dreamed of being a great man, probably a great artist like Michelangelo. He borrowed Duchesne's outlines of the Old Masters, bought the Bohn translation of Vasari, prowled for hours through Dublin's deserted National Gallery dragging McNulty with him – two schoolboys, one short and dark, the other tall and fair, going from picture to picture, full of argument, until they knew every work there. They also enrolled together for late afternoon courses at the Royal Dublin Society's School of Art and passed examinations in perspective, practical geometry and freehand drawing. But Sonny was not satisfied and, taking McNulty back to his room in Hatch Street, he announced a bolder plan. 'I was to be his naked model,' McNulty remembered, 'and, in return, he was to be mine . . . but I was adamant and Shaw's long-cherished dream of an inexpensive model was rudely shattered. I was very sorry for him at the time but I would have been more sorry for myself if I had had another attack of bronchitis.'

Sonny eventually renounced the artist's life because 'I could not draw'. He had decided instead, he told McNulty, to found a new religion.

At an early age Sonny had tried to build a fanciful world in which to forget the miseries of the real one – 'a sort of pale blue satin place,' as Broadbent describes it at the end of *John Bull's Other Island*. This dream of heaven presented itself as a small square apartment in which he was sitting with his ankles dangling, poorly dressed and filled with fears because

'I knew that I should presently be brought up for judgment by the recording angel before some awful person in the next room; and I had good private reasons for anticipating that my career would not be found up to the mark . . . on the only occasion on which I ever dreamt myself in heaven, I was glad when I woke. I also dreamt once that I was in hell; but I remember nothing about that except that two of my uncles were there and that it did not hurt. In my waking hours I thought of heaven as a part of the sky where people were dressed in white, had golden harps, did not eat or drink or learn lessons, and were wholly preoccupied in being intensely good.'

When very young he had used the Lord's Prayer as a spell against thunderstorms. But one evening on Torca Hill 'I suddenly asked myself why I went on repeating my prayer every night when, as I put it, I did not believe in it. Being thus brought to book by my intellectual conscience

I felt obliged in common honesty to refrain from superstitious practices.' By the third night, he tells us, his discomfiture vanished 'as completely as if I had been born a heathen . . . this sacrifice of the grace of God, as I had been taught it, to intellectual integrity synchronized with the dawning of moral passion in me which I have described in the first act of *Man and Superman*.'

What Sonny had done was to transfer his religious energy from day-dreaming to his actual life. He had come to recognize that, as an unlovable boy, he could expect nothing from other people. His 'moral passion' was a means of producing, independently of other people, the self-respect he lacked. Though he might not make himself into the sort of person his mother loved, he could become the sort of person she was: insensible to public opinion and a Bohemian without Bohemian vices. Before this 'I was such a ridiculously sensitive child,' he wrote, 'that almost any sort of rebuff that did not enrage me hurt my feelings and made me cry'. This new-found Stoicism reached its heretical peak in 1875 with a letter he wrote to *Public Opinion* attacking the Moody and Sankey revivalist meetings then being celebrated in Dublin. He ridiculed the vanity of their 'awakenings' which created 'highly objectionable members of society', and announced that he had given up religion.

He was by this time a committed Shelleyan. Shelley, who was to make Shaw into a momentary anarchist and lifetime vegetarian, cleared away the refuse of supernatural religions and prepared him for the planting of Creative Evolution. Sonny was a voluminous reader. Before he was ten he was saturated in Shakespeare and the Bible. But he had no access to a library and no money with which to buy books. Nobody at Hatch Street read. Lee, who made a habit of falling asleep at night over Tyndall on Sound, had been perplexed at hearing that Carlyle was an author and not Dublin's Lord Lieutenant, the Earl of Carlisle, and was puzzled by his failure to find, even in the large-print edition of Shakespeare, *The School for Scandal*. But his pupils often presented him with books – anything from Byron's works to Lord Derby's translation of Homer's *Iliad* – and to these were added pirated editions of novels brought back from America by Walter Gurly.

Sonny read all of these. He relished *The Arabian Nights*, *The Pilgrim's Progress*, *The Ancient Mariner*, *John Gilpin*, and fled from his own life into the adventures of Scott and Dumas. 'The falsifications of romance are absolutely necessary to enable people to bear or even to apprehend the terrors of life. Only the very strongest characters can look the facts of life in the face.' But he was determined to become one of this band of 'strongest characters' and started choosing his books accordingly. 'At twelve or thereabouts,' he remembered, 'I began to disapprove of highwaymen on moral grounds and to read Macaulay, George Eliot, Shakespeare, Dickens and so on in the ordinary sophisticated attitude.' He went through John Stuart Mill's autobiography, studied Lewes's *Life of Goethe* and every translation of *Faust* he could lay his hands on. 'No child should be shielded from mischief and danger, either physical or moral, in the library or out of it. Such protection leaves them incapable of resistance when they are exposed, as they finally must be, to all the mischief and danger of the world.'

Shaw's ingenious form of self-protection is best seen in his use of Dickens and Shakespeare. Beginning as a Dickensian disciple, he went on to convert Dickens, as the unconscious prophet of revolution, into an early attempt by the Life Force to produce an authentic Shavian. This sympathetic feeling sprang from the comparison he made between their early unhappiness, and the theatrical methods by which they later superimposed success upon unhappiness. Shaw wrote of his time at the Central Model School as being equivalent to 'what the blacking warehouse was to Dickens'; and his description of Dickens's outward life as 'a feat of acting from beginning to end' is a variation of his self-portrait: 'the real Shaw is the actor, the imaginary Shaw the real one.' By converting his schooldays into a Dickensian episode he gave them a sense of drama and a context in which they could be treated with humorous detachment. This was the power of comedy.

For a time he replaced his own life with the fictions of Dickens and Shakespeare. He knew some of Shakespeare's plays by heart. 'Hamlet and Falstaff were more alive to me than any living politician or even any relative.' In the reading of Shakespeare there was all life except the actual presence of the body from which, as a vehicle of emotion, Sonny had become alienated. In separating the word-music from the meaning he was to become, like Ulysses, tied to the mast and listening to the sirens. For Shaw's prejudice was optimism. To expose yourself to feel what wretches feel could lead to the 'barren pessimism' that Shakespeare himself might survive, but Shaw could not. Shakespeare's celebration of the splendours and miseries of sexual love paralysed Shaw who described it as 'folly gone mad erotically', and used all his wit and critical intelligence to reduce it to 'platitudinous fudge'. He could allow himself to respond to the passionate language only by insisting that it swept literature 'to a plane on which sense is drowned in sound'. So Sonny listened and was comforted by these sounds that filled the place of his captivity.

7

MUSIC IN DUBLIN

Without music we shall surely perish of drink, morphia, and all sorts of
artificial exaggerations of the cruder delights of the senses.
'The Religion of the Pianoforte', *Fortnightly Review* (February 1894)

'My university has three colleges,' Shaw used to say. They were Dalkey
Hill, the National Gallery, and Lee's Amateur Musical Society. Hatch
Street was full of music. 'I was within earshot of a string of musical
masterpieces,' Shaw wrote, 'which were rehearsed in our house right up
to the point of the full choral & orchestral rehearsals.' Before he was
fifteen he knew Beethoven's Mass in C, Mendelssohn's *Athalie*, Handel's
Messiah, Verdi's *Trovatore*, Donizetti's *Lucrezia* and above all Mozart's
Don Giovanni from cover to cover. After seeing Gounod's *Faust*, he decorated the walls of his room at Dalkey with watercolour heads of
Mephistopheles. 'We made of Mephistopheles a familiar, almost living
character,' McNulty recalled.

In music Sonny's senses came alive. He felt he was experiencing all
manner of impossible emotions: the 'candour and gallant impulse of the
hero, the grace and trouble of the heroine, and the extracted quintessence
of their love'. But he could neither play nor read a note of music, for
'nobody dreamt of teaching me anything'. When an amateur player named
Phipps offered to teach him the oboe, George Carr Shaw objected that
the price of an oboe and tuition fees put it out of the question. Sonny
did what he could. Presented by one of his uncles with an ancient cornet-
à-piston ('absolutely the very worst and oldest cornet then in existence'),
he took lessons twice a week from an English guardsman, walking to his
house in Mount Pleasant Street with the obsolete instrument wrapped up
in brown paper under his arm.

'My elder sister had a beautiful voice,' Shaw wrote. '. . . it cost her no
effort to sing or play anything she had once heard, or to read any music
at sight.' This contrast to himself irked Shaw. Lucy sang, he wrote,
'without the slightest effort and without the slightest point, and was all
the more desperately vapid because she suggested artistic gifts wasting in
complacent abeyance'.

Although it was Agnes of the hazel eyes and gorgeous curtain of red
hair who received most attention within Hatch Street, Lucy was the
star. Her expression charmed and interested people, and she had a faint
resemblance to Ellen Terry to which she drew attention by wearing

25

Lyceum-style clothes and feather hats. One of her admirers was Sonny's friend McNulty who later 'asked her to marry me: but she refused on the grounds that she was five years older: and that when I was forty-five she would be "a white haired old woman of fifty". So, that little romance faded.' Away from home, she was 'everybody's darling,' Shaw wrote: 'she broke many hearts, but never her own.' She longed not for a lover, but for a mother and father: a family. Not finding one, she affected a defensively low opinion of men. 'Brothers don't matter to their sisters,' Shaw commented; 'at least I didn't matter to mine: it is the stranger who is loved. The natural dislike for near relatives is ordained to save frightful complications. So presto vivace . . . and away with melancholy!'

Italian opera seemed what Lucy was heading for even before she sang Amina in Lee's production, at the Theatre Royal, Dublin, of Bellini's *La Sonnambula*. Lee had begun to organize musical evenings in the Antient Concert Room at 42¹/₂ Great Brunswick Street. These were often in aid of hospitals and would include a popular overture, some ballads and choruses, and the strengthening contribution from a regimental band. For the Shakespeare Tercentenary of 1864, having worked up a programme of Purcell and Schubert, Lee emerged at the head of his Amateur Musical Society as an orchestral conductor. He had no scholarship but, conducting from a first violin or vocal score, gave the right time to the band. 'There was practically no music in Dublin except the music he manufactured,' Shaw wrote.

'He kept giving concerts . . . and he had to provide all the singers for them. If he heard a flute mourning or a fiddle scraping in a house as he walked along the street, he knocked at the door & said "You come along & play in my orchestra." If a respectable citizen came for twelve lessons to entertain small tea parties, he presently had that amazed gentleman, scandalous in tights & tunic, singing as "il rio di Luna" to my mother's Azucena, or Alfonso to her Lucrezia, as the case might be. He coached them into doing things utterly beyond their natural powers.'

'This favourite Society,' reported the *Irish Times* on 30 May 1865, ' . . . includes many of the most distinguished amateur vocalists in the city . . . On few occasions has the Ancient Concert's Music Hall contained a larger and more fashionable attendance . . . and the concert was in every respect most judiciously carried out.' This was typical of the notices that the Amateur Musical Society received in the late 1860s. But Lee wanted to conduct oratorio festivals and operas; and his ambitions were set upon London.

*

It was probably in 1869 that Lee first began to dream of a conquest of London. He appears to have taken Bessie Shaw into his confidence. On 30 October that year Bessie and her brother made an agreement with their father whereby the son received £2,500 (equivalent to £97,500 in 1997) and Bessie £1,500 paid to her at the rate of £100 a year 'for her own sole and separate use and free from the debts control or engagements of her husband'. This was in addition to £400 settled on Agnes either through the estate of Ellen Whitcroft or Mrs Shaw's own trust of 1852. Bessie now had the maximum financial independence it was in her power to command.

Six weeks later, Lee published a book entitled *The Voice: Its Artistic Production, Development, and Preservation*. Encased between heavy dark green boards elaborately stamped in gold, with a woodcut on its cover from Maclise's *Origins of the Harp*, this volume of 130 pages of 'agreeably tinted' paper represented Lee's passport to a larger musical world. It had been ghosted, Shaw tells us, 'by a scamp of a derelict doctor whom he entertained for that purpose' – probably Malachi J. Kilgarriff, Demonstrator at the Ledwich School of Anatomy, a Catholic and one-time neighbour of Lee's in Harrington Street.

Not long after this, while still thirteen, Sonny was sent off to be interviewed by a firm of cloth merchants, Scott, Spain & Rooney, on one of Dublin's quays. His employment in the warehouse loading bales was on the point of being settled when the senior partner walked in and declared that 'I was too young, and that the work was not suitable to me. He evidently considered that my introducer, my parents, and his young partner, had been inconsiderate . . . I have not forgotten his sympathy.'

Unable to convert him from an expenditure at school to a source of income in the warehouse, they had failed to get him off their hands. He returned for another year to the Dublin English and Scientific Commercial Day School. Then, through the influence of his Uncle Frederick he was found employment as office boy in a 'leading and terribly respectable' firm of land agents, Uniacke Townshend & Co. He started work there on 26 October 1871 with an annual salary of £18 (equivalent to £875 in 1997). He was no longer Sonny to his family, but the name he most loathed: George.

Six weeks later an odd, apparently insignificant thing happened: Lee changed his name. In all press notices and legal documents he had been George J. Lee, the J. sometimes appearing as John. After 2 December 1871 the J. is replaced by a V. often lengthened to Vandeleur. This flowering of his name coincided with a fresh thrust to his musical ambitions. Since the publication of *The Voice*, Lee had been extending his Society beyond the giving of charitable concerts for the poor – increasing his advertisements in the press together with the number and glory of his patrons which, by 1871, included His Excellency the Lord Lieutenant. He had by now begun producing Italian Opera (mixed into the menu with burlesque and miscellaneous band music) at the Theatre Royal and the newly opened Gaiety Theatre – taking these productions on tour to Limerick and Cork, and making a reconnaissance himself to London.

The opposition to Lee was led by Sir Robert Prescott Stewart, an ambitious academic who had won many prizes for his glees and rose to become the most highly regarded Irish musician of his day. Stewart made his first move in the summer of 1871 – persuading the more eminent members of Lee's committee to resign. At a meeting on 11 November, following the congratulations on increased membership and money, the *Irish Times* reported that 'some misunderstanding has arisen as to members of the Society performing in English or other operas at the theatre [the Theatre Royal], and in consequence of which a considerable number of the committee refused to offer themselves for re-election'.

Lee acted immediately. He reconstituted his Society into the Amateur Musical, Operatic and Dramatic Society, replaced the various Lords and Generals with a sixteen-man Committee that included a Colonel, two Majors and ten Captains, and announced: A GRAND MILITARY, DRAMATIC AND OPERATIC PERFORMANCE WILL BE GIVEN AT THE NEW GAIETY THEATRE.

In January 1872, Lee transformed his amateurs into the New Philharmonic Society – a title that signalled his ambition to replace the almost fifty-year-old Philharmonic – and, under one title or another, led them indefatigably through concerts, oratorio festivals and truncated operas. Bessie, as his musical adjutant, was indispensable to him, arranging orchestral accompaniments, copying out band parts, composing songs ('The Parting Hour', 'The Night is Closing Round, Mother') under the *nom de plume* 'Hilda' and singing with what the *Irish Times* described as 'artistic grace and expression'. Her voice, which 'never expressed eroticism', was particularly thrilling in the interpretation of songs about bereaved lovers seeking reunion in the next world.

So successful had Lee become that on 19 September he bought the lease of Torca Cottage (which up to then he had merely rented). Though many of his concerts were advertised as being in aid of charity, only what was termed 'the Surplus' found its way to various hospitals. This usually amounted to about £25 – whereas Lee himself, so John O'Donovan has calculated, 'would have pocketed a sum not far off £200 for each concert'.

Early in 1873 Lee fulfilled one of his major ambitions by conducting the Dublin Musical Festival. 'The crowds of persons who besieged each portion of the hall soon filled to its utmost capacity, every particle of available space obtainable . . . the large doors leading into the building at the end of the Hall had to be thrown open and numbers were content to obtain standing room in the outer galleries,' reported the *Irish Times*. After congratulating Lee on his splendid results, the reviewer predicted that with patience he would surely 'reap the rewards his energies and abilities deserve'.

Eager for these rewards, Lee prominently advertised two benefit concerts of 'Amateur Italian Opera' for himself and the leader of his orchestra, the violinist R. M. Levey, in late March or early April. But Robert Prescott Stewart was already at work; with his encouragement the debenture holders availed themselves of their right to one free ticket and crowded the theatre. On 5 April, Lee and Levey published a sarcastic announcement in the *Irish Times* in which they begged 'to return their grateful thanks (?) to the many debenture holders who honoured their BENEFIT . . . by making use of their FREE admissions'.

The deciding battle was fought over the 1873 Exhibition the following month. In his opening concert, Lee, having assembled a combined chorus and orchestra of over five hundred, gave a performance of Mendelssohn's *Athalie*. Three thousand or more people attended the Concert Hall and the *Irish Times* reported that 'the five hundred voices blended most harmoniously'. Stewart was in the audience and next day in the *Daily Express* he published a scathing criticism of the performance, anonymously. Although Mr Lee had been 'heartily applauded' by his own chorus, Stewart concluded: 'Indiscriminate praise is worthless, and e'er long, heartily despised, even by those who are the objects of it.' In private Stewart was more outspoken. On page 50 of his copy of *The Annals of the Theatre Royal, Dublin*, he noted in the margin next to Lee's name: 'an impostor, who traded successfully on the vanity of amateur singers: he had a few aliases; now Mr Geo. Lee; again Mr Geo. J. Lee: and also J. Vandeleur Lee; at last he was Vandeleur Lee simply'. In a letter to Joseph Robinson, he admitted: 'I did in my time one good work in Dublin. I unmasked one arrant impostor and drove him away.'

The details of this 'unmasking' are unknown. On 26 May Lee gave his last concert in Dublin. The attendance was disappointing. At the beginning of June, having abruptly cancelled another concert, he left Dublin for ever and his place as conductor of the New Philharmonic was taken by Sir Robert Prescott Stewart.

Lee had gone to London. A few days later, on 17 June, her twenty-first wedding anniversary, Bessie Shaw followed him, taking Agnes on the boat with her, and at Hatch Street 'all musical activity ceased'.

8

MARKING TIME

The worst sin towards our fellow creatures is not to hate them, but to be indifferent to them; thats the essence of inhumanity.

The Devil's Disciple

'We did not realize, nor did she, that she was never coming back.' But there was much that the young George must have realized, and the later Shaw misremembered. The only suggestion that he had known of Lee's losing battle with Stewart is an acknowledgement in the 1935 Preface to *London Music* that 'Lee became the enemy of every teacher of singing in Dublin; and they reciprocated heartily'. But he gave as the reason for Lee's departure from Ireland his having reached the Dublin limit of excellence: 'Dublin in those days seemed a hopeless place for an artist; for no success counted except a London success.'

In the Shavian version, therefore, 'Lee did not depart suddenly from Dublin . . . there was nothing whatever sudden or unexpected about it.' George obviously knew that his mother had left within a fortnight of Lee but in answer to one of his biographers Shaw wrote: 'As to your question whether Lee's move to London and my mother's were simultaneous, they could not have been. Lee had to make his position in London before he could provide the musical setting for my mother and sister. But the break-up of the family was an economic necessity anyhow, because without Lee we could not afford to keep up the house.' It was towards this 'economic necessity' Shaw pointed his biographers.

'My father's business was not prospering: it was slowly dying. Then there was my eldest sister Lucy . . . She seemed to have a future as a prima donna; and this was about the only future that presented itself as an alternative to a relapse into squalid poverty, and the abandonment of the musical activity which had come to be my mother's whole life.

There was only one solution possible, granting that my mother and father could be quite as happy apart as together, to say the least. Lee was soon able to report a success: all the West End clamoring for lessons at a guinea, and his house in Park Lane a fashionable musical centre. This was clearly the opening for Lucy. It did not take very long for my mother to make up her mind. She sold up Hatch St., after a reconnaissance in London; settled my father and myself in furnished lodgings; and took a house for herself and her two daughters in Victoria Grove, Fulham Road . . . a couple of miles from Park Lane.'

As to George Carr Shaw: 'I should think it was the happiest time of his life.'

When Lee arrived in London he put up in lodgings at Ebury Street where he remained a year. A mile away, at 13 Victoria Grove, Bessie and Agnes were presently joined by Lucy. Though Bessie continued to sing and work for Lee, who was in and out of Victoria Grove very much in the old fashion, it was probably important that they lived apart. According to McNulty, George Carr Shaw initiated court proceedings citing Lee 'not as a criminal offender against the sacredness of Holy Matrimony but rather as an object of jealousy to the Petitioner'. Their 'reconnaissance', as Shaw calls it, lasted nine months during which time they were paying the rent for two separate premises in addition to the rent at Hatch Street which must partly invalidate the argument of 'economic necessity'. It was not until the beginning of March 1874 that Bessie returned to Dublin to sell up the furniture in Hatch Street, raise what money she could, and move her husband and son into rooms at 61 Harcourt Street. Then for the last time she left Dublin with her two daughters and returned to London. Perhaps because of some out-of-court arrangement with George Carr Shaw who agreed to pay her one pound a week, she did not live at the same address as Lee. In April he was to cut his last connection with Ireland by selling the lease of Torca Cottage to a musical colleague, Julian Marshall, from whom he afterwards rented 13 Park Lane in London.

The departure of his mother and Lee was a tragedy for young George. From the pictures in the National Gallery, the hills and bays of Dalkey and Killiney, the music that filled Hatch Street he had woven 'a sort of heaven which made the material squalor of my existence as nothing'. Shaw represents this daydream world as having been extinguished when he was ten, but the evidence suggests that, especially in his ambitions to be an artist or musician, they persisted until his mother finally left him at the age of sixteen. Instead of an artist, he was a clerk; he would enjoy no more summers at Torca; and 'I heard no more music'.

But his mother had not sold the piano. So he bought a technical handbook and taught himself the alphabet of musical notation. He learnt the keyboard from a diagram; then he got out his mother's vocal score of *Don Giovanni* and arranged his fingers on the notes of the first chord. This took ten minutes, 'but when it sounded right at last, it was worth all the trouble it cost'. What he suffered, 'what everybody in the house suffered, whilst I struggled on . . . will never be told'. But he acquired what he wanted: 'the power to take a vocal score and learn its contents as if I had heard it rehearsed by my mother and her colleagues'. From this practice and his reading of textbooks, he also mastered the technical knowledge he would need to become a music critic in London. It was a wonderful example of the advantages of deprivation.

His desk and cash box at the 'highly exclusive gentlemanly estate office' gave him 'the habit of daily work'. For fifteen months, during which his salary was increased from £18 to £24, he filed and manufactured copies of the firm's business letters, kept a postage account, bought penny rolls for the staff's lunch and combined the duties of office with errand boy. In February 1873, after the cashier absconded, George was employed as a substitute. The work gave him no difficulty. 'I, who never knew how much money I had of my own (except when the figure was zero), proved a model of accuracy as to the money of others.' His salary doubled to £48. He bought himself a tailed coat, remodelled his sloped and straggled handwriting into an imitation of his predecessor's compact script and 'in short, I made good in spite of myself'.

He became accustomed to handling large sums of money, and to collecting weekly rents by tram each Tuesday, tiny sums from slum dwellers in Terenure – an experience he had not forgotten when he came to write *Widowers' Houses*. But 'my heart was not in the thing'. He was never uncivil, never happy. He felt orphaned. Thirty-five years later he poured out his bitterness through the nameless clerk in *Misalliance* who seeks to avenge his mother's shame of bearing him out of wedlock:

'I spend my days from nine to six – nine hours of daylight and fresh air – in a stuffy little den counting another man's money . . . I enter and enter, and add and add, and take money and give change, and fill cheques and stamp receipts; and not a penny of that money is my own: not one of those transactions has the smallest interest for me . . . Of all the damnable waste of human life that ever was invented, clerking is the very worst.'

Uniacke Townshend 'was saturated with class feeling which I loathed'. The office was overstaffed with gentleman apprentices, mostly university men, who had paid large premiums for the privilege of learning a genteel profession and who were called Mister while George was plain Shaw. It was his involuntary feeling of inferiority among these colleagues that drove him to excel.

Art was the great solvent of bigotries and snobberies. George found he was most popular with the apprentices in his role as *maestro di cappella*. In his imagination he had become a Lee-like presence, replacing Townshend, and providing the young men there with operatic tuition as value for their premiums. 'I recall one occasion,' he wrote, 'when an apprentice, perched on the washstand with his face shewing above the screen . . . sang *Ah, che la morte* so passionately that he was unconscious of the sudden entry of the senior partner, Charles Uniacke Townshend, who stared stupended at the bleating countenance above the screen, and finally fled upstairs, completely beaten by the situation.' This represented a victory for George over Townshend whom, McNulty recalled, he disliked 'chiefly because he put an "H" in his name, flagrant evidence, in Shaw's opinion, of middle class snobbery'. Townshend was 'a pillar of the Church, of the Royal Dublin Society, and of everything else pillarable in Dublin'.

In his need for someone to look up to and learn from he had fastened at Harcourt Street on another Superman. Chichester Bell took the place of Lee in George's life. He was a far more sophisticated man: physician, chemist, amateur boxer and accomplished pianist. Where other boys collected stamps or trailed girls, George lusted after information. With Bell, who was responsible for converting him to Wagner, George studied everything from physics to pathology, universal alphabets and 'Visible Speech', and completed his education in Ireland.

He saw almost no one else, for he was intensely shy. 'I had no love affairs,' he confessed to Frank Harris. Late in 1877 Shaw came across a letter he had written to Agnes, describing what he was to call 'The Calypso Infatuation', and referring to a girl he had met in 1871. He does not seem to have fallen in love with her until the beginning of May 1875 when he was almost nineteen. A retrospective diary note he made under the heading 'The Lxxx [Love] Episode', in which he records burning his letter to Agnes two days after finding it, ends with 'The Catastrophe, or the indiscretion of No. 2', and is dated at 'about the beginning of August'. He celebrated this aborted romance with a hymn to stupidity. The 'indiscretion of No. 2' may have been her scheme to engage him to a sister after her own marriage to another man, for the poem tells that 'she succumbed to the cruel old fashion' and went to live with her husband not far from Torca Cottage. The poem ends with a tribute to the spell she had laid on him.

> I thought her of women the rarest
> With strange power to seduce and alarm
> One beside whose black tresses the fairest
> Seemed barren of charm . . .
> Then farewell, oh bewitching Calypso
> Thou didst shake my philosophy well
> But believe me, the next time I trip so
> No poem shall tell.

He felt most when he was rejected, because that was the only love he knew. But he recoiled from searching for happiness in others because their rejection of him carried behind it the annihilating force of his mother's initial rejection.

Work became his mistress. He kept no other company. McNulty, who was employed by a bank, had been sent to Newry. 'Shaw wrote to me every day. Otherwise I was absolutely alone.' The written word was threaded into their friendship. At school some of their favourite reading had been a boys' paper called *Young Men of Great Britain*. McNulty recalled that 'it was meat and drink to us and almost as vital to our existence as the air. We awaited each weekly instalment with feverish impatience.' Here Shaw sent a dramatic short story, involving piracy and highway robbery, that had as its main character a wicked baritone with a gun. He also wrote, in September 1868, asking a question, to which the answer was: 'Write to Mr Lacey, theatrical publisher, Strand, London W. C.' A neighbour remembered him sitting alone 'absorbed in the construction of a toy theatre'. He had a play (perhaps part of *Henry VI*) for this theatre about the fifteenth-century Irish rebel Jack Cade, for which he would cut out scenes and characters bought at a shop opposite the Queen's Theatre. Among his own early works was a gory verse drama, 'Strawberrinos: or, the Haunted Winebin', full of extravagant adventures in which our hero Strawberrinos is constantly bested by a Mephistophelean demon.

At the Theatre Royal in Dublin he had been used to seeing pantomimes, farces and melodramas involving villainous disguises and the convolutions of dense intrigue. In 1870 the great touring actor, Barry Sullivan, had arrived. George joined the crowds, emerging from the theatre with 'all my front buttons down the middle of my back'. Of all the travelling stars, Sullivan seemed to him incomparably the grandest. A man of gigantic personality, he was the last in a dynasty of rhetorical and hyperbolical actors that had begun with Burbage.

'His stage fights in Richard III and Macbeth appealed irresistibly to a boy spectator like myself: I remember one delightful evening when two inches of Macbeth's sword, a special fighting sword carried in that scene only, broke off and whizzed over the heads of the cowering pit (there were no stalls then) to bury itself deep in the front of the dress circle after giving those who sat near its trajectory more of a thrill than they had bargained for. Barry Sullivan was a tall powerful man with a cultivated resonant voice: his stage walk was the perfection of grace and dignity; and his lightning swiftness of action, as when in the last scene of Hamlet he shot up the stage and stabbed the king four times before you could wink, all

provided a physical exhibition which attracted audiences quite independently of the play . . .'

This was not a spectacle to George, but an experience. He could feel his
blood quickening during the performance, his mind beating, hurrying.
This was vicarious living at its most vigorous, where 'existence touches
you delicately to the very heart, and where mysteriously thrilling people,
secretly known to you in dreams of your childhood, enact a life in which
terrors are as fascinating as delights; so that ghosts and death, agony and
sin, became, like love and victory, phases of an unaccountable ecstasy'. He
forgot loneliness in this palace of dreams. When he came to write plays
himself, he instinctively went back to the grand manner and heroic stage
business he had seen from the pit of the Theatre Royal.

In 1874 George spent his summer holidays at Newry with his friend
McNulty. McNulty had developed what he called 'a morbid condition of
nerves'. He was so sensitive to the earth's rotation that he could not trust
himself to lie down on a sofa without falling off. 'I fancied I could see
the sap circulating in plants and trees,' he wrote. George's scepticism,
though not always comfortable, helped to reduce this tension. On their
second day the two of them had their photographs taken and they talked
of the inevitability of fame. Every evening they would write something
different – 'a short story, a comedy, a tragedy, a burlesque and so forth,'
McNulty remembered, 'and the real joy of the event lay in reading and
forcefully criticizing each other's work. This series we called: "The Newry
Nights' Entertainment".'

The following year McNulty was transferred back to Dublin and the
two of them saw a good deal of each other. McNulty would call round at
Harcourt Street to stagger through duets on the grand piano. George, he
observed, 'took little or no notice of his father who still spent his evenings
poring miserably over his account books'. Otherwise, his glasses low on
his nose, his head tilted back, he browsed before a newspaper or smoked his
one clay pipe a day, breaking it when he had finished and throwing the
fragments in the grate: 'a lonely, sad little man,' McNulty concluded.

George had resolved never to allow the diffidence he shared with his
father to cripple him. He looked to his father as a warning; otherwise,
like Lee, he looked to London.

His opportunity came early in 1876. Agnes, suffering from consumption, had been taken down to Balmoral House, a sanatorium on the Isle
of Wight. Though he was now getting £84 a year at Uniacke Townshend,
George felt more than ever unsatisfied there. One of his colleagues, an
old book-keeper, had confided that he 'suffered so much from cold feet
that his life was miserable,' Shaw recorded. 'I, full of the fantastic mis-

chievousness of youth, told him that if he would keep his feet in ice-cold water every morning when he got up for two or three minutes, he would be completely cured.' Shortly afterwards the man died. To his horror George was then offered his job. Charles Townshend wanted to install a relative as cashier and boot George upstairs to make room for him. But George refused and had to be moved, with an increased salary, to the position of general clerk. On 29 February 1876 he gave a month's notice. 'My reason is, that I object to receive a salary for which I give no adequate value,' he wrote. 'Not having enough to do, it follows that the little I have is not well done. When I ceased to act as Cashier I anticipated this, and have since become satisfied that I was right.'

This letter shows the paradoxical device of his new authority. It has the regretful air of an employer dismissing an employee. Its succinct superiority must have been galling. But anxious not to offend George's Uncle Frederick at the Valuation Office, Charles Townshend offered him his job back as cashier. George thanked him – however 'I prefer to discontinue my services'.

In retrospect G.B.S. applied a blinding Shavian polish to his arrival in England. Armed with the English language he proposed to advance on London and become 'a professional man of genius'. 'When I left Dublin I left (a few private friendships apart) no society that did not disgust me,' he wrote. 'To this day my sentimental regard for Ireland does not include the capital. I am not enamored of failure, of poverty, of obscurity, and of the ostracism and contempt which these imply; and these were all that Dublin offered to the enormity of my unconscious ambition.'

'Like Hamlet I lack ambition and its push,' he wrote. Yet it was not ambition he lacked: it was (like Hamlet) advancement. He insisted that he never struggled, but was pushed slowly up by the force of his ability. 'It is not possible to escape from the inexorable obligation to succeed on your own merits,' he confessed. He did not cross the Irish Sea for love of the English. 'Emigration was practically compulsory,' he told St John Ervine.

Agnes died of phthisis on 27 March. Between the two opportunities offered by her death and that of the book-keeper, George had never hesitated. Looking back on his twenty years in Ireland he summed up: 'My home in Dublin was a torture and my school was a prison and I had to go through a treadmill of an office.'

He packed a carpet bag, boarded the North Wall boat and arrived in London. It was a fine spring day and he solemnly drove in a 'growler' from Euston to Victoria Grove. Shortly afterwards he travelled down to Ventnor on the Isle of Wight following Agnes's funeral there. The family selected a headstone and an epitaph to be cut on it: 'TO BE WITH CHRIST WHICH IS FAR BETTER' – from a passage in Paul's Epistle to the Philippians where Paul compares the folly of living with the wisdom of dying. Nearly sixty years later Shaw was to write to Margaret Mackail, exposing what he felt about his own childhood: 'as the world is not at present fit for children to live in why not give the little invalids a gorgeous party, and when they have eaten and danced themselves to sleep, turn on the gas and let them all wake up in heaven?'

TWO

THE GHOSTING OF VANDELEUR LEE

I am afraid you will find London a drearily slow place to make a beginning in. Every opening is an accident; and waiting for accidents is rather discouraging.

Shaw to Rhoda Halkett (14 August 1894)

'Unoccupied': this was the word Shaw used to describe his first summer in London. He gave everyone to understand that 'on no account will I enter an office again'. But by September, he was submitting to a crammer's course for admission to the Civil Service. His mother and Lucy breathed out with relief – then in with alarm as, less than two months later, he gave up this 'tutelage of a grinder' and accepted the occupation of Lee's amanuensis.

Lee's credit with the Shaws had fallen dramatically since they came to London. It appears that, having grown so infatuated that 'he wanted to marry her', Lee was bullying Lucy into acting as the principal singer in a musical society he had started called the Troubadours. Lucy intensely disliked working under Lee's direction, and had written to her brother telling him of a huge rumpus. George, at his most paternal, replied: 'As to Lee, I would decline to listen to him. We all know what his tirades are worth, and I think his coming to Victoria Grove and launching out at you as he did, simply outrageous.' Matters between the pair deteriorated and, before George arrived in London, Lucy wrote to explain that 'Lee and I are bitter enemies now; we are frostily civil to each other's faces, and horribly abusive behind backs'.

Lee was no writer, 'and when he was offered an appointment as musical critic to a paper called *The Hornet* . . . in consideration of his praising the neighbourhood in the newspapers, I had the job of writing the criticisms and the articles,' Shaw explained. 'It was to some extent on my account that he undertook such pretences of authorship.'

Shaw provided *The Hornet* with careful criticism and careful jokes that do not carry the generosity of the mature G.B.S. The concert hall becomes a blackboard on which he scrupulously chalks up his remarks. If his writing is a little priggish, it still achieves wonderful confidence for someone aged twenty-one. Carl Rosa's first violin is accused of having played flat 'from beginning to end'; Herr Behrens is spotted frequently substituting 'semiquaver passages for the triplets' and betraying his ignorance of English by selecting the middle of a phrase as a suitable opportunity to take breath. Shaw castigates the timidity of other music critics twice or three times his age who 'can only judge one performance by reference to another'.

Although there is only a hint of G.B.S. in these apprentice buzzings, some Shavian notes are starting to sound towards the end of his *Hornet* life. Signor Rota is complimented as 'a master of the art of shouting'; and Madame Goddard is recorded as fascinating her hearers 'with a strikingly unpleasant imitation of a bagpipes'. In place of military drum and cymbals, Shaw advises the management of Her Majesty's 'to employ a stage carpenter to bang the orchestra door at a pre-arranged signal'. And after a performance of Donizetti's *Lucia* he deplored the Master of Ravenswood's habit of flinging his cloak and hat on the ground as 'ridiculous in the first act, impolite in the second, and only justified by the prospect of suicide in the third'.

Shaw would hand Lee these criticisms and Lee would hand him the fees, 'contenting himself with the consciousness of doing generously by a young and forlorn literary adventurer, and with the honor and glory accruing from the reputed authorship of my articles'. In later years G.B.S. exaggerated the 'vulgarities, follies, and ineptitudes' of these pieces for *The Hornet*. 'I did not know even enough to understand that what was torturing me was the guilt and shame which attend ignorance and incompetence.' But his shame proceeded less from their demerits than from the deception of ghost writing. He had arrived in London determined never to act on second-hand principles or submit to external circumstances. But in his first encounter he found himself in a conspiracy that formed part of the polite fraud he was attempting to demolish. It felt like a step back into cowardice.

By May 1877 the editor of *The Hornet* believed he had uncovered the truth. 'I have frequently rec'd "copy" palpably not your style,' he complained to Lee, 'but that in composition, idea and writing of a Lady.' By September, all was over. 'I must tell you candidly that *our* agreement is not being kept by you,' the editor told Lee. 'I stipulated for *your* production and not that of a Substitute. I can't insert the class of writing I have rec'd the last 2 weeks . . . Please send word to your man to send no more copy.' Shaw's last sting was delivered on 26 September 1877 when Lee was in Scotland. Two years later he reviewed the episode that had made him so miserable: 'I threw up my studies, and set to work to reform the musical profession. At the end of a year my friend [Lee] was one of the most unpopular men in London, the paper was getting into difficulties, and complications were arising from the proprietor's doubts as to a critic who was not only very severe, but capable of being in two places at the same time.'

*

Lee's faltering career, Shaw believed, 'disguised as it was by a few years of fashionable success, was due wholly to the social conditions which compelled him to be a humbug or to starve'. In order to keep going, he advertised himself as being able to make fashionable ladies sing like Patti in twelve lessons. To Bessie, Lee had been 'the sole apostle of The Method: the only true and perfect method of singing: the method that had made her a singer and preserved the purity of her voice in defiance of time'. She knew that the Method required two years of patient practice. The 'moment she found that he had abandoned "the method",' Shaw wrote, ' . . . she gave him up'.

Shaw gave as the particular cause for breaking with Lee, a sexual sentimentality which, ripening in London, had turned towards Lucy. 'My sister, to whom this new attitude was as odious as it was surprising, immediately dropped him completely . . . He came no more to our house; and as far as I can recollect neither my mother nor my sister ever saw him again.'

To G.B.S., this sexual sentimentality and the economic perversion of his musical talent were symptoms of the same disease. He invented a new Lee, an English Hyde who emerged from the Irish Jekyll. Lee was, he tells us, 'no longer the same man'. He was unrecognizable. 'G. J. Lee, with the black whiskers and the clean shaven resolute lip and chin, became Vandeleur Lee, whiskerless, but with a waxed and pointed moustache and an obsequious attitude.' So the Dublin genius collapses into a London humbug. Lee is the victim of a pantomime with Capitalism its bad fairy.

Lucy quickly escaped. She turned professional in 1879 and five years later joined the Carl Rosa Opera Company. For her mother, now nearing fifty, it was less easy. Though she 'despised' Lee, it is impossible to know in what measure her contempt was emotional, financial or moral. Her son makes it exclusively a matter of musical principle. But the language he uses carries other suggestions. 'The result was almost a worse disillusion than her marriage . . . that Lee should be unfaithful! unfaithful to the Method! . . . with all the virtue gone out of him: this was the end of all things; and she never forgave it.'

A symbol of Lee's days of vanity in London was his smart Park Lane house. Number 13 Park Lane lay at the less fashionable end of a street 'sacred to peers and millionaires'. It was half a house (part of number 14) and, because of a murder committed there two years before Lee moved in, less expensive than Shaw imagined. Here, Lee organized a few charity concerts and performances of amateur opera, and it was at one of these that the *Punch* cartoonist George du Maurier, making some sketches of the Shaws and what G.B.S. was to describe as their 'damaged Svengali', conceived his idea for *Trilby*. When, in 1895, du Maurier's novel was adapted for the stage, Shaw was to write:

'Svengali is *not* a villain, but only a poor egotistical wretch who provokes people to pull his nose . . . Imagine, above all, Svengali taken seriously at his own foolish valuation, blazed upon with limelights, spreading himself intolerably over the whole play with nothing fresh to add to the first five minutes of him – Svengali defying heaven, declaring that henceforth he is his own God, and then tumbling down in a paroxysm of heart disease (the blasphemer rebuked, you see), and having to be revived by draughts of brandy . . . surely even the public would just as soon – nay, rather – have the original Svengali, the luckless artist-cad (a very deplorable type of cad, whom Mr du Maurier has hit off to the life).'

Shaw was to try his own hand at creating such a figure in *The Doctor's Dilemma*.

By the time Shaw finished with *The Hornet*, his mother had left Park Lane and, appropriating 'the Method' (much as Eliza Doolittle threatens to make off with Professor Higgins's speech methods), set herself up as a private singing teacher. But Shaw 'remained on friendly terms' with Lee, playing the piano at some of his rehearsals and saving him the cost of a professional accompanist. Once or twice he even sang. Those smart people who had taken Lee up on his arrival in London had moved on to newer sensations, and his later recruits were less exalted. Shaw, who had begun by playing Mozart, ended by rehearsing the Solicitor in Gilbert and Sullivan's *Patience*.

Lee continued living with 'the young lady who had rescued him from entire loneliness', renting his rooms to bachelors and the music chamber for dubious supper parties. He kept in touch with Shaw, offering him odd jobs as *répétiteur* for the occasional lady who wished 'to try over her songs' and asking him to draw up a Prospectus on 'How to Cure Clergyman's Sore Throat'. On the evening of 27 November 1886, while putting his arm through the sleeve of his nightshirt, he dropped dead.

On the morning of the inquest, three days later, one of Lee's musical group told Lucy the news and she passed it on to her brother. Next day, 1 December, he called at 13 Park Lane to verify the report. 'Heard from servant,' he noted in his diary, 'that he was found dead of heart disease on Sunday morning. Went back home to tell Mother . . .' At the inquest on

30 November the jury returned a verdict of death by natural causes. Shaw, who had not gone to this inquest, adds that it 'revealed the fact that his brain was diseased and had been so for a long time'. Neither the newspaper reports nor the death certificate ('Angina Pectoris. Found dead on floor') corroborate this statement which nevertheless enabled Shaw to comfort himself that the mischief converting Lee from Jekyll to Hyde had begun its work years before. 'I was glad to learn that his decay was pathological as well as ecological,' he concluded, 'and that the old efficient and honest Lee had been real after all.'

2

EXPERIMENTS WITH THE NOVEL

What inexpensive pleasure can be greater than that of strolling through London of an evening, and reconstructing it in imagination? . . . you make Notting Hill low and exalt Maida-vale by carting the one to the other . . . you extend the embankment from Blackfriars to the Tower as an eligible nocturnal promenade . . . you build an underground London in the bowels of the metropolis, and an overhead London piercing the fog curtain above on viaducts, with another and another atop of these, until you have piled up, six cities deep, to Alpine altitudes with a different climate at each level . . . For purposes of transit you will devise a system of pneumatic tubes, through which passengers, previously treated by experienced dentists with nitrous oxide, can be blown from Kensington to Mile-end in a breath . . . What a London that would be!

'Ideal London', *Pall Mall Gazette* (5 October 1886)

Having escaped from Dublin, Shaw expected to find things ordered differently in London. Oscar Wilde who, though he had visited London before, came to live there two years later, was to inhale an air 'full of the heavy odour of roses . . . the heavy scent of the lilac, or the more delectable perfume of the pink flowering thorn'. The parks and gardens, squares and palisades sprouted their green between the seasoned brick and wedding-cake stucco of the West End where Wilde sauntered. But Wilde had come from respectable Merrion Square via Oxford to Mayfair and did not see the ill-smelling London Shaw was getting to know – a London of primitive streets with clinging red mud, miserably treated animals, and a sullen population storming the pubs at nightfall. Below the prim pattern of bourgeois life that Wilde was so delightfully to shock lay a vast reservoir of squalor and brutality. Drury Lane, the charming ambience of *Pygma-*

lion, was a derelict area until 1900, the territory of men and women in tatters, who crawled the streets like animals.

'Shelley . . . described Hell as "a city much like London". Dickens, who knew London, depicted it as full of strange monsters, Merdles, Veneerings, Finches of the Grove, Barnacles, Marshalseas indigenous to the Borough but cropping up sporadically among the monuments of Rome and Venice: all dreadfully answering to things that we know to be there, and yet cannot believe in without confusion and terror. How pleasant it is to shrink back to the genial Thackeray, who knew comparatively nothing about London, but just saw the fun of the little sets of ideas current in Russell and Bryanston-squares, Pall-mall, Fleet-street, and the art academies in Newman-street.'

The economics of London were to turn Shaw into a socialist. No new planning, he believed, could be achieved without a change of attitude in the country. 'The problem, unfortunately, is not one of realignment and patent dwellings,' he wrote in 1886:

'It is one of the development of individual greed into civic spirit; of the extension of the *laissez-faire* principle to public as well as private enterprise; of bringing all the citizens to a common date in civilization instead of maintaining a savage class, a mediaeval class, a renaissance class, and an Augustan class, with a few nineteenth-century superior persons to fix high-water mark . . . we must be content with the . . . periodical washing of the Albert Memorial . . . until London belongs to, and is governed by, the people who use it.'

*

Number 13 Victoria Grove stood on the east side of a cul-de-sac off the Brompton Road. The houses were semi-detached, with tiny gardens, and they occupied, along with those in a number of parallel groves, a countrified area, still with plenty of orchard and market garden, between Fulham and Putney. Here, for two years after *The Hornet*, Shaw did little but write short stories, literary reviews, articles, essays. It was 'mere brute practice with the pen . . . as a laborer digs or a carpenter planes'.

By February 1878 he was at work on a profane Passion Play in blank verse 'with the mother of the hero represented as a termagant'. Judas and Jesus in this play represent two sides of Shaw. Judas is

a man unblinded
And trained to shun the snare of self delusion

who sees in his corrupt surroundings a 'beastly world'. Jesus, who looks towards an invisible future, embodies hope. In the combination of the two, Shaw argues, the observer and the man of imagination, we reach reality. Judas's advice to the young Jesus is the lesson Shaw himself was endeavouring to master:

> Then must thou
> Learn to stand absolutely by thyself,
> Leaning on nothing, satisfied that thou
> Can'st nothing know, responsible to nothing,
> Fearing no power and being within thyself
> A little independent universe.

After forty-nine pages – 1,260 lines – the play breaks off in the second scene of Act II. Across one abandoned passage he wrote: 'Vile Stuff.' Fifty-five years later, in his Preface to *On the Rocks*, he explained that a modern Passion Play was impossible because 'the trial of a dumb prisoner, at which the judge who puts the crucial question to him remains unanswered, cannot be dramatized unless the judge is to be the hero of the play . . . If ever there was a full dress debate for the forensic championship to be looked forward to with excited confidence by the disciples of the challenged expert it was his trial of Christ. Yet their champion put up no fight.'

Also finished in February 1878 was *My Dear Dorothea*, a didactic pamphlet modelled on George Augustus Sala's squib *Lady Chesterfield's Letters to Her Daughter*, which Shaw had read the previous year. He subtitled his work: 'A Practical System of Moral Education for Females Embodied in a Letter to a Young Person of that Sex'. Much of the advice (including a warning against taking advice) would later become familiar furniture of Shavian philosophy: never be peevishly self-sacrificing; arm yourself with politeness which is a mark of superiority over unpleasant people; cultivate hypocrisy with others for kindness' sake, but never with yourself; read anything except what bores you; leave religion alone until you've grown up; get into mischief, but do not look for pity. Finally: 'Always strive to find out what to do by thinking, without asking anybody.'

The most closely autobiographical passages refer to Dorothea's mother:

'If your mother is always kind to you, love her more than you love anything except your doll . . . If you had indeed such a mother, my dear Dorothea, you would not need my advice at all. But I must not forget how seldom little girls have such guardians; and I will therefore take it for granted that your mother . . . thinks of you only as a troublesome and inquisitive little creature . . .

For such a parent, you must be particularly careful not to form any warm affection. Be very friendly with her, because you are in the same house as she, and it is unpleasant to live with one whom you dislike. If you have any griefs, do not tell her of them. Keep them to yourself if possible . . . You will soon be sent to school, and so get rid of her.'

Shaw's advice was a prescription against suffering. 'It is a most illuminating and sorrowful self-portrait,' Stevie Smith was to write, ' . . . because it shows that Shaw was as proud as the devil and put pride in the place of love. And why should a bright creature of such mercurial wits and fighting frenzies so limit himself if not for fear? . . . every now and then the heart limps in, but he is ashamed of it and begins to bluster.'

In March 1879 he began a novel called, 'with merciless fitness', *Immaturity*. 'As I could not afford a typewriter nor a secretary, I had to write directly and legibly for the printer with my own hand.' Five novels and part of a sixth he got through in this way. His handwriting, neat and spindly, sloping slightly backwards, is that of the chief cashier of Uniacke Townshend. He condemned himself to a daily reckoning of five pages – and so scrupulously that if his fifth page ended in the middle of a sentence he did not finish it until the next day. 'I have drudged year after year until I have very little patience left for anything but work,' says one of the characters, ' . . . it is the holding on day after day only a hair's breadth from failure.'

Immaturity was his 'first attempt at a big book'. The character of Robert Smith is Shaw himself at twenty with 'the culture that is given by loneliness and literature'. Unable to make contact with other people, Smith polishes his isolation to a virtue. His infatuation with a ballet dancer, releasing energy to be used for work, illustrates Shaw's susceptibility to women and his determination not to let them occupy his mind. Mlle Bernadina de Sangallo, as she is called in this first draft, takes her dream-like existence from Ermina Pertoldi, a dancer whom Shaw used to see at the Alhambra and who filled his night thoughts.

Like Smith, Shaw sometimes 'relapsed into that painful yearning which men cherish gloomily at eighteen, and systematically stave off as a nuisance . . . in later years'. Work, with which Shaw began to stave off this nuisance, becomes the hero of *Immaturity*. 'What is there to live for but work?' asks Cyril Scott, an artist modelled on the landscape painter Cyril Lawson. 'Everything else ends in disappointment. It's the only thing that you never get tired of, and that always comes to good.'

Shaw allows another worthy end: marriage. 'There is no gratification which a woman can afford you, that will not be sweeter when that woman is not your wife, except the possession of boys and girls to continue the record when you are in your coffin. Therefore marry the woman who will bring you the finest children, and who will be the best mother to them; and you will never find out that you might have done better elsewhere.'

Since hereditary factors are incalculable, Shaw places his bet on sexual instinct. In the debate he sets up between common sense and romance, it is common sense that is seen to lack courage, and romance, arguing against 'the folly of prudent marriages', that triumphs. 'The chief objection to fictitious romance,' he writes elsewhere in *Immaturity*, 'is that it is seldom so romantic as the truth.'

Smith is repeatedly accused, as Shaw was to be, of matter-of-factness. 'You are really very matter-of-fact, Mr Smith. You rub the gloss off everything.' It is this artificial gloss, reflected by the fashionable poet Hawkshaw (a sort of Shaw gone wrong who owes something to Oscar Wilde) that he dislikes. 'Matter-of-fact people are a great nuisance,' Smith concedes, 'and always will be, so long as they are in the minority.' The implication is that the days of Hawkshaw are numbered. He has not strength enough to resist the applause of a society that is, below its glossy surface, uncaring and uncomprehending. It is society that is the villain of the novel.

In this 'book of a raw youth', there is the outline of a Shaw who existed before his conversion into the fantastic personality of G.B.S. Like Hawkshaw, he was to take on a public gloss. But whereas Hawkshaw acquired his gloss from the caressing of society, the brilliant Shavian creature that emerged and flew away from the chrysalis of Smith wanted to outshine society and lead us to another place ruled over by 'one of my most successful fictions'. Like the 'Vandeleur Lee' who developed from G. J. Lee, 'G.B.S.' was a manufactured identity: not a victim of capitalist society – a weapon to be used against it.

*

Shaw finished *Immaturity* on 28 September 1879 and completed his revisions six weeks later. It was now a question, in the words of his father, of 'thrusting it down the throats of some of the publishers and so getting it into the hands of the mob'. On 7 November Shaw called on Hurst & Blackett and the following day sent them the manuscript. Next week they declined it.

Of his disappointment he showed nothing. At Victoria Grove he was reproached with laziness – his father in Dublin adding to the chorus and, to George's exasperation, obtaining a testimonial from Uniacke Townshend. Now and then he had gone half-heartedly out to look for work –

for example, after an introduction by the poet Richard Hengist Horne, to the Imperial Bank at South Kensington. 'Your son must *not* talk about religion or give his views thereon,' Horne warned Mrs Shaw, '& he must make up his mind to work & do what he is told – if not there is no use his calling.' In such circumstances it was not difficult to avoid employment. But as the pressure from his family tightened he was driven to more elaborate means of escape, and eventually these failed him. From his cousin Mrs Cashel Hoey he had received an introduction to the manager of the Edison Telephone Company, Arnold White, to whom on 5 October 1879, while still revising *Immaturity*, he wrote the sort of devastatingly honest letter he could usually rely on to extricate himself:

'In the last two years I have not filled any post, nor have I been doing anything specially calculated to qualify me for a business one . . .

My only reason for seeking commercial employment is a pecuniary one. I know how to wait for success in literature, but I do not know how to live on air in the interim. My family are in difficulties . . . However, I should be loth to press you for a place in which I might not be the right man.'

Arnold White, who liked Shaw, was not put off by this letter and offered him employment in the Way-Leave Department of the Edison Telephone Company. Shaw began working there on 14 November, immediately following the rejection of *Immaturity*. After six weeks he had earned two shillings and sixpence, and forfeited by way of expenses two guineas, having agreed to be paid on a commission basis. His job was to persuade people in the East End of London to allow insulators, poles and derricks to bristle about their roofs and gardens. 'I liked the exploration involved,' he remembered, 'but my shyness made the business of calling on strangers frightfully uncongenial . . . the impatient rebuffs I had to endure [were] . . . ridiculously painful to me.'

The truth appeared to be that he could not afford regular employment: 'I am under an absolute necessity to discontinue my services forthwith,' he told the head of his department. As a result of this threatened resignation he was given a basic wage of £48 (equivalent to £2,080 in 1997) a year and, two months later, promoted at a salary of £80, to be head of the department and 'organize the work of more thick-skinned adventurers instead of doing it myself'. He was now stationed in one of the basement offices of a building in Queen Victoria Street, loud with Americans who all adored Mr Edison, execrated his rival Mr Bell, worked with a terrible energy out of all proportion to the results achieved, and dreamed emotionally of telephone transmitters patented to their own formula.

Shaw waited patiently for his novel to rescue him. But *Immaturity* was rejected by every British and American publisher to whom he sent it. Sampson Low begged to be spared the pleasure of reading it. 'No,' wrote George Meredith for Chapman & Hall; 'unattractive', decided John Morley at Macmillan. *Immaturity* was 'a museum specimen of the Victorian novel,' Shaw later decided, which had been written at the wrong time.

'The Education Act of 1871 was producing readers who had never before bought books . . . and publishers were finding that these people wanted not George Eliot and the excessively literary novice Bernard Shaw, but such crude tales of impossible adventures published in penny numbers only for schoolboys. The success of Stevenson's *Treasure Island* and Jekyll and Hyde fairy tale, forced this change on the attention of the publishers; and I, as a belated intellectual, went under completely . . . Had I understood this situation at the time I should have been a happier novice instead of an apparently hopeless failure.'

3

SOME FURTHER EXPERIMENTS

The progress of the world depends on the people who refuse to accept facts and insist on the satisfaction of their instincts.

Back to Methuselah

Something was wrong with the Edison telephone: it 'bellowed your most private communications all over the house instead of whispering them with some sort of discretion,' Shaw wrote. 'This was not what the British stockbroker wanted . . .' On 5 June 1880 the Company amalgamated with the Bell Telephone Company and gave its employees one month's notice. Shaw, turning down an invitation to apply for a job with the new United Telephone Company of London, re-entered the literary world.

Immaturity was to lie 'dumb and forgotten' for fifty years; the *Passion Play* and *My Dear Dorothea* remained unpublished during Shaw's life. Of more than a dozen other stories and articles he had written in 1879 on 'subjects ranging from orchestral conducting to oakum picking' most were rejected, some were lost. The two that were eventually published earned him fifteen shillings. In the summer of 1880 he approached John Morley, the new editor of the *Pall Mall Gazette*, enclosing some examples of his work and asking whether he might make a music or theatre critic. 'I cannot hesitate to say,' Morley answered, 'that in my opinion you would do well to get out of journalism.' Describing this period later on, G.B.S. wrote:

'I did not throw myself into the struggle for life: I threw my mother into it. I was not a staff to my father's old age: I hung on to his coat tails . . . People wondered at my heartlessness . . . My mother worked for my living instead of preaching that it was my duty to work for hers: therefore take off your hat to her, and blush.'

Despite the failure of *Immaturity,* a career in novels seemed the only one open to him. Everyone wrote novels in the 1880s. Drama, economics, philosophy were unsaleable. He began to teach himself shorthand; he studied harmony and counterpoint; he persuaded his mother to train his voice by 'the Method' until he could sing 'as well as a man without twopennorth of physical endowment can be made to sing'; he persisted in playing the piano; he read greedily and, worst of all, he wrote.

He started on his second novel that summer, marching through it at the rate of a thousand words each day. 'The only test of competence is acceptance for publication,' he later wrote: 'friendly opinions are of no use.' But every opinion seemed unfriendly. His father was constantly fretting at him to find 'something to do to earn some money. It is much wanted by all of us.' Mrs Shaw unsuccessfully sought interviews for him; and Lucy, having failed to get their mother to turn George out of the house, had persuaded McNulty (as the only person likely to have influence) to write imploring him to take a job. Though sweet on Lucy, McNulty felt uneasy over this commission which put an end to their correspondence for nine months.

Shaw deafened himself to everything, wrote steadily, using some of his experiences at the Edison Telephone Company and some retaliatory observations of Lucy, and finished the novel which he called *The Irrational Knot* on 1 December 1880.

The inventor-engineer hero of this book, Ned Conolly, is not a self-portrait in the sense that Smith had been, but he embodies much that Shaw had learnt to admire since coming to London, and expresses many of his newest ideas. As a workman, a man of talent and integrity, Conolly opposes the perpetual falsehood of London society. 'You seem to see everything reversed,' one character tells him; and another, a clergyman, describes his opinions as being 'exactly upside down'. In sympathy with this upside-down view, Shaw inverts the conventional plot of the Victorian novel by having his heroine marry Conolly near the start and lose him at the end of the book.

Conolly is one of Nature's gentlemen, recognizing excellence by achievement, never by rank. The story throws up almost every situation that could shock society, from illegitimacy and alcoholic marriages to adultery and death. Aiming his attack on the 'villainous institution' of marriage, Shaw later described *The Irrational Knot* as having been 'an early attempt . . . to write *A Doll's House* in English'. In a deceitfully conducted world, it is the half-dead who flourish: men like tailors' dummies, and women like dolls to be gaped at in glass cages. Conolly will not accept such fashionable deception even if it means giving up a woman who sexually attracts him.

Shaw spent a fortnight revising the 641 'prodigiously long' pages of the novel. On 15 December 1880 he sent the manuscript to Macmillan whose reader reported that it was 'a novel of the most disagreeable kind . . . There is nothing conventional either about the structure or the style . . . the thought of the book is all wrong; the whole idea of it is odd, perverse and crude . . . So far as your publication is concerned, it is out of the question. There is too much of adultery and the like matters.'

'The better I wrote,' Shaw concluded, 'the less chance I had.' As an extreme measure, Shaw eventually sent *The Irrational Knot* to an American publisher 'who refused it on the ground of its immorality'. British publishers took a more sophisticated line. Smith Elder regretted that a book 'possessing considerable literary merit' was 'too conversational'; William Heinemann not only declined to publish it but advised the author not to submit it to anyone else: 'the hero is a machine like working man without any attractive qualities – an absolutely impossible person too.' Shaw agreed, in his fashion. Reviewing his novels himself in 1892 – a need arising 'through the extreme difficulty of finding anyone else who has read them' – he wrote of *The Irrational Knot*: 'This was really an extraordinary book for a youth of twenty-four to write; but, from the point of view of the people who think that an author has nothing better to do than to amuse them, it was a failure . . .'

4

RESPECTABLE HABITS

What people call health – appetite, weight, beefiness – is a mistake.
Fragility is the only endurable condition.

Shaw to Charlotte Payne-Townshend (4 April 1898)

On 23 December 1880, a week after *The Irrational Knot* had been sent
to Macmillan, the Shaws moved out of Victoria Grove to an unfurnished
apartment on the second floor of 37 Fitzroy Street.

The advantage for George was its proximity to the British Museum.
He had recently started to use the Reading Room, and now began going
there regularly. Here, in what Gissing called 'the Valley of the Shadow of
Books', he found a home. It became his club, his university, a refuge, and
the centre of his life. He felt closer to strangers in this place than to his
own family. He worked here daily for some eight years, applying for more
than three hundred books each year, advancing through the *Encyclopaedia
Britannica*, medical and municipal statistics for future articles, writing
lectures and letters to the press, adding to his musical knowledge and
completing his long literary apprenticeship. 'My debt to that great
institution . . . is inestimable.'

It was partly as a result of his reading that in January 1881 he became
a vegetarian. Shelley had first 'opened my eyes to the savagery of my
diet,' he recorded.

Never again may blood of bird or beast
Stain with its venomous stream a human feast!

While investigating the art of eating out cheaply, Shaw came across a
number of the inexpensive vegetarian restaurants that had recently opened.
During his first five years in London he had grown 'tired of beef and
mutton, the steam and grease, the waiter looking as though he had been
caught in a shower of gravy and not properly dried, the beer, the prevailing
redness of nose, and the reek of the slaughter-house that convicted us all
of being beasts of prey. I fled to the purer air of the vegetarian restaurant.'

Shaw hoped that vegetarian food might relieve the severe headaches
that had started to attack him each month. In one sense, vegetarianism
came easily to him. A symptom of his neglect in Ireland had been the
poor diet; the only food he had liked was the stoneground bread which
his mother had occasionally buttered for him. To reject all this – the

evidence of his own rejection – was no hardship. 'I am no gourmet,' he wrote: 'eating is not a pleasure to me, only a troublesome necessity, like dressing or undressing.' He looked forward to a time when people would subsist on an ecstatic diet of air and water. This was Shaw's ambrosia, and the food of his gods.

'If I were to eat it [meat], my evacuations would stink; and I should give myself up for dead,' he wrote in the last year of his life. Too little, he felt, was made of the fact that a frightened animal, terrified by smelling blood and seeing other animals killed in the slaughterhouse, stank. The flesh of such an animal, Shaw suggested, was tainted with poison and to eat it involved abusing the adaptiveness of the digestive system.

The sense of being a living grave for murdered animals filled him with repugnance. Part of this horror arose from the kinship he felt for animals – a fellow-feeling reinforced by the argument of Darwin and other naturalists establishing man's connection with animals. After which the practice of meat-eating became 'cannibalism with its heroic dish omitted'.

Having found from his experiments in the side-street restaurants round Bloomsbury that he could make a financial saving from putting his principles into practice, he went on to recommend vegetarianism as a means of world economy. 'My objection to meat is that it costs too much,' he wrote many years later, 'and involves the slavery of men and women to edible animals that is undesirable.' His campaign was to be an example of his dialectical skill.

Abstinence from dead bodies did not necessarily produce longevity, he argued, but affected the quality of living. He reminded those Englishmen in whom the superstition persisted that 'by eating a beefsteak he can acquire the strength and courage of the bull', that the bull (like an elephant) was vegetarian. He was sensitive to a need for scotching the popular myth that vegetarians were effeminate. Abstention from meat eating 'seems to produce a peculiar ferocity,' he noted. ' . . . And it is the worst form of ferocity: that is, virtuous indignation.' All his life he promoted vegetarians as the most pugnacious of people: 'Hitler, they say, was a vegetarian; and I can well believe it.'

G.B.S. had an air of knowing what was best for people. He calculated that, when the unappetizing truth was coated with Shavian sauce, it would go down a treat. So we often get from him fewer statements of truth than statements designed to hoodwink us into the truth. In private he could write: 'I am a vegetarian purely on humanitarian and mystical grounds; and I have never killed a flea or a mouse vindictively or without remorse.' This was the essential Shaw. But G.B.S. became the most unsentimental of vegetarians. 'He has no objection to the slaughter of animals as such,' his printed card on Vegetarian Diet reads. 'He knows that if we do not kill animals they will kill us . . . But he urges humane killing and does not enjoy it as a sport.'

From the nitrogenous point of view, and in line with Swift's modest proposal for the Irish, he saw no objection to a diet of tender babies, carefully selected, cleanly killed and gently roasted. Eaten with sugar, or a little beer, such a dish would, he estimated, leave nothing to be desired in the way of carbon, but: 'I prefer bread and butter.' If eating people was wrong, so was eating pigs. Bringing millions of disagreeable animals into existence expressly to kill, scorch and ingest their bodies was a monstrous practice which made our children callous to butchery and bloodshed.

Shaw needed courage to insist on his new diet in these early years. Usually it was wiser not to tell anyone he was vegetarian; otherwise he would be confronted with alarming quantities of breadcrumb preparations. At home he ate those vegetables the others took with their fish or meat. Some mornings a housemaid deposited among his books and papers a bowl of glue-like porridge and this often remained there for days while Shaw occasionally spooned a sticky mouthful or two. When travelling, he liked to carry lunch with him, diving his hands into his pockets and coming up with a fistful of almonds and raisins. He enjoyed advising vegetarians to avoid as much as possible all vegetables – particularly asparagus which gave one's urine a disagreeable smell – but it was imposs-ible in England to do without potatoes and brussels sprouts. The vegetarian foods, with names ending in -ose, which were variously dis-guised forms of oil cake, revolted him; but he liked cheese and fruit, tolerated omelettes for many years, and developed an increasingly sweet tooth for chocolate biscuits, fruit cake, honey, even heaped spoonfuls of sugar.

He drank water, soda water, barley water, an innocent beverage named Instant Postum, ginger beer, milk, cocoa, and 'I dont refuse chocolate in the afternoon when I can get it'. But no tea, 'however mediocre', very little coffee and never alcohol. He had been watching the effect of alcohol with the eye of an expert. 'My father drank too much. I have worked too much.' It was probably as much a weakness in his character, he later acknowledged, as a strength that compelled him to be such a strenuous teetotaller. But that was not the point. Reviewing his first nine years in London – 'years of unbroken failure and rebuff, with crises of broken boots and desperate clothes . . . penniless, loveless, and hard as nails' – he concluded that 'I am quite certain that if I had drunk as much as a single glass of beer a day . . . my powers of endurance would have been enormously diminished'.

Characteristically, he was to ridicule prohibition, assert that 'tea does more harm in the world than beer', buy shares in a municipal public house and eventually advocate the Russian method of piping vodka ('a comparatively mild poison') into society under efficient government control.

Shaw's attitude to drink recalls Dr Johnson's dictum that 'Life is a pill which none of us can bear to swallow without gilding.' In his copy of Bunyan's *The Life and Death of Mr Badman*, Shaw wrote: 'Living is so painful for the poor that it cannot be endured without an anaesthetic.' He saw drunkenness as a symptom of the malignant disease called poverty. To his mind alcohol was a trick, a depressant in the disguise of a stimulant, falsely associated (like corpse-eating) with virility. Drink seldom propelled us into melodramatic ruin and madness; it was a chloroform that lowered our self-criticism and self-respect.

Shaw needed self-respect to withstand the low esteem in which he was held among publishers and at home. Perhaps the new diet he shared with saints and sages would help to change him into a different person. 'The odd thing about being a vegetarian is, not that the things that happen to other people don't happen to me – they all do – but that they happen differently: pain is different, pleasure different, fever different, cold different, even love different.'

5

ON GROWING A BEARD

Think of my circumstances and prospects getting worse and worse until they culminated in smallpox next year (81) when I forced 'Love Among the Artists' out of myself.

Shaw to Charlotte Payne-Townshend (1 April 1898)

Each day he read at the British Museum and as an extra form of language tuition sang in French three nights a week with a *basso profundo* called Richard Deck in his single room off the Camden Road. He felt peculiarly fond of Deck and, following his death in the autumn of 1882, remembered him as 'a remarkable man, offering me advice concerning pronunciation, directing my attention to the aim of gymnastics . . . and introducing me to the ideas of Proudhon'.

On 19 May he started a new novel. He had been at work on this for about a week when he began to feel ill. In the belief that he was spending too much time indoors, he prescribed for himself a number of rides round

London on the top of omnibuses. A few days later he discovered he had smallpox.

Smallpox was then one of the most dreaded diseases in Western Europe partly because 'the bad cases were so disfiguring, and partly because the increase of population produced by the industrial revolution, and the insanitary conditions in which the new proletariat lived, had made it much commoner and more virulent'. In 1853 Parliament had made compulsory the vaccination of every child in Britain within three months of birth. Sonny had been vaccinated in infancy and the vaccination had taken well. This form of vaccination (which in 1898 was to be banned) meant the injection of cowpox matter from the pustule of a diseased cow or the diseased substance from the inflamed arm of a recently vaccinated person. Shaw makes little reference to his illness except to say that he emerged from it a convinced anti-vaccinationist.

Once, when his mother had been seriously ill in Dublin, Shaw recounts, Lee had taken 'her case in hand unhesitatingly and at the end of a week or so gave my trembling father leave to call in a leading Dublin doctor, who simply said "My work is done" and took his hat'. From this Shaw learnt a lesson he continued to apply. Lee's prescription had been fresh air, extreme cleanliness and a good diet, and these became for him the ingredients of political good health: 'it is now as plain as the sun in the heavens,' he wrote towards the end of his life, 'that pathogenic microbes are products of the zymotic diseases; and that these diseases are products of ugliness, dirt and stink offending every aesthetic instinct . . . that dirt and squalor and ugliness are products of poverty; and that . . . zymotic diseases can be abolished by abolishing poverty, the practical problem being one of economic distribution.'

'You have been vaccinated in your infancy,' a friend wrote, 'so ought if the doctors are to be believed, to have nothing to fear.' But were they to be believed? Or were they to be feared? It was less his helplessness as a smallpox patient that Shaw hated than the unpleasantness of the disease itself into which, he felt, he had been medically tricked.

Shaw externalized Evil. In his world there were no evil men and women except the insane; but there were evil circumstances which he could identify, attack and eliminate. Vaccination let the enemy in and allowed evil to circulate within the body. The method of inoculating children with casual dirt moistened with an undefined pathogenic substance obtained from calves impressed Shaw as being morally insane. His sense of contamination became part of his socialist dogma and a warning against substituting faith in an experimental prophylaxis for a full-scale sanitation programme ensuring good conditions of public health.

After three weeks confined to his room in Fitzroy Street, he went down to recuperate at Leyton in Essex with his uncle Walter Gurly who, having married an English widow during one of his trips to the United States, was living a life of precarious respectability as a country physician near Epping Forest.

Shaw was left with a scar on his right cheek. Whether the disfigurement was slight or he merely made light of it, he felt extremely sensitive. 'I was sorry to hear of your illness,' Aileen Bell wrote to him, 'and the idea of your telling Mrs Horne not to describe your personal appearance – as if I should like you the less . . .'

'I have a rather remarkable chin and would like to let the public see it; but I never had time to shave.' This joke, and several others on similar lines, covered up the initial motive for the beard which was to hide his sensitivity. It became exactly the right beard – a good red socialist affair and vastly conspicuous. Few people who had their attention arrested by this irrepressible flag waving at the head of the Shavian talking-machine, would have known that G.B.S. was publicly concealing something.

Shaw represented himself as the passive partner to his beard: he simply followed it wherever it went. So bewitched had he been with the figure of Mephistopheles that 'when Nature completed my countenance in 1880 or thereabouts . . . I found myself equipped with the upgrowing moustaches and eyebrows, and the sarcastic nostrils of the operatic fiend whose airs (by Gounod) I had sung as a child, and whose attitudes I had affected in my boyhood'. There could be few better examples of G.B.S.'s beard doing the talking.

'Like a Victorian matron I experimented with my brushes and comb.' The face that he designed for himself was startling. 'It is the face of an outlaw,' wrote one woman; 'it is full of protest: wild and determined, a very brigand of a face.' Another woman, observing him among the socialists at William Morris's converted coach-house in Hammersmith, noted:

'His face came out very distinctly in the unshaded light of the stable-room, and as he listened it seemed to me to be lit up not only by that outside light but also, and in a particular way, by some inner lamp, as if Morris's words had lighted a candle of great and incandescent power within him. Shaw's face that night burned itself in on me; I have never seen any face like it since . . . His pale skin, his hair that the light above it turned to gold, and his strong, gleaming teeth, made a picture that no one, I think, could ever forget.'

His taut body seemed wound up with energy, and his movements were rapid. He walked with long springy strides on the front of his feet. When seated he seemed to relax all over, huddling and stretching, sticking out his long legs then pulling them up to his chest as if embracing himself. In this position he chattered and swayed with laughter. Then he stood up, thin, erect, well-pleased with himself it appeared, the head upraised, body tilted back, beard pointed. The impression of this figure, combative and audacious, was often invaded by comedy. It was his comic spirit that, for all the Satanic twirls and flourishes, encouraged a friend to describe his face as an 'unskilfully poached egg', and enabled Shaw himself to write: 'My own beard is so like a tuft of blanched grass that pet animals have nibbled at it.'

The private face shows itself in the novel, *Love Among the Artists*, he forced out of himself while at Leyton. Love among artists is different from love among other people, for artists love their work more than they love other people. Shaw's novel plots social against artistic values. 'I am in a worldly sense an unfortunate man,' says Owen Jack, the hero-composer of the book, 'though in my real life, heaven knows, a most happy and fortunate one.' Jack defines worldly success as 'the compensation of the man who has no genius'. Some men, he says, 'begin by aiming high, and they have to wait till the world comes up to their level'. With such *obiter dicta* Shaw, giving a backward look at Lee's failure, kept his confidence afloat.

Jack (who Shaw asks us to believe was based partly on Beethoven but who reflects something of Richard Deck and something of Vandeleur Lee), and the pianist Aurelie Szczymplica, are the two geniuses of *Love Among the Artists*, and they inhabit the classless world of music in which Shaw felt happiest.

Since marriage 'kills the heart and keeps it dead', it is better, Jack concludes, to 'starve the heart than overfeed it. Better still to feed it on fine food, like music.' Another character, Mrs Herbert, who owes something to Shaw's mother, wonders if there is 'any use in caring for one's children? I really dont believe there is.' The effect of such a mother on her children is described by her son (the blissfully unhappy husband of Aurelie Szczymplica) in a speech that reflects Shaw's feelings about himself and Lucinda Elizabeth:

'Can you understand that a mother and a son may be so different in their dispositions that neither can sympathize with the other? It is my great misfortune to be such a son ... She is a clever woman, impatient of sentiment, and fond in her own way. My father, like myself, was too diffident to push himself arrogantly through the world; and she despised him for it, thinking him a fool. When she saw that I was like him, she concluded that I, too, was a fool, and that she must arrange my life for me in some easy, lucrative, genteel, brainless conventional way ... She did not know how much her indifference tortured me, because she had no idea of any keener sensitiveness than her own . . . She taught me to do without her consideration; and I learned the lesson.'

Shaw came to believe that *Love Among the Artists* marked 'a crisis in my progress as a thinker'. He had 'come to the end of my Rationalism and Materialism'. This conversion has an air of paradox. The discovery of knowledge did not emerge at the end of reasoning and as a result of it, but occurred by instalments in the form of fiction, hypotheses or jokes – after which we set about finding reasons for it.

'A man has his beliefs: his arguments are only his excuses for them. Granted that we both want to get to Waterloo Station: the question whether we shall drive across Westminster Bridge or Waterloo, or whether we shall walk across the Hungerford foot bridge, is a matter for our logic; but the destination is dogmatic. The province of reason is the discovery of the means to fulfil our wills; but our wills are beyond reason: we all will to live . . . we only see what we look at: our attention to our temperamental convictions produces complete oversight as to all the facts that tell against us.'

Shaw had returned to 37 Fitzroy Street in October and finished *Love Among the Artists* on 10 January 1882. 'I have a much higher opinion of this work than is as yet generally entertained,' he admitted. The eminent publisher's reader, Edward Garnett, in a report for Fisher Unwin, advised against publishing the book if they could 'get something else from the author'. *Love Among the Artists*, he wrote, *deserved* publication, but would probably fall flat with the general reader. 'The literary art is sound, the people in it are real people, and the fresh unconventionality is pleasing after the ordinary work of the common novelist: but all the same – *few people would understand it, & few papers would praise it.*' Garnett contrasted the novel with W. B. Yeats's first book of verse, *The Wanderings of Oisin*, 'which with certain faults shows a sense of *colour* & *softness* that betrays the artistic mind,' he concluded. 'There is a little genius in Yeats: there is an individuality of mind in Shaw's work, but neither are likely to command much attention.'

While at Leyton, Shaw had finally taught himself Pitman's Shorthand. This, 'probably the worst system of shorthand ever invented', suited him best, he decided, because Greg's was known only in America and Sweet's Current Shorthand had been made 'illegible by anyone except himself'. Pitman himself was everything a man should be – a teetotaller and vegetarian, a radical well-whiskered man of business.

Shorthand enabled Shaw to intensify his programme of self-education at the British Museum and to write at a speed that kept pace with his thoughts. It also raised the family's hopes of his employment. While *Love Among the Artists* was being returned to him by the London publishers, Shaw proposed himself for the job of preparing the work of another unpublished novelist, Ethel Southam, who had advertised for a copyist. From Shaw she received many hundreds of words of advice about punctuation, the use of prepositions, and avoidance of adjectives – after which the partnership collapsed and G.B.S. was deprived of the amusement of pointing to a ghost-written collaboration as his first book.

Pressed again by his family, he read the advertisement columns and applied for employment as secretary to the Smoke Abatement Institute and as secretary to the Thames Subway Committee. He was careful not to conceal his politics ('those of an atheistic radical'), his lack of university education, mathematical and linguistic inabilities ('no German whatsoever'), and experience as secretary or shorthand clerk ('I can write longhand rapidly – in fact more rapidly than I can yet write shorthand').

On 12 April 1882 he began his fourth novel.

6

COURTING MISS LOCKETT

Which yet my soul seeketh, but I find not: one man in a thousand have I found; but a woman among all these have I not found.

Ecclesiastes vii.28

In a notebook he kept during his first six or seven years in London, Shaw copied down this passage. He described himself at this period as 'a complete outsider'. During his convalescence from smallpox, he had even thought of emigrating to the United States where his friend Chichester Bell was going. The bleakness of these years grew so unbearable that he afterwards translated it into a hatred of his novels.

Though the place was full of culture, London society contrived to get along on an intellectual diet of sport, party politics, fashion and travel. It seemed as if a mighty harvest had left the soil sterile. In Dublin the professions had formed the aristocracy, and without any great income and no experience of horses or guns, one could enjoy the best company without the taint of social inferiority. In London there were different rules and far greater importance was attached to money. 'The real superiority of

59

the English to the Irish,' Shaw was to write, 'lies in the fact that an Englishman will do anything for money and an Irishman will do nothing for it.' But this was a later discovery to which, since for the time being he had no money, 'I had to blind myself'. There were times when he longed for people to blind themselves to him. He was a scarecrow catapulting himself along the streets with a professional habit of cheerfulness, but in broken boots, a tall hat so limp he wore it back to front to avoid doubling the brim when raising it, cuffs whose margins had been refined with his mother's scissors, trousers whose holes were hidden by a tailed coat fading from black to green. He was an example of poverty. 'It is my practice to make a suit of clothes last me six years,' he explained. 'The result is that my clothes acquire individuality, and become characteristic of me. The sleeves and legs cease to be mere tailor-made tubes; they take human shape with knees and elbows recognizably mine. When my friends catch sight of one of my suits hanging on a nail, they pull out their penknives and rush forward, exclaiming, "Good Heavens! he has done it at last." '

His plight was so glaring that people hinted they were good for loans. But he never borrowed, having no reason for believing he could repay them. He was conscious of the charm of his conversation if it never led to a request for five shillings. 'When you borrow money, you sell a friend,' he wrote.

He went to the National Gallery on its free days and, when he had a shilling in his pocket, to the theatre. Almost the only social gatherings in which he was included had been Lee's *soirées musicales*. But by the 1880s, largely through his sister Lucy, he also began to receive invitations to the 'At Homes' of Lady Wilde and of Elizabeth Lawson, mother of the landscape painter Cecil Lawson on whom he had modelled the artist Cyril Scott in *Immaturity*. They were the sort of engagements that make a man long for death. To equip himself for such ordeals he sought out from the catalogue at the British Museum volumes on polite behaviour.

He liked the Lawsons, and the artistic atmosphere of their house in Cheyne Walk was congenial, but he had not mastered the art of pleasing, could not dance, spoke hesitantly though usually to disagree, and occasionally made a jarring exhibition of himself. 'I sometimes walked up and down the Embankment for twenty minutes or more before venturing to knock at the door,' he remembered. ' . . . The worst of it was that when I appeared in the Lawsons' drawingroom I did not appeal to the good-nature of the company as a pardonably and even becomingly bashful novice. I had not then tuned the Shavian note to any sort of harmony.'

He saw very little of anyone with whom he did not work. Politics was to provide him with new colleagues. Otherwise he had few companionships.

Among these were the writer and adventurer Richard Hengist Horne and his wife Sophie; a person of mild exterior, Edwin Habgood, from the Edison Telephone Company; James Lecky, an exchequer clerk from Ireland interested in phonetics, keyboard temperament and Gaelic, who was also a big noise in the English Spelling Reform Association (signing himself 'jeemz leki'), who was to introduce him to the philologists Alexander John Ellis and Henry Sweet; and J. Kingston Barton, a doctor with whom Shaw passed many of his Saturday evenings. On Sundays he saw the Beattys.

Pakenham Beatty – Irish playboy, amateur pugilist, minor poet – was a moustachioed perpetual boy of a man. Born in Brazil, he had spent part of his childhood in Dalkey, been educated somewhere between Harrow and Bonn, and got to know Shaw as a fellow-exile in London. He belonged to a breed of troubadour-entertainers that was to include Frank Harris and Gabriel Pascal, for whom Shaw had a special fondness. Beatty enabled him to enter a life very different from his own. He was not 'sensible' about money. He spent it in the Irish manner, generously, spontaneously, without thought, until everything was gone and he was left with nothing but the settled habit of spending. His source of money was a small inheritance that, before it ran dry, allowed him to flirt with fine art. At the end of 1878, he published a volume of verse entitled *To My Lady and Other Poems*. One of his ladies, Edith Dowling, married him early the following year and became known as 'Ida' Beatty. They had two daughters and a son christened Pakenham William Albert Hengist Mazzini Beatty whom Shaw nicknamed 'Bismarck'.

In this company Shaw became a figure of attention and authority. He had no money but he spent all his advice on them, nuggets of information laboriously quarried out at the British Museum about the children's books, boots, careers, clothing, diet, education, illnesses, pianos and so on; and later, when he was earning money, he gave it to them in sums ranging between £10 and £200 and underwrote a good part of the children's schooling. 'Old grandfather Shaw', as Ida Beatty called him, was a father and a friend to them all.

Shaw made his appearance among them as a practical man, a part invested by his imagination with much glamour. He judged them to be *hopeless*, in which condition they *needed* him. But he also had need of them, since, for all their hopelessness, they had something almost entirely lacking in the Shaws: an atmosphere of family affection. Pakenham Beatty was extravagantly fond of his two sisters-in-law and even went on to shower his attentions jointly on Shaw's sister Lucy and a friend of their mother, Jane Patterson. But Shaw refused to be shocked. One afternoon he came across his friend recovering from delirium tremens and surrounded by whispering relatives who, having bullied him into making a will, were assembled as if for a funeral. 'I dispersed them with roars of laughter and inquiries after pink snakes &c, an exhibition of bad taste which at last converted the poor devil's wandering apprehensive look into a settled grin . . . Tomorrow he goes to a retreat at Rickmansworth, to be reformed.'

Shaw was a rock in this Bohemian whirlpool, splashed, invigorated and unchanged. The Beattys added to his education outside the British Museum. He loved Beatty for his bad verses ('something too awful') and for presenting such an atrocious advertisement for the romantic life. He re-christened him 'Paquito', a name that would serve as an alias for the eponymous hero of *Captain Brassbound's Conversion*. 'My plays are full of your jokes,' he told him.

Paquito's letters to Shaw were mostly in high-flown and facetious verse. His non-poetic intervals were devoured by the ambition to be an amateur light-weight champion. 'I am about to take boxing lessons from the scientific Ned Donnelly, a very amiable though powerful person in appearance . . . If you wish,' he invited Shaw, 'these lessons which I learn from Donnelly I will teach unto you.' Shaw couldn't resist. The comedy of all this was serious business for Shaw. He did his initial training at the British Museum, battling with Pierce Egan's *Boxiana* and other expositions. Paquito had presented him with a copy of Donnelly's *Self-Defence* ('the best book of its kind ever published') and 'insisted on my accompanying him to all the boxing exhibitions'. In consequence Shaw was to gain among his political acquaintances the reputation as 'a tall man with a straight left' whose knowledge of pugilism might prove valuable if it came to revolution.

There were times when Shaw himself seemed to accept such fantasies. He showed up at a school-of-arms in Panton Street called the London Athletic Club where he obtained tuition from Ned Donnelly himself who, as Professor of Boxing, had instructed the most brilliant light-weight of his day, Jack Burke, on whom Shaw based the hero of the novel he was writing. A month after finishing this book, on 17 March 1883, he entered the Queensberry Amateur Boxing Championships on the turf at Lillie Bridge. At a weight of ten stone (140 lbs) he applied to take part in both Middle and Heavyweight Classes, and was given a place for both categories in the programme, but not in the ring. It was the climax of his prize-fighting career, a paper apotheosis, after which he found he 'had exhausted the comedy of the subject'.

Shaw's long affair with boxing was to worry some of his admirers. How could this champion of the vegetable world involve himself in brute pugilism? 'Paradoxing is a useful rhyme to boxing,' he once thanked a journalist. 'I will make a note of it.' He saw at once the great publicity in pugilism. Newspapers, he believed, were 'fearfully mischievous', yet they were creators of public opinion. So what could be more natural than to marry one such brute profession to another? Since the public were more interested in sport than serious politics, Shaw was to spread his political views through the sports pages as he would the music and art columns. Under his treatment boxing was to become an allegory of capitalism, the prize-ring a place where he could exhibit Shavian theories on distribution of income and award a points decision to socialism.

Shaw's knowledge of boxing formed part of an armoury that, by the end of the 1880s, was to make him, in Max Beerbohm's opinion, 'the most brilliant and remarkable journalist in London'. Unlike bicycling, it didn't get you anywhere, and it was not as pleasant as swimming which, with its cleansing effect and the sensation of rendering the body weightless, almost non-existent, became 'the only exercise I have ever taken for its own sake'. But his shadow boxing, even before it was converted into words, was the essence of Shavianism.

For almost six years he visited the Beattys most Sundays, sparred several platonic rounds with Paquito the poet, then sat at the feet of his wife Ida, practising French. This was the first of numerous triangular relationships in which he re-created his mesmeric but chaste version of Vandeleur Lee with Lucinda and George Carr Shaw, and kept those ghosts at peace. 'Dont talk to me of romances: I was sent into the world expressly to dance on them with thick boots – to shatter, stab, and murder them,' he challenged Ida. 'I defy you to be romantic about me . . . and if you attempt it, I will go straight to Paquito; tell him you are being drawn into the whirlpool of fascination which has engulfed all the brunettes I know.' This was shadow boxing from which Shaw emerged very much in control of a situation that did not really exist. He could not exclude dreams of more orthodox affairs, but 'all these foolish fancies only want daylight and fresh air to scatter them,' he instructed Ida, as if the fancies had been hers and not his.

Shaw made himself attractive to women by informing them he was attractive – then warning them against this damnable attractiveness. He converted the neglected Sonny into a besieged G.B.S., who would have fainted with surprise 'if a woman came up to me in the street and said "I DONT adore you" '.

Being in love with Shaw could be a bewildering business. 'You are very contradictory,' Aileen Bell complained. ' . . . What am I to do?' He teased and tested; he loved you and he loved you not. He achieved an air of confidence by taking away your own confidence. 'When we did fight in the old days,' Aileen Bell wrote to him, 'I used to go upstairs afterwards, &

stamp about my room & abuse you, saying "I hate George Shaw".' His talent was to disconcert. He charmed you, then made you too angry for words and (since the affair was one of words) impotent. On paper, where he held absolute authority, he was promiscuous. He attributed to others the romantic daydreams he suppressed in himself, and encircled them in fantastical webs of jealousies and misunderstandings.

Shaw's relations with women during his first four or five years in London are cryptically recorded in his diary notebooks. At the end of 1876, he noted: 'Inauguration during the year of the Terpsichore episode. Also La Carbonaja.' Terpsichore was his codename for Ermina Pertoldi, the ballerina of the Alhambra Theatre and a character in *Immaturity*. La Carbonaja was the daughter of a London hostess who gave him a medal of the Virgin Mary, hoping to convert him to Catholicism. The following year La Carbonaja is 'in the ascendant' and in 1879 'La C flickers until 11th [January] When the star of Leonora gains the ascendant (Terpsichore evaporated) . . . Made the acquaintance of the Lawson family on 5th [January], and met Leonora on the 11th.' From 'Leonora' he preserved a pressed flower together with an odd note: 'These flowers were plucked from the garden of a millionaire by one of his would-be brides as a memento of a sweet prelude to a "might have been".'

Unable to come to terms with women except in make-believe, Shaw conducted his most successful affairs from the galleries of theatres or his gymnasium in the British Museum, and worked himself eventually to sleep at night. Confusion began when this make-believe came in contact with the actual world. Between 1878 and 1894 he kept a correspondence in play with Elinor Huddart, author of *My Heart and I* and other novels that would have won her notoriety 'if I could have persuaded her to . . . use the same pen name, instead of changing it for every book'. She had been impressed by his kindness and good sense. 'How you manage to pick my work to pieces from end to end,' she wrote to him on 16 September 1878, 'and yet never hurt me (and I am rather easily hurt) I cannot conceive.' One reason she was not hurt was that Shaw had invented an Elinor of his own, possessed by his spirit and made into a new creature. 'You are the only man friend I have ever made,' she told him. ' . . . I am content to be your friend and no man's wife.' For someone who appeared so frivolous it was astonishing how persistent he could be. He beat down on her like a sun, warming her, blistering her, trying to blow a new climate round her and imbue her with fresh life as a writer. But 'I can put forth no new leaves,' she objected. 'I am not a beech tree . . . Leave my ashes in peace, they can do you no good.' But he would not leave her. He wanted to pour his will-power into women so that their achievements became the children of the union.

In his exertions to work his will vicariously through women his flirtations became those of a schoolmaster. 'I beg of you,' Aileen Bell once wrote to him, 'not to lecture quite so much.' However much he did lecture, urge, flatter, coax, he could not make the worlds of fantasy and actuality coalesce.

Shaw's love eliminated many things to which women were accustomed. In his plays he was to create a stereotype, Woman-the-Huntress, whom he sent into battle against the Victorian Woman-on-a-pedestal. Debarred by his childhood from forming close emotional attachments, he gave his allegiance to ideas – but saw women as vehicles for those ideas. Shaw took the body away from women and addressed their minds. His own mind was astonishingly fast, but emotionally he was lame. The result was that women found themselves continually out of step with him. When Shaw looked at a woman, he appeared to turn his back on her and raise a mirror. It was a disconcerting stare, positive, remote, and appearing so bold while actually in retreat.

*

Sonny had wanted love; G.B.S. soared wittily above it; and Shaw was pulled between the two. The tug-of-war moved critically backwards and forwards over his first serious girl friend, Alice Lockett. In February 1882 he returned to Leyton and, while recuperating from scarlet fever, was introduced to her. She was twenty-three and robustly good-looking. He fell violently in love – which is to say, he was strongly attracted to her. After his convalescence he managed to return to Leyton by the uncharacteristic means of getting temporary employment there, earning six guineas in as many days counting votes during the election of Poor Law guardians. He saw her, walked in the moonlight, talked, flirted. By 17 April, he felt able to report to Elinor Huddart that 'Alice thinks I am in love with her'. The honeymoon was almost over and the contest between them ready to begin.

Alice and her sister Jane had been conventionally brought up and educated at a Victorian ladies' college. In 1879 their father had died and the next year their elder brother also died. Their mother suffered a paralytic stroke, and her two daughters, transferred to the care of their grandmother, prepared to take up professions. Jane, who was experimenting with a novel called *Yeast* (exorbitantly condemned by Shaw), studied for a career in education; Alice, who enrolled in a nursing course at St Mary's Hospital in Paddington, was taking singing lessons from Mrs Shaw.

The affair was carried on between the railway station and piano stool ('Oh the infinite mischief that a woman may do by stooping forward to turn over a sheet of music!'). Alice felt she had been relegated in the social order by her family misfortunes, and nursed dreams of a dramatic ascent up the ladder of society; Shaw was determined to kick that ladder away. Alice sensed a power in Shaw, but one which he was often misusing. In place of manly leadership, he presented her with exhibitions of clever indecisiveness. Quarrelling between them was inevitable. 'I hate people to hesitate,' she chided him.

In one of his early notebooks Shaw had jotted down his observations on the typical society woman. 'Clever, frivolous, vain, egocentric,' he wrote. 'Pretty & knows it. Sits silent and affects the scornful. Also a morbid sensitiveness and a consequent pleasure in inflicting hurts on others. Effect of this type of egotist in making others seem intolerably egotistical . . .'

It was to save Alice from becoming this woman that Shaw exerted all his powers. He re-created her as a figure from his novels and she became someone through whom he attacked the London society that had lured Lee and Lucinda away from him and, when he followed, rejected him.

Shaw divided Alice into two people. Miss Lockett had been stiffened by the starch of society and was full of protective scorn and attempted sarcasm. Towards men she bore herself tyrannically, having no notion that any interest of men in women might exist apart from a desire to marry. But sometimes Miss Lockett forgot to be offended, scornful, pretentious – and Alice emerged. Alice was the child in her, sympathetic, unspoilt, spontaneously generous, someone capable of considering her own instinctive judgement a safer guide than the formulated rules of society. Alice was capable too of Shavian improvement; the proud and foolish Miss Lockett had gone too far down the hackneyed road of her own dignity to be brought back. Between these two beings Shaw enacted a perpetual drama. Miss Lockett 'is the dragon that preys upon Alice,' he told her, 'and I will rescue Alice from her'.

Shaw dramatized in Miss Alice Lockett a division he knew to exist within himself. In one corner there was G.B.S., 'resolved . . . to walk with the ears of his conscience strained on the alert, to do everything as perfectly as it could be done, and – oh – monstrous! – to improve all those with whom he came in contact'. In the opposite corner stood Sonny, the Irish contender, who was not afraid to become 'as a little child again and was not ashamed to fall in love with Alice'.

But the voice that lectured Miss Lockett on the importance of becoming Alice was that of G.B.S., not Sonny who could seldom 'snatch a few moments from his withering power'. G.B.S. worked day and night; he was seldom out of love with his work – in which condition he accused

Alice of taking advantage 'of the weakest side of my character', and warned
her to believe nothing that Sonny whispered to her.

The crisis in Shaw was real. Before a caress with Alice had time to
cool, he longed to return to his ascetic life, to his books, his developing
socialism. But then the memory of her beauty could prevent him going
to bed in peace, and gave him a thrill that could last 'through a political
meeting and four hours of private debate on dry questions of economy'.
Shaw's appeals to Alice were often the means by which he tried to offend
her so as to save himself from falling in love. But sometimes he did not
have the heart to succeed – and then Sonny would whisper things that
G.B.S. would have to shatter with his laughter.

Shaw had hit on the device of pretending to be what he was – but with
a comic exaggeration that prompted disbelief. He pretended to be 'in love'
with Alice and she, congratulating herself on not being taken in, accused
him of insincerity. Sometimes it seemed as if she were only speaking the
lines he had prepared for her. It was oddly unreal. 'We are too cautious,
too calculating, too selfish, too heartless, to venture head over heels in
love,' he wrote to her. 'And yet there is something – ' Both tried to limit
their vulnerability to the other. But Alice did not understand where her
power lay – she never realized into what extraordinary suspense her beauty
put him. In attempting to hurt him with deliberate cruelty, she merely
became the stubborn and timid Miss Lockett of his hostile imagination,
squaring up to her impregnable enemy G.B.S.

'George Shaw, I consider you an object to be pitied – but the truth is I
might just as well speak to a stone. Nothing affects you . . . Now your
book has failed – for which I am truly sorry for your sake, although it is
perhaps better for other people. I suppose you mean to begin another and
be another year dependent on your mother. Why on earth don't you
work?'

Alice had been in the marriage market since leaving school and looked
on 'love-making' as the most serious business in life. It was because Shaw
believed that Sonny was incapable of inspiring love in women that he
invented G.B.S. Alice tried to understand him – but he took care that she
should not. In serious moments he could make her see with his eyes,
flattering her ('Must I eternally flatter flatter flatter flatter flatter?') by his
apparent conviction – which she shared – that she was capable of a higher
life. But his political dreams had no meaning for her so 'it is my small
troubles that I go to you with,' he told her.

Alice Lockett's challenge to Shaw had been to make him feel his
loneliness most painfully. At moments his self-command wavered. 'Write

to me,' he asked her, 'and I will make love to you – to relieve the enormous solitude which I carry about with me. I do not like myself, and sometimes I do not like you; but there are moments when our two unfortunate souls seem to cling to the same spar in a gleam of sunshine, free of the other wreckage for a moment.'

Miss Lockett's social ambitions would not allow her to be stranded in this way; she wanted to travel first class. As for Shaw, it was Sonny who was left senseless and G.B.S. who appeared 'too strong for you. I snap your chains like Samson.'

On two occasions they returned each other's letters; several times they decided never to see each other. The affair lasted until 1885 when all love had gone out of it and they drifted apart. In 1890 Alice married a former house-surgeon at St Mary's, William Salisbury Sharpe. Obliged during the Great War to borrow some money from Shaw, she lived on to witness the halo of world renown encircle G.B.S. But in many criticisms of his books and plays she would have been able to read of an absent quality – and to have recognized in this absence the departure of Sonny over which she had helplessly watched.

7

DEATH AND A RENEWAL

It was lonely to be myself; but not to be myself was death in life.

Cashel Byron's Profession

On 22 April 1882, ten days after starting his fourth novel, Shaw moved with his mother to 36 Osnaburgh Street, on the east side of Regent's Park. This was an improvement on the insalubrious rooms in Fitzroy Street where he had often been ill.

They saw little of Lucy. From the Carl Rosa Opera Company she transferred to a D'Oyly Carte group and in 1884 went off with them on tour.

Lucinda Elizabeth Shaw continued methodically to give private tuition in singing. In 1885 she suddenly struck a new vein of work as music instructor at Clapham High School, and the following year became choirmistress and teacher of class singing at the North London Collegiate School for Ladies where she remained until her retirement in 1906.

Shaw went his own way – to the British Museum – and finished his fourth novel on 6 February 1883. *Cashel Byron's Profession*, as he called it, is a fairy-tale about power. Its hero, Cashel Byron, a prize-fighter as clever with his fists as Shaw was with words, embodies Shaw's fantasy about action. To him is given the first Shavian speech (which goes the distance of three thousand words) on the superiority of 'executive power' over 'good example'. It is a dialectic on the philosophy of winning, and a hymn to skill and science over incoherent strength.

Taking a profession that society officially repudiated, Shaw uses it as a metaphor for the way people unofficially live their lives – a formula he was to try again in *Mrs Warren's Profession* and *Major Barbara* (which he thought of calling 'Andrew Undershaft's Profession'). His make-believe leads the hero and heroine from love at first sight through all supposed social barriers to marriage in the last chapter. The Lady is Cashel's prize – in a way that Ida Beatty or any of the other women with whose husbands G.B.S. sparred would never be Shaw's. In the book, romance won by a knock-out and 'my self-respect took alarm'.

'The lower I go, the better I seem to please,' Shaw wrote hopefully to the publisher Richard Bentley. But though in later years *Cashel Byron's Profession* was so much enjoyed by R. L. Stevenson, W. E. Henley and others that Shaw marvelled at his escape from becoming a popular novelist, it was turned down by the London publishing houses. 'It flies too decidedly in the face of people's prejudices to make it likely that it will be a popular book,' advised the reader for Macmillan. ' . . . well and brightly written, but the subject is not likely to commend itself to any considerable public.'

Reviewing the book himself, Shaw pointed out that one of the fights in the novel was a restaging of the wrestling match in *As You Like It*, and hints at the effort he made to write a book as the public liked it. His reaction to what he called his 'shilling shocker' became studded with the glittering contradictions which formed part of his insulation against failure. In 1886, following at least seven rejections, he recommended it as 'one of the cleverest books I know'. But in 1888, when welcoming another publisher's rejection of it, he burst out: 'I hate the book from my soul.' He hated the conditions in which he had written it and the London publishers for whom he had written it: he hated the person who had written it; he hated failure. He had sailed as near compromise as he dared – too near and to no effect. Next time (for he was not ready to give up) there should be no compromise.

He called his fifth novel *The Heartless Man* – later changing the title to *An Unsocial Socialist*. As with the two previous novels he drafted most of it in shorthand at the British Museum, and then transcribed it in longhand. The plot revolves round Sidney Trefusis, the heartless socialist of both titles. At the beginning of the book, Trefusis shocks everyone by running away from his newly married wife. By accepted standards it has been a brilliant match, full of money and romance. But accepted standards have made women into a class of person fit only for the company of children and flowers. With a man like Trefusis they can have no connection, except sex. Unfortunately the sexual attraction between them was so strong, Trefusis gravely complains to his wife Henrietta, that 'When you are with me I can do nothing but make love to you. You bewitch me.'

As Shaw's mouthpiece for Socialism, Trefusis recognizes the natural inequality of human beings but condemns England's social inequality for exploiting it. This artificial inequality will vanish, he claims, once 'England is made the property of its inhabitants collectively'. The choice is 'Socialism or Smash'.

Most people preferred Smash because it looked safer. To open their eyes, British socialists needed to study feminism, for it was women who, by giving Socialism respectability, could make it grow. Shaw's women are sympathetically drawn but, as custodians of Society's standards, they embellish the capitalist philosophy of Smash. Trefusis's aim, whether through sermonizing or seduction, is to head them off from this course. It is the old struggle to release natural vitality from an unnatural system of morality. The most attractive of these girls, for whose socialist souls he wrestles, is Gertrude Lindsay, Shaw's portrait of Alice Lockett. It is a hostile portrait, done in the colours of revenge, of a discontented girl who counts 'the proposals of marriage she received as a Red Indian counts the scalps he takes', and who treats her dog (a St Bernard) with more kindness than 'any human being'.

It is not Gertrude who becomes Trefusis's second wife, but Agatha Wylie – a Shavian Becky Sharp who was inspired by a glimpse of 'a young lady with an attractive and arresting expression, bold, vivid, and very clever, working at one of the desks' in the British Museum Reading Room. She is a symbol of the future.

By separating his socialist hero into two people, Shaw reflected the division he felt existed in his own character. Some of the most entertaining pages of the novel are those where Trefusis, reluctant heir to a fortune, takes on the role of a talkative labourer – a Dickensian character called Smilash (a compound of the words smile and eyelash). In this partnership, Shaw the comedian and Shaw the reformer are brought together for the same ends. The character of Smilash appeals to the 'vagabond impulse' in Trefusis, and the actor in Shaw. 'I am just mad enough to be a mountebank,' Trefusis explains. 'If I were a little madder, I should perhaps really believe myself Smilash instead of merely acting him.'

Trefusis is the great man who had lain asleep in Smith, the tentative hero of *Immaturity*, and who wakes up by the light of Marxist economics.

Shaw's novels had been experiments to find a political framework in which to develop his thought and personality. Conolly, the engineer of *The Irrational Knot*, had been 'a monster of the mind' embodying rationalism; Owen Jack, the composer from *Love Among the Artists*, was 'a monster of the body' representing unconscious instinct; in *Cashel Byron's Profession* Shaw had toyed with a romantic fusion of mind and body in the marriage of his prize-fighter and educated lady. In *An Unsocial Socialist* the union takes place not between two people but within one. Trefusis is Shaw's first socialist hero and Don Juan figure in whom he attempts to reconcile his sexual and political attitudes. The novel foreshadows *Man and Superman*, with Trefusis a prototype of Tanner.

It was an extraordinary book to have produced in the early 1880s – 'the first English novel written under the influence of Karl Marx with a hero whose character and opinions forecast those of Lenin,' Shaw later declared. He finished his revisions on 15 December 1883. 'We are afraid that the subscribers to the circulating libraries are not much interested in Socialism,' wrote Smith Elder & Co. David Douglas of Edinburgh and Chatto & Windus in London excused themselves from looking at it. For Macmillan, John Morley (not realizing that he had previously advised the author to give up writing) reported that 'the author knows how to write; he is pointed, rapid, forcible, sometimes witty, often powerful and occasionally eloquent'. But, Morley concluded, the socialistic irony would not be attractive to many readers and 'they would not know whether the writer was serious or was laughing at them'. In refusing the book, Macmillan wrote that they would be glad to look at anything else he might write 'of a more substantial kind' – a request that, Shaw replied, 'takes my breath away'. In his correspondence with Macmillan, he came as near making an exasperated appeal for sympathy as he could.

'All my readers, as far as I know them, like the book; but they tell me that although they relish it they dont think the general public would. Which is the more discouraging, as this tendency of each man to consider himself unique is one of the main themes of the novel. Surely out of thirty millions of copyright persons (so to speak) there must be a few thousand who would keep me in bread and cheese for the sake of my story-telling, if you would only let me get at them.'

His new political friends were to give Shaw his chance of getting at the public. *An Unsocial Socialist*, he claimed, 'finished me with the publishers'. Instead of adding it to the pile of rejects, Shaw sent it off to J. L. Joynes, one of the editors of *To-Day*, a new 'Monthly Magazine of Scientific Socialism'. Joynes recommended the serialization of the novel to his fellow-editor, the philosopher E. Belfort Bax, who replied: 'Go on and prosper with Shaw . . .'

An Unsocial Socialist appeared in serial form between March and December 1884. Shaw was not paid, but for the first time he had an audience. 'William Morris spotted it and made my acquaintance on account of it. That took me into print and started me.' Between April 1885 and March 1886 *Cashel Byron's Profession* was also serialized, due largely to the enthusiasm of the magazine's printer, H. H. Champion, a clever, epileptic man who was later to become Shaw's dramatic agent in Australia. Champion stereotyped the pages from *To-Day* and published them in a misshapen 'Modern Press' edition of 2,500 copies in March 1886. This was Shaw's first published book, costing a shilling and carrying a royalty of one penny a copy. Two of his other novels, *The Irrational Knot* (April 1885–February 1887) and *Love Among the Artists* (November 1887–December 1888), were to be published serially in Annie Besant's *Our Corner*.

Shaw's political interests soon devoured his ambitions as a novelist. In 1887 he abandoned an attempt at a sixth novel because 'I could not stand the form: it is too clumsy and unreal. Sometimes I write dialogues; and these are working up to a certain end.' His disenchantment with the novel is apparent in *An Unsocial Socialist*. In the appendix to this book, which takes the form of a letter to the author from Trefusis, Shaw writes: 'I cannot help feeling that, in presenting the facts in the guise of fiction, you have, in spite of yourself, shewn them in a false light. Actions described in novels are judged by a romantic system of morals as fictitious as the actions themselves.' This opinion he shared with Defoe who, in *Serious Reflections*, had described the 'supplying of a story by invention' as 'a sort of lying that makes a great hole in the heart, at which by degrees, a habit of lying enters in'. Like Defoe, Shaw resolved to make his fiction as much like fact as possible.

Now that it was too late, publishers were urging him to go on. His books would reach a good circulation, Swan Sonnenschein encouraged him, providing he 'stick to novels, or go in for plays (which are even more suited to you, in my opinion) . . .' Shaw acknowledged that he might 'descend as low as that one day', but five failures had been 'enough to satisfy my appetite for enterprise in fiction'.

Since he could not marry his story-telling to his socialism, Shaw relinquished story-telling. From his socialist philosophy he was to harvest optimism, while the novels, representing his first nine years in London, remained like dead fruit on the bough. Over fifty years later he wrote that his 'failure to find a publisher for any of them was for me a hardening process from which I have never quite recovered'. Although they carry many ideas that were to be developed in his plays, these novels seemed to Shaw to have been written by someone else – someone with his roots in Ireland who once dreamed of a grand literary conquest in London. That Shaw was almost dead.

*

One final tie with his past was cut when on 19 April 1885 George Carr Shaw died. They had had little communication over the last five years. 'I have nothing else to say that you would care about,' his father had written on 2 September 1880; and again, on 4 December 1882: 'I have nothing else particular to say.' Of his son's published works he read only *An Unsocial Socialist*, liked it, but warned him: 'dont get yourself into Holloway Jail.' Though he often asked for letters, 'whether you have anything to say or not', he seldom heard from George who he felt did not 'have anything sentimental left in you'. Years later, Shaw wrote: 'When I recall certain occasions on which I was inconsiderate to him I understood how Dr Johnson stood in the rain in Lichfield to expiate the same remorse.' But he had never fought his father, so all the battles of his adult life would seem bloodless.

George Carr Shaw died suddenly of congestion of the lungs while recovering from pneumonia in a bed-and-breakfast lodging house in Leeson Park Avenue. 'I hastened there, and was ushered upstairs into a bedroom,' McNulty recorded. '. . . He had died in his sleep: and his lips wore a smile.' He had not been wanted, dead or alive, and he was not missed. Lucy was in Ireland at the time, but she did not go to the funeral. When the news reached Shaw, he sent a note, with two staves of music headed 'Grave', to his friend Kingston Barton:

'Telegram just received to say that the governor has left the universe on rather particular business and set me up as

An Orphan.'

From the insurance on his father's life, Shaw was able to buy that summer his first new clothes for years – an all-wool Jaeger suit, a black coat, vest, collar, cravat and pants, all for £11 1s. 'In short, I had become, for better for worse, a different man.'

73

THREE

IN SEARCH OF A FAMILY

> I was a man with some business in the world . . . my main business was
> Socialism.
>
> Shaw to Archibald Henderson (3 January 1905)

The London in which Shaw had been living was like a City of Revelation. From anarchists and atheists; dress- and diet-reformers; from economists, feminists, philanthropists, was the socialist revival of the late nineteenth century to be drawn. This was the last age of the religious and political tract. One, by a clergyman of the Established Church, proved that Jehovah was a small red venomous snake; a second, by a German, replaced this snake with a fish; yet a third, by a Methodist professor, abolished both snake and fish, explaining that Jehovah was a widower. Such scholarly confusion was intensified by the crumbling of known structures. Science, like a great steam engine, having crashed through the infallibility of the Bible, was being garlanded with the dogmas and symbols of mythology and made the Idol of a new religion.

A fresh urgency entered the progressive movement. New clubs and societies sprang up in London, catering for all talents and temperaments. Many working-class socialists joined the street parades of the Social Democratic Federation; anarchical socialists with a taste for sexual radicalism were attracted to the glamorous Socialist League; while the Fabian Society was filled by middle-class intellectuals who wanted to rewrite the economy and rearrange the social patterns of the country without a shot fired. All were agreed that there was a crisis in the land. Thirty per cent of the population of London – the richest city in the world – were living in poverty. Such was the magnitude of capitalism's failure.

Shaw felt relief at entering this turmoil. His personal need coincided with the need of the age. The 'power to stand alone', which Smith had acquired in *Immaturity*, 'at the expense of much sorrowful solitude', was no longer necessary. G.B.S. stood shoulder to shoulder.

The man who, in 1885, could admit that 'I hate all fraternity mongering just as heartily as any other variety of cant' and go on to declare himself the 'member of an individualist state, and therefore nobody's comrade', had decided at the beginning of 1887 that 'it is time for us to abandon the principle of Individualism, and to substitute that of Socialism, on pain of national decay'. By 1891 he had reconciled his instinct with his practice by discovering that 'the way to Communism lies through the most resolute and uncompromising Individualism' – 'pragmatic' individualism, but not *laissez-faire* 'economic' individualism. So he could still reassure a friend: 'Believe me, I always was, & am, an intense Individualist.'

His first manoeuvres towards shedding his neglected self aimed at replacing his family with a community of his own choosing. 'I haunted public meetings,' he remembered, 'like an officer afflicted with cowardice, who takes every opportunity of going under fire.' Towards the end of 1880 he had joined the Zetetical Society, which met weekly in the rooms of the Women's Protective & Provident League in Long Acre. Though 'nervous & self-conscious to a heartbreaking degree . . . I could not hold my tongue. I started up and said something in the debate, and then felt that I had made such a fool of myself . . . I vowed I would . . . become a speaker or perish in the attempt . . . I suffered agonies that no one suspected . . . my heart used to beat as painfully as a recruit's, going under fire for the first time. I could not use notes: when I looked at the paper in my hand I could not collect myself enough to decipher a word.'

The Zetetical Society was a junior copy of the London Dialectical Society which Shaw joined in 1881, reading his first paper there (on the virtues of Capital Punishment over Life Imprisonment) early the following year. Women took an important part in the debates of both societies and helped to insist upon uncensored speech. From the practice of examining each speaker with questions at the conclusion of his paper (heckling was also part of the menu), Shaw began to sense his formidable debating powers.

He also experimented with some literary groups, passing calm evenings with the New Shakespere Society, and more breezy ones with the Browning Society. In 1886 he acted as press officer for the Shelley Society's private production of *The Cenci*. This five-act blank-verse tragedy was, Shaw wrote, 'a strenuous but futile and never-to-be-repeated attempt to bottle the new wine in the old skins'.

He was surprised to find that the Shelley Society presented the poet 'as a Church of England country gentleman whose pastime was writing sermons in verse'. When he announced to the Society that 'I am a Socialist, an Atheist and a Vegetarian', two members resigned. Having begun to submerge his self-consciousness into a social conscience, he wanted, like Shelley, to pierce the illusions that made the present order seem eternal, and show the world its future. He wanted 'a cause and a creed to live for'.

He found them on the evening of 5 September 1882 at the nonconformist Memorial Hall in Farringdon Street where the American economist, Henry George, was speaking on Land Nationalization. George spoke with an appealing American intonation. He was simple, he was sentimental; and, like the best avant-garde Americans, he was fifty years behind the times in most of Europe. But he gave to politics the powerful orchestration of religion.

George's *Progress and Poverty*, which Shaw bought that evening for sixpence, offered an explanation as to why increasing economic progress brought increasing poverty. The ownership of land had always been a precondition of power in Britain. These few landowners monopolized the birthright of the people, but the nationalization of this land would give the people back their birthright.

For the first time it flashed on Shaw that all this controversy between Science and Religion, Darwin and the Bible, was barren ground. 'The importance of the economic basis dawned on me.' George's book helped Shaw come to terms with his own past. He had been betrayed into his one exhibition of feeling (seizing and kissing his mother's hand) over the possession of Torca Cottage – and that had led to disillusion. Now he could find an impersonal reason, bleached of grievance, for his loveless home and miserable years in the estate office of Uniacke Townshend. All had been part of an inhumane system of property-owning.

Henry George was to reduce Land Nationalization to a single tax on land - a casting back to the *impôt unique* of Honoré Mirabeau. His Single Tax was a stepping stone to socialism, and socialists stepping over it did not take it with them. They were converted by George, but not to him. Shaw, who played Voltaire to George's Mirabeau, had no sooner read *Progress and Poverty* than he went on to Karl Marx, and finally 'devoted about four years to the study of abstract economics so as to get my foundations sound for my work as a socialist in devising practicable methods of industrial and political reconstruction'.

He spoke at clubs; he read in the British Museum. He searched among new organizations for a political headquarters. He tried out his voice at the Bedford Debating Society organized by an Irish Unitarian preacher, Stopford Brooke (on whom Shaw partly modelled the Reverend James Morrell in *Candida*); he joined two discussion groups in Hampstead, and he went to meetings of the Democratic Federation, the first political organization of socialists in Britain.

The Federation was led by H. M. Hyndman who saw himself, in his immaculate frock-coat, fine gloves and silk hat, leading his rough proletarian army to a revolutionary dawn. But it was ballet rather than revolution. His drilling of the unemployed and parading of the working class in the streets appeared to be rehearsals for the Apocalypse which was fixed for 1889, the anniversary of the French Revolution. With his high-chested carriage, he already looked like a prime minister. Hyndman had known Marx and, when leaving his house one day, put on his hat by mistake and found that it fitted. In 1881 he had published a book, *England for All*, that, while introducing Marxist doctrines to English readers, did so without mentioning Marx's name – except (a point that failed to satisfy Marx) in a Preface. But it was Hyndman's connection with Henry George that had attracted Shaw to what became known as the Social Democratic Federation. At his first meeting, he mentioned George and was told to go off and read Marx. There was no English version available so he studied the first volume of *Das Kapital* in Deville's French translation, working during the autumn of 1883 at the British Museum. 'That was the turning point in my career,' he told Hesketh Pearson. 'Marx was a revelation . . . He opened my eyes to the facts of history and civilization, gave me an entirely fresh conception of the universe, provided me with a purpose and a mission in life.' *Das Kapital*, he wrote, 'achieved the greatest feat of which a book is capable – that of changing the minds of the people who read it'.

But when, brimming with Marxism, he returned to the SDF, he found that Hyndman's lieutenants had not read him themselves. He was now a 'candidate member' of the SDF, but for two reasons decided not to join. The first was Hyndman's own incapacity for teamwork. His famous temper was responsible for driving away many socialists – Edward Aveling, Belfort Bax, Walter Crane, Eleanor Marx and William Morris, who formed themselves into an anti-parliamentary group called the Socialist League, soon to be infiltrated by the anarchists.

But there was a second reason why Shaw turned his back on Hyndman. 'I wanted to work with men of my own mental training.' It was then that he came across the first tract, *Why are the Many Poor?*, of the newly formed Fabian Society. Here was an educated body appealing to the middle-class intelligentsia: 'my own class in fact.' From this tract he discovered the Society's address and on 16 May 1884 turned up for its next meeting.

*

The nominal founder of the Fabian Society had been Thomas Davidson, the illegitimate son of a Scottish shepherd. Davidson was an inspired talker and very strong on immortality. In 1881 he had blazed through London, inflaming miscellaneous agitators and idealists with what William James called his 'inward glory'. On his next visit two years later some of these acolytes formed 'a sort of club'. Members were of two conditions: those whose impulse was primarily religious; and others, more politically minded, who wished to reconstruct society. Soon the club split up into two branches – 'The Fellowship of the New Life' attracting the former and the Fabian Society the socialists.

'What does the name mean? Why Fabian?' asked Edward Pease, the first secretary of the Society. The Fabian Society's motto was printed as an epigraph to the Fabian Tract that Shaw read in the spring of 1884.

'For the right moment you must wait, as Fabius did, most patiently, when warring against Hannibal, though many censured his delays; but when the time comes you must strike hard, as Fabius did, or your waiting will be vain and fruitless.'

When critics asked the name of the history from which this quotation came, Pease answered gleefully that the work of the Fabian Society was not to repeat history, but to make it. Since the instincts of the early Fabians were literary as well as political, their business – chiefly under Shaw's influence – was to alter history by rewriting it.

The Minutes of the meeting of 16 May had a famous mauve-ink side-note in unmistakably Shavian hand and style – the careful signature with its incongruous flourish of defiance: 'This meeting was made memorable by the first appearance of Bernard Shaw.' On 5 September he formally enrolled and before the end of the year had published an unsigned two-page leaflet entitled *A Manifesto*, listed as Fabian Tract No. 2. Never again was Shaw so succinct. His seventeen propositions have a trenchancy and wit giving it a different tone from other socialist documents. Under present circumstances, he wrote, 'wealth cannot be enjoyed without dishonour or foregone without misery'; the result of nineteenth-century capitalism in Britain had been to divide society 'into hostile classes, with large appetites and no dinners at one extreme and large dinners and no appetites at the other'; under *laissez-faire*, competition 'has the effect of rendering adulteration, dishonest dealing and inhumanity compulsory'; instead of leaving National Industry to organize itself, the State should compete 'with all its might in every department of production'; and there should be equal political rights for the sexes, since 'Men no longer need special political privileges to protect them against Women'. The Manifesto ended with the proposition: That we had 'rather face a Civil War than such another century of suffering as the present one has been'.

By the beginning of 1885 two things had been achieved. The Fabians had found a programme – and Shaw a platform.

2

HEROES AND FRIENDS

> I found that I had only to say with perfect simplicity what I seriously
> meant just as it struck me, to make everybody laugh. My method is to
> take the utmost trouble to find the right thing to say, and then say it
> with the utmost levity. And all the time the real joke is that I am in
> earnest.

During 1884 and 1885, Shaw had taken on two gruelling jobs. Between November and April he edited for H. H. Champion's Modern Press an edition of Lawrence Gronland's *The Cooperative Commonwealth*, an exposition of socialism that had recently appeared in the United States. 'By God, I never read [such] English!' he exclaimed to Champion. Shaw's editing gave the book a sparkling tone. He polished it with optimism. His payment for this editing was to be £5, 'if the book ever produces anything over the costs & advts' – a figure that became more remote once Gronland, repudiating Shaw's version, published his American 'authorized' edition, with a preface addressed 'To the British Reader'.

Even less profitable was a commission Shaw had accepted as early as January 1884 to provide a glossary and index for the Hunterian Club's edition of Thomas Lodge's Works. 'I wasted the year deplorably,' he noted in his diary. At intervals over the following year he would receive imploring letters from the Club, and these would result in desperate resolutions to buy an alarm clock. In July 1885 he transferred the commission to Thomas Tyler, a 'rectangular, waistless, neckless, ankleless . . . man of letters of an uncommercial kind' who had previously made a translation of Ecclesiastes. Tyler completed the job but not long afterwards died, 'sinking unnoted like a stone in the sea' – though remaining for the grateful Shaw 'a vivid spot of memory in the void of my forgetfulness'.

During 1885 Shaw 'slipped into paid journalism'. This had come about through his friendship with William Archer who, two months younger than Shaw, had already made his name with a charming series of articles on theatre in the *London Figaro*. Working at the British Museum Reading Room in 1883, Archer's attention had been drawn to what appeared as an undelivered brown paper parcel on the next seat. This was Shaw. 'There I used to sit day by day,' Archer recalled, 'beside a pallid young man with red hair and beard, dressed in Jaeger all-wool clothing which rather harmonized with his complexion. My interest was excited . . . by the literature to which he devoted himself day after day. It consisted of Karl Marx's *Das Kapital* in French, and a full orchestral score of Wagner's

Tristan und Isolde.' Before long they were introduced. 'We had many interests in common,' Archer recalled, 'and soon became intimate friends.'

Shaw loved Archer and Archer reciprocated this love. They shared an intimacy of humour, and neither mistook the other's emotional reticence for lack of feeling. When emotional, Archer grew so wooden that, on the point of tears, he looked like a piece of mahogany. Shaw admired him for his unpretentiousness and integrity. They teased and chided and fathered monstrous advice on each other freely. The candour of their exchanges was a relief to them both, for they inflicted no malice and received no wounds. Under the device of open disagreement they made a secret code of their affection.

They disagreed most on whatever interested them most. As dual champions of Ibsen they each regretted that the other was not an Ibsenite. Each wanted the other to succeed – and felt that he alone knew how this quality of success was to be come by. Archer might not be able to combat his high cheek-bones or the outline of his jaw, but he could unbutton the collar that gave 'his head the appearance of being wedged by the neck into a jampot' – and, in doing so, Shaw counselled, 'consent to make an ass of yourself publicly'. Shaw had to do the opposite thing: quell all that reckless extravaganza, grow up, and cease from making an ass of himself in public. 'He loses influence by being such an incorrigible jester,' Archer lamented, 'by wearing the cap and bells in and out of season.'

Both had made one awful error: Shaw in writing plays, and Archer in not writing plays. 'Why the devil dont you write a play instead of perpetually talking about it?' Shaw demanded. Goaded by the perpetual stings, when just short of his sixty-fifth birthday, Archer woke up one morning from a dream of a Rajah in the depths of the Himalayas accompanied by his valet – obviously a 'complete scheme for a romantic melodrama,' he revealed to Shaw, 'which only needs your co-operation to be infallibly THE PLAY OF THE CENTURY.' But Shaw collaborated only to the extent of helping him to transform the dream into a lurid plot 'about an Asiatic Rajah made cynical by a western education, and a Green Goddess who had to be propitiated by blood sacrifices'. *The Green Goddess* became a melodramatic success because, Shaw felt, 'collaboration between us was impossible'. He had learned this when, in the late summer of 1884, he set to work on an earlier theatrical notion of Archer's.

With our knowledge of Shaw's success in the theatre, it is easy to ridicule Archer's cordial discouragement. But Shaw's plays were *not* plays. Archer had no trouble in spotting this. His friend had dispensed with plot, with character, with drama and the red corpuscles of life, to demonstrate that argument squeezed into a well-built dramatic machine was as good as any play. So: 'Let us be grateful for him as he is, and . . . enjoy and applaud him. He is not, and he never will be, a great dramatist; but he is something rarer, if not better – a philosophic humorist, with the art of expressing himself in dramatic form.'

Archer's criticism, presented as friendly and despairing advice, required Shaw to change into someone else (or to reverse the change into G.B.S.). 'I doubt whether there has ever been a more extraordinary and fascinating combination of gifts in one single human brain,' he acknowledged. He saw through Shaw's optimism; he did not see Shaw's need for optimism. It was the urgency of this need that was driving Shaw to hammer together, like a magical raft, his philosophy and float lightly upon it over the sea around him. Archer wanted him to abandon this whimsical craft and plunge into the water. But Shaw's nourishment came not from reality as Archer witnessed and experienced it, but from a fantasy that, for all its hard businesslike style, slid along a slice of invisible air. His word-addiction kept him incredibly suspended, and he seldom allowed himself to fall victim to events. But Archer believed this limited his appeal. He would never get a ducking. His audiences might not be able to ignore him but, resenting his superiority, they were resolved never to take him seriously.

Archer would occasionally slip along to Shaw's little room on the second floor of 36 Osnaburgh Street. Troubled by what he saw, he 'took my affairs in hand,' Shaw recorded, planting him among the reviewing staff of the *Pall Mall Gazette*, where he contributed book reviews from May 1885 to December 1888. He also procured him a place on the *Magazine of Music*, which applied to Shaw for articles pretty regularly during the later months of 1884; and he introduced him to an Irishman named Edwin Palmer who, in February 1885, started the *Dramatic Review* and employed Shaw as his music critic.

But Shaw was not an easy man to help. 'I am making more money than I have any present need for, and shall always be glad to help you to keep going until one or other of your argosies comes home,' Archer wrote to him. Such help, which Shaw was frequently to offer others in a similar manner, he could never receive himself. Archer, however, had hit on a more delicate ruse. He had been prevailed upon by Edmund Yates, editor of *The World*, through whose columns he had recently begun what Shaw called 'his victorious career' as theatre critic, to double as a critic of art. Knowing nothing about pictures, yet knowing Shaw, Archer invited his friend to accompany him round the galleries. Shaw agreed and, as Archer had expected, poured forth a stream of comment and suggestion. Archer listened, then wrote the article and forwarded to Shaw a cheque for £1 6s. 8d., being half his fee. But Shaw, recommending more exercise and earlier hours, sent it back. Archer, exasperated by his friend's stubbornness, told him he was a 'damned fool not to accept the money,' adding,

'I certainly should in your position.' Since Archer's incorruptibility was notorious this should have served as a telling argument when he sent the cheque back to Shaw: 'If you took the trouble to read what I do write you would see that every second idea is yours ... So be a good fellow and stow your logic.'

But Shaw was proof against this plea. He re-returned the cheque, 'and if you re-re-return it,' he warned, 'I will re-re-re-return it'. He then treated Archer to an outpouring of Shavian economics that, by way of Ricardo's Law of rent and Lassalle's Law of wages, concluded that it paid him famously to go without remuneration: 'I have the advantage of seeing the galleries for nothing without the drudgery of writing the articles.' Archer was adding to his schooling in the National Gallery of Ireland, with a free education and: 'we all grow stupid and mad to just the extent to which we have not been artistically educated.'

Archer had no way of telling that the arrangement he was proposing reproduced for Shaw those ghost-writing days with Lee on *The Hornet*. It was as if Shaw was being given an opportunity to scrub away that tainted year when he had submitted to polite fraud. It was particularly ingenious that he should be tempted by his closest and most honourable friend, and from the worthiest motives. As an admirer of *The Pilgrim's Progress*, Shaw would not have had it differently. It was a soft and amiable corruption to which he was being beckoned, and the first major test of whether his socialism was making a new man of him. Archer, the innocent implement of this trial, is a siren voice: everything he says is reasonable, well-intentioned and brimful of sense. But Shaw steadfastly refuses. He is impoverished and free.

Archer, however, was not free. For some weeks he continued to work laboriously as art critic for *The World* 'until my conscience could endure it no longer'. He then persuaded Shaw to do a specimen article which he sent to Yates and which secured him the post. In Shavian language, Archer had 'rescued me by a stratagem', having deliberately planned to resign his post as soon as Shaw got a firm hold on it. This, so Archer held, was a lovely essay in *a priori* Shavianism, where true belief becomes a matter of will over chronology.

*

Shaw held the post of art critic on *The World* from the spring of 1886 to the autumn of 1889. He had in June 1885 started to contribute an 'Art Corner' (covering all the arts) to *Our Corner*, having met its editor Annie Besant at the Dialectical Society that January, and he continued this column until September 1886. 'On art I am prepared to dogmatize; on traffic, ask a policeman,' he wrote. It was his comic dogmatism that made these catalogues of pictures so entertaining to readers of *Our Corner* and *The World*:

'Concerning Mr Poynter's "Difference of Opinion", with its expanse of closely-clipped grass glittering in the sun, one can only suggest, not disrespectfully, that it would make a capital advertisement for a lawn-mower . . .'

'Mr Phil Morris's "Storm on Albion's Coast" contains a raging ocean made of what I think is called "tulle" . . . Mr Kennedy has spent much careful work to doubtful advantage on something resembling an East End starveling stuffed into the tail of a stale salmon, and called a mermaid. Miss Dorothy Tennant is reviving the traditional "brown tree" with a vengeance, as a background to her dainty little nude figures. The humorous picture of the year is Mr C. Shannon's "Will he come in?" a group of primeval men in a pond, where they have taken refuge from a red-haired mammoth . . .'

' "Disaster" is the title given by Mr Walter Langley to his scene in a Cornish fishing-village; and, on the whole, I agree . . . The tiger in "Alert" is sitting for its portrait with immense self-satisfaction . . .'

'The President's [Walter Crane's] design, in which Mr Gladstone axe in hand, cuts down a serpent a thousand feet high, is allegory reduced to the desperation of mixed metaphor . . .'

Shaw's two gods in matters of art were Ruskin and Morris. Of Ruskin, 'a really great artist-philosopher,' he was to write: 'He begins as a painter, a lover of music, a poet and rhetorician, and presently becomes an economist and sociologist, finally developing sociology and economics . . . to an almost divine condition.' Even in a small way Shaw considered himself as carrying on Ruskin's business. 'In a society in which we are all striving after the thief's ideal of living well and doing nothing,' he said, ' . . . and in which the only people who can afford to buy valuable pictures are those who have attained to this ideal, a great artist with anything short of compulsory powers of attraction must either be a hypocrite . . . or starve.' We looked for no valuable advance in art, he argued, 'until we redistribute our immense Wealth and our immense Leisure so as to secure to every honest man his due share of both in return for his share of the national labour'.

Shaw enjoyed affronting picture-gallery conventions. He advised artists to sell their paintings 'by the foot'. 'Did they never teach you that the frame is the most important part of the picture, and a good "trade finish" (like Van Eyck's) its most indispensable quality?' he innocently asked Austin Spare.

Shaw followed Ruskin's taste as well as his example. 'I went into the National Gallery and spent more than an hour over the Turner drawings in the basement with deep pleasure in them,' he noted in his diary. But he claimed to be as much a politician at the press-view as a Member of Parliament on the hustings: 'I am always electioneering.' Recalling his work as art critic half a dozen years later, he wrote: 'Certain reforms in painting which I desired were advocated by the Impressionist party, and resisted by the Academic party. Until these reforms had been effectually wrought I fought for the Impressionists . . . [and] did everything I could to make the public conscious of the ugly unreality of studio-lit landscape and the inanity of second-hand classicism.'

Shaw criticized the 'insistently mundane' exhibitions at Burlington House and championed the Society of British Artists led by Whistler who 'must be at least as well satisfied as any propagandist in London,' he commented. 'The defeat of his opponents at the [1887] winter exhibitions is decisive.' This was an example of Shavian electioneering by a critic who privately believed Whistler to be a gentleman painter clever enough to make a merit of his limited ability. Yet his work was preferable to that of the future President of the Royal Academy, Sir Frederick Leighton, who specialized in 'the arts of the toilet as practised by rich ladies'.

Shaw was ideologically committed to progress and sensed that the notations of Whistler's 'symphonies' and 'harmonies', dashed off in an hour or two, were shorthand messages from the future. At the same time Whistler was Ruskin's enemy, and had declared in his famous *Ten O'Clock* lecture that art was 'selfishly preoccupied with her own perfection only . . . having no desire to teach'. Shaw's art criticism is impressive in its political dexterity: he treats Whistler more as a campaigner-artist than an artist-philosopher. Closer to his natural taste were the Pre-Raphaelites. The prize painter of the Brotherhood was Burne-Jones, who 'has the power to change the character of an entire exhibition by contributing or withholding his work'.

At least three times a week Shaw would abscond from literature and art, go down among the Fabians and, like a man bathing himself, 'talk seriously on serious subjects to serious people. For this reason . . . I never once lost touch with the real world.' The real world without art was deeply unsatisfying to Shaw, but the art world without reality seemed worse. As a compromise he supported the Arts and Crafts movement:

'It has been for a long time past evident that the first step towards making our picture-galleries endurable is to get rid of the pictures – the detestable pictures – the silly British pictures, the vicious foreign pictures, the venal popular pictures, the pigheaded academic pictures, signboards all of them of the wasted talent and perverted ambition of men who might have been passably useful as architects, engineers, potters, cabinet-makers, smiths, or bookbinders. But there comes an end to all things; and perhaps the beginning of the end of the easel-picture despotism is the appearance in the New Gallery of the handicraftsman with his pots and pans, textiles and fictiles, and things in general that have some other use than to hang on a nail and collect bacteria. Here, for instance, is Mr Cobden Sanderson, a gentleman of artistic instincts. Does Mr Cobden Sanderson paint wooden portraits of his female-relatives, and label them Juliet or Ophelia, according to the colour of their hair? No: he binds books, and makes them pleasant to look at, pleasant to handle, pleasant to open and shut, pleasant to possess, and as much of a delight as the outside of a book can be.'

Shaw promoted artists as people who, while apparently providing something that few people wanted, anticipated a demand. Whether it preached or argued, exposed, assured, revealed, consoled, art was a magic and, like Prospero's Ariel, it commanded kings. Through new combinations of sound, new bridges of feeling and rhythms of colour, people absorbed information that, presented merely as information, they would reject from prejudice or boredom. This was the penetrating power of art, and when Shaw spoke of it he turned naturally to music. 'And great artists, in order to get a hearing, have to fascinate their hearers; they have to provide a garment of almost supernatural beauty for the message they have to deliver. Therefore, when a man has a message to deliver in literature, with great effort and toil he masters words until he can turn them into music.'

This formed part of Shaw's case against Whistler's concept of art. We must not limit art, he argued, to the satisfaction of our desire for beauty. People cannot endure beauty any more than they can endure love. The paradoxical triumph of romanticism was to have drugged us into believing that we worshipped love and beauty even as we struggled to avoid their demands. Self-respect curdled into self-love, in Shaw's prescription, unless preserved by seriousness: the dilettante was *always* narcissistic. Oscar Wilde appeared the pre-eminent dilettante; the best example of the serious man was William Morris. His love of the medieval world sprang from a longing to regain those happy years 'when I was a little chap'. He summoned up a vision of the long past, a garden of happiness where nature, in the pattern of leaves and flowers, invaded the rooms: 'it was a positive satisfaction to be in his houses,' Shaw remembered. Morris had set his heart on founding a brotherhood that, by seeking medieval cures for the malaise of capitalism, would crusade against industrial squalor and replace it with a regenerated Britain – a green-tree land of gardens, fields and forests. His revolutionary politics followed a revolution in his own life to which Shaw's attitude is revealing.

Like Shaw, Morris had an extreme fear of emotional suffering; like Shaw, he identified schools as prisons, locking him out of Eden. But he returned to Eden when, in 1859, he married 'an apparition of fearful and wonderful beauty', Janey Burden, the daughter of a groom. For her, as for Augustus John's Dorelia, beauty had been a means of emancipation. She looked like a 'figure cut out of a missal,' Henry James said, and had been raised from her simple working-class life to be Queen of the Pre-Raphaelite kingdom, a Blessed Damozel, tragic, imposing, silent. Morris's developing interest in the working class seemed to threaten her with a return to the mean conditions of her past. Shaw observed no unhappiness. 'Their harmony seemed to me to be perfect. In his set, beauty in women was a cult.' When Morris, in old age, covered the forests of his wallpapers with whitewash, Shaw recognized not the extinction of something essential but an advance in 'his need for the clean, the wholesome, & the sensible'.

To Shaw, it was as if Morris had woken up from an impossible dream of fair women, opened his eyes on a Ruskinian landscape and strode out to reach the communism that 'was part of his commonsense'. He had transferred his hopes from an individual to a collective sphere, achieving fulfilment through the integration of politics and art. No matter that he had little natural aptitude for politics. Shaw acknowledged his position as head of the Socialist League to be 'absurdly false', recommending that he be treated with marked consideration as 'a privileged eccentric and in no way an authority as to socialist policy' – almost exactly in the same manner as the Labour Party was later to regard G.B.S. himself.

Morris was the clearest example of a hero in the Shavian iconoclastic world. Shaw felt wonderfully at home at his house on Hammersmith Terrace where he met many kindred spirits – men such as Sydney Cockerell and Walter Crane. In place of Wilde's aesthetics for the élite stood a man who worked with others on behalf of everyone – a man who wanted to bring applied arts and the perspective of beauty into all life. The 'idle singer of an empty day' had grown into the busy singer of a bursting day. Shaw believed that the artist's wares had to be marketed in the knowledge that most customers hated beauty because, as a reflection of love, it could hurt them. Though his capacity for loving was undeveloped, Shaw did not lack emotion. Cunningly fenced off behind some of the most brilliantly unsentimental prose in the language, is plenty of feeling. His faith in the employment of the arts is expressed in a puritan encyclical:

'The claim of art to our respect must stand or fall with the validity of its pretension to cultivate and refine our senses and faculties until seeing, hearing, feeling, smelling and tasting become highly conscious and critical acts with us ... The worthy artist or craftsman is he who serves the physical and moral senses by feeding them with pictures, musical compositions, pleasant houses and gardens, good clothes and fine implements, poems, fictions, essays and dramas which call the heightened senses and ennobled faculties into pleasurable activity. The great artist is he who goes a step beyond the demand, and, by supplying works of a higher beauty and a higher interest than have yet been perceived, succeeds after a brief struggle with its strangeness, in adding this fresh extension of sense to the heritage of the race.'

3

THE PROSPECTIVE LOVER

People who are much admired often get wheedled or persecuted into love affairs with persons whom they would have let alone if they themselves had been let alone.

These words appear in a short story, 'Don Giovanni Explains', that Shaw wrote in the summer of 1887. He makes use in this story of his experiences with women over the past three years to find the best truth available to him. Like Shaw, Don Giovanni had been born a shy man.

'On rare occasions, some woman would strike my young fancy; and I would worship her at a distance for a long time, never venturing to seek her acquaintance ... At last a widow lady at whose house I sometimes visited, and of whose sentiments towards me I had not the least suspicion, grew desperate at my stupidity, and one evening threw herself into my arms and confessed her passion for me. The surprise, the flattery, my inexperience, and her pretty distress, overwhelmed me. I was incapable of the brutality of repulsing her; and indeed for nearly a month I enjoyed without scruple the pleasure she gave me, and sought her company whenever I could find nothing better to do. It was my first consummated love affair; and though for nearly two years the lady had no reason to complain of my fidelity, I found the romantic side of our intercourse, which seemed never to pall on her, tedious, unreasonable, and even forced and insincere except at rare moments, when the power of love made her beautiful, body and soul.'

There were three categories of relationship in Shaw's life: flirtations with single women, usually at this time young Fabian girls; philanderings with the wives of friends, usually socialist colleagues; and a consummated love affair with a divorced or separated lady. With Alice Lockett he had tried to combine all his emotional needs in one person, and concluded that it could not be done. On 29 September 1888, more than three years after they had parted, Alice spent the day with Shaw in London. 'I sang some of the old *Figaro* bits with Alice, who presently went home,' he noted in his diary, 'overcome, I think, by old associations.'

There was no chance of Shaw being overcome: he overcame. He had plumed himself into a dazzling lecturer, enthralling audiences with his vitality and wit. He was marvellously adroit too in debate, catching his opponents' sallies in mid-air like a conjuror and returning them with amazing speed. The expectations he raised are beautifully caught by a young Fabian called Grace Black. 'People are so exceedingly miserable in every class, that I should lose hope if I did not know there are many who devote themselves entirely to trying to make things better,' she wrote to him.

' . . . you have a greater power of seeing truth than most people: you can do more than most. It is impossible to help expecting a great deal from you and now is the point – don't fail – please don't. For one thing I don't know how I could bear it – but that is not the point. What I fear is that you do not care for nor believe in people sufficiently . . . do care more for people for that is where you seem to fail.'

Shaw recognized at once a case of Fabian love. He could diagnose love as efficiently as a doctor identifying death. His objection to it was part of his hatred of private property. People said that all the world loved a lover: the truth was that a lover loved all the world, and therein lay his crime. Providing we were in love, the world was a fine place, and we condoned its awfulness. That we needed to love, he knew. But he represented the *partiality* of romantic love as a perversion of our deepest desire. For it was not to this person, then to that person, but to the whole world that we owed the comprehension of love. The world, however, was not ready for love. To renounce the indulgence of loving was in itself an act of love – the act of deferred love we call faith.

Grace Black had asked for no answer – 'if you sent me one, you might make me unhappy,' she told him. But Shaw could not let this alone. He sent his first letter to her by return of post. Her reply was a rebuke:

'I guessed you would think I was in love with you. So I am, but that has nothing to do with my letter and it is a pity if that thought has clouded my meaning. My personal happiness is certainly connected with your success as a teacher of socialism, & in a less degree by that of Hyndman & Morris, because I care very much for what is implied to me by socialism. But apart from that I do love you, & why do you wish to dissuade me from that and from believing in you? . . . There is nothing in my attitude of humility, dependence or expectancy which would give reason for irritation . . . But it is true that I wish that love were an easier simpler thing than it is now; but that is to wish for heaven . . . You are not much older than me, but all experience is to the bad. I am serious.'

Shaw's experience of love had been 'to the bad', and from Grace Black's feelings he took care to protect himself. His description of Grace's announcement in 1889 of her marriage is a good example of inverted Shavian romanticism: she 'sent me a note to say what she was going to do,' he wrote, 'adding, by way of apology for throwing me over, that she could never marry a man she loved'. The letter he actually received read as follows:

'You know that the reason I began to love you was because I believed you cared more for truth and would do more to help socialism than any other man . . . Long ago I saw that my love for you was a waste of force, because you were so different to me: but it is only lately I have been able to love anyone else. I do now, and am engaged to marry Edwin Human a Socialist . . . You have a place deep in my heart: my feelings have run through all the personal currents in respect of you & can't go back but have ended as they began in something quite impersonal, rather painful but in a way sacred.'

Meeting Grace some years after her marriage, he records: 'She looked extraordinarily youthful; she has children; her marriage is obviously as happy as it is possible for a marriage to be; her husband no more grudges her her adorations than he grudges her a motor car.' In casting himself as a piece of extra-marital machinery, Shaw re-creates what he hoped were the circumstances of his own Dublin household.

One family to have benefited from Shaw's interference had been the Beattys. Among others by now were the Avelings and the Blands. At the head of all three families was a husband notorious for his illicit love-affairs. Shaw, who was to place Edward Aveling on the stage as Louis Dubedat in *The Doctor's Dilemma*, described him as the man who 'seduced every woman he met and borrowed from every man', and yet would have 'gone to the stake bravely rather than admit that Marx was not infallible or that God existed'. As his interest in politics deepened he turned his attention to Karl Marx's youngest daughter, Eleanor. Shaw used to see this clever dark-haired girl at the British Museum, working for eighteen pence an hour as a literary hack. In June 1884 she decided to go and live with Aveling on the understanding that they would marry if his wife died. For Shaw, who regarded himself as unattractive, here was a revelation. 'Though no woman seemed able to resist him,' he wrote of Aveling, 'he was short, with the face and eyes of a lizard, and no physical charm except a voice like a euphonium.' Like Wilkes, he was only a quarter of an hour behind the handsomest man in Europe. Shaw seemed determined to pursue this mystery. Aveling worked on the staff of the *Dramatic Review* and Shaw often called at his home, but his diary reveals that it was Eleanor (or 'Mrs Aveling') he came to see. She was not sure what to make of him. 'If you are mad,' she wrote, 'there is marvellous method in your madness & penetration that sanity wd gambol from . . . oh, most amiable and sympathetic of cynics.' She would appeal to him to save her 'from a long day and evening of tête-à-tête with myself', and he responded.

17 February Called on the Avelings . . . Talked with Mrs A between 17 and 18 (A went out shortly after I came in).
28 February Mrs Aveling asked me to call in the afternoon and have a chat. Went at 17 and stayed until 20 nearly. Aveling absent at Crystal Palace concert. Urged her to go on the stage. Chatted about this, death, sex, and a lot of things.
28 March Went to Mrs Aveling and discussed *Love Among the Artists* with her.
14 April Called on the Avelings – A[veling] at Ventnor: Eleanor at home: stayed with her from 17 to 19.45.
20 June After meeting on musical pitch called on Mrs Aveling. Aveling came in later on. Went home and played all the evening.
24 August Rumour of split between the Avelings mentioned by [J.M.] Robertson.

Shaw recoiled at the news that the Avelings might separate. His instinct whispered retreat. The Avelings' later history exposed everything he most feared about sexual passion. In 1897, following the death of his wife, Aveling secretly married Eva Frye, and following an anonymous letter telling her of this marriage, Eleanor poisoned herself. 'My last word to you,' she wrote in her suicide note, 'is the same as I have said during all these long, sad years – love.' But Shaw could not endure the agony of such love. In his tight little note on her death, he referred to 'the news of Eleanor Marx's suicide in consequence of Aveling having spent all her money'.

As he began easing out of the Avelings' home, so he started to infiltrate the marriage of the Blands. Hubert Bland had been a founder of the Fabian Society, and its first treasurer. He was a man of Norman exterior, imperialist instincts, and huge physical strength, though to Shaw he seemed 'an affectionate, imaginative sort of person'. Like Hyndman, he wore Tory clothes and 'never was seen without an irreproachable frock coat, tall hat, and a single eyeglass which infuriated everybody'.

'Hubert was not a restful husband,' Shaw conceded. He had married his wife, Edith Nesbit, in 1880, when she was twenty-one and seven months pregnant, and subsequently had children by two other women. The first of these women Edith befriended; the second, Alice Hoatson, already was her friend and a part of the Bland household, where her daughter Rosamund was brought up by Edith as her own child. The Blands' home was a disorganized ménage and the conglomeration of parties, charades, music and children formed a refreshing contrast to sterner Fabian entertainments. Shaw would slip on boxing-gloves and dance round the short-sighted Bland who was incapable of deliberately hurting anyone. 'I was taller by a couple of inches and with longer reach,' Shaw calculated. And Edith watched.

According to Edward Pease, Edith was acknowledged as 'the most attractive and vivacious woman of our circle', though burdened with spectacular fainting fits and, at supreme moments of Fabian drama, the habit of calling sensationally for glasses of water. She abstained from corsets (a false method of 'girding the loins'), rolled her cigarettes which she smoked from a long holder, and looked every inch an advanced woman. 'On the other hand,' Shaw believed, 'she is excessively conventional; and her ideas are not a woman's ideas, but the ideas which men have foisted, in their own interest, on women.'

She was soon confiding her ideas to Shaw. Sometimes she would invite him to tea, but more often she met him at the British Museum, and they would go for long striding walks. By the summer of 1886 these meetings had grown longer and more intricate. 'On the whole the day was devoted to Mrs Bland,' Shaw wrote on 26 June 1886. 'We dined together, had tea together, and I went out to Lee with her and played and sang there until Bland came in from his volunteer work. A memorable evening!'

Edith, who was to become famous as a writer of stories for children, appealed to Shaw partly because she retained so much of the child in her. In the 1880s she wrote poetry. 'The faults of the poems are so directly and intimately the faults of the woman,' Shaw wrote in a review of her Lays and Legends (1886), ' . . . there is too much of the luxury of unreal grief, of getting into the vein by imagining churchyards and jiltings and the like.' Shaw composed music for some of these verses, among which were love poems to himself.

She called him 'the grossest flatterer (of men women and children impartially) I ever met'. He 'repeats everything he hears, and does not always stick to the truth, and is *very plain* . . . and yet is one of the most fascinating men I ever met'. She would pursue him to his lair in the British Museum, and he would hurry her out to pretty scenes on the river and in the park; give her tea in the Wheatsheaf; see her on to buses and trains. On their way to Baker Street Station one day, they called in at Shaw's home. From then on it became a struggle for her to get into his house, and for him to keep her walking in the open air. If, on their way to some bus stop or railway station, he needed to leave his books at home, she accompanied him inside and beckoned him upstairs; at other times he went on grimly walking through all weathers, hour after hour, till she dropped exhausted and veered off home. It was an exercising business.

It became increasingly difficult to detect in Bland the overflowing gratitude Shaw claimed such husbands lavished on him. He hoped, by everything short of a sexual relationship, to give Edith compensation for her husband's infidelities. But she protested to him: 'You had no right to write the Preface if you were not going to write the book.' He had made her determined to bring matters to a climax. On 11 May 1887, finding him hunched over More's *Utopia* in the Reading Room, she marched him out to tea at the Austrian Café and insisted on leading him off to his home. Believing his mother to be there, he agreed. His mother was out. There followed 'an unpleasant scene caused by my telling her that I wished her to go, as I was afraid that a visit to me alone would compromise her'. She went: but the friendship survived and the marriage endured. For Shaw, in his fashion, was a true friend of this marriage, rather than the ally of one partner. In 1914, when Bland was dying and felt troubled as to whether there would be enough money for the education of one of his sons, he told his daughter: 'If there is not enough, ask Shaw' – and indeed it was Shaw who paid for John Bland to go to Cambridge.

'I was, in fact, a born philanderer,' he later told Frank Harris. In his play *The Philanderer* he was to portray himself in the part of Leonard Charteris, whom he described as 'the real Don Juan'. With married women and Fabian girls, Shaw philandered. But Mrs Jane Patterson was to make a Don Juan out of him.

*

'Jenny' Patterson was a particular friend of Shaw's mother – indeed she was closer in age to Mrs Shaw than to her son and may have known the family in Ireland where she had been married to a well-to-do country gentleman. After his death, she moved to London and by 1885 was living in Brompton Square. Coming home from the British Museum, Shaw would find the two women together. Sometimes he joined them singing, sometimes he escorted Mrs Patterson to her bus home; but there seems to have been no romantic interest on his part until after his father's death on 19 April 1885. Almost at once their relationship changed. On 20 April, finding Mrs Patterson at home when he returned, he 'wasted all the evening' with her – the first entry of this sort in his diary. Seven days later occurs a note of his visiting her alone in Brompton Square: 'Went to Richter concert in the evening, but instead of waiting for the symphony went on to Mrs Patterson. Found her alone, and chatted until past midnight.' Up to the time he was twenty-nine, he told Ellen Terry, 'I was too shabby for any woman to tolerate me . . . Then I got a job to do & bought a suit of clothes with the proceeds. A lady immediately invited me to tea, threw her arms round me, and said she adored me . . . Never having regarded myself as an attractive man, I was surprised; but I kept up appearances successfully.'

The clothes with which Shaw tells his story, while fashioning an outline of the truth, also conceal something. At the beginning of his 1885 diary he had written: 'Took to the woollen clothing system, and gave up using sheets in bed.' He had been persuaded to 'rational dress' by a friend of William Morris, Andreas Scheu, an advocate of Dr Gustave Jaeger's sanatory system. Jaeger expected to regenerate the world by wool. He claimed to have tried out his wool-theories on himself and to have been restored by them from a sick creature – 'fat and scant of breath' with haemorrhoids and tendencies to indigestion – to a man who everywhere inspired affection. Shaw, who recognized in Jaeger another Vandeleur Lee, was enthusiastically converted.

He ordered his first Jaeger outfit on 19 June 1885 – 'the first new garments I have had for years'. They were 'paid for out of the insurance on my father's life,' he noted in his diary. The reddish-brown Jaeger suit was to become part of his physical personality – 'as if it were a sort of reddish brown fur,' G. K. Chesterton observed. The uniform was finished off with correct knee-breeches and stockings after a formula devised by Dr Jaeger to replace the insalubrious tubes of trousers. This was the Shavian equivalent to Oscar Wilde's aesthetic costumes.

Many of Jaeger's most faithful 'Woolleners', as they were called, came from among the Fabians who paid fastidious attention to diet and clothes, eating vegetables and wearing animals. Shaw advertised his brown combination as being 'the plumes and tunic of Don Juan' and so irresistible to women that almost anyone could knit himself into popularity. In fact it seems to have been less a matter of women regarding him so favourably in wool as of the woollen Shaw looking at women more confidently.

On 30 June, he 'got clothes from Jaeger's and put them on'. Next day he caught a cold but by 4 July was sufficiently recovered to call on Mrs Patterson and stayed with her till one o'clock. 'Vein of conversation decidedly gallant,' he logged in his diary. Over the next three weeks he visited her constantly. She provoked him, taunted him, half-defying and half-inviting him to advance, and he seemed spellbound. 'Supper, music and curious conversation,' he noted on 10 July after another evening in Brompton Square, 'and a declaration of passion. Left at 3. *Virgo intacta* still.' But only just. For these evenings were unlike his visits into other people's love lives. There he had been Vandeleur Lee, the chaste wizard; here, dressed in the clothes from his father's life insurance and with his mother's closest friend, he could re-enact and improve on the romance of George Carr Shaw and Lucinda Elizabeth. On 18 July he bought some contraceptives ('French letters 5/–') which, on examination, 'extraordinarily revolted me' – so much that in the evening at Jenny's there were 'forced caresses' instead of love-making. Much of this must have been known to Lucinda Shaw. She and Jenny had spent most of 25 July together. In the evening, Shaw came across them walking along the Brompton Road 'looking for a bus, but they were all full,' he noted. 'So, on the corner of Montpelier St. Mother went on by herself, and I returned to the Square with JP, and stayed there until 3 o'clock on my 29th birthday which I celebrated by a new experience. Was watched by an old woman next door, whose evil interpretation of the lateness of my departure greatly alarmed us.'

He had been starved of sex. 'I was an absolute novice,' he wrote in his diary. 'I did not take the initiative in the matter.' During his 'teens and twenties he was 'perfectly continent except for the involuntary incontinences of dreamland'. All these years he exercised his imagination in daydreams about women, but not until Jenny Patterson broke through his celibacy did he know the power of sex. Sometimes he resented this power she had over him. 'The spell of your happiness has been potent.' But when the spell evaporated, he was filled with mortification. Love un-Shavianized him, robbed him of his authority and the hard discipline of work through which he was trying to re-create himself. In retrospect his embraces with Jenny became part of a wrestling match between her possessiveness and his independence. His diary entries over the next weeks indicate the ambivalence of his feelings.

27 July No work done. Went to Museum and wrote a letter to JP . . .
3 August Wrote full circumstantial account of affair with JP to E.

McN[ulty] . . . Spent the evening with Sidney Webb at Colonial Office. He told me about his love affair and disappointment. Wrote a rather fierce letter to JP on my return.

4 August Did nothing practically. Called on Eleanor Aveling in the afternoon. Resolved to begin new *Pilgrim's Progress* at once . . . Wrote JP in reply to her answer to yesterday's explosion.

5 August Wrote the beginning of *Pilgrim's Progress* . . . to JP to eat and make love until 1.20.

10 August . . . JP came. To dinner at 16 then to Jaeger's where I ordered a knitted woollen suit. Mother and JP at Jaeger's too. After tea went home with JP & stayed until five minutes before midnight.'

He saw her every week, ending the day with her at Brompton Square and walking back home in the early hours. There would be intervals when she went out of town, usually to her cottage in Broadstairs, but when she returned, the entries in Shaw's diary would start up again: 'Called on JP'; 'Went to JP in the evening'; 'JP here when I came home. Walked to Brompton Square with her.' He turned up whenever he could not stay away – she hardly knew when it might be. Sometimes he came when she would have preferred him not to: 'You will not believe me I know,' she was to write to him, 'but it is absolutely true that often my body has been an unwilling minister to you.' At other times he would arrive so late that she was asleep and he would stand in the square looking up at the unlit windows.

In the shorthand diaries where he listed his expenditure on food and travel, he also noted in code the number of times he and Jenny made love: once on the 2 and 10 August; twice on 16 and 22 August – and so on. 'Sexual experience seemed a natural appetite,' G.B.S. wrote forty years later, 'and its satisfaction a completion of human experience necessary for fully qualified authorship.' The author learned about the demands and excitements of loving; and the wiles of self-protection. 'Only by intercourse with men and women,' he reasoned, 'could we learn humanity. 'This involves an active life, not a contemplative one . . . you must . . . give and receive hate, love, and friendship with all sorts of people before you can acquire the sense of humanity.'

'I wanted to love,' he wrote, 'but not to be appropriated.' He wanted Jenny to take the edge off his lust so that he was unassailable in his Fabian flirtations and with those wives into whose marriages he had introduced himself as the favourite son. Whenever he felt restless, he looked to her to settle him; but 'I was never duped by sex as a basis for permanent relations, nor dreamt of marriage in connection with it,' he insisted. 'I put everything else before it, and never refused or broke an engagement to speak on Socialism to pass a gallant evening.' But once the Fabian meetings were over, he would find himself, like a sleepwalker, back at her house. 'Went to JP's,' he wrote in his diary on 9 January 1886. 'Revulsion.' But three days later he was there making love to her again. 'Went to JP in the evening and there met T. Tighe Hopkins. He was bent on seduction, and we tried which should outstay the other. Eventually he had to go for his train . . . To bed late.'

'What a fascinating & charming lady your friend Mrs Patterson is!' May Morris told Shaw. 'I wonder why you professed to be reluctant to introduce me to her.' He *was* reluctant – but not to talk about her. 'Are you not a rather disloyal friend?' May questioned him. 'I confess I should hate to be scoffed at behind my back as you profess to scoff at Mrs Patterson.' But Shaw admitted to betraying everybody's confidences in the most exaggerated way. It was a sample, he explained, of Irish tact. Everyone branded him a mischief-maker but thought no worse of the people gossiped over.

Shaw's natural tendency to put Jenny Patterson in a compartment was strengthened by her jealousy. She accuses him of having 'kissed & mauled about' other women. She assails him with her need for reassurance. 'Are you thinking of me? Wanting me? . . . I wish you were here now! Good-night my darling love – when shall I see you?' Then came apologies for her 'awful' rages – 'You know how hard it is to master oneself and it is doubly hard for one like myself who has never been educated or controlled – in fact a savage.' She woos him back to Brompton Square with fresh grapes, honey, cocoa, brown bread, strawberries and the promise that they could both be fast asleep by 2 a.m. 'You are absolutely free to do as you please,' she instructs him. But not for long. 'You will run many dangers from my abandoned sex. You will be hardly safe without me . . . don't fall in love with anyone but me . . .'

Early in 1886 Shaw made an effort to end their relationship. 'Do you wish never to see me again?' she asks him, and adds, with truth: 'I could never make you see me if you did not want to . . . You have done me no harm. Nor have I harmed you.' But Shaw felt he had harmed her; he had used her body and only he knew what he felt when he did so. His urge to make a confession to McNulty and to start a 'new Pilgrim's Progress' were symptoms of his dissatisfaction. 'Be happy,' he had written to her in the first week of their affair, 'for I have not the fortitude enough to bear your misfortunes.' 'Let me be happy,' she wrote back to him. 'I love you.' But the currency of their love was different, and there could be no exchange between them that seemed fair. He could not make her happy for long. 'When a woman does what I have done & expects either consider-ation or love from her lover she is a fool. I am one for I believed in you &

loved you. I alas love you too much now . . . You are the one man in all the world to me & this I feel I know after nearly ten months of intimacy.' This letter was written on 8 May and preceded a 'violent scene' between them at Brompton Square the following day. When Shaw got home that night he wrote to tell her that 'our future intercourse must be platonic'. In this letter, which made Jenny 'unutterably unhappy', Shaw tried to explain his own guilt: 'I see plainly that I have played a very poor part for some time past . . . I have sacrificed you and am so far the better for it – but you are the worse . . . I had nothing to lose – but I had something to gain and therein lies the rascality of it.'

Jenny was unhappy, but by no means 'unutterably' so. In page after page over the next two days she went through her fears and regrets: 'You make me suffer tortures. Have pity on me. I have some little right to ask it of you. I write in despair . . . oh my love, my love, be good to me . . . do not abandon me . . . I said leave me but you would not. The parting then would have been less hard for me . . . You tell me to take other lovers as if I took them as easily as a new pair of gloves . . . I deeply deplore Sunday's work – but I am the sufferer. I couldn't help it. My grief is for your loss to me.'

She feared to open his letters, writing to ask whether they were unkind – and not daring to open the answers. He filled the backs of her envelopes with notes for political speeches. But what he wrote to her was not unkind. 'I do not mean to abandon or desert you – I will not change – but in one thing [sex]. All shall be as before – but that.' Knowing she still had some physical influence over him, Jenny decided to go and see him. 'JP called here in the morning distracted about my letter,' Shaw jotted in his diary on 13 May. 'There was a scene and much pathetic petting and kissing, after which she went away comparatively happy', and Shaw, with intense relief, settled down to the economic study of Jevonian curves of indifference. A few days later she wrote to him accepting 'all you offer. It will be for you to prove that it [sex] was not "the" one thing that brought you here, that nothing is altered betwixt us really except the thing you hold so cheap.' But, she added, 'I do know that you are outraging nature.'

He continued visiting her, but less often; and he left earlier. This had been one of the difficulties between them: whether he should stay the night and neglect his work, or return home at night and neglect her. Fearing that they would drift apart she promised to be 'as good as I possibly can if you will come, not even try to kiss you – unless you wish it'. So he began seeing more of her, sometimes walking her to the door of her house, sometimes going in. Seven Sundays after their platonic intercourse had begun they made love – twice – and things were calmer. 'My Friend & Lover,' she wrote to him at the end of July 1886, 'I am content that there are no barriers betwixt us – that you have taken me back. I will try to make you content with me.' But over the next eighteen months they made each other deeply discontented. When she went off to her cottage at Broadstairs, he felt 'much indisposed for her society'; when she returned to London he found himself 'much out of humour with her and things in general'. On 16 December, their relationship exploded in a quarrel that lasted till one o'clock in the morning.

'I am so happy when I am with you. Be as platonic as you will,' she had written to him. ' . . . I can care for you without any sensuality.' What he apparently wanted was a platonic experiment with full sexual intercourse. The uncertainty of her position swept Jenny into a variety of distracted moods. She would demand that he 'sacrifice something or someone for me'; plead with him: 'Where are you? . . . its a million years since I have been in your arms'; cross-examine him: 'Have you been faithful? Absolutely faithful??' The thought of his unfaithfulness made her ill. 'I am consumed by all sorts of fancies about you.' During platonic intervals, Shaw would drop in on her to change his clothes, plunge into a bath or dash off letters to other women. Once, after she caught him writing to Annie Besant, she followed the two of them next day in the street and was soon plastering him with reproaches. 'You belong to me,' she insisted.

*

At the beginning of his diary for 1886 Shaw recorded that 'my work at the Fabian brought me much into contact with Mrs Besant, and towards the end of the year this intimacy became of a very close and personal sort, without, however, going further than a friendship'.

Annie Besant was nine years older than Shaw. Though separated from her husband she was still legally tied to him and, better still, 'had absolutely no sex appeal'. Like Shaw, she had endured a loveless childhood, but at the age of twenty propelled herself into a painful marriage with a clergyman, Frank Besant, by whom she had two children, and from which she emerged with a fascination for celibacy and a devotion to atheism. Expelled from their home, she set out on an extraordinary pilgrimage, moving from one cause to another, each embodied by a man. The first had been the great secularist saint, Charles Bradlaugh, with whom she had 'fought all England in the cause of liberty of conscience'. Then she veered towards the insidious Aveling, but he had left her for Eleanor Marx. She had then persuaded a dependable young Scottish secularist, John Mackinnon Robertson, to take Aveling's place on Bradlaugh's *National Reformer* as well as her own new journal *Our Corner*.

She and Shaw met formally in January 1885 at the Dialectical Society near Oxford Circus where Shaw was to deliver a socialist address. It was rumoured that Annie, as the most redoubtable champion of individualist free-thought, had come down to 'destroy me,' Shaw recalled, 'and that from the moment she rose to speak my cause was lost'. Public meetings were the elixir of life to her. From the platform her voice, low and thrilling, seemed neither that of a woman nor of a man, but godlike and of irresistible authority. To Shaw's mind she was the greatest orator in England. Everyone waited for her that night to lead the opposition against Shaw, but she did not rise and the opposition was taken up by another member. 'After he had finished, Annie Besant, to the amazement of the meeting, got up and utterly demolished him,' Shaw remembered. '. . . At the end she asked me to nominate her to the Fabian Society and invited me to dine with her.' She was, he concluded, 'a woman of swift decisions'. And she was an 'incorrigible benefactress'. She arranged the serialization of *The Irrational Knot* and *Love Among the Artists* in *Our Corner*; and it was she who launched him there as an art critic. But she found, as Archer had previously done, that Shaw was extremely difficult to help. He had 'a perfect genius for "aggravating" her'. When he declared, after her death, that she had had no sex appeal, he meant that she was without a sense of humour. 'Comedy was not her clue to life,' he admitted:

' . . . no truth came to her first as a joke. Injustice, waste, and the defeat of noble aspirations did not revolt her by way of irony and paradox: they stirred her to direct and powerful indignation and to active resistance . . . the apparently heartless levity with which I spoke and acted in matters which seemed deeply serious . . . must have made it very hard for her to work with me at times.'

At the beginning of his diary for 1887 he noted that their intimacy had reached 'a point at which it threatened to become a vulgar intrigue, chiefly through my fault. But I roused myself in time and avoided this.' Such Shavian rousing was signalled from his side by the despatch of his photograph, and from hers by the composition of a number of fevered poems which, her sympathetic biographer Arthur H. Nethercot comments, 'perhaps fortunately, have not survived'. They orchestrated their incompatibilities over a series of piano duets on Monday nights. 'Shaw always came in, sat down at the piano, and plunged ahead,' Nethercot records, 'but Mrs Besant whenever possible practised for hours to perfect her parts in advance. The neighbourhood resounded with their efforts to keep in time.'

Annie Besant seemed to borrow everything from other people, adding nothing except the wonder of her voice. Beatrice Webb, who disliked her, nevertheless felt that she was 'the most wonderful woman of her century'. To Shaw also she was wonderful, but as someone on stage. 'Like all great public speakers she was a born actress,' he wrote. He tried to make her a good Fabian. 'I ought to have done much more for her,' he concluded, 'and she much less for me, than we did.' Annie, too, had hoped for more. In August 1887 she wrote in the *National Reformer*: 'Life had nothing fairer for its favourites than friendship kissed into the passion of love.' Shaw's love had two qualities – extreme levity and extreme tenacity. In December 1887 she presented him with a contract setting forth the terms on which they were to live together. When he refused to sign it ('I had rather be legally married to you ten times over,' he cautiously fulminated) she produced a casket in which she kept all his letters and handed it to him. Next day, 24 December, he returned her side of the correspondence, and on reaching home found that Jenny Patterson had been to his room 'and had read my letters to Mrs B. which I had incautiously left on my table'. Some of these letters mentioning herself she had taken with her. 'I make no excuse for taking the letters,' she wrote.

'You have taken advantage of . . . my belief & trust in you . . . I am ill & numb . . . & [my] loneliness is almost unbearable. I try to think what it is I have done to deserve this evil . . . I have a thousand memories of you that I can't forget . . . I feel ashamed beyond telling when I try to imagine what she must think of me. You have humbled me in the dust.'

On the morning of Christmas Day, Shaw was woken by a hammering at the door. It was Jenny Patterson, bristling with letters. They argued about it all, and then 'I at last got those she had taken and destroyed them'. The following evening they passed together, and so far mended matters that a few days later they saw in the New Year by making love.

Jenny still engaged his body as Annie Besant faded to a luminous voice in his memory. She flung herself violently into street socialism and then surrendered to the masculine charm of Madame Blavatsky, 'one of the most accomplished impostors in history'. 'Gone to Theosophy,' Pease noted on his Fabian list, and crossed out her name.

As for Shaw: 'Reading over my letters before destroying them rather disgusted me with the trifling of the last 2 years with women.'

4

INTRODUCING SIDNEY WEBB

> The Fabian lecturers are famous throughout the world. Their women
> are beautiful; their men brave. Their executive council challenges the
> universe for quality . . . Say to the horseleech, 'I have joined the Fabian,'
> and he will drop off as though you have overwhelmed him with salt.
>
> Shaw to Pakenham Beatty (27 May 1887)

'Whatever Society I joined,' Shaw wrote, 'I was immediately placed on
the executive committee.' The Fabians had elected him to their executive
on 2 January 1885, and Hyndman came to accept that he was lost for
ever to the Social Democratic Federation. In selecting a political partner
for himself, Shaw was guided by the need to discover someone as unlike
Hyndman as possible, someone vividly unheroic and unfrockcoated, who
would never play at soldiers in the street. He had already spotted the
man: a crushingly plain clerk from the Colonial Office, his bulky head set
on a dumpy body, graceless in movement, and as a public speaker inaud-
ible. According to his future wife, he looked something between a London
tradesman and a German professor. 'This was the ablest man in England,'
Shaw decided: 'Sidney Webb. Quite the wisest thing I ever did was to
force my friendship on him and to keep it.'

He had first met Webb in October 1880 at the Zetetical Society. 'He
knew all about the subject of debate,' Shaw recalled; 'knew more than the
lecturer; knew more than anybody present; had read everything that had
ever been written; and remembered all the facts that bore on the subject.
He used notes, read them, ticked them off one by one, threw them away,
and finished with a coolness and clearness that seemed to me miraculous.'
Though Webb was to laugh away this recollection, he acknowledged fifty
years later that their meeting led to a friendship 'which has been most
fruitful to me. I look back on it with wonder at the advantage, and indeed,
the beauty of [it] . . . Apart from marriage, it has certainly been the biggest
thing in my life.' And Shaw, in his ninetieth year, wrote in a letter to
Webb that 'I never met a man who combined your extraordinary ability
with your unique simplicity and integrity of character . . . you knew
everything that I didn't know and I knew everything that you didn't
know. We had everything to learn from one another and brains enough to
do it.'

Webb was indefatigably packed with information. But in Shaw's
opinion, his simplicity of character was a political disadvantage. He was
not mean, he had no envy, he was never a Party man. He had little

humour, was impatient with people less clever than himself, and incapable of dramatizing himself or his subject. 'I did all that for him,' Shaw told Kingsley Martin, and in a letter to Lady Londonderry he explained: 'All I could do for Webb was to beat the big drum in front of his booth, as he would not master that useful instrument himself.' The description he gave of Webb as one who 'never posed, never acted . . . and was never in danger of becoming a humbug and a living fiction, not to say a living lie', points to the disgust felt by the fastidious Shaw at the gyrations G.B.S. went through to gain public attention. He produced a fountain of sparkling illustrations to make the dullest subject entertaining. And people listened. For the first time Webb's arguments began to command an audience. Shaw had become his loudspeaker. From the other side of a Fabian screen that hid his physical defects, Webb planned to get his ideas implanted in the smart, the powerful, rich and successful figures of the world. People who felt chilled by Webb's programme of national efficiency adored Shaw's jokes, his acting, and gift for addressing two boys, a woman and a baby in the rain as if they were the greatest demonstration in the world. And behind him, invisible to the public, Webb was whispering the researched facts. But who had really 'permeated' the other was more difficult to know.

According to Webb, the Fabians always expressed Shaw's 'political views and work'. According to Shaw, Webb was 'the real inventor of Fabian Socialism'. Each was a wonder to the other. Writing in the third person for his biographer Archibald Henderson, Shaw declared that 'they valued and even over-valued one another'. But in overvaluing each other they overlooked one quality, essential in politics, that neither of them possessed: the ability to take action. Neither of them wanted to go directly into national politics, and it was this side-stepping that gave the Fabians their peculiar obliqueness.

Webb, the man of numbers, gave the Fabians their policy; Shaw, the man of letters, their tactics; and the two of them created the Fabian legend. From Webb came the distinguished Fabian tradition of research and education. In Shaw, they had a propagandist of brilliance. Everything he touched was given a bewilderingly cheerful coherence. Under their joint management, the Fabian Society became a club, a debating chamber, an ideas factory for the Labour movement in Britain, a focus for sociological research and literary-political propaganda. In place of the old revolutionary notion of attracting recruits until they were numerous enough to defeat capitalism at the barricades, the Fabians substituted the novelty that socialists should join other groups and permeate them with socialist ideas. They took socialism off the streets and sat it down in the drawing-room. They made it respectable by dealing it out as a series of parliamentary measures designed to merge political radicalism with economic collectivism. Shaw offered revolution without tears – you would hardly know it had happened. 'A party informed at all points by men of gentle habits and trained reasoning powers may achieve a complete Revolution without a single act of violence,' he stated.

Fabianism came to mean 'permeation'. In the political vocabulary it was the Fabians who patented the word. This policy gradually gave the Society its identity. Shaw and Webb believed in argument on paper. Other leading Fabians were also men of paper, for example Graham Wallas, a schoolmaster and political scientist who eventually lost his capacity for agreeable companionship in the grind of public service. A more attractive figure was Sydney Olivier. 'He was handsome and strongly sexed,' wrote Shaw, 'looking like a Spanish grandee . . . I believe he could have carried a cottage piano upstairs; but it would have cracked in his grip.' Shaw recognized in Olivier the powerful man needed by the Fabians.

Olivier joined the Fabians with Webb in May 1885, and Wallas enrolled the following year. They became known among Fabians as 'the Three Musketeers', with Shaw taking the role of d'Artagnan. This small group directed the affairs of the Society. The 'fifth wheel' on the Musketeers' coach was Annie Besant: 'a sort of expeditionary force,' in Shaw's words, 'always to the front when there was trouble and danger . . . founding branches for us throughout the country, dashing into the great strikes and free-speech agitations of that time . . . generally leaving the routine to us and taking the fighting on herself.'

With the support of Hubert Bland, Annie Besant urged the Fabians to advance boldly into front-line politics. But Shaw resisted this appeal and persuaded her that society must be reformed 'by a slow process of evolution, not by revolution and bloodshed'. This was a preliminary to Webb's famous phrase, first uttered in 1923: 'the Inevitability of Gradualness' – a philosophy that, by emphasizing the practical nature of their socialism, surrounded the Fabians with the glow of constitutional power and postponed for many years Shaw's disillusion with parliamentary politics in Britain.

*

Shaw calculated that if the Fabian Society was to become the centre of British socialism then its independence from other groups must be established not only in tone and tactics, but also in the dismal matter of economic theory.

The job of shifting the Fabians out of the shadow of Marx had begun late in 1884. Marx's value theory defined the value of a commodity as being determined by the labour involved in producing it. But Philip

Wicksteed, a Unitarian minister devoted to the works of Ibsen and the study of economics, had argued that Marxist economists failed to account for the obvious dependence of prices on supply and demand and concluded that value depended on the utility of the commodity to the consumer. From 1885 to 1889, Shaw went to the meetings of a group which, under Wicksteed's leadership, later grew into the British Economic Association. It was composed mainly of professional economists and members of the faculty of University College, London, and 'was the closest Shaw had ever come to a university education'. A controversy with Wicksteed 'ended in my education and conversion by my opponent,' Shaw later concluded, 'and the disappearance of the Marxian theory of value from the articles of faith of British Socialism'.

This was the first step for Shaw in getting rid of Marx's inevitable class war. Marx, he insisted, had been a foreigner who, though he could analyse capitalist policy like a god, did not understand the British social system. As someone outside that system, he had lusted after its violent destruction. Those who swallowed Marxism whole were possessed by a need for war. Shaw's need was for peace – to an extent where he made war (in *Arms and the Man*, for example, or in his journalism on boxing) unreal by mockery. Instead of a Marxist class war, he saw a conflict of interest between producers and the privileged unemployed – those who earned money and those who lived off rent. Such lines of battle did not run neatly between social classes, he pointed out, but through them. A continual civil war (as to some extent envisaged by Marx) could only come about if the Trade Unions and Employers' Federations were determined to play the capitalist game of labourer versus employer, particularly through free collective bargaining.

On alternate weeks, Shaw attended another group, later known as the Hampstead Historic Society, that met at Wildwood Farm, a house on the northern edge of Hampstead Heath belonging to a stockbroker, Arthur Wilson. At the centre of this group was his wife Charlotte Wilson, a firebrand bluestocking from Merton Hall, Cambridge.

The Hampstead Historic Society became the chief policy-making forum of the Fabian cabinet. They would stride up to Hampstead and argue between themselves so forcefully that other socialists could not believe they would remain friends. For Shaw, the elimination of the traditional class war took the political initiative from the socialist body and gave it to the socialist head – a transference from the proletariat to the intellectual. If Shaw's and Webb's analyses of capitalism were right, then such men as they were to have the power in the twentieth century. The sense of this power gives Shaw's Fabian writings their tone of authority, and Webb's social investigations their extraordinary persistence.

But as Shaw admitted: 'The fact is, 1886 and 1887 were not favorable years for drawing-room Socialism and scientific politics.' These were the years in which the Tories, under Lord Salisbury, swept back to power, replacing Gladstone's promise of Home Rule with the continuation of British dominance over Ireland, and replacing Chamberlain's programme of land and housing reform financed by higher taxes on the rich with a policy of expanding the Empire abroad and protecting property at home. The new order was without authority in Parliament. The trade depression of these years had thrown many out of work. 'They were years of great distress among the working-classes,' Shaw wrote. In many large towns throughout the country stones were thrown, railings uprooted, windows smashed, shops looted. The times seemed to belong to the militants – in particular to Hyndman, who had created in the SDF 'a machine that could mobilize up to twenty thousand demonstrators'. Compared with that, what was this stage army of Fabians – sixty-seven strong in 1886 and with an income of £35 19s.? The Fabian voice, insisting that true socialism was a matter of justice to the poor and not envy of the rich, was drowned. For the unemployed had begun to march and the Fabians, protesting their respectability, had no choice but to tag along behind them.

In the autumn of 1885 a police attempt to shut down a traditional 'speakers' corner' had led to a socialist demonstration in which Shaw, as one of the volunteer speakers, had pledged himself to be imprisoned. 'The prospect is anything but agreeable.' But no arrests were made and the battle for free speech was won. The following February, the SDF paraded in Trafalgar Square and there was a 'monstrous riot,' as Queen Victoria described it, ' . . . a momentary triumph for socialism and a disgrace to the capital'. London seemed open to a 'French Revolution'.

The SDF planned the largest demonstration of all to take place once more in Trafalgar Square, on Sunday 13 November 1887 – a week after Sir Charles Warren, the new chief of the Metropolitan Police, had closed it for further meetings. Originally a protest against the Government's Irish policy, it became another trial of strength over free speech. Every radical, socialist and anarchist body united to confront the forces of public order.

That day groups from all over London attempted to force their way into the square and were met by 1,500 police, 200 mounted Life Guards and a detachment of Grenadier Guards. Shaw, having studied the Act under which Warren had closed Trafalgar Square and decided that it was being illegally applied, joined the group at Clerkenwell Green. After speeches from William Morris, Annie Besant and Shaw himself, exhorting the people to be orderly and to press on in their irresistible numbers if attacked, the drums rattled, banners nodded, and they set off.

Shaw's various descriptions of what became known as 'Bloody Sunday' are exultant. In every avenue leading to Trafalgar Square, the forces of Labour were broken up by squads of police. At High Holborn, Shaw and Annie Besant were swept aside by the front ranks of their own procession in counter-revolutionary retreat. 'Running hardly expresses our collective action,' he reported. 'We *skedaddled* . . . On the whole, I think it was the most abjectly disgraceful defeat ever suffered by a band of heroes outnumbering their foes a thousand to one.'

The scene at Trafalgar Square was a débâcle. The red-haired adventurer Cunninghame Graham, rising like a Scottish Mephistopheles from the sulphurous smoke of Charing Cross Underground, was truncheoned to the ground and, along with the engineer John Burns, arrested and imprisoned. Annie Besant rushed everywhere trying to organize a defence line of carts and wagons against the Foot Guards. The mild-mannered Edward Carpenter was manhandled, he furiously wrote, 'by that crawling thing a policeman'. Stuart Glennie, a Scottish philosophic historian whose special period was 6000 BC, charged the thin red line of Grenadiers with his raised umbrella as they were fixing bayonets. Shaw arrived unostentatiously with his vegetarian friend Henry Salt who, discovering his watch had been stolen, realized he could not complain to the police since he was there to complain against them. Shaw consulted his own watch and, deciding it was tea-time, walked home. After tea, he went with Annie Besant to Farringdon Hall where she chaired his evening lecture on 'Practical Socialism'.

There were many lessons to be derived from Bloody Sunday. William Morris withdrew from outdoor militancy to the converted stable of his house on the Thames and the gatherings of his Hammersmith Socialist Society. For Hyndman it was the beginning of the end, as popular support hesitated, and veered elsewhere. To Shaw and Webb the retreat seemed a victory, not for capitalism over socialism, but for Fabian tactics over those of their socialist rivals. Once the Local Government Act of 1888 was passed, they set about turning defeat into success by working in municipal politics – a programme Hyndman called 'gas and water socialism'. But two people, Annie Besant and John Burns, learnt another lesson for the twentieth century.

Amid all the vengeful growlings over their rout it was Annie Besant who acted most constructively, collecting funds, organizing newspaper support, arranging for the bail and legal defence of prisoners, storming the courts, contradicting witnesses, browbeating the police and overawing magistrates. She was all for returning the following Sunday to the Square, and made an impassioned appeal to the Fabians to do so. But Shaw, speaking in opposition, carried a reluctant meeting with him. 'I object to a defiant policy altogether at present,' he explained to William Morris. 'If we persist in it, we shall be eaten bit by bit like an artichoke. They will provoke; we will defy; they will punish. I do not see the wisdom of that.'

Annie Besant was left with a conviction that success would have to depend on efficient planning and precisely calculated aims, on influencing public opinion through newspapers and the power of organization through the unions. Her leadership of the match-girls' strike in 1888, which ended with improvements in working conditions and pay and led to the formation of a Matchworkers' Union, was recognized as a triumph for these new orderly tactics.

Of the many strikes of 1889, the greatest, beginning on 14 August, was the London Dock Strike led by John Burns, which was won with the aid of funds from Australian unions and London demonstrations planned in consultation with the police. Burns emerged from the Dock Strike victory as a potential leader of British socialism. The future belonged to such people – a working-class man who represented Battersea on the London County Council, went into Parliament in 1892 and became the 'first artisan to reach cabinet rank'.

The great Fabian success of these years was the publication, in December 1889, of *Fabian Essays in Socialism*. Shaw had been appointed editor and given the job of preparing the book from a number of Fabian lectures. Having been told by the publishers that the book was 'commercially unproducible', the Fabians decided to bring out a subscription edition themselves – a thousand copies at six shillings. It had decorations in dark green by Walter Crane on the front and by May Morris on the spine, and was distributed from Pease's flat. The preface and two of the eight essays were supplied by Shaw, who also compiled the index, chose the paper and type, and drafted a handbill announcement. Within a month the entire edition was sold out – 'it went off like smoke'. A year later, over 20,000 had gone and it was still selling at the rate of 400 copies a week. By becoming a best-seller, socialism was made respectable in capitalist terms.

Fabian Essays became a socialist bible. Suddenly Fabianism was famous. In 1891, 335,000 tracts were distributed; by 1893, the membership, which included many influential figures (Keir Hardie, Ramsay MacDonald, Emmeline Pankhurst), rose to over five hundred and, in addition to the metropolitan groups, seventy local societies had sprung up.

One of the reviewers of *Fabian Essays* was William Morris. He regretted that such lucid economic analysis and exposition of socialist principles was no longer at the service of the revolutionary movement. Instead the Fabians advocated 'the fantastic and unreal tactic' of permeation which 'could not be carried out in practice; and which, if it could be, would still leave us in a position from which we should have to begin our attack on capitalism over again'. Morris blamed Webb for this 'somewhat disastrous move'. Webb had falsified the class struggle, substituted pieties about state regulation and reduced socialism to the mechanism of a system of property-holding. For Morris himself, socialism remained a 'complete theory of human life, founded indeed on the visible necessities of animal life [which] . . . will not indeed enable us to get rid of the tragedy of life . . . but will enable us to meet it without fear and without shame'. He wrote warmly, if regretfully, of Shaw. 'If he could only forget the Sidney-Webbian permeation tactic . . . what an advantage it would be to us all!'

Morris and Webb were Shaw's political mentors. Morris was a great man and Webb a great brain; Morris a hero for all time and Webb a man of the times. Shaw wanted to unite the applied arts with the social sciences and use Webb's logic to circumvent Morris's sense of history. But they remained two heralds beckoning Shaw in different directions. So he continued speaking of the Fabians with two voices. His most persistent voice aggrandized the Fabian achievement. The other voice sounded his despair that they had not achieved more. He insisted that 'Webb made no mistake'. But he was also to acknowledge by the 1930s the possibility that 'Morris was right after all'. He turned to one and then to the other: and eventually he turned to Soviet Russia.

FOUR

THE PERFECT IBSENITE

I attack the current morality because it has come to mean a system of strict observance of certain fixed rules of conduct . . . intensified by the addition to the ten commandments of sentimental obligations to act up to ideal standards of heroism. Now what Ibsen has done is to call attention to the fact that the moment we begin to worship these commandments and ideals for their own sakes, we actually place them in opposition to the very purpose they were instituted to serve, i.e. human happiness.

Shaw to Jules Magny (16 December 1890)

On 7 February 1887, their landlord having gone bankrupt, the Shaws had received notice to leave their flat at 36 Osnaburgh Street. 'Looking for lodgings in Marylebone and Gray's Inn,' Shaw noted in his diary on 26 February, 'where my feelings were somewhat hurt by the brusqueness with which the steward received my question as to whether ladies were permitted to reside within the precincts.'

Towards the end of March he joined his mother on the third and fourth floors of 29 Fitzroy Square. A big room overlooking the square became his bedroom, and he turned one of the rooms on the top floor into a study. Here, in grand disorder he was to write his first seven plays, his literary, music and theatre criticism, and carry on his most active political campaigning.

Number 29 Fitzroy Square had a handsome façade, but was in poor condition. Shaw, who later bought the lease for his mother, described it as 'a most repulsive house'. There was no bathroom and 'the sanitary arrangements had had no place in the original plans,' he discovered. 'In impressive architecture it is the outside that matters most; and the servants do not matter at all.' It was a fine place for the flowering of his socialism. After a series of humiliating interviews, he established himself as being not his mother's lodger but head of the household, so that in November 1888 he was able to register 'the first vote I ever gave in my life at an election, though I am over 32 years of age'.

Wherever he spoke his words were 'straight as a ray of light,' wrote H. M. Tomlinson, 'such as we get once or twice in a few centuries, as the result of a passionate morality that happens to be gifted with the complete control of full expression'. Many who heard this 'tall, thin man with a very pale and gentle face' speaking with deadly playfulness, and denouncing as robbers those usually regarded as the ornaments of society, were convinced that here was the leader of 'a revolutionary rising which would upset many of our conventions and bring a new dispensation, political and economic, into the London world'.

In 1887 he delivered sixty-six public lectures; by the end of ten years he had given nearly a thousand. Every Sunday he spoke, sometimes against the blaring of brass bands, often at workmen's clubs and coffee houses, arguing from squalid platforms in dens full of tobacco smoke, to a little knot of members whom he had pulled away from their beer and billiards. The 'ubiquitous Mr Shaw', as *The Star* called him, was soon well known: 'a strange and rather startling figure', erect and agile in his serviceable suit of tweed, red scarf, wide-brimmed felt hat and jauntily swinging umbrella – 'a tall, lean, icy man,' reported the *Workman's Times*, 'white-faced, with a hard, clear, fleshless voice, restless grey-blue eyes, neatly-parted fair hair, big feet, and a reddish, untamed beard'.

He preferred speaking in the open air – under lamp-posts, at dock gates, in parks, squares, market places – and in all sorts of weather. He never wrote or read his speeches. By the late 1880s he had laboriously perfected his technique 'until I could put a candle out with a consonant'.

Whether it was 'Capitalism' at the Wolverhampton Trades and Labour Council, 'Communism' at the Dulwich Working Men's Club, 'Socialism' at Plumstead, or 'Food, Death and Civilization' at the headquarters of the London Vegetarian League, he spoke, stretching his long fingers to reach out to his audience, as if all their lives depended upon it. He packed the halls with crowds of people; he made them listen, made them laugh. It is clear from the text of those lectures he later wrote up for publication that Shaw was passionately serious.

'Your authorised system of medicine is nothing but a debased survival of witchcraft. Your schools are machines for forcing a spurious literary culture on children in order that your universities may stamp them as educated men when they have fairly got hold of the wrong end of every stick in the faggot of knowledge. The tall silk hats and starched linen fronts which you force me to wear, and without which I cannot successfully practise as a physician, clergyman, schoolmaster, lawyer or merchant, are inconvenient, insanitary, ugly, pompous and offensive . . . your popular forms of worship are . . . only redeemed from gross superstition by their obvious insincerity . . . Under color of protecting my person you forcibly take my money to support an armed force for the execution of barbarous and detestable laws; for the urging of wars I abhor . . . Your tyranny makes my very individuality a hindrance to me: I am outdone and outbred by the mediocre, the docile, the time-serving. Evolution under such conditions means degeneracy.'

This was the voice of a man who had raised the torch of revolution. No wonder there was sometimes violence – and he had to escape through a window or back door.

'Your slaves are beyond caring for your cries . . . In the midst of the riches which their labor piles up for you, their misery rises up too and stifles you. You withdraw in disgust to the other end of the town from them; you appoint special carriages on your railways and special seats in your churches and theatres for them; you set your life apart from theirs by every class barrier you can devise; and yet they swarm about you still . . . they poison your life as remorselessly as you have sacrificed theirs heartlessly . . . Then comes the terror of their revolting; the drilling and arming of bodies of them to keep down the rest; the prison, the hospital, paroxysms of frantic coercion, followed by paroxysms of frantic charity. And in the meantime, the population continues to increase!'

Henry Sidgwick, Professor of Moral Philosophy at Cambridge, who heard him speak at Bath, noted in his diary that the speaker was 'a live Socialist, redhot "from the Streets"' who

'sketched in a really brilliant address the rapid series of steps by which modern society is to pass peacefully into social democracy . . . It is now *urban* ground-rent that the municipal governments will have to seize, to meet the ever-growing necessity of providing work and wages for the unemployed . . . There was a peroration rhetorically effective as well as daring, in which he explained that the bliss of perfected socialism would only come by slow degrees, with lingering step and long delays, and claimed our sympathy for the noble-hearted men whose ardent philanthropy had led them to cut these delays short by immediate revolution . . . Altogether a noteworthy performance: – the man's name is *Bernard Shaw.*'

Shaw's oratory was like a spur to insurrection, and if he stopped short of calling for the bombardment of the London slums by the new dynamite, it seemed only with reluctance. Gradualness might be inevitable, but it was not welcome: 'if we feel relieved that the change is to be slow enough to avert personal risk to ourselves; if we feel anything less than acute disappointment and bitter humiliation at the discovery that there is yet between us and the promised land a wilderness in which many must perish miserably of want and despair: then I submit to you that our institutions have corrupted us to the most dastardly degree of selfishness.'

For his thousand lectures over these years Shaw received no payment. 'He gives up willingly time, labour, the opportunities of self-advancement,' reported *The Star*. 'To such men we can forgive much.' At the election of 1892, while Shaw was speaking at the Town Hall in Dover, a man rose and warned his audience not to be taken in by someone whose opinions were purchased: 'I immediately offered to sell him my emoluments for £5,' Shaw recalled. 'He hesitated; and I came down to £4. I offered to make it five shillings – half-a-crown – a shilling – sixpence. When he would not deal even at a penny I claimed that he must know perfectly well that I was there at my own expense. If I had not been able to do this, the meeting, which was a difficult and hostile one . . . would probably have broken up.'

The art of public speaking answered his need for attention, though much of it was 'terrible tongue work'. He never admired this need in himself. The development of his public manner had forced brashness on to a nature that was ordinarily sensitive. 'Oratory is a vice,' he complained to the actress Lena Ashwell. He could not delude himself: the applause that rose through his meetings was an empty sound. 'My career as a public speaker was not only futile politically,' he later concluded: 'It was sometimes disgraceful and degrading . . . I suffered agonies of disgust at the whole business and shame for my part in it.'

The success of *Fabian Essays* in 1889 soon led to a train of provincial lectures, particularly in the north of England, and Shaw's flame-coloured beard and illuminated white face were seen in places that had never before borne witness to socialism. He worked eighteen hours a day and on the seventh day he worked. 'My hours that make my days, my days that make my years,' he wrote, 'follow one another pell mell into the maw of Socialism.'

*

He had hoped to convert some of this lecture-work into book-work: 'It is quite possible to get into a volume of 200 pages an adequate and bright explanation of the law of rent and the law of value, which really cover the laws of production and of exchange, and so, in a fair sense, cover the whole field of economics,' he explained to Havelock Ellis. ' . . . I could produce such a book before the middle of next year.' But early in 1889 he wrote to Ellis: 'I see about as much prospect of having "Production & Exchange" ready by June as of establishing the millennium . . . I have to keep up my lectures (five this week); and I have to keep myself alive by journalism all the time. This is not "Production & Exchange".'

In the summer of 1890, the Fabians found themselves committed to a programme of addresses under the heading 'Socialism in Contemporary Literature'. Between May and July Shaw worked on a paper about Ibsen which he delivered on 18 July at the St James's Restaurant. The minutes record that 'the effect on the packed audience was overwhelming'. But not all the Fabians were happy. 'It is very clever,' Sidney Webb wrote, 'and not so bad as I feared . . . But his glorification of the Individual Will distresses me.'

It was probably the Parnell case that decided Shaw to expand his lecture into a book. This *cause célèbre* had resulted in November 1891 in Captain O'Shea being granted a decree nisi against his wife, naming Charles Stewart Parnell, leader of the Irish Party in the House of Commons, as co-respondent. Both in private letters and letters to *The Star*, Shaw had defended Parnell against the outcry 'Parnell Must GO!' following this flouting of domestic ideals by a public figure. On the same day, 16 December, that he wrote to Sydney Olivier, criticizing the opposition to Parnell from within the Fabian Society, he decided to publish *The Quintessence of Ibsenism*.

The book was a product of Shaw's friendship with Archer through whom he had first got to know Ibsen's work. Meeting Ibsen in Denmark in 1887, Archer had observed that he 'is essentially a kindred spirit with Shaw – a paradoxist, a sort of Devil's Advocate, who goes about picking holes in every "well-known fact"'. It was this similarity that helped to give Shaw such an instinctive insight into Ibsen's plays. These plays had the power to move Shaw more than the work of any other living dramatist. Of a performance of *The Wild Duck*, he was to write:

'To sit there getting deeper and deeper in that Ekdal home, and getting deeper and deeper into your own life all the time, until you forget you are in a theatre; to look on with horror and pity at a profound tragedy, shaking with laughter all the time at an irresistible comedy; to go out, not from a diversion, but from an experience deeper than real life ever brings to most men, or often brings to any man: that is what The Wild Duck was like last Monday at the Globe.'

The joy of his *Quintessence* is that of feeling Shaw's agile and ingenious mind working with such vitality on material so sympathetic to him. He prefaced the book with the warning that he is not concerned here with Ibsen as a dramatist, but as a teacher; that this is not literary criticism but analysis of the philosophy of which Ibsen was an exponent. In seeking a symbolic leader who would unite the contradictory impulses within himself, Shaw leads him into battle against those conventional ideals that he felt formed the chief obstacle to progress.

By the early 1890s, following productions of *A Doll's House* and *Ghosts*, the name of Ibsen (who was sixty-three when the *Quintessence* appeared) had emerged from obscurity into huge contention in Britain as the playwright who was forcing a whole generation to re-evaluate its ideas. Shaw assumed the generalship of the British campaign.

As a model for his argument Shaw had adapted Matthew Arnold and used a threefold division of mankind into philistine, idealist and (pending the word superman) realist. He proposes a hypothetical community of one thousand people in which seven hundred are easygoing philistines, two hundred and ninety-nine dangerous idealists ('the idealist is a more dangerous animal than the philistine just as a man is a more dangerous animal than a sheep'), and there is one realistic pioneer essential to the evolution of the species. The philistine, substituting 'custom for conscience', is satisfied with the social system as it is. The irony of his position is that, though he sees any interference with the social machinery as highly dangerous, the real danger comes from allowing that machinery to grow outdated. The philistine employs the idealist to think for him and to 'idealize' his lack of thought. The idealist, though higher in the ascent of human evolution than the philistine, is a moral coward coerced by the majority into conformity. Ideals, in Shavian terminology, are therefore illusions which have their origin in fear; idealism is life by the rule of precedent, and the idealist a pedlar of fancy pictures which advertise this rule. Shaw likens these pictures to beautiful masks which the idealist puts for us on the unbearable faces of truth: the poetic mask of immortality on that king of terrors, death; the mask of romantic happiness, within the prison-house of marriage, on the sex instinct.

But the realist, bolder than the rest, believing in the 'unflinching recognition of facts, and the abandonment of the conspiracy to ignore such of them as do not bolster up the ideals', lays hold of a mask that we have not dared to discard and reveals the disagreeable truth. So he helps to relieve us from sacrifice to the tyranny of ideals: for 'the destroyer of ideals, though denounced as an enemy to society, is in fact sweeping the world clear of lies'. This was the Ibsen-impulse: 'to get away from idolatry and get to the truth regardless of shattered ideals'; and it became Shaw's philosophy of democratic élitism.

In a number of passages added to the 1913 edition Shaw makes clear that he is enshrining individual will only when it works in harmony with the world-will (or Life Force as it would become known). Although society needs to be shocked pretty often, he argues that the 'need for freedom of

evolution is the sole basis of toleration, the valid argument against Inqui-
sitions and Censorships, the sole reason for not burning heretics and
sending every eccentric person to the madhouse'. So the heretic of today
(Galileo, Darwin, Marx and perhaps Shaw himself), striving to realize
future possibilities, becomes the pillar of the community tomorrow. But
pillars of the community are idealists. So realism has constantly to be
kept up to date.

Some of the confusion surrounding the *Quintessence* arose from Shaw's
choice of one word. In the same way as 'superman', with its Nietzschean
associations, was to suggest not a symbol of synthesis but an immature
dictatorship, so the word 'Will', with its Schopenhauerian associations,
indicated not 'our old friend the soul or spirit' but an assertion of power.
In neither case did Shaw originally intend this, but the ambiguity of these
words points to an impulse that was gradually to gain possession of him.

'Life is an adventure, not the compounding of a prescription.' Human
conduct must 'justify itself by its effect on happiness'. By 'happiness'
Shaw meant human welfare and for the 1913 edition he changed
'happiness' to 'life'. In the interval between the first publication and his
preparation of the 1913 edition, though he maintained the same apparatus
of argument, Shaw's attitude shifted. In 1891 he had used the word
'idealist' pejoratively to cover all those who inhabited too exclusively the
world of ideas, whether they were blinded by illusions or held a fixed
vision of a better life. Such people, by preferring fantasy to the actual
world, risked being made prisoners of abstractions, he argued, since
morality was relative and must be continually tested by experience. But
his experience as a Fabian would drive him, as a source for optimism, to
a metaphysical creed depending on the ideal formula of equality of income.

The 1891 *Quintessence*, which aims its ingenious attack at the man he
was to become, is a paradoxically prophetic work – and nowhere more so
than in the pages about *Emperor and Galilean*, where Shaw begins to
explore the synthesis of relations that Ibsen's Maximus called 'the third
empire' – 'the empire of Man asserting the eternal validity of his own
will,' Shaw wrote.

'He who can see that not on Olympus, not nailed to the cross, but in
himself is God: he is the man to build Brand's bridge between the flesh
and the spirit, establishing this third empire in which the spirit shall not
be unknown, nor the flesh starved, nor the will tortured and baffled.'

Within *Emperor and Galilean* Shaw was to find the theme and dialectical
pattern of his middle plays. Yet the habit of segregation persisted like a
hereditary trait, and finally established itself in the flesh-starved Ancients

at the end of *Back to Methuselah*. In these almost bodiless fantasies the author of the original *Quintessence* might have seen a dramatic example of the failure of an idealist to accept man as he is.

2

A CRUST FOR THE CRITICS

> Some time in the eighties ... the New Journalism was introduced. Lawless young men began to write and print the living English language of their own day ... Musical critics, instead of reading books about their business and elegantly regurgitating their erudition, began to listen to music and distinguish between sounds ... The interview, the illustration and the cross-heading, hitherto looked on as American vulgarities imposs-ible to English literary gentlemen, invaded all our papers.
> 'Van Amburgh Revived', *Saturday Review* (7 May 1898)

The Quintessence of Ibsenism was the most sustained and sophisticated work Shaw wrote before the age of thirty-five. His care in guarding the book against being 'swept into an eddy of mere literary criticism' reflects his own experience of criticism up to this time. It was 'literary criticism' in the form of readers' reports that had put a stop to his novels; it was 'literary criticism' – over a hundred anonymous notices for the *Pall Mall Gazette* – on which he had become financially dependent from the spring of 1885 to Christmas 1888.

The *Pall Mall Gazette* was the centre of what Matthew Arnold called 'the New Journalism'. It was edited by W. T. Stead who altered the character of daily journalism in Britain during the mid-1880s. Papers became simpler – as he wished the world to be. He popularized interviews, added illustrations, invented picturesque headlines, pursued virtuous crusades.

Shaw was a contributor to the *Pall Mall* under Stead's editorship, 'but as my department was literature and art, and he was an utter Philistine, no contacts between us were possible'. Yet the paper had Oscar Wilde, George Moore and William Archer writing on the arts pages, and it was a sign of Stead's journalistic flair that he should also employ there this 'satirical contributor with a turn for prophecy'.

Shaw insisted that literature and the arts must not be segregated from politics. He deplored the editorial habit of the literary department of giving 'a page and a half of vapid comment to a book destined to be forgotten without having influenced the conduct or opinions of a single human being; whilst pamphlets that circulate by thousands, dealing with vital questions of national economy and private morals, are tossed aside into the waste-paper basket . . .' But the publication of the truth about anything or anyone 'is attended with considerable risk in English society,' Shaw explained.

'We have agreed to keep up a national pretence that the black spots in human nature are white; and we enforce the convention by treating any person who even betrays his consciousness of them . . . as a prurient person and an enemy of public morals . . . the convention rigorously exacts – under pretence of not speaking evilly of the dead – that biographers should exhibit great men, not as they were, but as ideal figures . . . That the very worst sort of evil speaking, whether of the living or the dead, is the telling of lies about them . . . is not taken into account in judging biography . . . The censors will tolerate no offence against hypocrisy, because . . . an offence against hypocrisy is an offence against decency, and is punishable as such.'

Shaw's prescription for biography looks forward to the biographical revolution of Lytton Strachey thirty-five years later, and is most ironically expressed in his review of a Jubilee chronicle of Queen Victoria:

'With her merits we are familiar . . . We know that she has been of all wives the best, of all mothers the fondest, of all widows the most faithful. We have often seen her, despite her lofty station, moved by famines, colliery explosions, shipwrecks, and railway accidents; thereby teaching us that a heart beats in her Royal breast as in the humblest of her subjects. She has proved that she can, when she chooses, put off her state and play the pianoforte, write books, and illustrate them like any common lady novelist. We all remember how she repealed the corn laws, invented the steam locomotive, and introduced railways; devised the penny post, developed telegraphy, and laid the Atlantic cable . . . in short, went through such a programme as no previous potentate ever dreamed of. What we need now is a book entitled "Queen Victoria: by a Personal Acquaintance who dislikes her".'

But it was through the world of the Victorian novel that his route mainly lay. 'The most dangerous public house in London is at the corner of Oxford St,' Shaw told one of his audiences, 'and is kept by a gentleman named Mudie.' The books in Mudie's Library were uniform, and by recommending any novel as 'very popular at Mudie's' Shaw meant that it was another mammoth romance. 'Such books,' he concluded, 'are not fair game for the reviewer: they are addressed to children of all ages who are willing to shut their eyes and open their mouths.' Second-rate fiction, he concluded, might be good enough for some adults but 'first rate fiction is needed for children themselves'.

'Many of our worst habits are acquired in an imaginary world,' Shaw warned.

'... we have got the nation corrupting fiction, and fiction reacting on the nation to make it more corrupt ... Hence springs up a false morality which seeks to establish dignity, refinement, education, social importance, wealth, power and magnificence, on a hidden foundation of idleness, dishonesty, sensuality, hypocrisy, tyranny, rapacity, cruelty, and scorn. When the novelist comes to build his imaginary castle, he builds on the same foundation, but adds heroism, beauty, romance, and above all, possibility of exquisite happiness to the superstructure, thereby making it more beautiful to the ignorant, and more monstrous to the initiated.'

Looking out from Shaw's imprisonment in this castle, we may catch a splendid view of popular late Victorian fiction. What journeys its characters make! Their route lay encumbered by avalanches, attacks of consumption, unmuzzled dogs, ghosts, lunatics, Chinese executions, runaway trains, fire engines, daggers and gunpowder. Outside towers a background of crag and fortress, cloud and sea, with green walls of pine and a mountain torrent. Within, aged hounds lie stretched on the carpet, curtains are continually tweaked aside by jewelled fingers and ropes of roses adorn the staircases ascending to the boudoirs. These strongholds, which in the last chapter are all burnt to matchwood, are inhabited by a throng of murderers, bigamists, coquettes and so on. Nearly everything takes place at night (to the cry of owls, nightingales and cat-birds), except for a little cockfighting perhaps and the regular afternoon calls which usually carry on the business of the second volume. There are a few old people past love-making, but they have all had prehistoric turns at it and each carries a sorrow to the grave. The villains, who break out under stress into uncouth scraps of French, are consumed by earthquakes or engulfed in shipwrecks carrying many innocuous travellers down with them. The hero is easily recognized by his faculty for alighting on haystacks when flung from continental expresses, for inheriting fortunes, and for tracking diamond smugglers to their doom. A composite photograph of the heroines at Mudie's would have shown golden tresses, a pair of blue eyes occasionally changing under degrees of emotion to green or hazel, and a plain white dress with a flower at the throat. For three volumes intransigent relatives and designing reprobates block her way to the altar, only to be arbitrarily removed in the last pages by violent Acts of God or the Devil, the sympathetic reader breathing more and more freely as the slaughter proceeds.

With such caricatures of the love he had once longed for himself, Shaw spent many hours, months, years of his time, first as a book reviewer and subsequently as a theatre critic. In this world of reviewing he needed to fasten his talent to a stimulating purpose: the creation, by use of irresistible ridicule, of a revolution in the habits of the book-reading, theatre-going public in Britain. The bookshop or theatre should no longer be an oubliette with its trap-door sealed against reality. 'Whilst the slums exist and the sewers are out of order, it is better to force them on the attention even of the polite classes than to engage in the manufacture of eau-de-cologne for sprinkling purposes.'

Shaw's voice in the columns of the *Pall Mall Gazette* was one of exasperated geniality, below which moved a current of resentment at being obliged to spend his time reading trivial books brought out by publishers who had rejected all his own novels. It was particularly galling to see that the other Irishmen on the paper were given major writers to review: George Moore wrote on Huysmans and Zola; Oscar Wilde on Dostoevsky, William Morris, Tolstoy and Turgenev. Occasionally Shaw was allowed a minor work by an interesting writer: J. M. Barrie's *Better Dead*; Wilkie Collins's *The Evil Genius*; and *A Mere Accident* by George Moore, whose 'commendable reticence' in evading the realities of a rape 'might have been taken further, even to the point of not writing the book'.

Shaw's long sojourn in this world of reviewing later enlivened his picture of hell in *Man and Superman*. He used the stock-in-trade of the novelist and playwright as a block against which to sharpen his prose style. 'A true original style is never achieved for its own sake,' he wrote. 'Effectiveness of assertion is the Alpha and Omega of style. He who has nothing to assert has no style and can have none: he who has something to assert will go as far in power of style as its momentousness and his conviction will carry him.' What he gave up in texture, he gained in pace and authority. His writing is luminous with conviction and humour. He seldom weeds out the clichés: when in love, his heart is as 'hard as nails'; his longer plays are inevitably 'cut to the bone'. 'The more familiar the word, the better,' he told his translator, Sobieniowski. Elsewhere he announced: 'I also am a journalist, proud of it, deliberately cutting out of my works all that is not journalism, convinced that nothing that is not journalism will live long as literature, or be of any use whilst it does live.' This was part of a cleansing exercise against his long immersion in pretentious literature.

It was a bright smiling instrument, his typewriter, a marvellously efficient machine for turning all the difficulties and despairs of life into an argument – not a bad-tempered argument, but an exchange of point and counterpoint that beats down relentlessly until the rough places are made plane. In his diaries, where Shaw is unprotected by the brilliant shell of this style, we see him several times accidentally coming close to some dreadful event and feeling the shock waves: 'In Wigmore [Street] we saw a young rough beating a girl and I disturbed myself for the rest of the evening by flying at him.' 'Was much upset by having to interfere in an altercation between a young couple and a private watchman who was apparently trying to blackmail them.' Though he attacked the substitution of literature for life, his own battery of words, eliminating suffering, was in some sense a replacement for action. 'A writer,' he advised Norman Clark, 'must have a gift of intimacy, which is dangerous and offensive without good manners or tact.' Shaw had outrageously good manners, but in place of intimacy he gives us a whirling informality. The effect of his prose is like alcohol upon the nerves: we are exhilarated, intoxicated, breathless and, before the end, exhausted – and still the talkative spirit, the ascending wit, drive on. For it is a style that is always in top gear: emphatic, industrious, omniscient, studded with surprises, and better-trained for shorter distances than discursiveness.

Shaw's columns in the *Pall Mall Gazette*, though without a byline, were soon making his name notorious in the trade. Two or three times an exceptional book fell his way: the *Rural Rides* of William Cobbett ('probably more dangerous to corrupt Governments than any single man known to English history, excepting only Jonathan Swift'); *A Handbook of the History of Philosophy* by Belfort Bax, and Samuel Butler's *Luck or Cunning*, both of which (as he indicates in his Preface to *Major Barbara*) influenced his thought. But for the most part, he was kept to heart-throb fiction. He seemed to fill his reviews from a magic well that never ran dry or lost its sparkle provided he pumped hard enough. But he chafed against the restriction. In the summer of 1887 he sent Stead a long letter in which he tried to palm a socialist programme on to him. Stead read it, kept it, and did nothing: its campaign for social reform was too bleak for him. Besides, as an instrument of persuasion, there was a quality in Shaw's letter that was to mar so much of his dazzling propaganda: it was too knowing – everything it said was correct and calculated to be flattering to Stead, but the calculations showed. To act on Shaw's advice so often meant parading one's inferiority to him. His tact was like a brilliant varnish: one saw straight through it.

However much he wrote, since he could not get what he wanted, he still searched for opportunities elsewhere. Letters editors of *To-Day*, *Justice*, *The Echo*, *St James's Gazette*, *Truth*, were harried with correspondence from George Bunnerd, Shendar Bwra, A. Donis, Redbarn Wash, G. B. S. Larking, Amelia Mackintosh, Horatia Ribbonson and the Reverend C. W. Stiggins Jnr, as well as from the 'milkman', an 'English mistress', 'Inveterate Gambler' and 'A Novelist'. Under one name or another, or no name at all, he was everywhere, pleading for the retention of the split infinitive and the abolition of Christmas, protesting against the Russian use of Siberian exile for dissidents and the prosecution of Henry Vizetelly for publishing an English translation of Zola's *La Terre*. As G. Bernard Shaw he wrote of Jack the Ripper as an 'independent genius' who by 'private enterprise' had succeeded where socialism failed in getting the press to take some sympathetic interest in the conditions of London's East End.

The power Shaw felt within him seemed everywhere to be blocked. In the summer of 1888, he accepted a proposal from H. W. Massingham, deputy editor of *The Star*, that he cover occasional musical events which 'Musigena', the paper's regular music critic E. Belfort Bax, could not attend. Towards Massingham Shaw felt lifelong gratitude and respect – he was 'the perfect master journalist,' he wrote. When Bax went on holiday in August, Shaw acted as his substitute; after which he carried on as the anonymous second-string critic until, Bax resigning in February 1889, Shaw took his place at two guineas per week.

Later that year, 'I did a thing that has been in my mind for some time,' he noted in his diary, ' – wrote to Edmund Yates asking him to give the art-criticship of *The World* to Lady Colin Campbell, as it is no longer worth my while to do so much work for so little satisfaction, not to mention money.' Yates replied admitting that Shaw had been 'cavalierly treated', but concluding: 'I have no idea of loosening my hold on you.'

But Shaw had made up his mind to give himself the sack as a reviewer of pictures for *The World*. Preparing to bow out of the galleries, he told his readers on 23 October 1889: 'I cannot guarantee my very favourable impression of the Hanover Gallery, as I only saw it by gaslight. This was the fault of Sarasate, who played the Ancient Mariner with me. He fixed me with his violin on my way to Bond Street, and though, like the wedding guest, I tried my best, I could not choose but to hear.'

3

MYSTICAL BETROTHAL

The pleasure of the senses I can sympathise with and share; but the substitution of sensuous ecstasy for intellectual activity and honesty is the very devil.

Preface to *Three Plays for Puritans*

Money was one measurement of success. In 1885, his first full year in journalism, Shaw had earned £112. At the end of each year he would note in his diary what he had made from contributions to papers: £150 in 1888; £197 6s. 10d. in 1889; £252 13s. 2d. in 1890; £281 16s. 10d. for 1891. Much of this money he would hand to his mother, 'asking her for a pound when my pockets were empty'. Ten years later he was earning almost £800 (equivalent to £43,000 in 1997). He trained hard, buying coloured spectacles, a pair of dumb-bells and a pendulum alarm clock. He took regular cold baths; he went on spectacular walks. At night he opened his windows so wide that cats and birds sailed through, interrupting his sleep. He dieted, logged his weight, kept himself at about ten stone ten pounds. To his shelves he added volumes on algebra, Danish and German; on his desk he stood a modern typewriter bought from H. W. Massingham for £13 and, 'as our rent was reduced and our earnings rather enlarged, we got a new piano on the hire system, and began to live a very little more freely'.

Behind this programme of self-improvement lay a history of backsliding. He sleeps through the alarm clock, or if it wakes him, takes a nap in the British Museum. Despite his diet, he cannot resist a heap of cherries, a few overripe bananas, some indiscreet mushrooms, and sweetmeats from a machine, to which are attributed fits of indigestion, plagues of gumboils and terrific nightmares. However icy his baths he breaks out in sweats and spells of influenza. He increases his walks, but trips and falls; he starts off again, but ends up lame; he bellows out songs 'rather violently' at the piano, 'for the sake of my lungs', and loses his voice; he covers page after page and sees them all swoop and vanish under the wheels of a train. Despite the grimmest of attempts, he learns no languages, no algebra. His letters to the press are returned, his private correspondence placed in the wrong envelopes. He develops a tendency of 'clean forgetting' to turn up at rallies where he is principal speaker and at meetings where he is chairman; of arriving at theatres without his tickets, mistaking matinées for evening performances, and presenting himself at the Steinway Hall instead of the Princes Hall and vice versa; he believes it to be Thursday when it isn't; he calls on people who by arrangement are calling on him and attends At Homes where everyone is abroad. He recklessly gives away money to drunkards and minor poets, crossing-sweepers and 'Street Arabs'. Outdoors he watches a squirrel playing in a tree and a huge spider making a web, indoors he dawdles over the piano harmonizing the *Marseillaise* – all when he should have been forming a committee for the municipalization of land. Suddenly unable 'to face more political cackle', he rushes off from an important conference to a performance of *Cymbeline* – 'and enjoyed it much more than I should have enjoyed the meeting'.

More unShavian still are the adventures with his typewriter. Within a month he has mastered the brute and declares himself 'much pleased' with it. Yet his expertise is oddly hypothetical, having come to him (as with bicycling and photography) by way of accidents. Despite everything, the machine won't 'settle'. At last 'to my great annoyance' he is obliged to ask for professional advice, but when he tries to put this advice into practice the typewriter breaks down altogether and he is 'furious over it'.

The diaries become strewn with Johnsonian lamentations over 'my inveterate laziness and procrastination'. 'Not up till 10 (curse this laziness),' he writes and chides himself for doing nothing except utter good resolutions. 'Very tired and greatly disposed to curse my fate,' he notes. For Shaw to be off his work has all the pathos of a domestic animal not eating. He loses strength; he loses authority over himself. 'For weeks now I have been going to bed at 2 and not getting up until 11,' he admits. Often he starts towards his desk, only to find himself seated at the piano. 'Restless and full of work in the morning,' he writes for 9 October 1889; 'but only sat down at the piano after all and played *Parsifal* with a very deep sense of it all.' He is disgusted with this waste of time but goes on playing and singing nonetheless. When he shakes off this idleness and works strictly to timetable, he is overcome by fits of giddiness. Even his mother notices how his hands shake and his nerves are stretched. Is his diet insufficiently austere? he wonders. Perhaps his teeth are at fault. Finally, he admits: 'Am driving myself too hard,' and tries, unsuccessfully, to take it easy by means of more exercise.

Anything in the style of a holiday unnerved him. Early in 1888, he experimented with a Sunday on the Surrey Hills.

'The uneven, ankle-twisting roads; the dusty hedges; the ditch with its dead dogs, rank weeds, and swarms of poisonous flies; the groups of children torturing something; the dull, toil-broken, prematurely old agricultural laborer; the savage tramp; the manure heaps with their horrible odor; the chain of mile-stones from inn to inn, from cemetery to cemetery . . . From the village street into the railway station is a leap across five centuries from the brutalizing torpor of Nature's tyranny over Man into the order and alertness of Man's organized dominion over Nature.'

The following year he went on his first trip to the Continent: a week in April to the Netherlands, reporting on an opera for *The Star*. 'My worst forebodings have been realized,' he assured William Archer. Antwerp was 'exactly like Limerick, only duller'; and, like the Liffey in Dublin, the 'smell of the canal disgusted me with the Hague'. On the way back he sat on deck all night and was ingloriously sick. 'Nature conspires with you in vain to palm off the Continent on me as a success,' he wrote to Archer.

Three months later *The Star*'s music critic was sick *en route* for Bayreuth. 'Carried out my program successfully,' he noted in his diary – four articles on Wagner, and such vigorous sight-seeing through Germany that he split his mackintosh 'like a trick coat in a farce'. Returning from a six-day ordeal in Paris the following spring, Shaw's admission of having been 'Very sick crossing . . . thoroughly wet and cold' was turned by the music critic into a plea for the Channel Tunnel, but for the want of which *The Star* 'would be as great a musical power in Europe as it is in England'.

In August 1890 he attempted a summer holiday with Sidney Webb, the one man whose dislike of all holidaymaking exceeded his own. Their destination was the Passion Play at Oberammergau where, in a downpour of rain, Shaw bounded up the mountainside leaving Webb, seated among trees at its base, apparently 'writing an article on municipal death duties . . .'

Though he gradually grew bolder, he quickly regretted it. From Italy, where he went on a tour organized by the Art Workers' Guild in the autumn of 1891, he wrote complaining to William Morris of 'the fearful solitude created by these 27 men, most of whom have taken up art as the last refuge of general incompetence'. This was an untypical rebuke from Shaw, indicating the extent of his irritation at having to travel as a devout Catholic in order to obtain vegetarian meals. 'On reflection,' he added, 'I doubt if this remark will bear examination: I suppose it is in the nature of such an expedition that we should all appear fools to one another.'

If there was anything Shaw learnt, it was how travel narrowed the mind. His one weapon, language, broke in his hand and he concluded that the only country you could learn about by going abroad was your own. He also came to recognize how much closer you could feel to those whom you had left behind. There was an increasing number of people for him to feel close to in this way: for example, Grace Gilchrist. 'I have no doubt

Miss Gilchrist fell in love with you,' another Fabian, Marjorie Davidson, assured him.

It seemed impossible for a young man and woman to have a friendship in Victorian Britain that was not tainted by assumptions of marriage. Shaw's attentions to Grace Gilchrist were much whispered over. He singled her out for long talks; he addressed letters to her and noted each sighting in his diary; he wrote music to Browning's 'I go to find my soul' for her. But by 1888 they were joined, not in marriage, but in a bond of misunderstanding. On Easter Day, Grace's friend the novelist Emma Brooke called on Shaw and 'heaped abuse on me'. It was like a plot from one of his novels: Shaw embodying the new morality; Grace, struggling unhappily through socialism to escape the marriage market; and Miss Brooke valuing her friend's happiness above Shaw's principles. 'Write no more letters,' Emma Brooke instructed him after he had tried to explain himself. 'In letters we do not seem able to touch any point of mutual comprehension.' Eventually she infuriated Shaw by returning his letters unopened. But by then, he had come to realize that there was 'Great Gossip about Grace Gilchrist' and even her family had counted on their marriage. It was exasperating.

On Hampstead Heath nine months later, Grace and Shaw hurried past each other without a word. Both felt that injustice had been done, Grace to her genuine feelings, Shaw to his good intentions, and no words had been able to reconcile such feelings and intentions. If Shaw treated Grace's unhappiness rather easily, this was partly because, compared with the awful poverty which was the chief concern of the Fabians, her romantic disappointment seemed almost an indulgence. He had enjoyed Grace's company and he seems to have found her good-looking. But he had never proposed marriage; he had never compromised her sexually; and if he had compromised her socially then it was due to absurd mores which she should have been too intelligent to accept.

'Someday a pair of dark eyes, a fierce temperament and a woman will obtain your body and soul,' Elinor Huddart had written to him. If he was on the lookout for such a creature, it was in order to avoid her. Even before the Gilchrist excitement was over, Shaw was gazing at 'a pretty girl named Geraldine Spooner'. He neither pursued the 'fair and fluffy' Miss Spooner nor ignored her but, after two years doing neither, decided that he was 'rather in love with Geraldine' – after which he saw a good deal less of her. He seemed to her 'a strange and very wonderful looking man, tall, and thin as a whipping post'. He had walked her to railway stations and they had eaten lunches at an Aerated Bread Shop. Each seemed to be presenting the other with opportunities for taking the initiative and neither of them took it – until, Shaw's lack of initiative growing excessive, Geraldine married the philosopher Herbert Wildon Carr. As soon as it was too late Shaw plunged into action, advancing on 'my old love Geraldine', in spite of the desperate fact of her now living in Surrey.

> If I could truly now declare
> I love but you alone . . .

But he couldn't. The visit had been in the nature of a reconnaissance – to learn whether the Carrs might grow into another of those families where he could act the Sunday husband. When Geraldine drove him off to the station in the horse cart, he made straight for the Salts where his Sunday husbandship was by now well-established.

Shaw was a lifelong admirer of Henry Salt. They shared many tastes – Ruskin and Shelley, vegetarianism and anti-vivisection. But though Shaw described his Old Etonian socialist colleague as 'a born revolutionist' he seemed more of a born naturalist, armed only with binoculars and eventually 'working all day at my profession which is looking for, and at wildflowers'. Salt, who was 'the mildest-mannered man that ever defied society', made a centre for his reforming spirit in the Humanitarian League of which he was a co-founder and whose journals, dedicated to the abolition of blood sports, corporal punishment, the death penalty and the commercial vulgarization of the countryside, he edited for a quarter of a century.

At the Salts Shaw bathed, rode on a tandem tricycle, made friends with Cosy, 'a cat of fearful passions', put into practice his special theories of bed-making and washing-up, cheated outrageously at an exhibition of table turning, gossiped, sang and played a great quantity of piano duets with Mrs Salt – and that was all he did. There was no need for 'gallantries' with Kate Salt since she only fell in love with other women. She treated Shaw as a confidant but she felt an idealized love for Edward Carpenter who was homosexual. This preference sometimes riled Shaw. 'Attacked Carpenter rather strongly over his lecture – perhaps too strongly,' he confessed in his diary. In Shaw's opinion, Carpenter exalted Kate's lesbianism into a cult (she called herself an *Urning*, one of the chosen race). Her problems would vanish when she had two or three children to look after. Kate hated this chilling cheeriness of Shaw's. 'Mrs Salt complained considerably of me,' he revealed after a breezy visit in 1896:

' . . . said she believed I had been practising scales (an unheard-of accusation); said I was in a destructively electrical condition and made her feel that she wanted to cry; said that if I undressed in the dark when going to bed, sparks would come out of me; and generally made me conscious of a grinding, destroying energy, and a heart transmuted to adamant . . . I am really only fit for intercourse with sensitive souls when I am broken and weary.'

*

Shaw counted his friendship with the Salts as one of the most successful of his triangular liaisons. More questionable were the appearances he was making in the family life of William Morris's daughter, May.

For years he had enveloped May Morris in a romantic haze that emanated from his feelings for what she called 'the father'. 'Great men are fabulous monsters, like unicorns, griffins, dragons, and heraldic lions,' Shaw was to write. ' . . . William Morris was great not only among little men but among great ones.' He still saw Morris as a crusader, struggling to make nasty people nice and ugly places beautiful. To go from the barren places of the Fabians to the 'Morris paradise' at their house in Hammersmith was wonderfully refreshing. Shaw went there often and sometimes, he owned, 'to see May Morris'. In what was to become a famous passage Shaw tells of a particular incident between them that took place in 1886.

'One Sunday evening after lecturing and supping, I was on the threshold of the Hammersmith house when I turned to make my farewell, and at this moment she came from the diningroom into the hall. I looked at her, rejoicing in her lovely dress and lovely self; and she looked at me very carefully and quite deliberately made a gesture of assent with her eyes. I was immediately conscious that a Mystic Betrothal was registered in heaven, to be fulfilled when all the material obstacles should melt away, and my own position rescued from the squalors of my poverty and unsuccess . . . I made no sign at all: I had no doubt that the thing was written on the skies for both of us.'

Characteristically, this metaphysical episode contains and conceals the truth. When Shaw submitted it fifty years later as part of his Introduction to the second volume of May's book on her father, she allowed its publication. 'People who don't count will view it as an amusing romance in the Shaw manner, and those who count – so few left – will read it understandingly.'

The Shaw manner suggests that he treated May as an ornament in her father's Pre-Raphaelite world. She was a picture, not real; something to look at and never touch. But she had never occupied the jewelled place he ascribed to her in the William Morris world. 'Yes, well, of course I'm a remarkable woman,' she later told him, ' – always was, though none of you seemed to think so.' The affair was one of suppers, songs, socialism. He wooed her politically, tried to seduce her from the Socialist League to the Fabians: 'I shall have to overcome my shyness of the Fabians – they are all so gruesomely respectable,' she protested. It was Shaw's respectability that made her shy. It was like a strait-jacket and he an inspired lunatic, tied hand and foot. Sometimes he made her laugh so much she felt enfeebled the next day; and it was beautiful to hear him lecture so passionately. 'I don't know if you are aware that our audiences love you very much,' she told him; 'their faces broaden with pleasure when we promise them that if they are good Bernard Shaw shall be their next teacher.' Did he love her? It seemed impossible to tell. 'You have succeeded in perplexing *me*. I don't believe I know you a bit better now than when we were first acquainted,' she wrote to him, after they had known each other for more than a year. 'Inscrutable man! I suppose this is *your* form of vanity.'

He seems to have been terrified of the unhappiness he would risk if she became real. Instinctively he countered fear with fear, making her feel that, although she wanted to be close to him, 'you keep me in a constant state of terror by your fantastic sarcasms, so I suppose it is impossible'. Sometimes, in her frustration, she was short-tempered: 'I do not know what possesses me to be always so rude when you are invariably kind and courteous to me,' she apologized. In another letter she referred to 'our harmless personal relations'. After a year or more of harmlessness, she turned elsewhere. Early in April 1886, Shaw wrote in his diary: 'Came back with Sparling, who told me of the love affair between him and May Morris.' Henry Halliday Sparling was a socialist colleague, 'a tall slim immature man,' Shaw decided, 'with a long thin neck on champagne bottle shoulders'.

Shortly afterwards May wrote Shaw a letter accepting, as it were, his mystic rejection of her the previous year. 'Your resolution when we became acquainted not to make love was most judicious and worthy of all praise, having, as you say, the most entirely satisfying results. I dont think our intercourse could have caused you more pleasure than it has me.'

Her irony was well-merited. By treating May Morris as a woman-on-a-pedestal, Shaw exhibited all the sentimental idealism he later attacked so vividly in *The Quintessence of Ibsenism*. The insignificance of Sparling amounted almost to an invitation for Shaw to supplant him. But still he could not escape the strait-jacket. 'So nothing happened,' he wrote, 'except that the round of Socialist agitation went on and brought us together from time to time.' They spent almost a week together at Kelmscott

Manor in August 1888, Shaw rowing and sailing on the river, playing hide and seek, shooting bows and arrows, guessing 'animal, vegetable or mineral' with various children, and feeling very happy. But on 14 June 1890, May married Sparling.

'This was perfectly natural, and entirely my own fault for taking the Mystical Betrothal for granted; but . . . [Sparling] was even less eligible than I was; for he was no better off financially; and, though he could not be expected to know this, his possibilities of future eminence were more limited.'

Yet Shaw, who had accepted the love affair, could not accept the marriage. In fantasy, he saw May as belonging to her father: William Morris was her man. By marrying her, Sparling had violated the idyllic union between father and daughter that Shaw in 'my limitless imagination' had dreamed into existence, with himself understudying the great William Morris.

He continued seeing the Sparlings, playing the piano with May sometimes till past midnight, as if nothing had happened. One evening, in the summer of 1891, after leaving Hammersmith for Jenny Patterson's house in Brompton Square, he noted: 'May only appeared as I was leaving . . . Gloomy evening. Sorry I left Hammersmith.' But was there any need to leave? That autumn he began staying at Hammersmith odd nights; and then having, as it were, placed one foot in the door, he felt obligated to call on the other foot to follow. Fitzroy Square seemed 'unbearable' when, late in 1892, the building was being redecorated. To escape the smell of paint, and of the drains, he moved to Hammersmith Terrace for part of November, December and January 1893. This was the nearest he came to impersonating Vandeleur Lee and reproducing the Dublin *ménage à trois*. His description of these months, though revealing the satisfaction this arrangement gave him (he even borrowed 'a change of clothes from Sparling'), is skilfully disingenuous. The 'young couple . . . invited me to stay with them awhile. I accepted, and so found myself most blessedly resting and content in their house . . .

'Everything went well for a time in that *ménage-à-trois* . . . It was probably the happiest passage in our three lives.

But the violated Betrothal was avenging itself. It made me from the first the centre of the household; and when I had quite recovered and there was no longer any excuse for staying unless I proposed to do so permanently and parasitically, her legal marriage had dissolved as all illusions do; and the mystic marriage asserted itself irresistibly. I had to consummate it or vanish.'

Reader, he vanished.

Like George Carr Shaw, Sparling had been reduced to nullity in the house. Shaw's explanation for what happened went naturally back to his childhood. 'My mother was enabled to bear a disappointing marriage by the addition to our household of a musician of genius,' he wrote. ' . . . I had therefore, to my own great advantage, been brought up in a *ménage à trois*, and knew that it might be a quite innocent and beneficial arrangement.' In Shaw's scheme, the music critic of the 1890s must do nothing that the musician of genius had not done in the 1860s. 'I was perfectly content to leave all that to Sparling and go on Platonically,' he added, 'but May was not.' So there was no alternative but to leave.

But Shaw left less convincingly than Sparling. For having gone, he often returned to Hammersmith, admiring her embroidery, reading poetry and 'playing all the evening with May'. Soon she started calling for tea at Fitzroy Square – 'the worst of it was she always wore her heart on her sleeve,' Lucy Shaw remembered, 'and everyone knew about her madness for G[eorge]'. They seemed to go everywhere together – to concerts, theatres; on long walks in the park; for skating and sculling along the river together between Chiswick and Barnes ('and got abominably blistered').

Shaw's conviction that this *ménage à trois* 'was probably the happiest passage in our three lives' has the same Panglossian ring as his description of George Carr Shaw's last years in Dublin after Bessie and the children had left: 'the happiest time of his life'. Sparling apparently believed that Shaw and May had slept together. In the summer of 1893 they had even gone to Zurich – with sixty other members of the British delegation to the International Socialist Workers' Congress. In any event, Shaw captivated May who 'might have been an iceberg so far as her future relations with her husband went'. Sparling finally went to live in Paris. 'The *ménage* which had prospered so pleasantly as a *ménage-à-trois* proved intolerable as a *ménage-à-deux*,' Shaw wrote. 'Of the particulars of the rupture I know nothing; but in the upshot he fled to the Continent and eventually submitted chivalrously to being divorced as the guilty party, though the alternative was technically arranged for him.'

Shaw made Sparling into a Hardyesque figure pursued by the remorseless Fates, while he himself is an observer of this retribution. But it is difficult to credit that he knew 'nothing' of the particulars of the rupture he had caused. How, for example, did he know that Sparling had legal grounds for obtaining a divorce against May – the 'alternative' that had been 'technically arranged for him' – unless perhaps that technicality had been arranged on one of the nights he slept at her house? But by the time Sparling left, Shaw had entered a new triangular liaison. In his imagination, May had returned to the immortal William Morris and her predestined place for all time. Even Morris's death in 1896 could not alter this: 'You can lose a man like that by your own death,' Shaw wrote, 'but not by his.' May's divorce (decree nisi) from Sparling became law on 18 July 1898. 'May and I discontent one another extremely,' Shaw admitted, 'carefully avoiding the subject we are both thinking of. I mount my bike and fly.'

May reverted to her maiden name, and never remarried. 'I made a mess of things then,' she wrote, 'and always, and [have] only myself to blame for a waste of life.' But thirty years later she could accept Shaw's re-creation of their relationship because by then it was 'a story out of another world', as it always had been for him.

4

CORNO DI BASSETTO

Only a musician's appreciation has any gratification for me.
Shaw to Neville Cardus (6 January 1939)

The first duty for '*The Star*'s Own Captious Critic' was to invent a resounding pseudonym: Corno di Bassetto.

The basset horn had been used by Mozart in his Requiem because of its 'peculiar watery melancholy'; Shaw's musical journalism was designed to drive melancholy away, as music itself had driven melancholy from his Dublin home. Lee's music had not unified Shaw's mother and father, but under its spell Sonny had been able to forget the divisions in the house. If there was love during those years, it was love conveyed by the play of musical instruments and the coming together of voices. The miraculous world of opera became a necessity in Shaw's life. What others found in loving relationships, Shaw believed he experienced in music. The years of self-tuition from mastering the classics in piano transcription in Dublin to the study of musical treatises in the British Museum, the lessons in harmony and counterpoint, and the long variety of piano duets with everyone's wife, amounted to an unsentimental labour of love. For him words were the 'counters of thinking, not of feeling', and music 'the sublimest of the arts'.

Between February 1885 and February 1889 he had written some ninety thousand words of music criticism for the *Dramatic Review*, the *Magazine of Music*, the *Pall Mall Gazette*. In these papers the spirit of 'Corno di Bassetto' was conceived. The readership of *The Star* was 'the bicycle clubs and the polytechnics', not 'the Royal Society of Literature or the Musical Association'. The collaboration he now started between *Star*-writer and *Star*-reader, and the changes he imposed on himself to make this collaboration effective, were part of the human engineering behind his development into a public man. What had begun with almost-an-apology was to become almost-a-boast. In a letter to the conductor August Manns two months before the birth of Bassetto, he had written: 'The writer who ventures to criticize you in a public newspaper is . . . a person of no consequence whatever . . . and he was never more astonished and flattered in his life than when he learned that his irresponsible sallies had attracted your attention.'

This, the voice of Shaw's father, appeared to be drowned in later years by a clamour of self-approval, and was only heard again when he confronted people such as Rodin or Einstein, who had not made the sort of public compromise at which G.B.S. excelled. His attitude to this compromise sometimes betrays the self-disgust that was one side of his nature. 'I daresay these articles would seem shabby, vulgar, cheap, silly, vapid enough if they were dug up and exposed to the twentieth century light,' he wrote of his Bassetto pieces in 1906. In his Preface, written in 1935, to the publication of *London Music in 1888–89 As Heard by Corno di Bassetto*, Shaw's tone has shifted: 'Vulgarity is a necessary part of a complete author's equipment; and the clown is sometimes the best part of the circus . . . I purposely vulgarized musical criticism, which was then refined and academic to the point of being unreadable and often nonsensical.'

To perform his job of making 'deaf stockbrokers read my two pages on music' it was vital to convince everyone that he knew nothing.

'When people hand me a sheet of instrumental music, and ask my opinion of it, I carefully hold it upside down, and pretend to study it in that position with the eye of an expert. When they invite me to try their new grand piano, I attempt to open it at the wrong end; and when the young lady of the house informs me that she is practising the 'cello, I innocently ask her whether the mouthpiece did not cut her lips dreadfully at first.'

This is the voice of the irresistible G.B.S./Bassetto – and Shaw means us not to resist, but to laugh and swallow his words and then discover that what we have assimilated is his burning sense of undervaluation and the resentment he felt at having to overcome it with such imposture. Bassetto's business 'is not to be funny, but to be accurate'; he explains that 'seriousness is only a small man's affectation of bigness', but that 'there is nothing so serious as great humor'. Though spoken of as severe,

Bassetto speaks of himself as 'lenient, almost foolishly goodnatured'. He never indulges in the cruel practice of giving misleading flattery. He has his passions: he hates the banjo ('If it be true that the Prince of Wales banjoizes, then I protest against his succession to the throne'); he hates the interruptions of encores and the habit of bouquet-throwing (the poor artists having to take the same vast bouquet to performance after performance to have it spontaneously hurled at them); he hates the old (Mendelssohn) when used as an obstacle to the new (Wagner); and he hates audiences, especially the practised coughers who should be removed to Piccadilly where their ailment can be treated 'by gently passing a warm steam-roller over their chests'. More annoying still were the men who beat time – one actually did it by shooting his ears up and down. 'Imagine the sensation of looking at a man with his ears pulsating 116 times per minute in a quick movement from one of Verdi's operas.'

But his chief objection to aristocracy-ridden London audiences was their imposition on music of artificial social standards. A wastefully competitive system obliged managers to convert opera houses and concert halls into fashionable post-prandial resorts. Intervals, which for many were the main events of the evening, were extended so that part of the audience was still chattering at full blast while the music was being played. Bassetto did not lack for a solution. The soldiers at present placed for show purposes in the vestibule should be moved into the stalls where they could turn their rifles on anyone who disturbed a performance. He urged the use of convict labour for the chorus and scene-shifting, and the taxing of private box-holders at twenty shillings in the pound to finance a Public Entertainments Trust under the chairmanship of Corno di Bassetto. After which they could get rid of the sham classical performances that had made the British into a race of cultural humbugs. 'The hypocrisy of culture, like other cast-off fashions, finds its last asylum among the poor,' he wrote.

Shaw calculated that the sort of social criticism that the editor T. P. O'Connor had found unendurable on the political pages of *The Star* would be acceptable when paraded through its musical columns. His objections to the tyranny of evening dress were famous. Bassetto disliked wearing the uniform of an idealist 'class of gentlemen to which I do not belong, and should be ashamed to belong'. In his eyes, it acted as a false passport. 'Next season, I shall purchase a stall for the most important evening I can select,' Shaw threatened Augustus Harris, the cautious manager of Covent Garden Opera House. 'I shall dress in white flannels.

'I shall then hire for the evening the most repulsive waiter I can find in the lowest oyster shop in London. I shall rub him with bacon crackling, smooth his hair with fried sausages, shower stale gravy upon him, season him with Worcester sauce, and give him just enough drink to make him self-assertive without making him actually drunk. With him I shall present myself at the stalls; explain that he is my brother; and that we have arranged that I am to see the opera unless evening dress is indispensable, in which case my brother, being in evening dress, will take my place.'

Shaw admitted the easy advantages of a compulsory costume that was cheap, simple, durable. It 'prevents rivalry and extravagance on the part of the male leaders of fashion,' he wrote, 'annihilates class distinctions, and gives men who are poor and doubtful of their social position (that is, the majority of men) a sense of security and satisfaction'. Such arguments applied equally to women's clothes: yet they were free to pursue private enterprise with horrible consequences:

'At 9 o'clock (the Opera began at 8) a lady came in and sat down very conspicuously in my line of sight. She remained there until the beginning of the last act. I do not complain of her coming late and going early: on the contrary, I wish she had come later and gone earlier. For this lady, who had very black hair, had stuck over her right ear the pitiable corpse of a large white bird, which looked exactly as if someone had killed it by stamping on its breast and then nailed it to the lady's temple, which was presumably of sufficient solidity to bear the operation . . . I presume that if I had presented myself at the doors with a dead snake round my neck, a collection of blackbeetles pinned to my shirtfront, and a grouse in my hair, I should have been refused admission. Why, then, is a woman to be allowed to commit such a public outrage? . . . I suggest to the Covent Garden authorities that, if they feel bound to protect their subscribers against the danger of my shocking them with a blue tie, they are at least equally bound to protect me against the danger of a woman shocking me with a dead bird.'

Bassetto's 'Musical Mems' were a continual protest against distractions from good musical performance. The worse the music, the more Bassetto diversified. Readers liked to hear of the voice trainer who hit his pupils, declaring that it was the only method to make them produce the vowel *o*; they liked to discover Bassetto himself, after a visit to the ballet, at dawn the next day with a policeman, a postman and a milkman ('who unfortunately broke his leg') attempting *pirouettes* and *entrechats* in Fitzroy Square; they liked, as part of a teetotal campaign, his plea for dancing in church, which just stopped short of converting Westminster Abbey into a ballroom; they even accepted his rank socialism: 'What we want is not music for the people, but bread for the people, rest for the people, immunity from robbery and scorn for the people, hope for them, enjoyment, equal respect and consideration, life and aspiration, instead of drudgery and despair. When we get that I imagine the people will make tolerable music for themselves.'

Almost the only person not to be diverted was T. P. O'Connor. Bassetto had fabricated for the public a very pretty relationship between critic and editor. But the reality was unpleasant. 'I find it impossible to continue as I have been doing lately,' Shaw told Massingham early in 1890. 'This week I have had to attend five concerts; have advanced fourteen shillings from my exhausted exchequer; and have written the Bassetto column, all for two guineas.' But T. P. O'Connor refused to increase Bassetto's salary. He wanted to be rid of him and of his attempts to turn his Liberal paper into a Socialist one. But to do so would make him one of the most unpopular editors in London. So he starved him out. Bassetto had sometimes made fun of his own resignation – 'this threat never fails to bring Stonecutter Street to its knees,' he told readers; 'though, lest too frequent repetition should blunt it, I am careful not to employ it more than three times in any one week.' In private, Shaw was driven by destitution to walk to and from many of the concerts and to wait a year for the repayment of some of his expenses.

By the early summer of 1890 their relationship had grown so strained that 'we came to the very grave point of having to exchange assurances that we esteemed one another beyond all created mortals'. The day O'Connor had been looking forward to arrived in the middle of May 1890, when Bassetto of *The Star* became G.B.S. of *The World*. It was William Archer who persuaded Yates to re-employ Shaw. 'Arranged to take the musical criticship of *The World*,' Shaw wrote in his diary on 14 May, 'if T. P. O'Connor has nothing to say to the contrary.' In his own style, O'Connor had everything to say in its favour. 'I am extremely glad to hear you have got the excellent offer of *The World*,' he congratulated Shaw the next day. '. . . Take the offer by all means.' Above Corno di Bassetto's last column which appeared on 16 May, O'Connor stuck a discordant adieu: 'The larger salary of a weekly organ of the classes has proved too much for the virtue even of a Fabian.' 'After the malediction, the valediction,' Bassetto countered, and went on to show how all grievance (though not forgotten) could be submerged in humour:

'A man who, like myself, has to rise regularly at eleven o'clock every morning cannot sit up night after night writing opera notices . . . I ask some indulgence for my successor, handicapped as he will be for a time by the inevitable comparison . . . I hope he will never suffer the musical department of the Star to lose that pre-eminence which has distinguished it throughout the administration of "Corno di Bassetto".'

*

The character adopted by G.B.S. in *The World* was less dramatic than Bassetto. Anyone who made him laugh melted most of the criticism out of him. By offering the most far-fetched comparisons and analogies as stepping stones to his conclusions – the training of circus horses to compose dance music or the installation on the site of the prompter's box of a steam crane to hoist despairing critics out of their seats and drop them at the refreshment bar – G.B.S. amused the deaf stockbrokers, but also encouraged them to overlook what lay behind these fantasies, and to dismiss his serious recommendations as more absurdity. For the first time in his writing a note of exasperated despair sounds over the misreading of his careful statements. 'It has taken me nearly twenty years of studied self-restraint, aided by the natural decay of my faculties, to make myself dull enough to be accepted as a serious person by the British public; and I am not sure that I am not still regarded as a suspicious character in some quarters.'

Shaw's method of judging music, he once stated, was to do with his ears what he did with his eyes when he stared. Some critics imposed on the public by displays of 'scientific analysis'. G.B.S. resented this fashion for 'silly little musical parsing exercises to impress the laity'. In one of his most effective debunking feats, he parodied this scholarly pretentiousness with a comparable 'analysis' of Hamlet's soliloquy on death:

'Shakespear, dispensing with the customary exordium, announces his subject at once in the infinitive, in which mood it is presently repeated after a short connecting passage in which, brief as it is, we recognize the alternative and negative forms on which so much of the significance of repetition depends. Here we reach a colon; and a pointed pository phrase, in which the accent falls decisively on the relative pronoun, brings us to the first full stop.'

Academic preconceptions, G.B.S. argued, had encouraged a ruck of 'barren professors of the art of doing what has been done before and need not be done again'. He detected a gentlemanly gang at work in the musical world, and it was with outcast irony that he asked: 'who am I that I should be believed, to the disparagement of eminent musicians?' Commenting on Professor Stanford's *Eden*, he continued:

'If you doubt that Eden is a masterpiece, ask Dr Parry and Dr Mackenzie, and they will applaud it to the skies. Surely Dr Mackenzie's opinion is conclusive: for is he not the composer of Veni Creator, guaranteed as excellent music by Professor Stanford and Dr Parry? You want to know who Dr Parry is? Why, the composer of Blest Pair of Sirens, as to the merits of which you have only to consult Dr Mackenzie and Professor Stanford.'

As early as 1885 Shaw made out his historical case against the persisting influence of these composers. 'Our really serious music is no longer recognized as religious,' he wrote, 'whilst our professedly religious music . . . is only remarkable as *naïve* blasphemy, wonderfully elaborated, and convinced of its own piety.

'It was Mendelssohn who popularized the pious romancing which is now called sacred music; in other words, the Bible with the thought left out. M. Gounod proved his capacity in this direction by giving us Faust with all Goethe's thought left out, the result having been so successful (and, it must be confessed, so irresistibly charming), it is natural that he should turn his attention to the Bible, which is worshipped in England so devoutly by people who never open it, that a composer has but to pick a subject, or even a name, from it, to ensure a half-gagged criticism and the gravest attention for his work, however trivial.'

G.B.S. was merciless on the 'flagrant pedantry . . . and waste of musical funds' which the oratorio market produced for English festivals. 'I do not know how it is possible to listen to these works without indignation, especially in circumstances implying a parallel between them and the genuine epic stuff of Handel.' Had oratorio been invented in Dante's time, 'the seventh circle in his Inferno would have been simply a magnified Albert Hall, with millions of British choristers stolidly singing, All that hath life and breath, sing to the Lord, in the galleries, and the condemned, kept awake by demons, in the arena, clothed in evening dress'.

He was obliged to listen to a good deal of work by contemporary composers: Sir Frederick Cowen, Sir Alexander Mackenzie, Sir Hubert Parry, Sir Charles Stanford, Sir Arthur Sullivan, and other knights and bachelors of music, most of whose works he would happily have committed 'to the nearest County Council "destructor"'. Sullivan, a musician of care and refinement, who had spent over twenty years composing for the drawing-room and the Church, achieved success through a burlesque of the classics he revered. 'They trained him to make Europe yawn; and he took advantage of their teaching to make London and New York laugh and whistle.' In Stanford, G.B.S. detected a similar division exposed by the 'somewhat scandalous' success of his Irish Symphony, into which Shaw read 'a record of fearful conflict between the aboriginal Celt and the Professor'.

Here was a beginning in his quest for a formula that, with its symbol of a reconciled England and Ireland, would integrate inherited factors in such deep conflict that they had forced his parents to occupy separate countries and were eventually to neutralize himself as a man without nationality. For who was Shaw to censure Stanford for not displaying his emotions in public? Yet it is partly as self-censure, self-analysis and self-encouragement that we should read such passages:

'When Professor Stanford is genteel, cultured, classic, pious, and experimentally mixolydian, he is dull beyond belief. His dullness is all the harder to bear because it is the restless, ingenious, trifling, flippant dullness of the Irishman, instead of the stupid, bovine, sleepable-through dullness of the Englishman . . . Far from being a respectable oratorio-manufacturing talent, it is, when it gets loose, eccentric, violent, romantic, patriotic, and held in check only by a mortal fear of being found deficient in what are called "the manners and tone of good society". This fear, too, is Irish: it is, possibly, the racial consciousness of having missed that four hundred years of Roman civilization which gave England a sort of university education when Ireland was in the hedge school.

In those periods when nobody questions the superiority of the university to the hedge school, the Irishman, lamed by a sense of inferiority, blusters most intolerably . . . Then the fashion changes; Ruskin leads young Oxford out into the hedge school to dig roads; there is general disparagement in advanced circles of civilization, the university, respectability, law and order . . . This reaction is the opportunity of the Irishman in England to rehabilitate his self-respect, since it gives him a standpoint from which he can value himself as a hedge-school man . . . If he seizes the opportunity, he may end in founding a race of cultivated Irishmen whose mission in England will be to teach Englishmen to play with their brains as well as with their bodies; for it is all work and no play in the brain department that makes John Bull such an uncommonly dull boy.'

His few aberrations in judgement usually arise from treating music historically, that is, with the type of academic measuring-rod he scorns. He placed Hermann Goetz 'above all other German composers of the last hundred years, save only Mozart and Beethoven, Weber and Wagner', partly because his Symphony in F was technically and intellectually more symphonic in form that any by Schumann or Schubert. He undervalued Schubert and considered him overplayed because 'I could not see that

Schubert added anything to Mozart & Beethoven except sugar: and though the sugar was extraordinarily rich and sweet, I rather jumped over him to Mendelssohn'. Music composed out of the dramatic instinct (such as Goetz's *Taming of the Shrew*) attracted him far more than anything intimate. He was sometimes a poor judge of chamber music because it tended to conflict with his commitment to twenty-four-hours-a-day cheerfulness.

He sniped at Brahms, insisting that with all his great powers of utterance he had nothing to say ('Brahms' enormous gift of music is paralleled by nothing on earth but Mr Gladstone's gift of words'). Shaw's hostility to Brahms focused on his Requiem ('patiently borne only by the corpse'). In 1947 he explained that 'the first performances of Brahms's Requiem in London were dreadfully and insincerely mock-solemn and dull. Now that I know the work, its fugal bits and march music amuse me; and its one Mendelssohnic chorus is a favourite of mine.' But this explanation cannot conceal Shaw's antipathy to all near-contemporary religious music, especially when connected with death. He empties these works of poetry and makes them colossal monuments to boredom. He literally cannot listen to them.

But when he listens to other music it is with acute attentiveness. Whenever possible before a performance he studied the score and would expose cuts, interpolations and other textual deviations, as well as derivations from the work of other composers. His descriptions of performers have an exactness that enables us to differentiate one from another precisely: the exuberant hammer-play of Paderewski, the cool muscular strength of another musical gymnast, Slivinski, a prodigiously rapid pianist of the Leschetizky school, and the hugely energetic Rubinstein, a player of marvellous manual dexterity limited by his narrowness of intellectual sympathy. Among violinists he discriminates so finely between the judgement of Reményi, the sensitive hand of Sarasate, Joachim's peculiarly thoughtful style and the self-assertiveness of Ysaÿe that we can almost hear their playing. He analyses the varying styles of the conductors from Richard Wagner and Richter to Henschel's London Symphony Orchestra, Charles Hallé's Manchester concerts, and the Saturday concerts led by August Manns at the Crystal Palace. He brings in reports from music halls and from amateur events in the country such as the brass band of shoemakers playing on a racecourse at Northampton – the sort of place where the music of the country was kept alive. He argues that public opera houses are as essential to people as public museums and public galleries, and a powerful competition to public houses. He wants to transform this brainless country 'where you cannot have even a cheap piano provided for the children to march to in a Board School without some mean millionaire or other crying out that the rates will ruin him'. Among his targets for criticism are charity concerts that promoted bad music for well-meaning ends, as if a good orchestra was not as 'important to a town as a good hospital'.

The critic who amused stockbrokers in the 1880s and 1890s was to become one of our best guides to the history of music performed in England during the late nineteenth century. He had perfected the Shavian note – assertive, audacious, fantastic, expertly wrapped round with the illusion of intimacy – until he became his own description of the confident journalist-critic: 'magnificently endowed with the superb quality which we dishonor by the ignoble name of Cheek – a quality which has enabled men from time immemorial to fly without wings, and to live sumptuously without incomes'.

'The critic who is modest is lost,' Shaw wrote. But he also knew the damage that could be done to those who, to gain the popular ear, force 'vulgarity upon a talent that is naturally quiet and sympathetic'.

5

EXITS AND ENTRANCES

Very few people in the world have ever had a love affair.
'Beethoven's "Unsterbliche Geliebte"', *The World* (1 November 1893)

Florence Farr was 'an *amiable* woman, with semicircular eyebrows' whom Shaw describes in his portrait of Grace Tranfield from *The Philanderer*: 'slight of build, delicate of feature, and sensitive in expression . . . but her well closed mouth, proudly set brows, firm chin, and elegant carriage shew plenty of determination and self-respect'. She was four years younger than Shaw and unlike any woman he had met. She seemed to resemble some of the New Women he had optimistically invented in his novels. It was partly her feminism that had brought her to William Morris's house in Hammersmith where she was learning embroidery with May through whom, in about 1890, she met Shaw.

He had seen her act in John Todhunter's *A Sicilian Idyll*, remarking on her 'striking and appropriate good looks'. Then, on 4 October 1890, he 'had a long talk' with her at the private view of an Arts and Crafts exhibition, after which they went 'gadding about' to plays and recitals together, to the Pine Apple and Orange Grove restaurants and, for long teas, to ABC shops where he 'chatted and chatted' and she 'laughed and laughed'. He would turn up out of the night at her lodgings in 123

Dalling Road, only half a mile from May Morris, play a little, sing a little, and take her for walks round Ravenscourt Park. 'First really intimate conversation,' Shaw recorded after an evening with her on 15 November. As the daughter of a sanitary reformer who had tried to persuade his countrymen that England was dying of dirt, her Shavian provenance was impeccable. She had been schooled in Shakespeare and tap-dancing, then married a handsome actor, Edward Emery, who spent much of his time resting. Florence was not an observant woman: it was almost four years later, in 1888, that she noticed that Edward was no longer there. He had gone to America, leaving her an independent married woman.

Like Jenny Patterson Florence took the initiative over Shaw. 'As she was clever, goodnatured, and very goodlooking, all her men friends fell in love with her,' he recalled. Before the end of the year they had become lovers. Shaw made no secret of his love for Florence. 'Went over to FE in the evening,' he wrote in his diary on 30 December 1890: and added uncharacteristically, ' – a happy evening.' He told his friends he was in love with her; he told Florence herself she was 'my other self – no, not my other self, but my very self', and 'the happiest of all my great happinesses, the deepest and restfullest of all my tranquillities, the very inmost of all my loves'.

Whenever he felt incapable of further work and craved for exercise, he would leap away from his desk and usually find himself six miles off at Florence's lodgings, where he 'let time slip and lost my train back'. One night he arrived to 'find the place in darkness'. He 'wandered about disappointed for a time', then returned to Fitzroy Square, put down the feelings released in him by her absence, and sent them to her as a letter: 'I have fallen in with my boyhood's mistress, Solitude, and wandered aimlessly with her once more . . . reminding me of the days when disappointment seemed my inevitable & constant lot.'

Florence promised him a future he had believed to be impossible. 'Women tend to regard love as a fusion of body, spirit and mind,' he later told one of his biographers. 'It has never been so with me.' Yet for a time, perhaps a year, it seemed as if it could be so. Florence had, according to W. B. Yeats, 'three great gifts, a tranquil beauty . . . an incomparable sense of rhythm and a beautiful voice'. For Shaw, her attractiveness lay partly in her beauty and partly in her attitude. Though unpuritanical she was fastidious, 'claimed 14 lovers', but retained her independence. 'When a man begins to make love to me,' she admitted, 'I instantly see it as a stage performance.'

Almost before they knew themselves that they were in love, Jenny Patterson knew it. Towards the end of 1890 she had gone abroad, and for almost four months Shaw and Florence saw each other freely. But then, on 27 April 1891, Shaw 'went in to JP's. Fearful scene about FE, this being our first meeting since her return from the East. Did not get home until about 3.' These scenes grew fiercer, but each time she won a battle she won less. 'Not for forty thousand such relations will I forgo one forty thousandth part of my relation with you,' Shaw promised Florence. '. . . The silly triumph with which she [Jenny Patterson] takes, with the air of a conqueror, that which I have torn out of my own entrails for her, almost brings the lightning down on her . . . Damnation! triple damnation! You must give me back my peace.'

Once Jenny Patterson too had given him peace, but it had been a peace of the body only, as she well understood: 'Any other woman would have brough[t] you the sleep I did.' After the Annie Besant rumpus, she expected their sexual relationship to go on as before: and to some extent it had. Shaw was neglectful, long-suffering, and passionate by turns. 'You are beginning again the old games,' she had warned him in January 1888. But the next month she wrote: 'Be as ardent as you were last week, it is your place to be so – I adore to be made love to like that. It takes my breath away . . .'

Yet she could not conceal from herself that his feelings for her were not what they had been 'when I was dear Mrs Patterson & worth seeing . . . oh les beaux jours'. Her expectations of him seemed to fade. 'How my lover is becoming less my lover every month . . . just thinking of me as a sucking baby does of its mar when it is hungry!' she had complained on 20 October 1888. 'Adieu most disappointing of men.' She could say goodbye, she could not leave him; and the next month she is begging him to 'write me again so that I may have something to live on until I see you'.

But their relationship had become stale to Shaw. He tried not to hurt her – 'You are gentle and good nearly always to me,' she allowed – but increasingly recoiled from the physical centre of their liaison. Nevertheless, though he flirted with Fabian girls and other men's wives he had made love only to Mrs Patterson and perhaps May Morris until he fell in love with Florence. His love affair with Jenny Patterson had separated sex from other interests. She repeatedly writes of it as if it were a commodity like some bargain at a shop. 'My boy you got all for nothing – it was not to be bought at any price.' Sex was everything she had to bargain with, and through it she gave her whole self. She loved him in a way he could not love her. Hers is a small world and her feeling for him so fills it that there is no place for interests or enthusiasms beyond her infatuation. 'You are my love, my life & all the world to me,' she writes.

This love was Shaw's small private hell. Jenny may have been going through the change of life. She weeps, rages, flings a book at his head, provokes quarrels over imaginary offences, breaks off their relationship, arranges a luxurious reconciliation. In his chapter called 'The Womanly Woman' from *The Quintessence of Ibsenism*, Shaw was obviously using his experiences with Jenny Patterson when he describes 'the infatuation of passionate sexual desire'.

'Everyone who becomes the object of that infatuation shrinks from it instinctively. Love loses its charm when it is not free ... it becomes valueless and even abhorrent, like the caresses of a maniac. The desire to give inspires no affection unless there is also the power to withhold; and the successful wooer, in both sexes alike, is the one who can stand out for honorable conditions, and, failing them, go without.'

Only with his New Woman could he achieve these honourable conditions. Shaw never explained that Florence was infertile. This may help to account for her list of lovers, and why Shaw entered his name on it so prominently. By implication it may also elucidate a mysterious passage from a letter he wrote in 1930 to Frank Harris and later published in *Sixteen Self Sketches*: 'If you have any doubts as to my normal virility, dismiss them from your mind. I was not impotent; I was not sterile; I was not homosexual; and I was extremely susceptible, though not promiscuously.' How then did he know that he was not sterile? The evidence, though meagre, suggests that in the first half of 1886 Jenny Patterson may have had a miscarriage. She had gone to see Shaw's medical friend Kingston Barton early in February. 'I have seen "the" Barton,' she told him and followed this with an enigmatic row of dots. On 10 May, in the first of her desperate pleas to him not to abandon her, she writes of having to hide her predicament from 'Lucy's sharp eyes' and play at being her 'old self' to Shaw's mother: 'I dread being ill it will all come out I fear then.' But it is clear from Shaw's diary that his mother and sister knew of Mrs Patterson's attachment to him. So there must have been something more to come out. During the spring Jenny Patterson had complained of illness, and her letter of 11 May contains a definite allusion to pregnancy. 'You cant help wronging me. I trusted you entirely. Had there been results I should have had to bear that also alone.' So by the second week of May two things were established: that there was now no pregnancy and that they would henceforward experiment with a platonic relationship. The fear of pregnancy and the revulsion caused by a miscarriage could only have been extra brakes to Shaw enjoying sexual intercourse with other women until he met one who was herself sterile. It would also deepen the sexual guilt with which, despite all his freethinking morality, Jenny Patterson had encircled him.

With Florence there was no tyranny or guilt; and from his gratitude arose a dazzling overestimation of 'the magnetic Miss Farr'. There were times when she could make him feel 'more deeply moved than I could have imagined'. But she also brought him something deeper than the 'revulsion' he had noted against Jenny Patterson's name, and this, as he put in his diary, was 'Disillusion'.

After her husband's disappearance Florence had turned simultaneously towards two writers: W. B. Yeats and Shaw.

> Great minds have sought you – lacking someone else
> You have been second always . . .

Ezra Pound assured her:

> You are a person of some interest, one comes to you
> And takes strange gain away:
> Trophies fished up: some curious suggestion;
> Fact that leads nowhere: and a tale or two,
> Pregnant with mandrakes, or with something else
> That might prove useful and yet never proves . . .
> No! there is nothing! In the whole and all,
> Nothing that's quite your own.
> > Yet this is you.

Both Shaw and Yeats fashioned castles in the air with Florence, their amiable Princess, waving airily from them. While Shaw beckoned her towards a bright future, Yeats serenaded her back to the magical past. To Yeats she could 'tell everything'; from Shaw she heard everything. Like him she had sent herself to school in the Reading Room of the British Museum, and absorbed a fine store of facts that led nowhere. 'It is impossible to mention anything she does not know,' Shaw exclaimed in astonishment. He felt a tremendous challenge to discover some purpose within the debris of her knowledge. She had flirted professionally with the stage before her marriage, and was now preparing to float back to it by way of Ibsen's *The Lady from the Sea*. But Shaw 'delivered to her so powerful a discourse on *Rosmersholm* that she presently told me that she was resolved to create Rebecca or die'.

Shaw's fascination with the stage had been intensifying during his fifteen years in London. He had taken part in the copyright performances of one or two plays, acted in various amateur theatricals produced by the Socialist League and a '3rd rate comedy' with May Morris. He had been able to express his feelings for May more accurately on the stage than in real life: 'I do not love her – I have too much sense for such follies; but I hate and envy the detestable villain who plays her lover with all my soul.'

The stage appealed to Shaw as a place where actions were governed by words. His interest in Florence rapidly concentrated on her acting. 'I have an extraordinary desire to make the most of you – to make effective & visible *all* your artistic potentialities,' he told her. During February 1891 they went through *Rosmersholm* and from Shaw's diary come whispers of their excitement.

6 February Went over *Rosmersholm* (first few scenes) with FE. Found it hard to leave . . .
11 February . . . to FE's. She gave up her intention of going out to dinner and I stayed all the evening. We were playing, singing, trying on *Rosmersholm* dresses, going over the part etc.

The success of *Rosmersholm* was moderate and Shaw redoubled his efforts to make Florence's originality blaze forth. He became her tutor, calling round at Dalling Road to 'work on her dramatic elocution' and prepare her during the summer of 1892 for playing Beatrice in *The Cenci*. The scenes where Owen Jack coaches Madge Brailsford for the stage in *Love Among the Artists* had invaded life and were to return to fiction in *Pygmalion* (later Shaw was to advise Florence to study phonetics with Beerbohm Tree, the first Professor Higgins, at his school of drama). The name Doolittle irresistibly suggests Florence. She did not lack intelligence or feeling or beauty; she did not lack voice. But there seemed a 'frightful vacuity' at the centre of her life. Shaw strove to plant in this void the seeds of a vigorous and improving energy. She needed will-power, and it was his role to supply this power vicariously from the batteries of his own will.

During rehearsals at the Bedford Park Club on 30 June, Florence fainted but stood up bravely at the opening a fortnight later when 'the white robe and striking beauty of Beatrice' were favourably noticed by the anonymous critic of the *Daily Chronicle*, G. Bernard Shaw. But there were still Himalayas to cross before she could pass as an important leading lady. Behind the beating of Shaw's optimism emerges a bathos whenever he insists too much on the success of their collaboration: 'She actually realized greater possibilities than she had (what a sentence!).'

At the same time he had prudently invested his hopes in another actress. 'Interesting young woman,' he observed on 16 June 1889, after sitting next to Janet Achurch at a dinner in the Novelty Theatre celebrating the English première of *A Doll's House*. Shaw's mother, who accompanied him to this production, had also been struck by Janet, remarking with conviction: 'That one's a *divil*.' But Shaw found himself 'suddenly magnetized, irradiated, transported, fired, rejuvenated, bewitched', and sat up till 2 a.m. the following night writing to his 'wild and glorious young woman'.

Janet was married to another actor, Charles Charrington Martin. Together they had played in a company managed by F. R. Benson, a splendidly incomprehensible actor whose mission to spread Shakespeare through the country was aided by the widespread belief that he was related to the Archbishop of Canterbury.

There was no conventional prettiness to Janet. She was Amazonian. Shaw could never think of her noble outline 'without imagining myself lost at sea in the night, and turning for refuge toward a distant lighthouse, which, somehow, is you'. Others contemplating her voluptuous appearance thought of Helen and Guinevere and 'those Northern beauties who strangled the souls and bodies of heroes in the meshes of their golden tresses'.

She and Charles Charrington had signed an agreement to tour Australia and New Zealand for two years. It was with money borrowed in advance of their salary that they had financed one week's performance of *A Doll's House* at the Novelty Theatre.

That Janet was to leave for the other side of the world in less than three weeks stirred Shaw's feeling magnificently. He saw *A Doll's House* five times, and sent her two of his novels. On the morning of 5 July he went to Charing Cross to see them both off on their Australian tour. He had pledged himself to work in Janet's absence but would find himself wasting time with a long letter to her. She sent him her photograph and asked for his news. He replied, telling her of all the 'nibblings at Ibsen' in London and of his own *Quintessence*. William Archer's criticism was gaining wonderfully in its recklessness, he added, while 'I am getting middle-aged and uninteresting. Political drudgery has swamped my literary career altogether. Still, as all the follies of love and ambition fall off from me, my soul burns with a brighter flame.' Then there was the music criticism: Corno di Bassetto of *The Star* was dead – long live (on five pounds a week) G.B.S. of *The World*! 'Since I began to write for the World, revising my work with great labor and going to great numbers of performances, I have become more and more a slave to art, and can by no means be satisfied with intellectual interest,' he divulged.

'. . . Consequently, my last word tonight shall be said to you, with whom I have no ignoble or unlovely associations . . . I see you quite distinctly – on the stage of the Novelty . . . Take courage then; for if you can cast these magic spells on a man thousands of miles away, after years – centuries – of absence, what can you not do to those only separated from you by a row of footlights, with Ibsen to help you?'

The music, his preoccupation with Ibsen and the spell exercised on his imagination by Janet Achurch and Florence Farr, were combining to move him towards the theatre. But when 'the fearsome Charringtons', as Henry James called them, returned to England early in 1892 and revived *A Doll's House* at the Avenue Theatre, something had changed. Janet exploded into fortissimo and tightened her lower lip 'like an India rubber band'. But 'my admiration is in nowise abated,' G.B.S. reassured her. Admiration was the form Shaw's love for Janet was now taking. 'I am actually less enamoured than before,' he wrote, 'because my admiration elbows out the commoner sentiment. I speak as a critic, not merely as a miserable two legged man.'

To move his emotions on to the stage was a new experiment for Shaw. But in 1893, turning down an opportunity of producing *Rosmersholm*, Janet and Charrington mounted their own season of plays in London: Richard Voss's *Alexandra*; Brandon Thomas's *Clever Alice*; and Scribe and Legouvé's *Adrienne Lecouvreur*. Shaw was appalled. 'Those old stalking horses are no use: the better you do them the more hopeless do they appear,' he reprimanded them.

Part of the trouble had to be Charrington. As Helmer in *A Doll's House* his failure had been complete. But he was more dangerous off the stage where, in addition to being Janet's husband, he played the more serious role – one obviously intended for Shaw – of her business manager. A man with a considerable knowledge of pawnbrokers, he developed a talent for converting other people's investments into thin air. Shaw, who often insisted that he was 'not fit to be trusted with money', handed him a good deal of his own over the years.

Charrington's debt-collecting was obviously an 'incurable neurosis'; Janet's neurosis took Shaw longer to identify. On their long way back from Australia she had fallen ill, getting through her parts only with the help of morphia which the doctors had prescribed after she nearly died in childbirth. Previously she had had a tendency to alcoholism; now she added an addiction to morphia. As her condition became clear to Shaw, a method of driving out her disabling addiction by means of a more ingenious drug, distilled upon the stage, began to form in his mind.

The Charringtons appealed to his instinct for turning failure into success. Janet's happy prior attachment obliged Shaw to direct almost all his emotional energy towards her stage life. 'I had to be sensible about Janet,' he explained.

'I have two sorts of feeling for you . . . one is an ordinary man-and-woman hankering after you . . . you are very handsome and clever, and rich in a fine sort of passionate ardor which I enjoy, in an entirely selfish way, like any other man. But I have another feeling for you. As an artist and trained critic, I have a very strong sense of artistic faculty and its value. I have as you know, a high opinion of your power as an actress; and just as I want to have my own powers in action and to preserve them from waste or coarsening, so I have sympathetically a strong desire to see your powers in action . . . This is the side on which you may find me useful.'

Charrington's impracticalities opened the way for Shaw's most romantic role – that of the expert businessman, crackling with exasperated energy. 'Mind you do exactly what I tell you,' he instructed Charrington. But the Charringtons, while valuing his financial help, tested his instinct for success to its limits. 'Why were you ever born?' he burst out. 'Why did you get married?' And, echoing his mother: 'Oh Charles and Janet, what a devil of a pair you are!'

The Charringtons did not rest at dissipating Janet's genius: they conspired to tip the frailer talent of Florence Farr over the precipice, having persuaded her to play the Princess in their production of *Adrienne Lecouvreur*. 'The unspeakable absurdity of that performance is only surpassed by the unparalleled blastedness of the play,' Shaw admonished.

At the same time Shaw felt committed to Florence and still hoped to produce from that commitment a miraculous transformation. His loyalty to her was intensified by his final break with Jenny Patterson. Between the spring of 1891 and of 1893 the scenes with Jenny had grown worse until both of them looked like caricatures of themselves – he stonily refusing to 'sentimentalize' while Jenny, pretending to open none of his letters to her, scrutinized as many of other people's letters to him as she could put her hands on. In the intervals of remorse they behaved with studied kindness to each other. They got on best while she was away in Australia, Egypt and Ireland – and Shaw could spend more evenings with Florence. 'We read a lot of Walt Whitman and were very happy,' he noted simply in his diary on 26 January 1893. But when Jenny came back all her jealousy revived. She besieged him in his room so that he had to make his way out by physical force, take up asylum in the British Museum and telegraph his mother to clear the house before he returned. But 'the scene upset me,' he admitted.

Jenny's hounding of him at Fitzroy Square had probably been an inducement for Shaw to go and stay with the Sparlings, so near to Florence's lodgings. Nevertheless her emotional influence over him was waning. Something spectacular was needed.

Something spectacular happened on 4 February 1893. 'In the evening,' Shaw wrote in his diary:

'I went to FE; and JP burst in on us very late in the evening. There was a most shocking scene, JP being violent and using atrocious language. At last I sent FE out of the room, having to restrain JP by force from attacking her. I was two hours getting her out of the house and I did not get her home to Brompton Square until near 1, nor could I get away myself until 3. I was horribly tired and shocked and upset; but I kept patience and did not behave badly nor ungently. Did not get to bed until 4; and had but a disturbed night of it. I made JP write a letter to me expressing her regret and promising not to annoy FE again. This was sent to FE to reassure her.'

Next day he wrote letters to both Florence (which he got May Morris to deliver) and to Jenny. There was an embattled pause. Then on 22 February 'Got a letter from JP, which I burnt at the first glance. Wrote to tell her so, feeling the uselessness of doing anything else.' It was the end. Jenny never forgave him; and he never forgot her – he even remembered her in his will by leaving her one hundred pounds, though she successfully avoided this by dying first.

They corresponded once more – in *The Star* about the case of a police constable condemned to be hanged for the murder of his mistress. This tragedy 'will recur tomorrow or the next day with some other pair,' Shaw predicted. 'We shall never be rid of these butcheries until we make up our minds as to what a woman's claims exactly are upon a man who, having formerly loved her, now wishes to get free from her society. If we find that she has some claims, let us enforce them and protect the man from any molestation that goes beyond them.' In a letter signed E four days later, Jenny Patterson replied: 'I know too well the feeling when a girl knows she is no more loved by the one she has given her all to, but is only a thing to be cast aside like a toy which has been tired of.' Shaw concluded the correspondence by describing this as showing precisely the 'unreason that has got the woman killed and the man hanged. At the bottom of all the unreason, however, will be found the old theory that an act of sexual intercourse gives the parties a lifelong claim on one another for better or worse.'

FIVE

I

THE COURTSHIP OF THE WEBBS

In politics, all facts are selected facts . . . To put it another way, the very
honestest man has an unfair mind.
'Why a Labor Year Book?', *The Labour Party Year Book* (1916)

While Shaw had been leaping up the mountains at Oberammergau, in the
heather down below Webb had not after all been writing on municipal
death duties, but pouring out love letters to a woman called Beatrice
Potter. 'I do not see how I can go on without you,' he implored. Shaw,
he added, 'does not suspect my feeling for you'. Later on G.B.S. would
claim to have sleuthed out the facts from Webb's complexion ('Sidney
used to come out in spots when he fell in love').

Beatrice was then in her early thirties. Handsome, with huge black eyes,
sweeping brown hair tortured into a knot at the back of her head, a wide
rather sensuous mouth, she had what was known as a 'beautiful carriage'.
Her origins, Beatrice admitted, 'lie in my sensual nature'. But she had
sought to quell this nature, feeling it wicked to crave from men the love
and attention she had missed as a child. 'My childhood was not on the
whole a happy one,' she wrote. She was scrupulously ignored by her
mother who had wanted a son instead of her eighth daughter, and who
considered her 'the only one of my children who is below the average in
intelligence'. As she grew up, Beatrice turned to the informal warmth of
the servants' quarters, curling up among the sheets and tablecloths in the
laundry or sitting on the ironing board and confiding to the maids her
intention of becoming a nun. 'I must pour my poor crooked thoughts into
somebody's heart,' she wrote, aged fifteen at the beginning of her diary,
'even if it be my own.'

To one man she did give her heart – Joseph Chamberlain. He was
'intensely attractive to me,' she confessed, yet she could not overlook his
'personal ambition and desire to dominate'. Sexual passion and the attraction of power divided her – it seemed impossible to reconcile her sensual
with her intellectual needs. 'I don't know how it will end,' she wrote.
'Certainly not in *my happiness*.' Chamberlain's rejection drove her into
suicidal depression. 'If Death comes it will be welcome,' she wrote. ' . . .
It is curious this feeling of life being ended.'

Another life came to her through social work which moved her emotional energies into politics. She brooded over statistics, went on a study of Sweating in the tailoring trade, kept company with trade unionists. 'At last I am a Socialist,' she exulted in January 1890.

That month she had met Sidney Webb – 'a London retail tradesman,' as she described him, 'with the aims of a Napoleon'. Though she liked to claim that she was without a sense of beauty, she had an almost voluptuous appreciation of ugliness. 'His tiny tadpole body, unhealthy skin, lack of manner, Cockney pronunciation, poverty, are all against him,' she noted. He strutted round the room with an expression of inexhaustible conceit. But despite his 'bad habits' she liked him. Beneath the bourgeois black coat, inside the bulky head, lurked an improbable monster of romance who wanted to marry a beauty and to see his ideas command the lives of Cabinet Ministers such as Joseph Chamberlain. 'You have it in your hands to make me, in the noblest sense, great,' he informed her. And Beatrice responded. 'One grasp of the hand,' she recorded, 'and we were soon in a warm discussion on some question of Economics.' He wooed her with charts and equations. As he lay in bed at night, a vision of her face flashed before him 'in the guise of a co-worker . . . between the lines of the despatches'. She had devised a concordat to hoist their 'camaraderie' from 'the predominance of lower feeling' to the pinnacles of high-mindedness. 'The agony is unendurable,' he assured her. She urged him to consider his clothes, and the string to his pince-nez. 'Take care of your voice pronunciation,' she commanded: 'it is the chief instrument of influence.' Her heart seemed imprisoned by its past attachment to Chamberlain. 'I am not capable of loving,' she insisted.

The courtship grew so desperate as to bewilder them both. 'The question is,' Beatrice urgently demanded, 'what is the present position?' Whatever it was, suddenly it changed and she began to brood on matrimony. One day, after Sidney had finally given up all hope, she failed to withdraw her hand from his. 'I am still a little in a dream,' he owned.

Marriage, they were agreed, was the waste-paper basket of the emotions. Optimistically he sent her his full-length portrait, but: 'No dear,' she chided him, 'I do not even look at your photograph. It is too hideous . . . it is the head only that I am marrying.' 'You have made a splendid beginning,' he responded. Their engagement was cemented, in Sidney's phrase, over the death of Beatrice's father, and on 23 July 1892, in 'a prosaic, almost sordid ceremony', they were married at St Pancras vestry hall, spending their honeymoon in Dublin investigating Irish trade unionism. 'We are very very happy – far too happy to be reasonable.'

'If all marriages were as happy,' Shaw concluded, 'England, and indeed the civilized world, would be a Fabian paradise.'

*

Beatrice initially disliked Shaw. 'We embarrass each other frightfully when we are alone together,' he observed, 'without some subject of keen and immediate interest to discuss.' His philanderings riled her. 'His stupid gallantries bar out from him the friendship of women who are either too sensible, too puritanical or too much "otherwise engaged" to care to bandy personal flatteries with him,' she noted contemptuously in her diary. 'One large section of women, comprising some, at any rate, of the finest types, remains hidden from him.' 'Nothing annoyed her so much,' Shaw recognized, 'as being suspected of any sensual attachment to me.' Nor could he resist playing on this until she found a way of neutralizing him. 'You cannot fall in love with a *sprite*: and Shaw is a sprite in such matters, not a real person,' she explained. And Shaw himself agreed: 'It is certainly true.'

They came to understand each other well because of the Fabian 'dry goods' they shared. 'We are committed for life to Socialism,' Shaw acknowledged. It was after her that Shaw created Vivie Warren in *Mrs Warren's Profession* – an 'attractive . . . sensible . . . self-possessed' woman in whom William Archer (not knowing Beatrice) could see nothing 'but a Shaw in petticoats'. It was Shaw's 'most serious play,' Beatrice decided.

Each summer the Webbs would take a house in the country for three months – first an enlarged Jacobean mansion called Argoed, at Penallt in the Wye Valley; subsequently a rectory in Suffolk or a farm in Surrey – and here they would invite Sidney's friends on the Fabian executive. 'The Fabian old gang can only afford a country house for a holiday,' Shaw bluntly put it, 'because one of us has a wife with a thousand a year.' They passed their mornings, each in separate rooms, writing; stopped for a ravenous plain meal ('we do not have butter for Sidney's breakfast'); strode off on crushing walks during the afternoon and spent the evenings arguing violently over politics. By the mid-1890s they had changed from walkers into bicyclists.

'My new toy is my bicycle,' Shaw proclaimed in 1895. That spring, to the convulsions of the coastguards, he started learning to ride this new hobby horse with the Webbs on Beachy Head: 'I will do twenty yards and a destructive fall against any professional in England,' he told Janet Achurch. 'My God, the stiffness, the blisters, the bruises, the pains in every twisted muscle, the crashes against the chalk road that I have endured – and at my age [39] too. But I shall come like gold from the furnace: I will not be beaten by that hellish machine.' Beatrice, who scudded into a wasps' nest but managed to cure herself with whisky, calculated that 'One's "byke" is a great addition to the pleasure of life.'

And Shaw, lying exhausted in a deep ditch near Argoed, the moonlight filtering onto him through the revolving spokes of the wheels and the laced thorn twigs of a briar, reflected: 'Bicycling's a capital thing for a literary man.' On wheels, the Fabians appeared to become schoolboys and girls again. Beatrice (until Sidney had one smash too many) rigorously prescribed it during the long Fabian summer afternoons; and Shaw hygienically explained: 'Unless I seize every opportunity of bicycling off into the country, if only for a couple of hours, I get beaten by the evil atmosphere in which I have to pass so much of my time.'

For a dozen years, until 1908 when he took dangerously to cars, the bicycle was a prime article of Shavian equipment. Its effect was enormous, he reasoned, since the bicyclist could extend a day's travel from the pedestrian's few miles to the region of a hundred miles. So, by increasing the efficiency of existence, the bicycle which was popularly attacked as the terror of horses and a temptation to women, became a symbol of modernity. As such it was wheeled by way of metaphor and analogy into many Shavian arguments.

By 1896 he had enrolled as the 621st member of the Cyclist Touring Club whose Annual General Meeting he considerably lengthened by a plea against improving the tone of the Club's *Gazette* (where fiction, he thought, should be found only among the advertisements). To actresses, parents, schoolboys, he poured out information about the varieties of crack machines. 'Do not expect to improve with practice,' he recommended. 'You wont. The change from hopeless failure to complete success is instantaneous and miraculous.' One miracle was staying alive, though 'if you keep on bicycling long enough,' he promised, 'you will break your leg'.

For someone physically timid, Shaw's experiments by bicycle were extraordinary. He would raise his feet to the handlebars and simply *toboggan* down the steep places. Many of his falls, from which he would prance away crying 'I am not hurt', with black eyes, violet lips and a red face, acted as trials for his optimism. The surgery afterwards was an education in itself. Each toss he took was a point scored for one or more of his fads. After one appalling smash (hills, clouds and farmhouses tumbling around drunkenly), he wrote: 'Still I am not thoroughly convinced yet that I was not killed. Anybody but a vegetarian would have been. Nobody but a teetotaller would have faced a bicycle again for six months.' After four years of intrepid pedalling, he could claim: 'If I had taken to the ring I should, on the whole, have suffered less than I have, physically.'

*

He saw a good deal of the Webbs during the first half-dozen years of their marriage. The income that Beatrice inherited from her father enabled Sidney to retire from the Colonial Office; and together they planned to give unpaid service to society in return for this unearned income. Beatrice immediately put Sidney to work, writing their books on trade unionism, industrial democracy and English local government. This work established the Fabian tradition of research. It was complemented by their 'permeation' policy of infiltration and persuasion. Under Beatrice's direction, this was to take a more social turn. She was not a good hostess. Like Shaw, her achievement was built on the repression of the body. She grew addicted to fasting, weighing herself regularly at Charing Cross Station and gloating over each little loss of weight. Her bare lunches and dinners, though feasts of intellect, never added an atmosphere of seduction to the manipulating activity of permeation.

Beatrice was to be the *salonnière* of the Fabian Society, with Shaw its instant historian. What his audiences heard from him on the platform, what they read by him in their newspapers, kept morale sparkling with the sense that political events were going their way. It also enabled them the more easily to accept decisions in their name that had been made exclusively by the Webbs and Shaw.

Only one Socialist, Keir Hardie, had been returned to Parliament at the General Election of 1892. The Fabians generally supported the Liberals on whom, by means of what was called the Newcastle programme, they believed that they had imposed a detailed plan for constructive social reform. At the beginning of 1893, the future of a Labour Party in Parliament was remote; but implementation by Gladstone's Liberal Government of the Fabian-inspired Newcastle Programme, involving new factory legislation, the extension of free education, municipal reform, payment of MPs and the 'mending or ending' of the House of Lords, seemed imminent. Six months later, it had become clear that Gladstone had abandoned almost all radical reforms and handed Parliament's time over to an Irish Home Rule Bill. To the Fabians, this was a waste of time (literally so, since the House of Lords halted the Home Rule Bill), and a betrayal of election promises. 'We must,' Shaw wrote to a hesitant Graham Wallas, ' . . . satisfy the legitimate aspirations of the ardent spirits by getting out a furious attack on the Government.'

This furious attack, written by Shaw with Webb's assistance and signed 'By the Fabian Society', appeared in the November *Fortnightly Review* using the Biblical call to revolt, 'To Your Tents, Oh Israel!' Acknowledging that legislative reforms might have been limited by the small Liberal majority, Shaw's manifesto examined each of the departments of State and showed what administrative reforms, not subject to this limitation, might have been effected so that individual ministers could redeem some of their Government's pledges. 'Had the will existed,' the manifesto concluded, 'there would have been no difficulty about the way.' This was a triumphant piece of political journalism, which Shaw elaborated in January 1894 into Fabian Tract No. 49, *A Plan of Campaign for Labor*, which called for the trade unions to raise 'a parliamentary fund of at least £30,000, and the running of fifty *independent* Labor candidates at the next general election'. But this manifesto produced two reactions: it alienated the Liberal Party and all those Fabians who still saw in Liberalism a means of introducing a progressive programme into Parliament; and it came too late to kindle sympathy with men such as Keir Hardie, who was to lose his seat in the 1895 General Election, and who described the Fabians as 'the worst enemies of the social revolution'. For though *A Plan of Campaign for Labor* proposed similar measures to those of the Independent Labour Party, Shaw feared that any amalgamation would lead to the extinction of his Fabian family. Already by the spring of 1894 the Society, which Shaw was to urge not to 'waste another five minutes on permeation', was drifting back to the idea of grafting collectivism on to Rosebery who had then succeeded Gladstone as Liberal Prime Minister. At the 1895 General Election, 'sitting with their hands in their laps', the Fabians neutrally committed themselves to the principle of a Collectivist Party, distinct from Liberals, Conservatives and the ILP. The large Conservative victory that summer seemed to mark an end to the socialist resurgence in Britain. The trade-union movement had faltered, the ILP had done badly, and the Fabians had done nothing at all.

Fabian strategy during the 1890s exemplified Shaw's dogma of adaptability. He excelled at seizing the initiative in retrospect. In whichever direction history plunged, there was the Fabian waiting to guide and explain. To some extent these twists and weavings were the natural trials and errors of Shaw's political education. He felt strongly convinced that the humane and reasoned voice of the intellectual must not be lost amid the struggle of party politicians and the rough and tumble of popular democracy. To be heard, seen, and valued as advocates of progress with safeguards against revolution, the Fabians needed someone to play these political games and command popular appeal – while leaving the central concept of egalitarian English socialism uncontaminated. It was on such an understanding that Shaw was exploiting his dialectical skills.

2

PLAYS UNPLEASANT

Widowers' Houses seemed to me better worth printing than burning . . .
I am not burning it: I am just finishing another play . . . Then I shall
write another; and I have no doubt that when I have written ten or
eleven more or less simple and crude plays I shall be able to write a
complex and perhaps powerful one.

Shaw to Karl Pearson (20 June 1893)

He had been hovering on the edge of writing plays for a long time. This
fascination with the stage, deriving from those visits in Dublin to the
Theatre Royal and the new Gaiety Theatre, had hidden itself in his novels,
for he was (so he confessed to readers of the *Pall Mall Gazette*), 'a sufferer
from that strange brain disease which drives its victims to write long
stories that are not true, and to delight in them more than in any other
literature'.

In 1884 he had begun his first serious attempt to write a full-length
play in collaboration with Archer. The plan was for Archer to borrow a
plot from a domestic 'cup-and-saucer comedy' by Emile Augier called
Ceinture Dorée, Archer doing it into English scene by scene and ladling it
out to Shaw who would set about reconciling it, in sparkling dialogue,
with his Marxist passion for political economy. It was to be called *The
Way to a Woman's Heart*, though they soon began calling it *Rheingold*
(later anglicized to *Rhinegold*). Shaw started on 18 August and by 12
September completed the first act. A month later, the second act was also
completed; but in mid-November, after writing twenty-three lines of Act
III, he stopped, with the explanation that he had exhausted all Archer's
plot. In fact he was able to find use for all too little of it. His difficulty
lay in matching this contrived Parisian structure to an analysis of contemporary slum landlordism. Increasingly he was driven away from Augier's
story to plunder other sources – *Little Dorrit*, some scenes from his own
last novel, *An Unsocial Socialist*, and a penny pamphlet called *The Bitter
Cry of Outcast London* that was to lead to a Royal Commission. But
eventually he 'gave up fiction and took to Socialism,' as he explained to
Janet Achurch.

There were occasions over the next two or three years when, coming
across his notebooks, Shaw would copy out some pages of *Rhinegold* in
the hope of regaining his momentum. But the play still lacked direction.
'Wrote no new fiction,' Shaw noted at the beginning of his 1886 diary.
He felt the lack of creative writing, and by 14 April 1887 observed himself

to be 'hovering on the confines of beginning a novel'. A month later he registered in his diary that he 'began a new novel and sat up till 3 at it. Hooray!' But after two months there is no further mention of it. Having put aside the novel he again picked up his play. Early that autumn he made a fair copy in longhand of the first two acts which he left with Archer on 4 October. 'They are not supposed to be complete,' he told him, 'but they present a series of consecutive dialogues in which your idea is prepared and developed . . . but I have no idea of how it is to proceed.'

Two days later Shaw read Archer the first act of their unfinished drama. A long argument followed, and when Shaw began reading the second act, Archer closed his eyes. 'I softly put the manuscript away,' Shaw wrote, 'and let him have his sleep out.'

Archer believed that realism represented 'the hope of the dramatic future'. Ibsen had told him that there was always a stage when his writing might as 'easily turn into an essay as a drama'. What his playwriting experiment taught Archer was that his own future lay in writing realistic essays. There was not even money to be made from a collaboration with Shaw who was a fantasist rather than a realist. So he closed his eyes on a playwriting dream.

Archer's opinion was important to Shaw. Though he had trained himself to do without encouragement, he needed the support of this man who had given him so much of his theatrical education. Not receiving it, he was lost.

The following year he tried something new. 'Worked at the plan of the play which has come into my head,' he noted in his diary on 29 June 1889. The idea of this play had been stimulated by an incident involving Janet Achurch and the Archers. Frances Archer had apparently objected to Shaw having declared his love for Janet, a married woman. Shaw replied that conventional marriage stifled, the imagination. He even told Archer that his wife was spoiling him and that he would be 'a lost man' unless he broke free. Archer replied that Shaw must not visit their home while he held views so disparaging to his wife.

But the notion that marriage had meant 'checkmate' to Archer as a playwright 'for years to come' persisted in Shaw. Why else had Archer let him down over *Rhinegold*? The idea began to infiltrate a new work. At odd moments, in parks and restaurants, on trains and political platforms – even during the intervals of other people's plays – he would write passages of dialogue for what was turning out to be a comedy of intrigue, called *The Cassone*, with characters based on the Archers, the Charringtons and himself. It was a revenge for *Rhinegold* and a precursor to *Candida*, a battle of the artistic versus the domestic instinct. But his life was so pell-mell with politics and journalism he had no opportunity to complete *The Cassone.*

After the failure of his collaboration with Archer, Shaw had despaired of writing an actable play. 'I wish I could write you a real play myself,' he told the actress Alma Murray, 'but unfortunately I have not the faculty.' But he did not completely give up. 'I was surprised one day when he told me that he had been trying his hand at a new sort of stuff, some of which he showed me, written lengthwise in a reporter's note-book in his exquisite handwriting, unaffected by the vibration of railway travelling, and which I realized was a dramatic dialogue,' Sydney Olivier remembered.

'. . . I was surprised, because the quality of British play-wrighting, and the deadly artificiality and narrow conventions of native contemporary British Drama were at that time so repellent to me that I could not imagine any man of the intelligence of Shaw . . . conceiving that there was any possibility . . . for expressing himself in that medium.'

What nerved Shaw to continue was the example of Ibsen who had demonstrated how serious business (such as the working out of a new system of social values) could be conducted from the stage. After seeing Archer's translation of *A Doll's House* acted by the Charringtons, he had written:

'I find people enjoying themselves there who have been practically driven from the other theatres by the intolerable emptiness of the ordinary performances. I miss the conventional lies of the stage there; and I do not droop, wither, and protest I am being poisoned for want of them . . . [I] see a vital truth searched out and held up in a light intense enough to dispel all the mists and shadows that obscure it in actual life. I see people silent, attentive, thoughtful, startled – struck to the heart, some of them.'

From the affinity he felt with Ibsen, Shaw emerged with new confidence. 'But not only has the comedy to be made, but the actors, the manager, the theatre, the audience. Somebody must do these things,' he wrote.

It was a Dutchman, J. T. Grein, who did this thing by starting what Shaw called 'the most important theatrical enterprise of its time'. Hiring a cheap hall ('the nearest thing to a barn left in Tottenham Court Road'), Grein announced a performance of Ibsen's *Ghosts* in 1891 to inaugurate 'The Independent Theatre', with Thomas Hardy, Henry Arthur Jones, Meredith, George Moore and Pinero among its members. 'Result – barn too small; performance transferred gloriously' to the Royalty Theatre, and Grein, suddenly the most famous theatrical entrepreneur in Britain.

It was Grein who, the following year, struck the spark of encouragement Shaw needed. While the two of them were walking one autumn night from Hammersmith, Grein mentioned his disappointment at the absence of new British playwrights for his theatre; and Shaw replied that he had written a new British play 'that you'll never have the courage to produce'. Grein answered the challenge by asking for the manuscript. It came, a few days later, 'written partly in a large notebook and for the rest on loose sheets,' Grein recalled, 'and I spent a long and attentive evening in sorting and deciphering it. I had never had a doubt as to my acceptance . . . But I could very well understand how little chance that play would have had [with] . . . the average theatre manager.'

The two acts of *Rhinegold* had lain among Shaw's discarded manuscripts for over four and a half years until, on 29 July 1892, while attempting to set his papers in order, he came across them. Next day he had 'set to work to finish the comedy'. On 31 July he was 'still amusing myself finishing the comedy', and by 2 August he 'began to revise the comedy'. That he was now to solve the problem that had baffled him in the 1880s was due to his education by Ibsen. The hero of the play, Harry Trench, proposes to Blanche Sartorius and is accepted by her in Act I. But in Act II, finding that her money comes from slum properties, he breaks off their engagement. How then was Shaw to bring the lovers together without violating his own and his hero's principles? His solution, by the summer of 1892, was to make the hero less 'heroic', and by showing the slum landlord Sartorius to be not a villain but the symptom of a social system in which everyone was implicated.

'I think, by the bye, that the title Rheingold ought to be saved for a romantic play,' he had suggested when leaving the first two acts with Archer. 'This is realism.' On 20 October 1892, while working at a new scene near the end of Act II, he decided on the 'far-fetched Scriptural title', *Widowers' Houses*. From its conception over seven years earlier the play had changed so fundamentally as to make Archer a collaborator only in the sense of having set Shaw's imagination to work.

The ramshackle rehearsals, scheduled for 14 November, started punctually the following day at a public house, 'the Mona Hotel'. Sometimes there were not enough actors to carry through a rehearsal at all. When they did turn up they vied anxiously with one another to avoid various parts – in particular Lickcheese, the Dickensian rent collector, who was played by James Welch after entering the pub for a drink. Shaw was there, he was everywhere, until begged to stay away so that the actors could get their words.

Widowers' Houses opened at the Royalty Theatre in Dean Street, Soho, on 9 December, the most obvious vocal part that evening being the prompter's. It was a curious example, commented Archer in *The World*, 'of what can be done in art by sheer brainpower'. At the end of the performance, Shaw hurried before the curtain to make a speech and was acclaimed with hisses. At the second and final performance, a matinée on 13 December, he again climbed on to the stage and, there being no critics present, was applauded.

If it had not achieved success, it had 'made a sensation,' Shaw contended. After more than eight years, he squeezed out the stimulus he needed. *Widowers' Houses* had been born: its job now was to give birth to him as a professional dramatist.

*

The novelty of *Widowers' Houses* lay in the anti-romantic use to which Shaw put theatrical cliché. When the father discovers his daughter in the arms of a stranger, he omits to horsewhip him, but pitches into negotiations over the marriage – and these negotiations reveal a naked money-for-social-position bargain. It is the young girl, not the young man, who takes the initiative in the love scenes, and when her fiancé initially refuses to accept his father-in-law's dowry because it has been acquired from appalling exploitation of the poor, she does not forsake all for love – in fact, she does the opposite. Unlike Augier's hero, who tips his tainted gold into the Rhine, Shaw's hero comes to accept it ('We're all in the same boat it appears'); and the final happy ending is a lustful surrender to corruption. In relation to the Victorian theatre, this 'was a prodigious feat,' wrote the critic Eric Bentley some fifty years later; 'it remains the most revolutionary act in modern English drama.'

Standing on stage that first night in his dazzling Jaeger wool, Shaw welcomed the turbulent hooting by agreeing that, 'yes', it was a disgraceful state of affairs they had just witnessed, a true picture of things then going on in middle-class society that he hoped would soon become unintelligible to London audiences. Later on, Shaw would instruct producers that Lickcheese, the reptilian rent-collector, should be played with pathos and sincerity, even geniality. 'There should be absolutely no unpleasantness at all about him . . . The audience should delight in him in a thoroughly friendly way: and he should wallow in their friendliness.' Shaw's point was that Lickcheese, the other characters, and the audience itself, were all incapable of being better than the world around them: it is a cast of philistines, with Sartorius the idealist at their head.

But 'friendly', in the Shavian vocabulary, is a dangerous word. What gives *Widowers' Houses* its power is Shaw's anger. He was writing here from personal experience, as the young man who had 'collected slum rentals weekly with these hands' in Dublin, and who in London was immersing himself in municipal politics. Shaw wanted to make his audience 'thoroughly uncomfortable whilst entertaining them artistically'. This philistine audience retaliated through its idealist critics by calling the play 'not a play' and the playwright 'no playwright'. He was, they allowed, a fine speaker and would have done well in comic opera or the Church. So began Shaw's lifelong battle with the critics for whom he was (in the words of A. B. Walkley), 'a detestable dramatist', having started his career with 'a singularly bad piece of work'.

Widowers' Houses contains the stereotype figures (heavy father, low comedian, *femme fatale*), but displaced by Shaw from their familiar roles. Lickcheese was to develop into Doolittle; the slum landlord Sartorius into the armaments manufacturer, Undershaft; Blanche Sartorius into Ann Whitefield. But they present themselves more crudely here, and without self-mockery or Shavian guile. In a sense this is Shaw's most human play. Nowhere else is his dislike of the world as it exists more plainly felt. The perfect embodiment of this world is Blanche Sartorius, over whom the pact between aristocratic respectability and financial exploitation is made. 'I see I have made a real lady of you, Blanche,' says her father a little wistfully. She is an enslaving woman, a landlady of the emotions who betrays, more clearly than anywhere else in Shaw's work, the results of Jenny Patterson's rigorous devotion. Here, on paper, was his revenge; and given on the stage an ironic twist by the casting of Florence Farr in the part. The predatory Blanche, with her terrifying temper, prompted Oscar Wilde to congratulate Shaw: 'I admire the horrible flesh and blood of your creatures.'

Though *Widowers' Houses* presents a socialist view of life, there is no socialist in it. Trench is an innocent Conservative who decides that he is not called upon to remake the world at his own expense. But his adaptability to facts becomes merely an acquiescence to corruption and his innocence is lost. To what extent socialism made compromise honourable was a question that was to be tested on Shaw with his next play.

*

With the press-cuttings crammed into his bag, Shaw caught a train to join William Morris's Christmas house party at Kelmscott Manor, in Oxfordshire. Over the holiday he began pondering his first Preface and dreaming of his second play. He would do such things . . . He would sail, all guns smoking, into the topical storm that was engulfing the New Woman; demolish the marriage and divorce laws, expose the evil of vivisection, violently assault modern doctors for reducing human beings to chemical machines. It was to be a grand cleaning-up operation. In his exhilaration he opened a wider window, cracked thicker ice, that winter.

For Easter 1893 he went to Oxted to stay with the Salts. His travelling companion on the train was Sydney Olivier who, it seemed, was also writing a play – which was surprising in view of the dismay he had shown over Shaw's writing of *Widowers' Houses*. Olivier read part of his play to the Salts one day, and was generally 'very full' of it, Shaw observed. Here was the pacemaker he needed to get going. His diary entry for the next day, 29 March, reads: 'After breakfast went up to the Common by Rickfield Rd and selected a spot on the West Heath, near the orphanage, where I lay down and got to work on the new play which I have resolved to call *The Philanderer*.'

Much of the play was written on trains to and from his various lectures and speeches, and (sometimes under an umbrella) in Hyde Park and Regent's Park, on the Embankment and on the top of Primrose Hill – whenever he could snatch an hour or two. Then he suddenly got stuck. On 23 May, he wrote in his diary: 'After dinner I went out to Putney and walked by way of Roehampton to Richmond Park, where I tried to get to work on the third act of the play, but could not think of a subject for it.'

The following day he went to William Archer's house to hear the reading of Olivier's play. Afterwards, on a bus to Shepherd's Bush, 'I hit on the third act of my new play.' The idea he had hit on was the marriage and divorce question. He continued intermittently working on this act and discussing it with Janet Achurch.

On the afternoon of 17 June he read a revised text to Lady Colin Campbell. What then happened changed the content of the play and the course Shaw's work was to follow. Lady Colin Campbell, he explained, 'pointed out to me that the third act at which I have been working ought to be put into the fire. This opened my eyes for the first time to the fact that I have started on quite a new trail and must reserve this act for the beginning of a new play.' A few days later, on 22 June, 'I went up to the top of Primrose Hill and there wrote a new scene for the beginning of the new third act of the play, as suggested by Lady Colin.'

Lady Colin Campbell was a formidable woman. She rode, she swam, she wrote books on etiquette and was Shaw's successor as art critic on *The World*. She was also Irish. But she was best known for having obtained, in a sensational series of court actions, a judicial separation from her husband, the youngest son of the eighth Duke of Argyll. She was a practical woman and a sensitive judge of public opinion. What she told Shaw was that no audience in the early 1890s would accept the last act as he had written it. He was in his thirty-seventh year. After that tiny taste of success with *Widowers' Houses*, he hungered to have his play produced. But by substituting her suggestion for his original inspiration he was going against much that he claimed for himself as a dramatist.

This may help to explain the revulsion that sometimes overtook him with this play.

In the original third act there is one extra character, a comic butler called Spedding. It takes place at the house of Dr Paramore on his third wedding anniversary to Julia Craven (the character based on Jenny Patterson). Only a man with the name Paramore and the inventor of a non-existent illness, 'Paramore's Disease', would marry Julia. But now he is a changed man, as tired of his wife as she is of him, and in love with Grace Tranfield (the character based on Florence Farr). He is – and this gives a nice symmetry to the play – in very much the same position as the philanderer Charteris in Act I: that is, on with the new love before he is off with the old, but with the additional complication of being married. It is this subject of marriage and divorce that occupies this act, during which they decide to go to South Dakota where the divorce laws have been better adapted to human nature.

The plot is carried forward by means of conversation. It is, in fact, Shaw's first discussion drama. There is an interweaving of ideas, an elegance of argument pushed to the point of comic exasperation, and a dissolving of action into talk – all innovations in the theatre that were not actually to reach the stage for more than another ten years.

By the end of June, *The Philanderer* (with Lady Colin Campbell's last act) was finished and early the following month Shaw had his chessmen out and was experimenting with the stage positions of his characters. As the second of what he was to call his 'unpleasant' plays, *The Philanderer* dealt with sex – with the power game of sex that was played in the society of the 1890s. Charteris, we are meant to understand, has had sexual intercourse with Julia Craven and Grace Tranfield. He is 'making love' to Grace on a sofa before Julia arrives early in Act I. In a letter to his Swedish translator, Shaw explained:

'A philanderer is a man who is strongly attracted by women. He flirts with them, falls half in love with them, makes them fall in love with him, but will not commit himself to any permanent relation with them, and often retreats at the last moment if his suit is successful – loves them but loves himself more – is too cautious, too fastidious, ever to give himself away.'

The Philanderer was an unlucky play. Shaw had wanted to include 'everything that is supposed to be hopelessly undramatic, and make them the most amusing part of the piece,' he told Charles Charrington. 'It will be unspeakably improper: so I expect it will only see the light at the Independent Theatre. Grein is already after it eagerly.' But Grein was

unimpressed. 'Shaw was probably much amused at our lack of appreciation, and took his manuscript away.'

That Grein suspected him to have been 'amused' at this rejection shows
how well Shaw could conceal his feelings. At the last moment he had
compromised – and his compromise had led nowhere. He had told Archer
that *The Philanderer* was to be 'a step nearer to something'. It was
true that 'the ideas and atmosphere of it belonged to a new world as yet
undiscovered at the West End Theatres', but at the last moment he had
taken a pace back.

*

After his failure with *The Philanderer*, Shaw returned to the vein he had
worked in *Widowers' Houses*, writing a problem play that was to reveal the
corruption produced by compromising too readily with society. Once
again the theme is one of social inheritance and the profit motive; once
again he shadows his audience with guilt.

'Do you think you are guiltless in the matter? Take care ... The wages
of prostitution are stitched into your button-holes and into your blouse,
pasted into your matchboxes and your boxes of pins, stuffed into your
mattress, mixed with the paint on your walls and stuck between the joints
of your water-pipes ... you will not cheat the Recording Angel into
putting down your debts to the wrong account.'

Writing in 1901 a Note for the end of *Cashel Byron's Profession*, he was
to explain that 'the word prostitution should either not be used at all, or
else applied impartially to all persons who do things for money that they
would not do if they had other assured means of livelihood'. In his play,
which he called *Mrs Warren's Profession*, he used the same formula as in
Cashel Byron's Profession, that of taking 'a profession which society
officially repudiates as a metaphor for the way in which that larger
society is really conducted'.

Ever since the licensing of continental brothels in the 1870s and the
subsequent discovery that British girls were being exported to Brussels
and Vienna (where Mrs Warren conducted her business), 'The Great
Social Evil', as the Victorians called prostitution, had begun to exceed
slum-landlordism as the most controversial topic for the press. In 1885,
W. T. Stead launched his sensational series, 'The Maiden Tribute of
Modern Babylon' in the *Pall Mall Gazette*, his first article revealing how
Mrs Armstrong had sold her daughter for £3. 'I am quite willing to take
as many quires of the paper as I can carry and sell them (for a penny) in
any thoroughfare in London,' Shaw wrote to Stead. On discovering that

Stead had doctored his facts, Shaw felt that he had been betrayed: 'he [Stead] was so stupendously ignorant that he never played the game.' Stead's game had been to force the Criminal Law Amendment Bill (the chief provision of which was to raise the age of consent from thirteen to sixteen) through Parliament.

The immense press coverage gave Shaw an insight into the nineteenth century's attitude towards its 'unfortunates'. Victorian domestic virtues were represented by the middle-class family with its many children and dominating paterfamilias. The wife-and-mother, guardian of the hearth, who ran the household and bore the children, was a sexless being whose gentility (physicians were agreed) was outward proof of the absence of a female orgasm. For sexual satisfaction, the husband-and-father had to explore the lesser breeds, such as working-class women earning a shilling a day in the sweatshop, for whom prostitution could bring a vital addition to their income. London was honeycombed with houses of assignation illegally maintained through police bribery; but only on the Continent had the brothel become an established social institution. The more superior of these brothels were run as clubs and they offered businessmen, such as Mrs Warren's Sir George Crofts, opportunities of forming profitable syndicates. These syndicates, which would purchase premises, secure licences and supply girls, provided investments similar to those made in the eighteenth century by city merchant houses in the slave trade.

In representing prostitution as an economic phenomenon ('Prostitution is not a question of sex: it is a question of money') Shaw was writing from the point of view of women; but he also wrote as a socialist ('Every increase in women's wages produces a decrease in prostitution') who prescribed as his remedy a living wage for women ('a Minimum Wage law and . . . proper provision for the unemployed'); and finally he wrote as a man struggling to supplant the sex instinct in himself.

It was Janet Achurch who fired the starting gun by telling Shaw the story of a play she was then writing called *Mrs Daintree's Daughter* based on Maupassant's *Yvette*. On 30 August 1893 he announced to Archer: 'I have finished the first act of my new play, in which I have skilfully blended the plot of The Second Mrs Tanqueray with that of The Cenci. It will be just the thing for the I[ndependent] T[heatre].'

Beatrice Webb suggested that he 'should put on the stage a real modern lady of the governing class – not the sort of thing that theatrical and critical authorities imagine such a lady to be'. To which Shaw added: 'I did so: and the result was Miss Vivie Warren.' Reporting his progress on 4 September, he wrote to the woman he hoped would play Vivie, Janet Achurch:

'The play progresses bravely; but it has left the original lines. I have made the daughter the heroine, and the mother a most deplorable old rip (saving your presence). The great scene will be the crushing of the mother by the daughter. I retain the old roué, but keep him restrained by a continual doubt as to whether the heroine may not be his daughter. The young lover's father, an outrageous clergyman, is in the same perplexity, he also being an old flame of the mother's. The lover is an agreeable young spark, wholly good-for-nothing. The girl is a quite original character. The mother, uncertain who the girl's father is, keeps all the old men at bay by telling each one that he is the parent.'

He continued working on it between visits to the Jaeger Wool Shop and the British Museum. He set out for walks with the play in his pocket, camping from time to time on wayside seats to write up the speeches. He called on his friends and, for purposes of revision and casting, delivered his lines. By the time he had finished all four acts on 2 November, he had tried it out on Archer, the Charringtons, Florence Farr, Sydney Olivier, the Salts, the Webbs and Mrs Theodore Wright, who being London's first Mrs Alving in Ibsen's *Ghosts* would, Shaw hoped, take the title role. He also read it to Lady Colin Campbell who, ironically, was going into collaboration with Janet Achurch over her version which, though licensed the following year, was never professionally performed. After all this preparation *Mrs Warren's Profession* was ready for the Independent Theatre by the second week of December.

Unlike Maupassant's *Yvette*, Vivie Warren neither attempts to kill herself nor becomes a courtesan like her mother; unlike Pinero's Mrs Tanqueray, Mrs Warren declines to step into the next room and commit suicide. She is 'a counter-portrait to the general image of the romantic, sentimentally attractive courtesan of the stage'. The cast is largely made up of prostitutes like Mrs Warren herself, and their clients: Sir George Crofts the big-time client; the old vicar who has sold himself for his benefice and turned from rake into sanctimonious humbug; and his son Frank, the nearest to an authorial presence in the play, who almost sells himself in marriage to Vivie. Below the talking surface of the play move mysterious undercurrents of incest.

This theme of incest (deriving from *The Cenci* as well as from Ibsen's *Ghosts* and *Rosmersholm*), was muted after Shaw's corrections to the first draft. Originally Frank and Vivie were established as half-brother and sister, and Vivie welcomes this fact as saving her from 'the sort of relation my mother's life had tainted for ever for me'. She returns to the moonlight illusion of being 'babes in the wood . . . covered up with leaves'; but as the curtain descends at the end of Act III she 'lifts her face & presses his lips on hers'. The confusing remnants from such incestuous moments suggest that Shaw felt all sex to be tainted for Vivie. 'I am like you,' Vivie tells her mother. But by focusing his play on the daughter and not (like Pinero and Maupassant) on the mother, Shaw seeks to convert sexual destiny into work destiny. 'There's no alternative,' says Madame Obardi, the prostitute mother, to Yvette who is shown as unable to avoid her fate in the 'world of gilded prostitution'. But for Vivie Warren there is an alternative: 'my work is not your work,' she tells her mother, 'and my way is not your way.' She gains integrity through sexual isolation – 'away from it all – away from the sentiment of the tie I formed under the spell of that ghastly moonlight, away from the very air breathed by my mother and that man, away from the world they are part of'. These words of Vivie's Shaw dropped from the published version: but they still lie between the lines and provide an uneasy sub-text to the play.

Shaw's case is that there are two ways of preventing the present from repeating the errors of the past: love and work. In love we forget, are reborn, speak like infants. Then the good moment goes, for the world is not lovable. But if what we call love also supplies the future generations, it is work that decides what sort of life those generations will follow. Instinct tells us whether we should love, and what work we should do; and will-power gives us the vitality to carry through this work.

Shaw places his emphasis on the gospel of work and against the religion of love. When Frank sees Vivie with her arm round her mother's waist, he is revolted: 'Dont it make your flesh creep.' But when he appeals to the love-instinct in Vivie ('Come and be covered up with leaves again') she gives a 'cry of disgust' and tells him: 'You make my flesh creep.' Is this because of the revelation that she is Frank's half-sister as well as the revelation of how her mother's money is made? That Frank's father had gone through some sexual involvement with Vivie's mother seems probable; but in such an atmosphere of consanguinity (like the atmosphere of Sonny's home), uncertainty prevails. Arising from Shaw's doubts about his parenthood and ambiguous feelings for his mother, incest is made to cover us all, like the leaves. Something of Mrs Shaw can been seen in Mrs Warren, and this may help to account for the uncertainty and aggression of the play. 'I can't stand *anybody* as Mrs Warren, because I can't stand the play itself,' he told Gertrude Kingston in 1925. ' . . . Ugh!'

When Vivie Warren 'buries herself luxuriously in her actuarial calculations as the curtain falls we are conscious that she has experienced horror and a sense of contamination'. This was the reaction, too, of G.B.S. who tried to turn himself from his mother's son into an immaculate speaking and writing machine. There is autobiographical passion and pathos in the final stage directions:

[*Mrs Warren goes out, slamming the door behind her. The strain on Vivie's face relaxes; her grave expression breaks up into one of joyous content; her breath goes out in a half sob, half laugh of intense relief. She goes buoyantly to her place at the writing table; pushes the electric lamp out of the way; pulls over a great sheaf of papers . . . Then she goes at her work with a plunge, and soon becomes absorbed in its figures.*]

'I do not think there is the least chance of the play being licensed,' Shaw wrote cheerfully to Grein. He had not foreseen that Grein would feel that *Mrs Warren's Profession* was unfit 'for women's ears' and that, since it might lead even strong men to 'insanity and suicide', he could not allow a private production. 'I am at my wits end about this unlucky play of mine,' Shaw told the actress Elizabeth Robins.

Mrs Warren's Profession had to wait until 1902 for the first of two private performances by the Stage Society and until 1925 for its first public production in Britain: 'too late,' Shaw remarked. He failed to get a copyright performance in Ireland, and after its world première in the United States in 1905, it was prosecuted in the courts. Even as late as 1955 the play was banned as 'amoral' from the Salle Luxembourg in Paris by the selection committee of the Comédie Française.

Shaw had taken immense trouble to tailor his play to the conventions of the stage. The difficulties preventing its performance thrust him deep into a vigorous campaign against theatre censorship; and it changed his orientation as a dramatist. Slum-landlordism, the marriage laws and prostitution had all proved 'unspeakable' subjects on the Victorian stage, and Shaw made the decision to write no more plays with a social purpose, and to become a writer of plays with no purpose 'except the purpose of all poets and dramatists' – that is 'plays of life, character and human destiny'. In order to get his words spoken on the stage he moved the emphasis 'from the public institution to the private imagination'; set out to make his audiences laugh rather than feel uncomfortable (though sometimes to laugh at themselves); and resolved to 'sport with human follies, not with crimes'. Having put aside *Mrs Warren's Profession*, he went back to the beginning and started again – this time with a nursery play. His diary entry for 26 November 1893 reads: 'spent the evening beginning a new play – a romantic one – for F[lorence] E[mery].'

3

ARMS AND THE MAN

> I greatly regret that my play, 'Arms and the Man', has wounded the
> susceptibilities of Bulgarian students in Berlin and Vienna. But I ask
> them to remember that it is the business of the writer of a comedy to
> wound the susceptibilities of his audience. The classical definition of his
> function is 'the chastening of morals by ridicule' . . . When the Bulgarian
> students, with my sincerely friendly assistance, have developed a sense
> of humor there will be no more trouble.
>
> *The World Wide News Service Inc.* (16 November 1924)

By the mid-1890s, despite all his reverses, Shaw had become thoroughly
well known. Scurrilous attacks, disguised as interviews, were regularly
made on him by the press. Extra-special reporters, athletic rather than
intellectual, would force their way into his room apparently for no purpose
other than to bully and insult him. Shaw would defend himself in heart-
rending tones. 'I have kept my temper for eighteen years, and have never
been uncivil to an interviewer,' he explained. Many readers felt that here
was an astonishing example of Christian forbearance. Only a few realized
that the interviews had been written by himself.

'I presume, Mr Shaw,' one imaginary reporter asked before the opening
of his new play, 'that when the eventful night comes, the most enjoyable
part of it will be your speech after —.' Stepping out before the curtain
after the first performance of *Arms and the Man*, Shaw addressed his short
speech to the solitary man who in a cheering audience had uttered a loud
'Boo!' 'My dear fellow,' he exclaimed, 'I quite agree with you, but what
are we against so many?'

In this Wildean *mot* Shaw placed his true feelings. Writing to his fellow-
playwright, Henry Arthur Jones, some eight months later, he explained:
'Like you, I write plays because I like it, and because I cannot remember
any period in my life when I could help inventing people and scenes.'
But, he went on:

'I am not a storyteller: things occur to me as scenes, with action and
dialogue – as moments, developing themselves out of their own vitality . . .
my quarrel with the conventional drama is that it is doctrinaire to the
uttermost extreme of dogmatism . . . clever people predominate in a first
night audience; and, accordingly, in 'Arms & the Man', I had the curious
experience of witnessing an apparently insane success . . . and of going

before the curtain to tremendous applause, the only person in the theatre who knew that the whole affair was a ghastly failure.'

Part of the 'intelligent misunderstanding' of Shaw's plays arose from his method of dressing himself in the strait-jacket of theatrical conventions and performing tricks of elastic unconventionality. But it came too from the discrepancy between a sophisticated intellect and emotions that still responded to the adult world from the doorway of the nursery. Of the horrors of war *Arms and the Man* conveyed as little as *Mrs Warren's Profession* did the pleasures of sexual intercourse. 'I do not yet feel grown up,' he wrote when almost fifty.

Mrs Warren's Profession had derived from Janet Achurch: *Arms and the Man* revolved round Florence Farr, who had received a sum of money via an occult society to promote a theatrical season at the Avenue Theatre in London. Her backer, whose identity was kept secret from Shaw for another dozen years (it came to him, he would claim, in a dream), was Annie Horniman. Thin and medieval in appearance (she wore a huge jewelled dragon in oxidized silver round her neck), Annie Horniman smoked cigarettes and bicycled in slacks (she had a black eye when Shaw finally met her). 'She was wonderful about the money really,' Florence Farr later told Shaw, '& just gave it me to do anything I liked with in the way of advertising myself.'

Florence asked both Yeats and Shaw to write plays for her. 'I have made a desperate attempt to begin a real romantic play for F.F. in the style of Victor Hugo,' Shaw reported to Janet Achurch. 'The first act is nearly finished; and it is quite the funniest attempt at that style of composition ever made.' But he was too dilatory for Florence. By way of encouragement she would read to him from her own novel, *The Dancing Faun* (at the end of which her Shavian cad, George Travers, is most satisfactorily shot by his titled mistress); and she invited him to Dalling Road to hear Yeats read his verse play, *The Land of Heart's Desire*, in which a wife escapes domestic drudgery, through death, into fairyland. Following these goadings, Shaw would surge onwards.

In its first version, tentatively entitled *Alps and Balkans* (Salt had suggested *Battlefields and Boudoirs*), he had given the play no geography – 'nothing but a war with a machine gun in it' – the names of the places being left blank and the characters simply called the Father, the Daughter, the Heroic Lover, the Stranger and so on. He then went to Sidney Webb and asked him to find a good war for his purpose. Webb 'spent about two minutes in a rapid survey of every war that has ever been waged and then told me that the Servo-Bulgarian was what I wanted,' Shaw remembered. 'I then read the account of the war in the *Annual Register* with a modern railway map of the Balkan peninsula before me, and filled in my blanks, making all the action take place in Servia, in the house of a Servian family.' He also got a good deal of information from Admiral Serebryekov, who had commanded the Danube flotilla for the Bulgarians, as a result of which the 'play proved impossible from beginning to end,' Shaw told Charles Charrington. 'I have had to shift the scene from Servia to Bulgaria, and to make the most absurd alterations in detail for the sake of local color,' which, Shaw added, would convince people that 'I have actually been in Bulgaria'.

All this research and rewriting meant that the play, now called *Arms and the Man* from the first line of Dryden's heroic verse translation of Virgil's *Aeneid* ('*Arma virumque cano*'), was not ready for the opening of Florence Farr's season. Instead, using Yeats's *The Land of Heart's Desire* as a *lever de rideau*, she produced *A Comedy of Sighs* by the Irish pastoral playwright, John Todhunter. Shaw, who attended the first night on 29 March, noted that 'the play at the Avenue Theatre failed rather badly'. Yeats was to describe the fiasco more voluminously. 'For two hours and a half, pit and gallery drowned the voices of the players with boos and jeers that were meant to be bitter to the author who sat visible to all in his box surrounded by his family, and to the actress struggling bravely through her weary part,' he remembered. Todhunter sat on 'listening to the howling of his enemies, while his friends slipped out one by one, till one saw everywhere their empty seats'. Archer described Florence's performance as 'panic-stricken' – and this was the most excruciating part of the evening for Shaw: 'have you ever seen so horrible a portent on the stage as this transformation of an amiable, clever sort of woman into a nightmare, a Medusa, a cold, loathly, terrifying, grey, callous, sexless devil?' he asked Elizabeth Robins.

'What madness led Todhunter to write her a part like that? – what idiocy has led me to do virtually the same thing in the play which I have written to help her in this hellish enterprise? . . . Had she been able to give full effect to herself, the audience would have torn her to pieces. I lay under harrows of red hot steel.'

The next day Shaw received a telegram summoning him to the theatre where he found Florence with *Widowers' Houses* open before her, contemplating its production in despair. Dissuading her from this he took 'my new play out on to the Embankment Gardens and there and then put the last touches to it before leaving it to be typewritten'.

Arms and the Man went into rehearsal on 11 April, three days before Todhunter's play was withdrawn. Among the audience on the first night were Archer, Henry Arthur Jones, H. W. Massingham, George Moore, Oscar Wilde and W. B. Yeats, whose little play was again used as a curtain raiser. Sidney Webb, who 'might possibly bring a cabinet minister if he has a box', was joined by fellow-Fabians Sydney Olivier and Graham Wallas. The Charringtons came, Janet being specially seated 'where her beauty will not be lost'. Edith Bland, too, Shaw estimated, 'will be worth a thousand posters in Blackheath'. 'Chuckers out' were hired, and the only group Shaw forgot to invite was his family.

Shaw himself arrived towards the end of Yeats's play. His chocolate cream soldier forced his way into Raina's bedroom some twenty minutes later, in what seemed to be the start of a stereotype military melodrama. 'The whole pit and gallery, except certain members of the Fabian Society, started to laugh at the author and then, discovering that they themselves were being laughed at, sat there not converted – their hatred was too bitter for that – but dumbfounded, while the rest of the house cheered and laughed,' Yeats later recalled. ' . . . I listened to *Arms and the Man* with admiration and hatred. It seemed to me inorganic, logical straightness and not the crooked road of life, yet I stood aghast before its energy as to-day before that of the Stone Drill by Mr Epstein or of some design by Mr Wyndham Lewis . . . Presently I had a nightmare that I was haunted by a sewing machine, that clicked and shone, but the incredible thing was that the machine smiled, smiled perpetually.'

No one forgot this opening performance. 'It was applauded,' wrote G. K. Chesterton, 'by that indescribable element in all of us which rejoices to see the genuine thing prevail against the plausible.' Yeats described this venture as 'the first contest between the old commercial school of theatrical folk and the new artistic school'. The Prince of Wales (later Edward VII) came and kept repeating: 'The man is mad, the man is mad.'

Arms and the Man presents the adult world of warfare through the eyes of a child. Shaw contrasted the child's simplicity with the farcical sophistication of parents trying to escape the consequences of their own childhood. *Arms and the Man* is a 'play' in the sense of it being a childish activity. Every stage trick in its clockwork machinery 'suggests a puppet play for human actors, or a moving toy shop,' writes Margery Morgan. ' . . . The ease with which Shaw regressed to childishness can be regarded as a sign of psychological weakness and emotional immaturity . . . [but] released within the frame of the play, it is this childishness that constitutes Shaw's genius. He used it as a means of attacking insidiously and openly every form of humbug and pretentiousness, including the unnaturalness of moral virtue that children . . . instinctively detect.'

Shaw was particularly exasperated when his deconstruction of heroism – professional soldiers who carry chocolates instead of cartridges and weep when scolded; battles waged mostly by paperwork and won through ludicrously lucky errors – was treated not in the tradition of Cervantes but as Gilbertian cynicism. Gilbert was the child who mimicked the adult world; Shaw was the child who saw through it. In a letter to Archer, Shaw explained what he felt was the difference:

'Gilbert is simply a paradoxically humorous cynic. He accepts the conventional ideals implicitly, but observes that people do not really live up to them. This he regards as a failure on their part at which he mocks bitterly. This position is precisely that of Sergius in the play . . . I do not accept the conventional ideals . . . and no longer use them even for dramatic effect. Sergius is ridiculous through the breakdown of his ideals, not odious from his falling short of them. As Gilbert sees, they dont work; but what Gilbert does not see is that there is something else that does work, and that in that something else there is a completely satisfactory asylum for the affections.'

'On my honor it was a serious play,' Shaw protested. But the 'tragedy' with which he insisted he had replaced Gilbertian 'heartlessness' was a petit tragedy – though a delightful comedy. The attempt to show pragmatism and instinct in triumphant league against idealism and rationalism was ingeniously outflanked by the public's instinctive, and the critics' reasoned, misunderstanding. Shaw changed the subtitle from 'A Romantic Comedy' to 'An Anti-Romantic Comedy', but the joyous misapprehension continued to swell, finally exploding in Oscar Straus's comic opera *The Chocolate Soldier* ('that degradation of a decent comedy into a dirty farce,' as Shaw called it).

Arms and the Man ran for fifty performances between 21 April and 7 July, and was followed by a provincial tour and a production in the United States. But Shaw had doubts over the play. In the contest between 'the old commercial school of theatrical folk and the new artistic school', G.B.S. the new artist suspected he had borrowed too much from the armoury of the old commercial school. It was not quite the masterpiece he needed.

His royalties from *Arms and the Man* at the end of 1894 came to £341 15s. 2d. (equivalent to £17,000 in 1997). That autumn, after seven years of continuous musical criticism, he dropped his column in *The World*. 'I had not before realized the severity of the strain on the attention involved by musical criticism,' he noted in his diary. It seemed as if, in entering his thirty-ninth year, he had at last achieved popularity. 'When you take a theatre of your own,' he told the manager of the Avenue Theatre, 'just bring me pen and ink, a ream of paper, a bottle of ginger beer, and a few beans, and you shall have the most brilliant play of the century to open with.' But privately he knew the quicksand on which he was advancing. 'I have taken the very serious step,' he confided to McNulty, 'of cutting off my income by privately arranging to drop the World business at the end of the season; and now, if I cannot make something out of the theatre, I am a ruined man.'

4

THE PLAYWRIGHT AND THE ACTRESS

I hereby warn mankind to beware of women with large eyes . . . and a love of miracles and moonshees. I warn them against all who like intellectual pastimes; who prefer liberty, happiness and irresponsibility to care, suffering and life . . . who reject the deep universal material of human relationship and select only the luxuries of love, friendship, and amusing conversation.

Shaw to Florence Farr (14 October 1896)

Florence Farr's performance in Todhunter's play had been shocking, and Shaw's relegation of her from the part of Raina, the romantic lead, to that of Louka, her maidservant, in *Arms and the Man* represented a fall in his estimation, almost from grace. Florence was aware of this. Walking back from the Avenue Theatre in the evenings with Yeats, they would often discuss Shaw. What feelings lived under his bright surface and, among all that rattle of words, what poetry? For all his knowledge, his vitality, his busy politics, there seemed (except for its impenetrable absence) no mystery, no beating of a religious pulse. Florence, like Yeats, had been caught up in the stream of occultism flowing over traditional Western religion. She had looked into Egyptology and Babylonish lore, hovered over astral projections, investigated alchemy, covered the walls at Dalling Road with Oriental drapery, practised the hermetic arts; and she was about to be promoted to Praemonstratrix in the ineffable Order of the Golden Dawn. The chasm separating her aspirations from her abilities, starkly illuminated by the footlights, vanished amid these mysteries.

Shaw had been pressing Florence to get herself divorced from the ever-absent Edward Emery; and eventually in 1894 she agreed. The procedure, which involved an accusation of adultery, was unpleasant but by February the following year the decree was made absolute. Shaw used the technicality of her freedom to chide Janet Achurch: 'There will be a mail in tomorrow, I suppose: and if I hear nothing then, F.F. shall be Mrs Bernard

Shaw at the earliest date thereafter permitted by statute.' But to Florence, as to May Morris, he said nothing. Two days after this divorce, it was not Shaw but Yeats who travelled to Dalling Road. He came bearing esoteric apparatus and escorted by a mediumistic chemist's assistant. Together they drew the curtains and unwrapped their miracles. It was a relief to turn from the hectic Shavian vocabulary to the less demanding presence of Yeats. Florence's consonants withered, her phonetics fell away and the athletic articulation drilled into her by Shaw sighed to a stop. Yeats provided for her a single twanging instrument. She plucked interesting discords, meditated on colours, muttered verse invocations that intensified 'ordinary twaddling,' Shaw protested, 'into a nerve destroying crooning like the maunderings of an idiot-banshee'.

It was now Yeats's turn to see Florence as a 'great success'. Her tranquillity dazzled him. She was a fairy child and would make his poetry a garden for magical thought, and the Chanted Word. 'Cats do the same thing when they are serenading one another,' advised Shaw; and even Yeats spoke of her giving 'the worst performance on the psaltery I have ever heard' – adding: 'There are times when she makes me despair of the whole thing.'

In time Florence dismissed both her Irish champions as 'half-baked'. 'And now you think to undo the work of all these years by a phrase & a shilling's work of exoteric Egyptology,' Shaw had railed at her.

'Now a great horror & weariness comes on me. I cannot help anyone except by taking help from them; and you cannot help me. You have brains and imagination – the means of deceiving yourself, without faith, honor, heart, holiness – the means of saving yourself. I have the greatest regard for you; but now to be with you is to be in hell: you make me frightfully unhappy . . . Forgive me; but you have driven me to utter desperation.'

What had gone wrong? When he called on her he found 'her windows were dark [and] I did not go in'. He began sleeping badly – and waking late. In November 1894 they ceased being lovers. Fabian and Occult forces had pulled them apart. They were still friends. Strolling pleasantly through Richmond Park in the spring of 1895, they chatted about bicycling and literature, but kept what they really cared for to themselves. She lured him with a casual reference to the quarter of a million pounds that Annie Horniman might give her for another theatrical enterprise; but her heart was not in it, and he was not seriously tempted. Their excitement in each other's company had evaporated, leaving vacancy. His sense of loss was painful. He had so little heart, he told another actress, 'that when it kindles for ten minutes once a year I hasten to cry out what I feel, lest I should die without having once done anything to save life from emptiness'.

They continued to see or correspond with each other, amiably but with longer intervals almost until 1912, when Florence travelled to Ceylon and, at the request of Sir Pannamballam Ramanathan, was appointed the first principal at his College for Girls. There she died in 1917; and thirty years later, after reading her story in the *Ceylon Daily News*, Shaw (then in his nineties) confessed himself astonished. 'I thought that Yeats and I knew her through and through, as far as there was anything to know,' he wrote. 'I now see that we did not know her at all.' To Yeats she had appeared to move 'upwards out of life' to her 'unnoticed end'. But Shaw suspected that Pannamballam Ramanathan had 'opened her mind and developed the real woman. I should have said that she was the last woman on earth to become the authoritative head of a college, or to break her way out of the little cliques in which she figured in London, and find a spiritual home in philosophic India. I was wrong. I was the wrong man for her, and I am deeply glad that she found the right one after I had passed out of her life.'

5

CANDIDAMANIA

It is only the people who have the courage and independence to let themselves go without scruple who discover what a terrifically powerful instinct chastity is.

Shaw to Barbara Low (17 September 1917)

In leaving Jenny Patterson for Florence, Shaw had renounced a love that was exclusively sexual; in turning from Florence to Janet Achurch in the mid-1890s he was replacing sex and planting his words in the woman he loved so that she could bring his plays to life. Florence had been sterile – but sterile on the stage. 'I renounce spiritual intercourse with you,' he told her. But it was sexual intercourse he was renouncing and spiritual intercourse with Janet he was taking up. 'I have become a sort of sublime monster,' he wrote to Janet early in 1896.

'. . . Do you know who will buy for twopence a body for which I no longer have any use? I have made tolerable love with it in my time; but now I have found nobler instruments – the imagination of a poet, the heart of a child, all discovered through the necessity – the not-to-be denied inmost necessity – of making my way to an innocent love for Janet.'

*

There had been a moment when, quailing before the challenge of Janet with her interfering husband, her heavy drinking, her drugs, Shaw turned to 'a destroying angel in a bonnet', the Ibsen actress Elizabeth Robins. Elizabeth was an enigma. For two years she had been married to an American actor, George Parks, who one midnight (wearing a suit of stage armour) had stepped into the Charles River in Boston, and drowned. Dressed in black, Elizabeth had sailed to England. Wonderfully impressed by Janet Achurch in *A Doll's House*, she had gone in 1891 with her chaperon to see William Archer about a translation of *Hedda Gabler*. Her performance as Hedda that April at the Vaudeville Theatre was described by Archer, reviewing it in *The World*, as 'the finest piece of modern tragedy within my recollection. Sarah Bernhardt could not have done it better.' The anti-Ibsenites had been equally re-assured. 'It was like a visit to the Morgue,' declared Clement Scott in the *Daily Telegraph*. Shaw, who saw the production two or three times, assured Elizabeth Robins that 'you may safely accept all the compliments you get about the play and the part. I never had a more tremendous sensation in a theatre.'

In the battle over Ibsen, Shaw knew where his loyalties lay. But Elizabeth was Archer's protégée and therefore a rival to Shaw's Janet. Both Archer and Shaw were attracted to Elizabeth. She was a hardworking actress, ambitious and businesslike; and, now in her late twenties, she was dramatically beautiful, with hypnotic blue eyes, chestnut hair and an erotic southern American voice. But she seemed nervous of men and fearful of male sexuality. She was to make an exception of Archer for whom she became the love of a lifetime. But Shaw's flattery-and-effrontery alarmed her. He implied that Archer was not unaware of her sex appeal; he begged her not to mind his Irish suggestiveness; he boasted that her 'lustrous eyes' would never turn his head; he even called informally at her apartment, before her production of *The Master Builder* in 1893, for the purpose of interviewing her – and she was obliged to threaten him with a revolver.

Shaw promised to play no more pranks on her. But he suspected that she and Archer were lovers, and he could not resist interfering. Both of them were used to suppressing their sexual instincts, and they sealed their relationship from him. Someone who had dramatized his own love affairs in *The Philanderer* might play havoc with their lives.

Elizabeth had glorified the brother-and-sister relationship, and Shaw dreamed of supplanting a wife with a mother. Both wanted to free one sex from the power of the other. But the only way Shaw could overcome his vulnerability to women who interested him was to envelop their bodies with his words, and then fall in love with his own verbal clothing. What attracted him to Elizabeth was that, like his mother, she was at best indifferent to him. It was difficult for an actress to make a successful career in the theatre, but she did not believe Shaw would ever succeed as a playwright and when he offered to write a leading part 'especially designed for you & all the other parts about six lines long', she heard only the voice of the seducer. Her apprehensions were confirmed when he sent her *Mrs Warren's Profession*, a play about prostitution. 'It was black ingratitude to try and let you in for this villainous play which is quite unworthy of you,' Shaw admitted. Yet, granted that she could not endure him, could they not for stage purposes use each other? 'What has frightened you?' he asked. What had frightened him? This fear was what they shared, and it prevented them from becoming what Ibsen would have called an 'episode' in each other's lives.

*

While Shaw was still involving himself with Florence and hazardously experimenting with Elizabeth Robins, the Charringtons had been sinking. A quintuple bill they presented at Terry's Theatre in 1893 including, besides plays by J. M. Barrie, Conan Doyle and Thomas Hardy, a farce by Lady Colin Campbell, had prompted some critical acclaim; and closed after a week. 'Then smash!' Charrington explained; cheaper lodgings, unsuccessful scripts, smaller parts, shifty deals.

Unlike Nora in *A Doll's House* (after whom she had christened her daughter), Janet could not slam the door on her husband – though he would ruin her if she continued to trust in him. But from the practical consequences of his own advice Shaw instinctively shrank. He was obsessively replaying the old triangular liaison. Until the autumn of 1894 he could find no way of dissolving his sexual attraction for Janet into his admiration for her talent. Then, on 2 October, following another visit to Italy with the Art Workers' Guild, he began *Candida*, his 'modern pre-Raphaelite play'. 'Titian's Virgin of the Assumption in the Accademia in Venice, and Correggio's in the dome of the cathedral in Parma,' he afterwards remembered, 'boiled down into Cockney Candida.'

It was to be their play, his and Janet's. It was to be their salvation. Candida derived from his mother who was to be replaced by Janet. 'I have been no saint myself – have hunted after one form of happiness occasionally,' he confided. 'Janet *recreates* me with an emotion which lifts me high out of that.' *Candida* had been conceived as a spiritual orgasm.

Janet would re-create herself by playing the 'clean dry, strong and straight heroine', the 'true Virgin Mother' Candida, and feel no further need for the stimulants prescribed by Charrington.

The Reverend James Mavor Morell, the cocksure Christian Socialist clergyman, is Shaw's pre-Raphaelite; his Raphaelite is Marchbanks, the shy, aristocratic, unconvincing poet. Shaw claimed to have based Marchbanks on De Quincey, though Shelley and Yeats were also to be mentioned as models. 'I certainly never thought of myself as a model,' he objected. Nevertheless, Marchbanks was the vehicle for Shavian beliefs and a silhouette of the almost twenty-year-old Sonny. The rivalry between Marchbanks and Morell over Morell's wife Candida carries echoes from several of Shaw's three-cornered affairs, in particular that of May Morris and Sparling, but was intended as an interpretation of the current drama between himself and the Charringtons. The writing and production of *Candida* was to be a spell, no less magical than the spells of Yeats and Florence Farr, through which Shaw would manifest his will. He had designed the play as *A Doll's House* in reverse, showing the household doll to be the husband. In Candida herself he had written a part at which Janet would excel. Its success, he hoped, would nerve her to separate her interests from Charrington's, emerging from domesticity as an independent actress of genius. That, at any rate, was the play he intended to write; what he actually wrote was something else. 'Candida does not change, as Shaw believed Janet must,' Margot Peters has written.

'She is at the end of the play what she was at the beginning, the mother-sister-nurse-wife of her boy husband Morell, trapped by the very altruism that Shaw was trying to root out of Janet so that she could put herself and her art first. It is Eugene Marchbanks who experiences the metamorphosis from sensuality to spirituality and artistic dedication ... he concludes that domesticity, security, and love are inferior ends compared with the sublime and lonely renunciation of the artist. Shaw thus washed his hands of Janet.'

The 'pure' (as her white name indicates) and patronizing Candida is not Janet: she was 'entirely imagined'. But she shares with Janet a sexual charm that she can use to get her own way – and from which Marchbanks disengages himself. But his escape is not a sublimation of lust into admiration; it is rejection, an optimistic re-writing of Lucinda Shaw's rejection of Sonny.

The crisis between Candida and Marchbanks comes early in the third act when Candida offers herself ('Do you want anything more?') to Marchbanks. We have been prepared for this and told how to interpret it in her conversation with Morell in the previous act – and the words and situation were as much as the Examiner of Plays would allow. The poker that Candida holds 'upright in her hand . . . looking intently at the point of it' until it 'must have hypnotised me', is converted from an obvious phallic image into an emblem of knightly chastity: 'a flaming sword that turned every way, so that I couldnt go in; for I saw that that was really the gate of Hell'. The affinity between them is that of mother and son, and the weapon that guards them from Hell is the taboo of incest. It is because the Virgin Mother outlaws sex that she is Shaw's ideal. Candida reduces all men to children by emotional castration. In providing other explanations Shaw falls into the error that he himself had defined so brilliantly in *The Quintessence of Ibsenism*. He idealizes. It is the minor characters who provide the corrective, in particular the secretary, 'a brisk little woman of about 30', Miss Proserpine Garnett, nicknamed Prossy. She, as her classical name suggests, represents amorousness unanswered. She is secretly – though it is an open secret – in love with Morell, and her only expression of love is to make herself his idolizing slave. Others, with whom she is not in love, she can see clearly.

Shaw romanticized Marchbanks's chastity. He has not blown away illusions but transferred them from people to work. *Candida* was a prophecy rather than a catalyst in Janet Achurch's life; and that prophecy was to find its proof in the negotiations over the play's production.

*

Candida is the most tightly constructed and economical of Shaw's plays. Driven on by the Charringtons' debts, he finished writing it on 7 December 1894, and before the end of the year had tried it out on two leading actor-managers. Wiping his eyes at the end of the final scene, Charles Wyndham, the most accomplished performer of light comedy parts at the Criterion Theatre, told him that, dear God, it would be a quarter of a century before the London stage was ready for such matter. Shaw also took it to George Alexander, whose St James's Theatre, as the most fashionable playhouse in London, specialized in dramas featuring peers of the realm. One of the handsomest men in England, who had recently caused a sensation with Mrs Patrick Campbell in Pinero's *The Second Mrs Tanqueray*, Alexander offered to play the eighteen-year-old aristocratic Marchbanks if Shaw, to combine an easier disguise with a larger claim for sympathy, would render the poet blind.

By reserving the part of Candida for Janet, Shaw had created an extra obstacle for the London actor-managers. But he would not be moved on this, and in February 1895 he decided instead to try the play in the United States.

There were good reasons for his decision. *Arms and the Man* had been taken the previous year to the United States by the actor-manager Richard Mansfield. Mansfield was an Englishman two years older than Shaw who had appeared on the London stage between 1877 and 1882 before emigrating to New York. He was a man who spoke plainly. He believed that life was for living, and plays were for playing; and he was seldom afraid to say so. He had slipped one evening into the Avenue Theatre to see *Arms and the Man* and decided to put it on. Shaw was summoned to see him at the Langham Hotel and an invigorating antipathy sprang up between them. Each knew better than the other about everything; but each valued the other as a property. A contract, drafted by Shaw, was signed on 9 June 1894 and, some three months later, *Arms and the Man* opened at the Herald Square Theatre in New York where, after sixteen performances, it 'produced reputation, discussion, advertisement', and put Shaw 'to the inconvenience of having a bank account'. By retaining the play in his repertory for the rest of the season and sending it on tour, Mansfield gave Shaw a new theatrical experience: 'It was not an absolute failure.'

It was to Mansfield, on 22 February 1895, that Shaw sent a tantalizing letter about *Candida*. 'Now let me ask you whether you can play a boy of eighteen – a strange creature – a poet – a bundle of nerves – a genius – and a rattling good part,' he wrote.

Shaw challenged him to sail over to London, play the poet for half a dozen matinées opposite Janet's Candida, and, having set all London buzzing, 'disappear in a flash of blue fire'. There was need for haste. Already Janet was growing obstreperous; she had made a drunken scene when he took her to the theatre, had brazenly dyed her hair a heartbreaking yellow and was smoking cigarettes. Shaw warned her that 'you will grow fatter; and your flesh instead of being braced and healthy will be slack and open to chills; and you will have heavy sensual eyelids and swimming eyes instead of a clear, open, divine brow'. There was nothing for it, until Janet was reborn in *Candida*, but to wag his finger in this way. His lectures offended her and were a terror to himself lest they ended their relationship.

It was Richard Mansfield who, barely in time, thundered to their rescue. He had been intrigued by Shaw's description of *Candida* ('I still play youths of 18. The only trouble is I look too young for the part'). In the first week of March he cabled his acceptance to Shaw.

'WILL PLAY CANDIDA WILL ENGAGE JANET WILL COME TO LONDON CONTRACT JANET NOT LESS THAN THREE SEASONS . . . ALL MUST COME NEW YORK QUICK – MANSFIELD'

Shaw had promised the Charringtons that he would get his plays performed; and now 'it is all settled and our fortunes are made'. The next ten days were hectic. Despite a swirling Fabian programme of lectures and articles on other people's plays, Shaw finished his minutely detailed plan of the stage action ('the full score of Candida and the band parts'), arranged for the prompt copies to be typed and corrected, and had everything ready for the boat on Saturday 16 March. At the station, Janet was so overcome as to take an affectionate farewell of Mansfield's brother Felix (who was travelling with her) under the impression he was her husband Charrington; and Shaw tottered back shakily to his bed like an exhausted dog.

Janet was now on her own: 'the time for pupilage is past.' Yet wherever she went Shaw's voice went with her. He seemed unable to leave his pupil alone. He prescribed distilled water, oatmeal bannocks, walnuts, honey and peaches. 'I urge you to go to church once a day at least to tranquillise your nerves . . . Read the gospel of St John and the lives of the saints: they will do everything for you that morphia only pretends to do.' She must not seek bold type; she must not purr or smoke; she must not place New York at her feet; she must not be fringy or fluffy. He recommended she part her hair in the middle – better still, send for a barber and 'have your hair shaved absolutely bald. Then get a brown wig.' She would become like the Madonna by Antonio Rossellino he had seen at Santa Croce in Florence.

Having told her what way to go, he told Mansfield to let her go her own way. 'She comes from Manchester,' he explained, 'she will grab everything you try to keep from her . . . Give her everything she dares ask . . . I hereby authorize you to announce her as the authoress of the play, if that will please her.'

Having condescended to everyone's follies, Shaw awaited the results. They came swiftly: a cablegram from Janet telling him and Charrington that *Candida* had been withdrawn. It seemed that she and Mansfield, far from being transformed by Shaw's words, had never been more themselves. In Mansfield's opinion there were two things wrong: Shaw's play and Shaw's actress. Mansfield could see too that Shaw had put a lot of himself into the play, and there, perhaps, lay the fault. Now, as Mansfield knew, the world was tired of all this morbid philosophy and womanish whatnot – a bustling, striving, pushing, stirring American audience wouldn't stand for it or sit through it, and Mansfield wholeheartedly agreed with them. 'All the world is crying out for deeds – for action!' he informed Shaw.

On the subject of Janet, too, Mansfield was obligingly frank. 'I couldn't have made love to your Candida (Miss Janet Achurch) if I had taken ether,' he began.

'I detest an aroma of stale tobacco and gin. I detest intrigue and slyness and sham ambitions. I don't like women who sit on the floor – or kneel by your side and have designs on your shirt-bosom – I don't like women who comb their tawny locks with their fingers, and claw their necks and scratch the air with their chins.'

Mansfield represented everything that Shaw was to pit his strength against over the next three years. But his success in the theatre, begun with *Arms and the Man* and soon to be established with *The Devil's Disciple*, was to be achieved by a man with whom he could not remain on speaking terms.

He did not show Mansfield's letter to Charrington who, his face swelling alarmingly, was fingering Atlantic time-tables and rehearsing the strangulation of Mansfield in New York. Shaw envied Charrington in that moment. 'Charrington is right because he *is* a fool . . . hating what he doesn't like and loving what he likes, fighting the one and grudging it its crust, backing up the other in the teeth of all justice.'

But over *Candida* Shaw conceded defeat. 'I have played my last card, and am beaten, as far as I can see, without remedy,' he told Janet. For once his equanimity seemed to falter. Mansfield produced an unusual effect on him. 'He drives me out of my senses.' Since this often prevented them from addressing each other, Shaw conducted much of his business with Mrs Mansfield, 'which is much pleasanter'. The rivalry that Shaw neutralized with this stratagem had begun to show itself in the two men's struggle over Janet. Mansfield offered to produce *Candida* with her in the leading role 'if I need not appear'. But Shaw, believing that Mansfield was looking to put on the play with a bad cast so as to establish its failure 'and prevent Janet from making a success in New York', forbade him from producing it 'on any terms whatever'. Despite his dislike of Janet, Mansfield invited her to join his company knowing how hard Shaw would be hit if she accepted. But Shaw's influence persisting, she refused and, surrounded by many exciting rumours of her plans, she sailed in the second week of June back to London.

SIX

I

LIVING WITH THE *SATURDAY*

We all swore by the *Saturday* . . . Life was not worth living without it;
it gave us the latest news from the front. And we craned our necks
nightly over the gallery rails to see Shaw our champion take his seat
among the well-groomed critics in their 'glad rags'. Shaw played up well
to us in the gallery.

Dan Rider, *Adventures with Bernard Shaw* (1929)

'The first man I wrote to was George Bernard Shaw,' wrote Frank Harris.

Harris had been editor of the Conservative *Evening News* in direct
competition with W. T. Stead's *Pall Mall Gazette*. He had quadrupled its
circulation by sending his New Journalists to the police courts, and
startling his readers with alluring headlines: 'Extraordinary Charge
Against a Clergyman'; 'Gross Outrage on a Female'. It was Harris who
had reported in scabrous detail the divorce case of Lady Colin Campbell,
receiving an indictment for obscene libel that assisted the paper's Tory
proprietor in dismissing him in 1886. From this crisis he quickly recovered, replacing John Morley as editor of the *Fortnightly Review*, a sober
literary magazine that (as its title somehow fails to suggest) appeared once
a month. The sensationalism of the *Evening News* was unknown to the
editor of the *Fortnightly*. 'Every month the review appears regularly,'
complained Whistler, 'just what one looks for, a work of high-class English
mediocrity: lamentable . . .' Yet from time to time Harris would pluck
aside the skirts of respectability by printing Verlaine's poems, or Wilde's
The Soul of Man Under Socialism, or his own short story about the
adulterous passion of a Baptist minister for one of his deacons' wives.

It was at this period that Harris first asked Shaw to write for him: 'Is
there no subject on which you would like to unbosom yourself in the
Fortnightly?' Intermittently during the early 1890s, Shaw would hand
him contributions on subjects ranging from Home Rule to 'The Religion
of the Pianoforte' and including early drafts of Fabian tracts such as
Socialism and Superior Brains. None of these could have pleased Frederick
Chapman of Chapman & Hall, the proprietor-publisher of the *Fortnightly*,
to whom 'Bernard Shaw was anathema'. Worse still were Harris's flirtations with anarchism, reflected in an article that praised two bomb-

throwers, 'the sweetest and noblest of men', and led, in the autumn of 1894, to Harris being fired. But in next to no time he was back in London and had taken over the editorship of the *Saturday Review*, a moribund magazine that, at £560, was being hawked around for the price of one pound per reader.

While editor of the sensational *Evening News* he had been torridly in love with 'Laura', the obsessive passion of his life. As editor of the dignified *Fortnightly* he lived smartly in Park Lane as the husband of a woman of 'high position', often entertaining the Duke of Cambridge. But in 1895 the new editor of the *Saturday Review* was a single man, who had turned his back on advancement through marriage and decided to become immortal through his genius as a man of letters. He wished to raise the *Saturday Review*, then known as the *Saturday Reviler*, from a finder of faults to a finder of stars. But the stars he gathered round him were irresistible fault-finders. Shaw's theatre criticism ('Happy is the nation that has no history, and happy the play that has no criticism in this column'), led to some managements withdrawing their free seats; and several of the book reviewers were so severe that publishers cancelled their advertisements, obliging Harris to fill the spaces with publicity for pneumatic tyres and South African mining companies.

Shaw had been summoned to the *Saturday Review* office in Southampton Street during the late afternoon of 4 December 1894. He was, Harris observed, 'thin as a rail, with a long, bony, bearded face. His untrimmed beard was reddish, though his hair was fairer. He was dressed carelessly in tweeds with the inevitable Jaeger collar. His entrance into the room, his abrupt movements – as jerky as the ever-changing mind – his perfect unconstraint, his devilish look, all showed a man very conscious of his ability, very direct, very sharply decisive.' They were as ill-matched as Don Quixote and Sancho Panza. And yet, Shaw decided, Harris was 'the very man for me, and I the very man for him'.

Although he had been happy to resign as *The World*'s music critic, Shaw was soon missing the bustle and involvement of weekly journalism. Harris's offer came at exactly the right time (as he was finishing *Candida*) and guaranteed him a salary of £6 a week – £1 more than Edmund Yates had given him: 'not bad pay in those days'. He would end up 'a ruined man,' he had predicted to McNulty, 'if I cannot make something out of the theatre'. It was as theatre critic rather than playwright that he was to make his basic income over the next three and a half years.

He had long wanted to have a regular theatre column. 'I wish for the sake of Ibsen that I could get a turn at dramatic criticism,' he had told Janet Achurch when still employed by *The World*. There was one qualm that delayed his acceptance of the job: the question of whether a playwright should also play dramatic critic.

'The cardinal guarantee for a critic's integrity is simply the force of the critical instinct itself. To try to prevent me from criticizing by pointing out to me the superior pecuniary advantages of puffing is like trying to keep a young Irving from going on the stage by pointing out the superior pecuniary advantages of stockbroking. If my own father were an actor manager, and his life depended on his getting favorable notices of his performance, I should orphan myself without an instant's hesitation if he acted badly ... So stubborn is the critic within me, that with every disposition to be as goodnatured and as popular an authority as the worst enemy of art could desire, I am to all intents and purposes incorruptible.'

On New Year's Day 1895, he went to the Garrick Theatre to see *Slaves of the Ring* by Sydney Grundy. Next week, readers of the *Saturday Review* were able to share the experience with him.

'It is not a work of art at all: it is a mere contrivance for filling a theatre bill ... Mr Grundy somehow managed to plunge me into the densest confusion as to who was who, a confusion which almost touched aberration when I saw a double leading lady walk on to the stage, both of her in full wedding dress ... The spectacular effect alone of so much white silk was sufficiently unhingeing. But when the two brides proceeded solemnly to marry one another with a wedding ring, I really did feel for a moment a horrible misgiving that I had at last broken through that "thin partition" which divides great wits from madness.'

2

SOME DRAMATIC OPINIONS

The whole world is ruled by theatrical illusion ... The great critics are those who penetrate and understand the illusion: the great men are those who, as dramatists planning the development of nations, or as actors carrying out the drama, are behind the scenes of the world instead of gaping and gushing in the auditorium after paying their taxes at the door.
'Toujours Shakespeare', *Saturday Review* (5 December 1896)

'I enjoy a first night,' Shaw wrote, 'as a surgeon enjoys an operation.' Sometimes the evening would open with a curtain raiser, 'to keep the gallery amused whilst waiting for the plutocracy to finish their dinners and get down to their reserved seats'. Then came the main play – a never-ending melodrama or all-conquering farce. Melodramas were equipped with 'French windows' and misdirected bottles of poison, and kept going with soliloquies (accompanied by harps, horns and violins writhing 'like a heap of trodden worms' in its pit). The action was waged immaculately off-stage, being announced to the audience by telegrams or reported by characters staring wildly through the wings. What the melodrama lacked in reality it tried to make up in verisimilitude. Real water cascaded; a couple of horses were led on for the race or polo match; and some actual guns for the battle in the fourth act. Why not, Shaw eagerly enquired, a mad bull to exercise the hero? Real babies, ostentatiously dandled, were popular; and no drawing-room dared reveal itself without an elaborate display of spirit stands, siphons and decanters, combining 'the charms of the private and the public house'. The gentleman-hero, husky with emotion, would have his knuckles imprinted with the kisses of kneeling ladies and his back resoundingly thumped by manly men. The villain, with his accomplice the comic Jew, knew he was performing well if the theatre filled with hisses whenever he presented himself before his arrest in the ballroom at the final curtain. Farces were not so different from melodramas, though the humour usually depended on the under-clothing of the ladies, such 'abject little naughtinesses furtively slipped in under cover of the tamest propriety'.

Upright and silent in the stalls sat Shaw, isolated in his boredom from the starched and sweating audience; acutely conscious of the bad smells, bad music, humbug and snobbery playing round him; his spirits sinking as the hour grew late until 'at such moments I pull out handfuls of my hair, and sit contemplating them vacantly, asking myself what I am doing in such an absurd place as the British theatre'.

The real question that Shaw was asking himself was how, without abandoning all hope, could such idiocy be explained. Money-making in the theatre was founded on the assumption that it was 'impossible to underrate the taste and intelligence of the British public'. To enter a theatre was to go back two hundred years. Theatrical art had become an exploitation of the public – what was called giving the public what pleased it. But audiences did not want to be pleased.

'They want to be excited, and upset, and made miserable, to have their flesh set creeping, to gloat and quake over scenes of misfortune, injustice, violence, and cruelty, with the discomforture and punishment of somebody to make the ending "happy". The only sort of horror they dislike is the horror that they cannot fasten on some individual whom they can hate, dread, and finally torture after revelling in his crimes.'

In a number of devastating passages Shaw's anger brings forth the misery and disgust he feels with his fellow human beings. This is not sexual disgust – he strongly attacks the secretary of the National Vigilance Association for that form of misanthropy ('Human nature and the human body are to him nasty things. Sex is a scourge. Woman is a walking temptation which should be covered up'). Shaw's horror derives from people's brutality and silliness exploited for profit by theatre managers. He used all his ingenuity to escape the Shakespearian pessimism to which these reflections naturally led. The British public could not stand being given what it wanted for long. The indiscriminate bawling and booing, hissing and hooting of the audiences ('like dogs who had been purposely run over'), the riots and uproars lasting up to half an hour were all evidence of their dissatisfaction.

The monopoly of the star system, Shaw argued, was being broken and only progress was safe. 'Let their flatterer slip, as he always does sooner or later, and they are at his throat mercilessly before he can recover himself,' he gloatingly warned. As with critics so with dramatists: 'there is nothing the public despises so much as an attempt to please it.' Obsequiousness never created beauty, it aped fashion, did not produce drama, but a fuss. 'No great play,' he declared, 'can ever be written by a man who will allow the public to dictate to him.' He assured his readers that the business of the playwright, as of the politician, was 'to strive incessantly with the public; to insist on earnest relations with it, and not merely voluptuous ones; to lead it, nerve it, withstand its constant tendency to relapse into carelessness and vulgar familiarity; in short, to attain to public esteem, authority, and needfulness to the national welfare (things undreamt of in the relations between the theatrical profession and the public today), instead of to the camp-follower's refuge of mere popularity'.

This was Shaw bringing the philosophy of his *Quintessence of Ibsenism* to the practical matters of stage business. He tried to persuade theatre managers that there was money in Ibsen and the German playwright Hermann Sudermann; he urged British dramatists to raise their courage in the face of that legendary dragon, the great British donkey of the public. He waved his pen and the philistine brute disappeared. The way was clear for masterpieces – and yet it was not clear after all. One man stood obstructing: the Lord Chamberlain in the person of his Examiner of Plays. 'He is the Tsar of the theatres, able to do things that no prime minister dare do,' Shaw explained. Early in 1895 the holder of this office, E. F. Smyth Pigott, died, and the press teemed with tributes to his 'admirable discretion', his 'kindly blue pencil'. To these plaudits, Shaw added his own citation in the *Saturday Review*:

'The late Mr Pigott is declared on all hands to have been the best reader of plays we have ever had; and yet he was a walking compendium of vulgar insular prejudice . . . He had French immorality on the brain; he had American indecency on the brain; he had the womanly woman on the brain; he had the Divorce Court on the brain; he had "not before a mixed audience" on the brain; his official career in relation to the higher drama was one long folly and panic . . . It is a frightful thing to see the greatest thinkers, poets, and authors of modern Europe – men like Ibsen, Wagner, Tolstoi, and the leaders of our own literature – delivered helpless into the vulgar hands of such a noodle as this amiable old gentleman – this despised and incapable old official – most notoriously was.'

This is quintessentially Shavian – and oddly courageous since, while attracting the charge of being 'a cowardly attack on a dead man', it risked a good deal of unpopularity from among the living. Shaw insists that the late censor, a 'stupendously incompetent' man, uttering bushels of 'immoral balderdash', was invincibly well-intentioned, that his 'personal character' was never in question – indeed that he was 'as excellent a man for all private purposes as Charles I'.

It was Pigott who had told the Royal Commission in 1892 that all the characters in Ibsen's plays were 'morally deranged' and that William Archer's praise of Ibsen had been a device to make money out of him. Pigott it was who had banned the centenary performance of *The Cenci*. Shaw's 'obituary' was a plea for the appointment of a censor prepared to take responsibility for licensing those plays on which the growth and vitality of the theatre depended. It made an excellent impression on Frank Harris – and none at all on the Lord Chamberlain. Pigott's successor as his Examiner of Plays was G. A. Redford, an ex-bank manager, who, during his sixteen years in the post, refused licences to *Mrs Warren's Profession*, *The Shewing-up of Blanco Posnet* and the original version of *Press Cuttings*.

Several battles in Shaw's long war against this 'Malvolio of St James's Palace' were fought out in the *Saturday Review*. It was clear to Shaw that if his post were abolished, the theatre would revert to being the social and political power it had been before Walpole instituted censorship, and stopped Fielding's stage exposure of parliamentary corruption. From the 'idealistic' point of view, which regarded new opinions as dangerous, almost everything written by Shaw, whose instinct was 'to attack every idea which has been full grown for ten years', strengthened the case for censorship. So he continued firing off brilliant salvoes at the enemy – though with the suspicion that he was armed with chocolates rather than real ammunition.

*

The censor became a symbolic figure in Shaw's imagination. When in 1886 a licence had been refused for *The Cenci*, the Shelley Society had taken over the Grand Theatre in Islington to give a 'private' performance for its members, headed by Robert Browning. Technically, since no money was taken at the door, no licence was needed for what was in law a meeting of a society rather than the public representation of a play. But the censor was not to be so easily cheated. When the annual licence of the Grand Theatre came to be renewed, the lessee found himself obliged to accept a new clause forbidding performances of unlicensed plays on the premises. This warning had been well understood by other managers. After that, the blockade had been run chiefly by the Independent Theatre, which was technically 'private' like the Shelley Society and which operated mainly by using various halls for its theatrical 'At Homes'.

In addition to Grein's Independent Theatre Shaw reported on such academic-revolutionary bodies as the New Century Theatre, started in 1897 by an aspiring combination of enthusiasts – Archer and Massingham, Alfred Sutro and Elizabeth Robins. These painfully evolved little organs were free both from actor-managership and censorship. Indifferent to public demand, yet wishing to create a taste for the work of those playwrights who seemed to be the most advanced of the time, these enterprises functioned like laboratories where experiments could be tried out on a particular audience. 'The real history of the drama for the last ten years,' Shaw wrote, 'is not the history of the prosperous enterprises of Mr Hare, Mr Irving, and the established West-end theatres, but of the forlorn hopes led by Mr Vernon, Mr Charrington, Mr Grein, Messrs Henley and Stevenson, Miss Achurch, Miss Robins and Miss Lea, Miss Farr, and the rest of the Impossibilists.'

Shaw argued for the infiltration of the experimental stage repertory into the repertory of the fashionable theatres. It was useless to appeal to Augustin Daly or Henry Irving, who seemed 'fit for nothing but to be stuffed and mounted under glass to adorn the staircase of the Garrick Club'; but if more imaginative actor-managers – George Alexander, for instance, or Herbert Tree at the magnificent new Her Majesty's Theatre – were to insert a series of matinées of serious plays into their popular farce-and-melodrama seasons, they might lay the foundations of a genuine classic theatre. It was in the context of this need for artistic and financial co-operation that he fashioned his own plays and judged the work of contemporary dramatists.

Shaw the dramatist continued to make use of the rickety mechanisms he ridiculed as a critic: *Widowers' Houses* had derived from *Ceinture Dorée*; for *Mrs Warren's Profession* he had borrowed the plot of Pinero's *The Second Mrs Tanqueray*; the mechanics of *Arms and the Man* were Gilbertian; *The Man of Destiny*, which he wrote during his first summer as dramatic critic, was 'an old-fashioned play, as completely pre-Ibsen as Sardou or Scribe'; while *You Never Can Tell* he described as 'a frightful example of the result of trying to write for the *théâtre de nos jours*'. What Shaw objected to were the limitations imposed by these theatrical constructions, but he reluctantly accepted some of this machinery as being unavoidable for those who wanted their plays produced commercially. He valued such work by how skilfully it permeated the commercial theatre with social and artistic truth.

This method of evaluation is most lucidly seen in his comparative criticism of Pinero and Henry Arthur Jones. It was Pinero's 'aptitude for doing what other people have done before that makes him a reactionary force in English dramatic literature,' Shaw asserted. To destroy the legend of his mastery of stagecraft Shaw devastatingly analysed the structure of *The Second Mrs Tanqueray*, concluding that it amounted to little more than 'recklessness in the substitution of dead machinery and lay figures for vital action and real characters'. The purpose of much of his criticism of Pinero was to combat the popular belief that he embodied a new spirit in the theatre. This popularity derived from his subtle powers of flattery – he was 'simply an adroit describer of people as the ordinary man sees and judges them' – and a bogus reputation for courage: 'he has had no idea beyond that of doing something daring,' commented Shaw of *The Notorious Mrs Ebbsmith*, 'and bringing down the house by running away from the consequences.' Only for *The Benefit of the Doubt* did Shaw praise Pinero's honesty of perception: 'Consciously or unconsciously, he has this time seen his world as it really is.'

Pinero was a darling of the drawing-room world, while Henry Arthur Jones merely had one foot in its door – and principally for that reason, Shaw affirmed, 'I unhesitatingly class Mr Jones as first, and eminently first, among the surviving fittest of his own generation.' He saw in Jones's plays, which were regularly produced in the West End, the best available chance of beginning the reformation of that fashionable theatre and making it a force for change. Jones, he wrote, was the only popular dramatist whose sense of real life 'has been deep enough to bring him into serious conflict with the limitations and levities of our theatre'.

Shaw's support of Jones involved much special pleading. Shaw knew that Jones's heroines were apt to die of 'nothing but the need for making the audience cry'; he recognized the tendency of his last scenes to collapse, and his characters to act as if hypnotized by public opinion. But there was a detachment in Jones – 'he describes Mayfair as an English traveller describes the pygmies' – that Shaw laboured to encourage. Yet sometimes he would feel a revulsion from all this special pleading.

'Those safe old hands Pinero, Grundy, and Jones, cautiously playing the new game according to the safe old rules, fail to retrieve the situation . . . the public are getting tired of the old-fashioned plays faster than the actors are learning to make the new ones effective . . . The managers do not seem to me yet to grasp this feature of the situation. If they did, they would only meddle with the strongest specimens of the new drama, instead of timidly going to the old firms and ordering moderate plays cut in the new style.'

This complaint was written in the same month, July 1895, that he made an abortive attempt, with *You Never Can Tell*, to fashion a moderate play for the West End, cut in its new style. After the experience of having his first five plays turned down by every commercial theatre in London, he had gone to these theatres as a dramatic critic and seen productions of awful plays. Humiliation and grievance had fuelled his criticisms; he had mocked, goaded, tiraded in the *Saturday Review*. As a dramatic critic he was revolutionary; and as a dramatic critic he had represented himself as a revolutionary dramatist. 'Some plays are written to please the author,' he wrote; 'some to please the actor-manager (these are the worst); some to please the public; and some – my own, for instance – to please nobody.'

Yet between the author of *Widowers' Houses* and *The Devil's Disciple* (written in 1897), some compromise had begun to take place. In an article published in *The Humanitarian* in May 1895, Shaw argued that, at periods when political institutions lagged too far behind cultural changes, it was natural for the imagination of dramatists to be set in action on behalf of social reform. But despite this, 'the greatest dramatists shew a preference for the non-political drama . . . for subjects in which the conflict is between man and his apparently inevitable and eternal rather than his political and temporal circumstances'. In writing this, Shaw may have had in mind his own move from 'unpleasant' to 'pleasant' plays. But Pinero also wrote pleasant plays. How then must the critic differentiate between great drama and merely professional plays? In a passage from the *Saturday Review*, Shaw gave his answer.

'Vital art work comes always from a cross between art and life: art being one sex only, and quite sterile by itself. Such a cross is always possible; for though the artist may not have the capacity to bring his art into contact with the higher life of his time, fermenting in its religion, its philosophy, its science, and its statesmanship . . . he can at least bring it into contact with the obvious life and common passions of the streets.'

As a critic Shaw had banished the bogey of public opinion and invented a new audience to whom he addressed his plays. For this mythical public – and bypassing so far as he could the requirements of the censor – he adapted the artificial conventions of nineteenth-century theatre, eventually permeating the old traditions of the theatre with curious new sounds. 'The present transition from romantic to sincerely human drama is a revolutionary one,' he announced, but then added: 'those who make half-revolutions dig their own graves.' In the *Saturday Review* between 1895 and 1898 there are many passages in which the critic seems to be warning the playwright about the possible dangers of his work: 'Let us have the new ideas in the new style, or the old tricks in the old style; but the new ideas combined with the old tricks in no style at all cannot be borne.'

Shaw's dramatic criticism lies in the classic tradition of Hazlitt and G. H. Lewes. Shaw himself believed that 'Lewes in some respects antici-pated me'. He pointed to Lewes's flexibility, fun and particularly 'his free use of vulgarity and impudence whenever they happened to be the proper tools for his job.

'He had a rare gift of integrity as a critic. When he was at his business, he seldom remembered that he was a gentleman or a scholar. In this he shewed himself a true craftsman, intent on making the measurements and analyses of his criticism as accurate, and their expression as clear and vivid, as possible, instead of allowing himself to be distracted by the vanity of playing the elegant man of letters, or writing with perfect good taste, or hinting in every line that he was above his work.'

Shaw had established a model for himself in Lewes whose 'combination of a laborious criticism with a recklessly flippant manner' reminded him of a certain Corno di Bassetto. Then, almost as an afterthought, he threw in one further trait: Lewes, he added, 'wrote plays of the kind which, as a critic, he particularly disliked'.

3

TILTING WITH HENRY IRVING

I shall never be able to begin a new play until I fall in love with somebody else.

Shaw to Janet Achurch (30 March 1895)

The Fabian social critic; the anonymous literary critic of the *Pall Mall Gazette*; the art critic of *Our Corner* and *The World*; the variously named musical critics of the *Dramatic Review*, *The Star* and *The World*: all were given a voice in the dramatic opinions of the *Saturday Review*. It was the Fabian who called for the establishment both of a National Theatre and of local theatres supported by local government, claiming for the drama 'as high a place in the collectivist program as municipal gas, water and tramways'. It was the Fabian, too, who campaigned for better wages for supporting actors and actresses, and who proposed a Royal College of the Drama 'with scholarships, and a library scantily furnished with memoirs and reminiscences, and liberally furnished with technical works, including theatrical instruction and stage mechanism'.

Shaw the art critic felt able to recommend George Alexander to dye his upholstery and curtains green (a more restful colour than crimson for entertainments lasting four hours); to review *King Arthur* as if it were an occasion for enjoying Burne-Jones's sets; or suddenly to surrender almost all the theatre page to the paintings of Watts and Ford Madox Brown.

But more persistent than any of these is the voice of Corno di Bassetto. As a dramatist Shaw was to claim that 'my method, my system, my tradition, is founded upon music'. He went back to nineteenth-century opera, which contained its counterpoint of spoken sequences, and concluded that operatic music was essentially a drama of the passions. 'Drama can do little to delight the senses: all the apparent instances to the contrary are instances of the personal fascination of the performers. The drama of pure feeling is no longer in the hands of the playwright: it has been conquered by the musician, after whose enchantments all the verbal arts seem cold and tame . . . there is, flatly, no future now for any drama without music except the drama of thought.'

As a critic Shaw was primarily a listener rather than a watcher. He was not imposed upon by Beerbohm Tree's profusion of stage pageantry, preferring the careful readings of William Poel's Elizabethan Stage Society, assisted by the authentic pipe and tabor of Arnold Dolmetsch, which could do for sixteenth-century blank verse, he believed, what conductors such as Richter and Mottl had successfully done for Beethoven and Wagner. It was to the orchestration of words, 'a rhetorical notation based on musical pitch and dynamics', that he was particularly attentive.

Shaw's dramatic criticism is itself dramatic writing, supplying cries from the audience and giving contrasting transcriptions of the comedian's technique – for example, between Coquelin and John Hare in Sydney Grundy's *Mamma*, where the hero discovers that his elaborate labours to murder his mother-in-law have been in vain.

'Coquelin clowned it, even to the length of bounding into the air and throwing forward his arms and legs as if to frighten off some dangerous animal. But he did not produce the electric effect of Mr Hare's white, tense face and appalled stare, conveying somehow a mad speed of emotion and a frightful suspense of action never to be forgotten by any playgoer with the true dramatic memory.'

But Shaw's imagination was most vividly awakened on the stage by women. He mocked himself for this susceptibility. 'Woman's greatest art is to lie low, and let the imagination of the male endow her with depths,' he warned. He had transferred into the theatre his struggle to be master of himself in the company of women. For Shaw the greatest actress was Eleanora Duse.

Duse had no obvious sex-appeal. She was a plain little woman, with genius: 'a most laborious artist hard at work, and not a pretty woman making an exhibition of herself', was how Shaw described her. He refers to her 'exquisite intelligence', and represents her as the finest exponent of the new drama, where emotion existed 'to make thought live and move us'. He uses her acting against which to measure the performances of other actresses – most famously in the beautiful passages comparing her playing of Sudermann's *Magda* with Sarah Bernhardt's. The two crucial words Shaw uses to explain Duse's 'vigilant sense of beauty of thought, feeling and action' were 'integrity' and 'integration'. She did not trade in flattery, solicit applause, manufacture a sham appeal for journalists. Most good actresses created themselves, Shaw believed, but were incapable of superimposing another character on top of that creation. 'Duse's greatest work is Duse,' he wrote, 'but that does not prevent Césarine, Santuzza, and Camille from being three totally different women, none of them Duses, though Duse is all of them.' And in *Magda*, her face shadowed and lined ('they are the credentials of her humanity'), it seemed to him that she spoke and acted for every woman 'as they are hardly ever able to speak and act for themselves'.

In contrast to Duse stood Mrs Patrick Campbell, a magnificent animal

of a woman, perilously bewitching, whose talent depended upon her
'irresistible physical gifts'. It was away from the excitement of Mrs Pat
and towards the non-sexual appeal of Duse that Shaw was trying to move
Janet Achurch 'whose playing of Alexandra, in Voss's play,' he wrote,
'came nearer to Duse's work in subtlety, continuity and variety of detail,
and in beauty of execution, than anything I have seen on the English
stage.

'But Duse has been helped to her supremacy by the fortunate sternness
of Nature in giving her nothing but her genius . . . Miss Terry or Miss
Achurch, if they had no more skill than can be acquired by any person
of ordinary capacity in the course of a few years' experience, would always
find a certain degree of favor as pretty leading ladies.'

This was not the first time that Shaw had slipped Ellen Terry's name
in next to Janet's. News of Mansfield's withdrawal of *Candida* reached
him in April 1895. The following month, while Janet still lingered in
America, he began to write a new play for Ellen Terry.

*

He thought her unique. Her voice, slightly veiled, seemed to enfold herself
and those to whom she spoke in a glow of happiness. Shaw described her
as 'heartwise', meaning perhaps a little cautious since, nearing fifty, she
knew where her tender heart might still lead her. He admired her for her
charm and beauty, but most of all for her refusal to trade on them with
the public. Her acting 'reminds me of my imaginary violin-playing,' he
wrote; 'she seems utterly innocent of it, and yet there it is, all happening
infallibly and delightfully.'

Ellen Terry was over nine years older than Shaw and had been brought
up 'healthy, happy and wise – theatre-wise at any rate'. At the age of
sixteen she had abruptly left the theatre to marry the middle-aged painter
G. F. Watts. The marriage had failed and she returned to the stage but
absconded again two years later to live with the man she loved, the
architect Edward William Godwin, by whom she had two children,
Gordon and Edy Craig. The need for money had taken her back into the
theatre after six years; and in 1877, largely to give her children legal
status, she married Charles Wardell, 'a manly bulldog sort of man', who
had walked in from soldiering on to the boards. Making him her leading
man, she had scored a huge success with *New Men and Old Acres* at the
Court Theatre in 1878. Shaw, who was in the stalls, dismissed the play
as 'piffling'. But Ellen Terry had enthralled him: 'I was completely conquered.'

The public too was conquered and granted her a place, as its popular darling, set apart from Victorian standards of morality. For her emotional life had become increasingly unconventional. Before the end of 1878 she had joined Henry Irving at the Lyceum; then her marriage to Wardell began to deteriorate and in 1881 they separated. 'I should have died had I lived one more month with him,' she later told Shaw.

With Irving, Ellen Terry had tried to unite 'the great happiness of occupation' with the great excitement of romance – 'I doted on his looks,' she said. She helped to manage the Lyceum cast as if they were a family of children, acting as Irving's hostess at public banquets, touring with him, and leaving the theatre with him at night. But though he bought a house and made it ready, they never lived together: and eventually the house was sold. 'We were terribly in love for awhile,' she said. 'Then, later on, when it didn't matter so much to me, he wanted us to go on, and so I did, because I was very very fond of him and he said he needed me.'

In one of his early notices for the *Saturday Review*, Shaw wrote indignantly of Ellen Terry as 'a born actress of real women's parts condemned to figure as a mere artist's model in costume plays which, from the woman's point of view, are foolish flatteries written by gentlemen for gentlemen'. She 'OUGHT to have played in the Lady from the Sea,' he claimed, though at the same time acknowledging that she 'was never called an advanced woman' – perhaps forgetting that he had himself described her in the *Saturday Review* as 'the only real New Woman'. In their *Correspondence*, while parading his feminist credentials ('no male writer born in the nineteenth century outside Norway and Sweden did more to knock Woman off her pedestal and plant her on the solid earth than I'), he called her 'goddesslike' and raised her onto a stage pedestal, explaining: 'I was steeped in the tendency against which I was reacting.'

In Shaw's mind such contradictions reflected two Ellen Terrys, one inside the other. *His* Ellen of the 'ultra-modern talent' was waiting to be released from Henry Irving's leading actress. For almost twenty years she had lain locked in the ancient dungeons of the Lyceum Theatre, guarded by an ogre called 'His Immensity'. Up to this castle, in the year 1895, Shaw pranced in his Ibsenite armour, and flung over the battlements a strange challenge: *The Man of Destiny*.

*

They had sent each other a few letters haphazardly, but it was not until near the end of 1895, when he revealed his 'beautiful little one act play for Napoleon and a strange lady', that their flirtatious correspondence really opened. She demanded to be given the play ('Lord, how attractively tingling it sounds'), and on 28 November he despatched it to her.

'I really do love Ellen,' he was to write. He loved her for helping to move his romantic feelings from a bruising world on to the stage, from the body to the page. She gave him love without physical life and therefore without threat of death. They *acted* love. She drew his imagination out into 'a thousand wild stories and extravagances and adorations' while he sat solitary at his desk 'blarneying audacities'. They protected each other and were safe – but: 'Only the second rate are safe.'

In *The Man of Destiny* Shaw had written of 'one universal passion: fear'. It was this fear that confined them to an island of enchantment where there was no pain or regret and no growing old. They knew about such things and, when the atmosphere of charm lifted a little, could spy them far off; then go back to their play-acting together.

'Let those who may complain that it was all on paper,' Shaw later cautioned, 'remember that only on paper has humanity yet achieved glory, beauty, truth, knowledge, virtue, and abiding love.' Like soldiers, these strong and rather beautiful words guarded his frightened soul, concealing the truth that we may not put more courage, virtue, love into our words than we practise in our life. It was for this reason that he could not write for Ellen 'one of my great plays', but offered her instead this trifle, *The Man of Destiny*, 'a perfectly idiotic play' that itself revolved around a piece of paper, a supposed love letter.

The Man of Destiny was a token, plucked from his involvement with Janet Achurch and handed over to Ellen Terry as a symbol of his new engagement. 'If I make money out of my new play I will produce *Candida* at my own expense,' he told her, 'and you & Janet shall play it on alternate nights.' When turning down *Candida*, Richard Mansfield had taken the trouble to instruct Shaw that the stage was for romance. 'You'll have to write a play that a *man* can play and about a woman that heroes fought for and a bit of ribbon that a knight tied to his lance.' *The Man of Destiny*, which Shaw began less than a month after receiving Mansfield's letter, is this bit of ribbon – 'a harlequinade,' he told Janet Achurch, 'in which Napoleon and a strange lady play harlequin & columbine'.

The contest between Napoleon and the Strange Lady – a tactical duel between the man of action and a woman of words – was to be parodied by a duel of actor-manager versus playwright. 'Just read your play. Delicious,' Ellen telegraphed. She loved Shaw's shrewdly inserted description of herself as the Strange Lady:

'. . . extraordinarily graceful, with a delicately intelligent, apprehensive, questioning face: perception in the brow, sensitiveness in the nostrils, character in the chin: all keen, refined, and original . . . very feminine, but by no means weak: the lithe tender figure is hung on a strong frame . . .

She enters with the self-possession of a woman accustomed to the privileges of rank and beauty.'

The Strange Lady had Ellen's appearance; but did she have her character? In the play she succeeds in persuading the twenty-seven-year-old general to let her burn unread a letter that might compromise Josephine and the Director Barras. Ellen Terry's task, to persuade Irving to read and produce *The Man of Destiny* at the Lyceum with the two of them in its star roles, was hardly less daunting.

She began well. Irving read it and, despite the difficulty of fitting a one-act play into the Lyceum bill, positively did not turn it down. 'H.I. quite loves it,' Ellen translated, 'and will do it finely.' But Shaw was suspicious. A production at the Lyceum 'would of course be quite the best thing that could happen to it'. But did he dare hope for this? 'As long as I remain a dramatic critic,' he asked Ellen to tell Irving, 'I can neither sell plays nor take advances. I must depend altogether on royalties and percentages on actual performances. Otherwise, you see, I should simply be bribed right and left.' This followed his familiar tactic of moving to high moral ground from which to cross swords. He was fighting two battles: first to get his 'opera bouffe' produced; and secondly to win Ellen's allegiance from Irving. Behind these battles lay the warfare he was conducting against the late Victorian theatre.

*

Shaw had first seen Irving on stage at the Theatre Royal, Dublin, in *The Two Roses*, and 'at once picked him out as the actor for me'. Irving seemed 'born to play ultra-modern parts' – that is to bring to life 'the Shavian drama incipient in me'. Then he saw Ellen Terry in the first glory of her talent and beauty – and 'there I had my leading couple'.

Beside Sonny's hero, the splendid Barry Sullivan, Irving seemed a meagre presence with spindly legs, a shambling dance for a walk and 'a voice made resonant in his nose which became a whinny when he tried to rant'. Yet he had triumphed over these limitations to become the unchallengeable leader of the British stage.

Ever since arriving in London, Shaw had been studying Irving's performances. Between April and July 1879, he had seen him as Hamlet, as Claude Melnotte in *Lady of Lyons*, as Cardinal Richelieu and Charles I. 'Richelieu had been incessantly excruciating: Hamlet had only moments of violent ineptitude separated by lengths of dullness,' Shaw reported.

'. . . Before Claude Melnotte had moved his wrist and chin twice, I saw that he had mastered the rhetorical style at last. His virtuosity of execution soon became extraordinary. His Charles I, for instance, became a miracle of the most elaborate class of this sort of acting. It was a hard-earned and well-deserved triumph; and by it his destiny was accomplished.'

A man of two destinies, Irving had harnessed his new style of acting to no new dramatist of talent. He had returned to the much older rhetorical art that, while not itself false, was given over to acting versions that were falsifications of old plays, particularly spurious Shakespeare. Had he persisted in producing studies of modern life and character, 'we should have had the ablest manager of the day driven by life-or-death necessity to extract from contemporary literature the proper food for the modern side of his talent, and thus to create a new drama instead of galvanizing an old one and cutting himself off from all contact with the dramatic vitality of his time'.

By the 1890s the 'great possibilities' of Ellen Terry, that Shaw accused Irving of sacrificing, seemed little more than a gallant Shavian hypothesis. The symbolic choice with which Shaw apparently presented Irving – either Sardou's Napoleon, 'the jealous husband of a thousand fashionable dramas', or his own 'baby comediatta' – was never a real one. Shaw claimed to bear Irving 'an ancient grudge which I never quite forgave him . . . So I was never really fair to him . . . for, scrupulously judicial as my criticisms were . . . you can smell a certain grudge in them.' His real grudge lay against Irving's power based partly on something that Shaw himself lacked: money. Money was freedom of action and the power to limit other people's freedom. Money was a substitute for generosity, even for affection. Money was false romance.

'It was part of H.I.'s mixture of policy with sardonic humor to buy everybody. He liked to see them selling themselves, and bought them partly to gratify that taste. He knew he was being robbed; but would not sack the robbers because it put them in his power and at his command. He tried to buy me, and believed I had come to sell myself. But he did not always buy the right people.'

*

What Shaw interpreted as Irving's attempt to 'buy me in the market like a rabbit', took place between the summer of 1896 and late spring the following year. For over seven months *The Man of Destiny* had lain at the Lyceum: and nothing had happened. Yet Ellen Terry refused to let up and in the first week of July 1896 Irving wilted, indicating that he would 'agree to produce The Man of Destiny next year, or forfeit rights, if that must be an imperative condition,' Ellen reported to Shaw. 'He wants the play very much (and so do I want him to have it), and he would like to buy it.'

Shaw communicated the following week with Irving, regretting that his play was 'so trivial an affair; but when I wrote it I had no idea it would be so fortunate'. Even now he felt it could be little more than 'a fancy of Miss T's', in which case 'a performance or two on some special occasion' would meet the case. 'I should of course be delighted to license any such without any question of terms.'

Irving countered this with his standard payment of £50 (equivalent to £2,700 in 1997) for a year's exclusive option – a proposal Shaw politely described as 'reasonable' but which, he repeated, 'raises a lot of difficulties for me . . . it is impossible for a critic to take money except for actual performances without placing both himself and the manager in a false position.' He therefore suggested that a few performances be given in 1897 without any guarantee as to fees, adding as an apparent 'concession' that 'If you produce a play by Ibsen . . . then I will not only consent to a postponement of "The Man of Destiny" but will hand over the rights for all the world to you absolutely to do as you like with until your retirement without fee or condition of any kind.'

With Ellen Terry looking on laughing, there was nothing much Irving could do but (with the deletion of Ibsen) appear to accept the Shavian counter-proposal. Shaw had won a paper victory.

Irving could not have taken kindly to being lectured *de haut en bas* on financial ethics. Yet he could not afford to look mean, so he grandly did nothing for a further two months. Then, with Shaw in the audience, he announced from the stage that the Lyceum would be producing Sardou's Napoleon show, *Madame Sans-Gêne*, in the spring of 1897. This, the actor's riposte to the writer, was a wonderful provocation to Shaw, who sent an over-polite enquiry as to whether he was 'for the first time' free to submit *The Man of Destiny* elsewhere. Irving's response was to invite him to the Lyceum.

So, at half-past twelve on 26 September 1896, the two men met in Irving's office. There was no one with a more imposing presence than Irving; no one bolder with words than Shaw. Both had been provoked. That morning the *Saturday Review* published Shaw's ferocious analysis of Irving's *Cymbeline*. 'In the true republic of art Sir Henry Irving would ere this have expiated his acting versions on the scaffold,' Shaw had written.

'He does not merely cut plays; he disembowels them ... This curious want of connoisseurship in literature would disable Sir Henry Irving seriously if he were an interpretative actor. But it is, happily, the fault of a great quality – the creative quality ... The truth is that he has never in his life conceived or interpreted the characters of any author except himself.'

Like royalty, Irving rose above Shaw's journalism, knew nothing about it, extinguished it. Though Shaw was able to hold to his principle of not accepting money, Irving was magnanimous here too. He tolerated Shaw's eccentricities. Fifty pounds was nothing to him. Of course he would stage *The Man of Destiny* – notwithstanding Sardou's play – sometime. The man whom Shaw had that day accused in public of having no literary judgement was pleased to think highly of *The Man of Destiny*. So the interview, which Shaw was never to describe, ended with what seemed an uneasy truce; and a stage victory for Irving.

*

The two men had met, but the man and the woman, even after a year of letter writing, had not. Ellen came to the door where Shaw and Irving were talking, heard their voices, and skedaddled. 'I think I'd rather never meet you -- in the flesh,' she had written to him, and he had replied: 'Very well, you shant meet me in the flesh if you'd rather not. There is something deeply touching in that.' It was lack of confidence that kept them apart. She felt old. Her body ached, sometimes even disgusted her. She could regain her attractiveness only through an illusion. 'They love me, you know!' she wrote. 'Not for what I am, but for what they imagine I am ... I never *feel* like myself when I am acting, but some one else, so nice, and so young and so happy, and always in-the-air, light, and bodyless.' She felt he understood. And he confirmed this understanding: 'Our brains evidently work in the same way.' For he too felt better bodyless. In body he was 'a disagreeably cruel looking middle aged Irishman with a red beard' who, in the *Saturday Review*, turned into a magic Shaw. So they sent out their imaginary selves to meet each other, she so schoolgirlish, he so cocksure. He entertained her, made her 'fly out laughing', and sometimes strengthened her stage confidence. 'You have become a habit with me,' she acknowledged. She gave him 'that lost feeling of unfulfil-ment'. He thought he had found someone like himself, vulnerable yet determined to be self-sufficient: 'you are a fully self-possessed woman and therefore not really the slave of love.' Each enabled the other to keep these illusions, and each was aware of this conspiracy. 'I, too, fear to break the spell,' he wrote, 'remorses, presentiments, all sorts of tendernesses wring my heart at the thought of materialising this beautiful friendship of ours by a meeting.' It was the same for her: 'I love you more every minute,' she owned. 'I cant help it, and I guessed it would be like that! And so we wont meet.'

What he called 'silly longings . . . waves of tenderness' almost broke the spell. He slipped the words 'I love you' into one of his letters, and she admitted not being able to 'cure' herself of him. Sometimes, in bed at night, she felt the need 'to touch you, to put my hand on your arm'. Then he too would grow impatient at the row of footlights separating them and want to hold her in his arms: 'Don't let us break the spell, *do* let us break the spell – don't, do, don't, do, don't, do, don't – ' And the spell did not break.

In place of their bodies they put their work. 'I *must* attach myself to you somehow,' he had written: 'Let me therefore do it as a matter of business.' And she agreed: 'I'm not going to write any more 'cept on business.' His business was to make her 'the greatest actress in the world'.

Much of his correspondence is an attempt to undermine Ellen's faith in Irving. 'Has he ever loved you for the millionth fraction of a moment?' he wondered. Such questions worried Ellen. She had always been in awe of Irving – his beauty, his distinction – but felt frustrated in the patriarchy of the Lyceum. Irving was so crafty. 'I wish he were more ingenuous and more direct,' she confided in her diary. ' . . . I think it is not quite right in him that he does not care for anybody much.' But to Shaw she wrote: 'I wish you were friends – that *you knew each other* . . . I think everything of him (is that "love"?). He can do everything – except be fond of *people* . . . but that's his great misfortune . . . Love him & be sorry for him.'

*

Irving's magisterial 'Governor' at the Lyceum was an equivalent self-production to Shaw's phenomenal G.B.S. of the *Saturday Review*. 'I really care deeply for nothing but *fine work*,' Shaw had insisted, and the same was true of Irving. Since their work stood opposed they appeared implacable enemies. It is hard not to feel sympathy for Irving. 'The artist sacrifices everything to his art, beginning with himself,' Shaw had written of Irving. 'But his art *is* himself; and when the art is the art of acting, the self is both body and soul.' It was Irving's body and soul that Shaw held up to ridicule in the *Saturday Review*. 'Mr Irving must remember that we now applaud him, not critically, but affectionately,' he reminded him.

' . . . We indulge him, every evening at the Lyceum, with a broadsword combat the solemn absurdity of which quite baffles my powers of description. If we treat his orations as lectures, do we not also treat Mr Gladstone's tree-felling exploits as acts of statesmanship? No one can say that we are not indulgent to our favorites.'

What could have exasperated Irving more than the Shavian endorsement of his knighthood conferred on him, *Saturday Review* readers understood, 'by his own peremptory demand, which no mere gentleman would have dared to make lest he should have offended the court and made himself ridiculous'. It was a battle of author versus actor, dramatist against theatrical manager. Who should rule the theatre?

'The history of the Lyceum, with its twenty years' steady cultivation of the actor as a personal force, and its utter neglect of the drama, is the history of the English stage during that period. Those twenty years have raised the social status of the theatrical profession, and culminated in the official recognition of our chief actor as the peer of the President of the Royal Academy, and the figure-heads of the other arts. And now I, being a dramatist and not an actor, want to know when the drama is to have its turn. I do not suggest that G.B.S. should condescend to become K.C.B.; but I do confidently affirm that if the actors think they can do without the drama, they are most prodigiously mistaken.'

In the *Saturday Review* Shaw dramatizes the ghastly struggle between Irving and Shakespeare, urging his readers to bear in mind the venerable actor's deep sincerity in preferring his own treasons 'to the unmutilated masterpieces of the genius' on whom he had 'lavished lip-honor'. For these treasons Shaw recommended a small penalty: 'my regard for Sir Henry Irving cannot blind me to the fact that it would have been better for us twenty-five years ago to have tied him up in a sack with every existing copy of the works of Shakespeare, and dropped him into the crater of the nearest volcano.' By such tricks did Shaw hope to arrange for Irving's entrances on stage to be greeted with bursts of laughter – a fitting penalty for the actor who (in one sense or another) had played the dramatist off the stage, and become 'the despair of all authors and true Shakespeareans'.

Shaw is here classing himself among the true Shakespeareans. He had kept up to date with new textual criticism of Shakespeare, and his attack on the Lyceum's mutilated versions complemented the philological and photographic facsimile scholarship of F. J. Furnival (whom he had met at the New Shakespere Society), and the austere Elizabethan production methods of William Poel (which he had studied as a dramatic critic). As Sonny, he had lived in Shakespeare's world more vividly than his own, and to the extent that something of Sonny persisted in Shaw, to that extent there lived on in him a legacy of love for Shakespeare. But when Sonny had turned to Dickens, he had taken his first step into the theatricality of the stage where G.B.S. now enshrined Ellen Terry. His emotional instincts tended to despair; but his mind needed optimism as the oxygen with which to go on breathing. The Shavian theatre became a factory for the manufacture of this life-supporting tonic.

At their best Shaw's tirades against 'the poor foolish old Swan' were part of theatre politics, and an attempt to cleanse the Victorian theatre of its snobbish bardolatry. But at their worst they dissolve into a stream of puerilities as irrelevant to Shakespeare's work as anything performed at the Lyceum by Henry Irving; and as self-advertising: 'With the single exception of Homer, there is no eminent writer, not even Sir Walter Scott, whom I can despise so entirely as I despise Shakespeare when I measure my mind against his.' Irving had reduced Shakespeare to a pantomime pet; Shaw fashioned him into a journalistic Aunt Sally whose politics 'would hardly impress the Thames Conservancy Board'. Whenever this rain of abuse against Shakespeare's 'economics' abates, Shaw's scrupulous knowledge of the poetry gleams through. 'It is as though he resented his own susceptibility,' Hilary Spurling was to observe, as though he had to punish him before he could 'admit how deeply he has been moved – overpowered is his own word – by the beauties of the play in question'.

Shaw's attitude to Shakespeare and Irving reflect his attitudes to sex and power. As there are two Shakespeares in Shaw's world, so there were two Irvings: the dictatorial actor-manager and the man with humours parallel to Shaw's own.

'All attempts to sustain our conduct at a higher level than is natural to us produce violent reactions . . . I remember years ago going into the Lyceum Theatre under the impression that I was about to witness a performance of Richard III. After one act of that tragedy, however, Mr Irving relapsed into an impersonation of Alfred Jingle. He concealed piles of sandwiches in his hat; so that when he afterwards raised it to introduce himself as "Alfred Jingle, Esq., of No Hall, Nowhere," a rain of ham and bread descended on him . . . He was simply taking his revenge on Shakespear and himself for months of sustained dignity . . . I am the last person in the world to object; for I, too, have something of that aboriginal need for an occasional carnival in me.'

Through absurdity we become human. It was this humanity that Shaw warmed to whenever he could change their positions and make Irving the clown or outsider. 'Does H.I. really say that you are in love with me?' he asked Ellen. 'For that be all his sins forgiven him! . . . I am also touched by his refusing to believe that we have never met.'

*

Shaw's article on Irving's *Richard III* had appeared in December 1896, and like a time-bomb exploded four months later under *The Man of Destiny.* The play had seemed fated to bring Shaw and Ellen Terry together. But in April 1897 the Lyceum decided after all not to stage his play.

It was almost a relief. 'I hate failure,' Shaw had once confided to Ellen. So did Irving. It seemed important to each man that he should be judged by Ellen to have acted the better. She was their referee, and in her reaction was success to be sought. For many Saturdays Shaw had been prodding out his dramatic opinions and trying to goad his opponent into committing some moral foul. For eighteen months they had circled each other while Ellen, believing it actually was a dance and not a fight, looked on.

Irving's sudden action took Ellen by surprise. At first he gave Shaw no reason, allowing the great paradoxer to make a conventional deduction. 'I am in ecstasies. I have been spoiling for a row,' Shaw told Ellen. But Ellen felt irritated. Why were these men quarrelling? They were like schoolboys. 'My dear, this vexes me very much,' she reproved Shaw. 'My friends to fight! And I love both of them, and want each to win.

'Henry has been much vexed lately (I only learned this last evening) by what he calls "your attacks" upon him in the Saturday Review, the Olivia article especially annoying him . . . I said I believed he had another reason . . . I believe he was ashamed and I felt strangely powerfully sorry for him . . . he and I are going for a long drive this afternoon, and he shall tell me all then.'

Shaw did not wait to be told more. 'Of course I knew all about it,' he answered:

'a good surgeon knows when his knife touches a nerve; a good critic knows the same with his pen. There was a terrible thing in that "Olivia" notice . . . if he is clever enough to tell you on that afternoon drive – as I should in his place – that he is giving up the play because he is jealous of me about you, take his part and console him: it is when a man is too much hurt to do the perfectly magnanimous thing that he most needs standing by.'

Shaw then proceeded to what he assumed must be a quick magnanimous victory. He informed Irving's manager that if the Lyceum broke its pledge on no other grounds than that his *Saturday Review* criticism had been impolite, then the only conclusion to be made was that Irving had used *The Man of Destiny* to purchase good notices. 'I am not likely to put myself in the wrong,' he assured Ellen, 'with you standing between us.'

By the time she read this Ellen realized it was to be a more complicated business. On their drive that Sunday, Irving indicated that Shaw's article on *Richard III* was an accusation of drunkenness on stage. With someone who used his journalistic position for such a libel no gentleman's agreement was binding.

Shaw's criticism in the *Saturday Review* contains too many oblique references to drunkenness to be accidental.

'He [Irving] was not, as it seemed to me, answering his helm satisfactorily; and he was occasionally a little out of temper with his own nervous condition. He made some odd slips in the text . . . Once he inadvertently electrified the house by very unexpectedly asking Miss Milton to get further up the stage in the blank verse and penetrating tones of Richard. Finally, the worry of playing against the vein tired him. In the tent and battle scenes his exhaustion was too genuine to be quite acceptable as part of the play. The fight was, perhaps, a relief to his feelings . . . If Kean were to return to life and do the combat for us, we should very likely find it as absurd as his habit of lying down on a sofa when he was too tired or too drunk to keep his feet during the final scenes.'

On 10 April Sardou's Napoleon play had opened at the Lyceum, where the box-office manager, making a half-hearted attempt to refuse admission to Shaw, was brushed aside. Shaw's notice, treating *Madame Sans Gêne* almost as a rehearsal for *The Man of Destiny*, had come out on the same day as he received the Lyceum's rejection. It had been nicely timed. *The Era* suggested that previous reports of the Lyceum having accepted the play were false; the *Glasgow Herald* announced that Irving, having found Shaw's Napoleon unsuited to him, 'has thought it best to return the manuscript to the author with, it is understood, a handsome compliment and a present'. Suddenly Shaw found himself in a flurried situation where his own moral supremacy seemed unclear. It was, he told a friendly journalist, 'enough to make a saint swear'.

'For the first time in all my long long life I am most frightfully dispirited,' Ellen wrote to him. 'Oh God, how frightful it is . . . Dont quarrel with H[enry]. That would add to my unhappiness.' 'This is at heart a tragic business,' Shaw admitted. ' . . . Dont be anxious: I'll behave nicely and nothing particular will happen.' By behaving nicely Shaw meant that instead of going to the press he would try to settle matters privately with Irving. On 29 April he wrote to him in brisk and embattled fashion. There had been no imputation of drunkenness, he stated: 'I never dreamt of such a thing.' Irving's reply was unaccommodating. 'I had not the privilege of reading your criticism – as you call it – of Richard. I never read a criticism of yours in my life. I have read lots of your droll, amusing, irrelevant and sometimes impertinent pages, but criticism containing judgement and sympathy I have never seen by your pen.'

With journalists clamouring for some riposte, it was becoming increasingly difficult for Shaw to remain silent. But for Ellen's sake he decided to make one more appeal to Irving. Either the Lyceum must announce the production of *The Man of Destiny* later that year; or they must concoct together an explanation, highly creditable to them both, for the abandonment of the play. For this second course Shaw had ready a scenario involving Mrs Patrick Campbell and Johnston Forbes-Robertson as an alternative cast. 'If you can think of anything better than this, let me know,' he offered. But for Irving anything was better – even nothing was better. To accept such a plan would reduce him to a Shavian puppet. So he simply arranged for his manager to send back the manuscript of Shaw's play with a brief note of rejection, followed by a more indignant expostulation drafted by his secretary.

Ellen had begged Shaw not to quarrel with Irving. Quarrel he would not; but a 'mild tussle,' he advised, would clear the blood. To Ellen it appeared that Irving was behaving much the worse. She had not seen his first performance in *Richard III*, and could find nothing wrong with Shaw's notice of it in the *Saturday Review*. His rudeness to her friend and lack of consideration for herself made her feel 'tired and sad and hopeless'. After all those years together, she still could not penetrate the elegant-grotesque veneer of his personality. Sometimes she found herself hating him – and immediately hated herself for doing so. 'H and I are out! A little bit,' she confided to Shaw. For the first time she began to criticize one man to the other. 'I've spoiled him! I was born meek. (Ugh) . . . I do assure you it is *I* all along who wished so hard for the play. He never wishes for anything much outside his own individual effort. I admire him for it, and I hate him for it, that he appreciates NOTHING and NOBODY . . . He wants a good slapping, but *you* must not do that, and *I* wont.'

The men had had their tussle and Shaw, by not going to the newspapers, would win her tribute. But as she turned to him, so he turned to his public.

The Lyceum door had been slammed in his face for all to see. Ellen, after all, did not seem to be his Strange Lady; Irving, when not acting (like Napoleon when not soldiering), was nobody – and in respect of Shaw's plays would remain nobody. 'Forgive me; but your Henry is not a hero off the stage,' he wrote to Ellen. He was almost forty-two and he had written eight plays. *The Man of Destiny* had been one more battle lost. He needed two things as his spoils of defeat: to revenge himself on Irving through Ellen; and to rewrite the whole history of the event through the press.

He felt safe in attacking Irving because Ellen had already begun to criticize him herself. '*You* must not take his part now: I declare him unworthy of my Ellen,' he wrote to her.

'Your career has been sacrificed to the egotism of a fool: he has warmed his wretched hands callously at the embers of nearly twenty of your priceless years; and now they will flame up, scorch his eyes, burn off his rumbathed hair, and finally consume him ... He tries to hide himself from himself with a rampart of lies; and he got behind it to hide himself from me. That was why he became an actor – to escape from himself.'

This was sent to Ellen on 13 May, by which day he had already drafted a long interview with himself for the *Daily Mail*. It was characteristic of Shaw to make this the occasion for helping a young office clerk in his ambition to become a journalist; and that this man, Reginald Golding Bright (later to become Shaw's London theatrical agent), should turn out to have been that solitary member of the audience who had heckled *Arms and the Man*. 'Vengeance I leave to Destiny,' Shaw announced to Ellen. What better evidence of this superiority to vengeance could there now be than his helping hand to Golding Bright? Their 'interview' in the *Daily Mail* contained no obvious malice at all, though by describing Irving as 'still obstinately under the spell of my genius' he converts him to a comic Shavian invention.

But Ellen wasn't fooled. She could tell from Irving's furtive expression how much he was affected. His last letter to Shaw was in effect a cry of 'For God's sake, leave me alone!' How much more human this seemed than all Shaw's acrobatics. 'My poor Henry!' she exclaimed. Why hadn't Shaw been able to leave him alone – for her sake? 'Well, you are quite stupid after all and *not* so unlike other people. You should have given in and said, "Take the play and do it when you can ..." I'm angry with you.'

Shaw had told Ellen that sometimes on Sundays he used to see her and Irving driving along Richmond Terrace 'like two children in a gigantic perambulator, and [I] have longed to seize him, throw him out, get up, take his place, and calmly tell the coachman to proceed'. What Ellen had learnt from this quarrel was that Shaw wanted to let her proceed alone. 'And NOW – well go your ways,' she decided. They were self-centred impractical men, and jealous.

She could not always remember her lines; she was on the verge of breaking down – and yet at a sound or a touch, she could still feel a throb of her heart. 'I fly from "throbs" in these days. It is not becoming. It's absurd.' She flew to her work, which was another sort of love. 'Work hardens and alerts me,' she confirmed in Shavian style. But the discipline of work without a little bit of real love became mechanical. Neither Irving nor Shaw could give her real love; neither would touch her, produce that throb.

From the wreckage of those hopes they had placed in each other, kindness persisted. And from that kindness came an honesty; and from honesty a muted revival of hope. Shaw's letters to Ellen tell of his childhood, of his dilemma of loving and the escape from incest into fantasy.

'I have only one thing to say to you . . . wanting to sleep, and yet to sleep with you. Only, do you know what the consequences would be? Well, about tomorrow at noon when the sun would be warm & the birds in full song, you would feel an irresistible impulse to fly into the woods. And there, to your great astonishment & scandal, you would be *confined* of a baby that would immediately spread a pair of wings and fly, and before you could rise to catch it it would be followed by another & another and another – hundreds of them, and they would finally catch you up & fly away with you to some heavenly country where they would grow into strong sweetheart sons with whom, in defiance of the prayerbook, you would found a divine race. Would you not like to be the mother of your own grandchildren? If you were my mother, I am sure I should carry you away to the tribe in Central America where – but I have a lot of things to say . . .'

In such passages, and without ever stating openly that the need he felt for his mother's love had set a pattern for his relationships with women, Shaw tried to indicate why he had supplanted the physical act of love with 'a lot of things to say'. In his fashion he loved Ellen; at any rate he wanted to love Ellen; but he could more easily hurt than touch her and felt he must 'get beyond love'. However much of this Ellen understood, she recognized the integrity and limitation of his feeling for her: 'You are a dear old kind fellow, as well as everything else.'

So they laid the preparations for a second chapter of their love, in

1 Vandeleur Lee, with Shaw's mother on his right and Shaw's father behind on his left

2 Lucinda Elizabeth ('Bessie') Shaw

3 George Carr Shaw

4 Bernard Shaw, aged nineteen, c. 1875

5 Jenny Patterson

6 Alice Lockett

7 Shaw, 1891

8 Charlotte Payne-Townsend, shortly before her marriage, 1898

9 Elizabeth Robins,
aged twenty-nine, 1891

10 William Archer, c. 1900

11 W. B. Yeats, mid 1890s

12 Florence Farr, 1890

another place than the Lyceum. For he had promised her: 'Nevertheless you shall play for me yet; but not with him, not with him, not with him.'

4

CANDIDA REFINISHED

> Here am I, the god who *has* been happy, among people who say 'I want to be happy just once'. The result, though, is alarming – desiring nothing further, I have become a sublime monster, to whose disembodied heart the consummation of ordinary lives is a mere anti-climax.
>
> Shaw to Janet Achurch (29 January 1896)

Four months after her return from New York, Janet Achurch stepped onto the stage of the Metropole in Camberwell in the revival of Wilkie Collins's *The New Magdalen*. It was a fashionably sentimental drama of the sort that had once provoked Shaw's 'unpleasant plays'. But he was in the mood to be generous. Describing her as 'the only tragic actress of genius we now possess,' he wrote that 'Miss Achurch [has] taken this innocent old figment of Wilkie Collins's benevolent and chivalrous imagination, and played into it a grim truth that it was never meant to bear . . . so that the curious atmosphere of reluctance and remonstrance from which Calvé use to wring the applause of the huge audiences at Covent Garden when the curtain fell on her Carmen, arose more than once when Miss Achurch disturbed and appalled us.'

Shaw had designed his notice so as to help re-establish Janet's career. While she was abroad he had kept her name before the public by linking it to Ellen Terry's. Ellen and Janet held twin attractions for him. Under their spell he was like a child playing at mothers-and-fathers. About business affairs they needed a stream of fatherly advice; and while he handed them this advice they encircled him with such powerful maternal appeal that, by 1896, he was imagining them performing on alternate nights in *Candida* which he described as 'THE Mother Play'.

Janet had talent but, as Ellen Terry noticed, she would '*overdo*' it'. She had barely grasped her words from the prompter than she fell ill. On 10 November Shaw's medical friend Kingston Barton diagnosed typhoid fever. Her illness 'occupied me a good deal during the last two months of the year [1895],' Shaw noted in his diary, 'partly because of its bearing on all possible plans for the production of *Candida*, and partly because I have come into relations of intimate friendship with the Charringtons'.

He was under tremendous strain. The money he earned from his journalism was absorbed by his family, but whatever small change he could squeeze out he handed over to Charrington; and whatever time he could scratch together, often from his hours of sleep, he spent with Janet at Onslow Square. The atmosphere in the house was appalling. But Shaw, though suffering from terrible headaches, refused to admit pessimism – even when Charrington, rousing himself with a bout of hostility, objected to his closeness to Janet in her bedroom. A nurse was installed, but Janet grew worse until, her death appearing possible, Shaw was denied her room altogether.

But Janet did not die: and with her recovery Shaw's hopes took off again. Perhaps she might play his Strange Lady. From her illness had come health; but after her convalescence she began to slip back into 'your brandy and soda self, your fabling, pretending, promising, company promoting, heavy eyelidded, morphia injecting self,' he admonished her.

With Shaw's help, Charrington had succeeded J. T. Grein as managing director of the Independent Theatre. It was a calculated gamble, aimed at helping Charrington's chances of achieving a stage career separate from his wife, whom Shaw had once more exhorted to 'live out your own life in your own way, and leave him [Charrington] to do the same'. This was Shaw's way of forbidding Janet's bedroom to her husband. But his confidence in Janet was diminishing as his interest, denied access to Elizabeth Robins, mounted in Ellen Terry. The plot of *Candida* was being enacted in his own life. In a letter he wrote to Janet while Charrington was away in April 1896 can be heard again the accents of Marchbanks at the end of the play. 'The step up to the plains of heaven was made on your bosom, I know; and it was a higher step than those I had previously taken on other bosoms,' he warned her.

'But he who mounts does not take the stairs with him . . . I have left the lower stairs behind me and must in turn leave you unless you too mount along with me.'

What Shaw had achieved for himself through will-power, he wanted to achieve for Janet vicariously. He wanted to become her guide and the source of her power; he wanted to replace her ordinary husband-and-wife liaison with Charrington by a motherly communion with himself.

Janet gave Shaw her answer the following month by revealing that she had been faithless to his principles 'to the extent of making "Candida" impossible until after next February [1897], when she expects to become once more a mother'. Watching Janet, seeing her beauty (her eyes like moons in a wet fog), Shaw understood what physical joy she took in her pregnancy. It was for her, as it had been for Ellen Terry, a voluptuous confinement. But Ellen was not pregnant and never would be again; while Janet's pregnancy moved the plot of their lives back from the stage into life. In short: she could not act in 'THE Mother Play' because she was to be a mother. 'I daren't be devoted now,' he told her in a moment of rare pathos. 'The appeal of your present experience to my sympathy is too strong to be indulged. So don't be angry with Shaw, Limited.'

*

Late in 1896 Janet seems to have had a miscarriage. 'Poor Janet,' Ellen Terry commiserated to Shaw. 'But tell her to wait. One gets everything if one will only wait, and she can. She is young and clever.' Early the next year, 1897, in her home town of Manchester, she enjoyed a 'glorious rampage', playing Cleopatra opposite Louis Calvert's 'inexcusably fat' Antony. But Shaw could not share her enjoyment. She had abandoned the experimental drama for which members of the Independent paid their subscriptions and replaced it with a thirty-year-old acting version of Shakespeare that might be seen any evening at the Lyceum. For the first time Janet was made an object for the hilarious sarcasm Irving knew so well:

'She is determined that Cleopatra shall have rings on her fingers and bells on her toes, and that she shall have music wherever she goes . . . The lacerating discord of her wailings is in my tormented ears as I write, reconciling me to the grave . . . I am a broken man . . . I begin to have hopes of a great metropolitan vogue for that lady now, since she has at last done something that is thoroughly wrong from beginning to end.'

What did he do to these women? He had laughed at Archer's susceptibility to Elizabeth Robins and its effect on his criticism in *The World*, but what of his own *Saturday Review* writings on Janet?

That May, Janet put on *The Doll's House* again, enabling Shaw to compare her performance with the one that had so hypnotized him eight years before. She had lost, he thought, her naturalness – a loss comparable to that of Alice in Miss Lockett, and matching the disappearance of Sonny within G.B.S. Their story was ending with a curious reversal. 'At last I am beginning to understand anti-Ibsenism,' Shaw told his *Saturday Review* readers:

'I no longer dwell on the awakening of the woman, which was once the central point of the drama. Why should I? The play solves that problem just as it is being solved in real life. The woman's eyes are opened; and instantly her doll's dress is thrown off and her husband left staring at her, helpless, bound thenceforth either to do without her (an alternative which makes short work of his independence) or else treat her as a human being like himself, fully recognizing that he is not a creature of one superior species, Man, living with a creature of another and inferior species, Woman, but that Mankind is male and female . . . We see a fellow-creature blindly wrecking his happiness and losing his "love-life", and are touched dramatically.'

The sympathy he feels for Helmer reflects a new sympathy for Janet's husband, and his rising fear of being imprisoned himself within a secure and happy marriage. The Independent Theatre's next production, *The Wild Duck*, did not feature Janet, and gave him the opportunity to declare that it had been Charrington who struck the decisive blow for Ibsen in England.

'Mr Charrington, like Mr Kendal and Mr Bancroft, has a wife; and the difference made by Miss Janet Achurch's acting has always been more obvious than that made by her husband's management to a public which has lost all tradition of what stage management really is, apart from lavish expenditure on scenery and furniture . . . Now, however, we have him at last with Miss Janet Achurch out of the bill. The result is conclusive . . . there is not a moment of bewilderment during the development . . . The dialogue, which in any other hands would have been cut to ribbons, is given without the slightest regard to the clock . . . That is a real triumph of management. It may be said that it is a triumph of Ibsen's genius; but of what use is Ibsen's genius if the manager has not the genius to believe in it.'

Shaw still believed that Janet and Charrington ought to part – but now it was for his sake more than hers. During 1897 Shaw used his *Saturday Review* column to persuade his readers that Charrington was 'the only stage-manager of genius the new movement has produced . . . [an] adventurer who explores the new territory at his own risk and is superseded by commercial enterprise the moment he is seen to pick up anything'. Here was a handsome apology to Charrington, transformed in Shaw's public imagination from the friend of pawnbrokers, who only cared for 'a pipe, a glass of whisky, a caress from a respectable woman', into a dedicated man-of-the-theatre crippled by obsessive love for his wife.

So when, having achieved success nowhere else, Shaw finally consented in the summer of 1897 to let the Independent Theatre produce *Candida*, it was into the 'capable hands' of Charrington, not to Janet, that he gave it. Ellen would not act for him: but why should her daughter, Edy

Craig, not play Prossy in the production? 'Would she go, do you think?' Shaw asked Ellen. ' . . . she might pick up something from Charrington; and Janet would keep her in gossip for a twelve-month to come.' So Shaw proposed; Ellen consented; and Edy was signed up for £20 a week.

Ellen felt tantalized by Shaw's friendship with her daughter. She had sent him a picture of both her children; Shaw had responded with one of himself – but with his eyes averted. So the photograph had not looked at her. But some evenings when Ellen was at the Lyceum, he would call at her home in Barkston Gardens and read his latest play to Edy and her friend Sally Fairchild. By the time Ellen returned, he was gone. They still had not met. He was, it seemed, 'the vainest flirt'. 'He'd coquet with a piece of string,' Sally Fairchild volunteered. But they had seen the dreadful fatigue behind his teasing.

'Oh, I'd love to have a baby every year,' Ellen had written to Shaw. Of course it was a fantasy: all men were babies to her. But to her own children she was not a good mother, spoiling her son, dominating her daughter. She had rejected Edy's suitors, and she welcomed this tour. Her daughter's watching eyes, that cool voice, unsettled her.

Candida was first presented to the public for one performance on 30 July 1897 in Aberdeen. The *Aberdeen Daily Journal* called it a 'risky business', though the drunken scene had been 'much appreciated'. 'I don't think we'll be much troubled with Mr Shaw's comedy,' predicted the *Northern Figaro*. 'I am sorry for Miss Achurch, she had such an uncongenial part to play, she certainly did her best with it, but I don't think she will ever say that "Candida" is her favourite part.'

When the Charringtons' tour reached Eastbourne, Ellen went to see it. 'It comes out on the stage even better than when one reads it. It is absorbingly interesting every second . . . Even the audience understood it all.' As for Janet, Ellen would write to her 'about one or two trifling things in her acting, suggestions which she may care, or not care, to try over'.

But 'I daren't face it,' Shaw told Janet. He was out of love with the theatre, with theatrical people, and with Janet. She had tried to borrow money from Ellen Terry and, worse still, from Edy. She had even tried to take advantage of a new friend of Shaw's, a 'public spirited Irish Lady' called Charlotte Payne-Townshend. Once he had retreated before the 'moral vacuity' of Florence Farr; now he backed away from Janet, accusing her of being 'a moral void – a vacuum'.

Eventually he saw his 'unhappy play' when the Charringtons did a London performance for the Stage Society in the summer of 1900. Edy 'pulled off the typist successfully,' he assured Ellen. But Janet, he decided, 'wasnt the right woman for it at all'.

She still had power to charm him. Calling round one evening at the end of 1897 he had found her as adorable as ever. But soon she grew loud and, after dinner, fuddled – reminding Shaw of his father. He knew then what he must do. He must walk out into the night.

'I held up a mirror in which Janet was beautiful as long as I could, in private and in print: now I've held it up with Janet inarticulate and rowdy. Avoid me now as you would the devil . . . it's sufficient that I loved you when I was young. Now I can do nothing but harm unless I say farewell, farewell, farewell, farewell, farewell, farewell, farewell, farewell.'

5

A FIRST PLAY FOR PURITANS

My reputation as a dramatist grows with every play of mine that is *not* performed.
'The Man of Destiny', *Daily Mail* (15 May 1897)

Between the end of 1895 and the beginning of 1897 Shaw gave the West End stage two more chances of discovering him. *You Never Can Tell* was a farce, and *The Devil's Disciple* a melodrama. Both were conventional as to form but extraordinary in style. 'When I got to the end,' wrote George Alexander, returning the text of *You Never Can Tell*, 'I had no more idea what you meant by it than a tom-cat.'

In his Preface to *Plays Pleasant* Shaw described *You Never Can Tell* as an attempt to answer the many requests of managers in search of fashionable comedies for West End theatres. 'I had no difficulty in complying,' he explained,

'as I have always cast my plays in the ordinary practical comedy form in use at all the theatres; and far from taking an unsympathetic view of the popular preference for fun, fashionable dresses, a little music, and even an exhibition of eating and drinking by people with an expensive air, attended by an if-possible-comic waiter, I was more than willing to shew that the drama can humanize these things as easily as they, in the wrong hands, can dehumanize the drama.'

You Never Can Tell has all the extravagant materials of farce: lost parents, antiphonal twins, outrageous coincidences, transparent disguises and the crowning emblem of a comic waiter. With dentistry as his meta-phor, Shaw used laughing gas (specifically identified in the original manuscript version) to 'pluck from the memory a rooted sorrow', and refill theatrical comedy with new material.

In his Preface to *The Shewing-up of Blanco Posnet* he was to liken the nation's morals to its teeth ('the more decayed they are the more it hurts to touch them'), and he once wrote to a dentist comparing their pro-fessions. 'I spend my life cutting out carious material from people's minds and replacing it with such gold as I possess. It is a painful process and you hear them screaming all through the press. I cannot give anaesthetics, but I do it as amusingly as I can.'

You Never Can Tell was his attempt to write for, without succumbing to, the theatre of Oscar Wilde's *The Importance of Being Earnest*. He had criticized Wilde's comedy for the *Saturday Review* at the end of February 1895 and begun his first attempt at *You Never Can Tell* some four months later.

'I cannot say that I greatly cared for The Importance of Being Earnest. It amused me, of course; but unless comedy touches me as well as amuses me, it leaves me with a sense of having wasted my evening . . . though I laugh as much as anybody at a farcical comedy, I am out of spirits before the end of the second act, and out of temper before the end of the third, my miserable mechanical laughter intensifying these symptoms at every outburst.'

This reaction is so singular that some critics have attributed it to envy. But *The Importance of Being Earnest* seems to have pressed on a concealed bruise that unsettled Shaw.

One morning, before Sonny's first birthday, his father had gone down to the railway station to see his wife as she went through on the train. But 'there you were with your head stuck down into a Book and of course you did not pretend to see me,' he complained. ' . . . there is a queer feel over me today, I did not mind it yesterday but I feel so forlorn, forsaken, alone.' Wilde's comedy, involving the identity of a handbagged baby in the cloakroom at Victoria Station, seemed to stir in Shaw the same 'queer feel' experienced by his father, against which G.B.S. had hardened his adult mind. There are echoes in *You Never Can Tell* of *The Importance of Being Earnest*. The recommendation of Valentine, the five-shilling dentist, to his patients, the young Clandons, to acquire 'a father alive or dead' for social respectability, is close to Lady Bracknell's recommendation to Jack Worthing to 'produce at any rate one parent, of either sex, before the season is quite over'.

Both plays use the theatrical device of the chance reunion of a separated family. The long-lost father in *You Never Can Tell* appears to have stepped out of a standard Victorian farce. But his drinking and outbursts of temper are seen as deriving from marriage to a woman who did not love him; and he has most to gain from the affectionate pantomime atmosphere Shaw works up at the end. This dance from grimness into gaiety represents the humanity Shaw found lacking in Wilde's play.

The autobiographical interest in *You Never Can Tell* is never literal, but is part of the reshaping of facts Shaw made while hammering out his philosophy of optimism. In the first version the play was set not in Devon but the Isle of Wight, where he had gone with Lucy and his mother after his sister Agnes had died there. The cast included improved versions of his father and mother, Lucy, Agnes ('Yuppy') and himself: they are Fergus Crampton, the abandoned father with 'an atrociously obstinate ill-tempered grasping mouth, and a dogmatic voice'; his wife, now calling herself Mrs Clandon who rules out 'all attempt at sex attraction'; and the three children she has brought up by herself: Gloria, 'the incarnation of haughty high-mindedness', and the twins, a 'darling little creature', Dolly, who is spoilt by her mother, and the 'handsome man in miniature', Philip, whose self-consciousness would be 'insufferable in a less prepossessing youth'. All of them are transferred from their Shaw family background into the landscape of Shakespearian romantic comedy, while the imposing Finch McComas, who twenty years before fired the imagination of Mrs Clandon, occupies the place of Vandeleur Lee, but is now made an agent for the reunion of the family.

On stage his family is in Shaw's power. He can dress them up, make them move to his music, manhandle them into pleasant reconciliation. His characters all carry the germs of real suffering. Bohun, the lawyer, speaks for everyone when he says: 'It's unwise to be born; it's unwise to be married; it's unwise to live; and it's wise to die.' And his father, the waiter, gives Shaw's answer: 'so much the worse for wisdom!'

But in an unwise world what can human beings do? First, Shaw suggests, they can use their intelligence. Bohun, even in a false nose and goggles, represents the 'terrifying power' of the trained mind, and demonstrates how tragedies may be avoided *in advance* by using intelligence freely; the encouraging presence of the waiter shows how we can avoid giving pain *at the time* by exercising tact and the spirit of acceptance recommended by Shakespeare's *As You Like It* and *What You Will* (*Twelfth Night*); and in Valentine the dentist we are given an example of how to deal with pain *in retrospect*, extracting it with magical ease. He is the only character without a surname and therefore a character without a past.

You Never Can Tell is Shaw's attempt to enact Valentine's philosophy.

Mr Crampton acknowledges '*in sudden dread*' that feeling is 'the only thing that can help us'. But the emotions are dangerous. 'Stop. Youre going to tell me about your feelings, Mr Crampton. Dont,' Bohun interrupts. And Gloria too interrupts Valentine: 'Oh, stop telling me what you feel: I can't bear it.' The sea ('You can imagine that the waves are its breathing, and that it is troubled and stirred to its great depths by some emotion that cannot be described') was used by Shaw to indicate the unconscious feelings and is a remnant from the imagery in *The Lady from the Sea*. But he eliminated much of this imagery from the published version of his play and presents us for the most part with a happy seaside spectacle. And for this, he implies, our response should echo the first two words with which Dolly opens the play after her successful operation in the dentist's chair: 'Thank you.' The dentist's anaesthetic at 'five shillings extra' is Shaw's own numbing of emotion ('I have never felt anything since').

The title, with its Shakespearian associations, summed up most people's reactions to the play. They couldn't tell: and Shaw, perhaps because he flinched from this violation of his own past, was politely unhelpful. There was always hope. 'Cheer up, sir, cheer up . . . You never can tell, sir: you never can tell.'

By 18 May 1896 it was officially finished, though three months later he was still toiling 'to get it ready for the stage'. This stage was the Haymarket Theatre whose 'exceptionally brilliant' management, he told Ellen Terry, 'appear to be making up their minds to ruin themselves with it'. He had designed it for the West End; and the West End had apparently accepted it. On 26 February 1897 a memorandum of agreement was finally signed with Frederick Harrison and the actor-manager Cyril Maude who was to play the waiter in the Haymarket production.

The rehearsals started badly and grew worse. Shaw prowled the theatre getting on everyone's nerves. He was particularly disliked by Alan Aynesworth, a young man who had played Algy in *The Importance of Being Earnest*, and to whom Cyril Maude was anxious to give the lead. Shaw had suspected that the Life Force love scene at the end of Act II was beyond Aynesworth, and now found his suspicions confirmed. At one moment of exasperation Aynesworth turned on Shaw and demanded: 'Let us see you play it yourself.' Shaw sprang up on to the stage and delivered his lines. 'But that,' protested the actor, 'is comedy!' Why had no one told him they were in a comedy? Both of them turned to Cyril Maude who seemed affably paralysed.

After a fortnight Shaw went to Frederick Harrison, the manager of the Haymarket, telling him he must come to the next rehearsal. 'After the rehearsal,' Shaw later recounted, 'Harrison joined us with such a long face that Maude saw it was all up.

'It was a miserable moment: they had been a thoroughly happy family; and my confounded play was going to break it up . . . I rescued them by saying that "we" had better withdraw the play and wait for another opportunity. They were enormously relieved.'

'I don't know how to express my appreciation of the way in which you met us over the withdrawal of your play,' Frederick Harrison wrote to him. Shaw was adept at concealing disappointment. His behaviour was impeccable. But a fear had been planted in him as to whether his plays were unactable. Could any actor play Valentine? 'There is no difficulty about You Never Can Tell,' he told Mrs Mansfield eighteen months later, 'except the difficulty of getting it acted. The end of the second act requires a consummate comedian; and that comedian has never been available.' Only occasionally did he reveal the keenness of his disappointment. 'It maddens me,' he burst out to Ellen Terry. 'I'll have my revenge in the preface by offering it as a frightful example of the result of trying to write for the *théâtre de nos jours.*'

You Never Can Tell was not presented in public for another three years when it was staged at the Strand Theatre. Once again 'the rehearsals lacerated my very soul', and he refused to let it proceed beyond six matinées. He had believed *You Never Can Tell* to be what he later called 'a champion money-maker'. But for eight years it made him almost nothing.

In one respect he was successful. When in 1903 Cyril Maude was writing his history of the Haymarket Theatre, he sent Shaw the chapter dealing with this period and Shaw replied with his own version, written as if from Maude's point of view, which was tipped into the book as Chapter XVI, under the transparent guise of it having been composed by Maude. The narrative describes how Svengali-Shaw hypnotized Aynes-worth into confusion over the end of Act II; how he almost caused a divorce between Mr and Mrs Maude; how, using 'a certain superficial reasonableness', he took over the whole business of stage-managership: and then surveyed the wreckage he had created 'with that perfidious air of making the best of everything which never deserted him'. Finally, having unnerved them all, he entered the theatre *in a new suit of clothes* bought in anticipation of the play's royalties.

The burlesque into which he turned his disappointment was a counter-part of the pantomime at the end of the play, and proof that he could dissolve bitterness and grievance into 'lightness of heart'. But it was also evidence of how he excelled at overcoming rather than confronting truth. For the truth was devastating. 'I sincerely hope that you will bring us another comedy presently,' Frederick Harrison had written to him, 'which we can carry to a successful issue.' But for Shaw, now in his early forties, the time for comedy seemed over. He had finished with the stage.

*

You Never Can Tell, the last of Shaw's pleasant plays, advocated lightness of heart; *The Devil's Disciple*, the first of his plays for Puritans, advocated seriousness of instinct. The Life Force which appears in *You Never Can Tell* as a biological current moving mainly through women, changes its course in *The Devil's Disciple* and works politically through the men.

The form of melodrama was suggested by William Terriss, a member of Irving's company who had moved to the Adelphi Theatre, which, by the 1890s, had reached the summit of its glory as the home of melodrama. Terriss himself, now in his fiftieth year, invariably played the hero; his mistress, Jessie Millward, was the heroine; and comic relief came from Harry Nichols. On the afternoon of 7 February 1896, Shaw went to the Adelphi where Terriss informed him that he intended to make a world tour and would like to add to his repertoire a play that should contain 'every "surefire" melodramatic situation' – a series of hair-raising adventures with (between the acts) miraculously unexplained escapes. These would culminate in a hanging that, to preserve the happy ending, turned out to be the nightmare of a sleeping bridegroom shortly before his marriage – the tolling death bell at the hero's execution developing as he woke into a brilliant peal of wedding bells. From Terriss's cupboard of ingredients, why should Shaw not cook up a masterpiece?

Shaw judged the scenario to be not quite 'in my line'. In a letter the following morning, he explained that what Terriss needed for a world tour was not another Adelphi melodrama but 'something like Hamlet – on popular lines'.

That autumn Shaw agreed to have his portrait painted by a Slade School artist, Nellie Heath, and turned the sittings to account by scrawling his play in a series of pocket notebooks. 'The play progresses,' he told Ellen Terry on 16 October 1896, ' . . . such a melodrama! I sit in a little hole of a room off Euston Road on the corner of a table with an easel propped before me so that I can write and be painted at the same time.' It was more than melodrama; it was all the plots of all the melodramas he had ever sat through for the *Saturday Review*. 'The whole character of the piece must be allegorical, idealistic, full of generalisations and moral lessons,' he had written, describing the ideal Adelphi production; 'and it must represent conduct as producing swiftly and certainly on the individual the results which in actual life it only produces on the race in the course of many centuries.' It was in this last concept that Shaw believed there was room for original ideas. The danger was that, attempting simultaneously to exploit and subvert the stage melodrama, he would get trapped within its conventions. 'I finished my play today,' he wrote to Ellen Terry on 30 November, ' . . . but I want your opinion; for I have never tried melodrama before; and this thing, with . . . its sobbings & speeches & declamations, may possibly be the most monstrous piece of farcical absurdity that ever made an audience shriek with laughter.'

He had written it round the scene of Dick Dudgeon's arrest 'which had always been floating in my head as a situation for a play' and which had probably floated in from Sydney Carton's heroic sacrifice at the end of *A Tale of Two Cities*. Dickens's novel was regularly dramatized for the Victorian stage which, though it never dared exhibit sexual love, always alleged that love was the motive behind noble action. Like all theatrical heroes, Sydney Carton went to the gallows for the sake of the heroine. Shaw took this situation and gave it another motive. Judith Anderson, who embodies the love motive, concludes that Dick Dudgeon has taken the place of her husband and let himself be arrested 'for my sake'. But Dick Dudgeon, like Hamlet, is a 'tragic figure in black'. He has 'no motive and no interest', and denies acting out of love. Everyone, he tells Judith from prison, could 'rise to some sort of goodness and kindness when they were in love [*the word love comes from him with true Puritan scorn*]. That has taught me to set very little store by the goodness that only comes out red hot. What I did last night, I did in cold blood, caring not half so much for your husband, or [*ruthlessly*] for you [*she droops, stricken*] as I do for myself . . . I have been brought up standing by the law of my own nature; and I may not go against it, gallows or no gallows.'

Like Shaw, Dick appears a mountebank, mixing instinctive good manners with the desire to shock by acting *impersonally*. That Shaw recognized himself in Dick can be shown by comparing Dick's prison speech to Judith with a letter Shaw himself wrote over ten years later: 'The only aim that is at all peculiar to me is my disregard of *warm* feelings. They are quite well able to take care of themselves. What I want is a race of men who can be kind in cold blood. Anybody can be kind in emotional moments.'

He placed the action during the American Revolution, and he fixed the date in October 1777 with the surrender of General Burgoyne at Saratoga. This, he implied, like the distant background of Madeira in *You Never Can Tell*, was culturally equivalent to modern Ireland. Shaw's Burgoyne is a fabricated figure through whom the Shavian comedy works best and who, making his entrance in the last act, often steals the show. In *The*

Devil's Disciple (as in his next play, *Caesar and Cleopatra*) Shaw rewrote history and set it on course for the future he wanted. 'What will History say?' Major Swindon asks Burgoyne as he contemplates the defeat of Britain by the Americans. 'History, sir, will tell lies as usual,' Burgoyne assures him. For these schoolroom lies Shaw substitutes a dramatic narrative that eliminates evil and identifies the real enemy of human progress as 'Jobbery and snobbery, incompetence and Red Tape'. The America of 1777 is a man's world full of crude notions that women can see through but do not have the legal or political status to alter.

'The Devil's Disciple has, in truth, a genuine novelty in it,' Shaw later wrote. But he was careful not to let this novelty spoil the story. It is, in that sense, one of the least Shavian of his plays. He took it to Terriss even before it was completely finished. But Terriss's dreams of a world tour had failed and he had no recollection of his arrangement with Shaw. The reading took place at Jessie Millward's flat and was probably, Shaw believed, at her insistence. His account of what happened in some respects resembles his story of reading *Widowers' Houses* to Archer. Terriss 'composed himself dismally' as if Jessie Millward 'had taken him to church', listening in deep perplexity as Shaw plunged into his play. At the climax of the first act, he suddenly interrupted to ask whether 'this is an interior?' Then, a short way into the second act, he again apologetically broke in: 'I beg your pardon: but *is* this an interior?' Shaw's answer, he declared, had set him 'completely at rest'. This seemed to be true, for a few minutes later he uttered a long drawn snore.

After that nothing seemed to go right for *The Devil's Disciple*. 'I think I shall die lonely,' Shaw wrote to Ellen Terry, 'as far as my third acts are concerned.' He still believed that Terriss would be the best person to do it, but on 16 December 1897 Terriss was motivelessly assassinated on the steps of the Adelphi and died in Jessie Millward's arms. So he became 'only a name and a batch of lies in the newspapers', while the history of *The Devil's Disciple*, Shaw told Charrington, 'has given me such practice in hardening my heart that I have lost all human sympathy'.

*

He was not to start another play for fifteen months, when he gave up his drama criticism for the *Saturday Review*. 'What is the matter with the theatre, that a strong man can die of it?' he was to enquire in his Preface to *Three Plays for Puritans*. He had been attracted to the stage by the opportunities it seemed to offer him of overriding his private life with a public career. He wanted to be reborn through his work and use the theatrical world to develop his new identity, fulfilling what he called 'my instinct . . . to turn failure into success'. His rejection by the West End hit the same spot made sensitive by all his early neglect – though this was now a well-bandaged wound. He had looked to the stage for another existence but as Terriss's assassination suggested, the insidious illusion of the theatre flowed out and contaminated ordinary life. 'When we want to read of the deeds that are done for love, whither do we turn? To the murder column: and there we are rarely disappointed.'

There is anger and disgust in Shaw's condemnation. He had entered a paradise of fools where the actor-manager was enthroned as god, the actress as star: and the author was merely its word-carpenter. Everyone, even his friend Archer, insisted that he could not write plays. Yet he persisted. 'Here am I, after 20 years drudging away, at last venturing to tell myself that if I *begin* writing for the stage, I will master the business by the time I am fifty or so,' he wrote to Janet Achurch in the spring of 1896. But the rejection of his last two plays seemed to have cracked this confidence. He had risked prostituting his talent. His thought was far more subtle than his orchestration of it for trumpet and big drum suggests. The rhetoric, the overstatement, the ear-catching tricks, jokes to the gallery, all proceeded from his need to be heard; but they masked what he wanted to say and enabled the public, whose ear he eventually caught, to hear only the voice of an Irish paradoxer who did not mean half of what he said.

Even his sentimental loyalties, it seemed to Shaw, had played him false. He had failed to liberate Ellen Terry from the hypnotic rule of Irving; he had failed to separate Janet Achurch from Charrington or to free her from the dominance of alcohol and morphia; he had failed to make an actress of Florence Farr. In all these endeavours he had sent his plays out to do his work, but the scarcity and poor quality of their performances gave life no chance to imitate the Shavian drama. 'Give up *wanting* to have the plays produced,' he advised another dramatist, 'if you value your happiness as a man and your dignity as an artist.' Early in 1897 he took this advice himself. On being elected a member of the St Pancras Vestry he plunged into local politics, recognizing 'that there is better work to be done in the Vestry than in the theatre'. At about the same time, in another essay at turning failure into success, he decided to publish his plays.

It was not an easy decision. Only two categories of drama were commonly published as books: non-dramatic plays by poets such as Browning and Tennyson; and acting editions, using a good deal of technical stage business.

Towards the end of 1896, one of W. T. Stead's young men, Grant Richards, having set up a new publishing company, offered to become 'publisher in ordinary and publisher extraordinary' of his dramatic works. Shaw replied categorically that 'the public does not read plays'. But

Richards was not put off: 'I went after G.B.S.' He caught up with him after a theatrical first night and together they walked back, Shaw in a baggy Jaeger suit, Richards in evening dress, to Fitzroy Square.

Shaw had been longing for someone to take no notice of him. All his sensible arguments had been taken from others. Richards had borrowed £700 (equivalent to £37,500 in 1997) from his uncle, Grant Allen, and another £700 from his bank, and was now presenting himself to various authors he admired: Wells, Bennett, Chesterton, Masefield, Housman. He was blatantly monocled, had a taste for Monte Carlo, and a charm that reconciled friends to his lack of scruples. Shaw's threats of the Bankruptcy Court left him amiably unruffled. The struggle between them went on through the winter, Shaw resisting, Richards never tiring; and in the spring of 1897 Shaw suddenly succumbed. 'I am being pressed to publish my plays,' he wrote to Ellen Terry. 'I think I will, and give up troubling the theatre.' The decision in some ways reflected his disenchantment with the stage as a place on which to conduct his love affairs. Fifteen months earlier, in a letter to Janet Achurch, he had predicted that if he could not find beautiful women to play his roles, 'then I will do what I am often tempted to do – publish my plays and appeal to the imaginations of those who are capable of reading them without wasting myself on trying to have them performed without utter profanation'. That time had now come.

Richards and Shaw combined well. 'You are the most incompetent publisher I ever heard of,' Shaw told him. And Richards replied: 'You are just about as businesslike a man as I have ever met in my short life.' Shaw seemed to recognize in Richards the sort of 'young villain' that Sonny might have turned into had he remained in Ireland. He had 'allowed himself to fall in Love with Literature', which was tragic in a publisher.

Shaw, Richards acknowledged, was 'the born man of affairs'. In fact it was like an affair of love for Shaw; while for Richards it was an education. 'Make yourself pleasant, no matter what provocation you may get,' Shaw later recommended him, 'and you will not only be doing what you do best usually, but you will be pursuing the only possible policy under the circumstances.' This was roughly how their partnership worked. Shaw ordered him to 'sit tight' and 'trust my judgment'; and Richards complied.

So G.B.S. got to work. He issued injunctions on punctuation (which often indicates where the actor shall breathe), demanded narrow margins, made proposals on pagination, introduced experiments with the title page. He employed lower-case italics in square brackets for stage directions, abolished apostrophes from contracted words and substituted spaced letters for italic in underlined words. He selected a green binding and went in search of the blackest printing ink. He let it be known that a single misprint upset him more than the deaths of his father and his sister 'with whom I was on excellent terms'. He threatened proof corrections on the scale of Balzac and Carlyle ('you may charge me for all corrections over and above 95% of the total cost of production'), and prescribed the price and print run. In short, he enjoyed himself extravagantly.

Shaw's ideas on book design derived from William Morris. He looked at a page as a picture and at a book as an ornament that could be admired by a man who could not read a word of it, 'as a XII century chalice or loving cup may be cherished by a heathen or a teetotaller'. By the end of August 1897, Shaw reported to Richards that he had sent three plays to the printer 'transmogrified beyond recognition, made more thrilling than any novel'. In re-forming these plays for the press Shaw treated the pen and the *viva vox* as different instruments, the one producing a literary language for the eye, the other sounds mainly intelligible to the ear, and each needing separate scoring to blend into an unbroken narrative. To attract the novel-reading public he made it a rule with his stage directions never to mention the stage, proscenium or spectators; to discard all technical expressions and insert plenty of descriptive matter; to give sufficient guidance to the theatre management and information to the actor of *what* but not *how* to act – without spoiling anything for the reader.

Shaw took a further step away from the stage with his Prefaces, which 'have practically nothing to do with the plays'. The Shavian Preface was to be a treatise on the social problems with which the plays were connected. 'Every play, every preface I wrote conveys a message,' he told an interviewer. 'I am the messenger boy of the new age.'

By adding the publication of his plays to his Fabian activities and theatre reviewing, Shaw filled up each day with sixteen hours of work 'that nobody should ever touch after lunch'. He felt exhausted even in the morning. 'I get out of bed so tired that I am in despair until I have braced myself with tubbing,' he told Ellen Terry. 'When I sit down my back gets tired: when I jump up, I get giddy & have to catch hold of something to save myself from falling.' The plays crept through the press with Shaw scanning every item in the proofs.

He had decided to divide the plays into two books, 'Pleasant' and 'Unpleasant'. He began the Unpleasant Plays (*Widowers' Houses, The Philanderer* and *Mrs Warren's Profession*) with a Preface, 'Mainly About Myself', which he continued without further title at the beginning of the Pleasant Plays (*Arms and the Man, Candida, The Man of Destiny* and *You Never Can Tell*). Only *The Devil's Disciple* was laid aside for another volume, *Three Plays for Puritans*.

These first two books were to inaugurate a long series of Shaw's plays in the same format, and change the fashion in play publishing. 'I was as proud as Punch,' declared Grant Richards. 'The look and feel of it gave me intense pleasure. But it did not make me rich.'

Plays Pleasant and Unpleasant were published in April 1898. Archer, in the *Daily Chronicle*, called *Candida* a work of genius, *Mrs Warren's Profession* a masterpiece, *Widowers' Houses* a crude 'prentice work, and *The Philanderer* 'an outrage upon art and decency, for which even my indignation cannot find a printable term of contumely'. Henry Arthur Jones, whose plays Shaw had consistently overpraised in the *Saturday Review*, wrote that 'much of them is not dramatic and would never be interesting in any circumstances to any possible audience'. But the most devastating response came from Shaw's *Saturday Review*:

'The men are all disputative machines, ingeniously constructed, and the women, who, almost without exception, belong to the strange cult of the fountain-pen, are, if anything, rather more self-conscious than the men . . . Mr Shaw is not, as the truly serious dramatist must be, one who loves to study and depict men and women for their own sake, with or without moral purpose. When Mr Shaw is not morally purposeful, he is fantastic and frivolous, and it is then that his plays are good . . . his serious characters are just so many skeletons, which do but dance and grin and rattle their bones. I can hardly wonder that Mr Shaw has so often hesitated about allowing this or that theatrical manager to produce one of his serious plays. To produce one of them really well would be almost impossible at any ordinary theatre.'

This criticism had been composed by Max Beerbohm, and appeared in the same issue of the *Saturday Review* (21 May 1898) in which Shaw, writing his valedictory as the paper's theatre critic, welcomed his successor 'the incomparable Max'. It was a characteristic example of Frank Harris's editing: lazy but provocative. His booming voice awed his staff, from whom he excited the loyalty due to a sea-rover, but by 1898 the 'little old pirate ship', Max Beerbohm wrote to Shaw, was already 'going down into the waves, with you (Admiral of the Moral Fleet) suddenly perceived standing, in full uniform, with folded arms and steadfast eyes, on the bridge; and with me and other respectable people clinging to the rigging'.

Harris was bought out of the *Saturday Review* six months after Shaw left. There had been a number of libel cases and rumours of blackmail – later put down by Shaw to Harris's innocence of English business methods. But though Shaw was to take this mitigating stance, his description of Harris as 'neither first-rate, nor second-rate, nor tenth-rate . . . just his horrible unique self', indicates how much he disliked sharing his professional life with him. His work for the *Saturday Review* had seriously reduced his health and offered little 'to the enormity of my unconscious ambition'. His valedictory shows at what exorbitant human cost he had overcome the poverty, obscurity, ostracism and contempt that infected his Dublin years. 'I have been the slave of the theatre,' he wrote.

'It has tethered me to the mile radius of foul and sooty air which has its centre in the Strand, as a goat is tethered in the little circle of cropped and trampled grass that makes the meadow ashamed. Every week it clamors for its tale of written words; so that I am like a man fighting a windmill: I have hardly time to stagger to my feet from the knock-down blow of one sail, when the next strikes me down . . . Do I receive any spontaneous recognition for the prodigies of skill and industry I lavish on an unworthy institution and a stupid public? Not a bit of it: half my time is spent in telling people what a clever man I am. It is no use merely doing clever things in England . . .

Unfortunately, the building process has been a most painful one to me, because I am congenitally an extremely modest man. Shyness is the form my vanity and self-consciousness take by nature. It is humiliating, too, after making the most dazzling displays of professional ability, to have to tell people how capital it all is. Besides, they get so tired of it, that finally . . . they begin to detest it.

. . . I can never justify to myself the spending of four years on dramatic criticism. I have sworn an oath to endure no more of it. Never again will I cross the threshold of a theatre. The subject is exhausted; and so am I.'

'Now the playwrights may sleep in peace,' observed the actor-manager of the Criterion, Charles Wyndham, 'and the actor may take his forty winks without anxiety.'

SEVEN

ST PANCRAS VESTRYMAN

People think of me as a theatrical man, but I am really proud of having served six years as a municipal councillor.

New York Times (24 March 1933)

Fabian progress through the north of England after the success of *Fabian Essays* had been helped by an elderly supporter, Henry Hunt Hutchinson. Crusty and querulous, exuberantly describing his marriage as a penal servitude, he reminded Shaw of Samuel Butler. 'I liked the man,' he decided. But 'Old Hutch' did not much like Shaw. He would alternate with his cheques to the Fabians cantankerous letters complaining of Shaw's rudeness. The Fabian executive, banking the cheques and applauding Old Hutch's public spirit, would deplore his advancing age and infirmity. What would happen, they wondered, to Fabian finances when he died?

In the summer of 1894 they had their answer when Old Hutch shot himself. The Webbs were staying in the Surrey hills, with Shaw and Wallas, when Sidney received a letter informing him that he had been appointed one of Hutchinson's trustees. Old Hutch had been a solicitor and had made a will that was almost certainly invalid. To his wife he bequeathed £100; his two sons and two daughters received smaller bequests; and Fabianism was to benefit, over a period of ten years, by almost £10,000. This money had been left to trustees (of whom Sidney became first Chairman), to be used for 'the propaganda and other purposes' of the Fabian Society 'and its Socialism', and for promoting Fabian goals 'in any way' that the trustees thought 'advisable'. At breakfast the next morning, the Webbs told Shaw and Wallas of their decision to found in London a School of Economics and Political Science, similar to the Massachusetts Institute of Technology or the Ecole Libre des Sciences Politiques, where experts could be specially trained for the purpose of reforming society. Shaw, who believed that Hutchinson had 'left his money for Red propaganda by Red vans', would have preferred using it to enliven Fabian campaigns. Yet it was he who acted as Webb's spokesman and cleverly avoided antagonizing Olivier and Bland, both of whom objected to Webb's plans.

Sidney had to placate the Hutchinson family and the Fabian executive.

He had to win support both from the London County Council and from businessmen by representing his school as an institution with commercial courses, though dedicated (despite its socialist propaganda) to disinterested research. Knowing that disinterested research inevitably led to socialist conclusions, Sidney detected no discrepancy in this – especially since small amounts of the Hutchinson money were to be segregated for the promotion of Fabian lectures and an increase in the secretary's salary. But it was too paradoxical for Shaw. Always scrupulous in financial affairs, he warned Beatrice that Sidney was antagonizing the Fabian executive by what looked like a plan to bribe them in return for permission 'to commit an atrocious malversation of the rest of the bequest'.

As Webb had once frowned on Shaw's individualism, so Shaw now worried over Webb's idealism, fearing that his love for this new invention could cause a break-up in the Fabian family. Nevertheless, for reasons of unity, Shaw reluctantly supported his friend's dream of a centre for sociological research.

So, by means of a suspect will, at variance with anything Old Hutch could have envisaged, and amid a good deal of Fabian grumbling, one of Webb's lasting achievements was begun. 'It is honestly scientific,' Beatrice pronounced after the school had opened in the summer of 1895. And Shaw later admitted that 'Sidney Webb performed miracles with his money which I should never have done'.

*

The London School of Economics became another instrument for long-term permeation (particularly valuable since Lord Salisbury's Tory Government was elected), and for the introduction of collectivism by educationists rather than political partisans. Before their marriage, Beatrice had revealed her doubts as to whether Sidney was 'a really big man' like Chamberlain, but assured him that he might be capable of doing 'first-rate work on the London County Council'. After their marriage she supported his refusal to go into Parliament, partly because she believed that 'the finest part of his mind and character' would be unemployed in the House of Commons, and partly because she recognized in a parliamentary career the 'enemy of domesticity'. They had moved at the end of 1893 to an austere ten-room house at 41 Grosvenor Road on the Embankment. It was a short distance from Spring Gardens, where the London County Council held its meetings, and from Adelphi Terrace, where in 1896 the London School of Economics moved. After his meetings and lectures Sidney would return in the evening to Beatrice's simple meat suppers with cigarettes.

At first sight Shaw's maverick figure does not find a part in the undramatic plans Webb had made for revolution through research. He had refused in 1889 to stand for the London County Council in Deptford – the seat Webb was to win from the Tories three years later. But his experiences in the theatre over the next eight years made him see that it was no longer a grand choice between Parliament and the West End, but a means of combining a limited commitment to municipal politics with a limited success in provincial theatres. Early in 1894 he had refused an invitation to put himself up as the parliamentary candidate for Chelsea; but he stood in the School Board elections at the end of that year for the St Pancras Vestry – and was handsomely defeated. Then, letting his name go forward as a Progressive candidate at an uncontested election in May 1897, he was appointed to the Vestry Committee of Ward 7 of St Pancras, together with an architect, barrister, builder and tea-dealer.

London local government in the 1890s was an 'archaic patchwork' of vestries. The St Pancras Vestry, stretching from Islington to Marylebone and from Holborn to Hampstead and Hornsey, contained almost two hundred thousand inhabitants. Their culture 'may be inferred from the fact that there was not a single bookshop in the entire borough,' Shaw recorded. But it clustered with 'houses of ill-fame', especially in the side streets off Tottenham Court Road (one of which was named Warren Street). And there were slums often owned by landlords like Sartorius and managed by rent-collectors such as Lickcheese.

On behalf of their constituents the vestrymen looked after an elastic range of matters from manure receptacles (maintenance of), horns (blowing of), graves (purchase of) and noxious literature (sale of), to the management of ice cream notices, street cries, the sampling of milk-in-transit and all business involving public baths, lighting, tramways. The strength of local government was planted, Shaw believed, in its independence from Parliament. The St Pancras Vestry had a Chairman and 116 vestrymen. They did not operate under the party system. 'Every member can vote as he thinks best without the slightest risk of throwing his party out of power and bringing on a General Election,' Shaw explained. 'If a motion is defeated, nobody resigns: if it is carried, nobody's position is changed.' Reviewing his six years as a vestryman and borough councillor at the age of eighty, he recalled that 'I never had to vote on any question otherwise than on its specific merits . . .

'in Parliament I should have been a back row chorus man, allowed to amuse the House with a speech occasionally . . . [the] perversion of parliament has produced all the modern dictatorships . . . The little socialism we have is gas and water Socialism. And it is by extension of Gas & Water Socialism that industry will be socialized.'

Shaw's first meeting took place at the Vestry Hall, Pancras Road, on 26 May 1897. He was soon joined by a young Methodist minister named Ensor Walters;

'the vestry, as far as it knew anything about me, classed me as a Socialist and therefore an atheist, sure to differ with the Methodist minister on every question. What actually happened was that he and I immediately formed a party two strong all to ourselves. And we troubled ourselves about no other party . . . He was out to make a little corner for the Kingdom of God in St Pancras; and nothing could have suited me better.'

Shaw served on the Health Committee of which Ensor Walters became Chairman, on the Officers Committee and the Committee for Electricity and Public Lighting. These were three of ten sub-committees which met separately and 'set forth their conclusions as to what the Council ought to do in their departments in a series of resolutions. When the whole Council meets, these strings of resolutions are brought up as the reports of the Committees, and are confirmed or rejected or amended by the general vote.'

This system impressed Shaw as being so sensible that he wondered why parliamentary business should not be conducted on similar lines. He discovered local government, however, to be undermined by two factors: the inadequacy of the men who were elected and the paralysing poverty of the municipalities. His fellow-vestrymen were well-intentioned people but 'absurdly unequal to the magnitude of our task.

'Our ablest leaders were a greengrocer and a bootmaker, both of them much more capable than most members of Parliament; for it needs considerable character and ability to succeed as a shopkeeper, especially as a publican, whereas persons with unearned money enough can easily get into Parliament without having ever succeeded in anything. I found them excellent company, and liked and respected them for their personal qualities . . . but in the effective lump we were as ignorantly helpless politically as the mob of ratepayers who elected us, and who would never have elected me had they had the faintest suspicion of my ultimate political views.'

By their policy of under-rating, these men had by 1900 put the St Pancras Vestry in debt to the bank by £17,000. It was this insolvency that weakened the local authority. A weak vestry, Shaw argued, was at the mercy of its officials and of parliamentary rule. 'He saw in municipal government a valuable decentralizing balance and counter-check to Parliamentary government,' wrote H. M. Geduld. 'It existed to ensure that local necessities were not sacrificed to national interests . . . Unfortunately, Parliamentary government frequently forces its inefficient decisions upon weak municipalities.'

The vestrymen deliberately kept the rates down because they themselves, and the people who had voted for them, could not afford a rating figure that would ensure municipal solvency. Shaw strove unsuccessfully to alter the rating system so as to relieve ordinary ratepayers and arrest reckless overdrawing on the bank. 'There is only one remedy,' he wrote, 'and that is to take the burden off the shoulders of the men who do the work & conduct the business of London, & throw it on to those who take enormous sums in rent and interest out of our business to squander in idleness.' He proposed to do this by the taxation of ground values ('or, as I want it, taxation of unearned incomes'), with a rating exemption limit and a series of abatement limits as in the case of income tax.

The London Government Act of 1899 replaced the forty-two vestries with twenty-eight Metropolitan Boroughs each with a Mayor and Council. Wards 7 and 8 of the old Vestry were amalgamated into the Southern Division of the new St Pancras Borough and ten candidates stood for the six available seats at the election on 1 November 1900. For Shaw (who with 704 votes came second only to a clergyman, beating a bootmaker, removal contractor and store proprietor), this was the one successfully contested political election of his career. He campaigned hard, armed himself against failure ('the relief will be enormous'), and described his success as 'a sentence of hard labor'.

He had opposed the London Government Act in that it disqualified women, who had been part of the vestries, from sitting on the Borough Councils, and he attempted to give publicity to the need for women on public bodies, but *The Times* declined to publish a letter he wrote that threw off 'the customary polite assumption that women are angels'.

'English decency is a . . . string of taboos. You must not mention this: you must not appear conscious of that . . . everything that must not be mentioned in public is mentioned in private as a naughty joke. One day, at a meeting of the Health Committee of the Borough Council of which I was a member, a doctor rose to bring a case before the Committee. It was the case of a woman. The gravity of the case depended on the fact that the woman was pregnant. No sooner had the doctor mentioned this than the whole Committee burst into a roar of laughter, as if the speaker had made a scandalous but irresistible joke. And please bear in mind that we were not schoolboys. We were grave, mostly elderly men, fathers of families . . . There is only one absolutely certain and final preventive for such indecency, and that is the presence of women. If there were no other argument for giving women the vote, I would support it myself on no other ground than that men will not behave themselves when women are not present.'

In the Borough of St Pancras women had two unmentionable grievances: first, there were few public lavatories for them; secondly, where these had been provided they necessarily consisted not of urinals. but separate closets, entrance to which traditionally cost one penny – 'an absolutely prohibitive charge for a poor woman'. The grotesque struggle for free lavatories raged for years, and with particular heat round a site in Camden High Road. Some councillors objected that persons who so far 'forgot their sex' did not deserve a lavatory; one suggested that the water supply would be used by flower girls to wash the violets that he occasionally purchased for his buttonhole. The site was also assailed as a terror to traffic and a feature so gross as to contaminate the value of all property in the neighbourhood.

It is not easy to chronicle Shaw's work as a vestryman and borough councillor. Fearing that his own proposals might not be listened to seriously, he often filtered them through other councillors. Nevertheless, a pattern to his municipal work can be picked out. He voted in favour of more free time for workers employed by the Council (every other Sunday off instead of every third Sunday for lavatory attendants) and for trams against underground railways in the interests of shopkeepers; and he introduced a motion to raise the salaries of the Council's clerical staff by means of promotion through independent tests of their qualifications. After St Pancras became a metropolitan borough, the Chairman of the Vestry was translated into a Mayor. The Vestry Chairman had been unpaid, and the first Mayor of St Pancras, Alderman Barnes, proposed continuing this magnanimous tradition. Shaw objected, warning the Council against making a new precedent:

'It was, of course, very handsome of Mr Barnes to say he would not accept any salary, but at the same time a definite sum of money ought to be placed at his disposal . . . He [Shaw] moved that this question of the paying of the Mayor be adjourned for further consideration, because it would not be a proper or democratic thing to pass a resolution that might prevent a poor man accepting the office of Mayor.'

Shaw's motion was defeated, but when in 1903 the Council appointed as their second mayor W. H. Matthews, a greengrocer (and the model for Bill Collins in *Getting Married*), the matter of a salary was again discussed,

£200 a year being proposed. Shaw made a strong speech, emphasizing that 'it was quite legal to pay the Mayor, and no other method would place every man there on a footing of absolute equality.

'But 200 pounds a year was a ridiculous sum; he would multiply it by five. There was no sounder democratic principle than that a man should be paid for public services. At present in that Council when they wanted a man to be Mayor they had first to find out if he could afford it.'

But he was again outvoted and the office of Mayor continued unsalaried.

Shaw annoyed his fellow-councillors by a persistent campaign against badges of office, regalia and robes that converted the St Pancras aldermen into 'animated pillar boxes'. Were not such grandiose uniforms an obvious misuse of public money? Even on issues he supported Shaw looked carefully at expenditure. When the Mayor proposed spending £40 to send a delegation of councillors rambling into the countryside to report on the public installation of a crematorium in St Pancras, Shaw intervened to say that he

'sometimes spent his week-ends near Woking, and if they would lend him a councillor for the purposes of cremation (much laughter) he would bring up a report of all that happened (laughter) without cost to anyone (laughter)'.

Shaw's advocacy of cremation was part of a campaign for public hygiene he pursued on the Health Committee. He urged that 'if earth-to-earth burial was to be continued, the depth below the surface ought not to be more than a couple of inches, and the coffin of the flimsiest material it was possible to have'. As a member of this committee he visited workhouses, hospitals, sweatshops and the homes of the poor, and saw the destitution and disease. Many of the tenements were lice-ridden; there were epidemics of smallpox, and occasional cases of typhoid fever, and even bubonic plague. Houses were disinfected with sulphur candles, on the fumes of which pathogenic bacilli actually multiplied. On asking the Medical Officer of Health why ratepayers' money was spent on a useless fumigant, Shaw was told that, though the real disinfectants were soap, water and sunshine, no stripper or cleaner would dare enter an infected house unless it was filled with the superstitious stink of sulphur.

Shaw accepted sulphur but not vaccination which, he believed, was seen as a cheap prophylactic and employed as an alternative to a decent housing programme. During the spread of smallpox in 1901 Shaw battled with the medical advisers in St Pancras, who were urging on the Council a compulsory vaccination scheme. But he found limited support from the Borough Medical Officer, Dr Sykes. The difference was one of private practice versus socialized medicine. The Council paid half a crown for each revaccination. 'No doubt the doctors were honestly convinced that vaccination is harmless and prevents smallpox; but the half-crown had more to do with that honest conviction than an unbiased scientific study of the subject.'

Dr Sykes's position was dependent on the good health of the district – it was what Shaw called 'the position that one wants Socialism to place all doctors in'. He could be dismissed only by the Local Government Board which judged his efficiency by the health statistics.

'Dr Sykes's income did not get larger when the district got sick. The private practitioners' did . . . you could see the private practitioners getting new ties and new hats. When the death-rate went up they always looked better off and happier. That was not the case with the medical officer of health: he looked more worried: it was a bad time for him.'

What he heard passed in Council convinced Shaw that medical opinion was often little more than a conspiracy to exploit public credulity. Over two years, in a series of what were called 'curious pathological effusions' to *The Times*, the *British Medical Journal*, the *Saturday Review* and *Vaccination Inquirer*, he pressed for an independent re-examination of statistics, and for a socialized health service as a replacement to the money motive in medicine.

Shaw treated the press as a democratic instrument through which he poured information and advice to the public and from which he hoped to get instructions formed by that advice. The principles by which he tried to reach a workmanlike relationship with voters are revealed by some remarks he made to vestrymen and borough councillors. 'Never do anything for the public that the public would do for themselves,' he told them. And: 'Give the public not what they want but what they ought to want and dont.' It was the responsibility of councillors and Members of Parliament to persuade the public to want what was best in the long term.

What Shaw wanted was to command political action without the horror of submerging himself in political life. The need to earn money from his other work made it impossible for him to attend all meetings. Of the possible 321 council and sub-committee meetings he was eligible to attend between November 1900 and September 1903, he turned up at 192.

In public, Shaw's attitude to his municipal duties was one of undisguised optimism – which is to say, disguised pessimism: 'I love the reality of the

Vestry,' he told Ellen Terry, '. . . after the silly visionary fashion-ridden theatres.' But that had been at the start of his vestry duties. An almanac Shaw kept in the early spring of 1898 shows under what strain this municipal work, with its hours of talk (no less fashion-ridden than the theatre) 'about our dignity & respectability', was beginning to place him. 'Vestry beyond all endurance,' he recorded on 30 March.

Shaw was to use his experience in local politics as raw material for his plays. Of *Man and Superman* he wrote: 'The mornings I gave to it were followed by afternoons & evenings spent in the committee rooms of a London Borough Council, fighting questions of drainage, paving, lighting, rates, clerk's salaries.' Such occupation, he maintained, had enabled him to create realistic dramas so unrecognized in the fashionable London theatre that critics believed them to be fantastical – in fact not plays at all. But what are the picturesque tramps of the Sierra Nevada doing at the opening of 'Don Juan in Hell' but holding a St Pancras Vestry meeting? Who are the municipal characters in *Getting Married* but the aldermen and borough councillors with whom Shaw had sat those long unventilated hours? And where do the conflicting opinions of the medical specialists in *The Doctor's Dilemma* come from but the Health Sub-Committee? All this he took from St Pancras; and if he gave back no dramatic triumphs of municipal legislation, he presented it with a theatre of entertainment.

After half a dozen years, Shaw concluded that the theatre, after all, was a vehicle for social and cultural change better suited to his abilities. Shortly before his fiftieth year, he 'faded out of vestrydom having,' he wrote, 'more important work'.

In a speech supporting Alderman Matthews as Mayor of St Pancras, Shaw gave an oblique notice of his retirement from local politics, in the parentheses of which we may hear that 'universal laughter' drowning Tanner's words at the end of *Man and Superman*.

'Councillor G. Bernard Shaw was glad, speaking from the Progressive part of the chamber, to support the nomination of Alderman Matthews, although it was difficult for them to realize the extent of his (the speaker's) self-sacrifice in taking that course (laughter) . . . He regarded him as a respectable gentleman (laughter), with little to say and with no political opinions whatever (much laughter). He never was more astonished than when Mr Matthews was out of the chair, because then he found him an active politician with a great deal to say for himself (laughter). In the chair he was most admirable and orderly, out of it he was the most disorderly man he had ever met (laughter). His (the speaker's) self-sacrifice he told them was very great, because he wanted to be the man for Mayor (laughter). He had looked forward to the time very fondly when he would find his life crowned by becoming Mayor of St Pancras (laughter). He had carefully calculated the number of years it would take him to get it, and came to the conclusion that when all the Aldermen of the present Council, all the chairmen of the old Vestry, and some of the more prominent Councillors, had their turn, that the number of years would be 22 (laughter). That was the prospect before him (laughter), and thus it would come to pass that in the year 1924 an old man, with white hair, dim of sight, and hard of hearing, would be elected Mayor of St Pancras and would pass up the Council chamber to the chair amid encouraging cries of 'Good old Shaw!' and sympathetic murmurs of 'Poor old chap!' (laughter). Having said that, he had now to say that nobody supported the nomination of Alderman Matthews more heartily than himself (applause) . . . He (the speaker) had spent the greater part of the preceding day with Sir James Hoyle, the Lord Mayor of Manchester, who like their out-going Mayor, Councillor Barnes, had become a distinguished public man in connection with education. They had a technical school in connection with the City Council of Manchester . . . on the school was spent 30,000 pounds a year out of the rates. The population was not more than twice as large as St Pancras, where they had not the courage to make sufficient rates to cover their liabilities. As time went on he hoped their ideals would expand, and instead of trying to resist the County Council they should enter into competition with it, and try as far as they could to take this part of London off their hands. In the name of the Progressives he supported the nomination from that intellectual part of the Council chamber (laughter and applause).'

2

COURTSHIP DANCES

His sensuality has all drifted into sexual vanity – delight in being the candle to the moths – with a dash of intellectual curiosity to give flavour to his tickled vanity. And he is mistaken if he thinks that it does not affect his artistic work. His incompleteness as a thinker, his shallow and vulgar view of many human relationships . . . all these defects come largely from the flippant and worthless self-complacency brought about by the worship of rather second-rate women . . . Whether I like him, admire him or despise him most I do not know.

The Diary of Beatrice Webb (8 May 1897)

If Shaw could settle down to marriage as she and Sidney had done,

Beatrice Webb felt certain she would come to like him better. Already, almost in spite of himself, she was beginning to see 'a sort of affectionateness' beneath his layer of vanity. He was so extraordinarily good-natured, spending days over Sidney's and her *Industrial Democracy* and *Problems of Modern Industry*. His method, which turned everything inside out to see whether the other side wouldn't do as well, was genuinely interesting. 'If only he would concentrate his really brilliant intellect on some consecutive thought.'

Shaw was seeing a good deal of the Webbs in the mid-1890s. But this was different from his previous triangular relationships. He could not flirt with Beatrice and retain his friendship with Sidney; and so he could not flirt. He felt painfully excluded watching them petting each other as if, he noted, they were still honeymooning. 'I – I, George Bernard Shaw – have actually suffered from something which in anyone else I should call unhappiness.' His body ached for 'a moment of really sacred intimacy'. He was physically attracted to Beatrice and sensed that she found him attractive, in much the same hostile way as Judith Anderson in *The Devil's Disciple* is unconsciously drawn to Dick Dudgeon. Feeling her embarrassment, her antipathy, he also felt the strain of all that was unspoken between them rising to 'a perfectly devilish intensity'.

What he was witnessing in the Webbs' marriage was the merging of passion into a shared obsession for work. That was a marriage he could understand. But could he ever make such a partnership for himself? Beatrice decided to find out.

Bertha Newcombe looked a good candidate. That she was Fabian was essential; that she was 'lady-like' no disadvantage; and that she was 'not wholly inartistic' an unlooked-for bonus. She was in her thirties and, despite her aquiline features, thin lips and a figure that put Beatrice in mind of a wizened child, not perhaps lacking absolutely in all attraction. At least she was quite smartly turned out, *petite* and dark, with neat, heavily fringed black hair. And she was devoted to Shaw.

He had sat to Bertha for his portrait as early as 1892. She had painted him as the platform spellbinder, full-length, hand-on-hip, his mouth slightly open as if uttering one of his formidable ripostes, his red-gold hair and Irish blue eyes adding to the impression of easy confidence – 'a powerful picture,' Beatrice decided, 'in which the love of the woman had given genius to the artist'.

She had painted him as a spellbinder, then fallen under his spell. Later, while he was writing *The Man of Destiny*, lying in a field with his fountain pen and a notebook, she painted him again: *A Snake in the Grass*. He had not deceived her, but he had bewitched her. He was so easy, delightful; almost intimate, though not quite. Not understanding him, she complained that he did not understand her, and doubted whether he had the gift of sympathetic penetration into any woman's nature.

He seems to have liked her, but was protected from deeper involvement by her obvious obsession with him. It was an obsession he helped to rouse. He had told her of his adoration for Ellen Terry and introduced her to Janet Achurch – 'the wonderful woman who absorbed Shaw's leisure to an extent of which I was only half-conscious'. He also joked about Beatrice Webb's zeal to see him married. Though he felt the power and pleasure of love, he was determined never to repeat his experiences with Jenny Patterson.

Bertha sensed the latent passion that Jenny Patterson had aroused in him, but she could not reach it herself. Her love awoke his apprehensions. 'The sight of a woman deeply in love with him annoyed him,' Bertha commented.

'Unfortunately on my side there was a deep feeling most injudiciously displayed . . . I realize how exasperating it must have been to him. He had decided I think on a line of honourable conduct – honourable to his thinking. He kept strictly to the letter of it while allowing himself every opportunity of transgressing the spirit. Frequent talking, talking, talking of the pros and cons of marriage, even to my prospects of money or the want of it, his dislike of the sexual relation & so on, would create an atmosphere of love-making without any need for caresses and endearments.'

What she did not see was that his talk was a method of testing her strength. Everyone was recommending him to marry Bertha. But were they really well-matched? If he married it must be to someone whose love was threaded with shared interests. Bertha and he could never be useful partners like the Webbs. 'She ought to marry someone else,' he told Janet.

'She is only wasting her affections on me. I give her nothing; and I do not even take everything – in fact I dont take anything, which makes her most miserable . . . she would like to tie me like a pet dog to the leg of her easel & have me always to make love to her when she is tired of painting . . . I wish somebody could come along & marry her before she worries herself into a state of brokenheartedness.'

Shaw's campaign to steer Bertha away from 'this lunacy of hers' employed every means except one: he could not absent himself from her infelicity. 'Heavens! I had forgotten you – totally forgotten you,' he reminded her. He would not let her alone. In desperation she wrote to

Beatrice who, on Shaw's instructions, had stopped inviting them together to the Fabian countryside. For five years Bertha had been loyally devoted to Shaw. She had endured rumours of flirtations, largely because she knew that Beatrice was counselling him to marry her. Now she was dismayed to hear that Beatrice was encouraging him to marry someone else. Why?

Beatrice came to the dark wainscoted studio in Cheyne Walk to give her answer. So long as there had seemed a chance of marriage she had welcomed her as Shaw's prospective wife. But now she realized he would never marry her she had backed out of the affair. As Beatrice proceeded with her explanation, Bertha's small face seemed to shrink; and, remembering perhaps her own pain over Chamberlain, Beatrice suddenly raged against Shaw. 'You are well out of it, Miss Newcombe,' she said. ' . . . You know my opinion of him – as a friend and a colleague, as a critic and literary worker, there are few men for whom I have so warm a liking – but in his relations with women he is vulgar – if not worse.'

'It is so horribly lonely,' Bertha answered. 'I daresay it is more peaceful than being kept on the rack – but it is like the peace of death.'

Partly because of the inconclusive nature of their romance, Bertha was never at peace over Shaw. She remained at Cheyne Walk and never married. By 1909, having taken the post of Honorary Secretary of the Civic and Dramatic Guild, she found herself responsible for the private production of his *Press Cuttings*. They met; he read her this 'ghastly absurdity', then went home to write her a letter.

'I expected to find a broken hearted, prematurely aged woman: I found an exceedingly smart lady, not an hour older, noting with a triumphant gleam in her eye my white hairs and lined face. When I think that I allowed those brutal letters to hurt me – ME – Bernard Shaw!! Are you not ashamed?'

But Shaw's teasing, even when intended to be supportive, never amused Bertha. The following month they were quarrelling and she was calling him a 'villain'.

'It is far better that I should again efface myself for another 11 years. Possibly we may all die before then . . . Do you still continue to think of yourself as an idol for adoring women? That idol was shattered for me years ago – – – Inadvertently when you mention the care that has been taken of you, you touch upon the lasting grievance.'

And her grievance did last. A World War came and went. Bertha was approaching sixty, approaching seventy; and still it lasted. 'B[ertha] *wont* accept the situation,' Shaw protested to Charrington, who had taken the part of go-between, ' . . . [it] is beyond human patience.' He tried to present himself as unappealing, but could not resist the paradoxical flourish, the shattering joke – then would recover himself, too late. 'I am still the same writing speaking machine you know of old,' he assured her in 1922.

'I am in my 66th year; my hair is white, and I am as heartless a brute as ever . . . women adore me more, and are less ashamed of it than when you painted The Snake in the Grass. Hearts can be heard breaking in all directions like china in the hands of a clumsy housemaid . . . You have my books – the best of me.'

It was not enough, the shattered idol and the broken china. From such debris it had once seemed possible to piece together something valuable. But their correspondence, reviving past expectations, tormented Bertha with these ruined images, and much of it she destroyed. 'Your memories terrify me,' Shaw wrote to her in 1925. 'Thank God there will be no letters.'

That was their future.

So Beatrice Webb rose to go. 'Come and see me,' she told Bertha, ' – someday.' There seemed nothing else to say. She kissed her on the forehead and escaped downstairs. 'I doubt,' she confided in her diary, 'whether Bernard Shaw could be induced to marry.'

*

But it was Beatrice who had inadvertently put an end to Shaw's interest in Bertha. At a luncheon party in the early autumn of 1895 she and Sidney had met an Irish lady named Charlotte Payne-Townshend, 'a large graceful woman with masses of chocolate brown hair,' Beatrice later described her. 'She dresses well, in flowing white evening robes she approaches beauty. At moments she is plain.

'By temperament she is an anarchist, feeling any regulation or rule intolerable, a tendency which has been exaggerated by her irresponsible wealth. She is romantic but thinks herself cynical. She is a Socialist and a Radical, not because she understands the Collectivist standpoint, but because she is by nature a rebel . . . She is fond of men and impatient of most women, bitterly resents her enforced celibacy but thinks she could not tolerate the matter-of-fact side of marriage. Sweet tempered, sympathetic and genuinely anxious to increase the world's enjoyment and diminish the world's pain.'

Beatrice interested Charlotte in the London School of Economics, and was rewarded with a subscription of £1,000 for the library and the endowment of a woman's scholarship. Charlotte also agreed, at a rent and service charge of £300 a year, to take rooms on the two upper floors above the School when, in October 1896, it moved to 10 Adelphi Terrace. Beatrice soon began to absorb her 'into our little set of comrades', nominating her for the Fabian Society, with a note to the secretary that the amount of her cheque testified to the degree of her convictions.

Shaw was introduced to her on 29 January 1896. She noted the event without comment; and he did not go two months later to her At Home at LSE. But he was apparently 'prepared to take my part' in a plan Beatrice had formed to marry Charlotte off to Graham Wallas. In the late summer of 1896 the Webbs rented a Spartan rectory at the village of Stratford St Andrew in Suffolk; and Wallas and Charlotte were invited. Shaw was there as a matter of course. Everything seemed in train for a satisfactory Fabian match.

But Wallas, who left early, arrived four days late; and in those four days the pantomime ostrich spread before Charlotte his most brilliant plumage. They were constant companions, pedaling round the country all day, sitting up late at night talking. 'They are, I gather from him, on very confidential terms,' Beatrice noted in her diary, 'and have "explained" their relative positions . . . I am somewhat uneasy.'

*

'I had a perfectly hellish childhood and youth . . .' There was much in what Charlotte said about herself to interest Shaw. She was six months younger than he and her family came from County Cork; at least her father's did. Horace Townsend had been 'a marvel of patience'. Charlotte, who 'was always attracted to men of action', longed for him to assert himself. It was astonishing how his gentleness provoked everyone – especially his wife, a domineering English lady fretted by social ambitions. She got hold of him, hyphenated and then aspirated his name, dug him up from Rosscarbery. If only he had quelled her. But she 'could not bear opposition; if it was offered she either became quite violent or she cried.'

Early in February 1885 Horace decided to die. There was nothing much wrong with him and he was comparatively young. But his patience had given out, and for a polite man there was nothing else to do.

His wife was incredulous, but Charlotte understood. She understood that her mother had killed him – not legally, of course, but in fact. By everything she now did she sought to avenge his death. Her mother had one ambition left: to see her two daughters brilliantly married. Charlotte refused to give her mother that satisfaction. 'Even in my earliest years I had determined I would never marry.'

Mother and daughter were determined women. In a furious dance they struggled across Europe, always in 'the best circles' and seldom anywhere for more than a week. Inevitably Charlotte blundered into offers of marriage. J. S. Black proposed in 'as few words as I can' in a note from his club; Count Sponnek declared himself in South Kensington and, being rebuffed, rushed off in an emotional state to St Petersburg; Finch Hutton sent her the skin of a bear shot in Wyoming and twelve dressed beaver skins: but 'I cannot marry you,' Charlotte replied; Herbert Oakley, a barrister, died before completing his case; the wife of Arthur Smith-Barry also died, leaving Arthur Smith-Barry wondering whether Charlotte would take her place. She didn't. And there were others. Majors and Generals and Major-Generals. Mrs Payne-Townshend watched them all, her hopes pumping up and down. The hatred between the two women was by now 'almost a tangible thing'. For the first time in her life Mrs Payne-Townshend was not going to get her own way. She felt ill. A doctor was called but he could find nothing wrong with her except 'nerves'. A few days later she died. 'It is really awful to think how glad I was,' Charlotte admitted.

She was thirty-four and at last free. For the first time in her life she allowed herself to fall in love. Dr Axel Munthe, hypnotist and story-teller, caught her in the immense web of his vanity and left her there. Extricating herself had been painful, and it was then that she had flown into the Webbs' parlour.

Graham Wallas arrived, bored Charlotte, then left. Shaw and she resumed their companionship.

'If the walls of this simple-minded rectory could only describe the games they have witnessed, the parson would move, horror-stricken, to another house,' he wrote to Janet Achurch.

'We have made many bicycling expeditions together *à deux*. Also, instead of going to bed at ten, we go out and stroll about among the trees for a while. She, being also Irish, does not succumb to my arts as the unsuspecting and literal Englishwoman does; but we get on together all the better, repairing bicycles, talking philosophy and religion and Shaw table talk, or, when we are in a mischievous or sentimental humor, philandering shamelessly and outrageously. Such is life at Stratford St Andrew.'

The loneliness and irritation Shaw had felt at watching the Webbs caressing each other evaporated. Falling out of love with actresses, he was suddenly able to make them an audience for his own romantic play-acting opposite this 'Irish lady with the light green eyes and the million of money'. 'I am going to refresh my heart by falling in love with her,' he announced to Ellen Terry, ' . . . but, mind, only with her, not with the million; so someone else must marry her if she can stand him after me.' It *was* play-acting. What else could it be? They were genuinely fond of each other, but Charlotte was no slave to romance and 'she doesnt really *love* me'. Kissing in the evening among the trees was very pleasant, but 'She knows the value of her unencumbered independence, having suffered a good deal from family bonds & conventionality before the death of her mother & the marriage of her sister left her free,' Shaw confided to Ellen Terry. 'The idea of tying herself up again by a marriage before she knows anything – before she has exploited her freedom & money power to the utmost – seems to her intellect to be unbearably foolish.'

He liked her honesty; he liked her involvement with the political side of his life; and he liked her independence. 'You don't love me the least bit in the world,' he informed her. 'But I am all the more grateful.'

Watching them uneasily over these weeks at Stratford St Andrew, Beatrice reached a different conclusion. 'These warmhearted unmarried women of a certain age are audacious and almost childishly reckless of consequences.'

*

On 17 September, Shaw and Charlotte, Sidney and Beatrice, ascended their machines and wheeled off back to London, which they reached in pouring rain four days later. Shaw was immediately engulfed in business. There was time for only the most tantalizing note to Charlotte who missed him and rather miserably told him so. 'You look as if you had returned to your old amusement of eating your heart,' he reproved her, remembering Axel Munthe. ' . . . you must get something to do: I have a mind to go upstairs & shake you, only then I should lose my train.'

He was determined that she must remain strong. 'Don't fall in love: be your own, not mine or anyone else's.

'From the moment that you can't do without me, you're lost, like Bertha. Never fear: if we want one another we shall find it out. All I know is that you made the autumn very happy, and that I shall always be fond of you for that. About the future . . . let us do what lies to our hands & wait for events. My dearest!'

Fearing that she was falling in love with him, Charlotte suddenly left for Ireland. Shaw felt nonplussed: he was unused to people taking his advice. The kick of his disappointment took him aback. She had surpassed his expectations. He began by welcoming her journey ('I had rather you were well a thousand miles away than ill in my wretched arms'), then complained of her removal ('oh for ten minutes peace in the moonlight at Stratford! . . . keep me deep in your heart . . . I wish I were with you among those hills'). But his eloquence and even his teasing seemed to lose itself in her absence.

On the day before Charlotte's return from Ireland, he sent her an exactly truthful letter. 'I will contrive to see you somehow, at all hazards,' he wrote: 'I *must*; and that "must" which "rather alarms" you, TERRIFIES me.

'If it were possible to run away – if it would do any good – I'd do it; so mortally afraid am I that my trifling & lying and ingrained treachery and levity with women are going to make you miserable when my whole sane desire is to make you hap – I mean strong and self possessed and tranquil. However, we must talk about it . . . let's meet, meet, meet, meet, meet: bless me! how I should like to see you again for pure *liking*; for there is something between us . . .'

He saw her the night she returned. For hours beforehand he had felt curiously agitated. Then they were together and 'I really was happy . . . I am satisfied, satisfied, satisfied deep in my heart.' He had found with Charlotte a real friendliness mixed with some sexual interest. But that sexual interest put a faint shadow over his happiness. 'I wish there was nothing to look forward to,' he wrote to her later that night, 'nothing to covet, nothing to gain.' What he actually feared was that there was something to lose. Charlotte, he had told Ellen Terry, 'knows that what she lacks is physical experience, and that without it she will be in ten years time an old maid'. But he could not stay away from Adelphi Terrace. He came – 'and now, dear Ellen,' he confided, 'she sleeps like a child, and her arms will be plump, and she is a free woman, and it has not cost her half a farthing, and she has fancied herself in love, and known secretly that she was only taking a prescription, and been relieved to find the lover at last laughing at her & reading her thoughts and confessing himself a mere bottle of nerve medicine, and riding gaily off'.

Often before Shaw had implored women to *use* him. 'All my love affairs end tragically because the women *can't* use me.' Charlotte had used him and 'in the blackest depths' he felt robbed of 'that most blessed of things – unsatisfied desire'. From this desire he conceived the make-believe of his plays. Now, he told Charlotte, 'I have squandered on you all the material out of which my illusions are made'. Once again Charlotte had confounded his expectations. Prim and socially self-effacing, she could take off her inhibitions once she selected a man for intimacy. It was one of those 'volcanic tendencies' Beatrice had detected in her.

Charlotte had an apprehension of sexual intercourse, deriving from what Shaw later described as 'a morbid horror of maternity'. She was in her fortieth year and 'there was never any question of breeding'. Over the next eighteen months they seem to have found together a habit of careful sexual experience, reducing for her the risk of conception and preserving for him his subliminal illusions. To such muted sexuality Shaw could give assent. 'ALL CLEAR NOW YES A THOUSAND TIMES,' he had cabled Charlotte in October. That autumn too he started to terminate his relationship with Bertha Newcombe; blow away Ellen Terry's daydreams of becoming his mother-in-law; renounce retrospectively 'spiritual intercourse' with Florence Farr; and tell Janet Achurch that her maternity had made her 'stark raving mad'. Then, turning back to Charlotte he resumed his intrepid *doubles entendres*: 'Cold much worse – fatal consummation highly probable. Shall see you tonight . . . What an exacting woman you are! Is this freedom?'

*

Charlotte soon made herself almost indispensable to Shaw. She learnt to read his shorthand and to type, took dictation and helped him prepare his plays for the press. Her flat above the London School of Economics became 'very convenient for me' – more convenient than Fitzroy Square. There was no question of turning up there at any time in the casual way he had dropped in on Jenny Patterson, Janet Achurch, Florence Farr and others. He would invite her to theatres and picture galleries; and she invited him to lunch or dinner, seeing to it that her cook became expert in vegetarian dishes. There were interruptions: his migraines, her neuralgia; his work, her journeys. And there was a momentary crisis when she threatened to buy a poodle – which drew from him the panicky suggestion that she 'have (or hire) a baby' instead. In a spirit of compromise she attended lectures at the School of Medicine for Women.

Between April and June 1897 Charlotte shared with Sidney and Beatrice the expenses of a pretty cottage called Lotus on the North Downs, near Dorking. Shaw went down as frequently as he could. But he had less time than at Stratford the previous year – 'tired and careworn' he described himself. But the Webbs were in excellent working form. The sun streamed through the dancing leaves and they revelled, almost childlike with excitement, in the economic characteristics of Trade Unionism; while Charlotte sat upstairs miserably typewriting *Plays Unpleasant*, and the playwright himself strode the garden forming his Dramatic Opinions. Beatrice watched with concern. It was obvious that Charlotte was deeply attached to Shaw, but 'I see no sign on his side of the growth of any genuine and steadfast affection,' she noted.

Though she found everything 'very interesting', Charlotte could take only a modest part in what Shaw called 'our eternal political shop'. On Sundays they enlisted a stream of visitors – young radicals, mostly: William Pember Reeves and his wife Maud; Bertrand and Alys Russell; Herbert Samuel; Charles Trevelyan; Graham Wallas – and Charlotte sometimes felt excluded. She hung on, but her face showed at times 'a blank haggard look'. Beatrice felt that Shaw must share her own irritation at Charlotte's lack of purpose. 'If she would set to – and do even the smallest and least considerable task of intellectual work – I believe she could retain his interest and perhaps develop his feeling for her.'

Charlotte struggled to make an occupation out of Shaw's work. On Sundays in London she had made her way to the dock gates and street corners to hear him speak. But these experiences mortified her. She hated the roughness of the crowds. 'It appears that my demagogic denunciations of the idle rich – my demands for taxation of unearned incomes – lacerate her conscience; for she has great possessions. What am I to do: she won't stay away; and I can't talk Primrose League. Was there ever such a situation?'

Although the author of *The Philanderer* believed it was better for 'two people who do not mean to devote themselves to a regular domestic, nursery career to maintain a clandestine connection than to run the risks of marriage', Charlotte was surprised to find that his advice to women was to 'insist on marriage, and refuse to compromise themselves with any man on cheaper terms'. He considered the status of a married woman as 'almost indispensable under existing circumstances to a woman's fullest possible freedom.

'In short, I prescribed marriage for women, and refused it for myself. I upset her ideas in many directions; for she was prepared for conventional unconventionality, but not for a criticism of it as severe as its own criticism of conventionality.'

Within this argument seems to lie the biological politics that were to vitalize *Man and Superman*. In fact the philosophy of this play was one of the 'illusions' that Shaw substituted for actual experience. For Charlotte did not want marriage in order to have children; she was beginning to want it as a partnership that, though different from the Webbs', would be no less satisfactory. At that level Shaw had little to say. Eventually she began to run out of patience with him.

Charlotte had surprised Shaw before by taking his advice. Now, she attempted to do so again. If it was her job to marry, he would not object to her making the proposal. This it seems is what she attempted to do in the second week of July 1897. Shaw described the scene as 'a sort of earthquake'. He received the golden moment, he told Ellen Terry, 'with shuddering horror & wildly asked the fare to Australia'. This description, given a fortnight after the event, is a good example of the replacement of 'Shaw Limited' by 'G.B.S.'. Pain, regret, tenderness are dissolved in the triumphant playing of a Shavian scherzo. 'I have an iron ring round my chest, which tightens and grips my heart when I remember that you are perhaps still tormented,' he wrote to her the day after the proposal.

'Loosen it, oh ever dear to me, by a word to say that you slept well and have never been better than today. Or else lend me my fare to Australia, to Siberia, to the mountains of the moon, to any place where I can torment nobody but myself. I am sorry – not vainly sorry; for I have done a good morning's work, but painfully, wistfully, affectionately sorry that you were hurt; but if you had seen my mind you would not have been hurt . . . Write me something happy, but only a few words, and don't sit down to *think* over them.'

She was rich, he was poor. Marriage for property, he had written, was prostitution; to marry her would be the act of an adventurer. This financial scruple had the advantage of being kindly; it was not a *personal* rejection. Yet it was a prevarication, and did not protect Charlotte from being 'inexpressibly taken aback'. It was absurd for him to turn his back on a richer woman simply because people might regard him as a fortune-hunter.

Politically, Shaw had put his faith in the power of words to inspire action. But in his personal life he employed words to avoid taking action. His letters to Ellen Terry and others had developed into an oblique device for this avoidance. He talked himself out of emotional danger. Advancing to the front of the stage he put his case mockingly to the audience:

'I will put an end to it all by marrying. Do you know a reasonably healthy woman of about sixty, accustomed to plain vegetarian cookery, and able to read & write enough to forward letters when her husband is away, but otherwise uneducated? Must be plain featured, and of an easy, unjealous temperament. No relatives, if possible. Must not be a lady. One who has never been in a theatre preferred. Separate rooms.'

Such a monologue, though it floods the auditorium with amusement, does not advance the event-plot of the play. And does it convince? At least one member of his audience with a shrewd knowledge of such performances thought not. 'Well,' Ellen Terry responded, 'you two will marry.'

*

Superficially the rupture between Shaw and Charlotte healed quickly. But added pressure was now being placed on him to marry. Webb had uncharacteristically given him a talking to; and then, at the end of July, Graham Wallas unexpectedly announced his own engagement to a high-principled short-story writer, Ada Radford. With this 'desertion' Shaw was to become the only unmarried member of the Fabian Old Gang.

That August he had arranged to stay at Argoed with Charlotte and the Webbs. He was more deeply exhausted than ever – too tired to fix up the hammocks Charlotte had brought, too tired to draw rein from writing even for a day. The days flew past, 'like the telegraph poles on a railway journey', and he worked on. But 'I am in the most disagreeable humor possible,' he complained to Florence Farr. His 'victory' over Charlotte had disappointed him. They lived an irreproachable life, the writing machine and the typist, in the bosom of the Webb family. It was apparently everything he had wanted. Yet a dialogue began to develop between G.B.S. and Shaw Limited in his correspondence.

'I am fond of women (one in a thousand, say); but I am in earnest about quite other things. To most women one man and one lifetime make a world. I require whole populations and historical epochs to engage my interests seriously . . . love is only diversion and recreation to me.'

Shaw Limited sees G.B.S. as a bragging emotional bankrupt playing timidly with the serious things of life and dealing seriously with the plays. His appeal to the audience carries a far-off echo of Sonny's voice:

'It is not the small things that women miss in me, but the big things. My pockets are always full of the small change of love-making; but it is magic money, not real money.'

For his mother's elopement with Vandeleur Lee, G.B.S. had substituted an economic for the emotional necessity; and he had used a financial argument to trick himself out of marrying Charlotte. So now Shaw Limited brings a money metaphor to expose the unreality of G.B.S. If only Charlotte had had the confidence to tear up that ridiculous Shavian balance sheet. Instead, unknown to Shaw, she had committed herself to him on the very terms by which he had rejected her, making a will that (barring a bequest to a cousin) left him her entire fortune.

But after their return to London at the end of August, Charlotte's behaviour changed. Suddenly she seemed less anxious to be with Shaw. Early in October she absconded to Leicester to visit her sister, Mary Cholmondeley who, Shaw knew, disliked him. 'Where am I to spend my evenings?' he complained. Charlotte returned, but suddenly veered off again back to her sister. 'It is most inconvenient having Adelphi Terrace shut up,' he pointed out. 'I have nowhere to go, nobody to talk to.' When Charlotte returned again, she was curiously unavailable. When he called one afternoon he was told by the maid that Charlotte was out. She always seemed to be 'out'. But three days later, on his way to dine at the Metropole, he suddenly found 'to my astonishment my legs walked off with me through the railway arches to Adelphi Terrace', where he saw the lights on in Charlotte's bedroom, signalling (he assumed) *her* unhappiness; but hardly had he written triumphantly to tell her so than she had disappeared to Paris. 'I miss you in lots of ways,' he wrote. ' . . . I wish you could stay in Paris & that I could get there in quarter of an hour. I feel that you are much better & brighter there; but it is damnably inconvenient to have you out of my reach.'

Charlotte came back early in November – but not to London. Instead she went straight to Hertfordshire to stay with some rich Fabian friends, Robert and 'Lion' Phillimore. This was too much for Shaw who pursued her on his bicycle and, travelling back at night, took one of his formidable tosses down a hill. He put the accident to instant use in an article for the *Saturday Review*, 'On Pleasure Bent'. All the same, Charlotte did not return at once.

When she did get back to London, he was almost cumbersomely tactful. 'I shall not intrude on my secretary tomorrow. If she desires to resume her duties, doubtless she will come to me.' A week later the tone was brisker: 'Secretary required tomorrow, not later than eleven.' But, for Charlotte, typing and shorthand had been a means to an end that seemed to be fading. She was not amused by his evasive joking. 'Charlotte can not only resist jokes, but dislikes them,' Shaw later explained to Pinero. 'Hence she was not seduced, as you would have been, by my humorous aberrations.' He made ready for Charlotte's arrival next morning to continue her secretarial work. He swept the hearth and made the fire; he laid out Charlotte's shawl and footwarmer; and then he waited – and she did not come. She had gone to Dieppe! 'What do you mean by this inconceivable conduct?' he demanded. 'Do you forsake *all* your duties . . . Must I also go back to writing my own articles, and wasting half hours between

the sentences with long trains of reflection? Not a word: not a sign! . . .
Are there no stamps? has the post been abolished? have all the channel
steamers foundered?'

He was genuinely put out. So, after making fun of himself, he turned
on Charlotte and accused her of everything she would most dislike. 'Go,
then, ungrateful wretch,' he wrote, 'have your heart's desire:

'find a Master – one who will spend your money, and rule in your house,
and order your servants about, and forbid you to ride in hansoms because
it's unladylike, and remind you that the honor of his name is in your
keeping, and . . . consummate his marriage in the church lest the housemaid should regard his proceedings as clandestine. Protect yourself for
ever from freedom, independence, love, unfettered communion with the
choice spirits of your day . . . But at least tell me when youre *not* coming;
and say whether I am to get a new secretary or not.

G.B.S.'

This letter points to one of Charlotte's hidden attractions for Shaw:
she was a member of the same family as the 'terribly respectable' land
agents, Uniacke Townshend, that had employed him as an office boy
twenty-five years ago in Dublin. His attitude seems divided: the socialist
responding ironically, the Irishman romantically to this fact. He knew
that, though the Irish might grudgingly admit him to be (in Edith Somerville's words) 'distinctly somebody in a literary way', it was assumed that
socially 'he can't be a gentleman'. Marriage to Charlotte would shock
some of those who had looked down on the office boy and who (if he ever
returned to Ireland) would have to open their doors to him. Such things
would of course never influence him; but it was pleasant to speculate on
them.

Though he repeatedly insisted on the independence of women, Shaw
continued to make them dependent on him. He excited interest: then ran.
But Charlotte, who had money and the habit of travel, ran first and
ran further. She was emotionally dependent but financially independent.
Such manoeuvres gave Shaw the appearance of pursuing her.

The New Year bristled with good intentions. Charlotte was particularly
attentive, rubbing vaseline on his bicycle wounds and encouraging him to
use Adelphi Terrace as office and convalescent station. Shaw struggled
to be reasonable.

That March 1898, the Webbs planned to be off on a tour round
America and the Antipodes, 'seeing Anglo-Saxon democracy', and they
invited Charlotte to go with them. 'If she does,' Shaw told Ellen Terry,
'she will be away for about a year, just time enough for a new love affair.'

Perhaps because she felt the danger of this herself, Charlotte did not take up the Webbs' invitation, but accepted instead an offer from Lion Phillimore to go for seven weeks to Rome. 'Charlotte deserts me at 11,' Shaw noted in his almanac. He felt 'quite desperate' and put it down to 'lack of exercise'. His friend Wallas was away with his new wife; Sydney Olivier had decided to go to the United States; his audience of actresses had dispersed and he was alone.

3

A TERRIBLE ADVENTURE

> By the way, would you advise me to get married?
>
> Shaw to Henry Arthur Jones (20 May 1898)

'Sisterless men are always afraid of women,' Shaw was to write; yet his own fears proceeded from the women in his family. He had seen their contempt for men – for his father and himself, even for Vandeleur Lee once his usefulness was exhausted.

On 25 November 1886 his sister Lucy had brought home a young man called Harry Butterfield to meet her mother. The purpose of this introduction was to announce her engagement – to Harry's brother, Charles, who may have been unavailable that evening because he was having an affair with another woman.

Besides his couple of 'wives', Charles had two names. As 'Cecil Burt' he travelled with a band of wanderers called 'Leslie's No. 1', performing as a cherubic tenor. 'He sang with difficulty,' Shaw remembered. He and Lucy Shaw sang together in Alfred Cellier's popular comedy-opera *Dorothy*, which had opened in London late in 1886. Shaw missed the first night; he also missed their wedding ('did not get to the church until the ceremony was over') and the small wedding party at Fitzroy Square a year later. But (as Corno di Bassetto) he caught up with them at Morton's Theatre, Greenwich, in the autumn of 1889 for the 789th performance of *Dorothy*'s provincial tour. His brother-in-law, Shaw observed, 'originally, I have no doubt, a fine young man ... was evidently counting the days until death should release him from the part'.

Into the description of *Dorothy* he poured his long-standing resentment at having to submit to Lucy's alleged superiority. He knew her mind was commonplace, her talent little more than a trick of facility, her attractions superficial. It had been Lucy whom Bessie had taken with her to London;

and Lucy whom Lee had favoured; and Lucy who had been welcome at some of the London salons where George felt so *gauche*; and again Lucy whom people thought so lovable and entertaining. Great things had been expected of her; great things by the age of thirty-six had led to *Dorothy* at Morton's Theatre, Greenwich.

'She will apparently spend her life in artistic self-murder by induced Dorothitis without a pang of remorse, provided she be praised and paid regularly. Dorothy herself, a beauteous young lady of distinguished mien, with an immense variety of accents ranging from the finest Tunbridge Wells English (for genteel comedy) to the broadest Irish (for repartee and low comedy), sang without the slightest effort and without the slightest point, and was all the more desperately vapid because she suggested artistic gifts wasting in complacent abeyance.'

The impulse behind what Lucy called this 'typically fraternal – Irish fraternal – act' was part of the Shaw family feeling from which Lucy wanted to escape. 'She was more popular outside the family than inside it,' her cousin Judy Gillmore explained, 'and . . . she preferred people who would look up to her to those who would stand up to her.' Like her brother, Lucy had largely substituted theatre for home life; like him too she tried to replace her own family with another. Shaw had made use of the Fabians; Lucy used her husband's relatives. It was these relatives she had married. That was the significance of announcing her engagement in the presence of her future brother-in-law. Both George and Lucy, having grown up in a matriarchal family, instinctively cast about for a mother elsewhere.

Charles Butterfield was not an immediately attractive man. But he had an exceptional mother who knitted Lucy into the pattern of the Butterfield family with its comforting social world in the suburbs of Denmark Hill. But after Mrs Butterfield died, Lucy had drifted back to Fitzroy Square. 'LOVE,' she wrote, ' . . . is dead sea fruit, whether it is parental, fraternal or marital, and anyone who sacrifices their all on its altar plays a game that is lost before it is begun . . . it's a damnable world.' She seemed little more now than a figure of derision to her mother. Much of the money Shaw squeezed out from journalism went towards the maintenance of this unhappy household, which included Bessie's hunchback sister, Kate Gurly (whose 'state of unparalleled inclination' preceded her final plunge into Roman Catholicism), and from time to time her brother Walter Gurly, who would arrive at Fitzroy Square paralytically drunk, threatening to leave his nephew his heavily mortgaged Carlow property.

From this 'damnable world', with planchette and ouija, Shaw's mother had ridden away to parlay with the dead. She found them more congenial company than the living. First there was her favourite child Yuppy; and even her husband and her father seemed faintly less intolerable since their deaths. But on the whole she preferred chatting with people she had never known, the more remote the better, eventually settling for intercourse with a sage who had visited the earth in 6000 BC.

Bessie's spiritualism was an embarrassment to her son: '[I] held my tongue because I did not like to say anything that could worry my mother.' In his diary he had privately dismissed spiritualism as a 'paltry fraud'. At a session of spirit-rapping and table-turning with Belfort Bax and H. W. Massingham, he had cheated from the first and 'caused the spirits to rap out long stories, lift the table into the air, and finally drink tumblers of whisky and water, to the complete bewilderment of Bax . . . I have not laughed so much for years.' He released some of this laughter anonymously into the *Pall Mall Gazette*.

'Every Englishman believes that he is entitled to a ghost after death to compensate him for the loss of his body, and to enable him to haunt anybody that may have murdered or otherwise ill-used him in the days when he was solid.'

Bessie's wishful writings appeared like a non-malignant growth in an otherwise healthy body. But the escapist illusions of spiritualism raised in his mind the whole question of the morality of fiction. 'A person who describes events that never happened and persons that never existed is generally classed as a liar – possibly a genial and entertaining liar,' he wrote. 'And what is the business of a novelist if not to describe events that never happened and to repeat conversations that never took place.' To such an uncomfortable conclusion had his failure as a novelist driven him; and his comparative failure as a dramatist was persuading him to look on his plays too as methods of extending his self-deception.

'When we are young our inordinate fondness for theatrical and novel-writing leads us to simulate and describe emotions which we do not feel. Later, when the struggle for existence becomes too serious for such follies, real emotions come to us in battalions; but we take as much trouble to conceal them as we formerly did to affect them . . . [and] Life comes to mean finance.'

He had kept up the appearance of a realist; but who could say whether he too had not been misled by illusions? Asking himself why his mother had chosen to practise such an apparently senseless activity as spirit writings, he added another question: 'Why was I doing essentially the same as a playwright?' And answered: 'I do not know. We both got some satisfaction from it or we would not have done it.'

Lucy had made a brief escape from Fitzroy Square to the United States in 1897, playing in Villiers Stanford's *Shamus O'Brien*. This, the last small success of her career, merged with the first large success of her brother. *The Devil's Disciple* had opened at the Fifth Avenue Theatre on 4 October 1897, running to full houses for sixty-four performances until, early in 1898, Richard Mansfield took it off on a popular Mid-West tour. From this production of *The Devil's Disciple* Shaw earned £2,000 (equivalent to over £100,000 in 1997) and came to be recognized 'as a possible winner in the box office gamble'. It was a turning point of his career. For more than twenty years he had lived from hand to mouth. By the time Charlotte was preparing to return from Rome, he was suddenly in easy circumstances and 'with every reason to believe that things would improve'.

One result of this affluence had been his decision to give up drama criticism. Another result was his decision to write plays again. He chose Shakespeare's birthday, 23 April, on which to compose a Puritan prelude to *Antony and Cleopatra*. 'Snatch up my note book & make a start at last on "Caesar & Cleopatra",' he wrote. 'Lifelike scene in the courtyard of the palace at Alexandria among the bodyguard of Cleopatra. Screamingly amusing . . . [it] is going to save my life.'

Something was needed to save his life, for he was now in his own words 'a fearful wreck'.

*

During Charlotte's absence Shaw had struggled to maintain his self-sufficiency, working until 'I got into a sort of superhuman trance'. He had engaged Henry Salt's wife, Kate, to do his typing and dictation. Now that he was alone, he claimed to be 'no longer unhappy, and no longer happy: I am myself.' Mrs Salt would arrive, carrying a brown paper parcel containing a three-legged stool, some bananas and biscuits. 'We achieve a phenomenal performance with the arrears of correspondence,' Shaw wrote to Charlotte. ' . . . Your memory is totally obliterated . . . This is indeed a secretary.' But it was 'frightful not to be able to kiss your secretary'.

The longer Charlotte remained in Italy, the more unstable Shaw grew. He felt he was growing old and breaking up. 'I want a woman & a sound sleep,' he exclaimed. ' . . . Oh Charlotte, Charlotte: is this a time to be gadding about in Rome!'

He dared not trust his feelings. He missed her; but felt relieved that she was gone, as if a crisis had receded. So there must be two Charlottes, as there had been two Alice Locketts. In her absence, he could plant her neatly in his fantasy world. 'You count that I have lost only one Charlotte,' he wrote to her; 'but I have lost two; and one of the losses is a prodigious relief.

'. . . the terrible Charlotte, the lier-in-wait, the soul hypochondriac, always watching and dragging me into bondage, always planning nice, sensible, comfortable, selfish destruction for me, wincing at every accent of freedom in my voice, so that at last I get the trick of hiding myself from her, hating me & longing for me with the absorbing passion of the spider for the fly. Now that she is gone, I realize for the first time the infernal tyranny of the past year, which left me the licence of the rebel, not the freedom of the man who stands alone. I will have no more of it . . . *That's* the Charlotte I want to see married . . . yet I have her in my dreamland, and sometimes doubt whether the other devil ever had anything to do with her.'

This letter shows the extent to which Shaw had been unable to absorb Charlotte into his private mythology. So solid, yet elusive, she occupied his dreamland but threatened him with everyday experience. His letter seems deliberately hurtful, as if he is provoking her to break it off. But she would not.

To marry, or not to marry: that was the question: and he answered it differently each hour. 'I probably will marry the lady,' he told the Pakenham Beattys that April. But to the mathematician and biologist Karl Pearson he maintained that he was 'as firmly set against such a step as ever I was in my most inveterate youth and bachelordom'. Walking through the park, bicycling into the country: doing anything that awakened him from the oblivion of his work-addiction, exacerbated the dilemma. Charlotte still lingered in Rome, but her companion Lion Phillimore had returned in April and she and her husband invited Shaw to their home for Easter. Once there they started to bully him for his stupidity in not marrying Charlotte. One of the chief delights of married life, they told him, was the avoidance of the pre-nuptial obligation to be constantly paying amorous attentions to one another. Against such a Shavian device, 'I was totally incapable of self-defence'.

The length of Charlotte's Italian visit and the infrequency of her letters to him was not due, as Shaw suggested, to 'some Italian doctor'. Though Dr Axel Munthe was then in Rome, Charlotte had avoided seeing him. She was busy, in Fabian fashion, with a study of the municipal services of the city and could not return to London until she had properly collated her notes. Shaw, who had so often complained about her incapacity for work, could not now complain over the reason for her extended absence. It was as if everyone had learnt the Shavian game, and was playing it against him.

In the middle of April, while lacing one of his shoes too tightly, Shaw pinched his left instep. A week later, when riding his bicycle to see the Beattys, the foot expanded 'to the size of a leg of mutton'. He felt confident of curing it 'with hot water', and had just succeeded when, under stress of theatre reviewing in the evenings and vestry meetings during the day, the foot swelled up 'to the size of a church bell'. Some of his friends suggested 'vegetarian gout'. Walking soon became so excruciating that 'I now simply hop,' he wrote to Charlotte, 'my left foot being no longer of any use'. On 23 April he called in Dr Salisbury Sharpe, Alice Lockett's husband, who told him that his two toe joints had slipped over each other and become inflamed. 'My medical skill is completely vindicated: I have been doing exactly the right thing,' Shaw congratulated himself after the doctor had left. The hot water treatments continued and these were of great benefit to *Caesar and Cleopatra*. 'Finished whole scene of Cleopatra,' he noted in the almanac he was keeping each day and sending to Charlotte, ' . . . quintessence of everything that has most revolted the chivalrous critics Ha! Ha! Julius Caesar as the psychological woman tamer.'

Shaw, as woman tamer, had been letting Charlotte have almost daily reports on his foot with the result that she came 'back from Italy to nurse me'. She left Rome at the end of April. She was due to arrive in London on the evening of 1 May. Shaw limped down Tottenham Court Road, descended at Charing Cross, and went on slowly to Adelphi Terrace. 'With a long gasp of relief, I lay my two-months burden down & ring the bell.' Martha, the parlourmaid, answered the door. Charlotte was not there! He could do nothing but leave her a note of protest and hobble all the way back to Fitzroy Square. 'Wretch, devil, fiend ! . . . Satan's own daughter would have telegraphed.'

Travelling from Naples by sea, Charlotte arrived later that night and replied next day on the back of Shaw's note:

'Yes, I *might* have telegraphed: it was horrid of me. I am a wreck, mental and physical. Such a journey as it was! I don't believe I shall ever get over it.

My dear – and your foot? Shall I go up to you or will you come here and when? Only tell me what you would prefer. Of course I am quite free.

Charlotte'

*

'Come when it is most convenient to you . . . the sooner the better (for the first moment at least).'

She went at once to Fitzroy Square and was appalled. His room was a shipwreck. Correspondence and miscellaneous manuscripts, agitated by his perpetually open window, lay fluttering among the solid debris of cutlery, saucepans, apples, cups of trembling cocoa, plates of half-finished hardening porridge and a drifting surface of smuts and dust. Charlotte could only squeeze in sideways. Unshoe'd, his mobility had 'contracted itself to within hopping distance of my chair'. He could no longer look after himself and no one else there had any interest in him. For over twenty years mother and son had lived under the same roof in London, seldom communicating, and in such conditions that Charlotte's horror turned at once to a hatred of his mother and sister.

Something needed to be done. Charlotte demanded back the post as his secretary – and he refused. Kate Salt, he said, was looking after his secretarial needs very well; she was excellent at dictation and eminently bullyable. He did not want to bully Charlotte. He wanted her to bully him. He did not want a replacement for Mrs Salt but for Mrs Shaw. Charlotte retired to consider how best she might deal with his predicament. His foot looked terrible, and he appeared haggard with strain. Ellen Terry had sent them tickets for a new play at the Lyceum on 5 May, and he 'nearly killed myself' getting in a review on time.

The day after the Lyceum Charlotte suddenly took the initiative, calling at Fitzroy Square and taking Shaw back to Adelphi Terrace for a long talk. There is little record of what they said to each other. Three days later he underwent an operation on his left foot. An anaesthetist arrived at Fitzroy Square at half-past eight in the evening together with nurse Alice Lockett and her physician husband. After coming round from the chloroform, Shaw was told by Dr Sharpe that an abscess had formed on his foot. An attempt had been made to scrape the necrosed bone clean, but until it healed he would be on crutches.

He made this the subject of his penultimate article, 'G.B.S. Vivisected', for the *Saturday Review.* 'A few weeks ago one of my feet, which had borne me without complaining for forty years, struck work,' he wrote.

'The foot got into such a condition that it literally had to be looked into . . . My doctor's investigation of my interior has disclosed the fact that for many years I have been converting the entire stock of my energy extractable from my food (which I regret to say he disparages) into pure genius. Expecting to find bone and tissue, he has been almost wholly disappointed . . . He has therefore put it bluntly to me that I am already almost an angel and that it rests with myself to complete the process summarily by writing any more articles before I have recovered . . . It is also essential, in order to keep up the sympathy which rages at my bedside, to make the very worst of my exhausted condition.'

This notice of his operation in the theatre pages of the *Saturday Review* was part of the relentless Shavianizing of these strange weeks. Having planted his injured foot in the middle of Frank Harris's paper, he made it the ludicrous substitute for a broken heart. There was nothing pedestrian about Shaw's foot. It was part of the theatrical traffic in what reads like the scenario for a miracle play, helping prepare the public for the extraordinary happening of his marriage.

'For the first time in my life I tasted the bliss of having no morals to restrain me from lying, and no sense of reality to restrain me from romancing. I overflowed with what people call "heart". I acted and lied in the most touchingly sympathetic fashion . . . I carefully composed effective little ravings, and repeated them, and then started again and let my voice die away, without an atom of shame. I called everybody by their Christian names . . .

At last they quietly extinguished the lights, and stole out of the chamber of the sweet invalid who was now sleeping like a child, but who, noticing that the last person to leave the room was a lady, softly breathed that lady's name in his dreams. Then the effect of the anaesthetic passed away more and more; and in less than an hour I was an honest taxpayer again, with my heart perfectly well in hand. And now comes the great question, Was that a gain or a loss?'

This question invites us to see his marriage to Charlotte (which he refers to elsewhere as 'the second operation he has undergone lately') being performed under ether. The starting point was the reversal of a cliché: that marriage is a fate worse than death. 'I found myself without the slightest objection to death, and stranger still, with the smallest objection to marriage.' Nevertheless 'death did not come; but . . . Marriage did,' he told the economist Philip Wicksteed. The following year, in a letter to another of his correspondents, Richard Mansfield's wife Beatrice, he presented the story epigrammatically. 'I proposed to make her [Charlotte] my widow.' The Shavian paradox appears with the fact that the union produces not a mother of children but the father of plays.

Some eighteen years later Shaw was still insisting that he had considered the situation, 'from the point of view of a dying man'. In fact he had considered it as a method of prolonging active life. Work was his life; as he lived so he must write. But if he persisted working and writing in Fitzroy Square, 'nailed by one foot to the floor like a doomed Strasburg goose', he would become an invalid – that was Charlotte's verdict, and there can be little doubt that she put it to him strongly that day at Adelphi Terrace. The moment for a decision had come; she took it and he acceded. It was agreed between them that he was starved, if not of red meat, then of fresh air and rest. Charlotte proposed renting a house in the country, hiring two nurses and a staff of servants, and superintending his recovery however long that might take.

Charlotte's sister, Mary Cholmondeley – or 'Mrs Chumly' as Shaw liked to write her name ('I forget the full spelling') – refused to meet her future brother-in-law and, 'as a last kindness to me', requested Charlotte to secure her money. Lucinda Elizabeth Shaw seemed less interested in their news, making no comment beyond saying that it would be difficult to call Miss Payne-Townshend 'Charlotte' since she looked more like a 'Carlotta' – the mockingly glamorous name by which Lucinda and Lucy Shaw were always to know her.

Charlotte had spoken that day in Adelphi Terrace of Shaw's health and they must have spoken too of her money. The success of Mansfield's American production of *The Devil's Disciple* had removed Shaw's financial scruple against marriage. 'It did not make me as rich as my wife; but it placed me beyond all suspicion of being a fortune hunter or a parasite.' In 1896 he had earned £589 5s. 1d. (equivalent to £31,000 in 1997); in 1897 his income had risen to £1098 4s. 0d. of which £674 8s. 3d. had come from the opening weeks of *The Devil's Disciple*. One of the financial matters they seem to have discussed was a marriage settlement to enable 'my mother, if I died, to end her days without having to beg from my widow or from anyone else'. In fact Shaw safeguarded Lucinda, who was now in her sixty-ninth year, by means of an annuity and a private understanding with Charlotte that, if he were unable to meet the payments, she would make them without revealing herself as the source. In May 1899 Charlotte's solicitors drew up a settlement that guaranteed the income from two trust funds (administered by Sidney Webb and a clerk in the Bank of England and founder of the Stage Society, Frederick Whelen) to Shaw himself – these funds reverting to Charlotte in the event of his predeceasing her. Two years later, on 1 July 1901, Shaw was to make a will, appointing Charlotte as his sole executrix and trustee, bequeathing her his literary manuscripts and copyrights and all the estate not otherwise disposed of. Among his specific bequests was an annuity of

£600 to be paid to Lucinda Elizabeth Shaw, and, in the event of her death, an alternative annuity of £300 for his sister Lucy.

Between themselves they agreed to share basic expenses, but to keep their unequal incomes mainly apart. 'Her property is a separate property,' Shaw later notified the Special Commissioners of Income Tax, to whom he refused to file a joint income-tax return. 'She keeps a separate banking account at a separate bank.'

Besides health and money what else was there – except the crucial question of a marriage proposal? This was slipped into the agenda by Shaw as an item of social etiquette and accepted by Charlotte 'without comment'. It has the air of 'any other business'.

By presenting his marriage contract as a document of social intercourse, Shaw underlined the fact that it was not primarily a sexual arrangement he had entered into with Charlotte. Only with this proposal, he told Beatrice Webb, had the relation between them 'completely lost its inevitable preliminary character of a love affair'. Now, as patient and nurse, they were nearer to being parent and child, and with the possibility of beginning a new life.

Shaw continued to screen their feelings behind a rattling extravaganza. 'My disabled condition has driven Miss Payne Townshend into the most humiliating experiences,' he exulted in a letter to Graham Wallas. 'I sent in for the man next door to marry us; but he said he only did births and deaths.

'Miss Payne Townshend then found a place in Henrietta Street, where she had to explain to a boy that she wanted to get married. The boy sent the news up a tube through which shrieks of merriment were exchanged . . . Miss Payne Townshend then had to suffer the final humiliation of buying a ring . . . at last she succeeded, and returned with the symbol of slavery . . . of such portentous weight and thickness, that it is impossible for anyone but a professional pianist to wear it; so my mother has presented her with my grandfather's wedding ring for general use.'

He had asked Graham Wallas to act as one of the witnesses and, following a refusal from Kate Salt ('who violently objects to the whole proceeding'), invited as his second witness her husband Henry Salt. 'CAN YOU MEET US AT FIFTEEN HENRIETTA STREET COVENT GARDEN AT ELEVEN THIRTY TOMORROW WEDNESDAY TO WITNESS A CONTRACT.'

Shaw arrived on crutches and in an old jacket with armpits patched with leather that the crutches had badly frayed, and was taken by the registrar for 'the inevitable beggar who completes all wedding processions.

'Wallas, who is considerably over six feet high, seemed to him the hero of the occasion, and he was proceeding to marry him calmly to my betrothed, when Wallas, thinking the formula rather strong for a mere witness, hesitated at the last moment and left the prize to me.'

They were married in the afternoon of 1 June 1898. A week before Shaw had written that if 'ever I get married, it will have to be done very secretly'. In fact the newspapers pounced on the event 'as eagerly as the death of Gladstone' – largely because of a report in *The Star* drafted by G.B.S. himself.

'As a lady and gentleman were out driving in Henrietta-st., Covent-garden yesterday, a heavy shower drove them to take shelter in the office of the Superintendent Registrar there, and in the confusion of the moment he married them. The lady was an Irish lady named Miss Payne-Townshend, and the gentleman was George Bernard Shaw.
. . . Startling as was the liberty undertaken by the Henrietta-st. official, it turns out well. Miss Payne-Townshend is . . . deeply interested in the London School of Economics, and that is the common ground on which the brilliant couple met. Years of married bliss to them.'

With these Shavian flourishes, G.B.S. started on the 'terrible adventure' that was to turn him into 'a respectable married man'.

EIGHT

THE HAPPY ACCIDENTS OF MARRIAGE

Every busy man should go to bed for a year when he is forty.
Shaw to Hesketh Pearson (25 October 1918)

The adventure began between Haslemere and Hindhead. After recon-noitring several places in Surrey, Charlotte had taken Pitfold, a rather 'small, stuffy house' on the south slope of Hindhead. The air was so fine that 'our troubles seemed to be over,' Shaw told Beatrice Webb. Charlotte and Shaw had different ideas about air. It was a convalescent substance, soporific, supportive – that was Charlotte's opinion. But on Shaw it appeared to act as an intoxicant. Air went to his head. He had emerged from the London smoke into the ventilation of the country on 10 June 1898 and, despite his invalidism, set fiercely to work on his metaphysical study of the *Ring* cycle, *The Perfect Wagnerite*. Then, on the morning of 17 June, hurrying downstairs on his crutches, he fell into the hall, breaking his left arm and making 'a hopeless mess of the Wagner book'. Charlotte rushed forward with some butter pats, fastened them into splints and called the doctor.

This was the first of several accidents over the next eighteen months that were to keep Shaw largely convalescent. On 27 July an illustrious surgeon named Anthony Bowlby, attended by three doctors, came down to perform a double operation. He dug out most of the bad bone from the instep, charged Shaw 60 guineas and instructed him he would be healed in three weeks. Then he went away: but – *he had forgot the arm*. 'I am so unspeakably tickled by this triumph over the profession that I cannot resist the temptation to impart it to you,' Shaw wrote the next day to his vegetarian friend Henry Salt. Charlotte added a postscript: 'He is doing very well – but must be kept absolutely quiet.'

Shaw was discovering that his wife had a genius for worrying. Her mind ran largely on sickness and travel, diagnosing one, prescribing the other. Shaw represents these smashes as keeping her 'in a state of exhausting devotion'. His prolonged disablement seemed to emphasize certain elements in their marriage. He felt 'as helpless as a baby'. Sex was postponed until its absence became part of the habit of their lives. But having scarcely possessed him sexually, Charlotte felt peculiarly insecure.

She dreaded having to *act* an effusive friendship with his theatrical friends, and wanted to assert her predominance over his past. After a visit in the spring of 1900, Beatrice Webb noted that 'Charlotte Shaw did not want to have us. Perhaps this is a morbid impression. But it is clear that now that she is happily married we must not presume on her impulsive hospitality and kindly acquiescence in our proposals.'

Work was another subject about which Shaw and Charlotte could not agree. She took dictation and prepared copy for his typist (Ethel Dickens, a granddaughter of the novelist). But, as she later admitted to Nancy Astor, 'I don't really like work.' G.B.S. liked nothing better – especially the sort of 'creative work,' Charlotte complained, 'that pulls him to pieces'. Unfortunately 'it is the only occupation he really cares for'.

Shaw's illnesses gave Charlotte an occupation that seemed to unite his needs with her wishes. He did not underrate what she had done: she 'brought me back to life,' he told Beatrice Mansfield. But it was dismaying for her to see how tenuously her husband was attached to life. 'She has an instinctive sense that there is a certain way in which I do not care for myself,' Shaw wrote to Sidney Webb, 'and that it follows that I do not care, *in* that way, for anybody else either; and she is quite right.' He was going through a change of life, he believed, a little death. Whether it actually killed him, or helped to fortify him for another forty years, 'I do not greatly care,' he told Sidney Webb; 'I am satisfied that, on the whole, I have used myself economically and fired my whole broadside.'

The independence he had fixed upon before marriage had been shattered by his accidents. His income during the first year of marriage came to only £473 and by 1902 it had shrunk to £90 (equivalent to £24,000 and £4,400 in 1997). He lived almost entirely from Charlotte's money. To safeguard himself from going 'soft with domesticity and luxury', he began to separate his work from the experience of his life. These early years of his marriage were marked by a burst of creativity. 'I no longer sleep: I dream, dream, dream,' he told Charrington. Once he had confided to Ellen Terry that his childhood had been 'rich only in dreams, frightful and loveless in realities'. Now he began to manufacture from his dreams another world locked deep in himself and fortified against the encircling love and invalidism of his marriage. This was another reason for Charlotte's opposition to his work: it gave him a legitimate escape from her loving custody. She always knew where he was, but not what he was thinking. As his existence grew more comfortable, his work became oddly anarchical. 'He still writes,' Beatrice Webb noted after a visit to Hindhead, 'but his work seems to be getting unreal: he leads a hothouse life, he cannot walk or get among his equals.'

After six months, Shaw's foot was no better – indeed it seemed to

Charlotte decidedly worse. At the beginning of November, they went up to London to consult Bowlby, the specialist who that previous summer had predicted a three weeks' cure. He examined the foot and recommended a further period of disuse – about three weeks. To Charlotte's horror, Shaw decided that he would prefer to have his toe amputated than to endure a longer spell of inactivity. At the end of the month he returned to Bowlby and demanded an immediate removal of the whole bone and toe. To his surprise, Bowlby observed that if it were his toe, he would stick to it. 'He declares that my health is improving visibly; that I am pulling up from a breakdown . . . So I am waiting.'

While Shaw waited and worked, Charlotte acted, moving them both from Pitfold to Blen-Cathra, a larger house with 'lofty, airy rooms,' she told Beatrice Webb, on the main Portsmouth–London road between Hindhead and Haslemere. 'This place beats Pitfold all to fits,' Shaw told Henry Arthur Jones. 'I am a new man since I came here.' A week later, on 9 December, he completed *Caesar and Cleopatra*.

Shaw's health improved throughout 1899. By 23 March he reported himself in a doubly accurate phrase as being 'fed up' to eleven stone, a gain of five pounds. On 12 April he announced that 'the vegetables have triumphed over their traducers', an X-ray having shown a 'perfectly mended solid bone'. He began in May and completed in July *Captain Brassbound's Conversion* – after which Charlotte insisted on an unmitigated holiday.

In the middle of August they arrived at a rented house in Ruan Minor. 'I am down here, wallowing in the sea twice a day,' Shaw wrote, 'swimming being the only exercise I ever take for its own sake.' Not liking him to float off too far, Charlotte allowed Shaw to teach her to swim 'with nothing between her and death but a firm grip of my neck'. His publisher Grant Richards came down and Shaw, with his recently broken arm and sprained ankle, swam him out to sea and brought him back in terror of drowning.

So beneficial was the sea air that Charlotte felt justified in having ordered a recuperative cruise round the Mediterranean in an Orient steamer, the SS *Lusitania*. 'Anything better calculated to destroy me, body & soul, than a Mediterranean cruise on a pleasure steamer in October & Sept (the sirocco months) it would be hard to devise,' Shaw told Beatrice Mansfield. Like Lady Cicely in *Captain Brassbound's Conversion*, Charlotte was in her element coping with these pleasures. She tackled the rigorous sightseeing, digested the rich food, paid their bills and calculated the gratuities in complicated currencies. Trapped on this 'floating pleasure machine' as it moved through a sickly sea, the band striking up perpetual polkas and skirt dances, Shaw came to feel that every condition of a healthy life was being violated. He was at the plutocratic centre of capitalism. 'It is a guzzling, lounging, gambling, dog's life,' he cried. Passing through the Greek archipelago he was violently sick; in the overwhelming damp heat between Crete and Malta he sat at sunset in his overcoat, shivering, with the mercury as high as seventy-five Fahrenheit. 'I wake up in the morning like one in prison,' he wrote, 'realizing where I am with a pang.'

They arrived back in London at the end of October. At the time of their marriage they had agreed to retain their separate addresses in town, and Shaw openly speculated as to whether he would 'revert to my old state of mind & my bachelor existence'. Now, at the beginning of November 1899, he moved some of his belongings at 29 Fitzroy Square into Charlotte's double-decker apartment at the south corner of Adelphi Terrace. It seemed a pleasant place to live, overlooking the river and Embankment Gardens and, except for the occasional hooting of the boats, undisturbed. Shaw slept in a converted box-room off Charlotte's bedroom. 'The dining-room and large drawing-room were on the second floor, with the bedrooms, a study for G.B.S., and the kitchen on the third floor. There was no bathroom; the maids took cans of hot water into the bedrooms and filled a hip bath.' On the staircase Shaw installed a huge wicker gate with a bell-push on the gatepost, marking the Shavian frontier and reinforced by a hedge of pointed steel spikes attached to the balustrade, making the place, he claimed, look like a private madhouse. He worked in a small plain oblong room, above the river, his desk planted near the window which, summer and winter, remained open. There was a little Bechstein piano; an etching by Whistler, drawings by Sargent and Rothenstein, stuck like stamps on the flowered Morris paper which covered the ceiling as well as the walls, giving the impression of an inside-out box. The drawing-room mantelpiece had been designed by the Adam brothers: over the fireplace was cut the sixteenth-century inscription *Thay say. Quhat say thay? Lat Thame say* – the morality of which Shaw reckoned to be 'very questionable'. He was to live here almost thirty years 'before I realised how uncomfortable I was'. For £150 a year he leased Fitzroy Street for his mother who was joined there by her half-sister Arabella Gillmore and her half-niece Georgina ('Judy') Gillmore.

Shaw's foot was now completely mended following treatment of the sinus by pipe water in place of idoform gauze, and he was 'diabolically busy'. The new century seemed full of promise and activity. He had two new plays on his hands, a preface to write and text to revise for his second collection; he was beginning to involve himself with the newly formed Stage Society ('a sort of Sunday night Independent Theatre') which had chosen *You Never Can Tell* for its opening performance. The Boer War had started, forcing the Fabian Society 'to a new birth pang with a foreign policy' and Shaw to act as midwife with a manifesto, speeches and letters.

The honeymoon was over. 'I spent eighteen months on crutches, unable to put my foot to the ground,' he summed up. Within that period he had produced *The Perfect Wagnerite*, *Caesar and Cleopatra* and *Captain Brassbound's Conversion*: and, though he had not married for happiness, 'I cannot remember that I was in the least less happy than at other times'.

2

ON HEROINES AND HERO-WORSHIP

Charlotte and Shaw have settled down into the most devoted married couple, she gentle and refined with happiness added thereto, and he showing no sign of breaking loose from her dominion . . . It is interesting to watch his fitful struggles.

The Diary of Beatrice Webb (30 October 1899)

When William Archer first noticed Shaw in the Reading Room of the British Museum, he had observed how the young Dubliner was balancing Deville's French translation of *Das Kapital* against the orchestral score of *Tristan und Isolde*. Shavianizing Marx had been a matter of pulling politics off the barricades and into the tract. But Shaw also wanted to pull Wagner out of his antiquated heavens and place him in the contemporary socialist scene. *The Perfect Wagnerite* is an extraordinarily lucid exposition that uses Wagner as he had previously used Ibsen to work out his own philosophical position.

During the seven years that separated *The Quintessence of Ibsenism* from *The Perfect Wagnerite*, Shaw had begun to revise his political philosophy. In the earlier work he had divided human beings into three classes: philistines, idealists and those realists on whom progress depended. In the sequel he again makes a threefold division, representing the Wagnerian dwarfs, giants and gods as 'dramatizations of the three main orders of men: to wit, the instinctive, predatory, lustful, greedy people; the patient, toiling, stupid, respectful, money-worshipping people; and the intellectual, moral, talented people who devise and administer States and Churches'.

This change (subdividing the philistines into dwarfs and giants) reflects a shift towards a deeper pessimism arising from his greater experience of national and local politics. He had begun to feel that progress by instalments through the permeation tactics of the Fabians was too slow. A more romantic figure than that of the civil servant and political researcher was needed to fire the imagination of the philistine. The quietist should dress himself in a loud coat – a magical garment, its pockets rattling with the fool's gold of those idealistic illusions Shaw had derided in *The Quintessence of Ibsenism*. For most people had to be paid in such coin. Change the appearance of things and you were a long way to changing the reality. Acknowledging this, Shaw appears to accommodate a fourth class of human being into his philosophy: 'History shews us,' he writes, 'only one order higher than the highest of these: namely, the order of Heros.'

In fact Shaw's heroes are his realists from the *Quintessence* in disguise; they are Wagner's blond warriors, raised out of recognition into a higher organization of man ready to do their work in the twentieth century. Wagner's cycle of music dramas had told a story of love lost and regained; Shaw's commentary is a retelling of the story as love lost and replaced by something else. His 'frightful & loveless' childhood, followed by his years of poverty and social unacceptability in London, made him immediately sympathetic to Wagner's view of human history. There is no mistaking his personal involvement. Man, he writes, 'may be an ugly, ungracious, unamiable person, whose affections may seem merely ludicrous and despicable to you.

'In that case you may repulse him, and most bitterly humiliate and disappoint him. What is left to him then but to curse the love he can never win, and turn remorselessly to the gold?'

From Shaw's reading of the *Ring* we see human beings in loveless desperation as giant philistines succumbing to the corrupt millions of the Rhinegold. He also portrays them as dwarf philistines exploiting the malign systems of capitalism. These systems displace the need for human love with a love for the machinery of power. They establish their dominion over the world through the majesty and superstition of the Church, and guard them with the terrifying powers of the law. Only one quality can defeat this tyranny of religion and law, and that is the quality of fearlessness. The redemption of mankind therefore depends upon the appearance in the world of a hero or the spirit of heroism.

Wagner's Siegfried is a symbol of love, the original deprivation of which had been the genesis of man's tragic story. For Shaw, love was not a romantic solution to social difficulties because it could have little place in the down-to-earth conflict between humanity and its gods and governments. Love belonged to heaven where Wagner transported us once the *Ring* changed with *Götterdämmerung* from music drama into opera – which Shaw regarded as a decline, almost a betrayal. Shaw does not seek to lead us from earth to heaven, but to conduct a marriage of heaven and earth, religion and politics. He was to supplant Siegfried as a dramatic symbol with a succession of eccentrically inspired common-sense figures from

Julius Caesar to St Joan and to experiment with ways of substituting the Shavian Life Force for Wagnerian resurrection. 'The only faith which any reasonable disciple can gain from The Ring is not in love,' he wrote, 'but in life itself as a tireless power which is continually driving onward and upward.' From this faith emerged the creed of Creative Evolution Shaw was to explore in the dream sequence of *Man and Superman*. It is a moral commitment to progress through the Will, answering the need for optimism in someone whose observation of the world was growing more Pessimistic.

Concurrently with *The Perfect Wagnerite* he had been creating his own Puritan hero. His Caesar was more directly descended from Parsifal than Siegfried, a protagonist conventionally seen less as a hero than a fool: 'one who, instead of exulting in the slaughter of a dragon, was ashamed of having shot a swan. The change in the conception of the Deliverer could hardly be more complete.'

*

Shaw's Caesar was born from his longing that such men should exist and be thought great; and that in our better liking of them might lie a seed for our advancement. Caesar is a man of words – an author rather given to preaching – a politician, financier and administrator who, in middle age, has turned his hand to 'this tedious, brutal life of action' because public expectation has made it necessary. His battles are like Christ's miracles: 'advertisements for an eminence that would never have become popular without them'. At fifty-four he is 'old and rather thin and stringy' to Cleopatra's eyes. But his victories (particularly his paradoxical knack of turning defeat into victory) have given a sheen of heroic idealism to his pragmatic nature. He is plainly dressed, drinks barley water, works hard ('I always work') and rules 'without punishment. Without revenge. Without judgment.' He is rather vain, wears an oak wreath to conceal his baldness and is 'easily deceived by women'. Yet he 'loves no one . . . has no hatred in him . . . makes friends with everyone as he does with dogs and children'. This indiscriminate kindness is part of his avuncular superiority – what Shaw called his 'immense social talents and moral gifts'. Such was the man whom Shaw believed might initiate evolutionary progress for mankind.

He had come initially from Mommsen's *History of Rome*, from the fifth volume of which Shaw made extensive notes. 'I stuck nearly as closely to him,' he wrote, 'as Shakespeare did to Plutarch or Holinshed.' Shakespeare was a contributory influence in the shaping of the play. In his appraisal of *Julius Caesar* for the *Saturday Review* Shaw had expressed his indignation 'at this travestying of a great man as a silly braggart'. Lifting

Caesar from Plutarch, Shakespeare had added the qualities of vacillation and conceit from his general knowledge of dictators and his particular observation of Queen Elizabeth. Shaw replaced this Elizabethan stage tyrant by adding to Mommsen's Caesar something of Christ – a paraphrase, for example, at the climax of the play of the Sermon on the Mount.

The play was composed for Forbes-Robertson, 'the only actor on the English stage capable of playing a classical part in the grand manner without losing the charm and lightness of heart of an accomplished comedian'. What he looked for, and eventually received from Forbes-Robertson, Shaw was to set out in an article written at the time of the play's first presentation in London. *Caesar and Cleopatra* was 'an attempt of mine to pay an instalment on the debt that all dramatists owe to the art of heroic acting. . .

'We want credible heroes. The old demand for the incredible, the impossible, the superhuman, which was supplied by bombast, inflation, and the piling of crimes on catastrophes and factitious raptures on artificial agonies, has fallen off; and the demand now is for heroes in whom we can recognise our own humanity, and who, instead of walking, talking, eating, drinking, sleeping, making love and fighting single combats in a monotonous ecstasy of continuous heroism, are heroic in the true human fashion: that is, touching the summits only at rare moments, and finding the proper level on all occasions.'

Shaw was engaging the best Shakespearian actor of the time to help him make obsolete Shakespeare's *Julius Caesar* and undermine *Antony and Cleopatra*. His Caesar is a hero for the realists: Shakespeare's Antony is the idealistic hero created for the philistines. 'You are a bad hand at a bargain, mistress,' Rufio tells Cleopatra at the end of the play, 'if you will swop Caesar for Antony.'

Between the attractions of love and power Antony seems perpetually divided. Caesar is subject to no such struggle. By reducing Cleopatra's age from twenty-one to sixteen and ignoring Caesarion, the legendary child of Caesar and Cleopatra, Shaw is able to write off the threat of sex. 'It is extremely important that Cleopatra's charm should be that of a beautiful child, *not of sex*,' he wrote years later. 'The whole play would be disgusting if Caesar were an old man seducing a child.' Shakespeare's Cleopatra was a physically mature woman drawn from life, a dramatic portrait of the 'black' mistress of the Sonnets from whom he created a role so consummate, Shaw judged, 'that the part reduced the best actress to absurdity'. Shaw's Cleopatra is based on his observation of 'an actress of extraordinary witchery', Mrs Patrick Campbell. It is a part conceived from the stalls, yet with some faint foreknowledge perhaps of their emotional involvement to come. That involvement, which was to impair the Shavian Will in his mid-fifties, offers an ironic comment on Caesar's untroubled control of his sexual susceptibility.

Whatever was taken from Mommsen, anticipated as Christ, or dressed up as Johnston Forbes-Robertson, Caesar is Shaw: a figure to promote his way of life and dramatize his philosophy. Caesar is as fearless in life as Shaw was on the page, and becomes a fantasy image of Shaw himself upon the Fabian stage and in the theatre of politics.

The ancient Briton of the play, Britannus, Julius Caesar's loyal secretary, is like a modern Englishman. Shaw never wrote costume drama for its own sake: his plays were always addressed to the present. The figure of Britannus keeps the audience imaginatively half in the present (which was one of the ways Shaw became a model for Brecht). Since there had been such little progress through generations of sexual reproduction we are left with example as the stimulus for improvement. But Caesar's example is not followed by anyone in the play and will lead, we know, to 'his assassination by a conspiracy of moralists'. His schoolmastering of Cleopatra is easily defeated by her egocentricity ('But me! me!! me!!! what is to become of me?'). At the beginning she is a child full of fear ('*She moans with fear . . . shivering with dread . . . almost beside herself with apprehension*'). 'You must feel no fear,' Caesar instructs her. But when he leaves her at the end she is, he acknowledges, 'as much a child as ever'. All she has added to herself is the trick of imitating Caesar and this trick (unlike a similar trick learned by Eliza Doolittle) has not altered her.

Caesar is as alone at the end as when, at the beginning of Act I, he confronted the Sphinx:

'I have wandered in many lands, seeking the lost regions from which my birth into this world exiled me, and the company of creatures such as myself. I have found . . . no other Caesar, no air native to me, no man kindred to me, none who can do my day's deed, and think my night's thought . . . Sphinx, you and I, strangers to the race of men, are no strangers to one another.'

This is Shaw's own isolation. Caesar's address to the Sphinx anticipates a passage from the Preface to *Immaturity*, written over twenty years later, in which Shaw tells of a 'strangeness which has made me all my life a sojourner on this planet rather than a native of it'. That strangeness seemed intensified by his life with Charlotte. For, as his next play would continue to protest, he was unfitted for the institution of marriage.

*

Lady Cicely Waynflete is the female equivalent in Shaw's world of Caesar. 'If you can frighten Lady Cicely,' her brother-in-law Sir Howard Hallam tells Captain Brassbound, 'you will confer a great obligation on her family. If she had any sense of danger, perhaps she would keep out of it.'

Lady Cicely has walked across Africa with nothing but a little dog and put up with six cannibal chiefs who everyone insisted would kill her. In fact: 'The kings always wanted to marry me.' Her power lies partly in the authority of a mother over her children: 'all men,' she insists, 'are children in the nursery.' Her far-sightedness and tact being so much more effective than their conventional logic, she constantly runs rings round these men. 'Strong people are always so gentle,' she announces, but her own air of gentleness is an obvious imposture. Like Caesar she is surrounded by bullies whom she must constantly outwit. She re-educates them by a mixture of shrewdness and an attraction that does not depend on the erotic use of sex. She is Shaw's ideal of womanhood.

The interest of *Captain Brassbound's Conversion* focuses upon the character and performance of Lady Cicely. She is the only woman in the play. Her adventures give Shaw the opportunity of making a statement about the policy of British Imperialism that was increasingly occupying the Fabian Society at this time. Captain Brassbound had served under General Gordon before he was killed by the Mahdi. Britain had then re-annexed the Sudan from the Mahdi and was about to annex the two Boer Republics. It was for this reason that Shaw set his play in Morocco, 'the very place where Imperialism is most believed to be necessary'.

Shaw wanted to contrast travellers with conquerors, to show Europe's *mission civilisatrice* carried forward by the 'good tempered, sympathetic woman' who rules by natural authority against 'physically strong, violent, dangerous, domineering armed men' who shoot and bully in the name of Imperialism. In a letter to Ellen Terry, he spelled out this opposition between the male and female principles in human nature, telling her to read two books: H. M. Stanley's *In Darkest Africa* and Mary Kingsley's *Travels in West Africa*. 'Compare the brave woman, with her common-sense and good will, with the wild-beast man, with his elephant rifle, and his atmosphere of dread and murder, breaking his way by mad selfish assassination out of the difficulties created by his own cowardice.'

Lady Cicely's historical model was Mary Kingsley; her literary model Shelley's 'The Witch of Atlas'; her actress model Ellen Terry; and her model from life Charlotte whose passion for tourism had persuaded Shaw to read a number of travel books and to pick up, after completing *Captain Brassbound's Conversion*, his only first-hand knowledge of Morocco: 'a morning's walk through Tangier, and a cursory observation of the coast through a binocular from the deck of an Orient steamer'.

It was to Ellen, he let it be known, that the play owed its existence. Lady Cicely is not a portrait of Ellen Terry but a vehicle that incorporates something of her manner and magnifies it hugely. This is how he wanted her to be; this is how he believed she might become if she grew into the part. For the motive behind *Captain Brassbound's Conversion* was similar to that behind *The Man of Destiny*: to make one last effort to infiltrate the Lyceum with Shavian drama or, in failing, to detach Ellen Terry from Henry Irving.

The Lyceum had in 1898 been turned into a limited liability company. It was a step that, though designed to ease Irving's financial burdens, precipitated the end by making it more difficult for him to obtain credit. Early in 1899 Shaw approached Max Hecht, the principal investor in the new 'Lyceum Ltd' ('which I understand to be a benevolent society for the relief of distressed authors & actors'), and made the 'entirely interested suggestion' that the newly managed theatre should put on his 'recklessly expensive play' *Caesar and Cleopatra*, with Forbes-Robertson and Mrs Patrick Campbell in the title roles. 'On the whole, Forbes Robertson & Mrs Pat look more like the heir & heiress apparent to Irving & Ellen Terry than any other pair,' he wrote.

The copyright performance of *Caesar and Cleopatra* had taken place on 15 March 1899 at the Theatre Royal in Newcastle with Mrs Pat reading Cleopatra. But she 'was not attracted by her part' and did not accept Shaw's invitation to 'bring Caesar down to lunch' at Hindhead. Forbes-Robertson by himself could not risk such a production and Shaw's scheme for entering the Lyceum by the back door while Irving was abroad stuck. It was at this moment that he started 'Ellen's play'.

For years Ellen had supported Irving's romantic one-man dramas; now Shaw was presenting her with a non-romantic drama for one woman. 'I dont think that Play of yours will do for me at all!' she answered. Yet it was just the sort of thing she had consistently been helping Irving to produce. There was, in her abasement to him, a curious sense of superiority. She felt he depended on her far more than he could acknowledge; and she had come to rely on his dependence. After she had complicated their relationship by introducing Shaw with his Napoleon play showing how a real Man of Destiny rises above jealousy, Irving had begun to turn to Mrs Aria. He said nothing to Ellen. 'But who is Mrs A?' she had asked Shaw.

Eliza Aria was a social journalist and *salonnière* who had contrived to make herself the perfect companion. Attractive in appearance, generous with her praise, she was able to give Irving an encouraging reflection of himself. Ellen could see how Irving was renewed by Mrs Aria – and she determined to feel pleased for him. She did feel pleased: but she also felt betrayed. For she had the power to help him more than anyone, if only he would let her. But Irving was almost impossible to help – a presence that cocooned itself in silence. She wondered how his other friends and lovers felt. 'I have contempt and affection and admiration. What a mixture!' He was curiously tortured: 'a silly Ass,' Ellen called him. Sometimes she was frankly impertinent like this: at other times in awe. He still had the power to wound her. Appearing 'stouter, very grey, sly-looking, and more cautious than ever', he had informed her early in 1899 that he was ruined. He intended to mend his fortunes by touring the provinces with a small company. As for Ellen she could 'for the present' do as she liked. Ellen was furious. She had contemplated leaving him: 'I simply must do something else.' But she did not leave.

This was why she wanted something special from Shaw, something to bring back the glorious days of the old Lyceum. She had first wanted *Caesar and Cleopatra*: Irving, she was convinced, 'could have done *wonders* with that Play'. But Shaw had not seen her as his Cleopatra: 'She is an animal – a bad lot. Yours is a beneficent personality.' Also Irving made it clear that he would never produce a play by Shaw – in which case, Shaw retaliated, the only feasible alternative would be to produce his next play at the Lyceum when Irving was away.

He sent Ellen *Captain Brassbound's Conversion* at the end of July 1899 and she read it with disappointment. 'I couldnt do this one,' she told him, ' . . . it is surely for Mrs Pat.' He was dismayed. *Captain Brassbound's Conversion* had been conjured out of the last four years of their letter-writing love-affair: and she had not recognized it. 'Alas! dear Ellen, is it really so?' he wrote back. 'Then I can do nothing for you.

'I honestly thought that Lady Cicely would fit you like a glove . . . I wont suggest it to Mrs Pat, because I am now quite convinced that she would consider herself born to play it, just as you want to play Cleopatra . . . And so farewell our project – all fancy, like most projects.'

It was almost the end, a divorce between her acting and his playwriting skills. But he would not let them separate without a protest. 'Of course you never *really* meant Lady Cicely for me,' she had written to him. 'Oh you lie, Ellen,' he answered, 'you lie:

'never was there a part so deeply written for a woman as this for you . . . Here then is your portrait painted on a map of the world – and you . . . want to get back to Cleopatra! . . . do you think I regard you as a person needing to be arranged with sphinxes & limelights to be relished by a luxurious public? Oh Ellen, Ellen, Ellen, Ellen, Ellen. This is the end of everything.'

How much of this impassioned letter could Ellen afford to understand? In her autobiography she was to advise her readers that 'it doesn't answer to take Bernard Shaw seriously. He is not a man of convictions.' Here certainly were the methods of Lady Cicely Waynflete, but used for the opposite ends: to keep out the truth. Yet Shaw's letter unsettled her. She *did* know what he meant: 'the horridness of it all is, that all the time I think exactly as you do!' But to convert his words into her actions would mean emerging from the womb of the Lyceum and becoming independent – and it was too late. 'Of course I know it's *me* all the while . . . What is the good of words to me?' But words were all Shaw had to give her: the power of words to change our lives. And she could not change. All Shaw had done was to force her to recognize this fact.

So *Captain Brassbound's Conversion* went back on the shelf. As a consolation, Irving allowed Ellen to go through the copyright ceremony with the Lyceum company at the Court Theatre in Liverpool before they sailed for the United States in the autumn of 1899. But nobody liked Lady Cicely. 'It's because I read it wrong,' Ellen reasoned. But her daughter Edy, sitting out in front, remarked that she couldn't have read the lines differently, and that it seemed Shaw had thought his Lady Cicely one sort of woman but had written another.

The other woman was Charlotte. When she commanded him to go travelling, he went as obediently and unwillingly as Sir Howard Hallam and Captain Brassbound and his crew followed Lady Cicely into the Atlas Mountains. Robbed of his Old Testament religion of revenge for what he imagined had been done to his mother, the idealistic Brassbound proposes to fill this emptiness with love. 'I want to take service under you,' he tells Lady Cicely. 'And theres no way in which that can be done except marrying you. Will you let me do it?' But love is rejected as the solution as it had been earlier by Caesar and by Shaw himself in *The Perfect Wagnerite*. It is not Ellen Terry or Charlotte or any other woman who gives Lady Cicely's answer to Brassbound: 'I have never been in love with any real person; and I never shall. How could I manage people if I had that mad little bit of self left in me? Thats my secret.' By forestalling their marriage with warning gunfire ('Rescue for you – safety, freedom!'), Shaw is asserting his own 'mad little bit of self', and his intellectual isolation from Charlotte.

In Brassbound's saturnine features, grimly set mouth, dark eyebrows, his wordless but significant presence, we may also see something of Henry

Irving – and the imaginary conversion of Irving to Shavianism. Ellen had pretty well decided to leave Irving – but not quite. She was frightened of poverty – and then Henry could always weaken her resolve when she was most determined to go by appealing for her help. 'I appear to be of strange *use* to H, and I have always thought to be *useful, really* useful to any one person *is* rather fine and satisfactory.' So Shaw was persuaded to give up the struggle.

'Now for one of my celebrated *volte-faces*. I hold on pretty hard until the stars declare themselves against me, and then I always give up and try something else . . . now I recognize that you and I can never be associated as author and player – that you will remain Olivia, and that Lady Cicely is some young creature in short skirts at a High School at this moment. I have pitched so many dreams out of the window that one more or less makes little difference – in fact, by this time I take a certain Satanic delight in doing it and noting how little it hurts me. So out of the window you go, my dear Ellen; and off goes my play to my agents as in the market for the highest bidder.'

This letter reveals in what depth of disappointment Shaw lit his candle of optimism and converted its spectral shadows into a world of solid reality. In the open market only Charrington's Stage Society was interested in presenting his play with (the final shuddering irony) Ellen's role given to Janet Achurch. Ellen had had to choose: and she had chosen Henry. Was it loyalty or lack of courage? 'Ah, I feel so certain Henry just hates me!' she wrote to Shaw.

Here was Shaw's consolation. Into his love for Ellen had been poured a hatred of Irving. Like two stage monsters, Dracula and Svengali, they had fought with all their magical powers over the leading lady, both claiming victory at the final curtain. 'Of course he hates you when you talk to him about me,' Shaw burst out. 'Talk to him about himself: then he will love you – to your great alarm.'

Captain Brassbound's Conversion was first presented by the Stage Society at the Strand Theatre on 16 December 1900. Ellen came, and after the performance, on her way to the dressing-room of Laurence Irving (who played Brassbound), passing under the stage, she spoke to Shaw for the first time. They had been corresponding with each other for more than five years, and had feared that a meeting would rub the bloom off their romance. And now, having met briefly and parted, they apparently did not send each other a loving letter for almost a year and a half. 'They say you could not bear me, when we met, that one time, under the stage,' Ellen went on to explain in December 1902. Her self-esteem, undermined and exploited (with her own co-operation) by Irving, had to be fed by the persistent reassurance of her usefulness. What Shaw had said that could have reached her in this form and who carried such words to her is unknown. But it is difficult not to suspect that her daughter Edy was involved: Edy who had watched their long-running romance while two of her own had been ended by Ellen; Edy whose jealous gossip (Ellen went on to warn Shaw that same December) needed a 'little salt'.

It was at the end of this silent period that Ellen began to separate from Irving. 'She broke loose from the Ogre's castle,' Shaw wrote, ' . . . only to find that she had waited too long for his sake, and that her withdrawal was rather a last service to him than a first to herself.'

Ellen's last service to Shaw was to play Lady Cicely at the Royal Court Theatre in 1906, eighteen months after Irving's death. 'Sooner or later I know I'll play Lady C.,' she had promised him. It had been a hope: and finally it was a fact. She was fifty-eight, could not remember her lines, felt easily demoralized. Shaw made certain that the producer treated her with gentleness and to Ellen herself he wrote: 'Behave as if you were more precious than many plays, which is the truth . . . The only other point of importance is that you look 25; and I love you.'

When the play opened on 20 March, *The Times* drama critic noted that 'Miss Terry is, as always, a little slow, the victim of a treacherous memory'; and Desmond MacCarthy in *The Speaker* observed that 'there was a hesitation in her acting sometimes, which robbed it of effect'. She recognized this herself. 'You try to keep up your illusions about me,' she wrote to Shaw, 'about my acting, altho' you know all the while – ' But Shaw refused to know. He had no time for this 'saintly humility'. The marriage of her acting with his playwriting had at last taken place and its beauty was manifest. 'She is immense, though she is 58, and cant remember half my words,' he wrote. ' . . . now that she has at last actually *become* Lady C, and *lives* the part, saying just what comes into her head without bothering about my lines, she is very successful.'

The following year Ellen took *Captain Brassbound's Conversion* on her farewell tour of the United States. On 22 March, in Pittsburgh 'of all places in the world' she married James Carew, the American actor who played Captain Kearney in the play. Though Dame Ellen would never become Lady Cicely, 'her history has become your history,' Shaw acknowledged. ' . . . Why could you not have been content with my adoration?' But most people preferred conventional romance to Shavian adoration and would attempt to infiltrate it into his plays. When in 1912 Gertrude Kingston acted the role of Lady Cicely, she replaced in rehearsal Shaw's final line – 'How glorious! And what an escape!' – with her own: 'How glorious! And what a disappointment!' But the disappointment, brilliantly concealed, was Shaw's. 'Lady Cecilys [*sic*] no longer exist,' he conceded in a letter to Gertrude Kingston, ' – if they ever did.'

*

Shaw was developing into an ingenious 'Ladies' Tailor'. But what was the use of this if no lady would wear his clothes? The late Victorian theatre was so different from any living world, that he could see 'no real women in the plays except heavily caricatured low comedy ones,' he later wrote to Edy Craig; 'and what the leading actresses had to do was to provide an embodiment of romantic charm . . . without having a single touch of nature in the lines and gestures dictated by the author's script . . . unless they could smuggle in something of their own between the lines.'

Shaw had been at this smuggling game now for ten plays and was almost always caught, either by the Lord Chamberlain's office, or by the male actor-manager's régime of the West End. Together, they policed a theatre-going public that was not yet ready for the New Drama as a vehicle for the New Woman. Shaw's huntresses and persons 'exactly like myself' peopled the army he had called up to invade the *fin de siècle* theatre, topple the womanly women from their stage pedestals, then march down from the boards to the stalls and out into the world. But finding the doors of the theatre heavily barricaded, his regiment veered off instead to the offices of Grant Richards. Having failed as a novelist and, it seemed, also as a dramatist, from these two failures Shaw proposed to manufacture success with a literary genre composed of essay, play and novel.

By November 1900 *Three Plays for Puritans* had been passed for the press and in January 1901 an edition of 2,500 copies was published. 'The effort has almost slain me,' Shaw admitted. He had not done it for money; he had not worked sixteen hours a day with Charlotte's approval; and he had gone directly against the advice of William Archer who predicted popularity for at least one of these plays leading to an inevitable Shaw boom if he would give it 'a chance, by waiting at least two years for somebody to produce it before publishing it'. Why then had he done this?

Shaw was acutely aware of the continuous current of sex in the Victorian theatre because, like the sex in his own life, it was suppressed. He argued that the sensuous conventionality of Victorian stage sex was pornographic in that it was not frank. This lack of frankness, he added, had been what 'finally disgusted me'. With such passages – and there are many of them in his Preface – he disclaims being a prude and identifies himself as a proponent of the realistic treatment of sex in contemporary drama. But for Shaw realistic sex meant less sex. He passes in his preface almost unnoticeably from demolishing the genteel assumptions of the sex instinct as shown on the stage, to a demolition of the sex instinct itself.

Before marriage, in his three-cornered affairs with women, Shaw's part had been an impersonation of George Vandeleur Lee, the interloper in his parents' marriage. In marriage he had taken on a double role, that of George Carr Shaw and George Vandeleur Lee together. He was legitimately married but it was a *mariage blanc*. The dominant role was that of Lee whose 'potency' arose from his public life – as did Shaw's. Casting off the ambiguous skin of 'George', Shaw had literally 'made a name for himself' as a writer, the magnificently impersonal G.B.S. (his equivalent of Lee's 'Vandeleur'). His frustration at not getting the work of G.B.S. performed manifested itself as an impotence. From this impotence came his impatience – his inability to take Archer's advice to wait – and his confusing paradoxes in the Preface between celibacy and pornography. He had already waited too long. His only channel for reaching the public was the book world. But this outlet was unsatisfactory since he could not put his potent words into the mouths of actresses, could not direct them on a stage, could not witness their effect on audiences, could only, with the aid of his written narrative, transport them into his imagination. It gave him only temporary relief.

'No: it is clear that I have nothing to do with the theatre of today,' he had written to Ellen Terry. To create a family of plays for future generations was still Shaw's ultimate aim. In the short term, however, there was another theatre where he could perform: the theatre of politics. 'It is time to do something more in Shaw-philosophy, in politics & sociology. Your author, dear Ellen, must be more than a common dramatist.'

3

BOER WAR MANOEUVRES

If I were not a politician I would be a Fabian.
R. B. Haldane to Bernard Shaw (15 October 1900)

Shaw was with Charlotte on board the 'floating pleasure machine' SS *Lusitania* when on 11 October 1899 the war in the Transvaal broke out. When he arrived back in England he found the country in a state of civil war over South Africa. The prosperity of the Empire, the longevity of the widowed Queen herself, seemed to have sunk Britain in the doldrums of peace and the public was more than ready to take off for some foreign adventuring. The novels of Trollope, with their solid domestic themes, were beginning to lose popularity and being replaced in the public imagination by Kipling's Indian stories, the adventures of R. L. Stevenson and the historical romances of Conan Doyle. Doyle shared with thousands of 'men in the street' an attitude that converted warfare into sport. 'If ever England gets into a hole,' he had declared, 'you may depend on it that her sporting men will pull her out of it.'

Shaw had wanted to have nothing to do with it. But the eruption of hostilities was of such violence, shifting the landscape of British politics, that non-involvement became impossible. The atmosphere in Britain of conflicting imperialist and pro-Boer passions, gathering up the vague discontents of years, was considerably less sportsmanlike than on the smoke-filled battlefields of South Africa. John Burns, 'the Man with the Red Flag' who ten years earlier had led the Dock Strike, was obliged to take up his cricket bat one night to defend himself against a crowd attempting to break into his home.

The Conservative Party, saw Englishmen riding 'the white steed of destiny' all over South Africa. Most socialists joined in opposition to the war – Keir Hardie, for example, picturing the Boers as pure-living, God-fearing farmers grazing peacefully under the Christ-like guardianship of President Kruger. Between the romanticism of the right and the sentimentality of the left floundered the Liberal Party with its cautious new leader Campbell-Bannerman. It was the middle ground of British politics that was torn apart by the South African war; and since the Fabian Society, with its policy of permeation, had been cultivating this middle ground, it now found itself at the centre of a crisis.

The Webbs' attitude to South Africa was simple. They did their best to ignore it. Beatrice, who described the war as an 'underbred business', was determined that the Fabians should be 'so far removed from political influence that it is not necessary for Sidney to express any opinion'.

It was Sidney's lack of interest in foreign politics – despite his years at the Colonial Office – that had dictated the Fabian silence over Imperialism. But since it was impossible any longer to smother things in silence, he handed over the 'show' to the Fabian literary expert. Shaw's brief was complicated. He had to discover some honourable method by which, while the war issue dominated British politics, the Fabians could legitimately continue to produce tracts on municipal bakeries, fire insurance and the milk supply.

His attitude had begun to change over this year until, with the publication of *Fabianism and the Empire*, it seemed to invert the traditional socialist standpoint, supporting pacifist permeation tactics at home while tolerating a good deal of bloodshed overseas. He urged all Fabians to stick together. No party or society could entirely discharge the soul's message of every member; and no member, he added, 'can find a Society 800 strong which is an extension of his own self – even the society of 2 called marriage is a failure from that point of view'.

Shaw tried to suffocate the moral issue of the war by spreading over it his theory of pragmatism. In its most negative phase Shaw's pragmatism meant that socialism should not touch any problem that it did not have a reasonable chance of solving; more positively it meant in this case waiting for the inevitable annexation of the Transvaal, and then introducing there the social organization on which the Fabians had been working. In a letter to Ramsay MacDonald he explained, 'I have done my best to avert the fight for which the democratic spirit and the large grasp of human ideas is always spoiling, and for which the jingo spirit is no doubt equally ready. If you wont take my way, and wont find a better way, then punch one another's heads and be damned.'

Of what use, he asked, were ethics that were taken out of the cupboard from time to time and that led to conclusions no one could act on? 'I am a revolutionist in ethics as much as in economics,' he told Walter Crane;

'and the moment you demand virtuous indignation from me, I give you up . . . the Fabian ought to be warproof; and yet Capitalism has only to fire a gun, and split a great shaving off us.'

In fact Shaw was extraordinarily successful in keeping the Fabian peace. By the time the Treaty of Vereeniging was signed in 1902 (leaving the enfranchisement of the native population to be settled in due course) 22,000 British soldiers had been killed and £223,000,000 spent – but no great shaving had been split off the Fabian Society. In steering them out of war-range, Shaw had removed the Fabians from the rest of the socialist fleet, taken them, it seemed, out of politics and stranded them on the high ground of political philosophy. He had also plucked from politics the 'heroic' quality he had so recently inserted into his plays.

Shaw hated war; he hated the human beings who were attracted by war; and he felt that every human being, whatever his moral stance, was implicated. His revulsion at the Boer War, and the policy he formed based on this revulsion, is most succinctly expressed in a letter to a fellow-Fabian, George Samuel. 'The Boer and the Britisher are both fighting animals, like all animals who live in a chronic panic of death and defeat,' he wrote.

'. . . Do you expect me solemnly to inform a listening nation that the solution of the South African problem is that the lion shall lie down with highly-armed lamb in mutual raptures of quakerism, vegetarianism, and teetotalism? . . . Let us face the facts. Two hordes of predatory animals are fighting, after their manner, for the possession of South Africa, where neither of them has, or ever had, any business to be from the abstractly-moral, virtuously indignant Radical, or (probably) the native point of view ... The moral position of the Boers and the British is precisely identical in every respect; that is, it does not exist. Two dogs are fighting for a bone thrown before them by Mrs Nature, an old-established butcher with a branch establishment in South Africa. The Socialist has only to consider which dog to back; that is, which dog will do most for Socialism if it wins.'

Fabianism and the Empire was produced as a Fabian foreign policy document, one hundred pages long, published at one shilling by Grant Richards and directed at the 'Khaki' election in the autumn of 1900. The first draft, which took Shaw three months to complete, was sent to every member of the Fabian Society, 134 of whom returned comments which, with extraordinary ingenuity, he attempted to stitch into his text. The final version was such a 'masterpiece' of literary craft that no more than fourteen Fabians voted against its publication. 'By this time the controversy over the war had reached an intensity which those who cannot recollect it will find difficult to believe,' Pease remembered, 'and nobody but the author could have written an effective document on the war so skilfully as to satisfy the great majority of the supporters of both parties in the Society.'

He recommends reforms for the army, the Consular Service and the administration and social justice of Imperialism, drafting what Beatrice Webb called 'the most prescient and permanently instructive public document of its date'. But on the General Election, the Treaty of Vereeniging and the subsequent social conditions in South Africa, *Fabianism and the Empire* had no influence at all, and 1,500 copies were remaindered the following year.

In the new Parliament the Tories had won 402 seats, the Liberals 186 and the Nationalists 82. Keir Hardie was the only independent Labour politician to survive the election, but it was not through him that the Fabians sought to operate. As Beatrice noted, 'a Conservative Government is as good for us as a Liberal Government'. The Fabians were ascending in society, becoming friendly with Bishops and Tory Cabinet Ministers, while among the Liberals they chose Lord Rosebery as their man – partly on account of his admiration for Shaw's manifesto. '*Our* policy is clearly to back him for all we are worth,' Shaw urged Beatrice who noted in her diary: 'We have succumbed to his flattery.' A few weeks later, in the autumn of 1901, Sidney published 'Lord Rosebery's Escape from Houndsditch' – an invitation for him to lead the progressive Liberals in their campaign to raise each department of national life to its maximum efficiency.

NINE

SOME UNEXPECTED CHARACTERS

I stand just now at a point where a failure would put me quite out of court, and a success would 'chair me ever'.

Shaw to William Archer (26 March 1902)

After six years' 'Borough Councilling', Shaw concluded in 1903, 'I am convinced that the Borough Councils must be abolished'. His method of quitting local politics was characteristically 'Shavian'. In the spring of 1904 he stood as a Progressive candidate for one of the two London County Council seats in South St Pancras. 'The Shaws have been good friends to us,' Beatrice wrote in her diary, 'and we would not like them to have a humiliating defeat.' The party organizers however had long ago given up the seat as lost and even Beatrice admitted 'he is not likely to get in'. But this was not good enough for G.B.S. He needed, while campaigning with tremendous gusto and geniality, to make *absolutely certain* of not getting in. Every day of the campaign he showed himself as 'hopelessly intractable' – except to his enemies, to whom he was 'the most accommodating candidate that was ever known'. He insisted that he was an atheist; that, though a teetotaller, he would 'force every citizen to imbibe a quartern of rum to cure any tendency to intoxication . . . chaffed the Catholics about transubstantiation; abused the Liberals, and contemptuously patronized the Conservatives – until every section was equally disgruntled'. As a result, he was triumphantly beaten into third place. And so, with honour high, Shaw paraded out of party politics. 'We are not wholly grieved,' Beatrice wrote. 'His . . . quixotic chivalry to his opponents and cold drawn truth, ruthlessly administered, to possible supporters, are magnificent but not war.'

Shaw's election defeat was probably more disappointing to Charlotte than to the Webbs. She wanted to find him a respectable career in politics. Though she believed in his gifts as a playwright she could not blink the facts. In the summer of 1903, he was in his forty-eighth year and still almost wholly unknown to British audiences. From such facts and her conflicting reactions to them, Charlotte hit on a curious programme of nudging him into professional politics at home while furthering his reputation as a dramatist abroad.

Her opportunity to help Shaw's plays on to the European stage came with a visit early in 1902 of a young Austrian writer, Siegfried Trebitsch. Trebitsch was a sentimentalist of wonderful persistence – the sort of person Shaw had been sent into the world to quell but who in practice so often got the better of him. 'I held forth for quite a while about his plays,' Trebitsch remembered.

'What do you mean to do with me?' Shaw interrupted.

Trebitsch knew the answer to this. He meant to become Shaw's 'apostle in Central Europe' and conquer the German stage for him. In short he allowed himself to 'speake straight forward' and give his 'dear adored Shaw' what he called 'a peace of my mind'. The result was that Shaw jumped up and ran out of the room, crying out for Charlotte to 'try to calm' this 'young lunatic'.

Obediently Charlotte appeared and Trebitsch 'expounded my intentions to her'. The grandeur of these intentions, contrasted with the inadequacy of the language in which they were expressed, did not strike Charlotte as funny. She summoned her husband back into the room and Shaw spoke forbiddingly about the 'extremely important matter of copyright' of which Trebitsch knew nothing. Trebitsch left soon afterwards and a few days later received a letter from Charlotte inviting him to lunch. It became clear to him during this meal that, though she took no part in the conversation, Charlotte approved of him and that this approval had been responsible for a change in her husband's manner.

For Trebitsch to translate his plays into German involved Shaw in mastering the German language – or at least buying 'a devil of a big dictionary, also a grammar'. He teased and tutored Trebitsch terrifically. His translation of *Caesar and Cleopatra* was stuffed with misunderstandings; *Arms and the Man* 'full of hideous and devastating errors'; and *Candida*, Trebitsch's favourite, was worst of all. 'You didnt understand the play: you only wallowed in it . . . I tore out large handfuls of my hair and uttered screams of rage . . . I plucked up my beard by the roots and threw it after my hair.'

From such comments, over several years, Trebitsch began to sense that something was not quite right. 'I have just met the most beautiful Shavian I have ever seen,' Trebitsch deciphered at the end of one of Shaw's letters to him. 'She is the wife of one of our diplomatic staff, who is joining the British Embassy in Vienna very soon. I think I will ask her to correct your translations: you can make mistakes on purpose.' What could this mean? 'You must learn to laugh,' Shaw suggested. Was it all some joke? Perhaps not, since Shaw had also advised him: 'I have no objection to being taken seriously. What ruins me in England is that people think I am always joking.'

To be the perfect translator of Shaw's plays Trebitsch needed to be resolved into a German edition of G.B.S. Shaw spelled out the prescription minutely. Trebitsch must use the same menu as Shaw himself. 'Never eat meat or drink tea, coffee, or wine again as long as you live,' he warned. ' . . . If you are very very very bad, become religious, and go . . . round all the Stations of the Cross on your knees, and pray incessantly. When you begin to feel sceptical you will be getting well.'

It was agreed that Trebitsch should translate three plays and hold exclusive rights in them for one year. He chose *The Devil's Disciple*, *Candida* and *Arms and the Man*, and kept them 'ceaselessly circulating among publishers, theatrical people, producers'. The proprietor of the Entsch theatrical publishing firm in Berlin refused 'to have anything to do with this crazy Irishman' whom he described as 'a lost cause'. Trebitsch was advised to 'stop being so obstinate' or he would endanger his own career. 'I was somewhat desperate,' he wrote. 'But I did not lose heart.' He continued working 'feverishly, usually the whole day, and often half the night as well, for, after all, I had a time limit'.

Within the year Trebitsch began to accomplish what Shaw had been failing to achieve in Britain over more than a decade. He persuaded the director of the Raimund Theatre in Vienna to stage *The Devil's Disciple* in February 1903, and the Stuttgart publishers Cotta to bring out all three plays, *Drei Dramen*, in the same year. In 1904 the Deutsches Volkstheater produced *Candida* and *Arms and the Man*; and within the next three years there were productions by leading directors of *You Never Can Tell*, *Mrs Warren's Profession* and *Man and Superman*, all in Trebitsch's translations. Germany came to recognize Shaw's 'importance to the modern stage,' Thomas Mann wrote, 'indeed to modern intellectual life as a whole, earlier than the English-speaking world.

'His fame actually reached England only by way of Germany, just as Ibsen and Hamsun conquered Norway, and Strindberg Sweden, by the same roundabout route, for London's independent theatre fell short of doing for Shaw's reputation – soon to grow to world-wide dimensions – what men like Otto Brahm and Max Reinhardt . . . were able to accomplish, for the simple reason that at that time the German stage was ahead of its British counterpart.'

Trebitsch recorded that it 'made a very great impression on Shaw that I had kept my word and accomplished what I set out to do'. What Shaw felt for Trebitsch was naked gratitude – the emotion he usually denied and invariably distrusted. Trebitsch in his autobiography presents a chronicle of unchecked success. The first night of *The Devil's Disciple* 'was one of the most remarkable I have ever experienced,' he writes. *Mrs Warren's Profession* 'was the greatest success of the season'. The production of *Candida* 'turned out to be a sensation' and so on. The stream of Shaw's letters along this triumphant passage form a curious undercurrent. Over a period of two and a half years, he writes:

'Give up all anxiety about those plays . . . let this experience cure you of your excessive sensitiveness to reviews . . . If I bothered about such things I should go mad three times a week, and die on the alternate dates . . . you must not lie awake and get neuralgia . . . As to the play being ruined for all German stages, do not trouble about that. When you have been ruined as often as I have, you will find your reputation growing with every successive catastrophe. Never ruin yourself less than twice a year, or the public will forget about you . . . Dismiss it from your mind now: there is no use bothering about a commercial failure . . . we can say that it is the public that failed . . . let us laugh and try again . . . nothing succeeds like failure . . . We shall be hissed into celebrity if this goes on.'

Shaw developed a paternal tenderness for Trebitsch. For many years Trebitsch was violently attacked in Germany for knowing neither German nor English. He never learned what Shaw called 'the grand style of fighting', falling upon your opponent and clubbing him dead with the weapons of generosity and politeness. In spite of Shaw's work with the dictionary, many misunderstandings persisted, the most notorious being Trebitsch's interpretation of the Waiter's remark in *You Never Can Tell*: 'I really must draw the line at sitting down' – after which, following Trebitsch's stage directions, he goes to the window and, before taking his seat, draws the curtains. Shaw knew all about these howlers. 'Never join in attacks on translators,' he advised one of his biographers. His loyalty to Trebitsch took the form of claiming for these 'so-called translations' the status of 'excellent original plays'. Had they been the least like his own, he explained, they could never have succeeded so well.

Shaw's experiences with Trebitsch influenced his arrangements with other translators. 'I calculated that the only way to make the job really worth doing was to catch some man in each country who would undertake *all* my work, and thus get something like an income out of half the fees,' he wrote to Henry Arthur Jones in 1908. 'At last I succeeded everywhere except in Portugal . . . Sometimes I picked a man who had never dreamt of the job and hypnotised and subsidised him into it. Whenever possible, I got a man with an English or American wife . . . The results have been very varied.'

He chose his translators because they charmed him, touched his sense of humour or presented impeccable political credentials. His most extreme translators were Augustin and Henriette Hamon. He was a socialist and an anarchist of 'terrific intellectual integrity . . . whose main means of subsistence has always been borrowing money'; she knew some English, which was helpful. Hamon did what he could to wriggle away. He was not a literary man, had never written a play and knew little of the theatre. It was true that he had published a number of works on hygiene and sociology. It was also true that he was the radical editor of *L'Humanité Nouvelle*, a periodical frequently visited by the police. Yet Shaw seemed determined to prove Hamon 'a born homme de théâtre'. That Hamon was an individual bicyclist and a revolutionary with exemplary collectivist principles pleased him. As evidence of his good choice, Shaw pointed to the 'dramatic liveliness' of Hamon's reports on various socialist congresses.

So Shaw bought a Larousse dictionary and set about becoming a co-translator of his plays into the French language. He enjoyed firing off letters in a French that was so 'extremely Britannic' that it 'must be positively painful' to any man of literary sensibility to read them. ' "Hard as nails" – "dure comme un clou" – is an expression which ought,' he judged, 'to enrich the French language.' The Hamons were able, he discovered, to concentrate into ten amazing lines of their translated text 'all the errors which I spend my life in combating'. Hamon had no notion that he might be translating comedies, and was once seen rushing from the theatre when the audience began to laugh, crying to his wife, '*Mon Dieu! On rit. Tout est perdu.*'

All Shaw's schooling could not make these translations good. They were caustically attacked in France as forming a permanent barrier to the acceptance of Shaw's plays by the French public. Hamon never fathomed 'the utter illiteracy of the playgoing public', to prepare for which, Shaw reminded him, Molière used to read his plays aloud to his cook. The great failing of the Frenchman, Shaw maintained, was his academicism. 'Every Frenchman is a born pedant,' he advised Hamon. 'He thinks it a crime to repeat a word – the crime of tautology.'

Despite the pleas of many eminent translators, Hamon went on to translate almost all Shaw's plays. Only seven or eight of these plays were produced in Paris, not at the commercial *théâtres du boulevard* but the small *coterie* theatres. 'I have given up all hope of getting into touch with France,' Shaw conceded in the 1920s, shortly before the success of *Saint Joan*.

'This is all the more annoying as I do not believe for a moment that the French reading public is less accessible to my methods than any other public . . . I still believe that if only I could have secured a pulpit in

France, I could have amused the inhabitants quite as effectively as the Germans.'

In the words of Vicomte Robert d'Humières, Shaw became attached to his translator 'like a criminal is attached to the rope which hanged him'. It was 'a defiant and heroic act', intensely Shavian, that would end in 'suicide on the threshold of our admiration'. To a perpetual gunfire of criticism Hamon dug in for the rest of his life with the work he had never wanted to do. He and his wife remained desperately poor. Feeling perhaps his own part in the Hamons' poverty, Shaw purchased their house in Brittany for them and in the 1930s bought 'an annuity for his own and his wife's life, of £12 a month,' Shaw revealed to Trebitsch. 'And this enables him to live comfortably according to his standard of comfort.'

Trebitsch and Hamon were two principal members of Shaw's family of translators over whom he exercised great power and generosity. The antagonism which their amateur status and exclusive rights brought them in their own countries intensified their loyalty. They became part of a special Shavian clan (their intimacy seldom tested by an actual meeting) through which, like pollen on the wind, Shaw's words were eccentrically spread across the world.

2

HOME LIFE AND HOLIDAYS

A true dramatist should be interested in everything.
Shaw to Trebitsch (16 August 1903)

Charlotte treated her husband partly as an employer, partly as her child. It was the employer whose correspondence she dealt with, whose manuscripts she took to the typist. She also arranged lunches with people he should meet and protected him from other people who would worry him needlessly. It was on behalf of this employer, too, that she still sat on committees at the London School of Economics and the School of Medicine for Women, and had joined the play-reading committee of the Stage Society.

But it was the child who exercised her talent for anxiety. Some of his young hobbies – photography or the piano – were harmless. She didn't mind him taking her picture in the least (though she hated others doing so) and she grew to like his playing to her in the evening. Bicycles were dangerous; and he did very naughty things in newspapers – writing, for example, after the Queen died to denounce the rapturous lying-in-state as 'insanitary'.

She had given instructions to the servants to vary his diet as much as possible, and from time to time felt half-persuaded to try it herself. Whenever she was unwell she would pick at something of his vegetarian food, washed down with a glass of whisky. 'My wife has at last become a convinced vegetarian,' Shaw reported to Henry Salt in the summer of 1903, ' . . . and she now eats nothing but birds & fish, which are not "butcher's meat".'

Charlotte regarded G.B.S.'s lust for publicity as part of the odder equipment of his genius. There was no other respectable way of explaining it. He literally *asked* for what he got sometimes, arriving at Max Beerbohm's house on his bicycle and requesting the cartoonist to do a drawing of him. 'Max was less gratified by this than might have been expected,' Lord David Cecil wrote, ' . . . and suspected that Shaw was actuated less by admiration than by a desire for the publicity the cartoon might bring him. Max also found Shaw's appearance unappetizing; his pallid pitted skin and red hair like seaweed. And he was repelled by the back of his neck. "The back of his neck was especially bleak; very long, untenanted, and dead white," he explained.'

Max did over forty caricatures of G.B.S.'s 'temperance beverage face' and, as dramatic critic, reviewed more than twenty of his plays. 'My admiration for his genius has during fifty years and more been marred for me by dissent from almost any view that he holds about anything,' Max was to acknowledge in a letter written for Shaw's ninetieth birthday. And G.B.S. endorsed this: 'Max's blessings are all of them thinly disguised curses.' Max reinforced the disgust Shaw himself felt at the Shavian publicity phenomenon. After a couple of highly successful speeches in Glasgow during the first week of October 1903 he wrote to Trebitsch: 'I have hardly yet quite recovered from the self-loathing which such triumphs produce . . .

'I always suffer torments of remorse when the degrading exhibition is over. However, the thing had to be done; and there was no doing it by halves . . . I am not at all ashamed of what I said: it was excellent sense; but the way I said it – ugh! All that assumption of stupendous earnestness – merely to drive a little common sense into a crowd, like nails into a very tough board – leaves one empty, exhausted, disgusted.'

Max and Charlotte found themselves in agreement over G.B.S. He was never an artist, they said, but a reformer. 'That is what I always tell him,' insisted Charlotte. But in their married life it was she who attempted to reform him. Since it was only on holiday that, as he put it, 'I prefer to leave my public character behind me and to be treated as far as possible as a quite private and unknown individual', she tried to lead him on a succession of long holidays. During April and May 1901 she had him touring through France with her; and in July and August she planted him in Studland Rectory at Corfe Castle in Dorset. 'This is a very enchanting place – to look at,' Shaw informed Beatrice Webb. 'It also has the curious property of reviving every malady, every cramp, every pain, every bone fracture even, from which one has ever suffered.'

Next year Charlotte packed them both off to a safe hotel on the Norfolk coast for the summer. 'The only way to rest and get plenty of work done at the same time is to go to sea,' Shaw later concluded. This was not what Charlotte had in mind. She wanted to take him away from all his work. She wanted to banish the employer and make him wholly, for a time, her child.

In the spring of 1903 she rushed him through Parma, Perugia, Assisi, Orvieto, Siena, Genoa and Milan. 'I am getting old and demoralized,' he confessed to Janet Achurch, 'I have been in Italy for three weeks.' Three months later she placed him in Scotland, and held him there for ten weeks. 'There is no railway, no town, no shops, no society, no music, no entertainments, no beautiful ladies, absolutely nothing but fresh air and eternal rain,' Shaw wrote. 'Our house is primitive; our food is primitive; we do nothing but wander about, cycle against impossible winds, or pull a heavy fisherman's boat about the loch . . .'

For most Christmases Charlotte would board him out with her at a bracing hotel or in one of the houses she had rented. In April 1902 they had given up Piccard's Cottage at Guildford and the following year took instead a country house, Maybury Knoll, in a favourite part of Surrey, near Woking. Here they spent winter weekends and the whole of Christmas at the end of 1903, after which Charlotte was to rent a grander place at the top of a hill overlooking Welwyn which she liked better.

No sooner had Charlotte marched him up to the top of the hill than she marched him down again – and back to Italy. They started out on 1 May 1904 and arrived back in London on 10 June. A week later Shaw began a new play, his thirteenth, to be called *John Bull's Other Island*. Charlotte shuttled him between Adelphi Terrace and Welwyn, and then returned him, protesting, for the summer to Scotland. 'Our expedition has been so far a ruinous failure,' he calculated. 'The place is impossible – no place to write – no place to bathe . . . Oh these holidays, these accursed holidays!'

For fourteen years they were to go through every holiday side by side, despite his belief that married people 'should never travel together: they blame one another for everything that goes wrong.' It was particularly irritating for him to see how she preened herself on toning up his health while really driving him mad; it was exasperating for her to find, however exorbitant their journeys, he never failed to carry his work with him everywhere. But still they manacled themselves, each for the sake of the other. 'I am overacting the part of a respectable married man,' Shaw admitted. 'But I am only rehearsing for my old age: my guiltiest passions are still glowing beneath the surface.'

3

SHAKES VERSUS SHAV

I am not writing popular plays just now.

Shaw to Alma Murray (19 February 1901)

'You know all about "The Admirable Bashville", or at least you would know if you ever read my books,' Trebitsch read in one of Shaw's letters.

The Admirable Bashville or *Constancy Unrewarded* was itself a translation from Shaw's novel, *Cashel Byron's Profession*, into a three-act play in 'the primitive Elizabethan style'. This was Shaw's eleventh play and he had finished it in a week on 2 February 1901. Hearing rumours that there were several pirated stage versions of his novel in the United States, and that one of these productions was coming to Britain, he 'took the opportunity to produce a masterpiece' in order to protect his copyright. He squeezed out of this exercise all the fun he could, using it as another squib against bardolatry and claiming that he had been forced to employ the rigmarole of Shakespearian verse (of which 'I am childishly fond'), occasionally patching in actual lines from Shakespeare and Marlowe, because he did not have the time to write it all in prose. Having plagiarized his own work and parodied Shakespeare's, he produced a caricature of his advertising methods. It was, he assured Trebitsch, 'my greatest play'. But this delight in what was 'my only achievement in pure letters' began to recoil once other playwrights hit on the notion of agreeing with him.

A number of Shaw's 'serious intentions' are planted in the burlesque. He has some fun with phonetics; he airs his expertise on self-defence; he owns up to the loneliness of excellence and devotes some mighty lines to family and filial sentiment. There is a surge of real feeling when Cashel contrasts the presumed barbarities of boxing with the concealed cruelties of polite life.

> . . . this hand
> That many a two days bruise hath ruthless given,
> Hath kept no dungeon locked for twenty years,
> Hath slain no sentient creature for my sport.
> I am too squeamish for your dainty world,
> That cowers behind the gallows and the lash,
> The world that robs the poor, and with their spoil
> Does what its tradesmen tell it. Oh, your ladies!
> Sealskinned and egret-feathered; all defiance
> To Nature; cowering if one say to them
> 'What will the servants think?' Your gentlemen!
> Your tailor-tyrannized visitors of whom
> Flutter of wing and singing in the wood
> Make chickenbutchers. And your medicine men!
> Groping for cures in the tormented entrails
> Of friendly dogs. Pray have you asked all these
> To change their occupations? Find you mine
> So grimly crueller? I cannot breathe
> An air so petty and so poisonous.

Shaw assisted Harley Granville Barker in directing the first professional presentation of the play, put on by the Stage Society on 7 and 8 June 1903 at the Imperial Theatre in London. It was an early instance of the working association between the two men, and laid down the lines for their later collaborative work at the Court Theatre. Barker was (in the modern sense) stage-manager and Shaw arrived fairly late in the preparation of his play. He hunted enthusiastically for bird-whistles, some soft-nosed spears, a white beaver hat, post-horn, one enormous blue handkerchief with white spots, a throne: also 'We shall want a crowd'); and directed it in the Elizabethan stage manner with traverses, and two beefeaters with placards denoting the scenes. He insisted that it should be announced as 'Bernard Shaw's celebrated drama in blank verse with, possibly, an epigraph: "If you have tears, prepare to shed them now." Shakespeare.'

As in his subsequent 'Interlude', *The Dark Lady of the Sonnets*, the humour depends upon the audience's familiarity with Shakespeare. Those with no Shakespearian knowledge would sit bewildered or else, in all earnestness, break into applause. Despite its awkward playing length, the Stage Society production 'went with a roar from beginning to end'. The policeman (played by the cricketer C. Aubrey Smith, later to become famous as a Hollywood film actor) was made up as G.B.S. so effectively that his mother, sitting next to him, was deeply perplexed.

Also performed was the copyright trick of upstaging all American dramatizations of the novel – including one by Stanislas Strange (who was to write the libretto for *The Chocolate Soldier*) and starring, as Cashel Byron, former world heavyweight champion 'Gentleman Jim' Corbett.

The Admirable Bashville was published by Grant Richards in October 1901 as part of a new edition of *Cashel Byron's Profession* that also included Shaw's essay 'A Note on Modern Prizefighting'. The book was reviewed at length, and disconcertingly, by Max Beerbohm.

'As a passage by steam is to a voyage by sail, so is Mr Shaw's fiction to true fiction . . . he wants to impress certain theories on us, to convert us to this or that view. The true creator wishes mainly to illude us with a sense of actual or imaginative reality. To achieve that aim, he must suppress himself and his theories: they kill illusion. He must accept life as it presents itself to his experience or imagination, not use his brain to twist it into the patterns of a purpose. Such self-sacrifice is beyond Mr Shaw.'

Here was the most coherent argument so far raised against the Shavian art. Shaw could not create: his characters were all victims of Shavian theses, all parts of himself differentiated only by quick changes and superficial idiosyncrasies. On another level, as a personality, G.B.S. was immortal. There was no one like him. Seriousness and frivolity were the essence of Shavianism. 'He is not a serious man trying to be frivolous,' Beerbohm explained. 'He is a serious man who cannot help being frivolous, and in him height of spirits is combined with depth of conviction more illustriously than in any of his compatriots.' It did not matter what he wrote. All his writing was filleted with Shavianism – that quality whose deep seriousness served artistically to raise the humour. 'As a teacher, as a propagandist, Mr Shaw is no good at all,' Beerbohm joyfully concluded. It was as a comedian whose frivolity, vampire-like, sucked the seriousness from his work, that he was unique. So when he claimed apropos his next play, *Man and Superman*, that 'the matter isnt really in my hands. I have to say the things that seem to me to want saying', everyone sharing Beerbohm's view of G.B.S. drew in their breath and prepared to greet it with a good laugh.

4

MAN AND SUPERMAN

You must not translate it, as you would get six years in a fortress for the
preface alone.

Shaw to Trebitsch (7 July 1902)

The characters had started talking inside Shaw's head over two years
before. In May 1900 he began outlining a Parliament in Hell between
Don Juan and the Devil. Around the Socratic debate he composed a
three-act comedy, completing the scenario between 2 July and 8 October
1901. He worked between accidents and on journeys, in hotels and at
home: he worked whenever Charlotte took her eye off him until, in June
1902, this many-layered work, now called *Man and Superman. A Comedy
and a Philosophy*, was finished – when the business of revision immediately
began. In January 1903 Shaw read it aloud to the Webbs at the Overstrand
Hotel at Cromer in Norfolk. 'To me it seems a great work; quite the
biggest thing he has done,' Beatrice wrote in her diary. 'He has found his
form: a play which is not a play; but only a combination of essay, treatise,
interlude, lyric – all the different forms illustrating the same central idea.'

Since it was 'useless as an acting play', he explained to Hamon, being
'as long as three Meyerbeer operas and no audience that had not already
had a Shaw education could stand it', he had decided to publish *Man and
Superman* himself, abandoning Grant Richards and signing an agreement
with Archibald Constable to act as distribution agent for his works – an
agreement that lasted the remaining forty-seven years of his life.

Man and Superman was published on 11 August 1903. 'I cannot be a
bellettrist,' Shaw wrote in his Preface. 'Effectiveness of assertion is the
Alpha and Omega of style. He who has nothing to assert has no style and
can have none: he who has something to assert will go as far in power of
style as its momentousness and his conviction will carry him. Disprove
his assertion after it is made, yet its style remains.'

Between style and art and power and reality Shaw crossed the lines of
his argument with such dexterity as to bring almost everyone into confusion. Critics were fixed in his net of words – though not Max Beerbohm
who seemed to slip between the meshes. Max was to draw a caricature of
Shaw bringing a bundle of clothes to the Danish critic, Georg Brandes
(who is represented as a pawnbroker), and asking for immortality in
exchange for the lot. Brandes protests: 'Come, I've handled these goods
before! Coat, Mr Schopenhauer's; waistcoat, Mr Ibsen's; Mr Nietzsche's

trousers – .' To which Shaw answers: 'Ah, but look at the patches!' As for style, Max astutely judged his Alpha and Omega to be 'more akin to the art of oral debating than of literary exposition. That is because he trained himself to speak before he trained himself to write.'

For the same reason, Max conceded, Shaw excelled in writing words to be spoken by the human voice. 'In swiftness, tenseness and lucidity of dialogue no living writer can touch the hem of Mr Shaw's garment,' Max wrote. 'In *Man and Superman* every phrase rings and flashes. Here, though Mr Shaw will be angry with me, is perfect art.' For Shaw *used* art 'as a means of making people listen to him . . .

'He is as eager to be a popular dramatist and . . . willing to demean himself in any way that may help him to the goal . . . I hope he will reach the goal. It is only the theatrical managers who stand between him and the off-chance of a real popular success.'

Man and Superman, Max concluded, was Shaw's masterpiece so far. This 'most complete expression of the most distinct personality in current literature' showed G.B.S. able to employ art without becoming an artist and excelling in dialogue without developing into a playwright. From this opinion Max somewhat recanted two years later when he saw *Man and Superman* (in its three-act version) performed on stage. It was not only the humanizing of Shaw's words by living actors that changed his mind. He also appears to have been swayed by Shaw's argument that, as a caricaturist, Max also did not 'see things and men as they are', but that his distortions, far from disqualifying him as an artist, were the essence of his art. The artist creates his own reality and his own epoch: and Britain was about to enter a Shavian epoch. Max sensed this. Shaw was one of those for whom the visible world had largely ceased to exist and was being replaced by a world seen through his mind's eye. That it was a world disliked by Max was partly the reason why he had denied its creator artistic capacity. The production of *John Bull's Other Island* in 1904 was to convince him that Shaw had 'an instinct for the theatre'. And when he saw *Man and Superman* on stage in 1905, he prepared to make way for the coming Shavian revolution in the British theatre:

'Mr Shaw, it is insisted, cannot draw life: he can only distort it. He has no knowledge of human nature: he is but a theorist. All his characters are but so many incarnations of himself. Above all, he cannot write plays. He has no dramatic instinct, no theatrical technique . . .

That theory might have held water in the days before Mr Shaw's plays were acted. Indeed, I was in the habit of propounding it myself . . . When

Man and Superman was published, I . . . said that (even without the philosophic scene in hell) it would be quite unsuited to any stage. When I saw it performed . . . I found that as a piece of theatrical construction it was perfect . . . to deny that he is a dramatist merely because he chooses, for the most part, to get drama out of contrasted types of character and thought, without action, and without appeal to the emotions, seems to me both unjust and absurd. His technique is peculiar because his purpose is peculiar. But it is not the less technique.'

*

Man and Superman is the first in a trilogy of plays in which Shaw's thesis and antithesis of fact and fantasy produced the synthesis of evolutionary progress. Creative evolution had the potential for replacing his lonely sense of being 'a sojourner on this planet rather than a native of it' with the feeling of being part of the collective consciousness 'up to the chin in the life of his own time'. The Life Force was not a rival scientific theory to Darwin's Natural Selection, but a different outlook on life. By making external a division he felt to exist within himself Shaw was able to use an intellectual method – the Hegelian triad which he had picked up from the British socialist philosopher Belfort Bax – of reconciling opposites and bringing harmony to his life. He wished to create the new drama in which, as in a series of parables, he could rewrite history and set it on a new course.

The Hegelian structure became a model for his thought. Reviewing a novel by Moncure Conway early in 1888, he had written of Hegelianism as never having been positively 'adapted and translated into practical English politics'. In the hands of Marx, it had been 'chiefly effective as a scathing but quite negative criticism of industrial individualism'.

It was positive Hegelianism that Shaw wanted to import into English politics. This is made explicit in a letter he sent some fifteen years later to the Labour Member of Parliament Charles Trevelyan. 'A Government . . . if it is really to govern and propagate its species . . . must have a common religion, which nowadays means a philosophy and a science, and it must have an economic policy founded on that religion.

'Well, I contend that such a nexus exists . . . you will find it in Thomas Hardy's poems at one extreme of literature and in the blitherings of Christian Science at the other. But take two expositions that may be known to you: the third act of Man and Superman and Bergson's Creative Evolution. These are totally independent of one another: Bergson and I would have written as we did, word for word, each if the other had never been born. And yet one is a dramatization of the other. Our very catchwords, Life Force and Élan Vital, are translations of one another . . . why not a creative-evolutionist party? . . .

The economic policy of the party is clear enough. Everyone who can see the sun shining at noon can also see that there is only one main problem to be solved, and that is the redistribution of income. Also that it is not only an economic question, but a political and biological one. Here you have a body of doctrine on which a party could be built literally over a whole epoch.'

Towards the third act of his play Shaw felt especially protective. Its long second scene, staged as a dream and held in a chronological paradox 'Beyond Space, Beyond Time', is a science fiction made from Shaw's retrospective longings. It is a contest between his optimism for which the Tanner-surrogate Don Juan speaks, and his pessimism which is represented by Mendoza's counterpart, the Devil. Agreeing on much, they are divided in their debate over the need and practicality of human progress. Both are contemptuous of the morality of pretence which filled the Victorian theatre and reflected the conventions of life outside. But what are the alternatives? The Devil says fantasy and play; Don Juan says the evolution of a higher type of human being.

Heaven and hell are not states of afterlife but metaphors for opposing temperaments, values and philosophies. Juan defines hell as 'the home of the unreal and of the seekers for happiness . . . Here you escape this tyranny of the flesh; for here you are not an animal at all: you are . . . in a word, bodiless . . . here there are no hard facts to contradict you, no ironic contrast of your needs with your pretensions, no human comedy, nothing but a perpetual romance.'

This aspect of Shaw's hell was to become a factor of his theology almost twenty years later in *Back to Methuselah* where the tyranny of the flesh disappears in a whirlpool of pure thought. Here was a three-hundred-year romance by an extremely fastidious man whose disgust with the physical condition of human beings compelled him to eliminate them from his philosophy. 'There are no social questions here, no political questions, no religious questions, best of all, perhaps, no sanitary questions.' Shaw's formula for hell in *Man and Superman* has enough in common with the bodiless Utopia of *Back to Methuselah* to suggest that the Devil may surreptitiously be going to win a good part of his case.

Conventional morals will always succumb to the Devil's attractions. To resist his hell, Juan argues, we need evolutionary morals. If reality is worry, ugliness and age, sadness and tragedy and death, why not, asks the Devil, use your ingenuity to create a life of endless escape from it? For two reasons, answers Juan. Nature has given man a brain; he needs the

power of self-awareness and understanding. The direct pursuit of happiness and beauty leads to misery – happiness may only be gained as a by-
product of other endeavours. Secondly, life is not composed as the Devil
would like us to believe. It is an illusion to think that we can solve our
problems. From each problem solved springs some new challenge. So life
must forever progress upwards: or end. Man's quest for knowledge has
set him off on the great adventure of transforming his environment and
understanding the universe. He may not stop the world and go off on a
perpetual holiday.

Juan's belief in brains provokes the Devil into his first great counter-
attack. 'Have you walked up and down upon the earth lately?' he enquires.
What have human brains done but produce more awful weapons of
destruction? It is when we become too ambitious on behalf of the human
race that we end up destroying ourselves. His monologue amounts to a
conservative attack on the illusions of progress and a recommendation of
the aristocratic principle of cultivated living.

Don Juan's reply reveals his belief that salvation depends upon the urge
to transcend past achievements. It is easily conceivable that the world will
blow itself up, or Western civilization peter out, unless this human urge
is renewed. But the Devil is no vulgar hedonist. 'I am also on the
intellectual plane,' he says. It is the credulous strivers after perfection in
the social organization, he insists, who slaughter millions. He, the Devil,
stands for moral principles in that he treats people as ends, not means.

The resolution to their debate comes through Doña Ana with her cry
at the end of the scene: 'a father for the Superman!' And so, from the
two ways of serving the Life Force, the biological and the intellectual,
Shaw gives priority in time to the first. Evolutionary progress, he suggests,
depends on sexual instinct; on the coming together of opposites to produce
through generations a better human combination of mind and body. In
The Quintessence of Ibsenism and *The Perfect Wagnerite*, the battle had been
fought between realist and idealist for the mind of the philistine; in *Man
and Superman* the evolutionary need for greater intelligence lies in the
sexual conquest of the realist by the philistine. So the dramatic pursuit
of the intellectual Tanner by the predatory Ann is not a defeat for
intelligence after all. Tanner's dream and disquisition with the Devil is
Shaw's attempt, through operatic argument, to achieve the 'drama of
thought'. But Don Juan's speeches grow too long and, behind their
resolute optimism, reveal Shaw's panic.

There is no doubt that Shaw intended Don Juan to win the debate.
Against the common belief in a God who looked at the world and saw
that it was good, he postulated a God who looked and saw it could be
bettered. 'I tell you that as long as I can conceive something better than

myself I cannot be easy unless I am striving to bring it into existence or clearing the way for it,' says Juan. 'That is the law of my life.' That this purpose is Shaw's own is made clear by a parallel passage in the 'Epistle Dedicatory', where he writes: 'This is the true joy in life, the being used for a purpose recognized by yourself as a mighty one.'

Tanner wins all his word-battles. Ann wins the actual battle between them. Shaw's Superman was a symbol for the synthesis between word and deed.

Only the obtuseness of theatre managers, as Beerbohm had said, was able to postpone Shaw's success as a playwright. The younger generation of theatre audiences was waiting for him. Almost two years after publication of the book the three-act play was first performed. This version, full of melancholic autobiographical undertones, has a precise theatrical unity. It is a romantic courtship comedy about the stock subjects of marriage and money, and has all the farcical episodes of the love-chase. The Victorian and Edwardian theatregoer would easily recognize the situations and characters. There is a love-pursuit through Europe, a capture by brigands and a rescue; there is a clandestine marriage, an emotional triangle, the reading of a will, a happy ending; the stage is peopled by standard figures – the romantic artist, the heavy father, the lover and the servant in a long line from Leporello and Sancho Panza to Sam Weller and Jeeves.

Yet nothing is what it seems to be and everywhere romantic expectation is confounded. Shaw replaces the woman-on-a-pedestal with the female huntress; the new woman with the technological man. The play is crowded with paradoxical reversals. His brigands are vestrymen and Fabians, their leader a love-afflicted sentimentalist; the rich and difficult father turns out to be a social eccentric who wants a misalliance for his son and is reconciled to his marriage not by his daughter-in-law's purity and sweetness but her business acumen. A daughter dominates her mother; a servant rules his employer; and the governing action of the play is the woman's pursuit of her lover. Hell is revealed as a sentimentalist's picture of heaven.

In this skill at inverting popular conventions and creating genre antitypes lay the special power of Shaw's 'heretical' plays. He welcomed his audience into a world where everything was familiar to them, then upset all its values and forced it to 'reconsider its morals'.

5

JOHN BULL'S OTHER ISLAND

The object of the play is to teach Irish people the value of an Englishman as well as to shew the Englishman his own absurdities.

'Author's Instructions to the Producer', *John Bull's Other Island*

Two years separated the completion of *Man and Superman* from the composition of Shaw's next play. Shortly before the publication of *Man and Superman*, Shaw confided to Yeats that he had it 'quite seriously in my head to write an Irish play (frightfully modern – no banshees or leprechauns)'; but he did nothing further until what seemed a fair chance appeared.

It was Yeats who gave him this chance. Together with Lady Gregory and Edward Martyn, he had founded the Irish Literary Theatre which proposed to create in Dublin 'a Celtic and Irish school of dramatic literature . . . [with] that freedom to experiment which is not found in theatres of England'. They must 'escape the stupefying memory of the theatre of commerce' which clung to London's West End.

There was much that was familiar in this to Shaw and much that appealed to him. Lady Gregory was to his mind 'the greatest living Irishwoman'; Edward Martyn, an owl-blinking misogynist, lover of wine and caviar, and first president of Sinn Fein, was an admirer of Ibsen; and Yeats manoeuvred his theatre colleagues with all the skill Shaw devoted to the Fabians. In 1902 Yeats fell in with the Fay brothers, Frank and Willy, and their little band of Irish actors. From this association, the following year, the Irish National Theatre Society was born with Yeats himself as president, and a new set of colleagues, Maud Gonne, Douglas Hyde and the poet, theosophist and visionary painter George Russell (known as A.E.) its vice-presidents. In the spring of 1904, the Society was invited to play at the Royalty Theatre in London, and Shaw went along to watch them. They played Synge's *In the Shadow of the Glen* and *Riders to the Sea*; Yeats's *The King's Threshold* and *A Pot of Broth*; and Padraic Colum's *Broken Soil*, all showing the influence of Gordon Craig's revolt against the elaborate productions of Irving and Beerbohm Tree. It was then that Shaw opened his eyes to a renaissance in the Irish theatre.

Yet it had been, until this year, a hole-and-corner affair not dissimilar, in its fashion, to the Stage Society. What changed matters was the involvement of Annie Horniman who bought a ninety-nine-year lease on a small music-hall theatre within the Mechanics Institute on the corner of Lower Abbey Street, and adjacent premises in Marlborough Street that 'had served as a bank, the home of a nationalist debating society, a recruiting centre for the Fenian movement, and the City Morgue'. She now offered Yeats, as president of the Society, use of the new theatre cost-free. The Abbey Theatre was to open its doors at the end of 1904, and it was for this opening, 'as a patriotic contribution to the repertory of the Irish Literary Theatre', that Yeats invited Shaw to write his next play.

'Not a word of the play yet on paper,' Shaw promised Lady Gregory on 20 June. In fact he had begun writing it, under the provisional title *Rule Britannia*, in a pocket notebook three days earlier while staying with Charlotte at Hindhead. It continued seething in his mind and filling his notebooks over the next ten weeks.

On 7 September Shaw sent the completed play to Ethel Dickens with instructions to type it out and forward a copy to Yeats. He had been horrified to find that the autograph manuscript, scattered through four pocket notebooks, contained about 32,000 words. Henry Arthur Jones, he recollected, had put 18,000 as the correct length, 'but I am too exhausted to attempt to cut it,' he told Yeats.

In *John Bull's Other Island* Shaw contrasted the twenty years of his upbringing in Dublin with the twenty years of his career in London. At one level, which he later developed in his Preface, the play is about the opposing political histories and national characteristics of the two countries. But Ireland and England are also metaphors for differing philosophies: and Shaw's experiment at reconciling them is the theme of this self-revealing work.

'Live in contact with dreams and you will get something of their charm: live in contact with facts and you will get something of their brutality. I wish I could find a country to live in where the facts were not brutal and the dreams not unreal.' This wish, voiced by Larry Doyle, the exiled Irishman working in England, was the motive-power behind these middle-period plays. Larry Doyle is the vertex of a triangle at one corner of which stands the successful English businessman Tom Broadbent, and at the other Peter Keegan, the unfrocked Irish priest, who meet over Broadbent's plan to form a Land Development Syndicate.

In Broadbent Shaw created, for Irish audiences, the stage-Englishman, having in the first scene chased the stage-Irishman Tim Haffigan off as an impostor. Broadbent represents the world of facts, however brutal; Keegan the world of dreams, however unreal. Broadbent is the perfect philistine, a 'robust, full-blooded, energetic man in the prime of life'. His kingdom is the material world. He feels happy in what Keegan describes as 'very clearly a place of torment and penance'. On the contrary, Broadbent declares, it is 'quite good enough for me: rather a jolly place, in fact'.

The key to Broadbent's success is his narrowness of intelligence and imagination. He simplifies everything for profitable use. 'The only really simple thing is to go straight for what you want and grab it,' says another philistine, Ann Whitefield, in *Man and Superman*. Broadbent is the acquisitive man. Within twenty-four hours of arriving at Rosscullen he has collared the parliamentary seat, taken up Larry's sweetheart Nora Reilly and acquired the land for development. He brings to Ireland a terrible corruption of Shaw's belief in improvement, but he brings it cheerfully. The stage directions picture him as 'always buoyant and irresistible'.

Everything that is absent from Broadbent goes to make the character of Peter Keegan. Broadbent could be played by a Falstaffian performer; Keegan needed 'a poetic actor'. Broadbent is a land speculator interested in the modern technology of motor cars, neat golf links, new hotels. Keegan, who loves the land, speaks with grasshoppers and calls the donkey, the ass and the pig his brothers. In contrast to Father Dempsey, the parochial reality, Keegan is 'an ideal Catholic', the first and most convincing of Shaw's mystical sages, who retreats at the end of the play to the Round Tower and will reappear briefly as Androcles and later as the damaged Captain Shotover in *Heartbreak House*.

Into Keegan's mouth Shaw put his own fastidious sense of horror at Broadbent's world –

'[a] place where the fool flourishes and the good and wise are hated and persecuted, a place where men and women torture one another in the name of love; where children are scourged and enslaved in the name of parental duty and education; where the weak in body are poisoned and mutilated in the name of healing, and the weak in character are put to the horrible torture of imprisonment, not for hours but for years, in the name of justice.'

Broadbent's schemes for the future ('this place may have an industrial future, or it may have a residential future') do not impress Keegan who replies that it 'may have no future at all'.

Broadbent embodies action, Keegan speaks for the emotions and Larry Doyle represents the intellect. Throughout the play there is a bias in favour of action. Larry has had only two ideas: 'to learn to do something; and then to get out of Ireland and have a chance of doing it'. Ireland 'produces two kinds of men in strange perfection: saints and traitors,' we are told. If Keegan is the saint, Larry Doyle is the traitor. He has repressed everything he shares with Keegan: he has rejected Ireland. Shaw's stage directions throughout Larry's long speech on 'the dreaming! the torturing, heart-scalding, never satisfying dreaming, dreaming, dreaming, dreaming!' of Ireland underline the personal feeling he put into these pages: '*With sudden anguish ... Savagely ... bitterly, at Broadbent ... With fierce shivering self-contempt ... Dropping his voice like a man making some shameful confidence.*'

Not sharing Keegan's self-sufficiency, Larry must borrow his strength from Broadbent's self-confidence. Otherwise, he says, 'I should never have done anything'. It is Broadbent who sees clearly the price Larry has paid. 'He has absolutely no capacity for enjoyment,' Broadbent tells Nora: 'he couldn't make any woman happy. He's as clever as be-blowed; but ... he doesn't really care for anything or anybody.'

Keegan is the man Sonny might have grown into if he had been able to endure the anguish of living in the Land of Dreams; Larry Doyle, with his 'clever head', his 'suggestion of thinskinnedness and dissatisfaction' and determination to be ruthless, must have been Shaw's nightmare. The syndicate which Keegan and Broadbent have formed (in which Larry owns a 'bit of the stock') is not the synthesis between dreams and facts for which Shaw was looking. It is a business partnership in which Larry's intellectual powers are used to serve Broadbent's philistine aims.

The second partnership in the play, that between Broadbent and Nora, is not a marriage of body and spirit, but a devouring of the spirit by the body. A 'frail figure', she is 'almost sexless' and he, with his 'good broad chest', promises to 'plump out your muscles and make em elastic and set up your figure'. She is his ethereal 'ideal' and he will make her into the housewife of 'a solid four-square home'.

Everyone remains separated in the play and no one is converted. Broadbent takes charge of the world; Keegan retires to his tower; and the conflict within Larry is not reconciled. He has split life into dreams and facts, and chosen facts as reality.

But was the world of facts real? Shaw's insistence that it was is continually interrupted by his subversive humour and a pessimism that undermines much of what he dedicated his career to establishing. 'Every dream is a prophecy: every jest is an earnest in the womb of Time,' says Keegan who explains to Nora that 'my way of joking is to tell the truth'. It is Keegan who sees reality in dreams and strikes an apocalyptic note over Shaw's own Fabian territory of statistics: 'For four wicked centuries the world has dreamed this foolish dream of efficiency; and the end is not yet. But the end will come.'

*

The play was 'a wonderful piece of work' and 'full of good things,' William Fay, the Abbey Theatre manager, reported to Yeats. Synge, too, believed it would 'hold a Dublin audience, and at times move them if even tolerably played'. And Yeats wrote to Shaw: 'I thought in reading the first act that you had forgotten Ireland, but I found in the other acts that it is the only subject on which you are entirely serious . . .

'You have said things in this play which are entirely true about Ireland, things which nobody has ever said before . . . It astonishes me that you should have been so long in London and yet have remembered so much. To some extent this play is unlike anything you have done before. Hitherto you have taken your situations from melodrama, and called up logic to make them ridiculous. Your process here seems to be quite different, you are taking your situations more from life, you are for the first time trying to get the atmosphere of a place . . . a geographical conscience . . . You have laughed at the things that are ripe for laughter, and not where the ear is still green . . . we can play it, and survive to play something else.'

Yet there were difficulties. The company met to discuss these difficulties in the second week of October 1904: the difficulty of length; the difficulty of getting a cast; the difficulty of handling modern appliances such as grasshoppers and hydraulic bridges. These difficulties accumulated as they argued, silencing a more fundamental difficulty: that (to use Shaw's words in the Preface to the 1906 edition) 'it was uncongenial to the whole spirit of the neo-Gaelic movement, which is bent on creating a new Ireland after its own ideal, whereas my play is a very uncompromising presentment of the real old Ireland'. Yeats was to concede when he saw it performed in London that 'it acts very much better than one could have foreseen'. Like Max Beerbohm, he had underrated Shaw's instinct for the theatre partly because 'I don't really like it,' he wrote. 'It is fundamentally ugly and shapeless.'

The shape of the play, loosely constructed round a string of character-turns with the emphasis directed away from the action and focused on a parallel series of discussions that occur at rather unremarkable moments (the after-breakfast pause, the after-tea stroll) makes use of the conventional props of Irish Romance to explode the Irish romantic ideal. Yeats instinctively felt opposed to such extravaganza. Yeats's writing was oblique and Shaw's assertive; and Yeats wrote poetry where Shaw laughed. All they shared were the same enemies. 'If I had gone to the hills nearby to look upon Dublin and to ponder upon myself, I too might have become a poet like Yeats, Synge and the rest of them,' Shaw stated. 'But I prided myself on thinking clearly, and therefore could not stay. Whenever I took a problem or a state of life of which my Irish contemporaries sang sad songs, I always pushed it to its logical conclusions, and then inevitably it resolved itself into comedy.'

Such a passage helps to explain Yeats's description of Shaw as a 'barbarian of the barricades'. When Shaw made Larry Doyle deride Keegan as sentimental, chastise the eternal dreaming in himself, and question the holy ground on which they both stood, he uprooted the Irish legends from which sprang Lady Gregory's and Yeats's plays. His 'queer elephant' of a play seemed antagonistic to everything the Abbey Theatre was to achieve. 'We all admire it,' Yeats wrote: and between them all a polite understanding was kept up that it had merely been too large and difficult a work for the Abbey to handle.

Yeats could recognize the wonderful power of Shaw's pen – its logic, justice, audacity, conviction. But Shaw represented 'the spirit of the press, of hurry, of immediate interests' over what Yeats felt was the slow-burning spirit of literature. He was consuming his own talent with superficial theatricality, the unnerving tic of his wit, rambling vulgarity – anything that seemed to stiffen the purpose of the moment.

6

GRANVILLE BARKER COMES TO COURT

We shall have to play off the piece as a very advanced and earnest card
in the noble game of elevating the British theatre.

Shaw to Granville Barker (24 August 1904)

Looking around for an actor suitable to play Marchbanks for a Sunday performance of *Candida* at the Strand Theatre in the summer of 1900, Charrington had proposed the name of Harley Granville Barker. At the sixth 'meeting' of the Stage Society, Barker played Marchbanks and was 'the success of the piece', Shaw told Archer. This performance of *Candida* completed the Stage Society's first season. The Society was now the principal rallying point for things modern in the theatre. On 16 July 1900 the maximum membership was increased from three to five hundred (each paying a yearly subscription of two guineas) and a decision was taken to add to the private Sunday evening presentation a weekday matinée to which the press (though required to pay) would be admitted. Performances were still described as 'meetings'; no scenery was employed and no salary offered to the actors who all received the same nominal sum – one guinea – for expenses. These rules enabled the Society legally to present new British plays as well as classical and contemporary foreign dramas (for some of which the Censor had refused a licence).

The Stage Society's Sunday evening and Monday afternoon performances gave Barker some experience as a director as well as actor, particularly in the presentation of his own four-act comedy, *The Marrying of Ann Leete*. 'Do you realise that he is a great poet and dramatist,' Shaw asked Henry Arthur Jones. ' . . . His *The Marrying of Ann Leete* is really an exquisite play. I truckle to G.B. in order to conciliate him when he is forty.' Behind this half-frivolous tone was the feeling that he was no longer alone: at last he had a successor in the theatre, someone to share, inherit and modify the Shavian stage experiment. Before *Ann Leete*, Barker had written other plays. Like Shaw's, they had seemed unplayable. But Shaw 'found them fascinating'. At first he had doubted whether Barker's 'delicacy of style' would travel across the footlights. But on seeing *Ann Leete* performed under Barker's own stage management, 'I had to confess that he had succeeded,' Shaw wrote.

'There is a sort of dainty strangeness about it that fits its eighteenth century period and costumes; and the curious way in which it begins in a garden at midnight takes it so effectually out of the Philistine key that its quaint fantastic conversation, consisting mostly of hints and innuendoes, seems to belong to it naturally.'

Here lay the theatre of the future. Shaw felt a special tenderness towards the young man, as if his own blatant qualities, obliterating much that was sensitive in himself, had served to protect him. After all, it had been to bulldoze Irving's execrable Lyceum mutilations off the stage that the phenomenon of G.B.S. had been partly manufactured. That Barker could afford to take no notice of Irving was partly due to G.B.S.; and partly, of course, a matter of age.

Shaw was twenty-one years older than Barker, 'old enough', he wrote, 'to be his father'. This was indeed the peculiar kinship he felt for him. He had grown up in an atmosphere of good speech and drama and with a thorough knowledge of Dickens and Shakespeare. He scored his first stage success in 1899 playing Richard II for William Poel, but was to be no happier as a successful actor than Shaw was as a successful platform speaker. Beatrice Webb observed him to be 'a most attractive person . . . good looking in a charming refined fashion – with a subtle intellectual expression – faculties more analytic than artistic?

' . . . with varied interests, good memory, a sharp observer of human nature and above all a delicate appreciation of music, poetry and art – a medley of talents of which I do not yet see a very definite whole. He has not yet emancipated himself from G.B.S.'s influence or found his own soul.'

Barker's incompleteness fascinated people. What Beatrice thought of as the influence of G.B.S. was probably a similarity of temperament. 'I am an intellectual, but by no means a dramatic disciple of G.B.S.,' Barker declared. 'We have quite different ideas . . .' G.B.S. agreed. 'We were as different as Verdi from Debussy.' Yet there was a natural intimacy between them. They talked much in quotations from Dickens and Shakespeare, using them as a private code. But they seldom discussed their own plays. 'We took them as they came, like facts of nature.' Shaw was able to watch and direct Barker in a number of his roles during the early stages of their friendship: he was Marchbanks, the poet Shaw had repressed in himself; he was Father Keegan, the best self Shaw had sealed up in the Round Tower; he played Jack Tanner made up with a beard to look like a younger G.B.S.; and in Shaw's next play *Major Barbara*, he was to play Adolphus Cusins, the foundling academic who is adopted as his heir by the Shavian father figure of Undershaft, also a foundling. From this succession of sympathetic roles a whisper arose that Barker was Shaw's natural son. The notion appealed to Shaw who observed that most people rejected the hypothesis 'on the ground that I am physically incapable of parentage'.

Barker fulfilled the imaginative role of son to Shaw's father and Charlotte's mother, replacing the natural child they never had. He seemed all things to all people – whatever they wanted most. Charlotte was one of several childless women in whom he prompted a maternal instinct. For G.B.S., Barker became someone to scold and schoolmaster, encourage and idealize; he was the juvenile lead with whom G.B.S. shared the family companionship of work.

In the summer of 1901 Barker and Shaw had joined the management committee of the Stage Society which had decided to put on *Mrs Warren's Profession* towards the end of that year. Because the play had not been granted a licence, however, thirteen theatres, three hotels, two music halls and the Royal Society of British Artists refused to lend their premises. From these difficulties and delays Shaw and Barker drew differing lessons. Shaw felt that the Stage Society was capable of putting on a 'tomfoolery' such as *The Admirable Bashville*; but a performance even of the first act of *Caesar and Cleopatra* was too large an enterprise: the Society could not scrape together 'the price of a sphinx & an old pantomime wardrobe for the Egyptian & Roman soldiers'. It was for this reason that he had turned to the Abbey Theatre.

For Barker, the cap-in-hand, door-to-door experiences over *Mrs Warren's Profession* had emphasized the need for a permanent theatre. His chance came early in 1904 when he was invited to produce *Two Gentlemen of Verona* at the Court Theatre in Sloane Square. The lease of this theatre had recently been bought by J. H. Leigh, a wealthy businessman and amateur actor, to stage a series of 'Shakespearean Representations' featuring his wife Thyrza Norman. The first two productions had been unsatisfactory and Leigh, coming to William Archer for help, was advised to employ Granville Barker for his next play. Leigh struck up an arrangement with Barker that allowed him to give six matinées of *Candida* at the Court. The play was well-received by the critics and actually made a profit.

Three weeks later Barker was producing Gilbert Murray's rhyming translation of Euripides' *Hippolytus* at the Lyric Theatre. 'J. H. Leigh has expressed himself bitten with the idea of doing Greek plays,' Barker confided to Murray. 'Not a word – but let us talk anon.' This talk between Barker, Leigh and the Court Theatre's manager J. E. Vedrenne 'led to the most important development in Barker's career'. He suggested giving regular matinées at the Court on those afternoons when the London West End theatres were closed. The management would then be able to engage first-class professional actors who would not be playing at those hours and, because they were interested in this new work, would be prepared to act for a nominal salary. Vedrenne took charge of the management and, with the backing of small sums of money from friends, they agreed to begin the experiment that autumn.

As the opening performance at the Court Theatre, he repeated the Murray–Euripides *Hippolytus*. The second Court play, after a good deal of negotiation, was *John Bull's Other Island*.

Nominally it was Barker who produced *John Bull's Other Island*; in fact it was Shaw. 'You can imagine the state I am in with rehearsing,' he wrote to the actress Ada Rehan. 'It is great fun; and I have got them all to the point of believing that this is the turning point of their careers, and that something immense is happening.' He had got himself to believe this too.

Shaw had strong opinions as to how all the parts should be played. But these opinions were for the actors to interpret and adapt: 'Dont worry yourself by trying to carry out my suggestions exactly or hampering yourself in any way with them,' he advised J. L. Shine, who was playing Larry Doyle. 'Very likely when you study them over you will be able to improve on them.

'That's all they're for. I think I am probably nearly right as to the best changes and stopping places on the journey; but as to the way of making

them, follow your own feeling and make the most of your own skill: turn
the whole thing inside out if you like . . . dont hesitate on my account to
make the part entirely your own.'

He was full of advice, but also ready to learn; and his tirades, being
comic performances themselves, did not shrivel the actors' self-confidence.
'I know very well that it is often the artists who give the author least
trouble who get the least acknowledgement and have their virtues taken
as a matter of course,' he wrote to Ellen O'Malley, who took the part of
Nora. 'This is not so, I hope, with me: I am very sensible of how good
you have been in every way, though I have had no opportunity of saying
so.'

The reviews, though sometimes niggardly, were good, and the best
critics wrote most enthusiastically. Max Beerbohm's notice in the *Saturday
Review* was headed 'Mr Shaw at his Best'. Desmond MacCarthy declared
the play to be 'an absolute success'; and William Archer in *The World*
wrote that Shaw 'has done nothing more original'.

To the fifth matinée, on 10 November, Beatrice Webb brought the
Conservative Prime Minister, Arthur Balfour. To her surprise he liked
the play so much that he eventually saw it five times, bringing with him
two leaders of the Liberal Opposition, Campbell-Bannerman and Asquith.
Most people in London saw it as a largely affectionate satire on the
Liberal Party's attitude towards Ireland, and Balfour himself praised it
for clearing away humbug. His interest led to a special evening performance being given, on 11 March 1905, for King Edward VII. The King
laughed so belligerently that he broke the special chair Vedrenne had
hired for the evening and, in falling, flung Shaw's dramatic reputation
high into the air. Here, a few months short of his fiftieth year, was success.
Yet he felt uneasy. What was it worth? What had been the cost? The
Prime Minister had told the King, and the King had told his countrymen,
and now they were all telling the world that G.B.S. was the funniest of
Irishmen. He began to react against the play, and gave his answer to his
King's heehawing by adding to the programme of a later production a
'personal appeal' to the audience not to demoralize the actors with shouts
of laughter and noisy applause.

'Would you dream of stopping the performance of a piece of music to
applaud every bar that happened to please you? and do you not know that
an act of a play is intended, just like a piece of music, to be heard without
interruption from beginning to end? . . . Have you noticed that people
look very nice when they smile or look pleased, but look shockingly ugly

when they roar with laughter or shout excitedly or sob loudly? Smiles make no noise.'

Eleven days after the royal command performance of *John Bull's Other Island*, he began a new play. In this, the last of his 'big three', he would challenge his own popularity and present himself as a moral revolutionist. 'The play is wildly impossible,' he told the actress Eleanor Robson. ' . . . It would run for a week. But what a week that would be!'

7

CURTAIN UP ON *MAJOR BARBARA*

It seems to me that what Barbara finds out is that the ancient Greek (whoever he was) who said 'First make sure of an income and then practise virtue' was rightly preaching natural morality.
Shaw to Gilbert Murray (5 September 1941)

Father Keegan had been a saint, 'and now I want to see whether I can make a woman a saint too,' Shaw wrote to Eleanor Robson. 'The heroine is so like you that I see nobody in the wide world who can play her except you.'

Charlotte was not happy with the way her husband corresponded with actresses. But he believed that Eleanor Robson would be striking in the piquant role of his Salvation Army officer. She was little more perhaps than a professional model for the part: the biographical model was Beatrice Webb. Like Barbara, Beatrice was a rich man's daughter and had gone East Ending with the gospel of social salvation. Her violent reaction to the play ('a dance of devils . . . hell tossed on the stage, with no hope of heaven . . . the triumph of the unmoral purpose') registered her involvement in the ruin of Barbara's salvationism.

Barbara, as a prototype of St Joan, is a woman apparently converted from religion to a creed of action. But hers is not really a conversion: it is a growing-up. She is a chip off the old block, her father Undershaft having a genius for action that Barbara inherits. The man who stands between Barbara and Undershaft, Adolphus Cusins, is the real convert. Modelled on the classicist Gilbert Murray, Cusins represents Shaw's own position: that of the fastidious scholar trying to find his place in the political world. He is attracted to Undershaft as the only man who can make him effective through marrying his intellect to power.

There are more false starts, deletions and drastic changes in the holograph manuscript of *Major Barbara* than in any of Shaw's previous plays. In the intervals and 'mostly in Great Northern express trains', he polished off a 'new and original tragedy' early that summer. *Passion Poison and Petrifaction or The Fatal Gazogene* completed a trilogy of 'tomfooleries' done while still at work on his 'big three'. The invitation had come from Cyril Maude on behalf of the Actors' Orphanage which each year commissioned a playwright to compose a burlesque of old-time melodrama to be performed in the Royal Botanical Gardens of Regent's Park during the Theatrical Garden Party. Shaw's idea came from a story he had once told the Archer children about his aunt, who liked making plaster of Paris figures, and her cat which one day mistook the liquid plaster of Paris for milk and, while asleep, turned into a ponderous mass of cement – to be used by the aunt as a doorstop. From the beginning when the cuckoo clock strikes sixteen (signifying eleven o'clock at night) to the moment when Lady Magnesia Fitztollemache's lover is obliged to eat part of the ceiling (containing lime) as an antidote to the jealous husband's poison, we are, as Irving Wardle writes, 'into Ionesco territory'.

This 'brief tragedy for Barns and Booths' by the 'Chelsea Shakespeare' was performed 'for the first time in any tent' at intervals during the afternoon of 14 July. The author, who was absent, described it as a 'colossal success', and arranged for the royalties on all performances for the rest of its copyright life to be paid to the Actors' Orphanage Fund. 'Charities are remorseless,' he explained.

He returned to, but could not finish, *Major Barbara*. At the beginning of July Charlotte took charge. She proposed returning G.B.S. to Ireland. It was twenty-nine years since he had boarded the North Wall boat for London. Like Larry Doyle, he had 'an instinct against going back to Ireland'. Nevertheless, like Larry Doyle, he went. It was not of course on his own initiative. 'I went back to please my wife; and a curious reluctance to retrace my steps made me land in the south and enter Dublin through the backdoor from Meath rather than return as I came, through the front door on the sea.'

They were to stay at Charlotte's father's house three miles out of Rosscarbery, a little market town in County Cork. It was a solid grey stone structure built on rising ground with gardens that sloped down to a lake. From the terrace, facing south, they 'could look out on a great sweep of the bay, with a lighthouse rising like the stub of a pencil on the farthest point of land'. But could he work there? Did the house have a sitting-room well away from the drawing-room? This was vital since they were to be joined by Charlotte's sister, Mary Cholmondeley, and her husband who was a colonel. It was important to be out of earshot.

G.B.S. spent much of the next three months in that sitting-room getting on 'scrap by scrap' with his new play. It progressed very slowly – 'a speech a day or so,' he informed Vedrenne. 'I have not yet finished the play,' he wrote to Eleanor Robson on 21 August; 'and my inspiration, as far as the heroine is concerned, is gone. I shall finish it with my brains alone.' On 11 September he reported that it was 'just finished': but he had been left 'in a condition of sullen desperation concerning it'.

He had turned back from autobiography to politics – from his marriage and the country of his childhood to the economic questions that had first provided the themes of his *Plays Unpleasant*. Over twenty years separated the beginning of *Widowers' Houses* from the completion of *Major Barbara*, and though the living standards of the middle class had risen in this period there were now almost a million people in the country receiving Poor Law relief. In London at the beginning of 1905 the number of paupers had risen to 150,000, of whom 1,500 were 'casual paupers' sleeping in the streets or the casual wards of workhouses and living, according to William Booth, 'below the standard of the London cab-horse'. Booth had founded the Salvation Army in 1878 to make war on poverty. Though Britain was still at the summit of her imperial power, much of her population existed on the edge of destitution. It was this paradox that Shaw investigated in his play using, as a symbol of Imperialist prosperity, the armaments industry.

'One never really makes portraits of people in fiction,' he wrote: 'what happens is that certain people inspire one to invent fictitious characters for them, which is quite another matter.' The millionaire munitions capitalist, Andrew Undershaft, seems to have had a composite inspiration: there was the dramatist Charles McEvoy's father, a benign grey-haired gentleman who, after fighting on the side of the Confederacy in the American Civil War, settled down quietly to establish a torpedo factory; there was Hans Renold, a businessman who came to lecture the Fabian Society on the principles of 'service before self' in the manufacture of high explosives. Another prototype was Alfred Nobel, 'the gentle Bolshevik' who had patented dynamite in 1867 and in 1901 endowed the Nobel Peace Prize which, as the critic Louis Crompton commented, 'challenged the humanitarian liberals among his personal friends to solve the problems his discoveries had created'. William Manchester has argued that Shaw's model was Friedrich Alfred Krupp, the Prussian 'Cannon King' whose paternalistic welfare arrangements for his workers in Essen may have suggested Undershaft's model town. Krupp had died in 1902 and was succeeded by his daughter Bertha. 'In 1906 – the year after the publication of *Major Barbara* – she married Dr Gustav von Bohlen und Halbach,' wrote Maurice Valency, 'who later assumed the name of Krupp, and took over the management of the Krupp combine, thus fulfilling in reality the role of Dr Cusins in Shaw's play.' Shaw himself wrote that Undershaft emerged into the world as Henry Ford. Other critics assumed that he derived from the legendary Basil Zaharoff, chief salesman of Vickers, who 'made wars so that I could sell arms to both sides'.

Such a multiplicity of candidates attests to the rise of arms traffic throughout the world at the turn of the century. Some, like Zaharoff, made no apology for their merchandise. Others, such as Britain's largest arms maker Sir William Armstrong, placed the responsibility for 'legitimate application' of weapons on the buyer and speculated that better armaments might well render war less barbarous. Others again, such as Nobel, argued for the deterrent effect of explosives.

Undershaft expresses all these attitudes. But when he challenges Cusins to 'make war on war' he is deliberately tempting him with the conventional paradox of those times which soon led to German, French and British soldiers being shot down with guns made by their fellow-countrymen in a 'war to end wars'.

The first act of the play is a drawing-room comedy set in the library of Lady Britomart's house in Wilton Crescent which displays the wealth of capitalist society; the second act is a Dickensian melodrama showing capitalism's destitution at the West Ham Shelter of the Salvation Army. Shaw had got as far as Undershaft's arrival at West Ham when he took his manuscript to Ireland. From then on Undershaft begins to take control of the play and in the third act, a political fantasy set in Perivale St Andrews, a futuristic model town, he dominates the stage.

On 8 September Shaw scribbled 'End of the Play' at the conclusion of the third act. But Undershaft's annihilation of everyone else had left him feeling dissatisfied. Why had it happened? He appeared to have let his unconscious Will, with its fantasies of violence, speak through Undershaft. That name itself brings together the wishes of the unconscious and the underground kingdom of the Devil.

In London earlier that year he had blamed the pressure of business for his difficult progress on the play; at Rosscarbery he attributed his difficulties to the moisture of the Irish climate. His aggressive instincts, however, are more likely to have been aroused by 'Mrs Chumly', Charlotte's sister. Mary Cholmondeley's determination never to see her brother-in-law had gradually wavered. She had heard a good deal about him and, pricked by curiosity, allowed Charlotte to persuade her after half a dozen years to meet him. For the first week or two, perhaps feeling her disapproval, G.B.S. stayed working all day in the sitting-room. Charlotte joined him there in the mornings to do secretarial work; and in the afternoons she would visit friends in the neighbourhood with 'Sissy'. Soon G.B.S. was accompanying them on these walks. 'Mrs C and I, in view of our previously rather distant relations, laid ourselves out to conciliate one another, and rather more than succeeded,' he confided to Beatrice Webb.

'I have the important advantage in such matters of not being nearly so disagreeable personally as one would suppose from my writings. I am now completely adopted on the usual lunatic privileged terms in the Cholmondeley household. I have taken several photographs of Mrs C and taught her to swim. The Colonel has presented me with a watch which tells the date and the phases of the moon. I play accompaniments to Mrs C's singing and the past is buried.'

From that past and behind the patina of politeness the sinister figure of Undershaft expanded. So favourable an impression meanwhile was G.B.S. making on the Cholmondeleys that they invited him to go with them on a round of Irish peers in their castles and only accepted his refusal ('the worm turned at last') on the understanding that he would rejoin them the following month at Edstaston, their home in Shropshire.

Shaw arrived back in London alone on 30 September and the next day went down to read his play at Gilbert Murray's house in Oxford. The ostensible reason for his visit was to ensure that those people on whom his characters were modelled would not be offended. He had written to Murray asking whether Murray himself minded being represented as a foundling. Murray replied that the only thing that Shaw did at his peril was to fasten on him the Christian name Adolphus. In Shaw's first draft the professor had been called Dolly Tankerville. But he changed this Wildean surname to Cusins, suggesting the foundling's curious relationship (his own cousin) to himself.

His audience at Oxford that day included Murray and Granville Barker who was shortly to play the part of Cusins. At the end of the second act they were, Murray remembered, 'thrilled with enthusiasm, especially at the Salvation Army scenes. Act 3, in which the idealists surrender to the armaments industries, was a terrible disappointment to us.'

Shaw returned to London and that night wrote to Murray confessing that he felt 'quite desperate about my last act: I think I must simply rewrite it.'

To encourage himself he went next day to the Albert Hall where the Salvation Army was holding a festival to commemorate dead comrades. As the band played

'When the roll is called up yonder
I'LL BE THERE'

he stood in the middle of the centre grand tier box, in the front row, 'and sang it as it has never been sung before,' he told Vedrenne. 'The Times will announce my conversion tomorrow.'

The following afternoon he joined Charlotte and the Cholmondeleys at Edstaston. He had received a letter from Gilbert Murray enclosing some ideas set down in dialogue for the third act. 'What I am driving at, is to get the real dénouement of the play, after Act ii,' Murray explained. ' . . . It makes Cusens come out much stronger, but I think that rather an advantage. Otherwise you get a simple defeat of the Barbara principles by the Undershaft principles.'

The rewriting of his last scene took Shaw eleven days. 'I want to get Cusins beyond the point of wanting power,' he replied to Murray. The Edstaston manuscript was completed on 15 October 1905. It is perhaps the most complex and ambiguous scene Shaw ever wrote. The debate between Undershaft, Barbara and Cusins takes place at many levels. Barbara, who represents evangelical Christianity, has lost her faith by the end of Act II, using Christ's words upon the cross: 'My God: why hast thou forsaken me?' Cusins represents scepticism, a purely negative force by itself; and Undershaft embodies Shaw's concept of the Life Force, a mindless power for good-or-evil depending (like all technology) on what human beings themselves decide to do with it.

Barbara's transfiguration must come through a resurrected faith that involves Cusins and Undershaft – her future husband and her father: three in one and one in three. While she occupies the position of the Son, Cusins is the Holy Ghost and Undershaft God the Father. But Undershaft is also the Devil – 'You may be a devil; but God speaks through you sometimes,' Barbara admits. In the religion of Creative Evolution, life arises from the anonymous concept of energy. It is a force without morality and, as Barbara discovers, 'there is no wicked side: life is all one.'

Cusins recognizes in Undershaft the mysterious spirit of Dionysus, capable of creation and destruction. Human beings therefore 'create' God or the Devil according to the way in which they employ Divine Energy. On the psychological level Barbara is the superego, Cusins the ego and Undershaft the id: three in one and one in three. According to the system laid out in *The Quintessence of Ibsenism*, Barbara is the idealist, Cusins the realist and Undershaft the philistine. In his last scene Shaw attempts to unite all three: Cusins is to be Barbara's husband and, as the foundling inheritor of his father-in-law's munitions factory, will become Andrew Undershaft VIII. He will be able to join his intelligence and Barbara's spiritual passion to his father-in-law's money and material strength.

For all his pragmatism and lack of hypocrisy, Undershaft is a limited man. He writes up UNASHAMED as his motto and is contemptuous of democratic shams. The 'ballot paper that really governs,' he says, 'is the paper that has a bullet wrapped up in it'. But though he exults in his power he is also its prisoner. Armaments are the instruments of revolutionary change and also the means by which authoritarian governments repress change. The will to live must do battle with the tendency to self-destruction.

The ambiguity of the play partly derives from the conflict of Undershaft's motives. By inviting Cusins to be his successor is he tempting him, as Mephistopheles tempted Faust, to his damnation? Or is he an instinctive agent for the Life Force seeking in Cusins a better use of the power he commands? In fact he is doing both: that is how life operates. 'You cannot have power for good without having power for evil, too.'

Cusins believes that he will reject the armourer's faith and 'sell cannons to whom I please and refuse them to whom I please'. To this Undershaft replies: 'From the moment when you become Andrew Undershaft, you will never do as you please again.' This seems to be the percipient voice of the Devil having recruited a partner in his hellish trade. But elsewhere Undershaft appears to challenge Cusins and Barbara to use this power in a fundamentally different way: 'Society cannot be saved,' he says (paraphrasing Plato's *Republic*), 'until either the Professors of Greek take to making gunpowder, or else the makers of gunpowder become Professors of Greek.'

In the earlier manuscript Undershaft had posed a conundrum for Cusins: 'Why is a government a government?' And Cusins answered: 'Because the people are fools.' In the Edstaston manuscript Cusins states his belief in the common man:

'I love the common people. I want to arm them against the lawyer, doctor, the priest, the literary man, the professor, the artist and the politician, who, once in authority, are the most dangerous, disastrous and tyrannical of all the fools, rascals and impostors. I want a democratic power strong enough to force the intellectual oligarchy to use its genius for the general good or else perish.'

Cusins enshrines something of Gilbert Murray's political idealism – it is not surprising that Murray's later work for the League of Nations should be in line with Cusins's decision to 'make war on war'. Shaw and Barker felt the excitement of working in the theatre with this brilliant young Oxford professor. He was, Shaw told Pinero, a 'genuine artistic anarchic character'. Shaw wanted to bring Murray's classical scholarship to bear on twentieth-century politics and he uses Undershaft to give muscle to a man D. H. Lawrence was to call 'all disembodied mind'. The passionate thinking Shaw put into *Major Barbara* was partly the result of this association with Murray; and their friendship became a bonus added to the successful breakthrough of Shaw's plays at the Court. Both these factors helped to make the positive ending to *Major Barbara* – an ending with the 'inconsequence of madness in it'.

This hard-won optimism had survived the initial effects of Shavian irony, but there are signs of rejection to the graft. Beatrice Webb records Shaw as arguing 'earnestly and cleverly, even persuasively, in favour of what he imagines to be his central theme – *the need for preliminary good physical environment before anything could be done to raise the intelligence and morality of the average sensual man*'. But Undershaft's general attitude towards life continued to trouble people.

Of all the play's aphorisms and ideas echoing from Plato, Euripides, Nietzsche, the most significant derive from Shaw's reading of Blake's *Marriage of Heaven and Hell*. What Shaw believed to be the central theme of *Major Barbara* – that 'the way of life lies through the factory of death' – is similar to several proverbs of Blake, with whom Shaw shared a religious faith in Energy. He could expound this faith so well that even Beatrice Webb 'found it difficult to answer him'. Yet, she added, 'he did not convince me.

' . . . the impression left is that Cusins and Barbara are neither of them convinced by Undershaft's argument, but that they are uttering words, like the silly son, to bridge over a betrayal of their own convictions.'

Shaw's genius went into the creation of Undershaft. The armaments manufacturer loves his enemies because they have kept him in business. Like Christ, he comes 'not to send peace but a sword'. Cusins he had constructed 'with my brains alone' – and with Gilbert Murray's. 'But you are driving me against my nature,' Cusins protests to Undershaft. 'I hate war.' Shaw, too, seems to be driven against his nature. He had wanted to move Cusins and Barbara 'beyond the point of wanting power'. But their final permeation of the Undershaft firm lacks conviction on stage. Shaw knew this. He continued tinkering with this last scene up to 1930 when the Standard Edition of the play was published, trying to make Barbara and Cusins 'more prominent' and giving them 'more commanding positions on stage and stronger movement'. But as he told Robert Morley ten years later during the making of the film version of the play: 'That's always been a terrible act. I don't think anyone could do anything with it.'

'You have learnt something,' Undershaft tells Barbara at a genuinely touching moment. 'That always feels at first as if you have lost something.'

Shaw himself seems to have felt this sensation of loss. 'But oh! Eleanor between ourselves, the play, especially in the last act, is a mere ghost, at least so it seems to me ... It was a fearful job ... Brainwork comes natural to me; but this time I knew I was working – and now nobody understands.'

This lack of understanding proceeds from the complexity of what Shaw was questioning. Is socialism at odds with human nature? Are the self-destructive impulses of human beings ineradicable? Are there ways of disarming oppressive power that do not betray the cause that uses them? Though the affirmation comes out strongly, getting through to it had been the hardest work the playwright had done. And the chance that he is wrong remains. The Devil's Force of Death speech in *Man and Superman*, with its more efficient engines of destruction ('of sword and gun and poison gas') leads straight to Undershaft's weapons factory with its 'aerial battleships' that eventually will fly over Captain Shotover's villa at the climax of *Heartbreak House*, threatening with its *'terrific explosion'* the end of humankind.

Shaw's optimism was a perilous act of faith focused on the future. He had looked in *John Bull's Other Island* for a country where the 'facts were not brutal and the dreams not unreal'. In Perivale St Andrews nothing is achieved 'by words and dreams': killing is 'the final test of conviction'. It is the nightmare of a man with 'honour and humanity on my side, wit in my head, skill in my hand, and a higher life for my aim', who has a vision of world war to come. In the aftermath of this war, through the fantasy of *Back to Methuselah*, he will refashion humankind in the image of his heart's desire.

*

The Salvation Army lent uniforms for the production at the Court Theatre. The audience for the first performance on 28 November 1905 included a box full of uniformed Salvation Army Commissioners who for the first time in their lives had entered a theatre. Among 'the intelligentsia of London' sat the Prime Minister, Arthur Balfour, in the last week of his Government, with Beatrice Webb, whom five days before he had appointed to the new Royal Commission on the Poor Law. The foyer of the Court was crowded to bursting – hundreds of people had to be turned away – and above the excitement floated a rumour that the play was blasphemous. The curtain rose.

TEN

I

FABIAN BEDFELLOWS

> What a transformation scene from those first years I knew him: the
> scathing bitter opponent of wealth and leisure, and now! the adored one
> of the smartest and most cynical set of English Society . . . our good
> sense preserve us!
>
> *The Diary of Beatrice Webb* (14 October 1905)

'Politics are very topsy-turvy just now,' Beatrice Webb wrote at the end
of December 1903, 'and one never knows who may be one's bedfellow!'
Many of the Fabians were suspicious of the social glamour with which
the Webbs surrounded themselves. Sidney himself warned Beatrice that
they should not be 'seen in the houses of great people'. But the Fabian
policy of permeation made it obligatory for them to enter the drawing-
rooms of Edwardian polite society.

This permeation was taking the Webbs away from the evolution of the
Labour Party. They took little notice of the attempts to bring socialism
and the trade unions together as a parliamentary Labour Party. As Shaw
warned Pease, 'any sort of amalgamation means, for us, extinction'. Power,
they believed, still resided with the traditional parties in Parliament and
access to power must still lie through persuading them.

Among the Liberals, they had chosen Lord Rosebery, an enigmatic
figure who had left the leadership of the party in 1896. The speech he
made in Chesterfield at the end of 1901 owed much to 'Lord Rosebery's
Escape from Houndsditch', the article that Sidney Webb had written, and
Shaw toned up, the previous September. Using this as his brief, Rosebery
attacked the record of party politics and called for a 'clean slate' on which
to draft a programme of national efficiency.

At the top of this clean slate, the Webbs hoped to chalk up housing
and education. But what did Rosebery himself intend? He was grateful to
Sidney Webb for giving him something to say, but he had taken off his
'Gladstonian old clothes' and, instead of putting on the new collectivist
garments that Sidney Webb handed him, he simply put himself to bed
and switched out the light. 'Why are we in this galley?' Beatrice wondered.
And Shaw himself was driven to concede the emptiness of their Rosebery
campaign.

But permeation did seem to work with the Conservatives. Their Tory bedfellow was Arthur Balfour who succeeded his uncle Lord Salisbury as Prime Minister in the summer of 1902 and 'will I think,' Beatrice predicted, 'make no ripple of change'. Quietly scintillating at the dinner table, he was well-spoken and precise-sounding in the House of Commons, and as a political thinker elegantly indecisive. Like Beatrice, he sometimes felt he would have preferred a contemplative to a public life – in fact it struck Beatrice as 'the oddest fact' that he should be 'mixed up . . . with democratic politics'. Really he had gone into politics to please his mother and then developed the knack of pleasing all sorts of people. He was at home on the golf course, in the concert hall and among the 'gallants and graces' of the fashionable world; popular too with the finer minds of the universities, the pick of the clergy, the flower of the bench: and also with the Webbs.

It seemed to them incredible that a Prime Minister in his mid-fifties should have preserved an open mind on so many political questions. His opinions shifted uneasily between the need for action and the futility of taking it. Unlike Rosebery he was not to be persuaded by what might be popular but by whether he was bored or not. He was easily bored – so much politics was without refinement of thought or sensibility. It was here that the Webbs saw their opportunity. Between 1902 and 1905 they 'slipped into' friendship with him. 'He comes in to dinner whenever we ask him, and talks most agreeably,' Beatrice noted. Balfour responded to these Fabians as a connoisseur might respond to an unusual wine. He believed Shaw to be 'the finest man of letters of to-day' – though he would not read his *Plays Unpleasant* because 'I never read unpleasant things'. He counted on the Fabians painlessly fitting such unpleasant things into the perfect equilibrium of his life, and the Webbs endeavoured to oblige. 'I set myself to amuse and interest him,' Beatrice wrote. And he was so responsive intellectually, so courteous, that 'we found ourselves in accord on most questions'.

But Beatrice distrusted her attraction to Balfour. She had with difficulty walked away from the social world to which her family belonged and dedicated herself to disinterested public service – and now found that this service was leading her back into the milieu she had abandoned. For Balfour belonged to 'the Souls', that exquisite group of intellectuals with artistic and aristocratic tastes who were to find an obituary in *Heartbreak House*.

This immersion in party-giving-and-going seemed justified by what the Fabians achieved over the Education Acts of 1902 and 1903. Sidney's Fabian Tract No. 106, *The Education Muddle and the Way Out*, recommended the abolition of School Boards and the passing of control for education to the local government bodies. The Education Act of 1902 (which did not apply to London) 'followed almost precisely the lines laid down in our tract,' wrote Edward Pease. 'Our support of the Conservative Government in their education policy caused much surprise.'

It caused more than surprise: it caused misgivings at the invasion of education by party politics, and Webb's proposal to give assistance out of public funds to reactionary Church schools fomented outright opposition. It was far from being the 'clean slate' other socialists wanted. Over the Education Act of 1903, which transferred the School Boards' powers to the London County Council, Webb experienced still greater difficulties. To Ramsay MacDonald it seemed that Sidney was collaborating with Balfour in order to get a Government post.

The Fabian success had been achieved at a dismaying price. There was, as Beatrice put it, 'a slump in Webbs' on the political market. After the local elections of 1904 Sidney was voted off the Progressive Party Committee and denied all positions of authority on the London County Council. He had hoped to be brought back into communication with the trade union world through his appointment by Balfour to a new Royal Commission on trade union law. But this became a 'fiasco' when the trade unions boycotted the Commission. Suddenly the Fabians seemed isolated. Through their educational reforms they had lost much of the interest they had spent years nurturing among the Liberals; and by their pronouncements on tariff reform they were to assist in the downfall of their one political ally, Balfour.

*

Webb had conducted the Fabian policy on education; it was Shaw who stage-managed their fiscal policy. The rightfulness of Free Trade had been taken for granted. But following Chamberlain's speech in May 1903, 'Free Trade versus Fair Trade', tariff reform suddenly became a controversial electioneering issue. 'I think we are clearly called upon to oraculate on the present crisis,' Shaw wrote to Pease: and Webb reluctantly agreed. At a Fabian meeting in June 1903 he had given a tentative analysis of the situation, on balance against tariffs, but in effect recommending more Fabian research into the subject.

Shaw's attitude was more dramatic. Following instinct rather than research, he had come out as 'a Protectionist right down to my boots', at one with Ruskin and Carlyle in his belief that 'Free Trade is heartbreaking nonsense'.

Over the last six months of 1903, Fabian opinion had come to lodge halfway between tariff and Free Trade. To give commanding expression to such mixed opinion needed unusual dexterity. Shaw was convinced that the Fabian Society 'must say something that nobody else is saying'. He had wanted to demonstrate that sensible tariff reform involved, as a preliminary step, the introduction of socialism. He proposed an agreement where, in exchange for their support of Chamberlain's protectionist scheme, the workers were guaranteed a minimum wage. He also proposed that Chamberlain be invited to give a pledge that any extra revenue arising from tariffs would be applied to 'public purposes' and not 'to still further reduce the existing shamefully inadequate taxation of unearned incomes'.

Shaw argued that, in principle, there was no objection from a socialist point of view to 'State interference with trade, both to suppress sweating at home and to guide and assist our exporters abroad'. Socialists were therefore necessarily anti-Free Trade as they were anti-Laissez-faire, both systems being historical counterparts of each other and idealizing the exploitation of market forces.

At a Fabian meeting on 22 January 1904 the draft of Shaw's Tract No. 116, *Fabianism and the Fiscal Question*, was fought over page by page. With numerous amendments, it was published on 31 March. 'Though I am the pen man of this Tract, its authorship is genuinely collective,' Shaw explained in a Preface. It was as adept a performance as *Fabianism and the Empire*. Both tracts submerge immediate election questions and extreme Fabian differences in the creed of international collectivism and a lucid exposition of the practical benefits of domestic socialism that might be wrung out of an imperial policy.

Shaw did not believe that the Labour Party would win seats at the next election. He expected Chamberlain to become Prime Minister, and if Chamberlain could be persuaded to accept a minimum wage for workers, the Fabian work on tariff reform would not be in vain.

But in the election following Balfour's resignation on 4 December, the Liberals won an unprecedented majority. Their leader, Sir Henry Campbell-Bannerman, that 'weak, vain man' whom 'nobody will follow', became Prime Minister and various Liberal friends of the Webbs (Asquith, Grey and Haldane), making their peace, accepted office under him. Balfour was never again to lead the party in office; and Joseph Chamberlain (who suffered a stroke not long afterwards) never again held political office.

There was one further surprise at the election: fifty-three seats were captured by Labour men. Of these, twenty-four were trade unionists (mostly textile and mining men) who owed their primary allegiance not to Ramsay MacDonald and Keir Hardie, but to the Liberal Party which had pledged to restore protection of union funds from liability for loss caused through industrial disputes. The complexion of British politics was changing. A successful pact had been made between socialism and trade unionism that gave the Labour movement a parliamentary base in national politics. In *The Clarion* Shaw laid down some 'Fabian Notes' on the election. The Labour members had provided nothing more than 'a nominally independent Trade Unionist and Radical group,' he wrote. '. . . I apologise to the Universe for my connection with such a party.'

2

WELLS JOINS THE CAST

We have always been misunderstood, mistrusted, and from time to time roundly denounced and vilified not only by the other Socialist Societies but even by a minority of the Fabian Society . . . From William Morris in 1890 to H. G. Wells in 1906, all the able, energetic and impatient spirits have begun by demanding an abandonment of the Fabian policy, and have ended by perceiving that it is the only possible policy under the circumstances.

Discarded section of Shaw's leaflet, *Election of Executive Committee 1907–8* (8 February 1907)

The unease felt by growing numbers of Fabians swelled after the General Election of January 1906 into a tumour of discontent. Their policy of permeation looked like a series of little interferences and minor activities that had wasted resources and produced dubious results. What was the point of Sidney Webb ingratiating himself with Tories and Liberals at the dinner table while Shaw drastically insulted both parties in his tracts? 'I quite understand that you can so define permeation as to cover all forms of Socialist activity,' S. G. Hobson wrote to Shaw. 'But that won't help us.'

Hobson and others felt that the Fabian Society was in danger of counting for very little in politics. During its first twelve years, it had lined up what was potentially a great following in the country. Then it had 'ossified'. The last ten years seemed to be a history of lost opportunities. They had been supplanted by Ramsay MacDonald and Keir Hardie, by the Independent Labour Party and the Labour Representation Committee.

Like Fabius, the Fabians had waited. But when the new century arrived they had not struck hard – they had gone on waiting. Rising numbers of them however were insisting that the waiting game must end. 'Webb has repeatedly told me that he does not believe in the possibility of a Socialist Party,' Hobson told Shaw. 'On the contrary, I think that an organised

Socialist Party which shall include the LRC and the ILP is quite feasible and in every sense desirable.'

Shaw was not unsympathetic to this argument. The Fabian tracts gave the new Labour Party a programme for a decade of electioneering. Shaw argued that the Fabian Society must nevertheless continue with the policy of placing its work at the disposal of 'anybody and everybody, including the established capitalist governments, who can and will carry out any instalment of it'. If, however, socialism precipitated itself into a genuine political party, then the Fabian Society must back it for all it was worth. But if trade unionism and traditional radicalism prevailed, then the next job for the Fabians would be to detach socialists from the Labour Party and 'form a Socialist party in parliament independent of all other parties, but leading the advanced elements in all of them by its ideas and its political science'.

He envisaged the bulk of this new party coming from the middle-class proletariat, and substituting middle-class methods of business and conceptions of democracy for trade union methods – representative government in place of bodies of delegates. Their socialism (what Shaw would later call communism) would work to reverse the policy of capitalism by transferring private property into common wealth. The question was whether such a revolutionary programme could be carried out by Parliament, the municipalities and parish councils.

'Do not let us delude ourselves with any dreams of a peaceful evolution of Capitalism into Socialism, of automatic Liberal Progress . . . The man who is not a Socialist is quite prepared to fight for his private property . . . We must clear our minds from cant and cowardice on this subject. It is true that the old barricade revolutionists were childishly and romantically wrong in their methods; and the Fabians were right in making an end of them and formulating constitutional Socialism. But nothing is so constitutional as fighting.'

Once a true socialist party was born in Britain, the Fabian Society 'would shrink into a little academic body'. Shaw had been on the Fabian executive now for twenty years. He felt loyalty; he felt weariness. He wanted freedom as well as ownership – his child must grow up, become independent and powerful: *his child*. 'We cannot sit there any longer making a mere habit of the thing,' he advised Webb.

He dreamt sometimes of a Fabian party in Parliament. If the thing caught on it would prove the 'right climax of the whole Fabian adventure' – and if it failed what was there to lose? 'This is the psychological moment,' Shaw told Webb late in 1906. He had been convinced of this by a new leader that the Fabians had thrown up – a brilliant intellectual prospector on whom he might unload his political burden, as he hoped one day to hand over the theatrical future to Harley Granville Barker.

*

H. G. Wells was ten years younger than Shaw. He had seen the aggressive Dubliner with his 'thin flame-coloured beard beneath his white illumined face' at Kelmscott House. Like other students, Wells had been converted to socialism under the aesthetic influence of Blake, Carlyle and Ruskin. Late at night, walking back from Hammersmith through the gas-lit streets, or travelling by the sulphurous underground railway, their red ties giving zest to frayed and shabby costumes, he and his fellow-students would speak enthusiastically of Morris and Shaw – how fierce they were in spirit, how sage in method. A revolution seemed to be breaking out around them.

But by the time Wells and Shaw met almost a decade later, this revolution seemed to have become a cultural event. Wells, at the beginning of 1895, was suddenly given the post of theatre critic for the *Pall Mall Gazette*. On 5 January he turned up at the St James's Theatre to see *Guy Domville*, 'an extremely weak drama' by Henry James. There were two audiences in the theatre that night. When the curtain came down 'jeers, hisses, catcalls were followed by great waves of applause . . . The two audiences declared war.'

Wells, in his new evening clothes, had noticed how Shaw 'broke the ranks of the boiled shirts and black and white ties in the stalls, with a modest brown jacket suit, a very white face and very red whiskers'. The new drama critic of the *Pall Mall Gazette* accosted the new drama critic of the *Saturday Review* as a colleague and, as Wells had to pass Fitzroy Square to reach his home near Euston, the two writers walked back together, a lean spring-heeled marcher and a valiant sparrow hopping beside him.

'Fires and civil commotions loosen tongues,' commented Wells, who described Shaw as talking 'like an elder brother to me'. His conversation was a 'contribution to my education,' Wells recalled. But Wells felt out of place in the theatre, whereas Shaw understood that the pandemonium at the St James's, likened by Henry James to a set of savages pouncing on a gold watch, had been a warning of what might happen in Britain if Fabian tactics failed.

After four months on the *Pall Mall Gazette* Wells decided to throw over theatre reviewing. During the next half-dozen years, he created a new genre of scientific fairy-tale with his vivid fantasies, allegories, fables and adventures – *The Time Machine, The Island of Dr Moreau, The War of the Worlds, The First Men in the Moon.* He wrote one book, then another, and then half a dozen more. They came like magic. 'It did not take us long to recognise that here was Genius,' wrote Ford Madox Ford. ' . . . And all great London lay prostrate at his feet.'

Shaw too had been impressed. A natural story-teller, with a fertile imagination, Wells spoke directly to the people and was 'our nearest to a twentieth century Dickens'. His romances of time and space stimulated Shaw's optimism. Dickens's world 'becomes a world of great expectations cruelly disappointed,' he wrote. 'The Wells world is a world of greater and greater expectations continually being fulfilled.'

Wells was the modern man who accepted nothing of the past and could hardly wait to experiment with the future. He wanted to write history before it happened. It was after his next book, a 'prospectus' called *Anticipations*, that Shaw asked Graham Wallas (whose sister-in-law was Wells's neighbour at Sandgate) formally to introduce them. 'He [Wells] interests me considerably.'

Wells had also begun to interest the Webbs. Beatrice Webb confided in her diary that *Anticipations* was the 'most remarkable book of the year . . . full of luminous hypotheses and worth careful study by those who are trying to look forward'. She gave the book to Sidney. Wells had imagined a technocratic élite called 'the New Republicans' that could regenerate the nation. I 'find myself in sympathy with many of your feelings and criticisms and suggestions,' Sidney wrote.

The Webbs seemed to stand for the more disciplined, better-informed expression of all that Wells was eager to achieve. 'We discovered each other immensely; for a time it produced a tremendous sense of kindred and co-operation,' he wrote. This was the beginning of a pincer movement by the Webbs and the Shaws to recruit him to the Fabian Society. Wells is 'a good instrument for popularising ideas,' Beatrice noted in her diary, ' . . . it is refreshing to talk to a man who has shaken himself loose from so many of the current assumptions, and is looking at life as an explorer of a new world.'

Wells was nervous of the Webbs. Sidney was so excessively devoted to the public service; and the handsome figure of Beatrice alarmed him. But he liked the notion of meeting influential people – Members of Parliament such as Asquith, Haldane and Grey, philosophers such as Bertrand Russell, and Pember Reeves, soon to be made High Commissioner for New Zealand – at their political dinners.

In February 1903 Wells joined the Fabians. The Society 'is always open to new ideas,' Charlotte innocently encouraged him, '& to criticism of its past action.' Sidney Webb had listed Wells's *Anticipations* as one of his favourite books of 1901. Wells had chosen *Three Plays for Puritans*. 'You are, now that Wilde is dead, the one living playwright in my esteem,' he wrote to Shaw. He went to see *John Bull's Other Island* at the Court Theatre, pretended that the figure of Broadbent had been a 'disgusting caricature' of himself ('even my slight tendency to embonpoint was brought in'), and concluded: 'The play has some really gorgeous rhetoric, beautiful effects, much more serious Shaw than ever before & I'd rather see it again than see anyone else's new play.'

But underlying Wells's admiration of Shaw boiled a vast irritation. In the mid-1890s he had been prepared to learn from the older writer as from an elder brother: he was not content to do so ten years later – especially on subjects about which he was educated and G.B.S. was not. 'I was a biologist first and foremost, and Shaw had a physiological disgust at vital activities,' he was to write. '. . . He detected an element of cruelty, to which I am blind, in sexual matters.' Shaw's main impulse towards other human beings was to establish a dominant relationship over them – something which Wells fiercely resisted. He regretted having fallen in with these Fabians.

A year after joining the Society, Wells attempted to resign. He was working so hard at his new books – *A Modern Utopia* and *Kipps* – he did not have time to attend the Fabian meetings. At once the prevailing influences of the Fabians, the Webbs and the Shaws closed in on him. And Wells capitulated.

He now felt trapped. For he was an escapologist, and this need to escape lay at the centre of his politics, utopias and love affairs. The claustrophobia of marriage was to become endurable for him only after he had set up an alternative household with a mistress and could oscillate between two homes. 'He is a romancer spoilt by romancing,' Beatrice decided in her diary, ' – but in the present stage of sociology he is useful.'

Of the two romances he published in 1905, *Kipps* was an affectionate glance backwards at what had moved him in the past, and *A Modern Utopia* a blue book vision of the future disinfected of pain. His anxiety to escape from the present fitted perfectly with the mood of a country travelling from Victorian traditions into the complex territory of the twentieth century. He had made converts to socialism by translating the Fabian creed of national efficiency into popular fiction. In *A Modern Utopia* he reinvented the 'New Republicans' as a benevolent dictatorship of noblemen called 'the Samurai' who preside as social engineers over the ideal state. 'The chapters on the Samurai will pander to all your worst instincts,' he assured Beatrice Webb. But he had done what the Webbs had wanted. 'He is full of intellectual courage and initiative,' Beatrice observed.

A Modern Utopia made Wells a hero among the more radical Fabians.

'I'm going to turn the Fabian Society inside out,' he promised Ford Madox Ford, 'and then throw it into the dustbin.'

*

Wells's campaign opened on 6 January 1906 with a Fabian lecture, 'This Misery of Boots', using the shoe trade to satirize the condition of England. It was both an illustration of what he wanted from the new Fabians, and an indictment of Shaw and the Webbs, 'who will assure you that some odd little jobbing about municipal gas and water is Socialism, and back-stairs intervention between Conservative and Liberal is the way to the millennium'.

He launched his main attack in a second lecture a month later on 9 February. 'Faults of the Fabian' was Wells at his most comic-destructive. Almost everything in the sphere of thought had changed in the last twenty years – unless it was the Fabian Society. 'I am here to-night to ask it to change.' A great deal of work, 'with a certain lack of charm perhaps', had been invested in permeation. Some of it was gratuitous, some of it unfortunate; and almost all of it was removed from socialism. Their indirect methods were a senile conceit of cunning: 'something like a belief that the world may be manoeuvred into socialism without knowing it; that . . . we shall presently be able to confront the world with a delighted, "But you *are* socialists! We chalked it on your back when you weren't looking . . ."'

'The mouse decided to adopt indirect and inconspicuous methods, not to complicate its proceedings by too many associates, to win over and attract the cat by friendly advances rather than frighten her by a sudden attack. It is believed that in the end the mouse did succeed in permeating the cat, but the cat is still living – and the mouse can't be found.'

Wells's next criticism of the Society was its size. It had an air of arrested growth, as if by the effort of taking an office in a cellar in Clement's Inn, it had exhausted its energy. From this cellar, through the burrowings of one secretary and his assistant, the Fabian Society was to shift the indus-trial basis of civilization. Amid the jungle of politics it looked to Wells like 'a pot-bound plant'.

They were also poor, the Fabians, always in debt. 'You have it from Mr Bernard Shaw that poverty is a crime, and if so, then by the evidence of your balance-sheet ours is a criminal organization.'

Wells spoke on, adding to his catalogue of defects and accusations. The Fabians had evolved into a conservative society, and were collectivist only by definition of their collective inactivity. 'We don't advertise, thank you;

it's not quite our style. We cry socialism as the reduced gentlewoman cried "oranges": "I do so hope nobody will hear me." '

After an hour and a half Wells had nearly concluded his Fabian indictment. He had just one more vice to nail. 'Our society is small; and in relation to its great mission small minded; it is poor; it is collectively, as a society, inactive; it is suspicious of help, and exclusive,' he summarized. And, he added: 'it is afflicted with a giggle.'

Of all the faults of the Fabians, he declared, this juvenile joking was probably the worst. No wonder they were never taken seriously by politicians. The giggling excitement that ran through their meetings 'flows over and obscures all sorts of grave issues, it chills and kills enthusiasm,' he said. 'Its particular victim in this society is Mr Bernard Shaw.

'It pursues him with unrelenting delight, simply because he is not like everybody else, as he rises, before he opens his mouth to speak it begins. Shaw has a habit of vivid statement . . . and he has a natural inclination to paradox. Our accursed giggle lives on these things. Now Bernard Shaw is at bottom an intensely serious man, whatever momentary effect this instant dissolution of sober discussion into mirth may produce on him, he does in the long run, hate this pursuit of laughter . . . you will not suppose that in attacking laughter I am assailing Bernard Shaw. But I do assail the strained attempts to play up to Shaw, the constant endeavour of members devoid of any natural wit or wildness to catch his manner, to ape his egotism, to fall in with an assumed pretence that this grave high business of Socialism, to which it would be a small offering for us to give all our lives, is an idiotic middle-class joke.'

The timing of this attack on the political insidiousness of Shavianism, and the humorous requiem over permeation, was perfect and during the discussion afterwards, and in the weeks that followed, Wells was engulfed by support. 'People in the provinces think H. G. Wells is a great man,' the secretary of a Socialist League branch in a Yorkshire mill town wrote to him, 'and I can assure you they pay great attention to anything you say. Your audience is assured already, let the prophet appear.'

The prophet's chariot took the form of a Special Committee – a squadron of Wells-picked men and women whose mission was to increase the 'scope, influence, income and activity of the Society'. Wells had wanted them to move fast, finishing their work before he left at the end of March for a lecture tour in the United States. But Shaw and the Webbs, word-perfect in gradualism, entangled him with their assistance. The Webbs believed that, lacking the capacity for co-operation, he would not have the stamina to carry through his revisionist programme.

'The more I think of Mr Wells's Fabian Reforms the more do I welcome them & if only everyone will be sensible & broadminded I foresee a new era for Fabianism,' wrote Marjorie Pease. Shaw too believed Wells was vitally important to the future of Fabians. But below his admiration lay resentment, almost envy. He saw Wells as attractive, gifted with intimacy and lovable while he was fated to be unloved. Wells had succeeded at once and (so it seemed to Shaw) without effort. 'He was born cleverer than anybody within hail of him,' Shaw wrote, using his own upbringing as an invisible comparison. 'You can see from his pleasant figure that he was never awkward or uncouth or clumsy-footed or heavy-handed . . .

'He was probably stuffed with sweets and smothered with kisses . . . He won scholarships . . . The world that other men of genius had to struggle with, and which sometimes starved them dead, came to him and licked his boots. He did what he liked; and when he did not like what he had done, he threw it aside and tried something else.'

Shaw knew nothing of the illnesses and insecurities of Wells's early years. He simply saw, in contrast to himself, someone who had 'never missed a meal, never wandered through the streets without a penny in his pocket, never had to wear seedy clothes, never was unemployed'. And now he was being fussed over by the whole family of Fabians.

Wells arrived back from the United States still eager to put 'woosh' into the Fabians. The contrast between the go-ahead Americans and recalcitrant Englishmen had stimulated his radical energies. He wanted to change permeation into propaganda: to make the Society into a bigger, richer, simpler, less centralized organization. He wanted to obliterate Shaw's influence, to fade him out of its past by rewriting the Fabian tracts himself, and by realigning Fabian loyalties with the Labour Party and Keir Hardie who had fought the battle for socialism while Shaw had been making jokes elsewhere. He proposed changing the name of the Society to the British Socialist Party – but this was unanimously rejected by the executive which also rejected (by six votes to five) Wells's redefinition of the purpose of the Society as forwarding the progress of socialism 'by all available means'.

His report was published in November together with a Counter Report and Resolutions on behalf of the executive which had been written by Shaw. To Wells it seemed the most 'mischievous piece of writing I have read for a long time', destined, with its preposterous fables of Fabian foresight, to become 'a classic in the humorous literature of Socialism'.

Most of the issues which divided these two teeming documents were matters of internal reorganization and not difficult to reconcile. But beneath this administrative business lay a hidden agenda. The Fabians were a family, with Wells their rebel son. They had prevented him leaving and he now turned murderously back on them. He wanted to kill off the parents and, in his own image, father a new breed of this family. His fantasy of omnipotence, with its current of sexual energy, attracted crowds of excited Fabians for his dramatic confrontation with G.B.S.

Their first crossing of swords took place on 7 December at Essex Hall. Shaw moved the executive's resolution. His tone was friendly, his argument ominously reasonable.

Then Wells rushed up and began to address the meeting. Until then it had seemed as if, like the magical hero in his story 'The Man Who Could Work Miracles', he might perform anything he wished. But he spoke badly. His proposals for reorganizing the Society degenerated into a list of accusations against Shaw and the Webbs. He moved an amendment calling for the abolition of the executive and its replacement by a larger representative body that would endorse the 'spirit and purport' of his Special Committee's proposals. There had been a swell in favour of his amendment at the start; by the time he ended it had sunk. A second-reading debate was arranged one week later.

During the interval both parties prepared. Wells had described as 'shabby and unwise' the Fabian failure to co-operate with Keir Hardie. What he did not reveal was that he had written to Keir Hardie and been advised by him not to waste time bullying these steady-going Fabians 'who would continue to do their own useful work'. It was 'not quite fair' to the Society. 'Why not leave it to pursue its own way by its own methods,' Keir Hardie suggested, 'and come in and take your part in the political side of the movement as represented by the ILP?'

The answer to this was that Wells wanted to capture the Fabian army from Shaw, lead it over to Keir Hardie, and then go off to do something else. But Keir Hardie had been critical of Shaw too. Had his report been 'more accurate historically and less bombastic,' he wrote to G.B.S., 'the task of averting a menace to the movement wd have been easier.

'That apart what I wd like to see passed wd be a declaration of loyalty to the Labour Party which wd be binding on the Society and on its officials [who] . . . shall not support the candidates of other political parties . . . in this respect members of the Fabian Society are sad sinners.'

Neither Wells nor Shaw mentioned their letters from Keir Hardie when Wells turned up at Adelphi Terrace the day after the Essex Hall encounter. He came with an offer of compromise. 'Why dont you see how entirely I am expressing you in all these things?' he had asked G.B.S. But Shaw had scented victory. He proposed leading this second debate. It would be a peculiarly Shavian exercise – a 'terrific' verbal victory achieved without 'saying anything unkind'. He retreated into the country to gather his superiority. 'All I dread is being in bad form,' he wrote; 'for I am overworked.'

The crowd was even larger for this second contest. At nine o'clock Shaw rose to speak. If Wells's amendment abolishing the executive were passed, he said, the executive would obey it 'by not offering themselves for re-election'. It would be dismissal with dishonour: they would be drummed out. But this amendment, he reminded the audience, had nothing to do with the two reports. Over the serious business of the proposals in these reports, the executive would never resign, even if defeated on every resolution, but would faithfully carry out the decisions of the Society. Above the uproar Wells was heard pledging himself not to resign. 'That is a great relief to my mind,' continued Shaw. 'I can now pitch into Mr Wells without fear of consequences.'

He then offered up Wells for Fabian entertainment. 'During his Committee's deliberations he [Wells] produced a book on America,' Shaw told his audience. 'And a very good book too. But whilst I was drafting our reply I produced a play.' Shaw paused and there was silence. S. G. Hobson in the audience noticed his eyes vacantly glancing round the ceiling. 'It really seemed that he had lost his train of thought,' Hobson remembered. 'When we were all thoroughly uncomfortable, he resumed: "Ladies and gentlemen: I paused there to enable Mr Wells to say: 'And a very good play too!'"'

Wells had paid the penalty for having attacked the Shavian joke. For it was this joke which seemed to dissolve him into sustained laughter. The chairman took it for granted that the amendment was withdrawn by consent: and Wells made no protest. 'Keats was snuffed out by an article,' commented Hobson; 'Wells was squelched by a joke.'

'No part of my career rankles so acutely in my memory with the conviction of bad judgement, gusty impulse and real inexcusable vanity,' Wells afterwards admitted. But: 'I was fundamentally right.' He had reacted with imaginative enthusiasm to the future; and to the past with splenetic irritation. The present had been turned into theatre, which he had never liked or understood. 'Now we shall see whether he will forgive G.B.S.,' commented Beatrice.

This was not how G.B.S. saw it. He had arranged everything so that Wells could 'come up smiling' again among the Fabians. His purpose extended not a frown further. For he recognized that 'Wells is a great man'. He was a glamorously popular figure, particularly among the women of the new Fabian nursery. 'Tell the dear man that it is almost impossible to do anything without him,' Maud Reeves wrote to Wells's wife. Other Fabians, too, begged him not to desert them. To Shaw it seemed that the worse Wells behaved the more he was indulged.

No one knew what Wells would do next. The past still rankled: he felt a grievance. It seemed to him that Shaw's mind had been corrupted by public speaking and destroyed by the committee habit. Nevertheless he told Shaw: 'you are always sound hearted & I am always, through all our disputes & slanging matches, Yours most affectionately, H.G.' And Shaw agreed that Wells had played a 'great game' with 'immense vitality and fun'. There was no excuse for quarrelling – yet it seemed inevitable.

'I'm damnably sorry we're all made so,' wrote Wells.

'To complain of such things is to complain that the leaves are green and the sky blue,' wrote Shaw.

But what good came of it in the end? The issue had been shifted from a comparison of reports and policies to a gladiatorial contest of personalities. To Wells's frankness, his raging desire to discover the truth, Shaw had opposed something polemically formidable and professionally correct, yet somehow dubious. 'I incline to the prophecy that five years will see H. G. Wells out of the Society,' Beatrice Webb wrote. ' . . . It will be interesting to watch.'

3

A REVOLUTION AT THE COURT

As a matter of fact, I am overrated as an author: most great men are.

When the curtain came down on 28 November 1905, it was clear that *Major Barbara* was to be Shaw's most controversial success. The critics were impressively divided. Desmond MacCarthy told his readers: 'Mr Shaw has written the first play with religious passion for its theme and has made it real. That is a triumph no criticisms can lessen.' But the anonymous critic of the *Pall Mall Gazette* found that the play betrayed 'an utter want of the religious sense' and that its author was 'destitute of the religious emotion'. In the *Sunday Times*, while acknowledging G.B.S. to be 'the most original English dramatist of the day', J. T. Grein recoiled from Bill Walker's punching of the down-and-out Rummy Mitchens and his assault on the young Salvation Army lass Jenny Hill; this 'double act of brutality literally moved the audience to shudders. It was beyond all bounds of realism in art. It was ugly and revolting.' But Max Beerbohm

335

saw that 'the actor impersonating the ruffian aimed a noticeably gentle blow in the air, at a noticeably great distance from the face of the actress impersonating the lass'. Critics who professed themselves outraged, Beerbohm concluded, 'must have been very hard up for a fair means of attack'.

These critics felt inconvenienced on several counts. The play's 'lack of straightforward intelligible purpose' (*Morning Post*) made it spectacularly difficult for them to calculate its effect on audiences. Collectively they offered the choice between 'an audacious propagandist drama' (*Clarion*), 'one of the most remarkable plays put upon the English stage' (*Speaker*), a work of 'deliberate perversity' (*Morning Post*) or of the 'keenest insight and sense of spiritual beauty' (*Saturday Review*). There was no consensus as to whether G.B.S. was 'ephemeral' (John Galsworthy) or 'a high genius' (Oliver Lodge).

The war that had opened between the two audiences at Henry James's *Guy Domville* was now breaking out between critics and the public. Against all odds Shaw had become a fashionable craze. 'The old order is changing,' calculated one of the *Clarion* writers. Shaw's message to society 'to cast all its obsolete creeds and moral codes to the scrap heap' matched the new order.

Yet Shaw's career was now being blessed by the guardians of a society he was working to destroy. On the first night of *Major Barbara* there were almost as many carriages and motor cars outside the Court 'as there are in the Mall on a Drawing-room day'. Shaw was box office at last. Rupert Brooke, after flying visits to the Court from Rugby and then Cambridge, described *John Bull's Other Island* as 'unspeakably delightful', *Candida* 'the best play in the world' and *Major Barbara* 'highly amusing & interesting, & very brutal'. G.B.S. had been voted 'one of our leaders in the revolutionary movement of our youth,' wrote Leonard Woolf. Though Shaw's dramas did not have the grandeur of Ibsen's, they were played at the Court Theatre with relentless gusto, like a hurricane sweeping into the alley of Victorian morality and scattering the accumulated litter. Shaw, the champion of free speech and free thought, of paradoxical common sense and the ingenious use of reason, had 'a message of tremendous importance to us'. Along with Wells and Arnold Bennett, he had become one of the idols of young intellectuals. Many of the young men and women who attended the Court Theatre entered as *fin de siècle* Bohemians and emerged as twentieth-century radicals. Even A. B. Walkley, the reactionary critic of *The Times*, was obliged to admit that 'there is no such all-round acting in London as is nowadays to be seen at the Court theatre'.

The ensemble playing at the Court handed over the actor-manager's authority to the dramatist-producer. For over two centuries, from Thomas Betterton to Beerbohm Tree, the history of the British theatre had been the history of great actors. The Court Theatre set up a different standard of merit, bringing the acting and production of plays more in line with that of the contemporary Scandinavian and German stage. It changed the public's attitude. They went to see the play rather than an actor; and they had confidence in the all-round excellence of the cast.

Because the actors recognized Barker and Shaw as practical men of the theatre and respected their choice of plays, knowledge of stagecraft and skill at casting, they were willing to work as a team, accepting the smallest parts however successful they had earlier been in major roles. Barker believed that a variety of parts extended an actor's range, and he believed in repertory as a method of sustaining a school of actors.

Barker was a more literary and autocratic producer than Shaw. He liked to question his actors over the past history of their characters. 'You are not, I hope, going to tell me that the fellow drops from the skies, ready-made, at the moment you walk on the stage?' The biographies he provided became green-room legends. 'I want when you enter to give the impression of a man who is steeped in the poetry of Tennyson,' he was reputed to have told Dennis Eadie. For a scene in one of his own plays, he advised an actress that 'from the moment you come in you must make the audience understand that you live in a small town in the provinces and visit a great deal with the local clergy; you make slippers for the curate and go to dreary tea-parties.' Her one line in this scene was: 'How do you do?' Though a target for jokes, Barker was introducing a form of Stanislavsky's method of psychological realism which, he claimed, had been forced on actors by the bare dialogue of Ibsen with so much implicit in it.

Shaw was more matter-of-fact. If the producer, watching rehearsals, noted 'Show influence of Kierkegaard on Ibsen in this scene' or 'the Oedipus complex must be very apparent here. Discuss with the Queen', then 'the sooner he is packed out of the theatre the better'. If he noted 'Ears too red', 'Further up to make room for X', 'He, not Ee', 'This comes too suddenly', then, Shaw concluded, 'the producer knows his job and his place'.

Shaw would read his plays, first to friends, then to the company. Before the first rehearsal, he worked out on a chessboard with chessmen and a boy's box of assorted bricks, every entry, movement, rising or sitting, disposal of tambourine and tennis racket. The first rehearsals at the Court were always choreographic, the actors having their books in hand and the producer on the bare stage with them (the exits marked by a couple of chairs) teaching them their movements. Once these had been mastered, the words learned, and the actors made comfortable with what was going on, the books were discarded and the producer would leave the stage to sit front of house with a notebook and torch. 'From that moment, he should watch the stage as a cat watches a mouse,' Shaw advised, 'but never utter a word or interrupt a scene during its repetition no matter how completely the play goes to pieces, as it must at first when the players are trying to remember their parts and cues so desperately that they are incapable of acting.'

The producer at the Court (whom we would now call director) involved himself in reading plays, choosing casts, inventing the machinery, arranging the lighting, designing scenery and costume, adding incidental music, and co-ordinating everything except finance, which belonged to Vedrenne. Shaw liked to take a week over the stage movements, a fortnight for memorizing, and a final week for the dress rehearsals, when he would come on the stage again, going through passages that needed finishing, and interrupting now whenever he felt like it. Barker liked longer but in the crowded Court schedule this was seldom practicable.

Shaw had come to the theatre with the twin aspirations of giving the British public a political education and creating verbal opera; Barker's aim was to discover, through fractured syntax, crafted inarticulateness, oblique dénouement, the naturalistic dialogue to express a new stage situation. From those different aims as composers of plays arose their different styles of conducting the players.

Barker had never witnessed the heroic acting of old-timers. His taste for low tones, which worked perfectly for his own plays and those of Galsworthy, did not seem to suit Shaw who entreated him to 'leave me the drunken, stagey, brassbowelled barnstormers my plays are written for'. Barker's restrained style 'makes me blush for the comparative blatancy of my own plays,' Shaw conceded.

Shaw was patient and persistent, used a good deal of flattery, and took advice from some of the better actors. Barker was more persistent and less patient. Shaw set a limit of three hours (preferably between breakfast and lunch) and ensured that actors with only a few lines to speak were not kept hanging around all day while the principals rehearsed. Barker was a perfectionist and sometimes refused to leave off rehearsing until, according to Shaw, 'the unfortunate company had lost their last trains and buses and he had tired himself'. He also got alarmingly annoyed. 'His curses are neither loud nor deep: they are atmospheric,' one actor remembered. 'It is what he doesn't say that paralyses one. He *looks*; and having looked, he turns his back to the stage – and you can still see him looking through the back of his head.'

But it was exciting to work for Barker. If he did not spare his actors, he did not spare himself. They had the sense of collaborating at the beginning of a revolution in British stage production. The plays Barker presented had the appearance of being more natural, more lifelike, than anything else being performed in London and gave audiences a sensation of participating in the drama, rather than watching it from the auditorium.

Shaw's fatherly feelings for Barker spilled over on to the whole company at the Court. They felt part of a family, working to restore the English theatre to its rightful place in national life. A vivid example was the career of Lillah McCarthy. Shaw had seen her first in 1895 as a sixteen-year-old Lady Macbeth, 'immature, unskilful, and entirely artificial'. Yet she had gone at it bravely, her instinct and courage helping where her skill failed, and produced an effect that was 'very nearly thrilling'. 'She can hold an audience whilst she is doing everything wrongly,' he wrote in the *Saturday Review*. ' . . . I venture on the responsibility of saying that her Lady Macbeth was a highly promising performance, and that some years of hard work would make her a valuable recruit to the London stage.'

After ten years of hard work she wrote and asked to see Shaw. He was at this time looking for someone to play Ann Whitefield in *Man and Superman*. When she arrived at Adelphi Terrace ('a gorgeously good-looking young lady in a green dress and huge picture hat . . . in which she looked splendid, with the figure and gait of a Diana'), he gave her a broad smile of recognition: 'Why, here's Ann Whitefield.'

As one of the principal players at the Court, Lillah 'created the first generation of Shavian heroines with dazzling success'. Her technique, which combined the manner of 'the grand school with a natural impulse to murder the Victorian womanly woman', fell in perfectly with his stage needs. 'And with that young lady,' he wrote a quarter of a century later, 'I achieved performances of my plays which will probably never be surpassed.'

Working at the Court was a revelation for Lillah. She seemed hypnotized by G.B.S. 'With complete unselfconsciousness he would show us how to draw the full value out of a line,' she wrote. ' . . . With his amazing hands he would illustrate the mood of a line. We used to watch his hands in wonder. I learned as much from his hands, almost, as from his little notes of correction.' During rehearsals they often lunched together at the Queen's Restaurant in Sloane Square – apples, cheese, macaroni and salads with chilly milk and soda. 'I ate it because everything he did seemed right to me,' she remembered.

Lillah worshipped Shaw: but she did not understand his plays. Mrs Pankhurst was to tell her that Ann Whitefield had 'strengthened her purpose and fortified her courage' and many other women told her that Ann had 'brought them to life and that they remodelled themselves upon Ann's pattern'. Lillah played Ann Whitefield at the Court in May and June 1905, and again in October and November, and bore witness that 'she made a new woman of me'. She acted the part of Ann with earnest intensity. Barker, in the role of Tanner, 'carried the thing through remarkably well'. But it was difficult to keep Lillah's feet on the ground. 'Her life was rich in wonderful experiences that had never happened, and in friendships with wonderful people (including myself) who never existed,' Shaw remarked. She pursued Barker across the Court Theatre: and on 24 April 1906, at the West Strand Registry Office, she caught and married him.

The marriage had the air of being a brilliant success. 'She was an admirable hostess; and her enjoyment of the open air and of travelling made her a most healthy companion for him,' Shaw explained. Marriage suited Barker, who was no Bohemian. 'The admirations and adorations the pair excited in the cultured sections of London society could be indulged and gratified in country houses where interesting and brilliant young married couples were welcome.' Why then was Shaw 'instinctively dismayed'? As his Court 'children', their marriage was that of brother and sister. They had no children, and were not well cast for what the other needed: a mother for him, a father for her. 'There were no two people on earth less suited to one another,' Shaw wrote. It was the marriage of actors and actresses, a stepping aside from reality, an escapade.

That summer after their marriage they went to stay with the Webbs. 'I think what he [Barker] lacks is warmth of feeling – he is cold, with little active pity or admiration, or faithful devotion,' Beatrice wrote in her diary. 'A better acquaintance than a friend, a better friend than a husband . . .

'She is a strikingly handsome lady, also hard-working and dutiful – a puritan, I think, by temperament . . . Otherwise, I fear she is . . . commonplace, and he has all the appearance of being bored by her after two months' marriage.'

By the end of October 1906, they were back on stage as Tanner and Ann Whitefield. Next month they stepped into a new Shaw play at the Court: a tragedy in which Barker was an artist dying of consumption, with Lillah his wife – 'the sort of woman I hate', Shaw notified her.

4
CONCERNING *THE DOCTOR'S DILEMMA*

> Here am I, for instance, by class a respectable man, by common sense a
> hater of waste and disorder, by intellectual constitution legally minded
> to the verge of pedantry, and by temperament apprehensive and economi-
> cally disposed to the limit of old-maidishness; yet I am, and have always
> been, and shall now always be, a revolutionary writer.
>
> Preface to *Major Barbara*

Over the early summer of 1906 Shaw wrote prefaces to *John Bull's Other Island* and *Major Barbara*. The first, discursively favourable to Home Rule, ridiculed nationalism and the military and bureaucratic imagination that supported it. The second, in celebration of social equality, included some powerful invective against the malicious injury of judicial punishments and the social damage resulting from an inequitable distribution of money. Both prefaces were assaults on institutions of power. Then over the late summer, he wrote *The Doctor's Dilemma*, a play aimed at another powerful institution, the medical profession.

It was Charlotte who reminded him of a good dramatic subject he had come across earlier that year at St Mary's Hospital, Paddington. The Principal of the Institute of Pathology there was Almroth Wright who had recently created a scientific sensation by claiming to have found a method of measuring the protective substances in the human blood. Wright 'discovered that the white corpuscles or phagocytes which attack and devour disease germs for us do their work only when we butter the disease germs appetizingly for them with a natural sauce'. The chemical condiments ebbed and flowed like the tide. Wright believed he had invented a means of calculating the periodical climaxes. Vaccine therapy could now proceed, he announced, on a scientific basis.

Shaw was keen to let the London drama critics know that the 'scientific side' of his play was 'correct and up to date'. Sir Colenso Ridgeon, the hero, 'is, serum pathologically, Sir Almroth Wright, knighted last birthday (May [1906]) for his opsonic discovery,' he informed A. B. Walkley. Some of Sir Almroth's friends would drop in to his research institute at St Mary's at night and, among the glass tubes, bottles, powders, plasters, discuss the newest theories of 'Vaccinotherapy'. Shaw was present at one of these late-night tea parties when a discussion arose among the physicians over admitting an extra tuberculosis patient who had arrived that day for experimental treatment. Wright's chief assistant objected: 'We've got too many cases on our hands already.' Shaw then asked: 'What would happen if more people applied to you for help than you could properly look after?' And Wright answered: 'We should have to consider which life was worth saving.'

This weighing of human worth on the scales of life and death is superficially the problem at the centre of Shaw's play. Whose life is of greater value: the unprincipled artist of genius or the honest sixpenny doctor? If there is an air of unreality about this choice it is because, as G. K. Chesterton pointed out, nobody at sea shouts 'Bad citizen overboard!' In real life, the doctor 'doesn't fool himself that the moral value of the characters comes into it,' James Fenton was to write. 'He chooses the people he has the best chance of saving.'

The real dilemma in the play, and the pivot of Colenso Ridgeon's choice, involves the nature of our unconscious motives and the idealizing process of logic by which we justify them to ourselves and represent them to one another. Almroth Wright was a misogynist who had concluded in *The Unexpurgated Case Against Woman Suffrage* that the feminine mind 'accepts the congenial as true, and rejects the uncongenial as false: takes the imaginary which is desired for reality'. In *The Doctor's Dilemma*, Shaw takes Wright's view of the inferior and irrational feminine mind and applies it to his gallery of scientific men. In particular he focuses on the unconscious sexual motives of Sir Colenso Ridgeon, the fashionable physician modelled on Wright who, listing his symptoms, innocently takes medical advice when he is about to fall in love.

Shaw liked Wright and disagreed with him about almost everything. Lord Moran, who heard some of their contests at St Mary's, remembered feeling sorry for Wright once Shaw had finished speaking. 'I felt that he had been pulverized, but at the end of Wright's reply I blushed to think that Shaw, who was after all a guest, had been so mercilessly shown up. The devastating effect of such speech depends on the art of selection. Every single sentence was a direct hit; there was not a single word which did not contribute to the confusion of the enemy.'

Here is a source and echo of the medical crosstalk in *The Doctor's Dilemma*. Shaw's sense of vulnerability to the power of this medical élite, displacing a fear of death, gave his satire its edge; his sparring matches with Wright also enabled him to parody his own habit of presenting himself as morally superior to human frailty and devastatingly up to date with scientific fashion. Unlike Wright, who had won an extraordinary pile of medals, honours and academic prizes, Shaw had never learned anything at school. 'I could not pass an examination and win a certificate in an elementary school to this day.' He was an academic *manqué* and resented his exclusion from university excellence – that nest of singing birds.

Behind these years of controversy with Wright, and the play that derived from their association, there lay a wish to take authority from the orthodoxly educated and give it to outsiders. Like the scholastic profession, the medical freemasonry was a closed circle of privileged people whose mesmeric power over other human beings angered Shaw. 'It is awful how these scientific men wallow in orthodoxy, when they get the chance,' he complained to Gilbert Murray. ' ... Free thought really depends on the men of letters – and progressive thought, too.'

*

The Doctor's Dilemma shows us a cabal of physicians driven into the position of private tradesmen, abjectly dependent upon their patients' incomes and delusions. Beneath the invented drama of the play with its surface tension of ethics versus aesthetics, lies a theme that confronts the philosophies of science for science's sake with the social usefulness of art, balancing Wright's way of looking at the world against Shaw's. Sir Colenso Ridgeon's choice, which is intended to illustrate the subjective foundations of scientific reasoning, exposes him at the end of the play as having been so emotionally self-deluded as to have 'committed a purely disinterested murder!'

The most effective sections of the play depended on Shaw's instinct rather than his research. He sensed that something was wrong with Wright's reputation. The War Office, wanting to use Wright's anti-typhoid injections, 'first had him knighted and then used his knighthood as evidence of the unassailability of his theories' – a similar process to that of Ridgeon's knighthood in Act I of the play. One reason for the popularity of Wright's treatment seems to have been its novelty. No Harley Street specialist could afford to see his patient leave him for someone more 'up to date'. But looking back from 1970, W. D. Foster concluded in *A History of Medical Bacteriology*: 'It is doubtful if this form of treatment produced any good results and certainly in most instances, it was valueless to the point of fraudulence.'

Shaw said of Wright that it was 'useful to know a man who has discovered the philosopher's stone but does not know the value of gold'. It was a percipient statement. The concept of certain body cells reacting in a measurable way to an invasion by bacteria 'had great importance for the future development of bacteriology and immunology,' wrote Dr Gregory Scott in *British Medicine*. But the significance of this discovery was taken up by Wright's junior at St Mary's, Alexander Fleming. While accidentally finding a drug that would take the place of vaccine therapy, Fleming was financed by money raised from the use of Wright's vaccine, and obliged to pay perpetual lip-service to the man who became nicknamed 'Sir Almost Wright'. The story was to end with the renaming of St Mary's laboratory as the Wright-Fleming Institute and the development of the wonder-drug penicillin by Florey and Chain. Shaw's instinct had alerted him to recurring and timeless patterns within the medical community.

There were several models for the artist Dubedat. Chief among them was Edward Aveling, the basilisk-eyed 'blackguard' whom Eleanor Marx had idolized. When Ridgeon assures Jennifer Dubedat that 'your hero must be preserved to you', he is protecting her from Eleanor Marx's suicidal destiny by ensuring that her illusions survive her husband's death. Shaw also recycled some of his feelings for H. G. Wells and Charles Charrington, used the case histories of Beardsley and Rossetti, as well as a scandal from the career of Sir Alfred Gilbert, sculptor of Eros in Piccadilly Circus, and cast a backward look at Vandeleur Lee.

In the play Dubedat becomes the figure through whom 'the Shavian devil is most active,' writes Margery Morgan. 'For the debate reflects a division that ran deep in the author himself.' Critics have proposed that since Dubedat admits 'I'm a disciple of Bernard Shaw', he represents G.B.S. But he had taken this statement from a court case. A youth called Rankin, sentenced early that year to six months' imprisonment for attempting to blackmail his father, a schoolmaster, had pleaded guilty to being a disciple of Bernard Shaw as the explanation of his crime. In Wormwood Scrubs he refused the ministrations of the chaplain, and asked that G.B.S. be sent for. As Shaw was abroad, Stewart Headlam visited him in gaol. 'It was quite clear that he was under the impression that my teaching was simply an advocacy of reckless and shameless disregard of all social and moral obligations,' Shaw later reported, 'an error which he owes, I should say, not to reading my works unsophisticatedly, but to reading the follies which the press utters about me . . . It was as a reductio-ad-absurdum of this error and partly as a warning against it that I made Dubedat in the play use Rankin's defence.'

Shaw subtitled his play 'A Tragedy'. To peddle self-delusion and advertise it as a happiness-drug was to manufacture human tragedy. Shaw recommended people to 'stop taking any opiates or palliatives if you can endure life without them'; and he used the medical profession as a metaphor for every conspiracy of self-deception that worked against the public interest. The doctors in his play are all amiable men. It is public fear that insists on their omniscience, public superstition that equips them with their hocus-pocus of charms and cures, public ignorance that obliges them to trade in hypochondria. They are the idealists of Shaw's philosophy, who are paid to give the philistines what they want and will be out of a job unless they do so.

Shaw believed that most progress depended on heretics but that most heretics were not vehicles for progress. In Dubedat we are shown a realist infected by poverty and the atmosphere of idealism. Ridgeon, the physician, romantically idealizes Jennifer who romantically idealizes her artist-husband Dubedat who idealizes his work as the murderous doctors idealize theirs.

The embodiment of romanticism is Jennifer. 'Provisionally I have called her Andromeda; but Mrs Andromeda Dubedat is too long,' Shaw wrote to Lillah McCarthy from Cornwall. 'Here in King Arthur's country the name Guinevere survives as Jennifer.' The names reveal Shaw's intention to parody the Greek and Arthurian myths of chivalry. Ridgeon sees himself as a Perseus rescuing his beautiful Andromeda by killing her monster-husband. By calling her Jennifer and preserving the connection with Arthurian legend, Shaw recalls his own 'Mystic Betrothal' to May Morris whose mother Jane had been painted as Guinevere by William Morris. The more recent case of Guineverism, Shaw implies, had been Lillah and Barker.

Shaw wrote his play, he said, in response to a challenge from Archer who had written that G.B.S. was incapable of writing a convincing death scene. 'It is not the glory but the limitation of Mr Shaw's theatre that it is peopled by immortals,' he wrote. Shaw intended *The Doctor's Dilemma* to be a 'tragic comedy, with death conducting the orchestra'. To assist the critics, who had not yet heard of black comedy, Shaw issued a press release in which he prophesied 'it will probably be called a *farce macabre*'; and as an aid for his audiences he added a quotation to the programme: 'Life does not cease to be funny when people die, any more than it ceases to be serious when people laugh.'

The death of Dubedat is usually more interesting to scholars than spectators. The serious artist in Dubedat is already dead and the tragedy over. What remains is an actor performing a death scene for his audience on stage. The long operatic farewell, with its comic chorus, has none of the sordidness of death from tuberculosis.

Shaw was fond of his death scene. He described it as 'none the worse because its climax is "derived" (not to say stolen) from Wagner's End of a Musician in Paris'. The scholarship in which he wrapped the King of Terrors round becomes the weapon for a perfect riposte to charges of bad taste and cheap art.

'The creed of the dying artist, which has been reprobated on all hands as a sally of which only the bad taste of Bernard Shaw could be capable, is openly borrowed with gratitude and admiration by me from one of the best known prose writings of the most famous man of the nineteenth century. In Richard Wagner's well known story, dated 1841 . . . the dying musician begins his creed with the words, "I believe in God, Mozart and

Beethoven". It is a curious instance of the enormous Philistinism of English criticism that this passage should not only be unknown among us, but that a repetition of its thought and imagery 65 years later should still find us with a conception of creative force so narrow that the association of Art with Religion conveys nothing to us but a sense of far fetched impropriety.

I am, Sir, your obedient servant

G. Bernard Shaw.'

5

INVASION OF THE WEST END

Touchstone: Wast ever at the Court, shepherd?
Corin: No, truly.
Touchstone: Then thou art damned.

Shakespeare, *As You Like It*

The materials for his play had accumulated gradually: but the writing was fast. Shaw had begun it on 11 August 1906 at Mevagissey on the coast of Cornwall. By 21 August, on Polstreath Beach, he finished the first act. A week later another act was completed. 'It springs into existence impetuously with leaps & bounds,' he told Trebitsch; 'the only trouble is to get it inked.'

He wrote everywhere, ending the third act on St Austell Station in Cornwall and starting the fourth the same day after joining the train from Exeter to London. He came to the end of this act at the village of Moulsford in the Thames Valley, then started the last on the train from Reading to London. The first draft was completed at twenty minutes past six in the evening aboard a steamer on the Thames, as it docked at Cherry Garden Pier below Tower Bridge.

Shaw's revisions ('a slower job than the writing was') persisted, through rehearsals, almost up to opening night on 20 November. From the Carfax Gallery the Court leased pictures by Augustus John, William Orpen and Will Rothenstein, suggesting an extraordinary diversity in Dubedat's style.

Again the critics were divided. But Shaw himself noticed how they were beginning to compare him somewhat unfavourably to himself. 'In the future, instead of abusing the new play and praising the one before, let them abuse the one before and praise the new one,' he recommended. He was genuinely anxious for the press to act as a helpful patron to the

Court. The 'atmosphere of good humour' which the newspapers could promote, he told Vedrenne, was 'next to an atmosphere of solid money' the most precious possession they could own. He felt a commitment to their enterprise not simply because it had given him an audience and made his name as a dramatist of performable plays, but because it represented a step towards establishing the theatre in England. 'It is a huge factory of sentiment, of character, of points of honour, of conceptions of conduct,' he wrote later when appealing for the building of a National Theatre, 'of everything that finally determines the destiny of a nation.'

*

Barker used these years at the Court to test some of the ideas he and Archer had proposed in their book, *A National Theatre: Scheme and Estimates*. This book, 'the blueprint and the bible for the National Theatre movement', envisaged a large repertory of plays, both ancient and modern, foreign and English. The Court was more avant-garde than anything that, for pragmatic reasons, they were recommending to the general public. But its success was an excellent advertisement for the scheme. Privately printed and circulated before the Court pilot project began in October 1904, their book was published shortly after the Vedrenne–Barker management left the Court in June 1907.

Barker and Shaw had introduced repertory into the London theatre and achieved what the young actor Hesketh Pearson called 'the most famous epoch in theatrical management since the days of the Globe on Bankside'. But besides Barker and Laurence Housman, none of the contemporary playwrights (who included Galsworthy, St John Hankin, John Masefield and W. B. Yeats) wrote work that was really popular. The only outstanding success was G.B.S. himself. Of the thirty-two plays by seventeen dramatists presented at the Court over almost three years, eleven were his; and of the 988 performances altogether, Shaw's plays made up 701. Everything could be explained away as having depended upon one man. After June 1907, when *Don Juan in Hell* and *The Man of Destiny* were presented in a double bill, Shaw's portfolio was pretty well exhausted. There was a feeling that he had been rather too successful. John Quinn, the American patron and collector, reported that the theatre was 'brimming over with Shaw and Shaw's plays at present . . . Yeats says he will soon become a public nuisance.'

But the reputation of the Court partly owed its solidity to 'the prudent pessimism' of Vedrenne. 'Barker, aiming at a National Repertory Theatre, with a change of program every night, was determined to test our enterprise to destruction as motor tyres are tested, to find out its utmost possibilities,' Shaw wrote. 'I was equally reckless. Vedrenne . . . was like a man trying to ride two runaway horses simultaneously.' Vedrenne wanted to make money out of the theatre. Barker felt constantly balked by his subtle economies, his greeting of all fresh ideas with extravagant horror. Shaw represented their mutual dislike as a miraculous bonus. 'The partnership of V & B has every aspect of permanence: you are exactly on the terms which bind men to one another for ever & ever,' he promised Vedrenne, 'each with a strong grievance against the other to give interest & life to what would otherwise be a tedious & uneventful routine.'

Everything was enlivened by what Barker felt to be Vedrenne's 'vendetta' against Lillah McCarthy. 'My position between you is very fearful,' Shaw warned Lillah. 'I ask myself repeatedly Is Lillah the greatest liar known to history, or is Vedrenne?' And he cautioned Vedrenne: 'You will end by busting up Vedrenne & Barker.' Under this pressure they were all driven to abuse each other. 'What with Barker gradually losing all desire to act, and Vedrenne gradually losing all desire to do anything else but act, the position has become more & more impossible,' complained Shaw. 'If I could only get V on the stage & B off it, I should amaze the world.'

In Shaw's opinion, the job of producing plays was ruining Barker's acting. But Shaw minimized Barker's distaste for public performance. 'I do believe my present loathing for the theatre is loathing for the audience,' he was to write a decade later. 'I have never loved them.' He wished to retire and write for a more refined theatre – the National Theatre of his imagination. Shaw's advice seemed partly to assist the first step in this retreat. 'The next thing *you* have to do is to finish the play [*Waste*] & produce it,' he had urged in the summer of 1906; 'then publish it with Ann Leete & Voysey in a single volume.'

But Barker needed money to write at his ease and produce his plays fastidiously. By 1907 two possibilities lay open to him. 'There is to be a new theatre in America financed by 23 millionaires; and I have been asked whether Barker will go over and manage it,' Shaw announced to Lillah. This Millionaire's Theatre, between 62nd and 63rd Streets on Central Park West, was being built to run on the repertory principles described in Barker and Archer's blueprint, and it offered Barker an opportunity to cut free from Vedrenne and join a more intellectual partnership with Archer. 'America looks rather real at moments,' he wrote to Archer, 'and it would be a correct sequel to the blue book if we went together.'

But the Millionaire's Theatre was still under construction and other arrangements had to be made for the coming season of 1907–8. Shaw believed that repertory meant playing in London for advertisement and then playing on tour for money. Vedrenne wanted to capitalize on their success at the Court by advancing straight into the West End of London. Perhaps because touring was such a helter-skelter business, Barker mainly supported Vedrenne and together they leased the Savoy Theatre in the Strand. Shaw did not intend to join their partnership: 'I shall act simply as usurer,' he told them. To enable the Savoy season to open he put up £2,000 (equivalent to £94,500 in 1997) at five per cent interest – to which was added £1,000 each from Vedrenne and Barker who were both to draw salaries of £1,000 a year. 'My own salary – another thousand – ' added Shaw, 'is to be taken out in moral superiority.'

The Savoy was twice the size of the Court and had become celebrated for its Gilbert and Sullivan productions. But the audiences from the Court never took to the Savoy where the management actually played the National Anthem and made them stand up. In his excitement Vedrenne appeared to Shaw to have thrown aside all his prudence; while Barker, his hopes focused on New York, would have been content with Restoration comedy. Shaw complained of his reluctance 'to tackle anything but easy plays and easy people – easy, that is, to his temperament'. He also objected to the many revivals of his own plays, which were losing their sparkle. 'The thing to aim at now,' he insisted to Barker, 'is a season without a single Shaw evening bill.' He wanted Galsworthy's new play *Joy* and Barker's *Waste* to take up the running. But Galsworthy's sentimental work was a disappointment; Barker's *Waste* was banned by the Censor; and even the weakly cast production of Gilbert Murray's version of Euripides' *Medea* appeared lustreless. The Savoy season, which closed on 14 March 1908, had turned out a failure.

Immediately afterwards Barker took off with Archer for New York. But they found the New Theatre, 'with an enormous, gaping, cavernous proscenium', to be 'fit only for old-fashioned, nineteenth century spectacle'. They returned in disappointment to London.

In the spring of 1908 Vedrenne leased another theatre, the Haymarket, to present Shaw's new 'dramatic masterpiece' *Getting Married*. This was to be followed in the summer with *The Chinese Lantern* by Laurence Housman whose *Prunella* (in collaboration with Barker) had been one of the Court's non-Shavian successes, and a new play called *Nan* by John Masefield whose *Campden Wonder* Shaw felt had been seriously underrated at the Court.

'The Vedrenne and Barker enterprise then is as much alive as ever?' Shaw made a *Daily Telegraph* reporter ask him in May 1908 – to which he answered: 'it seems to be immortal.' In fact Barker and Vedrenne longed to be free of each other, but (being so heavily in debt to him) could not come to any arrangement without Shaw's consent. And Shaw, reluctant to announce their separation, succeeded in delaying it until early in 1911. Barker had by then written *The Madras House*, directed a season of plays at the Duke of York's Theatre with the American producer Charles Frohman and begun a theatrical partnership with his wife. Vedrenne was starting on a new partnership, 'Vedrenne and [Dennis] Eadie', at the Royalty Theatre. To reunite them was no longer possible. Shaw, who had advanced £5,250 to them over the years and arranged for Barker to be repaid his loans first, agreed to accept £484 3s. 10d. (plus some assets from the sale of scenery) as a final settlement.

It had been 'worth the cost a hundred times over,' he declared; 'but the cost fell on us, and the benefit went to the nation'. In 1909 he had joined the Organizing Committee of the Shakespeare Memorial National Theatre, and converted his Vedrenne & Barker loss into an investment in the campaign. What could be done by private enterprise, he argued, had been exhaustively tried at the Court. 'Messrs. Vedrenne & Barker were not rich men,' he wrote. 'They voluntarily forewent the opportunity of turning the enterprise into a lucrative commercial speculation and left themselves at the end with all their resources mortgaged. My own income falls very far short of the point at which the loss of sums of four figures becomes a matter of no importance . . . I had to stop.'

ELEVEN

I

SITTING TO RODIN

Do you know Shaw's writings? That's the man who has quite a good way of coming to terms with life – of putting himself into harmony with it (which is no small achievement). He is proud of his work, like Wilde or Whistler but without their pretension, rather like a dog that is proud of its master.

Rainer Maria Rilke to Elizabeth von der Heydt (26 April 1906)

'We are in the agonies of househunting,' Shaw had appealed to Wells in April 1904. 'Now is the time to produce an eligible residence, if you have one handy.' Charlotte had grown more ingenious at braking her husband's flow of work. Early in 1906 she encouraged him to sit for his portrait by Neville Lytton. It was an extraordinary picture, owing much to an observation by Granville Barker that the Velázquez portrait of Pope Innocent X in the Doria Palace at Rome was uncannily similar to G.B.S. Working in imitation of Velázquez, and placing his subject in papal vestments and throne, Neville Lytton achieved what Shaw was to call a 'witty jibe at my poses'.

These poses multiplied over the last half of Shaw's career – as busts, statuettes, medallions, stamps, portraits in oils, watercolours, crayon and needlework; as wooden marionettes, caricatures on posters and in papers, on film, as photographs (poised either naked or eccentrically tailored) on land, in cars, under parasols, at sea; and as likenesses rendered in stained glass, from a simple stick of shaving soap, as a brass door-knocker or waxwork tricyclist and, most extreme of all perhaps, in grisaille with hands held to ears on a Chinese *famille rose* vase decorated with dense peony, chrysanthemum, lily and vine . . .

People were aghast at Shaw's Everest of vanity. But, admitting his addiction to public attention, he tried to employ it usefully. His commissioned portraits and busts may be seen as evidence of generous patronage. He was curious too about the public phenomenon he had manufactured to replace the unloved Sonny.

But Charlotte was not amused. Taking advantage of a visit to England by Rodin, she invited the French sculptor to visit her at Adelphi Terrace on the afternoon of Friday 1 March 1906. He came, they talked, and the consequence was that, as Shaw wrote to Trebitsch later that day, 'my wife insists on dragging me to Paris for twelve days at Easter so that Rodin may make a bust of me!!!!!'

They stayed at the Hôtel Palais d'Orsay, and after meeting Rodin on 16 April began the sittings at his private studio in Meudon. 'He had, I believe, a serious friendship for us,' Shaw was to write. They were at his house all day, most days, until they left France on 8 May. Talking to Rodin as he was preparing to begin, Charlotte complained that other artists and photographers had automatically produced the sort of mephistophelean figure they assumed her husband to be, without taking the trouble to look at him. Rodin replied that he knew nothing of Shaw's reputation: 'but what is there I will give you.'

G.B.S. was determined to prove a champion sitter, putting immense vitality simply into standing still. 'The portrait makes tremendous strides, thanks to the energy with which Shaw stands,' wrote Rainer Maria Rilke, then Rodin's secretary. 'He stands like a thing which has the will to stand, over and above its natural capacity for it . . .

'Shaw as a model surpasses description. He . . . has the power of getting his whole self, even to his legs and all the rest of him, into his bust, which will have to represent the whole Shaw, as it were, that Rodin has before him. something quite unusually concentrated, which he absorbs into himself and into his work (you can imagine with what zest).'

Rodin's studio seemed transformed into a theatre. Each day an audience assembled and sat in mesmerized silence as Shaw ('*ce modèle extraordinaire*') collected and concentrated himself and Rodin filled the place with 'his raging activity, his gigantic movements', and volleys of unintelligible sound. In the intervals Charlotte played about G.B.S. 'like a spring wind about a goat'. In a letter to his wife, Rilke sent a beautifully exact description of the work's development. 'After rapidly cutting out the eyebrows so that something like a nose appeared, and marking the position of the mouth by an incision such as children make in a snowman, he began to make first four, then eight, then sixteen profiles, letting the model, who was standing quite close to him, turn every three minutes or so . . .

'In the third sitting, he placed Shaw in a low child's chair (all of which caused this ironical and mocking spirit, who is however by no means an unsympathetic personality, exquisite pleasure) and sliced the head off the bust with a wire – (Shaw, whom the bust already resembled very strikingly, watched this execution with indescribable delight.)'

What appealed to Shaw was Rodin's monumental matter-of-factness. He never pretended to a knowledge of his plays ('he knows absolutely nothing about books,' Shaw commented, ' – thinks they are things to be read'), his eyes never twinkled, his hands did not gesticulate: he worked, and 'like all great workmen who can express themselves in words, was very straight and simple'. Shaw's words, according to Rodin, were less straight but even more simple: '*M. Shaw ne parle pas très bien,*' he said; '*mais il s'exprime avec une telle violence qu'il s'impose.*'

These *séances* at Meudon became one of the features of Paris's spring season. People as various as G. K. Chesterton and Gwen John were reported to have bulged or peeped in for a moment. From Vienna came Trebitsch to marvel and absorb the 'lofty mind' of Charlotte in 'profound talk about God and the universe'.

To other acquaintances – including the young American photographer Alvin Langdon Coburn – Shaw sent invitations for the unveiling of Rodin's sculpture 'Le Penseur'. Coburn had photographed Shaw two summers earlier, and in 1906 Shaw had written a preface to the catalogue for an exhibition of his work in which he compared Coburn's photograph of Chesterton to Rodin's statue of Balzac. The inauguration of 'Le Penseur' outside the Panthéon took place on the afternoon of 21 April. Next morning Shaw surprised Coburn with the suggestion that 'after his bath I should photograph him nude in the pose of Le Penseur' on the edge of his bath. With this parody of 'Le Penseur' he came close to sabotaging his purpose in going to Rodin for evidence of himself 'just as I am, without one plea'. He wanted to feel cleansed of the revulsion that periodically rose up in him over his own notoriety. But this Shavian fame arose from so deep a need that he sentimentalized his humility towards Rodin when famously remarking: 'at least I was sure of a place in the biographical dictionaries a thousand years hence as: "Shaw, Bernard: subject of a bust by Rodin: otherwise unknown".'

They went to Ibsen's *Canard Sauvage* and to the Grand Guignol with Trebitsch. The more blood-curdling these plays, Trebitsch observed, the more of an effort Shaw had to make 'not to burst out laughing'. He particularly enjoyed the guillotine. Nothing, it seemed to Trebitsch, could frighten G.B.S., not even the evening newspaper predictions of a revolution in Paris on May Day which he looked forward to as 'the next instalment of the horror-play we have just been seeing'. Shaw spent the afternoon of May Day with Charlotte on the Place de la République and afterwards sent a message to the *Labour Leader* commenting that the French Government wanted to win the General Election 'by suppressing a revolution. Unluckily there is no revolution to suppress. The Government therefore sends the police and the dragoons to shove and charge the lazy and law abiding Parisians until they are goaded into revolt. No use: the people simply WON'T revolt.

'But several respectable persons have been shoved and galloped over and even sabred. Surely it ought to be within the resources of modern democracy to find a remedy for this sort of official amateur revolution making. It is a clear interference with our business as scientific revolutionists.'

In a letter to Granville Barker he admitted there had been a little more activity, describing Charlotte as clinging to lamp-posts in order to see over people's heads and growing 'so furious when she saw a real crowd charged by real soldiers that she wanted to throw stones'. After being 'pushed roughly hither and thither' she was led back by Shaw ('by dignified strategy which did not at any time go to the length of absolutely running away') to their hotel 'bursting into fresh spasms of rage all the way'. They had quitted the field without wounds and Shaw insisted that Charlotte had 'rather enjoyed being part of a revolution'. 'We finished up in the evening with a very stirring performance of Beethoven's 9th symphony at the Opera,' he told Trebitsch; 'so the day was a pretty full one.'

On 8 May Shaw sat to Rodin for the last time, then he and Charlotte caught the four o'clock train back to London. She carried with her two pencil-and-wash sketches of herself inscribed by Rodin '*Homage à sympathique Madame Charlotte Shaw*'. From London she sent him chocolates and her photograph of him (none of Shaw's had come out) and in October the curiously tame marble bust arrived at Adelphi Terrace; '*maintenant je suis immortel*,' wrote Shaw in a letter to Rodin that was returned to him as insufficiently addressed.

Within six weeks of returning to London Shaw was turning his head to William Strang for a good tight portrait. The following year, 1907, began with a couple of quick sittings for a bust by Troubetzkoy and ended with a preliminary one for Epstein. Shaw was to use these busts (and others by Sava Botzaris, Kathleen Bruce, Joseph Coplans, Jo Davidson, Sigismund de Strobl and Clare Winsten) to pull faces at his 'reputation'. Prince Troubetzkoy, being paternally Russian, 'made me flatteringly like a Russian nobleman'; and in the hands of Jacob Epstein, an American expatriate, he later became 'a Brooklyn navvy . . . my skin thickened, my hair coarsened, I put on five stone in weight, my physical strength trebled'. It followed that his plaster reputation lay in the imaginations of other people, not within himself.

Charlotte welcomed the respite from work these sittings and standings and posings obtained for him. But Epstein's ungentlemanly bust (completed in 1934) was 'like a blow in the face' and she told everyone who mentioned it to her that if this object 'came into our house she would walk out of it'. As Rodin had not understood his humour so Epstein had overlooked his Shavian veneer: and 'without my veneer I am not Bernard Shaw'.

This veneer, he had sometimes argued, was his reputation. In these busts and portraits, Shaw often felt he recognized part of himself; but never could he find all parts combined. Perhaps there was no method, even in his own work, of allying the opposing forces within himself. At the age of fifty he had proposed 'to furnish the world with an authentic portrait-bust of me before I had left the prime of life'. The nearest he came to this was perhaps Strobl's work - Charlotte certainly thought so. But the search for comprehensive authenticity continued almost to the end of his life. It was impossible, H. G. Wells complained, to move around Europe without being stared at by these Shavian images which seemed at the same time to mock and celebrate his rising success.

In the summer of 1906, as if in sympathy with this success, Shaw ascended from Wandsworth Gas Works in a balloon (a happening he would later re-compose for his play *Misalliance*). He rose and floated and descended over two and a half hours, without Charlotte's knowledge yet in the company of her sister, Granville Barker and the aviator-actor Robert Loraine. Loraine was a combination of artist and man-of-action Shaw particularly admired. 'I was never free from the impression when Shaw was speaking to me,' Loraine had written in his diary, 'that he might at any moment ascend to Heaven like Elisha on a chariot of fire.' They were guided in their balloon by an aeronaut Percival Spencer (who was translated into Joey Percival in *Misalliance*) to a height of 9,000 feet. After forty minutes' drifting 'very pleasant and seraphic with nothing happening, except that Shaw would peer through a hole in the boarding at his feet which made him feel rather sick, we discussed landing,' Loraine wrote. ' . . . I thought the people would be rather interested to receive visitors from the air, and especially flattered when they discovered Shaw's identity. "Don't be so certain," said Shaw. "They may think my works detestable." ' In the event they bumped down in a field near Chobham and were met by a purple-faced landowner, unacquainted with Shaw's *oeuvre* and waving a shooting-stick. 'The welcome he gave us was a curt direction as to the quickest way off his property.'

2

A CAT AND DOG LIFE

I was born to do odd jobs.

Shaw to Beatrice Webb (9 December 1910)

Their agonies of house-hunting ended when they came across the Rectory at Ayot St Lawrence, not far from Wheathampstead in Hertfordshire. The Rector, who could not afford to keep up the grounds, had no need of such a large house himself, and Charlotte decided to rent it. She did not plan to stay there long. They continued renting the place for fourteen years and shortly after the First World War bought it – following which it became known as 'Shaw's Corner'.

Ayot was a remote twelfth-century village where 'the last thing of real importance that happened was, perhaps, the Flood'. It had two churches, one shop, no omnibus or train service and, even by the 1930s, no gas or water supply, no delivery of newspapers and no electricity – the Rectory itself making use of a private generating plant. The house, which had been built in 1902, was a plain dark-red building standing in a sloping two-acre plot with scraps of kitchen-garden, orchard, lawn and a belt of conifers. Besides the dining-room, study and a small drawing-room, there were eight bedrooms.

Shaw and Charlotte moved in at the beginning of November 1906, with a married couple, Henry and Clara Higgs, to look after them. Higgs took over the garden, with an odd-job man to help him; and Charlotte engaged two maids to assist Mrs Higgs indoors. The Higgses, who had already been with them at Adelphi Terrace, were to remain in their service for some forty years. 'Mrs Shaw looked upon my wife almost as a daughter,' Higgs reckoned; 'they were like a father and mother to us.' Shaw recognized their value to him with an inscription in one of his books: 'To Harry and Clara Higgs, who have had a very important part in my life's work, as without their friendly services I should not have had time to write my books and plays nor had any comfort in my daily life.'

The Rectory was a fairly comfortable, fairly dismal house. Charlotte filled it with stiff armchairs, bureaux, beds: lodging-house objects with hardly a good piece among them. They had grown tired of house-hunting and this was one of the few houses about which they were agreed: neither of them liked it. Every day at Ayot felt like a Sunday. Once they had settled in, they were free to move out and around.

*

They had kept their maisonette in Adelphi Terrace, went regularly between London and Hertfordshire, and erratically everywhere else. At the end of March 1907, Charlotte carried Shaw off to France and they whirled through town after town for twelve days of hectic relaxation. 'I shall go to Beauvais probably tomorrow or next day,' Shaw wrote from Rouen, 'and shall either do the cathedral in ten minutes & hurry on Lord knows where, or stay there a day or two.' But, he owned, 'the cessation of writing & talking has done me a lot of good'.

To lighten the load of correspondence he had devised in 1906 a series of five stereotyped postcard messages. Over the next years the range of these cards greatly expanded. He attempted to give them a series of coloured codes, though eventually running out of colours. His views on capital punishment, on temperance, and the forty-letter British 'alfabet' were to be relayed in tones of green, orange-brown and blue. Neat piles of these coloured cards lay on his desk and, as he read through his mail each day he was able to cap many letters with an appropriate card. Snap! Politely and with force, they spelled out his reasons for being unable to read and report on unpublished manuscripts, give spoken interviews, inscribe books that were not his personal gifts, or comply with requests from strangers for his signature (with or without a photograph); why he could not receive visitors, acknowledge gifts, encourage people to celebrate his birthdays, respond to appeals founded on the notion that he was a multi-millionaire, open bazaars, speak at public dinners, write prefaces, read or write letters. In short: why he could not do so many of the things he spent his life doing.

'The only way to avoid giving offence by refusing is to refuse everybody by rule.' But Shaw consistently disobeyed his rule – even his authoritative refusals to provide autographs were sometimes signed. The cards were a method of saving time. He invested many hours in drafting variant texts. But always there was an ample margin that he could fill with commentary, outwitting the purpose of a printed message.

In 1907 he engaged Georgina Gillmore, daughter of his mother's half-sister Arabella, as his secretary. Charlotte and Shaw were fond of 'Judy'. She was eighteen and lived with Lucinda Shaw in Fitzroy Square when she started work for G.B.S. He sent her to secretarial college and she worked for him until her marriage in 1912.

Even with her help, Shaw complained that only 'the fear of my wife' was keeping him from a breakdown. Throughout the year, more than fifty of his articles, statements, interviews and letters appeared in the newspapers. There was Shaw on disarmament in the *Evening Standard*, on polygamy in *The Times* and on diet in the *Daily Mail*. His most common subjects were marriage, censorship and women's suffrage. But readers of the *Daily Graphic* could pick up what he had to say on 'the imperfections of phrenologists'; and *Clarion* subscribers could learn about 'the Gentle Art of Unpleasantness', a social exercise in three parts. He fired off a piece on Delacroix to the *Saturday Review*; composed a famous essay on Belloc and Chesterton for the *New Age*; and published a review of A. R. Orage's book on Nietzsche in *Fabian News*. The variety seemed infinite, the quantity endless.

In July 1907 the Shaws and the Webbs went off to a large house in Llanbedr, a village on the Welsh coast between Barmouth and Harlech, where the first Fabian Summer School took place. The event was under-written by Charlotte who saw it as a method of ventilating their studies with fresh air and a holiday atmosphere.

The Fabian Summer Schools, which later came to be seen as a found-ation of the intellectual wing of the Labour Party, were originally designed to get country members to meet metropolitan Fabians, and grey-haired socialists to mingle with the Fabian nursery. Occasional romances glim-mered, but the exhilarations were generally those of a 'joyous monastery'. The day would begin with Swedish Drill led by Mary Hankinson, a much-loved muscular games mistress and leading Fabian cricketer, who was to be a prototype for Shaw's St Joan. Breakfast, an experimental meal, was followed by a venture into co-operative washing-up. Cold baths were free (hot baths cost sixpence); rooms were set aside in which to practise silence, and no smoking was permitted (except, literally, in the smoking-room). There were courses of lectures available on the National Debt and the Modern Novel. Additional fixtures included swimming and tugs-of-war (Vegetarians versus Meat-eaters); and people were allowed to bring bicycles and eventually tennis balls – though never dogs or children. Highly organized games were discouraged, but there was always some tonic recreation such as country dances with the aid of Cecil J. Sharp's *The Country Dance Book* (3 vols.). Lights went out and doors were bolted at 11 p.m., and Fabians were requested 'to refrain from loud talk and noises' in the dormitories.

'The Fabian School is sleeping five in a room, and apparently enjoying it,' Shaw wrote to Granville Barker. G.B.S. was the chief attraction. He lectured on marriage, education and foreign politics; gave readings from his plays; and chatted with everyone. Thirty-nine Fabians camped in the old schoolhouse down the road from the Shaws, who had been joined in their house by Charlotte's sister and Robert Loraine. After one day's hike Shaw failed to return. Dressed in convenient drill-costumes and equipped with lanterns, a party of almost a hundred Fabians streamed across the mountains and valleys: and he was discovered asleep in a hotel.

More alarming were his exploits at sea. Each morning he swam and one morning, after a storm, almost drowned. Pressing him later as to what thoughts had come to mind during what might have been his last few moments alive, Loraine was told that he had been almost completely preoccupied by the business inconveniences of his death. How would Charlotte understand the arrangements with his translators? How would she cope with his lateness for lunch? 'Then my foot struck a stone, and instead of saying "Thank God!" I said, "Damn!" '

It was against this terrible capacity for endangering himself, and his instinctive 'Damn!' rather than 'Thank God!' on reaching safety, that Charlotte had to be so fiercely on guard. Increasingly, as Arnold Bennett noticed, she looked 'like the mother of a large family'. For Christmas she tucked Shaw up again in her sister and brother-in-law's house, where it was pretty well impossible for him to get into scrapes. And she kept him under her supervision and out of the country for three summer months of 1908 while the drains at Ayot were being replaced. First they went to Stockholm. To help preserve its exclusiveness, he promised to 'perpetrate the notion that Sweden is a frightful place, where bears wander through the streets and people live on cod liver oil'. He then descended to Bayreuth where he heard Richter conduct Wagner's *Ring* as well as 'the most perfectly managed performance [of *Parsifal*] I ever saw (and I had seen six before)'. Finally, Charlotte escorted him round the railway hotels of Ireland, from Galway to Dublin, where he was to present the Municipal Art Gallery with one of his Rodin busts.

The visit marked a change from their previous tours of Ireland when they had stayed with the 'Brandons and Castletowns and Kingstons & other Irish peers in their castles'. These families regarded G.B.S. as a jumped-up Dublin office boy. 'Charlotte seems perfectly happy and delighted with her cad,' reported Edith Somerville, 'for cad he is in spite of his talent.' For Charlotte's sake Shaw made himself 'very agreeable and quite affable,' as Edith Somerville admitted, but this affability cost him a good deal in patience and energy, and after 1907 (when he declined to accompany Charlotte to Castle Haven) they stayed at hotels or with more recent friends such as Lady Gregory.

Their motor tour of Europe had been an ambitious excursion. 'I was crushed, I am now exasperated,' Shaw cried out in a letter to Granville Barker, ' . . . another day's motoring will murder me.' But the next day's motoring near Rothenburg had almost murdered Charlotte, the motor having 'backjumped,' Shaw explained, '& sent Charlotte like a rocket to the roof of the car (a limousine, unluckily)'. Her symptoms (a bad throat) made her uncertain whether or not her neck was broken. 'She leans to the belief that it is,' observed Shaw who had the advantage, while she recuperated, of remaining four days in the same place. Pathetically he signalled his friends for business letters, and confided to Granville Barker how fed up he was with 'the cat and dog life I lead with poor Charlotte . . . Another month of it would end in a divorce.'

Their most curious holiday episode had been an encounter with Strindberg. 'I thought it my duty to pay my respects to a great man whom I considered one of the great dramatists of Europe,' Shaw afterwards remembered. 'People told me it was not of the slightest use. He is absolutely mad, they said, he won't see anybody, he never takes walks except in the middle of the night when there is nobody about, he attacks all his friends with the greatest fury. You will only be wasting your time.' Nevertheless, 'I achieved the impossible,' Shaw wrote to Archer. Strindberg was 'quite a pleasant looking person,' Shaw recalled, 'with the most beautiful sapphire blue eyes I have ever seen. He was beyond expression shy.' Shaw had prepared some conversational material in French, but Strindberg took the wind out of his sails 'by addressing me in German'. Their exchange developed by way of some embarrassed silences, a 'pale smile or two' from Strindberg and an undercurrent of polite French from Charlotte.

Strindberg had arranged for them to see that morning a special performance of *Miss Julie* at his Intimate Theatre, having summoned August Falck and Manda Björling back from their holiday in the archipelago to play the two protagonists. The absence of an audience and the presence of Strindberg had been unsettling – this astonishingly being 'the first time Strindberg had accepted to see the play in the 20 years of its existence,' Anthony Swerling records, 'so much did he shy from the theatre'. Though Strindberg had proudly shown the Shaws round his theatre beforehand, shortly afterwards, in a celebrated spasm of gloom, he consulted his watch and, noting it was almost half-past one, remarked in German that at two o'clock he was going to be sick. 'On this strong hint the party broke up.'

How much did they comprehend each other, the author of *Married* which Strindberg called 'the reverse side of my fearful attraction towards the other sex'; and the author of *Getting Married*, a tentative 'conversation' with feminist implications dramatizing the economic relations of marriage? Shaw was to describe what he had seen at the Intimate Theatre as one of Strindberg's 'chamber plays'. With the emotional intimacy of chamber music he had never felt easy. But generally he knew where Strindberg stood. 'I was born too soon to be greatly influenced by him as a playwright, but,' he was to write 'he is among the greatest of the great.' In the Preface to *Three Plays for Puritans* he had described him as 'the only genuinely Shakespearean modern dramatist', a resolute tragi-comedian, logical and faithful, who gave us the choice either of dismissing as absurd his way of judging conduct or else, by accepting it, concluding that 'it is cowardly to continue living'.

The suffering men and women inflict on each other in the name of love never appears in Shaw's work as it does in Strindberg's. Greatness 'implies a degree of human tragedy, of suffering and sacrifice,' wrote Thomas Mann. 'The knotted muscles of Tolstoy bearing up the full burden of morality, Atlas-like; Strindberg, who was in hell; the martyr's death Nietzsche died on the cross of thought; it is these that inspire us with the reverence of tragedy; but in Shaw there was nothing of all this. Was he beyond such things, or were they beyond him?'

Shaw's tragedy lay in the need to suppress such things; Strindberg's in the need to re-enact them. But Shaw felt the force of that re-enactment. He tried to persuade Beerbohm Tree to put on *Lycko Pers Resa* at His Majesty's (the play closest to Ibsen's *Peer Gynt*), but without success. Almost none of Strindberg's plays had been translated into English before Shaw's sister Lucy, with Maurice Elvey, produced a version of *Miss Julie* that was first presented in London by the Adelphi Play Society in 1912. That year, the Swedish newspaper *Dagens Nyheter* circulated a letter eliciting opinions of Strindberg's role in European culture to be published in the event of his death from cancer. 'Strindberg is a very great dramatist: he and Ibsen have made Sweden and Norway the dramatic centre of the world,' Shaw replied. '. . . Time may wear him out; but Death will not succeed in murdering him.' Strindberg died a fortnight later.

3

GETTING MARRIED AND STAYING MARRIED

> This multiplicity of motives is, I like to think, typical of our times. And if others have done this before me, then I congratulate myself in not being alone in my belief in these 'paradoxes' (the word always used to describe new discoveries).
>
> Strindberg, Preface to *Miss Julie*

'On the question of technique, I have, by way of experiment, eliminated all intervals,' wrote Strindberg in his Preface to *Miss Julie*. For *Getting Married* Shaw used a similar experiment. 'The customary division into acts and scenes has been disused,' he wrote, 'and a return made to unity of time and place as observed in the ancient Greek drama.'

By directing critics to the play's Aristotelian rules, Shaw swept their attention past an embarrassing parallel. For years in the *Saturday Review* he had made fun of the plays of Victorien Sardou, full of a 'bewildering profusion of everything that has no business in a play'. *Getting Married* is in places an ingenious adaptation of Sardou's *Divorçons*. The parallels are 'not only in the overall fusion of Farce with a genuine discussion of marriage and divorce,' observed the critic Martin Meisel, 'but in particulars and details'. Sardou's plan of playwriting, Shaw had written, 'is first to invent the action of his piece, and then to carefully keep it off the stage and have it announced merely by letters and telegrams'.

The Shavian play structure too moved the action off stage, and reversed the relationship between dialogue and incident. *Getting Married* progresses by means of a series of conversations: duologues and trios that form and dissolve one into another. It is as if a conventional well-made play were being performed backstage, and we witness the performers discussing its event-plot during the intervals. 'It is the wedding day of the bishop's daughter,' he wrote. 'The situation is expounded in the old stage fashion by that old stage figure the comic greengrocer, hired for the occasion as butler.

'The fun grows fast and furious as the guests arrive, invited and uninvited, with the most distracting malaproposity. Two are missing: the bridegroom and the bride. They have each received anonymously a pamphlet entitled "*Do you know what you are going to do? By one who has Done It*," setting forth all the anomalies and injustices and dangers of marriage under the existing British law. They refuse to get up and dress until they have read this inopportune document to the last word. When at last they appear they flatly refuse to face the horrors of the marriage law. Thereupon the whole company plunges into a discussion of marriage, and presently sits as a committee to draw up a form of private contract, as in the later days of ancient Rome, to supersede the legal ceremony. They are utterly unable to agree on a single article of it.'

Though Shaw claimed a classical provenance for *Getting Married*, it actually represented 'a new dramaturgy' as Eric Bentley wrote, 'and not, as its critics thought, a mere pamphlet in dialogue form'. Like *The Doctor's Dilemma*, it stages an institution. 'The play is about marriage as an institution and about nothing else.' His method of treating it was one that he had first attempted, and been persuaded to abandon, fifteen years before in the original last act of *The Philanderer*. It had been the celebrated divorcée Lady Colin Campbell who opened Shaw's eyes to 'the fact that I have started on quite a new trail and must reserve this act for the beginning of a new play'. With *Getting Married* Shaw finally started out on that trail.

The Philanderer had been one of Shaw's most directly autobiographical plays; with *Getting Married* he had grown more oblique. Nevertheless there is an autobiographical undercurrent. The scene in which the whole company sits as a committee ineffectually attempting to draft an English Partnership Deed comes from Shaw's memory of the contract Annie Besant presented to him over their piano duets.

More complex in derivation are the characters of Mrs George Collins and St John Hotchkiss. Mrs George, as she is called, is a mayoress, a coal merchant's wife and also 'Incognita Appassionata', the mysterious writer of love letters to the Bishop of Chelsea: altogether 'a wonderful interesting' woman, her brother-in-law the greengrocer tells everyone. The others believe she is 'too good to be true' until her appearance, described in Shaw's stage directions at the moment of her entrance as a 'triumphant, pampered, wilful, intensely alive woman ... But her beauty is wrecked, like an ageless landscape ravaged by long and fierce war ... The whole face is a battle-field of the passions, quite deplorable until she speaks, when an alert sense of fun rejuvenates her in a moment, and makes her company irresistible.'

She represents three women in one. Her age is approximately Charlotte's, but Shaw adds the qualities of two other women covered by Mrs Collins's other names. As 'Incognita Appassionata' she embodies the sexual passion that had been excluded from his marriage. For more than two years Shaw had been receiving a series of extraordinary letters from 'Poste Restante, Godalming', signed 'Miss Charmer'. He replied saying that love was an infinite mystery 'like everything else'; and that she had better 'marry and have children: then you will not ask from works of art what you can get only from life.' The result was that the girl, who revealed herself as Erica Cotterill, a cousin of Rupert Brooke's and daughter of a respectable Fabian schoolmaster, Charles Clement Cotterill, transferred her infatuation from the plays to the playwright whose unorthodox theories of sexual intercourse outside marriage for the procreation of babies she urgently wanted them to put into practice together. She challenged Shaw to confront all he had turned his back on: which he obliquely attempts to do by transferring them to Mrs Collins's correspondence with the Bishop.

Then as 'Mrs George' Shaw summons up a third woman: the figure of his mother who appeared in his dreams as 'my wife as well as my mother'. These dreams elevated his affection for Charlotte and intensified his feelings for his mother since, Shaw explained to Gilbert Murray, there was 'the addition of the filial feeling and the redemption of the sexual feeling from "sin" and strain'.

Shaw's practice of obscuring the self-portraits of his plays by giving the characters a superficial resemblance to other people – Marchbanks to

De Quincey, Tanner to H. M. Hyndman, Professor Higgins to Henry Sweet – extends to St John Hotchkiss who is ostensibly modelled on his fellow-playwright St John Hankin. But when the 'St John' falls away and he confesses to Mrs George that 'my own pet name in the bosom of my family is Sonny' the pretence becomes transparent. In Hotchkiss we may see something of the reaction that Shaw produced on his contemporaries: 'He talks about himself with energetic gaiety. He talks to other people with a sweet forbearance (implying a kindly consideration for their stupidity) which infuriates those whom he does not succeed in amusing.'

When Hotchkiss meets Mrs George on stage he recognizes her as the coal merchant's wife with whom ('when I was a young fool') he had fallen in love. 'I felt in her presence an extraordinary sensation of unrest, of emotion, of unsatisfied need,' he remembers. It is not fanciful to feel in this 'unsatisfied need' Shaw's own response to his mother when in Dublin. In *Getting Married* Shaw makes Hotchkiss run away abroad in place of his mother leaving for England. And now that they meet again, Hotchkiss again falls in love. The relationship is essentially that of an adopted son. 'I want to talk to him like a mother,' says Mrs George who tells Hotchkiss that 'Sonny is just the name I wanted for you'.

So Shaw provides another scenario for the Dublin *ménage à trois*, now that his mother, merged with the figure of Charlotte, has returned to him in his dreams. His sense of the incompleteness of his marriage pervades this play. It was an incompleteness for which Charlotte was to compensate with mystical hoverings comparable to Mrs George's Blakean 'inspir-ations'; and from which Shaw escaped by taking on the authority of the Bishop who wants to 'make divorce reasonable and decent'. From the abnormality of his own marriage he argues with the tolerant voice of the greengrocer Collins that 'theres almost as many different sorts of marriages as theres different sorts of people'.

The cast of characters has been assembled to illustrate this observation. At one level they are the stereotypes of the Victorian theatre: crusty old general, thundering priest, dashing philanderer and so on. But there is another level where they are shown, wearing their official costumes, as representatives of the Church, the Army and the Landed Gentry. Finally Shaw removes their masks to reveal them as ourselves and the people we know. He wants to show us the varieties of human nature that must share the earth. The individual temperaments range from the enemies of marriage to the personification of domesticity; from the woman who loves children but not men, to the woman who wants lovers but is not interested in babies. From the interweaving of all these public and private voices Shaw conducts his symposium and arrives at the conclusion that marriage

as a legal institution must be reformed as part of the general transformation of our society.

*

'It will improve by keeping,' Shaw had told Granville Barker. But Vedrenne
needed a new play and Shaw was persuaded to place the action of *Getting
Married* on 12 May 1908, the day of its first performance at the Haymarket. Five days before the opening he published in the *Daily Telegraph*
the most extreme of his self-drafted interviews. 'There will be nothing
but talk, talk, talk, talk, talk – Shaw talk,' he promised.

'. . . Shaw in a bishop's apron will argue with Shaw in a general's uniform.
Shaw in an alderman's gown will argue with Shaw dressed as a beadle.
Shaw dressed as a bridegroom will be wedded to Shaw in petticoats. The
whole thing will be hideous, indescribable – an eternity of brain-racking
dulness. And yet they will have to sit it out . . . they will suffer – suffer
horribly . . . I am not a vindictive man . . . We shall not be altogether
merciless. The curtains will be dropped casually from time to time to
allow of first-aid to the really bad cases in the seats allotted to the Press.'

Getting Married was greeted with what Shaw called a 'torrent of
denunciation'. Desmond MacCarthy was to question how we could take
seriously characters who are presented to us merely as knockabout figures
of farce: why should we be attentive to their opinions or moved by the
absurdity of their passions? The 'scenes between Hotchkiss and Mrs
George seem to me deplorable,' MacCarthy was to write; 'too funny to
be serious, and too serious to be funny'. Lord Alfred Douglas, under the
heading 'For Shame, Mr Shaw' in *The Academy*, called for the censor to
put a stop to such insidiously feminine work making 'serious inroads on
the British home'. Shaw challenged anyone to name a play that was not
all talk, and enquired whether they had expected ballet. 'The cast finds
out more every time of what it is all about; and so, consequently, does the
audience.'

Yet he was uncertain about *Getting Married*. 'Poor people!' exclaims
the Bishop. 'It's so hard to know the right place to laugh, isnt it?' Max
Beerbohm and Desmond MacCarthy judged that he had orchestrated the
laughter in the wrong place. And J. T. Grein believed that the play traded
on Shaw's peculiar weakness: 'His loquacity is literally torrential.' In the
play he makes Reginald Bridgenorth impatiently exclaim: 'It's no good
talking all over the shop like this. We shall be here all day.' In a work
aiming to preserve all the unities of time and place, this spasm of

impatience articulated a genuine qualm which he submerged in a battle with the critics.

4

SLAVE OF THE AUTOMOBILE

I am a slave of that car and of you too. I dream of the accursed thing at night.

Man and Superman

'I shall take to motoring presently,' Shaw threatened in the summer of 1908. He had already studied at the National Motor Academy and subjected himself to lessons from a professor of driving, H. E. M. Studdy, from whom Charlotte also took tuition. By the end of 1908 the household at Ayot St Lawrence stood ready to receive the Shaws' first automobile, a 28-30 hp Lorraine-Dietrich. 'It is a double cabriolet, with detachable hind part,' reported *The Autocar*. ' . . . The lines of the car are uncommon and graceful.' They became a little more uncommon after the first day when Charlotte, attended by Mr Studdy, crashed it mildly into a local obstruction, scattering the splashboards and other impedimenta; and Mr Studdy, accompanied by Charlotte, knocked off the paddle-box against the gate on their way back.

Since Charlotte's career as motorist was brief and Shaw was rather too fond of reading in the car, a trained chauffeur, Albert James Kilsby from Notting Hill, was employed. In Kilsby's opinion the De Dietrich was 'a proper bugger' to start. But the car was also, Shaw reckoned, awkward to stop, the accelerator pedal being placed on the left with the brake to the right of it. He never lost the habit of treading on the right pedal to arrest a vehicle.

The two men, dividing the fun-and-labour of it, would swap driver and passenger positions fairly evenly. After three weeks, it was reported that G.B.S. was seriously disabled. 'Say I'm dead,' he cabled the *Daily Mail*. He was extraordinarily chivalrous to the injured, especially when the fault was theirs. He was also shockingly reckless at the wheel, sometimes (when Charlotte was not travelling) giving lifts to tramps, and presenting them with money. The De Dietrich was a car for all seasons and subjects: a philosophical vehicle. He reported on its capacity to penetrate Swiss avalanches and its place in the future of Ireland; on its moral claims versus the road dog, its tax-generating properties, and the lessons it gave (such as 'How to Narrow a Road by Widening It') in Shavian engineering. Of the detachable wheels, movable hood and electric klaxon horn, its cork and brass, the invisible locks and variable speed dynamo, Shaw grew pedantically fond. For a man entering his mid-fifties this was more appropriate than the bicycle. He still used the train for long political journeys, but for serious holiday-making the car was essential.

They took it first to Algeria and Tunisia for five spring weeks: Kilsby and Shaw jostling up front; Charlotte and her sister Mrs Cholmondeley occupying the back. Among the luggage they had room for the Koran, but no spare parts. 'Now I come to think of it, it's a wonder we got anywhere,' Shaw remarked. At Biskra he rode for two hours on a camel and 'my seat on this most difficult of mounts was admitted to be superb'. Next day he was stiffly back in the driver's seat and, careering a hundred miles north into Constantine, achieved a dramatic change of climate (something inconceivable on a camel): 'rain in colossal blobs instead of drops; and a wind against which I had to hold the car straight by main force'. Kilsby's time was much filled with repairing burst tyres and then veering melodramatically away from wonderful seas with islands rising out of mirror-like waters and other mirages in which he could not bring himself to disbelieve.

For the summers of 1909 and 1910 they accompanied the car on holidays to Ireland, parking at an extraordinary turreted hotel, the Great Southern, by the woods of Parknasilla on the Kerry coast. It was a place of long sea views and intricate walks between ferns and fuchsias, rock and rhododendron, to burnt-out castles, and along the various fingers of land that pointed south-west into the Atlantic. Sometimes they would try out the Irish roads with an expedition to Lady Gregory at Coole or, on Shaw's fifty-fourth birthday, an exploration of the Giant's Causeway where 'I sat under my umbrella in my aquascutum, like a putrid mushroom,' he told Barker, 'whilst a drenched mariner rowed me round the cliffs and told me lies about them'. Further out to sea he was rowed by ten men in an open boat and landed on the legendary Skelligs. 'At the top amazing beehives of flat rubble stones, each overlapping the one below until the circles meet in a dome – cells, oratories, churches, and outside them cemeteries, wells, crosses, all clustering like shells on a prodigious rock pinnacle . . . An incredible, impossible mad place.'

Upon this cathedral of the sea, the man who generally seemed a stranger on the planet felt at home. Standing in the graveyards at the Skellig summit, he recalled the summers of his early years when Sonny roamed over the rocks and goat-paths of Dalkey, and gazed across the blue waters to Howth Head; or had lain on the grassy top of the hill above the bay – then raced down to the shore known as White Rock and plunged into the waves. Sonny had been a product of Dalkey's outlook: there was little place for him in the bustling world where G.B.S. moved. But he breathed again in the magic climate of this island. 'I tell you the thing does not belong to any world that you and I have ever lived and worked in,' Shaw wrote next day to Frederick Jackson, a political journalist and solicitor: 'it is part of our dream world.'

They rowed him back in the dark, without a compass, the moon invisible in the mists: two and a half Atlantic hours. Then he drove to Parknasilla, to Charlotte, and the world he lived in.

During April 1910, in more orthodox style, the car had taken them for a spin in France, Shaw having undertaken to write reports for the Royal Automobile Club. In the first five and a half days they whizzed along 660 miles, going for all they were worth despite Shaw's view that, owing to the lethally cambered roads, it was unsafe to pass anything without first slowing to a halt. 'I am already twice the man I was when I left,' he reported to Barker. Charlotte felt less cheery. 'G.B.S. does not allow us one moment of peace – we are *harried* from place to place!'

From their cards Barker could feel a struggle developing between Shaw and Charlotte. 'I drive half the day,' Shaw exulted; 'lie deliciously awake half the night; and am visibly waning towards my grave.' At each shattering explosion of the exhaust, his spirits soared. His plan appears to have been to cure Charlotte for ever of their compulsory holidays. 'Charlotte positively loathes me, and is, as usual pathetically unable to dissimulate,' he told Barker at the end of the month.

Back in England, Charlotte diverted some of her loathing from her husband to his car. Their next holiday abroad would be, not yet apart, but separated from his roving machine. As for Shaw, he reported to the Royal Automobile Club that motoring in France was rather like driving along the roof of St Pancras Station.

5

A TREATISE ON BIOGRAPHY

People like to back a winner ... However, nothing succeeds like failure ... Even nonsense is sometimes suggestive.
Shaw to Ensor Walters (1 November 1903), to Trebitsch (20 July 1903),
to Lady Gregory (16 April 1920)

'The villagers all thought he was a rum one – a *very* rum one,' remembered his neighbour Mrs Reeves. Sitting bolt upright in his car, he would career very fast (over 20 miles per hour) through the village, leaving behind him a wake of grumbling. But Edith Reeves never heard of him knocking anyone down. Living so near, she had got to know the Shaws quite well. They would put the mown grass over the wall as fodder for the Reeves's livestock, and give them cabbages and other vegetables from the garden. And Mr Reeves sold the Shaws raspberries and cherries.

Mr and Mrs Reeves named one of their sons Bernard. Shaw and Charlotte took great interest in the small Reeveses. During Mrs Reeves's confinements, while Mr Reeves was out with his sandwiches working in the fields, they would send cooked meals in to her – chicken or fish with fresh vegetables from their garden. Charlotte confided that she would have liked children of her own: and Mrs Reeves was given to understand that it was on account of her asthma that she had none.

Shaw's fondness for animals was notorious. Mr and Mrs Reeves would feel quite uncomfortable loading their squealing pigs into the cart for market – though Shaw never said anything. He had a pigeon-cote and several hives of bees in the garden; and there was an erratic little white dog, Kim, which would streak in and out of the house, sometimes barking, sometimes rolling on its back. Shaw never bought a dog, though 'I always own a dog in the country'. He was glad there had been a dog in his home in Dublin since this put him on easy terms with what was often a pleasant extension of human society. 'I have no lies to tell about dogs,' he declared. He had a fellow feeling for them, as well as for cats: any species of animal in fact. But he did not claim to like all dogs and cats.

The Shaws were good neighbours but they minded their business; and, since they were often away, the villagers regarded them as 'characters' rather than native people. They attached little importance to Shaw's literary fame.

*

This fame, though it stopped short at Ayot, had been spreading round the world with the publication of several books about him. Eighteen critical and biographical volumes appeared before the war. The most brilliant of them was by G. K. Chesterton; the most persistent of his biographers was Archibald Henderson.

Henderson was twenty-five and an Instructor in Mathematics at the University of North Carolina when, early in 1903, he had been 'electrified' by a performance of *You Never Can Tell* in Chicago. He spent the next year studying Shaw's writings and then sent Shaw a letter threatening to write his life: 'it never occurred to me,' he afterwards admitted, 'that perhaps I was wholly unfitted for the job.' Shaw added Henderson's name to an extensive card index marked 'Disciples' and wrote a postcard asking him to 'send me your photograph!' Henderson put himself to a good deal of bother over this, all of which amounted to placing himself in line for a kindly Shavian joke: 'You look like the man who can do the job.'

'I began making notes,' Henderson noted. For the next fifty years he continued making notes that Shaw orchestrated into a semi-Shavian melody. Henderson's first book on Shaw (*His Life and Works*) appeared in 1911. By 1932, in his blockbuster *Playboy and Prophet*, he reported having published 'the eighth book of mine devoted, in part or in whole, to interpretation of your life, character and significance'. He reached his apotheosis six years after Shaw's death and seven years before his own in *Man of the Century*, when the century only had forty-four declining years to run. Of Henderson it may literally be said that no man could have done more. But why had G.B.S. encouraged him to do so much?

He wanted to use his biographer to re-create the life of G.B.S. 'who is up to the chin in the life of his own times'. In his fashion G.B.S. was a truth-teller; but the fashion was far from literal. It needed ingenious interpretation and independent checking – and neither temperamentally nor geographically was Henderson able to supply these. He was a 'disciple' rather than a scholar, who manufactured what Shaw himself was to call 'a colossally expanded extract from Who's Who', and then went on manu-facturing it. The surviving galley proofs of *Playboy and Prophet* reveal how large a part of this narrative was actually drafted in the third person by G.B.S. himself. He did not do this for facile self-aggrandizement, but to provide his ideas with the endorsement of biographical authority. If his childhood had been 'rich only in dreams, frightful & loveless in realities' this was because the social and economic conditions of those times were frightful. After leaving Ireland, Shaw believed he had turned his back on dreams and set out through the body of his literary and political work in England to make the realities of his times less frightful. He feared that if his instincts, like a compass, were seen as having been eccentrically affected by his early experiences, then his thinking itself might be regarded as eccentric. He used biography therefore as adjustments to the rudder, keeping his work in the mainstream. From these secret collaborations he learned how to ghost his own life through later biographers until he became the very author of himself.

'You are threatened with more than one competitor,' Shaw had written to Henderson in 1907. The chief competitor seemed to be G. K. Ches-terton. Shaw completed the comic circle by reviewing Chesterton's book in *The Nation*, describing it as 'the best work of literary art I have yet provoked'. This compliment was not all it appeared to be. Shaw separated art from information rather as he divided feeling from thought. Henderson had the information; Chesterton was the literary artist: one book complemented the other. He was reasonably happy with Chesterton's *Shaw* because, despite its title, it 'has little to do with me'. 'My last word must be,' Shaw concluded, 'that gifted as he is, he [Chesterton] needs a sane Irishman to look after him.' In other words, Chesterton needed Shaw to write the book for him. Reviewing it was the next best thing.

'I have found that if I invent all my facts on a basis of my knowledge of human nature I always come out right, whereas if I refer to documents and authorities they weary me and set me wrong,' Shaw was to write to another biographer, St John Ervine. 'Trust to your genius rather than to your industry: it is the less fallible of the two.' This is what Chesterton did – and what Shaw complained of his having done. He represented Chesterton's commentary as a washing-line on which hung all manner of crucified shirts and dancing trousers. But none of them fitted him. Indeed, some more nearly fitted G.K.C. For biographers, like portrait painters, 'put something of themselves into their subjects and sitters when there is anything of themselves to put in,' Shaw explained.

'The truth is I have a horror of biographers,' Shaw admitted to Frank Harris. Chesterton had loaded his gun with guesses, but from time to time his aim was true. In his review, Shaw gave a wonderfully clownish performance, trying on all the conjectures that were 'madly wrong'. On others he turned his back, leaving them strung out along the line of Chesterton's impressions:

'quick-witted [and] . . . long-winded . . . the very forest of the man's thoughts chokes up his thoroughfare . . . if there is anything that Shaw is not, it is irresponsible. The responsibility in him rings like steel . . . a kind of intellectual chastity, and the fighting spirit . . . . Shaw is like Swift . . . in combining extravagant fancy with a curious sort of coldness . . . benevolent bullying, a pity touched with contempt . . . sincere, unsympathetic, aggressive, alone . . . He never gives his opinions a holiday . . . Socialism is the noblest thing for Bernard Shaw; and it is the noblest thing in him . . . he cares more for the Public Thing than for any private thing . . . This is the greatest thing in Shaw, a serious optimism – even a tragic optimism . . .'

Shaw recognized in Chesterton, as he had in Wells, a quality absent in himself. Wells, who claimed to 'have got Great Britain Pregnant', had the power of sexual attraction; Chesterton, as champion of the common people against intellectuals and politicians, could magically elicit affection. People adored him for his wit and extravagance, his whacking style. His creation of the jolly toby-jug Chesterton had similarities with Shaw's invention of the pantomime ostrich. These cheery images displaced for both what Chesterton called 'the morbid life of the lonely mind'.

Shaw developed a proprietary interest in Chesterton. In a discarded segment of *Back to Methuselah*, he pictures him as Immenso Champernoon, 'a man of colossal mould, with the head of a cherub on the body of a Falstaff . . . friendly, a little shy, and jokes frequently enough to be almost always either still enjoying the last or already anticipating the next'. Shaw thought of Chesterton as a marvellous boy who never grew up, a political innocent who, by prodigious literary journalism, had taken the position created in the eighteenth century by Dr Johnson. In short: he was 'the greatest publicist we possess'. For over a quarter of a century, Shaw struggled to convert him to socialism and creative evolution.

Their debates began in 1911. On 29 May, in the Victoria Assembly Rooms at Cambridge, Shaw addressed the Heretics Society on 'The Religion of the Future'. He told his audience that superstitious religion had died in the Middle Ages, though it was artificially kept in existence by the stimulants of idolatry and intimidation. The English, he declared, had no fundamental religion: they simply made idols of people who were capable of giving orders and resorted to the stage management of them. Such people were given crowns, or gold lace on their collars, a certain kind of hat, a different income and a particular kind of house to live in. Their sons and daughters could not marry common people: and we pretended to believe that they were agents of a loftier idol. But in our democratic age we were gradually getting rid of idols. 'As for my own position, I am, and always have been, a mystic,' Shaw announced. 'I believe that the universe is being driven by a force that we might call the life-force.

'We are all experiments in the direction of making God. What God is doing is making himself, getting from being a mere powerless will or force. This force has implanted into our minds the ideal of God. We are not very successful attempts at God so far, but . . . there never will be a God unless we make one . . . we are the instruments through which that ideal is trying to make itself a reality.'

'The Religion of the Future' was one of a series of heterodox sermons Shaw had started to give after the writing of *Major Barbara*. His new theology redefined the terms and vocabulary of Christianity. God was impersonally reshaped into the Life Force; the Trinity was interpreted as 'You are the father of your son and the son of your father'; and the Immaculate Conception made an everyday happening: 'I believe in the Immaculate Conception of Jesus's mother, and I believe in the Immaculate Conception of your mother.'

The effect of Shaw's addresses on the public was extraordinary. They sat appalled, fascinated, squirming and twisting in their seats. 'The sight of his tall, tense figure in the pulpit, electrical in its suggestion of vital energy completely under the control of his will ... compelled a similar intensity of interest and attention from his hearers,' wrote a reporter on the *Christian Commonwealth*. ' ... Several times I looked round upon my fellow-auditors to mark the effect of his words. I saw consternated faces, hostile faces, faces which bore an expression of alarm and even horror.'

Many who heard him were convinced that here was the finest public speaker in England. He was admired, especially by the young; but he was not loved. His intellectual authority on the platform provoked extreme reactions from the press. *The Academy*, which described his lecture as a 'Detestable Outrage ... vile and blasphemous ravings', protested against his 'dissemination of poisonous theories amongst young persons' and regretted that Shaw had not been 'kicked out of the window, or ... thrown into the Cam'.

When they invited Chesterton to reply with a speech entitled 'Orthodoxy', the Heretics at last found a Christian champion capable of standing up to Shaw. Chesterton delivered his reply on 17 November at the Guildhall, Cambridge, and the first thing he did was to defend his adversary from newspaper attacks. *The Academy* report had been 'not merely written by an idiot but by an idiot who had no belief in the Christian religion,' he pronounced. ' ... How could Mr Shaw blaspheme by saying that Christ or the Christian religion had failed in England when the remark is obviously true.

'The majority of the governing classes believe in no religion. I have known many editors and newspaper proprietors but I have yet to meet one who believed in religion ... Mr Shaw is living in a comparatively Pagan world. He is something of a Pagan himself and like many other Pagans, he is a very fine man.'

This was characteristic of the intellectual magnanimity existing between the two men. 'I enjoyed him and admired him keenly,' Shaw was to write of Chesterton in the late 1930s; 'and nothing could have been more generous than his treatment of me.' And at about the same time Chesterton was saluting Shaw in his autobiography. 'I have never read a reply by Bernard Shaw that did not leave me in a better and not a worse temper or frame of mind; which did not seem to come out of inexhaustible fountains of fair-mindedness and intellectual geniality.'

When they moved from religion to politics, the contest was between Shaw's socialism and Chesterton's distributism, of equality of income against peasant proprietorship. Shaw defined socialism as 'that state of society in which the income of a country would be divided exactly equally amongst all the people of that country, without reference to age, sex or character'. Chesterton warned against the totalitarianism and artificiality within socialism.

'You cannot draw the line across things and say, You shall have your garden hose, but not your garden; your ploughshare, but not your field; your fishing rod, but not your stream; because man is so made that his sense of property is actually stronger for such things as fields or gardens or water than for such comparatively unnecessary things as garden hoses or rakes or fishing rods . . . if you want self-government apart from good government you must have generally distributed property. You must create the largest possible number of owners.'

Shaw conceded that collectivism without socialism might indeed be a system of tyranny – the tyranny that was later to emerge as fascism. He suggested therefore that the difference between Chesterton and himself appeared to be that one wanted distribution of property and the other *equal* distribution of property. 'This is not the normal definition of the term [socialism],' Chesterton objected. 'That the State should be in possession of the means of production, distribution, and exchange was always called Socialism when I was a Socialist.'

It was a good and serious contest. Their jousting over the years developed into a perfect balance of contrasting styles, with breathtaking displays of analogy and tricks of paradox. Chesterton's bulky swaying presence matched the immense range of illustration he gave his ideas, lit up by a spirit of enjoyment and comic inventiveness. Shaw was more incisive, his emphatic eyebrows like two supplementary moustaches, an assured and wiry figure standing with arms folded who could speak with a force thrilling to all who heard it. But to Chesterton's eyes, Shaw's strengths were limited in their humanity. 'Shaw is like the Venus de Milo,' he declared: 'all that there is of him is admirable.'

Chesterton's conversion to Catholicism in 1922 showed how far he was from agreeing with Shaw. 'If I wandered away like Bergson or Bernard Shaw,' he wrote at the end of his life, 'and made up my own philosophy out of my own precious fragment of truth, merely because I had found it for myself, I should soon have found that truth distorting itself into a falsehood.' Chesterton's truth seemed to Shaw a blind alley up which he had been led by Hilaire Belloc, 'with the odd result,' Shaw wrote to Wells, 'that he is now dreadfully in earnest about beliefs that are intellectually impossible'.

The two warriors met for their last public exchange at Kingsway Hall in the final week of October 1927. Tumultuous crowds struggled in the corridors, burst open the doors, flowed round the building like hot lava. Belloc presided and the British Broadcasting Corporation relayed their words through the country. 'Do We Agree?' was the question they debated. Both spoke well. They spoke of socialism and distributism, income and property – of all they had spoken about sixteen years and one world war earlier in the Memorial Hall. And they said similar things. The change was in the audience, baying for good sport. 'This is not a real controversy or debate,' Chesterton admitted. What they said was what they could most effectively perform as actors. 'I suspect that you do not really care much what we debate about,' Shaw said, 'provided we entertain you by talking in our characteristic manners.' This they did. 'Obviously we are mad,' remarked Shaw, taking what seemed a good embarkation point for a voyage of agreement. But it was when Shaw drew on his reservoirs of optimism that Chesterton felt dispirited. Shaw insisted on agreement. 'I find that the people who fight me generally hold the very ideas I am trying to express.' He tried to wrap Chesterton up in a jacket of agreement. The agreement of two mad people (in the East they would be reverenced) was important.

'If you listen to them carefully and find that at certain points they agree, then you have some reason for supposing that here the spirit of the age is coming through, and giving you an inspired message. Reject all the contradictory things they say and concentrate your attention on the things upon which they agree, and you may be listening to the voice of revelation.'

And did they agree? 'Ladies and gentlemen. The answer is in the negative.' Chesterton did not agree with Shaw and 'nor does Mr Shaw'. And the people watching and listening did not experience a voice of revelation. The spirit of the age had moved from the platform to themselves: it would be heard in their interruptions, their urging for disagreement to flourish, and their belief that none of it any longer mattered. 'In a very few years from now,' Belloc concluded, 'this debate will be antiquated.'

6

SHEWING UP THE CENSORSHIP

Success in the theatre is very largely a matter of being able to flirt with
the public.

Shaw to Maud Churton Braby (18 May 1908)

Shaw had joined a society 'for the Prevention of Cruelty to Authors' in
1897 when deciding to publish his plays as books. Soon afterwards he
started making his views and experiences known through the Society of
Authors' Journal. He paid *The Author* the compliment of treating it as a
serious business paper. He wrote there of the beauties of phonetic spelling
and simplified punctuation; warned schoolmasters against inflicting literature compulsorily on children; described the pathos of British bookselling,
calculating that 'the average man wears out over fifty pairs of boots whilst
he is reading a single book'; and he gave advice on publishers: 'Whenever
a publisher gives me literary advice I take an instant and hideous revenge
on him. I give him business advice . . . and I urge him to double his
profits by adopting my methods.' Some of these contributions to *The
Author* – such as his recommendations to novice playwrights on the
submission of manuscripts – were printed as circulars.

In most matters of negotiation, it seemed to him, authors presented
themselves as a flock of sheep bleating to be fleeced. 'Nothing will save
the majority of authors from themselves,' he declared, 'except a ruthlessly
tyrannical Professional Association.'

He had been elected to its committee of management in February 1905,
and joined its dramatic subcommittee the following year. He took this
work seriously, believing that the literature of a country created its mind
since each country largely took its ideas from what it read. What he looked
for within the Society was the creation of a corporate consciousness. In
Shaw's perfect world there would have been no law of copyright, no
advances or retreats, no giving or receiving of royalties (the very word
sounded dreadful to a republic-minded person). Pending this, authors
were necessarily capitalists and literature a sweated trade. As an artistic
and learned profession, it had to be defended against the presumption
that its interests must give way to the most trivial political consideration.

Authorship was a good example of a profession that was helpless without
collective action. A writer who was poor, Shaw argued, had no means to
defend himself; and when, suddenly, he became famous, his time was so
valuable that it was not worth his while wasting it on bad debts. It was

pitiable to see these 'professional men on whom the Copyright Acts have conferred a monopoly of enormous value unable to do for themselves what is done by porters and colliers and trade-unionists generally with no monopoly at all at their backs'. Although unionism was most practicable in trades where the members worked together in large bodies, lived in the same neighbourhoods and belonged to the same social class, Shaw believed that the Society of Authors should be careful how it disclaimed the idea of being unionized. He looked on trade unions as conspiracies against the public interest that would become unnecessary in a socialist society, but that acted meanwhile as a corrective to the capitalist account.

Shaw was prepared to spend hours drafting and revising documents. It was admirable: but did he succeed? On the whole, he concluded, the ten years he spent on the Society's 'two big committees' might have been passed at the top of Everest. Over such matters as the model treaty with West End managers, on which he negotiated interminably, no progress was made. His frustration led him eventually to lose faith in the validity of unrefined democracy. For who, in their efforts to make improvements, had used the democratic process more thoroughly than himself? Had he not earned the right to a dissenting opinion? In the interests of getting things done much had been suppressed and little accomplished. His deepest disenchantment sounded from suppression itself: the censorship laws. What a heartbreaking business it had been. 'I had ten years of it; and I know.'

*

Shaw was to write more than fifty articles against the censorship, reinforced with many speeches and letters to newspapers. As late as 1950 he could still be heard objecting to the appointment of 'an ordinary official with a salary of a few hundreds a year to exercise powers which have proved too much for Popes and Presidents'. In fact the Lord Chamberlain never read plays but delegated this job to a series of under-paid clerks. These officials fell back on making a list of controversial subjects (religion, sex) that must not be mentioned, and words that must not be used: they then worked to this list automatically. Professional pornographers soon learnt these inventories and how to get round them, with the result that the commercial theatre had become a prostitution market masquerading as theatre.

Shaw argued that the censorship was damned both by the pernicious trash it allowed, and by the good work it suppressed. Its purpose was to suppress immorality: but what it meant by immorality was deviation from custom. It was assumed that every Englishman knew the difference between wicked and virtuous conduct. But Shaw reasoned that what was wanted from dramatists, and all other writers, was a constant challenge to such accepted knowledge. The notion that everything uncustomary was wicked helped to keep people in line with their neighbours and gave Government what appeared to be a moral basis for penalizing change. But without change there could be no development. Progress depended upon the toleration of unexpected behaviour, and heresy was essential to the welfare of a community. A nation that did not permit heresy was stagnant.

Shaw realized that he must not only discredit this function of the Lord Chamberlain's office, but also propose a better control of the stage by the community. The alternative was not anarchy, he wrote, but control by local authorities. 'The municipality will not read plays and forbid or sanction them,' he explained. 'It will give the manager both liberty and responsibility . . . Let him manage how he pleases, knowing that if he produces utterly vile plays, he will find himself without a defender in council when the question comes up as to whether his licence shall be continued.' It was important, Shaw stressed, to license the management, not the theatre. A manager could then pursue his business as any other professional man, while the annual licensing system would ensure that he could be struck off like a solicitor. Shaw was therefore taking a moral line more democratic than the official guardians of morality by recommending a transference of the care of the nation's morals from a few paid clerks to the county councils and city corporations, with watch committees to warn them when managers were conducting their theatres as disorderly houses.

He was propelled into the front line when Granville Barker's new play *Waste* was refused a licence late that year. This ban, and another in respect of Edward Garnett's *The Breaking Point*, led to a renewed attack by the playwrights. 'Stiffen your back,' Shaw exhorted Gilbert Murray. Throughout 1908 he kept up this campaign, luring the censorship into a serious blunder.

*

For half a dozen years Beerbohm Tree had been prompting Shaw to write him a modern stage version of *Don Quixote*. As a rather startling variation on this theme, and reverting to his method in *The Devil's Disciple*, Shaw dashed off *The Shewing-up of Blanco Posnet* between 16 February and 8 March 1909. This one-act 'Sermon in Crude Melodrama', as he subtitled it, was commissioned for a matinée performance at His Majesty's to benefit a children's charity. 'I wrote a perfect triumph of this made-to-measure art for Tree in *Blanco Posnet*, and he was simply shocked by it, absolutely horrified,' he remembered. Tree was then three months short of his knighthood. What worried him were Blanco's references to God as 'a sly one . . . a mean one', and his statement that the chief witness in the trial had had 'immoral relations with every man in this town', including the Sheriff. He appealed to Shaw to 'cut that bit about God and that other bit about the prostitute'. But Shaw convinced him there was nothing to fear. If the Examiner of Plays passed the words, Tree would have obtained official blessing; and if he didn't the actor would never have to utter them. So Tree submitted the play to the Censor: and the Censor, on the grounds of blasphemy, refused to license it.

Set in a Town Hall 'in a Territory of the United States of America' sometime during the nineteenth century, *Blanco Posnet* is pervaded with an air of unreality. 'Let the imagination play,' Shaw advised Martin-Harvey. 'There never was no such place and no such people.' His own imagination was literary and showed its derivations from Bret Harte, Dickens and Tolstoy's play *The Power of Darkness*. What he wanted was a respectable provenance for a piece of moral propaganda that had as its point the protest of a horse-thief against his punishment for an admitted crime. From the consequence of this crime he would have escaped but for his yielding to the first good impulse of his life: the giving up his plunder to an unhappy woman in order to save her sick child. By using some phrases from the Lord Chamberlain's proscribed list, he adapted this blameless drama into a ten-inch gun in the censorship war. 'I have taken advantage of the Blanco Posnet affair to write a tremendous series of letters to The Times,' he informed Trebitsch that summer; 'and the result has been that the Prime Minister has promised to appoint a Select Committee of both Houses of Parliament to enquire into the whole question of Censorship.'

Shaw's methods were to harass the enemy as a dramatist by all ingenious means: then hurry to their rescue as a responsible committee man. The opportunity of performing *Blanco Posnet* to the maximum embarrassment of the Censor came after a visit by Lady Gregory to Ayot. Shaw gave her the play, and she took it back to Coole where Yeats read it and agreed to put it on at the Abbey Theatre – Dublin being the one place in Britain beyond the Lord Chamberlain's jurisdiction.

As soon as the Abbey production was announced, the Under-Secretary of the Lord Lieutenant of Ireland wrote from Dublin Castle threatening to revoke the Abbey Theatre's patent. Lady Gregory and Yeats were summoned to the Castle by the Viceroy Lord Aberdeen, and one of the Castle lawyers warned their solicitors that if *Blanco Posnet* was performed, the authorities would use against the theatre all the legal powers at their command. Yeats found himself forced into a position where he had either to abandon the principle of theatrical freedom or risk, by the closure of the Abbey, the livelihood of its players and the fruit of half a dozen years' work. He and Lady Gregory decided to confront the Lord Lieutenant's precautionary notice with a manifesto.

'If our patent is in danger it is because the English censorship is being extended to Ireland, or because the Lord Lieutenant is about to revive, on what we consider a frivolous pretext, a right not exercised for 150 years, to forbid at his pleasure any play produced in any Dublin Theatre . . . we must not, by accepting the English Censor's ruling, give away anything of the liberty of the Irish theatre of the future . . . what would sooner or later grow into a political censorship cannot be lightly accepted.'

The issue had now been adroitly spread from blasphemy to cover almost the whole area of Anglo-Irish politics. Having defied the Castle, Lady Gregory tactfully offered the Lord Lieutenant a small face-saver in the way of two tiny omissions. It was essential, Shaw pointed out, that such concessions should be ridiculous. As he explained in a programme note:

'To oblige the Lord Lieutenant, I have consented to withdraw the word "immoral" as applied to the relations between a woman of bad character and her accomplices. In doing so I wish it to be stated that I still regard these relations as not only immoral but vicious; nevertheless . . . I am quite content to leave the relations to the unprompted judgement of the Irish people. Also, I have consented to withdraw the words "Dearly beloved brethren", as the Castle fears they may shock the nation.'

The Shewing-up of Blanco Posnet opened at the Abbey, with Lady Gregory's *The Workhouse Ward* and Yeats's *Cathleen Ni Houlihan*, on 25 August 1909. It was Horse Show Week in Dublin, the peak of the summer season, which 'draws to the Irish capital a vari-coloured crowd, of many languages,' wrote James Joyce. ' . . . For a few days the tired and cynical city is dressed like a newly-wed bride. Its gloomy streets swarm with a feverish life, and an unaccustomed uproar breaks its senile slumber. This year . . . all over town they are talking about the clash between Bernard Shaw and the Viceroy . . . between the representative of the King and the writer of comedy . . . while Dubliners, who care nothing for art but love an argument passionately, rubbed their hands with joy.' Many people now entering a theatre for the first time in their lives were offering guineas for standing-room in the wings. Foreign newspapers had sent their critics – James Joyce sent in a review to *Il Piccolo della Sera*. Charlotte was there with her sister but G.B.S. stayed strategically in Parknasilla. Lady Gregory's fear was that there might be a hostile demonstration, or complaints from the Church, that would give the Viceroy an excuse for taking legal action.

The reception of the play must have disappointed many who had come looking for a disturbance. The audience took to *Blanco Posnet*

enthusiastically, laughing at its humour, passing over the dangerous passages with sympathetic blankness, and at the curtain interrupting their
applause with vain calls for the author. There was general agreement that
Mr Posnet was a very mild-spoken ruffian in comparison with the reports
of him; and some people questioned whether they had been victims of an
Abbey hoax. 'There is no feeling in Dublin except amusement about the
more or less false pretences by which a huge audience was attracted last
night to the Abbey Theatre,' reported *The Times*. 'Everybody today is
enjoying the story of Mr Shaw's cleverness and the Censor's folly ... The
play is perfectly innocuous; it could not shock the most susceptible
Irish feelings.' The Churches refused to make a protest (some clergymen
actually preached sermons celebrating the play); and the *Irish Times*
commented that if ridicule were as deadly in Britain as in France, the
censorship would be 'blown away in the shouts of laughter that greeted
Blanco Posnet'.

Shaw sent his congratulations. 'You and W.B.Y[eats]. handled the campaign nobly,' he wrote to Lady Gregory. 'You have made the Abbey
Theatre the real centre of capacity and character in the Irish movement:
let Sinn Fein and the rest look to it.' The Abbey had vanquished the
Castle, but no one could tell what effect this Irish victory would have on
the Censor in England.

It was this that Shaw set out to test by applying for a licence to produce
Blanco Posnet at Annie Horniman's repertory theatre, the Gaiety, in Manchester. The play was submitted in its Irish version which, as George
Redford noted, was 'practically identical' to the text sent to him by
Beerbohm Tree. Under these circumstances, Redford added, 'there is no
ground on which I could ask the Lord Chamberlain to reconsider his
decision'. But Shaw was able to remind him that plays could be considered
more than once. The performance in Dublin, which had elicited good
opinions from critics and clergymen, was ample evidence, he contended,
that an error of judgement had been made. He therefore requested a re-
submission to the Lord Chamberlain. This Redford was obliged to do:
but the Lord Chamberlain gave the same decision. 'What the Censorship
has actually done exceeds the utmost hopes of those who, like myself,
have devoted themselves to its destruction,' Shaw wrote in *The Times*.

There was one more move for him to make. He allowed *Blanco Posnet*
to be performed in London by the Abbey Theatre Company under the
protection of the Stage Society. The English could now see for themselves
that his reputedly blasphemous piece was no more than a 'sentimental
tract,' as Desmond MacCarthy was to describe it. The whole affair,
including Shaw's publication in a newspaper of the words to which the
Lord Chamberlain took offence, had dramatized the full absurdity of

the system. 'Let us all dance on the prostrate body of Mr Redford as violently as we can,' exhorted Max Beerbohm in the *Saturday Review*.

*

'Mr Redford has a fixed delusion that I am a dangerous and disreputable person, a blasphemer and a blackguard,' Shaw wrote to the manager of the Gaiety Theatre, Ben Iden Payne.

He used Payne for an extra skirmish that summer. Between the end of March and the beginning of May 1909, he had composed a one-act satirical farce called *Press Cuttings*. Exploiting his own fear of women and merging it with the general fear of a German war, he coupled the cause of feminism to his fight against the censorship by naming two of his characters General Mitchener and Prime Minister Balsquith (who enters dressed as a woman). On 24 June Redford returned the manuscript in order to give its author 'the opportunity of eliminating all personalities, expressed or implied'. He called attention to the rule: 'No offensive personalities, as representation of living persons to be permitted on the stage.'

This was what Shaw calculated would happen. In various newspapers, he assured the public that he had been 'careful not to express a single personality that has not done duty again and again without offence in the pages of *Punch*'. Privately he let it be known that he had used the name Mitchener 'in order to clear him of all possible suspicion of being a caricature of Lord Roberts'. As for the well-worn *Punch* figure of Balsquith, it was neither Balfour nor Asquith 'and cannot in the course of nature be both'.

Two 'private receptions' of the play were given under the auspices of the Women's Suffrage movement at the Court Theatre early that July. Shaw then altered the names of Mitchener and Balsquith to Bones and Johnson (the ringmaster and clown of the Christy Minstrels) and Iden Payne re-submitted the play which was licensed for public performance on 17 August, and opened the following month at the Gaiety in Manchester. 'In the crucial scene the Prime Minister forced his way into the War Office disguised as a militant suffragette,' wrote Iden Payne. ' . . . When he had removed his woman's attire, Bones exclaimed, "Great Heavens, Johnson!" When the innocuous name was heard there was a roar of laughter, followed by loud ironic applause, which was repeated when Johnson could be heard to answer "Yes, Bones".'

There were some who felt that Shaw was prostituting his talent in these forays against the censorship. Yet many playwrights agreed that some liberalization of the law was needed. It was important that those interviewed by the Select Committee should speak with a reasonably unanimous voice. In various multigraphed letters to members of the Society of Authors, Shaw assigned to himself the job of voice-trainer. 'Witnesses must be careful not to put forward the contention that the freedom of the stage would be absolutely safe. The proper reply is that its risks would be no greater than the risks of the freedom of the press, freedom of speech, and freedom of public meeting . . . they are the price of liberty and progress.'

These letters to fellow-writers were accompanied by an 11,000-word statement that Shaw had prepared as his own evidence. His examination was to consist of questions on this written evidence which, at the Committee's invitation and his own expense, he had distributed beforehand. However, the Committee informed him that it could not admit his printed statement into the record since to do so would be acting against precedent. Shaw argued that some of the distinctions he wished to make were not easy to bring out simply in replies to questions, and he cited three precedents from the 1892 Committee which had accepted written evidence in favour of the censorship. At this the Committee cleared the room, discussed the matter in camera, and then repeated without explanation that 'it would not be permissible to print the statement as part of the evidence'.

Shaw was completely taken aback. 'The sudden volte face when I cited precedent, the dramatic secret conclave, the point blank refusal without reason given, are too good to be thrown away . . . I shall fly to the last refuge of the oppressed: a letter to The Times.'

Shaw's letter appeared on 2 August; and three days later, when he arrived to resume his evidence, he was told that the Committee 'have no further questions to ask you'. It was hard to conceal his resentment. He incorporated his rejected evidence, as a form of minority report, into his Preface to The Shewing-up of Blanco Posnet which Conrad judged to be 'somewhat imbecile – in the classical meaning of the word'. Shaw had sought to inflict imbecility on those members of the Committee who supported the censorship: to embezzle them of their wits. He was acting the modern Don Quixote Tree had wanted him to dramatize in Blanco Posnet, the man who 'is always right and always apparently wrong with smaller and more practical people round him'. He had turned his plays into the accoutrements with which the Don set out to fight his battles.

'I saw that I had to deal with a hostile majority,' Shaw excused himself, ' . . . so I misconducted myself.' His words spilled out all over the place. He could not stop. The Committee had treated Redford – 'the filter that my life's work has to pass through' – most decorously. He felt aggrieved; he felt aggravated. He had made himself better informed on censorship than any member of the Committee. Then he had worked by the rules, won every round fairly and been counted out.

The Report was published on 8 November 1909. What comes out strikingly is the evidence of what Shaw would call the idealists. Theatre managers' organizations argued that censorship had not inflicted any injury on serious drama in England; actors' associations spoke of the desirability of maintaining a censorship which protected their members from taking unpleasant parts in undesirable plays; A. B. Walkley, drama critic of *The Times* and President of the Society of Dramatic Critics, believed the censorship to be justifiable because it reflected the common sense of the man in the street, while Lena Ashwell, lessee of the Great Queen Street Theatre and soon to play the Polish aviatrix in *Misalliance*, wanted the Censor as protection against the man in the street; W. S. Gilbert thought it imperative that audiences be protected against 'outrages' – the theatre was 'not the proper pulpit from which to disseminate doctrines possibly of anarchism, of socialism, and of agnosticism'. Many authors too, if they were doing well, did not really want to change the system. 'A censorship of any kind acts inevitably as a protection to the average author,' Shaw explained. 'He is never censored; and those who are censored are not only his commercial rivals, but are generally putting up the standard on him and changing the fashion.'

Archer, Granville Barker, J. M. Barrie, Chesterton, Galsworthy, Gilbert Murray and Pinero gave evidence against the censorship. Some of their recommendations were attached to the Report which proposed that future licensing be optional and that unlicensed plays take their chance in the courts; that music halls be treated equally at law; and that doubtful cases be referred to a special committee of the Privy Council. But no legislation was passed to implement these proposals. Instead, an advisory committee was appointed the following year to assist the Censor. So matters stayed as they were.

Shaw had tried to improve things by letter and by law: this was temperamentally the most natural way for him to act. He was a scholar-revolutionary. His tactics for changing society had not been to break its laws, but to obey them pedantically, ingeniously, literally, until by laughing consent they were finally rendered impractical. But for the first time it seemed as if all the thought and feeling of this work was issuing nowhere. He was in his fifty-fifth year; as he grew older this sense of powerlessness was to intensify. Looking back, he came to believe that it had been this Censorship Committee that altered his views on how to obtain political results. He was forced into a belief in the inevitability of violence: 'the whole ridiculous transaction,' he wrote, ' . . . was a lesson to me on the futility of treating a parliamentary body with scrupulous courtesy and consideration instead of bullying them and giving them as much trouble as possible.' He had forgotten how much trouble he gave.

The philosophy of violence that makes its appearance in Shaw's later life was a product of his sexual and then his political neutering; a reaction to having been made to feel as ineffectual as his mother had believed him to be. This was the true misery of life, the being used up for no purpose. The means were not justified that brought no ends: he had no children and he had no power. Increasingly he was to find compensation in the world of his imagination. His fantasies of longevity and dictatorship, which in the actual world did harm to no one, brought some relief to his despair, acting like Prospero's prayer

> Which pierces so that it assaults
> Mercy itself, and frees all faults.

TWELVE

I

THE GODS AND *MISALLIANCE*

> I am a specialist in immoral and heretical plays. My reputation has been
> gained by my persistent struggle to force the public to reconsider its
> morals. In particular, I regard much current morality as to economic and
> sexual relations as disastrously wrong; and I regard certain doctrines of
> the Christian religion as understood in England today with abhorrence.
>
> Preface to *The Shewing-up of Blanco Posnet*

'To me God does not yet exist; but there is a creative force constantly
struggling to evolve an executive organ of godlike knowledge and power;
that is, to achieve omnipotence and omniscience; and every man and
woman born is a fresh attempt to achieve this object,' Shaw wrote in a
letter to Tolstoy accompanying *The Shewing-up of Blanco Posnet*. ' . . .
Whoever admits that anything living is evil must either believe that God
is malignantly capable of creating evil, or else believe that God has made
many mistakes in His attempts to make a perfect being.'

The incomprehensibility of life was comforting to Tolstoy on whom
Shaw's 'intelligent stupidities' jarred painfully. 'Life is a great and serious
affair,' he rebuked him. Whatever G.B.S. could not reduce to intelligibility,
he expelled as a joke. 'Why should humour and laughter be excommunicated?' he had asked. 'The problem about God and evil is too important
to be spoken of in jest,' answered Tolstoy. But as Shaw had previously
told Henry James, 'Almost all my greatest ideas have occurred to me first
as jokes.'

Shaw had made a similarly painful impression on Henry James. James's
god was art. But Shaw 'would not lift my finger,' as he wrote to Tolstoy,
'to produce a work of art if I thought there was nothing more than that
in it'. When the Reading Committee of the Stage Society rejected James's
one-act adaptation, called *The Saloon*, from his story 'Owen Wingrave',
Shaw was asked to write and tell James.

'Shaw's writing – Bernard Shaw,' he began. James's adapted ghost story
about a young pacifist in a military family who dies from an act of self-
assertion is an exploration of the irreversible forces of the past – 'one of
the most "deterministic" [tales] James ever wrote,' his biographer Leon

Edel calls it. It was this horror of inevitability that Shaw found 'sticking in my gizzard ever since'.

James seemed a man of the past and Shaw of the future – the novelty of the future. James believed that the imagination of the artist reached back and, planting itself in unconscious motives, gave the artist psychological energy with which to create beautiful things. 'It is art that *makes* life,' he instructed H. G. Wells. James recognized in art a force as mysterious and unalterable as Tolstoy's God. It was this fatalism, breaking out at the word of Darwin in the 1860s, and purveyed through the novels of George Eliot and Thomas Hardy, that was gaining new intellectual ground and, so Shaw protested, persuading people who had lost their faith in a Tolstoyan God 'that Man is the will-less slave and victim of his environment'. Shaw wanted to replace God with a more positive substitute. 'What is the use of writing plays?' he demanded, ' – what is the use of anything? – if there is not a Will that finally moulds chaos itself into a race of gods with heaven for an environment.' To Tolstoy this was impious vanity. And to James, the advice that proceeded from it – that he stick on a happy ending to his play since he 'could give victory to one side just as artistically as to the other' – revealed a wholly 'shallow and misleading' conception of what art was.

Shaw wanted more control over his destiny. 'You have given victory to death,' he accused James. Tolstoy had given victory to the next world. But Shaw wanted to win battles for this world. *Blanco Posnet*, no less than *Widowers' Houses* or *Mrs Warren's Profession*, had been written for contemporary use – even *Press Cuttings* was a farce designed to blow up a farcical situation. Yet all Shaw's works, however topical, had been determined in form by precedents from the past.

The Bernard Shaw not writing to Henry James was a playwright who had lost his sense of pragmatic certainty as to what his plays were saying and whose unconscious processes filtered into these plays layers of suppressed autobiography. This mysterious *alter ego* was a ghost that mocked the champion of free will and floated free of the scholar bent over his theatrical formulas. He seemed invisible to the writer of prefaces. For he was not obviously an executive organ of a creative force, but a dreamer of the absurd, wondering whether 'the world were only one of God's jokes'.

*

In April 1909 advertisements had begun to appear for a new repertory scheme opening in the West End of London. The man behind this enterprise was a powerful Broadway impresario Charles Frohman and the man behind Frohman was J. M. Barrie. Frohman was 'my kind of man,' Barrie decided – someone shy and successful who had tumbled in love with the stage and converted one of his London theatres, the Duke of York's, to experimental repertory. Productions of plays new, revived, and unwritten were placarded there, including works by Granville Barker, Henry James, John Masefield, Somerset Maugham, Gilbert Murray, Pinero, Shaw and Barrie himself – though not Galsworthy's *Justice*, with which, almost a year later, the season actually began.

People had faith in Frohman. He was a man of sumptuous generosity and wonderful schemes. They entrusted their capital to him, confident that here was a hard-headed businessman who would look at nothing that didn't pay. 'If Mr Frohman were really that sort of man, I should not waste five minutes on his project,' wrote Shaw in a dissenting opinion. 'He is the most wildly romantic and adventurous person of my acquaintance.'

The play, called *Misalliance*, Shaw wrote for Frohman between early September and early November 1909, was a return from the melodrama Frohman had hoped for after *Blanco Posnet* to the disquisitory tactics of *Getting Married*. 'I have again gone back to the classic form, preserving all the unities – no division into acts, no change of scene, no silly plot, not a scrap of what the critics call action,' Shaw wrote.

According to Barrie's biographer, Andrew Birkin, Frohman 'worshipped mothers and children'. Shaw had chosen the theme of parents and children because it was close to Frohman's heart but treated it comically. 'We cant all have the luck to die before our mothers, and be nursed out of the world by the hands that nursed us into it,' says one of the characters mocking Frohman's reverence for the family. ' . . . No man should know his own child. No child should know its own father,' he adds, matching Shaw's doubts against Frohman's ideals.

Shaw told Archibald Henderson that *Misalliance* 'is on the plan of *The Taming of the Shrew*'. Characteristically he reverses matters. If Shakespeare's farce is the chastening of a woman whose moods tormented him, Shaw's 'debate in one sitting' is a humbling of men from the governing classes at whose homes he had felt miserably ill at ease when he came to England, and who had recently humiliated him over the censorship. *Misalliance* is also a re-working of Barker's play *The Madras House*. Barker used the metaphor of the drapery trade, with its *haute couture*, to represent the decadent culture of contemporary Western civilization: Shaw uses Tarleton's Underwear.

Contemporary critics, to whom these derivations were not apparent, responded to *Misalliance* as an oddly disintegrating work. 'The debating society of a lunatic asylum – without a motion, and without a chairman,' was *The Times* critic's description. Desmond MacCarthy, too, was to feel that Shaw 'had not a clear notion where his perceptions in this case were leading him. It is inconclusive.' And Max Beerbohm, on whom it produced 'a very queer effect', objected to 'the unreality, the remoteness from human truth, that pervades the whole "debate" '.

Monitoring a revival of the play in 1939, *The Times* critic commented: 'With the lapse of time inconclusiveness comes to seem a positive merit.' With a further lapse of time these qualities of unreality and madness, and the fracturing of standard plot procedures, may be seen as having affinities with the drama of Pirandello, where events 'erupt on the instant, arbitrarily,' as Eric Bentley described them, 'just as his characters do not approach, enter, present themselves, let alone have motivated entrances; they are suddenly there, dropped from the sky.'

The extravagant ideas and incidents that cluster within the second part of *Misalliance* – an abrupt descent from the skies of a Polish equilibrist demanding a Bible, music-stand and six oranges ('billiard balls will do quite as well'); the emergence from a portable Turkish Bath of a cringing homicidal clerk, pistol in hand, crying 'I am the son of Lucinda Titmus' – all help to establish Shaw's kinship with Ionesco (who was not born until late in 1912) and show him to be, in R. J. Kaufmann's words, 'the godfather, if not actually finicky paterfamilias to the theatre of the absurd'. G.B.S. was familiar with early modernist experiments and had his own agenda for clearing away the dominance of the well-made play.

The house of *Misalliance* (which owes something to his sister-in-law's home at Edstaston) is an arena where incompatible aspects of Shaw's personality confront one another. Julius Baker, alias Gunner, arises from the Turkish Bath, prophesying revolutions despite being unable to fire a single bullet, to speak for the loveless ineffectual Sonny. Bentley Summerhays exhibits Shaw's thin-skinned capacity when young for provoking dislike (and occasionally protectiveness) from others; Joey Percival shares with him the culturally advantageous experience of having three fathers (his natural one, a tame philosopher in the house and his Italian mother's confessor corresponding to George Carr Shaw, Uncle Walter Gurly and Lee); Lord Summerhays, the experienced man who feels 'still rather lost in England', voices some of Shaw's political convictions about government and reveals a shrinking Shavian sensitivity to sexual matters ('Can no woman understand a man's delicacy?'); John Tarleton has Shaw's money-making abilities and a self-educated obsession with book-learning ('Have you learnt everything from books?' he is asked); and his son and daughter, Hypatia and Johnny, convey something of Shaw's contempt for these Shavian characteristics, in particular the actionless vacuum with its polished walls of 'Talk! talk! talk!'

Into this Shavian mansion comes the heavenly invader Lina Szczepanowska (pronounced [fi]sh-ch[urch]-panovska). She comes in answer to Shaw's prayer for positive action as much as to Hypatia's plea for 'adventures to drop out of the sky'. Like a bird she lands from above: the authentic superwoman who, arriving from the future, is to have her second coming in *St Joan*. Lina's appearance 'in full acrobatic trapeze dress, as dazzling as possible, to make her effect when she throws off her masculine cloak' is the most astonishing entrance to be made in a Shaw play. Up to this point the audience has been at an Edwardian country house party and heard the capitalist middle class in conversation with the aristocracy. It is a conventional drawing-room comedy of manners – Johnny even has the celebrated query popularly supposed to have been coined in the 1920s: 'Anybody on for a game of tennis?' The old are divided from the young, the rich from the poor, men cut off from women, parents from children: almost everyone is inhibited from any kind of initiative.

Lina comes from a different world: she is a foreigner to the class system whose manners and values look absurd. 'Wont you take off your goggles and have some tea?' enquires Mrs Tarleton after Lina has crashed into the greenhouse. The tone of the play now changes from realism into magic realism. 'These woods of yours are full of magic,' exclaims the aviator Joey Percival to John Tarleton. 'I must be dreaming,' remarks John Tarleton. 'This is stark raving nonsense.' Mrs Tarleton agrees: 'Well, I'm beginning to think I'm doing a bit of dreaming myself,' she says. But their dreams explode the British class system into fragments of comedy. 'It should be clear by now that Shaw is a terrorist,' wrote Brecht. 'The Shavian terror is an unusual one, and he employs an unusual weapon – that of humour.'

The play is obsessed with action, though the characters themselves are unable to change anything. The captain of industry and the colonial administrator have grown obsolete. John Tarleton is incensed that his human destiny should be restricted to underwear. 'I ought to have been a writer. I'm essentially the man of ideas,' he insists. Lord Summerhays (the name deriving from Wells's Samurai) also feels redundant in the twentieth century. 'I dont understand these democratic games; and I'm afraid I'm too old to learn . . . Democracy reads well; but it doesnt act well, like some people's plays.' Tarleton's two children representing sex (Hypatia) and money (Johnny); and Lord Summerhays's son representing fear – the emotional and economic fear of growing up – are the poisoned fruits of capitalism.

Capitalism is threatened in *Misalliance* by two types of invader. Julius Baker, alias Gunner, comes as revolution fuelled by personal grievance and carried out by force of arms. 'I came here to kill you and then kill myself,' he tells John Tarleton, his mother's alleged seducer. In the behaviour of the various inhabitants of the house we see the tactics bourgeois society uses to tame potential revolutionaries – how it tricks and intoxicates them, how it torments them with assistance: 'Let me hold the gun for you,' John Tarleton politely offers. And when Mrs Tarleton hears of Julius Baker's attempt on her husband's life, she exclaims: 'Oh! and John encouraging him, I'll be bound!' In such a contrived atmosphere the political terrorist sounds ridiculous: 'Rome fell. Babylon fell. Hindhead's turn will come.'

Shaw's other invaders represent salvation from the future not the past, the air and not the earth. Lina brings Joey Percival, the best mate for Hypatia who demands that her father 'buy the brute for me'. This is the biological method of serving the Life Force. The intellectual method is advanced by Lina's invitation to take Bentley Summerhays off in the aeroplane. Bentley's terrified acceptance of this is comparable to the birth of 'moral passion' in Sonny, lifting him above the religious climate of Ireland.

The part of Lina went to Lena Ashwell. She was celebrated for playing heavily emotional roles that called upon her 'to bear an illegitimate child or stab someone to death and then suffer gorgeously for her sins'. But though Yeats believed she had brought to the role something 'extremely rare: *beautiful gaiety*', she disliked the goggles, tunic and pants, and felt thrown off balance by the craziness of the play. Her imperviousness to G.B.S. was warmly approved by Charlotte and she became one of the few actresses whom Charlotte befriended.

Frohman's season opened on 21 February 1910. Barker's production of Galsworthy's *Justice* was a major contribution to the campaign for prison reform – the impact of a wordless scene in a cell was used by Churchill when introducing a provision into Parliament for more humane legislation. But a play dealing with solitary confinement was a brave choice for an evening's entertainment in London's West End. Shaw's country house burlesque, opening two nights later, made a confusing contrast. *The Globe* judged it to be 'absolutely his worst play', and *The Standard* doubted whether it would have ever reached the stage if written by someone else.

Instead of the capacity houses he anticipated, Frohman was getting less than half. He sat there paralysed, amazed, caught between his investors who wanted quick returns and big profits, and his new colleagues in the drama who, explaining that repertory needed time to accumulate its audience, congratulated him on doing so well. A triple bill of two small plays by Barrie and a posthumous comedy, partly in verse, by Meredith, was introduced at the beginning of March, and followed nine days later by *The Madras House* which Barker had been slow in finishing. The confusion deepened. Desperately, Frohman fell back on two popular revivals, Pinero's *Trelawny of the Wells* and Barker and Laurence Housman's Court Theatre success *Prunella*, which helped to restore the confidence of his backers.

Eventually King Edward VII came to the rescue. He died. And Frohman, his commercial and sentimental interests at last coinciding, joined the general shutting-down of theatres.

The season had lasted ten weeks and *Misalliance* was performed eleven times, *The Madras House* ten. But Frohman grew proud of having created 'an imperishable monument of artistic endeavour'. In a lecture called 'The Theatre: the Next Phase' delivered in London on 9 June, Barker argued that Frohman's experiment had shown that, though a repertory theatre could not be made to pay in the commercial sense, 'the practicability of modern repertory had been proved'. In concert with this speech, Shaw published a self-drafted interview three days later in the *Observer*. 'The season at the Duke of York's was well worth doing,' he wrote, ' . . . because I shall never be able to persuade English men of business to endow the National Theatre unless I am in a position to say that I have exhausted all the resources of private enterprise.'

2

FURTHER PARTICULARS ON MR WELLS

> I rejoice in life for its own sake. Life is no 'brief candle' to me. It is a sort of splendid torch which I have got hold of for the moment; and I want to make it burn as brightly as possible before handing it on to future generations.
>
>   'Art and Public Money', *Sussex Daily News* (7 March 1907)

H. G. Wells had been one of those to whom Shaw, emerging from the rough Welsh seas off the coast of the Fabian Summer School, had reported his near death from drowning. 'Wasted chances! You shouldn't have come out,' Wells returned. 'There you were – lacking nothing but a little decent resolution to make a distinguished end . . . As for me I could have sailed in with one or two first class obituary articles.'

Shaw claimed to be 'dead against this exhibition sparring' because 'I do it so well that the sympathy goes to my opponent'. But on this occasion Wells had done it better. Neither of them enjoyed these knockabouts for long – they turned too deadly. But Wells found himself pressed forward into the ring by a new supporters' club among the Fabians. His spirits rose: he felt game enough. His potent spell promised a new era for Fabianism. 'He is a man of outstanding genius,' wrote Edward Pease. ' . . . his energy and attractive personality added radiance to the Society only equalled in the early days.' During 1907 the membership doubled.

There was an influx of younger women and men from the universities, many of them drawn by what Rupert Brooke called 'the wee fantastic Wells'.

The political climate of the country was changing. Shaw's plays and Wells's novels had helped to create a middle class with expectations of swift social change. The failure of Campbell-Bannerman's Government to initiate any policy of reform soon led to middle-class discontent with Liberalism and a swelling support for the Labour Party. It was this switch of allegiance by progressive intellectuals that had given rise to the new Fabian boom.

These new members were joining the Society of Shaw and Wells, rather than of the Webbs. This was one of the reasons why Beatrice suspected this sudden Fabian popularity. Their new recruits 'lived the most unconventional life,' she observed during the Fabian Summer School, 'stealing out on moor or sand, in stable or under hayricks, without always the requisite chaperon to make it look as wholly innocent as it really is'. Could she be certain that it was innocent? Their conversation was surprisingly free. And their gym costumes gave several of the elderly Fabians some bad quarters of an hour. Beatrice felt apprehensive, too, when the economics had to stop, of where their 'larky entertainments' could lead. There was danger in innocence. There was danger everywhere.

Beatrice knew the undiscriminating power of sex. She suspected Shaw and Granville Barker, no less than Wells, of letting themselves go 'pretty considerably' with women. But she had so curbed her 'lower desires' that she seemed unaware of how controlled the erotic motive was in Shaw's *Misalliance*, which she described as 'disgusting'. 'I think probably the revelations with the H.G.W. various sexual escapades largely suggested the play,' she wrote. She seemed to have no means of telling, as could the young Fabians, the difference in such matters between Shaw and Wells.

Among the young Fabians, Shaw behaved benignly, his conversation mixing instruction with unflagging public entertainment. 'He was personally the kindest, most friendly, most charming of men,' remembered Leonard Woolf.

'He would come up and greet one with what seemed to be warmth and pleasure and he would start straight away with a fountain of words scintillating with wit and humour . . . but if you happened to look into that slightly fishy, ice-blue eye of his, you got a shock. It was not looking at you . . . it was looking through you or over you into a distant world or universe.'

Wells's eyes were more penetrating and when they looked at you they looked at no one else. As if to make up for early emotional loss, he was hungry for sex. He seemed vulnerable; but even his uncertainties were endearing – so often they were your own. He appeared 'nearer and more sympathetic than other men,' wrote Dorothy Richardson.

Wells was happy among the young Fabians. They were mostly women. There was a good-looking flirtatious writer, Violet Hunt, whom he entreated to 'be nice to a very melancholy man'. There was Hubert Bland's plump and beautiful illegitimate daughter Rosamund, who was said to enjoy the admiration of men. 'I have a pure flame for Rosamund,' Wells admitted. There was Amber Reeves, sweet, pretty, coaxing, who loved visiting the Wellses at Spade House. 'She adores you both,' her mother confided to Jane Wells. Lucy Masterman too remembered her holiday at Sandgate as an 'impression of perpetual sunshine, health and ease'. 'I am ready to go on working for [socialism],' Wells wrote, ' . . . in the meantime having just as good a time and just as many pleasant things as I can.'

Women now numbered more than a quarter of the Fabian membership and they wanted the Society to turn its attention to supporting votes for women. Shaw was appointed to discuss the matter with the Fabian spokeswoman, Amber Reeves's mother Maud Pember Reeves. There were few differences between them: Shaw supported women's suffrage and believed that women themselves should have the principal place in the suffrage campaign. He therefore returned to the executive with a recom-mendation that it agree to the women's wishes. As a result, 'the establishment of equal citizenship between men and women' was added to the Objects of the Society. A Women's Group (with Jane Wells on its executive) was formed – also a Biology Group and a Socialist Medical League – and the Fabian women arranged themselves into a useful platoon in the fight for enfranchisement.

The backbone of Shaw's feminism was financial self-respect: he spoke in particular of equal pay for actresses and the economic independence of wives. He wanted the Fabian Society to stand for political equality as the universal relation between citizens without distinction of sex, colour, occupation, age, talent or hereditary factors; and he advocated 'the explicit recognition by legally secured rights or payments of the value of their domestic partners and to the State as housekeepers, child bearers, nurses and matrons'. He wanted to see them, in equal numbers with men, on all political organizations, including the House of Commons.

It was his political 'discovery' that 'a woman is just like a man', that enabled Shaw to replace the Victorian stereotype of the womanly woman with Woman the Huntress. But 'the pursuit has about as much sex appeal as a timetable,' complained Frank Harris. Though the sexual 'syringeing' of women by men had 'compensations which, *when experienced*, overwhelm all the objections to it,' Shaw admitted to St John Ervine, ' . . . I always feel obliged, as a gentleman, to apologise for my disgraceful behaviour'. This 'apology' infiltrated his writing, against which some women reacted even when admiring the moral elegance of his argument.

'I am a woman,' says the man in one of Shaw's plays to the girl; 'and you are a man, with a slight difference that doesnt matter except on special occasions.' Wells did not feel this difference to be slight, and the occasions were frequent. Like Shaw, Wells defended the rights of women, condemning conventional sexual morality and the marriage laws founded on it. But he dared to do what he advocated. Several rebellious young women, oppressed by Edwardian conventionality, sought him out. He was not simply on the side of the young, he was in many ways one of them.

Although no scandal about his affairs had yet broken into public view, Wells had been accused in the press of having manufactured through his books a paramour's Utopia. Shaw and the Webbs feared that 'Fabian Free Love' might set socialism back a decade – Wells was not at liberty to throw his emotional match-ends about in powder-magazines. There had almost been an explosion over his relationship with Rosamund Bland. The Society had hummed with rumours of how Hubert Bland had intercepted the pair at Paddington Station. But these rumours were confined within the Society and did not reach the public. Shaw had circled round emitting advice but, knowing few of the facts, he was not well employed. 'What an unmitigated moral Victorian ass you are,' Wells accused him. 'You play about with ideas like a daring garrulous maiden aunt but when it comes to an affair like the Bland affair you show the instincts of conscious gentility and the judgement of a hen . . .

'You don't know, as I do, in blood & substance, lust, failure, shame, hate, love & creative passion. You don't understand & you can't understand the rights & wrongs of the case into which you stick your maidenly judgment any more than you can understand the aims of the Fabian Society that your vanity has wrecked. Now go on being amusing.'

Only Shaw among the Fabian elders had really wished Wells to stay on the executive. Webb and Bland plainly wanted him to leave – and Wells too was eager to go: all they differed on was the manner of his going. At a by-election in the spring of 1908, Wells supported the Liberal candidate, Winston Churchill, whose 'rapidly developing and broadening mind . . . [was] entirely in accordance with the spirit of our movement'. His motives for this action seem to have been mixed between a natural preference for Churchill over a dull socialist candidate incapable of winning the contest, and a wish to strengthen opposition to the Tory candidate, William

Joynson-Hicks, who had accused him of being 'a nasty-minded advocate of promiscuous copulation'. At the annual meeting of the Fabian Society on 22 April 1908, Wells was accused of betraying socialism and took the opportunity to resign. 'It is to other media and other methods,' he wrote, 'that we must now look for the spread and elaboration of those collectivist ideas which all of us have at heart.' He would go back to writing novels.

This resignation, which the executive accepted ten days later, was an act of mercy. During the winter of 1908–9 what Beatrice called 'a somewhat dangerous friendship' developed between Wells and Amber Reeves. Amber graduated with a double first in moral sciences and conceived Wells's child at about the same time. What made it worse for Beatrice to contemplate was that they had enjoyed sexual intercourse, so she heard, in the girl's rooms 'within the very walls' of Newnham College. The events, as they emerged over the year 1909, began to unsettle Beatrice. First she was irritated that Wells could intermittently go on living with his wife as if nothing were wrong; she was also affronted when Amber ran for the cover of a marriage of convenience to a chivalrous barrister with the tautologous name of Blanco White, giving Wells's daughter a 'legitimate' birth; then she felt exasperated on hearing that they were persisting with the liaison following that marriage; finally the publication of *Ann Veronica*, Wells's novel advertising the affair, drove her frantic.

Amber's father was Director of the London School of Economics; her mother was prominent among the Fabian Women's Group; her lover was a Fabian; her husband was a Fabian; and she herself had been treasurer of the Cambridge University Fabians. Even Jane Wells, the complaisant wife, was on the Fabian executive. Worse still, it was the Webbs who had introduced Wells to the Reeves family. 'I wish we had never known them,' Beatrice exclaimed. Something would have to be done. Pulpits were shaking with denunciations of *Ann Veronica*, and the National Social Purity Crusade brandished the novel at the head of its campaign for formal censorship in circulating libraries. Reviewers who knew something of Wells's biography took the opportunity to treat Ann as if she were Amber. The criticism overflowed from the book and cascaded into Wells's life. 'I can't stand this persecution,' he cried out. 'He will disappear,' Beatrice predicted, 'for good, from reputable society.' He did resign from the Savile Club; and Jane was asked to quit the Fabian executive.

Beatrice felt intensely involved. She insisted that Wells would be permanently wretched. 'I doubt whether he will keep his health – and he may lose his talent'; and she believed that Amber was 'a ruined woman, doomed to sink deeper into the mire'. Once Beatrice had been anxious lest Wells, after his resignation from the executive, became a Fabian enemy like Ramsay MacDonald. 'Don't shake us off altogether,' she had appealed. 'It won't be good for either the Webbs or the Wells and will be very bad for the common cause.' But now he was a danger, an abomination. 'The end of our friendship with H. G. Wells,' she noted in her diary in the summer of 1909.

Beatrice had done what she could. She had written letters to Fabians with teenage daughters; she had spoken to Blanco White and counselled Amber. She had also been in touch with Shaw. But Shaw took a different view. Now that Wells was only a subscriber to the Fabian Society, it was permissible to view the affair as part of that fine art of private life which consisted in taking liberties. Wells excelled at this kind of social experiment. 'The situation can be saved by letting it alone,' he instructed Beatrice. ' . . . I aim at the minimum of mischief.'

Shaw had already written sympathetically to Wells. 'Occasionally,' Wells responded, 'you don't simply rise to a difficult situation but soar above it & I withdraw anything you would like withdrawn from our correspondence in the last two years or so.' For despite everything, there was part of Shaw that warmed to Wells's escapading. Some writers had to act foolishly in order to write well. 'Mr Wells does not shirk facts because they are considered scandalous, especially when the conventional foundation of that view of them is becoming more and more questionable,' Shaw was to write a dozen years later; 'but I cannot find in his books a trace of that *morbidezza* which . . . is very largely produced by the fact that the writers have no real experience of what they are writing about, and are the victims of a baffled *libido* rather than a Casanovesque excess of gallantry.' The mixed vocabulary of this tribute indicates the changing culture through which these Fabians were passing. In this shifting landscape it was difficult finding one's way. 'All this arises because we none of us know what exactly is the sexual code we believe in,' observed Beatrice, 'approving of many things on paper which we violently object to when they are practised by those we care about.'

*

Wells's place as Fabian activist was almost immediately occupied by Beatrice herself. Until recently she had not acted as much more than an aide to Sidney. Her deeper involvement arose in part from a changed attitude to the role of women in politics. Some twenty years before she had signed an anti-suffrage manifesto drafted by Mrs Humphry Ward. It 'is the spiritual function of a woman to be the passive agent bearing a man's life!' she had emphatically instructed Sidney before their marriage. Her impatience with some of the militant pioneers of women's suffrage was overtaken by a feeling of distaste over the 'coarse-grained things' being said by men opposed to emancipation. Towards the end of 1906 she sent Millicent Fawcett, president of the National Union of Women's Suffrage, her formal recantation.

Nothing did more to alter Beatrice's views than her experiences as a member of the Royal Commission on Poor Law. She had been appointed by Arthur Balfour during the last days of his Government at the end of 1905. Before that, as she admitted, 'I have never myself suffered the disabilities assumed to arise from my sex'. Three years' work on this largely man-dominated Commission left her wondering: 'Are all men quite so imbecile as that lot are? . . . It makes me feel intolerably superior.'

'Certainly the work of the Commission will be an education in manners as well as in Poor Law,' she wrote. She trained like an athlete for this work, rising for her cold bath and quick walk at six-thirty, feasting off bread and cheese and drawing on Sidney's 'blessed strength and capacity'. Yet her manners did deteriorate. 'From first to last she has declined whilst in the Commission to merge her individuality in it, but claims the right of unrestricted free action outside,' wrote the mild-mannered chairman. Her Minority Report, completed early in 1909, was signed by three other Commissioners.

Everyone had been dissatisfied with the ramshackle Poor Law of 1834. Some saw it as expensive and inefficient; others as inadequate and demoralizing. Beatrice wanted to break up the Poor Law altogether and replace it with a comprehensive scheme of welfare that allocated responsibilities for assisting those below a national minimum to a series of Government departments dealing with specific causes of poverty, such as chronic sickness, old age and unemployment. She was contemptuous of the Majority Report which sought by simple unemployment insurance to alleviate the circumstances only of the destitute and necessitous. Shaw sensed that the Minority Report was a more important document than most people realized. 'It may make as great a difference in sociology and political science as Darwin's "Origin of Species" did in philosophy and natural history,' he predicted. ' . . . It is big and revolutionary and sensible and practicable at the same time, which is just what is wanted to inspire and attract the new generation.'

The Report lies somewhere between Bentham and Beveridge. Beatrice's collectivist scheme was to be a blueprint for the Welfare State, but it also retained something of the puritanism of Bentham who had believed in the utilitarian device of the workhouse to 'grind rogues into honest men'. Beatrice was haunted by this problem of the able-bodied unemployed. 'I dream of it at night,' she wrote, 'I pray for light in the early morning.' For those who lacked capacity she recommended compulsory training; and for those who lacked will, disciplinary supervision. Believing that a grant from the community should be conditional on reasonable conduct from the individual, she was later to express criticism of Beveridge's proposed extension of unconditional unemployment doles on the grounds that this would encourage malingering.

It was the Majority Report that got the better press. But from the Fabian point of view, the political situation appeared to have improved. After Campbell-Bannerman suffered a heart attack in April 1908, a new Government was formed with Asquith its Prime Minister – a man 'inclined to carry out our ideas,' Beatrice thought. But Asquith left much of this work to Winston Churchill (President of the Board of Trade) and Lloyd George (Chancellor of the Exchequer): and neither of them was sympathetic to the Webbs. Sidney and Beatrice therefore decided to deploy the Fabian Society on a national campaign. This was the sort of enterprise Wells had been urging on the Fabians before his resignation – it was 'quite after my own heart,' he told Beatrice. Here was the 'new start' Beatrice had promised the Fabians: a missionary crusade of 'raging tearing propaganda' to change the mind of the country about destitution.

'As a preparation I practise voice presentation between 6.30 and 8 a.m. every morning on the beach – orating to the Waves!' she wrote after the Fabian Summer School. ' . . . It is rather funny to start on a new profession after 50!' The turmoil rather thrilled her. Yet it was a 'curiously demoralizing life'. She spurred herself on to be an itinerant agitator. 'It is no use shirking from this life of surface agitation, from this perpetual outgiving of personality.'

Beatrice had published her Minority Report in two volumes totalling 946 pages. Though it was extraordinarily far-seeing, it proved difficult to expound to electors; and it was impossible to convince governments that a complex bureaucracy would not be needed to set it up. After the last Liberal election win in 1910, people preferred Lloyd George's simple National Insurance Bill.

'Lloyd George and Winston Churchill have practically taken the *limelight*,' Beatrice conceded. She had needed the talents of Wells and Shaw to combat such brilliantly effective slogans as Lloyd George's 'Ninepence for fourpence' advertising contributory social insurance. But Wells, though he joined the campaign 'very much as a drop of water, when it encounters a pailful, lines up with the rest', was too busy working at his caricatures of the Webbs in *The New Machiavelli*; whilst Shaw seemed to have 'lost the power of doing anything except in imperative emergencies'.

Beatrice's Minority Report had a formative influence on Shaw's political thinking. It broke from the commercial tradition of the nineteenth century and went straight to the issue of public welfare. It was not enough, the Report stated, to secure every man a minimum wage for the work he found to do. 'You must provide the wage anyhow, and enable him to find all the work that exists, and if there is no work available you must still spend the wage on him in keeping him fit for work when it does come,' Shaw wrote in a review of the Report. 'His right to live, and the right of the community to his maintenance in health and efficiency, are seen to be quite independent of his commercial profit for any private employer. He is not merely a means to the personal ends of our men of business; he is a cell of the social organism, and must be kept in health if the organism is to be kept in health.'

From the Webbs' national minimum wage, Shaw's mind moved on to an annual salary that would in effect be an equal share of the national product. Then, in or about December 1910, he came up with a new definition of socialism. Ideally it meant equality of income – 'a state of society in which the entire income of the country is divided between all the people in exactly equal shares, without regard to their industry, their character, or any other consideration except the consideration that they are living human beings . . . that is Socialism and nothing else is Socialism.'

Though Shaw did not have much confidence in imposing this 'remoter solution' on the Fabians, he felt that Lloyd George's plans for pensioning the elderly and taxing unearned income made it imperative for socialists to regain the initiative in radical thinking about the redistribution of income. Equality was fundamental to socialism, he argued, and without it all Lloyd George's schemes to take from the rich and give to the poor would seem predatory. For without equality nothing could be done except to organize capitalism on a more commercially profitable basis. Shaw replaced Lloyd George's old age pension with a life pension, substituting social service for private profit as a motive for human action. 'We must proceed by taxation as Mr Lloyd George does,' he told the Fabians: 'but our object should [be] . . . the reduction of all excessive incomes to the normal standard.'

When, after their crusade, Beatrice arranged to take Sidney on a sabbatical voyage round the world, G.B.S. saw an excellent opportunity for retirement. He had always intended to resign, he reminded Edward Pease, 'when I had completed my quarter of a century service; but what with Wells and one thing and another the moment was not propitious . . . if we do not resign now, we shall never resign.' Neither Bland, nor he himself, nor Stewart Headlam would stand again. The clearing out of the Old Gang would be pretty well complete – so why not make it complete and simultaneous? 'I think Sidney *must* retire,' Shaw advised. 'We must all go together, with the limelight on, and full band accompaniment.'

At the executive elections in April 1911, Webb came top of the poll and stayed on: Shaw, Bland and three other members resigned. Looking back some years later, Shaw wondered whether the Old Gang should not have left half a dozen years earlier and taken the risk of handing everything over to Wells. 'In a way he [Wells] was fundamentally right in seeing that he could do nothing unless The Society would definitely accept him and trust him, and get rid of us,' he wrote.

3

SKITS AND FARCES

I confess I am getting old and childish and easily amused.
Shaw to Greenhaugh Smith (29 December 1904)

In the half-dozen years before the war Shaw whipped up more than half a dozen one-act skits, farces, extravaganzas for the stage written mostly in a style which Virginia Woolf described as that of 'a disgustingly precocious child of 2 – a sad and improper spectacle to my thinking'. The event-plots of these pieces tell the story of Shaw's contribution to magic and absurdity, and rearrange fragments of his life into revealing patterns.

The Fascinating Foundling was knocked off early in August 1909 for a charity performance at the request of Elizabeth Asquith, daughter of the Prime Minister. Shaw provided the piece with a subtitle – 'A Disgrace to the Author'.

The story revolves round the destiny of orphans. A smart and beautiful young man forces his way into the ante-room of the Lord Chancellor's office, and engages his elderly clerk in a broadsword combat (fire tongs versus poker). This parody of a Shakespearian duel is interrupted by the indignant appearance of the Lord Chancellor. The young man explains that he is Horace Brabazon, a foundling, and has come to the Lord Chancellor as 'father of all the orphans in Chancery' to ask for a wife – 'someone old enough to be my mother,' he explains, ' . . . not old enough to be your mother . . . I attach some importance to that distinction . . . One mustnt overdo these notions.' After he leaves a second caller arrives. She is Anastasia Vulliamy, a superior foundling who had been discovered 'on the doorstep of one of the very best houses in Park Lane'. She too wants the Lord Chancellor 'to be a father to me' and find her a husband, 'someone I can bully'. Horace Brabazon returns for his walking-stick, and she proposes to him, recommending a three-week engagement: 'You are only on approval, of course.' He agrees because she is a foundling and will bring no family to make him miserable.

The Glimpse of Reality was a more sombre tomfoolery which took Shaw nearly eighteen months to complete and eighteen years to see performed, chiefly because he kept mislaying it. It is set in the fifteenth century and takes place at an inn on the edge of an Italian lake. A devout friar aged one hundred and thirteen is hearing the confession of a young girl, Giulia. He urges her to press close to him as he is deaf. She does so, telling him that in order to win a sufficient dowry for her to marry a fisherman she is to decoy young Count Ferruccio ('a devil for women') to the inn. The Count will then be killed by her father who will claim the reward. The venerable friar flings off his gown and beard and reveals himself as the young Count. Giulia's father, the innkeeper, and her fiancé, the fisherman, appear, and all four of them sit down to supper. The Count negotiates for his life, but in a complicated tactical game is defeated. 'There is nothing like a good look into the face of death,' he says, '. . . for shewing you how little you really believe and how little you really are.' With this glimpse of reality his terror of death falls away. He speaks so fearlessly that the innkeeper and fisherman, believing him mad and therefore under the protection of God, refuse to murder him.

Among the other playlets of this period were 'An Interlude', 'A Thumbnail Sketch of Russian Court Life in the XVIII Century', 'A Piece of Utter Nonsense', and 'A Demonstration'. The 'Interlude', which was Shaw's subtitle for *The Dark Lady of the Sonnets*, is a miniature work of art composed between 17 and 20 June 1910, to support the appeal for a British National Theatre.

It is a midsummer night on the terrace of the Palace at Whitehall, overlooking the Thames, in the spacious times of Elizabeth I. A Beefeater is approached by a ghost. 'Angels and ministers of grace defend us!' he cries. The cloaked figure stops and writes, then speaks. He is no ghost, but a man come to keep tryst with his Dark Lady. The Beefeater relaxes: he knows this dark lady well enough. She is always making trysts with men. 'You may say of frailty that its name is woman,' he casually remarks. The man turns pale at this information, yet luxuriates in the phrase and makes a note of it – at which the 'well-languaged' warder dubs him 'a snapper-up of such unconsidered trifles': and down that goes too on the man's tablet.

The Beefeater moves discreetly off and a sleepwalking lady wanders along the terrace cursing the cosmetics that have peppered her with freckles: 'Out, damned spot . . . All the perfumes of Arabia will not whiten this Tudor hand.' The man, enchanted by this word-imagery, mistakes her for his mistress, the mysterious 'woman colour'd ill'. He wakes her but discovers that she is a stranger. By way of introduction he tells her that he is 'the king of words', and rhapsodizes over her own word-skill – he has so bad a memory, he adds, he must catch them on his tablets. He

13 Sir Henry Irving

14 Lillah McCarthy

15 Shaw and Harley Granville Barker, 1901

16 Himself and herself at Adelphi Terrace, photographed by Shaw, c. 1905

17 Ellen Terry

puts his arms round her, but the two of them are knocked sideways by the Dark Lady who has been jealously listening. During this falling-about the three characters are revealed as Shakespeare, Queen Elizabeth and Mary Fitton.

Mistress Fitton is terrified. Only fear strikes any words out of her that Shakespeare finds worth taking down and she is eager to leave the scene of danger. But Queen Elizabeth is a *femme inspiratrice* and practically every word she utters is Shakespearian. 'I am not here to write your plays for you,' she eventually rebukes him. Prospero-like, Shaw has called her there, together with Shakespeare, as history's two most commanding witnesses to plead the cause of endowing a National Theatre.

To the play Shaw attached a Preface warning readers against using the past as a refuge from the present. Shakespeare lives in each of us and all Shakespearian criticism is a form of autobiography. Shaw's Shakespeare makes comedy out of his own misfortunes, is inspired by his love of music, grows immune to the weaknesses of passion and becomes superhuman. He is also a master of irony. 'I am convinced,' Shaw concludes, 'that he was very like myself.'

The 'state of levity' which Shaw insists buoyed up Shakespeare's life floats through almost all these playlets whose subtitles have a similar mutinous tone to Shakespeare's popular comedies – *Much Ado About Nothing*, *As You Like It*, *What You Will*. His 'Piece of Utter Nonsense', otherwise called *The Music-Cure*, is a topical skit written as a curtain-raiser for the play he had finally persuaded G. K. Chesterton to write. Chesterton's drama, which shows love miraculously conquering diabolical evil, was called *Magic*. Shaw's variety turn is a piece of magic realism suggesting that this miracle of love is a hallucination, like the concept of evil.

Lord Reginald Fitzambey, Under-Secretary in the War Office, cannot stand very much reality. 'I am not fit for public affairs,' he confesses. ' . . . I have a real genius for home life.' But because his father is a Duke he has been obliged to enter Parliament, and is suffering from a breakdown. A doctor gives him some opium and he 'sees' a laughing crocodile about to play the piano with its tail – which is Shaw's unconvincing version of evil. The doctor concludes that he should double the dose after which 'if anything comes it will be something pretty this time'. He leaves, and a lovely lady pianist, Strega Thundridge, appears. She tells Reginald that his mother has engaged her for a terrific fee to play the piano in his room for two hours. There follows, as she plays Chopin's Polonaise in A flat, an optimistic essay on the effects of opium upon the romantic imagination. 'Ever since I was a child I have had only one secret longing,' declares Reginald, 'and that was to be mercilessly beaten by a splendid, strong, beautiful woman.' Strega Thundridge, whose natural strength has been marvellously expanded by her playing of left-hand octave passages, is that splendid creature. She too has a dream: 'It is a dream of a timid little heart fluttering against mine, of a gentle voice to welcome me home . . . of someone utterly dependent on me, utterly devoted to me' whom she would beat sometimes to a jelly, before casting herself into an ecstasy of remorse. They play the Wedding March, embrace fiercely and confront their terrible destiny together.

The Music-Cure, Shaw revealed, 'is not a serious play'. It took him almost nine months to bring himself to complete it, during which time (between 29 July and 13 August 1913) he had also written *Great Catherine*. She is, he tells us in his 'Author's Apology', the Catherine whom Byron had celebrated in *Don Juan*.

> In Catherine's reign, whom glory still adores
> As greatest of all sovereigns and w----s.

Shaw's Catherine is a woman set in authority over men. There is no real plot in the play. It is an eighteenth-century encounter, spread across four bravura scenes, between some extreme personalities. There is the genial and gigantic Shavian villain Prince Patiomkin; there is a caricature Englishman, the stiff and insular Captain Edstaston of the Light Dragoons (who is Britannus escaped from *Caesar and Cleopatra* and now named after Shaw's sister-in-law's house) and his invincibly snobbish fiancée Claire – all comic stereotypes with whom Shaw felt at ease. 'This is carrying a joke too far,' protests the Captain as the semi-drunken Pati-omkin carries him into the Empress's *petite levée* and dumps him on her bed. And that is what Shaw is doing, carrying the joke as far as it will go and further. 'This is perfectly ridiculous,' says Claire surveying the Empress's court which, after Shaw's juvenile rearrangement, has been converted into a nursery. In this nursery the pain and fear of adult life evaporate. The Captain, though threatened with five thousand blows of the stick, with being skinned alive, having his tongue ripped out or his eyelids cut off, is actually trussed up and tickled by the Empress's toe.

That rulers behave like children is an adult observation and one that was confirmed when the Lord Chamberlain's Comptroller recommended (besides modification to the captain's uniform) that Patiomkin be made a teetotaller and Catherine a monogamist so as to avoid giving offence to Grand Duke Vladimir of Russia, a friend of the British Royal Family. Such absurdities support Shaw's point that 'the fiction has yet to be written that can exaggerate the reality of such subjects'. Yet Shaw did not so much exaggerate as overrule reality. His characters behave badly out of fear, and it is this fear that these playlets replace with fun and games. But they show too, in a childlike way, the sources of his fear: physical cruelty and the dominance of death, but also infant sexuality and its bearing on the adult operation of the sex instinct. In the secret place of Shaw's fantasies, all prescriptions against sex are inoperative. 'The truth is that a man (or a woman) should never take his (or her) innocence for granted in matters of sex,' he wrote to Edith Lyttelton, 'in which ANYTHING is possible and even probable.'

It is this guilty world of ANYTHING that these playlets invade. The role of Strega Thundridge, for example, was written for an actress who had started her career as a talented pianist whom Shaw had encircled with erotic dreams. This affair, which virtually began by her bedside while she was ill, is comically retold in *Great Catherine* after the fastidious Captain Edstaston is deposited on Catherine's bed by Prince Patiomkin.

Shaw had given a 'demonstration' of this affair in another of his short plays. Its first title, *Trespassers Will Be Prosecuted*, had been suggested by a notice posted on the gate of Edith Lyttelton's house (she being a confidante of Shaw's erotic actress). After three weeks' work in the summer of 1912, he finished the play on a 'Gt Northern train passing Holloway', removed the warning, *Trespassers Will Be Prosecuted*, and substituted *Overruled*.

He believed his little play to be 'really a work of some merit'. For years he had been objecting to the teasing versions of adultery presented on the stage. In *Overruled* he claimed to have dramatized marital infidelity and introduced the act of sexual intercourse itself (so far as this was practicable) to the theatre. Mysteriously no one noticed.

The plot of the play explains some of the mystery. It is a summer night at a seaside hotel. A lady and gentleman are sitting together on a chesterfield in a corner of the lounge. He throws his arms round her but suddenly he discovers she is married. She too is astonished to learn that he has a wife, particularly since they have been cruising round the world each believing the other to be single. At that moment they hear the voices of a man and a woman in the corridor, and spring to opposite sides of the lounge. These voices belong to their respective husband and wife who enter, occupy the still-warm chesterfield and begin to enact a similar love scene. It transpires that both married couples had decided to enjoy a holiday away from each other and go round the world in opposite directions. The second flirtation is interrupted by the first couple, and there follows what Shaw calls in his Preface to the play 'a clinical study' of how polygamy actually occurs 'among quite ordinary people'.

Conceived as a one-act burlesque of Sydney Grundy's fashionable three-act 'tissue of artificialities' *Slaves of the Ring*, which involved 'a quadrille of lovers instead of a pair', *Overruled* was offered as a 'model to all future writers of farcical comedy'. Twenty years later this option was to be taken up by Noël Coward in his own version of Shaw's world-cruising quartet, *Private Lives*, where the couples once again meet in a hotel with each other's partners.

Overruled demonstrates certain truths about the married man who was now entering his late fifties. 'You see, it's a great many years since Ive been able to allow myself to fall in love,' explains one of the husbands. ' . . . I thought I had lost the power of letting myself fall really and wholeheartedly in love.' And the second husband confesses: 'Year after year went by: I felt my youth slipping away without ever having had a romance in my life; for marriage is all very well: but it isnt romance.' In his optimistic fantasy Shaw assigns the wives of these marriages a perfect tolerance of adultery. 'If you will be so very good, my dear, as to take my sentimental husband off my hands occasionally, I shall be more than obliged to you,' says one wife to the other who is perfectly willing to comply since, she says, 'I like to be loved. I want everyone round me to love me.'

But Charlotte was far from feeling this. Shaw's comedy was an outlet for his wishes rather than a clinical study of how polygamy was soon to threaten their marriage. In the Preface, where he maintains that those who profess advanced views are mostly 'the last people in the world to engage in unconventional adventures of any kind', he opposes the 'demonstration' of his play. Was the play to overrule the Preface, or the Preface overrule the play? The dilemma registers the tension and uncertainty with which he entered the great romance of his life, for which *Overruled* had served as curtain-raiser.

4

ON THE SUB-TEXT OF SUCCESS

I can't stand people who will not believe anything because it might be false nor deny anything because it might be true.

Shaw to Cliff Keene (12 June 1914)

The quantity of objects, duties, events from which Charlotte had to remove G.B.S. was mounting. 'Anything to avoid Christmas in England!' he had exclaimed on 23 December 1910. For a fortnight Charlotte and he rolled on the rough seas, arriving on the evening of 6 January at Kingston,

Jamaica. They were met by their old Fabian friend Sydney Olivier, the Governor-General, who put them up at his post-earthquake palace, 'a masterpiece of *nouveau* art' in reinforced concrete. 'I am taking photographs in 100th of a second through yellow screens & watching the lizards and dragon flies,' Shaw wrote to Granville Barker. ' . . . The trees & mountains look pleasantly theatrical through the mosquito curtains.' After six days on the island, they embarked for another fortnight at sea. 'On the whole it was a good move, this,' Shaw concluded, though he'd hardly had time to get used to the novelty of 'bananas and sugar canes and coloured villages and eighty in the shade in January'.

An enormous parcel of work and his first commercial stage success awaited him in London. *Fanny's First Play*, which he finished on 5 March 1911, had been born of Shaw's interest in some of the most topical events in England. But he had worked on it anywhere but in England: in the remote Gothic hotel at Parknasilla on the south-west coast of Ireland; and at sea while steaming to and from Jamaica. One consequence of writing in such far-off places about up-to-the-minute issues seemed to be a strange unfastening of the theme from its treatment – a dislocation which was to produce what some critics would later see as 'the type of alienation which Brecht thought necessary to a dispassionate argument'.

The play depicts two middle-class families, the Gilbeys and the Knoxes, associated in business and by their strictly brought-up son and daughter, Bobby and Margaret, who are engaged to be married. After short spells of imprisonment for assaulting the police, they are released from their social prison and acknowledge that their feelings for each other are those of brother and sister. Bobby then marries a prostitute and Margaret a footman who (in characteristic Shavian reversal) reveals himself as the younger brother to a Duke. Both are acting in accord with the natural morality of sexual instinct rather than the rules of an enclosed system.

That was the complete play when Shaw and Charlotte arrived from their holiday in Jamaica at 10 Adelphi Terrace, and when Lillah McCarthy (who could spy their arrival from her rooms at 5 Adelphi Terrace) came to see Shaw. She told him that she had borrowed some money from Lord Howard de Walden; that she was setting herself up as an actress-manager at Gertrude Kingston's Little Theatre below her apartment: and she asked him for a play. *Fanny's First Play* was too short. But on the plan of *The Taming of the Shrew*, Shaw ingeniously added an Induction and an Epilogue, and early in March handed Lillah this 'Easy Play for a Little Theatre'. 'The idea of the Induction is this,' Shaw explained to Charles Ricketts who designed the costumes. 'A certain Count O'Dowda . . . loathes modern industrial England, and has spent his life in Venice, in the footsteps of Byron, Shelley, and the Brownings.

'He has lived the perfect artistic life, with his daughter, tolerating nothing later than the XVIII century. But he has consented to send his daughter to Cambridge for two years as it is his own university, and he feels quite sure that it is still untouched by the XIX century. The young lady . . . writes an ultra modern suffragette play – Fanny's first play – the perform-ance of which nearly kills the unfortunate old gentleman.'

Fanny O'Dowda has persuaded her father to have her play anonymously performed, 'with real actors and real critics', at his country house for her nineteenth birthday. The differences separating father from daughter reinforce the conflict of the parents and children in Fanny's play; and the sexual liberation of the young people in her play is complemented by Fanny's intellectual liberation from the rule of the theatrical critics, who are a police force of the mind. In the Epilogue these critics debate the authorship of the play they have just seen, offering scholarly comparisons with *The Admirable Crichton*, *The Madras House* and *The Second Mrs Tanqueray*. 'I believe it's Shaw,' blurts out Flawner Bannal. 'Rubbish!' retorts Gunn. 'Rot!' exclaims Vaughan. They all agree that Shaw is incapable of writing a play. All he wants is to 'set us talking about him', which to their disgust he makes them do.

Fanny's First Play had evolved in much the same way as had the full version of *Man and Superman*, and it takes to the point of caricature the Shavian practice of ending the drama in the middle of the play and letting the discussion take over. 'I have not put my name to it,' he told Lillah McCarthy when handing her the typescript, and he urged her to reveal that the author's name began with a *B*, so encouraging the rumour that it was by Barrie.

Fanny's First Play by Xxxxxxx Xxxx opened at the Little Theatre on 19 April 1911. 'It was like old time at the Court,' Shaw told Vedrenne two days later, 'except for the void left by Vedrenne.' But this was not repertory: they ran the play continuously for as long as the public wanted it – the way Vedrenne had always wished to run Shaw's plays at the Court. 'It is really amusing – considering who wrote it,' Shaw admitted: and the public agreed. The Shavian drama seemed to have won through to genuine popularity. On 1 January 1912 it transferred to the Kingsway Theatre and later completed a run of 622 performances. 'I thought that . . . you touched your highest, often striking the human note,' wrote Herbert Beerbohm Tree.

*

The coronation celebrations of King George V and Queen Mary that summer provided a good incentive for Shaw and Charlotte to get abroad again. Shaw's diary lists some forty towns in France, Switzerland, Austria, Germany and Italy that he and Charlotte saw over the next sixteen weeks. They travelled with the patient Kilsby and his boisterous motor car and spent many hours motor-mountaineering along impassable tracks over the Alps and Dolomites. 'In the valleys, in the towns, in the hotels, in the hideous heat, I have been wretched,' he informed Trebitsch; 'but on the mountains I revive.'

He was back in harness in the second week of October. Charlotte kept him gently on the move between Ayot and Adelphi Terrace, then boarded him up at Edstaston with her sister and brother-in-law for Christmas and the New Year. Here, on 2 January 1912, he began a new play, 'a religious harlequinade,' he described it to Frances Chesterton. 'Do you know anyone who can play a lion well, with a practicable tail, for the Christian Martyr scene in the arena?' he asked Pinero three days later. The last of the seventy-eight pages of shorthand manuscript was finished on 6 February and sent to his secretary Judy Gillmore for typing.

Androcles and the Lion was an offshoot from *Major Barbara*. Desmond MacCarthy's description of it as a 'religious pantomime' recalls Count O'Dowda's execration of this genre in *Fanny's First Play*: 'that vulgar, ugly, silly, senseless, malicious and destructive thing the harlequinade of a nineteenth century English Christmas pantomime!' This was a view that Shaw could share, having as Corno di Bassetto written that, rather than sit out another pantomime, 'I should choose death'.

Death was the subject of Shaw's pantomime. MacCarthy believed that in *Androcles and the Lion* Shaw had invented a new form, the nearest equivalent to which were 'those old miracle plays in which buffoonery and religion were mixed pell-mell together'. Shaw, who subtitled the work 'A Fable Play', turned his Roman arena into a variety theatre with a Call Boy announcing the successive entertainments: 'Number six. Retiarius versus Secutor ... Number eleven! Gladiators and Christians! ... Number twelve. The Christian for the new lion.' It was a flourish of Shavian extravaganza.

Androcles and the Lion was born of two other plays. The first was J. M. Barrie's *Peter Pan*, written for idealized children and then in its first great vogue. Max Beerbohm had drawn a caricature of Barrie 'reading it to a circle of elderly people and children,' Shaw remembered. 'The elderlies were beaming with enjoyment; the children were all asleep. I agreed, and wrote "Androcles" to show what a play for children should be like.'

The play was also intended as an antidote to Wilson Barrett's enormously popular religious melodrama *The Sign of the Cross*. Shaw had reported on this production in the *Saturday Review*. 'The whole drama lies in the spectacle of the hardy Roman prefect, a robust soldier and able general, gradually falling under the spell of a pale Christian girl, white and worn with spiritual ecstasy,' he wrote. ' . . . As she gradually throws upon him the fascination of suffering and martyrdom, he loses his taste for wine; the courtesans at his orgies disgust him; heavenly visions obsess him; undreamed-of raptures of sacrifice, agony, and escape from the world to indescribable holiness and bliss tempt him; and finally he is seen, calm and noble, but stark mad, following the girl to her frightfully voluptuous death.'

'Depend on it,' G.B.S. alerted readers of the *Saturday Review*, 'we shall see Mr Wilson Barrett crucified yet.' Prior to crucifixion, he had been festooned with praise by the most celebrated writer of the day, author of *The Sorrows of Satan*, Marie Corelli, who had found in his 'choice and scholarly' language, 'the unpurchasable gift of genius'. 'I must either hold my tongue or else re-write the play to shew how it ought to be done,' Shaw responded. Holding his tongue was never in the Shavian line.

Wilson Barrett's scripture-drama had traded on the whip, the stake and the lions. But the audience at *Androcles* is forbidden these sensations. 'It is a crime to gratify that passion,' the Roman Captain tells Lavinia. Shaw renounces too the fairy-tales of Christianity which had been the substance of *The Sign of the Cross* but which Lavinia, as she waits for death, finds 'fading away into nothing'. 'Are you then going to die for nothing?' the exasperated Captain demands. And Lavinia answers that she is dying for something greater than dreams, something too big to give a name to. This is the same undefined decision to die as Dick Dudgeon made in *The Devil's Disciple*. The fact that Shaw's spokesman and spokeswoman for the Life Force should both volunteer for death and be saved only by the improbabilities of extravagant event-plots, reflects a pessimism that needed the constant somersaulting of paradox to turn up at the surface so courageously cheerful – like the Christian prisoners in *Androcles* who are 'determined to treat their hardships as a joke'.

After leaving the Fabian executive Shaw fixed his imagination on far-off solutions to political problems. To Beatrice Webb, still active in the Fabian campaigns, he seemed fantastically impractical. But this was what Shaw meant by the term 'religious'. He set his gaze over the horizon at a time when Christianity would have expressed itself politically as communism; when our system of punishments had been abandoned; when we had established an equal income for everyone and could trust our future to a sense of fellow-feeling with all living beings. This distant view, imbued by what Shaw understood as the essence of Christianity, was what moved him to take up Aulus Gellius' ancient legend of Androcles and set his play some sixteen hundred years off from the contemporary world.

In the Shavian sense Jesus was one of a number of Supermen who appear in history to show us the future of human evolution. It was a future for which Shaw was to make his appeal in the sombre Preface to *Androcles*: 'Why Not Give Christianity a Trial?' Jesus had been the first Christian, but by choosing a death that was not to be avoided by any Shavian manipulations of event-plot, he had become the last Christian too. 'Christianity was a growing thing which was finally suppressed by the crucifixion.' Since then all civilizations had been elaborate organizations for the prevention of Christianity.

Shaw's imaginary journey gave him the distance to comment dispassionately on the twentieth century. The Roman centurions are our own police and soldiers; the Emperor, who is 'a divine personage', is our monarchy; Lavinia and Androcles embody aspects of a religious spirit, but 'the saint is always embarrassed by finding that the dynamiter and the assassin, the thief and the libertine, make common cause with him'. The powerful and choleric Ferrovius, whose 'sensibilities are keen and violent to the verge of madness', is a human lion in the prime of life whose kingdom is very much of this world: which is to say he belongs to the present. In the hour of trial he reverts from passive Christianity to the warrior's faith that sees God in the sword. 'Mars overcame me and took back his own,' he says. 'The Christian god is not yet. He will come when Mars and I are dust; but meanwhile I must serve the gods that are, not the God that will be.'

As the chocolate soldier gets the better of the professional cavalry officer in *Arms and the Man*, so the 'small, thin, ridiculous little' Greek tailor Androcles triumphs over the Roman Emperor who behaves like the Mayor of Toy Town. Androcles is a Wellsian hero, recognized by Wells himself in a letter to Shaw as 'one of your greatest creations, the holy silly man . . . I could almost find it in me to try an imitation.' The dreadful monster of death is reconstituted as a nursery animal called Tommy, a frisky, clever, coquettish creature which 'purrs like a motor car' and transforms the ghastly arena of death into a dance hall. 'What a pretty liony-piony situation it is, with no thought at all for the realities of Christian martyrdom,' Stevie Smith later wrote. 'And underneath there beats a heart of fear that cannot allow suffering.'

In the lion that 'holds up his wounded paw and flaps it piteously before Androcles', Brigid Brophy has seen a likeness to the literary lion who once boasted to Beatrice Webb he was 'untameable' and who had then been tamed by Charlotte into marriage 'on one leg' and led off for a honeymoon on crutches.

But there is another way of seeing the paradisiacal dance that Androcles and this wonderful animal perform in the forest at the end of the Prologue. Androcles is a long-suffering married man 'addicted to Christianity' (as his wife Megaera complains) in much the same way as Shaw was addicted to work. The journey through the forest with his wife has all the tension and bickering that were beginning to fill the Shaws' holidays. When Androcles 'embraces the lion' and 'the two waltz rapturously round and round and finally away through the jungle', he is expressing Shaw's desire to be off on some escapade. When he triumphantly dances again with the lion at the end of the play in the Roman arena, his wife Megaera has gone – no one cares where. Her last words of the Prologue – 'you havnt danced with me for years; and now you go off dancing with a great brute beast that you havnt known for ten minutes' – are a comic variation of a complaint Shaw was soon to hear from Charlotte.

*

Early in 1912 there had been an eruption of labour disputes among railway workers, cotton operatives and dockers. The coal miners were on strike; feminists were breaking windows; there was fresh agitation in Ireland for Home Rule and new legislation covering military emergencies. Shaw exercised himself over everything: making political speeches at Coventry and Southampton; discussing Ireland with Winston Churchill and corresponding with Keir Hardie; writing on free speech for the *Fabian News* and, as an illustration of free speech, letting it be known in the *Saturday Review* that he would be prepared to shoot industrial malingerers. Malingerers, of course, were not miners or feminists, but ladies and gentlemen living the lives of social parasites on unearned incomes. Their social disadvantages of family, public schooling and vaccination had given them little chance.

There was little time for Charlotte. When alone they hardly spoke; when they did speak they broke out into quarrelling. Charlotte was making a selection of passages from Shaw's writings. By April the work for this compilation, arranged alphabetically under a hundred and ninety-five headings, was pretty well complete, and it was obvious to her that the time had come for a resounding holiday. She proposed that they go to Rome – and G.B.S. said no. In the fourteen years of their marriage, this was unprecedented. Charlotte made it clear that she needed a change; but still he would not go with her. What she needed, he believed, was what they both needed: a change from each other. How stupid, then, to change everything – air, language, meals, habits, country – except that main condition of their lives, and to intensify that condition violently by isolating themselves in a foreign place where they knew practically no one else. Their nerves would never stand it. Eventually she decided to sail alone. 'She took leave of me,' Shaw told Beatrice, ' . . . in a way that left Charles I taking leave of his family simply nowhere.'

Charlotte sailed on 12 April, and Shaw spent part of the time 'motoring about the country'. As if to punish G.B.S. Charlotte clung to her coughs and colds. G.B.S. sent her every two or three days a narrative-through-letters of his motoring tour round England. 'I feel fearfully incomplete, though I rather like the novelty of being a bachelor too,' he told her the day before he set out.

The motor party consisted of co-drivers Kilsby and G.B.S., and passengers Judy Gillmore (who was shortly to get married to a naval officer and give up her job as Shaw's secretary) and Granville Barker who was to catch up with them later. They advanced, sometimes bounding forwards at the rate of a hundred miles per day, by way of Cambridge, Peterborough and Lincoln, to York, where they stopped to wait for Barker.

Shaw and Barker together were like two schoolboys, endlessly and idiotically quoting Shakespeare, while Judy had developed into a fast and indefatigable walker. 'She flies up hills, leaving us gasping and trudging after in our elderly manner.' At Windermere they went by motor boat down the lake and were caught in the tempest and uproar of the hydro-aeroplanes which 'nearly blew us into the lake'. Then Barker suspended himself from a nail to calculate his weight and 'fell with an appalling bang on his back on the stones'.

They pressed on as far north as Carlisle where Judy went down with an overwhelming cold; Barker limped off home exhausted; Kilsby was left with his 'pet bag of scrap iron' doctoring the car; and Shaw was struck down by a vigorous lumbago which he sent off to Rome to compete with Charlotte's influenza. 'Lumbago is a fearful thing. Possibly it is appendicitis. Possibly spinal paralysis.'

The perils of road-journeying grew extreme when at a fork in the road Kilsby found himself steering while his employer reversed, and the car toppled over a bank: 'she slid down gracefully like the elephant on the chute at the Hippodrome – backwards – without the slightest shock, except one of surprise to Kilsby . . .' But nothing deterred Shaw. Producing a map, he pointed to a road which looked all that a road should be, but which soon ascended so steeply that the car again refused. Shaw and Judy jumped out and began searching for stones to arrest the descent, but the monster rolled backwards over Judy's finger and she fainted. 'Kilsby got his shoulders under her like a fireman; I heaped her up on him,' Shaw recounted to Charlotte, 'and he carried her up the hill to an open place where we laid her down and laid our by no means clean handkerchiefs, dipped in mountain water mud, on her forehead . . . This is a shocking country for motoring.'

Proceeding more cautiously they came to Blackpool, which was in festivity. Princess Louise had opened a new promenade and everything was illuminated, 'a triumph of crimson and gold fire'. This was Blackpool's first taste of royalty. Thousands of dancers moved to the tempo of band music over acres of parquet floor. 'The sentimental solemnity of the waltzing is beyond description,' Shaw exulted. 'The two-steps are more joyous; and the lancers approach, by comparison, delirium . . . Kilsby says he will bring Mrs Kilsby here for their next holiday.'

To heighten Judy's morale Shaw introduced her to a socialist hair-dresser. 'Judy is all right,' he predicted. But shortly afterwards she admitted that she wanted to return to London. Since her naval officer was soon to be landing there 'I did not dissuade her,' Shaw wrote, and reluctantly put her on the train back.

So now there were two. They raced on to Edstaston where 'Mrs Chum' and her husband, the Colonel, put Shaw to work chopping down gorse, adding cramp to his other ailments. But: 'the place is looking delightful, all leaves & blossoms, and soft summer airs,' he informed Charlotte.

Charlotte returned on 22 May and Shaw met her at Southampton. Now that they were together, what had their separation shown? Charlotte could hardly have envied Judy's predicament which might so easily have been her own. G.B.S. had endured the same headaches, cramps, accidents, lumbagos as ever. Nevertheless, the difference had been Judy. 'The chief fun of the tour is her enjoyment of it,' he had explained to Charlotte. 'I never realized how very staid she is as secretary in Adelphi Terrace until I saw her gambolling like a rabbit or a lamb in the open.'

By early June two ingredients had been added to Shaw's career: a new woman and a new play. The new woman was Ann M. Elder. Approved of by Charlotte – she put G.B.S. in mind of 'a very attractive bullfinch' – Ann took Judy's place as his secretary and was to work with him for seven years before marrying.

The new play was *Pygmalion*. Shaw took it round that month to read to George Alexander. The professor of phonetics appealed to him so well that he told Shaw he could settle his own terms and name any actress he liked for the flower girl – except the actress for whom Shaw had written it, Mrs Patrick Campbell. 'I'd rather die,' he appealed to Shaw. But Shaw had set his heart on her. Eliza Doolittle was as good a fit for Stella Campbell as Lady Cicely had been for Ellen Terry: 'for I am a good ladies' tailor, whatever my shortcomings may be'.

5

DEAREST LIAR

I badly need some sort of humanizing . . . I have loved – and have
survived it . . . I shall never quite get over it.
Shaw to Mrs Patrick Campbell (20 March 1913, 8 February 1914,
23 October 1912)

He had been 'violently in love' with Mrs Patrick Campbell from the start:
and fearfully on his guard. Her sexual power was more compelling than
Ellen Terry's charm, and when he used it as a warning to Janet Achurch
he had been warning himself.

He had seen her in many plays. 'It is impossible not to feel that those
haunting eyes are brooding on a momentous past, and the parted lips
anticipating a thrilling imminent future . . . Mrs Patrick Campbell is a
wonderful woman.' She had been 'wonderful' as Juliet, though unable to
act the part; and a disquietingly mad Ophelia; and he had been delighted
by her also as the heroine of 'the celestial bed' in *Nelson's Enchantress*.
'You will tell me, no doubt, that Mrs Patrick Campbell cannot act,' he
lectured his *Saturday Review* readers. 'Who said she could? – who wants
her to act? . . . Go and see her move, stand, speak, look, kneel – go and
breathe the magic atmosphere that is created by the grace of all these
deeds.' She would cast an extraordinary glamour round such plays as *The
Second Mrs Tanqueray* or *The Notorious Mrs Ebbsmith*. 'Clearly there must
be a great tragedy somewhere in the immediate neighbourhood,' Shaw
concluded. ' . . . But Mr Pinero has hardly anything to do with it.'

Shaw was envious of Pinero. He wanted Mrs Pat for his own play-
world. He had written his Cleopatra for her, but she only read the
copyright performance. She was better formed for the mature Cleopatra of
Shakespeare's world than Shaw's marvellous child. *Caesar and Cleopatra*
had been a dramatization of their relationship thus far as critic and actress.
The dazzled Caesar who retains his full self-possession is G.B.S., sworn
critic of the *Saturday Review*, who names Mrs Pat as Circe, and states his
intention of making 'the best attempt I can to be Ulysses'. He believed
that he had the antidote to romance; that he could, like Ulysses, drink
from the cup unharmed – and without harming others. He wanted to re-
enact the Greek legend, with no descent to Hades before sailing on
escorted by favourable winds. He wanted to serenade his Circe, through
his acts on stage – to direct her, fill her with his words.

As early as September 1897 everything 'has been driven clean out of
my head by a play I want to write . . . in which he [Forbes-Robertson]

shall be a west end gentleman and she an east end dona in an apron and three orange and red ostrich feathers'. Fifteen years later he wrote this play. The liaison between Forbes-Robertson and his 'rapscallionly flower girl' as Shaw had called her was long over, and Mrs Pat had returned briefly to the St James's. Sir George Alexander would have made as good a West End gentleman as Sir Johnston Forbes-Robertson: but what mattered to Shaw was that Mrs Pat should become the cockney flower girl: a Galatea to his Pygmalion.

But would she stand for such a vulgar role? Not daring to offer it to her directly, he formed a stratagem. This involved Mrs Pat's close friend Edith Lyttelton at whose house he arranged to read his play on 26 June 1912, when Mrs Pat was expected to be present. She came: heard Shaw's amazingly awful cries of 'Nah-ow' and even 'Ah-ah-ah-ow-ow-ow-ow!'; recognized his clever mimicry of her own voice: and realized that this part of Eliza Doolittle was meant for her. She might have interrupted. She could have left. But Shaw read with spellbinding power and she listened.

Next day she wrote to thank him for 'thinking I can be your pretty slut' and inviting him to come and discuss the business proposals for *Pygmalion*. 'I wonder if I could please you,' she wrote. ' . . . We said so little yesterday. I mustn't lose time – my days are numbered surely.'

He went at once to her house in Kensington Square. It was now her turn to put forth spells. Shaw scorned the danger. But taking his hand she touched his fingers against her bosom and 'I fell head over heels in love with her,' he confessed to Granville Barker, ' – violently and exquisitely in love – before I knew that I was thinking about anything but business.' They were together for an hour. He walked on air all afternoon and the next day 'as if my next birthday were my twentieth,' he told Ellen Terry. His beard was going white, he was on the verge of fifty-six but 'I have not yet grown up'. She was forty-seven and still beautiful. 'Is there no age limit?' he wondered. He was determined, however, that his infatuation should last no longer than a day, or perhaps two, and by the end of the month declared that G.B.S. was himself again. 'I did not believe that I had that left in me,' he acknowledged in a letter to Mrs Pat – or Stella as he was to call her. 'I am all right now, down on earth again with all my cymbals and side drums and blaring vulgarities in full blast; but it would be meanly cowardly to pretend that you are not a very wonderful lady, or that the spell did not work most enchantingly on me for fully 12 hours.'

Shaw's recovery was signalled by a frightful migraine and pages of 'horrid' business practicalities about producing *Pygmalion* 'behind which my poor timid little soul hides'. Yet his feelings kept interrupting his professional literary manner. 'I wish I could fall in love without telling everybody,' he wrote. He told Lillah and Barker; he told Barrie, Edith Lyttelton, Ellen Terry, Lady Gregory . . . and he told Charlotte. 'I must now go and read this to Charlotte,' he concluded one of his letters to Stella. 'My love affairs are her unfailing amusement: all their tenderness recoils finally on herself.'

*

Charlotte had already experienced enough recoil over the business of Erica Cotterill. G.B.S. had encouraged that young girl disgracefully, she sometimes thought. They had actually been forced to threaten her with the police. But Shaw felt Charlotte's accusations were unjust. Was it his fault that, having received his advice to 'join some Socialist Society', Erica had become a Fabian and followed him devotedly back from his lectures to Adelphi Terrace? Could he seriously be blamed for not having foreseen that, after accepting tickets to his plays, she would write a play herself in which the heroine declares her passion to have 'some gorgeous thing to live for and love with every atom of my whole soul', and that she would point to G.B.S. as this 'gorgeous thing' and hand the play to Charlotte? Had he acted wrongly by informing Erica that her letters (which he scrupulously showed his wife) were illegible, simply because she was to go off, employ a printer, and begin publishing her correspondence to him as a series of 'accounts' totalling a quarter of a million words, dedicated to Shaw 'whom I love'? And where was the harm in inviting her to lunch and introducing her to some friends – unless it had lain in her decision to camp in the woods nearby and come racing up to Ayot on her motor-bicycle under the trance-like conviction that Charlotte's house belonged to her? No: he had done no wrong.

Yet her exasperating naïveté touched him at times with its loneliness and oddity so that, after almost seven agonizing years, he was still locked in correspondence with her in the summer of 1912. Her hypnotic style, undivided, ecstatic, insistent, was as unstoppable as his own. She wrote in one key identified by Shaw as E flat minor. This was a letter missing from the Alpha and Omega of his own prose. Her pages were emotional orgasms: she lived upon the page as if it were her body. Reluctantly he counselled her to adopt literature as a profession. Shaw would have to guide her.

He sent for her: bullied her with his high-speed opinions. But: 'I didnt want to be scolded,' she wrote, 'I wanted to be loved, and perhaps I nearly cried.' Then something happened. He pulled away, and laughed. 'What would have come if you had not held me back and I had knelt down to you?' she wanted to know. 'Would you have laughed then? . . . would you have felt nothing ... and what would have come if you had felt it? ... were you hidden deep from your conscious mind *afraid* of feeling it?'

He sent her away: and started his correspondence course. 'Now listen to me.' She was an adult not a baby; strong not weak; and exquisite. But everything was made impossible by her nymphomania. He pointed to his wife, and the iron laws of domestic honour. Then he explained about seducers and socialist orators; and then about divine sparks and ultimate goals. And after the explanations poured forth the advice. She should marry; she should marry as quickly as possible. Marriage was an acquired taste, but if she chose someone by the same rule as (for example) she might choose a horse, someone of the right size, shape, complexion and (in the horsedealer's sense) without vices, she could become fond of him – after which she could put her energy into work. Then after the advice came the education. 'When an adult woman and an adult man caress one another, the result is entirely different from the result of your kissing your mother.' The person to whom she behaved in that perfectly happy way would lose all power of doing anything but the thing that would result in her having a baby. 'People who do these natural things are socially impossible.'

But Erica *was* socially impossible and the woman least fitted in the world to be Eliza Doolittle to his Henry Higgins. 'You hardly yet know how to behave yourself at all,' he complained. He identified Erica with Sonny. He had been 'just as shy & sensitive as you are'. So now he tried to give this 'terrified child' all the parental help he had missed himself. But no amount of Shavian coaching could change her. For she had her own insights: 'youre a child all the while acting that youre a man,' she countered. '*Why* do you act – what *use* is it – it deceives no deep parts ...

'in all the whole stream of people that have come out of you theres not one that moves me first and last for itself – you watch and study and get behind and master things in them ... and then you suddenly do a thing – you suddenly *use them* ... *consciously* youre using them to expose some evil or falsehood or whatever its chosen to be called ... cant you feel that everything of any kind that comes from you, work speeches plays letters ... comes *at its root* from a pose or attitude of some kind.'

Erica would not smarten up her writing, or learn her biology, or master the simplest obligations of society. She wanted the creative fire to leap into activity within their bodies. The strain was too much. 'I would not stand it from Cleopatra herself.'

But, in Stella Campbell, he had become involved with a modern Cleopatra, and to Charlotte's mind there was no telling what he would not stand. Over the Erica Cotterill affair, she had interceded by sending a letter (drafted by G.B.S.) forbidding the girl her house and her husband. To separate him from Mrs Pat she reintroduced their motoring holidays with her sister and Kilsby on the Continent. This time Shaw could not refuse, and they started on 27 July.

*

'All I ask is to have my own way in everything,' Shaw had reasoned with Stella, 'and to see my Liza as often as possible.' Charlotte's tactics in removing G.B.S. were somewhat nullified when Stella's taxi had 'a blinding bang' with another vehicle and she decided to recover in France, leaving three days after the Shaws. For part of August they were tantalizingly close. 'I have only to push on to Tresenda,' Shaw wrote from Bad Kissingen, 'turn to the right, skirt Lake Como, hurry through Milan, dash through the Little St Bernard (being myself the Great St Bernard), make through Albertville to Chambery, and then be in your arms in an hour. But back I must turn for all that, leaving your arms empty.'

No one had their way that summer. The waters at Aix and the air of Chamonix were of little benefit to Stella who arrived back in London feeling less well than when she set out. Meanwhile, the tonics in Bad Kissingen proved poisonous to G.B.S. – one mouthful and he made a dash for the Alps, and at fall of evening on 6 August, ruptured the car. This was largely Stella's fault since, instead of minding the road Shaw had filled his head with a thousand letters he wanted to write her with 'millions of additional verses'.

They returned to Bad Kissingen and deposited the two women for three further weeks of voluptuous cures. Charlotte 'gasps in rarefied air whilst her sister wallows in mud,' Shaw notified Stella. ' . . . Charlotte wants to get thin; and her sister wants to get plump; so they have both agreed to be asthmatic and have treatments.'

The two men then launched themselves across Europe until, ploughing through ruts of limestone mud, the car 'seemed to get its teeth full of paving stones . . . and finally reduced us . . . to admit that our journey was over . . . Tomorrow we shall attach a couple of brewery horses to her and have her hauled to the railway station.'

While the car was being put to rights at Luneville, Shaw and Kilsby waited twenty-seven kilometres off at Nancy where G.B.S. corrected the proofs of a new Prologue to *Caesar and Cleopatra*, and made final revisions to his study of marital infidelity, *Overruled*. 'It has an air of being outrageous,' he advised Charlotte; 'but it really does drive in its moral, which is that four reasonably amiable people in a matrimonial difficulty find themselves with nothing to guide them but a morality which will not work.'

His letters to Charlotte were regular, amusing, friendly, informative – he even asks her to send a rough proof of *Pygmalion* to Mrs Pat who 'now says that her notion of bliss is to travel for a year and have a letter from me every week'. Shaw's letters to Stella were of a kind that Charlotte had never received. 'Stella, do not ever bully me: you don't know how easily frightened I am,' he wrote from Nancy. ' . . . Let us take life as it comes, and love and hate and work without dramatizing it more than we can help.' But it was impossible for Shaw not to dramatize it. He had been born with the instinct to show off which his mother, feeling no pride in his tricks, had stifled. His hunger for love fed on his imagination and found consummation in his dreams. 'If you knew all the adventures we have had already in the imaginary world which is my real world,' he told Stella, 'you would blush to the remotest contours of your enchanting person.' Stella fulfilled an important adolescent need in Shaw untended by the years of his marriage. 'You are a figure from the dreams of my boyhood,' he told her. Their relationship took him back to 'the indescribable heartbreak of Ireland' and reminded him of that 'bewitching Calypso' with the beautiful 'black tresses' with whom he had fallen in love shortly before leaving Dublin. 'Once, in my calfish teens,' he told Stella, 'I fell in love with a lady of your complexion; and she, good woman, having a sister to provide for, set to work to marry me to the sister.'

The Calypso whom he originally loved was married and, being taken care of in reality, able to inhabit his imagination freely. His retreat from the sister was in effect a flight from reality, with which his emotions could not cope. But Stella, alias Mrs Pat, seemed to represent both sisters and threatened to bring the real and his imaginary worlds into collision. His letters to Stella have none of the artistry of the Ellen Terry correspondence: Shaw's relationship with Ellen had been on paper. But to Stella 'I dont know why: I cant write. Writing is no use . . . It is past letter writing with me. There are things one cannot put on paper . . . All that paper love is nothing: the real thing is in the marrow of my bones and the roots of my nerves.' The spoken not the written word was Stella's art ('I have always been an odious letter writer'). Their love affair therefore 'was acted, not written' and the correspondence incidental. But 'I must break myself of this,' he wrote.

Stella 'was the beauty of the moonlight,' wrote Rebecca West, 'as Ellen Terry was the beauty of the sunlight'. Like him, she was reckless yet fundamentally respectable. He was attracted by strong women, she to weak men. She had married Patrick Campbell when she was twenty and pregnant. It seemed romantic, but however handsome he looked Patrick

Campbell was not a creature of romance. After his death she had not remarried, but recently, unknown to Shaw, involved herself with a well-connected, insolvent officer, 'a bit short on brains', called George Cornwallis-West, unhappily married to the famous American beauty Jennie Jerome, widow of Lord Randolph Churchill.

Mrs Pat wanted to be loved and she wanted to act great roles; but she was impossible to live with and almost impossible to act with. The late Victorian and Edwardian theatre had very few good roles for actresses. She needed a playwright who believed in the equality of women and men in the theatre to write for her. But though Shaw's child-play made her laugh, so that she nicknamed him Joey after Grimaldi the clown; and though she was attentive to the commercial undertones of what he wrote to her, she underrated the emotional fires she had lit up in him.

But it was a delightful game and Stella played it beautifully. As for Shaw, he was feeling his part so deeply he sometimes forgot they were on stage. 'Playing Romeo has given me an ill-divining soul,' he told Edith Lyttelton: 'I cannot foresee the happy ending.'

*

By the time they scrambled back to England, Shaw had made up his mind to sell the car. It was four years old, had covered 70,000 miles, and gave him lumbago. But being fond of it, he postponed the sale for another eleven years and added to his stable a brisk little motor-bicycle in green enamel. This machine which he rode 'like a thunderbolt' suited his new spirit of recklessness which seemed to gain in response to everyone else's illness. Stella was confined to bed: Charlotte had fallen down; neither seemed able to recover from their continental cures.

More serious still was his mother's illness. While at Nancy he had heard from his sister Lucy that 'the Mar' had suffered a stroke. Over the next six months, she had two more strokes. She had continued into her seventies as a peppery music teacher at the North London Collegiate School for Girls; and she had continued living at 29 Fitzroy Square until the lease gave out, when Shaw bought for her the lease of 8 Park Village West, near Regent's Park. In her retirement she became economically more dependent on G.B.S., as did Lucy. 'I have now stock enough of my own to secure my mother & sister against all contingencies,' Shaw told Beatrice Webb that summer. He wanted to revoke the marriage settlement which, should he die first (in a car or motor-bicycle accident perhaps), made his family dependent on his wife. It was inappropriate, especially since they disliked Charlotte. Not that Bessie and Lucy seemed troubled: they spared George their gratitude. However hard he worked he was still 'a dreadful procrastinator' to his mother and a 'prosperous idler' to his sister.

Yet Lucy could not help associating herself with her brother's success. She liked to claim that he stole his best witticisms from her. Fate ('with her usual inscrutable workings and apparent lack of discrimination as to deserts') had raised up the brother and 'dealt her blows' to the sister. It was difficult not to feel bitter. 'The good things of this world which have poured into George's lap in the last three or four years are rubbing the sharp edges and crisp individuality off his intellect,' she cautioned a friend. ' . . . My worst dread about him is that he may become commonplace – I could stand anything but that. I still wish for his own sake that he had not married.' Such wishes derived from the sense of insult she felt after the break-up of her marriage. In her early forties she had got pneumonia, then pleurisy, 'and the result is tuberculosis'. She had spent her convalescence in Jenny Patterson's house. When the doctor broke the news to her that she might be going to die, her reaction had been 'absolute relief, rest and even exaltation'.

There seemed little to live for. She had lost her voice. For almost a decade she exiled herself in Germany while her husband, Charles Butterfield, carried on in London. Then, one October evening in 1908 shortly after returning to England, she had been stopped in the foyer of the Coronet Theatre, Notting Hill, and told by the manager, Eade Montefiore, that her husband had been living with an actress during Lucy's years abroad. 'Although I had taxed him with almost every failing a man could have, I never for one moment suspected him of infidelity.'

Shaw advised divorce and paid the costs – £91 13s. 8d. (equivalent to £4,200 in 1997) – needed to prevent Charles Butterfield from contesting the action. 'I can find money for you as soon as you want it,' he told her early in 1910. She needed some money to pursue good health. She spent much time by the sea but kept coming back to her mother's Park Village house.

Mother and daughter had a patchy but strong relationship. Bessie was 'a great old war horse' and could never see what Lucy was making such a fuss about. A disappointing career, a broken marriage, chronic ill-health, almost no money – these were hardly things to complain of. As for herself, Bessie put her trust in spiritualism. She preferred her friends when dead and would spend an hour each day chatting to them at the ouija board. They liked to tell her of the death of other friends: and she would hurry out for the wreaths. They told her, too, what she suspected: that the sort of success which had come to George 'doesn't count for anything up here'. Lucy too experimented with the planchette and received some extraordinary communications from Rajah Mahattan,

Knight Oliphant, Master Bariole and other unknown exotics on the subject of the planet Mars which she sent, with disappointing results, to the Astronomer Royal. Bessie when 'influenced' filled the house with drawings though she could hardly hold a pencil at other times. G.B.S. didn't trouble Bessie with his scepticism. But he had been somewhat useless to his mother, as men were. No wonder she had kept no 'photo of my son as a boy or child,' as she informed Archibald Henderson. ' . . . Nor have I a single letter.'

Now as she lay dying she shocked everyone, getting 'ridiculously cured . . . by a Christian Scientist who broke into the house and meditated on her whilst she slept,' Shaw reported. This cure did not prevent her death. Lucy was with her most of the time, and George (who came and went) provided two nurses. 'I have been watching her trying to die for five weeks since the last seizure,' Lucy wrote. 'Her body and all her organs are so sound that she seems unable to get away . . . the strain has been terrible.' Shaw too, in his fashion, felt the strain: 'my mother is dying, they say, but *wont* die – makes nothing of strokes – throws them off as other women throw off sneezing fits,' he wrote to Lady Gregory. Lucy had reported on 6 December that 'it is a question of days or even hours now', but Bessie held on for another ten weeks. On 19 February 1913 Lucy telegraphed George with the news: 'All over.'

To Lucy it seemed as if all was over for her too. 'My mother's exit has made an astonishing abyss in our little kingdom,' she told a friend. ' . . . consciously and subconsciously she guided and influenced everything I ever did. I feel as if the rock had vanished from under my house and I was tumbling about in the sand.' When her mother's body was taken from the house Lucy 'completely broke to pieces'. George put her in the care of a chest specialist and he insisted that she stay in bed. 'A halt had to be called if I did not want to follow Mama,' Lucy wrote, 'which I certainly did.'

She was not well enough to go to the funeral service and cremation at Golders Green on 22 February. Four people turned up: the chaplain, the undertaker, Shaw and Barker – whose presence revived the rumour that he was Shaw's natural son.

The only person to whom Shaw could write about this day was Stella 'who understands about one's mother, and other things'. The words of the burial service had been altered a little for a cremation. 'A door opened in the wall; and the violet coffin mysteriously passed out through it and vanished as it closed,' he told her. ' . . . I went behind the scenes at the end of the service and saw the real thing . . . it is wonderful.

'I found there the violet coffin opposite another door, a real unmistakeable furnace door. When it lifted there was a plain chamber of cement and firebrick. No heat, no noise, no roaring draught. No flame. No fuel. It looked cool, clean, sunny, though no sun could get there. You would have walked in or put your hand in without misgiving. Then the violet coffin moved again and went in, feet first, And behold! The feet burst miraculously into streaming ribbons of garnet colored lovely flame, smokeless and eager, like pentecostal tongues, and as the whole coffin passed in it sprang into flame all over; and my mother became that beautiful fire.'

They were told they should return in thirty minutes. 'When we returned we looked down through an opening in the floor to a lower floor close below,' Shaw wrote that night to Stella. 'There we saw a roomy kitchen, with a big cement table and two cooks busy at it.

'They had little tongs in their hands, and they were deftly and busily picking nails and scraps of coffin handles out of Mamma's dainty little heap of ashes and samples of bone. Mamma herself being at the moment leaning over beside me, shaking with laughter. They swept her up into a sieve, and shook her out; so that there was a heap of dust and a heap of calcined bone scraps. And Mamma said in my ear, "Which of the two heaps is me, I wonder!" '

For the first time she was behaving as her son commanded. The relief was enormous. He realized how little he had known her. They made dust of the bone scraps, then scattered the remains over a flower bed. The day had had some 'wildly funny' moments and been 'a complete success'. He made a note to buy some shares in the cremation business. That afternoon he drove to Oxford and at Notting Hill Gate (the car being in 'a merry mood') 'accomplished a most amazing skid, swivelling right round across the road one way and then back the other, but fortunately not hitting anything . . .'

*

His mother's death seemed to promise him emergence from the long shadow of his Dublin childhood, as his sea holidays at Dalkey had once done. To Stella 'I opened the grave of my childhood'. He expected a miraculous resurrection. Stella became everything he had once looked for in Lucinda Elizabeth Shaw and tried to replace with Alice Lockett, Jenny Patterson, Florence Farr, Janet Achurch and Charlotte too. She was his Virgin Mother and his Dark Lady, his playmate and working-partner, his magical friend. He had become a mass of wants that now rushed out towards her. He wanted to 'have a woman's love on the same terms as a child's,' he implored, '. . . to hear tones in a human voice that I have never heard before, to have it taken for granted that I am a child and want to be happy . . . and suddenly find myself in the arms of a mother – a young mother, and with a child in my own arms who is yet a woman: all this plunges me into the coldest terror as if I were suddenly in the air thousands of feet above the rocks or the sea . . . And yet I am happy, as madmen are . . .'

Stella's mysterious illness heightened their affair. She wrote saying that the doctor had forbidden her to see anyone except himself. He would go galloping up the stairs, three at a time, with beard flying, to 'my most agitating heart's darling'. He was 'most frightfully in love with you'. Sitting by the bed, he was allowed to put his arms round her waist, and they would kiss and kiss.

Sometimes, on account of her illness, she begged him to 'be patient with me', then she urged him on: 'I think if you don't come and see me rather soon there won't be me to see.' He went backwards and forwards. 'I love you for ever and ever and ever, Stella,' he wrote. Her deteriorating health made him desperately anxious. 'I will get into the bed myself and we shall perish together scandalously.'

Early in 1913 she had entered a nursing home in Hinde Street for an exploratory operation. Shaw continued to visit her whenever possible. At his most sympathetic, he charmed and flattered her, made her smile, made her forget the illness and the operation. 'Himself living in dreams,' she testified, 'he made a dream-world for me.' In return she let him play 'in the nursery of my heart' where he felt happy beyond reason – 'I shall never be unhappy again.' Had she been well perhaps she might not have let their fantasy-attachment go so far, but it was now too late, she acknowledged, 'to do anything but *accept* you and *love* you'. He basked in this acceptance. 'I have slipped out of the real world,' he told her.

But Stella never lost sight, as Shaw seemed to, of the traps in their relationship. Shaw wished to remain loyal to Charlotte while loving Stella. 'I throw my desperate hands to heaven and ask why one cannot make one beloved woman happy without sacrificing another,' he cried out. He recognized that Charlotte, with her sensitiveness, her susceptibility to worry, needed protection; and he had tried to explain this to Stella. Only that February Charlotte had said that she never knew where George spent his afternoons. Once she had given no thought to such things. Now she was full of doubts. So he told her what the rest of London already seemed to know: that he had been at Stella's bedside.

Charlotte was devastated. Shaw had not continued reading to her his correspondence with Stella. His wish to protect her seemed no more to Charlotte, however, than the keeping of a guilty secret. No wonder she had felt so anxious, had lain gasping in bed with asthma and bronchitis. She refused to meet this 'middleaged minx' or leave calling cards on her – and this offended Mrs Pat's sense of propriety. She began to grow hostile to what she called the 'suffragette' figure of Shaw's wife.

Early in March Stella left the nursing home and went to convalesce in Brighton. As she began to recover so the romance clouded. She resented this marriage-attachment of 'Mr and Mrs Mouse' and chided Shaw on his timidity. His advances could have led to love-making if – 'if only you'd eat red steaks and drink beer your spirit would be meet, I mean meet to mate – no I dont mean that . . .' But she did mean it. Since Shaw's 'Mother is dead & Charlotte is your wife I'll be your grandmother,' she mocked him.

'Dearest Liar,' Shaw addressed Stella, not wishing to believe some of the things she was saying to him. There was no need for him to warn her against falling in love with him as he had warned other women. He sensed that she could beat him at his own game 'and revenge his earlier victims'. He knew the unhappiness he risked. But 'I am still in love with Stella . . . Cannot help it,' he found himself writing, ' . . . my first defeat, and my first success.'

Late in March Shaw and Charlotte left for two weeks in Ireland. It seemed a safe move: except that in this country of his childhood, 'all the old longing for beauty and blessing get stirred up in me' so that he switched his emotional focus back to 'my girl, my beauty, my darling, barefooted, dusty petticoated, or my mother of angels, or a dozen lovely wild things . . .'

They were staying not far from Dublin with Horace Plunkett, founder of the agricultural co-operative movement in Ireland, who 'devoted his life to the service of his fellow-creatures collectively; and personally . . . disliked them all,' G.B.S. later recalled. ' . . . He remained a bachelor for the sake of Lady Fingal, and was unquestionably in love with her; yet I never felt convinced that he quite liked her.' There seemed nothing for G.B.S. to do but 'work, work, work', and this now pleased Charlotte who suddenly got well and, he wrote to Stella, 'changed from a fiend into a green-eyed mermaid, smiling & fascinating & dressing in diamonds & generally dispensing charm and childish happiness . . . Dont grudge her.'

But Stella had not been pleased by Shaw's efforts to strike some balance between the two women 'I was born to love'. That April, after they had all returned to London, she began to exploit what she saw as the limitation of Charlotte's marriage to G.B.S.: its childlessness. Stella knew that Shaw felt a reverence before the fact of childbirth. 'A sort of pang goes through me from the base of my heart down to my very entrails,' he had written to Sylvia Brooke, Ranee of Sarawak, when she was pregnant with her first child. ' . . . you are going to be torn to pieces and come to life again with a terrible contempt for fragile male things that would be broken by such creative miracles.'

Shaw had denied himself a share in this miracle, and been joined by Charlotte in a conspiracy of denial they called their marriage. Stella, who had 'suffered her suffering' and given birth to a son and daughter while her husband was alive, now informed Shaw that 'I could have 6 more children' when all he apparently wanted to create with her was a new play. Sometimes Stella could be merciless over his 'being addicted to work and neglecting your hearts love'.

Shaw had warned her that only on paper was he brave. Sometimes she felt pinned to his sheets of paper like a Painted Lady. She seemed to exist only in the make-believe of his mind. 'I think you are mad,' she told him. 'I think I am pretending to be what it amuses you to think I am.' He had been generous with offers of money, but she had no status in his life – all that belonged to Charlotte; and she had no future.

In the second week of June, Stella summoned Shaw to her house and told him that she was thinking of marrying George Cornwallis-West. He had touched her with his helplessness and dependence when Shaw had merely been amusing: besides he was prepared to divorce his wife and Shaw was not.

In the train travelling back to Ayot that night Shaw wrote that Stella's marriage to 'the other George' would cut him off for ever from what was still young in his humanity. 'I say he is young and I am old; so let him wait until I am tired of you,' he wrote. ' . . . It is impossible that I should not tire soon: nothing so wonderful could last . . . I will hurry through my dream as fast as I can; only let me have my dream out.'

It was a relief to Shaw to leave the country at the end of the month and spend a few days in Germany with Granville Barker. Though there were still delightful moments with Stella – making up verses for her (though he was lost for any rhyme to her name except umbrella), or teaching her to jump from the ground on to a bench in Richmond Park as part of her convalescence – he had felt 'all torn to bits' behaving so artificially with Charlotte. She had accidentally come upon a list of meetings mischievously entered by Stella in Shaw's pocket diary and there were dreadful scenes. Another time Charlotte had caught him speaking to her on the telephone and flared up into an appalling rage. Seeing someone suffer like this gave Shaw 'a sort of angina pectoris,' he told Stella. ' . . . It hurts me miserably . . . I must, it seems, murder myself or else murder her.'

To help her resist these lacerating scenes Charlotte had taken up with a spiritual healer. James Porter Mills was a bad-tempered old man who had travelled the world perfecting what he called the 'Teaching'. His personality had a profound effect on Charlotte. She felt a compulsion to apply his principles, whatever they might be, to the painful upheaval of her emotions. The result was that, in the middle of some terrible quarrels with G.B.S., she would convulsively recover her balance, smile dizzily, and be changed back into 'the happy consort of an easygoing man'. But damage had been done, and in the priority she gave to Dr Mills's 'Teaching' over Fabianism and the Life Force, Charlotte was being unfaithful to G.B.S. in the only way open to her.

'This is a terrific romance,' remarked J. M. Barrie, 'and at last Shaw can blush.' Living opposite G.B.S. in Adelphi Terrace, Barrie witnessed Mrs Pat courting them both for plays. That summer she decided to appear in Barrie's *The Adored One* which was to open in September – and Shaw was grateful. To go into rehearsals now with Stella in *Pygmalion* would 'probably kill me,' he had calculated. It was as much as he could do to go round to her house on his return from Germany. But she shut the door in his face. He had thought that he could only experience the suffering of others, never his own. But now he felt it, and he was shocked. A little later that July, he found to his astonishment that he was crying. Everything except his adoration of Stella seemed tedious. 'This clown misses Joey,' she relented. But she must be alone to study the Barrie play. 'I will hide in the sands somewhere.'

'When I am solitary you are always with me,' he answered. 'When you are solitary by the sea, where shall I be?' She did not want him with her. 'Its getting difficult not to love you more than I ought to love you,' she reassured him. ' . . . But by the sea I must be alone – you know.'

He did not want to know. On the afternoon of 8 August he took Charlotte to Liverpool Street Station to catch the boat train for Marseilles. He intended to join her at the end of the month for a six-week tour of France. On leaving the station he went straight down to the Kent coast where he knew Stella had borrowed the theatrical producer Nigel Playfair's cottage at Ramsgate. But she was not there. Answering the door late that night, the Playfairs' housekeeper informed him that Mrs Campbell, her maid, chauffeur and dog, had gone to the Guildford Hotel on Sandwich Bay. Shaw walked off into the dark, an exhausted figure in his Norfolk jacket, making his way back across the sands.

Stella was not pleased to see him next morning. He had made his entrance in the wrong scene. The Guildford Hotel was far from being the private tomb of love they had created in her London bedroom. She intended to marry George Cornwallis-West and Shaw's presence could be compromising. 'Please will you go back to London today,' she wrote to him, ' – or go wherever you like but dont stay here – If you wont go I must . . . Please dont make me despise you.'

But Shaw would not go. He had come so far and there would never be another chance like this, with Charlotte out of the country – a chance to spend some days with Stella and perhaps one or two nights. After reading the note he searched the hotel and went looking for her in the darkness along the sands. Eventually he found her and they ordered a nightcap. Tired herself, Stella noticed with irritation how sleepy he was. They arranged to meet next morning before breakfast for a bathe in the sea – though not before eight o'clock, she insisted. But by half-past seven she was speeding along the coast, with her chauffeur, maid and dog, towards Littlestone-on-Sea. At eight o'clock punctually Shaw knocked at her bedroom door. 'Come & bathe,' he called. A cheerful chambermaid answered, telling him that they had gone – and he pretended to have muddled the dates. She had left him a note: 'Goodbye. I am still tired – you were more fit for a journey than I – .'

He returned to his room and tried to write away his distress. 'I am deeply, deeply, deeply wounded . . . I cannot bring you peace, or rest, or even fun.' The world was horribly changed. He looked up at her room where he had imagined happiness, and there was nothing. 'I shall die of thirst after all.' The truth was inescapable. Of his fifty-seven years 'I have suffered 20 and worked 37'. 'Then I had a moment's happiness: I almost condescended to romance. I risked the breaking of deep roots and sanctified ties . . .' and now, on that desolate strand, 'what have I shrunk into?'

He kept mailing letters to Stella wherever she was: again that night ('Sandwich. Darkness') then next morning ('Another day that might have been a day!') and after he returned to London ('back from the land of broken promise'). It seemed to him that she had been gratuitously cruel, and he turned all the blame on her. She used her sex appeal irresponsibly, furtively, without care. He felt the need of some monstrous retribution. 'I have not said enough vile things to you.'

But Shaw's rhetoric was not hurtful for, as Stella understood, 'you have no claws'. Nevertheless she needed to defend her action, and her retaliation was more piercing than anything he had written to her. 'No daughters to relieve your cravings – no babies to stop your satirical chatterings, why should I pay for all your shortcomings,' she demanded. ' . . . You lost me because you never found me – I who have nothing but my little lamp and flame – you would blow it out with your bellows of self.' Yet the depth of his feelings startled her, and she felt his suffering as he had felt Charlotte's. 'You are trying to break my heart with your letters,' she appealed. ' . . . What other thing was there for me to do? I had to behave like a man.'

Because they were 'useless, these letters; the wound will not heal', she agreed to see him once they were both back in London. He occupied himself as best he could, swimming at the Royal Automobile Club, visiting the zoo and stroking a lion as part of the preparation for Granville Barker's production of *Androcles*. He was to join Charlotte in France in the second week of September and he welcomed this. For the romance with Stella had confirmed all his beliefs about love. It was a hideous business: 'the quantity of Love that an ordinary person can stand without serious damage,' he measured, 'is about 10 minutes in 50 years.'

THIRTEEN

CONCERNING FAME AND ANONYMITY

I am a Mr Jorkins on the New Statesman; Clifford Sharp is Mr Spenlow.
Shaw to St John Ervine (1912)

Beatrice Webb was one of those who had viewed this emotional business
between G.B.S. and his 'somewhat elderly witch' with distaste. Charlotte
had told her all about it: and the two women shook their heads.

Beatrice, in her fashion, felt caught up in the wreckage of this affair.
During the summer of 1912, she had begun appealing to G.B.S. to help
her and Sidney launch a new Fabian weekly journal. But he had displayed
little enthusiasm. Unless they established in the mind of the railway
traveller, he told them, a certainty that he would be amused and interested
by their paper for the next hour of his journey they would never capture
the sixpenny public.

It was as bait for this public that Beatrice wanted Shaw's name as a
regular contributor. Yet he was reluctant to give up the time and energy.
He would hand over some money, but 'I wont write'. He believed they
were too old. 'Unless you can find a team of young lions . . . and give
them their heads, the job cannot be done,' he answered Beatrice. ' . . . I
should not serve you by attempting to lag superfluous on the stage I once
adorned.'

But Beatrice persisted. The *New Statesman*, as it came to be called,
was to be a platform for the reformist middle class, and her and Sidney's
last venture before their retirement. There was need for a well-informed
pugnacious journal voicing Fabianism in the contemporary political debate
– one that featured G.B.S., instead of leaving him to permeate their
opponents.

So Shaw was persuaded. He became one of the *New Statesman*'s original
proprietors and directors, put up (with a cheque for £1,000, equivalent
to £43,000 in 1997) one fifth of its capital, purchased approximately
2,400 shares and sent out a series of letters soliciting subscribers. And
Beatrice was pleased.

Almost everything, Shaw told Beatrice, would depend on the tact and
dash of their editor. The Webbs had chosen Clifford Sharp whom Sidney
thought a 'weak, timid and slow' man, but Beatrice believed to be 'a good

man of business'. His credentials were faultless. He was a steadfast
member of the Fabian executive, had married H. G. Wells's ex-love
Rosamund Bland, and had helped the Webbs' anti-Poor Law campaign as
editor of the *Crusade*. But no one really liked him. He was like 'an old,
mangy, surly, slightly dangerous dog,' wrote Leonard Woolf. Imperialist
by temperament, Sharp did not share many of the radical preoccupations
of socialism such as removal of the House of Lords, and introduction of
proportional representation; he was not pro-birth-control or anti-vivisection. But he was a thoroughgoing collectivist: and that was what mattered
most to the Webbs.

'The first number has been a huge success,' Shaw reported following
its publication on 12 April 1913. Not wishing to find himself presiding
over a raucous weekly symposium, Sharp relied on the anonymity of his
contributions to help him achieve a single tone and unity of style
throughout the paper. 'It is not usual for a journal to communicate to the
public the names of those of its staff who contribute unsigned articles,'
he wrote in the first number.

'We feel, however, that, in view of the promises which have been made,
and which have possibly induced many persons to subscribe to *The New
Statesman*, we owe it to our readers to explain that Mr Bernard Shaw and
Mr Sidney Webb will as a rule write editorially in our columns, and that
the present issue includes, in fact, more than one contribution from each
of these gentlemen.'

Shaw's unsigned contributions on feminism and income tax, the performance of motor cars, the ethics of prize-fighting and the duties of the
poet laureate were too surreal to blend into the mood of didactic common
sense that Sharp wanted to establish. The two of them, it was said, saw
eye to eye on nothing except Ireland and Death Duties – 'we did not even
agree about the Income Tax,' Sharp added. He therefore proposed that
G.B.S. should be treated as an exception to the rule of anonymity and be
allowed to sign his contributions. But Shaw refused. 'I have had enough
of being the funny man and the privileged lunatic of a weekly paper.' As
a result 'the *New Statesman* is in fact the one weekly in which Shaw's
name never appears,' Beatrice complained in her diary that summer, 'and
it is Shaw's name that draws ... He will not cooperate on terms of
equality.'

But he had agreed to co-operate on terms of equal anonymity. Collectivism did not mean to him a regimentation of opinion, but the release of
differing individual talents for a generally harmonious purpose. Sharp
reminded him somewhat of his father. He was a moral teetotaller who

drank: a man of late hours and cloudy scandals. Though it was impossible for Shaw to trust him, 'I never felt inclined to resent in the least the good-humoured contempt which he never concealed,' Sharp told Beatrice. 'I think he is much the most generous and sweetest-tempered person I ever came across.' Sharp met the difficulties with courage and ingenuity. 'I am very favorably impressed by his standing up to me,' Shaw admitted.

The differences between the two men were to be exacerbated by the war, during which, Sharp wrote, the *New Statesman* represented Shaw's views 'in scarcely a single particular'. He needed fortitude against Shaw's magnanimous and subversive tactics. Their battle was for authority. Sharp believed that authority belonged to him as editor: but Shaw needed this authority for his iconoclastic opinions. 'The time has come for me to be old and savage,' he asserted. He used everything except his money and his position as proprietor in their struggle. His weapons were words.

Beatrice, though she and Sidney were themselves to sever their relationship with Sharp later on ('your turn will come,' Shaw predicted), tended to support the editor. 'The New Statesman enjoys the distinction of being the only paper in the world that refuses to print anything by me,' Shaw was to write in the autumn of 1916, ' . . . and I am compelled, as I have been more or less all my life, to depend for publicity on the more extreme Conservative organs of opinion.'

*

Beatrice had wished for closer intellectual intimacy with Shaw through the *New Statesman*. But his 'big brain', she became convinced, had been spoilt by Mrs Patrick Campbell. 'He is the fly and the lady the spider.'

Shaw had been unusually subdued during the autumn of 1913 as he flew round France on what Stella called his 'honeymoon' with Charlotte. 'I am horribly unhappy every morning,' he wrote to her, ' . . . you have wakened the latent tragedy in me.' On his return he tried to keep hidden from their friends the memory of Stella that 'tears me all to pieces'. Now that the affair had ended, Beatrice began to feel more sympathetic towards him. Instead of hanging around Mrs Pat's bedroom he 'has attended every one of our six public lectures, and taken the chair twice,' she approved. It was not wholly displeasing to Beatrice that Shaw's recent plays, of which she did not think much, had been unsuccessful. *The Music-Cure* was presented for just seven performances at the Little Theatre; *Great Catherine* ran for thirty performances at the Vaudeville and had not been very well reviewed. More surprisingly, Barker's production of *Androcles and the Lion*, with shimmering Post-Impressionist designs by Albert Rothenstein, had come off after fifty-two performances at the St James's Theatre. The play had puzzled people. 'An English audience has not as a rule sufficient emotional mobility to follow a method which alternates laughter with pathos, philosophy with fun, in such rapid succession,' explained Desmond MacCarthy in the *New Statesman*.

Everyone had loved the lion, a delicious beast with the most alluring howls and pussycat antics, and 'the one character in the whole range of Shavian drama,' commented A. B. Walkley warmly, 'who never talks'. But it was the lion's evening rather than the playwright's. The *Manchester Guardian*'s critic reported that the words 'vulgarity', 'blasphemy', 'childish' were to be heard at the end of the performance, and predicted that 'Mr Shaw's new play will scandalise . . . the most characteristic part of the English public [which] . . . cannot understand being passionately in earnest about a thing and in the same breath making fun of it.' And so it proved.

For Christmas and the New Year he went to Devon and Cornwall for a fortnight's tour with the Webbs. The scenery had 'an almost Irish charm'. Each day they would set off walking over ten or thirteen miles of researched country, with the car panting in attendance to take them, when exhausted, to the most luxurious hotel in the neighbourhood. 'Our old friend and brilliant comrade is a benevolent and entertaining companion,' Beatrice allowed. But he was 'getting rapidly old physically, and somewhat dictatorial and impatient intellectually, and he suffers from restlessness,' she observed. 'We talked more intimately than we have done for many years.'

Shaw's life was changing – everything was changing – from comedy to tragedy. From Cornwall he wrote to Charlotte: 'I miss you, as you would be happy here, and I like to be with you when you are happy.' From Devon he wrote to Stella, reminding her of their love a year ago: 'I believe we were both well then, and have been ill ever since.' He could not conceal these divisions from the sharp eyes of Beatrice. 'He is still fond of Charlotte and grateful to her,' she noted, 'but he quite obviously finds his new friend, with her professional genius and more intimate personal appeal, better company.'

Stella had taken little notice of Joey's letters this winter. 'I ought to have written,' she acknowledged. Barrie's *The Adored One* had not been a success. She began to look differently at Shaw. 'Be quite serious in your friendship for me,' she appealed. Though not knowing whether Shaw still wanted her to play Eliza, she had recently approached Beerbohm Tree about *Pygmalion*. Having already heard from George Alexander that this play was 'a winner', Tree asked Shaw to come to His Majesty's and read it to him. The reading took place high up in the dome of the theatre, and before the end of the third act Tree had made up his mind to stage it. Rehearsals were to begin in February 1914. Tree's 'admiration for you and the play is ENORMOUS,' Stella wrote to Shaw. 'I'll be tame as a mouse and oh so obedient – and I wonder if you'll get what you want out of me . . .'

2

THE HISTORY OF *PYGMALION*

> Ibsen was compelled to acquiesce in a happy ending for A Doll's House in Berlin, because he could not help himself, just as I have never been able to stop the silly and vulgar gag with which Eliza in Pygmalion, both here and abroad, gets the last word and implies that she is going to marry Pygmalion.
>
> Shaw to William Archer (19 April 1919)

Pygmalion marks the climax of Shaw's career as a writer of comedies. It is a return in feeling and form to the period of his *Plays Pleasant*, an integration of Faustian legend and Cinderella fairy-tale, a comedy of manners and a parable of socialism. Written so near to his mother's death and to the flowering of his romance with Stella, the play weaves together a variety of Shavian themes and obsessions, imaginatively rephrasing the relationship between his mother and Vandeleur Lee, and casting Mrs Pat as the emotional replacement for Mrs Shaw. Its vitality and charm endeared *Pygmalion* to audiences, with whom it has remained Shaw's most popular 'romance'. 'There must be something radically wrong with the play if it pleases everybody,' he protested, 'but at the moment I cannot find what it is.'

He enjoyed describing *Pygmalion* as an experiment to demonstrate how the science of phonetics could pull apart an antiquated British class system. 'The reformer we need most today is an energetic phonetic enthusiast,' he was to write in his Preface. This was Shaw's gesture towards removing the power for change from fighting men who were threatening to alter the world by warfare, and handing it to men of words whom he promoted as 'among the most important people in England at present'. In this context, the character of Henry Higgins (who appears as a comic version of Sherlock Holmes in Act I) takes his life from the revolutionary phonetician and philologist Henry Sweet, who had died while the play was being written. Writing to Robert Bridges in 1910 about the need for a phonetic institute, he had described Sweet as the man 'I had most hopes of'. It was Bridges who, the following year, retained Shaw to speak at the Phonetic Conference on spelling reform at University

College, London. 'It is perfectly easy to find a speaker whose speech will be accepted in every part of the English speaking world as valid 18-carat oral currency,' he wrote to Sweet afterwards, 'NOT that the pronunciation represented is the standard pronunciation or ideal pronunciation, or correct pronunciation, or in any way binding on any human being or morally superior to Hackney cockney or Idaho american, but solely that if a man pronounces in that way he will be eligible as far as speech is concerned for the post of Lord Chief Justice, Chancellor at Oxford, Archbishop of Canterbury, Emperor, President, or Toast Master at the Mansion House.'

It was this experiment that Shaw transferred to Higgins's laboratory in Wimpole Street, with its phonograph, laryngoscope, tuning-forks and organ pipes. This is a live experiment we are shown on stage, and as with all such laboratory work it is necessary for the Frankenstein doctor to behave as if his creation were insentient. 'She's incapable of understanding anything,' Higgins assures his fellow-scientist Colonel Pickering. 'Besides, do any of us understand what we are doing? If we did, would we ever do it?' When Pickering asks: 'Does it occur to you, Higgins, that the girl has some feelings?', Higgins cheerily replies: 'Oh no, I dont think so. Not any feelings that we need bother about. Have you, Eliza?'

Shaw conducts a second social experiment through Eliza's father, Alfred Doolittle, an elderly dustman of Dickensian vitality. Doolittle is any one of us. When asked by Higgins whether he is an honest man or rogue, he answers: 'A little of both, Henry, like the rest of us.' Being his name, he does as little as possible – some bribery here or there, a little blackmail, more drinking, an occasional change of mistress: and he provides positively no education at all for his illegitimate daughter 'except to give her a lick of the strap now and again'. Yet he has the quick wits and superficial charm of the capitalist entrepreneur. He is society's free man – free of responsibilities and conscience. 'Have you no morals, man?' demands Pickering. 'Cant afford them, Governor,' Doolittle answers. Undeserving poverty is his line: 'and I mean to go on being undeserving. I like it,' he adds. His disquisition on middle-class morality is intended by Shaw to have the same subversive effect as Falstaff's discourse on honour.

Yet this is the man whom Shaw chooses as the first recipient of what he calculates to be a reasonable income-for-all. As the result of Higgins's joking reference to Doolittle as the most original moralist in England in a letter to an American philanthropist, the undeserving dustman is left £3,000. In Act II he had made his entrance with 'a professional flavour of dust about him'. In Act V when his name is announced and Pickering queries, 'Do you mean the dustman?', the parlourmaid answers: 'Dustman! Oh no, sir: a gentleman.' He is splendidly dressed as if for a fashionable wedding. Shaw's point is not that a gentleman is merely a dustman with money in the same way as a flower girl with phonetic training can be passed off as a duchess: it is that moral reformation depends upon the reform of our economic system. As Eric Bentley writes: 'He was giving the idea of the gentleman an economic basis.' It is this that Doolittle dreaded and derided, and now finds himself dragged into. 'It's making a gentleman of me that I object to,' he protests. ' . . . I have to live for others and not for myself: thats middle class morality.'

Under Higgins's tutelage Eliza becomes a doll of 'remarkable distinction . . . speaking with pedantic correctness of pronunciation and great beauty of tone', which Mrs Higgins tells her son is 'a triumph of your art and of her dressmaker's'. This dummy figure replaces the 'draggle tailed guttersnipe' whose life Higgins acknowledges to have been real, warm and violent. The classical Pygmalion had prayed to Aphrodite to make his ideal statue come alive so that he could marry her. Shaw's flower girl, whom Higgins has manufactured into a replica duchess by the beginning of Act IV, is transformed into an independent woman whom Higgins refuses to marry. However, the transformation scene, in which Higgins lays his hands on Eliza like a sculptor's creative act, is a struggle the implications of which are sexual:

'*Eliza tries to control herself . . . she is on the point of screaming . . . He comes to her . . . He pulls her up . . .* LIZA [*breathless*] . . . *She crisps her fingers frantically.* HIGGINS [*looking at her in cool wonder*] . . . LIZA [*gives a suffocated scream of fury, and instinctively darts her nails at his face*]!! HIGGINS [*catching her wrists . . . He throws her roughly into the easy chair*] LIZA [*crushed by superior strength and weight*]. HIGGINS [*thundering*] Those slippers LIZA [*with bitter submission*] Those slippers'

These stage directions contain many sado-masochistic undertones. But Higgins himself resists every innuendo. This was important to Shaw. For, remembering Sweet's genius for 'making everything impossible', he turned his mind to another 'genius' as a model for Higgins, the author of *The Voice*, Vandeleur Lee. Higgins's asexual association with Eliza is consequently authorized by Shaw's faith in his mother's 'innocence', and written as an endorsement of his own legitimacy. The platonic arrangement depends on the professional circumstances of their relationship. 'You see, she'll be a pupil,' Higgins explains to Pickering, 'and teaching would be impossible unless pupils were sacred.' Higgins's voice tuition of Eliza takes the place of the singing lessons Lee had given Bessie (Lucinda Elizabeth Shaw) and to reinforce this substitution Shaw provides Higgins's pupil with the same name as Lee's pupil:

HIGGINS   Whats your name?

THE FLOWER GIRL   Liza Doolittle

HIGGINS   [*declaiming gravely*] Eliza, Elizabeth, Betsy and Bess,
        They went to the wood to get a bird's nes'.

'I've never been able to feel really grown-up and tremendous, like other chaps,' Higgins tells Pickering. He explains the reason to his mother who has regretted his inability to fall in love with any woman under forty-five. 'My idea of a lovable woman is somebody as like you as possible,' he tells her. 'I shall never get into the way of seriously liking young women: some habits lie too deep to be changed.'

In his final act, Shaw was rewriting the legend of Svengali and his pupil Trilby. When Svengali dies of a heart attack, Trilby's voice is silenced, she cannot sing at her concert, and she follows Svengali into death. In Shaw's version Eliza's true voice is heard once she emerges from Higgins's bullying presence and walks out to a separate life. But other forces were at work in the final act obliging Higgins himself to speak increasingly with the voice of G.B.S., the public figure that had developed from Vandeleur Lee; while Eliza comes to represent the emotions that Stella Campbell was introducing into his life. Higgins's description of Eliza as a 'consort battleship' has something of the armoured impregnability Shaw attributed to his mother ('one of those women who could act as matron of a cavalry barracks from eighteen to forty and emerge without a stain on her character'). But no one else in the play regards Eliza in this light. Mrs Higgins calls her 'naturally rather affectionate'; Doolittle admits she is 'very tender-hearted'; and Eliza herself demands: 'Every girl has a right to be loved.'

What Higgins wants is less clear. He claims he has created an ideal wife – 'a consort for a king' – yet he must resist her emotional appeal: 'I wont stop for you . . . I can do without anybody.' The purpose of Higgins's experiment has been 'filling up the deepest gulf that separates class from class and soul from soul'. It is half successful, half a failure. The class gulf is filled at the garden party, dinner party and reception: the gulf between Eliza and Higgins remains. Eliza has changed, but Higgins admits 'I cant change my nature.' He seems 'cold, unfeeling, selfish' to Eliza. 'I only want to be natural,' she says. But can Higgins be natural? Where will things lead if she accepts his invitation to go back to him 'for the fun of it'?

The original ending of the play is carefully ambiguous, reflecting Shaw's uncertainties over his romance with Stella. He could not marry her: she could not remain for ever his pupil as an actress learning from his theatrical direction. But might they become lovers? The question is left open to our imagination:

MRS HIGGINS   I'm afraid youve spoilt that girl, Henry. But never mind, dear: I'll buy you the tie and gloves.
HIGGINS   [*sunnily*] Oh, dont bother. She'll buy em all right enough. Good-bye. *They kiss. Mrs Higgins runs out. Higgins, left alone, rattles his cash in his pocket; chuckles; and disports himself in a highly self-satisfied manner.*

This, as Eric Bentley argues, 'is the true naturalistic ending'. But Shaw's subsequent attempts to clear up its ambiguity have blurred the outline of its elegant structure. The faint poignancy of the ending lies in the half-emergent realization that there is to be no satisfactory marriage for this Cinderella; while a feminist reading tells us that Higgins cannot be approved of as a husband. But the public wanted the Miltonic bachelor to be transformed into the beautiful lady's husband. 'This is unbearable,' Shaw cried out. Once his love affair with Stella had ended, he could not bear to speculate on what might have happened when 'I almost condescended to romance'. 'Eliza married Freddy [Eynsford-Hill],' he told Trebitsch; 'and the notion of her marrying Higgins is disgusting.' In other words Eliza married a double-barrelled nonentity like George Cornwallis-West, and Higgins's agonizing boredom with the Eynsford-Hill family reflects Shaw's own impatience with the smart visitors who sometimes crowded him out of Stella's house.

The history of *Pygmalion* was to develop into a struggle over this ending. For the play's first publication in book form in 1916, Shaw added a sequel recounting 'what Eliza did'. Her decision not to marry Higgins, he explained, was well-considered. The differences between them of age and income, when added to Higgins's mother-fixation and exclusive passion for phonetics, was too wide a gulf to bridge. He told the story of Eliza and Freddy, Mr and Mrs Eynsford-Hill, as invitingly as he could: but the public went on preferring its own version. Shaw made his final version of the end on 19 August 1939:

MRS HIGGINS   I'm afraid youve spoilt that girl, Henry. I should be uneasy about you and her if she were less fond of Colonel Pickering.
HIGGINS   Pickering! Nonsense: she's going to marry Freddy. Ha ha! Freddy! Freddy!! Ha ha ha ha ha!!!!! [*He roars with laughter as the play ends*]

But by now this laughter sounded as hollow as Higgins's prediction, and even Shaw's printers had begun to query his intentions.

The English-language film of *Pygmalion* gave Shaw an extra opportunity to remove 'virtually every suggestion of Higgins's possible romantic interest in Liza'. His screenplay even omits the word 'consort' and leaves Higgins calling Eliza a 'battleship'. But the producer of the film hired other screenwriters who added a 'sugar-sweet ending' which Shaw found out for the first time at a press show two days before its première.

But one battle he apparently did win. 'Hamon, my French translator, says that it is announced that Lehar is making an operetta of Pygmalion,' he notified Trebitsch in the summer of 1921. ' . . . Can you warn him that he cannot touch Pygmalion without infringing my copyright, and that I have no intention of allowing the history of The Chocolate Soldier to be repeated.' For almost thirty more years he made the same reply to all composers. 'I absolutely forbid any such outrage,' he wrote when in his ninety-second year. *Pygmalion* was good enough 'with its own verbal music'.

*

Pygmalion, which was first published in book form in Germany, Hungary and Sweden (plus an unauthorized edition in the United States), received its theatrical début at the Hofburg Theater in Vienna on 16 October 1913, and was played a fortnight later at the Lessingtheater in Berlin. *The Times* on 17 October 1913 reported that the opening night in Vienna 'met with an excellent reception from the audience, which among a number of distinguished personages included the Archduke Francis Ferdinand'.

Shaw described this première as a compliment paid to him by German and Austrian culture 'which I value very much'. *Pygmalion* had been performed in a beautiful theatre splendidly subsidized and free of rent. 'I am handsomely paid for my work,' he reported. 'In London, with an equally popular play, the ground landlord leaves less than nothing for me and for the management . . . Meanwhile, huge endowments are proposed for football, pedestrian races, and throwing the hammer.'

However, there was a small cloud floating over this foreign production.

The central situation of the play also appears in Shaw's novel *Love Among the Artists* where the Welsh Beethoven, Owen Jack, gives elocution lessons to Madge Brailsford. But an alert German critic pointed out the extraordinary resemblance of Shaw's story to the adventures of Smollett's hero with a sixteen-year-old beggar girl in Chapter 87 of his novel *Peregrine Pickle* – and the British press immediately took this up as the reason why Shaw had produced his play out of the country. It showed 'an amusing ignorance of English culture,' Shaw countered. 'The one place where I should have been absolutely safe from detection is London.' He had read *Peregrine Pickle* in his youth and not cared for it and he did not realize that 'Smollett had got hold of my plot'. Later he was to speculate on the likelihood of this incident having 'got lodged in my memory without my being conscious of it and stayed there until I needed it'. None of this affected the morality of his position. 'If I find in a book anything I can make use of, I take it gratefully,' he stated. ' . . . In short, my literary morals are those of Molière and Handel.' Shakespeare too had taken his goods where he could find them. 'Do not scorn to be derivative,' Shaw urged his friends, ' . . . the great thing is to be able to derive – to see your chance and be able to take it . . . Read Goldsmith on originality.'

There was a rumour that the actor playing Higgins in Berlin had introduced a 'horrible gag' suggesting that he and Eliza shared the same bedroom. In London, where Shaw was producing the play himself, such travesties would not be permitted. But when he turned up for rehearsals in the second week of February he found His Majesty's a madhouse.

Famous for his absent-mindedness, Tree was the despair of playwrights. He greeted Shaw warmly, but with obvious surprise. It was as if he believed himself to be the author of *Pygmalion*. His head hummed with plans. For he had experience of collaborating with other dramatists – for example, Shakespeare into whose *Richard II* he introduced a very effective pet dog, and whose *Twelfth Night* he had improved by the addition of four miniature copycat Malvolios. His performances were hugely entertaining to his fans, but they relied on a good deal of improvisation especially when he was not quick enough to reach the stage furniture in time and pluck from its niches the pieces of paper on which he had written out his more troublesome lines. He loved to disguise himself with beards, uniforms, vine leaves, ear-trumpets. In this respect, Professor Higgins was a disappointment. It seemed he was required to do little more than dress and speak normally: and this bewildered him. In vain did he plead with Shaw to let him take large quantities of snuff, to vault onto the piano from time to time, to indicate an addiction to port by walking with a limp and a stick.

Delays were often caused by Tree's brainwaves for taking over other roles (such as Doolittle) or filling the theatre with philosophical dustmen and flower girls. To Shaw's businesslike mind it seemed miraculous that any production ever took place at His Majesty's. Tree had with dignity assured him that 'I will not place myself in the position of receiving a rebuff', and was taken aback when Mrs Campbell hurled a slipper bang in his face. His morale shattered, he collapsed into a chair while the cast tried to get him to understand that this was part of the play. The worst of it was, Shaw wrote, that 'it was quite evident that he would be just as surprised and wounded next time'.

Shaw was strangely convinced that Tree was a tragedian and Stella a comedian. 'I am sending a letter to Tree which will pull him together if it does not kill him,' he informed Stella. But Tree reflected in his note-book: 'I will not go so far as to say that all people who write letters of more than eight pages are mad, but it is a curious fact that all madmen write letters of more than eight pages.'

In her fashion, Stella worked hard at Eliza Doolittle. Her prompt copy of *Pygmalion* was pencilled with encouraging scribbles: 'My hand is held out Joey ... I'll do my level best ... Your delicious play needs real greatness ... gentle Joey.'

But Shaw was not always so gentle. Though often maddened by Tree, 'I could never bring myself to hit him hard enough,' he regretted. But on Stella he believed that 'no poker was thick enough nor heavy enough to leave a solitary bruise'. He had been partly persuaded of this by the knowledge that she thrived on conflict. She would put out her tongue, turn her back on Tree ('But it's a very nice back, isn't it?') and finally drive him screaming from his own stage.

Stella's tantrums masked a lack of confidence. She had never played in comedy before and she was thirty years too old for the part. 'Dreadfully middle-aged moments,' Shaw observed in his rehearsal notebook. Occasionally he did not keep such observations to himself. At one moment, as he knelt before Stella imploring her to speak the lines as he directed, she told the actors: 'That's where I like to see my authors, on their knees at my feet.'

Opening night was set for 11 April 1914. The week before was marked by two spectacular disappearances. Instead of going to the theatre on Monday 6 April, Stella took off for the Kensington Registry Office where she married George Cornwallis-West two hours after his decree absolute came through. From there they went on a three-day honeymoon to a golfing resort near Tunbridge Wells, returning in time for Stella to take part in the dress rehearsal at His Majesty's on Friday evening. 'Of *course* I knew about the marriage,' Tree lied to the press assembled in the dress circle bar, 'and I'm very happy for both of them, but naturally I was sworn to secrecy ... contrary to popular rumour there have been no quarrels between us, in fact rehearsals have progressed with the most delightful smoothness & harmony.'

Shaw could reflect now on the consequences of his own timidity. The day before the news of Stella's marriage appeared in the papers, Charlotte had sailed for the United States. She did not know that her husband's affair with Mrs Pat was over – how could you ever tell such things? The long rehearsals of *Pygmalion* had been agony for her. She did not want to witness their first night climax. On 8 April she left England with her friend Lena Ashwell to join their guru James Porter Mills and his wife. These last months, while G.B.S. occupied himself at His Majesty's, Charlotte had been preparing an abstract of Mills's 'Teaching' which he persuaded her to publish as a business prospectus entitled *Knowledge is the Door: A Forerunner.* It was a comfort to her that Dr Mills was not brilliant or literary. She felt calmed by his assurance that '*there is no need to give way to human feeling* . . . we can gradually quiet the waves of emotion.'

There was a great swell of excitement round the first night. Shaw sat by himself in the teeming theatre: not far off was the other George, Stella's 'GOLDEN man'. The curtain lifted on the first act. All went smoothly and well. In the second act Edmund Gurney, who had been listening to Lloyd George's speeches in the House of Commons to pick up the right tone of contempt for the aristocracy, scored a colossal success as Doolittle. Stella 'ravished the house almost to delirium' throughout the third act, and 'Tree's farcical acting was very funny'. But Eliza's sensational exit line, 'Not bloody likely,' nearly wrecked the play. The audience gave a gasp, there was a crash of laughter while Mrs Pat perambulated the stage, and then a second burst of laughing. The pandemonium lasted well over a minute. 'They laughed themselves into such utter abandonment and disorder,' Shaw wrote to Charlotte in the United States, 'that it was really doubtful for some time whether they could recover themselves and let the play go on.'

Tree had been in a pitiful state of nerves, begging Shaw to substitute 'blooming' or 'ruddy' for Eliza's dreadful word. Now he felt frightfully pleased. He relaxed. He expanded. 'He was like nothing human.' Much of the dialogue between Higgins and Eliza held special meanings for Shaw – echoes from the controlling influence of his mother ('I cant change my nature') and overtones of his unhappy romance with Stella ('I hadnt quite realised that you were going away . . . I shall miss you Eliza'). Tree made it all absurd; 'For the last two acts I writhed in hell,' Shaw wrote to Charlotte. ' . . . The last thing I saw as I left the house was Higgins shoving his mother rudely out of his way and wooing Eliza with appeals to buy ham for his lonely home like a bereaved Romeo. I went straight home to bed and read Shakespear for an hour before going to sleep to settle myself down.'

Stella had followed his directions as if she were Eliza imitating Higgins. To thank her, and because he could not endure going backstage after the performance, Shaw invited her and her new husband down to Ayot next day. 'You *must* consent to receive Cornwallis-West in the country,' he wrote to Charlotte that night. 'He has a dog Beppo, a huge black retriever, who plays hide & seek, distinguishes between right & left when he is given instructions, takes people's hats off when ordered, and is withal a grave & reverend signor. I believe you would ask them both to stay for a month on condition that Beppo came too . . . They treat me as a beloved uncle.'

Shaw doubted if *Pygmalion* could succeed. Once its success became apparent, Tree chivvied him to come back and see it. But Shaw was adamant. 'Come soon – or you'll not recognize your play,' Stella appealed. But he would not. 'Never no more.' But at last he relented and came to the hundredth performance on 15 July.

It was awful. It was appalling. It was worse than anything he had imagined. His directions had been wonderfully circumvented. Instead of flinging the ring down on the dessert stand at the end of Act IV, Eliza on her knees clutched and gazed on it feelingly – there were no words because the emotion was obviously too deep. In the brief interval between the end of the play and fall of the curtain, the amorous Higgins threw flowers at Eliza, a theatrically effective gesture, as Nicholas Grene has observed, 'reversing the image at the end of Act I where Eliza threw her flowers at Higgins'.

Tree claimed that his improvements delighted the audience: and it was this public that Shaw really blamed. What had happened to its serious instincts, its sense of proportion? During these hot summer months there had been turmoil in Ulster over Asquith's Home Rule Bill, and hunger strikes among the militant suffragettes in London. Then on 28 June, the Archduke Franz Ferdinand, who had been at the première of *Pygmalion* in Vienna, was shot: and Europe moved to the edge of war. But for much of this time 'all political and social questions have been swept from the public mind by Eliza's expletive,' Shaw reported. The Bishop of Woolwich cried out for it to be banned; Bishop Weldon felt saddened that such a vulgar word had to be uttered by a married lady with children. Scholars and intellectuals duelled in the columns of *The Times* over the origin of 'bloody'. The Oxford Union met and voted in favour of a motion declaring 'a certain sanguinary expletive' to be 'a liberating influence on the English language', but the Debating Society at Eton deplored 'the debasement and vulgarization of the commercial theatre'. The *Daily Express* got hold of an authentic Covent Garden flower girl called Eliza, took her to the play and reported her as being shocked. At 10 Downing Street the Prime Minister received a letter of protest from the Women's Purity League.

The summer days persisted hot and sunny; the public continued to come to *Pygmalion*: but Tree was bored. He wanted a holiday and took off the play late that July. He had attributed the bloody rumpus over

Pygmalion to 'the flatness of the political situation'. 'Triviality,' Shaw wrote, 'can go no further.'

3

WHAT HE DID IN THE GREAT WAR

As for going mad, dont you wish you could? The trying thing is to be sane with everyone else (except the rogues who are taking advantage of it) as mad as hatters.

Shaw to Rowley (7 January 1916)

The Fabians were unprepared for war. Most of them believed that modern war was caused by the capitalist struggle for markets and could be discouraged by means of the General Strike. Besides, as Sidney Webb said, 'it would be too insane'.

Shaw also thought it insane – and all the more likely for that. Militarism in all countries had developed, he argued, 'not from the needs of human society, but because at a certain stage of social integration the institution of standing armies gave monarchs the power to play at soldiers with living men instead of leaden figures'. German culture in particular had got stuck in this obsolete *Roi Soleil* system. This was why Shaw did not favour unilateral disarmament. 'All nations should be prepared for war,' he was to write. 'All houses should be protected by lightning conductors.' Until there existed a European police force, Britain must be prepared 'to make war on war' if she wanted to exercise an effective foreign policy. Sidney Webb's pacifism was that of the sane man. But at a time of war 'sanity is positively dangerous'.

Europe was ready for fighting, as if surfeited with the material gains of the previous hundred years. Germany's militarism was apparent. Thomas Mann was to speak of the hearts of poets standing in flame 'for now it is war! . . . Nothing better, more beautiful, happier could befall them in the whole world.' In England, where Rupert Brooke was to thank God for matching us with His hour, romantic militarism was dressed up to fit the righteous Christian, the hard-headed businessman, travelling adventurer, puritan character-builder. In a letter to *The Times* Lord Roberts had written: ' "My country right or wrong and right or wrong my country", is the sentiment most treasured in the breast of any one worthy of the name of man' – which Shaw paraphrased as 'teaching a Christian to disobey Christ at the commands of a non-commissioned officer'. His

Preface to *Androcles and the Lion*, written late in 1915, amounted to a denunciation of war as a method of solving international disputes.

Once war started, countries surrendered every other consideration except victory. 'It is one of the horrors of war,' he reminded Carl Heath, secretary of the National Peace Council, 'that both parties abandon the ground of right and wrong, and take that of kill or be killed. That is a reason for making an end of war, and in the meantime keeping political power out of the hands of bellicose persons.' He hated the silence of diplomacy. Laughter was one of his devices for shattering this silence: the mystique that in the public interest the public must know nothing. Preparation for war necessitated so much lying on the part of belligerent Governments as to develop an unthinking habit: 'if anyone remarks at noon that it is twelve o'clock, some minister automatically articulates a solemn public assurance that there is no ground for any such suspicion,' Shaw later wrote, 'and gives private orders that references to the time of day are to be censored in future.'

The secret of Britain's foreign policy was that there was no foreign policy. In an article for the *Daily Chronicle* on 18 March 1913 he proposed one: a triple alliance against war by England, France and Germany, the terms being that 'if France attack Germany we combine with Germany to crush France, and if Germany attack France, we combine with France to crush Germany'. From that starting point, he continued, the combination might be added to from Holland and the Scandinavian kingdoms 'and finally achieve the next step in civilization, the policing of Europe against war and the barbarians'. He repeated this formula, which was another magical trinity for achieving self-integration, in an article on the comity of nations entitled 'The Peace of Europe and How to Attain It' in the *Daily News* on New Year's Day 1914. 'I want international peace,' he stated. Those barbarians within our frontiers, who advocated war as a tonic, should not be let loose on foreigners but rather sent for annual war sports to Salisbury Plain, he suggested, to 'blaze away at one another' until the survivors (if any) felt 'purified by artillery fire'.

Lunching with the German ambassador Prince Lichnowsky, Shaw asked what he thought of his peace proposals and was told that such problems were better left to politicians and diplomats – which might have been a better answer if politicians and diplomats were required to do the fighting. 'Can anybody suggest an alternative policy?' Shaw had asked. But there seemed no alternative. 'Complete failure of my campaign,' he noted. This failure, together with his feeling of isolation from other Fabians, contributed to the somewhat aggrieved tone and massive outpouring of Shaw's writings on the war. A war symposium published by the *Daily Citizen* on 1 August he described as 'about as timely and sensible as a symposium on the danger of damp sheets would be if London were on fire'. But, he added: 'it is important that our statesmen and diplomatists should understand that there is a strong and growing body of public opinion to which all war is abhorrent, and which will suffer it now only as a hideous necessity arising out of past political bargains in which the people have had no part and the country no interest . . . We muddled our way in and we may have to fight our way out.'

*

Shaw and Charlotte were at a hotel at Salcombe in Devonshire on 4 August. Shaw first heard of the declaration of war on coming down to breakfast. A middle-aged Englishman 'after a fairly successful attempt to say unconcernedly "I suppose we shall have to fight them" suddenly changed "them" into "those swine" twice in every sentence'. It was an early symptom of the epidemic that was soon covering the country: 'the ordinary war-conscious civilian went mad.' People rejoiced at the prospect of a first-rate fight. The excitement, the dread of being thought unpatriotic even by fools with white feathers for brains, was to leave the country at the mercy of anyone in authority. 'This is the greatest fight ever made for the Christian religion,' the Bishop of London declared, ' . . . a choice between the nailed hand and the mailed fist.' Kitchener's finger was to point at everyone. The upper and the upper-middle classes were exhorted to sacrifice their butlers, chauffeurs, gamekeepers and grooms for service at the front. Old men postdated their births, dyed their hair, and lined up at the recruiting offices; old women lamented that their ineligibility to serve as nurses would prevent their killing the German wounded; mothers hustled their sons into uniforms and off to the trenches; a fifteen-year-old cadet at the Royal Naval College was publicly flogged when he tried to go home.

People needed enormous doses of self-righteousness to endure the shock of war. A chauvinistic industry, manufacturing foreign monsters, quickly expanded. A general in France, writing to a journalist, apologized that 'there has been only one atrocity lately and that was not a good one'. Not everyone was so meticulous. Newspapers competed for German atrocities to answer the clamour of their readers – 'like the clamor,' Shaw reported, 'of an agonizingly wounded combatant for morphia'. The whole country buzzed with stories of Germans tossing babies on the points of their bayonets; Germans burning field hospitals full of British wounded; Germans going into battle driving crowds of women before them; Germans making collections of fingers. Shaw searched for some practical line of reasoning to set against this hell. Would it really encourage recruitment? Surely it was kinder to those who had sons and husbands at the front *not* to insist that they must be horribly mutilated if they fell into enemy hands? 'Since you expect to go out soon, I really refuse to leave you troubled in spirit by that man with his eyes gouged out,' he reassured George Cornwallis-West. It was amazing how this totally blinded refugee careered around – he was far too quick for anyone to have seen, though all had heard of him. Elsewhere, a number of Belgian nurses whose hands everyone knew to have been scissored off by the Huns had, he was glad to see, grown new ones.

Among the baying patriots were the British disciples of Dr Mills. They could not tolerate Charlotte's refusal to assist this righteous war in any capacity 'except that of a reluctant taxpayer'. Worst of all in their eyes were her anxieties over poor Trebitsch. She felt a spring of joy on hearing that he had failed his medical examination. 'You will die prematurely,' G.B.S. assured him, 'at the age of 98 in a hotel lift, from ascending too rapidly.'

Shaw felt concern for all his translators – those other selves shredded in conflict. 'YOU AND I AT WAR CAN ABSURDITY GO FURTHER,' he had wired Trebitsch on 4 August. 'MY FRIENDLIEST WISHES GO WITH YOU UNDER ALL CIRCUMSTANCES.' Next day he and Charlotte went on to Torquay where they were to stay for a couple of months at the Hydro Hotel. 'This suits me pretty well too, as I have a lot of work in hand,' he told Beatrice Webb.

In a statement, drafted on 6 August, he set out the predicament as he saw it.

'We shall have to fight and die and pay and suffer with the grim knowledge that we are sacrificing ourselves in an insane cause, and that only by putting up a particularly good fight can we bring ourselves out of it with credit . . . For the present time there is only one thing to be done besides fighting . . . And that one thing is to set to work immediately to draft the inevitable Treaty of Peace which we must all sign when we have had our bellyful of murder and destruction.'

He accused the generals and politicians of being unable to think further ahead than the length of a bayonet, and he urged Beatrice Webb and other Fabians to cultivate 'long range firing more than you do, or you will leave forts unreduced in your rear which will undo half your work later on'. The real enemy was not Germany, he maintained, but jingoists and junkers in all countries. Therefore, in moments of optimism, he would represent the war as an opportunity of victory for the Suffragettes, the Irish volunteers and socialists everywhere.

Shaw judged the responsibility for war as lying almost evenly between British commercial adventurers and Germany's militarists, and denied that violation of Belgian neutrality was a *casus belli*. Using his new American literary agent Paul Reynolds, he placed an 'Open Letter to the President of the United States of America' in *The Nation* and the *New York Times*, appealing to him as 'the spokesman of Western Democracy' to rally the neutral powers for the purpose of demanding both sides to withdraw from Belgium ('the effect of our shells on Belgium is precisely the same as that of the German shells') and fight out their quarrel on their own territories. Behind this invitation lay a warning that history would judge Germany to have been the wrong side on which to intervene, and that Washington ('still privileged to talk common humanity to the nations') would inevitably chair the world conference that settled the peace.

The British press had been eager for Shaw's war contributions. But after three months, when he had vented his disgust on England and Germany as 'a couple of extremely quarrelsome dogs' and advised the soldiers in both armies to 'SHOOT THEIR OFFICERS AND GO HOME', many newspapers blacklisted him. 'In any ordinary time I should have been delighted to publish your letter with every word of which I agree,' wrote the editor of the *Manchester Guardian*, C. P. Scott, 'but at this horrible time one has to consider so many things which one would like to ignore . . . your letter would be highly disturbing to many minds. That of course is the object of it and a very excellent object. But I suppose one's duty now is to encourage and unite people and not to exercise and divide.' Shaw recognized the power of this call for suspending controversy in the face of national danger, but countered it with the argument that able-bodied soldiers in the trenches depended on able-minded civilians at home to guard their constitutional liberties. Soldiers must be protected while their backs were turned from those abuses of power – such as the suspension of by-elections – not necessary for the defeat of the enemy.

'I have sat at England's bedside during her delirium,' Shaw was to write. He saw himself as a doctor who reluctantly admits that his horror-struck patient may need chauvinistic drugs, but believes that the quality of his recovery depends upon their withdrawal as soon as possible. 'I do not grudge a mother the shelter of a lie any more than I grudge a soldier the shelter of a clump of briars,' he wrote; 'but the more thoroughly we realize that war is war, and death death, the sooner we shall get rid of it.' After the monthly casualty figures began to arrive affecting almost every family in the country (already in November there were 89,954 British casualties), then people would need some antidote. His *Common Sense about the War* was a complicated prescription prepared for those emerging from these bloody fantasies. On 14 November it appeared as a monumental supplement to the *New Statesman*. 'I have told the truth about the war,' Shaw claimed; 'and stated the democratic case for it.'

*

Until noon each day Shaw worked in the roof garden of the Hydro Hotel. Before lunch he would swim and after lunch continue working in his suite. Sometimes he went for rides in the car along the coast; sometimes he went and listened to Basil Cameron's concerts at the pavilion. After dinner he read.

It was impossible to think of anything except the war. Never can there have been a war in which the belligerents had such correct cases. Austria had the assassination of an Archduke; Germany the mobilization of Russia and the threatening articles of the Franco-Russian alliance; Britain the impeccable Treaty of 1839. All the provocations were valid according to the most accredited precedents. Academically, on all sides, the war was perfectly in order. 'I had to slave for months getting the evidence,' Shaw wrote to Alfred Sutro. ' . . . It makes me sick to recollect the drudgery of it all.'

The mood of the country was beginning to infiltrate Torquay. When a depressed Granville Barker came down for a few days, he and Shaw were threatened with shooting by a panicky coastguard as they walked along the beach. The hotel porter, a German who had registered as an enemy alien, was suddenly handcuffed and 'deported to the innermost centre of Britain – to Exeter, in fact' – so that he could not signal to German submarines.

Shaw needed to feel up to his chin in what was going on. Neither Asquith nor Grey, he believed, were the real spokesmen of their times. He hated Grey – 'a Junker from his topmost hair to the tips of his toes . . . [with] a personal taste for mendacity' – for his part in the sensational horror at the Egyptian village of Denshawai in 1906, when the British colonial power administered floggings, hangings and penal servitude for life after a rumpus arising from some pigeon shooting. This governing class was above listening to him. Shaw wanted his own class of men, Chesterton and Wells, Bennett and Bertrand Russell, to rise at the head of a popular movement and replace Asquith with someone such as Winston Churchill. He recognized that Churchill's anti-German pugnacity was enormously more popular in the country than the moral babble of Asquith. So he kept his eye on Churchill. Meanwhile 'our job is to make people serious about the war,' he wrote to Bertrand Russell. 'It is the monstrous triviality of the damned thing, and the vulgar frivolity of what we imagine to be patriotism, that gets at my temper.'

Shaw's position in *Common Sense about the War* was that of the Irishman who, when asked for directions, replies that he wouldn't start from here. It was given the Shavian dimension by the fact that England had not asked for directions. He was therefore obliged to step out dangerously into the traffic and transmit unsolicited signals.

He attempted to answer the question: what is the war about? It had erupted from a prodigious evil: that of mounting wealth throughout Europe untapped by any corresponding equitable distribution of this wealth. Borne on the soils and sighs of monstrous inequality this war had become a crude method of advancing social organization. Politicians still believed it was a question of Union Jacks and tricolours and Imperial Eagles – but 'there are only two real flags in the world henceforth,' Shaw wrote: 'the red flag of Democratic Socialism and the black flag of Capitalism.' The militarists of Europe had used this energy of dissatisfaction for their sport of war, and all the adventurous young men joined in. Shaw reasoned that the militaristic case led to what the militarists themselves most dreaded – a dramatic example was to be the collapse of tsardom and the rise of communism in Russia. 'The Democratic case, the Socialist one, the International case is worth all it threatens to cost,' he predicted. 'Democracy without equality is a delusion more dangerous than frank oligarchy and autocracy.'

Shaw's long-term aim was straight. He foresaw that the enormous demand for coal, cloth, boots, army rations, weapons, ammunition, transport vehicles, ships and all other accessories of war, would arrest the huge exports of capital and transform them into wages – besides doubling taxation on unearned incomes. He pointed out how the Government had already taken control of railways, bought up all the raw sugar, regulated prices, guaranteed the banks and achieved many of 'the things it had been declaring utterly and eternally Utopian and impossible when Socialists advocated them'.

During war we live in a political truce; in peacetime the political war begins again. Shaw wanted socialists to prepare for this struggle by ensuring that on enlistment labourers found themselves better fed, paid, clothed than before. He recommended the appointment of working-class representatives to the War Office, and the reform of the 'tyrannical slave code called military law' so that the soldier could serve as a citizen with all his rights intact.

This was Shaw's case for open diplomacy, full civil rights, a fair livelihood for the soldier and his dependants, and genuine working-class democracy in place of Asquith's Mutiny Acts which, even in time of peace, 'imprison Labour leaders and muzzle the Labour Press'. In his thirty years of public work Shaw had seen 'man after man in the Labour movement sell out because he could not trust his future to the loyalty of the workers,' he wrote, 'and I should perhaps have had to sell out myself long ago if I had not possessed certain powers as a writer which made me a little more independent than others'. Armed with this independence, 'I have put my best brains and skill at the service of the Labour cause'.

*

Shaw had modelled his *Common Sense about the War* on Tom Paine's *The Rights of Man*, and it blew up a similar dust-storm of abuse. Libraries and bookshops removed his works from their shelves; newspapers instructed their readers to boycott his plays. The editor of *The Clarion*, Robert Blatchford, described his manifesto as 'the meanest act of treachery ever perpetrated by an alien enemy residing in generous and long-suffering England'. At the Royal Naval Division the Prime Minister's son, 'Beb' Asquith, announced that he 'ought to be shot'. And former President Theodore Roosevelt called him a 'blue rumped ape' and lumped him with 'the unhung traitor Keir Hardie' among a 'venomous' herd of socialists, all 'physically timid creatures'. 'You are not so loved here as you were,' Granville Barker reported from New York. 'The "Common Sense about the War" raised you up many enemies and turned some of your friends very sour.'

Feeling themselves implicated, some writers reacted dramatically. The best-selling novelist W. J. Locke suddenly sprang up screaming: 'I will not sit in the same room with Bernard Shaw!' J. C. Squire put it to his readers that G.B.S. should be tarred and feathered. In an open letter, subtitled 'A Manual for the Haters of England', Henry Arthur Jones blasted him with an enormous vituperative sentence:

'The hag Sedition was your mother, and Perversity begot you. Mischief was your midwife and Misrule your nurse, and Unreason brought you up at her feet – no other ancestry and rearing had you, you freakish homunculus, germinated outside of lawful procreation . . .'

More painful to Shaw was the response of those he loved. Archer's son, whom from childhood Shaw had known as 'Tomarcher', sailed home from New York on the first available steamer to rejoin his volunteer corps and was sent to Flanders. 'It is a sickening business this sending lambs to the slaughter,' Shaw commiserated. But Archer, fiercely patriotic, felt differently.

Shaw had also hoped to get support from G. K. Chesterton. But Chesterton, who had been ill during late 1914 and early 1915, was 'hungry for hostilities'. The war excited the dark side of his nature. 'I have always thought there was in Prussia an evil will,' he wrote to Shaw. 'Of course there is an evil will in Prussia,' Shaw agreed. 'Prussia isn't Paradise. I have been fighting that evil will, in myself and others, all my life.' Chesterton's hatred seemed to Shaw the product of a mind in which the war had lodged as medieval fantasy. And to Chesterton, Shaw appeared equally unreal. 'I think you are a great man; and I think your first great misfortune was that you were born in a small epoch,' he wrote. 'But I think it is your last and worst misfortune that now at last the epoch is growing greater: but you are not.'

Wells too chimed in with the public outcry, describing G.B.S. as 'one of those perpetual children who live in a dream of make-believe . . . that he is a person of incredible wisdom and subtlety running the world.

' . . . It is almost as if there was nothing happening in Flanders. It is almost as if there was no pain in all the world . . . [he] flings himself upon his typewriter and rattles out his broadsides. And nothing will stop him. All through the war we shall have this Shavian accompaniment going on, like an idiot child screaming in a hospital . . . He is at present . . . an almost unendurable nuisance.'

'If I were a German, I should criticize the Berlin Government with equal fierceness for having made the war,' Shaw wrote to Trebitsch. In fact he did write 'The German Case Against Germany' in May 1916, but by that time he was widely regarded as a German sympathizer. 'I am not what is called pro-German,' he wrote, ' . . . neither am I an anti-German.' He insisted that a gentleman refused to hate his enemy in wartime. But this attitude had no comfortable place in a country exulting in the announcement that all German music was to be banned at concerts. People reminded one another how he had championed Wagner. Even 'his Fabian ideas of social reconstruction,' claimed the *Daily Chronicle*, 'are inspired by Berlinese notions of symmetry'.

His reasoning was impeccable; his offence emotional. 'In the right key one can say anything,' he wrote to Bertrand Russell, 'in the wrong key, nothing: the only delicate part of the job is the establishment of the key.' But many writers felt he had gone off-key. Henry James, who was soon to become a British citizen, claimed that he had not been able to read Shaw's *Common Sense* at all because 'his horrible flippancy revolts me'. Arnold Bennett, too, described as a 'disastrous pity' Shaw's 'perverseness, waywardness, and harlequinading'.

Shaw's jokes, such as his tip to those who wanted unconditionally to smash Germany that they should go about killing all her women, were his natural method of expression. 'If we did not die of laughter at the humours of war we should of horror,' he admitted to Robert Loraine; and to his sister Lucy he confessed: 'one has to learn to laugh at such things in war or else go mad.' He asked those who objected that his jokes did not fit the hour to ignore the 'imbecilities' of his style and fix on the content. But this was impossible. 'Shaw is often ten minutes ahead of the truth,' wrote Woodrow Wilson's brother-in-law Stockton Axson, 'which is almost as fatal as being behind the time.'

He felt his isolation. 'Thanks for your friendly hail,' he wrote acknowledging a letter from Bertrand Russell. 'It really is necessary for people who can keep their heads to pass the time of day occasionally lest they should begin to fear that they, and not the others, are the madmen.' Most members of the Dramatists Club refused to meet him at their lunches; and when James F. Muirhead, editor of *Baedeker*, resigned from the Society of Authors, because 'I cannot consent that any part of my affairs should be in any way under the control of a man of whom I think as I do of you', Shaw stepped down himself from the two committees at the Society of Authors where for the past ten years he had been the chief source of energy and initiative. Muirhead was an admirer of Shaw, counting the shocks he had given Britain over the past thirty years 'among the most salutary influences brought to bear on that country'. But by 1915 he was writing of his 'myopia of genius ... you really do not understand why you are at present a cause of offence to 99 out of every 100 people that I meet.'

It had needed courage to go on writing as he did. 'It was not easy,' Shaw admitted. 'I know of no other literary man of anything like his eminence who would have taken such treatment so good-naturedly,' wrote Desmond MacCarthy. Almost he seemed unperturbed. 'I am not afraid of unpopularity,' he told Beatrice Webb. He could not get angry with people he met – 'it breaks my back completely,' he explained in a letter begging not to be introduced to Lloyd George. But he was long-lastingly affected. Below the surface of his forbearance, layers of disillusion were forming. He would take imaginative revenge against this society by threatening it with his Zeppelin raid at the end of *Heartbreak House*, and by scoring victories over the 'Goddams' in the person of St Joan. He would recharge his optimism, too, by gazing through the heartbreaking facts into a haze of Shavian hypotheses. 'I don't expect anybody but myself to see as far as I do,' he told the Webbs – an expectation amply to be justified by the public's blindness over *Back to Methuselah*. Meanwhile, he kept his spirits whirring with colossal swanking. 'The longer I live the more I see that I am never wrong about anything,' he admitted to Wells.

He protected himself too with brighter paradoxes. The war, he complained, 'has made me excessively popular'. He became expert at converting every rebuff into another victory. 'All the forts opened fire on me,' he had reported to Stella Campbell who was touring *Pygmalion* in the United States; 'and they have capitulated one after the other . . . my enemies are my footstool.'

About those matters that might have stirred approval – his cheque for £200 to the Belgian refugees; his £20,000 (equivalent to £700,000 in 1997) contribution to the British War Loan – he kept uncharacteristically quiet. Partly it was a matter of self-respect, partly of outmanoeuvring those who wished to surround him with obloquy. 'Unless you make a reputation at once for being utterly impossible, implacable, inexorable, you are lost,' he was to advise his French translator, Augustin Hamon. But by making such a reputation, Shaw was becoming a lost man in politics.

'When war comes the time for arguing is passed.' But Shaw could not keep from arguing. He argued as other people in another war were to dig: for victory. Whenever he was criticized, he counter-attacked. When accused of giving propaganda ammunition to Germany he retorted that it was his accusers themselves who had done that, Germany having attacked him bitterly until it noticed similar attacks in England.

He had an answer for everything: often a wonderfully exasperating answer, formed in the conviction that it was as much his duty to face criticism as it was the soldiers' to face bullets. Full of the appalling slaughter at Neuve Chapelle and at the Gallipoli landing, he mocked the outcry that arose in the spring of 1915 over the sinking of a popular Atlantic liner, the *Lusitania*. Here at last was something small enough – the killing of saloon passengers – for the public imagination to grasp. He heartily welcomed it, and the execution of Nurse Edith Cavell, for the effect it would produce on the United States, the moral centre of the neutral world. 'I even found a grim satisfaction,' he afterwards wrote, 'very intelligible to all soldiers, in the fact that the civilians who found the war such splendid British sport should get a sharp taste of what it was to the actual combatants.' During the first Zeppelin raids he advocated that movable metal arches should immediately be placed in school play-grounds so that children might know where to run when the Zeppelins came. But before this suggestion was implemented, people accused him of defeatism, goading him into recommending a judicious bombardment of London. 'In fact if we had any sense we would bombard London ourselves, and demolish the Houses of Parliament and all the new government offices for aesthetic reasons just as we should demolish the slums for sanitary reasons.'

The most difficult long-term problem for Shaw was recruitment. There could be no denying that the Government's painting of the war as a simple scene of knight errantry, with England as Lancelot-Galahad, Germany as the wicked giant and Belgium as the beautiful maiden, had been wonderfully popular. But after three months of war fever, recruitment had begun to fall off, and with it, Shaw claimed, the justification for keeping the nation in its fool's paradise disappeared. 'The recruiting got on its feet again,' he wrote, once the War Office 'withdrew the silliest of its placards, and faced the necessity for higher pay and better treatment of recruits'.

Shaw wanted to bring the same people up to the same guns equipped with a far better arsenal of attitudes, motives, opinions; to place them in the same trenches looking forward without detestation to the soldiers opposite, and looking back with scepticism at the politicians who had arranged this grotesque firing line. 'The newspapers are so stupid that, simply because he's Mr Shaw, they won't report him – instead of running him as our leading patriot,' wrote Lytton Strachey.

The newspapers did send their reporters to his speeches, but only to see him hissed and mobbed. The German press had already described him as being persecuted in London, fearful of assassination, and living under house arrest with sentries at his doors. The failure of his speeches to provoke mobbing – 'reporters who were sent to see me torn limb from limb withdrew copyless' – was partly due to the nature of his audiences which mingled 'smart persons of the soulful type – Lady Diana [Manners] for example' with clusters of prominent Fabians. They were, in short, very like theatre audiences, full of young people in bright clothes, for whom he gave excellent performances without benefit of reviews.

Most people did not know by now whether he was a pacifist or a conscriptionist – in fact he was neither. 'It seems to me that all Socialists should advocate compulsory national service, both civil and military,' he wrote. 'But compulsory soldiering is another matter.' It was agonizing to see the short, red-faced, Cecil Chesterton got up in khaki and looking as if he could camouflage himself 'as a beetroot on a sack of potatoes by simply standing stock still'. Shaw himself would have cut a far sharper figure in uniform. In the first days of the war he had witnessed a company of volunteers come swinging along Gower Street and 'to my utter scandal I was seized with a boyish impulse to join them'.

As a 'superannuated person' he felt the inappropriateness of urging young people to take up arms. He criticized the Derby Scheme, which was bullying and cajoling men into voluntary service, for its 'appalling bad stage management' as well as the perverted economic and emotional basis on which it was founded. 'If the decision is to be Conscription, let it be faced, not as a temporary expedient,' he wrote in the *Daily News*, 'but as an advance in social organization.' But the second Conscription Act, which became effective on 25 May 1916, a week before the Battle of Jutland, was an emergency measure, with little considered legal character. Every military authority now became a press gang. The superstition that all Britons were free was kept up by a clause in the Act which reserved the liberty of people to refuse service on conscientious grounds, but neither the qualifications nor the treatment of this category of exempt person were defined. The result was that conscientious objectors were in practice rancorously persecuted.

All over the country there were cases of ill usage and vindictive sentences: and though Shaw 'should not have objected myself if I had been liable to serve', he was greatly exercised by this widespread maltreatment. He intervened in the case of an employee in the Education Department of the London County Council who was sent for miscellaneous duties to a military barracks, because the decision meant that 'public education is of no service to the country'. How could the Government reasonably claim that 'to take an educated man of special literary talent and aptitude from the work of national education, and to set him to sweep barracks, dig latrines, or wait at table on an officers' mess is to effect a stroke of national economy which will materially help to win the war'? He objected to the composer Rutland Boughton's work being described as 'not of the least national importance'. Despite all the musical entertainments for the troops it was as if military tribunals believed that fine art was frivolous and out of place in wartime, 'and that all a man needs to be a complete Englishman is football in peace, fighting in war, and a formula about his duty to King and Country to save himself the trouble of thinking'. He appeared as a character witness at a court martial on behalf of Clarence Norman, a journalist whom he had employed to make verbatim reports of his speeches in shorthand and who was imprisoned for two and a half years for ignoring his call-up papers. And he used the cases of two other conscientious objectors of recognized integrity, Stephen Hobhouse and Clifford Allen, to demonstrate the common misuse of the Government's legislation by military tribunals. 'If Mr Hobhouse is imprisoned for a single hour,' he wrote in Massingham's *Nation*, 'the law is broken and the good faith of the Government discredited.'

Shaw studied the evidence, took trouble to be legally exact, and chose each case with care. Repeated sentences for the same offence could with hard labour become sentences of death. A new crime had been created. 'It is worth noticing that Quakers have been persecuted with the utmost ferocity,' Shaw wrote, 'whilst pugnacious objectors who simply objected to this particular war and openly declared that they would fight in a class war have been treated with comparative indulgence.'

He also gave sympathetic advice to one or two deserters, destroying the letters for their protection and writing confidentially so as not to undermine his own position as 'an old advocate of compulsory service'. According to Rebecca West, he was like Swift rather than Shelley, and whatever he said, the effect of his words was to question rather than inspire the prosecution of the war. Watching him as he walked on to the platform and began speaking, she perceived that his virtue was getting thin with dilution. 'The passing of middle age has wiped the aggressive strangeness from his face, by mitigating with silver the redness of his hair and the pirate twist of his eyebrows, and has revealed a predominant quality of noble and unhysteric sensitiveness,' she wrote. 'In public life there is not time for such sensitiveness . . . when he began to speak, and the Irish accent shivered over his musical voice like the wind over a lake, one perceived another reason why he should not enter into politics.'

But Shaw always worked against the grain of his natural sensitivity. 'I go back to politics, religion & philosophy,' he had written to Stella Campbell. 'They give me frightful headaches, but satisfy my soul.' He felt that he knew now 'why Shakespeare and Swift were so bitter' after the wars against Philip II and Louis XIV. To overcome early bitterness he had removed himself from the intimate thing and forced his way into politics, but now felt uncertain of his place in public life: 'I no longer have any confidence in my notions of what this generation needs to have said to it,' he told Wells.

It seemed impossible to go on writing plays. In these days of clashing events, art could 'only be carried by the deaf,' Rebecca West acknowledged. 'And the artist who, like Mr Shaw, abandons it, at least shows that he has good hearing and is listening to the world.'

But he wanted a world that listened to him. The Fabian Research Department had commissioned Leonard Woolf to investigate the causes of the war. Against a background of Bloomsburgian scepticism, Woolf records, 'I did an immense amount of work on this.' His conclusions were published in 1916 as a book, *International Government*, to which Shaw supplied an American Preface.

Leonard Woolf argued that the first step towards the prevention of war must be the creation, as part of international government, of a supranational authority. His examination of the minimum requirements for such a body and his description of its probable structure comprised the first detailed study for the League of Nations. Shaw wanted to amplify this project. 'I find myself installed as a great prophet,' he pointed out. But he was a prophet without disciples, disestablished, needing affirmations. Shaw's League of Nations floats with its dreaming spires like an academy for supermen and superwomen, a sublime factory where Undershaft's weapons are manufactured by a professor of Greek and his wife, charged with defending democracy from those who, seeking mob popularity, sacrifice the eternal to the temporal. It is a Palace of Revolution, shimmering across the wilderness where Shaw preached, in which international matters are taken from those whose outlook is formed by official habits and given over to the welfare of us all. Finally, this visionary League stands as a temple for Shaw's paradoxes, his Abbey of Theleme, where all is magnificently opposed to the ordinary world.

4

TOURING THE TRENCHES

To a man who has produced a modern comedy, a campaign is child's play.

'Joy Riding at the Front', *Daily Chronicle* (7 March 1917)

The ordinary world, over which crawled tanks, U-Boats and Zeppelins, appeared scarcely less fantastical than Shaw's *phalanstère*. At the end of 1916 Lloyd George's new War Cabinet rejected Germany's peace proposals: but public opinion was veering more sympathetically towards 'Dearest G.B.S. (who is splendid about the war)' as Ellen Terry called him.

He had always found some supporters. Keir Hardie had 'felt the thrill' of his *Common Sense* and there had been the suggestion that a popular edition should be prepared by Arnold Bennett. When purged of the satirical absurdities readers accepted so literally, Bennett believed that Shaw's writing, which contained 'the most magnificent, brilliant, and convincing common sense that could possibly be uttered', would inaugurate a period of open discussion. Nothing came of this plan, though Shaw himself endorsed it. 'You, and I and Wells and Webb should be working together,' he urged Bennett late in 1916. '... However, it can't be helped – we must do the best we can ploughing our lonely back gardens.' Shaw had looked for a coalition of the intelligentsia, believing it was the duty of representatives of art and literature in all countries to keep moral considerations above the nationalistic level of the war. But though these writers gained no authority beyond what each could separately extort by the persuasiveness of his or her pen, at least the atmosphere had eased. Both J. C. Squire and W. J. Locke had come up and shaken Shaw's hand. Wells, too, having gone through 'disillusionment about the beneficence of our war-making', had reached conclusions similar to Shaw's.

Adelphi Terrace had been damaged in an air raid; at Ayot St Lawrence an anti-aircraft station, with searchlights and soldiers' sheds, was put up.

Shaw continued, as in peacetime, to divide his weeks between the two places. The villagers suspected him of being a spy. After all, he had been there less than a dozen years. They knew his car and motor-bicycle well enough; they knew his dog Kim, 'the village terror': but they did not know what to make of his remarks about this 'most *maddening* war'. Their suspicions began to blow away after the famous Hertfordshire Blizzard of 1915. 'He came out and worked hard with the other menfolk for days on end, sawing up trees which had been torn up by their roots and lay blocking the road,' one of them remembered.

It was the Zeppelin raids above all else that gave everyone a subject of conversation. One Zeppelin, after voyaging majestically over the Shaws' house on its way to London, was shot down near Ayot on 1 October 1916. Next morning Shaw rode off through the rain to see the wreckage – two lumps of twisted metal framework in a watery field splashed over all day by happy crowds. 'The police were in great feather,' he reported, 'as there is a strict cordon, which means you cant get in without paying.' But admission was cheap and well worth the price. 'I didnt half cheer, I tell you,' Shaw heard one girl remark. Nineteen bodies lay in a barn at the edge of the field. 'May I go in?' asked one woman. 'I would like to see a dead German.'

He had been enchanted by the sky-spectacle against the stars, with its magnificent orchestration. Having seen the Zeppelin fall like a burning newspaper, 'with its human contents roasting for some minutes (it was frightfully slow)', he had gone back to bed and was asleep in ten minutes. Reflecting on this, he confided to the Webbs: 'One is so pleased at having seen the show that the destruction of a dozen people or so in hideous terror and torment does not count . . . Pretty lot of animals we are!'

Charlotte wrapped herself round with remoter preoccupations. She felt proud of her husband's fame, but shared few of his interests; was wreathed in smiles, but seemed out of it all. To Virginia Woolf she appeared like a 'fat white Persian cat', which had rolled itself up on a cushion of Indian mysticism and gone to sleep. 'When she got me alone she tried to convert me,' Virginia wrote after a weekend together in the summer of 1916, 'and lent me little books about the Seutras, which she had to hide from Mrs Webb.' Unluckily for Charlotte, Beatrice Webb spied these little books beside her bed and nosed out their contents. 'The thesis is that by continuous meditation, or self-hypnotism, you will rise above the self-conscious self and realize the "God Power" within you,' Beatrice noted sceptically. Charlotte confided to Virginia Woolf that Beatrice, though a wonderful person, 'had no idea of religion'. She reacted with irritation to Charlotte's easy answers and (according to Virginia) 'jeered at poor old Mrs Shaw'. But it was the spectacle of *rich* old Mrs Shaw that aggravated

Beatrice – this woman whose decent restlessness had been stilled by a religious placidity removing her from 'all efforts to make things better for those who are suffering from their heredity or environment'. Beatrice had felt sympathetic to Charlotte when she was suffering over her husband's intrigue with Mrs Pat: what antagonized her now was Charlotte's lack of suffering. It was exasperating to see her beaming with overflowing contentedness in the middle of this appalling war: she appeared so little *inconvenienced* by it all.

At the beginning of 1917 Shaw began a new diary. 'I am going to try to keep it for a year,' he noted, 'as a sample slice of my life.' Altogether he kept it for ten days, and the sample slice it cut from his Ayot routine shows why he did not prolong it. There was no time. Every morning he was hectically occupied pouring out his 'intolerable opinions' to readers of the *Woman's Dreadnought*, *Somerset County Gazette*, and much of the American press. In the afternoons he and Charlotte would go into the garden where she sawed logs and he split them with a beetle and wedges. Sometimes he hurried through the village with his West Highland terrier; when he needed to go further he would set off for a spin and a spill on his motor-bike, and come rushing back to tighten nuts on the front wheel. At half-past four he allowed himself a cup of chocolate, while Charlotte drank tea. Then he would press on with his writing, often dealing with letters that Ann Elder had sent down from London. The second interval of the day – called dinner – began at half-past seven: then he would read and end the evening singing and playing the piano – Strauss's *Elektra* and Liszt's transcription of Beethoven's Ninth Symphony, Gounod's songs, arias from Mozart and Wagner operas, and a good deal of miscellaneous Berlioz, Elgar and Schumann. Finally he would go up to Charlotte's room to say good-night, and retire to his own bed with the *Economic Journal*.

Early that month he received an invitation from Douglas Haig, Com-mander-in-Chief of the British army, to visit the Front. 'Charlotte said I must go, as I ought to see this terrible thing for myself,' he noted. 'I grumbled that I should see nothing except a conventional round on which all the journalists are sent; but . . . my interest increased as the day went on.' By the following week he had come to feel that he 'was not free to refuse'.

In the blunted landscape, with its splintered trees, its signposts without villages, Shaw found some devastating material. Privately he confided to Lady Gregory that his week at the Front had been 'a most demoralizing experience'. Publicly in the *Daily Chronicle* he reported: 'I enjoyed myself enormously and continuously.' Both statements contained truth, and were a shorthand for his translation of a demoralizing early life into a career of sustained and serious comedy. He set out to console those who had husbands, brothers, sons, friends in the trenches, or who were themselves in training for that ordeal, with a display of black entertainment. He confidently assured everyone that there was no inevitability at the Front of being killed. On the contrary, death was very uncertain: the gas was crazily blown in the wrong direction, the high explosives were so appallingly imprecise that the 'Somme battlefield was very much safer than the Thames Embankment with its race of motors and trams'. The devastation was terrific yet many of the old towns had been badly in need of demolition. The cathedral at Arras looked finer as a ruin than when he had last seen it intact; the Little Square, too, had been most 'handsomely knocked about' and many old buildings, such as the Cloth Hall at Ypres, would gain a more beautiful existence in the memory than they had ever achieved in actuality.

Drudgery was one of the hardships of war: but the military provided many colourful diversions. Whenever an aeroplane sailed across the blue, delightful white puff-balls blossomed in the sky around it. Every night was Guy Fawkes Night. The guns hurled their fiery shells joyously into the air and set up a bombardment finer than Tchaikovsky's *1812*. He had difficulty believing that the man lying by the roadside was not a tramp taking a siesta during the booming and whizzing of this band music, but a gentleman who had lost his head. Behind the lines bayonet practice was conducted without the least blood lost, and imparted a bank holiday air to the place which really looked magnificent in the snow and sunshine. The trenches were crammed with pacifists, socialists and internationalists, all freed from theoretical illusions, all damning the party politicians with the greatest heartiness, and despite uncomfortable conditions, 'no more hopelessly wretched than I'. Fighting men, Shaw explained, escape the perpetual money worries of their civilian counterparts and the egotism of their preoccupation with commerce. At the Front something exciting was always happening that satisfied man's heroic instincts.

The horror is forced invisibly between the lines of Shaw's writing. War could do many things, he argued, but it could not end war. 'A victory for anybody is a victory for war.' He predicted that economic rather than military forces would eventually end it all, and that the only benefits of this vast calamity would lie in the employment of military virtues for a decently organized civilian life. For in the army, instead of your hand being against every man's and every man's hand against you, 'you are continually trying to get things done in the best possible way for the benefit of your comrades in arms, of your country, of the whole of which you are a part . . . whereas commerce is normally competitive and places your individual pocket before all the higher objects of ambition'.

Shaw's 10,000-word report of his experiences as a war tourist revived questions of his loyalty. One Member of Parliament demanded if this were the sort of man who should be officially invited to the British front line. 'I have always found that when any gentleman visits the front in France,' replied the Government spokesman, 'he comes back with an added desire to help the British Army and is proud of it.' The House of Commons filled with cheers – this time on Shaw's behalf. Many who had accused him of German sympathies now wondered whether he was actually in the service of the British Government to advertise the country's celebrated freedom of speech. Observing him to be 'an interesting man of original views', Haig had taken G.B.S. to a demonstration of experimental weapons. But though he later voted Haig 'the most interesting new writer of the past twelve months', Shaw privately judged him to be an academician of war 'trained socially and professionally to behave and work in a groove from which nothing could move him, disconcerted and distressed by novelties and incredulous as to their military value, but always steadied by a well-closed mind and unquestioned code . . . He made me feel that the war would last thirty years, and that he would carry it on irreproachably until he was superannuated.'

Though he greeted the news of the first revolution in Russia that March as 'a gain to humanity', and described the entry of the United States into the war on 6 April as a 'first class moral asset to the common cause against junkerism', Shaw felt politically gloomy. The Prime Minister had struck out his name from the 'list of persons with ideas' proposed for the Reconstruction Committee to advise on post-war social problems. He was still an outsider.

That July he was sixty-one. 'Any fool can be 60,' he explained to Trebitsch, 'if he lives long enough.' Charlotte had taken off for Ireland that summer for the sake of her lumbago, leaving G.B.S. to revert somewhat to his bachelor ways. He was seeing much of Kathleen Scott, formidable widow of the Antarctic explorer Robert Falcon Scott – a model Shavian heroine 'adventurously ready to go to the ends of the earth at half an hour's notice with no luggage but a comb with three teeth in it, and always successful'. Her job was sculpting – she made a bust and full-length statuette of G.B.S. in bronze. During periods of grass-widowhood G.B.S. was sometimes allowed to stay with Kathleen, especially after her marriage in 1922 to Hilton Young. 'We got on together to perfection,' he recorded.

After Stella had gone off to marry Cornwallis-West 'I really thought I was a dead man,' Shaw admitted, 'until I recovered my sanity by going right back to my economics and politics, and put in a hard stint of work on this abominable war.' But by 1917 he had come to feel that 'my bolt is shot as to writing about the war', and that he 'must get away for a moment from Fabians & politics or I shall go mad'. He decided to make for Ireland and enjoy the open skies of Parknasilla where Charlotte had been staying with her sister.

He arrived on 10 September and early the following month reported that he had been 'boating and bathing and making butter in a dairy ever since'. Work was impossible. 'In the Atlantic air one grows big and rank and Irish,' he wrote to Beatrice Webb. ' . . . this is the Land of the Free compared to England.'

5

THE RECRUITING OFFICER

> The art of the dramatic poet knows no patriotism.
>
> Preface to *Heartbreak House*

Early in the war Shaw's box office appeal had plummeted. 'The moment is not happily chosen for resuming the old Shavian capers, which were among the strangest by-products of the long peace,' declared A. B. Walkley in *The Times*. There were many who felt that theatres, museums and picture galleries should be converted into hospitals and barracks. To their surprise the stage grew incomparably popular between 1914 and 1918. Initially there were recruiting plays with patriotic songs which featured a harangue in the interval by the fire-eating chauvinist (and fraudulent financier) Horatio Bottomley. Shaw, who went to see one of Bottomley's perorations, reported: 'It's exactly what I expected: the man gets his popularity by telling people with sufficient bombast just what they think themselves and therefore want to hear.' For a specialist in the unexpected there was no audience. Producers and actor-managers ransacked their memories for out-of-date musicals and revues to exploit the bliss of soldiers who were happy to be no longer under fire and ready to be delighted by every young girl they saw, old joke they heard. London suddenly reverted to antique farces played in bedrooms with four doors and a window, identical to the bedrooms of flats above and below them, and all occupied by jealous husbands and wives mistaking one bedroom for another.

Shaw's contribution to this wartime theatre was four playlets that caricature, in juvenile fashion, the economic and social changes brought about in Germany, England and Russia by the Great War: and the lack of any change in Ireland. His characters are preposterously named –

464

Archdeacon Daffodil Donkin, Ermyntrude Roosenhonkers-Pipstein – and preposterously re-cast. Wives of fashionable architects take jobs as tea ladies; eminent medical men become waiters in hotels. Shaw made the plots of these playlets more ludicrous and their action more knock-about than any bedroom farce – then having appealed to the popular nonsensical mood, he tried to introduce a few moments of serious reflection. At the end of *The Inca of Perusalem*, for example, the absurd Inca, whose athletic moustache 'is so watched and studied,' we are told, 'that it has made his face the political barometer of the whole continent', ceases to be a lampoon on the Kaiser, and speaks in the tones of the Devil from *Don Juan in Hell*. Shaw wanted to remind his audiences that war had long been a favourite food of their imagination – when men had no battles to fight they played at war in their films and magazine stories. Since all of us were partly infected by the same passion, we could not simply blame one man, the Kaiser, for making us fight.

Shaw's satire against wartime England was an exaggerated stunt, *Augustus Does His Bit*, which he threw off in August 1916 to be performed in aid of the Belgians. This skit on high-born officialdom and crass bureaucracy at home (Lord Augustus Highcastle produces a bullet which had been flattened by contact with his skull) was well recognized at the Front, but it did not gain much recognition in London. 'He has simply evolved an idiot out of his own consciousness,' noted *The Times*, 'and ascribed to him the follies of his own imagination.'

Annajanska, his 'revolutionary romancelet', is a half-hour bravura piece written during three December days in 1917 – a month after the Bolshevik Revolution and a week before Russia signed an armistice with Germany. Shaw hands the derelict power created by the fall of tsardom back to a 'wild grand duchess'. He wanted to exploit the apparent paradox of the most radical event in his lifetime having erupted in the most politically backward country. The extravaganza may best be regarded as a present to Lillah McCarthy. It enabled her to make a startling entrance dragging in two exhausted soldiers, fire off several fusillades and dominate the Coliseum stage in a magnificent green and black Russian fur coat designed by Charles Ricketts. 'I went home very tired,' she wrote happily.

O'Flaherty, V.C. had been conceived in the summer of 1915 while staying with Lady Gregory at Coole ('the scene is quite simply before the porch in your house'). He had intended a four-handed light comedy (with small but important additional roles for a thrush and a jay) that would appeal to what he called 'the Irishman's spirit of freedom and love of adventure'. But as he wrote, a portrait emerged of the Irish character that 'will make the Playboy seem a patriotic rhapsody by comparison,' he apologized to Lady Gregory. ' . . . *C'était plus fort que moi*. At worst, it will be a barricade for the theatre to die gloriously on.'

Having been asked by Sir Matthew Nathan, Under-Secretary for Ireland, for help over Dublin Castle's disappointing recruitment campaign, he had taken a famous recent Irish exploit – the killing of eight German soldiers and capture of fifteen others singlehanded by Private Michael O'Leary – and Shavianized it for the stage. 'Incomprehensible as it seems to an Englishman, Irish patriotism does not take the form of devotion to England and England's king.' More effective, he reckoned, would be to advertise the war as an opportunity to travel abroad at the British Government's expense.

The enlargement of O'Flaherty's experience at the Front induces in him an unbearable realism. 'Knowledge and wisdom has come over me with pain and fear and trouble,' he says. 'Ive been made a fool of and imposed upon all my life.' He sees everything for what it is: Irish patriotism is mindless ignorance; Irish family life grows more terrible than life in the trenches; his Irish sweetheart, no longer the angelic colleen, is ruthless and mercenary; and his mother becomes an appalling termagant whose 'batings' at home have proved good training for O'Flaherty's acts of bravery in the army.

Shaw's happy ending was hardly adequate compensation for a recruiting play that has its hero exclaiming: 'Dont talk to me or any other soldier of the war being right. No war is right.' And: 'Youll never have a quiet world til you knock the patriotism out of the human race.' This was not what Sir Matthew Nathan had been expecting. He consulted General Sir John French, Commander-in-Chief of Home Forces and soon to be made Lord Lieutenant of Ireland, and, having brooded on it with him, wrote to say that they both believed the production should be postponed. It was a tactful letter. Any performance, he suggested, might lead to 'demonstrations' smothering the 'fine lessons' of the play.

O'Flaherty, V.C. received its first presentation on 17 February 1917 at Treizennes in Belgium. Robert Loraine was O'Flaherty and the other parts were played by officers of the Royal Flying Corps, while the men put on a performance of *The Inca of Perusalem*. Later that year Shaw himself read the play to a hospital full of wounded soldiers near Ayot. 'They gave me three cheers, and laughed a good deal,' he told Lady Gregory; 'but the best bits were when they sat very tight and said nothing.'

Though *O'Flaherty, V.C.* was not performed by the Irish Players until it had softened into 'A Reminiscence of 1915' at the end of 1920 – and then only in London – Shaw's reputation seemed to have come alive in Ireland. After seven years without a Shaw production, the Abbey Theatre staged what amounted to an extraordinary festival – seven Shaw plays between the autumn of 1916 and the summer of 1917. And what was happening in Ireland appeared to be happening in other parts of the world. The American manager William Brady had presented *Major Barbara* in New York; the British-born actor William Faversham had broken the box office records set by *Pygmalion* with his United States tour of *Getting Married*. Throughout Europe all manner of Shavian productions were appearing – *Androcles* in Stockholm, *Candida* in Budapest, *Pygmalion* in Warsaw, *Mrs Warren's Profession* in Helsinki, *Widowers' Houses* in Prague and *The Devil's Disciple* pretty well simultaneously in Copenhagen and Vienna.

In Britain too there was a recovery of interest in his work – *Man and Superman* had been performed in its entirety in Edinburgh, and half a dozen other plays were touring the country from Plymouth to Birmingham. The London theatre stood ready at last for a new drama from G.B.S. But he felt oddly undecided. He had begun a shorthand draft of a play, provisionally called *The Studio in the Clouds*, on 4 March 1916. 'I dont know what its about,' he wrote to Stella over thirteen weeks later. By the end of that year he had written a first act, 'filling the stage with the most delightful characters under the pleasantest circumstances,' he told William Archer. ' . . . I have left them there for months and months, hopelessly stuck. This has never happened before.' Later he changed the title to *Heartbreak House*. 'We must be content to dream about it,' he advised Lillah McCarthy in the summer of 1918. 'Let it lie there to shew that the old dog can still bark a bit.'

6

ANGLO-IRISH POLITICS

The government of one nation against its will by another nation raises no question of whether such government is good or bad: it is itself misgovernment, and would be bad even if it produced perfect order and mutual material prosperity . . . I object to being governed by a superior race even more than by an inferior one, so that the Englishman may take it as he likes, as superior, inferior or equal: I object to his governing me.

Shaw to Sá (4 November 1917)

'If you want to bore an Irishman, play him an Irish melody, or introduce him to another Irishman,' Shaw had written. ' . . . Abroad, however, it is a distinction to be an Irishman; and accordingly the Irish in England flaunt their nationality.' His original motive for leaving Ireland, like his mother's, had been economic: 'a necessary transfer of my business to a European metropolis'. The Irish Renaissance had changed the literary business potential of Dublin. But Dublin was still the city of his discontent. Returning there after more than thirty years, he saw that 'the houses had never been painted since and the little shops had eggs in the windows, with mice and rats running over them'. Later, after reading parts of *Ulysses*, he was to congratulate Joyce: 'It is a revolting record of a disgusting phase of civilization; but it is a truthful one,' he wrote in a letter to the book's publisher Sylvia Beach; 'and I should like to put a cordon round Dublin; round up every male person in it between the ages of 15 and 30; force them to read it . . . I have walked those streets and know those shops and have heard and taken part in those conversations. I escaped from them to England.' He wanted to dissolve that squalid past into a radiant future: and he advised Ireland to cease puffing her sails with the rhetoric of stale grievances, and replace her preoccupation over national divisions with an overall political emancipation.

Shaw separated Dublin from Ireland and overlaid biography with history. 'I am an Irishman and I have not forgotten.' What other person could have demanded, but be refused, membership of the Irish Convention; be offered, but decline, nomination to the Irish Senate; and accept the first presidency of the Irish Academy of Letters. He recommended that Ireland be established as a sanatorium where the English should be sent to gain flexibility of mind: and advised Britain to sell Ireland to the United States in order to pay off her national debt. He was to leave the country to 'stew in her own juice' by not returning there after 1923: then registered as a citizen of the Irish Free State twelve years later.

His career was studded with illuminating acts of generosity to Ireland. He campaigned with Lady Gregory to recapture Hugh Lane's pictures according to the wishes expressed in an unwitnessed codicil to Lane's will; and he promised the Lord Mayor of Dublin a donation of 100 guineas as his contribution towards a good municipal gallery to house them. He presented the Assembly Rooms at Carlow, which he had inherited from his uncle Walter Gurly, to the Catholic Bishop of Kildare and Leighlin for conversion into a technical school and was largely responsible for the Technical College which later developed on that site. He attempted to set up an Irish film industry to which he offered to give *Saint Joan*, being 'desirous that his plays shall employ and develop the dramatic genius of his fellow-countrymen and make Ireland's scenic beauties known in all lands'. Later he would hand the manuscripts of his novels to the National Library of Ireland and finally leave the National Gallery of Ireland one third of his residuary estate.

But Shaw's words spoke louder than his actions. He described Ireland's political debates as 'baby talk', her papers 'comics', her history mere 'police news', and her education a hellish training that prolonged the 'separation of the Irish people into two hostile camps'. He condemned the Censorship of Publications Act as an 'exhibition of Irish moral panic', and castigated her lack of birth control and sex education as a monstrous folly. He ridiculed the Gaelic League for loosening the country's hold on a vital twentieth-century acquisition, the English language, and counselled all patriots 'to go to bed and stay there until the Irish question is settled'. Nevertheless the fact that he was an Irishman 'has always filled me with a wild and inextinguishable pride'. He would have preferred to be 'burnt at the stake by Irish Catholics than protected by Englishmen'. And as a cure for the bad blood flowing from the unhappy historical marriage of England and Ireland, he prescribed a parting by consent rather than absolute divorce, together with a legal wand of oblivion moved over all past warring. To nurture malice, Shaw warned, 'is to poison our blood and weaken our institutions with unintelligent rancor'.

Shaw used 'every device of invective and irony and dialectic at my command' to assuage Ireland's longing for freedom. He had merged the subjects of divorce legislation and the constitutional independence of nations when covering the Parnell scandal of 1890. Home Rule had suddenly come within reach when a majority of Irish Members of Parliament pledged to the issue had been returned to Westminster. But at the height of his leadership of the Irish Party, Charles Parnell had been cited as co-respondent in a divorce case involving the wife of another Irish Member of Parliament and his political future seemed ruined. In letters to *The Star*, Shaw had argued that 'the whole mischief in the matter lay in the law that tied the husband and wife together and forced Mr Parnell to play the part of clandestine intriguer, instead of enabling them to dissolve the marriage by mutual consent, without disgrace to either party'. He advised Parnell to 'sit tight' and urged the Irish Party to unite behind him – otherwise the Liberal Government would exploit the disunity and abandon its commitment to Home Rule. The verdicts of antiquated laws, he added, 'can produce no genuine conviction of its victims' unfitness for public life'. Similarly repugnant was the legally enforced tie between England and Ireland, he implied, where under the Coercion Act 'constitutional reformers are driven to employ all the devices of criminals'.

In the 'Preface for Politicians' which he attached to *John Bull's Other Island* in 1906, Shaw had predicted that 'we can do nothing with an English Government unless we frighten it . . . under such circumstances reforms are produced only by catastrophes followed by panics in which "something must be done".' Ireland's catastrophe was the 'ghastly' Easter Rising of 1916. Shaw made clear his support for 'any Irishman taken in a fight for Irish independence against the British Government, which was a fair fight in everything except the enormous odds my countrymen had to face'. He felt anxiety lest relations between the two countries be fatally poisoned by acts of reprisal from the frightened English Government. 'The men who were shot in cold blood after their capture or surrender were prisoners of war,' he objected, after twelve of the insurgents had been executed.

Shaw's most quixotic intervention into Anglo-Irish politics was on behalf of Roger Casement. Casement had taken advantage of the war to seek help from Germany for the cause of Irish independence, but on the eve of the Easter Rising he was captured by the British as he stepped ashore in Ireland from a German submarine. Feeling in England ran high against Casement who, as a British subject, would inevitably be found guilty of high treason. Much of the money for his defence was raised in the United States. In England writers as various as Conan Doyle and Arnold Bennett appealed for clemency on grounds that ranged from Casement's mental health to Britain's political expediency. Beatrice Webb noticed that, when Charlotte spoke in support of him, her 'eyes flashed with defiance'. So Beatrice took Casement's old friend, Alice Green, who was helping to organize his defence, to see the Shaws. It was a painful meeting. Alice Green desperately needed money to engage a first-rate defence lawyer: Shaw insisted that, since no credible denial of the facts was possible, paying lawyers to come up with technical ingenuities and exchange legal compliments would be throwing money down the drain. Instead he proposed a 'daring frontal attack on the position of the Crown'. Casement was to conduct his own case, admit the facts, plead not guilty and apply as an Irish Nationalist to be held as a prisoner-of-war. Alice Green explained that Casement was extremely ill and incapable of handling a court full of lawyers: in which case, Shaw retorted, 'we had better get our suit of mourning'. So the meeting broke up: Alice Green retiring in tears; Beatrice feeling a fool for having intervened; and G.B.S. striding into his study to compose a speech for Casement which would 'thunder down the ages'.

Beatrice accused Shaw of conceitedly playing word games with the life of this poor man as if it were a 'national dramatic event'. But Casement himself was delighted with the speech. 'I shall be so grateful if you will convey to Bernard Shaw my warmest thanks,' he told the Sinn Fein sympathizer Gavan Duffy; 'his view is mine, with this exception – that I should never suggest to an English court or jury that they should let me off as a prisoner of war, but tell them "You may hang me, and be damned to you".'

Such a man was beyond saving. Casement later regretted not using what he called 'the only defence possible, viz., my own plan and that of G.B.S.' There had been nothing to lose: but he was dissuaded by Alice Green and other friends, found guilty, and sentenced to be hanged. Only then did 'the virtually dead man' rise to make his own lengthy speech from the dock, using a portion of what G.B.S. had written for him. In the fortnight between the court's verdict and the date of sentence, Shaw tried hard to win Casement a reprieve. 'I cannot make matters any worse than they are,' he told H. W. Nevinson, 'and there is just an off chance that I might make them better.' He wrote to *The Times* which rejected his letter, published correspondence in the *Manchester Guardian* and the *Daily News*, and anonymously drafted a petition to Asquith warning him that hanging would make Casement a national hero. Casement was hanged on 3 August 1916.

To those claiming that the unification of Ireland would result in Protestants and Catholics cutting one another's throats, Shaw had replied that 'civil war is one of the privileges of a nation'. Such extermination was 'too much to hope for,' he added darkly, though mankind 'still longs for that consummation'. If 'hatred, calumny, and terror have so possessed men that they cannot live in peace as other nations do, they had better fight it out and get rid of their bad blood that way'.

'What I have dreaded all along,' he told Horace Plunkett, 'is the usual political expedient of a settlement that is no settlement.' To argue for his own federal solution, he accepted an invitation from the editor of the *Daily Express*, a newspaper specially hostile to him during the war, to tell its readers how to unravel the Irish problem. His series of articles, which were later issued in Dublin and London as a pamphlet, *How to Settle the Irish Question*, assembled a brilliant array of arguments for the inevitability of federation. This conclusion, which he described as 'Home Rule for England', possessed similar magical properties to the triple alliance in *Common Sense about the War*, and he frequently edged Wales out of the equation to achieve his mystical three-in-one – 'the federation of the three nations (four if you count the Welsh)'. He then reinforced this combination by building three parliaments – National, Federal and Imperial – in his imagination for 'the three kingdoms alike'.

After eight deliberating months Plunkett's Convention, which had been set up by Lloyd George, voted for an Irish Parliament with authority over the whole country. 'The story becomes more thrilling as it draws to an end,' Shaw wrote to Plunkett in March 1918 after reading the proof sheets of his secret report to the King. '. . . I await the report with some nervousness.' The moment came: the report made no sound. The Government had 'funked it', and Shaw was left feeling that it had been another instance of the unreality in Dublin politics.

The extreme nationalist party Sinn Fein, which had refused to partici-
pate in Plunkett's Convention, rapidly evolved into a political power as
Parnell's old Irish Party passed away. Sinn Fein refused to attend Westminster and formed their own assembly (Dáil Éireann) in Dublin, representing
a completely independent Republic of Ireland which was immediately
declared illegal by the British Government.

Shaw had advocated federation as early as 1888 and he was still advocating it more than thirty years later. The flaw in his logic, as he had once
expressed it himself, lay in the problem not being 'one of logic at all, but of
natural right'. England's extreme procrastination had produced Ireland's
extreme reaction, leaving Shaw's consistency as a remnant of historical
academicism. He disliked Sinn Fein's glorification of nationalism: yet
thirty years before he had written of nationalism being 'an incident of
organic growth [which] . . . we shall have to accept'. The young Shaw
believed that 'like Democracy, national self-government is not for the good
of the people: it is for the satisfaction of the people.' The older Shaw
warned against national independencies and neutralities which were set
up 'not by the internal strength of a nation's position, but by the interested
guarantees of foreign Powers'.

In his 'Preface for Politicians' he had diagnosed the condition of Ireland
as being like that of 'a man with cancer: he can think of nothing else . . .
A healthy nation is as unconscious of its nationality as a healthy man of
his bones. But if you break a nation's nationality it will think of nothing
else but getting it set again. It will listen to no reformer, to no philosopher,
to no preacher, until the demand of the Nationalist is granted . . . That
is why everything is in abeyance in Ireland pending the achievement of
Home Rule.'

Ireland's cancer had worsened and now demanded the fiercer remedies
of separatism. Shaw regarded the policies of Sinn Fein as symptoms of
the disease and not parts of a homoeopathic medicine. 'Sinn Fein means
We Ourselves: a disgraceful and obsolete sentiment, horribly anti-Cath-
olic,' he wrote in *How to Settle the Irish Question*. ' . . . Ireland is the
Malvolio of the nations, "sick of self-love", and . . . Sinn Fein's delight is
to propagate this morose malady.'

Ireland eventually placed its future in the hands of the quacks and
windbags of the two rival religions, and in tearing itself away from England
tore itself apart. Watching this process was to be intensely painful for
Shaw. In his fashion he was devoted to Ireland. But he had become the
reformer, philosopher and preacher to whom no one listened.

7

CASUALTIES OF WAR

Literature should never be at war.
Shaw to Henry Newbolt (25 July 1920)

The Shaws did not enter the revelry on Armistice Day. They stayed at Ayot. These years of helplessness seemed to have made a cavity within G.B.S. 'Every promising young man I know has been blown to bits lately,' he told Lady Mary Murray; 'and I have had to write to his mother.' He had written to Stella Campbell at the beginning of 1918 when her son Alan Campbell was killed by the last shell from a German battery. 'My beloved Beo is killed,' she had scribbled to him – but he could not find words of polite consolation. 'I cant be sympathetic: these things simply make me furious,' he burst out. ' . . . Oh, damn, damn, damn, damn, damn, damn, damn, damn, DAMN DAMN! And oh, dear, dear, dear, dear, dear, dearest!'

A month later the news reached him that Robert Gregory had been shot down in his plane and was dead. In a letter prefiguring Yeats's two poems 'An Irish Airman Foresees His Death' and 'In Memory of Major Robert Gregory', he wrote consoling Lady Gregory: 'To a man with his power of standing up to danger – which must mean enjoying it – war must have intensified his life as nothing else could . . . I suppose that is what makes the soldier.' He used Alan Campbell's death – used Stella's reaction – to bring Augusta Gregory comfort. 'Like Robert he seemed to find himself in doing dangerous things. His mother thinks he got all the life he wanted out of the war and nothing else could have given it to him.'

'I was hoping for a letter from you,' Lady Gregory replied. 'I knew it would be helpful.'

Most griefs were beyond help. 'I know you will be very sorry for us,' J. M. Barrie had written after his much-loved godson George Llewelyn Davies had been shot dead near Ypres. Though also living in Adelphi Terrace, he could not bear to give the news in person, but pushed his note through the door of the Shaws' apartment. When he read it, Shaw wept.

William Archer was another who suffered bereavement. His son 'Tom-archer' was wounded at Mount Kearnel and died in a German hospital not long before the Armistice. 'He left his young widow to take his place in his parents' affection, the newly beloved daughter succeeding to the newly lost beloved son,' Shaw recorded. 'Yet Archer was loth to let the son

go . . . and even experimented unsuccessfully in those posthumous conversations in which so many of the bereaved found comfort. And so, between
daughter and son, the adventure of parentage never ended for Archer.'

And there were others, such as the hopelessly unsoldier-like Cecil
Chesterton who had visited Shaw before leaving for the Front and died
soon afterwards from trench fever. 'It is impossible to describe what I
used to feel on such occasions.'

Whenever possible Shaw used his comic energy to overcome his feelings. He lectured Robert Loraine who had been shot in the small of his
back ('the bullet coming out of his collar bone after going up through
his lung and knocking his heart into his left elbow') on the importance of
being kept 'in the lowest spirits, as laughing cannot be good for shrapnel
in the lung'. In the summer of 1918 Loraine was again wounded, and his
left kneecap being shattered, advised that his leg might have to be amputated. 'If the worst comes to the worst, I suppose one can play Hamlet
with a property leg,' Shaw calculated. ' . . . an artificial leg of the best
sort will carry you to victory as Henry V. If you . . . are lame, it means a
lifetime of Richard III, unless I write a play entitled *Byron*.' As for flying,
'when it comes to aerial combat, the more of you that is artificial the
better'.

Loraine's leg was saved. But to St John Ervine, who did lose a leg that
summer, Shaw sent hasty congratulations on his being 'in a stronger
position'. Having two available legs, when had Shaw himself ever groused
because he did not have three? 'You will have all the energy you have
hitherto spent on it to invest in the rest of your frame. For a man of your
profession two legs are an extravagance,' G.B.S. assured him. ' . . . You
are an exceptionally happy and fortunate man, relieved of a limb to which
you owed none of your fame, and which indeed was the cause of your
conscription; for without it you would not have been accepted for service.'

Such black parodies of the Shavian dialectic were 'the cheering remarks
one makes now to the sacrifice of this horrible war'.

*

The war also finished off the marriage between Granville Barker and
Lillah McCarthy. They had gone to the United States where Barker 'fell
madly in love – really madly in the Italian manner'. The Helen who had
enchanted him was an occasional poet and minor novelist, the wife of
Archer Milton Huntington, heir of a railroad fortune, who had provided
a guarantee against loss for Barker's theatrical season in New York.

Barker had returned to England in June 1915 promising Lillah that his
affair with Helen Huntington was over. He was some £5,000 (equivalent
to £170,000 in 1997) in debt, but £2,000 of this was owed in royalties to

G.B.S. who immediately wrote it off. After joining a Red Cross unit, Barker drove over to France – then in September headed off back to the United States, this time to give a series of lectures paying off his debts. He had made what Shaw called a resolution to devote himself to poverty and playwriting. 'I cannot very well remonstrate, as I have been for years urging him to stick to his own proper job of writing plays and leave production and management to people who cant do anything else,' Shaw explained to Pinero that October. ' . . . Meanwhile Lillah is at a loose end.'

On his way to the States, Barker had written to Lillah: 'my dear wife – I love you very much if you please – and I'm not very far from you. Distance doesn't mainly count.' But he was also corresponding with Helen, and instead of returning to England at the end of the lecture tour he sent Lillah a letter asking for a divorce. She went, 'all frozen on a cold January night', to Shaw's flat in Adelphi Terrace. He 'made me sit by the fire. I was shivering . . . presently I found myself walking with dragging steps with Shaw beside me . . . up and down Adelphi Terrace . . . he let me cry. Presently I heard a voice in which all the gentleness and tenderness of the world was speaking. It said: "Look up, dear, look up to the heavens. There is more in life than this. There is much more." '

Back with the Red Cross in France, Barker asked Shaw to act as his agent to procure the divorce. Since Lillah had already made him her confidant, he was placed in an awkward position. He went to work instructing Barker to write Lillah a letter her lawyers could use, advising Lillah what he had done, what Barker was doing, and what she should do – which was to get someone to counsel her as he was counselling Barker. Accordingly she chose J. M. Barrie. He, like Shaw, believed that the domestic crockery had been too badly broken to be worth mending, but his advice was swamped by Lillah's emotionalism. Was it likely, she demanded, that Barker knew his mind better than his own wife did? Once this affair was over, he would be coming back to her. This put Barrie's and Shaw's arguments into perpetual check, for it was impossible to recommend anything without offering Lillah a 'vulgar insult'. Shaw tried to hand her the initiative. 'Quite seriously, I have come to the conclusion that you had better get rid of Harley . . . as you are now at the height of your powers, and . . . I gravely doubt whether Harley is fit for married life at all . . . It is in your power to demand your release; he cannot refuse it.'

Barker had expected everything to be cleared up by the spring. He sailed back to the United States and continued fuming impatiently. 'What in heaven's name she is waiting for I don't know. I really believe she has some idea in her head that no divorce is complete without a scandal.'

Poised between Lillah's obduracy and Barker's exasperation, 'I had a difficult time of it,' Shaw afterwards admitted. Once conscription was brought in, Barker returned to Britain, and went to an officer cadet school in Wiltshire. Many of these summer and autumn weekends he spent at Ayot nervily plotting divorce tactics with G.B.S. and Charlotte or with Barrie in London. Driven mad by the delay he implored Shaw to offer Lillah a settlement of five or six hundred pounds a year for life. Since Barker had no money, Lillah immediately realized that he must be in collusion with Helen – and informed the unsuspecting Archer Huntington. 'There was an almighty explosion at the other end,' Shaw later reported, 'and Helen never forgave me for being, as she thought, solely responsible for Lillah's letter.'

Barker's decree was made absolute in the late spring of 1917; Helen's in the summer of 1918. On 21 June that year G.B.S. and Helen met for the first time: and detested each other. 'The guilty pair are not yet married,' Shaw reported to Lillah. ' . . . When it happens I will let you know as soon as I know myself.' They were married on 31 July, but let Shaw know nothing. 'I surmise that you are married; but it is only a surmise,' he wrote to Barker on 26 August. 'It is desirable that your friends should be in a position to make a positive affirmation on the subject. An affectation of ecstasy so continuous as to make you forget all such worldly considerations is ridiculous at your age.'

Shaw was not to know that they had both altered their ages, Helen reducing hers by almost eight years, on the marriage certificate. They wanted to free their lives from the sort of considerations he was emphasizing, and start again. Charlotte disapproved of Barker's divorce as setting a precedent for G.B.S., and she blamed Helen for introducing such unpleasantness into all their lives. Shaw tried to take the long-term view and, during a visit to them near the end of 1918, read out part of his new play *Back to Methuselah*. But 'it has never seemed quite so tedious before,' he apologized afterwards to Barker; ' . . . it was rather hard on Helen to have such a depressing beginning of my playreading.'

It was the end rather than a beginning. 'Virtually we never met again,' Shaw wrote. After her marriage in 1920 to the botanist Frederick Keeble, Lillah pretty well left the stage. 'You must begin a new career as a new woman,' Shaw was to tell her. And she responded: 'Life begins again. I find new delights every day & am re-born.'

But it seemed to Shaw that Barker's seclusion was a genuine loss to the theatre: and then there was the personal loss. 'I could not intrude when I was not welcome.' He was prepared to keep out of their way 'for six months or six years' if necessary. But after six years, 'the devil entered into me'. Though he had not seen them during this time, he had picked up various reports. They had bought a Jacobean mansion in Devon called Netherton Hall (renamed by Shaw Nethermost Hell). Here, his name newly hyphenated, his socialism cast off, and attended by fifteen servants (including a liveried footman) Granville-Barker completed his perfectionist work on the sociology of the stage, *The Exemplary Theatre*, and an unperformed play called *The Secret Life*. 'We shall have to keep on insulting him for his sterility,' Shaw commanded St John Ervine, 'or he will be dead before he gets another play on to the stage.' He tried to stir him up by likening him to Swinburne at Putney; by spurring William Archer on to 'tell him to do something thoroughly vulgar: he needs contact with earth'; and by inventing a Barker Relief Expedition consisting of Lawrence of Arabia, Thomas Hardy and J. M. Barrie.

In May 1925 Shaw was asked to give a vote of thanks after Granville-Barker's address on the theatre at King's College in the Strand. 'I praised Barker's speech to the skies and said that his retirement from the stage to become a professor was inexcusable,' Shaw told Hesketh Pearson. Barker was now placed in a very ticklish position. Lord Balfour, who was in the chair, rose to the rescue with a clever closing speech during which Shaw suddenly began to feel in great pain – 'as if my backbone had turned into a red-hot poker' was how he described it to Lady Rhondda. He was determined to sit it out. Somehow he reached home on foot. 'I really thought I was done for.' Charlotte removed him to Ayot where he lay helpless on his bed until one day, a month later, with a great effort of will he decided to walk down the road – and instantly the pain vanished. Later on he related this experience to Lady Colefax who revealed that Helen Granville-Barker had been sitting exactly behind him, not three feet away, leaning forward with her eyes glued to his backbone. 'I have never seen such hate in any eyes before.'

This story enabled Shaw to cast Helen as a witch who had placed her spell on Granville-Barker so that 'he ceased to be the independent human being we had all known'. This was less disconcerting to him than the belief that they were both perfectly happy. In his position 'I should regard myself as a damned soul,' Shaw remarked to Archer. But Barker had been retreating into his 'natural Henry Jamesism' before he met Helen. She re-created him as a fairy-tale Prince. Every syllable Shaw uttered threatened to dissolve this fantasy. All communication with him was therefore shut down until early in the 1930s when Lillah McCarthy invited Shaw to contribute a Preface to her memoirs. He arranged for the publisher to send Granville-Barker this Preface (which contained a celebration of Lillah's historic stage collaboration with Barker, as well as biographical sidelights on their marriage and divorce). As a result Barker suddenly turned up at Ayot demanding that the book be withdrawn.

Barker wished to forget Lillah whose very name disturbed Helen. 'Let it alone,' he had written to Shaw. Rather to his dismay, Lillah's book was to appear without any reference to him: his past had been obliterated. Twenty minutes after leaving Ayot he returned to take an effusive farewell of Charlotte: and this was the last time they saw him.

Shaw could not quench his pleasure on learning of Helen's fury when, Frederick Keeble being knighted, Lillah became Lady Keeble. Helen wanted a glittering knighthood for her husband, but had she not cut him off from all commerce with the theatre might he not have been given one? Or so G.B.S. believed. 'Cannot you persuade Mr Granville-Barker to stay here and produce Shakespeare,' Raymond Mortimer was to ask Helen years later during one of her last visits to London. To his horrified embarrassment the old lady burst into tears. 'Everyone blames me,' she answered, 'but it is not my fault: it is Harley's.'

Shaw blamed Helen. When Barker died in 1946 the shock 'made me realize how I had still cherished a hope that our old intimate relation might revive'. In a letter to the *Times Literary Supplement* enclosing an old photograph of his friend he had taken in the days of their intimacy, he was to quote Swinburne:

> Marriage and death and division
> Make Barren our lives.

*

This was a good epitaph for a war whose survivors would always be avenging their wounds. Many people have died 'in simple horror, mercifully without quite knowing it,' Shaw wrote to Henry Salt whose wife Kate died early in 1919. Janet Achurch had also died. 'So that adventure is over,' Shaw wrote to Charles Charrington, '. . . Now Janet is again the Janet of 1889, and immortal. Better that than half dead, like me.'

Another casualty was Shaw's sister Lucy. She had never wholly recovered from the death of her mother. Suffering from a 'nervous irritation' she was looked after by Eva Schneider, the daughter of the German family she had lodged with in Gotha. Shaw helped to arrange Eva's exemption from deportation through repeated applications to the Home Office establishing her as his sister's permanent nurse-companion. Financially he was conscientious over Lucy's needs, though otherwise 'I am forced to neglect her as I am forced to neglect everything else'. He had seen most of her when he was seeing most of Stella. They had used Lucy's home as one of their meeting places, enabling Lucy to boast that 'among my most frequent visitors is Mrs Patrick Campbell'. Shaw complimented Stella on having 'brought out the nice side of Lucy that I haven't seen since she was a girl'.

Lucy's tuberculosis was no longer active but her apprehension over the Zeppelin raids seemed to be killing her. 'She is in bed, fearfully ill,' Shaw notified Stella. ' . . . [Her] address for the moment is 2 Grove Park, Camberwell Grove . . . Later, the Crematorium, Golders Green.' Kept alive by the devotion of Eva, she somehow pulled through and in the Easter of 1917 the two of them moved to Sussex Lodge, a pretty house on Champion Hill in south-east London. Lucy had reckoned that, being close to an anti-aircraft battery 'we shall always know when the Zepps are on the way' and this would be a comfort. She had not realized that they were also near a bombing exercise ground and within sound of the gun testing at Woolwich Arsenal. Amid the continuous din, 'we didn't know whether a raid was on or not'. The booming of the big defence gun in the next field 'which seemed to blow the house away every time it went off', the noise of exploding bombs and the terrifying sight of a Zeppelin descending through the sky in flames was too much for her. 'I could not stand the strain.'

Shaw then rented a house at Okehampton in Devon where Lucy and Eva travelled in the summer of 1917. Despite eating almost nothing and going nowhere she had become 'a very expensive person,' she remarked wryly – '*my brother indulges me in any extravagance I express the least wish for*'. Shaw kept on Sussex Lodge with a caretaker and, a few weeks after the Armistice, Lucy returned in an ambulance to London. She was slowly starving herself to death. Eva did what she could to persuade her, spoonful by spoonful, to keep alive; and Mrs Pat sent all sorts of delicacies from Fortnum & Mason.

After Lillah's wedding on Saturday 27 March Shaw went round in the late afternoon and sat by Lucy's bed. 'I am dying,' she told him. 'Oh no,' he replied conventionally: 'you will be all right presently.' He took her hand and they were silent. 'There was no sound except from somebody playing the piano in the nearest house (it was a fine evening and all the windows were open), until there was a faint flutter in her throat. She was still holding my hand. Then her thumb straightened. She was dead.'

The doctor informed him that she had been suffering from shell-shock and become anorexic. 'My body to be cremated if possible and the ashes scattered,' she had noted in her will. 'No funeral, no flowers, no mourning.' Shaw arranged for a private cremation, like their mother's, at Golders Green. But finding the church crowded with people, he made up 'a sort of funeral service' of his own.

> Fear no more the lightning-flash
> Nor the all-dreaded thunder-stone.

Remembering the Zeppelins and awful guns that had made her want to die, Shaw ended the service with the dirge from *Cymbeline*. Lucy burnt with a steady white light, like a wax candle.

FOURTEEN

I

SOME HINTS ON THE PEACE

It is to be impressed on all officers and men that a state of war exists
during the armistice.

The Times (21 November 1918)

The Cabinet had already decided on a quick post-war general election. A
few days after the Armistice, Lloyd George dissolved Parliament and
announced 14 December 1918 as polling day. It was a degrading election,
exploiting people's hatred of the Germans and their delirious gratitude
for peace, to grab a renewed mandate for the old coalition of Tories and
Liberals. To cries of 'Vote for the Man who won the War', and 'Make
Britain a fit country for Heroes to live in', the electioneering was hurried
through before the heroes themselves had a chance of getting their
opinions known, or the opposition (silenced so long by the Defence of
the Realm Act) make itself effectively heard. 'I feel physically sick when
I read the frenzied appeals of the Coalition leaders . . . to hang the Kaiser,
ruin and humiliate the German people, even to deprive Germany of her
art treasures and libraries,' Beatrice Webb wrote in her diary. 'The one
outstanding virtue of the Labour Party . . . is its high sense of international
morality.'

Shaw, now in his sixty-third year, dropped almost all his engagements
to go campaigning. He toured the country, speaking every day to enormous
crowds of working people at Liverpool and Manchester, Birmingham and
Wakefield, Leicester and Wolverhampton. He spoke in support of Ramsay
MacDonald, who had preferred to resign his leadership of the Labour
Party rather than endorse Grey's foreign policy. He warned the electorate
against making it a Jingo versus Pacifist contest: voters must look for the
solid brickwork under all that political whitewash. He gave them facts; he
gave them figures: more than 50,000 German children had died in 1917
alone, the civilian mortality rate had increased by thirty-seven per cent –
and 'these are only the deaths'. He was to call for the raising of the Allied
blockade of Germany which Lord Balfour had declared 'cannot cause the
death of a single civilian' but which later caused 763,000 persons to die
of malnutrition, 'a polite name for starvation'. Did they want *more* revenge?
'When we break a German's leg with a bullet and then take him prisoner,'

he explained, 'we immediately set to work to mend his leg, to the astonishment of our idiots, who cannot understand why we do not proceed to break his other leg.'

Britain was vibrating with exultation over the most magnificent military triumph in her long record of victories. It was enormously important, Shaw insisted, that she should check the evil that could easily fester after the guns had stopped, and 'set the world an example of consideration for vanquished enemies'. Surely we wanted to prosper by restoring trade with our best customer?

Shaw's series of campaign speeches that winter was 'my greatest platform success'. But on 14 December, Lloyd George's coalition careered back to Parliament with 516 seats – a huge majority of 340 over the other parties. Most of the Labour candidates Shaw had championed – including Ramsay MacDonald – lost their seats because of their opposition to the war. However, with sixty-two seats over the twenty-seven of Asquith's Liberals, Labour now sat in the House of Commons as the official Opposition.

Shaw ended the war as he had begun it: with a brochure. Ten thousand copies of *Peace Conference Hints* were published on 12 March 1919. Partly an admonition to Britain against exploiting her self-righteousness at the Versailles Peace Conference, and in part a collection of 'hints' to nerve President Woodrow Wilson against the wiles of Clemenceau and Lloyd George, the pamphlet represents a continuation of Shaw's election campaign and the summation of his political writings about the war. It is a story retold and completed.

When asking for a mandate for his peace offensive against Germany, Lloyd George had demanded: 'Is no one responsible? Is no one to be called to account? Is there to be no punishment? Surely that is neither God's justice nor man's?' Shaw's answer invoked another justice and brought the matter before a different court of morality. He believed that by fixing the guilt of history collectively or individually on others, Lloyd George was making a classic evasion of the human spirit. Through this duplicity of mind Britain risked restarting the mechanism that would bring the same tragedies back into people's lives.

Peace Conference Hints is a Bunyanesque tract on the moral consequences of the war. He surveys botched-up British diplomacy between 1906 and 1914 to strengthen his case for the international acceptance of new rules of conduct in war and peace. He grinds out a history lesson to sharpen a moral point. 'The moral cleaning-up after the war,' he states, 'is far more important than the material restorations.' The Versailles Peace Conference must be made a nucleus for the League of Nations. Like an illuminated picture, the League of Nations that appears in Shaw's missal is a 'very vigorous organization of resistance to evil', protected by an international police force but making conquests through the power of conscience. 'Principle is the motive power in the engine,' Shaw explains: 'its working qualities are integrity and energy, conviction and courage, with reason and lucidity to shew them the way.' This technology for human progress is shown being forced upon us not only by the inevitable march of civilization but by our fear of Armageddon. For the next war, if permitted to occur, 'will be no "sport of kings" '.

Having raised up his Architecture of Nations, Shaw tries to set up as its mystical prophet from the New World, President Woodrow Wilson. With the rusty accoutrements of his fourteen points, he resembles a benighted Quixote of the Peace. The week after Wilson was to lay his patched-up rag of a treaty before the United States Senate, Shaw was declaring that he had known all along the Versailles Conference would come to nothing and that 'in spite of anything that could be urged by the wisest and most powerful statesmen, the victorious side would skin the other alive . . . I had no illusions on that subject when I backed Wilson for all I was worth; and therefore I am not disillusioned nor disgusted now.'

He may have had no illusions; he did have hopes. Woodrow Wilson's godlike procession through Europe before the conference had stirred people's goodwill. 'Nothing like this had ever been seen before,' records one witness. 'The full-throated acclamation of Londoners, Parisians and Romans was not the normal cordiality which crowds accord to a visiting monarch. The ovation surged from the depth of the wounded contrite universal heart to a deliverer, the shaper of a new world.'

Some echoes of these aspirations, like distant trumpets, sound through Shaw's pamphlet. For if the war had not gained new moral territory for human beings, then it had been a defeat for everyone. The possibility of defeat is in his text. Pessimism and optimism are cross-stitched into the narrative, and in his subsequent reaction to the incompetent document Woodrow Wilson took away from Versailles may be glimpsed the extent of Shaw's hopes. 'The treaty of Versailles, which was perhaps the greatest disaster of the war for all the belligerents, and indeed for civilization in general,' he wrote, 'left nothing to be done in foreign affairs but face the question of the next war pending the consolidation of the League of Nations.'

Like Bunyan, Shaw had urged the peacemakers to climb the hill Difficulty. But they had fallen into the pit Destruction. At the end of that year another work of moral tension and stylistic force, Maynard Keynes's *The Economic Consequences of the Peace*, was published. After a succession of dreadful weeks at Versailles, Keynes had quitted 'the scene of nightmare' and written up his account of 'the devastation of Europe'. 'A great sensation has been made here by Professor Keynes of Cambridge, who was at Versailles as economic expert, and resigned that position and came home as a protest against the peace terms,' Shaw reported to Siegfried Trebitsch. 'He has now published a book in which he demonstrates that the indemnity demanded from Germany is an economic impossibility.' Keynes's demonstration was Shaw's vindication.

In the urgency of his despair, Keynes, the informed insider, became 'an outlaw from British official circles', while Shaw was to occupy the position of enemy rather than outlaw. 'He felt that capitalism had caused the war,' commented William Irvine, 'and that democracy had lost the peace.' Keynes dedicated his book to 'the new generation [that] has not yet spoken and silent opinion [that] is not yet formed'. But Shaw, being a generation older than Keynes, felt his precarious faith in this generation diminishing. At the peace table, over the heads of his colleagues, Woodrow Wilson had appealed to the conscience of the public. But the public's conscience had been subtly changed by the European free press; and the man whom no one dared criticize during the war was now openly jeered at and called a 'dangerous radical' by businessmen who controlled the newspapers. 'He stood in great need of sympathy, of moral support, of the enthusiasm of the masses,' wrote Keynes. ' . . . And in this drought the flower of the President's faith withered and dried up.' Such personal reliance on applause, and journalistic manipulation of popularity, came as additional evidence to Shaw that government by the people was unworkable. Only 'government of the people and for the people' was practicable.

2

SHAW'S HEARTBREAK

Is this England, or is it a madhouse?

Heartbreak House

Shaw's response to the Great War is most deeply revealed in *Heartbreak House*. His depression had seeped into the play: his anger over what he saw at Versailles inflamed the Preface. It had 'begun with an atmosphere', the unjudgemental atmosphere of Chekhov's plays. 'An exquisite play by Tchekoff was actually hissed,' Shaw had reported to George Moore before the war. 'You cannot conceive how inferior we are (a small circle excepted) to the common playgoer.' He was to subtitle his own play 'A Fantasia in the Russian Manner on English Themes'. *Heartbreak House* is full of 'the same nice people, the same utter futility' as *The Cherry Orchard*. But, as the Preface makes clear, this is Shaw's view of 'cultured, leisured Europe before the war'.

At the centre of this atmosphere Shaw placed the supernatural story-book character of Captain Shotover. His model had been the actress Lena Ashwell's seafaring father, Commander Pocock, who in retirement went to live on a sailing vessel on the River Tyne, fitting out the stern as his own quarters, placing bars on Lena's nursery portholes, and equipping the upper deck with a drawing-room and greenhouse.

Heartbreak House was intended as tragedy. 'Behold my Lear,' he later gestured from his puppet play, *Shakes versus Shav*. He regarded *King Lear* as pure tragedy: 'even the fool in Lear is tragic'. Like Lear, Captain Shotover's heartbreak has apparently been caused by his two daughters, Ariadne and Hesione.

Ariadne Utterword, who is 'as strong as a horse', speaks for Horseback Hall which is mentioned in the Preface as 'the alternative to Heartbreak House', a very Irish alternative 'consisting of a prison for horses with an annex for the ladies and gentlemen who rode them'. At the age of nineteen, Ariadne escaped from the overheated atmosphere of Heartbreak House and became part of the wooden-headed, outdoor tradition of English life. The Preface prepares us for a Peacockian dialogue in the style of *Headlong Hall*. Having run away from the eccentricity of her upbringing and the world of her emotions, Ariadne has pursued respectability which is represented by her decorous 'numskull' of a husband, a colonial Governor of the British Empire. Sir Hastings Utterword could 'save the country with the greatest ease,' she boasts, once he was given the necessary powers and 'a good supply of bamboo to bring the British native to his senses'. Ariadne is an utter philistine. For much of the first act Captain Shotover has pretended not to recognize her. 'You left because you did not want us,' he eventually tells her. 'Was there no heartbreak in that for your father?'

Hesione is the opposite of Ariadne. As the chatelaine of Heartbreak House she is a siren of sexual infatuation who lures people into her web and leaves them suspended. She has disabled the two 'inventors' in the house, her husband and her father. Hector Hushabye is a man of action reduced from being a creator of exploits to an inventor of stories; Shotover is the thinker whose intelligence has been trivialized into money-making. 'Money is running short,' Hesione informs him after his patent lifeboat has failed to earn them more than £500. ' . . . Living at the rate we do, you cannot afford life-saving inventions. Cant you think of something that will murder half Europe at one bang?'

Shaw's Cordelia is Ellie Dunn, a spiritual offspring of Shotover's rather than his blood relation. She has been invited to the house by Hesione, and her unsentimental education is the play's single continuous thread of narrative. When the curtain rises she appears as a solitary figure on stage dreaming over *Othello*, only to find a few minutes later that her own Othello, a man of wonderfully adventurous stories whom she has known by the name of 'Marcus Darnley', is actually Hesione's husband Hector. She passes rapidly in the stage directions from '*great distress*', through anger to look '*curiously older and harder*'. She had been going to marry a fifty-five-year-old 'perfect hog of a millionaire' nicknamed Boss Mangan, acting from sentimental gratitude for the financial help he had given her father. In Act II, as part of her disillusioning education, she learns that Mangan has in fact made a profit out of her father by assisting him into bankruptcy. But she is still determined to marry him, her motive now being to gain use of the money he has tricked out of her father, even though Mangan, who has followed her to the house, has fallen in love with Hesione.

In the last act Ellie reveals to Mangan that she 'never really intended to make you marry me . . . I only wanted to feel my strength.' She has reached a mystical union with Shotover, who lies in her arms as fast asleep as a baby while she tells the others that she has given 'my broken heart and my strong sound soul to its natural captain, my spiritual husband and second father'. Her emotional transformation-in-a-day is an accelerated dash through the long pilgrim's progress of his life. All the optimism of the play centres on Ellie. 'Heartbreak is not what I thought it must be,' she says. For her it is the process of growing up and 'the sort of pain that goes mercifully beyond our powers of feeling'.

But Shaw also makes his Goneril and Regan victims of heartbreak. Hesione suffers from the dangerous after-effects of a love that came once in her lifetime, then passed. What she shared with Hector, whom she has now reduced to the 'household pet' of their marriage, cannot be regained. All her flirtations and seductions will bring no more than fading reflections of that dream. She is forty-four and has no other interests; what can she do but cry to dream again? For her sister Ariadne heartbreak is paradoxically lack of heart. She is as fearful of emotion as Mangan is of poverty, and has fashioned herself into a rigidly conventional woman of the world whose tragedy is that 'her heart will not break'.

Both sisters, we are given to understand, have been damaged by their wayward upbringing. 'Old Shotover sold himself to the devil in Zanzibar,' Hector romances. 'The devil gave him a black witch for a wife; and these two daughters are their mystical progeny.' In a letter to Trebitsch, Shaw explained that by heartbreak he meant the chronic effects of heredity and childhood, rather than the setback of an unhappy love affair. Shotover is prevented from advancing to his 'seventh degree of concentration' by forces that swamped Shaw's own childhood. He describes Heartbreak House itself as 'my kennel' – the word Shaw used for his birthplace in Synge Street – and, having retreated into 'my second childhood', he is diverted by habitual rum-drinking from pursuing his thought 'so long and so continuously' that it issues into action. 'To be drunk means to have dreams' – or Shavian fantasies. 'You must never be in the real world when we talk together,' Ellie soothes him. But this incapacity of the most gifted characters to use their abilities in the real world has by the last act developed into the collective heartbreak of the play. 'We sit here talking,' cries Hector, 'and leave everything to Mangan and to chance and to the devil.'

*

At the beginning, the house is 'a palace of enchantments, as in the second act of Parsifal'. It contains light and dark, land and sea, sleeping and waking, fantasy and fact. The first act, with its complicated jigsaw of almost sixty entrances and exits, its ensemble playing of what appears to be a chaos of informality, is 'as dependent on atmosphere as any of Tchekov's' plays. Shaw felt he had seen in *The Cherry Orchard* a method of advancing the disquisitory technique of *Getting Married* and *Misalliance* – which preserved the unities and removed the action outside the theatre – with the odd dramatic break-in by pilot, burglar or would-be assassin. In later acts he made a number of further references to Chekhov: the 'splendid drumming in the sky' accords with the snapping of the string in *The Cherry Orchard*; and the topsy-turvy burglar is the equivalent of Chekhov's ominous tramp. But Chekhov's world, with its fusion of impressionistic touches, is naturalistic; in Shaw's house, which is full of surreal and disorientating episodes, 'the very burglars cant behave naturally'.

From the moment the curtain goes up and the audience sees Ellie Dunn's copy of *Othello* sink to her lap, as she dozes in slumber on the draughtsman's chair, the theatre has moved into a world of dreams. Asleep in her bedroom upstairs lies Hesione, the mistress of *Heartbreak House*, who has changed her name from Shotover to the somnambulistic Hush-abye as the result of her 'enchanting dream' of love with Hector. In the second act Mangan is sent into a hypnotic trance, and in the third act, as the thunderous bombers approach, it is the Captain who sleeps. This sleeping and dreaming allows Shaw additional licence for exploring his characters' unconscious minds. In the pathetic scene in which Hector, left alone on stage, 'falls into a daydream' and performs a desperate duel with an imaginary opponent and then in 'another reverie' mimes a thrilling love scene with an invisible woman, we witness all the qualities of courage and imagination he has never been able to employ in waking life – qualities that, when Shotover enters, are immediately contracted into 'a series of gymnastic exercises'.

Growing-up becomes allied to a process of waking-up. Ellie Dunn has the strength to wake herself and the power to mesmerize Mangan so that he cannot resist hearing the truth about himself. He exhibits the essential babyhood of capitalism. This is a revelation to Hesione, who has accepted him as he has presented himself to the world: a businessman 'Boss' with plenty of money and no heart. 'It comes to me suddenly that you are a real person: that you had a mother, like anyone else.' But it is too late for Mangan to grow up.

'What is true within these walls is true outside them,' announces Shotover. Heartbreak House has splendid views of reality which no one inside can reach. For the Palace of Dreams is a revelation as well as a refuge, and recalls an earlier dream sequence in Shaw's plays: the hell scene in *Man and Superman*. Hector is the reluctant Don Juan of this hell and Hesione a Doña Ana who has long ago given birth to her children and now gives herself over to pleasure. Her house is a moral vacuum. 'What do men want?' she demands, reversing Freud's question on women. ' . . . Why are they not satisfied?'

Shaw shuffles the cards of identity with comic virtuosity. It is a matter of Shavian orthodoxy that every person should contradict the pose he adopts. 'The great question is, not who we are, but what we are,' sententiously remarks Mazzini Dunn, little realizing that he is to be shown up as a gullible sentimentalist wrong about everything except his daughter ('you become quite clever when you talk about her,' Hesione admits). Even comfortable Nurse Guinness, who asks disbelievingly: 'now is it likely I'd kill any man on purpose', is shortly afterwards demanding why the burglar (who turns out to be her husband as well as one of the Captain's old crew) had not been shot. 'If I'd known who he was, I'd have shot him myself,' she swears. Shaw has her running at the end of the play 'in hideous triumph . . . laughing harshly' to the gravel pit where her husband has been blown up.

For Mazzini Dunn, Shaw borrowed some of the trappings of Ebenezer Howard, idealistic pioneer of the Garden City Movement. It had been Ebenezer Howard's book *To-morrow, A Peaceful Path to Rural Reform* that Tom Broadbent had carried round with him as a blueprint of heaven and model for his business expansion scheme in *John Bull's Other Island*. And it had been Ebenezer Howard's dream-town that Shaw put on the stage as Perivale St Andrews, 'beautifully situated and beautiful in itself', in *Major Barbara*.

Mangan is possibly the least sympathetic character in all Shaw's work. He is the alternative captain to Shotover: a captain of industry who sees his job as getting the better of 'other fellows in other departments'. His announcement that the Prime Minister had asked him to 'join the Government without even going through the nonsense of an election, as the dictator of a great public department', provokes a dismay which is part of the general humiliation of Mangan in *Heartbreak House* before his miserable death in a gravel pit. Nurse Guinness's 'Serves un right!' is the signing-off of Shaw's revenge on Mangan who was based on Hudson Kearley, head of a wholesale grocery firm, whom Lloyd George had brought into his Government at the same time as he rejected Shaw for a place on the Irish Convention.

Hesione is Shaw's first portrait of Mrs Patrick Campbell since the end of their affair. Hesione's talent for incapacitating those she seduces makes Hector liken her to a vampire. 'When I am neither coaxing and kissing nor laughing,' she says, 'I am just wondering how much longer I can stand living in this cruel, damnable world.' Mrs Pat had predicted that her life 'is sure to be a short one. I wish it to be.' Being denied her wish, she was to demand pathetically in old age 'who is there here who still *loves* me?' and receiving no reply, ask: 'Why am I alive – what for?' It is this emptiness that Hesione conveys, foreshadowing the career of a great actress who was to die '*sans profession*'.

Nobody could speak Hesione's lines as she could, Shaw told Stella, 'or give the quality of the woman as you could if you would'. But she fancied playing the eighteen-year-old Ellie – and that was impossible. For Ellie was conceived from Shaw's memories of that hypnotic young girl, Erica Cotterill, who had lived in 'a fanciful world of her own' and now occupied a special place within the fanciful world of his plays. As 'Incognita Appassionata' in *Getting Married*, she had embodied the sexual passion lacking in his marriage; and as Ellie Dunn she is his spiritual intimate, which may be one reason why *Heartbreak House* was 'loathed by Charlotte'.

Charlotte's loathing of this play is reproduced in Ariadne's disapproval of the house. Ariadne's emotional rigidity, as well as her early determination to make a marriage unacceptable to her living parent, were Charlotte's attitudes. Shaw had entered the world of Horseback Hall on visits to Charlotte's friends and relations, when he put up in the castles and big houses belonging to the county families of Anglo-Irish society. But Ariadne's affinity with Charlotte is well-disguised. Her appearance, it has been suggested, was taken from Virginia Woolf.

The Shaws, the Woolfs and the Webbs had come together during the weekend of 17 to 19 June 1916 at a house called Wyndham Croft in Sussex. 'We talked quite incessantly,' Virginia remembered. ' . . . I liked it better than I expected. At anyrate one can say what one likes, which is unusual with the middle aged.' In Shotover-style, Shaw slept, Virginia observed, 'and then woke up and rambled on into interminable stories about himself . . . Poor Mrs Shaw was completely out of it.' In the mornings Shaw would go into the garden where Leonard saw him writing his play 'on a writing pad on his knee'. From this garden could be heard the guns of the Somme offensive which he turned into the 'splendid drumming' that Mazzini characteristically identifies as the sound of a goods train.

This weekend, with its coming together of Bloomsbury and the Fabians, helped Shaw over some of his difficulties with the play – which he acknowledged in a letter to Virginia twenty-four years later when the bombs of the Second World War had begun to fall. Though the Bloomsbury Group had published and exhibited little of its work before 1916, the principles of aesthetic sensibility and personal relationships which animated that work, and to which it gave priority over the economic and political values of the Fabians, would have become apparent to Shaw during these days of incessant talking, and it is these Bloomsbury values which he now injected into the play. 'Shaw visits upon the age of Bloomsbury with its cult of sentimental personal relations the same scorn Carlyle visited upon the age of Brummel with its Byronism and its pococurantism,' commented the critic Louis Crompton. But the inhabitants of Heartbreak House are more convincingly made up from that coterie of gallants and graces known as 'the Souls', who were more aristocratic than Bloomsbury and went on polishing their veneer of culture, went on sipping the sweet life, even after the declaration of war. Shaw added Bloomsbury to his mixture so as to make his play contemporary, but he had earlier and better knowledge of the Souls than of Bloomsbury.

Shaw's pessimism had grown from his experience of contemporary history; his optimism was increasingly tied to a visionary future where the action of human will has broken the cyclical pattern of behaviour. *Heartbreak House* is less a visionary than a contemporary play, and Shotover wins only a misanthropic victory. 'I cannot bear men and women. I have to run away,' he cries out. ' . . . Old men are dangerous: it doesnt matter to them what is going to happen to the world.'

The throbbing pessimism, bolts of anger, shivers of violence that build to the ambiguously explosive climax are also ingredients active in the great apocalyptic works of the war: Eliot's *The Waste Land*, Lawrence's *Women in Love* and Yeats's 'The Second Coming'. Shaw is in surreal territory several years before the arrival of the surrealists who courted loss of control to explore connections between dream and reality. The sudden spiralling of his wit, the curious patches of farce, the sideslips of tone (such as the nursery incantation at the end of Act I which seems to sound from the world of T. S. Eliot), all fill gaps in the play's organic unity. He had written a revenge tragedy without blood. As they drift in and out of this visionary house, these elemental characters seem to grow disembodied, as if made of air and fire. It is the play of an older man. 'I have children,' says Hector. 'All that is over and done with for me' – as it is for Hesione and Ariadne. Larry Doyle in *John Bull's Other Island* had longed for a place where the facts were not brutal and the dreams not unreal; but the brutality of the war had driven Shaw deeper into dreams. The love charades of *Heartbreak House* are the games that go on in 'the house of the unreal and of the seekers for happiness' which is Don Juan's definition of hell in *Man and Superman*. He had come as close as he dared to 'the blasphemous despair of Lear'.

*

Some 20,000 copies of *Heartbreak House*, *Great Catherine*, and *Playlets of the War* were published in North America and Britain during September 1919. In Britain the critical response was generally unfavourable. A. B. Walkley doubted whether the 'fun' of *Heartbreak House* 'would stand the glare of the footlights', and other critics shared this doubt. Eventually, in the summer of 1920, Shaw signed a contract with the newly incorporated Theatre Guild of New York, where his volume of war plays had been less condescendingly received. The world première took place at the Garrick Theater in New York on 10 November 1920. It was well reviewed, and the production ran for more than 100 performances over almost five months.

In Vienna, where Trebitsch's translation was staged later that November 'with great respect for the intentions of the author', Shaw's loquaciousness seemed to weaken the power of the play. 'The audience at first listened with great interest,' one critic wrote; '... later, however, the interest lessened visibly, the signs of impatience were not wanting at the end.'

Shaw was to learn something of this difficulty for himself a year later during rehearsals of the English production which he directed with the new leaseholder of the Court Theatre, the Irish playwright and manager J. B. Fagan. 'I am rehearsing Heartbreak House at the Court Theatre,' he wrote to Edward Elgar. 'It was like old times rehearsing John Bull there.' But there was a difference. 'The book of the words has been so widely read and so much discussed,' wrote the critic of the *Westminster Gazette*, '... that the real hush of expectation was absent.' In the old times, publication of Shaw's plays had sharpened the public's demand for their performance; now it seemed to dull the curiosity of an audience that already knew about the eccentricities of Shotover and the climax of the bombing raid. It was retitled 'Jawbreak House' and the play which took place in 'a private lunatic asylum with many patients and no keeper' was classed as being 'about the worst there ever was'. The only reputation to be significantly lifted was Chekhov's. 'Tchekov always has an atmosphere,' commented the *Sunday Times*; 'this play has only a smell.'

Shaw blamed the lack of rehearsal time and immediately set about cutting it – exactly what he had forbidden the American and Austrian directors to do. 'I never cut anything merely to save time,' he told St John Ervine, ' . . . [but] there are always lines which are dud lines with a given cast. Change the cast and you get other lines dud.' This truth, however, obscured another truth: the play lacked the seventh degree of concentration. 'As an entertainment pure and simple it is dull and incoherent . . . [with] all the author's prolixities and perversities,' reported James Agate in the *Saturday Review*, and yet 'I found it quite definitely exhilarating and deeply moving, and it therefore ranks for me among the great testaments.'

3

MISS CROSS PATCH COMES TO STAY

You are becoming too famous.

Shaw to Blanche Patch

'Would you care to be my secretary?' Shaw enquired of a forty-year-old clergyman's daughter. Blanche Patch seemed perfect casting for the vacancy. In appearance she reminded Shaw of Harold Laski – and since he was a prominent socialist at the London School of Economics, this counted in her favour. It may even have influenced Charlotte on whom Miss Patch made a 'pleasant impression'. She had been a nurse, a hand-loom weaver, a pharmacist's assistant in Wales and was currently typing for a London optician. She was 'not a university woman', but came recommended by the Webbs. She knew pretty well nothing about the literary or political world.

As a non-Shavian, Miss Patch was unaware of her advantages. Shaw's 'quick, witty, friendly way . . . [which] was new to me then' increased her diffidence, and she wrote back declining his offer. Recognizing the uncertainty behind this refusal Shaw tried again. 'I hardly like to steal you away from another man. Still, I will not take your first No for an answer; so will you let me have a second one, or a Yes, before I let loose a general announcement that the post is vacant?'

This tactful renewal gave her confidence to do what she really wanted. She started work as Shaw's secretary at the end of July 1920 and remained with him until his death. During this time he treated her like a typewriter. 'Nothing that you could possibly write,' he told Stella Campbell, 'could produce the slightest effect on her.' Certainly nothing that he wrote ever affected her. She was completely 'Shaw-proof'.

Ann Elder had observed that 'my successor, Miss Blanche Patch, was older and more mature than I, but I'm not sure that her sense of humour was ever very strongly developed'. This lack of humour amused Shaw. 'Patch is a born comedian,' he insisted in a letter to Beatrice Webb, 'and shews me photographs of herself as a Pierrot.'

She had been nervous at first. 'Does he throw things at you?' she asked one of the maids. But what responsible employer would deliberately damage his office equipment? During her thirty years' employment only twice could she remember him losing his temper – and then it was not with her. 'Even-tempered he always was, and that made working for him easy; but never a word of praise came from him.' He was less a father to her than a maintenance inspector.

He never misused her, never spoilt her. 'No man knows your value better than I do,' he told her: and it was true she was wonderfully economic. 'Will you think £3–10s per week too much?' she had asked him and he immediately agreed to this, not telling her that it was ten shillings a week less than Ann Elder had been getting. Over the years, she was to witness him handing away many thousands of pounds, but such gifts were conferred 'without human warmth,' Miss Patch noted, and often to people she felt were undeserving. It struck her as odd too that he should be so spontaneous with strangers while remaining so cautious with herself. His scorn for capitalistic money-making affected her awkwardly. He had been paying Ann Elder more than union rates and would have paid her still more if she had asked. But by the time Blanche Patch took over he preferred to *calculate* his finances. These calculations, sometimes hampered by an elderly adding machine, seemed to her 'finicky'. 'The meaning to the ordinary worker of the increased cost of living never reached his conscious mind,' she complained. She was not to know that he added a codicil to his will in the late 1920s leaving her an annuity of £260, which he raised to £365 in the late 1930s and to £500 in 1950 (equivalent to £9,300 in 1997). For a long time she puzzled over his financial aberrations until it suddenly occurred to her that he simply had no head for numbers. 'He could never, for instance, remember how many brothers and sisters I had.'

Shaw had warned her that the Adelphi Terrace apartment was protected by a fortified obstacle giving it 'the appearance of a private madhouse'. When she had got through this barbed-wire gate, she ascended to the study, a long 'horribly pokey room' on the third floor overlooking the Water Gate arches upon Hungerford Bridge, with Shaw's desk at one end and hers at the other. His shorthand, which was without contractions or grammalogues, had all the vowel signs written in and difficult words spelt out in longhand, so it was easy for her to transcribe. He wrote 1,500 words of prime work a morning on blocks of water-lined paper with a green tint to rest his eyes, and would give her his shorthand draft in batches. 'I used to rest his manuscript on a stand, such as violinists have, placed behind my typewriter and raised to eye height,' she wrote. Very occasionally she made an error – 'the profiteers of the theatre' instead of 'the proprietors of the theatre', which struck Shaw as an improvement, and 'porter' for 'torture', which for some reason made him laugh.

Apart from swimming at the RAC, walking, motorcycling and motoring (with a little hedge-trimming and log-sawing in the country), Shaw did nothing but work, so far as Miss Patch could see. 'His industry was terrific,' she wrote. 'I have always thought that he wrote too much.' Privately she found *Back to Methuselah* 'hard pedalling' and *On the Rocks* 'dull', while *Too True to be Good* 'bored me a bit'. The first two plays she worked on were *Jitta's Atonement*, which was 'slight' and 'rather dismal', and *Saint Joan*, which she acknowledged to be not his best. She was still less enthusiastic about his non-dramatic work. 'He would be an uncommonly devoted Shavian who to-day would cheerfully set out again to read through *The Intelligent Woman's Guide*, followed by *Everybody's Political What's What* not to say explore once more the Sahara of the novels,' she wrote after Shaw's death.

Often she was obliged to put aside her 1,500 words of play-typing for the articles and long letters about Beethoven and Churchill, Walt Whitman and Santa Claus; on proposals for sex training and the question of rejuvenation by monkey glands, also whether dogs have an after-life and why he could not afford a peerage – all implacably typed out. Then there were the 'pests' and 'busybodies', who wanted autographs, prefaces, cheques, speeches, whom she would 'fob-off' with one of the printed cards from his coloured pack or a paragraph of careful explanation. 'To most of them,' she objected, 'he was much too polite.'

Miss Patch herself was not so polite. Some of those who had been enchanted by her name ('it suggests a vivacious person in a play by Sheridan,' proposed Charles Ricketts) were soon addressing her: 'Dear

Miss Cross Patch.' She referred to 'my pretended irascibility' as a necessary component of 'our firmness'. The only person who really exasperated
her was G.B.S. himself. 'Oh, go away and write another play!' she would
exclaim when he came pacing near her typewriter – 'he created a considerable draught as he swung past me'. His formal manners were invariably
courteous, she admitted, but he was a shy man who shrank from people:
how envious he must be of the way she herself got on with everyone. 'He
always appeared to be astonished that I knew much more about the
working classes than he did.'

But what exasperated her most was the way he took her for granted. 'I
resented being looked on simply as a shorthand typist.' Normally he
behaved as if she wasn't there at all. 'I might be away for a week or so
with influenza and he would receive me when I returned to work as if I
had been there all the time.'

Planted beneath the cool surface of their relationship was a perpetually
unflowering seed of emotion. Although she never showed it openly, Charlotte was 'jealous of the fact that I had to read and transcribe his
shorthand,' Miss Patch noticed. It didn't surprise her. Phonetic shorthand
was a form of intimacy that 'a lonely type of person' like Charlotte
would have loved. Miss Patch could appreciate that. What she could not
appreciate was Shaw's behaviour when, from time to time, he passed on
'certain of my duties' to another woman – by which she meant his former
secretary and relative, Judy Gillmore. That really put a spark in the
gunpowder. Why G.B.S. should still feel so fond of Judy Miss Patch could
never comprehend. Judy had made her bed with Harold Musters in 1912;
and that should have been that. Then there was the matter of the big toe
of her right foot. Miss Patch must have injured it in her school days, for
it had stiffened over the years and by the time she settled down at Adelphi
Terrace it had become an agony. News of her toe never failed to stimulate
G.B.S. By way of experiment, he even sent her at his own expense to a
'Scandinavian Naturpath' who applied hot fomentations to almost every
part of her body except the foot, bringing no relief whatever. Shaw was
anxious that she avoid 'the operation panacea' but all the extra walking
during the General Strike finally disabled her and she decided to go into
St Thomas's Hospital to have her toe joint removed. It was when she went
down to Frinton for what she hoped would be a peaceful convalescence that
Shaw exploded his surprise. He had engaged Judy Musters as *locum tenens*,
'so you need not hurry back if your foot needs a little more rest'. She
hurried back.

But to do him justice, he seemed greatly relieved to have her back. 'I
am distracted and lost without you,' he had appealed, and he had 'footed'
the bill for her operation. So they settled down again until the next

upheaval. Miss Patch realized that some people thought her attitude to G.B.S. was unfriendly; one of them (probably St John Ervine) was to send her an anonymous card marked JUDAS when she published her reminiscences of him. But Shaw himself understood the nature of their partnership. He cared for her as he did for his paste and scissors, which also contributed to the manuscripts and proofs of his life. And she looked after him as a matron of a nursing home might look after a long-term patient – with detachment and efficiency, occasionally telling him off when his foolishness went too far. 'The faithful Patch,' he once called her. She prized this tribute from one who had the tribute of the world.

*

'Travelling is still very troublesome,' Shaw had written to Trebitsch in the summer of 1919. For more than six years following the war the Shaws did not travel outside the United Kingdom, though Charlotte regularly hustled G.B.S. over England, Scotland, Wales and Ireland on a series of purposeful holidays, theatrical tours and to Fabian Summer Schools. Kilsby, going off to make aeroplane engines at Woolwich, had taken a long farewell of them during the war, and in May 1919 Charlotte engaged Fred Day from Codicote as their new chauffeur. G.B.S. was still a fiery motorcyclist, and he egged on Day to 'ginger up' his two-stroke machine – after which it would hurtle away, bucking him off and sometimes landing on top of him. Before Day's arrival he had taken hypothetical instruction from the local chemist, E. P. Downing, on how to steer this motorcycle round corners, but he could not bring himself to accept the theory that it was necessary to slow down and to lean over at an angle. The chemist was impressed by Shaw's 'outstanding deficiency in mechanical sense' and had no more luck with his hints on reversing motor cars, Shaw once taking half an hour to turn the car round, and demolishing some flower beds while doing so.

The village had grown proud of Shaw's notorious road exploits. Local dogs, knowing him well, would play dead under his car while he anxiously crawled after them – when they would bounce out, barking triumphantly. In Fred Day's opinion his employer was 'rather reckless' at the wheel, though 'always very considerate' afterwards. Whenever anything happened, such as a bump or a crash, he would leap out, offer to pay all expenses, scoop up the other driver and passengers and drive them trembling home.

Fred Day stayed on for thirty-one adventurous years and owned that he 'would do anything for Mr Shaw'. Once, during a storm, Shaw noticed Day give a small wave to a woman and child at a bus stop. 'Who's that?' he asked. 'My wife,' Day answered. 'Stop,' Shaw commanded, ' – turn round. We must take them home.' Day had schooled his family never to recognize him if they met him on duty since 'in those days [1925] it was definitely not usual for the gentry to have anything to do with the staff socially. But Mr Shaw was different. He put his arm round her shoulders and helped her into the car. She was terrified.' Later on, Shaw offered to pay for his daughter to train as a schoolteacher though admitting 'I'd rather be a crossing-sweeper'.

It was an interesting job being the Shaws' chauffeur. You got to drive all sorts of machines – a Vauxhall or a Bianca with mechanical windscreen wipers, a straight-eight Lanchester with a harmonic balancer (which Mr Shaw spoke of as if he believed it to be a musical contraption), followed by a 'run-about' Lanchester ten, then a chocolate-coloured Rolls-Royce and finally a 25–30 m.p.h. Silver Wraith. Mr Shaw would ask Day's advice on cars – such as the A.C. coupé they bought in 1923 – quiz him about helical pinions or differential gears and take him to the dealers. He liked to ride next to Day up front, and take the wheel until lunch, while Mrs Shaw preferred sitting at the back. Mr Shaw had the back seat specially upholstered for her, with the compartment sealed from draughts and fitted with a heater. Mrs Shaw designed the front seat for him, with a cushion at the head propping him bolt upright. In this manner, at various speeds, they travelled the country, very slow when Mrs Shaw was with them, very fast when she wasn't and Mr Shaw was driving. His favourite trick, Day noticed, was to mistake the accelerator for the brake. Sometimes, when visiting their friends, his employers would travel by train and arrange for Day to follow with the bags. It seemed to him a funny sort of logic, using a Rolls-Royce for carrying luggage.

4

TRAGEDY OF AN ELDERLY GENTLEMAN

I am doing the best I can at my age.

Preface to *Back to Methuselah* (1921)

'Messrs Constable & Co have to announce the publication early in the forthcoming season of an important and even extraordinary work by Mr Bernard Shaw,' wrote Shaw in a press release for his publishers in the spring of 1921. The book would, he promised, 'interest biologists, religious leaders, and lovers of the marvellous in fiction as well as lovers of the theatre'. It was 'his supreme exploit in dramatic literature'

He had begun this colossal affair, its 30,000-word Preface leading to a sequence of five plays under the collective title *Back to Methuselah*, more than seven months before the war was over, and completed it at the end of May two years later, though continuing to revise and prepare it for publication into the early months of 1921. Like *Heartbreak House*, it was struck out of him by the war; but where *Heartbreak House* exploits the forces of death, *Back to Methuselah* explores new powers of life. It is a vastly hopeful composition, and 'the last work of any vigor I shall produce'.

In his mid-sixties Shaw sensed the encroachments of age not in ill-health and sexual loss, but more obliquely as philosophical pessimism and financial threat, a sense of falling out of step with the contemporary world and losing contact with his audience. The Continent was miraculously transformed from a battlefield into a playground. Don Juan's picture of hell had been visited on earth. Below the whirling triviality, Shaw sensed a disillusionment. He was fighting disillusionment in himself. These terrible post-war years sometimes seemed to him more frightful than the war itself. Every day he received appeals to save babies who were starving overseas. Every week some unfortunate German author would 'write me the whole history of his life, more to console himself and persuade his wife that he was doing something that might bring them the price of a sack of coals, than in any real hope of escaping from his miseries,' he told the German playwright Julius Bab; ' . . . it became part of the day's routine to hear that So and So and his wife were starving and that there was not a child under 7 years of age left alive in Poland.' Before the war Shaw had been remarkably generous to all manner of people who appealed to him for money. But the financial calamity now seemed beyond all reckoning. His generosity persisted but, seeming almost pointless, grew capricious – one tragedy more or less was hardly noticeable when the whole world was breaking up.

It was an immense relief to work in the futuristic world of *Back to Methuselah*, phasing out the miseries of life around him. The expectation of death (with which *Heartbreak House* concluded) had utterly exhausted people who had learnt to feel, think and act as if there were no future. In *Back to Methuselah*, Shaw struggled to discover what this discouraged generation needed to have said to it. He wanted to give it back a future with new prospects of living, and restore the certainty of his own position.

His cycle of plays is a metaphysical (or what he called a metabiological) enquiry into the causes of pessimism in the development of thought since Darwin, and a search for a legitimate philosophical basis on which to re-engage optimism. His political experience suggested that men and women were incapable of solving the social problems raised by their civilization and had therefore been doomed to the poverty against which socialism vainly protested. But he insisted that this was no reason to abandon socialism. 'I take the view that the worse a job is the more reason for trying to make the best of it,' he wrote. 'But my creed of creative evolution means in practice that man can change himself to meet every vital need, and that however long the trials and frequent the failures may be, we can put up a soul as an athlete puts up a muscle. Thus to men who are themselves cynical I am a pessimist; but to genuinely religious men I am an optimist, and even a fantastic and extravagant one.'

Back to Methuselah is the vision of an extravagant fantasist, a *Paradise Lost* and *Paradise Regained* which seeks to demolish our concepts of normality, reintroduces the imaginative quality of free will as an unconscious process, and treats the present as a passing phase of history in which crisis and even collapse might be interpreted as vital changes for the future. There was a peculiar satisfaction for Shaw in responding to what he believed were the needs of the present by removing himself into the future. 'The present occupies all my time,' he wrote. But his chief contact with the historic present comes through newspapers and his animosity towards journalism – which pretends to be an organ and not the exploiter of public opinion – is partly the awareness of its inadequacy as a primary source. He dreamed of a renewal of faith that would measure conduct by the longest conceivable perspective, and of an imaginative rather than academic lens through which to regard history. He wanted to go as far as thought, and much further than facts, could reach. An instinctively trained eye was needed to recognize the tiny shoots and buds sent out by the Life Force – for example, the natural tendency for people in the twentieth century to live longer. Maynard Keynes caught the mood of the moment when in 1923 he wrote that in the long run we were all dead. But what would happen if, in the long run, we were still alive?

*

'Our will to live depends on hope,' Shaw was to write; 'for we die of despair, or, as I have called it in the Methuselah cycle, discouragement.' Christ had reformed the vindictive morality of Moses with his perception of the futility and wickedness of punishment and revenge. But after almost two thousand years another Reformation was needed to adapt Christian morality to the mental habits of modern times. Shaw believed it was necessary to redistil religion by scientific methods. This meant a change in vocabulary: a matter of replacing the word God with the concept of an evolutionary appetite operating by trial and error towards the achievement of greater power over the environment. From our past it was easy to prove that mankind was incorrigible. But though all known civilizations had collapsed, and contemporary civilization was showing all the recorded symptoms of collapse, nobody could prove that men and women would not succeed this time, or next time, or sometime. And even if the human species were scrapped, like the megalo-organisms which were known through fossils, that was no cause for pessimism. 'Man may easily be beaten: Evolution will not be beaten.'

Shaw called for the same sort of admission that Copernicus, Galileo and Darwin had demanded. He too removed human beings from their central position as unique instruments through which a divine will operated, but he restored to them their own will. As subjects of literary biographies will collaborate with their unknown biographers in the future writing of their lives, so our general history may be considered as part of an unfinished narrative that did not cater for our self-interest, but would be influenced by individual acts and thoughts. This collaborative hypothesis restored the value of instinct and the use of intelligence as controls for human destiny.

'If I must explain what I dont understand,' Shaw wrote, 'I prefer to do it in an inspiring way and not in a stultifying one.' His treatise is a modernizing of the first five books of the Old Testament (he subtitled his play 'A Metabiological Pentateuch') in which the Garden of Eden is comprehensively weeded. *Back to Methuselah* is Shaw's version of *Gulliver's Travels*, with longevity replacing size, and the element of the future added as a preventative against morbidity. For it had been a crude blunder, he argued, to treat causation as a process by which the present was determined by the past and would determine the future. 'The true view is that the future determines the present,' he wrote. 'If you take a ticket to Milford Haven you will do so not because you were in Swansea yesterday but because you want to be in Milford Haven to-morrow.'

Shaw encouraged everyone to treat themselves, under a strictly impartial rent act, as tenant-caretakers of this planet. He regarded the isolated figure of Samuel Butler as a pioneer in the crusade against the environmental consequences of Darwinism. Butler had revealed his genius to Shaw in *Life and Habit*, the essay on evolution where he compressed his objections to the dogma of Natural Selection into six words: 'Darwin banished mind from the universe.' In 1887 Shaw had been sent Butler's *Luck or Cunning?* for review by the *Pall Mall Gazette*. 'I was indignant because the review was not printed at full length,' he remembered, 'presumably because the literary editor did not consider Butler important enough ... From this time on I was acquainted with Butler's view of evolution, though I do not think I grasped its full significance until years afterwards when I had arrived at it in my own way.'

The review treats Butler's opinions as being of equal merit to Darwin's. 'The question at issue is – granted the survival of the fittest, were the survivors made fit by mere luck, or did they fit themselves by cunning?' he wrote. 'Mr Butler is for cunning; and he will have it that Darwin was all for luck.' Shaw leaves undecided the matter of whether the controversy was one of semantics or metaphysical truth. Yet the review had felt almost epoch-making to Butler himself. Butler 'admits pure luck as a factor in evolution,' Shaw wrote,

'but denies its sufficiency as an explanation of all the phenomena, and insists that organisms that have the luck to be cunning make further luck for themselves by the deliberate exercise of that cunning, and so introduce design into the universe – not design as we used to conceive it, all-foreseeing from the first, but "a piecemeal, *solvitur ambulando* design", which, as it becomes more self-conscious and intelligent, tends to supplant natural selection by functional modification.'

In the decade following this review, Butler and Shaw met on several occasions. In his *Notebooks*, Butler admits to having 'long been repelled' by Shaw, though 'at the same time attracted by his coruscating power'. At the Fabian Society, after Butler had advocated his ingenious theory that the *Odyssey* was written by a young woman living at Trapani, Shaw got up and 'spoke so strongly that people who had only laughed with me all through my lecture began to think there might be something in it after all. Still,' Butler continues, 'there is something uncomfortable about the man which makes him uncongenial to me.' Shaw did not mind being disliked: he had long been uncongenial to himself. He regarded Butler as the sort of person he himself might have turned into if he had not invented G.B.S. – someone who, having gone around 'undermining every British institution, shocking every British prejudice, and deriding every British Bigwig with irreconcilable pertinacity', was dismissed by the public as an oddity and a vulgarian, and could make no headway with his writings. 'He died in 1902,' Shaw wrote; 'and, outside a small but highly select circle, nobody cared.'

As 'one of the select few who read "Erewhon" and swore by it', Shaw counted himself within this circle. By suggesting that poverty should be attacked as a crime instead of being coddled like a disease, Butler 'made me reconsider a rather thoughtless contempt for money, and thereby led me towards the theme of Major Barbara,' he acknowledged. In the Preface to *Major Barbara* he had described Butler as being 'in his own department the greatest English writer of the latter half of the XIX century'. Thereafter he makes many references to Butler which reveal the kinship he felt for this uncomfortable man. He pictures Butler as being 'naturally affectionate' as a child, as having 'sought for affection at home' and gone on 'assuming that he loved his dear parents' whose good names he later slew in *The Way of All Flesh* 'so reasonably, so wittily, so humorously, and even in a ghastly way so charitably'.

In a letter to Butler's biographer Festing Jones, Shaw wrote: 'Butler can stand on his own legs and carry most of us on his shoulders as well.' It was as an evolutionist, and particularly in *Back to Methuselah*, that Shaw stood on Butler's shoulders. As a great moralist, a writer whose *Erewhon* Shaw called 'the only rival to Gulliver's Travels in English Literature', who used his instinctive knowledge of human nature instead of a collection of evidence based on guinea-pigs in laboratories, Butler had stood alone. But he had committed the strategic error of handling Darwin like a moral delinquent. In his *Methuselah* Preface Shaw comes to praise Darwin, not to dig him up and throw stones. He was 'an amiable and upright man' and an 'honest naturalist' who 'never puzzled anybody'. Shaw congratulates him on 'having the luck' to be everybody's good neighbour. 'Darwin, by the way, was no more a Darwinist than I am a Shavian,' he adds. But in order to separate Darwin from his followers and repair the damage done by Butler's insults, he advances into factual error. Darwin had declared himself 'convinced that Natural Selection has been the main but not exclusive means of modification'. Shaw paraphrases this by declaring that Darwin 'did not pretend' that Natural Selection 'excluded other methods, or that it was the chief method'. Taking this extra step enables him to get beyond range of Darwin and to concentrate on the Neo-Darwinians whose minds Darwin himself had influenced only 'unintentionally'.

In Shaw's Preface Charles Darwin becomes a figure from *The Doctor's Dilemma*: someone whose evolutionary 'discovery' had often been made in the past – by his own grandfather Erasmus Darwin among others. By describing Natural Selection as Circumstantial Selection, Shaw made it all seem rather unremarkable. He used all his dialectical skills to undermine the authority of determinism, accusing its adherents of having reduced Evolution to the level of external accident, 'as if a tree could be properly said to have "evolved" into firewood by the storm which blew it down'.

Shaw felt an aversion to 'the barren cruelties of the laboratories', and objected to 'manufactured evidence in a secret chamber' because it produced knowledge that, being based on constructed and controlled events, was necessarily mechanistic. If the central debate in a scientific age was to be limited to the laboratory findings of people who would 'guess eggs if they saw the shells', then he was once more the complete outsider. He wanted to erase the distinction between scientists and imaginative artists such as Leonardo and Goethe. 'I have made observations and experiments in the spacious laboratory of the world with a marvellous portable apparatus compactly arranged in my head.'

Shaw's Preface to *Back to Methuselah* is an example of that compound of Will and Hope called wishful thinking. He took his readers to a high place and made them look round. What better evidence was there of where a belief in the 'survival of the fittest' had led than the contest of a world war?

But was all this necessary? Shaw says not, if we regard such disasters as evidence of the results and not as evidence of the truth of Neo-Darwinism. For we are co-authors of our world and our 'imagination is the beginning of creation'. Organic Natural Selection was unrepeatable in our life-span. Shaw therefore used the time-scale of his imagination. But he thought less about the scientific origins than the social effects of Darwin, whose theory of competitive survival could so conveniently be used to justify individualistic capitalism. 'I argue out the statements until I reach a verdict – often comic in its simplicity – and then I give the verdict,' he declared. But Shaw's verdicts were to sound as predetermined and his statements, hammered out in the secret chamber of his head, as much 'put up jobs' as any laboratory trial.

'Posterity will believe what it wishes to believe; and if its wishes jump with my guesses I shall be among the prophets,' he concluded. 'If not, I shall be only Simon Magus.'

*

After this appeal to the intellect came a demand of the imagination. Even the history of science carried its tales of witchcraft and wonders, from Archimedes in his bath to Newton under his apple tree. Shaw had begun to make a dramatic parable of his religion in the dream sequence of *Man and Superman*; and in the science fiction of *Back to Methuselah* he attempted to provide it with an iconography. 'I abandon the legend of Don Juan with its erotic associations, and go back to the legend of the Garden of Eden,' he announced. 'I exploit the eternal interest of the philosopher's stone which enables man to live for ever.'

The hell scene in *Man and Superman* took a Mozartian form; the Methuselah cycle, though it quotes from Mozart, advances as a series of Wagnerian leitmotifs. 'Back to Methuselah is my Ring,' Shaw confirmed. Despite its machinery of ghosts and miracles, with a cast that includes a couple of lethal Pavlovian dolls, one huge badly-behaved egg, a hooded serpent and a terrifying Oracle, Shaw did not intend it as a work of remote antiquity or impossible futurism, but as a contemporary drama gathering up the styles of political satire and drawing-room comedy, disquisition and extravaganza he had developed in earlier plays, and pointing the way to his future mystical fantasies.

The long journey begins in the Garden of Eden, where Adam and Eve come across a fawn that has stumbled and broken its neck. It is their discovery of death, and Shaw's illustration of how accident controls dying rather than living. The discourse that follows this discovery between the two of them and the serpent is a wonderful seminar in which vocabulary and understanding advance together. In the beginning there was Lilith, the Mother of Creation. 'I was her darling as I am yours,' says the Serpent, which represents Shaw's evolutionary belief that all habits are acquired *and* inherited – inherited by infinitesimal instalments and, when discarded, recapitulated in leaps and bounds.

While Lilith remained alone, all humankind was vulnerable to extinction by a single accident. So, like the snake, she renewed herself and overcame death by the miracle of birth. She imagined; she desired; she dared; she willed – and then she conceived. But since the labour of renewing life was too dangerous for one, she divided herself in two and created Adam and Eve to share this burden in the future.

Adam and Eve are suspended between two terrifying possibilities – the prospect of living for ever, and the accidental extinction of themselves. But they have not been created equal. 'Fear is stronger in me than hope,' Adam says. 'I must have certainty.' But hope is stronger than fear in Eve. She identifies improvement with the species rather than with herself, and accepts uncertainty, even death, as an inevitable risk in the process of creation.

The first scene of the play ends with the Serpent whispering the secret of conception to Eve. The stage directions read: '*Eve's face lights up with intense interest, which increases until an expression of overwhelming repugnance takes its place. She buries her face in her hands.*' This passage was criticized by St John Ervine. Was it not more likely, he demanded, that Eve 'leapt with joy'? Shaw defended his representation of a woman 'in a state of complete pre-sex innocence as making a wry face when it was explained to her that in consequence of the indelicacy with which Nature, in a fit of economy, has combined a merely excretory function with a creatively ejaculatory one in the same bodily part (she knowing only the excretory use of it), she is to allow herself to be syringed in an unprecedented manner by Adam . . . It is true that the indignity has compensations which, *when experienced*, overwhelm all the objections to it; but Eve had not then experienced them.' Coming at the end of this magical first scene which shows life expanding in an atmosphere of strangeness, as idea gives birth to idea in the sunny stillness of that garden, Eve's repugnance is theatrically powerful.

In the second scene 'a few centuries later' at an oasis in Mesopotamia, Adam and Eve have given birth to their family. What had taken place is a series of moral descents. The moment Adam invented death, it was 'no longer worth his while to do anything thoroughly well'. That was the first step of the Fall; the second came as a result of inventing birth, before which Adam dared not risk killing Eve because he would have been 'lonely and barren to all eternity'. But the invention of birth has meant that anyone who is killed can be replaced. One of Adam's sons 'invented meat-eating. The other . . . slew his beefsteak-eating brother, and thus invented murder. That was a very steep step. It was so exciting that all the others began to kill one another for sport, and thus invented war, the steepest step of all.'

Which is the stage reached in Mesopotamia in 4004 BC. Adam's fear has stopped his development with the invention of the spade. Cain is an early example of the Superman who sets the standards for further human advancement. Like his brother Abel, whom he envied, copied and killed, he is 'a discoverer, a man of ideas, a true Progressive'. From his father he has inherited fear which he overwhelms daily with acts of courage and the ecstasy of fighting. From his mother, he has taken hope, but he has no imagination to make creative use of his will and daring. 'I do not know what I want,' he tells Eve, 'except that I want to be something higher and nobler than this stupid old digger.' In Cain, the first murderer, Shaw embodies his belief that what we have learnt to call evil is technically an error in the experimental process of trial and error by which the Life Force must advance.

Cain is the dominant man. His fearful inventions of murder and war are reducing life to its new brevity. 'Through him and his like,' Eve declares, 'death is gaining on life.' She blames Lilith's miscalculation in sharing the labour of creating so unequally between man and woman. 'That is why there is enmity between Woman the creator and Man the destroyer.'

The twentieth century is largely populated by Adam's successors. In 'The Gospel of the Brothers Barnabas', the second part of his cycle, Shaw stages his revenge on these mean material people whom he typifies in Joyce Burge and Henry Hopkins Lubin, his lampoons of Asquith and Lloyd George. These are his contemporary idealists. They have one quality, which is Will, necessary to the Life Force. But it is Will without imagination, loveless, and by itself destructive. 'The Gospel of the Brothers Barnabas' is designed as a humiliation of these two Liberal leaders who arrive at Franklyn Barnabas's house as a couple of campaigning political candidates. They have come on fools' errands, having carefully read between the lines of several newspaper reports and made the erroneous conclusion that Barnabas is going to enter politics and contest the approaching general election. Almost everything they hear they misunderstand; almost everything they say is trivial or untrue.

The play demonstrates the incompatibility between Adam's offspring and the children of Eve – that incompatibility which Shaw felt to be his own inheritance. Lubin and Burge cannot take a long view even of the possibilities of longevity. They imagine the gospel of Creative Evolution to be a marketable elixir ('The stuff. The powder. The bottle. The tabloid. Whatever it is. You said it wasnt lemons') which must be kept secret. When they discover it to be an idea (or 'moonshine'), they have no further use for it.

For half an hour in the third part of the cycle, 'The Thing Happens', almost no progress is detectable. We have edged forward another 250 years. The Lilliputian President of the British Islands is named Burge-Lubin, symbol of soldered fixity. Equally unchangeable is Barnabas, the Accountant-General with a likeness to his ancestor Conrad Barnabas, a bureaucrat who has made a god of statistics. Two other characters resemble figures in the previous play of the cycle: the Archbishop of York is 'recognizably the same man' as the Reverend William Haslam who was engaged to Franklyn Barnabas's daughter Cynthia; and the Domestic Minister, Mrs Lutestring, seems remarkably similar to Franklyn Barnabas's parlourmaid. A statistical survey leads accidentally to the dramatic revelation that they are indeed the same people, and since, 'like all revolutionary truths, it [longevity] began as a joke', this gives Shaw's absurdist talent excellent scope. He chose for this experiment two of the least promising candidates from 'The Gospel of the Brothers Barnabas' so as to demonstrate that the change would not take place as the result of individual self-interest. 'If the geniuses live 300 years,' Shaw explains, 'so will the chumps.' Since there are more chumps than geniuses, most of those to whom the thing happens will be ordinary people, like the parlourmaid.

It is the story of Adam and Eve once again, with a vital difference. When this new word is made flesh, the mother and father of the long-lived (their own ages presently totalling more than 557 years) are animated solely by hope. These two long-livers have experienced a hostility and strangeness among the short-lived that reflects Shaw's own isolation. 'I have been very lonely sometimes,' reflects Mrs Lutestring; and the Archbishop reveals that it is 'in this matter of sex [more] than in any other, you are intolerable to us'.

All this is reversed in the fourth part of the cycle, 'The Tragedy of an Elderly Gentleman', which propels us forward to a colony of long-lived people at Galway Bay in the year AD 3000. The deputation of short-lived visitors has come to consult their oracle. Among them is Napoleon, 'the finest soldier in the world' and Cain's most perfect descendant. 'War has made me popular, powerful, famous, historically immortal,' he explains. 'But I foresee that if I go on to the end it will leave me execrated, dethroned, imprisoned, perhaps executed. Yet if I stop fighting I commit suicide as a great man and become a common one.' The Oracle answers that his only escape is death, and he is immobilized. For this scene Shaw developed the electric emanation, Vril, with which the subterranean sages of Bulwer-Lytton's *The Coming Race* (a favourite book of his boyhood) slayed at sight. The invisible mesmeric field, naturally accumulating round the long-lived, is that same fantasy of intellectual power that Captain Shotover had struggled to invent. By using this force finally to arrest the progress of his own 'Man of Destiny', Shaw seals the destiny of the short-lived.

'The Tragedy of an Elderly Gentleman' is perhaps the weakest play of the cycle. It explains differences between the two species that could be more imaginatively charted through the use of differing languages. Shaw recognized this growing challenge of vocabulary: he would get round it in the final play by having an 800-year-old She-Ancient tell a three-year-old that 'we have to put things very crudely to you to make ourselves intelligible'. Yet the short tragi-comic scene with which the fourth play ends is peculiarly effective. This introduces the Elderly Gentleman who is Shaw's partial self-portrait. In the short-lived world he has prided himself on daringly advanced thinking which, in the long perspective, becomes mere obscurantism. At home in neither world, he must choose between the despair of living among people to whom nothing is real, and consenting to be phased out among the superior long-lived. 'I take the nobler risk,' he decides, like Gulliver seeking to escape the Yahoos. The Oracle offers him her hands. '*He grasps them and raises himself a little by clinging to her. She looks steadily into his face. He stiffens; a little convulsion shakes him; his grasp relaxes; and he falls dead.*'

The Elderly Gentleman's grasping of hands is a commitment to the spiritual future set out in the fifth and last play of the cycle. 'As Far as Thought Can Reach' combines past, present and future as paraded before a viewing platform set in the year AD 31,920. We are given 'a glimpse of the past' through a grotesque puppet play performed by two 'artificial human beings' that have been manufactured in the laboratory. This synthetic couple proclaim themselves to be the products of Cause and Effect, and offer a pantomime of the determinists' concept of human life. They are ourselves, motivated by fear, enveloped in illusions, playing fantastic tricks that kill their Frankenstein-creator, the fanatical scientist Pygmalion, and finally, though shrinking from death at any cost, dying of terror and discouragement.

The future is a stateless society inhabited entirely by the long-lived. They have been born from artificially hatched eggs in which they were incubated for two years, developing from all sorts of creatures that no longer exist, to emerge as newly-born human beings roughly equivalent to our sixteen-year-olds. Before them stretch four years of what is called childhood, devoted to arts, sports and emotional pleasures, during which they pass through the immaturity that members of the audience begin to shed at the age of fifty. But whereas the short-lived audience will soon die of decay, the long-lived cast are like the original Adam and Eve, and will evolve over hundreds of years into a breed of intellectual voluptuaries known as the Ancients, who are Shaw's version of Swift's Houyhnhnms.

Such a prospect appals the children, just as it appals the audience, for we cannot sense anything in the existence of these Olympians to enchant us. Shaw's artistic problem is one experienced by many creators of utopias. 'I could not shew the life of the long livers, because, being a short liver, I could not conceive it,' he wrote. The imaginative effect is handed over to the actors, directors and designers.

In the final minutes of *Back to Methuselah* the ghosts of Lilith, Adam and Eve, Cain and the Serpent appear. Cain acknowledges that there is no future role for his offspring in the world; Adam too can make nothing of a place where matter does not rule the mind. But the Serpent feels justified. She has chosen the knowledge of good and evil, and she sees a new world in which, hope having vanquished fear, 'there is no evil'. Eve too concludes that all is well: 'My clever ones have inherited the earth.' Finally, as an epitome of the whole cycle, Lilith delivers her testament.

'Is this enough; or must I labor again? . . . They did terrible things . . . I stood amazed at the malice and destructiveness of the things I had made . . . The pangs of another birth were already upon me when one man repented and . . . so much came of it that the horrors of that time seem now but an evil dream . . . Best of all, they are still not satisfied . . . they press on to . . . the whirlpool in pure intelligence that, when the world began, was a whirlpool in pure force . . . when they attain it they shall become one with me and supersede me, and Lilith will be only a legend . . . Of Life only is there no end . . . for what may be beyond, the eyesight of Lilith is too short. It is enough that there is a beyond.'

Earlier in the play, the She-Ancient defined art as a 'magic mirror you make to reflect your invisible dreams in visible pictures'. Lilith's speech is Shaw's magic mirror. Following his courting of disorder in *Heartbreak*

House, he had made a greater effort than in any play since *Major Barbara* towards a new coherence. The end of *Back to Methuselah* foretells the dissolution of matter and, with it, all that had vexed his mind. He sent his optimistic signal infinitely far beyond personal experience. The distant echo he received underscores Lilith's words with a poignancy that against all odds makes them perhaps the most moving of all Shaw's speeches for the theatre.

*

'The sale of the book here and in America has been greater than that of any other of my works,' Shaw told Karel Musek, his translator into the Bohemian language. *Back to Methuselah* seemed to answer a need of the times. 'Your mind was never more infernally agile, your intellectual muscle was never better,' William Archer reassured G.B.S. ' . . . When a man can walk on a tightrope over the Falls of Niagara, turning three somersaults to a minute, it's no use his appealing to the census paper to prove himself decrepit.' More surprising was Max Beerbohm's opinion – that *Back to Methuselah* was the best book Shaw had written because he had got away 'from representation of actual things . . . and thought out a genuine work of art'.

Shaw sent complimentary copies of the book to any number of old friends and comrades, including one inscribed to Lenin. Lenin seems to have found in the Preface confirmation of his view that Shaw was 'a good man fallen among Fabians'. In those places where the shortcomings of capitalism were exposed, Lenin wrote his favourite expression – *'Bien dit!'* – in the margin. But where Shaw appeared to be 'in the power of his Utopian illusions there are marks of disapproval'.

Almost everyone agreed with Shaw's eventual view that 'I was too damned discursive'. In the critical opinion of T. S. Eliot such garrulity had been a product of the 'potent ju-ju of the Life Force [which] is a gross superstition'. This 'master of a lucid and witty dialogue prose hardly equalled since Congreve, and of a certain power of observation,' he wrote, was now 'squandering these gifts in the service of worn out home-made theories, as in the lamentable *Methuselah*'.

Shaw had not counted on a performance in the theatre. He had calculated, however, without the 'lunatic' founder of the American Theatre Guild, Lawrence Langner, who came to Adelphi Terrace in the spring of 1921. He was examined, as Trebitsch had been, by Charlotte: 'a gentle gracious lady with plain, pleasant features,' Langner observed, 'of medium height and comfortable build'. G.B.S. had introduced her 'in the grand manner' as if she were a *prima donna*, then ostentatiously seated her in a chair and stayed unfamiliarly quiet. Once her mystic scrutiny of Langner was over, Shaw sprang from his chair and dashed 'like a sprinter to the door' which he held open 'with a deep bow until she had passed into the hall'. Herself being favourably impressed, Himself was free to give Langner a brief synopsis of his play, lasting two hours, at the end of which Langner concluded that 'Shaw had more than a touch of the fanatic about him'. But between fanatic and lunatic an oddly effective partnership developed. *Heartbreak House*, Shaw cautioned Langner, was like 'a musical comedy' compared with *Back to Methuselah*. But despite its eight changes of scene, a cast of forty-five characters, and a duration exceeding twelve hours, Langner decided it was 'just the kind of thing for the Theatre Guild to do'.

The rehearsals, which began early in 1922, called for a group of actors who were sufficiently talented to play several parts, and sufficiently flexible not only to play them on succeeding weeks but to rehearse them almost simultaneously – 'much as the Grand Central Station had to be built while the trains were run'. *Back to Methuselah* opened in New York on 27 February 1922 with a matinée of Part I and evening performance of Part II. The cycle was completed over three weeks. Over nine weeks, twenty-five performances of the complete cycle were given, at the end of which the financial loss had risen to $20,000. On the other hand, the Theatre Guild had nearly doubled its subscribers. 'The Garrick Theater was too small for us to make money out of the play,' Langner explained. 'If we had had a theater twice the size, there would have been a profit instead of a loss.' 'It isn't likely that any other lunatic will want to produce *Back to Methuselah!*' Shaw concluded.

He had seriously underrated his attraction for lunatics. Going up to Birmingham in 1923 for a matinée of *Heartbreak House* he met Barry Jackson, known locally as 'the Butter King' after the Birmingham Maypole Dairies founded by his father, from which he derived a large private income. Jackson's madness took the form of philanthropy: over a period of twenty-one years he was to spend more than £100,000 (over £2 million in 1997) of his own money on the Birmingham Repertory Theatre which he had founded in 1913. Jackson had been disenchanted by the fashion machine of the London West End theatre. His repertory staged both classical and contemporary plays including continental expressionist drama – he put on Georg Kaiser's *Gas* and the Čapeks' *Insect Play*. *Heartbreak House* was the ninth of Shaw's plays to be produced there since its opening, and Jackson now proposed a tenth, the impossible *Methuselah*. 'I asked him was he mad,' Shaw remembered. ' . . . I demanded further whether he wished his wife and children to die in the workhouse. He replied that he was not married. I began to scent a patron.'

Barry Jackson's patronage between the wars became the equivalent in

England of Lawrence Langner's promotion of Shaw's plays through the Theatre Guild in the United States. Almost twenty-five years younger than G.B.S., Jackson inherited Granville-Barker's kinship of the stage. 'Elegant, urbane, unselfconsciously dominating, always seeming to be a head taller than his companions', he appeared like one of the superior long-lived among the short-lived inhabitants of Birmingham. Though his theatre was one of the happiest places in which to work, it offended Birmingham's respect for profit-making.

Jackson appealed to Shaw as someone whose speciality was to make the impossible take place: a conjuror converting dreams into reality. He therefore handed over *Back to Methuselah!* (which at that time ended with an exclamation mark) and saw it staged in the autumn of 1923, with sets by Paul Shelving and featuring a cast of 'provincial nobodies' that included Gwen Ffrangcon-Davies, Cedric Hardwicke, Raymond Huntley and Edith Evans (who played the Serpent, the Oracle, and the She-Ancient). 'It is a mighty work,' Gwen Ffrangcon-Davies wrote during the rehearsals, ' . . . but opinion is divided about it in the theatre . . . I do not myself know whether it will be as enthralling to see as it is to read.'

Four consecutively played cycles were performed at Birmingham and produced a loss of around £2,500 (equivalent to £62,000 in 1997), of which a little was recovered from a further four cycles put on at the Royal Court Theatre in Sloane Square early the following year. But Shaw was happy. 'This has been the most extraordinary experience of my life,' he declared after the first performance.

From the sequence of secrets and revelations in the Garden of Eden to the terrible cry of the Elderly Gentleman receding into the distance, there were thrilling moments. Desmond MacCarthy, who had been told that, though marvellous, the play was rather boring, listened with riveted attention to the final part. He had learnt that those of Shaw's ideas which 'first struck me as silliest were the ones which I subsequently found had modified my thoughts most', and he recognized that G.B.S. was placing his ghostly faith out of reach of human discouragement. This kind of drama, with its chords of inspiration, flashes of moral passion, and searching chaos, was rare in the theatre. 'The superb merit of the play is that it is the work of an artist who has asked himself, with far greater seriousness and courage than all but a few, what is the least he must believe and hope for if he is to feel life is worth living.'

5

HOME RULE FOR ENGLAND.

What we need is not a new edition of rules of the ring but the substitution
of law for violence as between nations.

Shaw to Jerome N. Frank (13 April 1918)

In the first four and a half years of Fred Day's employment, the Shaws
made four journeys into Ireland. Usually they spent some weeks bathing,
boating, walking and writing at Parknasilla, which Charlotte had known
as a child and which to her mind always rejuvenated G.B.S. Near the
opposite coast, they would stay with Horace Plunkett of Foxrock outside
Dublin – 'the kindest and most helpful of my Kilteragh guests,' he called
them.

'One reason that I am anxious to get him here,' Plunkett had told
Charlotte, 'is that I feel it in my bones that the time has come for him to
do his great service to Ireland.' It was difficult for Shaw to resist such
unusual trust, and when Plunkett's new party, known as the Dominion
League, was formed in 1919, he began numerous contributions to its
paper, the *Irish Statesman* edited by AE.

In Shaw's imagination the Dominion League became a forum for all
extremists whose opposing views could be beguiled into a visionary Irish
Bill that none of the extremist factions could obtain separately. To pull
off this amazing trick 'the ace is the public opinion of the world,' Shaw
reckoned, 'especially the English-speaking world'. He promoted the
League as a sensible way forward for businessmen, an attractive vehicle
for patriots, and an honourable solution for the British Government.
'What the Irish want is the freedom of their country,' he declared. But
no one could agree what freedom meant. Was it complete independence,
or the gaining of a position similar to Australia and Canada, or the
occupation of a place equal to England's within the British Commonwealth, or the beginning of a federated partnership of the United
Kingdom?

Meanwhile Ireland continued to exist under a virtual state of martial
law. 'Laws are enforced, not by the police, but by the citizens who call
the police when the law is broken,' Shaw argued. ' . . . But in Ireland
nobody will call the police, nobody will give away another Irishman to
the policeman.' The result was a miserably weak British regime holding
on to power through Black and Tan coercion. In Ireland 'you have every
sort of liberty trampled on,' Shaw told the Fabians. ' . . . all these petty

persecutions, annoyance, these flingings of men into jail, putting down newspapers, charging political meetings with bayonet and baton charges have produced a condition of the most furious revolt against the British Government and, of course, you have the governing class in this country quite deliberately and unmistakeably going on with that in order to provoke revolts against them which will enable them to say it is impossible to give Ireland self-government.' Amid the raids, ambushes and weekly acts of terrorism, the attempted assassination at the end of 1919 of Lord French, the Lord Lieutenant of Ireland, which appeared to shock the English, came as no surprise to Shaw.

But what did take him by surprise was the sudden action of Lloyd George who announced a Bill for the 'better government of Ireland', partitioning six of the nine Ulster counties from the twenty-six so-called 'southern' counties, north and south being provided with separate home rule and a local Parliament. Lloyd George's Bill led to the Anglo-Irish Treaty and semi-finalization of the partition of Ireland at the end of the year. The Dáil ratified the treaty, but the minority opposing it, led by Éamon de Valera, attracted the support of a majority section of the Irish Republican Army. The Anglo-Irish war had ended: in June 1922 the Irish Civil War began.

'This is an impossible situation,' Shaw wrote in the *Irish Times* that summer. It was literally impossible in the sense that the men he had always called 'marginal impossibilists' had won the day. The IRA was flushed with success – though to Shaw's eyes it represented only 'the stale romance that passes for politics in Ireland'. His purpose throughout all these complicated Anglo-Irish troubles had been to promote any act of grace that could sweeten the atmosphere of this war-tortured country. 'We must all, at heavy disadvantages, do what we can to stop explosions of mere blind hatred.'

After the ratification of the treaty, whatever skirmishes went on between IRA and Irish Free State Army troops, the country would have to govern itself, 'which means that her troubles are beginning, not ending,' Shaw warned. He continued to come over, keeping himself up-to-date with political developments. On 19 and 20 August 1922 he and Charlotte had stayed once more with Horace Plunkett at Kilteragh where they met Michael Collins, one of the most attractive of the Free State leaders. Collins had been a member of the Irish delegation that negotiated the Anglo-Irish Treaty and now, as Commander-in-Chief of the Free State Army, was leading the fight against some of his ex-comrades in the IRA. A few days before this meeting, following the death of Arthur Griffith, he had been appointed head of the new government of the Irish Free State. To be dining with Michael Collins at Kilteragh seemed entirely appropriate to Shaw. With the political realignment between Irishmen, Collins had been moving from extremism to the moderate centre until he now occupied Plunkett's old role – the very change that Shaw had looked for, by non-violent means, in his proposals for the Dominion League.

The Shaws left Kilteragh next day; and a day later Collins was shot dead in an ambush near Cork. 'How could a born soldier die better than at the victorious end of a good fight, falling to a shot of another Irishman – a damned fool, but all the same an Irishman who thought he was fighting for Ireland – "a Roman to a Roman"?' Shaw wrote to Michael Collins's sister. 'I met Michael for the first and last time on Saturday last, and am very glad I did. I rejoice in his memory . . . So tear up your mourning and hang up your brightest colors in his honor; and let us all praise God that he had not to die in a snuffy bed of a trumpery cough, weakened by age, and saddened by the disappointments that would have attended his work had he lived.'

It was a handsome letter, masking Shaw's own pessimism under its shining style. Shaw had returned with Charlotte to Ireland for a couple of months in mid-July 1923, burning up the thirty miles of mountainous Cork and Kerry roads between Glengarriff and Parknasilla 'in a new 23–60 h.p.'. Despite alarms in the papers, excursions across the south of Ireland were safer than anywhere else in Europe, he reported to *The Times*. There was some outdoor economic socialism-in-action – 'the loot from plundered houses has to be redistributed by rough methods for which the permanent law is too slow and contentious' – but none of this was exercised at the expense of the errant Englishman. 'The tourist's heart is in his mouth when he first crosses a repaired bridge on a 30 cwt. car, for the repairs are extremely unconvincing to the eye,' he wrote; 'but after crossing two or three in safety he thinks no more of them.

'Since I arrived I have wandered every night over the mountains, either alone or with a harmless companion or two, without molestation or incivility . . . there is not the smallest reason why Glengarriff and Parknasilla should not be crowded this year with refugees from the turbulent sister island and the revolutionary Continent, as well as by connoisseurs in extraordinarily beautiful scenery and in air which makes breathing a luxury.'

On 12 September he fell on some rocks along the Kerry coast, damaging two ribs and badly bruising himself. He came back to England six days later, like an Irish hero himself, to be attended by an osteopath, a surgeon and radiographer.

This was his thirteenth visit to his country since he had emigrated from Dublin almost fifty years ago, and he would not go back again. His last political hopes for Ireland had appeared to go up in smoke when Horace Plunkett's house Kilteragh was burnt to the ground by the Republicans earlier that year. He had already written his valediction.

'I am returning to England because I can do no good here ... I was a Republican before Mr de Valera was born ... I objected to the old relations between England and Ireland as I object to the present ones, because they were not half intimate enough ... I must hurry back to London. The lunatics there are comparatively harmless.'

6

FREE WILL IN TRANSLATION

Nature must have a relief from any feeling, no matter how deep and sincere it is.

Jitta's Atonement

'The war is over,' Shaw wrote. ' ... All the literary, artistic and scientific institutions should be hard at work healing up the wounds of Europe.' What he advocated as public policy he tried to implement in his private dealings, seeking to invest his German royalties in German industry. 'It is with great pleasure that I find myself able to correspond with my German friends again,' he had written to Carl Otto in the autumn of 1919. 'I need hardly say that the war did the most painful violence to my personal feelings.' He felt a special tenderness for Siegfried Trebitsch. For much of the war they had hardly been able to communicate at all, and even during the long months of the Armistice Shaw had to obtain official authorization to write Trebitsch a letter – all his correspondence to Austria and Germany being inspected to make certain it was confined to business and 'expressed in terms suitable to the existing political relations between our respective countries'. When Trebitsch moved for a time to Switzerland, Shaw vented his relief: 'At last I have got you in a country which I can write to without being shot at dawn.'

Shaw instructed Trebitsch to hold on to all monies due and use them for himself and his wife. 'Spend my money: *steal* it: do anything you like with it as if it were your own until you are in easy circumstances once more.' But Trebitsch could not get the hang of these economic reversals. Despite all Shaw's urgings, he would convey strange sums by dubious routes at odd intervals, imperilling their licence to trade. Because he was aware of Trebitsch's dismay at becoming principally known as 'Shaw's translator' ('my name as a writer in my own right faded away'), G.B.S. hit on the corrective paradox of translating his translator. When Trebitsch sent him a copy of his latest play, *Frau Gittas Sühne*, shortly after the war, he accepted it as an opportunity to make this singular counter-reparationary gesture with *Jitta's Atonement*. 'I have read Gitta,' he wrote in May 1920, 'though most of your words are not in the dictionary.' Within this tangle of difficulties there opened a beautiful advantage for Shaw: 'I had to guess what it was all about by mere instinct.'

He took a year over the translation. Using 'some telepathic method of absorption, I managed at last to divine, infer, guess, and co-invent the story of Gitta'. He had asked Blanche Patch's German-speaking *locum tenens* to provide him with a literal translation of the play which served as a helpful departure guide. 'I hope my tricks wont make you furious,' he wrote uneasily to Trebitsch after completing the first act. 'Charlotte says I have made it brutally realistic; but this is an unintended result of making the stage business more explicit for the sake of the actress . . . The stock joke of the London stage is a fabulous stage direction "Sir Henry turns his back to the audience and conveys that he has a son at Harrow".'

Sending him this first act, Shaw advised Trebitsch to 'tear the thing up if it is impossible', but not to do so 'merely because it is disappointing' since all translations were that. 'It is much better than the original,' gallantly responded Trebitsch who had learnt Shaw's politeness without its component of irony. He eagerly exhorted G.B.S. to complete his version which 'proves again your stage-genious', and add his name as co-dramatist to increase its chances of production. 'I feel a childish delight reading Trebitsch in English,' he wrote happily. ' . . . Please handle that play like your own.'

This, increasingly, is what Shaw did. At the end of the first act, the fifty-year-old Professor Bruno Haldenstedt lies dead of a heart attack on the floor of an apartment where he had been keeping an assignation with his mistress, Jitta Lenkheim, the wife of a medical colleague. 'I was horribly tempted to make Haldenstedt sit up after Jitta's departure, and make a comedy of the sequel,' Shaw warned Trebitsch. His struggle to resist these temptations weakened in the second act and was joyously abandoned in the third where the cast, with 'a paroxysm of agonizing laughter', evolves into a hilarious troupe of Shavians. 'The real person always kills the imagined person,' announces Jitta as Trebitsch's characters die away; and the dead lover's daughter, Edith Haldenstedt, agrees that it is 'such a relief' to be acting sensibly at last.

Studying the typewritten transcription from Shaw's shorthand turned out to be a strange experience for Trebitsch. 'I was puzzeled very much reading your bold alterations,' he admitted. ' . . . The III Akt is in your version almost a comedy!' Shaw was quick to provide healing explanations. It was true, he acknowledged, that he had not done justice to Trebitsch's poetry. But Trebitsch would be overjoyed to discover that by making the characters rather less oppressively conventional, and then inserting a little mild fun into their lives, he had managed to rescue the hero and heroine from their dark fates of misery and despair. 'That is the good news,' he confirmed. Then he had been obliged to replace Vienna (which still lay in the romantic haze of Strauss waltzes) with London and New York (where the delicious anaesthetic of romance was only tolerated in Italian opera). The hopeless gloom into which Trebitsch flung everyone would be fatal to the play in Britain and America. 'Life is not like that here,' he explained. Trebitsch was surprised to learn that even with such artificial aids as black clothes, the British exercised a reaction against grief over death – an irresistible reaction into cheerfulness. Also 'nine tenths of the adulteries end in reconciliations,' Shaw notified Trebitsch, 'and even at the connivance of the injured party at its continuation'.

The delight that had initially flowed through Trebitsch was by now rather confused. To what degree was *Jitta's Atonement* his own work? The tragedy of his first act and the melodrama of the second act had been dissolved in the sparkling comedy of Shaw's ending. It was true that he had been invited to refashion the play if he found these treacheries unbearable – but he trusted Shaw's 'diabolical skill' and his estimate of the play's increased chances of performance. So he gave the go-ahead to prepare an acting version of the text. 'What could I do but agree?'

'You will find that in this final acting edition of the play I have committed some fresh outrages,' Shaw wrote. ' . . . Nothing has been lost by this except the characteristic Trebitschian brooding that is so deliciously sad and noble in your novels but that I could never reproduce . . . My method of getting a play across the footlights is like revolver shooting: every line has a bullet in it and comes with an explosion . . . so you must forgive me: I have done my best.'

Lee Schubert's production in Washington and New York, with Bertha Kalich as Jitta, 'did not succeed even as a comedy,' Langner recorded. For two years Shaw held up *Jitta* in England in the hope of getting a West End production – then he handed it to Violet Vanbrugh who 'will try it at a rather nice suburban theatre at Putney Bridge, called the Grand Theatre'. Shaw was abroad for this first English production, but caught up with it two months later at Leicester. 'The funniest thing about it is that I was very much struck with your play when I saw it on the stage,' he told Trebitsch. Most of the reviews made it clear that (as the *Daily*

Telegraph reported) 'Mr Shaw conjugates the verb "to translate" very differently from most men'. But whenever the reviewers should have felt like 'holding up our hands in horror at the shameful way the original author has been manhandled,' wrote the *Nation & Athenaeum* critic, 'we are laughing too loud to remember to do so . . . it cannot possibly have been better entertainment.' One of those most deeply entertained had been Arnold Bennett. '*The thing is simply masterly*, & contains a *lot* of the finest scenes that Shaw ever wrote.' In his diary he recorded that the effect of re-engineering a machine-made drama with Shavian wit had been electrical. 'The mere idea of starting on a purely conventional 1st act and then guying it with realism and fun, shows genius.

'In the other acts there is some of the most brilliant work, some tender, some brutal, and lots of the most side-splitting fun that Shaw ever did – and he is now approaching seventy, I suppose. The "hysterics" scene of laughter between the widow and the mistress of the dead man is startlingly original. The confession scene between the mistress and the daughter of the dead man is really beautiful.'

Though none of his fantasies of film versions and West End triumphs became facts, Trebitsch had already decided that 'the play was indeed a success'. Shaw paid Trebitsch £100 (equivalent to £1,750 in 1997) for a perpetual non-exclusive licence to translate and publish *Frau Gittas Sühne*, and then diverted Trebitsch's interests elsewhere. 'Did I tell you that I am working on a play about Joan of Arc?' he asked. There was, he had supposed, 'no chance of your coming over here'. Not having seen Shaw now for some ten years, and feeling it was his 'destiny and privilege' to meet his friend again, Trebitsch swore 'a vow that in spite of all difficulties and all qualms I would receive the master's new work only from his own hand. *Saint Joan* summoned me, and I had to go and receive her.' Shaw provided information on the prices and standards of London hotels, added an unglamorous assessment of Ayot – 'a village where nobody dreams of dressing' – and noted some of the house rules: 'If you smoke cigars, you will give Charlotte asthma.' All the same, he conceded, 'I hope to be able to give you printed proofs of Joan'.

The main obstacle to his visit was what Shaw called 'a disgraceful Aliens Act'. The British Embassy had cautioned Trebitsch against trusting to his visa alone. To avoid the risk of being sent straight back across the Channel, he would need an authoritative letter from a British citizen. The letter Shaw sent him admirably fulfilled its purpose, disarming 'the austere passport control officials' at Dover with 'considerable merriment'. Shaw met him at Victoria Station, 'coming with long strides along the platform,'

Trebitsch remembered, ' . . . a laughing giant . . . I grasped the hand this long-missed man held out to me.' They drove to Ayot where, for the first time, Trebitsch heard Shaw read one of his own works out loud.

Afterwards they spoke of the dreadful war years – experiences, moods and opinions that could never have been sent through the mail. 'My generation has passed away and I shall soon have to follow its example,' Shaw said. The days passed all too quickly for Trebitsch. When they said *auf Wiedersehen* it seemed to him that the additional unspoken phrase 'in a better world' was plainly implied. He carried with him the latest work. 'There is no other new play,' Shaw told him: 'Joan is *the* new play.'

FIFTEEN

I

COLLABORATING WITH A SAINT

We want a few mad people now. See where the sane ones have landed us!
Saint Joan

Shaw had been long familiar with Joan of Arc in the theatre. In his Notes to *Caesar and Cleopatra* he had classed her with Nelson and Charles XII – all 'half-witted geniuses, enjoying the worship accorded by all races to certain forms of insanity'. Some ten years later, in the Preface to *Getting Married*, she is no longer a lunatic but gifted with 'exceptional sanity'. In the interval, Quicherat's factual testimony had been translated and published in England, providing authentic evidence of the real Joan.

Shaw does not seem to have considered adding to Joan literature himself until 1913 when, returning from Germany through the Vosges and 'pleasing myself as to my route, I took Domremy on my way for the sake of St Joan of Arc'. He had often travelled through 'Joan of Arc country', but never before visited Orléans. It was here, at the Musée Historique, that he saw the fifteenth-century sculptured head of St Maurice, traditionally believed by the inhabitants to have been modelled from Joan after her triumphant relief of their town from the English. Shaw was happy to embrace this belief. For the Gothic image showed a remarkable face – 'evidently not an ideal face but a portrait, and yet so uncommon as to be unlike any real woman one has ever seen,' he wrote. ' . . . It is a wonderful face . . . the face of a born leader.' This was the image before Shaw ten years later when he presented Joan in the turret doorway of his play – '*an able-bodied country girl of 17 or 18, respectably dressed in red, with an uncommon face: eyes very wide apart . . . a long well-shaped nose . . . resolute but full-lipped mouth, and handsome fighting chin*'.

From Orléans he wrote to Stella Campbell: 'I shall do a Joan play some day.' He imagined it beginning with the 'sweeping up of the cinders and orange peel *after* her martyrdom', and ending with Joan's arrival in heaven. 'I should have God about to damn the English for their share in her betrayal,' he wrote, 'and Joan producing an end of burnt stick in arrest of Judgment.'

The play's epilogue, a bedroom cabaret in Charles VII's dream, has some affinities with Shaw's original fantasy. But more significant is the change of surroundings in which Shaw places his 'masterful girl soldier' after the First World War, and the different task he assigns her. The chronicle play he wrote in 1923 is his 'one foray into popular myth-making,' Irving Wardle has written, 'undefaced by his usual ironic graffiti'; while the epilogue is a Shavian revue sketch which does not remove Joan up to heaven, but brings her forward from the fifteenth into the twentieth century – a move implicit in the previous six scenes.

Shaw felt he recognized in Joan the spirit needed for the regeneration of society in the modern world. A quarter of a century earlier in *The Perfect Wagnerite*, 'Siegfried as Protestant' had anticipated Joan, the first Protestant. Siegfried and Joan both quell their fear of fire, and are trans-figured by the flames. Describing Protestantism in the late fifteenth century as a 'wave of thought' that led 'the strongest-hearted peoples to affirm that every man's private judgement was a more trustworthy interpreter of God and revelation than the Church', Shaw concluded:

'The most inevitable dramatic conception, then, of the nineteenth century is that of a perfectly naïve hero upsetting religion, law and order in all directions, and establishing in their place the unfettered action of Humanity . . . This conception, already incipient in Adam Smith's Wealth of Nations, was certain at last to reach some great artist, and be embodied by him in a masterpiece.'

Saint Joan is Shaw's attempt at this masterpiece and the vehicle for a dialogue between ancient and modern worlds. If Joan's rehabilitation was an example of a modern show trial, the original court hearing seemed to Shaw one of history's secret trials – like those of the Star Chamber. 'Joan was killed by the Inquisition . . . The Inquisition is not dead,' he wrote in 1931. ' . . . when in modern times you fall behind-hand with your political institutions . . . you get dictatorships . . . and when you get your dictatorship you may take it from me that you will with the greatest certainty get a secret tribunal dealing with sedition, with political heresy, exactly like the Inquisition.'

The hero as victim transformed into saviour had been in Shaw's mind as early as the *Passion Play* he had started to compose at the age of twenty-one. Like Jesus, Joan was an agent for change inspired against the idealist *status quo* of the established Church. Cauchon's great cry – 'Must then a Christ perish in torment in every age to save those that have no imagination?' – makes the connection plain. So *Saint Joan* became Shaw's passion play and represents Joan's life as another coming of Christ to the world.

Shaw interprets Joan's voices as evidence of a living imagination – the 'inspirations and intuitions and unconsciously reasoned conclusions of genius' – which are miraculous not by virtue of their alleged source but because of exceptional consequences. These voices and visions, being the manifestations of Joan's instinct ('the voices come first,' she explains, 'and I find the reasons after'), operate similarly to Shaw's own methods of writing. 'I am pushed by a natural need to set to work to write down the conversations that come into my head unaccountably,' he had explained ten years before. 'At first I hardly know the speakers and cannot find names for them . . . Finally I come to know them very well, and discover what it is they are driving at, and why they have said and done the things I have been moved to set down.' By this telepathic process Shaw hoped to attune himself to Joan, he echoing her when following the court testimony, she echoing him when he departs from it, and together collaborating in the miraculous creation of the play.

To many it seemed that the miracle had been Saint Joan's transformation of G.B.S. Johan Huizinga claimed that she had brought Shaw 'to his knees'. But the wretched innocent who had 'talked with angels and saints from the age of thirteen,' Marina Warner reminds us, who had defended the 'external and objective reality of those voices' and 'turned to the Pope for help in her long and appalling trial', reappears in Shaw's play as a 'sharp-witted individualist, who attributes her motives and ideas to hard common sense . . . [and is a] protesting prophet, subverter, active agent of the Life Force, rational dresser'. To have succeeded in getting this 'pert spitfire' to enter English consciousness as the true Joan was the final miracle.

'The first thing he invariably does when his setting is in the past, is to rub off his period the patina of time,' wrote Desmond MacCarthy; ' . . . he will scrub and scrub till contemporary life begins to gleam through surface strangeness and oddities.' Shaw worked fast, filled with relief at having lifted himself free from the post-war débâcle and entered a previous century to fight another war against English imperialism. He translated his own assertion of style into Joan's inspired efficiency of action – 'She is so positive, sir,' Robert de Baudricourt's steward says to account for her effect on everyone. Shaw presents her as the warrior-saint he had sometimes thought of dramatizing as Cromwell and Mahomet, and had looked for in a play about the Unknown Soldier. But after *Saint Joan* he needed to write none of these works. 'It's a stupendous play,' Sybil Thorndike wrote to him, '& says all the things that the world needs to hear at the moment.'

*

Sybil Thorndike had felt destined to act St Joan and in 1923 commissioned Laurence Binyon to write a play for her about the Maid. Shaw, too, had begun writing his *Saint Joan* that year. On 27 August, he was able to write: 'Saint Joan is finished (except for the polishing) . . . and I thought I should never write another after Methuselah!'

It was not until he had finished the play that Sybil Thorndike and Lewis Casson got to hear of it. In some consternation they wrote, telling him of Laurence Binyon's work-in-progress and asking what should be done. G.B.S. was flatteringly adamant: 'Sybil is to play my Joan; let someone else play Binyon's.' In the event, Binyon gracefully withdrew and the difficulty lifted.

Charlotte seems to have been instrumental in Shaw's choice of subject. 'Yes, I sometimes find ideas for plays for the Genius,' she conceded. 'If we can find a good subject for a play, he usually writes it very quickly.' The same proposal had also been made by the man he had named as his literary executor, Sydney Cockerell, curator of the Fitzwilliam Museum in Cambridge, to which, early in 1922, the Shaws had presented one of Augustus John's portraits of G.B.S. 'I have always been under the impression that I was in a small way responsible for St Joan,' Cockerell wrote to Shaw twenty years later, 'by giving you or introducing you to Douglas Murray's book containing the full proceedings at her trial and rehabilitation and suggesting that you might do something with it.'

There was yet another begetter, a teacher at St Mary's College, Hammersmith, called Father Joseph Leonard, whom the Shaws had met in 1919 on holiday at Parknasilla. Shaw later sent him a letter asking where he could find a record of the proceedings of Joan's canonization. 'What I want to know is how the Church got over the fact, which must have been raised by the *advocatus diaboli* if he did his duty to his client, that Joan asserted a right of private judgment as against the Church,' he explained. ' . . . I may write a play about her some day; and this is the only point on which I do not feel fully equipped.'

This letter initiated a long exchange between Shaw and the priest who became his 'technical adviser' on the play, though not all his advice was accepted. Shaw held Joan's private judgement to be inspired and the Church's judgement banal. He took the evidence from the court – often in Joan's words – and dramatized it in the theatre as the speeches of a natural rebel against the Church's authority. Father Leonard declared Joan's loyalty to the Pope to be of far greater significance than any number of eccentric voices, for 'the Church is large enough to contain all sorts of queer fish'. But to have made Joan a queer fish within the Catholic aquarium would have destroyed the Protestant purpose of Shaw's play, which was to bring a realist heroine before a perfectly conducted court of idealists.

The play seemed almost to write itself. More difficult was the revision, in which he eliminated many tempting digressions. This was well advanced by the late autumn when Sybil Thorndike and Lewis Casson came down to Ayot to hear G.B.S. read his play. 'He read it beautifully – he ought to have been an actor really and from the moment he started we couldn't move!' Sybil Thorndike wrote to her son John. The reading lasted three hours and three minutes. 'When it came to the Epilogue Lewis and I were in tears,' Sybil Thorndike recalled.

*

Though Sybil Thorndike was the theatrical vehicle Shaw had in mind for the role, he had used another model as Joan's contemporary equivalent – the middle-aged Fabian Mary Hankinson. Hanky, as she was known, had been born in Cheshire, physically trained in Kent and employed as Head of a Sunday School. For thirty years she acted as Spartan hostess at the Fabian Summer Schools, captaining their cricket teams, drilling their country dancers and policing their morals. She was vividly remembered for teaching Shaw to waltz backwards: 'an unforgettable sight!' She seemed entirely sexless, pouring her energies into gymnastics and flute-playing, and sharing her domestic life with her friend Ethel Moor. Shaw had attended the Summer School in 1919 at Penlee where Hanky had miraculously quenched a Fabian uprising. But though a rigid discipli-narian, this

'maid with silver hair
With school-boy heart and skipper air'

as John Dover Wilson serenaded her, inspired much admiration, for she was a woman of 'unusual good sense,' St John Ervine observed. When *Saint Joan* was published in 1924, Shaw presented her with a copy inscribed: 'To Mary Hankinson, the only woman I know who does not believe she was the model for Joan, and also the only woman who actually was.'

'It is difficult,' wrote the critic Maurice Valency, 'to understand in what way Miss Hankinson . . . could have served as a model for Saint Joan.' But her feminism, which modulated Joan's speech so that it sounded to Desmond MacCarthy like the voice of 'a suffragette and a cry from a garden city', was the influence to which T. S. Eliot took exception when criticizing Shaw for having created 'perhaps the greatest sacrilege of all Joans' by turning 'her into a great middle-class reformer . . . [whose] place is little higher than Mrs Pankhurst's'. Shaw may have had Eliot in mind when, delivering a radio talk in 1931, he stated that although no modern

524

feminist was quite like St Joan, 'St Joan inspired that movement . . . If you read Miss [Sylvia] Pankhurst, you will understand a great deal more about the psychology of Joan.'

Shaw's play carries on the historical business of literature, reconstructing the roles of past figures and keeping the dead in perpetual employment. He uses Joan's symbolic dimensions to add credentials to his vitalist philosophy, as Voltaire and Anatole France had used her for their purposes, and as Shaw's contemporaries were themselves using her for opposing ends. Not long before, Charles Péguy had re-created Joan as a socialistic mystic and martyr who found her equivalent in the government-persecuted figure of Dreyfus; and Charles Maurras had rediscovered her as a proto-fascist emblem of the Action Française, reinforcing military and national authority as Joan had reinforced the French army and the King.

Shaw's Joan is the complete outsider who feels most lonely when she is in company with those who voice opinions of the day. Her own timeless voices echo her unworldliness and establish her kinship with the man who felt a stranger on this planet and at ease only with the dead. Shaw's methods of composition were too oblique and multifaceted for straightforward self-portraiture. To illustrate how the progress of humankind still depended on some people regarded by philistine society as sick and even lunatic, Shaw enlisted more than one contemporary parallel. In addition to Mary Hankinson there was Lawrence of Arabia.

Shaw had been introduced to T. E. Lawrence in March 1922 when Sydney Cockerell brought him along to help carry away the portrait by Augustus John. Shaw was one of Lawrence's heroes, and five months later he received a letter from Lawrence asking him to read 'or try to read, a book which I have written'. By the middle of September one of the eight copies of Lawrence's *The Seven Pillars of Wisdom*, cumbersomely printed on a linotype machine by the *Oxford Times*, arrived at Ayot. This awkward and prodigious work, 'about twice as long as the Bible', stood at the centre of Shaw's working life. 'You are evidently a very dangerous man: most men who are any good are,' he told Lawrence. ' . . . I wonder what, after reading the book through, I will decide to do with you.'

His detailed revisions (including virtuoso use of the semi-colon), which affected 'the spirit as well as the letter of the book,' Lawrence acknowledged, and 'left not a paragraph without improvement', were not completed until some two years later. But Shaw had read the book 'to the last morsel' much sooner. By the time he started on *Saint Joan* he had only forty pages left to read, and when he finished it early in the summer he felt convinced that here was 'one of the great books of the world,' he told Lady Gregory.

In the meantime he had found out some facts about this puzzling man. Lawrence had quit his Arabian adventures, left the Colonial Office, erased his old name and, having been discharged from the RAF following his public identification as 'Private Ross', enlisted in the Royal Tank Corps in Dorset using as his new alias – of all names – Shaw.

Lady Gregory visited Ayot St Lawrence that May, and her diary records that the two people most on Shaw's mind were Joan of Arc and Lawrence of Arabia. To some degree *The Seven Pillars of Wisdom* may be read as a cross-referring work to *Saint Joan*. Lawrence was what Shaw called 'a grown-up boy, without any idea of politics'. He had gone to the Paris Peace Conference expecting President Wilson to secure self-determination for the Arab peoples, and had come away full of the bitterness of defeat. His inspired leadership of the Arab revolt against the Turks, which kept the Arabs fighting for the Allies instead of among themselves, helped to redeem them from their Ottoman servitude. Like Joan, Lawrence had been 'in the grip of a nationalistic impulse to create a unified state from a feudal order, and to set a monarch representative of that unity upon the throne of the nation-state'. Joan had succeeded with the Dauphin and been martyred; Lawrence had failed with King Feisal and seemed, after Versailles, to be backing into oblivion.

As a man-of-letters in peacetime who became a man-of-action in war, Lawrence provided a living connection between G.B.S. and Joan that helped Shaw to bring his heroine 'close to the present day'. Lacking an adult sense of his identity, Lawrence invited his heroes to invade his character and link it with their own. His choice of Shaw's name, the opening he gave G.B.S. to edit and amend his vast first-person chronicle of the Arabian campaign, and the visits he began making that summer to the Shaws' village, the name of which so coincidentally sanctified his own, were part of the mechanics by which G.B.S. was encouraged to merge their destinies.

Already, by the beginning of 1923, Shaw was advising Lawrence to 'get used to the limelight', as he himself had done. Later he came to realize that Lawrence was one of the most paradoxically conspicuous men of the century. The function of both their public personalities was to lose an old self and discover a new. Lawrence had been illegitimate; Shaw had doubted his legitimacy. Both were the sons of dominant mothers and experienced difficulties in establishing their masculinity. The Arab revolt, which gave Lawrence an ideal theatre of action, turned him into Colonel Lawrence, Luruns Bey, Prince of Damascus and most famously Lawrence of Arabia. 'I note that you have again moulded the world impossibly to your desire,' G.B.S. wrote to him. 'There is no end to your Protean tricks . . . What is your game really?' It was natural to interpret it all as a Shavian game, and to see in the shy bird who had helped to carry the Augustus John portrait a version of Sonny. 'I was naturally a pitiably nervous, timid man, born with a whole plume of white feathers,' he confided to Lawrence; 'but nowadays this only gives a zest to the fun of swanking at every opportunity.'

But it is this swanking and fun that makes Shaw's Joan into the Principal Boy of a pantomime, and the play into a charade exhibiting 'all Shaw's most irritating stylistic habits,' as Irving Wardle wrote: ' . . . garrulousness, flimsy poeticism, and thick-skinned flippancy'. Like another of Pygmalion's experiments, he had constructed a likeness of Joan by grafting the eccentric muscle of Mary Hankinson, and framing her with the aura of 'an accomplished poseur with glittering eyes,' as Beatrice Webb described Lawrence. G.B.S. gave Lawrence several copies of *Saint Joan* – variously dedicated 'to Shaw from Shaw' and 'to Pte Shaw from Public Shaw' – but Lawrence, who mislaid these copies, was an unreliable chaperon for the rendezvous of G.B.S. with his saint and remained as much of a mystery to Shaw as Joan herself whom, he conceded, 'I do not profess to understand'.

*

'Mortal eyes cannot distinguish the saint from the heretic,' warns Cauchon in the Epilogue. From the perspective of history it may be easy to see that Joan is inspired and that the other fanatic, de Stogumber, who throws himself into Joan's chair after her burning, is heretical. But there exists a more sophisticated fanatic in the Inquisitor, who gives a warning of where the toleration of fanaticism may lead. His fearful condemnation of change is made with such idealistic sympathy that some critics have understood it to define G.B.S.'s own attitude. What Shaw intended to voice through this 'most infernal old scoundrel' was his audience's opinion of the Church and Empire, before demonstrating where such opinions led. The Inquisitor's attack on Joan's masculine dress is also a denunciation of Shaw's Jaeger costume. Changes in fashion exhibit how the unorthodoxy of one time becomes the convention of another, a point dramatically made in the Epilogue by everyone's amusement at the appearance of the clerical-looking gentleman wearing 'a black frock-coat and trousers, and tall hat, in the fashion of the year 1920'. The Inquisitor's court has reduced justice to the dictatorship of fashion.

Saint Joan is a tragedy without villains. The tragedy exists in human nature where the mad credulity and intolerant incredulity of religious and secular forces meet and fix the *status quo*. Against this social structure Shaw's heroine gains no victory; she can win a battle as Shaw can win a debate, but she will never change the social order until the world truly becomes a fit place for heroes to live in.

The Epilogue, which reflects the flames of Joan's burning in the summer lightning against the windy curtains and brings us into the present century, gave Shaw the chance to step forward and 'talk the play over with the audience'. What he tells us is that we too would burn Joan at the stake if we got the chance. It was not surprising that much of the hostile criticism of *Saint Joan* centred on this Epilogue, which 'shattered the historical illusion' – and made way for Brecht.

The historical illusion was cherished by the public. In vain did the American critics protest after the play opened in New York that it contained 'too little comedy' and 'a good deal of fustian', and was 'a mere historical scaffolding upon which the dramatist drapes the old Shavian gonfalons'. Alexander Woolcott warned readers of the *New York Herald* that 'certain scenes grow groggy for want of a blue pencil'; and in the *New Republic* Edmund Wilson was to complain that it had the characteristic over-explicitness of the social historian turned dramatist, giving the audience a sense 'that it is reading a book instead of witnessing a real event'.

On the opening night a number of these critics and some of the audience began leaving the theatre before the final curtain came down at 11.35 p.m. Lawrence Langner cabled urgently to Shaw stating that if he refused to shorten it, *Saint Joan* could not be a success. Shaw replied declaring the press notices, which had so frightened him, to be 'magnificent'. For it was true that Alexander Woolcott had also called the play 'beautiful, engrossing and at times exciting', and Edmund Wilson described it as 'a work of extraordinary interest'; that the *New York Times* critic who found the play 'monotonous' had nevertheless thought it a 'great triumph', that the *New York Post* critic who found it 'exasperating' still thought it 'brilliant'. All these favourable points seemed to have been gathered together in a long review for the *New York Times Magazine* by Luigi Pirandello. 'I have a strong impression that for some time past George Bernard Shaw has been growing more and more serious ... he seems to be believing less in himself, and more in what he is doing,' Pirandello wrote. ' . . . In none of Shaw's work that I can think of have considerations of art been so thoroughly respected as in *Saint Joan* . . . There is a truly great poet in Shaw.'

Shaw ranked Pirandello as 'first rate among playwrights', believing that he had 'never come across a play so *original* as Six Characters'. He advised the Theatre Guild to recover its nerve. 'It is extremely annoying to have to admit that you are right,' Lawrence Langner replied the following January. 'People are coming in droves to see *Saint Joan*, and it is a great success.' The production had to be transferred from the Garrick to the larger Empire Theater, and ran for 214 performances before being sent on tour.

The English production at the New Theatre in St Martin's Lane marked the culmination of Charles Ricketts's partnership with Shaw which had begun in 1907 at the Court Theatre with his 'inscenation' of *Don Juan in Hell*. His costumes there, modelled on Velázquez, had stood blazing against a stage dowsed in black velvet and appeared magical to Shaw. 'If only we could get a few plays with invisible backgrounds and lovely costumes like that in a suitable theatre,' he had written, ' . . . there would be no end to the delight of the thing.' He had again turned to Ricketts for *The Dark Lady of the Sonnets* in which Shakespeare, clothed in greys and russets, Queen Elizabeth in silver and black, and the Dark Lady, wearing crimson and black, appeared before an 'intense and abnormal starlit sky of a fabulous blue'. The following year Ricketts had attired the Venetian *père noble* Count O'Dowda after Thomas Lawrence's portrait of George IV and given his daughter a strict Empire dress to lend her the look of a fillette 'depicted on elegant pre-revolution French crockery' in the successful run of *Fanny's First Play*. The 'gorgeous white uniform, half covered by an enormous green overcoat trimmed with black fur' he designed for Lillah McCarthy's role as *Annajanska* seven years later had been so successful that Margot Asquith copied the overcoat for her dressing-gown.

For *Saint Joan*, Ricketts created costumes designed to be an 'intelligent blend between Pol de Limbourg and the Van Eycks, avoiding the bright fourteenth-century colour of the first and the rather prosy phase in dress in the second'. He 'flung himself into the job', authenticating heraldry on the magnificent tapestries, tents and curtains, designing the stained glass for Rheims Cathedral, and basing the sunny stone chamber in the Castle of Vancouleurs on the kitchen of a Norman keep at Chilham which he shared with Charles Shannon. In his history of British theatre design, George Sheringham was to describe the visual effect as being, within its conventions, 'one of the most beautiful things that has ever been seen on the London stage'.

Partly perhaps as a heritage from William Morris and partly in response to Gordon Craig's influence, Shaw had used artists such as Albert Rutherston and Ricketts to carry the theatre away from Victorian scene-painting into twentieth-century realms of stage design that could produce a style to match the director's view of a play. This had gradually become accepted as part of a Shaw play-in-performance by the time Barry Jackson took over the Vedrenne–Barker tradition and appointed Paul Shelving as his regular designer.

Both Shelving and Ricketts designed productions of *Saint Joan*. The public's delight in the beauty and vitality of Ricketts's designs for the first production helped to establish it as Shaw's most successful play. At last he had done what Archer had been goading him to do: he had written a realistic or symbolic work that 'should go to every city in the world and shake the souls of people'. In Berlin and Vienna, Max Reinhardt's production, presenting Elizabeth Bergner as Joan, scored 'the greatest theatrical success that I have ever known,' recorded Trebitsch. Before long, the play was being performed in Scandinavia, throughout Eastern Europe, and even in Paris where seven unsuccessful productions of his previous plays in the Hamons' translations were thought to have established complete 'barriers of language, thought and feeling between Shaw and the French'. The play's producer and star actress, George and Ludmilla Pitoëff, who were to revive it in Paris no less than a dozen times in ten years, had been appalled by the Hamons' version. In collaboration with Henri-René Lenormand they revised it so as to present a dreamlike vision of a miraculously sublimated Joan. For the first time, the French critics united in their praise of the Hamons' brilliant rendering; for the first time they praised Shaw for an innovative structure of hagiography that contrasted the saint with the farcical world of Shavian satire, and parodied the court in the manner of an Offenbach operetta, while leaving Joan spiritually uncontaminated. This original technique was hailed as an effective means of dramatizing the supernatural, and Shaw was credited with having invented a new type of historical drama.

'Woe unto me when all men praise me!' says St Joan in the Epilogue. Shaw greeted his own popularity with similar scepticism. He had sent out his play to rescue Joan from canonization and restore her heresy, but found it was to lead to his own canonization with the Nobel Prize for Literature. He had been put up, and turned down, for the Nobel Prize four or five times previously. But the literary adviser to the Swedish Academy, Per Hallström, was converted by *Saint Joan*: 'even if the real Saint Joan was a different figure,' he acknowledged, 'Shaw has created a great one.' Shaw was appalled. 'The Nobel Prize has been a hideous calamity for me,' he told Augustin Hamon. ' . . . It was really almost as bad as my 70th birthday.'

He had never encouraged prizes. 'You cannot give examination paper marks to works of art,' he had written in 1918. He had not changed his mind. 'If the prizes are to be reserved on Safety First principles for old men whose warfare is accomplished,' he wrote to his Swedish translator Lady Ebba Low, 'the sooner they are confiscated and abolished by the Swedish Government the better.' After politely describing the award as a reinforcement between British and Swedish culture that, especially after

W. B. Yeats's prize two years earlier, would not be lost on his native Ireland, he went on to discriminate between the award, for which 'I have nothing but my best thanks', and the prize of some £7,000 (equivalent to £175,000 in 1997) which 'I cannot persuade myself to accept'. His readers and audiences 'provide me with more than sufficient money for my needs,' he explained, 'and as to my renown it is greater than is good for my spiritual health.' He therefore proposed that the Swedish Royal Academy confer on him the 'final honor of classing my works in that respect *hors concours*', and use the money to commission good English translations of Sweden's literature. But the Swedish Academy refused this suggestion. He was therefore obliged to accept the prize, assist in the creation of an Anglo-Swedish Literary Foundation, and hand over to its Trust Fund all his prize money.

'He is now the most famous author in the world,' one newspaper declared. 'Such steps towards Mr Shaw's canonization are being made,' wrote an *Evening Standard* reporter, 'that people are forgetting that he was formerly almost always described as Mephistophelean.' Though the press announcement was made in 1926, he had officially been awarded the prize for the year 1925. 'I wrote nothing in 1925,' he told the newspapers, 'and that is probably why they gave it to me.' But everyone recognized that, as Shaw himself phrased it in a letter to Edith Evans, 'I am in the very odor of sanctity after St Joan.'

2

THE END AND A BEGINNING

I can scarcely believe that the septuagenarian in the looking glass is really G.B.S.

Shaw to Beatrice Mansfield (3 August 1927)

'On the 26th we sail for Madeira,' Shaw notified William Archer in mid-December 1924. 'My wife expects me to return in the middle of February; but my private intention is never to come back . . .'

He was in his seventieth year, 'too old' he told his publisher Otto Kyllmann, who nevertheless prevailed upon him to prepare a collected edition of his writings for Constable. 'I ought to be retiring,' he protested; 'and my business is advancing instead.' His passage to Madeira, with its 'flowers, sunshine, bathing, and no theatres' was not a retirement from business – he took with him a sack of correspondence. But since the war there were fewer people he liked to see. An exception was Archer. 'I don't know whether you are in England or not, and should be glad of a hail if you are,' he signalled him shortly before sailing. Earlier that year he had been invited to chair a lecture by his friend, enthusiastically entitled 'The Decay of Decency', and replied: 'As Archer and I are the same age (though he doesn't look it) I think we should be meditating on the Decency of Decay.' But the truth was that when he and Archer got together and relived their old campaigning days, they felt quite startlingly young. Archer still saw in the extravagance of G.B.S. a deep menace to the exercise of his friend's talent. It was still not too late, he felt, to get Shaw on to the right lines. He never wearied of attempting this feat and G.B.S. never wearied of retaliating. They had been at it now for forty years.

'Oblige me with a hammer, a saw, a beetle and a couple of wedges that I may operate on your all but impervious knowledge box,' Shaw had requested in the summer of 1923 after looking through Archer's new book, *The Old Drama and the New*. What lay between them was the name and nature of drama. Shaw believed that Archer treated the theatre as a fairyland. Archer believed that for all Shaw's sociological interests, he was a blatant fantasist. Where then lay reality? There was a chance of settling the matter, Archer urged, if Shaw would simply use different words. As a professional translator, Archer felt well-qualified to change Shaw's language, and generously offered to do so. 'I say a cat is a quadruped, with a brain, a backbone, and (unless of the Manx variety) a tail,' he explained. 'You say, "Oh no – a cat is a round, mushy iridescent object with long streamers, usually observed on the shingle at low tide." "Why," I reply, "that is not a cat but a jelly-fish." '

'The alternatives are not a cat and a jelly-fish,' Shaw countered, 'but a clockwork cat and a live cat.'

'It won't do,' Archer wrote.

'You haven't got it yet,' Shaw wrote.

But there was still time. In December 1924 Archer changed his tactics and published in *The Bookman* a long exegesis entitled 'The Psychology of G.B.S.'. Most readers, Archer believed, would be shocked to learn that G.B.S. was governed by a passionate sense of right and wrong. Though considering himself exceptionally skilful in the art of persuasion, he was 'so unique, so utterly unlike the overwhelming majority of his fellow-creatures, that he has never mastered the rudiments of that art'. He had gained the ear of the public, but he had never got at its will. 'Shaw, a professed revolutionist, will revolutionise nothing.'

Unless, that was, Archer could bring him into a new relationship with his public. In his *Bookman* essay, he was appealing to the public itself. He invited his readers to overlook the irresponsible tic of Shaw's joking, forgive the Shavian blunders of tone. For in G.B.S. they had among them an original thinker and artist, and where Archer himself had benefited, so could they. 'There is no man for the fundamentals of whose character I have a more real respect,' he wrote. 'I own myself deeply indebted to him for many lessons taught me in the years of our early intimacy.'

Shaw read 'The Psychology of G.B.S.' that December. He knew how much affectionate sensitiveness lay beneath Archer's reticence. Being emotionally reticent himself he sent off a letter simply asking for news of Harley Granville-Barker, and whether, before sailing for Madeira, there was any chance of seeing Archer. For he was someone of whom Shaw had 'not a single unpleasant recollection, and whom I was never sorry to see or unready to talk to'.

'G.B.S. has taken like an angel to my article,' Archer reported to Granville-Barker. 'I am especially glad in view of this operation business.' Archer had been told he had to undergo an operation for the removal of a cancerous tumour 'one of these days' – in fact he was going into hospital the following day. 'I feel as fit as a fiddle.' But because 'accidents will happen', for a few apologetic sentences, Archer suddenly broke their code of reticence. 'Though I may sometimes have played the part of the all-too candid mentor,' he wrote, 'I have never wavered in my admiration and affection for you, or ceased to feel that the Fates had treated me kindly in making me your contemporary and friend. I thank you from my heart for forty years of good comradeship.' It was said – and time to leap quickly back into a joke about the King of Norway.

Shaw played his part rather well: 'I was not seriously alarmed, and presently sailed for Madeira.' Actually Archer had got through his operation and was recovering by the time Shaw and Charlotte sailed. They arrived at Reid's Palace Hotel on 30 December, and saw as they entered the hall a news bulletin announcing Archer's death three days earlier. Now it was G.B.S.'s turn to break the code – but too late. Each morning after breakfast he would work frantically, emptily, then plunge into the Gulf Stream. In the afternoons, while others played roulette and tennis, he sat miserably in the glorious sunshine. 'This is one of those unnaturally lovely hells of places where you bathe amid innumerable blossoms in midwinter,' he wrote bitterly to William Rothenstein.

He had never been able to regard a death caused by an operation as natural death. 'My rage may have been unjust to the surgeons; but it carried me over my first sense of bereavement.' Later he overcame this anger with a whimsical piece of therapy on the dance floor, which would surely have impressed Archer as quintessentially Shavian. Having heard that the wife of the hotel proprietor Max Rinder had been successfully operated on for cancer, he joined her as a dancing partner and together they learnt the tango. A photograph of them, correctly positioned, still hangs in the hotel. They are preparing to put their best foot forward under the watchful instruction of Max Rinder, 'the only man who taught me anything,' the caption reads. But the lesson was symbolically Archer's. By recognizing the practice of modern operative surgery to be 'often more successful than its reasoning', Shaw was taking a step towards Archer's view that, outside the theoretical world of his own construction, a real world existed with which he should move in rhythm.

'All good wishes for 1925 – Ever yours, W.A.' These had been Archer's last words to him. But when Shaw returned on 16 February 1925 to London, 'it seemed to me that the place had entered on a new age in which I was lagging superfluous'.

*

To some extent life continued as it had before the war. The Shaws often stayed with the Webbs at Passfield Corner and with Charlotte's sister and brother-in-law at Edstaston; and Lady Gregory, the 'charwoman of the Abbey', sometimes came and stayed with them at Ayot. In London, Charlotte continued to give her lunches for old friends and new acquaintances. 'You can imagine how excited I was to be invited [to lunch] and how disappointed to find an old old gentleman and a cushiony wife,' wrote E. M. Forster in 1926. 'Shaw was pleasant and amusing, but I felt all the time that he'd forgotten what people are like . . . She wanted to talk mysticism, and denounced "atheists" with the accents of a rural dean. I came away with the hump.'

With the Trebitsches and the Hamons, Shaw maintained his literary-business relationships and replaced other translators as they fell away in exhaustion with still more exaggerated figures, such as the impoverished Polish adventurer Floryan Sobieniowski, who had been the lover and blackmailer of Katherine Mansfield. He remained in friendly communication with G. K. Chesterton and Gilbert Murray and continued to see Barrie, Arnold Bennett and Galsworthy. But he could not forget those who had died. 'I still feel that when he went he took a piece of me with him.' Archer's death had also closed Shaw's best means of access to Granville-Barker. He had written to G.B.S. after seeing *Saint Joan*, and they were both to compose obituaries of Archer, after which there followed years of silence. No single person could understudy Harley, though Barry Jackson, Lawrence Langner and T. E. Lawrence between them filled part of the vacuum.

While G.B.S. acted as editor of *The Seven Pillars of Wisdom*, Charlotte volunteered to be its proofreader. 'I devoured the book from cover to cover as soon as I got hold of it,' she told Lawrence. 'I could not stop. I drove G.B.S. almost mad by insisting upon reading him special bits when he was deep in something else.' It was an extraordinary experience, sending her back on a wave of excitement to her twenties when, 'reaching out for something that was beyond her understanding', she had become absorbed in Eastern religions. From the pages of his book, Charlotte had an impression of Lawrence as 'an Immense Personality soaring in the blue (of the Arabian skies)', and he became 'the strangest contact of my life'. She sent him honey and chocolates and *marrons glacés*, nectarines and peaches; records, particularly of Elgar's music, to play on the gramophone G.B.S. had given him. Usually 'a very grudging taker', Lawrence defended himself by giving her his manuscripts. But he accepted a motor-bicycle (from Charlotte and G.B.S. together) which he called Boanerges (a name he transferred from one bike to another), and would roar up in his goggles, gauntlets and peaked cap to arrive without warning at Ayot – Charlotte's Arabian Knight. Sometimes he stayed a weekend in what became known as 'the Lawrence room'. At other times the quietude induced such a terrifying reluctance ever to leave that, after an hour or two, he would have to jump on his machine and hurtle back to barracks or on to another of his sanctuaries – to Max Gate to see Thomas and Florence Hardy, or to Alderney Manor and Fryern Court to visit Augustus and Dorelia John. Charlotte, seeing his gleams of happiness, felt that 'Ayot is justified – it lifts its head'.

They grew closer when apart. After Lawrence went to India, they started up a 'tennis game' of correspondence. 'I want to tell you something about myself,' she wrote. She told him what she had once begun to tell G.B.S. about her parents and childhood, and after 'a fearful lot of cogitation' she told him about the 'teachings' and 'treatments', meditations and healings of her religion which were 'such a help'. Lawrence responded by confiding some of his secrets – the emotional disturbances with his mother and his sexual trauma at Deraa. He sent her poems, his private anthology *Minorities*, and the unexpurgated text of *The Mint*. 'It *is* a wonderful book . . . that no one but yourself could achieve,' she replied, ' . . . [it] has stirred me to the very depths of my being.'

To no other woman could Lawrence write quite so frankly. It was their solitariness that seemed to have brought them together. Lawrence felt curiously untaxed by their relationship. By unburdening his emotions to this anonymous wife of the celebrated G.B.S., he was also secretly communicating with posterity. Over thirteen years they were to exchange some six hundred letters in which Charlotte revealed to him things 'I have never told a soul'. She had never met anyone like him, though she had met all sorts of people, being now 'an old woman, old enough at any rate to be your mother'. This image, however, suddenly chilled Lawrence.

'Let me acquit you of all suspicion of "mothering me". With you I have no feeling or suspicion of that at all.' His mother's inquisitorial letters 'always make me want to blow my brains out' – no trust 'ever existed between my mother and myself'. At Ayot he was on neutral ground. 'I do not wish to feel at home,' he warned her. ' . . . Homes are ties, and with you I am quite free, somehow.'

They were not disloyal to G.B.S. Lawrence felt grateful for all his help as literary agent and editor, and curious over what G.B.S. might try to make of him in future plays. He was determined to evade a Shavian take-over, though his letters to Charlotte teem with praise of her husband's strength, confidence and mastery. 'He has given himself out to his generation year by year, without reserve or grudge.' When Lawrence compares his own career, the advantages all seem to be with Shaw. Yet it was strange how sympathetically Lawrence came out of comparisons so heavily weighted against himself ('he's great and I'm worthless . . . G.B.S. has brought forth twenty books; and I'm in a mess over one'). 'G.B.S. has become too famous any longer to be really great,' he suggests. 'His reputation is dwarfing him. However,' he adds with apparent tact, 'that will pass.'

The tone of these letters was perfectly judged. Charlotte was proud of her husband and his achievements, but hated the publicity that rose around their lives. Fame had been an emollient for G.B.S., but it 'has closed his pores'. And it was true, Charlotte agreed, that G.B.S. was not 'interested in anything but his work'. In Lawrence she saw again the suffering and loneliness that had been exposed in her husband at the time of his physical breakdown and their marriage. Now, feeling sometimes stranded in this marriage, she gazed towards Lawrence and formed a half-undisclosed friendship that counterbalanced her husband's letter-writing relationships with women. 'Marriage is not natural – but unnatural and disastrous,' she wrote to Lawrence. ' . . . The idea [of having children] was physically repulsive to me in the highest degree.' Yet these revelations, which she felt unable to disclose to another soul, could have appeared in *Man and Superman* or *Getting Married*. Her lack of reticence, however, did surprise Shaw. 'I realize that there were many parts of her character that even I did not know,' he later owned to Hesketh Pearson, 'for she poured out her soul to Lawrence.' Perhaps he had once known them, and forgotten.

Lawrence had approached the Shaws' marriage like an undercover agent. Charlotte and G.B.S. 'mix like bacon and eggs into a quintessential dream,' he eulogized. He was at his best in their company 'for they loved and comprehended him,' Osbert Sitwell observed; 'and there was, I noticed, a sort of audacity of mischief about his attitude and conversation when they were present, that was enchanting'. But the strange self-immolation that Lawrence sought in order 'to keep sane' reminded Shaw painfully of his own early obscurity. Their relationship became a teasing tug-of-war between Shavian possessiveness and assertion and Lawrentian waywardness and ambiguity. 'You and I,' Shaw told Lawrence, 'are worse than characters: we are character-actors.' 'You have read too much of yourself into me,' Lawrence warned, and 'Your advice would sink my ship.' But this was how G.B.S. went into operation. His friendship was a form of patronage. He ushered him into the Cliveden Set, introduced him to Elgar, and helped to elect him a Fellow of the Irish Academy of Letters which actually pleased Lawrence 'because it is a gesture on my part that I am Irish'.

Lawrence 'always had one eye on the limelight,' Charlotte admitted. Perhaps that was why she sometimes suspected that she had been used as a messenger service between him and G.B.S. But as a vehicle for Shaw's theories, he proved 'a most troublesome chap': a man of marvellous dual abilities who failed to unite literature with action, believing he could 'never quit myself of the consequences of my past actions till I am dead'.

Another candidate for this romantic synthesis was a neighbour of the Shaws at Ayot. Apsley Cherry-Garrard had been one of the youngest members of Scott's last expedition to the Antarctic. Cherry, as he was known, won golden opinions from Scott for his pluck and popularity, especially on the 'weirdest bird-nesting expedition there has been or will ever be', gathering the eggs of the Emperor Penguin at Cape Crozier. Their zoological jaunt was a wonderful example to G.B.S. of the evolutionary appetite.

Cherry was approximately the same age as Lawrence and some thirty years younger than G.B.S. His exploration of the Antarctic, with its awful outcome (he was one of the team that had found Scott dead in his tent on the Great Ice Barrier), marked the rest of his life, as the Arab campaign had marked Lawrence's. This legendary exploit, while he was still in his early twenties, had been the apotheosis of his career. 'Nature would be merciful if she would end us at a climax and not in the decline,' Lawrence wrote. It was the same for Cherry-Garrard.

Cherry became a great favourite of the Shaws. When Charlotte told Lawrence in December 1922 that 'both G.B.S. and I have lots of experience about books and we would both *like* to put it at your service', the joint experience she had in mind was over Cherry-Garrard's *The Worst Journey in the World*. After the Shaws' editorial advice and textual emendations, the book had been published by Constable earlier that month. This account of the journey was originally commissioned by the Captain Scott Antarctic Fund, but finding himself becoming critical of his leader,

Cherry had withdrawn from his official commitment and produced an independent narrative on which, Shaw believed, 'the expedition will be finally judged'. Several passages were drafted or rewritten by G.B.S.

Shaw's presentation of Cherry took no account of the Lawrence-like agonies of self-doubt that had prompted his writing of the book. 'Lawrence had never escaped himself nor his nerves which drove his muscles,' Cherry was to write. 'He knew that he had shot his bolt.' His own readjustment was complicated by the death of his father, a rival spirit who had spurred him with initiative. He had travelled to the end of the earth to find a separate identity his father could admire, and made Scott a temporary replacement for his father. He had worshipped Scott but, after his father's death, came to resent his influence. To reconcile these feelings of worship and resentment he divided Scott in two. 'He considers Scott a schizophrenic,' Shaw later told Lord Kennet, 'two different persons.'

Like *Seven Pillars*, *The Worst Journey* was partly the open-air theatre of boyish adventure in which G.B.S. retrospectively took part and, with great delight, almost took command. The two books attracted him strongly. 'Why should not sand have the same appeal as snow?' he demanded after Lawrence had demurred over the public interest in his own work. Cherry-Garrard had described his life-and-death experiences so effectively 'that the reader forgets how comfortable he is in his armchair, and remembers the tale with a shiver as if he had been through it himself'. Lawrence too possessed this power of re-creating action. He 'made you see the start of Feisal's motley legions as plainly as he saw it himself', and gave you a sense of the 'track underfoot, the mountains ahead and around, the vicissitudes of the weather, the night, the dawn, the sunset and the meridian [that] never leaves you for a moment'.

Shaw stole into these heroic landscapes but took care to conceal his literary stage management of them. 'It would be fatal to make any suggestion of collaboration on my part,' he advised Cherry-Garrard. '... As my experience on the ice dates from the great frost of 1878 (or thereabouts) when I skated on the Serpentine, my intrusion into the Antarctic Circle would be extraordinarily ridiculous.'

There was another reason for attempting secrecy. He risked losing the sympathy of Scott's widow Kathleen, 'a very special friend'. She had recently married Hilton Young who came to believe that Shaw denigrated Scott because Cherry-Garrard, 'an egotistical man, with a grievance against his leader', had worked his way into Charlotte's esteem and 'flattered Shaw by letting him rewrite [his] book, more or less'. Shaw wrote as gently as possible to Kathleen explaining that 'bringing a hero to life always involves exhibiting his faults as well as his qualities'.

In his imagination the appalling conditions of the Antarctic became a metaphor for the moral climate of Britain between the wars, and Cherry-Garrard's survival a triumph of human will over social adversity. The idealized adolescence of both Lawrence and Cherry-Garrard touched his own parent-damaged emotions. Over twenty years later he reported Cherry as having 'recovered his health rather miraculously' and escaped his pessimistic destiny. But Beatrice Webb, who met him in the 1930s, left a grimmer picture. 'He is at war with all his neighbours; he has closed footpaths, dismissed tenants, and cannot keep servants. Years ago he was personally attractive, a rather distinguished youth with artistic and intellectual gifts, today he is drab and desolate, looks as if he were drinking and drugging as well as hating. I should not be surprised to hear that a revolver shot had solved his problem.'

*

'On the very threshold of seventy I have fallen through with a crash into ninety,' Shaw told Kathleen Scott. As his vigour declined, so his need for vicarious exploits through younger men-of-action-and-letters intensified. Feeling as if 'I have left half of me behind', he replaced the missing half with a team of athletic candidates.

One of these was Cecil Lewis, a wartime flying ace with the Military Cross whose war memoirs, *Sagittarius Rising*, showed him also to be 'a thinker, a master of words, and a bit of a poet,' Shaw reckoned. Lewis submitted some of his early writings to G.B.S. and came to count him 'one of the great influences of my life'. As a founding member of the British Broadcasting Corporation, he arranged for Shaw to give a reading of *O'Flaherty, V.C.* (which was broadcast live on 20 November 1924) and fired his interest in radio technology. Before long, G.B.S. had bought a Burndept four-valve set with loudspeaker and was issuing the BBC with advice.

The 'invisible play' was a phenomenon that fascinated him, and he quickly recognized the unstoppable power of radio. It would enable those who could not bear the degradation of public speaking to address their fellow-countrymen in solitude and out of sight, 'using no art except that of giving each syllable its value'.

He asked no fees for his radio talks, regarding them as an extension of his political speaking in the 1880s and 1890s. The vast size and variety of his new audience delighted him, and he celebrated it grandiloquently. 'Your Majesties, your Royal Highnesses, your Excellencies, your Graces and Reverences, my Lords, Ladies and Gentlemen, fellow citizens of all degrees,' he began a talk in the BBC series 'Points of View' on 14 October 1929; 'I am going to talk to you about Democracy . . .'

Cecil Lewis records that Shaw had 'impeccable verve and artistry' as a broadcaster, and he made it his business to see that G.B.S. was given a modern platform. For years Shaw watched over his career 'with parental care and I grew to idolize him,' Lewis was to write, 'for, in those days when I was part of the spearhead of the exploding mass media which were changing the whole shape of society and in touch with many of the leading figures of the day, he was the only man among them who appeared to have any social conscience or any practical suggestions to offer to combat the Dragon's Teeth which I felt were everywhere being sown among us'.

To push his political ideas into renewed life Shaw needed to make contact with younger men and women. By his contemporaries he was celebrated for his past, and usually for his literary rather than his political past. At a 'Complimentary Dinner' for his seventieth birthday he declared that he did not care a snap of the fingers for this literary success in comparison with his pioneering work as one of the Fabian founders of the Labour Party – but the BBC refused to broadcast the speech, 'Socialism at Seventy', on the grounds that it was politically controversial (it was printed in full by the *New York Times* – and pirated throughout the country).

Shaw was not displeased to have his celebratory dinner at the St James Room of the Hotel Metropole hosted by the Parliamentary Labour Party and chaired by Ramsay MacDonald. He had admired MacDonald's courage in resigning from the Labour Party leadership to oppose the war, and campaigned for him in the coupon election of 1918 at Leicester in which MacDonald lost his seat. To many it appeared as if MacDonald were politically destroyed. But his oratory, and the polished humour with which he had defended himself against attacks, added to his credentials and on his re-entry into Parliament in 1922 he became a natural choice as Labour leader. His brief premiership two years later established the Labour Party as a valid alternative government to the Conservatives and himself as the first socialist of national stature.

When MacDonald first became Prime Minister in January 1924, with Sidney Webb as President of the Board of Trade, Shaw had hailed him as the 'ablest leader in England'. By the time he came to form his second Labour Cabinet in June 1929, with Webb now translated into Lord Passfield and Colonial and Dominions Secretary, Shaw like some others was already preparing to discard him. MacDonald was a Liberal at heart, though his position as leader of the Labour Party had been legitimately won during his days as a rebel and an outcast. At the peak of his career he struck Shaw as being politically dead. But who among the living should take his place? Shaw backed someone forty years younger than himself, Oswald Mosley.

Mosley's political career in the 1920s had the radicalism and unortho-doxy that Shaw admired. At the beginning of the decade Mosley had broken with the Conservative Party over its Irish policy and exhibited his superiority to the party system by standing as an independent candidate, and winning. After MacDonald first came to power, Mosley joined the Labour Party and, following two years in the wilderness during Labour's opposition, became a junior minister in MacDonald's second adminis-tration. He was tipped by many as a future Prime Minister, an outsider increasingly fancied to overtake the tiring leader in the 1930s.

Mosley was a wonderful manipulator of words. He sounded rational, he sounded omniscient, and when he vented his full powers of assertion it seemed as if heroic deeds were being performed. He was athletic and quick-minded, part child and part strong man – could this be the superman whose advent Shaw had been prophesying?

Mosley had come to see himself, his biographer Robert Skidelsky writes, 'acting out in real life the central dramatic situation of Shaw's plays: the vital man, with ideas and impulses, confronting the inert creature of ideology and habits'. By the beginning of the new decade he had become an amalgam of Keynesian economics and Shavian political philosophy. 'Has MacDonald found his superseder in Oswald Mosley?' Beatrice Webb wondered in 1930.

In January that year Mosley made his move with a memorandum to MacDonald proposing a recovery plan that called for the mobilization of national resources to combat unemployment. This programme of state intervention and large-scale public works was casually turned down by a Cabinet committee and on 20 May Mosley resigned – a 'melodramatic defection from the Labour Party,' Beatrice Webb called it, 'slamming the door with a bang to resound throughout the political world'. Using this memorandum as a political manifesto, in the spring of 1931 Mosley formed his New Party which was planned as a Labour ginger group but which evolved eighteen months later into the British Union of Fascists.

Shaw watched Mosley's operatic career with a mixture of emotions. 'Oh, if Oswald had only waited,' he wrote after the New Party had been created, ' – if only he had known that MacDonald was contemplating political suicide!' To some extent Shaw preserved his loyalty to Mosley by attacking the National Coalition Government that came to power in the summer of 1931. This, rather than Mosley's splinter group, seemed to Shaw the real danger. Twice the Labour Party had been elected, and still there was no socialism in Britain.

Shaw believed that the implementation of Mosley's programme (similar to Roosevelt's New Deal) would have gone some way to averting the financial crisis of 1931, which had been brought about partly by the cost of unemployment benefits. In his view, the government should have abandoned free trade and the gold standard. He thought that MacDonald had been imposed upon by American bankers and exploited by British politicians using the economic situation to split the Labour Party. MacDonald's 'clear course when the crisis came was to go into the Opposition and lead the Labour Party in a strenuous fight to balance the Budget at the expense of property instead of at the expense of Labour. That, at least, he could understand, if he could not understand the currency question,' Shaw wrote at the beginning of 1932. 'When he went over to the enemy and led the attack on wages and doles instead without ever mentioning the alternative, he was lost to Socialism for ever.'

Shaw interpreted the extraordinary rally to the Nationalist idea, which gave MacDonald his landslide victory in the autumn of 1931, as a sign that 'people are tired of the party system'. This was how he himself felt, though he knew that a coalition was the opposite of strong government. By his mid-seventies Shaw was disenchanted with the Fabian concept of weakness permeated by strength and the politician's empty head continually filled with other people's ideas. He had tried permeation all his life and it did not work – the ideas leaked away. 'The Fabian parliamentary program was a very plausible one,' he wrote in 1932, 'but, as MacDonald has found, parliament and the party system is no more capable of establishing Communism than two donkeys pulling different ways.'

While addressing an audience 'in praise of Guy Fawkes' at the Kingsway Hall in November 1932, Shaw singled out Mosley as 'one of the few people who is writing and thinking about real things and not about figments and phrases'. MacDonald was applauded by the people for his phrases; Mosley was feared because he represented change. Shaw translated the one into a Shavian idealist and the other into a realist. He ignored Mosley's layers of dissimulation and his uninhibited private ambition, and used his fascism ('the only visible practical alternative to Communism') as a stick with which to beat a philistine parliamentary system.

Shaw's speech was largely an attack on speech-making. The chief function of Parliament, he declared, had become the defeat of democracy through the art of fooling the public. His 'painfully incoherent tirade' (as Beatrice Webb called it) eloquently communicates a despairing sense of impotence. For almost fifty years he had been making political speeches and 'so far as I can make out, those speeches have not produced any effect whatever . . . I have come to see at last that one of the most important things to be done in this country is to make public speaking a criminal offence.'

In which case Shaw himself was a major criminal. This indeed was how he had come to feel. All Tanner's revolutionary 'talking' from *Man and Superman* had merged with 'this continual talk, talk, talk in Parliament'. What could be more appropriate in a speech praising the man who 'saw that the first thing to enable the Government to do anything was to blow up Parliament', than to *threaten* people with Mosley? 'The moment things begin seriously to break up and something has to be done, quite a number of men like Mosley will come to the front . . .' he warned. 'Let me remind you that Mussolini began as a man with about twentyfive votes. It did not take him very many years to become the Dictator of Italy. I do not say that Sir Oswald Mosley is going to become Dictator of this country, though more improbable things have happened . . . You will hear something more of Sir Oswald Mosley before you are through with him.'

What the public was to hear in the later 1930s was the stamp and chant of Mosley's Blackshirts. In Shaw's experience of British politics the only precedent for these rallies were the ineffectual marches of Hyndman's Social Democratic Federation. A measure of Mosley's political invalidity in Shaw's mind after 1933 is his absence from both *The Intelligent Woman's Guide to Socialism, Capitalism, Sovietism and Fascism* in 1937 and *Everybody's Political What's What?* in 1944. Even his campaign for Mosley's release from prison in the Second World War was to be based on the assumption of his political insignificance.

Shaw distanced himself from the unsavoury aspects of Mosley's British Union of Fascists. 'Anti-Semite propaganda has no logical connexion with Fascism,' he said. ' . . . Anti-Semitism is the hatred of the lazy, ignorant, fat-headed Gentile for the pertinacious Jew who, schooled by adversity to use his brains to the utmost, outdoes him in business.' He was to define fascism as 'State financed private enterprise' or 'Socialism for the benefit of exploiters'. From the 1930s onwards Shaw chose to call himself a communist: 'that is, I advocate national control of land, capital, and industry for the benefit of us all. Fascists advocate it equally for the benefit of the landlords, capitalists and industrialists.'

Beatrice Webb protested that Mosley, Mussolini and Hitler had 'no philosophy, no notion of any kind of social organization, except their own undisputed leadership instead of parliamentary self-government – what was the good of it all?' Admitting this lack of economic principle, Shaw asserted that they all had the *personality* to change the world. Britain was in decline because she did not recognize that social progress depended on leadership. But Beatrice was not convinced. 'This strange admiration for the person who *imposes* his will on others, however ignorant and ugly and even cruel that will may be, is an obsession which has been growing on G.B.S.,' she reflected a year later.

'. . . As a young social reformer, he hated cruelty and oppression and pleaded for freedom. He idealized the rebel. Today he idealizes the dictator, whether he be a Mussolini, a Hitler or a Stalin, or even a faked-up pretence of a dictator like Mosley . . . And yet G.B.S. publicly proclaims that he is a Communist . . . What he really admires in Soviet Communism is the *forceful* activities of the Communist Party . . . lifting the whole body of the people to a higher level of health and happiness.'

3

AN IDLE ROMANCE

Man is the occupation of the idle woman.

Shaw to Mary Hamilton (23 November 1918)

'Hello, Bernard Shaw.'

'Hello.'

'We've come to see you.'

In the late summer of 1921 an American girl had accosted G.B.S. on the sidewalk outside Adelphi Terrace. She was twenty-four with dark hair, eyes like muscatel grapes 'and a fine shape'. Her name was Molly Tompkins. She had come from Atlanta, Georgia, with her husband Laurence and their two-year-old son Peter to 'find' him, she explained; they had got his address at Hatchards. 'Then where is Laurence?' asked Shaw. He was round the corner nervously drinking coffee. Leaving him there, and under the spell of her good looks, Shaw invited her to 'come upstairs and tell me all about it'. She came and, over buttered crumpets, unfolded their plan. Laurence was rich and had ambitions as a sculptor; Molly herself had been in Ziegfeld's *Follies*. Together they dreamed of creating a Shavian theatre, he carving in stone the story of Creative Evolution, she interpreting it on stage.

He saw that Molly was 'as vain as a goldfinch' and reckoned that 'poor Tompkins' had 'taken on a fine handful'. Yet her eagerness 'softened my stony heart a little,' he admitted; 'and now I suppose I am in for taking some interest in you occasionally'. So it began.

He instructed Laurence to get a studio and arranged for Molly to take the written and oral examinations for the Royal Academy of Dramatic Art. He had been on the Council of RADA since W. S. Gilbert's death in 1911 and his bracing influence was largely responsible for broadening its constitution and liberalizing the students' education. But Molly did not think much of it. The two houses which comprised the Gower Street part of the premises (and which, with the help of £5,000 from G.B.S., were later replaced by a larger building) impressed her as being 'dim and dingy'; the director Kenneth Barnes was 'pompous'; and she took an 'instant dislike' to her first teacher, the actor Claude Rains. Indeed, she behaved so badly that Kenneth Barnes threatened to expel her. 'You are a disgrace to me,' Shaw admonished her. ' . . . [they] ask me despairingly what they are to do with you and why I didn't bring you up properly.'

But he could not help being tickled by his protégée's goings-on or conceal his entertainment at the *beaux gestes* with which, at the very last moment, she would avoid their consequences. For every quality, she seemed to have some infamous defect. 'You are worse than the tragédienne who rehearsed Pygmalion in the upper division for me some years ago,' he told her. This, perhaps, was her appeal. She challenged him to re-embrace past sentiments, improving his old performances and rephrasing some painful scenes, this time painlessly – for surely he was beyond pain now.

*

Recently Stella Campbell had been pressing Shaw to let her publish the 'dear letters' she had inspired him to write. 'What have you written?' he demanded. 'Your life or mine or both?' She called it *My Life and Some Letters*. Knowing how much she needed the money ('the poor woman can hardly lay her hand on a hundred pound note') he wrote to her publisher stating that he had made a 'gentleman's agreement' with her not to raise the question of copyright over his correspondence.

Awakened by Charlotte to the implications of what he had done, he asked Stella to send him the proofs: he might perhaps 'spot some dangers that you may not have thought of'. She did not dare let him see all her proofs, but had a copy made of the correspondence she proposed publishing. 'People talk carelessly, but nobody will *think* anything but what lovely letters and what a dear man you are,' she prompted him.

This 'terrible wadge of letters' arrived at Ayot St Lawrence shortly after Christmas 1921 and it appalled him. He dared not reveal its contents to Charlotte. 'Public exposure' of them would be as 'utterly impossible,' he warned Stella, as for 'you to undress yourself (or me) in the street'. Their only chance was for him to edit them. 'My treasure, my darling, my beloved, adored, ensainted friend of my very soul' was pared down to 'my adored ensainted friend', and his 'most agitating heart's darling' vanished altogether. What remained, he told himself, was ten times more than any publisher had the right to expect. 'There is the requisite touch to set Charlotte right without which I would have seen the whole universe

damned before consenting to the publication of a line,' he soothed Stella.
'It will be hard enough on her as it is to see her husband as the supreme
ass of a drama of which you are the heroine.'

But Stella was not soothed. 'You have spoilt my book,' she objected.
'You have spoilt the story . . . Lustless Lions at play . . . It is really sad:
you creep on the ground, instead of flying in the air – through taking
away those delicious letters.'

'You *must* have some more love letters,' he appealed desperately. 'You
cannot appear as a famous beauty who had only one catch: an old idiot
of 56. Will there be nobody to keep me in countenance?' The truth was
that she had been more feared by men than loved, and Shaw's correspondence with her was unique. This was partly why she felt so angry. These
'massacred' letters, she let him know, had become 'the only insincere thing
in the book'. And really he agreed with her. 'I hate the whole thing, because
it is impossible to present it in its simple truth to the public,' he explained,
'and it is dishonest to disguise it, and disloyal to pretend that it was all
play-acting. I felt a great deal more than you did; and I still feel a great
deal more about it than you. You are doing – if you only knew it – a
dreadful thing.'

Being unexpectedly hurt, Stella stretched forth her claws. 'You have
ceased to amuse me. You have *revoked* – that's your game always.' Her
book was to be serialized in May 1922 by the *New York Herald* to which
the corrected proofs had been sent with the lines Shaw had excised still
legible. 'Oh Joey – oh lor! oh Hell! I have just seen the *New York Herald*,
they have put in all the letters uncut, this in spite of all their promises,'
she apologized. ' . . . I feel *very* unhappy because I know how much you
will mind.'

He did mind – because of Charlotte. As for himself, he considered the
publication of a love letter as 'an indecent exposure'. But if Stella regarded
it as 'a splendidly courageous declaration . . . I have no argument to
oppose: it is instinct against instinct,' he explained to G. K. Chesterton.
'She has a right to her view, and to her letters. I cannot call a policeman . . .
I cannot control her . . . Besides, it was delightful while it lasted; one
cannot refuse gratitude when it has absolutely no damned nonsense of
merit about it; *and the money was very badly wanted*. Still, a dreadful thing
to do.'

He had always loved Stella's dreadfulness. 'I forgive you the letters
because there is a star somewhere on which you were right about them,'
he wrote to her, 'and on that star we two should have been born.' Molly
Tompkins too seemed to have arrived from that star. But perhaps he could
teach her to live on this one. Then he need not hurt Charlotte. He would
police their correspondence in exemplary fashion. 'I read your letters

diligently,' he assured Molly. 'I even read them aloud to my wife (with an occasional skip) . . . they make me feel romantic at times, which is pleasant at my age.' His friendship with Molly blossomed as the struggle over publication of Stella's love letters was warming up, and it appeared to offer him an opportunity for rewriting the past. 'If you knew the trouble those unlucky letters made for me you would understand a lot of things,' he later confessed to Stella. His exchange with Molly was intended as a simple series of letters between a 'delightful correspondent' and a 'useful bore' which would record a relationship as innocent as that of Higgins and Eliza. He had lost 'all *specific* interest in women,' he told a disbelieving Stella in 1923. ' . . . I can no longer tell myself love stories.'

*

Shaw was well aware that Molly Tompkins brought out qualities he shared with Professor Higgins. He sent her twice a week for lessons in diction to Professor Daniel Jones, who taught phonetics at London University. But principally he tutored her himself. 'You just do what I tell you,' he explained. He told her how to address an envelope and stick stamps on it; when to use make-up and how to order a vegetarian meal at a restaurant without risking early death. He described the correct manner of bargaining for white oxen when in Italy; went through the drill for curing a fear of bats; and strongly recommended parrots as preferable to dogs as pets for beautiful women. He instructed her in the art of having rows ('for heavens' sake make them as rowdy as possible') and of saying 'No!' with conviction ('It is the most useful accomplishment in the world'). Finally he provided hints on how to take all this advice: 'When you get a bit of advice, don't bolt it. Chew it fortyseven times; and then it will digest all right.'

It was curious that the more advice his 'Mollytompkins' heard, the more she appeared to need. 'The old should not prevent the young making fools of themselves,' he concluded. In this sense at least he was successful.

He went to see her at Gower Street, where she was learning eurhythmics and fencing as well as acting, and invited her to lunches at Adelphi Terrace where she met Barrie, Galsworthy and others who 'didn't register with me'. In the afternoons he sometimes gave her help with the lines she was learning. 'I was supposed to be able to go to Adelphi Terrace whenever I felt like it and make myself at home,' she remembered, 'but when Shaw wasn't there Charlotte was cool, and she could be very icy indeed . . . so I just went when I was invited.'

Molly was invited to spend part of the spring at Stratford-upon-Avon with the Shaws in 1922, and Laurence (her husband) came too. Then, when RADA broke up for the summer and Charlotte went to Ireland, G.B.S. invited them both to meet him at a Fabian Summer School at

Godalming and accompany him on a motor tour of English cathedral towns.

At Godalming Molly and Laurence acted as a shield against some of the more pressing Fabian ladies, especially one fiery redhead. And then there was a moment in the garden at Godalming when Molly spoke her feelings for Shaw. 'You will grow out of your Shavian infatuation (alas! for I hope it is a great pleasure to you),' he had told her. Later on he explained 'why I was so shy at Godalming'. Whatever age they might be in fairyland, in prosaic society (and what could be more prosaic than a Fabian garden) they were an old man and a young thing. 'La Rochefoucauld says that the very old and the very young, if they desire to avoid making themselves ridiculous, should never allude to the garden at Godalming.'

They began the tour, bowling along the English lanes in Shaw's car, 'open, high, doorless, with gears outside, and painted a hideous brown, but it was enchanting,' Laurence thought. ' . . . We took turns sitting up front with the chauffeur or in the back with Shaw.' They went to the music festival at Glastonbury, to Salisbury Cathedral, to Wells in Somerset and then diagonally across the country up to Northumberland. Shaw dressed for this adventuring in what Molly called 'old-fashioned knickers with stockings and a Norfolk jacket with pleats down the front and belt'. At night, while Molly and Laurence changed into evening clothes, Shaw presented himself in a buttoned-up, double-breasted, blue outfit, 'like a sailor's reefer'.

Molly was not an easy travelling companion, wanting to go off with G.B.S. to less historical sites and objecting to being booked into a separate hotel with Laurence. Their destination was Scarborough where another Fabian Summer School was taking place, and where they saw again the Fabian redhead. It was obviously she who had placed Molly in an annexe, sharing a cramped little room with Laurence far removed from Shaw. So 'just before dawn we packed and walked out,' Molly recorded, 'hired a car and went into Scarborough to catch a train to London'. But there were no London trains till the afternoon, so they took a room in a hotel and went out to 'a movie'.

Shaw came into Scarborough, searched the station, searched the hotels, and found them. There were no explanations. They sat through the film to its end, then he took them to their train, promising to see them in London that autumn. Laurence had thought Shaw would never speak to them again after they had run away without a word. But their bad behaviour actually seemed to have made him more friendly.

Shaw wanted Molly to finish her course and win the Gold Medal. But, hearing that the Plymouth Repertory needed a leading lady, she caught a train to Plymouth where the hypnotized manager engaged her. Kenneth Barnes and Claude Rains breathed with relief, and Shaw wrote to congratulate her. Yet there remained a problem. 'If you had a sense of humor . . .' Shaw began. But she hadn't. Unfortunately the stock company at Plymouth wanted comedies. 'I do not think she's any good for the stage,' the theatre manager notified Shaw. So she took to the road searching for a tragic lead.

Besides G.B.S., she had another champion in Johnston Forbes-Robertson, three years older than Shaw and soon to be knighted. A quarter of a century ago there had been a romance between Shaw's handsome Caesar and the girl Shaw had wanted for his Cleopatra and who became his Eliza. Now, for the second time, playwright and actor were led away by similar good looks. Forbes-Robertson 'seemed to ask me to every first night at the theatre,' Molly noticed, 'and to lunch or supper whenever I had a free moment'. A shadow-rivalry soon developed between her two septuagenarian suitors. 'I envy Shaw being so near you at the play, and seeing you in your lovely green dress,' Forbes-Robertson lamented: 'Oh, he doesn't like your earrings, doesn't he? Well *I* do, and I must come first, so there.' And Shaw enquired reprovingly: 'I gather that another gentleman of my age, and famous for his good looks and charm, was bolder.' Molly was always opening letters from these two fond old men. It seemed that G.B.S. wrote 'every day and Forbes-Robertson two or three times a day'.

These letters were also read by a Plymouth drama critic called Mollie Little, who had taken on the role of secretary and housekeeper to the Tompkins family in London, and who in 1925 tried to use them to blackmail Molly's admirers. With Forbes-Robertson, whose knighthood might have been imperilled by such revelations, Miss Little appears to have had some success. But, following the publication of his correspondence to Stella Campbell, Shaw was unable to take the threats seriously.

'Suddenly I was sick of the whole business,' Molly decided. ' . . . I wasn't supposed to be an actress.' She turned to Shaw for further advice. 'I see no reason on earth why you should not go to Italy,' he volunteered. 'Everybody should go to Italy.'

So Molly went to Italy, taking Laurence and inviting G.B.S. to join them. 'I will not come to Italy to share the fate of Achilles,' Shaw replied. In England – at Godalming for example – he had been 'bound to behave very well indeed for the credit of the [Fabian] Society,' he explained. But there were not the same constraints abroad.

*

During the late spring and early summer of 1925, Shaw's diary and letters record, he had been 'ill in bed' and 'crawling about a bit'; after which, between July and October, Charlotte raced him away on a bracing tour of the Orkneys and the Shetlands 'up to our eyes in scenery'. But by spring the following year his health had seriously collapsed. 'I had been ill for many months,' he later told Harriet Cohen. Charlotte was determined to take him somewhere so that he could get over his shivers. On 5 August 1926 they arrived at the Regina Palace Hotel at Stresa, overlooking Lake Maggiore.

It seemed an inspired choice. Before starting out by train, he had felt 'an obscure fire within me that craves for cold water'. At Lake Maggiore he was able to bathe every morning – '& I bathe sometimes,' added Charlotte in a letter to Apsley Cherry-Garrard. 'Altogether I think we have fallen on our feet & GBS is far more bright and happy.' They were particularly lucky to have found 'some gay bright young friends here'. She was referring to the conductor Albert Coates who owned a villa three miles from their hotel on the opposite side of the lake, 'a magnetically charming person,' Charlotte described him, with a 'wife [Madelon] we like too', and some interesting guests including Cecil Lewis and his wife 'Dooshka', who turned out to be a 'Prima Donna from Moscow'.

When not listening to music and bathing 'on the clean side' of the lake, Shaw was at the other side near Pallanza sitting for a statuette by Prince Paul Troubetzkoy who had 'a big studio & an astonishing wife,' Charlotte reported to Beatrice Webb. ' . . . It has kept GBS employed & amused going over day after day & sitting.' Much of the time 'we are on the lake in motor boats'. One of the Isole Borromee round which they boated – the tiny luxuriant island of San Giovanni – was advertised in their hotel as being available for renting from an Italian prince. In fact, it had been taken by Molly and Laurence Tompkins.

Shaw knew this before setting out for Stresa. 'At last an address!' he had written to Molly the previous month. But when he arrived, their palazzo was being renovated and Molly and Laurence were in Paris. 'I cannot tear myself away from the Isola Molli,' he wrote. 'I sailed round it again today . . .' On receiving his letter, Molly left Laurence and rushed down on the Orient Express. She arrived at the Regina Palace in a horse and carriage, the dust rising in the sunlight behind her.

She went bathing and picnicking with the Shaws' 'gay bright young friends', but could not enjoy herself. The presence of Charlotte, invariably dressed in black – sometimes in a black taffeta swimsuit with a stuffed canary on the shoulder – clouded her spirits. 'I like it best without Charlotte,' she stated. And when she was with Shaw alone, she found that Charlotte had been watching them through powerful binoculars. 'You and Charlotte have got to come to some arrangement,' Shaw insisted. But they could not. Molly hated Charlotte's air of ladylike superiority, and could not understand why everyone else seemed to like her. One day, Charlotte had accused her of having 'an evil mind'. Molly wondered as she lay in her lonely room that night what was making her so cross. Next morning she caught an early train back to Paris. Four postcards from Shaw pursued her: 'Your life seems to be one of considerable quite unnecessary friction,' he wrote. 'I didn't exactly want to leave,' Molly explained to Laurence. So, she despatched a telegram and let Laurence put her on the train for Italy.

Back at the Regina Palace, the concierge handed her a note from Shaw. They had not known when she was arriving, had stayed in till half-past two and were now on a previously arranged excursion to Orta, the silent green lake to the west, from which they would be back at dinner. 'Fury blazed up inside me,' Molly remembered. He had not detached himself and waited for her. 'So sorry to miss you this trip. Returning to Paris immediately,' she scribbled on a Tiffany card, and caught the afternoon train back. 'Return immediately to hell,' Shaw replied to her that night, '. . . and never dare write to me or approach me or mention your poisonous island to me again as long as you live.'

Even Laurence was 'almost beginning to lose patience'. There seemed only one thing to do. 'I suppose it's the only thing you *can* do,' Laurence agreed. So once more he put her on the train, the same train, and she checked into the Bellevue Hotel at Baveno on the edge of the lake two and a half miles from Stresa. 'Driving along the road to Stresa, which Shaw called the road to Baveno, I promised myself this time I'd be good.' And she very nearly was. After sun-filled days and quiet evenings, when they sat in a boat rowed by the leisurely stroke of the fishermen, Shaw would walk her back to Baveno, 'and then I would walk back with him halfway to Stresa and then he would return again to leave me at Baveno on the steps of the Bellevue, striding off into the night, the sound of his brogues fading into the lap-lap of wavelets from the lake'. On her last day, with autumn in the air, Molly accompanied the Shaws to a garden-party; then after they had taken Charlotte back to the hotel, Shaw 'came with me up to the station and put me on the train to Paris'.

*

He felt miraculously restored, 'better and much stronger than I had been for years before my illness'. This new vigour was 'partly you, I think,' he wrote to Molly. She had confided her growing adoration of him in a 'bothersomely honest letter' at Stresa, and this adoration was now 'an indispensable Vitamin in my bread of life'.

'I have still two years of youth left,' he had assured her when retreating from their tête-à-tête at Godalming: 'so make the most of them.' Now that he was seventy and she not yet thirty, it was time for some advice: 'Find your own way,' he tried to tell her; 'never mind me.' She must also mind Laurence who 'will certainly be vamped, and elope,' he warned. 'You have trained him to be imposed on.' Unless he found his roots back in the United States, Laurence would never do anything: the Jamesian era for 'deserting America to live in Europe as an artistic vagabond (like the sculptor Story, whom Charlotte knew quite well) is gone by'. But after this direct exhortation to Laurence came the irresistible afterthought: 'By the way, you might leave Molly behind if you are tired of her.'

He tried again. Molly was a coquette 'and the sooner you realize that what is fun to you is heartbreak and homebreak to your victims, the better,' he admonished her. 'Not that that will stop you; for the instinct which delights in dancing on the edge of a precipice when you have lured a giddy man there, knowing that your own head is sound and that you can get back in safety, is incurable.' In which case she had better leave all those young Italians she mentioned in her letters, and 'remain faithful to me, your ancient Shotover'.

Something had gone seriously wrong with the Shavian advice-machine. 'Love me as long as you can,' he wrote; 'but make young friends.' Yet he did not always want to shield her. 'You would get wearied if I were always nice and considerate of your feelings,' he wrote early in 1927. '... And anyhow, you must take me as I come ... I am beginning to let the mask slip occasionally and damn the consequences.'

Early in 1927 Charlotte took G.B.S. to stay with the Webbs at Passfield Corner. Beatrice and Charlotte appeared to be getting on more affectionate terms as they grew older. Charlotte interested Beatrice. 'She has developed admirable manners and a pleasing and cheerful personality ... there is fascination in an exquisitely clothed and cared-for person, if those artifices are combined with personal dignity and graciousness. Certainly she holds fast GBS's respect and affection.'

In her analysis of the Shaws' married happiness, Beatrice took no account of Charlotte's incurable arthritis and the pain she sought to rise above, through religious meditation; nor did Beatrice sense the dangerous restlessness that took possession of G.B.S. whenever he relaxed from his writing. In this state the attraction of Molly on her magic island grew 'very strong'. He knew that 'it is a mistake to go back anywhere' and that if he did go back to Lake Maggiore 'my infatuation would be suspected at once'. All the same, he still dreamed of the Baveno road.

To the Webbs, Charlotte had kept discreetly silent about Molly. Only to T. E. Lawrence did she show a glimmer of her feelings. 'She has no influence, but what she has is bad – you will understand.' Charlotte knew that G.B.S. wanted to return and felt another holiday in Italy would benefit his health. He could listen to music again with Albert Coates, and pose for a full-length statue this time by Troubetzkoy. By the first week of July 1927 they were back in the same corner suite at the Regina Palace.

Laurence and Molly were now living in their palazzo on the Isolino San Giovanni, and each morning Shaw and Charlotte came over the Bay of Pallanza in a small motorboat to swim. After lunch all four of them would return to the mainland and go off by car into the Lombardy hills. As the summer progressed and the heat intensified, Charlotte more often preferred to stay on the island during these afternoons: it was cooler to sit reading on one of the terraces under the trees in her black taffeta bathing dress than to bounce over the country roads at a mile a minute with Molly at the wheel. Laurence, too, was grateful to get back to his studio. So, while Charlotte read and Laurence worked, Shaw and Molly would drive off together into the mountains, sometimes staying late to eat supper at a trattoria or to watch movies in one of the towns round the lake, and coming home so late that Charlotte began to feel uneasy and 'even Laurence would frown'.

One day, as they were raising a cloud of white dust behind them, Molly turned off the road and bumped the Renault over the hollows and rough grasses of a field until they reached a copse of trees by a concrete emplacement 'just right for parking a car'. Not far from these trees flowed the river Toce, its smooth green surface concealing strong currents and treacherous whirlpools. They walked to the low sandy banks, and sat down under the eucalyptus trees. 'For a long time we lay on the river bank looking down at the water, or up at the tree limbs and sky, content and with no need to talk,' Molly remembered. 'All the million things I had to say to Shaw were forgotten.' Later, in his 'curiously enchanting voice', he began talking of what was 'uppermost in both our minds', and at the end Molly turned to him, 'so full of you, and the river, and trees, and sweetness' – but suddenly out of the landscape a soldier appeared and informed them that they were in a military zone, had perched their car on a gun emplacement and must remove it. *Subito!* He saluted and was gone.

This afternoon was the high point in their romance. Molly, who confessed to being 'dazed by the violence of my desire', went on to imply that there had been some sexual liaison between them that 'gave my body and my mind and my heart peace when I lay by the side of a river'. Shaw, too, appears to suggest that he may have come near to celebrating his seventy-first birthday that July as he had celebrated his twenty-ninth. 'I hoarded my bodily possessions so penuriously that even at seventy I had some left,' he reminded Molly eighteen months later, 'but that remnant was stolen from me on the road to Baveno and on other roads to paradise through the same district. Now they are all dusty highways on which I am safe because nobody can rob a beggar.'

Whatever happened, it led to different expectations. Shaw was to warn Molly against her erotic imagination because it could not make her happy. 'You thought that when you had secured your Ogygia and lured me to its shores you could play Calypso to my Odysseus and make a hog of me. Aren't you glad you didn't succeed?' But Molly was not glad. She wanted a fulfilled love affair with Shaw. That summer they all had a dreadful time: Shaw falling ill and Charlotte feeling wretched, Laurence like a helpless prisoner on the island and Molly a 'predestinate damned soul, a Vamp fiend'. 'You will prowl round that lake, making men's wives miserable, tormenting yourself whenever their glances wander from you for a moment,' Shaw wrote, 'until the lake water changes to fire and brimstone and rises up and scorches you into nothingness.'

During a sudden storm one night Molly and Laurence were almost drowned as they tried to reach Stresa in a canoe. The evening had been planned as a reconciliation. Arriving very late at the hotel, Molly was still trembling with fear and cold. Shaw picked up her shipwrecked figure in his arms and put her in his bed upstairs. Lying on his bed she told him she was pregnant, that she did not want another baby and was going to Milan for an abortion. 'Please don't go to Milano, Molly,' she remembered him saying. 'It will be my spiritual child at least.' But being in love with one man and apparently pregnant by another, Molly was determined. Later she noticed that Shaw's eyes looked old and tired 'and I felt I had committed a murder'. After this Shaw came every day to the island and would sit in the garden holding her hand. 'But there was little to say . . . it was almost a relief when the last day came.'

Shaw and Charlotte took the Orient Express back to London on 6 October. It had been a troubling episode. 'I must not think about you; for I cannot save you; I have done my best and only made matters worse,' he wrote to Molly, as he had written to Florence Farr and Janet Achurch. He asked her the same question he had asked Stella: 'Can you not learn how to live in the world?' But if he had taught them that, he would have destroyed what he loved in them. There seemed no future for Molly, though her future, like Stella's, was to stretch out as a long vexed sequel, shadowing their aborted romance. Molly's love-island, Shaw told her, was 'a place to spend six weeks a year in, but not a place to live in'. Yet it lingered like a sea fantasy over his last plays and continued to haunt his memory. 'Write oftener, far oftener, even if I cannot answer,' he appealed. 'The restless hands sometimes tire of the pen and remember the road to Baveno . . . angels will always love you, including G.B.S.'

4

INTELLIGENT WOMEN AND THE BODY POLITIC

> Such books are never written until mankind is horribly corrupted, not
> by original sin but by inequality of income.
>
> *The Intelligent Woman's Guide*

'My dear GBS

You will think me a dreadful bore when I tell you that I want you to send me a few of your ideas of Socialism. Unfortunately the Study Circle to which I belong have got hold of the fact that you are my brother-in-law, so I promised I would write to you. We want to know so many things . . . Will you answer my questions *quite plainly* . . .'

'It would be easy, dear madam, to refer you to the many books on modern Socialism which have been published since it became a respectable constitutional question in this country in the eighteen-eighties. But I strongly advise you not to read a line of them until you and your friends have discussed for yourselves how wealth should be distributed in a respectable civilized country, and arrived at the best conclusion you can.

For Socialism is nothing but an opinion held by some people on that point . . .'

So Shaw began *The Intelligent Woman's Guide to Socialism and Capitalism*, his 200,000-word reply to 'Mrs Chumly's' modest request. When the going was good he welcomed the challenge 'to do a real hard literary job, all brains, instead of writing plays'. But in other moods he would admit to having 'nearly killed myself' over 'my confounded book for women on socialism!' After three years, on 7 March 1927 it was 'within a chapter of its end,' he told T. E. Lawrence, and nine days later Charlotte wrote to Lawrence: 'The book – the Socialism book – is <u>finished</u>! Last words written this morning!'

There was a good deal more to follow these last words. He prepared two private copies of the *Guide* with special title pages: one for T. E. Lawrence and the other for his sister-in-law, Mary Cholmondeley, whose name he misspelt in the dedication. The four-colour dust-jacket was designed by Eric Kennington and showed a naked woman (actually Mrs Kennington) 'making a copious display of bare breasts and indolently scratching a swelling on her right forearm', protested a Dublin reader, as she peered in a well for the truth like a figure in a fairy story. The olive cloth binding had a woven-chain pattern by Douglas Cockerell in gilt and green; the laid paper was opaque and marked with wide vertical chains; there were green endpapers and a gilt top to the pages. Over 90,000 copies were published simultaneously on 1 June 1928 in Britain and the United States, costing 15s. and $3.00. 'The reception of The Guide has been overwhelming,' he reported four months later. 'I meant it to be.'

*

It should have been the work on socialist economics that Havelock Ellis had tried to commission from him in the 1880s. In or about December 1910, when first advocating 'the abolition of class by the abolition of inequality of income', he had composed what was in effect the opening chapter of this book as an exploration of how to get the economic basis of society right in a civilized country. Six years later, when resigning from the *New Statesman*, he wrote to Beatrice Webb that he would be taking 'my solution and my policy elsewhere. And there is nowhere else except in a book doing at long range what should be done by a journal at short range.' In one form or another his *Guide* to Socialism had been waiting in the wings for forty years.

Six weeks before publication an Act had been passed in Parliament lowering the voting age for women from thirty to twenty-one and giving them the same residence qualification as men. With the small exception of business and university franchises, the democratic equality of one adult one vote was finally reached in the 1929 general election. This extension of the franchise added five million newly qualified women to the electoral register. Since Labour increased its support in the country by three million votes, Shaw's special appeal to women had been perfectly timed. For its fifth reprint in May 1929 his publisher brought out a five-shilling 'popular' edition, called by Lord Lothian 'a Manifesto for the election of 1929'.

But otherwise Shaw had delayed too long. 'The sources of his intellectual creed are the tenets of the late Victorian era,' wrote Father Martin d'Arcy. His faith in government power and compulsory labour was unshadowed by auguries of totalitarianism. The *Guide* contained more John Eliot Cairnes than John Maynard Keynes and was addressed to women from his sister-in-law's class. He explicitly links his work to that of European authors of the nineteenth century, and admits his lack of involvement with post-war society:

'Ibsen's women are all in revolt against Capitalist morality . . . The modern literature of male frustration, much less copious, is post-Strindberg. In neither branch are there any happy endings. They have the Capitalist horror without the Socialist hope.

The post-Marxian, post-Ibsen psychology gave way in 1914–18 to the postwar psychology. It is very curious; but it is too young, and I too old for more than this bare mention of its existence and its literature.'

But the *Guide*'s merits did not depend on topicality. Here was the summary of a lifetime's thought, a work of eloquent insight and fantasy, and Shaw's political autobiography. As he marches forward on his pilgrimage the social landscape behind him is brilliantly lit up, while ahead the Promised Land glows with an eerie light. Only the marching figure himself is lost in the midst of current confusions, so that we cannot see whether he has struck an original route or is losing himself on some precipitous digression.

By making use of simple definitions, such as 'capital is spare money', Shaw had set out to demystify a subject that, like medicine, was increasingly viewed as being impenetrable to non-specialists. 'Economics is supposed to be an involved and abstruse subject,' acknowledged Martin d'Arcy, 'yet here we have the secrets of it set forth in a prose worthy of Platonic dialogue.' The *Guide* is a sustained act of teaching that aims at driving the reader back to the foundations of her own beliefs (Shaw uses throughout the feminine pronoun which in certain contexts, he points out, 'includes the masculine'). Most works on economics and political science had been addressed to an abstract reader conceived as aridly male: 'You might read a score of them without ever discovering that such a creature as a woman had ever existed.' He concluded that 'because there is nothing to sell, there is a very general disposition to regard a married woman's work as no work at all, and to take it as a matter of course that she should not be paid for it'.

Anyone who can manage her domestic economy, Shaw maintains, can understand the political economy of twentieth-century capitalism. He further raises the self-esteem of his readers by attributing the greater success of men in business and the professions to their sexual inferiority, the jobs of accountants, barristers, doctors, managers, shopkeepers and so on being generally neuter. Since women have a natural monopoly in bearing children, it followed that, 'being as it is the most vital of all the functions of mankind, it gives women a power and importance that . . . men cannot attain to at all. In so far as it is a slavery, it is a slavery to Nature and not to Man . . . The only disadvantage the woman is at in competition with the man is that the man must either succeed in his business or fail completely in life, whilst the woman has a second string to her bow.'

Feminism was only one aspect of his general theory of equality; nevertheless, as Margaret Walters has written in the 1980s, the *Guide* 'remains an important feminist document' which impressed politicians, historians and intellectuals. 'After the Bible this is in my eyes the most important book that humanity possesses,' Ramsay MacDonald remarked, an aside that revealed him to be 'more of a wit than I suspected,' Shaw granted. 'It is a very great book,' T. E. Lawrence wrote to Charlotte. ' . . . It is like the aged Hardy writing poetry.'

The poetry is in the dogma. In Shaw's Paradiso all citizens have as natural a right to equal incomes as they have to air and sunlight, justice and education. He examines seven ways of distributing wealth, exposing all but one of them as deadly sins. This logical annihilation, which appears to drive capitalism into a series of surrenders and retreats, is a bewitching display in the art of political pamphleteering. He surveys the nation's institutions, from the courts of justice and the institution of marriage to the usefulness of its schooling and the quality of its newspapers, and finds them all ingeniously bedevilled by the effects of dividing people into rich and poor.

Shaw's Purgatorio is here and now. He struggles to free himself from his own respectability and retrieve the power of anger, the sense of disgust, that had so impressed William Morris during their street-campaigning days. 'His criticism of the modern capitalist muddle is so damaging, his style so trenchant, and so full of reserves of indignation and righteous scorn,' Morris had written, 'that I sometimes wonder that *guilty*, i.e. non-socialist, middle class people can sit and listen to him.' Now that he was addressing an audience of Conservative matrons and obliged to be charming, reasonable, elementary, Shaw wondered whether his old fires were failing. 'I miss from its babytalk the sweep of my ancient periods,' he confessed. But in his early chapters, and again in the peroration at the end, he rekindles these flames of his youth. They rise most brilliantly when swept by the disillusions and betrayals of political events he had lived through, and when seen against the clouds of his own rising despair. He writes as one whose normal affections have been gouged out by capitalism and whose politics have rushed in to fill the emotional void. 'I do not want any human child to be brought up as I was brought up . . . Life is made lonely and difficult for me in a hundred unnecessary ways.'

Shaw's peroration to the Intelligent Woman is similar to Swift's 'unanswerable' indictment of mankind as 'the wickedest of all known species'. He finds his redemption in a formula that, substituting inequality of income for original sin, provides him with an abstract optimism. If moral triumphs, like mechanical triumphs, are reached by trial and error, he reasons, then it is possible to despair of capitalism without despairing of human nature. Under more benign conditions we would discover human nature to be good enough for reasonable purposes and would come to read *Gulliver's Travels* as a vivid clinical lecture on extinct moral diseases 'which were formerly produced by inequality as smallpox and typhus were produced by dirt'.

Capitalism diminished the collective well-being by directing so much of a nation's energies to maintaining the parasitic rich. Under these conditions we can see 'half-fed, badly clothed, abominably housed children all over the place; and the money that should go to feed and clothe and house them properly being spent in millions on bottles of scent, pearl necklaces, pet dogs,' he complained. ' . . . [This] is a badly managed, silly, vain, stupid, ignorant nation, and will go to the bad in the long run no matter how hard it tries to conceal its real condition from itself by counting the pearl necklaces and Pekingese dogs as wealth.'

Shaw's socialism was a means of achieving social responsibility by active interference in the production and distribution of the nation's income – that is, by a well-managed public service to replace the quarrelsome and divisive effects of private competition. The great basic industries needed to be managed for the benefit of all, though not, he urged, until an efficient organization was in readiness to take over control from private hands whose insatiable drive for profit had shown no concern with the public interest. The railways, the mines and, above all, the banks which were the chief factor in determining the level of prices and the use of capital for development, should be made community property.

Placing himself ahead of events, Shaw looked back at the contemporary world. Such a peculiar focus gave the *Guide* some of its originality, but also explains its lack of political impact. He is especially critical of Britain's complacent acceptance of the parliamentary circus as the best available type of government. 'If democracy is not to ruin us,' he warned, 'we must at all costs find some trustworthy method of testing the qualifications of candidates before we allow them to seek election.

'When we have done that we may have great trouble in persuading the right people to come forward. We may even be driven to compel them; for those who fully understand how heavy are the responsibilities of government and how exhausting its labor are the least likely to shoulder them voluntarily. As Plato said, the ideal candidate is the reluctant one.'

Shaw's economic proposals were not so much methods for changing the present as fantasies for escaping from it. He wanted the world to be controlled by dreams rather than experience. But when he draws close to contemporary politics his pen takes on a self-destructive cunning, as if the boy once neglected by his mother has grown into a man convinced he is neglected by his adopted mother country. Nobody understood what was happening except 'here and there a prophet crying in the wilderness and being either ignored by the press or belittled as a crank'. He threatens smug British democracy with all sorts of bogeymen dictators. In such recurring passages he invites the disrespect of which he is complaining. His tone wavers, his judgement narrows, and there is another symptom. 'To put the same thing in another way . . . I could go on like this for years.' All this was 'too boring for the intelligent man, if I'm any sample,' commented D. H. Lawrence. 'Too much gas-bag.'

Shaw was at his best when passionately defending his plan. When questioned as to what income would content him, he retorted: 'Who cares what I would or would not be content with? . . . We shall have to be content with our share . . . It is our public business to see that everyone shall have as much as possible, and not less or more than anyone else.' To a correspondent who had questioned the compatibility of socialism with foreign trade, he replied: 'I need not remind you that trade, home or foreign, is something to be minimized, not maximized and regarded as an index to prosperity,' he wrote.

'. . . the garden of Eden was happy without trade. But to many of our statisticians it seems as if Eve, instead of handing Adam the apple, had sold it for a bunch of Algerian dates, and the purchaser had sold it for a pound of Italian olives, and the olive sellers sold it for some Spanish figs, and the fig merchant sent it to Ireland in payment for a blackthorn stick, and so on round the globe until it came round to Mesopotamia again and was purchased by Adam for an ostrich feather, both Adam and Eve would have been much more prosperous.'

Harold Laski objected that 'for a man to tell you that the desirable thing is equality of income without telling you how to get it is simply irritating'. But Shaw had argued that people would win socialism by desiring it, and his *Guide*, like an alchemy, had been written to create that desire. 'The difficulty of applying the constructive program of Socialism lies not in the practical but in the metaphysical part of the business; the will to equality,' he wrote.

He was sometimes accused of attempting to banish evil from the world. He would respond that his *Guide* simply traced certain avoidable evils to inequality and suggested that they would not occur under his plan. 'No woman would have to turn her back on a man she loved because he was poor, or be herself passed by for the same reason. All the disappointments would be natural and inevitable disappointments; and there would be plenty of alternatives and consolations.'

Shaw's economic solution for uniting people in a true democracy was the invention of a man who believed his own disunities to have arisen from the marriage of his parents made under economic dictatorship. By changing the economic basis of society, he hoped to change natural behaviour. Beatrice Webb, who had thought it would 'be a marvel if it is not a bad book', came to marvel at its autobiographical sincerity and pathos. 'His acknowledged genius, his old age, the warmth and depth of his earnestness and his amazing literary brilliance have paralysed his would-be critics and opened the hearts of fellow-socialists, especially those on the left,' she wrote. 'He denounces society as it is, he gives no credit and no quarter, and he preaches a curiously abstract utopia, which eludes criticism because of its very unreality.'

SIXTEEN

I

STRIKING AN ATTITUDE

In fact all men are comic.
> Shaw to Stanley W. Bull (6 July 1926)

Adelphi Terrace was scheduled for demolition. While G.B.S. and Charlotte were in Stresa during the summer of 1927, the servants moved their belongings to a service flat in 4 Whitehall Court. This was a wonderfully turreted old building, with pavilion roofs and loggias, facing the Thames at Westminster between Charing Cross Bridge and Old Scotland Yard. Number 130 was a corner flat with five rooms and a surrounding balcony overlooking the Embankment and the river.

They moved in early that October. Shaw was determined not to like the place, but gradually Charlotte rearranged the furniture, positioned her Chinese pottery around it, and settled in the Dolmetsch clavichord, the Rodin bust, the Sartorio watercolour landscapes, the print of William Morris and other treasures. G.B.S. organized his study – a dozen filing cabinets, hundreds of books, a big flat-topped desk for himself opposite a smaller one for Blanche Patch, and between them a typing table. They were in business again.

'G.B.S. was not fond of Whitehall Court,' observed St John Ervine who was a neighbour there for the first year and a half, 'but Charlotte loved it.' There was positively nothing to do in the way of housekeeping, except to study the menu which was discreetly slipped under the door each morning from the restaurant downstairs. In the eight-storey block there were some 150 service flats as well as a selection of clubs – the Junior Army and Navy, Golfers & Lady Golfers and, with its separate entrance at the end of the building, the National Liberal Club. The ceilings were high, the floors of marble and the walls panelled. It was a world apart, a temple to the rich. The residents included tea-merchants, oil magnates and diplomats from around the world, as well as retired officers, the editor of *Punch* and various commuters to the House of Lords.

G.B.S. was always going in and out. The young bookshop assistant in the foyer would watch him striding across the hall. He was often followed, she noticed, by two women of contrasting appearance. The first, slightly behind him loaded with a bundle of papers and looking firmly ahead, was tall and austere; the second, who was older and more solid, wearing a squashy hat and carrying a travelling rug, smiled and nodded as she passed. One morning when G.B.S. was hurrying out alone, this young girl held the door open for him. 'Never hold open any door for a man,' he said to her. 'It embarrasses him and belittles you.' He seemed to think this all the more important as she had only one arm. After this introduction, he would sometimes come over and chat to her at the bookstall. He was interested in how 'she spent her time, where she had her lunch and how much it cost and other everyday details of daily life'. She took on jobs for him – selecting books for a journey, or ringing his bell when she saw newspaper reporters going up so that he could nip down the back stairs. Occasionally she went up and had tea in the flat and was surprised to find that the dumpier of the two ladies (whom she had guessed must be a housekeeper) was Shaw's wife, 'a very homey, comfortable person' who told her she was 'undernourished' and presented her with a tin of biscuits each month.

*

'I have seen very little of anyone who has not worked with me,' Shaw wrote early in 1928. 'Except with my wife I have no companionships: only occasional contacts, intense but brief. I spring to intimacy in a moment, and forget in half an hour.' One vital new companion for Charlotte and workmate for G.B.S. was Lady Astor. In 1927, Nancy Astor invited them to spend Christmas with her at Cliveden and they were snowed up there for eighteen days. It was for both of them a surreal expanse of time. 'We both agree that all that has occurred during the last 3 weeks is a wonderful & impossible dream,' Charlotte wrote to Lady Astor. ' . . . I feel as if I had known you and your husband all my life.'

Nancy Astor had acquired a taste for English country life in Virginia where it was assiduously imitated. She had apparently been attracted to her first husband, Robert Shaw, by his spectacular polo: he had an uncanny knack of tumbling off his one-eyed pony without damaging himself. Was he intoxicated? The teetotal Nancy left him several times, beginning on the second night of their marriage. Sex had come as a shock to her: it was so rude.

After the final break-up of her marriage and the death of her mother, Nancy had come to England, a politer country. Here in 1906 she married Waldorf Astor, a perfect gentleman of German origin who had a bad heart and plenty of excellent racehorses. She was to enter the history books as the first woman Member of Parliament to take her seat, though she achieved little in the House of Commons except a series of vivid interruptions.

'Charlotte is very fond of you,' Shaw wrote to Nancy. 'So am I. I don't know why.' Nancy's devastating personality guarded a rather frail character but admitted others to her protection. She was supported by a wilful belief in Christian Science and, unlike Beatrice Webb, was never derisive about Charlotte's mystical wanderings. She did not dream of flirting with G.B.S. The liberties she took with him were spectacularly safe – and rather tickled Charlotte. Once, approaching his shed at Ayot, she pulled open the door and seeing G.B.S. at work on a manuscript barked out: 'Come out of there, you old fool. You've written enough nonsense in your life!'

The tone they took with each other was part of what Nancy Astor's biographer, Christopher Sykes, called the 'freemasonry' of famous people. Nancy was a mixture of combustible qualities – a 'volcano', Shaw called her. He did not really expect to convert her to socialism. Occasionally he might try to permeate a Private Member's Bill or influence an amendment to some clause in a Government Bill, but what he chiefly wanted was to demonstrate how people of absolutely different ideological commitments could strike up a lasting friendship. Flourishing in the limelight rather than in sunlight, Nancy seemed like a Shavian creation. At Cliveden, a vast nineteenth-century Italianate mansion overlooking the Thames, she created a fantasy kingdom that surrendered to reality only under extreme pressure – such as the Great War, when it was converted into a hospital and convalescent home.

Nancy invited G.B.S. to this amphitheatre in Berkshire as a new star, and provided him with a new audience. 'I "peacock" here (Charlotte's expression) amid week end crowds of visitors,' he wrote to Molly Tompkins near the end of his first visit. 'The mutual liking of the Shaws and Astors grows apace,' Beatrice Webb noted disapprovingly in her diary.

Shaw brought such celebrities as Lawrence of Arabia to Cliveden and performed before people who belonged neither to his Fabian nor to his theatre worlds. He would hold reading parties for his new political comedies there, going through the supporting guest list with Nancy. 'What about Balfour? . . . what about Mosley & his Cynthia (to represent the Labor Party)?'

Cliveden appeared an ideal place for the presentation of Shaw's extravaganzas. It also became renowned as the headquarters of a secret conspiracy to make a second Western accord with Hitler. Shaw himself was contemptuous of this theory. He conspired with no one, treated his own opinions as unique, and was not secretive about them. 'Never has a more senseless fable got into the headlines,' he wrote. The fable had floated up from a series of articles by Claud Cockburn in his paper, *The Week*, re-creating Cliveden as a castle of plot and machination. Shaw resented his own theatre being converted into a branch of the Foreign Office, and ridiculed 'the silly notion that big historic changes can be effected by the country-house clique of a wicked British aristocracy'. In the wake of these rumours, Nancy Astor was referred to in the House of Commons as 'the honourable member for Berlin', and treacherous scandals were passed among the newspapers. Shaw went to her defence in the American magazine *Liberty*, pointing out that, far from being German fifth column agents, the Astors 'have become the representation of America in England; and any attack on them is in effect an attack on America'.

This defence of his friend – taken up after an uncharacteristic appeal from Nancy – was read by Beatrice Webb with a wry smile. 'Alas! poor Shaw, you have succumbed to Charlotte,' she had written in her diary. Arnold Bennett had observed that Charlotte 'plays the role of the super-celebrity's wife with much tact'. But this tact did not impress Beatrice. She disapproved of the Cliveden Set as she had disapproved of 'the Souls' before the First World War. Both were aspects of a world she had renounced in order to be a socialist. 'What troubles us is that this new intimacy will widen the estrangement of G.B.S. from the Labour Movement,' she wrote, 'build higher the barrier between him and the young intellectuals who are working out the better way of life for the bulk of the people – and dishearten and discourage his old admirers.'

Democracy, Shaw believed, meant the trial and error of political experiment through representatives of opposing ideologies exchanging thoughts independently of party political whips. Cliveden, where a 'vociferous Marxist Communist' such as himself could meet Colonel Lindberg (the friend of Hitler's chief-of-staff), a dyed-in-the-wool Liberal Lord Lothian, and Charlie Chaplin, was fundamentally more democratic than Parliament. Shaw did not flatter himself that he had influenced Chamberlain's appeasement policy; he had no special knowledge of Lord Halifax's visit to Goering and Hitler late in 1937. But he believed that, if denied war, both Hitler and Mussolini would fall: 'Twopence worth of manners may make all the difference.'

What discouraged young intellectual socialists and disheartened old Fabian admirers was Shaw's championing of Mussolini in the 1920s. People 'are so tired of indiscipline and muddle and Parliamentary deadlock,' Shaw wrote, 'that they feel the need of a strenuous tyranny, and think Mussolini the right sort of tyrant'. Certainly Mussolini's remarkable *coup de théâtre* could not have been brought off without popular support.

'All dictators begin as reformers and are encouraged by all sensible people until they find that their subjects do not understand their reforms and respond to nothing but military glory,' Shaw was to write. 'I applauded both Hitler and Musso while they were in their reform phase, just as

Churchill did.' On the road to dictatorship, with the official title *Il Duce*, Mussolini had begun a campaign of beating up his opponents. The murder in June 1924 of Giacomo Matteoti, Secretary-General of Italy's Socialist Party, led to a reign of oppression lasting until his fall from power nineteen years later. Shaw had picked up some bits and pieces of information about Mussolini from one of the neighbours at Stresa, Carlo Emanuele Basile, a novelist who had become Federal Secretary of the province of Novara in 1925, and would be condemned in 1945 to thirty years' imprisonment for war crimes. Shaw learnt that Mussolini was accepted as the only competent leader available. He was a 'Big Simpleton', in Shaw's view, and initially a man of the people.

Some people assumed that Shaw was unaware of the assassination of Matteoti and other atrocities. 'I knew about them,' he replied. Acknowledging that the dictatorship of *Il Duce* had been established with 'all the usual villainies', he assured the Austrian socialist politician Friedrich Adler that such brutalities 'which accompany the eternal struggle of government with anarchy . . . disgust me as much as they disgust you'. But he considered these savageries so customary in history as to be hardly worth remarking. 'The only question for us is whether he [Mussolini] is doing his job well enough to induce the Italian nation to accept him *faute de mieux*,' he wrote. 'They do accept him, some of them *faute de mieux*, several of them with enthusiasm.' Shaw placed himself in the first category: 'I have no "enthusiasm for Mussolini",' he insisted; 'but I back every ruler until he goes wrong.'

But Mussolini had gone wrong in the early 1920s, the historian Gaetano Salvemini argued, and Shaw had put himself in the wrong by openly accepting fascist Italy. Shaw replied that what he was accepting were facts: he would have preferred the Italian workers and liberals not to have been 'so hopelessly incompetent that Italy gave Mussolini *carte blanche* to extirpate them'. Italian exiles had the right to cry 'Tyranny! Murder!' British citizens, with no such *locus standi*, must insist on a practical foreign policy.

Shaw handled Mussolini as a theatrical director might, removing him in his imagination from Italy and making him perform before a crowd of anxious British onlookers. His Mussolini was the actor-scoundrel Britain would deserve if it continued to neutralize socialism with the procrastinations of sham democracy.

What made socialists indignant was the lack of moral perspective in someone who had asserted that progress depends on changing moral sensibility. The social critic who once challenged rule by historical precedent now appeared to slot fascist Italy into an inevitably recurring historical pattern going back to Caesar and Antony. Where was the sense of proportion in giving precedence to diplomatic courtliness over physical barbarity, to train times over terror? 'What G.B.S. has lost is any sympathy with the underdog,' Beatrice Webb was to comment after reading the 'Preface on Bosses' he wrote for *The Millionairess*. ' . . . He feels the frustration of old age and resents it.'

As a product of this frustration and resentment, Mussolini became a figure of make-believe whom G.B.S. could command to conquer old enemies. When Mussolini invades Abyssinia, Shaw goes with him – and invades Ireland, imposing on her all Mussolini's hypothetical improvements ('policed and water-supplied roads for a savage or waste country'). So, satisfying many urges, Mussolini appears on picture postcards on which Sonny draws bubbles and balloons, while G.B.S. is simultaneously extolling *Il Duce* as an emblem of national efficiency. 'He is still obsessed about Mussolini,' Beatrice Webb wrote, 'and his obsession takes queer forms.'

2

UPSETTING *THE APPLE CART*

> What takes place in a theatre is not always a simple matter of you please
> me and I'll pay you.
>
> *Malvern Festival Book* (1935)

Sitting alone in Whitehall Court, his typewriter on his knees 'like a sailor with his lass', Shaw would sometimes wonder whether he had finally shot his bolt. At least his migraines had gone after *The Intelligent Woman's Guide*: 'I transferred them to my readers.' While still at work on this book he had got a notion of a play which went on germinating in his mind. 'I slept very well last night; and the morning was all sunshine,' he wrote to his printer William Maxwell on 5 November 1928. '*Consequently I began a new play.*' He wrote it with extraordinary ease and swiftness. The subject matter and stimulus had been provided by Granville-Barker's long-maturing tragicomedy *His Majesty*. In less than eight weeks he had a complete play 'in the rough' – just in time for it to be read to Nancy Astor's guests at Cliveden over the New Year. 'The name of the play is *The Apple Cart*,' he wrote, 'and it is as unlike St Joan as it possibly can be.'

*

Shortly after mounting the British première of *Back to Methuselah*, Barry Jackson had announced that he was closing the Birmingham Repertory Theatre in Station Road. This ultimatum, which paradoxically saved the theatre, was a measure of his discouragement. 'The condition of the English Theatre has moved steadily downward, and today it may be said to have touched its lowest level on record,' wrote the stage-director William Poel in 1920. ' . . . The public has for so long seen theatrical amusements carried on as an industry, instead of an art, that . . . the plays of Shaw, Galsworthy, Barker, Masefield, with those of all men who respect themselves and their calling, are put on one side as being impossible compositions, written by those who do not understand the needs of the public, meaning those who are not with the Stock Exchange financiers.' Shaftesbury Avenue had been taken over by Threadneedle Street, driving the majority of Shaw's London productions in the 1920s to a drill hall out in Hampstead converted by Norman Macdermot into the Everyman Theatre; while his touring rights in thirteen plays were leased to the Macdona Players led by Esmé Percy 'with whom I never meddle'.

Barry Jackson shared Shaw's dislike of the West End which had contaminated so much of the repertory movement in London. He wanted to found a pastoral theatre, similar to the Three Choirs Festival at Gloucester. It was while walking with Shaw one day near Jackson's home at Blackhill that the idea came to him of fulfilling this dream in Malvern. The place had everything to recommend it. Malvern was a spa town built on terraces along a steep range of hills, and it had a newly reconstructed theatre. In the socialist England of Shaw's dreams, Barry Jackson would have found himself manager of a national theatre. But without public endowment there was nothing for it but to leave London and make a fresh start in the country where rents were comparatively low. While London's West End had become one of the most depressing growths of capitalism, Jackson's private enterprise impressed Shaw. So he made a pact. If Jackson went ahead with his scheme for a festival at Malvern, he would write a new play for it.

And Barry Jackson had gone ahead, assembling a company of more than sixty players who rehearsed for seven weeks at Lillian Baylis's Old Vic before the Malvern Festival opened. The pattern was to present a different play each evening for one week and then to repeat this programme over a second week. Visitors were encouraged to stay a whole week, enjoying the extra-theatrical enjoyments of morning lectures and concerts in the Winter Garden, donkey rides up the hills, gondoliering and night bathing in the pools. Afterwards the productions would transfer to Birmingham and only after that would the more successful ones advance into London.

Jackson realized that this venture needed a dramatic patron and he dedicated the festival to Shaw. 'We gather here, among the hills, to perform an act of homage to our greatest living dramatist,' Jackson wrote, 'to be amused and quickened by his humour and wisdom.' Six thousand people were to visit the Bernard Shaw Exhibition over the fortnight, and the cycle of plays included *Back to Methuselah*, *Caesar and Cleopatra* and *Heartbreak House*, as well as what Shaw called, in his flyleaf dedication to Jackson, 'the play which owes its existence entirely to you'.

Having laid the foundation stone of the Shakespeare Memorial Theatre in Stratford the previous month, Shaw arrived in Malvern on 18 August 1929. No other dramatist could have shifted the attention of the newspapers to a small town in the west of England on a sweltering Sunday afternoon in August. It was not even a world première (that had taken place, using Floryan Sobieniowski's translation, two months previously, at Warsaw's Teatr Polski). Nevertheless the first British production was treated as an international event. A special Sunday train was hired to carry down from London more than sixty drama critics who were delivered to the theatre doors in plain vans. Cedric Hardwicke was starring as a future King of England with Edith Evans as his mistress, and G.B.S. was able to assure everyone that, like the exciting new films beginning to fill the cinemas, his play was 'One hundred percent talking'.

*

The two acts of *The Apple Cart* are introduced by an overture and interrupted by an interlude. It is a burlesque of parliamentary government in the form of *opéra bouffe*. 'This music is a music of ideas . . . in which moralities are used as the motifs,' wrote Edmund Wilson. The chief role, taken by the King of England, is played against a children's chorus of uniformed Cabinet Ministers led by the head boy or Prime Minister. Initially there are two secretaries, or walking gentlemen, who begin a Mozartian overture which, Shaw told the playwright Alfred Sutro, had been part of a false start. 'I began with a notion of two great parties: the Ritualists and the Quakers, with the King balancing them one against the other and finally defeating a combination of them. But I discarded this, as there wasn't room for it.' What he retained was a duet that presents a mocking celebration of the ritualism that cherishes the philistine *status quo*, and this prepares us for an investigation into the appearance and reality of democratic power.

The Interlude, which precedes the second act and takes place in Orinthia's boudoir, is another exploration of power based on appearance. Shaw himself described this scene as 'a brief but intense sex interlude' and certainly it was intended to offer the audience an erotic interest absent elsewhere in the play. 'Orinthia, the proud, the aristocratic, the goddesslike, the woman of lofty enchantments and "strangely innocent relations"' had been modelled on Stella Campbell: 'the magnificence of the picture is due to you,' he was to tell her. But Stella in her middle sixties no longer felt magnificent.

Nothing seemed to have gone right since her beloved son's death in the war; her marriage to George Cornwallis-West had come unstuck, the roles she could take in the theatre were diminishing and, having paid her son's and her husband's debts, money was running out. But she refused to part with Shaw's 'lovely letters' (those letters over the publication of which she had behaved so badly), despite his advice to put them on the market before their price tumbled. A better solution, it seemed to her, would be to play a role in his new play.

'I wonder if you will come and read the new play to me,' she invited him on 12 February 1929, 'as you half promised you would.'

'I can't read plays to a starving woman,' he prevaricated – and offered instead to pay her telephone and electrical bills.

'Come and read your play to me,' she ordered him. ' . . . You cannot dare to make my poverty an excuse!'

But he had another excuse. 'I have just been smitten with a frightful and probably infectious cold . . . and I will not risk giving it to you this week, nor next.'

'I wonder if you are ever coming to read your play to me,' she tried again on 26 March.

This time he confessed to being 'too shy to read you the only scene in that play that would interest you. Its scandalous climax is a reminiscence of Kensington Square.'

'I know why you feel shy,' she responded. Her friend Edith Lyttelton had by now told her something about the scene and how Shaw had explained that Stella could not play Orinthia because 'no one could play themselves'. It was obvious to her that 'the scene isn't true, though it may amuse you to fancy it so'. He readily agreed with her: it was fiction, not fact – in short, a play. Still she pressed him and still he resisted.

Eventually Stella happened to encounter Edith Evans who 'gazed eagerly at me saying she was playing *me* in *The Apple Cart* at Malvern and in Birmingham and London'. 'You should have sent me your play to read,' she wrote to Shaw on 8 July. 'You are out of tune with friendship and simple courtesy.'

He had put off this dreadful confrontation for five months – too long, he now realized. On 11 July he went to her flat in Pont Street. Though they had kept in correspondence they had not met for the best part of fifteen years. He was conscious of no longer being her 'brilliant adorable

Irish lad' but a white-haired pink-cheeked skeletal figure on the eve of his seventy-third birthday. She had expanded from his 'blessedest darling' gypsy child into a woman of 'magnificent bulk . . . the chins luxuriant too . . . [and] noxious little dogs yapping at her heels'.

They still had their famous voices – hers more throaty than ever, his lilting Irish tones like the shivering of a wind across a lake – and with these voices they set out to repeat their *Pygmalion* duet in Edith Lyttelton's drawing-room before the war. He began the Interlude, and she listened until he came to the passage where Orinthia offers to give King Magnus 'beautiful, wonderful children' in order to win him from his wife and make herself Queen, and adds: 'have you ever seen a lovelier boy than my Basil?' Shaw then delivered the King's reply: 'Basil is a very good-looking young man, but he has the morals of a tramp.' This was too much for Stella. It was true that her pampered son had dissipated his life in gambling and affairs, but she loved him and felt she would never forgive Shaw. He registered the depth of Stella's mortification and conceded: 'I will let him go as a beautiful child . . . as he suffered for other people's sins, the balance of justice is struck.'

Stella also felt sensitive over references to her marriages. 'Not another word on the subject shall ever fall from my lips,' Shaw lied. The struggle between them went on into August. 'How troublesome you are!' he complained. His piecemeal revisions were no cure for the soreness in Stella's heart. 'Tear it up,' she commanded him. ' . . . Please do as I say – you will feel strangely relieved.' But he would not.

Shaw knew that her real objection sprang from the corrupted picture of their romance. 'My love for you was the love of a child who feels safe,' she wrote to him. Shaw echoes this sentiment when he makes King Magnus tell Orinthia that they were 'two children at play'. But there is nothing childlike in Orinthia and nothing 'innocent' about her relations with Magnus. She is a tyrant of the emotions who exploits the King's susceptibility to her beauty. 'Heaven is offering you a rose; and you cling to a cabbage,' she tells him. The cabbage is Magnus's wife, Queen Jemima.

The previous year Granville-Barker had published *His Majesty*, a play in which the Queen, who is a snob and a political idiot, irresponsibly precipitates a crisis which can only be resolved by the abdication of the King. Shaw reverses the situation. Though described as 'romantically beautiful, and beautifully dressed', Orinthia is without charm, except perhaps the charm of a precocious child. Stella Campbell did not know how unhappily his recollections of her had been disturbed by Molly Tompkins, who also, like Orinthia, had used her sexual powers to keep him from returning to Charlotte. King Magnus, who stands for 'conscience and virtue' in his dealings with the Cabinet, admits to Orinthia that with her he has no conscience – which is, in effect, what Shaw said to Stella about his writing of *The Apple Cart*: 'I am an artist and as such utterly unscrupulous when I find my model – or rather when she finds me.' This is the attitude of Louis Dubedat in *The Doctor's Dilemma*.

Stella's complaint was that conscienceless art led to falsification. It took away her talent and occupation, and robbed her of wit and sensitivity. By casting Orinthia as the King's platonic mistress, Shaw also negated her sexuality. 'I ran away from you at Sandwich because I wanted to remain Queen of the Kingdom of my Heart,' Stella explained, ' – but I suppose you mustn't humble the King in your play like that.' 'Yes: you were right, Sandwich and all,' Shaw confirmed. In the fantasy of the play, it is the King who struggles free of Orinthia. 'You are so abominably strong that I cannot break loose without hurting you,' he says.

Orinthia's bedroom is no fairyland. It is a battlefield for sexual politics. And it is this theme, ending with its skirmish on the floor and reaching back beyond Stella to Shaw's memories of Jenny Patterson, that connects the structurally intrusive Interlude to the rest of the play.

Orinthia is one of three queens in *The Apple Cart*. 'Everyone knows that I am the real queen,' she announces. '... I am one of Nature's queens.' By Nature's queens she means those who are naturally endowed with physical superiority, and by real she means the reality of appearance. What she offers the King is a pop-star dictatorship of the masses by beautiful people. But Shaw turns aside this temptation: 'you must be content to be my queen in fairyland,' he has King Magnus reply.

Magnus's conventional Queen is Jemima who rules over a domestic kingdom. She is what Orinthia calls a 'common housekeeper wife' who brings up 'common healthy jolly lumps of children'. She treats her husband as 'a good little boy' and imposes her own household priorities. 'You do not always know what is good for you,' she tells him.

The third Queen of the play is Amanda, 'a merry lady in uniform like the men' and Postmistress-General in the Cabinet. She can mimic people and sing funny songs, 'and that – with all respect, sir – makes me the real queen of England,' she tells the King. Amanda is a performer from the music-hall stage whose songs and mimicry cover all their targets with ridicule: even Breakages Ltd, the capitalist conglomerate that governs the country, is powerless against her. She is truly a democratic Queen in the sense that she answers the public's demand to have everything trivialized and turned into a sport – 'And thats how England is governed by yours truly,' she concludes.

But there are limits to Amanda's queenly power: she can stop anything; she can start nothing. If the country were governed responsibly, then its Queen would be Lysistrata, the Powermistress-General. She is a thinker

– 'a grave lady in academic clothes' – who combines Beatrice Webb's devotion to public service with Lady Astor's assertive patriotism. Lysistrata is the 'studious' King's one supporter in the Cabinet, his intellectual equal who in their first-act duet responds to his long oratorio on the condition of England by letting herself go with an impassioned denunciation of capitalism.

The England to which Shaw points his audiences is one that manufactures chocolate creams, Christmas crackers and tourist trophies, and that exports golf-clubs and polo ponies. Hardship and poverty have largely been abolished by sending capital abroad to places where they still exist so that Englishmen can live in comfort on the imported profits of their investments in cheap labour. The country is little more than a staging post for the movement of foreign capital: the heart has gone out of politics and into money-making. Less than seven per cent of the electoral register bother to vote. In such a country politics has deteriorated to Shaw's kindergarten Cabinet of squabbling nonentities. Presiding over this nursery school is Proteus, Shaw's cartoon version of Ramsay MacDonald. The job has brought him 'to the verge of a nervous breakdown'. At one moment he dashes from the room in a fit of contrived rage, knowing that the King will follow him and that they can settle their business in private. These were the exaggerated manoeuvres of Ramsay MacDonald who, according to Sidney Webb, 'always had neuritis' when things got difficult.

Shaw denied having 'packed the cards by making the King a wise man and the minister a fool'. Both, he wrote in his Preface, 'play with equal skill; and the King wins, not by greater astuteness, but because he has the ace of trumps in his hand and knows when to play it'. But it is G.B.S. who has slipped him this winning card.

For Proteus the fight is between royalty and democracy, and his aim is to come out on top. For Magnus the enemy is plutocracy. 'I stand for the great abstractions,' he declares: 'for conscience and virtue; for the eternal against the expedient; for the evolutionary appetite against the dog's gluttony; for intellectual integrity, for humanity, for the rescue of industry from commercialism and of science from professionalism.' This is the voice of the Shavian realist raised against the arch-idealist Proteus.

Some people assumed that King Magnus was a veiled portrait of King George V. 'I have a lot in common with the present monarch,' Shaw conceded, 'we are both human beings and we were both christened George, and I dare say he dislikes the name as much as I do.' Shaw's King is very like Granville-Barker's King in *His Majesty*; both are parts for an actor-manager. Shaw pointed to several historical precedents, but when cross-examined by his biographer Hesketh Pearson, he admitted, 'The real King Magnus is sitting within a few feet of you.' King Magnus belongs to the Shavian family tree of strong beneficent rulers. He is Caesar transported through history from *Caesar and Cleopatra*; he is Napoleon from *The Man of Destiny*. He combines the heroism of William Morris with the calculation of Sidney Webb: he is Shaw's fantasy of himself.

There are no Hitlers, Mussolinis, Stalins or Mosleys in *The Apple Cart*, for this is a play about the dangers of powerlessness. We are shown the conditions that favour the popular promotion of dictators. For the time being, power rests with Breakages Ltd which distributes accumulating wealth with capitalism's whimsical injustice. In Shaw's analysis, such inequality leads to a moral degeneration that can be cleared away only by revolution. 'I dread revolution,' says Magnus. All the Cabinet, except the women, laugh at him, but it is this dread that brings the extravaganza to a halt. 'I look on myself as a man with a political future,' Magnus informs Proteus as he contemplates forming a government in the House of Commons. But the King remains in his melancholy predicament as Shaw's fantasy peters out. 'This is a farce that younger men must finish,' Magnus tells Lysistrata. And the implication is that these younger men may have to finish it with violence.

*

'I imagine that Shaw has made the sensation of his life,' W. B. Yeats wrote to Lady Gregory. The Conservative press enthusiastically hailed *The Apple Cart*. 'The wonder is that GBS and Charlotte have not been invited to Sandringham,' Beatrice Webb drily observed. It appeared to some as if he had executed a political volte-face. 'All the tyrants in Europe will delight in the play,' warned H. W. Nevinson.

For the first time in his theatrical career Shaw had refused to give an even distribution of argument to both sides of a conflict. His Cabinet of clowns 'stand up like ninepins for his dialectical bowling,' complained Ivor Brown in the *Manchester Guardian* in 1929. ' . . . to idealize your unelected monarch is a pitiful approach to political philosophy.' The same objections were to be made fifty years later in the *Guardian* by the theatre critic Michael Billington, who found the play indefensible in theory – 'a snobbish endorsement of the inherent good breeding of royalty as against the bad manners of democracy' – and aggravating in performance – there was 'something dramatically unsatisfying about a play in which a clever king is allowed to run intellectual rings round . . . a collection of hare-brained boobies'.

Though G.B.S. was a great figure in the eyes of the general public, he no longer excited young intellectuals, who were turning to the new work of Eliot and Joyce, Pound and Proust, D. H. Lawrence and Aldous Huxley. Like Magnus, G.B.S. was 'old fashioned'. The modern literary periodicals of the 1920s and 1930s – T. S. Eliot's *Criterion* and F. R. Leavis's *Scrutiny* – had little interest in him. Yet it was by literary critics, rather than critics of the theatre, that *The Apple Cart* was later to be re-evaluated. In the judgement of Edmund Wilson, 'the fact that Shaw is here working exclusively with economic and political materials has caused its art to be insufficiently appreciated.' The contemporary view that Shaw was 'contemptuous as ever of shape and form' has given way to an understanding of what Margery Morgan calls the play's 'deliberately dislocated structure' and 'meticulous patterning of detail' influenced by cinematic technique.

The Apple Cart was to be the last of Shaw's plays to win a regular place in the standard repertory. Desmond MacCarthy ascribed the immediate success to its topicality in the late 1920s: it was about things that people happened then to be discussing. But over twenty years later Thomas Mann was to describe it as a 'stunningly clairvoyant political satire'. 'It is perhaps unfortunate that circumstances have not made the play date more,' complained a *Times* reviewer in 1965. For sixty years it retained an acute contemporaneity. '*The Apple Cart* delivers an exasperated uppercut to the trade unions and forecasts the economic rebellion of the Third World,' commented Irving Wardle in *The Times* after a revival in 1977. ' . . . The crisis he is writing about is still our crisis.' Revivals of the play were to come round each decade and 'each time it is rediscovered as a play for today,' added Irving Wardle in 1986.

Beatrice Webb, who had dismissed *The Apple Cart* in 1929 as frivolous and annoying, was to write in her diary on 6 September 1940: 'GBS's brilliant satirical play, *The Apple Cart*, his last popular success, seems today an amusing forecast.'

*

The success of *The Apple Cart* was a good omen for the Malvern Festival. On reaching London the play ran for 258 performances which exceeded the first London productions of *Saint Joan* and *Pygmalion* and everything else of Shaw's except *Fanny's First Play*.

'I always avoid places where my plays are being performed,' he had told Sobieniowski. But for Barry Jackson's Malvern he made an exception. He liked the vertical green hills, the quiet light, the air that 'would raise the dead' – though not the waters, 'one glass of which destroys my digestion for a week'. Over the 1930s he was to be seen almost every summer striding along the terraces and up the hills with his companions labouring after him. He was constantly on view. 'I have . . . created a general impression that I was born there,' he wrote in the 1937 Malvern Festival Book. 'In course of time visitors will be shewn for sixpence the room in which my first cries were heard.'

Charlotte enjoyed the hydro and sanatorium, but this was no holiday. 'GBS sails along & is charming to everyone, & they worship in crowds,' she told Nancy Astor, ' – but I have to plan & arrange & entertain & contrive meals & eliminate the worst undesirables! Oh!! . . . It is such a little place – and no refuge!' Nevertheless, 'it really is wonderful to hear the plays one after the other – these big things set off one another like the pictures at a one-man show which never look so well separated.' She felt comfortable, too, at the Malvern Hotel, with its automatic lift and suites of bed-and-sitting-rooms on every floor, each with a private bathroom. At the sound of the gong the elderly guests would rise up, like a *corps de ballet*, and rustle through to dinner. When Shaw strode in 'he was always clasping a travel book,' Beverley Nichols noticed. 'Mrs Shaw, in her turn, clutched a volume of economics.'

The atmosphere of the festival was that of an extended and overflowing country-house party. There were folk dances in the Assembly Rooms, people playing on the bowling greens, garden parties at the girls' school which Barry Jackson rented each summer, boating on the lake, Billy Gammon's syncopated band, starlight suppers and 'the scent and sounds from a thousand gardens'. G.B.S. would take the cast for drives around the hills and sometimes on to Droitwich, where he ducked into the brine baths, motoring back with the salt still in his beard. He read his plays to the actors before rehearsals in the town's Gas Office. In the auditorium itself, the actors could see his illuminated pen flashing as he made notes. He was determined to make the Malvern experiment another chapter in the reform of the English theatre. By 1931 its scope was broadened by the inclusion of works from other dramatists; in 1934 it was prolonged into a four-week occasion; between 1929 and 1939 it established itself as the major off-season theatrical event in England and an international showcase for playwrights. Sixty-five plays by forty British and foreign playwrights (evenly distributed between the past and the present) were produced over that period. They included world premières of *Geneva* (1938) and *'In Good King Charles's Golden Days'* (1939) and the first English productions of *Too True to be Good* (1932), and *The Simpleton of the Unexpected Isles* (1935).

In 1936 Shaw celebrated his eightieth birthday at Malvern accepting 'nothing over sixpence' from the cast. ('I gave him a coat-hanger from Woolworth's,' Wendy Hiller remembered.) He continued visiting Malvern until the following year which was the last time Barry Jackson directed the Festival.

Malvern was the forerunner of an age of festivals that was to flourish fifty years later and carry on the dramatic out-of-London development that Shaw and Barry Jackson had sought. G.B.S. had never wanted the festival to be a memorial to himself. 'Malvern must look to its present and future, not dream of its past. I am only one of Ibsen's Ghosts.'

*

'One of the choicest attractions' of Malvern was Edward Elgar. During rehearsals of *The Apple Cart* Shaw had invited him over from his home near Worcester, and later they discussed setting one of Shaw's plays to music, 'but I think we agreed to my view that he could do nothing with a play except what his Falstaff did with Shakespeare's,' Shaw told the composer Rutland Boughton.

Opening the Bernard Shaw Exhibition in the Malvern public library, Elgar told his audience that G.B.S. really knew more about music than he did. Shaw retaliated by admitting that 'although I am rather a conceited man I am quite sincerely and genuinely humble in the presence of Sir Edward Elgar. I recognize a greater art than my own and a greater man than I can ever hope to be.' Not to be outdone, Elgar informed the press that Shaw was 'a most remarkable man; he was the best friend to any artist, the kindest and possibly the dearest fellow on earth'.

These statements were more than reciprocal civilities for the public. 'The history of original music, broken off by the death of Purcell, begins again with Sir Edward Elgar,' Shaw had written in the *Morning Post* in 1911. After a century of imitation Handel, Mendelssohn and Spohr, Elgar's music had come as a new voice giving out a sound 'as characteristically English as a country house and stable are characteristically English'. All this had been written before they met in 1919 at a lunch given by Lalla Vandervelde, wife of the Belgian socialist leader.

A few days later Elgar invited the Shaws to Severn House, his home in Hampstead, to hear three of his chamber works including the Piano Quintet. 'The Quintet knocked me over at once,' Shaw wrote the next day. ' . . . There are some piano embroideries on a pedal point that didn't sound like a piano or anything else in the world, but quite beautiful . . . they require a touch which is peculiar to yourself.' It was this peculiarity that Shaw sought to define and celebrate. 'Elgar's Cockaigne overture combines every classic quality of a concert overture with every lyric and dramatic quality of the overture to Die Meistersinger,' he wrote at the end of that year. ' . . . You may hear all sorts of footsteps in it, and it may tell you all sorts of stories; but it is classical music as Beethoven's Les Adieux sonata is classical music: it tells you no story external to itself and yourself.'

Shaw's tribute delighted Elgar's wife, hitherto suspicious of what she thought of as Shaw's atheism. Her death three months later seems to have redoubled Shaw's championing of Elgar's work. In the summer of 1922, following a meagrely attended performance of *The Apostles* by the Leeds Choral Union, he erupted in the *Daily News*:

'The Apostles is one of the glories of British music: indeed it is unique as a British work ... The occasion was infinitely more important than the Derby, than Goodwood, than the Cup Finals, than the Carpentier fights, than any of the occasions on which the official leaders of society are photographed and cinematographed laboriously shaking hands ... I apologize to posterity for living in a country where the capacity and tastes of schoolboys and sporting costermongers are the measure of metropolitan culture.'

Elgar and Shaw had both initially been 'discovered' in Germany, and were now beginning to go out of fashion in Britain, the audiences for Elgar's oratorios disappearing in the 1920s as they were to disappear in the 1930s for Shaw's extravaganzas. Their friendship ripened in old age when, after the Malvern Festivals began, they saw each other regularly. Elgar, who could talk about every unmusical subject on earth, 'from pigs to Elizabethan literature', gave the impression of not knowing 'a fugue from a *fandango*'. And yet, Shaw wrote, 'Music was his religion and his intellect and almost his everything.' Elgar prided himself, however, on being a considerable playgoer. It was true that he had never stuck out *Romeo and Juliet* to the end, but he would travel almost anywhere to see the comedian Jack Hulbert perform, and he came to relish the Shavian productions at Malvern. As Master of the King's Musick, he was a martyr to conventionality, insisting that Shaw and Charlotte were correctly dressed for these occasions and for his own musical performances at Gloucester, Hereford and Worcester. 'The Protestant Three Choirs were the centre of his musical activities, especially Worcester,' Shaw later remembered: 'to hear The Music Makers conducted there by him was a wonderful experience.' In 1930 Elgar dedicated his Severn Suite to Shaw who was 'hugely flattered and touched'. After hearing the piece 'only eight times' at the Crystal Palace Band Competition in September that year, he wrote to Elgar, 'Nobody could have guessed from looking at the score and thinking of the thing as a toccata for brass band how beautiful and serious the work is as abstract music.'

'G.B.S.'s politics are, to me, appalling, but he is the kindest-hearted, gentlest man I have met ... to young people he is kind,' Elgar had written in 1921 to Sidney Colvin. But by the late 1920s, when they campaigned together against a restrictive new Music Copyright Bill, Elgar was beginning to look at Shaw's politics as a vehicle of Shavian generosity, and the Shavian merging of art with sociology as the basis of his comradeship with all artists. Elgar had opened himself up to a Shavian political education by rather nervously enquiring what 'capital' was. By way of explanation, Shaw replied that Elgar's products were infinitely consumable without limitation or deterioration. He then proposed an Elgarian Financial Symphony: 'Allegro: Impending Disaster. Lento mesto: Stony Broke. Scherzo: Light Heart and Empty Pocket. All⁰ con brio: Clouds Clearing.'

Whenever Elgar needed the clouds to clear, the Shaws shone down on him. 'Don't let yourself think dark thoughts,' Charlotte urged him. And G.B.S., who made him a present of £1,000 early in the 1930s (equivalent to £27,000 in 1997), persuaded the BBC to commission a Third Symphony for another £1,000. 'He [Elgar] does not know that I am meddling in his affairs and yours in this manner,' he wrote to John Reith, Director General of the BBC, ' . . . but I do know that he has still a lot of stuff in him that could be released if he could sit down to it without risking his livelihood.'

The Third Symphony was never finished because of the collapse in Elgar's health. Shaw recommended an American osteopath whose 'resemblance to an ophicleide would please you', though Charlotte preferred a Chinese acupuncturist from San Francisco. Alternatively, there was homoeopathy in the person of Raphael Roche, an unregistered practitioner from a well-known Jewish family of musicians (including Mendelssohn and Moscheles) who had healed a hydrocele of Shaw's, using what appeared to be a grain of powdered sugar. In 'the depths of pain' Elgar seems to have felt that the Shaws were trying to cure him with laughter. In 1933 he entered a nursing home and, resisting an impulse to rush down and rescue him from the 'damn doctors', Shaw was left trusting to Elgar's mighty Life Force.

'Having friends like you,' Charlotte had written in 1932, 'is the one thing in life worth having when one arrives at the age of GBS & myself.' The following year Elgar returned the compliment: 'the world seems a cold place to me when you are both away.'

Shaw described Elgar's death from cancer on 23 February 1934 as 'world-shaking' and far too early. But there was still the music. At the Gloucester Three Choirs Festival in the summer of 1934, he and Charlotte heard *The Kingdom*. 'I cannot tell you how we all miss Edward Elgar,' Charlotte wrote afterwards to Nancy Astor. 'We loved him . . . & when another man got up into the Conductor's Chair it was hard to bear.'

3

AUTHOR OF HIMSELF

I am honored and famous and rich, which is very good fun for the other
people. But as I have to do all the hard work, and suffer an ever increasing
multitude of fools gladly, it does not feel any better than being reviled,
infamous, and poor, as I used to be.

Shaw to Frank Harris (7 April 1927)

Shaw's travels abroad at the end of the 1920s became a sequence of flights
and explorations. In the summer of 1928 Charlotte arranged a holiday on
the French Riviera. They crawled into Cap d'Antibes at the crest of a
heatwave, 'hotter than I have ever imagined any infernal regions,' Charlotte
objected, and then dragged themselves off on excursions to Menton,
Monte Carlo, and the mountainous hinterland of Haute Provence; and
every day they plunged into the Mediterranean – 'even I can swim, swim,
swim – & never tire,' Charlotte discovered. 'You feel you cant sink in this
sea. And when you get out you can lie – nuda veritas – on the rocks &
bake. G.B.S. loves it – & that is why we stay.'

He loved it and hated it: 'one never knows whether the morning will
find us smiling in a paradise,' he wrote to Blanche Patch, 'or groaning in
a purgatory.' Lady Rhondda came, a feminist and the proprietress of *Time
and Tide* (for which Shaw wrote regularly in the 1920s and 1930s); and
so did Troubetzkoy, devastated by the death of his Swedish wife. There
were the Mosleys too, Oswald fresh from an International Congress in
Brussels, Cynthia an Atalanta who 'queens it with the best' on the beaches,
and both of them comically nervous of being photographed by the press.
It was 'Dear Mr Mosley,' Charlotte told Nancy Astor, who abetted her
plot to carry G.B.S. off to Geneva, 'a decent, proper town', for twelve
days early in September.

But the most significant meeting that summer was with Frank Harris,
now living in Nice. In England before the war he had been declared
bankrupt and sent on a libel charge to Brixton gaol. During the war he
had emigrated to the United States where he published a series of anti-
British articles that unfortunately tipped Germany as the victor. His
decline was accelerated by an erratic biography of Oscar Wilde that
brought him nothing but trouble, and a series of apocryphal 'Contemporary Portraits' first published in his new American magazine, *Pearson's*,
which, after threatening to fold each month, eventually did so.

'Your most interesting book will be your autobiography,' Shaw had
predicted in 1915. After the war, Harris set about retrieving his bank

balance by moving to France and acting on Shaw's advice. 'I am going to see if a man can tell truth naked and unashamed about himself and his amorous adventures in the world,' he wrote. The first volume of his notorious *My Life and Loves* had been burnt by customs officials; the second volume brought him to court on a charge of corrupting public morals. 'Il faut souffrir pour être Casanova,' Shaw reminded him.

G.B.S. was the one writer in England who remained loyal to Harris. He did not admire him, did not regard him as a fugleman for free speech, as he regarded Freud, Joyce, D. H. Lawrence and even Radclyffe Hall; he did not even like him. But he felt some kinship with Harris's sense of exile. The more Harris was cold-shouldered, the more G.B.S. assisted him – in his fashion. Instead of handing him money, he provided him with words. 'For God's sake give me deathless words,' Harris had appealed from the United States. Shaw responded with a fascinating account of his meetings with Wilde, which Harris was able to use in a cheap reissue of his biography. Then, when Harris sent over for correction a 'Contemporary Portrait' of Shaw, G.B.S. fired back a brilliant pastiche of Harris entitled 'How Frank Ought to Have Done It'. 'You are the first person I think in my journey through the world,' Harris wrote, 'who has shown any wish to surpass me in generosity.'

To be thus surpassed troubled Harris who knew himself to be twice the man Shaw was and could not frankly conceal this knowledge. And yet 'you have made more out of your worst play than I have made out of all my books put together'. How was this possible? They had, for example, both written plays about St Joan and yet for some reason theatres round the world persisted in staging Shaw's *Saint Joan* and never his own *Joan la Romée*.

'I have no one I can turn to except you,' Harris admitted. What he wanted from Shaw, he hardly knew. There was a limit to what he could raise from publishing or selling Shaw's correspondence: 'Letters are unsatisfactory,' he concluded. He wanted Shaw's help with publishers. 'I could surely do an Edition of Shakespeare better than any living man,' he hazarded, ' . . . you could get me this Shakespeare commission at once.' But such scholarly hack work 'would not keep you in bootlaces,' Shaw calculated. Harris also wanted to mine Shaw's good will and find some rich new vein. Shakespeare had failed him; Wilde had failed him; and in old age he was beginning to fail himself.

They met at Harris's villa in Nice in the second week of August 1928. Shaw came alone because Charlotte, he happily explained, could not be seen lunching with a pornographer. For Harris their day together was in the nature of a reconnaissance. A little later he took off for New York. 'Your vogue in America is extraordinary, almost incredible,' he reported.

'The *New York Times* declares that you are the greatest Englishman since Shakespeare, and this is the opinion one hears on all sides.' To this reputation Harris now proposed hitching his wagon by getting himself appointed Shaw's biographer. 'Abstain from such a desperate enterprise,' Shaw hastily replied. ' . . . I wont have you write my life on any terms: Nellie [Harris's wife] would do it far better.'

But Harris needed an old-age pension, and by 1929 was forced to accept the fact that only for a book about G.B.S., written with Shaw's co-operation, would any publisher give him a decent advance on royalties. Shaw's refusal was a desperate blow. All this exaggerated success, he protested, had gone to Shaw's head. Such insults delighted G.B.S. who wanted to know to what other part of his body success should have travelled. 'You are honoured and famous and rich – I lie here crippled and condemned and poor,' Harris pleaded. Shaw seemed briskly unaffected. Nevertheless the 'dreaded biography' began to encircle him. 'The truth is I have a horror of biographers,' he wrote. ' . . . Every man has a blind side; and I should catch you just on it . . . my heart is never in the right – meaning the expected – place.

'Besides, it is premature. Only two of the ladies are dead.

'Think no more of it. And forgive me.'

But Harris could not afford to be forgiving. As he began to give ground, Shaw divided the problem between Charlotte's interests and those of Nellie Harris. To put his Life into the hands of a writer whose own memoirs had been burnt by Charlotte, page by page 'so that not a comma should escape the flames', was surely too rich a paradox. She would never permit it. But Nellie's interests were a different matter and Charlotte had no answer when Shaw echoed Charles II's deathbed appeal: 'Let not poor Nellie starve.'

For G.B.S. himself there were further considerations. Archibald Henderson was proposing to put together another biography for the 1930s. Then there was the tragic case of Demetrius O'Bolger.

*

Demetrius O'Bolger 'is an Irishman: a professor of literature at an American university,' Shaw had told Harris. His study of Shaw's own plays had begun in 1912 as a thesis for the Graduate Department of the University of Pennsylvania. 'I determined to run out the thread of his home surroundings,' O'Bolger wrote. ' . . . I thought I saw not a few reticences . . . and I determined to penetrate them and systematize the results if Mr Shaw were willing to give me the necessary information.'

And Shaw was willing. O'Bolger would send him a sheet of paper with a question typed at the top, and G.B.S. would fill up the rest of the page with an answer sometimes extending to five or six hundred words. His help swelled into a positive obstacle. Often and often O'Bolger believed he had completed his book. He completed it, for example, in February 1916, only to receive a little later that month, twenty-nine closely type-written pages from Shaw, describing the circumstances of his youth and the household in which he grew up. 'The death of my mother set me free to tell O'B. more than I could allow Henderson to publish in her lifetime,' Shaw revealed to Harris, who was then struggling with his 'Contemporary Portrait' of G.B.S. Never had Shaw been so forthcoming – but 'I do not send you the stuff for publication as it stands,' he ominously added to O'Bolger.

O'Bolger had celebrated the end of the Great War by completing his book for the third time. Receiving an offer a few months after Armistice Day from Harpers to publish a revised text, he sat down to make a fourth draft, working 'till the nerves of my neck and the back of my head could no longer stand the strain'. Harpers seemed delighted: but Shaw was not delighted. Having examined the contract, he declared that he would treat direct quotation as an infringement of copyright 'and hand the stuff over to Frank Harris', whereupon Harpers cancelled their contract. Shaw had 'delivered a sound blow for principle's sake,' O'Bolger observed. 'He had saved me from being fleeced by saving me from being published.' In a frantic begging-and-abusing letter, O'Bolger appealed to G.B.S. to change his mind. 'Dont be scared,' Shaw responded. ' . . . Do not lose your head and try to drown your rescuer.'

Shaw felt a need after his mother died to gain control of his formative years, but he did not wish to see all he had spilled out immediately given away in print. So when O'Bolger sent him the yet-again-completed manuscript, he hung on to it, and it was still in his possession in the early 1920s. 'I somehow cannot make up my mind to send that blasted MS of yours back without another look at it.' O'Bolger, he informed Harris, 'was the son of an Irish inspector of police; and he proceeded to investigate the case precisely as his father would have done'. He also wrote like a policeman. This 'explains everything,' Shaw informed O'Bolger, ' . . . your treatment of my mother and father as suspicious characters in custody, your rejection of all my statements as unsupported by evidence and coming from a tainted source &c &c.' 'I am not qualified to advise you medically,' he went on, before advancing a diagnosis. His biographer was suffering from a Resentment Complex. He listed the symptoms. 'You have the resentment of the poor man against the rich man, of the Irish Catholic against the Irish Protestant . . .

'You have, in particular, achieved a portrait of a most horrible woman

whom you allege was my mother, with a sordid husband, and a disingenuous son, forming the sort of Irish interior which you most hate and
despise as typifying every social injustice from which you and your people
ever suffered.'

What this letter affirms is Shaw's genuine distress. O'Bolger's 'interior'
had turned the Shavian paradoxes inside out and come up with an ugly
picture of those Dublin years that Shaw himself had told Ellen Terry
were 'frightful in realities'. The 'worst of it was,' Shaw added in a letter
to Harris, 'that I could not deny that the information I had given him
bore his construction'.

So they reached deadlock until O'Bolger submitted to the process
of exhaustive Shavian editing that Archibald Henderson had accepted.
'Unfortunately this involved practically rewriting his book for him,' Shaw
pointed out; 'and for that it was impossible for me to find time.' So the
manuscript remained suspended. 'You will certainly be the death of me,'
Shaw cried out one of his most lethal paradoxes. In the summer of 1923,
O'Bolger suddenly died. 'The situation was a painful one for me,' Shaw
commented, ' . . . a great worry for him; and now it has helped to worry
him into his grave . . . A tragic business.'

Had there ever been such a cautionary tale for a biographer? 'The
unfortunate author died of disappointment,' Shaw told Harris, 'aided by
pernicious anaemia, cursing me for ruining him.'

*

O'Bolger had made no startling discoveries about Shaw's early years in
Ireland, but his enquiries had pressed on a bruise, disturbed G.B.S., and
made him deftly rearrange some of the facts. 'And now you want me to
start again,' he exclaimed to Harris. 'I had rather die misunderstood.'
Feeling like a 'dog returning to his vomit', he began early in 1930 a
succession of autobiographical letters to Harris.

Meanwhile there was no stopping Henderson from preparing an
expanded version of his biography called, to Shaw's disgust, *Playboy and
Prophet*. The market was saturated, he protested. Yet Henderson was not
to be deterred. The best compromise Shaw could negotiate was a delay
until 1932, plus an agreement that he should vet the text.

G.B.S.'s hand had been somewhat weakened in these negotiations by
his involvement with Harris. Harris had posted a letter to the *Times
Literary Supplement* soliciting 'quips, inscriptions, autographs'. He also
hired an editor by the name of Frank Scully, later an authority on flying
saucers. According to Scully, it was Scully who actually wrote the book;
certainly it is dedicated to him. At the beginning of May, the two Franks

had cobbled together over 100,000 words, a good fifteen per cent of which were by G.B.S. 'If you publish a word of mine I'll have the law on you,' Shaw threatened. Harris was panic-stricken. The lesson of O'Bolger had meant nothing to him – indeed, he had received an advance on royalties for the guarantee of Shaw's words rather than his own. So Shaw was obliged to relent, if only because Nellie and Frank 'were in rather desperate circumstances,' he explained to Henderson. However, he cautioned Harris that 'if there is one expression in this book of yours that cannot be read aloud at a confirmation class, you are lost for ever. Your life and loves are just being forgotten,' he went on. ' . . . This book is your chance of recovering your tall hat . . . So brush up your frock coat; buy a new tie; and remember that your life now depends on your being Francis Harris, Esquire.'

In this way the subject put himself in charge of his biographer's reputation. Frank, the ruffian, must be removed. 'Bury him,' Shaw commanded in April 1931. 'If you dont the parish will.' Four months later, Frank Harris was buried in the British Cemetery at Caucade. Shaw sent the widow Nellie a cheque: and Nellie Harris arranged for G.B.S. to be sent the galley-proofs.

'I have had to do many odd jobs in my time; but this one is quite the oddest,' he wrote in a postscript to the book, where he gives the impression of having corrected the finished proof sheets. In a letter to Nellie he comes nearer to explaining what he had actually done: 'Frank knew hardly more about my life history than I knew about yours; and the mixture of his guesses with the few things I told him produced the wildest results.

'I have had to fill in the prosaic facts in Frank's best style, and fit them to his comments as best I could; for I have most scrupulously preserved all his sallies at my expense . . . You may, however, depend on it that the book is not any the worse for my doctoring.'

Shaw made certain that the galley-proofs of Harris's book were destroyed since he did not want his shadowing of Harris's style to be detected. It had amused him, under the camouflage of Harris's reputation for mendacity, to insert several authentic passages and, as part of this strange collaboration, occasionally to slip the correcting pen over to Sonny:

'All through, from his very earliest childhood, he had lived a fictitious life through the exercise of his incessant imagination . . . It was a secret life: its avowal would have made him ridiculous. It had one oddity. The fictitious Shaw was not a man of family. He had no relatives. He was not only a bastard, like Dunois or Falconbridge, who at least knew who their parents were: he was also a foundling.'

'Ought Mr Shaw to Have Done It?' demanded the reviewers. It was a pity, they judged, that he had allowed himself to be bullied by such a pugilist-of-letters. What they could not observe, since it was invisible, was the extent of Shaw's vicarious presentation of himself which by the 1930s was becoming part of his dramatic production.

Harris's book sold well, which was bad news for Henderson whose first biography had been outshone by Chesterton and whose second biography appeared shortly in the wake of Harris. But the proofs of *Playboy and Prophet* were preserved, and they exhibit the cascading quantities of concealed rewriting done by G.B.S. in the persona of this friendly American mathematician who, without interest in politics or talent for writing, continued loyally to keep the pot boiling. Shaw, however, could not bring himself to write an endorsement. 'DAMN Bernard Shaw,' he wrote to Henderson, 'and his tedious doings and sayings!'

*

'For seven weeks I have been hiding within a day's ride ... I shall have left when this reaches you,' Shaw wrote to Molly Tompkins before moving on to Geneva; '... you should not drive me away to horrible hell-paradises like the Riviera by refusing to behave yourself tactfully.'

Searching for a paradise without hell, Shaw turned to the Adriatic in 1929, putting down on the island of Brioni off the Istrian peninsula. 'A settled melancholy, peculiar to the place perhaps, devours us,' he wrote to Blanche Patch: and this, Charlotte sharply added, suited them very well.

From here they sailed to Dubrovnik, then continued overland by way of Boka Kotorska to Cetinje, the capital of Montenegro, before going on to Split. The Royal Yugoslav Government, anxious to use his visit as an advertisement for tourism and an endorsement of its political regime, had greeted him with a two-hour press conference at Dubrovnik. 'There are good reasons for me to be careful about my political statements,' Shaw announced. He was angered by some of the misreporting of these statements and refused to meet the press a second time in Split.

The Shaws left Split on 27 May and sailed for Venice. Travelling back on the Orient Express he saw Molly's Isola from the train window, and hurtled on to London where, a fortnight later, he finished a 10,000-word Preface to his love letters with Ellen Terry.

Ellen had died the previous summer. For the last fourteen years of her life, since she played Lady Cicely Waynflete in *Captain Brassbound's*

Conversion, they had not often corresponded. 'I wonder shall I ever act in a Play of yours again!' she had written to him in 1910, and then, more than two years later: 'I suppose an old woman would not attract as a centre piece in a play, and that you never could write such a thing for – *me*?' Her enquiries filled him with dismay. 'It's as if Queen Alexandra came to me and asked me to get her a place as cook-housekeeper,' he wrote in a letter he was to exclude from their published correspondence.

Ellen was losing her eyesight, her memory for words, her stage confidence. 'Can you enlarge my prospect?' she had appealed to Shaw. ' . . . I must work.' When very young she had enlarged her prospect by escaping from an imprisoning marriage to G. F. Watts and eloping with William Godwin, 'the greatest aesthete of them all,' as Max Beerbohm called him. But having given birth to two illegitimate children, she found out what it was like to be a fallen and forgotten woman in nineteenth-century England. The partnership with Henry Irving had restored her reputation and the public happily identified her with the virtuous and sentimental roles Irving handed down to her. Shaw had then tried to enlarge their prospects together. But she had not wanted to risk public obloquy again.

In the late nineteenth century every Victorian gentleman who came to the Lyceum had fallen in love with Ellen Terry, and no wife had objected because she was regarded not as a notorious seductress like Mrs Patrick Campbell, but as the ideal embodiment of motherhood. Shaw knew how ironically this image fitted someone who, unleashing a power denied to her in the theatre, had given her children such a difficult and divisive upbringing. In the early twentieth century, following Irving's death, 'Our Lady of the Lyceum' had faded into 'Our Lady of Sighs', fiercely fought over by her son, the legendary theatre designer Gordon Craig, and by her lesbian daughter Edy Craig.

Edy Craig had read Shaw's letters when looking through the boxes of her mother's papers. At her request, Shaw sent her Ellen's letters, and she felt that both sides of the correspondence should be published. Shaw agreed to draft 'an explanation for posterity' that could be used as a preface whenever the letters were published. 'The rest lies practically with the executors,' he concluded.

Gordon Craig was not an executor. But Edy Craig was, and unknown to both men she had sold Shaw's letters to a publisher for £3,000 (equivalent to £82,000 in 1997). On learning this, Shaw wrote to Gordon Craig saying that it was 'no longer possible to pretend that we are under any pecuniary pressure to publish the letters'. He proposed sending Ellen's letters 'to the British Museum (say) with a copy of the preface to be placed with them when they are put into the catalogue at some future date'. In the meantime he forwarded Gordon Craig a proof copy, marked

'Very Private', of his 'Preface to be attached to the Correspondence of Ellen Terry and Bernard Shaw should it ever be published', with the request that he read it carefully because 'Edy tells me that you are at work on a memoir of Irving with incidental references to me'.

Gordon Craig had little intention of referring to G.B.S., whose part in Irving's career he believed to have been negligible. Irving was his hero, and he had now inherited the feud between 'my master', as he called him, and this 'literary gangster', as G.B.S. called himself. As he took the field under the banner of Shaw's old adversary, the faded colours once more unfurled, the dusty echoes stirred, and the ancient jousting was rejoined. But now it was Irving's champion and not G.B.S. who was banished from the arena of the commercial theatre. 'You were trying to make a picture frame of the proscenium to replace actors by figures, and drive the dramatic poet from the theatre,' Shaw accused Craig. 'And as I was doing precisely the reverse, and the Zeitgeist carried me to success, you felt that I was the arch enemy. So I was . . . the enemy who does not reciprocate your dislike – if you really dislike him.' But Gordon Craig really did dislike the man who had set out 'to damage my mother, Nelly Terry, my father, myself, my family, Irving, and a few more'.

Shaw also sent a copy of his preface to Edy Craig whose desire to see the correspondence quickly published – with the preface attached – was revitalized. Calculating that it would advance this end, she sold the copyright in her mother's letters for another £3,000 to the same publisher who had bought Shaw's side of their correspondence, and who promised that if he could not induce Shaw to allow the publication of his own letters he would publish Ellen Terry's alone. Since Edy Craig had now amassed £6,000 (equivalent to £00,000 in 1997) for the Ellen Terry Estate without the printing of a word, there seemed no need to publish Shaw's letters 'until we have all passed into history,' he confided to Gordon Craig ' – or out of it'.

But by the summer of 1930 Shaw had swung round to Edy's opinion. He had been largely excluded from Craig's book on Irving and now he was threatened with complete exclusion from Ellen Terry's published correspondence. He was passing out of history. Reading through both sides of their exchange for the first time, he saw that 'the moral of the whole correspondence' would be the 'justice done to the great woman E.T. sacrificed to the egotistical man H.I.'. Such a moral suited his own retrospective designs as well as the current feminist plans of Edy Craig and her lesbian lover 'Christopher St John' (with whom Shaw was silently to co-edit the volume). It also had the tactical advantage of forcing Gordon Craig to campaign simultaneously on two fronts.

Shaw's negotiations over the Ellen Terry correspondence were at once devious and honourable. He took care to omit all hurtful reference to living people, especially Gordon Craig himself; he gave all his own profits to the Ellen Terry Estate for the Memorial Museum that Edy was creating; and he agreed to the publication initially of a limited edition only, on the condition that Gordon Craig himself gave his consent – 'and he, swearing that he would ne'er consent, consented'.

Gordon Craig's consent took the form of a brief letter to Shaw in which he promised 'not to stand in the way' of the publication: 'you may rest assured that having said this I shall stick to it; and when the book containing my Mother's and your letters is published you can rely on me not to write about it in the papers or to give interviews.' Shaw was immediately generous in victory: 'I took it, and take it, that your consent to the publication is like mine, a very reluctant submission to circumstances over which we have no control.' Trying to align himself with both brother and sister, however, Shaw was caught between the fell incensed points of these mighty opposites. In his letter to Gordon Craig, he conceded, 'As to your complete liberty to write about those letters, about the Lyceum, about E.T. and G.B.S., you must continue to exercise that in all respects as before.' But when Gordon Craig did exercise this liberty in his book *Ellen Terry and Her Secret Self* the year after *Ellen Terry and Bernard Shaw. A Correspondence* was published, Shaw made devastating use of his earlier letter of consent.

Craig had given his consent to publication without seeing all the letters and his attitude changed after reading them through as a whole. The only honourable course, he now felt, was for Shaw and Edy to have destroyed everything, posthumously releasing his mother from this awful entanglement. After the publication of *A Correspondence*, he concentrated his anti-Shavian abuse in a curious pamphlet fitting into the back cover-pocket of *Ellen Terry and Her Secret Self*. 'Frankly, readers will suffer no irreparable loss if they leave it there,' commented *The Times*.

In *Ellen Terry and Her Secret Self* Gordon Craig evokes the golden mother of his country childhood in place of the mortifyingly powerful woman who had looked on him as a weak little boy. 'What makes this book of his so tragically moving,' Shaw acknowledged, ' – for if you disregard the rubbish about me, which is neither here nor there, it is a poignant human document – is his desperate denial of the big woman he ran away from and his assertion of the "little mother" he loved.' *A Correspondence* had revealed the Ellen Terry her son resented, 'an impetuous, overwhelming, absorbing personality,' Shaw remembered, '[who] could sweep a thousand people away in a big theatre; so you can imagine what she could do with a sensitive boy in a small house.'

Gordon Craig, however, had rightly observed that in regard to Ellen

Terry, 'we are all of us just children – and the naughtiest is often preferable to the good'. To one side of the battle over Irving's reputation raged a more intimate and childlike contest: a strange variation of sibling rivalry between the lost son, militant daughter, and claimant child from the theatre. In the marsupial annexe to his book, which is dedicated to Henry Irving and entitled 'A Plea for G.B.S.', Gordon Craig wrote as naughtily as he could, calling Shaw 'a very large, malicious, poke-nose old woman . . . with an idle and vindictive tongue quite fussily spreading falsehoods'. The 'falsehoods' were Shaw's claims to legitimacy with Ellen in a theatre world that had taken Craig's mother away and given her to everyone. He was an 'old woman' because he aligned himself with Edy's circle of feminists who had appropriated Ellen after her retirement from the theatre.

After the Shaw–Ellen Terry correspondence appeared in the autumn of 1931, everyone wanted their Shavian letters published. 'We have never had a correspondence in that sense,' Shaw explained to Frank Harris. Only one body of correspondence had suggested something more romantic. 'There is absolutely no comparison between Shaw's letters to Ellen Terry and his letters to me,' Mrs Patrick Campbell told American journalists when she arrived in New York that fall. 'I shall write my *own* preface to the edition, not Mr Shaw . . . I do not intend to give him the opportunity to say the last word. I don't trust him enough.'

Publication of the Shaw–Ellen Terry correspondence prompted Stella to mount one last campaign. His letters to her had been valued at £10,000 but (aside from the odd misdemeanour) she had behaved herself 'like a gentleman' and guarded them for nineteen years. Now times were hard, 'almost unbearable', she wanted this correspondence published for reasons of self-esteem as much as money. 'What objection can there be? Letters written so long ago, and all three of us on the verge of the grave!' But while Charlotte lived, Shaw could not agree. 'At all events for me you are an insoluble problem,' he admitted to Stella; ' . . . there is no use making myself unhappy about it.'

In 1937, suddenly coming upon all Stella's correspondence, Shaw parcelled it up in six registered envelopes and sent it to her in New York. He made no copies, 'as I should certainly die of angina pectoris during the operation'. 'There's a clutch at my heart,' Stella rejoined, ' . . . the desire to feel a child again will tempt me to read them.' Still nothing could be published while he and Charlotte remained alive, but 'as you are nine years younger than we are,' Shaw calculated, 'your chances of surviving both of us are fairly good'.

But it was Stella who died first, in April 1940. 'AND IT IS MY DESIRE,' she had written in her will, ' . . . that the Bernard Shaw letters and poems which are now in the custody of the Westminster Bank be published in their proper sequence and not cut or altered in any way, that they should be published in an independent volume to be entitled "The Love Letters of Bernard Shaw to Mrs Patrick Campbell" so all who may read them will realize that the friendship was "L'amitié amoureuse".'

Nothing more could happen until Charlotte's death three and a half years later. In his new will Shaw gave authority for Stella Beech 'daughter of the late eminent actress professionally known as Mrs Patrick Campbell to print and publish after my death all or any of the letters written by me to the said eminent actress and in the event of Mrs Beech's death before publication to give such authority (which is a permission and not an assignment of copyright) to Mrs Patrick Campbell's grandson Patrick Beech'. The proceeds of this correspondence he reserved 'as far as possible' for the secondary education of Stella Campbell's grandchildren.

There was another pause until Shaw died. Two years afterwards, their leftover letters finally appeared. Against her mother's wishes Mrs Beech cut a few passages and published the volume more prosaically as *Bernard Shaw and Mrs Patrick Campbell: Their Correspondence*. G.B.S. had placed himself *in loco parentis* to Stella's family and made this the only volume of his correspondence to be removed from the control of his executors. 'You would not come out of it with a halo like Ellen's,' Shaw had warned Stella. But Stella would hold her own in *Their Correspondence*. 'Like a cushion, she baffles the incisive blade of Shavian argument,' commented *The Times* reviewer.

There was to be one more ironic revolution in this 'Comedy of Letters' when Jerome Kilty lifted it off the page and transferred it into the theatre. '*Dear Liar* catches with remarkable theatrical assurance the spirit of the correspondence,' a critic in *The Times* wrote of the adaptation. ' . . . it brings out rather surprisingly how sweetly reasonable the actress who was the terror of Tree, Alexander and other actor-managers proved to be in her letters to Joey.'

To its end the relationship had pulled Shaw painfully between comedy and tragedy without ever reconciling the two. 'I can laugh with the comedian,' he had written to her; 'but with the tragedian – oh my heart! . . .

'Oh, Stella, Stella, Stella, Stella, *Stella!*'

4

THE CELTIC-HIBERNIAN SCHOOL

Them and their Academy of Letters – all in all, and in spite of all.
Sean O'Casey to James Joyce (30 May 1939)

'The Works of Bernard Shaw', which G.B.S. had been preparing intermittently since 1921, began to appear in two editions early in the 1930s. Twenty-one volumes of the Limited Collected Edition were published in 1930, starting on his seventy-fourth birthday with the five novels, embellished with Forewords and Postscripts, at the head of which he delivered the first printing of *Immaturity*, slightly revised after its fifty-year wait, and given a long autobiographical Preface. Thirty-two plays and playlets, many with emendations, followed in eleven volumes; and to these he added *Major Critical Essays* (*The Quintessence of Ibsenism*, *The Perfect Wagnerite* and *The Sanity of Art*), *The Intelligent Woman's Guide to Socialism* and various compilations ranging from *What I Really Wrote about the War* to the more distant *Short Stories, Scraps and Shavings*. 'We are unearthing all sorts of forgotten masterpieces!' Charlotte exclaimed. It involved what Shaw called 'appalling grave digging'. He went on digging up dramatic, literary, musical and political essays as well as critical pieces on education and medicine; and he added half a dozen new plays in the 1930s, bringing the total number of volumes to thirty-three. Nevertheless, he told Otto Kyllmann at Constable, 'I have conceived an extraordinary hatred to this particular edition, blast it!' and he later allowed it to be overtaken by what became known as Constable's 'Standard Edition' of his works, a cheaper set eventually rising to thirty-seven volumes uniformly bound in Venetian fadeless sail cloth. 'To the Standard Edition,' he wrote to Kyllmann, 'there is no limit but the grave.'

*

Rather unexpectedly, recognition was coming from Ireland. G.B.S. had never felt easy with Irish writers. 'We put each other out frightfully,' he wrote, recalling his meetings with Oscar Wilde; 'and this odd difficulty persisted between us to the very last.' Though Sonny and Oscar were born within two years and a couple of Irish miles of each other, no social contacts had been practicable in Victorian Dublin between families of such divergent histories. It was Charlotte's family that had lived opposite the Wildes in Merrion Square; while Shaw's father came to Sir William Wilde, 'Surgeon-Oculist in Ordinary to the Queen in Ireland', only as a patient. According to G.B.S., Sir William 'operated on my father to correct a squint, and overdid the corrections so much that my father squinted the other way all the rest of his life'.

In later years G.B.S. was seldom able to see Oscar Wilde as others saw him. He appeared to have two people in view: Oscar, the boyish romantic, chivalrously sympathetic to those less well-placed than himself and scrupulously well-mannered to others, such as Shaw, who were potentially his equals; and then Wilde, the arrogant Dublin snob encircled by acolytes. Shaw had met Oscar at one of Lady Wilde's richly eccentric at homes in London to which he sometimes went in the 'desperate days' between 1879 and 1885. 'Lady Wilde was nice to me,' he remembered. Oscar too had come up and spoken 'with an evident intention of being specially kind to me'. Lady Wilde's position, 'literary, social and patriotic, is unique and unassailable,' Shaw was to write in 1888 when reviewing her *Ancient Legends of Ireland* for the *Pall Mall Gazette*.

'She has no difficulty in writing about leprechauns, phoukas and banshees, simply as an Irishwoman telling Irish stories, impelled by the same tradition-instinct, and with a nursery knowledge at first hand of all the characteristic moods of the Irish imagination. Probably no living writer could produce a better book of its kind.'

This was partly because, Shaw manages to imply, the book belonged to a literature and sociology that were now dead. He had cut loose from this culture when throwing himself out of Ireland and into socialism, and he seems to have attributed what he saw as Wilde's false start as an apostle of art to the artificial prolongation of this dying tradition in the cult of aestheticism. Both Wilde, the complete dandy, and Shaw, the rational dress reformer, were showmen. The lilac puffs and frills, black silk stockings and tailored coats of braided velvet which made up Wilde's aesthetic presentation of himself were a 'coming out' of the superior cashmere combinations and other experimental underwear in which Shaw paradoxically showed off. Whenever these two noticeable figures met, they treated each other with elaborate courtesy, conscious that the British press resented their aberrations from ready-made Victorian behaviour. 'As far as I can ascertain, I am the only person in London who cannot sit down and write an Oscar Wilde play at will,' Shaw wrote in his *Saturday Review* notice of *An Ideal Husband*. ' . . . In a certain sense Mr Wilde is to me our only thorough playwright. He plays with everything: with wit, with philosophy, with drama, with actors and audience, with the whole theatre . . .

'All the literary dignity of the play, all the imperturbable good sense and good manners with which Mr Wilde makes his wit pleasant to his comparatively stupid audience, cannot quite overcome the fact that Ireland is of all countries the most foreign to England, and that to the Irishman . . . there is nothing in the world quite so exquisitely comic as an Englishman's seriousness.'

Wilde, too, made a point of treating Shaw's early work with true Irish seriousness. 'I like your superb confidence in the dramatic value of the mere facts of life,' he wrote after reading *Widowers' Houses*, ' . . . and your preface is a masterpiece – a real masterpiece of trenchant writing and caustic wit and dramatic instinct.' He let it be known that Shaw's *Quintessence of Ibsenism* had led him to write *The Soul of Man under Socialism*; and he supported Shaw's campaign against the 'ridiculous institution' of stage censorship. 'England is the land of intellectual fogs but you have done much to clear the air,' he wrote to Shaw in 1893: 'we are both Celtic, and I like to think that we are friends.' But on another occasion, he was reported to have said: 'Shaw is an excellent man. He has not an enemy in the world, and none of his friends like him'; while Shaw wrote that Wilde 'was incapable of friendship, though not of the most touching kindness on occasion'.

They were compatriots rather than friends. Their diffidence with each other masked what was probably an apprehension of their respective powers. Wilde was the one man in London capable of making the young Shaw sound comparatively dull. 'I had not to talk myself,' Shaw acknowledged, 'but to listen to a man telling me stories better than I could have told them.' But Wilde appears to have been nervous of Shaw's combative spirit and that 'caustic wit' which could pierce his own protective charm.

Their ways parted once Wilde's social aggrandizement seemed to implicate him in the very hypocrisies of Victorian society his absurdist wit had mocked. In Shaw's view, success brought out the snob in Wilde. This was one explanation for his reaction against *The Importance of Being Earnest* – Wilde's 'first really heartless play'. He wanted to believe that Wilde's talent for puncturing morals and manners fitted him for a place in 'a large public life' as a fellow socialist. Instead, Wilde appeared to succumb to flattery. His unconventionality was the very pedantry of convention, Shaw was to write; 'never was there a man less an outlaw than he.'

In fact, as his trial, imprisonment and exile showed, Wilde formed no more solid social foundations in England than G.B.S. Remembering that Wilde had been the only writer in London to sign his memorial in the late 1880s asking for the reprieve of the Chicago anarchists, Shaw drafted a petition seeking a remission of Wilde's prison sentence, but finding that his signature would stand almost alone he gave up the idea, concluding that the support would 'do Oscar more harm than good'.

He was able, however, to find a more sophisticated way of defending Wilde. His major critical essay, 'The Sanity of Art', had been aimed at Max Nordau's thesis *Degeneration*, which included as part of its 'Ego-Mania' section a hostile analysis of Wilde in the chapter 'Decadents and Aesthetes'. Shaw's response, originally entitled 'A Degenerate's View of Nordau', may be read as an intellectual rehabilitation of Wilde written during his second trial and published shortly after his sentence. In the happy days of the hugely successful *A Woman of No Importance*, which coincided with the shaky beginnings of *Widowers' Houses*, Wilde had paid Shaw the compliment of ranking their works together; in the days of Wilde's disgrace Shaw returned the compliment by ranking himself as a fellow 'degenerate'. He also went on favourably mentioning Wilde in his theatre reviews while Wilde was in prison; and six months after he was released, Shaw proposed his name – though that name was still taboo – as one of the 'Immortals' for an Academy of Letters. During the final period of Wilde's disgrace, they continued to send each other signed copies of their books, all works, as Oscar liked to say, of 'the great Celtic School' uniting socialism with aesthetics.

The great Celtic School had been held in place by its opposition to Victorian sexual and political ethics but, as the solid ground of Victorianism crumbled, it was to break up into two Hibernian tributaries. Shaw had rallied to Wilde in his misfortune, but switched off this support when he came to realize how tragedy was transforming him into a posthumous legend. Wilde's genius was for comedy, he declared, 'no other Irishman has yet produced as masterful a comedy as De Profundis'. By the 1930s Wilde was once again the more popular dramatist. 'My licence for the performance of my play Pygmalion . . . did not include an authorisation to advertise it as "the brilliant comedy by Oscar Wilde",' Shaw wrote in 1938 to the Grand Theatre in Wolverhampton. The manager of the theatre was disinclined to offer an apology, however, claiming that this substitution accounted for the play having attracted three times as much money as it did when billed as being written by Shaw. 'Beg him to continue the attribution, which was a most happy thought,' Shaw responded. 'I am not grumbling; I am rejoicing.'

Shaw's grumbles with Wilde arose less from personal rivalry than from their competing ideologies. By the 1920s and 1930s, Wilde's aesthetic creed had developed into the cult of personal relationships and artistic significance practised by the Bloomsbury Group, and would later lead to the 'flower power' of the 1960s and a branch of modernism in the 1990s. Shaw's economic opposition to Victorianism concurrently developed its programme of reforms towards the creation of a Welfare State which by the 1990s seemed no longer viable. He wanted egalitarian socialism to be accepted as the mainstream of twentieth-century culture in Britain. By giving his imprimatur to Frank Harris's inaccurate account of Wilde's life and by engaging for over a dozen years in a chastening correspondence with Alfred Douglas, Shaw sought to diminish the influence of a man whose memory was becoming an inspiration for the 'Artist Idolatry' he had attacked in the Preface to *Misalliance*, and whose ethics, with those of Beardsley, he had spotlighted in *The Doctor's Dilemma*.

Wilde was 'an original moralist' and it was his moral force that Shaw held in suspicion. This suspicion gave currency to the view of G.B.S. as a 'certain notorious and clever, but cold-blooded Socialist' whom W. B. Yeats depicts anonymously in an essay on Wilde.

Like Wilde, Yeats valued Shaw's fighting qualities. His 'detonating impartiality' had made him 'the most formidable man in modern letters' and was often used to 'hit my enemies'. Referring to his ballads on Roger Casement, Yeats was to tell Dorothy Wellesley in 1936: 'I am fighting in those ballads for what I have been fighting all my life, it is our Irish fight though it has nothing to do with this or that country. Bernard Shaw fights with the same object.'

Many years before, talking about G.B.S. as he walked back home in the evening with Florence Farr, the actress they both loved, Yeats had sometimes wondered 'whether the cock crowed for my blame or for my praise'. Finally he resolved the contradiction in a burst of Shavian-like humour: 'When a man is so outrageously in the wrong as Shaw he is indispensable.' He had accused Shaw of constructing plays like buildings 'made by science in an architect's office, and erected by joyless hands'; then he saw *Misalliance*, was delighted by the extravagant 'girl acrobat who read her Bible while tossing her balls in the air', and decided that her creator was 'irreverent, headlong, fantastic'.

But people lose their 'peace, their fineness in politics,' Yeats said, so it was no surprise to him that, fighting the political barbarians, Shaw had become something of a barbarian himself. Yeats responded to the mystical vein in Shaw, without believing it would ever quieten the 'Shaw who writes letters to the papers and gives interviews' and who had written *The Apple Cart*. 'He is haunted by the mystery he flouts,' Yeats wrote to George Russell. 'He is an atheist who trembles in the haunted corridor.'

Shaw had not liked Yeats's allegorical plays which seemed to float, full of 'treading-on-air' roles, within the twilight Ireland of Lady Wilde's legends. He hardly had the patience to tease out Yeats's dense and studied symbolisms. He had felt 'quite touched' by *Cathleen ni Houlihan*, 'but Ireland meant something then that cut no ice outside the island of saints'.

He had described *The Land of Heart's Desire* as 'an exquisite curtain raiser', but it had raised the curtain on *Arms and the Man*, a brisk modern comedy that Yeats likened to the hard-edged world of Epstein's *Rock Drill* and the Vorticism of Wyndham Lewis.

After they stayed as fellow-guests of Lady Gregory in the summer of 1910, Shaw had discovered 'what a penetrating critic and good talker' Yeats was, 'for he played none of his Bunthorne games, and saw no green elephants, at Coole'. He had also noticed the shrewdness with which Yeats handled the Abbey Theatre Company. 'The Abbey Players were enormously interesting, both technically and poetically,' he later wrote, 'and brought me into closer relations with him.'

In Chancery Lane one black night, Shaw remembered, 'into a circle of light under an arc lamp there suddenly stepped, walking towards me, Yeats with his wing of raven black hair swinging across his forehead and Maud Gonne, dazzlingly beautiful in white silk, both of them in evening dress. The pair were quite beyond description. I was invisible in the dark as they passed on; and of course I did not intrude.'

This was the only time Shaw saw Maud Gonne. He had not intruded on Yeats's Irish Movement, though somewhere else he was campaigning in the same war. He did not invade that pool of light, though from his courtly dance with Ellen Terry to his troubadour's pursuit of Stella Campbell he circled hypnotically round it, while Yeats, despite 'that girl standing there', had stepped into the shadows of politics as an Irish senator.

Between the poet of the emotions who believed that 'we begin to live when we have conceived life as tragedy' and the playwright of the intellect who thought that 'all genuinely intellectual work is humorous' there had once seemed to be no sympathetic meeting ground. But as Shaw's thought dissolved more into the surreal, he came to accept Yeats's visionary energies as being valuable for Ireland; and as Yeats moved 'closer to the common world' he understood the complementary value of the artist as politician.

On the Great Wheel of lunar phases round which Yeats charts the twenty-eight categories of human nature and the evolution of the soul through these categories, he places Shaw alongside Wells in phase 21 where writers are 'great public men and they exist after death as historical monuments, for they are without meaning apart from time and circumstance'. Yeats positioned himself at phase 17, an ideal phase except that the world was at phase 22 of its historical cycle and he was consequently fated to be one of its 'tragic minority'. So when seeking a vehicle of contemporary time and circumstance, he turned to the man whose moon almost exactly coincided with the age.

The Irish Academy of Letters was Yeats's version of Wilde's *politesse* about the 'great Celtic School'. It was to be an organization with the character of the Académie Française, bringing together those who had done creative work in Ireland, from the Celtic poet to the Cork realist, the Gaelic modernist and Big House novelist. He knew that the proposal would chiefly recommend itself to G.B.S. as a strengthening of forces against the censorship of the Catholic Church in Ireland; and indeed Shaw's participation was partly in acknowledgement of the help Yeats had given him in defeating British censorship at the Abbey with *The Shewing-up of Blanco Posnet*.

At the Academy's inaugural meeting in September 1932 Shaw was, in his absence, unanimously elected President, and Yeats became Vice-President. Twenty founding members accepted nomination plus eleven associates whose work was classified as 'less Irish'. Among the academicians was Shaw's future biographer, St John Ervine; among the associates Yeats's biographer, Joseph Hone. Most of the names were suggested by Yeats, though Shaw proposed T. E. Lawrence and Eugene O'Neill as associate members.

One nominee who refused the invitation was Sean O'Casey. Yeats had been O'Casey's spiritual father in Ireland when he was happy to be enveloped by 'the great glory of the Abbey'. But after the Abbey's rejection of *The Silver Tassie* in 1928 he turned to Shaw as his new protector and made Yeats his enemy. Shaw, who wished to support O'Casey and his family without antagonizing Yeats, urged conciliation. But O'Casey needed enemies as much as he needed heroes. The influences of Yeats and Shaw mingled uneasily in his plays. He could find no rapprochement between the Green Flag and the Red. Turning down the invitation to the Irish Academy was, he confessed, one of the hardest refusals of his life.

Another Irish exile, James Joyce, also refused the symbolic gesture, though warmly thanking Yeats through whom he also conveyed 'my thanks to Mr Shaw whom I have never met'. When reading parts of *Ulysses* in the *Little Review*, Shaw had been shudderingly reminded of his Dublin adolescence. 'I missed neither the realism of the book nor its poetry,' he later stated. Though admitting 'I could not write the words Mr Joyce uses', he acknowledged 'Joyce's literary power, which is of classic quality', adding, 'If Mr Joyce should ever desire a testimonial as the author of a literary masterpiece from me, it shall be given with all possible emphasis and with sincere enthusiasm.'

Shaw had received a prospectus for the Shakespeare and Company edition of *Ulysses* from Sylvia Beach who, believing he would relish the revolutionary aspect of the work, accepted Joyce's bet of a silk handkerchief to a box of cigars that Shaw's name would not be on the list of subscribers.

But, though praising Joyce's 'literary genius', Shaw had gone on to explain that 'I am an elderly Irish gentleman, and that if you imagine that any Irishman, much less an elderly one, would pay 150 francs for a book, you little know my countrymen'.

After that it was the turn of Ezra Pound to bully him into a subscription. 'I take care of the pence,' Shaw answered, 'because the Pounds will not take care of themselves.' Though this helped to earn him Pound's condemnation as a 'ninth-rate coward', it delighted Joyce himself. Having eyed their 'letter fight over me' through his cigar smoke, he thought he spied how matters stood. Echoing Shaw, he cautioned Pound that if he thought G.B.S. had not 'subscribed anonymously for a copy of the revolting record through a bookseller you little know my countrymen'. And Pound had conceded: 'Dear old Shaw has amused us.'

By 1920 Joyce's library contained thirteen volumes of Shaw, comprising seventeen works. In Zurich during the war he had become involved with the English Players' Company's presentation of *The Dark Lady of the Sonnets* (for which he wrote a darkly amusing programme note) and some unauthorized performances of the still-censored *Mrs Warren's Profession*. Shaw raised legal objections to this production, but although it was without benefit of royalties, Joyce may have thought he was engaged in defeating censorship as Yeats had done with *The Shewing-up of Blanco Posnet*.

Joyce's review of that play at the Abbey had been a 'shewing-up' of G.B.S. as a writer incapable of the 'noble and bare style appropriate to modern playwrighting'. In Joyce's eyes, Shaw was more preacher than literary artist. This was the obverse of Shaw's view of Joyce as a literary artist in danger of dwindling into a limited edition belletrist. 'I shall not do anything that may encourage him to be a coterie author,' he had warned Pound: 'Irish talent, when it is serious, belongs to the big world.'

That the world would venerate a linguistic experimenter like Joyce as well as a supernatural speculator like Yeats said something to Shaw of literature's removal from the streets into the universities. He did not keep up with Joyce's later work any more than with Yeats's. 'I have tried to read Finnegan but found it would take more time to decipher than it seemed worth,' he wrote in 1948. ' . . . I might have persevered when I was 20; but at 93 time is precious and the days pass like flights of arrows.'

'Allow me to offer my felicitations to you on the honour you have received and to express my satisfaction that the award of the Nobel Prize for literature has gone once more to a distinguished fellow townsman,' Joyce wrote in 1926. This was the only letter of congratulation Shaw kept. Had he persisted with *Finnegans Wake*, he would have found within its overlapping contexts many Shavian echoes and allusions from 'Sainte

Andrée's Undershift' to the injunction 'Plays be honest!' and the disarming 'Candidately'. Even Blanche Patch takes a bow in *Finnegans Wake*.

Wilde's great Celtic School found a symbol but never a centre in Yeats's Academy. Like Shaw, Yeats had thought in terms of synthesis. But the Celtic School depended on antitheses. It was a school of truancy, thriving on a pressure that drove people outwards, and on the tension and reproach of exiles 'too conscious of intellectual power to belong to party,' as Yeats wrote when describing Wilde and Shaw together. Joyce, whose imagination was lit up by a reference Shaw made to Wilde's gigantism, also coupled them in the Wildeshawshow of *Finnegans Wake* as brother opposites, like Sterne and Swift, of the same generation. From such half-admiring antipathies did the Celtic-Hibernian School gain its positive capability.

5

THE BOXER AND THE NUN

This is the way with us ageing men. In the decay of our minds the later acquisitions go first.
H.G. Wells's obituary of Shaw, *Daily Express* (3 November 1950)

'And now I have come from the burial of Thomas Hardy's ashes in the Abbey . . .' Charlotte wrote to T. E. Lawrence. Hardy had died aged eighty-seven on the evening of Wednesday 11 January 1928. 'He and I were on very friendly terms,' G.B.S. was reported as saying. ' . . . I always liked his poetry better than his prose.' Two days after his death, Shaw received an invitation to act as one of the pallbearers at Westminster Abbey. 'I desire to be buried in Stinsford Churchyard,' Hardy had written in his will; but according to Shaw he 'knew that he must ultimately come to the Abbey and he was quite reconciled to it'. As an extreme compromise his body was dismembered and the heart buried at Stinsford while the ashes were being laid to rest in the Abbey. Many people were horrified by this mutilation. But G.B.S. reassured Florence Hardy that, since her husband belonged to the nation as well as to himself, she had had no choice in the matter. 'Everything that could be done has been done to meet national sentiment,' he wrote in the *Daily News*. 'Wessex has the heart, the nation has his ashes.'

It was snowing hard on the day of the funeral, but sprawling crowds had assembled and lots were being drawn for tickets of admission to Poets' Corner. Shaw felt uncharacteristically nervous. Barrie, Galsworthy,

Edmund Gosse, A. E. Housman and Kipling were the other writers acting as pallbearers; there were Masters of two colleges that had made Hardy an Honorary Fellow, Queen's College, Oxford, and Magdalene College, Cambridge; as well as the Prime Minister and the Leader of the Opposition, Stanley Baldwin and Ramsay MacDonald. A young biographer who had journeyed down from Cambridge for the funeral observed that, in startling contrast to the weight and texture of the other pallbearers, Shaw seemed an ethereal presence. 'I have never seen so *transparent* a complexion; a pallor, very slightly tinged with the freshest rose – such as any girl or child alone normally has . . . His hair alone, still a glinting *gilt*, wire-like tangle of reddish threads, was material.'

Shaw attributed his success, despite almost falling over Kipling, to having posed for Troubetzkoy in a sublime attitude: 'I was in full practice,' he told Henry Salt. The clergy, full of worldly pomp and disdain, led the procession; and at the end, erect and calm, came Florence 'so completely swathed in crape that her face was invisible'. As the chords of the organ music swelled and burst out and the procession passed back, she hung on Sydney Cockerell's arm, Charlotte observed, and appeared 'completely broken'.

It was 'a fine show,' G.B.S. admitted, ' . . . but I didn't feel solemn a bit,' he afterwards wrote to Florence Hardy.

'If you only knew how I wanted at the end to swoop on you; tear off all that villainous crape (you should have been like the lilies of the field); and make you come off, *with him*, to see a Charlie Chaplin film! But of course we wouldn't have dared. I had to be content with nudging Cockerell disrespectfully as I passed him.'

In fact he had behaved with sensitivity, informing the press that Hardy 'had no enemies, at least that I know of', but in a letter to Florence Hardy revealing his awareness that her married life had not been easy. 'It is inconceivable that Thomas Hardy's widow should be unhappy or unblest. Only, don't marry another genius . . .'

*

'I cannot sympathize about his death,' Shaw remarked on hearing that the actor Robert Loraine had died, 'because I am going to die myself shortly.' He took the same line when James Barrie died eighteen months later in 1937. Far from being, as the public imagined, a genuine Peter Pan (like G. K. Chesterton) he had struck Shaw as having been born a thousand years old (like Max Beerbohm). He was one of the few people whom Shaw admitted to have been unhappy. 'Certainly he regretted that he had no children. Perhaps he ought to have had children . . .' But what was terrifying to Shaw was the way he had killed the child in himself. 'He gave you the impression that for all his playfulness he had hell in his soul.'

During the 1920s and 1930s the deaths of Fabian comrades, colleagues in the theatre and those who had influenced his early intellectual life were regularly announced in the newspapers, often with some tribute from Shaw. He and Charlotte were abroad when, in the early summer of 1935, they heard the news that T. E. Lawrence had been killed. Charlotte felt profoundly thankful to be away: the publicity would have been awful. Some of the evidence at the inquest had been contradictory and there were rumours of murder and suicide. The facts, as the Shaws understood them, were that he had been racing home from Bovington Camp on his Brough Superior 'Boanerges', a motorcycle with the same name as the bull-roarer in *The Apple Cart* that the Shaws had given him. He had swerved to avoid some boys on bicycles, gone into a skid, and been thrown over the handlebars. He was forty-six; but perhaps, Charlotte speculated, it was for the best. 'He always dreaded pain and the idea of death (as a sort of sign of defeat!) and now, you see, he had got off without knowing anything about it.'

Worst of all had been the news in May 1927 that H. G. Wells's wife Jane was dying of cancer. Jane 'is *valiant* & has been the gayest & pluckiest person I have ever known,' Charlotte wrote to Wells. A few days later they motored over to Little Easton. Jane lay exhausted on a sofa in the drawing-room while H.G. darted anxiously in and out. He was desperate to do anything that might make these last months easier for her, for he knew she was doomed. 'The doctors and the nurse, having committed themselves to the opinion that Jane is a goner, are naturally creating an atmosphere calculated to produce that effect even on a perfectly healthy woman,' Shaw protested in a letter to Beatrice Webb. ' . . . I am trying to make her defy science and have a turn at all the empiricisms as aids to curing herself. Charlotte was rather distressed . . .'

They visited Jane again that summer and saw her getting weaker. It was, as Charlotte said, 'beyond words' and Shaw agreed. 'There it is,' he had written with a tone of finality. But he could not leave it there. He advised Wells to take a gamble on anything from homoeopathy to osteopathy, and encouraged his old friend to 'grasp the horror of your own scientific education'. All this was meant to help Wells 'watch and wait with an undarkened mind'. But, though it probably had something of this effect on G.B.S., it can only have pushed Wells himself nearer the end of his tether. 'Charlotte says I can do no good by worrying you, as you will only be made more miserable,' G.B.S. ended his letter that August. 'But

I do not regard you as a miserable person . . . it would be very jolly to hear that Jane is all right. Send us a bulletin, however brief.'

But no bulletin came. 'Please H.G. dont be angry with him,' Charlotte wrote privately that September. 'You know he is like that – he must sometimes let himself go in this aggravating way – & he means it all so more than well! . . . Do – *do* – write a line – to *me*, even, & say you ar'nt angry.' So, within four weeks of his wife's death, Wells was obliged to comfort Charlotte over her husband. 'Your charming letter brought peace to me & a great deal of thankfulness,' Charlotte replied. ' . . . Perhaps now it will not be so very long before we meet.'

They met the following month for Jane's cremation at Golders Green. 'I haven't been so upset for a long time,' Charlotte wrote. The service was 'hideous – terrible and frightful'. Wells, dressed in a bottle-blue overcoat, came and sat with her and G.B.S. instead of with his family, and the organ started on an appalling dirge. At any second, Charlotte feared, G.B.S. might stride over and murder the organist in his loft. Wells, his handkerchief darting in and out of his pocket, 'began to cry like a child – tried to hide it at first and then let go'.

The funeral speech had been prepared by Wells and was delivered by T. E. Page, a classical scholar noted for his oratory. 'This oration was either not well done,' observed Arnold Bennett, 'or too well done.' Virginia Woolf, who had been looking forward to the outing ('What fun! How I love ceremonies') thought the presentation somewhat nondescript. To Charlotte it sounded like grief curdled by guilt. 'He drowned us in a sea of misery and as we were gasping began a panegyric of Jane which made her appear as a delicate, flower-like, gentle being, surrounding itself with beauty and philanthropy and love,' she wrote. ' . . . Then there came a place where the address said "she never resented a slight; she never gave voice to a harsh judgement". At that point the audience, all more or less acquainted with many details of H.G.'s private life, thrilled, like corn under a wet north wind – and H.G. – H.G. positively howled.'

At the end of the service the pale grey coffin with 'tassels like bell pulls' was 'shoved through the door into the furnace'. The chapel emptied. G.B.S. trotted out into the garden and encouraged Wells to take his boys into the furnace room. 'I saw my mother burnt there. You'll be glad if you go.' Wells did go, taking his two sons, and watched the quivering flames.

Charlotte remained in the chapel: 'I took a little time to get quiet.' When she came out into the yard most of the congregation was still there. 'Number of really A.1 people present, very small,' noted Arnold Bennett who saw only one man in full mourning and observed that G.B.S. who had no overcoat was wearing an amber handkerchief. The great world was no longer interested in Wells. 'It was desperate to see what a dowdy shabby imperfect lot we looked,' Virginia Woolf remarked.

Charlotte felt Wells had got his due. 'I am an old woman and there is one thing I seem, at least, to have learned,' she wrote grimly. 'The way of transgressors is hard.' Looking 'stately and calm, and remote', Virginia Woolf disengaged the tiny sobbing figure of Lydia Lopokova from Charlotte's arms while G.B.S. consoled her. 'You mustnt cry,' he said. 'Jane is well – Jane is splendid.' Then he began firing off 'jokes to everyone, and finally – putting H.G. into his car – he actually got a sort of grin out of *him*'. Wells had no wish to grin and resented being made to betray his grief in this way.

The occasion had a macabre postscript. In 1945 the *New Statesman* asked Shaw to draft an obituary of Wells and this was published when Wells died in the summer of 1946. It was an even-handed recollection of a spoilt man of genius, temperamental yet 'without malice'. Wells had also been asked at approximately the same time to write an obituary of Shaw for the *Daily Express*. His obituary was published over four years after his own death and came, St John Ervine remembered, like 'a piercing scream from the grave'. Shaw was an example of the 'mental and moral consequences of prolonged virginity' on a nervously active person. 'As a rule prolonged virginity means no real ascetic purity,' Wells had argued. ' . . . A furtive sexual system grows up detached from the general activities.' Needing to distance himself from reality, G.B.S. had grown forever out of adjustment to his environment. A secondary, vindictive personality took control whose method of self-assertion was 'to inflict pain'.

This was the danger of G.B.S.'s fantasies. Charlotte, 'that most lovable of women', had tried to prevent such vanities, and that was 'more and more her role as life went on,' Wells continued. 'She had married this perplexing being in a passion of admiration . . . and she found she had launched that incalculable, lop-sided *enfant terrible*, a man of genius, upon the world.'

*

'We were very good friends . . . On paper he died in despair; but I cannot believe that his gaiety ever deserted him,' Shaw was to write of Wells in 1946 to Gene Tunney. Tunney, the world heavyweight boxing champion, was more than forty years younger than Shaw, and famously unmarked, a scholar of the ring. Americans were puzzled on being told that he had been found, shortly before his first contest with Jack Dempsey, poring over Samuel Butler's *The Way of All Flesh*. They laughed openly at his contention that he would beat Dempsey by virtue of his superior mental training, and they never really forgave him for twice out-pointing their All-American Hero.

Tunney's career was a Shavian romance. 'Reputations cannot frighten him: personalities cannot hypnotize him,' Shaw wrote: 'he does not need to be a brilliant boxer like Carpentier or a terror like Dempsey; he wins by mental and moral superiority, combined with plenty of strength . . . You might say that he wins because he has the good sense to win.'

Here was Shaw's fantasy of action made real, Cashel Byron come to life. They met in December 1928. Earlier that year Tunney had retired as undefeated heavyweight champion, after which he delivered a course of lectures on Shakespeare at Yale, accompanied Thornton Wilder on a walking trip round Europe and married a young gentlewoman from Greenwich, Connecticut. 'My great work now is to live quietly and simply,' he announced to the world, 'for this manner of living brings me most happiness.' His pursuit of culture led him, by the end of this year, to 'an extremely pleasant' luncheon at Whitehall Court.

He spoke of his travels over many countries and it was then that he introduced the Shaws to Brioni in the Adriatic, where they all met up the following year. Tunney was 'so handsome & gentle & babyish that it refreshes one to look at him,' Charlotte wrote from Brioni to Nancy Astor. 'He takes G.B.S. for long walks (his boast is that you can walk 8 miles on the Island without repeating yourself!) & gazes at him, like a large dog at its master.'

On Brioni the Shaws passed many days at the Tunneys' villa. Charlotte had long suspected G.B.S. of taking advantage of her siestas to press secretly ahead with his work. The knowledge that he was being actively prevented from working by Gene Tunney came as a tremendous relief to her as she ascended to her bedroom. 'Mr Tunney is a most wonderful help,' she reported to Blanche Patch. 'He takes Mr Shaw off to the polo ground, or the golf course, or sailing, or something, and so keeps him from writing, which is splendid.'

When asked why he cultivated Tunney's friendship, G.B.S. was to reply: 'To plant my feet on solid ground.' Yet it was as airy a fantasy in its fashion as his island romance with Molly Tompkins – a magical relationship that enabled them to swap roles, G.B.S. being admitted as a champion boxing analyst in exchange for adopting Tunney as a very perfect literary scholar. Tunney met all manner of artists and writers at the Shaws' home, and they had to strain every nerve to match his sensitivity. 'Mr Tunney took me by the arm and led me to the windows and compelled my attention to the beauties of the sunset,' remembered Max Beerbohm.

By the early 1930s Tunney had 'got into the book-writing field myself' with his memoirs of the ring, *A Man Must Fight*. Shaw refused to contribute a Preface, explaining that 'when you want a publisher for your next book on the strength of this one they will all declare that your first book does not count as it was the Shaw preface that sold it'. Besides, Tunney was far more famous than any writer or artist. 'You may remember that at Brioni, when I was talking to Richard Strauss, nobody troubled about us until you joined us,' Shaw wrote to him; 'and then the cameras came with a rush.'

By the late 1930s, after Tunney had been retired for ten years, a change came over their relationship. G.B.S. was now the more famous of the two, and Tunney's confidence took a dive: 'I began to feel that I had no right to intrude on his time.' But out of the blue a letter was to arrive from G.B.S. at the end of 1946. 'I feel I must give you a hail to shew that I have not forgotten our old happy contacts.' He had now passed his ninetieth birthday and 'have only some scraps of wit left,' he wrote.

Tunney being once more the stronger of the two, their friendship was resumed. 'I am not worth the journey,' Shaw warned him in 1948, but Tunney came to Ayot and noticed how eager G.B.S. was to keep up-to-date and learn all there was to know about the new heavyweight wonder of the world, Joe Louis, who was reported as being anxious to exchange a few verbal rounds with him and the other champion of Britain, Winston Churchill.

That summer, in his last letter to Tunney, Shaw signed off: 'I hold you in affectionate remembrance.' Afterwards Tunney wrote to Stanbrook Abbey that Shaw had been 'the saintliest man I have ever known'.

The Prioress of Stanbrook Abbey, Dame Laurentia McLachlan, was another island of confidence in a doubting world. She had been officially received into the Order of St Benedict on the same day in 1884 that Shaw was enrolled in the Fabian Society. The Bishop had sheared off the long fair hair of the seventeen-year-old girl. Then the great enclosure door swung open in answer to the novice's importunate knocking, and presently closed behind her. For almost seventy years behind high walls and bolted doors, she was to follow the exacting codes of the enclosed Benedictine discipline, devoting each day to prayer, scholarship and the ceremonial worship of God.

The Abbey of Stanbrook was a Victorian Gothic pile not far from Malvern. By the 1920s it had become a place of pilgrimage for many exotic travellers. One of these was Sydney Cockerell, the astringent anti-quarian who had been a friend of Shaw's since his days as William Morris's secretary at Hammersmith. Cockerell first met Dame Laurentia in 1907, the year before he was appointed Director of the Fitzwilliam Museum at Cambridge. His curiosity was soon pricked by this nun with the beautiful voice in her 'rather nice cage' and he felt somewhat in awe of her great reputation as an authority on plainsong and liturgical ritual. The double grille through which they communicated seemed to simplify human relationships.

'Some I have to keep apart, others I wish to bring together,' Cockerell wrote to her. 'There are several I should very much like you to meet.' From the first, Shaw had been one of those Cockerell wanted her to meet. 'I wonder whether G.B.S's fame has got as far as Stanbrook,' he enquired in 1907.

'I have never heard of Mr Bernard Shaw,' Dame Laurentia replied.

But seventeen years later she gave Cockerell an opening. 'I hear Bernard Shaw has written a play about St Joan,' she wrote. 'I will lend you Shaw's play to read,' he offered. '. . . *Joan* is not yet published and mine is a very special copy.'

He sent her his special copy; she thought it 'a wonderful play' and on returning it wrote: 'Joan herself is beautifully portrayed.' But on a number of theological matters Shaw had gone astray and 'I should like to make some alterations'. Cockerell was sufficiently encouraged to show this letter to the Shaws themselves. Nine days later, on 24 April 1924, Dame Laurentia received a note from Charlotte enclosing two visiting cards: 'Our friend Sydney Cockerell has urged us very strongly to call upon you. We feel a little diffident about doing so, and hope you will not think us intrusive.'

After this formal opening came an impetuous rush as Charlotte and G.B.S. hurtled up to the Abbey. Cockerell was as eager as a marriage-broker to find out how the hour between them had passed. He pressed Charlotte, who eventually revealed that 'We like her *very* much.' From Dame Laurentia he learnt that the Shaws were 'charming'. All this was frustrating for Cockerell, a 'born intriguer and puller of strings', but an enticing relationship began to shimmer before him.

It had the air of a flirtation. That was how Charlotte saw it: a chaste flirtation. She seldom accompanied him on his jaunts to Stanbrook, prefer-ring to take the opportunity while he was at these tête-à-têtes of 'tidying his writing table'. Sometimes she turned up all sorts of naughtinesses there. 'He went off this morning with Sydney Cockerell – who is as bad as himself – to flirt with an "enclosed" nun at Stanbrook Abbey,' she wrote in the summer of 1929 to Nancy Astor.

'It was an immense treat to see you and Shaw together,' Cockerell wrote deferentially to Dame Laurentia following this visit. '. . . I think the encounter was a mutual tonic.' He was impressed by Shaw's manners. 'I never saw him so abashed by anyone but William Morris.'

Dame Laurentia agreed that 'Brother Bernard' was a 'delicious' tonic. She called him Brother Bernard ever since he had given her a copy of *Saint*

Joan with the inscription: 'To Sister Laurentia from Brother Bernard.' He had taken the trouble to answer her objections to the play, explaining that in 'heathen literature like mine', it was necessary to present Joan's visions in such a way as to make them completely independent of the iconography attached to her religion.

This letter, Dame Laurentia acknowledged, 'pleases me greatly in spite of its heresies'. 'I am delighted to learn that my St Joan is yours also,' he replied. She had not meant to go quite so far as that. Yet this elusive and complex man continued to impress her with his 'absolute sincerity and simplicity'. As Cockerell noticed, they complemented each other in various ways. 'I was greatly interested to meet such a famous man,' Dame Laurentia owned. She felt a special softness for famous people: they were a delightful disturbance in her seclusion. For Shaw Dame Laurentia was an enclosed nun without an enclosed mind whose private world he could approach, 'shake your bars and look longingly at the freedom at the other side of them'. Her place in his life was closer to that of the retiring humanist Henry Salt than of William Morris. 'My pastime has been writing sermons in plays, sermons preaching what Salt practised,' Shaw wrote; and in much the same tone, he confided to Dame Laurentia: 'you have lived the religious life: I have only talked and written about it.'

This attitude, Cockerell believed, accounted for Shaw's 'good behaviour' and seemed to admit 'that he was in the presence of a being superior to himself'. It came as no surprise to Dame Laurentia. Not being in possession of the true creed, Shaw was 'very much to be pitied'. And very much to be prayed for too. 'You expose yourself to the danger of being prayed for very earnestly,' she warned him. But he welcomed this current of goodwill ('it would be shockingly unscientific to doubt it'). He never felt any the worse for these prayers.

Though Laurentia was equally available to the poor and unknown, these rich and celebrated visitors to Stanbrook could be of special benefit. 'Do you remember when you gave me one of your plays, you advised me to sell it?' she reminded Shaw. 'I have been tempted to take your advice, for I am in great need of money – just £5,000 would be a fortune to me – but I know that a seller would advertise the owner's name & I should not be able to endure that.' She valued Shaw's generosity and would sometimes tuck in a discreet financial reminder with her prayerful inveigling of his soul. 'I am more glad than ever not to have a millionairess in my monastic family,' she told him after he sent her his play *The Millionairess*, 'useful as her cash would be.'

Shaw valued Dame Laurentia for some of the same overpowering qualities she shared with the heroine of that play. He saw her as a natural authoritarian. 'You would boss the establishment if you were only the scullery maid,' he told her. He relied on this strength; she was more a Mother Superior to him than a Sister. The centre of their relationship for her was the opportunity it offered for making a convert of G.B.S. to the divine doctrine of Catholicism. But catholicity for him meant comprehensiveness and a universality of interests. The essence of their relationship lay in the unchangeableness of their positions and the complementary views and uses they could offer each other.

Shaw was an eye-witness of the world providing visual confirmation for Dame Laurentia of what she already knew. The most dramatic use of his eye came on a journey he made with Charlotte in March 1931 to the Holy Land. She had asked him to 'bring me back some little trifle from Calvary'. But there was no credible Calvary, he discovered. Rosaries and testaments bound in 'the wood of the Cross', together with all sorts of sham relics, were thrust at him; the only genuine souvenirs of Gethsemane he found to send her were some olive leaves, with which she was well pleased. Then, from the threshold of the Church of the Nativity in Bethlehem, he picked up a pebble, a chip of the limestone rock 'which certainly existed when the feet of Jesus pattered about on it and the feet of Mary pursued him . . . In fact I picked up two little stones: one to be thrown blindfold among the others in Stanbrook garden so that there may always be a stone from Bethlehem there, though nobody will know which it is and be tempted to steal it, and the other for your own self.'

This second stone, which he presented to Dame Laurentia later that year, was set in a silver medieval-style reliquary designed by Paul Cooper. Cockerell, who had recommended the work of Paul Cooper, suggested adding an inscription explaining its purpose. But Shaw refused: 'If we could explain its purpose we could explain the universe,' he appealed to Dame Laurentia, ' . . . our finger prints are on it, and Heaven knows whose footprints may be on the stone. Isn't that enough?'

Besides, he had sent her letters enabling her to bring alive what she had imagined of the Holy Land:

'a region in which the miraculous is no longer miraculous but gigantically normal . . . with strange new constellations all over the sky and the old ones all topsy turvy, but with the stars soft and large and down quite close overhead in the sky . . . a hilly country, with patches of cultivation wrested from the omnipresent stones, which you instantly recognize with a strange emotion which intensifies when you see . . . a woman with an infant in her arms . . . It gives you the feeling that here Christ lived and grew up, and that here Mary bore him and reared him, and that there is no land on earth quite like it.'

'You have made me feel that I have seen the Holy Land through your eyes,' Dame Laurentia answered, 'and have revealed a great deal more than I should have seen with my own. I . . . continue to view the world from my cell at Stanbrook.'

*

These long-distance friendships with a heavyweight boxer and an enclosed nun were characteristic of someone who ran lines of communication between different disciplines. 'Nowadays a Catholic who is ignorant of Einstein is as incomplete as a thirteenth-century Dominican ignorant of Aristotle,' Shaw wrote. Science meant two things to Shaw. It was the algebraic hocus-pocus that had befuddled him at school and hypnotized so many adults. He viewed the priests of that science as an élite corps of idealists who had strengthened the philistines' citadel with inflexible axioms, giving it a brilliant technological façade. Shaw classed these renegade scientists with clairvoyants, diviners, hand readers and slate writers – all 'marvel mongers whose credulity would have dissolved the Middle Ages in a roar of sceptical merriment'.

The Shaw who believed in scientific advancement as a benefit to society was the author of *The Irrational Knot* whose hero had been an electrical engineer. This same Shaw was a life member of the Royal Astronomical Society and, in his nineties, would register his belief in the necessity of space travel by joining the British Interplanetary Society. 'The whole world has to be reorganized, has to be reset,' he stated during a speech early in 1920. 'That has to be done by thinkers, and men of science in the very best sense, and has to be done in the interests of humanity.'

This statement was made four months after *The Times* carried two articles on the verification of Einstein's General Theory of Relativity. 'Enough has been done to overthrow the certainty of ages,' *Times* readers were told, 'and to require a new philosophy of the universe, a philosophy that will sweep away nearly all that has hitherto been accepted as the axiomatic basis of physical thought.'

This was immensely exciting to Shaw. In *Back to Methuselah*, which was completed in May 1920, he made the scientist Pygmalion speak of children in the future possessing an innate 'sense of space time and quantity' and of knowing by instinct many things that the greatest physicists of the twentieth century 'could hardly arrive at by forty years of strenuous study'. For the first time in this play Shaw 'used mathematical speculation to characterize advanced intelligence,' observed the critic Desmond McRory. McRory argues that Shaw began writing futuristic plays after the Great War out of 'despair over the failure of his contemporaries and a desire to deal with a time distant enough to be hopeful'.

18 Mrs Patrick (Stella) Campbell

19 Beatrice and Sidney Webb

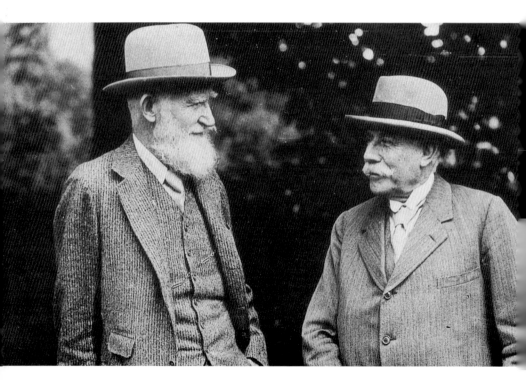

20 Shaw and Elgar at the Malvern Festival, 1929

21 The Ethical Movement, Miss Hankinson and G.B.S.
at a Fabian Society Summer School, 1922

22 In Hollywood, with l. to r. Charlie Chaplin, Marion Davies,
Louis B. Mayer and Clark Gable

23 Erica Cotterill

24 Molly Tompkins

25 G.B.S. with Blanche Patch

26 Charlotte photographed by Shaw

27 In the garden at Ayot St Lawrence, shortly before his 90th birthday, 1946

Shaw and Einstein first met at a dinner party early in June 1921 when Einstein was visiting London. In the nine years that passed before their second meeting in the autumn of 1930, their knowledge of each other had been advanced by Shaw's mathematical biographer Archibald Henderson. In 1923 Henderson had gone to the Institute of Physics at the University of Berlin to work with Einstein on relativity and atomic theory, and to instruct him on Shavian drama and politics in the evenings. On his return he resumed his schooling of Shaw on the latest advances in physics. By 1925 Shaw was speaking of Einstein as the great destroyer of scientific infallibility: 'he has upset the velocity of light, upset the ether, upset gravitation, and generally lit ... a fire among the gods of the physicists.'

Shaw and Einstein's second meeting, in October 1930, took place at a public dinner at the Savoy Hotel. Shaw's speech proposing Einstein's health, and Einstein's reply, were recorded by the BBC and broadcast to the United States. It was a singular moment for G.B.S. He could say exactly what he felt since his feelings, the polite occasion, and his ideological commitment to progress came naturally together. 'Suppose that I had to rise here tonight to propose the toast of Napoleon,' he said: 'undoubtedly I could say many flattering things about Napoleon, but the one thing which I should not be able to say about him would be ... that perhaps it would have been better for the human race if he had never been born!'

Shaw classed Einstein as belonging to a different order of great men whose 'hands are unstained by the blood of any human being on earth'. He explained, too, the affinity he felt for this man who had recently spoken of his need for solitude. ' ... My friend Mr Wells has spoken to us sometimes of the secret places of the heart. There are also the lonely places of the mind ... our little solitude gives us something of a key to his solitude ... his great and august solitude.

' ... I rejoice at the new universe to which he has introduced us. I rejoice in the fact that he has destroyed all the old sermons, all the old absolutes, all the old cut and dried conceptions, even of time and space, which were so discouraging ... I want to get further and further. I always want more and more problems, and our visitor has raised endless and wonderful problems and has begun solving them.'

Shaw's toast was a salute to the ultimate realist of the twentieth century. In the plays and books of Shaw's last twenty years, Einstein was to become a symbol of human possibility. 'You are the only sort of man in whose existence I can see much hope for this deplorable world,' Shaw wrote to him.

In his reply at the Savoy, Einstein described what he believed Shaw's achievement to have been as a dramatist. 'From your box of tricks you have taken countless puppets which, whilst resembling men, are not of flesh and bone, but consist entirely of spirit, wit, and grace . . .

'You make these gracious puppets dance in a little world guarded by the Graces who allow no resentment to enter in. Whoever has glanced into this little world, sees the world of our reality in a new light; he sees your puppets blending into real people . . . you have been able, as no other contemporary, to effect in us a liberation, and to take from us something of the heaviness of life.'

SEVENTEEN

I

ELOPEMENT TO RUSSIA

After exhausting the possible, he [Napoleon] had to attempt the impossible and go to Moscow . . . his failure made him the enemy of the human
race.

What I Really Wrote about the War (1930)

'Good news from Russia, eh?' Shaw had written to Frank Harris on
learning the news of Kerensky's revolution in February 1917. 'Not quite
what any of the belligerents intended . . . but the Lord fulfils himself in
many ways.'

The language Shaw and others had used to describe tsardom was to
become familiar ten and twenty years later in Western reports of Stalinism.
With its Siberian exiles, its pogroms, terrors, massacres, the Tsar's regime,
'under which women spent years in dungeons for teaching children to
read . . . laborers lived in cellars and . . . the dear princesses could hire a
droschky to take them to the Opera for four pence', was the most inequitable society in Europe. It should, Shaw recommended in 1915, be
excommunicated from international society as 'the open enemy of every
liberty we boast of'. He made what efforts he could to find out what was
happening during 1917, writing that spring in the *New York Times* of
'the enormous relief, triumph, and delight with which the news of the
revolution in Russia was received in England'. 'It not only at last justifies
the Franco-Anglo-Russian alliance (which in the days of the tsardom was
a disgrace to western democracy), but justifies the whole war,' he wrote
to Gorki in May 1917.

For most of this year Shaw found himself in unusual accord with liberal
opinion in Britain. 'Hail! The Russian Revolution,' proclaimed Ramsay
MacDonald. At the Albert Hall in London 20,000 people had to be
refused tickets for the celebration. 'Every person there was wanting a real
absolute change in everything,' Bertrand Russell affirmed, 'not the sort
of piecemeal niggling reforms that one is used to, but the sort of thing
the Russians have done . . . The Russians have really put a new spirit
into the world, & it is going to be worth while to be alive.' Many felt as
if they were living at the time of the French Revolution. It was 'a
tremendous event for me,' acknowledged Leonard Woolf, 'and for all those

whose beliefs and hopes had been moulded in the revolutionary fires of liberty, equality, fraternity'. People were filled with a sense of liberation. This 'giant stride from autocracy to republic-democracy astounded Western Europe,' wrote H. G. Wells. ' . . . Today Russia stands a gigantic challenge to every vestige of the dynastic system that has darkened, betrayed, and tormented Europe for unnumbered years.'

By the end of the year, however, what Wells called 'this banner of fiery hope' had been extinguished for many by Lenin's Bolshevik Revolution. There had been much in Kerensky's administration that was naturally appealing to Shaw. Kerensky's status as a lawyer and the presence in the provisional government of princes and historians gave these moderates a Fabian respectability. They had come to power by revolution, but it had been 'bloodless'.

Lenin described Kerensky as 'the boy braggart', which was exactly the sort of contemptuous dismissal people had flung at G.B.S. But everyone who saw him knew that Kerensky was a luminous orator: his 'words rose and fell in an inexhaustible, almost visible fountain of emotional sound,' one of his audience wrote; and another, who heard him deliver an impassioned address from the stage at the Alexandrinsky Theatre in Petrograd, observed that the 'theatrical setting' had 'spurred him on in his acting, a rôle that was natural to him'.

Kerensky's overthrow by Lenin represented a defeat for the sort of political activity Shaw had so long been conducting. In his study of fellow-travellers, David Caute was to question when Shaw had 'ever torn up paving stones, hidden in the marshes, carried a gun, plotted a coup?' He concluded that the neighbours at Ayot who knew him as a 'gentle old man' were 'closer to the truth' than Lenin who described him as a figure 'far to the left of those around him' who would never be mistaken for a clown in revolutionary conditions. But Shaw had made it plain that by the word revolutionist he did not mean 'a bloodstained man in shirt sleeves and a red cap of liberty' chopping aristocrats to pieces 'with an axe'.

After Kerensky's fall and Lenin's rise to power, Shaw began to reassess his own political function. Engels had praised him as 'a most talented and witty writer'; Gorki acclaimed him as 'one of the most courageous thinkers in Europe'. But what were witty writing and courageous thinking worth in the historical process? Was he 'absolutely worthless as an economist and politician', as Trotsky seemed to think?

Shaw's confidence in men of 'iron nerve and fanatical conviction' expanded and darkened as his own sense of political achievement shrank. 'I am tired of seeing Labor and Socialism rolling the stone up the hill with frightful labor only to have it rolled down again,' he complained in

1920. After forty years of political playwriting, speech-making, pamphlet-eering, permeation, he looked round Britain and saw little to be admired. The House of Commons was full of what Stanley Baldwin described as 'hard-faced men who look as if they have done very well out of the war'. 'The higher ranks of the learned professions,' noted the Conservative Member of Parliament J. C. C. Davidson, 'are scarcely represented at all.' How could change be effected through such a philistine legislative body? It seemed to Shaw that a democratic system designed to prevent tyranny had been exploited so that it arrested progress.

Until now, with some dramatic hesitations, Shaw had clung to a belief in 'gradual modifications of existing systems' rather than revolution from which 'all humane men recoil with intense repugnance and dread'. He had dedicated himself to creating a socialist conscience in the country. But 'there is no use in waiting,' he declared in 1920. They would wait for ever to get the majority of votes from people who 'knew a little about football and very much less about politics', and whom the newspapers were continually 'bemusing and bewildering and bedevilling'. Legislation must create rather than succumb to public opinion because, if no political measure could be passed until everyone understood and demanded it, then nothing could be passed at all. Lenin, the man of action, was a realist; Kerensky, the man of speeches, had been another theatrical romantic, like Ramsay MacDonald. 'People who really want to have something done, like Lenin, do not wait.'

Shaw felt he really wanted to have something done: this was the only source of optimism available to him. Socialists in the West had lost too many of their propaganda battles because capitalism had been promoted as the 'glorification and idolization of the rich,' he wrote in 1921. ' . . . it gives to every poor man a gambling chance, at odds of a million to one or thereabouts, of becoming a rich one . . . no one is condemned by it to utter despair.' But in Shavian terms, capitalism remained the last refuge of the idealist and 'the most unreal product of wishful thinking of all the Utopias'. Under assaults from the left the system had let in so much apparent change 'that superficial thinkers easily persuade themselves that it will finally progress into Socialism,' he argued; 'but it can never do so without making a complete *volte face*. Slavery is always improving itself as a system.'

Shaw made his own volte-face, switching his allegiance from Kerensky to Lenin, with the alacrity of one eager to abandon long-held lost causes and put himself in the vanguard of victory. 'Consistency is the enemy of enterprise,' he acknowledged, 'just as symmetry is the enemy of art.'

By the beginning of 1920 Shaw had settled on Lenin as the 'one really interesting statesman in Europe'. The following year he admitted Trotsky as a second world leader. 'They have had a terrific job to do,' he wrote; 'and the fact that after four years they are still holding Russia together shows that they are men of extraordinary quality.' He could point to only one potential leader in Britain: Lloyd George's Minister for War and Air, Winston Churchill. But Churchill 'has lost his head over Bolshevism completely,' he told a Russian journalist in 1920.

Shaw considered Churchill to be a politician without an ideology. Such a man, whose popularity was enhanced by big cigars, genial romantic oratory and an adventurous sense of patriotism, should have been the perfect vehicle for Shavian permeation. Churchill liked literature too, believing Shaw himself to be 'the greatest living master of letters in the English-speaking world'. But from his mid-forties onwards ('Every man over forty is a scoundrel'), Churchill moved to the right in politics, pursuing a policy of repression in Ireland, severing his connection with the Liberal Party and joining Baldwin's Conservative Cabinet in 1924. Nevertheless Shaw found it difficult to give Churchill up. 'You have never been a real Tory,' he informed him after he had been Conservative Prime Minister in the Second World War. The 'Blimps and Philistines and Stick-in-the-Muds' of the Conservative Establishment 'never understood and always dreaded' him.

Churchill compared G.B.S. to a 'continually erupting volcano' amid whose smoke and ashes there occasionally appeared 'a piece of pure gold smelted from the central fires of truth'. But the gold was literary, not political. In Churchill's view, literature existed as a great verbal firework display above the artistic fairground which kept everyone's spirits up in those lulls following chivalrous wars and during the intervals between the gladiatorial contests of politics. At such peaceful moments 'we are all the better for having had the Jester in our midst,' he acknowledged. So G.B.S. continued to live in Churchill's imagination as a 'bright, nimble, fierce, and comprehending being, Jack Frost dancing bespangled in the sunshine, which I should be very sorry to lose'. But there were other times, serious times, when such an 'irresponsible Chatterbox' was well lost.

'When nations are fighting for life, when the Palace in which the Jester dwells not uncomfortably, is itself assailed, and everyone from Prince to groom is fighting on the battlements, the Jester's jokes echo only through deserted halls, and his witticisms and commendations, distributed evenly between friend and foe, jar the ears of hurrying messengers, of mourning women and wounded men.'

Churchill paid lip-service to Shaw as a 'saint, sage' and 'thinker, original, suggestive, profound'; but after the curtain came down on his plays 'everything goes on the same as before'. It puzzled Churchill that he should try to struggle off the stage into a political world where he did not belong. 'The world has long watched with tolerance and amusement the nimble antics and gyrations of this unique and double-headed chameleon,' he wrote, 'while all the time the creature was eager to be taken seriously.'

This touched with lively contempt on the relationship between literature and politics that had been troubling Shaw. Politicians in Britain were like magistrates who reached the Bench through their superior social connections rather than by qualifications, and who appealed to the public simply as sportsmen might appeal to it. At his worst, Churchill exploited his popularity 'by telling people with sufficient bombast just what they think themselves and therefore want to hear'. He would have been better employed, according to Wells, as 'a brilliant painter' or, according to Shaw, 'as a soldier'. As a politician he was a century out of date, representing what was most ludicrous in British foreign policy. The failure to support Kerensky had let in Lenin; the Allied intervention had unintentionally provided the Red Army with British equipment and established Trotsky's credentials as a military campaigner; and the continuing refusal to trade with the Soviet Union helped to dig a deep moat of national paranoia round the country and establish it as another empire of conservatism.

Much of what Shaw wrote about the Soviet Union was designed to discredit Churchill's fearful picture of Bolshevism. He grew adept at taming the Soviet leaders' revolutionary language. What was totalitarianism after all but the State co-ordination of public welfare? The proletariat became a 'vast body of persons who have no other means of living except their labor', in contrast to the 'proprietariat' who lived 'by owning instead of by working' and were 'politically called the Capitalists'. He wanted Soviet Communism, like a good wine, to travel well. He told the Fabians that Democratic Socialism now spelt Communism. 'There is now nothing but Communism, and in future it is quite futile to go about calling yourselves Fabians.'

Shaw let his imagination play round Lenin's revolution until it flowered into a thoroughgoing Fabian event. For if words did not have the power to initiate political change as simply as he had once believed, they could still encircle events and change them mythologically. He remembered the shock of reading *Das Kapital*: it had been like lifting the lid off hell. But, in their obedience to Marxist principles, the worker-revolutionaries in Russia disenfranchised the educated classes and denied their children common schooling; they criminalized the intelligentsia; abolished private trading for commercial profit; expelled all managers without replacement by qualified directors; handed over the farms from the landlords to the peasants and generally 'went through a hellgate of mistakes'. The result was near starvation. 'Hordes of lost and deserted children, the aftermath of the war, wandered about Russia in little gangs, begging and stealing, following the seasons like migrating birds,' Shaw wrote in a chapter on Sovietism he added to *The Intelligent Woman's Guide*. Made desperate by the country's lack of government, Lenin was forced, under the title New Economic Policy, to introduce gas-and-water Fabianism. For what else was the electrification of Russia? He had adopted the Fabian device of allowing private enterprise to run the factories until their productive work could be taken over by public enterprise. 'That is to say,' Shaw concluded, 'Lenin was by the pressure of practical and immediate and imperative experience converted to what we call gradualism.'

For over a decade G.B.S. conducted an advanced Fabian course on Soviet Communism. He explained that Lenin had candidly admitted his mistakes – or 'atrocities', as they were sometimes called – and scrapped them. He gently guided the kulaks back at gunpoint to the farms from which they had been evicted; ushered the hordes of wandering thieves into well-appointed penal colonies; introduced compulsory labour to assist the unemployed; brought back ex-tsarist officers into the army to improve everyone's protection; and established the famous Cheka, a sort of Scotland Yard 'which took over the necessary shooting'.

But Shaw was critical of Soviet foreign policy which enmeshed itself in British domestic politics. The First International had been an Old Testament with Marx as its Moses. The New Testament of World Socialism was the Second International, a catholic narrative that included, besides Shaw himself, figures as diverse as MacDonald and Mussolini. But the Third International, which was founded in 1919 and was dedicated to crusades and *coups d'état* abroad, seemed to Shaw an apocrypha that had no place in evolutionary socialism. It reminded him of the extravagances of colonialism. He maintained that internationally 'the only objectionable Communist was the one who took his pay and orders from Moscow,' David Dunn wrote. The British Communist Party was losing public credibility by doing this, Shaw believed, as surely as he himself would have lost his integrity by accepting fees for his political speeches. He resigned in 1921 from the Labour Research Department, protesting that 'if the gaff is blown at the fatal time' about its banking of Russian funds, then 'the General Election will be wrecked for Labour'. The truth of this seemed to be borne out three years later when the notorious 'Zinoviev Letter', containing revolutionary instructions for a communist uprising in Britain, helped to bring Baldwin back for a second term as Conservative Prime Minister.

Between Lenin's death in 1924 and the economic débâcle of MacDonald's second Labour administration in 1931, Shaw added little to what he had already said about Soviet politics. He was in agreement with Sidney Webb's view that the job of the Fabians was 'simply waiting for Russia to prove its case' and then finding out how best to convey the consequences of this verdict into British life.

The slump of the early 1930s was in Shaw's eyes a sign of capitalism's old age (it 'has passed its climax here, and is getting unsteady on its feet of clay') rather than evidence of the Marxist crash that was to end in world revolution. He could see no justification for the faith of an 'unteachable doctrinaire' like Trotsky in the concept of permanent revolutions abroad, and described Stalin's victory as 'a triumph of common sense' because it represented the principle of 'Socialism in a single country' over the interventionary excesses of the Third International. Instead of relying on military invasions and economic subversion, Stalin's nationalism seemed to hand over to people like himself the vital missionary work of spreading communism 'to the rest of the world by permeation, example, and success'. As for Trotsky, exiled by Stalin in 1929, he should be 'warmly invited to favour us with his very interesting presence' in Britain.

'The Moscow Government may not be any fonder of really independent observers than other governments are,' Shaw wrote in 1922. ' ... We want something from a capable observer and effective writer who is neither a fanatical Communist nor a scandalized bourgeois.' He could have accepted handsome terms from the American newspaper owner William Randolph Hearst to report on events in Russia, but 'I did not go because people were expecting miracles from Soviet Communism,' he told the communist composer Rutland Boughton in 1928. Three years later, however, when the Astors 'challenged me to go with them', Shaw agreed. 'I felt, at my age, that if I did not seize the opportunity, I should never see Russia at all,' he told Horace Plunkett. As Hesketh Pearson observed, he was 'curiously dependent on external pressures for any activity outside his daily routine': Charlotte's friend 'Lion' Phillimore described him as 'an old tramcar, always on the same set of rails'. But to many people's minds he was about to go wildly off the rails.

*

It was a mercy he would be looked after by Nancy. 'But Nancy, I do trust you,' Charlotte wrote. 'You will take the right sort of care of him ... It will be difficult: but if anyone can keep him in hand *you* can!'

Nancy Astor was additionally in charge of her own husband and their nineteen-year-old son David, and was accompanied by two Christian Scientists: Charles Tennant, who fell ill during the trip, and Philip Kerr, eleventh Marquis of Lothian, who had been Lloyd George's private secretary and was later to be appointed Britain's ambassador to the United States. There was also a Russian-born, American-Jewish author Maurice Hindus, the only member of the party who spoke Russian. The Associated Press tended to overlook these minor characters and regularly wrote of Charlotte's appearance at Russian art galleries, railway stations and collective farms – an example for G.B.S. of inaccurate reporting on all things Soviet.

Charlotte was careful to see that he took cereals and biscuits. There were no single sleeping berths on Russian trains, so he paid double fares and secured compartments all to himself in which to stretch out during overnight journeys. He had sent a telegram to Bela Illesh, General Secretary of the International Federation of Revolutionary Writers, stating that though his visit would be brief, he was coming for 'serious business' and did not want to be 'burdened with parades, receptions or banquets'. Nevertheless, he warned Waldorf Astor, they could 'expect a salute of at least 101 guns on our arrival in Moscow'.

At eleven o'clock on the morning of 18 July, the party started out from Victoria Station, paused in Brussels for some sightseeing and, the following morning, arrived in Berlin. They were to be joined by Maxim Litvinov, Commissar of Foreign Affairs, who had timed his return from Geneva to coincide with their visit. That evening they all caught the night express to Warsaw, crossing the double frontier between Poland and the Soviet Union at 4 p.m. on 20 July. Armed guards mounted the train as they moved across the strip of no-man's-land, past flanks of sentries and fortifications, and under an arch inscribed 'Communism will do away with frontiers' to the areas of passport inspection, currency control and customs clearance. Here they were transferred to a wide-gauge Russian train. 'You are not hurried or fussed,' Shaw reported: 'the Moscow train will not start for ever so long.'

During the three and a half hours it took to refuel this train and attach a sleeping car, he wandered into the railway buffet, followed deferentially by a deputation of publishers, and was introduced to a couple of young waitresses familiar, the interpreter emphasized, with his plays. After pausing in wonderment, he rejoined his party and, there still being plenty of time, they strolled off into a village nearby called Negoreloje. This was simply a line of human kennels made of unpainted wood and spaced at wide intervals along both sides of a dirt track, a monument to the old Russia. 'Inside is a frowsy cupboard without a door, which is the family bed, and a kiln, politely called a stove, on the top of which you can sleep if you are chilly,' Shaw later wrote. 'The rest of the space is kept as free from furniture as possible for the accommodation of the live stock of the strip of land which the peasant cultivates.' The place reminded him of an impoverished Irish settlement.

Walking back to the station they came across half a dozen burly women with shovels. These 'volunteers' provided G.B.S. with the subject for his first ironically tinted essay in adulation.

'A bevy of girls were seated in two rows, one above the other, on some agricultural contraption that lent itself to this theatrically effective arrangement. They were armed with long-handled spades. There was neither stocking, sock, nor shoe among them; and their athletic freedom of limb and fearless air, which marked even the youthfully shy ones, had such a pleasant effect that we at once crowded round them . . .

Whilst we were talking and chaffing, a freight train came in. Instantly these girls sprang to their feet and bounded to the train with a rhythmic grace and vigour that would have delighted Diaghileff. It was the only Russian ballet we saw in Russia.'

Their arrival next morning at Belorussko-Galtiyskiy Station was everything a film producer could have dreamed: 'I hear that the only two other people who had anything like a similar reception were Gorky and Fairbanks (with Mary Pickford).' They were welcomed by an official body of 'authors, artists, men of science, industrial managers and the like who,' Shaw told readers in the West, 'with a little Savile Row or Conduit Street tailoring and here and there a touch of shaving cream, would have been at home in any of our West End bourgeois clubs'. Besides Karl Radek, a Jewish revolutionary with the aspect of a French Communard who was the leading commentator on foreign affairs, and the former Commissar of Enlightenment Anatoly Lunacharsky, the delegation featured Artashes Khalatov, president of the State Publishing House, a swarthy cartoon figure in breeches, high boots and with a deep black beard. 'The one thing they forgot was to put in his mouth a knife dripping with bourgeois blood.'

These Soviet characters were knocked across the platform by an onrushing American newspaperman, Henry Dana. Shaw was already getting used to this event. In each country, 'the official or deputation advancing to receive me was shoved aside by an enthusiastic American, beaming with hospitality, and shouting genially, "Mr Shaw: welcome to France (or Poland or Russia or Germany, as the case might be): I am an American."' Henry Dana was clutching a genuine Dubliner called Verschoyle, apparently born in Synge Street ('a fellow Scotsman,' *Izvestia* noted), who had come briefly to Moscow to work for the Writers' Union. 'If I were as young as you are I should move to Moscow altogether,' Shaw politely greeted him. Then he was whirled away to 'a salvo of fifty cameras', gliding through a corridor of Red Guards and out of the station. Walter Duranty of the *New York Times* caught an awed murmur through the crowd: 'What a noble old man!' The *Daily Herald* reporter conjured up 'wild applause' and shouts of 'Hail Shaw!' that could be heard, through the blaring of a brass band, from 'several thousands of people'. What was not clear from such accounts was that these crowds were football fans who had gathered at the station to see a team travelling on the same train.

They were driven to the Hotel Metropole where Nancy Astor, 'assuring everyone that I must immediately be left alone to sleep in the hotel, found me utterly out of control,' Shaw wrote happily to Charlotte. 'I insisted on sightseeing at express speed.' They hurried out to Lenin's mausoleum and on to the Kremlin. In the Council Hall G.B.S. climbed the speaker's podium and experimented with the acoustics by yodelling. He was like a schoolboy, suddenly springing on to a bundle of cannonballs to be photographed at the base of the giant tsarist cannon, then jumping off and slipping into a little church where he found a priest officiating.

'The congregation was a very devout one: their worship was so fervently demonstrative as they knelt and smote the ground with their foreheads, punctuating the priest's intonations with moans of intense faith, that in Westminster Abbey they would have been handed over to the police and charged with "brawling"; but there were very few of them, not more than fifteen at the outside, including myself.'

Having registered this freedom to worship, Shaw allowed Nancy to lead him back to their hotel.

Next day he started on an official programme of visits, accompanied by Litvinov and Lunacharsky, to Young Pioneer camps, Centres of Repose and Culture and model institutions. The Soviet establishment was nervous of Shaw. In 1925 Lunacharsky had responded to his criticism of the Third International by deriding him as an agile belletrist who had set the hearts of bourgeois ladies aflutter in Britain 'without shaking to any serious extent the basis of the solid affluence of their lords & masters'. But Lunacharsky has now modified his tone. In an article entitled 'Bernard Shaw is our Guest' he calls G.B.S. 'one of the freest-thinking minds of the civilized world', but cautions readers of *Izvestia* that 'people like Bernard Shaw – brilliant representatives of the intelligentsia, turn out to be too "free-thinking" . . . they start to get ironical'. The article is a skilful blend of welcome and warning, enabling his audiences to value Shaw's approval while discounting his criticism. His wit, 'like dazzling bursts of flame in the darkness, illuminates the dense twilight of the nightfall of capitalism', but his jokes at the expense of communism are the peculiar reflexes of an individualist outside the Party who cannot help 'treating everything with semi-seriousness'. Yet the Soviet people had a 'burning desire to achieve a closer understanding with this amazing old man,' Lunacharsky concludes, because he was coming to test his suspicions 'that the bourgeois press lies, that it gives a distorted view of our socialist set-up'.

Shaw's account of 'Touring in Russia' is as happy a fantasy as his 'Joy Riding at the Front' had been during the war. He likened the penal colony at Bolshevo to Battersea Park, salivating over its menus, applauding its entertainments and sympathizing with the criminals who 'will not leave at the expiration of their sentences'. He congratulated Soviet citizens engaged in compulsory labour on working for the public service and not for the private profit of a few individuals: 'I wish we had forced labour in England,' he added, 'in which case we would not have 2,000,000 unemployed.' His imagination bleached away all signs of pain and horror. He looks forward to a good performance at 'the torture chamber of the Tcheka ... [with] a victim or two ready, so that we may witness the process'. In place of 'shooting' he uses the word 'pistolling', a swash-buckling term such as might be used in *Arms and the Man* or *Annajanska*.

Below this parody of ideological engineering swarmed a mass of irregularities, as Lunacharsky had predicted. 'The interpreter groaned at the utter unexpectedness of my answers to questions,' Shaw noted. After visiting the Museum of Revolution he told nonplussed journalists that the government was 'mad' to allow such a dangerous exhibition. 'The moment a revolution becomes a government it necessarily sets to work to exterminate revolutionists ... For when the revolution triumphs revolution becomes counter-revolution. The young Russian fired with enthusiasm for the glorious old slayers of tsars, Grand Dukes, & chiefs of police, & finding their species as extinct as the buffalo, may try his hand on Stalin.'

Elsewhere he could not suppress the impulse to denounce a group of prettily dressed children singing about the glories of life in a farming commune as 'a parcel of insufferable little Marxian prigs'; or, after Nancy Astor had been heckled, resist exclaiming, 'the more I see of the proletarians the more I thank God I am not one'; or avoid calling for a 'Five-Year Aesthetic Plan' to remedy Moscow's shabbiness. To one questioner who presumed too far on his sentimental loyalty to the Soviet people he objected, 'I reserve the right to criticize every people – including the Russians.' He was also to qualify his statement on compulsory labour by recommending a four-hour working day, and he inscribed the visitors' book at an electrical plant that was completing its five-year plan ahead of schedule with the words: 'My father drank too much. I have worked too much. Comrades push the 5 years Plan through in 3 years, and *then* TAKE IT EASY.'

Nancy Astor was soon causing Lunacharsky unusual problems too. 'Lady Astor is positively flirting with me,' he noted in his diary. 'Preaching Christian Science at me. Very odd.' Her outspoken announcements – 'I am a Conservative. I am a Capitalist. I am opposed to Communism. I think you are all terrible' – were greeted with acclaim owing to the kindly mistranslations of the interpreter.

Moscow struck Shaw as a 'domestic sort of city . . . frightfully over-crowded and under-trammed' and he was glad to travel north to Leningrad. Soviet newsreels recorded a vast and welcoming crowd as the *Red Arrow* pulled into Moscovskiy Station on the morning of 24 July – not sports fans this time, but airship enthusiasts eager to see the Graf Zeppelin on its way to the Arctic Circle.

Shaw's first impression of Leningrad (or St Petersburg, as the communist leaders absent-mindedly called it) was that it looked 'as if it had been built by Mansard to the order of Louis XIV and laid out by Haussmann for greater convenience in shooting down insurgent mobs'. He was lodged in a 'grand-ducal apartment' at the Hotel de l'Europe and over the next forty-eight hours conducted through an intense programme of ceremonies and receptions of the kind he had asked to be spared. He also saw excerpts from Soviet films (including 'one of the very best films in existence', Eisenstein's *Battleship Potemkin*) and thought them all superior to Hollywood's 'sexual exploitations'.

At a home for retired people he met Stanislavsky, former director of the Moscow Arts Theatre; relaxed and animated, they chatted about Granville-Barker and were photographed over a glass of milk. He also met Gorki at his dacha outside Moscow. Shaw was fond of Gorki who was then ill, describing him as a sensitive 'hater of cruelty and injustice, the discoverer of touching virtues in the most impossible people', and adding: 'to him the revolution has not brought the millennium, though he can forgive it as he can forgive worse things.' Another 'angel of the revolution' who had not been made happy by Stalin's Russia was Krupskaya, Lenin's widow. After protracted difficulties, Shaw was taken to her shooting lodge for tea. He admired her 'beautiful ugliness' and described her as 'a woman to be adored by children'. The story had reached him that 'she had given the Soviet a piece of her mind so roundly that Stalin had threatened that if she did it again he would appoint another widow for Lenin'.

G.B.S. had little problem in accounting for such people's difficulties in the USSR. 'They would be unhappy in the Garden of Eden because the

cats played cruelly with the mice before devouring them.' Only the determination of his official hosts to honour and impress him seemed likely to
cloud his optimism. The endless greetings by audiences that 'had been
instructed to receive me with tumultuous applause', the tedium of 'faked
meals' held up by long toasts and forced orations 'washed the virtue out
of me'. 'I was exploited to the last inch,' he complained. Worst of all was
the special treat that had been prepared for his seventy-fifth birthday: a
horse race entitled 'The Bernard Shaw Handicap' at a racetrack outside
Moscow. 'I suppose there will be only one horse in the race,' he remarked,
'since there is no competition in a Socialist state.' Sitting in the sunlight
in his grandstand box he fell quietly asleep, his chin on his chest, while
the horses thundered past.

'Of course they don't realise that he is an Irishman,' remarked the
British ambassador Sir Esmond Overy, 'and he is growing more so every
day since he has been here.' The British Embassy had given a reception
for G.B.S. and his party on their arrival in Moscow. 'Noah's Ark had not
a more varied and bizarre collection of creatures,' wrote one of the guests.
'The Soviet leaders of those days, who as a rule never entered those
luxurious surroundings (Communism was still in its Puritan stage) have
shelved their prejudices in order to meet the great playwright, and are
sipping the dry Martinis and champagne cocktails presented to them on
brilliantly polished silver plates ... Suddenly, Lady Astor's red foulard
dress drops in a deep curtsey before Litvinov ...'

Both Nancy Astor and Shaw had been handed 'a piteous volley of
telegrams' from Dmitri Krynin, a professor of civil engineering at Yale
University, asking them to intercede on behalf of his wife who had been
refused an exit visa to join him and their son in the United States. Nancy
went into action at once. But after a flustered glance at the telegram
Litvinov brushed it aside: 'This matter is not within my jurisdiction.'

Shaw seemed more anxious over Nancy's distress than about the plight
of the Krynin family. 'Dont worry about the sorrows and terrors of the
poor things in Russia,' he tried to reassure her. But she did worry. Only
with difficulty was she dissuaded from going to worry the police. Later
she presented the cables to the Soviet authorities at the Kremlin, while
Waldorf Astor sought out Mrs Krynin, 'a pathetic sight terrified lest her
husband or son should be induced to return to Russia, evidently afraid
of what might happen to them if they did come,' he wrote in his diary.
'It seems to me that he probably must have gone to America with a permit
limited as to time and had not returned ... I wrote to Khalatov telling
him that the lady had no complaints to make against the authorities about
her treatment but was merely anxious to join her husband in America.'

And Shaw did nothing. It is not easy to sympathize with such unresponsiveness, especially when set against the Astors' courage and persistence. In the years following the war G.B.S. had increasingly detached himself from such appeals. He suspected that telegrams delivered on public occasions with newspapermen present were likely to be propaganda stunts. The Western press found Mrs Krynin, and reported the affair extensively. The Astors consoled themselves with the thought that, in the light of such publicity, the Soviet authorities were unlikely to contrive her 'disappearance'. Shaw reasoned differently. It was far easier to do harm than to do good. 'The notion that I am persona grata with the dictators is one of the Shaw myths,' he was to write to the novelist William Gerhardie who later appealed to him during the Stalinist purges on behalf of his brother-in-law, an expert in bee culture, who was imprisoned in Soviet Russia. '. . . foreign interference is not only resented as such, but taken as additional evidence of disaffection.'

Such a letter reveals the dark sense of reality that underlay Shaw's ideological make-believe and the spirit of pragmatism by which he reconciled reality with fantasy. The assertive language he cultivated sprang from his need to affirm a faith. In his essay 'A Short View of Russia', Maynard Keynes had analysed Leninism as a combination of two factors usually kept separate, business economics and religious conviction. The economics, he argued, were destined to fail; only the religious power could survive. When Shaw travelled to Moscow he was chiefly interested in Soviet methods of social and economic reconstruction; by the time he left he had been converted to the religion of communism. From Darwin to Einstein, the landscape of knowledge had been broken up during his lifetime, destroying many apparently absolute values that he had attacked, but leaving no solid ground of morality from which to survey the past and future. In their maze of anxieties people needed new rules of conduct. This was the appeal in the 1920s and 1930s of autocracies such as Mussolini's fascists and Hitler's Nazis whose dogmatic myths gave Italy and Germany a sense of national purpose. 'I doubt whether the mass of men can live without a common metaphysic and a common scale of values,' Beatrice Webb wrote in 1926. Advancing across the continent like a medieval religion, Soviet communism appealed to her emotional needs and seemed to satisfy her intellectual beliefs. 'I wish Communism to succeed,' she wrote in 1932. And Shaw agreed. 'In all the prophecies of Russia's failure the wish is father to the thought,' he said. 'We have a lot of foolish people who want the experiment to fail.'

Shaw was eager, while in Russia, to meet Stalin. He was granted an audience on the evening of 29 July and insisted on taking the Astors and Lord Lothian with him. Litvinov accompanied them, and two interpreters were present. During the interview, which lasted two and a half hours, the realities of Stalinist Russia were suspended and Shavian theatre prevailed. The set was simple: a large table and some chairs in an office. The costumes varied from Stalin's tunic and black top boots and Shaw's Norfolk jacket to Nancy Astor's spotted dress, Lord Lothian's lounge suit and the shirtsleeves of Litvinov. It was as if the encounter between Undershaft and Cusins from *Major Barbara* were being replayed in the Kremlin, with a remarkable transformation of the Soviet dictator. Like Undershaft, Stalin is UNASHAMED. He also believes that the 'ballot paper that really governs is the paper that has a bullet wrapped up in it'. Shaw grants Stalin an 'extraordinary military ability and force of character' but cloaks these iron qualities with the pious toga of Fabian respectability: 'he is said to be a model of domesticity, virtue, and innocence.' This is the priggish endorsement of Cusins which becomes sinister in the light of Stalin's wife's suicide.

In this staged seminar Stalin was also cast to play Shaw's Caesar opposite Nancy's spirited if elderly Cleopatra. 'The attempt to abash and silence Lady Astor was about as successful as an effort by a fly to make head against a whirlwind,' remembered Shaw. Stalin is shown as 'patient, assured, letting us talk back to our heart's content, and disarming us at every attack by a smile in which there is no malice but also no credulity'. But, to the audience beyond, it appeared that though Stalin, like Undershaft, deceived others he was not self-deceived. 'The Russians have always been fond of circuses and travelling shows,' wrote Churchill. 'Since they had imprisoned, shot or starved most of their best comedians, their visitors might fill for a space a noticeable void. And here was the World's most famous intellectual Clown and Pantaloon in one, and the charming Columbine of the capitalist pantomime ... Arch Commissar Stalin, "the man of steel", flung open the closely guarded sanctuaries of the Kremlin, and pushing aside his morning's budget of death warrants, and *lettres de cachet*, received his guests with smiles of overflowing comradeship.'

'The secret of Stalin is that he is entirely opportunist as to *means*,' Shaw was to tell Augustin Hamon, 'discarding all doctrinaire limitations, and confident that Russia is big enough to achieve Socialism by itself independently of the capitalist world, which can follow his example or go its own way to perdition.' But Shaw overlaid this realistic outline of Stalin with the image of 'Uncle Joe', head of the communist family.

For this brief period Shaw and Nancy Astor set the agenda and Stalin was obliged to respond agreeably. Though he never lost his self-command, it was for him a most disagreeable experience, and he later complained to his daughter Svetlana that Shaw was an awful person. On their return to the Hotel Metropole reporters crowded round. Shaw slowly mounted the marble staircase, turned at its summit, and crossed his arms. Everyone waited. 'Stalin,' he said, 'has splendid black moustaches.' Then he went to bed, leaving everyone seething.

From Shaw's writings Stalin emerges as a Soviet icon, an instrument needed to implement Leninism and to break the pattern of collapsing civilizations – the concept that Shaw had absorbed from the work of the archaeologist Flinders Petrie.

'We know from our recent historical researches that there have been many civilizations, that their history has been very like the history of our civilization, and that when they arrived at the point which Western capitalist civilization has reached, there began a rapid degeneracy, followed by a complete collapse of the entire system and something very near to a return to savagery by the human race. Over and over again the human race has tried to get round that corner and has always failed.

Now, Lenin organized the method of getting round that corner . . . if this great communistic experiment spreads over the whole world, we shall have a new era in history. We shall not have the old collapse and failure, the beginning again, the going through the whole miserable story to the same miserable end . . .'

For the first time anywhere, Shaw thought he saw the realists in command of the philistines. When progressive ideas appeared in Soviet Russia 'the entire state apparatus, all its organs, the press and public opinion set about realizing these ideas,' he said to Litvinov and Lunacharsky, 'whereas any progressive idea which appears in England is met not by sympathy, but by furious opposition from the powers that be and from the press'.

Shaw's pleasure at finding one of the forms of socialism he had preached almost fifty years before apparently coming to birth in Russia makes itself felt at the end of a speech he delivered on his seventy-fifth birthday at the Trade Union Central Hall (formerly the Hall of Nobles of the Nobleman's Club and later to be the showplace of Stalin's notorious treason trials). 'Tovarishchi,' he began, struggling to pronounce the Russian word 'Comrades'. It came out as a meaningless blur of Slavonic sounds and was lost in the storm of laughter and applause. He went on to joke about his British 'valour' in making this journey into Communist Russia.

'Our weeping families clung to us . . . they loaded us down with enormous baskets and parcels of food, so we wouldn't die here of hunger . . . The railway from the frontier to Moscow is strewn with the things we threw out [of] our carriage windows as we saw with what comfort, attention and kindness the new regime in Russia surrounded us.'

He then neatly changed this extravaganza into an elegant tribute.

'We don't know how to adequately express our gratitude for all that your country's Communist government has done for us. We can only say that if the Soviet government succeeds in providing to all the peoples of the Union those same conditions which it has provided us – and we believe this is one of the Soviet government's goals – then Russia will become the most fortunate country on earth.'

Halfway through his speech 'my mind went blank suddenly,' he wrote to Charlotte, 'and I had to frivol rather vulgarly'. He tried out one appalling pun: 'I have seen all the "terrors", and I was terribly pleased by them.' This was not the usual G.B.S. His wit had dried up. Then, suddenly, in a changed voice, he got going again. 'It is very difficult for me to end my speech,' he said. 'I can't talk to you as I generally do. As I look around I see in your eyes something I have never met in the audience of other countries . . .

'It is a real comfort to me, an old man, to be able to step into my grave with the knowledge that the civilization of the world will be saved . . . It is here in Russia that I have actually been convinced that the new Communist system is capable of leading mankind out of its present crisis, and save it from complete anarchy and ruin.'

He sat down disgusted at not having spread himself as imposingly as he wished. Yet for some listeners this hesitant sincerity was more effective than other polished presentations.

On their last night in Moscow they handed to the hotel staff the biscuits, cereals and tins of food which G.B.S. had pretended were littering the Russian railway tracks, and caught the night train to Warsaw. Shaw had warned Charlotte that 'I am at least 20 years younger' and he was soon busy denying rumours that his rejuvenation was due to a sexual gland transplant by the Soviet surgeon Serge Voronoff.

Charlotte was overjoyed to see him so well when he arrived back at Adelphi Terrace on the morning of 2 August. Nancy had obviously taken tremendous care of him: 'he never got a bite, or saw any sign of insects or infection,' Charlotte told a friend. And it was wonderful to hear him talk of Soviet Russia. 'He says,' she wrote, 'it all seems like a "splendid, sunny dream".'

*

The Webbs were particularly keen to question G.B.S. on his return. 'He was tired and excited by his visit to Russia; carried away by the newness and the violence of the changes wrought,' Beatrice wrote in her diary for 8 August. But she felt sceptical of his religious conviction, if such it was, after 'ten days' inspection of show institutions, surrounded with admiring crowds'. He was 'a supreme charmer' in old age, she reflected as she listened to him weaving his spell over the Fabians: 'appearance, voice, manner, gesture, outlook on other human beings, build up a perfect old man to be adored by the multitude.' But she soon came to realize that he was in earnest about Soviet communism. Its egalitarian principles, which aimed to do away with the disastrous motive of pecuniary self-interest and replace it with a way of life based on common property, were the Webbs' principles too; and Soviet brutalities, he argued, were manifestations of a backward country with a barbarous history. By the beginning of 1931 Stalin had not yet introduced any methods that would have raised an eyebrow during the tsarist regime; what he had done, Shaw said, was to build on Lenin's work in revolutionizing the purpose of government and the motives of human beings. This was the great adventure of transforming the environment of which Don Juan had spoken in *Man and Superman*. The only hope for the world was to change human nature – and that, Shaw claimed, was what the Russians were achieving.

'Putty is exactly like human nature. You cannot change it, no matter what you do. You cannot eat it, nor grow apples in it, nor mend clothes with it. But you can twist it and pat it and model it into any shape you like; and when you have shaped it, it will set so hard that you would suppose that it could never take any other shape on earth . . . the Soviet Government has shaped the Russian putty very carefully . . . and it has set hard and produced quite a different sort of animal.'

What becomes lost in this vision is the Devil's warning from *Man and Superman* that when we grow over-ambitious on behalf of the human race we threaten to destroy ourselves. Beatrice was aware of this danger. Yet she felt more inclined, after the fall of the Labour Government later that August, to place her faith in Soviet social engineering than in the haphazard ways of Western democracy. The economic depression signalled to many people the breaking-up of capitalism, and it was difficult for disillusioned socialists to place much hope in the Labour Party.

Shaw's challenge to Sidney and Beatrice was made at a critical moment in their lives. 'The tension between those who accept and those who denounce the USSR increases day by day,' Beatrice was to write. The Webbs could agree with the political diagnosis Shaw made when he pictured MacDonald, at the head of a Conservative-dominated National coalition, as having 'led his flagship, on the eve of Trafalgar, into the enemy's line, and hoisted the enemy's colors'. They also began to accept his prognosis: 'For really intelligent and longsighted leaders there is nothing hopeful now except a new departure to the left of the Labor Party to begin scientific communism with the experience of Russia to profit by.' There was a danger, Shaw believed, of members of the Labour Party abandoning socialism to gain power.

'Everybody who can possibly do so should go to Russia,' Shaw had said. The following year Sidney and Beatrice made the first of their own expeditions to 'the Russian show'. Shaw's reconnaissance had given him an impression based on instinct: their visit would be an investigation ostensibly based on facts. On 21 May 1932 Shaw came down to Hay's Wharf to see them off. For over forty years Shaw had been looking for a way of bringing together the two heralds of his political career – Webb, the constitutionalist, who 'made no mistake' and Morris, the revolutionist, who was 'right after all' – on the same territory. That territory was to be the Soviet Union.

The Webbs were Shaw's pre-eminent converts to Soviet communism. But numerous fellow-travellers in the 1930s took their inspiration from him.

'You happen to be the man who, nearly thirty years ago, gave me my first ideas of socialism, and . . . I am hoping that you will find a little of the thrill which I myself find in living here, and that it will draw you back again to see for a longer time . . . one of the forms in which the things you fifty-years ago prophesied, are coming to birth'

wrote an American journalist, Anna Louise Strong, whom David Caute depicts as thriving 'like a cactus in the desert, devoting her whole life to Russia and China during the most punishing phases of socialist construction'. Edgar Snow, whom Caute calls 'America's most widely read advocate of Chinese Communism', revealed the influence of G.B.S. on many left-wing intellectuals:

'It was Shaw who convinced me that the advancement of mankind beyond the predatory stage of human development and the replacement of existing systems of economic cannibalism by planned co-operation for the common good . . . were attainable and good ends and inevitable if men were to survive.'

Shaw's political position was aligned with that of Theodore Dreiser and Upton Sinclair in the United States, with Anatole France, Romain Rolland and with Ernst Toller on the European continent. In Britain he appeared to converge with a new literary movement that caught up Stephen Spender, Edward Upward, and other poets and novelists in their twenties. Big was beautiful and distance opened vistas of romance: electrification from the steppes was seen as a futuristic construct and the drumming of Soviet machinery heard as the sound of modernism. 'Beauty breaks ground, oh, in strange places,' C. Day Lewis wrote in celebration of the 'grain-Elevator in the Ukraine plain'; and Charles Madge bowed down before the spectacle when 'Power and the factories break flaming into flower'. Shaw formed no personal attachment with this new generation of writers who hardly heard his footfall just ahead of them on the stair. 'He's a kind of concierge in the house of literature,' Katherine Mansfield had written to Middleton Murry, ' – sits in a glass case – sees everything, knows everything, examines the letters, *cleans the stairs*, but has no part – no part in the life that is going on.'

Shaw had a more direct influence on such political ideologists and philosophers as John Strachey, the Labour Member of Parliament who published his polemical *The Coming Struggle for Power* in 1932; on the zoologist and film-maker Ivor Montagu; and on C. E. M. Joad, the naturist civil servant and teacher for whom G.B.S. became 'a kind of God'.

It had still been possible in the summer of 1931 to go to Moscow and see some evidence of an enthusiastic socialist country. But as the 1930s ticked away, the Shavian wonderland of Sovietism appeared more fanciful, and he was obliged to force his political views by way of letters, speeches, articles and interviews into a hostile press. He knew, as the American journalist Henry Dana admitted, that 'if he said nine things favorable to the Soviet Union and one thing hostile, the reporters would cable over to America the one hostile comment and suppress the nine favorable'. So he said 'ten favorable and not one thing hostile'. Such absolutism appeared to lead readers into politics of the absurd, so 'airily detached' (in Churchill's words) had he become from reality. Yet who can say whether Churchill's anti-Soviet obsession was not a factor in setting off reactionary Stalinism?

The Life Force seemed in league with the politics of death. Shaw's imagination flirted pleasurably with death and, in more extreme fantasies, killing. Yet people like himself were temperamentally unfitted for signing death warrants. There is nevertheless a misanthropic relish in his tone when he writes about such things. As he told Henry Salt at the end of 1934, he believed that 'really the human race is beyond redemption'. He knew well enough the dark side of Soviet Russia – the OGPU, for example, was 'an Inquisition pure and simple'. He realized that the Soviet Constitution of 1936 could properly be 'dismissed as a feat of window dressing to conciliate Liberal opinion in Europe and America'. Though lacking first-hand news, he described Stalin's show trials that same year as 'another witch burning epidemic'; and, although he refused to join the committee for Trotsky's defence, he dismissed the accusations against him as politically malicious, adding: 'I hope that Trotsky will not allow himself to be brought before a narrower tribunal than his reading public where his accusers are at his mercy.' In 1937 he went out of his way to salute André Gide's *Retour de l'URSS* as 'a really superfine criticism of Soviet Russia', praising Gide's 'complete originality and sincerity', and perhaps reflecting on his own wisdom in not returning. 'Charlotte and I are old and in our second childhood. We can no longer feel things (except little things) as you do,' he wrote to Trebitsch in 1940, 'which is very fortunate for us, because human misery is so appalling nowadays that if we allowed ourselves to dwell on it we should only add imaginary miseries of our own to the real miseries of others without doing them any good.'

Shaw's journey to Russia had been in the nature of a revelation – a revelation, some said, inspired by a hallucination. In 1932 he set out to bear witness to Soviet Communism using 'the famous execution on Calvary' as a metaphysical basis. The Crucifixion 'has never been challenged in respect of the two thieves who suffered on that occasion along with the Communist', he wrote in this work which he was never to finish.

'. . . All the controversies have arisen on the point whether the execution of the Communist was not a mistake – whether he was not rather the sort of person who should be encouraged rather than liquidated. Was he really an enemy of mankind or was he a saviour? Our general conclusion so far seems to be that, whether or no, we are well rid of him.

I think we go to the opposite extreme ourselves in glorifying thieves, provided their booty is big enough and they play the game according to the rules they have themselves made, meanwhile holding up that particular Communist as the prince of such thieves.'

'You must not expect a paradise,' Shaw would tell travellers to the Soviet Union. Yet his book, called *The Rationalization of Russia*, was an attempt to rationalize an ideal. Russian children in the future would be born without the original sin of inequality. He confided to the Reverend Ensor Walters that the absence of social and religious castes, which had so complicated his Dublin childhood, and of competitive commercial friction, which had oppressed his early years in London, was 'indescribable' in Moscow. He could not put into words the wonder of this equality; or describe how it uplifted and enchanted him during the Depression, the Second World War, and his old age. He wanted to rid human beings of 'the miserable delusion that we can achieve it [happiness] by becoming richer than our neighbours'. His writing glows and fades as it circles round this hope, then hesitates, repeats, and peters out. For what he feels is not directly communicable, but will find its way obliquely into memories, dreams, reflections: the fables, spells, extravaganzas, visions, miracles and marvellous history lessons of his final period.

2

A PILGRIM'S PROGRESS

> There is something fantastic about them, something unreal and perverse, something profoundly unsatisfactory. They are too absurd to be believed in: yet they are not fictions . . .
>
> *Too True to be Good*

Shaw began his first play of the 1930s as he and Charlotte left the coast of Marseilles on 5 March 1931 for a month's tour of the Mediterranean. By the end of May, Charlotte was writing to Nancy Astor that 'so far it is unlike anything I ever have read . . . only the 1st Act is done'. 'It is up to date and a little beyond,' Shaw notified his British publisher Otto Kyllmann, ' . . . I call it provisionally Too True to Be Good.' He completed the first draft on 30 June, and decided to keep the provisional title. 'I call it a Super Farce,' Charlotte confided in Nancy.

Working from unconscious impulses, Shaw had used one idea to summon up another in an apparently random sequence of impressions. In his dreamscape of land and sea Shaw places his apocalyptic vision of humanity poised between drowning in despair and making an awakening ascent. 'G.B.S. is like a Gulf-Stream: and I wondered where he would bring up,' T. E. Lawrence wrote to Charlotte. ' . . . I get up from reading dumb struck and rather scared.'

Shaw drafted a paragraph for *The Times*. 'It is not a sequel to the *Apple Cart*, and it is not a historical play like *Saint Joan*. Its main theme is the dissolution of established morals by the shock of the war; but the examples may prove unexpected.' The peculiar echoes and associations bring a transcendental air to Shaw's last plays, comparable in its heightened quality to Ibsen's *When We Dead Awaken* or Shakespeare's *The Tempest*, carrying audiences far from their familiar shores and out of sight of naturalism. It is the supernatural that Shaw exotically sets against the tropical jungles, islands, deserts, temples, and seas of these final period plays.

*

When the curtain goes up on *Too True to be Good* it is night in 'one of the best bedrooms in one of the best suburban villas in one of the richest cities in England'. The bedside table is congested with medicine bottles; a young lady lies heavily asleep under blankets and eiderdowns. Near her, reclining on an easy chair, sits a Monster made of 'luminous jelly with a visible skeleton of short black rods'. Nobody who enters the room will be able to see this Monster: it is a phantasm of the young lady's, and this is her dream that we are witnessing.

The Monster, who proclaims itself 'a poor innocent microbe', soliloquizes futuristically on the Rights of Microbes. 'These humans are full of horrid diseases,' the unfortunate bacillus complains: 'they infect us poor microbes with them; and you doctors pretend that it is we that infect them.' Throughout this act the Monster keeps up a subversive commentary on the common sense that kills.

The repository of this conventional common sense is the Patient's elderly mother, a 'maddening woman' named Mrs Mopply whose rule is Safety First and Last. She is spending a fortune on her daughter's illness, and her neurotic attitude brings to mind Charlotte's attitude to health.

Left alone with her charge, a young nurse begins behaving very oddly. She is signalling to her 'gentleman friend' who clambers through the window. But this is not an amorous tryst, as the Patient indignantly assumes. The young woman is actually the business partner of the gentleman who, wearing rubber gloves and a small white mask, introduces himself as a burglar somewhat in the fashion of E. W. Hornung's amateur cracksman, Raffles. Together 'Popsy' and 'Sweetie', as these Bright Young Things call each other, are after the Patient's celebrated pearl necklace. The Patient, however, springs from her bed and defends her jewel case with unexpected athleticism, before fainting from the exertion.

'Then I awoke and dreamed again.' Bewildering Shavian paradoxes, proliferating identities, shifting illusions and inversions now spring up. The Burglar peels off his mask and, revealing himself to be a clergyman, explains that he was secretly ordained while up at Oxford. But 'my father, who is an atheist, would disinherit me if he knew'. He proposes that the Patient steal the necklace herself and divide the proceeds among the three of them. 'Sell it; and have a glorious spree with the price.' His proposal 'may make another woman of you,' he adds, 'and change your entire destiny'. As he continues speaking, the Burglar's ideas grow more dazzling. 'Lets stage a kidnap,' he suggests. Mrs Mopply will then pay a ransom and her daughter 'will realize not only the value of the pearls, but of yourself'.

The stage is finally left to the Monster which has been luminously bounding about, perching on pillows and even getting into bed beside the Patient. It is transformed from a 'bloated moribund Caliban', the stage directions tell us, into 'a dainty Ariel'. Just as Ariel obeys Prospero's (and therefore Shakespeare's) commands, and Caliban represents Shakespeare's audiences, so Shaw uses this preposterous creature to speak for the most monstrous members of his own audiences: the critics. 'The play is now virtually over,' the Monster says, anticipating their notices; 'but the characters will discuss it at great length for two acts more. The exit doors are all in order. Goodnight.'

Shaw created Sweetie, the Burglar, and the Patient as the trinity of the capitalist religion: sex, intelligence and money. The Burglar conjures up an enchanting adventure: 'in dreamland generosity costs nothing,' the Patient reflects. ' . . . I'm going to make the most of this dream.' So her pilgrimage begins, in a capitalist nirvana at 'a sea beach in a mountainous country'. Also occupying these glaring sand dunes, and registering the colonial aspect of capitalism, is a British military cantonment. Here we are introduced to a couple of new characters, Colonel Tallboys VC DSO, and Private Meek.

Private Meek is famously modelled on Lawrence of Arabia. In a letter to G.B.S. Lawrence had written from India: 'I do what I am told to do, and rewrite the drafts [of routine orders] given to me, meekly.' Meekly, too, Lawrence persuaded G.B.S. to add almost two dozen 'squalid accuracies' to his play, strengthening the farce with authentic detail and guiding Private Meek between the dangers of servility and impudence.

Meek is a Shavian notion of genius. He is 'never at a loss': an omnicompetent, omnipresent human being who appears whenever the Colonel calls for an interpreter, quartermaster's clerk or intelligence orderly. Colonel Tallboys believes that the other men 'put everything on the poor fellow because he is not quite all there'. It takes an attack by local tribesmen, which Meek repulses with irresistible authority, to show the Colonel that the man whom it is socially correct to address as 'a very distant inferior', is in fact the commanding spirit. The Colonel rather than the Private is actually the halfwit because he has never followed his vocation. 'I have a passion of sketching in watercolours,' he tells the others. ' . . . Henceforth I shall devote myself almost entirely to sketching, and leave the command of the expedition to Private Meek.'

The British expeditionary force has been sent to this nameless country to rescue Miss Mopply from the brigands who have kidnapped her. It is not wholly the Colonel's fault that the three English tourists who have put themselves under his protection are actually the people he is supposed to be seeking, for they are spectacularly altered. Sweetie is now a flamboyantly unconvincing foreign aristocrat, the Countess Valbrioni, 'brilliantly undressed for bathing under a variegated silk wrap'; while the Patient is 'disguised *en belle sauvage* by headdress, wig, ornaments and girdle proper to no locality on earth except perhaps the Russian ballet'. The Burglar too has changed. He now uses, for the purposes of concealment, his real name, the Honourable Aubrey Bagot, and emerges from a bathing tent 'very elegant in black and white bathing costume and black silken wrap with white silk lapels: a clerical touch'.

The parts played by Shaw's characters multiply rapidly as their adventures proceed. While they are adjusting masks, confusing ranks, assembling disguises, aliases, nicknames, they gradually expose layers of biographical origins. Sweetie owes something to Molly Tompkins. She has soon become bored with this capitalist utopia. Aubrey, too, is without occupation in this sunny place. But the Patient is transformed: 'I have forgotten what illness means,' she says. She is also disillusioned: 'I am free; I am healthy; I am happy; and I am utterly miserable.' Shaw uses this second act of his play to demonstrate how even the rich in a capitalist society have to drug themselves into pretending they are happy when they are actually maddened with boredom.

Passing through a narrow gap between two grottoes and down a meandering path to the beach, they all assemble for Act III. Over the more gothic-looking of the grottoes soldiers have scrawled ST PAUL'S; over the wider grotto, which is illuminated rosily with bulbs wrapped in pink paper and contains a bench long enough to accommodate two people, is carved AGAPEMONE in Greek characters beneath which has been chalked in red THE ABODE OF LOVE to which is added in white chalk NO NEED TO WASTE THE ELECTRIC LIGHT. These two grottoes recall the preceding two scenes of the play: the house of decaying superstitions and the fairyland of pleasure.

St Paul's is occupied by a 'very tall gaunt elder' through whom Shaw presents the evolution of the fanatical Old Testament prophet into an imposing Victorian intellectual. His moral authority has suddenly collapsed with the coming of Einstein's relativity and 'his attitude is one of hopeless dejection'. These stage directions emphasize the Elder's resemblance to W. R. Inge, the most famous clergyman in the Church of England between the wars, and popularly known as 'the Gloomy Dean'. Inge 'detested the twentieth century', A. N. Wilson has written approvingly.

Shaw's own position in the play is surprisingly represented by Sergeant Fielding, the occupant of THE ABODE OF LOVE. He is a man 'completely absorbed in two books', the Bible and Bunyan's *The Pilgrim's Progress*. 'I carry them with me wherever I go,' he tells Sweetie who joins him in THE

ABODE OF LOVE. 'I put the problems they raise for me to every woman I meet.'

Shaw's dream play is a version of Bunyan's fable 'delivered under the similitude of a dream'. It is the pilgrimage of Hopeful rather than of Christian and pushes Shaw's spiritual autobiography into a land of allegory and abstraction, like Bunyan's Beulah, the illuminated country this side of death, near the Celestial City. He provides a 'narrow gap' between the grottoes, but his path is far from straight: it is an expressionist convolution. The profusion of mishearings, coincidences, accidents, illusions all suggest that dreams and the unconscious mind are as much aspects of reality as the familiar outlines of the known world. Our guide to reality is not the straight line of logical thought but an instinct that communicates, sometimes with crazy seriousness, from our buried selves.

This is the instinct that has brought Sweetie and the Sergeant together in THE ABODE OF LOVE. To the intelligent eye they look an extraordinarily ill-matched pair. 'God help the woman that marries you,' Sweetie tells him. Shaw's joke is that God will help Sweetie when she marries the Sergeant since theirs is a truly instinctive merging of complementary natures ('a top story as well as ground floor'). The Sergeant concludes that in this world of vanities neither the Bible nor Bunyan sufficiently values sexual love. 'That's a hard fact of human nature,' he says after kissing Sweetie; 'and its one of the facts that religion has to make room for.' The implication for G.B.S. himself is that Talkative and Mr Head-mind have had rather too much control over his career.

Only two characters in the play seem damned: the empty Aubrey and the unadaptable Elder. Shaw uses one of his more casual coincidences to make them father and son ('Hello, father, is it really you? I thought I heard the old trombone: I couldnt mistake it'). But Mrs Mopply who, dressed in black like the Elder, distractedly re-enters the play in Act III to urge on the rescue party, undergoes a miracle when she interrupts the Colonel's painting and so exasperates him that he whacks her sun-helmeted head with his umbrella – and literally knocks some sense into her.

At the end of the play, like a different species of Monster, Aubrey is left alone. 'I am by nature and destiny a preacher,' he declaims as the others hurry away. ' . . . I must have affirmations to preach . . . I must find the way of life, for myself and all of us, or we shall surely perish.' He has helped others; himself he cannot help. He has indeed lost his way while all but his father have begun to find theirs. But the pathos lies in the fact that they are finding their various ways without his guidance.

*

'EXPECT THE WORST,' Shaw cheerfully cabled the New York Theatre

Guild which was to produce the world première in Boston at the end of February 1932. Though it contained 'some of the funniest lines and situations Shaw ever wrote,' observed Lawrence Langner, for the most part it 'fell on indifferent ears in the depths of the depression period'. What success it achieved in the United States was attributed to the acting of Beatrice Lillie as Sweetie: it was a case, not of gilding the lily, Alexander Woolcott wrote, but of 'Lillie-ing the Guild'.

It opened at the Malvern Festival on 6 August. Ernest Thesiger, who had created the Dauphin in *Saint Joan*, became the Monster; Cedric Hardwicke, a successful King Magnus in the first British production of *The Apple Cart*, entered as the Burglar; and Ralph Richardson, who had recently played Zozim and Pygmalion as well as Bluntschli in revivals of *Back to Methuselah* and *Arms and the Man*, created the role of Sergeant Fielding. Barry Jackson chartered 'a sumptuous aeroplane' to carry London critics to the opening matinée. But the pilot lost his way in the mist and, overshooting their destination, deposited everyone at Hereford. From here they arrived by charabanc over an hour late, pale and disgruntled, one of them collapsing dramatically in the auditorium at the start of the second act.

'My new play will not, I am afraid, please everybody,' Shaw had promised. 'It is not meant to.' H. W. Nevinson, who hated *The Apple Cart*, found *Too True to be Good* 'one of his greatest and more unpopular plays'. But Charles Morgan scolded him in *The Times* for the 'fantastic irrelevance' of his 'leaky farce'; and even the sympathetic Desmond MacCarthy complained of his complete indifference to form: 'Here am I, an attentive playgoer, yet I can't tell you what the play I have just seen at the Malvern Festival is about.'

Never, it seemed to Charlotte, had there been such a discrepancy between the public and critics. She saw audiences *wriggling* with pleasure, and was convinced that this play was 'Deeper & more searching – & incidentally, much more amusing!' than *Heartbreak House*.

'*Too True* filled the cheaper seats and moved people as no play of mine has moved them before,' Shaw wrote. But it came off after forty-seven performances in London. Beatrice Webb had thought it despairing, and so did St John Ervine. His review of the London production drew from Charlotte an uncharacteristic retaliation. 'It is a play of *revolt*,' she countered. ' . . . it will be understood that this is among G.B.S.'s *big* plays.'

Desmond MacCarthy, who knew Shaw's work well and found Aubrey's peroration at the end 'an astonishing and moving feat' in the theatre, sensed that they were responding to G.B.S.'s own predicament. Shaw himself denied this. In the shell-shocked-young-gentleman-burglar-clergyman he had created an omen of capitalism whose spending-without-earning was leading to a moral bankruptcy not to be identified with someone who had placed his capital in the bank of communism. He had scattered aspects of himself through most of his characters, and made Aubrey a good preacher 'to warn the world against mere fluency'.

But this warning against fluency remains like a distant protest from Sonny against the pilgrimage of G.B.S.; and the law of equal action and reaction, which Shaw cites, tells us from what dark centre he had to call forth his affirmations.

3

MISSIONARY TRAVELS

I am myself a missionary.

Shaw to Clara M. Kennedy (27 September 1947)

Shaw's travels in the 1930s were planned as a series of evangelical missions. He journeyed as one who believed he had seen his conception of the good society being born. In the 1920s he was ready to dream of literary retirement; now in his late seventies he once more had affirmations to preach. He was determined to put his international fame to good use.

'English writers are not revolutionaries,' Shaw said while visiting South Africa. 'I, on the other hand, am.' He and Charlotte had discussed going to South Africa in the late 1920s, postponed a decision, and then 'in a moment of insanity' booked their passage on the *Carnarvon Castle* which sailed on Christmas Eve 1931. They steamed into Cape Town on Monday 11 January 1932 and were immediately encircled by crowds of journalists, photographers and a movie camera crew which persuaded G.B.S. to perform an on-the-spot 'talkie' up on deck ('Good Morning, South Africa ... Now that you have seen my face, I shall show you my left profile ... and the back of my distinguished head'), while Charlotte waited below in her cabin. 'Only the advent of Don Bradman or Mahatma Gandhi would have aroused greater interest,' commented the *Cape Argus*. Everyone was impatient to find out 'What Will G.B.S. Say to South Africa?'

This became clear the next day following an interview with the *Cape Times*. 'Our religious codes are obsolete in many ways,' he was reported as saying. 'Where will you get genuine religious fanaticism? You get it in Russia ... [The Russian] carries out the Christian doctrine that "all are equal" ... No one believes here that the black man is equal of the white.'

To the objection that a transformation from individual Christianity to collective communism might lead to tyranny such as was rumoured to be developing in Soviet Russia, Shaw answered that the Russian people had been hardened by tsarist persecution and needed to go to greater lengths than people in the West. 'In pursuit of knowledge and power men will suffer the most appalling sacrifices and endure terrible hardships.'

What were his plans? 'Seeing South Africa and saying nothing,' he replied. Yet he soon found himself criticizing the University of Cape Town for excluding women from its dining-club and advising students at the University of Stellenbosch to believe nothing they were told. Addressing a huge audience at the City Hall, he spoke of the example set by the Soviet march to prosperity through the pit of revolution. The *Cape Times* reported him describing communism as 'the absence of a competitive commercial system . . . There would be no greater crime, he declared, than to attempt to thrust Russia back to the conditions which existed in the majority of capitalist countries today. Your business is to study the experiment in Russia.'

Over his four weeks in Cape Town the newspapers put together an identikit picture of G.B.S.: a 'charming old gentleman', with 'the fresh complexion of a child', the 'springiness of an athlete' and a 'gurgling chuckle that is irresistible'. Readers liked to see him sitting on top of a famous escapologist's box at the Opera House declaring himself mystified; or advancing with his parasol from the tearoom and leaping among the rocks at the summit of Table Mountain. With its fruit gardens and its vineyards, hot and cold oceans, mountains, sunshine, Cape Town seemed enveloped by pleasantness. Charlotte bloomed in the climate like an autumn rose and Shaw swam frequently, allowing some children to duck him for a bet.

They had put themselves under the charge of Commander C. P. Newton of the Cape Town Publicity Bureau, and the publicity continued to roll jauntily along, with just a hint of menace to come. 'On the whole Cape Town has been extremely polite to Mr Shaw and has respected his wish for a restful holiday,' commented the *Cape Argus* after he had been there a week. 'Mr Shaw, for his part, has been quite exceptionally polite to Cape Town – so far.'

He tried his best to answer the large local mail he received each day, drafting replies in shorthand to be typed by Commander Newton's secretary. 'On the whole, I sincerely desire to say the best I can of it,' he pleaded. Rumours of his wit breezed spicily through Cape Town society. When General Smuts was retelling stories of his guerrilla exploits at lunch one day and happened to mention T. E. Lawrence, Shaw brought him to a confusing halt by mentioning D. H. Lawrence: 'Every schoolgirl of sixteen should read *Lady Chatterley's Lover*.' Smuts, suddenly outflanked, found himself agreeing: 'Of course, of course.'

South Africans relished Shaw's apparent enjoyment of their country. Topping everything was a flight over the Cape Peninsula in a Junker monoplane. 'It was one of the most thrilling experiences I have had,' he said to the waiting journalists at Wingfield Aerodrome. Charlotte too had reached for the skies. 'It was glorious!' she wrote to Blanche Patch in London. ' . . . We flew over two oceans, and back over a chain of mountains . . . we went about 120 miles an hour . . . I believe I shall be very sorry to leave!'

They accumulated much goodwill at Cape Town, and on the eve of their departure Shaw spent it all. 'Hullo, South Africa. Bernard Shaw speaking from Cape Town.' He was the first person to be given a simultaneous broadcast from all five stations in South Africa. 'I have been asked to say some nice things to you . . . But you must excuse me. Saying nice things is not my business.' Fifteen hundred miles of telephone wire carried his voice out of Cape Town to stations at Bloemfontein, Durban, Johannesburg and Pretoria. The advantage of having the finest sun trap in the world, he told his listeners, 'depends altogether on what you catch in it'. This was not the beginning his audience had expected.

'Sun traps have a powerful attraction for people with plenty of money and nothing to do; and you can prosper on the money they fling about – as long as it lasts.

You may easily, if you are short-sighted enough, become dependent on their expenditure, and put all your capital into splendid hotels, golf links, polo grounds and the rest of the elaborate and expensive machinery for fleecing them.

And you can devote all your skilled labour and professional resources into the arts of amusing them, doctoring them and burying them when they die of six meals and 20 cocktails a day.'

At the first sign of trouble, Shaw warned, these unproductive plutocrats would collect their money and go. He could hardly keep the joy from his voice as he imagined the hotels taken over by people from the slums and the golf links covered by playing children. 'Do not hesitate to fill your suburbs with delightful dwellings, which only the rich can now afford,' he urged. 'They will be wanted as much as ever when the rich of all lands have gone the way of the Russian grand dukes. What you have to do is to abolish your slums, for which, let me tell you, Cape Town deserves to be destroyed by fire from Heaven.'

This was appalling – and there was worse to come. 'One of the first things I noticed when I landed was that I immediately became dependent on the services of men and women who are not of my own colour. I felt that I was in a Slave State, and that, too, the very worst sort of Slave State.'

What he had seen in Cape Town during these four weeks had disturbed him. 'Darkies do all the work,' he wrote privately to his friend Emery Walker, ' . . . but the social problems . . . are insoluble.' The race war between blacks and whites was complicated by the other race war between Dutch and English. Thousands of Afrikaners had been forced off their farming lands and, migrating to the cities, became 'poor whites', in competition for jobs with the unskilled black population.

He knew that the affluent white population was uneasy over the danger of a violent uprising, and calculated that for the next half-century it had the power to suppress any such rebellion, with the help of black men if necessary. So he avoided making the usual threats of black revolution. 'If you let other people do everything for you you soon become incapable of doing anything for yourself,' he told his predominantly white listeners.

'You become an idler and a parasite, a weakling and an imbecile; and though you may also become a very pretty lady or gentleman you will be helpless in the hands of your slaves, who will have all the strength and knowledge and character that come from working and from nothing else.

The coloured man is terribly dangerous in this way. He can reduce you to a condition in which you cannot open a door for yourself or carry a parcel . . . He actually dictates your ideas of right and wrong, respectable and disreputable, until you are his mental as well as his bodily slave, while all the time you flatter yourself that you are his lord and master . . . If white civilisation breaks down through idleness and loafing based on slavery . . . then, as likely as not, the next great civilisation will be a negro civilisation.'

Though this moral rebuke was deeply insulting to the rich whites, Shaw had not been rude. He took care to remind his audience that he frequently criticized England's politics. He ended by giving his thanks 'from a heart full of gratitude and a stomach full of peaches. Good-night and good luck.'

He had advocated 'such control of the production and distribution of wealth as will ensure equality of opportunity to every member of the community regardless of race, colour, sex or creed'. Lacking such an economic basis, he believed that the South African regime was heading for moral degeneration. It was a widely unpopular message. Many white South Africans wrote angrily to the newspapers. But none of these protests answered his indictment of the slave state. As Leon Hugo was to write: 'Only Shaw could have said this – could have eschewed the platitude and seen the disturbing paradox in the master–servant, white–black relationship.'

Shaw left Cape Town with Charlotte the next morning and, sharing the motoring with Commander Newton, drove along the Garden Route towards Port Elizabeth. After three days they reached a pretty seaside place called Wilderness and then travelled towards Knysna. 'I negotiated several mountain tracks and gorges in a masterly manner,' Shaw later told Nancy Astor. Then he came upon half a mile of smooth road, 'and I let the car rip.

'Suddenly she twisted violently to the left over a bump. I twisted her violently to the right, and rising with all my energy to the sudden peril, stood on the gas hard as I held the wheel in a grip of iron. The car responded nobly. She charged and cleared a bank with a fence of five lines of barbed wire; carried the wires to a bunker (a sunken path) three feet deep; banged her way through; and was thrashing down a steep place to perdition when at last I transferred my straining sole from the accelerator to the brake and stopped her with the last strand of barbed wire still holding, though drawn out for miles.'

It was really the fault of the De Dietrich that he had bought back in 1908 which had its 'loud pedal' on the left. The Commander received a few negligible knocks and Shaw 'a clout on the jaw and a clip on the knee'. But 'oh! poor Charlotte! When we extricated her crumpled remains from the pile of luggage which had avalanched her I feared I was a widower,' Shaw wrote to Nancy Astor, 'until she asked were we hurt.

'Her head was broken; her spectacle rims were driven into her blackened eyes; her left wrist was agonizingly sprained; her back was fearfully bruised; and she had a hole in her right shin which something had pierced to the bone.'

They entered Knysna, fifteen miles away, and the Shaws took up quarters at the Royal Hotel. For once Charlotte was in the spotlight. 'She is still flat on her back with the shin hole giving no end of trouble,' Shaw wrote a week later. 'She put up a temperature of 103 yesterday (my heart jumped into my mouth) . . . She is very miserable.' He cancelled all his arrangements, and engaged a nurse to come in every day while he himself sometimes accompanied the doctor on his car-journeys to patients in the country districts. Early each morning he would go swimming in the lagoon;

and then, at 9 a.m., he settled down at a hard bench on the stoep of the hotel annexe. Cars hooted and screeched round him, people came up close to stare, but as one resident noticed 'he seemed to be in a dream'.

It was an opportunity to get ahead with his Soviet book. Instead, he found himself beginning a fairy tale: *The Adventures of the Black Girl in Her Search for God*. He had been set thinking about the contact of 'black minds with white religions' five years before by a missionary in Northern Rhodesia called Mabel Shaw, 'a woman with a craze for self torture, who broke off her engagement with a clergyman (he died of it) to bury herself in the wilds of Africa and lead Negro children to Christ'.

This is the starting point of Shaw's fable. The black girl does not share the masochistic excitement of her teacher who 'found in the horrors of the crucifixion the same strange joy she had found in breaking her own heart and those of her lovers'. She is as 'interesting but unsatisfactory' a convert as Lueli in *Mr Fortune's Maggot*, the novel which Sylvia Townsend Warner (another 1930s Stalinist) had written 'in a very advanced stage of hallucination' five years earlier. 'Where is God?' the black girl demands. And when the missionary tells her, 'He has said "Seek and ye shall find me",' she accepts this literally and strides off into the African forest. Each god she meets in the jungle of Old and New Testaments marks the Ascent of Man until she reaches Jesus's concept of a godhead that incorporates itself in human beings.

In the context of South African society, Christ is portrayed as 'a poor white' teacher who is obliged to play the conjuror in order to attract a following 'as they wont listen to his preaching but like his miracles'. Lying on a big wooden cross with his arms stretched out, he is being skilfully carved by a sculptor because, he tells the black girl, 'I am so utterly rejected of men that my only means of livelihood is to sit as a model to this compassionate artist'. This economic motive, Shaw suggests, reinforced by aesthetic power and the exploitation of something dark in human nature, has perverted Christianity and made the instrument of torture a symbol of faith. Using the method of Voltaire's *Candide*, Shaw attempted to replace this doped wine of religion with his own *élan vital*.

Christ's message that we should love one another is unsatisfactory to the black girl: 'our souls need solitude as much as our bodies need love,' she says. ' . . . We need the help of one another's bodies and the help of one another's minds; but our souls need to be alone with God.' Shaw reasoned that Christ's commandment was intended for his disciples and not the whole world. He makes Jesus tell the black girl that to find God 'you must go past me'.

Her pilgrimage leads to the garden cultivated by Candide, where she comes across a potato-digging Irishman. If G.B.S. looks something of a trespasser here, it is because he had cultivated a communal garden, seeing an author's business as minding everybody else's business. But he believed that 'Voltaire, Swift, Shaw make almost a special literary category', and likened Voltaire to Bunyan as one of the 'would-be saviors' of the world. What he shared with them was the threat of despair. Jesus says: 'I am the poorest of poor whites; yet I have thought of myself as a king. But that was when the wickedness of men had driven me crazy.' Shaw's craziness was his Soviet Communism which rose, like a magic carpet, lifting him above the darkness. In a letter to Mabel Shaw, he had written: 'we all have our superstitions and our complexes, the difference between a rather mad writer like Saint Paul and a rather sane one like Voltaire being only one of degree.' Shaw was both 'a rather mad writer' and 'a rather sane one'. In a work modelled on *Candide*, which Voltaire had ironically subtitled *Optimism*, he could not risk exposing the complex roots of a political ideology that protected him from Swift's despair but that could too easily be linked within his fable to Christ's exalted megalomania.

'Life is a flame that is always burning itself out; but it catches fire again every time a child is born.' Shaw's fable plants a series of prophecies: that 'the next great civilization will be a black civilization'; that future gods may be female rather than male; and that the biological solution to the race war between black and white is intermarriage.

Shaw wrote *The Black Girl* over seventeen days, giving his shorthand draft by instalments to a local stenographer, Dorothy Smith. Like many white Knysnaites, Dorothy Smith had imagined G.B.S. to be 'a terrible cynic'. She was surprised by his soft voice and considerate manner. During the five weeks Charlotte and the car were laid up for repairs, Shaw got to know a number of the rich whites and they found him charming. 'He never made me feel he was the great G.B.S., but always thanked me as if I were doing him a favour,' remembered Dorothy Smith. 'I must confess I liked him exceedingly.'

Shaw chartered a Union Airways Junker and on 18 March they flew back to Cape Town, the first passengers to make this three-hour journey by air. 'We were met at the Aerodrome – taken to the ship [the *Warwick Castle*] where we lunched & then there arrived such a crowd as I never saw,' Charlotte wrote to her doctor.

'There is a possibility that he will come back to South Africa,' reported the *Cape Times*. Shaw and Charlotte did return to South Africa three years later, 'rolling down' the Red Sea and along the east coast and disembarking at Durban at the end of April 1935. In celebration of King George V's Silver Jubilee, Shaw appeared as guest of honour at an Indian sports event between two celebrated wrestlers, the Masked Marvel and the Terrible Turk. He also escorted Charlotte to a Zulu war dance, joining in with a few ecstatic steps, chanting and clapping and delighting in the music which, he said, had probably inspired Wagner's *The Flying Dutchman*. 'All attempts to keep them [Zulus] in an inferior position,' he concluded, 'seem to break down before the fact that they are not inferior.'

On this second voyage he carried with him proofs of the Webbs' *Soviet Communism: A New Civilization?* which, like a prophetic text, took the place of his own aborted book on Russia and seemed to refuel his missionary fire. At a press conference on his departure a month later from Cape Town he proposed the introduction of collective farms which, operating like open-air universities, would contribute to a fusion of the races. 'I believe in fusion. The more fusion the better. All that talk of Hitler's about pure race is all nonsense.'

Shaw's ideas on racial fusion, which transported his coffee-coloured children from the end of *The Black Girl* onto the front pages of many newspapers, brought him notoriety round the world. While in Durban he had heard the pro-Nazi Minister of Transport and Defence, Oswald Pirow, make a public appeal to immigrants to keep up the white population, and it occurred to him that the effect of excessive sunshine on white skins might have something to do with white sterility. 'If so,' he reasoned, 'the remedy is clearly pigmentation, which can be brought about most easily by interbreeding with the colored races.' On his arrival back in England he announced himself to be 'an advocate of intermarriage between the white and black inhabitants' of South Africa. This was now his final solution to the racial problem.

'Marriages of White and Black', ran a *Daily Telegraph* headline. 'Startling Plan by Mr Shaw'. The South African press reported that Shaw's 'notorious' views were regarded in Britain as a bad joke. But in Germany they were described as 'blasphemy'. The *Deutsche Allgemeine Zeitung* reassured its readers that there was no danger of Germans on the African continent losing their political hold for want of reproductive vigour.

G.B.S. was unrepentant. 'The future is to the mongrel, not to the Junker. I, Bernard Shaw, have said it.'

*

The army of missionaries which had moved across the world during Shaw's lifetime offered a strange trinity of Christian God, modern medicine, and market capitalism. The road to a new heaven and a new earth led unexpectedly through a jungle of business civilization. In his Preface to *Major Barbara*, Shaw had made reference to the 'part played by Christian missionaries in reconciling the black races of Africa to their subjugation by European Capitalism'. During the 1930s he travelled as a counter-missionary armed with an opposing set of coercive myths and texts. He brought his message to mass-circulation newspapers, students at universities and politicians. The most ambitious of these proselytizing tours was a four-month world cruise on a Canadian Pacific liner, the *Empress of Britain*, sailing from Monaco in the middle of December 1932.

They travelled in a suite of two staterooms, carrying Shaw's vegetarian menus typed out by Blanche Patch which Charlotte would hand the chief steward and head waiter, and sometimes forward to their hotels. They did not join the Captain's table, but sat at a small one of their own in a corner, reading from a large bookbag of recent publications. While Charlotte stayed late in bed, Shaw would rise early, complete several laps of the outdoor pool and orbits of the deck and, after a breakfast of oatmeal porridge, grapefruit and refreshing 'Instant Postum', take up an isolated position on the lounge deck, wearing a cap with a large flap to protect his neck against the trade winds. 'All the time we have been on the ship he has done his mornings' work and there is a lot to show for it,' Charlotte reported back to Blanche Patch. He would hand his correspondence to the ship's stenographer for transliteration. But he was also writing plays again: 'you have to work or go mad'.

All aboard at Monte Carlo; first stop Naples. They gazed down the crater of Vesuvius, glanced at Pompeii, then sailed on to Athens where they were assailed by journalists. 'If you are ever tempted to go to Athens, I advise you not to bother,' Shaw had counselled. 'Just buy a few second hand columns, and explode a pound or two of dynamite amongst them, and there you are.' They plunged into Egypt under a blanket of heat. 'I did some *awful* journies,' Charlotte admitted. On New Year's Day 1933 they sailed from Suez and a week later came to Bombay.

It had been widely reported in the Indian newspapers that he might be visiting Gandhi, then in Yeravda Jail at Pune. They had met in November 1931 while Gandhi was in London attending the Second Round Table Conference on India. Though Shaw believed he was wasting his time keeping company with conference playactors, he saw in Gandhi a natural leader ('Superman = Mahatma') whose 'tactics like all tactics are subject to error and readjustment' but whose 'strategy is sound'. The two of them had taken an instant liking to each other ('Now look here, Gandhi, wouldn't you be comfortable on the floor'). Gandhi emerged from their interview in London paying tribute to G.B.S. as 'a generous ever young heart, the Arch Jester of Europe', adding later (after having read *The Black Girl*): 'In everything of his that I have read there has been a religious centre.' Shaw told Gandhi during their meeting that 'I knew something about you and felt something in you of a kindred spirit. We belong to a very small community on earth.' It was this kinship he stressed when later chiding Nancy Astor for reverting to the Churchillian view of Gandhi as a dangerous charlatan. 'Mahatma G. is not a crook: he is a saint, and as such under the covenant of grace,' he wrote.

Shaw viewed India as being in much the same political state as Ireland had been earlier in his life. 'India should be free to manage her own affairs,' he was to write. 'If she chooses to divide herself into fifty Pakistans and fight it out in fifty civil wars that is her business: not ours.' An editorial in the *Star of India* had warned Shaw to beware of Indian politics: 'there is nothing so dangerous as a sarcastic philosopher who tries to get a rise out of politicians.' Shaw concurred: 'the present situation in India will not bear being talked about,' he wrote to Rabindranath Tagore. 'I understand it only too well.' He understood it as part of a world-historical narrative, with each country poised at a different moment in the story. He refused to make statements about untouchability except when referring back to Britain: 'we have untouchability in England. Ask the labourer who wants to marry the duchess's daughter.'

Gandhi's existence was encouraging to Shaw because 'there might come a future when the whole population of India would be much more like Gandhi than they were at present'. He was also reported as saying: 'Mr Gandhi is the clearest-headed man in India, and he is so tired of you all that he goes on a "fast unto death".' From someone who was himself beginning to suffer from anorexia the kinship is transparent. After their meeting in 1931, Gandhi had said of Shaw: 'I think he is a very good man.' When Gandhi was assassinated in 1948, Shaw was to say: 'It shows how dangerous it is to be too good.'

While other passengers scurried across the country for five days and nights, Shaw and Charlotte remained on board. He was visited by Annie Besant's adopted son, the handsome Jeddu Krishnamurti. Shaw had kept intermittently in communication with Annie on her infrequent trips back to England. 'Do you consider me an intelligent or an unintelligent woman?' she had asked rhetorically on receiving a copy of *The Intelligent Woman's Guide*. 'Whichever I may be, I keep a corner for an old friend. I am ever a fighting Home Ruler and Socialist.' But she was many other things besides. 'What a forcing house of religious leaders the old atheists proved,' Henry Salt had written to Shaw: 'Annie Besant is now the leader of the Theosophists and looks, in her white robes, as though she sits on the right hand of God.' It was difficult for Shaw, contending with a world of superstition, to sympathize with Annie's aspirations, and he applauded Krishnamurti's refusal to be put forward as a new Messiah, the Star of the East. 'Do you ever see Mrs Besant now?' he asked.

'Every day,' Krishnamurti equivocated.

'How is she?'

'Very well; but at her great age she cannot think consecutively.'

'She never could,' whispered Shaw, and Krishnamurti smiled.

Later that year Annie Besant died. She had been in Shaw's estimate both intelligent and unintelligent – like himself – like everyone.

'I have been hung with flowers in the temples and drenched with rose-water and dabbed with vermilion in the houses; and the ship is infested with pilgrims to my shrine,' he wrote after five days at Bombay. According to Nirad Chaudhuri he had become 'almost an idol of educated Indians'. He was also, like his Black Girl, searching for something, and during his eight days at Bombay he appeared to find it unexpectedly.

Of all the religious denominations he had felt nearest to the Quakers, by temperament if not by faith. During the Great War he was impressed by their refusal to fight and willingness to serve as ambulance staff. He also liked their lack of ritual. 'When we want to talk with God,' he was to write, 'we use the same language that we ordinarily use, not prayers composed for us by other people, and we do not need a church to hold communion with him.' By the late 1920s he declared himself to be 'more nearly a Quaker than anything else that has a denomination'. But by the end of the 1930s, when he wrote a play 'In Good King Charles's Golden Days' that introduced the seventeenth-century founder of the Quakers George Fox onto the stage, he used it partly to chart the limita-tions of Quakerism: the denial of access to religion through music and the arts. Near the end of his life Shaw 'ceased to reply that my nearest to an established religion is the Society of Friends, and while calling myself a Creative Evolutionist, might also call myself a Jainist Tirthankava of eight thousand years ago'.

The ancient Jain religion, which recognized God as human-being-and-animal as well as man-and-woman, black-and-white, provided the presuppositions for Shaw's prophecies in The Black Girl, as well as the sublime Shavian double paradox of a temple that contained all the gods and a temple containing none. After visiting these Jain temples he came to believe that Hinduism must be 'the most tolerant religion in the world' because, he wrote to the Reverend Ensor Walters as he sailed away from India, 'Hinduism is so elastic and so subtle that the profoundest Methodist and the crudest idolator are equally at home in it . . . There is actually a great Hindu sect, the Jains, with Temples of amazing magnifi-cence, which excludes God, not on materialistic atheist considerations, but as unspeakable and unknowable, transcending all human comprehen-sion.' Shaw the worshipper and Shaw the iconoclast were joined in the Jainist understanding of all gods and no gods. Bergson, Butler, Lamarck share the Shavian temple with William Morris and Sidney Webb, Marx and Lenin.

Shaw had always accepted that religion was based on need and not dependent on evidence or reason, and that it must be feeling which set people thinking and not thought which set them feeling. He would refer to the Jains often in conjunction with Protestants and Catholics, indicating what he felt to be the Jain potential for healing. 'It is in these temples that you escape from the frightful parochiality of our little sects of Protestants and Catholics,' he wrote to Dame Laurentia McLachlan, 'and recognize the idea of God everywhere.'

Shaw liked to say that all his 'globe-trotting' left little mark on his later plays except for *The Simpleton of the Unexpected Isles* which he wrote in 1934. The Preface to that play, which called for 'greatly increased intolerance of socially injurious conduct', was strongly pro-Soviet, while the play itself was imbued with Jainism, 'the most tolerant religion in the world'.

*

Leaving Bombay, the *Empress of Britain* steamed south-east, via Ceylon and Singapore, into the Pacific area that was already a testing ground for the Second World War. The whole Pacific was afraid of Japan since she had invaded Manchuria. A League of Nations commission had laboriously toured the Far East and on the basis of its report Japan was rebuked early in 1933 for using force to restore peaceful conditions to the province before trying all other means – whereupon Japan resigned from the League.

The League of Nations had been the creation of a pre-war generation. 'There was no living man to whom the generations which came to maturity between 1900 and 1914 owed as much as to Mr Shaw,' Leonard Woolf was to write in 1934. '... Nothing less than a world war could have prevented [him] from winning the minds of succeeding generations ... ever since [the war] the barbarians have naturally been on top.' Shaw supported the work done by Woolf, which by 1920 had helped to set up the League of Nations. He also watched his friend Gilbert Murray's involvement with the League and was to witness his optimism change to disillusion. 'It seems to me clearer than ever,' Murray wrote in 1932, 'that public opinion is the real weapon of the League of Nations.' Shaw believed that collective security could only be achieved if its members pooled their military resources. For what could the League do otherwise?

On arriving in Hong Kong on 11 February, Shaw told the crowds of reporters who came scrambling on board that 'Japan is going to take Manchuria ... She pledged herself to the League of Nations that she would not declare war on anyone. Consequently she has not declared war on China, but has contented herself with fighting ... the League has funked the issues. And now it is gradually ceasing to exist ... Japan has called the League's bluff.'

He was to give one public speech in Hong Kong as the guest of Sir Robert Ho Tung, a picturesque Eurasian millionaire. The Shaws arrived at his house on Monday 13 February and were taken upstairs to a domestic temple that G.B.S. was later to incorporate into the third act of *Buoyant Billions*. 'It was a radiant miniature temple with an altar of Chinese vermilion and gold, and cushioned divan seats round the walls for the worshippers,' he remembered. 'Everything was in such perfect Chinese taste that to sit there and look was a quiet delight.'

On these world pilgrimages Shaw was trying to combine the long and short views of human nature. Such a combination would be essential to his foreign-policy thinking. But to professional politicians he looked dangerous: in dreams begin irresponsibilities. The Hong Kong Government could not prevent Shaw from saying what he wanted, but it did try to prevent the Chinese press from reporting what he said. 'You do not look very much like Chinese,' he welcomed a group of local journalists waiting to interview him, but even this remark was to smuggle its way into the *North China Herald*.

The Great Hall of the University where Shaw was to give his speech was overflowing as he arrived. As in South Africa, his political opinions were not affected by hospitality or vested interests. He began, as he had begun at the University of Stellenbosch in Cape Town, by exhorting the students to argue with their teachers, form their own opinions and read none of the books they were assigned. 'If you read, read real books and steep yourself in revolutionary books. Go up to your neck in Communism, because if you are not a red revolutionist at 20, you will be at 50 a most impossible fossil. If you are a red revolutionist at 20, you have some chance of being up-to-date at 40.'

From the prolonged applause they gave Shaw's peroration the students were 'clearly overwhelmed by the brio, the iconoclast gaiety . . . the metaphysical defiance of the man,' wrote a Senior Lecturer at Hong Kong University, Piers Grey.

In its correspondence to the press the British community in Hong Kong made it known that 'few people in Britain take Shaw's social or political views seriously and it is unfortunate that any of the British in Hong Kong should have done so'. The *Hong Kong Telegraph* accused him of endangering the lives of his student audience at a time when Chiang Kai-shek's nationalists were shooting and beheading communists in the streets. Shaw answered this charge during a talk to the PEN club in Shanghai four days later. 'I urged the students to start revolutions,' he explained. 'But please don't misunderstand.

'I didn't ask them to go to the streets and fight the police. When the police come to suppress revolutionaries with their clubs, the safest way is to run . . . for policemen are like the gun in a robber's hand . . . those with guns in their hands should still be beaten down. But this takes time and you cannot make it by sheer force.'

Despite tight censorship, a number of correspondents from the larger newspapers in China had slipped into his audience at Hong Kong University and telegraphed inflammatory accounts back to Shanghai. When the luxury liner with its dangerous cargo docked, 'the entire Shanghai foreign press was in hiding that morning for fear of coming into contact with him'.

Shaw had planned to stay on board with Charlotte during their short stop at Shanghai, but changed his plan on receiving an invitation from Soong Ching Ling ('Madame Sun'), the sister of Madame Chiang Kai-shek and widow of the revolutionary leader Sun Yat-sen. This was a risky initiative. Shanghai was then bursting into turmoil with many contending warlords – nationalists, communists, Japanese imperialists and European colonialists. At no distance from the night-clubs, banks and luxury restaurants were the prison-factories, miserable refugee camps, and dead babies in the gutters. Into this 'feast of human flesh' Madame Sun secretly brought the notorious *agent provocateur* G.B.S., conveying him by tender from the *Empress of Britain* at five o'clock in the morning of 17 February to her house in the rue Molière.

He was officially the guest of the Chinese League for the Protection of Human Rights, co-founded by Madame Sun and Cai Yuan-pei, a radical ex-Chancellor of Peking National University. Apart from these two, with their assistant Yang Xingfo and the historian Lin Yutang, the guests included Lu Hsun, China's celebrated short-story writer and essayist, the political historian Harold Isaacs, and Agnes Smedley, whose career was to range from promoting birth-control clinics in Germany (from where she had recently arrived) and the raising of funds for the Indian revolutionary movement against the British, to nursing wounded guerrillas in the Chinese Red Army and, at the end of her life, opposing McCarthyism in the United States.

All of them wanted something special from G.B.S. Harold Isaacs wanted him 'to denounce Kuomintang [nationalist] repression and make a world-wide propaganda score'; others wanted him to warn the world against the International Settlement under which they believed China was being handed over to the Japanese; Madame Sun herself pointed to Soviet infiltration into Jiangxi Province as a greater menace and wanted Shaw to point there too. 'So everybody hopes for different things,' wrote Lu Hsun observing them all close in on G.B.S. ' . . . You can tell the result is not too satisfactory by the great number of people who are complaining.'

But Lu Hsun was not complaining. He admired the composure with which, while perfecting his use of chopsticks, Shaw fielded the questions, and also his absolute refusal to please. He was able to make all the subgroups of Chinese intellectuals equally uncomfortable, and therein 'lies Shaw's greatness,' Lu Hsun concluded. G.B.S. was 'a great mirror' and 'from the antics of those who want to look in it or do not want to look in it, men's hidden selves are revealed'. Watching him being interviewed by journalists after lunch, Lu Hsun noticed that when Shaw spoke frankly, people roared as though he had made a satirical thrust; when he joked about not being infallible (at least not always), they insisted on treating him as an encyclopaedia; and when he excused himself as being on holiday, they besieged him the more earnestly to expound his political principles.

By reflecting in his own mirror a world comedian who forced paradox on to others, Lu Hsun was declaring his fellow-status with the legendary G.B.S. Harold Isaacs and Lin Yutang were later removed from the commemorative photograph taken in Madame Sun's garden that afternoon; Agnes Smedley's reputation was clouded by accusations of her involvement in a Soviet spy ring at Shanghai; Yang Xingfo was shot dead by a group of unidentified gunmen three months after this lunch; and Qu Quibai, the Marxist poet who compiled a book, *Bernard Shaw in Shanghai*, was executed by Chinese nationalists in 1935.

Shaw's day-trip into this nightmare was 'very jovial', Agnes Smedley recalled, 'filled with thought-provoking and witty remarks and Soong Ching Ling's [Madame Sun's] laughter'. 'But, as the situation outside was getting extremely tense, we were getting ready to be jailed by the Chinese fascists . . . Shaw said his Fabianism would probably collapse and he would become a revolutionary if he were tried by Chinese law and jailed in a feudal prison . . . Soong Ching Ling laughed so hard she cried and had to wipe away her tears with a handkerchief.' This was Shaw's role: to add the solvent of fantastic humour and to subdue divisive detail wherever he went.

Near Peking the *Empress of Britain* became icebound and they had to transfer to a heavy ice-breaking steamer and slowly smash their way to shore. Inland all the lakes and rivers were frozen hard. 'I have fallen in love with China,' Charlotte wrote to Nancy Astor. ' . . . I felt *at home* there – I belonged there!' Shaw attended his first classical Chinese theatre in Peking and later told a baffled Chinese novelist how deeply impressed he had been by 'the throwing and the catching of bundles and hot towels deftly performed from great distances in the auditorium by the ushers'. But to an English composer, he wrote:

'When there is a speech to be delivered, the first (and only) fiddler fiddles at the speaker as if he were lifting a horse over the Grand National jumps; an ear splitting gong clangs at him; a maddening castanet clacks at him; and finally the audience joins in and incites the fiddler to redouble his efforts. You at once perceive that this is the true function of the orchestra in the theatre and that the Wagnerian score is only gas and gaiters.'

In matters of art, Shaw felt, the Chinese had an instinct for doing things right. At Tientsin he heard 'a most lovely toned gong, a few flageolets (I don't know what else to call them) which specialized in pitch without tone, and a magnificent row of straight brass instruments reaching to the ground . . . They all played the same note, and played it all the time, like the E flat in the Rheingold prelude; but it was rich in harmonics, like the note of the basses in the temple.

'At the first pause I demanded that they should play some other notes to display all the possibilities of the instrument. This atheistic proposal stunned them. They pleaded that they had never played any other note . . . and that to assert that there was more than one note was to imply that there is more than one god. But the man with the gong rose to the occasion and proved that in China as in Europe the drummer is always the most intelligent person in the band. He snatched one of the trumpets, waved it in the air like a mail coach guard with a posthorn, and filled the air with flourishes and fanfares and Nothung motifs. We must make the BBC import a dozen of these trumpets to reinforce our piffling basses.'

Shaw and Charlotte ended the expedition in a Chinese air-marshal's biplane, its seats open to the skies as they soared high over the Great Wall where the Chinese and Japanese armies were fighting, and higher still on its flight back, so high they could see neither the Great Wall nor the fighting because 'the Chinese do not study identification marks before they fire'.

*

They arrived in Japan showing signs of exhaustion. Though the *Empress of Britain* made stops at Beppu, Kobe and Yokohama, Charlotte had withdrawn into her cabin like a snail in its shell. Shaw was using a walking-stick, but could still fence with fifty journalists for an hour or so. Dazzled by his pink cheeks and keen eyes 'like an airplane pilot', they conveyed to readers the wonder of his straight back, white tennis shoes, and all the other cheerful features of his seventy-seven-year-old boyishness.

One advantage of age was that it made you recklessly candid. Shaw's visit had been heralded by the first eruption for more than a century of Mount Aso, the world's largest active volcano, and coincided with an earthquake. To the Japanese authorities this seemed ominous. 'Foreigners with technical knowledge have always been welcome here, foreigners with ideas much less welcome,' explained a British resident in Tokyo. 'Now Mr Shaw is the "foreigner with ideas" par excellence, and from the Japanese point of view the worst possible ideas at that.' For a month the newspapers had been filled with explanatory and emollient articles about him. Now he spoke to them direct.

Turning his back on the beautiful Bay of Beppu, Japan's Inland Sea, he began what was to lengthen into a ten-day press conference, uttering seismic criticisms round a country where, as he later wrote in the Preface to *On the Rocks*, 'it is a crime to have "dangerous thoughts"'. He was referring to Japan's Peace Preservation Law under which the harbouring of 'dangerous thoughts' was punishable by imprisonment. The knowledge that he was speaking for those who could not freely speak for themselves charged his words with extra force.

He started by trying to weaken the heroic central spring of Japan's militaristic foreign policy. The conflict in Manchuria 'won't be won by courage and Bushido,' he warned; 'it will be won by machinery'. Like all wars it was being fought in 'self-defence', but of what value was such an alibi, he asked, when more women could be killed by bombs in modern warfare than soldiers by shells? All thinking people had learnt from the Great War that no one could control or predict the consequences of war in the twentieth century: even the victors risked revolution and bankruptcy. Though careful not to involve the Imperial Family in his criticisms, he trained his guns on imperialistic patriotism as a force that, though temporarily uniting Japan, must ultimately destroy it.

After a few days' reconnaissance at Kobe, Osaka, Nara and Kyoto, he switched his offensive to Japan's social and economic policies which were as much feared abroad, he said, as her militarism. The exploitation of men, women and children who were willing to work twice as long as people in other countries for half the wages made Japan the deadly enemy of workers throughout the rest of the world. Japan was 'measuring her prosperity by the magnitude of her exports instead of the well-being of her people'.

At Osaka he felt he was entering 'a huge industrial hell'. He noticed the dirty women and children, saw their squalid huts and breathed in the acrid fumes of the place, recognizing that 'Japanese cities are like our cities one hundred years ago'. They had abandoned their own feudal system and having been converted to Victorian values were 'busy making fortunes for half a dozen people'.

Shaw emphasized that he had 'no feeling against Japan where I was treated extremely well'. Though he was spreading a rash of embarrassment among ambassadors, consuls, cultural attachés and high commissioners in British embassies round the world, his popularity had soared. Diplomatically it was baffling. 'The more ruthless his statements, the more the public loved him,' a British consular official G. B. Sansom reported in an embassy memorandum.

'When, instead of praising the cherry blossom and the samurai spirit, he said that . . . Japanese cities were slums that ought to be blown up . . . everybody was delighted. In fact, one prominent journalist complained to me that Mr Shaw had been far too mild . . . On the other hand, a secretary in the Chinese Legation told me with great pride, that Mr Shaw had said far more awful things about China than about Japan.'

George Sansom was deputed to look after Shaw and arrange his programme in Tokyo. Arriving at Yokohama, his wife Katharine discovered 'an old man wandering with a slightly lost look on the deck of the ship' who became rejuvenated in conversation. 'G.B.S. will love to go with you,' Charlotte instructed her. 'But don't let him talk too much; he always does. And please, make him rest after lunch.' During lunch at the Sansoms' house in the British Embassy compound, he performed such antics while demonstrating points of musical instrumentation that the elderly butler and two maids 'gave up the struggle for correct deportment and fled from the room'. Protesting at being made to rest after lunch, he immediately fell asleep.

His appearance in the streets of Tokyo on his way to theatres, museums, Waseda University and the Upper House of the Diet (where he brought all business to a halt) was like the progress of a hero, interrupted yard by yard with 'old countrywomen climbing into buses, children, old men, chic girls, shop assistants – you could see each and every one with excited gaze and gaping mouth saying, "Shaw San!"'

Sansom had arranged for him to have a private meeting with the Prime Minister, Admiral Makoto Saito. A reporter in the next room overheard them laughing exuberantly as they discussed old age. Afterwards Shaw remarked to Sansom that he did not understand how state affairs could be conducted by such an 'amiable old nincompoop'.

'Above all,' he told one of his Japanese audiences, 'I am a man of the theatre.' His encounter with the fanatical Minister of War, General Araki, was remarkable theatre. The playwright and General introduced themselves in a grand waiting-room watched by some splendidly bemedalled officers. Suddenly large double doors sprang open and a pack of thirty snapping press photographers poured in, driving back the soldiers and encircling the two protagonists. The air filled with the explosions and smoke, as the chorus of cameramen 'grinning and snarling like wild beasts . . . mauled the general and Mr Shaw . . . It was an awful scene,' George Sansom later recalled.

Meanwhile the full cast assembled round a table: G. B. Sansom seconding G.B.S., a Japanese Colonel shadowing the General, and somewhat in the manner of Pamphilius and Simpronius, the Private Secretaries to the King in *The Apple Cart*, 'two ridiculously earnest young officers taking notes'. Each time their conversation started up, they were tantalizingly interrupted by a soubrette in the shape of the General's daughter, a pretty girl 'who kept on bringing cakes and tea and sandwiches at inconvenient moments'.

The comedy gave way to philosophy as General Araki strove to convert G.B.S. to his 'philosophy of earthquakes'. The General believed that earthquakes were good. They prevented people from becoming too attached to their possessions. They were deeper, the General ventured, than air-raids. In his reply, Shaw conceded that England was unhappily deficient in moral advantages of this kind. Possibly General Araki would favour the planting of dynamite by the British War Minister to provide artificial earthquakes periodically. 'But we have our earthquakes in England,' Shaw added. 'When people think that their institutions, their religions, their beliefs are firm and immutable, some disagreeable fellow like me comes along and upsets their cherished convictions. Now you need that kind of earthquake in Japan!'

In his conversation with Madame Sun, Shaw had described Stalin as 'a practical man' who paid 'little attention to theory' and was 'unscrupulous in trying to reach his goal'. Now, reflecting how closely General Araki resembled Stalin, he assured him that were he to visit Moscow he would return to Tokyo a devout Communist. He also offered the General a military tip: give priority to octogenarians, followed by septuagenarians then sexagenarians, when conscripting men for the army and sending them to the front.

In a memorandum sent by the British ambassador to the Foreign Secretary in London the occasion was judged to be 'a great success'. General Araki praised Shaw's epigrammatic 'life view'. But he still did not think Englishmen understood earthquakes: one 'does not just experience an earthquake and then forget about it'.

In Shaw's honour a special performance had been arranged at the Kudan Noh Theatre. Shaw had read some articles by his Japanese translator Yonejirō Noguchi on Noh theory and was quoted as saying: 'I understand though I don't understand.' In particular he had been struck by some of the contrasts in technique, such as the deployment of ghosts, use of chorus, and the sense of continuity suggested by the passageway of the thrust stage as opposed to the picture-frame of the proscenium stage in Western theatre.

Following the performance of the first work, a warrior-ghost play of the Komparu school called *Tomoe*, Shaw rose to give a short speech of thanks saying he had comprehended the 'artistic intention' of what he had seen. Artists and poets of the theatre would always do their work out of the necessity to follow a sincere impulse, he said, even if doing it meant destroying the human race – an outcome that might cause 'some of us' to follow it more enthusiastically. He seemed overcome by a sudden revulsion against all his trekking through the insincerities of international politics. In this theatre and among these actors he felt at home. 'I belong to it and it belongs to me.'

*

The climax of this world tour in March 1933 was Shaw's first visit to North America. In his twenties, Shaw had momentarily thought of emigrating to the United States. 'I could have come when I was young and beautiful,' he wrote when in his sixties he turned down an invitation from the New York chapter of the Drama League of America. 'I could have come when I was mature and capable.' But in his seventies, 'I cannot help asking myself whether it is not now too late'. Invitations had come in 'at the rate of 60 per minute all the time', but 'I am as far as ever from seriously contemplating it,' he wrote when refusing an offer in 1921.

These refusals masked a real and complicated fear. He was in some ways a natural American ('I'm like New York. It's hell and damnation for me to be doing nothing') who carried on a life-long quarrel with the United States very much in the manner of Charles Dickens. 'This pretence of being affectionate cousins is pure poison,' he wrote. ' . . . Better, where there is volcanic activity under the lid to lift the lid once in a while than sit on it until it blows off!' 'I do not want to see the Statue of Liberty,' he added. ' . . . I am a master of comic irony. But even my appetite for irony does not go as far as that!'

The Americans had pirated his early books and called him an 'Irish Smut Dealer' when issuing arrest warrants for disorderly conduct to the entire cast of *Mrs Warren's Profession* after its opening performance in New York. They had also removed *Man and Superman* and other volumes from the shelves of the New York Public Library; and actually imprisoned a man in Detroit for reading *An Unsocial Socialist* in a streetcar.

'Personally I do not take the matter so lightly,' Shaw had written to the *New York Times* when asked for his reaction to the withdrawal of his books from the state's libraries. 'American civilization is enormously interesting and important to me, if only as a colossal social experiment, and I shall make no pretence of treating a public and official insult from the American people with indifference.'

The resentment he felt at having his moral authority impugned, income cut, and early illusions extinguished sharpened his criticisms and gave them a vindictive edge. He argued that the anarchical plan of letting everyone mind his own business and do the best he could for himself was only practicable in a new country without any common industrial tradition. North America had been incapable of developing beyond this village stage. 'Every social development, however beneficial and inevitable from the public point of view, is met, not by an intelligent adaptation of the social structure to its novelties,' he wrote, 'but by a panic and a cry of Go Back.'

Before the Soviet Revolution Shaw had accepted that American politics had to be co-ordinated with the collective interest of civilization round the world. He took issue with revolutionaries who threatened the United States with the breakdown of capitalism for want of markets and who prophesied that socialism would build on its ruins. He preferred a more inviting evolutionary scenario. 'Socialism is only possible in the consummation of successful Capitalism,' he wrote, ' . . . only possible where Individualism is developed to the point at which the individual can see beyond himself and works to perfect his city and his nation instead of to furnish his own house better than his neighbor's.'

After 1917 he gave up these diplomatic manoeuvres with relief. 'I am not an American,' he admitted, 'but I am the next worst thing – an Irishman.' His tirades against Americans were partly self-inflicted criticisms – an involuntary response to the damage he sometimes felt he had done himself by manufacturing an ostentatious G.B.S., designed to travel in a world increasingly governed by the culture of the USA. 'For what has been happening during my lifetime,' he had written in 1912, 'is the Americanization of the whole world.'

When he returned from the Soviet Union he had used a special broadcast from Savoy Hill to give 'A Little Talk on America', heaping up his Dickensian invective to giddier, more ecstatic heights. The event was recorded by Movietone with G.B.S. at his most child-devilish encircled by immense lights like furnaces welcoming Americans into hell. 'Hello, America! Hello, all my friends in America! Hello, all you dear old boobs who have been telling one another for a month past that I have gone dotty about Russia . . .' Even Charlotte had to laugh. 'My dear!' she wrote to Nancy Astor. 'All the insults he sent over! Too bad – but so funny.'

Yet it was not all so funny. Lifting the lid on the volcanic activity within himself, he covered this 'most awful country' with colossal contempt. Sometimes in the past he had singled out the coast-to-coast desire for money as the most encouraging social aspect of American life. But since the accepted method of acquiring this money in the United States was theft, he liked to add, the country had grown rich only in paper dollars that were no protection against a real financial crash.

'That is what makes you so popular all over the world,' he persisted, moving into rare sarcasm: 'you make yourself at home everywhere; and you always have the first word.' Shaw wanted the last word. With his long-range artillery he aimed to smash the glitter of Western plutocracy and arm an infatuated British public against surrendering to its culture. When he lets off his word-fire at the United States he often has a Britain of the future in his sights.

He was happiest at long range and somewhat uneasy at the prospect of coming ashore and mixing with these 'uncommonly nice people person-ally'. His preliminary exercises in tact – 'Americans are conceited enough to believe they are the only fools in the world' – show his diplomatic skills to have been somewhat rusted. Free love and anarchism had given way after the war to alcohol and communism as the most dreaded social perils in the United States, enabling G.B.S. to use his awkward status as a teetotal communist to challenge American orthodoxy. He looked forward to obliging the immigration authorities with answers of the utmost frankness.

In matters involving others he was careful. He answered the appeal of Thomas Mooney, a militant American labour leader wrongly imprisoned more than fifteen years before in connection with a bomb explosion, by explaining that the interference of a 'Communist foreign celebrity' would do more harm than good. 'I do not consider it humane to use you as a stick to beat Capitalism,' he wrote to him in San Quentin prison. He would try to remain as non-committal with Mooney as he had over the Krynin family in Moscow, but 'I cannot pretend that I am not shocked at having any person put into a vault for 16 or 17 years,' he told reporters on landing at San Francisco. And he made it clear that his own political views were far more extreme than those of this fifty-year-old American who was to wait several years more for a pardon.

Leaving the *Empress of Britain* at San Francisco, Shaw and Charlotte were flown to San Simeon to stay with the millionaire newspaper owner William Randolph Hearst. 'I do not write for the people intelligent and instructed enough to share my views,' Shaw would later explain, ' . . . but to startle and wake up the readers of the H[earst] P[ress].' For four days they put up at his prodigious castle-ranch with the seventy-year-old Hearst and his young mistress, Marion Davies, together with more than forty starlets, sirens and swells of all sorts, as well as the apes, eagles and zebras that occupied the grounds outside.

Afterwards they flew by plane from Hearst's vivarium, swooping down as if 'to catch a fish' below a sudden thunderstorm and making a forced landing on the beach near Malibu. There they were picked up by a college sophomore who rattled them into Malibu Airport. Then, in a dignified cavalcade, they entered the MGM studio-village of Culver City – to be welcomed, as in a nightmare, by the people they had recently left, William Hearst and Marion Davies.

So far Shaw had refused all American offers to film his plays. He went out of his way to praise Eisenstein at the expense of Hollywood, offering him the film rights in *Arms and the Man* after meeting him in London in 1929, though refusing Mary Pickford the film rights to *Caesar and Cleopatra* in 1930. Eisenstein's disastrous experiences in Hollywood during the early 1930s strengthened Shaw's hostility.

Charlotte and G.B.S. were in Hollywood only two and a half hours, but 'bitterness and rancor of a kind hovered in their wake'. Years afterwards Marion Davies (who had wanted the film rights to *Pygmalion*) described Shaw as having 'that caustic Irish wit which is very detestable'. Though RKO Studios was also seeking the rights to *The Devil's Disciple* for John Barrymore and *Saint Joan* for Katharine Hepburn, 'I don't believe that Hollywood is within ten years of tackling my stuff,' Shaw wrote shortly after leaving. His relations with the United States film industry were commemorated by the 'caustic Irish wit' of his reply to Samuel Goldwyn who tried to flatter him into signing a contract for the screen rights of his plays: 'The trouble is, Mr Goldwyn, you are interested in art, whereas I am interested in money.'

They rejoined the *Empress of Britain* at Los Angeles, sailed down the Pacific coast to Panama, and up the Atlantic coast towards New York. Shaw had agreed to give one public lecture in the States – for the Academy of Political Science at the Metropolitan Opera House in New York. He was anxious for it to be known that 'I shall not take a cent out of America on this visit' so as to avoid the charges thrust at Dickens of grabbing as many dollars as he could.

He had agreed to give this formal lecture so as to produce an authentic record of his beliefs. 'I have been misquoted everywhere,' he was quoted as saying, 'and the inaccuracies are chasing me round the world.' The American freedom to tell lies worked like an ingenious form of censorship. He had forewarned the New York reporters that he would not be interviewed before his lecture. But when the *Empress of Britain* docked, two hundred journalists and photographers swarmed on deck in search of him. They found a message pinned to his cabin door which was guarded by the ship's master-at-arms:

'The New York press may return to its firesides and nurse the baby until tomorrow morning, except the enterprising section which came on board at Havana, and discussed everything with me for an hour and forty minutes. Today I am in training for the Metropolitan Opera House tonight, and may be regarded as deaf and dumb for the moment. With regrets and apologies. GBS.'

But they would not leave. After a couple of hours Shaw sent out his biographer Archibald Henderson, like a dove from the Ark, with a message that he would pose for photographs but say nothing. 'It was a terrible business for me,' he wrote afterwards to the actress Constance Collier, ' . . . I had to fight off a raging press to get some sleep and quiet before my big effort.' Eventually he was spirited away through the throng by his new American publisher, Howard Lewis, of Dodd, Mead. 'I can think of no private citizen with the exception of Lindbergh who had been greeted by more reporters and publicity than Mr Shaw,' he wrote to the British publisher Otto Kyllmann.

Charlotte had been getting increasingly worried over Shaw's 'big effort' at the Metropolitan Opera House. 'I do not feel he is up to it. It will be a terrible strain after all the exertions & fatigues of this amazing journey,' she had written to Nancy Astor. They arrived at the Metropolitan Opera House a little after 8.00 and were steered by police through the fast-flowing crowds. With 'the lithe step, all but prancing, of a cavalier', Shaw walked on to the platform led by his chairman – the President of the First National Bank – at 8.35. He had agreed to a national radio broadcast of his lecture on condition that it was not edited, and was now obliged to wait ten minutes for the National Broadcasting Company's schedule, while a standing ovation from the audience of more than 3,500 people changed into an impatient stamping of feet. Among this audience was Edmund Wilson, observing the 'arms folded of the schoolmaster' and 'the reddish nose of the old Irishman' dressed formally in his 'double-breasted black coat buttoned up high under the collar with an austere effect almost clerical so that it sets off the whiteness of his beard as his eyebrows against his pink skin look like cotton on a department-store Santa Claus'. Shaw stood up, a dark arrowy figure, slim and straight; and then his caressing accent began to permeate the auditorium, blending courtesy with irony, touching the imagination with a peculiar enchantment.

'Finding myself in an opera house with such a magnificent and responsive audience,' he began, 'I feel an irresistible temptation to sing.' But it soon became clear that he was not there to sing America's praises. He told them he had visited 'two plague spots' in the United States, Hollywood and New York. Hollywood was everywhere bringing public and private morals under its influence. But its philosophical answer to every challenge was a sock in the jaw. 'When shall we see a film issuing from Hollywood,' Shaw asked, 'in which the hero acts like a civilized man?'

The 'vast dumb audience', likened by Edmund Wilson to a 'demoralising aquarium of blind deep-sea creatures', was no better pleased by Shaw's picture of New York 'under the thumbs of your private racketeers, from the humble gunman to the great financial magnate'. His main target was the money kingdom of Wall Street whose power was 'so irresistible that it becomes a political and industrial power, not to say a religious power'. The United States had grown into 'a wonderful night clubby sort of nation; but there is nothing so helpless as a raided night club'.

Ostensibly Shaw's lecture was an examination of American government. He accurately predicted that private financiers would not allow Franklin Roosevelt to carry through his National Recovery Program, and that if necessary they would use the American Constitution to stop him. This Constitution had become a paradoxical symbol of Shaw's own frustration: 'a great protest against the tyranny of law and order', representing the struggle of his early career, that had been turned into a Charter of Anarchism guaranteeing 'to the whole American nation that it never should be governed at all', shadowing his sense of powerlessness in late middle age.

The United States did not want to be governed, Shaw reasoned, because it did not trust its own electoral system: 'those scandalous and disgusting spectacles that are called election meetings, at which sane and sober men yell senselessly until any dispassionate stranger looking at them would believe that he was in a lunatic asylum for exceptionally dreadful cases of mental derangement'. But Shaw is not a dispassionate stranger. He is painfully involved. 'I have never spoken nor listened at an election meeting without being ashamed of the whole sham democratic routine. The older I grow the more I feel such exhibitions to be, as part of the serious business of a nation, entirely intolerable and disgraceful to human nature and civic decency.'

In private he admitted to telling people 'all sorts of things that I do not believe, because I think it will please them'. But 'speeches made through the microphone to millions of listeners,' he later said, ' . . . take on a necessary sincerity'. It was as if the microphone could pick up the voice of Sonny using this climax to Shaw's missionary travels to make his objection heard to the fêted progress of G.B.S. around the world. Was not the spell of money on G.B.S. an American spell; his trick of overstatement 'an American trick; his gift for monologue, an American gift', as Blanche Patch was to suggest? Playing with these spells and tricks and gifts like sparks in the air, translating the child who had never grown up into the country that remained so juvenile, Shaw blinds and illuminates, angers and amuses his audience with this variety show of his dissatisfaction. In his urgent warning to Western civilization that it had 'reached the edge of the precipice' over which previous civilizations 'fell and were dashed to pieces' rose the anguish and relief of someone nearing the end of his own life.

'Mr Roosevelt, by a happy chance, got photographed with a baby. The baby was a success: Mr Roosevelt went to the White House in its arms.' There is a charm in such passages where the voices of Sonny and G.B.S. seem to blend, and a peculiar insight where they combine against a common enemy such as the financiers who 'live in a world of illusion'. Circling this illusory world Shaw presents a stereoscopic vision of the planet manoeuvred by the calculations of exchange value judgements from one great war towards another. All the gold in the world was being shipped to the United States – but what use was it? 'Ask your armies of the unemployed.' This question and command mirror Shaw's own position as someone financially successful, who felt politically 'unemployed' in the modern world.

'Whenever in the search for truth I hit the nail exactly on the head, there is always a laugh at first.' But in several places where he expected laughter in the Metropolitan Opera House there was a 'curious dead silence'. It was evident to Edmund Wilson that he had not been able to sense what kind of audience he was up against. His need for self-dramatization had delivered him into the hands of modern publicity, making the effect a little compromising, as if he were having to 'handle like hot potatoes convictions which were once incandescent,' Edmund Wilson judged. And yet 'he can still thrill us from time to time as he is able to make the timbre of the old daring, the old piercing intellectual clarity, ring out . . . in the pompous opera house . . . he continues to stand for something which makes us see audience and theatre as we have never quite seen them before.'

He had invited several people to come and see him next morning on board the *Empress of Britain* before it sailed, but they were quickly rushed aside by reporters and cameramen all over the ship. 'Evidently under instructions to "get Shaw's goat", they did everything possible to irritate and disconcert him,' Lawrence Langner observed. 'In one instance, a lout set off a flashlight bulb almost in his face, amid loud guffaws, and took advantage of Shaw's shocked surprise to snap an absurd picture of him which was later published in a New York journal. Not one of these hoodlums showed the slightest respect for the man.' Langner went up to a steward and asked whether some gangway could be made for Shaw. 'You'd need fixed bayonets, sir,' he was told. Eventually Shaw reached his cabin and 'literally had to throw his weight against his stateroom door'. 'We left the boat sadly,' recorded Lawrence Langner, 'wishing that GBS might have taken away with him a better impression of our national manners.'

As soon as the ship sailed, Shaw re-entered the world of his plays, and Charlotte was left reflecting on the 'very mixed business' of their wanderings: 'it is a sort of worthlessness that comes over one in this vagabond life.' On 19 April the *Empress of Britain* steamed up Southampton Water, her bunting flying, and the sirens hooting from the shore. Two days later they were 'off the map' back at Ayot.

They were to have another brief look at the United States early in 1936 as part of a second world tour – this one from west to east aboard the *SS Arandora Star*. Shaw was now in his eightieth year and this was a postscript to his missionary travels. He gave a 'low-keyed' interview to crowds of reporters at Miami and kept the rest of his trip private. Across a stormy Atlantic, between spasms of sickness, he wrote prefaces; along the Gulf of Panama, in temperatures of almost 90°F, 'I try to write plays falling asleep between every sentence'. At Honolulu they had lunch in a Chinese restaurant with Charlie Chaplin. At the Grand Canyon, startlingly covered with snow, they met J. B. Priestley.

'We have seen some glorious places & made some delightful friends & learned quite a lot of things,' Charlotte had written to Nancy Astor. Shaw would remember best the natives in Equatorial countries, who were the originals of Britain's Smiths and Browns, still unsmudged by commerce, and always looking carefree. But in the developed countries he had found people worried and anxious. Was it any wonder that he had paused to ask his audience at the Metropolitan Opera House: 'What is wrong with us?'

*

Between these two world cruises Shaw made one last evangelical venture, the most far-flung of all his sea-voyages, to New Zealand. By now he had perfected his boat drill. After early morning exercises, he would search the promenade deck for an 'unprotected lady who is ripe for a friendship with a celebrity. I plant my deck chair beside hers and ask her whether she minds my working at a new play instead of talking. She is so delighted at being given the role of protector of G.B.S. that whenever anyone comes near she makes agitated signs to warn him off, whispering that *Mr Shaw is at work on a new play*. So I make a new friend and get perfect peace during the entire voyage.' At the end of this trip he was able to present

Blanche Patch, who had as usual remained on duty at Whitehall Court, with shorthand drafts of three new plays: *The Simpleton of the Unexpected Isles*, *The Millionairess* and *The Six of Calais*.

New Zealand had passed a law enabling the government to refuse landing to 'persons who have recently visited Communist countries'. A few people had advocated that Shaw be disbarred from entry and there was 'some lively press discussion as to what would happen to me' before his arrival. As he and Charlotte came down the gangway the dockers began cheering – and so began 'a sort of Royal progress'.

'I shan't do it again,' he had promised after his lecture at the Metropolitan Opera House: 'I am too old for these feats of endurance.' But he could not quite hold to this resolution. In the event he gave one lecture to the hastily formed Wellington Fabian Society and a national broadcast, also relayed to Australia, entitled 'Shaw speaks to the Universe'. His address to the Wellington Fabians was a cheerful demolition of parliamentary democracy. In Britain, he told them, the House of Commons had become a House of Hypocrisy, which seemed to suit Ramsay MacDonald but had confounded Keir Hardie. 'He was the finest gentleman in Parliament. But that meant that he never understood that an English gentleman could get up in Parliament and tell a lie, or, still worse, convict him who never told a lie anywhere, of telling a lie in Parliament.' Shaw appealed to New Zealand socialists to free themselves from this lying model of government based on Westminster. If the sublime virtue of democracy was a mirage then so also was the black vice of totalitarianism. All law had to be totalitarian and everyone lived under a dictatorship of the proletariat or a dictatorship of the plutocracy. Shaw's advice was categorical: stick to socialism and let it dictate, rather than a clique of wealthy businessmen.

The New Zealand Government waived its broadcasting regulations which barred all controversial statements and allowed Shaw to say whatever he wanted. He was seeing a number of socialist politicians during his visit, including two future Labour Prime Ministers, Peter Fraser and Walter Nash, and he had briefed himself carefully. 'You have in Wellington a remarkable milk supply, which is the envy of the whole world,' he said.

'. . . But your milk I think costs too much. I just want to ask, why not distribute milk freely? . . . when you have distributed free milk, which is just as possible as free water, I would then suggest that you should go on from free milk to free bread . . . [then] such a thing as a hungry child will be impossible in New Zealand.'

The first Labour Government that came to power at the end of 1935 distributed half a pint of free pasteurized milk each school day to all schoolchildren. Shaw would receive grateful letters from New Zealand mothers (children themselves grew up feeling less grateful) but replied that the credit lay with the New Zealand Government for implementing his suggestion. The scheme lasted for thirty years and was expanded in 1941, not by free bread, but by free apples once the war had cut New Zealand's export market to Britain. This was therefore less of a socialist initiative than a solution to the problem of an unsaleable agricultural surplus.

To writers of a younger generation watching him stalk across the international scene like one of 'those big heads on stilts in carnival processions', it was astonishing how G.B.S. got away with his polemical feats. Fame was his passport. He had no job to lose and he exploited the world's fame-snobbery in order to break the conventions that harnessed other people. He aired unspeakable opinions vital to a democracy. With a prophetic eye on the German Olympic Games, he pointed to competitive sport as creating 'more bad feeling, bad manners and international hatred than any other popular movement'; he criticized the exclusivity of New Zealand's immigration laws which let in only Scandinavians, British and a few other people from north-west Europe; and he described as 'nonsensical' a system of employment that encouraged overtime from some workers and left others without jobs.

Above all, he begged New Zealand to stop acting as a dairy for the rest of the world (which was learning how to milk its own cows) and, once everyone in the country had plenty of cheese, cream, and butter on their bread, for pity's sake to 'produce something else'. Foreseeing something of what would happen with the European Common Market, he attacked the illusions of imperial-patriotic 'En-Zeds' who called England 'Home' and relied on this special relationship for trade protection to the end of the century. 'Keep your wool on your own backs; harness your own water power; get your fertilising nitrates from your own air; develop your own manufacturers and eat your own food; and you can snap your fingers at Britain's follies.'

Happy the country that would not be dependent on trade in the years to come, for she would not be dominated by foreign capitalists. After a reminder that 'all tourists are not exemplary characters like myself', he warned people against too much reliance on tourist traffic: 'If New Zealand wants to develop a big tourist industry it means that New Zealanders are to become hotel-keepers, waiters, cooks . . . the attractions of New Zealand are better kept for the recreation of New Zealanders themselves.'

After five days in Auckland they hired a chauffeur and sped off on a three-week motor tour of the North and South Islands. Charlotte was fearful that 'G.B.S. will get the bit in his teeth and drag me about travelling'. By travelling she meant walking. Herself, she 'never walks a yard when there is a vehicle – even a wheelbarrow – to be had for love or money,' G.B.S. had told Lady Gregory. Himself, he loved walking and, according to their breathless Maori guide at Rotorua, was the fastest walker in the Antipodes. Charlotte however could usually catch up by car, and together they examined strange thermal peaks, craters, and sulphurous steam holes reeking of brimstone like Hades – 'pure and boiling & bubbling & making the most absurd faces at one' – over which Charlotte could not help laughing and which Shaw complimented as being the most damnable spot he had ever visited, adding admiringly that he would have willingly paid £10 not to have seen it. They floated through the wonderful glow-worm cave at Waitomo, a firmament of blue shimmering lights that, since noise would extinguish them, completely silenced G.B.S. They motored beside the sub-tropical vegetation of the bush, climbed high up to the national park at Chateau Tongariro, and saw the sacred mountains covered in snow.

Wherever he went he had to combat a tendency to assume that he had come to New Zealand to study the Maoris. He could see nothing wrong with the Maoris – except that they were probably better off before the Europeans arrived. It was a pity that everyone had to study a pedantic treaty in differing versions from the last century to find out how to behave to one another rather than consult their own best instincts.

They ended their tour in Wellington. At the Truby King Karitane Hospital, G.B.S. spoke with the matron, mothers and nurses but unlike a politician, reporters observed, took little notice of the babies. Afterwards he was driven round to meet Sir Truby King. This pre-Spock revolutionary of infant care appealed to many facets of G.B.S. The socialist warmly approved the New Zealand system of free clinics for mothers; the adolescent who had been so impressed by Vandeleur Lee responded to Truby King's insistence on the health-giving properties of 'fresh air, light, warmth, proper food'; and the boy who had suffered from the neglect of his mother and transferred his loyalty to the adopted mother country applauded a reformer who placed more importance on nurse-educators than on motherly instinct.

Bouquets of flowers were passed through their portholes as the *Rangitane* cast off from Wellington on 14 April. Legendary stories were already floating in their wake: how G.B.S. had borrowed a lady's scarlet bathing-suit and plunged into the breakers at Mount Maunganui; how at Auckland he had presented Adolf Hitler's *My Struggle* to the Turnbull Library. It had been a carefree month – even the journalists were amiable, presenting this 'old elf in the zip-fastened jersey' as a brilliant social diagnostician and advocate of national welfare.

He had sensed that the country was on the verge of a political ascent to socialism. It was like looking at 'a growing child,' he said. On his arrival at Auckland he had announced that 'I have been in Russia. It is a very remarkable place. I want to see if New Zealand is any better.' In one respect he did find it better. 'Changes which have been made peacefully and reasonably in New Zealand have been made violently and even ferociously in other parts of the Empire.' One observer in Wellington noticed that 'Mrs Shaw, quietly knitting in the far corner of their Midland hotel sitting-room, stirred uneasily' as she heard her husband embark on a long eulogium of the Soviet system and that she 'ordered a mug of cocoa' to comfort herself. But as Charlotte later told a journalist: 'I only appear conventional on the surface . . . underneath I am the most unconventional of persons.'

After crossing the sea to what Mark Twain had called 'Junior England', Shaw experienced something of what Trollope had found the previous century – 'You are, as it were, next door to your own house.' So New Zealand came to suggest an idealized Ireland. 'If I were beginning life, I am not sure that I would not start in New Zealand,' he said. '. . . I, being an old Victorian, am much more at home here than in London. You are quite natural to me . . .' Such tributes suggest a mirage reflecting what his life might have been like in another Ireland without a tearful childhood and the divisive violence of Irish politics. 'If I showed my true feelings I would cry,' he told a photographer on board the *Rangitane* who had asked him to give his brightest smile on leaving New Zealand: 'it's the best country I've been in.'

4

PREFACES TO DEATH

I feel apologetic for my existence now that all decent men of my age are committing suicide . . . But I can still write to some purpose, and so must brazen it out until some assassin saves me the trouble of shooting myself.

Shaw to Mrs Patrick Campbell (16 April 1932)

The prefaces Shaw wrote in these years of travel are his missionary tracts. It is a loveless territory which these writings of the early 1930s illuminate. The prefaces to *On the Rocks* and *Too True to be Good*, the 'Preface on

Bosses' and the 'Preface on Days of Judgment' that precede *The Million-aires* and *The Simpleton of the Unexpected Isles* parade the history of the axe, the stake, the guillotine, garotte, electric chair, the disembowellings, floggings, burnings, hangings, lynchings that infest our history. He writes as one maddened by all this savagery. It was not true that it took all sorts to make a world, 'for there are some sorts that would destroy any world very soon if they were suffered to live and have their way'. Therefore, he asks: 'Is there really nothing to be done with such men but submit to them?' Why should we not treat these people 'as we treat mad dogs or adders'? For who can say that those granted premature retirement from the appalling misery of life would not be better off?

The problem of who should earn promotion into oblivion leads Shaw to a treatise on dictatorship. Dictators were thriving in the 1930s, he believed, because parliaments had removed themselves from the needs and feelings of the people. The capitalistic system, with 'its golden exceptions of idle richery and its leaden rule of anxious poverty', was a desperate failure. Shaw called for a new social creed and legal code, an economic Reformation in which the nobler coinage would drive out the baser currency. He wanted to draw up a set of conditions fundamental to human society and commission a new work of social philosophy to bring Mill's essay *On Liberty* into the twentieth century – what John Rawls was to attempt in *A Theory of Justice* in 1971.

Shaw had put his heart into politics and grown obsessed with dictators and by death. The peculiar tension of these prefaces arises from this relish and his recoil from it. Dividing himself into two voices, the old Shaw insists on the political necessity of killing people who are already pretty well dying from too much luxury; while the young Shaw raises the banner of tolerance and argues that there may be good biological reasons for the workshy. The old Shaw declares that no hostile critic of the existing social order should behave as if he were living in his own particular utopia: 'Not until the criticism changes the law can the magistrate allow the critic to give effect to it.' The young Shaw answers that 'civilization cannot progress without criticism, and must therefore, to save itself from stagnation and putrefaction, declare impunity for criticism'. The old Shaw writes that 'the community must drive a much harder bargain for the privilege of citizenship than it now does'. The young Shaw reminds us of Morris's saying that 'no man is good enough to be another man's master' and warns us that most 'autocrats go more or less mad'. The old Shaw points to 'the final reality of inequality'; the young Shaw insists that 'rulers must be as poor as the ruled so that they can raise themselves only by raising their people'.

So irreconcilable are Shaw's two voices that in his Preface to *On the*

Rocks he separates them in a dialogue between Pontius Pilate and Jesus. This experiment of a play-within-a-preface underscores the imaginative voice of the young Shaw which sounds clearer in the plays. The prefaces are increasingly dominated by the will of the old Shaw.

*

'I don't know what I shall do with this Black Girl story,' Shaw had written to his Edinburgh printers. But when William Maxwell suggested that, with the addition of some good illustrations, it might make an attractive little book, he began to see possibilities. After seeing a trial drawing, he picked a then unknown draughtsman and wood-engraver in his early thirties called John Farleigh who had been recommended by Maxwell. Shaw wanted pictures designed as part of the book, not 'illustrations' stuck into it. He was seeking to do something new in publishing that anticipated the Penguin paperback revolution of the later 1930s. 'Half a crown is the extreme limit,' he wrote to Otto Kyllmann.

By publishing the book on 5 December 1932 got up to look like a Christmas card, Shaw was scheming to enter thousands of Christian homes with a fable that exposed the contemporary state of religion. Describing G.B.S. as a wonderful 'weedkiller' and his *Black Girl* as an 'illustrated tract for the times', Beatrice Webb judged it to be a courageous indictment of a creed 'which is no longer practised or believed in by the majority of the citizens, rich or poor, enlightened or ignorant'.

A first printing of 25,000 copies was followed by five additional impressions before the end of the year, and in a letter to one of his translators the following summer Shaw reported sales as being 'roughly 100,000' – in addition to more than 50,000 copies brought out early in 1933 by Dodd, Mead & Company in the United States.

'If it were not for the author's prestige,' Beatrice Webb wrote in her diary, 'it would be considered blasphemous by all churchmen, conventional or genuine.' Six months after publication, the Irish Government banned all sales of the *Black Girl*, alleging its 'general tendency' to be 'indecent and obscene'. Shaw was curious to know whether the ban would be lifted if he issued a special Irish edition with the women draped in long skirts. 'The reverend censors are not nudists, and probably regard a nude negress as the last extremity of obscenity,' he wrote to W. B. Yeats who was marshalling the Irish Academy of Letters to challenge this censorship, which was revoked fifteen years later, in 1948.

'I shall not protest,' Shaw had written to Yeats, 'if the Churchmen think my book subversive they are quite right from their point of view.' But he was 'ridiculously surprised' by the hostility of Laurentia McLachlan. Dame Laurentia, recently elected Abbess of Stanbrook, had 'demanded to see the book', and Shaw sent her a proof inscribed on the flyleaf: 'An Inspiration which came in response to the prayers of the nuns at Stanbrook Abbey and in particular to the prayers of his dear Sister Laurentia for Bernard Shaw.' She had not finished reading the proof when she received a tiny playlet from him set in 'God's office in heaven' where God and the Archangel Gabriel are discussing the impasse between Dame Laurentia and G.B.S. It is God who represents Shaw's view ('I gave him a first class job in his own line') and merely the Archangel ('You'd better let her have her way') who speaks for the Abbess. Nevertheless Dame Laurentia took this to mean that Shaw was withdrawing the book. 'You have made me happy again by your nice little play and I thank you from my heart for listening to me,' she wrote ominously. ' . . . if you had published it I could never have forgiven you.'

Nine days after its publication, and just as he was setting out on his world cruise, Shaw sent her a copy. 'This black girl has broken out in spite of everything,' he wrote. It was as if he had thrown a bomb. As a natural authoritarian ('faithful servants are the worst of tyrants,' Shaw has God tell the Archangel Gabriel), Dame Laurentia was used to deference from her famous admirers. Indignation welled up in her at Shaw's incredible stubbornness. At the same time she felt humiliated. She had prayed that God might use her for the salvation of his soul, and now had to bear witness to a revolting profanity. Even her beloved crucifix had been twisted into the symbol of a neurosis.

Deeply displeased, she wrote to upbraid him. Her letter reached Shaw in Bangkok. He tried several times to reply from aboard the *Empress of Britain* but, fearing that his letters might wound her further, tore them up. 'I innocently took [it] to be a valuable contribution to the purification of religion from horrible old Jewish superstitions,' he pleaded on 29 June 1933 after returning to Whitehall Court. ' . . . I am afraid of upsetting your faith, which is still entangled in those old stories.'

This was additionally insulting to the Abbess. It was not her faith but her susceptibilities Shaw had upset. He had preferred his own wrongheadedness to the divinity of Christ; he had tried to analyse an experience that surpassed human understanding and reduced God to abstraction. 'The only way to comfort me would be for you to withdraw the Black Girl from circulation,' she answered.

This was obviously impossible. Shaw had hoped she might readmit him to her grace, but her mind was not 'unenclosed' after all. She had no intimation of Christianity as a revolutionary political idea. He wished to conciliate her, but could not falsify his own hope and faith. 'Laurentia: has it never occurred to you that I might possibly have a more exalted notion of divinity,' he appealed.

She did not answer. What was the point? Christ's divinity was not negotiable. After more than nine years their friendship was at an end, and when Shaw went to the Malvern Festivals he did not visit her. 'I never passed through Stanbrook without a really heartfelt pang because I might not call and see her as of old,' he later confessed. Then, in the autumn of 1934, after returning from Malvern to Whitehall Court, he found, among the correspondence waiting for him, a card.

IN MEMORY OF SEPT 6
1884–1934
DAME LAURENTIA MCLACHLAN
ABBESS OF STANBROOK

He wrote at once to 'the Ladies of Stanbrook Abbey' telling them that he had had 'no suspicion that I should never see her again in this world'. He had not dared to show his face at the Abbey, he explained, until Dame Laurentia had forgiven him for his little book.

'She has, I am sure, forgiven me now; but I wish she could tell me so. In the outside world from which you have escaped it is necessary to shock people violently to make them think seriously about religion; and my ways were too rough.'

This letter of condolence was answered by Dame Laurentia herself. 'My dear Brother Bernard, As you see, I am not dead,' she wrote. The card had been a souvenir of her Golden Jubilee. She did not tell him that she had been advised to send it by her archbishop. 'When next you are in the neighbourhood you must come and see me again . . . You have my daily prayers. I hope they will have nothing but good results in future.'

It was a miracle, a friendship resurrected. 'Laurentia! Alive!!' Shaw exclaimed. ' . . . I thought you were in heaven, happy and blessed. And you were only laughing at me. It is your revenge for that Black Girl.' They were back on terms of equal superiority. What is implicit in his letter to her is made explicit in a letter he sent Sydney Cockerell ten days later. 'But I felt as if a soul had been dragged back from felicity,' he wrote. 'Which is queer, as of course I dont believe anything of the sort.'

'I am not sufficiently fond of myself to wish for immortality,' he had told Virginia Woolf and Maynard Keynes. But he would have liked, he sometimes felt, to be dead. At least four times by the 1930s he had made positively his Last Will and Testament; and still he lived on. 'It seems the most ridiculous thing in the world that I, 18 years older than Gilbert, should be heartlessly surviving him,' he was to write to G. K. Chesterton's widow. ' . . . The trumpets are sounding for him.'

No trumpets had sounded for Shaw's fellow-playwright Pinero whose death on 23 November 1934 'passed almost unnoticed'. The following day, in the middle of a telephone conversation, Shaw himself suddenly dropped down dead . . .

EIGHTEEN

I

THE DEMANDS OF THE POLITICAL THEATRE

Didnt you know that English politics wont bear thinking about?

On the Rocks

It had always been a relief to get back to Ayot. The staff there were fiercely loyal. The new young Irish parlourmaid, Margaret Cashin, often came upon Shaw slipping money into envelopes and he always paid for her trips back to Ireland. He was a thorough gentleman. When she married he lent her the Rolls-Royce. 'It was grand.'

Out of doors he still looked spry and active. Chopping wood, making bonfires, sawing logs, collecting acorns, eyeing the strawberries while patrolling up and down with his notebook, camera and secateurs, he appeared 'like a magic gardener in a fairy story'. He would write in the garden too, stepping out from a veranda at the back of the house ('my Riviera') and hurrying past the flowers and trees to a small revolving hut, like a monk's cell, with its desk and chair and bunk. Here, in what some visitors mistook for a toolshed, he was conveniently out of the staff's way and the world's reach.

As for Mrs Shaw, she was 'one of the best', the assistant gardener Fred Drury reckoned. 'She used to help him a lot with his work.' The two gardeners often speculated over what was going on between Mr and Mrs Shaw as they watched them circumnavigating the lawn together. 'They had a special route round the garden which was just about a mile, and they put one stone down every time they passed,' Fred Drury observed. Henry Higgs noticed these stones too, and how they 'used to take them off the window sill on the way back, one by one'.

Such symmetry was particularly characteristic of Mr Shaw. He was a very tidy man. 'He always put chairs back in place, and his pyjamas on his bed in his room, neatly folded,' Margaret Cashin noted. ' . . . [He] was very particular about his erectness and appearance – proud of his person and figure . . . He always changed for the evening meal regardless of whether anyone was coming to see him or not.' Sometimes there were famous guests: heavyweight boxers, film actresses, war heroes, prime ministers – those sorts of person. But that didn't bother the staff who saw one of their prime jobs as protecting Mr Shaw from the outside world: by which they meant the villagers.

This became easier when, after his eightieth birthday, he more or less gave up driving. In recent years he had grown more reckless and Fred Day, his chauffeur, was often obliged to pull the wheel out of his hand crying 'Brake, sir!' and 'That will do sir'. It was an anxious time. 'I was fully occupied trying to keep him out of trouble,' Day admitted. 'I don't know why on earth they let me have a driving licence at my age,' Shaw complained one day after plunging into some hot water pipes at a garage.

As a pedestrian he went on into his mid-eighties disappearing downhill and updale for walks of up to six miles. He was supremely noticeable as he sailed by in his knee breeches, wide-brimmed hat and Norfolk jacket. For wood-chopping, to the delight of local children, he appeared helmeted. A bright mackintosh sometimes illuminated him at night.

He had some funny ideas too. When invited to present a prize at the village school for the best-conducted boy or girl, he suggested starting a rival prize for the worst-conducted boy or girl, 'and we will watch their careers and then find out which really turns out best'. After returning from South Africa, he came up with a notion that all the villagers should dance to the hymns in church and add to their repertoire 'O, You Must be a Lover of the Lord': he actually gave a demonstration for them in the street.

Then there was the rubbish dump a mile or so south of his house where the Wheathampstead refuse was deposited. His campaign to reclaim this acreage, which vented its poisonous gases through a layer of old trays, perambulators, bicycle wheels, umbrella frames and hovering flies, was sustained over ten years. In 1931 he informed the District Council that he had recently been cruising in the Mediterranean 'where I was very strongly reminded of the dump by the fumes of the island volcano of Stromboli'. Eventually, in 1932, changes were made and four years later Shaw received an enormous green apple that had grown from a tree on the site. 'I swallowed some of it before I was told what it was,' he wrote. 'I shall never be the same man again; but Mrs Shaw rather liked it.'

This was the bitter taste of success – success delayed too long. Would it have tasted sweeter, could he have achieved more, had he been capable of campaigning differently? The trouble was he seemed so strange to ordinary people. He had 'a funny way of expressing himself,' a fellow-villager objected after hearing him lecture for the local Women's Institute on 'How to Quarrel Properly'. It didn't sound like proper quarrelling at all. And he was so unpredictable. It was disconcerting for the chemist to be invited to 'try out' some of his bottles of medicine on himself so that his customers could witness how they worked; or for other villagers when greeting him in the street with a 'How are you?' to be answered: 'At my age, Sir, you are either well or dead.' You never knew where you were with such a person.

He had been living at Ayot now some thirty years. He was invariably courteous, but 'remote as a god'. And, like a god, he seemed made of mystifying contradictions. Why would someone rumoured to be an atheist contribute so generously to the cost of repairing the roof of the parish church, pay for the renovation of the organ, and keep up what he called his 'pew-rent' to the church's funds? And why would someone who attacked standard education for children arrange at his own expense to put Vitaglass into the school's windows? Finally, why did he keep so quiet about these things when he was well known to be a colossal publicity seeker?

There were various answers. According to the apiarist, a diffident man who came to give a hand with the bees, he seemed 'nervous and shy if anything'. To a local joker he appeared 'the greatest leg-puller the world has ever known'. And it was obvious to the Conservative party agent that he was no more a socialist than the man in the moon. 'Politics was not in his line,' said the barber who cut his hair.

But on one point there was general agreement: he had natural good manners. He 'made you feel you were his equal,' said the organist; he was 'prepared to engage in conversation on my level,' said the oculist; 'he always put you completely at your ease,' said the landowner. But few of them would really claim to know him. 'If you ignored Mr Shaw he took more notice of you than if you didn't,' recalled Mrs Harding. And Mr Williams observed that he was easier with children and animals. 'He always stopped and spoke to my little dog, Judy,' said Mrs Hinton to whom he did not speak much. 'He always talked to my children as an equal,' said another villager. Each year he sent the headmistress of the school a cheque to be spent on sweets. She would pass the money over to the village shop and the children were allowed to get their sweets, without paying, to a maximum of one shilling each.

'He never talked about his plays or anything like that,' one villager gratefully remembered. This was a mercy because, though they all accepted him as a great playwright, practically no one had actually seen his plays. It was a wonder he continued writing them. At the rate he was going he would soon ruin what reputation he had left. But he gave no sign of stopping. It must have been the love of money-making, people thought, that kept him working. His hairdresser did not think much of him as a dramatist; and in the view of Jisbella Lyth, the village post-mistress, some of his work 'lacked suspense'.

Mrs Lyth was a widow. She had started her career as a kennel-maid and, after some adventurous travelling, returned to England where in 1931 she and her husband took over the post office at Ayot. Almost immediately Mr Lyth had died of a heart attack in the garden. 'Oh! What a glorious death to die,' G.B.S. complimented her. 'I hope I die like that in my garden underneath the stars.' 'Yes sir,' Mrs Lyth replied, 'but not at fifty-four, surely.' On leaving, Shaw said: 'I hope we shall have you here in Ayot for many years.'

And they did. 'Mr Shaw wrote personally to me for every batch of stamps he needed,' Mrs Lyth recorded over twenty years later. ' . . . I've sold almost all those letters . . . I believe he meant them to be a sort of legacy to me.'

Shaw let his imagination play on this relationship. During January 1933, while steaming along between the Red Sea and the Indian Ocean, he wrote the first draft of a Comedietta for Two Voices in Three Conversations which he initially called *The Red Sea*. He had developed a habit of labelling his characters with sequences of letters, from *A* onwards for the males, and *Z* backwards for the females. He needed only two letters, *A* and *Z*, for this short play and when he completed the last draft that summer, changing its title to *Village Wooing*, he kept these letters in place of names.

'I do not see myself as the Man,' he told Lillah McCarthy: 'he is intended as a posthumous portrait of Lytton Strachey.' *A* represents the side of Shaw that most closely approximated to Strachey – a man of letters as opposed to a political writer. As for *Z*, she is not Charlotte but an approximation of Jisbella Lyth. 'Many's the time he's helped me with my crossword puzzles,' she said. Shaw's alphabetical characters may derive in part from the lettering of these puzzles, but the effect is to give general application to their ordinariness. They are any one and every one of us.

In the First Conversation on board the pleasure ship *Empress of Patagonia*, 'a literary looking pale gentleman under forty in green spectacles, a limp black beard, and a tropical suit of white silk' is crustily anxious not to be disturbed by *Z*, 'a young woman, presentable but not aristocratic, who is bored with her book'. *A* is an isolated intellectual obliged for financial reasons to write the popular 'Marco Polo' series of guidebooks; *Z*, who insists on interrupting his work with her life story, is the daughter of a 'man of letters' – a postman – who is using the money she has won in a newspaper competition to see the world. The Second Conversation takes place in a village shop and post office on the Wiltshire Downs where *Z* is putting through telephone messages. *A* enters as a customer on a hiking holiday, but does not recognize *Z*. She describes their cruise as having destroyed her romantic illusions of the world (partly created by

A's books). But in half an hour it is *A* who has surprisingly been persuaded to give up the occupation of literary gentleman and buy the village shop. In the Third Conversation *A* has been the shop's proprietor for three months and learnt more than he had over three years at Oxford. *Z*, who is working as his assistant, replies that he still has more to learn since the shop does not earn enough to keep three. The play ends with the Rector's wife, telephoning for vegetables, being asked by *Z* to fetch the Rector as she wants to put up the marriage banns.

Village Wooing is a celebration of change. The first conversation is ostensibly between an intellectual and a simpleton; the second is between a gentleman and a villager; and the third between an employer and employee. In all three scenes Shaw is demonstrating the need to break down these academic, class and economic barriers to change.

He is also speculating on change within himself. What might have happened if 'some habits [that] lie too deep to be changed' could be changed after all and, unlike Professor Higgins, the 'Complete Outsider' at ease only with the mighty dead could 'change my nature' and feel at home with ordinary living people?

*

Village Wooing encapsulates many Shavian themes and obsessions from phonetics to the Life Force, and forms a miniature pendant to *Man and Superman* and *Pygmalion*. The other play he composed at this time, *On the Rocks*, is a political fable in *The Apple Cart* line and 'a coda to *Heartbreak House*'.

The time is 'The Present' – still the Depression. Shaw takes us to the Cabinet Room at 10 Downing Street, and keeps us there throughout the two long acts of his play. Governing 'within democratic limits' the genial Prime Minister, Sir Arthur Chavender, presides over a dictatorship of democracy. 'I cannot go faster than our voters will let me,' he explains. The result is that the 'country isn't governed', his wife points out: 'it just slummocks along anyhow.'

Sir Arthur Chavender is an empty cavernous man who epitomizes the change wrought in Ramsay MacDonald by parliamentary life, as well as the change Shaw feared had taken place in himself. 'I make speeches,' he says: 'that is the business of a politician.' In the Shavian analysis, orators had once been powerful because, in their inspired utterances, they caught the spirit of the times. But the frivolity of public opinion turned these men and women of words into the exploiters of people's fears and prejudices.

Sir Arthur is responding to the unemployment crisis by preparing a soothing oration about the sanctity of family life. Shaw accompanies the rhetorical composition of this speech with interruptions from the Prime Minister's own family whose uncontrollable bickering (like the uncaring sounds from Sonny's Dublin home) gives the lie to every melodious phrase.

Sir Arthur is an emblem of the times. He has piloted not only England but himself on to the rocks. His wife, who sees that he will soon have a nervous breakdown, makes him promise to see a strange lady doctor who then mysteriously appears, in ghostly robes, near the end of the first act. This Lady Oracle, who was modelled by Shaw on the founder of Christian Science, Mary Baker Eddy, and influenced by Lady Astor, is a ghost from the future, a healer as well as a messenger of death.

In the unwritten interlude between the two acts, Sir Arthur passes three or four months at this lady's sanatorium in the Welsh mountains. 'It's amazing,' exclaims the Chief Commissioner of Police Sir Broadfoot Basham at the beginning of the second act. 'I could have sworn that if there was a safe man in England that could be trusted to talk and say nothing, to thump the table and do nothing, Arthur Chavender was that man. Whats happened to him?' What has happened is that he has been resurrected as a born-again Shavian. *On the Rocks* is Shaw's version of Malory's *Morte D'Arthur*, with Avalon (the Celtic Isle of the Blest) transposed into the Welsh sanatorium and the legendary Round Table remodelled as an imposing Cabinet table. Sir Arthur himself is a Once and Future Prime Minister and the second act his promised second coming in the hour of England's need. To lift the country off the rocks he brings with him a programme of regeneration which gathers together many of the political remedies G.B.S. had been picking up and putting out during his world travels.

The programme contains subtle ingredients to appeal to each section of English society. Since everyone approves the items which favour his own interests and regards all other items as caprices that will never be implemented, there seems to be some chance that the National Government will be able to introduce this programme by means of parliamentary democracy. But the plan is shipwrecked by the coming together of two political extremes: the bedrock of the far left and the rocklike uncompromising right.

The symmetry of *On the Rocks* comes from the attraction of opposites. The Duke is attracted to the factory girl; the Prime Minister's son is determined to marry a trade unionist and his daughter has sworn to marry a poor man (though she actually becomes engaged to an aristocrat who, as a member of the Labour deputation, dresses and talks as she imagines poor men dress and talk). The Prime Minister himself is married to a shadowy woman who apparently has no enthusiasm either for politics or for her children: her boredom with public life and inability to 'take an interest in people' derive from Lucinda Elizabeth Shaw's indifference to both Sonny and G.B.S. She is a complex woman nevertheless, capable of manipulating the plot and preparing the way for her husband's political illumination.

The dramatic opinions that fill the Cabinet Room are the voices that reverberate in Shaw's mind. The play exhibits Shaw's 'anarchic comic gift doing spirited battle with his authoritarian opinions,' Irving Wardle has observed, 'and the separate factions are orchestrated with effortless fluency and the ability to spring surprises'. The virtues of law and order match themselves against the vices of a police power state. 'I wonder should I find any bombs in your house if I searched it,' the Chief Commissioner of Police asks the elderly East End socialist, Hipney, who knowingly answers: 'You would if you put them there first, Sir Broadfoot. What good would a police chief be if he couldnt find anything he wanted to find?' The paradox of power, according to Shaw, is that *anciens régimes* are defended by oppressed and oppressors alike. 'Chained dogs are the fiercest guardians of property; and those who attempt to unchain them are the first to get bitten.'

After its opening in London Shaw reported a 'unanimously good press (for once)'. The *Morning Post* praised him for having 'made politics amusing'; *The Times* applauded his refusal to be canonized after *Saint Joan*; and Kingsley Martin in the *New Statesman & Nation* made the crucial observation that G.B.S. 'warns rather than advocates. Make up your mind, he says, that Parliament, as you know it, cannot be the instrument of salvation. Devise a constitution which gives scope to personal and national loyalty, but do not imagine that it can succeed without transformation of the social order.'

The play was to retain and renew its topicality. When it was revived at the Mermaid Theatre in the 1970s, Robert Cushman in the *Observer* called it 'quite the most topical play in London'; J. W. Lambert in the *Sunday Times* wrote of his 'astonishment at how little things, and people, have changed since 1933'; Irving Wardle in *The Times* pointed in detail to 'the numerous parallels between the Depression years and the economic ills of the 1970s'; and the critic J. C. Trewin summed up: 'What appeals to us now is the prophetic quality. The date is 1933, yet the dramatist could well have been thinking of 1975.' Again, when it was brought back at Chichester during the Falklands War in the 1980s, critics remarked on the play's contemporaneity – as if time had stopped and was pointing for ever at 'the Present'. *On the Rocks* seemed 'topical when I read it 10 years ago,' wrote Robert Cushman in the summer of 1982, 'prescient when the Mermaid staged it a couple of years after that, and positively uncanny at

Chichester now'. But the critic Benedict Nightingale, referring to the 'peculiarly bloodthirsty' Preface, described a performance of the play in 1982 as being 'precisely the sort of thing decent people should *not* have resurrected at a time like this, when unemployment is once again rife, party alignments confused, and parliamentary democracy itself under attack from both right and left'.

The writer of the play subverts the writer of the Preface. The artist in Shaw cannot accept the Shavian polemicist. He cannot abandon conscience for efficient action. 'I'm not the man for the job,' Chavender admits. ' . . . And I shall hate the man who will carry it through for his cruelty and the desolation he will bring on us and our like.'

But why should such desolation be necessary? Shaw believed that though Britain might be good at finding leaders in wartime when socialism advanced, her politicians were uninspired in peacetime, and the country instinctively felt the need for a peacetime fighter, whatever party he or she might lead. The Cabinet meetings in both *The Apple Cart* and *On the Rocks* 'are something Shaw *had* to give us some day,' wrote Eric Bentley, ' – a rounded picture of the political madhouse which directs our destinies'. These two plays are less surreal than his other plays of this period. The crash of breaking windows at the end of *On the Rocks*, like the bomb explosion near the end of *Heartbreak House* (or the Day of Judgment in *The Simpleton of the Unexpected Isles* and the planetary disaster in the last act of *Geneva*), are all symbols, as Eric Bentley indicates, of the atomic age and the global threat to our environment, as well as the anticipation of Hitler's Germany.

2

UNDERGOING A SEA CHANGE

Playwriting is becoming a Platonic exercise with me.
Shaw to Leonora Ervine (12 May 1934)

By the mid-1930s Shaw seemed to have become again what he had been in the 1890s: a versatile composer of experimental play-texts. *Village Wooing* received its world première at the Little Theater in Dallas, Texas, and was first presented in Britain by his fellow-dramatist Christopher Fry at the Pump Room in Tunbridge Wells. *On the Rocks* waited until the summer of 1938 before reaching New York when it was brought in by the government-sponsored Federal Theater which took over Shaw's plays from the Theatre Guild. In Britain the play was given its world première at the unfashionable Winter Garden Theatre in London where it was presented by Charles Macdona.

The Macdona Players, with Esmé Percy as their director, 'led the forlorn hope of advanced drama in England' between the wars and toured many of Shaw's plays through Britain, round the Continent (staging the long-banned *Mrs Warren's Profession* in Paris in 1925) and in South Africa, India and the Far East. *On the Rocks* was the only world première produced by Charles Macdona. Shaw had wanted Esmé Percy to direct the play, 'but now there is a nice man, a man G.B.S. likes nearly as well,' Charlotte wrote, '& I hope, later, G.B.S. will throw a good deal of work on to him'. This 'nice man' was Lewis Casson. He had worked with Shaw when directing the London production of *Village Wooing* which starred Casson's wife, Sybil Thorndike, as Z. Shaw enjoyed interfering with his own plays. He 'had a disgraceful appetite for "getting the laughs",' recalled Stephen Murray who played the part of the Prime Minister in the Malvern production of *On the Rocks* in 1936.

He also appeared a more dictatorial figure than in the Vedrenne–Barker days, talking more and listening less. He had been 'all eyes and ears,' remembered Cedric Hardwicke when rehearsing *Back to Methuselah*. Now his eyes and ears had dimmed, but not his opinions. According to Edith Evans, he was getting old-fashioned. One of the Macdona Players recalled that he made 'no attempt to help one to gain an imaginative feeling for the character and situations. Instead he went through the part line by line instructing me how he wanted every sentence emphasized and pronounced in his own, idiosyncratic Anglo-Irish accent.' He insisted on placing his dominant speaking character well up-stage to get absolute clarity, grouped the other actors decoratively round and gave a highly coloured orchestration to the vocal tempo and pitch. 'You've got to go from line to line, quickly and swiftly, never stop the flow of the lines, never stop,' he told Ralph Richardson when rehearsing *Arms and the Man* at the Old Vic. 'It's one joke after another, it's a firecracker. Always reserve the acting for underneath the spoken word. It's a musical play, a knockabout musical comedy.' Richardson remembered him as 'a wonderfully courteous, wonderfully polite man, I think perhaps the most polite man I've met in my life'. And John Gielgud, who played the Emperor in *Androcles and the Lion* 'with a red wig, a lecherous red mouth, and a large emerald through which I peered lasciviously', remembered that the cast was 'so amused that we forgot to be alarmed' when G.B.S. turned up to read his play to them. There were still characteristic outbursts of generosity. 'I dare say your words are as good as mine,' he told Phyllis Nielson-Terry who kept fluffing her lines during a revival of *Candida*.

On the day of the final rehearsal of *On the Rocks*, Shaw came into his own. After a morning 'word-rehearsal . . . which lasted until 3.p.m.,' wrote Stephen Murray. 'There was a photo-call at six, which Shaw insisted on attending. Dress-rehearsal at eight, and the curtain went up on it with Shaw on-stage. He never sat down for four hours, turning everything upside down and this way and that. At midnight he gave us vigorous notes for twenty minutes and then walked home. He had his eightieth birthday that week.'

As the opening night of *On the Rocks* approached, a current of excitement went through the Winter Garden Theatre. It was like the old days. 'An extraordinary evening,' Charlotte wrote. 'The way that enormous audience took the points and flung themselves into the whole thing was startling. I never met anything like it before.' Macdona and Shaw had experimented by charging 'popular prices' – between one and five shillings a seat, which was half the regular cost. They needed to fill the large out-of-the-way theatre to keep the play profitably running – and after the huge first night success and excellent notices it seemed they might succeed. The fans came over and over again, but the general playgoing public seemed to agree with Shaw's Prime Minister – 'This is not the time to talk about economic difficulties: we're up to the neck in them' – and stayed away. Beatrice Webb, who went to the theatre a fortnight after the play had opened, reported: 'the hall cold and cheerless, the cheap stalls not completely occupied, the gallery practically empty, a badly tuned gramophone playing during the one interval, did not constitute an attractive setting.'

After forty-one performances the shutters went up towards the end of January 1935. 'My popularity does not increase,' Shaw wrote to his publisher. But then he had never counted on commercial success. 'I shall not take any trouble to have them performed,' he had assured Trebitsch, 'but publish them in the same volume as *Too True*.' Early in 1934, 27,000 copies of this book containing *On the Rocks*, *Village Wooing* and *Too True to be Good* were published in Britain and the United States, and two years later it was joined in the Standard Edition by another volume, *The Simpleton, the Six, and the Millionairess*, containing the last three plays from his world travels.

*

'The greatest fact of your lifetime is that nothing has happened in the twentieth century except the impossible,' Shaw wrote to St John Ervine in 1932. ' . . . nothing has succeeded like impossibility.' *The Simpleton of the Unexpected Isles* is Shaw's enhancement of 'impossibility' far-advanced into some unspecified time he calls 'Approaching Judgment Day'.

The Unexpected Isles have recently risen out of the Pacific Ocean (where Shaw completed the play) and been occupied as a Crown Colony of the British Empire. In the three short scenes of the Prologue, past, present and future are brought together. A modern young woman arrives at the emigration office without her papers but with the catch-phrase (which becomes a theme of the play) 'Let life come to you'. She marches the Emigration Officer out of his office to show her round the island, leaving his clerk alone. This shabby clerk is recognizable partly as Shaw's father. Life has never come to him. He begins singing 'Rule Britannia', *blows his brains out and falls dead* – the fifth such suicide that month.

Meanwhile the Young Woman and Emigration Officer have progressed to Scene II – 'a grassy cliff top overhanging the sea' reminiscent of the Dover Cliffs in Act IV scene vi of *King Lear* where Gloucester, Edgar and the King himself meet within a foot of the extreme verge, and trifle with despair. The Emigration Officer too has reached despair: 'If you hadnt come in this morning I'd have done myself in,' he tells the Young Woman who is amazed that he should feel so wretched in this 'earthly paradise'. The explanation is given by a dark native Priest who rises into view up a concealed cliff path. The Emigration Officer, he says, comes from a country whose inhabitants 'die from their own hands to escape what they call the horrors' when 'in the midst of life and loveliness' they feel that only man is vile. The Emigration Officer, determined to go over the fearful cliffs, continues bending tremendously on the edge – until the Priest shoots out a foot against his posterior and he is sent catapulting into the sea. The Young Woman is appalled, but, as in *King Lear*, the cliffs are not simply what we have been led to expect; they mark the line of redemption as well as the abyss of death. 'There are nets below,' the Priest explains to the Young Woman as they advance into the third scene.

This is set in a temple made out of a shelf of rock halfway down the cliff, reminiscent of the Skelligs off the south-west coast of Ireland. Upon this cathedral of the sea, and representing the coming together of East and West, Shaw imposed the gigantic images of Oriental deities he had seen on Elephanta Island, off the coast of Bombay. The Priest and Priestess, perfectly attuned to their paradisiacal surroundings, treat visitors from the old country with something of the backward-looking contempt that British imperialists have treated natives of their annexed territories. 'I find these heathen idolaters very trying,' sighs the Priestess after encountering an affected English lady tourist, guidebook in hand. This turns out to be Lady Farwaters, the wife of Sir Charles Farwaters, a man of pleasant aristocratic appearance who owes a little to Shaw's Fabian friend Sydney Olivier.

What is to be done with such specimens? The Priest and Priestess decide they might be used in a eugenic experiment blending the flesh and spirit of East and West, and they all retire into a magical cavern (like the Abode of Love from *Too True to be Good*).

The Emigration Officer *rises into view in a spotless white robe* looking *pale* but *regenerated*. Writing of Shaw in the 1920s T. E. Lawrence had noticed 'some sea-change [that] has come over G.B.S. in the last ten years'. It is a sea-change, compressed into ten minutes, that Shaw has granted his Emigration Officer. Now 'the tables are turned', and just when the Young Woman thinks that life is 'coming a bit too thick for me', he rushes her screaming to the edge of the rock shelf and hurls her over. So ends a Prologue remarkable for its surplus of action over talk.

In a letter to Trebitsch, Shaw called *The Simpleton* 'an ultra-fantastic oriental modern (or futurist) play . . . contents indescribable'. With a peculiar blend of fantasy and satire, the two acts of the play survey the delights and drawbacks of the pantomime Utopia that arise from the Prologue. The first act takes up the story about twenty years later and carries it on through the experiences of an accidental traveller to this Otherworld: a young, highly credulous clergyman who, like the Elderly Gentleman in *Back to Methuselah*, gives an ironic view of Shaw's own pilgrim's progress from the perspective of the future. This simpleton has been kidnapped by pirates at Weston Super Mare and forced to sail round the world, making them ill with laughter by giving Church of England sermons. They are like the ex-criminals of Captain Brassbound's crew and use the clergyman to make people believe they are respectable. And Shaw uses them, the stock-in-trade crew of island litera-ture, to echo Captain Shotover's warning in *Heartbreak House* against capitalism's ship of fools and to remind us of its stranded destination in *On the Rocks*.

Suddenly released and set ashore, the simpleton wanders through the Unexpected Isles and comes to a terraced garden overlooking the port of Good Adventure. He is lost in enchantment. 'It's like the Garden of Eden: I should like to stay here forever.' The garden is given a hieratic aspect by four Oriental shrines at the corners of a raised flowerbed. As he gazes at the two magically beautiful girl-goddesses and two wonderful boy-gods, the simpleton's heart is filled with longing. 'How I wish you were alive and I could kiss your living lips,' he addresses the fair goddess. But in this wonderland wishes come true. The stage directions tell us what then happens: '*He does so and finds that she is alive. She smiles as her eyes turn bewitchingly towards him.*' In this variation of the Pygmalion legend, both the two goddesses and the two gods reveal themselves as four children from the Prologue.

'We formed a family of six parents,' explains Sir Charles Farwaters, who is now Governor of the Isles. His wife has changed from an affected tourist to a matronly silhouette of Charlotte Shaw; while the Emigration Officer is transformed into a *very different man, disciplined, responsible and well groomed* ' – and married (a distant image of the Webbs' marriage) to the Young Woman who is *still very much her old self* '. The other two parents are Pra and Prola, the Priest and Priestess.

But there is something lacking in the constitution of these four super-children. They are all, like Hitler's Aryan ideal, physically perfect, but they cannot muster 'between the whole four of them a scrap of moral conscience'. They are the embodiment of art for art's sake. From the idea of loving one another the superchildren have advanced to the ideal of being one another.

Shaw's Garden of Eden is unclouded by any evil. No serpent slides through the undergrowth, no original sin flowers in the grounds: this is a paradise without demons. We are shown a pure fairy story, like an adolescent's daydream, that joins Oriental fable to allegorical romance, and reflects Shaw's view of Edgar Allan Poe's poetic principle. 'His kingdom is not of this world,' he had written of Poe. ' . . . Life cannot give you what he gives you except through fine art.' Shaw's Unexpected Isles are located near *Eureka*, the prose poem in which Poe sought to relate poetic intuition to scientific thought. The first act is perhaps the nearest Shaw came to writing what is apparently art for art's sake in the theatre. The mood is celestially light – until the ominous ending in *black darkness*.

This eugenic experiment profoundly agitates the rest of the world. As their name suggests, the Unexpected Isles are islands of relativity, and the theory of relative values once formulated in Poe's *Eureka* and now per-fected by Einstein, is violently opposed by the fundamentalist forces of the contending mainlands. The simpleton learns what Shaw himself has learnt from his early search for love. 'It is a terrible thing to be loved,' he says. ' . . . Nothing human is good enough to be loved.'

With Act II comes Judgment Day, but it is 'hardly what we were led to expect'. The Angel, who has some difficulty in flying, apologizes: 'I am afraid you will find it very dull.' Judgment turns out to be the valuation of what the Young Woman and the clerk had discussed in the Emigration office: 'Dispensables and indispensables'. Those who wish to emigrate to God's Empire must be of value to the future. Others, the Angel off-handedly remarks, 'will simply disappear'. It is *Surrealpolitik*.

The simpleton finally learns what Shaw wants his audience to learn: that we create a fool's paradise by falling in love with our ideals. The quartet of exquisite superchildren, who recall the puppets created by the fanatical scientist Pygmalion in *Back to Methuselah*, have been the illusory ideals of Love, Pride, Heroism and Empire. Maya is love itself, the emanation of Shaw's young actress 'Mollytompkins' on her enchanted Isola, and the apparition created by the simpleton's inexpressible longing. 'I held Maya in my arms. She promised to endure for ever; and suddenly there was nothing in my arms.' When the simpleton ceases to believe in them, these ideals vanish so completely that no one can remember their names or even how many of them there seemed to be. The simpleton, too, vanishes back into his real self, an apprehensive clergyman nick-named Iddy who, released from the island spell, will go homing back to England.

The world advances to the foreground of the play at its conclusion. 'There is no Country of the Expected. The Unexpected Isles are the whole world.' It is a world of miracles but not of ideological Utopias and Millennia. 'We are not here to fulfil prophecies and fit ourselves into puzzles,' says Prola. The heaven on earth that Shaw has raised at the beginning has dissolved at the end but there is no despair. Left alone on stage Pra and Prola unite in a hymn to unexpectedness: 'Let it come.'

The Simpleton is the deepest and happiest of Shaw's fantasies, 'openly oriental, hieratic and insane' as he called it himself. This magical gathering on an island, with its dreams and illusions, and its departure to the real world after the political lessons have been delivered, is reminiscent of *The Tempest*.

Yet though there were plenty of literary signposts in these Unexpected Isles (to Coleridge, W. S. Gilbert, Goethe, Voltaire, and the Book of Revelation among others), though it drew on the prodigious literature of Utopias as well as on those romances and adventures which had taught Shaw how to dream as a boy, and though there were connections also with the popular Oriental extravaganzas that had played in Dublin and London theatres during the late nineteenth century, as well as with the fabulous *Chu-Chin-Chow* in the Great War, drama critics reacted to *The Simpleton* as if it were like nothing else.

Part of this confusion arose from the publication of Shaw's discon-certing Preface. But there were other difficulties too. Some of the sexual scenes shocked American audiences 'even in these days of theatrical impro-prieties'. In Austria, the play's strange divinities and eugenic impurities worried the censors, and it was banned. In Germany, where audiences burst spontaneously into cheering at such statements as Vashti's 'Obedi-ence is freedom from the intolerable fatigue of thought', the Nazi newspaper *Hamburger Tageblatt* commented that 'the applause of those eternally behind the times neither surprised nor frightened us . . . And just as little can Shaw upset us.'

But he had upset Stanbrook Abbey. Plainly the play was tinged with heresy. Sometimes Sister Laurentia wondered whether Brother Bernard really knew the difference between Truth and Error; then she would recollect that of course he must do. She had instructed him herself. So when his own Day of Judgment came round 'you will not be able to plead ignorance as the excuse of the evil that your books may do,' she warned him. 'I wish we could take Laurentia to the east,' Shaw confided to Sydney Cockerell, 'and make her pray in all the Divine Mother's temples.'

Shaw wished he could take all the directors and designers of his play to the East. In the West, the confidence of theatre directors was to be long undermined by Edmund Wilson's influential judgement, delivered in the late 1930s: '*The Simpleton of the Unexpected Isles* is the only play of the author's which has ever struck me as silly.' It *is* silly; but in such 'silliness', though it may be traced to a psychological weakness, lies Shaw's genius. 'Why don't you do "The Simpleton of the Unexpected Isles"?' he asked William Armstrong at the Liverpool Repertory Theatre in 1937. 'It is a lovely play; and you can let yourself go on the production.' But repertory theatres had settled into a routine of some dozen Shavian comedies, histories and pleasant plays.

*

Early in 1917, while joy-riding in France, Shaw had filled his 'last evening stretch of the journey by inventing a play on the Rodin theme of The Burgesses of Calais, which,' he told readers of the *Daily Chronicle*, 'like the play about the Rheims Virgin, I have never written down and perhaps never will'. What Quicherat's *Procès* supplied for his *Saint Joan*, Froissart's *Chronicles* now provided for *The Six of Calais*. In Froissart's story, Edward III agreed to lift the eleven-month Siege of Calais by the English in 1347 on condition that six starving hostages surrendered themselves to be hanged, wearing sackcloth and halters and carrying the keys of the town. Rodin's sculpture group (a duplicate of which stands at the Victoria Tower Gardens, Westminster) 'commemorates the bravery and selflessness – and misery – of the six burgesses who submitted themselves to Edward's humiliating conditions,' wrote Stanley Weintraub, 'and immortalizes the wretched men, half-naked and wearing halters at the moment of their surrender'.

But Froissart was an 'absurd old snob' and had 'got it all wrong'. Rodin had cast one of the burghers in an attitude that suggested a diehard even more extreme than the King. All that remained for Shaw to do was 'to correct Froissart's follies and translate Rodin into words'. In his comic-strip version of history, the mulish burgher and the donkey of a King ('Neddy') confront each other, sense an animal bond between them; and the play ends with a bray of hilarious laughter in which everyone joins.

He wanted to create a nursery world where cruelties arose, not from evil, but from the whims and reflexes of bored and frightened children. Like an imaginary entry in a child's encyclopaedia, complete with a King from A. A. Milne, this painless lesson shows us that the first step towards maturity is to cease playing at being adults and admit our childhood status.

*

'I was like a princess in a fairy tale,' exclaims Shaw's athletic millionairess, Epifania Ognisanti di Parerga. In a reversal of Portia's test from *The Merchant of Venice*, Epifania's late father, 'the greatest man in the world', had made her promise that whenever a man proposed marriage to her, she was to 'give him one hundred and fifty pounds, and tell him that if within six months he had turned that hundred and fifty pounds into fifty thousand, I was his'. Epifania has been led into an unsatisfactory marriage with a magnificent empty-headed sportsman, Alastair Fitz-fassenden, who won her by a mixture of pure luck and criminal 'kiting' – thieves' slang for a system of speedily raising money on false credit (later to be recycled from Shaw's play into Salman Rushdie's novel *The Satanic Verses*).

In Act I Epifania is making her will before committing suicide. She recounts this story to her solicitor whose office becomes filled with the dramatis personae – her estranged husband and his demure girlfriend as well as Epifania's own bland admirer – while the smart young solicitor vainly attempts to take instructions. His attitude to these clients is Shaw's attitude to the world: an incredulous striving to discover what advice he should give.

In the second act, which takes place that evening at a dismal riverside inn, the Pig and Whistle, Epifania throws her parasitical admirer over (over her shoulder, downstairs, and into hospital) and sets her cap at a serious-looking, middle-aged Egyptian doctor who keeps a clinic for penni-less Mahometan refugees. He has made his mother a solemn financial promise that forms the counterpart to Epifania's vow to her father. So a contract is struck between them: Epifania, 'the plutocrat of plutocrats', sets out to live for six months on his 35 shillings, while the doctor resigns himself to losing her £150.

Shaw's fairy-tale is a treasure hunt which begins next morning at a basement sweatshop along the Commercial Road where Epifania sets out to remake her fortune. 'The sweater and his wife speak Whitechapel Cockney,' Shaw wrote to the producer Matthew Forsyth in 1936. '. . . There is not a gleam of fun in these two poor devils.' This scene is unique in Shaw's plays and at the end, when Epifania has used her managerial genius to take over the business, the stupefied sweater rubs his eyes. 'It seems to me like a sort of dream,' he says – and we are about to re-enter Shaw's dream world.

His Cinderella soon wins her Egyptian Prince. Like the miller's daughter, she has learnt Rumpelstiltskin's secret of how to spin straw into gold; like King Midas she can turn everything, even her emotions, into money. Beginning as a scullery maid at the Pig and Whistle, Epifania has transformed the place within five months into an attractive riverside inn and appointed herself its new proprietor. 'It was cruel for us; but we couldnt deny that she was always right,' acknowledges the son of the previous owner, who is now its manager. ' . . . My father had a stroke and wont last long, I'm afraid. And my mother has gone a bit silly. Still, it was best for them; and they have all the comforts they care for.'

As in the first act, the characters assemble on stage round Epifania. The Egyptian doctor has given away his £150 to a widow whose husband had omitted to patent a successful invention – but this is interpreted by Epifania as a profitable retrospective investment, which meets her father's stipulation (and provides a nice example of Shaw's belief that logic is merely a device for getting what you want). The doctor too gets what he wants. He has fallen in love with Epifania's pulse 'like a slow sledge hammer . . . it is a pulse in a hundred thousand.' The play ends with the solicitor finally taking instructions.

Epifania is a monetarist heroine and the genius of capitalism. She dominates the play much as Undershaft dominated the action of *Major Barbara*. Shaw had been forced to rework the last act of *Major Barbara* and, for similar reasons, he offered a highly implausible alternative ending to *The Millionairess*. Here the happy couple contemplate going to Russia but decide instead to 'make the British Empire a Soviet republic'. Shaw was following the advice he had fathered on Henry James over his play *The Saloon*, as well as responding to those Marxist critics who 'since virtually the beginning of his career,' the critic Bernard Dukore wrote, had been urging him to 'provide an upbeat ending'. In Shaw's version for 'countries with Communist sympathies', Epifania's assets (not her life) will be liquidated, and her abilities converted into worthwhile social and political power. In this never-performed alternative Shaw abandons the last illusion of reality and floats his make-believe like a fragile soap-bubble in the air – without trying to satisfy his reader's credulity or appease his scepticism.

Epifania is an amalgam of every powerful woman Shaw had known. Though the cocks may crow, it is the hens that lay the eggs. 'People will say you are the millionairess,' he had written to Nancy Astor, ' – an awful, impossible woman.' The short third act in the Commercial Road uses some of Beatrice Webb's experiences in a tailor's sweatshop in London's East End; and the title itself is a reference to his ironic description of Charlotte at the time of their courtship and marriage – 'my Irish millionairess'.

Shaw's attitude to this superwoman is conveyed by his Egyptian doctor: 'You are a terrible woman; but I love your pulse.' Here is the irresistible beat of the Life Force reduced by capitalism to the rhythmic rise and fall of market forces. 'I have to take the world as I find it,' Epifania claims. To which the doctor replies: 'The wrath of Allah shall overtake those who leave the world no better than they found it.' In *The Millionairess* a great princess in prison lies. 'She has no sense of humor,' Shaw told Edith Evans. 'Except the solicitor, who is mildly amused at the follies of the others, everyone in the play is intensely in earnest.' Her tragedy lies both in the dissipation of her natural powers into pointless money-making and also in the fortress-like personality she shares with Shaw's mother which bars emotional relationships. G.B.S. knew her tragedy well. She is a person 'that no one can live with'.

'What makes the play rabidly distasteful is Shaw's patent admiration for the eroticism of wealth and power,' wrote Michael Billington in the *Guardian* after a revival of the play in 1988. This is much the same distaste felt by Beatrice Webb when she read the play in 1935 and saw in it a representation of her friend's 'admiration of what is *forceful*, however ugly and silly'. Unlike Shylock, humiliated at the end of *The Merchant of Venice*, or Volpone cast in irons at the end of Jonson's comedy, Epifania begins on the verge of suicide and ends triumphant.

'My third manner is going to be more trying than my second,' Shaw had predicted in a letter to J. C. Squire after the Great War; 'but then third manners always are.' His digressions and lapses into buffoonery had grown more frequent, his flights from reality more extreme. 'I was always in the classic tradition,' he explained. These plays depend for their effects upon the gargantuan acting tradition he had witnessed as a boy in nineteenth-century melodramas and music-hall entertainments. With their emphasis on vocal contrast, they all bear the marks of his musical knowledge. 'Opera taught me to shape my plays into recitatives, arias, duets, trios, ensemble finales, and bravura pieces,' he was to write towards the end of his life, 'to display the technical accomplishments of the executants.'

The Millionairess seemed an unlucky play for Shaw, but he continued to keep his eye out for the 'very vigorous actress' who could take on Epifania. 'The part requires just such a personality as Miss [Katharine] Hepburn,' he wrote to Lawrence Langner in 1940. 'Has she ever read the play?' In fact she had read it but decided she did not like it enough; then she read it again ten years later and persuaded the Theatre Guild in New York and Binkie Beaumont of Tennant Productions in London to produce it with her in the title role. Shaw had been dead for two years but, just as he 'had prophesied, Hepburn was superb in the part', recalled Lawrence Langner. This was the last new Shaw production by the Theatre Guild in New York and it played to packed houses. In London, too, it was welcomed with enthusiastic notices by critics unfamiliar with such prodigious acting. A young critic, Kenneth Tynan, describing it as 'that terrible hybrid, a didactic farce . . . written in the twilight of a civilization and of its author's life', and believing the part of Epifania to be 'nearly unactable', found himself carried away.

'Miss Hepburn took it, acted it, and found a triumph in it. She glittered like a bracelet thrown up at the sun; she was metallic, yet reminded us that metals shine and can also melt. Epifania clove to her, and she bestowed on the role a riotous elegance and a gift of tears . . . *The Millionairess* scores a bull's-eye on the target of her talents . . . in her last long speech, a defence of marriage and all the risks it implies, an urchin quaver invades the determination of her voice and coaxes the heart.'

3

SPONTANEOUS RESURRECTION

I cannot tell you the exact date of my death. It has not yet been settled.
Shaw to Hannen Swaffer (26 February 1938)

' . . . I dropped dead on the 24th Nov,' G.B.S. notified John Reith on 3 December 1934. The doctor had diagnosed a 'not serious' heart attack and Shaw slept continuously for almost three days and nights. It was 'the greatest pity,' he told his old friend Henry Salt 'that I revived like Lazarus. I was literally tired to death.'

It was a matter of Shavian pride to be sending Maynard Keynes within a week of his attack what Virginia Woolf was to call 'a long magnificently spry & juicy letter' done in his most breathtaking style with 'the whole of economics twiddled round on his finger'. Keynes, recognizing that 'the old gentleman is weak and ill', wondered why the great men of that generation went in for such stunts. Were these Shavian stage effects simply a box of cosmetics for colouring up morale as he grew out of date, or some acoustical gesture for catching the ear of the young? In the mid-1920s Virginia Woolf had sighed over her teenage nephews, Julian and Quentin Bell, for believing 'Bernard Shaw greater than Shakespeare'. By the mid-1930s Keynes was showing an 'unmitigated contempt,' Beatrice Webb noticed, 'for the Communist undergraduates'.

Beatrice and Sidney went up to London in the second week of January 1935 and found G.B.S. much recovered. But Charlotte lay ill in bed. Three doctors attended her, with a day nurse, a night nurse and a maid – 'yet she lives!' Shaw rejoiced. What would have happened to her had he died? 'The two old couples are each other's oldest friends,' Beatrice wrote in her diary, 'and we all dread the death of anyone of the quartet, and would feel responsible for the remaining partner.'

From the middle of the 1930s onwards Shaw struggled to reduce his volume of work. 'I Have Retired,' he insisted during a speech in the summer of 1936 at the People's Theatre, Newcastle. He did retire from the drudgery of directing his plays, but the bibliography of his writings lists thirty-seven contributions to the press that year; fifty-five in 1937; fifty-nine in 1938; and sixty-three in 1939. 'We cant take G.B.S. away from all his business & papers & interviews & usual occupations,' Charlotte admitted to Nancy Astor.

But how well was he writing? 'Give him a good situation, like Edward VIII's abdication, or the coronation of George VI, and his literary response is brilliant and wise, witty and worthwhile,' Beatrice Webb wrote in her diary. But she could not endure his late plays with all their slapstick and knockabout. Without this daily task of playwriting his life would be meaningless. 'There is no remedy for the defects of old age,' Beatrice concluded, ' – whether they take the form of continuous discomfort or poor quality of output – or both.'

But sometimes G.B.S. seemed to have found a remedy. The actress Irene Hentschel saw him entering the Globe Theatre in London at the end of 1936 'with the vigour of a hurricane'. Virginia Woolf too marvelled at his wires, his spring. 'What an efficient, adept, trained arch & darter!' she exclaimed. ' . . . And the hands flung out in gesture: he has the power to make the world his shape.' Visiting him in Whitehall Court, the Irish writer John Stewart Collis noticed how 'easy and ungrand' his manner still was. But he had grown terribly thin, his body supporting a white-bearded head 'like a long stem holding up a large flower'. Another Irish writer, the poet Brendan O'Byrne, watched him advancing along Pall Mall

'one long leg placed
Before the other as if he could – if he wished – so
Bestride the earth, his stout ash walking-stick
Striking the pavement before him as if
To teach it a lesson.'

Recently come over from Dublin and sleeping rough in the London streets, the young man

'had a hat I remember, and that
Is most important, for the whole point of this story is
That I raised my hat to Bernard Shaw, and he
Raised his hat to me.'

In such ways, for as long as possible, G.B.S. kept in touch with his own youth. 'But alas! we are *old*.' Old age brought the Shaws renewed problems. G.B.S. reckoned that 'the only way I can keep Charlotte up at present is by deciding that we are NOT going to do something'. Even so, she still fretted over his work and her own weakening ability to interrupt it. Each summer they would move to a country town hotel, usually by the sea, and declare themselves the better for it. 'We sleep like anything . . .'

When Beatrice had fallen ill earlier in the 1930s, Shaw arranged for £1,000 (equivalent to £29,000 in 1997) to be credited to Sidney's account at the Soviet Bank in London. 'We need, I think, have no scruple in accepting this most generous gift from my oldest friend,' Sidney reassured Beatrice who was then in a nursing home. In Sidney's letter to Shaw himself there is an unusual tremor of emotion. 'I am overwhelmed . . . It comes most timely to remove our anxieties [and] . . . as an immense relief to me,' he wrote. The Webbs and the Shaws continued their annual visits to each other's houses through most of the 1930s. In the summer of 1937 the Shaws went to Passfield and G.B.S. helped the Webbs with the proofs of their revised edition of *Soviet Communism* while Sidney helped the Shaws to redraft their wills. 'So continues the old unbroken comradeship in work, started forty-five years ago, between GBS and the Webbs,' observed Beatrice.

Though these were affectionate meetings, each one seemed to mark another stage on a downward journey. Early in the New Year, a few days after Beatrice's eightieth birthday, Sidney had a stroke. 'The inevitable has come,' Beatrice wrote in her diary. ' . . . So there he is lying in the bed . . . He will have care and love so long as I am strong enough to give it.' 'Sidney has given us rather a fright,' Shaw wrote to her, ' . . . we shouldnt do such things . . . we should arrange to die quietly in our beds of heart failure.'

Though he was able to read and follow conversations, Sidney remained a semi-invalid at Passfield, partially paralysed and with his speech impaired. 'I suppose it is best for you to be alone at Passfield with nobody to bother you, except your invalid,' Shaw wrote to Beatrice; 'but somehow it does not feel that way to us: the impulse to stand by is so strong that it needs an exercise of conscious reasoning to stifle it.'

'I dare say it's time for all us nineteenth century writers to clear out,' he was reported as saying when he learnt of Maxim Gorki's death. 'You'd better prepare my obituary,' he instructed the *New York Times*. In May 1938, he suddenly fainted under Charlotte's eyes. Sidney managed to send him one of his first short letters since his own illness. 'What a long life you and I have had, and done so much in it, with the aid of wifes!' But Charlotte found it almost impossible to aid him. He lay on a sofa claiming that he was curing himself by prolonged relaxation. 'I nearly went mad!' Charlotte protested.

He was diagnosed as suffering from pernicious anaemia. Until recently the treatment had been 'swallowing pounds of raw liver', as Gilbert Murray confirmed, 'but I think perhaps death is preferable to that'. A new remedy consisted of fifteen monthly injections of liver extract which he allowed the doctors 'to squirt' into 'my lumbar regions'. Almost at once the *Daily Express* reported 'G.B.S. Takes Meat'. 'I do not,' he answered, and he went on to reassure the *Vegetarian News* that 'My diet remains unchanged.' But he was not entirely happy. The liver extract had apparently set up a rejuvenated supply of red corpuscles, but 'my own view is that I am by nature a white-blooded man,' he confided to Henry Salt.

The weapons in Shaw's armoury were still bright from the last century and he took out all the old and glittering arguments. But the battleground was changing and he found himself having to combat not only Charlotte's anxieties and the doctors' conventionalities, but also the new militancy of vegetarians themselves. They bombarded him with queries and complaints. 'Poor G.B.S. just returned from death's door,' wrote Charlotte, ' . . . forced to write letter after letter when he could hardly hold the pen.'

He eventually replaced the liver injections with tiny grains, clean and tasteless, of a naturist's concoction called Hepamalt. 'Of this I have consumed tons to please the doctors and redden my blood counts, without as far as I can make out, producing any effect whatever,' he told Kathleen Kennet several years later. 'But the anaemia and all its symptoms are gone. The liver gets the credit, though I suspect I have cured myself. I believe in the Nature Cure.'

By the end of January 1939 G.B.S. was calling for research into vegetable hormones and developing a theory of protein poisoning which he later added to a new Vegetarian Diet postcard. But this was not good enough for vegetarian fundamentalists. Shaw was stung by their hostility. 'Liver extract you would take if you developed pernicious anaemia,' he answered one subscriber to the *American Vegetarian*. 'If you were diabetic you would take insulin. If you had edema you would take thyroid. You may think you wouldn't; but you would if your diet failed to cure you. You would try any of the gland extracts, the mineral drugs, the so-called vaccines, if it were that or your death.'

Shaw's anger was partly political. He believed that his own arguments were more honest than the claims of disease-free longevity made by radical vegetarians, and he felt convinced he was the better public advocate for vegetarianism. But privately he was in sympathy with some of their views. Though he was to claim that 'I had no more scruple about trying it [liver extract] than I have eggs and butter', the truth was that he had felt 'intense disgust' at being filled with such 'loathsome stuff'. He had made the unpleasant discovery that 'modern hormones have been arrived at by thousands of experiments on dogs, and that many of them are extracted from unappetizing materials which,' he wrote to Henry Salt, 'I shall not nauseate you by particularizing'. He was greatly relieved when he could bring 'this repulsive story' to an end and replace the hormones with yeast. His response to militant vegetarians was to seek an official assurance early in the Second World War that, when rationing began, special provision would be made for them. It was a fighting diet. 'Vegetarians are the most ferocious class we have; and any underfeeding of them would produce a reduction of our national fighting spirit out of all proportion to their numbers.'

Charlotte was the reason why Shaw consented to live. 'My most distressing complaint is Anorexia, or dislike of food,' he told Henry Salt: ' . . . if I were not a married man and could do as I pleased, [I] would not lift a finger to survive.' This was how Beatrice felt about Sidney. If he died, 'I would gladly sleep and rise no more,' she had written. But since his illness she slept less, rose earlier, and felt a greater stimulus to keep going. Visiting the Shaws during G.B.S.'s illness she had found him a 'white-skinned shadow' with Charlotte 'bending over him with motherly affection'. He was so delighted to see her that they 'actually embraced, and for the first time I kissed GBS!'

The war was to make travelling difficult, but in the early summer of 1940 Sidney prevailed on Beatrice to take him up to London for one last meeting with G.B.S. and Charlotte. 'Of the four I think I am the most willing to sink into nothingness and GBS least so,' Beatrice observed. If she felt resentment, it was quickly dissolved, as it always had been, by his admiration for Sidney and his wonderful kindness to them both. She felt more warmly now towards Charlotte too. Her stamina and loyalty were extraordinary. At lunch they spoke about politics which for fifty years had been the fabric of their friendship. 'They were delightfully affectionate,' Beatrice wrote. 'Why have we lived so long,' Shaw asked her. 'One war was enough.'

*

As his life lengthened so the *Lives* continued to multiply around it. Frank Harris's 'unauthorized biography' had been published in Britain in 1931, the year before Archibald Henderson's authorized *Playboy and Prophet* came out in the United States. These books, largely ghosted by G.B.S. himself and supporting in different ways his commitment to socialism, represent the aspects of his personality and career he was prepared to make visible to the public. But the public was not wholly satisfied and by the mid-1930s St John Ervine was preparing to show them how Harris and Henderson should have done it.

Shaw tried to head him off. He had known Ervine for twenty years and recognized him to be an aggressively independent man-of-letters. He was less likely to allow his book to be taken over and rewritten than Henderson had been; and he could not be humorously disparaged like Harris. 'Dont,' Shaw advised him. But Ervine was obstinate: 'I began to write it.' So Shaw was obliged to redouble his disparagement. He gave Ervine particulars as to why he was quite the wrong sort of chap. But as he began warming to this exposition of his friend's shortcomings, so he started to dig out some of the essential material Ervine needed for his book. It took Shaw until 1942 to abort this biography; and it took St John Ervine until 1956 to resurrect it for publication with a Foreword revealing how G.B.S. had 'hoped that I would one day finish what I had begun'.

Shaw's method of postponing this biography until after his death was peculiarly exasperating to Ervine. He made absolutely certain that the market was glutted by publishing at the Gregynog Press an autobiographical miscellany misleadingly entitled *Shaw Gives Himself Away* and then by helping into print another biography which he felt more confident of controlling: the celebrated *Life* by Hesketh Pearson.

Pearson, like Ervine, had known Shaw for many years. Before taking up biography he had been an actor and created the part of Metellus in the first production of *Androcles and the Lion*. His *Lives* of Hazlitt, Labouchère, Tom Paine and Gilbert and Sullivan were establishing him as the most popular British biographer of the 1930s. But he cared little for Lenin and Marx, and hinted that he would rather die than read *Das Kapital*.

Why then did Shaw prefer Pearson to Ervine? 'You will understand the Irish side of me better than anybody who is not Irish,' St John Ervine was later to quote Shaw as saying to him. But perhaps he did not want the Irish side of him 'understood': Demetrius O'Bolger's 'understanding' of his Irish years was a daunting precedent. Shaw needed to dissolve his Irish past into international socialism. Pearson would cover his politics skimpily and let G.B.S. augment it with his own version. He was in the line of previous biographers: G. K. Chesterton had written a friendly Introduction to his *Life* of Sydney Smith; Frank Harris had been his youthful literary hero. So it was really the old game all over again and a good way, in the last decade of Shaw's life, of forestalling any other game.

He tested his biographer with the customary shot across the bows and when in 1938 Pearson sent him a proposal for his book, replied: 'I shall dissuade you personally any time you like to see me.' Pearson called at Whitehall Court that autumn and over a long conversation, he tells us, demolished Shaw's innumerable objections. 'So you may go ahead with my blessing,' Shaw wrote to him at the beginning of December. 'There is no one else in the field' – which effectively disposed of St John Ervine.

Shaw liked Pearson. He liked his lack of formal education, his cheerfulness, his robust opinions – all Shavian attributes. 'It is far better to know nothing like me,' Pearson told him, 'than to know everything and get it all wrong like you.' Here was a man with whom Shaw could work. 'I find your company both restful and invigorating,' he wrote.

He was 'increasingly generous with help and advice,' Pearson remembered. But Charlotte felt uneasy. She thought Pearson was rather too assertively good-looking and suspected him of being a 'cad'. G.B.S. however assured her she would be omitted from the book. 'The biography is the usual thing,' he notified Beatrice Webb. ' . . . As he and I are old acquaintances since the days of Frank Harris I have promised to tell him anything he wants to know, and to recommend him to you, which I do accordingly, as anything is better than to leave biographers to their imagination and to press gossip.'

With this breezy assistance Pearson sailed along fast. 'My wife did most of the research work . . . and I took about a year to write it.' At the end of 1939 he had pretty well completed it but before sending off his typescript to the publisher he enquired whether Shaw would care to glance at it.

Over the next year Blanche Patch would come across chapters strewn all over the place as Shaw went to work altering, amplifying, editing and embellishing the biography. This revision of Pearson's text 'took me rather longer than writing the book myself,' he told Beatrice Webb who noted in her diary: 'G.B.S. insisted on correcting it – much to H.P.'s disgust.'

At first the corrections were fairly light and made in pencil. But as Shaw grew more interested in his *Life* so he turned to ink, using (as with Archibald Henderson) red ink for unpublishable outbursts: 'This is all poppycock . . . You jumping idiot.' Pearson had derived his technique as a biographer from his earlier career on the stage. To some degree he acted his characters on the page. Shaw's method of ghostwriting his Lives involved borrowing something of the character of his biographer. As Pearson's 'uninvited collaborator', he was faced with an intriguing linguistic exercise of impersonating someone who was Pearsonifying him. He saw in Pearson's stage career an opportunity to dramatize himself. He placed Charlotte out of bounds, revised the Fabian chapters heavily, and in two other areas suppressed or contradicted what Pearson had written.

'I came to the conclusion that the one event in his personal life that had brought him regret almost amounting to sorrow was his estrangement from Granville Barker,' Pearson recorded. ' . . . This break in their friendship was his most keenly felt loss . . . it was the only important matter about which he asked me to be reticent.'

But there was another important matter on which G.B.S. overrode Pearson. This was the chapter entitled 'Retreat to Moscow'. In the original typescript Pearson had distanced himself from Shaw's Stalinism, given an ironic description largely based on Nancy Astor's evidence of their 'Russian elopement', and traced a vein of insensitivity to suffering in Shaw's character. Here, momentarily, was a man who shifted the centre of gravity from the individual to the state, filled his emptiness with facts, and let collectivism come like a curtain between himself and reality. 'He praised and upheld the Russian dictatorship, which suppressed free speech, murdered its political opponents, starved its recalcitrant peasants to death,' Pearson wrote.

To Shaw's mind the danger of Stalin and the Russian Revolution to Britain was similar to the danger of Napoleon and the French Revolution at the beginning of the previous century. Reacting to bloodshed that had stained originally noble causes, the British became more insular, resistant to all experimentation and change. As Hazlitt and Shelley held to their vision of *Liberté, Egalité, Fraternité*, so Shaw clung to his belief in pure communism as the dayspring of a new era. Affecting less emotion than he felt, he treated Soviet atrocities as unnecessary boulders stopping the passage of fresh ideas in Britain, and simply rolled them away.

Shaw condensed Pearson's objections into a single paragraph and allowed a transitional passage ending with the sentence: 'But we must make an effort to see what happened from his own angle.' Then he eliminated the rest of Pearson's account and substituted more than 4,000 words of his own, painting an exhilarating picture of the Soviet political landscape. 'To Shaw it was better than he expected, and full of novelty and promise,' he wrote.

By the end he had given so much of what he called his 'unique private history' to the book that Pearson suggested that his contributions should be shown in the text between square brackets or by indentation. But Shaw was horrified at the thought of his collaboration being exposed. His reply to Pearson is a revealing description of his semi-autobiographical technique. 'Not on your life, Hesketh,' he wrote. 'What I have written I have written in your character, not in my own.

'As an autobiographer I should have written quite differently. There are things that you may quite properly say which would come less gracefully from me. I have carefully avoided altering your opinions except where you had not known the facts . . . But if a word is said to connect me with the authorship of the book or its first proposal or its commercial profits I shall be driven to the most desperate steps to disclaim it. It must appear as Harris's book did . . . [and] I strongly advise you to do what I did in the Harris case. When the book is safely in print, take the copy and burn every scrap of it.'

In fact Pearson did not burn the typescript. It is now in the Humanities Research Center at the University of Texas at Austin and betrays a similar quantity of rewriting to the Henderson proofs at the University of North Carolina at Chapel Hill. But Pearson's biography was far more entertaining than Henderson's. To the end of his life Shaw would refer readers to this biography ('there is nothing better than Hesketh Pearson'), using this recommendation as a deterrent to other potential biographers ('they are the plagues of my life') and as a protection against a third blockbuster from Henderson ('Drop it . . . are there not other geniuses . . . much less written-to-rags than I?'). He felt so pleased by Pearson's success that, having warned him never to reveal his co-authorship, he began speaking openly of his involvement. In Pearson's own copy, under the biographer's signature, Shaw added his own name: 'Also his humble collaborator G. Bernard Shaw.'

4

PAPERBACK AND CELLULOID

These accursed films are complicating life beyond endurance.
Shaw to Trebitsch (28 April 1931)

When planning to launch the *New Statesman* before the war Shaw had written to Beatrice Webb: 'I have no faith in the success of any sixpenny journal that cannot be bought by the casual railway traveller with the certainty that there will be something in it to while away an hour of his journey in a pleasant and amusing way.' It was a casual railway traveller, searching Exeter railway station one weekend for a pleasant and amusing book, who went on to create the sixpenny paperback revolution of the 1930s. Allen Lane's idea of mass-producing reprints of good contemporary writing in 'strong paper covers' and selling them for the price of ten cigarettes seemed to his cautious rivals a formula for bankruptcy. 'The steady cheapening of books is in my opinion a great danger in the trade,' the managing director of Chatto & Windus warned him at the end of 1934.

In several ways Lane was rather a Shavian character: leaving school at sixteen, pursuing his vision on Exeter railway station in opposition to all the experts, puzzling many employees with his superior claims to near-illiteracy, and rising to become (as the publishing historian Ian Norrie called him) 'a man of action in the world of words'.

Shaw bought many of these early Penguins – the novels in their orange covers, biography in blue and detective fiction in green – and in August 1936 he wrote to Lane recommending his friend Apsley Cherry-Garrard's *The Worst Journey in the World*. Lane replied that the book he really wanted was *The Intelligent Woman's Guide to Socialism*. He offered G.B.S. the same terms as other Penguin authors and G.B.S. did not quibble: he was eager to be part of this new paperback movement. Having arranged for his paperback to be set by his Edinburgh printer, R. & R. Clark, 'who is accustomed to my ways', Shaw added two new chapters 'dealing with events that have occurred since its first publication in 1928', extended the title to *The Intelligent Woman's Guide to Socialism, Capitalism, Sovietism and Fascism*, and drafted a note explaining that 'the present edition is in fact a better bargain than the first edition was, though the price is so much more modest'.

The Intelligent Woman's Guide, appearing in two pale blue volumes at sixpence each, heralded a parallel series of paperbacks called Pelicans.

This was an even more radical enterprise than the Penguin list, breaking the convention of reprinting only books already published by other houses, and aiming to extend adult education by making works on politics, economics, the social sciences, literature, the natural sciences and the visual arts cheaply available to 'the intelligent layman'. *The Mysterious Universe* by Sir James Jeans, *The Inequality of Man* by J. B. S. Haldane, Sigmund Freud's *Psychopathology of Everyday Life* and H. G. Wells's *A Short History of the World* were among the early Pelican titles, as well as works by Julian Huxley, R. H. Tawney, the Fabian economist G. D. H. Cole and Beatrice Webb. The future of this ambitious list, to which Clement Attlee credited the Labour Party victory in 1945, was guaranteed by the success of Shaw's two opening volumes in the summer of 1937.

This success also guaranteed his own future as a Penguin author which was to be celebrated on his ninetieth birthday by the 'Shaw Million' – simultaneous publication in Britain of ten titles in editions of 100,000 copies each. It was Allen Lane's most risky speculation yet: 'no venture which I have undertaken in thirty years of publishing has given me so much pleasure,' he later wrote. Nearly all the staff were involved in the project and they were in the office by eight o'clock on 26 July 1946. The first telephone call came from the manager of W. H. Smith's in Baker Street. He had been surprised by the length of the bus queue that morning outside his shop. Surprise swelled to amazement as he realized that these were members of a rare – perhaps dying – species, the general reader, lining up for the Shaw Million. In six weeks the Shaw Million was sold out.

*

Shaw's Penguins included 'screen versions' of *Pygmalion* and *Major Barbara* which were offshoots of his new career in the cinema. From the early years of the century he had loved silent films. He could not keep away from them. And the new motion picture companies could not keep away from G.B.S. The offers flowed in – from $50,000 for one play to $1 million early in 1920 for the rights to all his plays. He gave a variety of reasons for his refusals: that he was too old a dog to learn new tricks; that he had no wish to become a 'dumb dramatist'; that films killed plays and 'my plays are still alive'.

During the 1920s, films were suspected of being a threat to the work of novelists and playwrights in much the same way as photographers in the late nineteenth century had been seen as the enemies of Victorian painting. Shaw's enthusiasm for films was a development of his interest in photography. He predicted that the cinema would be an invention of even more revolutionary significance than printing. Films told their stories to the illiterate as much as to the literate – 'that is why the cinema is going to produce effects that all the cheap books in the world could never produce'. He foresaw a time when motion pictures would 'form the mind of England. The national conscience, the national ideals and tests of conduct,' he had written in 1914, 'will be those of the film.' One day pictures would be 'brought to my home for me' and it was in this direction, he told a journalist, 'that you must look for the most important changes'.

His cat and mouse tactics with the movie moguls partly reflected his sense of a film world in transition. The screen's silence had been 'the only reason I did not permit the filming of my plays, because their greatest strength was in their dialogue'. Meanwhile he did not want to sell his rights and lose control of his property.

The day he had long awaited began with *The Jazz Singer*, shown in the United States by Warner Brothers in the fall of 1927. Shaw had already conducted a studio experiment that summer at the DeForest Phonofilm Company employing Sybil Thorndike and Lewis Casson to test five minutes of the Cathedral Scene from *Saint Joan*, and in the next two years he made several appearances himself on Movietone newsreels and in screen interviews. 'I believe that acting and drama can be portrayed far more effectively as well as lucratively from the screen than from the stage,' he wrote in 1930. Yet he hesitated, did not proceed with the filming of *Saint Joan*, and three years later turned instead to his one-act skit, *How He Lied to Her Husband*.

The choice was significant. This *pièce d'occasion* had originally been composed in 1904 as a curtain-raiser 'to satirize those who took Candida to be a sentimental glorification of eroticism' and now came to serve its turn again, illustrating Shaw's contention that 'the whole history of the "movies" showed that "sex-appeal" was a thing that could be neglected almost altogether'. The heroine of Shaw's play is 'a very ordinary South Kensington female of about 37', and there are only two other people: her thick-necked City husband and a dreamy young admirer. The action, which revolves round a missing bundle of love poems (signifying the missing sex-appeal), takes place in a curtained room on the Cromwell Road and its shadowy simplicity reflects Shaw's view of the technical limitations of British films in 1930.

The question Shaw was examining with the film version of *How He Lied* was whether the best use of the medium lay in recording a perfect production of a play for showing round the world. He chose Cecil Lewis, the wartime flying ace who had been so helpful with his wireless career, to direct it, and persuaded British International Pictures to accept this 'absolutely unknown, untried man as director'. It was shot 'without transpositions interpolations omissions or any alterations misrepresenting the Author whether for better or worse except such as the Author may consent to or himself suggest' – a standard clause in Shaw's later contracts. Cecil Lewis rehearsed the cast of three until they were word and action perfect, worked out some camera angles for the cameraman, and completed the film in four days. But it 'was as much like a movie as a cow is like a pianola'. When it came to be shown in London in January 1931 *The Times* commented on 'the folly of those who suppose that the right use, and the commercial use, of the talkie invention is direct transference from stage to screen'.

Shaw defended this trial film as part of his campaign against the 'children's picture book' story-telling of Hollywood. The acting in Hollywood was good, the photography excellent and the expenditure one of the wonders of the world. But when it came to the script, Shaw liked to imagine, they called in the bell boy. 'The bell boy's vision of life is a continual arriving in motor-cars and going upstairs and disappearing through doors that immediately close and leave life a blank . . . 95 per cent of a film must consist of going up and down stairs and getting in and out of motor-cars . . . My plays do not depend on staircases for their interest.'

Shaw's guerrilla warfare against the big Hollywood corporations and movie moguls is a reminder of his embattled days fighting the West End theatre managements and actor-managers of the Victorian stage. Both were happy to mutilate texts to suit their star performers. The dialogue of *How He Lied* was continuous, he pointed out, and the entire action took place in the same room.

'The usual changes from New York to the Rocky Mountains, from Marseilles to the Sahara, from Mayfair to Monte Carlo, are replaced by changes from the piano to the sideboard, from the window to the door, from the hearth rug to the carpet. When the husband arrives he is not shewn paying his taxi, taking out his latchkey, hanging up his hat, and mounting the stairs. There is no time for that sort of baby padding when the action of a real play is hastening to its climax.'

Lewis's next film with Shaw was *Arms and the Man*. Shaw had received an offer from Sam Goldwyn who 'wants to cut the play down to forty minutes'. He trusted Lewis to make a full-length version, but the filming was a dismal experience. 'We were a little like a pilotless ship,' remembered Barry Jones who played Bluntschli. The actor cast in the part of Nicola, the manservant, died of a heart attack; and the prolonged attempts to re-create Bulgaria in North Wales were wonderfully unconvincing. In the end Lewis surrendered the film into the hands of what Shaw had called 'the business staff' who, no less philistine than their colleagues in the United States, cut it ineptly.

Working with Lewis's scenario, Shaw had this time made a real attempt to adapt his play into a film. His alterations to the script show that he was beginning to develop a film technique, and had come to accept that, though the dramatic principles of stage and screen might be the same, the methods must differ. 'The whole action of the play has to be confined to three scenes, two of them indoors,' he wrote.

'In the picture the battle is shewn, and the flight of the fugitive whom the heroine shelters. There is no pinning of the characters to one spot: they pass in and out of doors, upstairs and downstairs, into the gardens and across mountain country, with the freedom and variety impossible in the room with three walls which, however scene-painters may disguise it, is always the same old stage.'

This statement, contradicting what he had written after *How He Lied*, is Shaw's commitment to future film-making. 'My mind is always changing – it is not only a woman's privilege,' he said when asked in January 1933 to comment on his decision to allow RKO Studios in the United States to film *The Devil's Disciple* starring John Barrymore. British films were hopeless because 'they have no money,' he wrote that April to Kenneth MacGowan, an associate producer at RKO, 'and want to put in minutes (mostly wasted) where months are needed'.

The script by Lester Cohen arrived at Ayot St Lawrence in January 1934. A month later, Shaw called the deal off. Cohen's script was beyond rescue. 'I cannot be expected to lend a hand to my own murder.'

This episode left G.B.S. curiously stranded. 'Hollywood is not within half a century of knowing how to handle my stuff,' he wrote to Theresa Helburn, the executive director of the Theatre Guild. ' . . . I contemplate the popular Hollywood productions in despair.' But he did not despair of the future of films. His optimism soon appeared justified. By the summer of 1934 he was considering proposals from both Paris and Berlin for the filming of *Pygmalion*. In February 1935 he signed an agreement with Eberhard Klagemann, head of a Berlin film company. Helping Trebitsch was one of his incentives. He bought Trebitsch's half-share in the German language rights of *Pygmalion*, insisted that Klagemann should use his own screenplay and arranged that Trebitsch be employed to translate it.

The German film of *Pygmalion* (first shown in Berlin in September 1935) and the Dutch *Pygmalion* (first shown in Amsterdam in March

1937) were commercially quite successful: but Shaw loathed them. 'I don't know what they did with my scenario, but they certainly did not use it for the film,' he said after seeing the German version at the beginning of 1936. In fact Shaw was not credited with the screenplay and Trebitsch not listed as translator.

Almost immediately after finishing the *Pygmalion* script, Shaw had started on one of *Saint Joan*. At the end of November 1934 he handed it to the Viennese actress Elizabeth Bergner who had created the role of Joan ten years earlier in Max Reinhardt's Berlin production. Bergner had recently married the Hungarian producer-director Paul Czinner who planned to form a syndicate including Twentieth Century-Fox and produce the film of *Saint Joan* starring his wife. But Czinner, who professed himself delighted with this screenplay, then sent it without consulting G.B.S. to the Scottish dramatist James Bridie for rewriting; and Bridie contacted Shaw to ascertain whether this was being done with his approval. The cat was out of the bag.

Worried that Twentieth Century-Fox would not put up money if there was a risk of *Saint Joan* being subjected to a Catholic boycott, Czinner had also submitted Shaw's scenario to a newly created organization at the Vatican, called Catholic Action, which monitored the lay activities of the Church. Their report condemned the film as 'a satire against Church and State', and an 'attack to the R.C.C.' by the 'mocking Irishman'. Unless the film script was substantially altered, the film would be met by a Catholic veto.

Shaw knew that during the Depression film speculators in the United States traded in near-pornography and that there had been a counter-attack from such organizations as the Legion of Decency. To regain control of their industry, American movie producers formed a Production Code Administration in 1934 which was already leading to what Shaw called 'an epidemic of censorships'. He saw Hollywood as being in a pitiable condition, and urged film corporations in the United States to 'pluck up enough courage and public spirit to insist on the control of film morality being made a federal matter, independent of prudes, of parochial busybodies, and doctrinaire enemies of the theatre as such'.

'I have now cried off the film, and excommunicated Czinner with bell, book, and candle,' Shaw informed James Bridie in the summer of 1935. How long would he have to wait for an independent director who would carry his films to victory over these 'goddams' of Hollywood?

*

After more than fifteen years with G.B.S., Blanche Patch was an expert at fobbing off pests. The mail bulged with petitions from burglars, chemists, coffin makers, sailors, schoolboys, all of them 'howling to be answered'; and Miss Patch typed out the answers.

Those who wanted money were tiresome. They would demand anything from £2 to £20,000 and for all sorts of far-flung reasons: to save fifteen repertory theatres; help thousands of refugees; marry off an Indian gentleman's six daughters. It vexed Miss Patch to see the amounts of money her employer simply handed away – often, she thought, to the most undeserving. Such people, 'greedy for a flicker from the flame', were trying to 'poach on his reputation'. At a distance he seemed all things to all people, a father- and eventually a grandfather-confessor to the whole world.

Everyone turned to him: men who were thinking of entering the priesthood or taking up carpentry; women wondering whether to risk a divorce or send their daughters on the stage; children who wanted to name a pig or hedgehog after him. There were explorers needing radio apparatus for a whaling expedition; importers eager to bring a frost-resistant potato into Britain; inventors seeking Shaw's endorsement to promote schemes for causing clouds to dissolve and distilled water to consolidate into stone, or his testimonial to prevent cures for cancer, lunacy and hallucinations being stolen.

'I believe you have always had a warm corner in your heart for women and fanatics,' wrote a woman. 'I am a non-entity, you an entity,' wrote a man. G.B.S. was peculiarly the saint of the isolated, the odd, drowning women, desperate men – 'a doctor of the human soul,' one correspondent called him. Like Sherlock Holmes, he had a reputation for solving people's problems. They wrote to enquire where they should live, what they should do in retirement, how they should get out of jail. A number of people on the verge of murder or suicide tried him as their penultimate resort. 'I feel a little lonely,' admitted a twenty-one-year-old girl from New York, ' . . . I love you very dearly.' 'I am rather stout and ugly,' explained a boy in South Africa, ' . . . how should I go about getting friends.' 'I think your patronage was the greatest pleasure my poor father ever had,' claimed the son of a Colchester newsagent after his father's death.

'Irresponsible nonsense had an attraction for Shaw,' Miss Patch observed, 'which would lure him into correspondence of the most futile sort.' She found herself conveying his views on world slaughter, the fourth dimension, the existence of fairies. 'Why are you silent on public affairs?' demanded one man. That was a tricky one to answer. So was the woman who wrote regarding the forceps inside her, and the London busman who objected to Shaw's lack of interest in King George V and threatened to run him over with his bus.

Though it was all water off a duck's back to Miss Patch, much of what she fingered on to the paper and sealed into envelopes had that mixture of rare sense and inspired nonsense the world had learnt to call Shavian. A cheque for £400 to a poet whose clothes had gone up in smoke was accompanied by a note explaining how much Shaw disliked his poems. Someone in search of shock therapy was recommended to shave her head, put on a white wig and stand in front of a mirror. One fan who wanted a lock of his hair was advised to 'cut a wisp off the nearest white dog'. A family called Shaw who had christened their son George Bernard was accused of perpetrating a 'shocking outrage on a defenceless infant'.

Some of Miss Patch's typed replies were to gain fame. When he was asked 'Have we Lost Faith?', she sent back: 'Certainly not, but we have transferred it from God to the General Medical Council.' When G.B.S. came across one of his works in a second-hand bookshop with his hand-written inscription on the flyleaf, Miss Patch was able to pack it up carrying a Shavian postscript – 'With the author's renewed compliments. G.B.S.' – and post it back to the original dedicatee. She rather relished some of their point-blank rebuffs. To a hostess who sent a card stating that on a certain day she would be 'At Home', the succinct reply had been: 'So will G. Bernard Shaw.' Then there was the matter of the Prime Minister: 'Absence from town and a strong sense of humor,' she typed, 'will prevent me from accepting your invitation to dine in acknowledgement of the political eminence of Ramsay MacDonald.'

Over the worst period Miss Patch had to cope with up to three proposals of marriage a week. She helped to see off an actress from Zurich who claimed that since she had the greatest body in the world and Shaw had the greatest brain, they ought to produce the most perfect child, with a celebrated transposition: 'What if the child inherits my body and your brains?' But not all the famous stories were true. For example she had never sent Winston Churchill two tickets for the first night of a Shaw play inviting him to bring a friend 'if you have one'; and she had never received an answer from Churchill saying that he could come to the second night 'if there was one'. That was a journalistic invention.

Among Miss Patch's skills was the making of parcels. People liked to send things to Whitehall Court and, if they were not mislaid, she could send them back. 'I hate presents,' Shaw had said and on the whole she agreed with him, because they received such silly presents. A few presents, such as the rather handy axe, she could see he actually liked; but the bits of coal garnished with ivy, the seaweed, the bison-foot inkstand and enamel washing-bowl with its base deeply registering the G.B.S. profile were nothing but trouble.

More often people wanted things from Whitehall Court – hats, handkerchiefs, trousers, really anything at all. One man of the streets demanded

G.B.S.'s boots, and despite the awkwardness of packing them up, Miss Patch was actually obliged to post them off to him. But they had not reckoned on this pedestrian returning them whenever they were in need of repairs. Such episodes, Miss Patch noticed, seemed to amuse G.B.S.

But she was not so easily amused, particularly by the hordes of time-wasters who arrived at the door. Right up to the end they came. She didn't mind Charlotte's lunch guests – Barry Jackson, Apsley Cherry-Garrard, the aviator Amy Johnson, the actress Ellen Pollock, though Lady Astor rather overrated herself, she was inclined to think. She quite liked some of the more casual visitors, such as Maurice Chevalier who seemed 'exceedingly nervous' in her company, or even Charlie Chaplin who was 'quiet and serious' when she took him round the flat. When people were separated from her and got stuck with G.B.S., they had to take their chances. 'Shaw talked knowledgeably about Kemal Atatürk,' remembered the Hungarian actress Zsa Zsa Gabor who had been invited to London by the British Council. Of course there was no accounting for tastes and all tastes seemed to be catered for at Whitehall Court. 'There was such a wonderfully free atmosphere about, you were sure that nothing you said or did would shock or surprise them,' D. H. Lawrence's widow Frieda declared. 'If you had suddenly turned a somersault they would have taken it along with the rest.' Blanche Patch was rather glad she hadn't. 'You have no notion,' she typed, 'of the hosts of people who knock at my door every day . . . because my picture in the papers resembles their grandfathers.' There was the young man who had been directed in a *séance* to make off with the doormat in case 'some benefit might accrue to me' and landed up in an asylum; and, perhaps worst of all, the climbing American who, after publishing letters to them in the personal columns of *The Times*, scaled his way into the flat and had to be arrested by Scotland Yard.

After all this it was hardly a great surprise for Miss Patch to find on the doorstep one day towards the end of 1935 a swarthy Transylvanian gentleman commanding her to 'go and tell your master' that the film producer from Rome he had once met at Cap d'Antibes was here. 'Tell him,' he added, 'the young man with the brown buttocks.' How did he get past Miss Patch? 'He had no appointment, and we knew nothing of this caller who was obviously a foreigner,' she objected. But there was something appealing about him. At any rate, perhaps because 'his name made Shaw curious' too, he agreed to see this stranger and she ushered Gabriel Pascal into the study.

*

'The man is a genius,' Shaw announced ten years later. Like Vandeleur

Lee, Pascal was a charlatan genius 'quite outside all ordinary rules'. He made Shaw laugh with his whole body, throwing his shoulders about 'while the laughter ran up his long legs and threatened to shake his head off'. As Blanche Patch saw, 'G.B.S. never met a human being who entertained him more'.

Pascal was a short, powerful-looking man with broad shoulders, high cheekbones, a strong head and dense black hair. When he smiled he gave an enormous grin with a gap at the centre of his front teeth. He entered Shaw's study like a gorilla.

Their previous meeting had been something Pascal would have shrugged off had it not already entered the repertoire of his legendary past. One blue and golden summer morning, his story went, he had been swimming naked in the Mediterranean and, coming across G.B.S. treading water far out from shore, made himself known as the person whose destiny it was to make wonderful pictures from the Shavian playground. As he swam away, revealing his buttocks, Shaw had called out: 'When you are utterly broke . . . come and call on me . . . and I will let you make one of my plays into a film.' So here he was. He spoke in low solemn tones and with a strong Central European accent – then cracked open his enormous grin like an urchin. It was impossible to resist him.

'He reminds me of Frank Harris,' Shaw wrote to Trebitsch. Pascal was to gain a reputation in films similar to Harris's in journalism: that of a Svengali who discovered new stars while remaining curiously in need of discovery himself. In fact his name was not Pascal any more than Harris's name had been Frank. He was born Gabor Lehöl, yet 'Gabriel Pascal' was not so much an invention as a mutation – as Samuel Goldwyn was a mutation of Schmuel Gelbfisz.

When Pascal recalled his early years, the air would fill with fleeting images and sounds – the bright flames of a burning house, the despairing cries of women, a ramshackle gypsy caravan sauntering across the Alps; then cut to the life of a poor shepherd boy deeply attached to the earth; and afterwards to a daring circus acrobat who miraculously defied gravity, a rebel cadet at a famous military academy, a prodigy at the Imperial Hofburg Theatre in Vienna . . . and behind all these sets and scenes hovered the mysterious Jesuit priest who was his patron. Did Royal Blood course through his veins? Had he been kidnapped? Everything depended on the translation, the direction, and the rewrites.

He knew he had been born for great things but (again like Frank Harris) might be stopped from reaching them by his lack of height. 'Someday,' he promised, 'I shall try to figure out why this incomprehensible world confuses heroism with height.' He gained in mythical stature from his tall stories. To Shaw, who knew so well the springs of self-dramatization, there was a gallantry about adventures that could turn failure, poverty, obscurity and the ostracism and contempt which these invite, into such gorgeous entertainment. When he spoke of his wartime escapades either as a cavalry officer advancing along the Italian Front accompanied by two dachshunds, or hosting sumptuous banquets for his prisoners on the Russian Front, he brought back the innocent world of *Arms and the Man*. His favourite play was Shaw's melodrama *The Devil's Disciple* with its picturesque hero; but the talk in Shaw's study turned to the filming of *Pygmalion*.

There had been little in Pascal's career since the war, except perhaps his production of Franz Lehár's operetta *Friederika* in Germany, to raise confidence. 'I believe that the prospect of too much success frightened me,' he explained. Around the time of Hitler's rise to power he had left Germany (for he could have been a Jew as well as a Catholic and a Jesuit) and began roaming the world. 'I loved the California climate, but I did not like the coldness of Hollywood, where they called me the hobo producer.' He went to India to see his 'awakener' Meher Baba. But though he was presented with Baba's magic sandals, Pascal could not find his way to the Oriental film he longed to make on reincarnation. At last his vagrant path led to Whitehall Court.

He claimed that 'only a foreigner could translate Shaw into films'. But Shaw had received plenty of these proposals from foreigners – Samuel Goldwyn, Alexander Korda, Louis B. Mayer, Harry Warner – all immigrants or the children of immigrants from Eastern Europe, now creating from gangster and horror movies, musicals and westerns, a vast national fantasy for native-born Americans. Pascal was the joker in this pack. He was driven by a similar need to bury his unstable past under an empire made from other people's dreams. Only this time it should be an empire of Shavian myths and dreams.

At their first interview on 8 December Shaw had asked Pascal what capital he had – 'How are you fixed for money?' – and Pascal, emptying his pockets, cracking open his smile, pointed to one or two small coins. At their second meeting at Whitehall Court, G.B.S. decided to take a big chance. 'I have disposed of the English film of *Pygmalion* to Gabriel Pascal,' he wrote to Trebitsch two days later.

As for Pascal, 'I was the happiest man in the world.'

'I have had to forbid Pascal to kiss me,' Shaw wrote again to Trebitsch, 'as he did at first to the scandal of the village.'

*

Shaw estimated that his *Pygmalion* contract was worth £60,000 (equivalent to over £1.5 million in 1997) to Pascal. But although there 'wasn't a studio in the world that wouldn't have given its gold teeth for the rights to Shaw's plays', S. N. Behrman wrote, '... Pascal found it seemingly impossible to get the money to screen them'. His headlong optimism carried him over two miserable years during which his gift for lighting up people's enthusiasms was regularly quenched by what one of his wives was to call 'Gabriel's genius for messing up anything'.

Shaw's letters of agreement, which were always confined to one play at a time, gave Pascal only restricted rights to produce the film and retained for himself the contractual rights with all those clauses (five-year licence, author's control of script and a royalty of ten per cent of the gross receipts) to which film companies objected. Pascal felt corralled by these bristling business habits. For G.B.S. did not want extra fame and money. He wanted victory over Hollywood and had chosen Pascal as his champion.

So Pascal rode desperately on. But he appeared to be permanently riding into a setting sun. His head blazed with visions of a dozen simultaneous schemes and whenever he was on the verge of roping one of them, he would utter his jubilant refrain: 'I go now see the old man to talk cast.' After a year of galloping activity he had got nowhere. As one studio after another turned him down, Pascal looked shabbier and shabbier. He kept visiting Shaw and one day brought with him a financial backer who had made his fortune in flour. This was Joseph Arthur Rank. Suddenly he had the beginnings of a syndicate.

Pygmalion was finally scheduled for production at Pinewood Studios on 11 March 1938. 'I do not propose to interfere in the direction of the picture,' Shaw notified Pascal, 'since I cannot, at my age, undertake it myself.' He interfered as much as possible from a distance and whenever Pascal came 'to talk cast'. Wendy Hiller had been Shaw's choice for Eliza and he predicted that she would be 'the film sensation of the next five years'. He had wanted Charles Laughton to play Higgins and felt that Pascal's choice of Leslie Howard was 'fatally wrong' – 'the trouble with Leslie Howard is he thinks he's Romeo'. In his screenplay Shaw had tried to strengthen the role of Freddy Eynsford-Hill to make him a romantic second lead, but he suspected that the public would love Leslie Howard 'and probably want him to marry Eliza, which is just what I don't want'.

It was Anthony Asquith who made *Pygmalion* a success. Pascal as producer was a whirlwind. There was 'a terrible row and throughout the whole shooting of the picture we were never on speaking terms,' remembered Wendy Hiller. 'But as the direction was in the expert hands of Anthony Asquith we managed remarkably well.'

Shaw's scenario cut down the dialogue and opened up the play for the screen. He also added some extra scenes at Pascal and Asquith's suggestion, but did not accept all their proposals for giving the film more exteriors, greater movement and visual variety. It was then modified by various unseen hands which came together to sweeten the story and glamorize Higgins. Nevertheless, by Hollywood standards it was faithful to Shaw's work.

And Charlotte liked it. Two days before the première she and G.B.S. came to a preview and at the end Charlotte told everyone: 'This is the finest presentation of my husband's work.' Pascal had been trembling with nerves, clutching Charlotte's hand and almost wringing these favourable words from her. He had shot three alternative endings to the film and chosen the romantic one anticipating the marriage of Higgins and Eliza. When questioned about this happy ending, Shaw answered that apparently some '20 directors seem to have . . . devised a scene to give a lovelorn complexion at the end to Mr Leslie Howard: but it is too inconclusive to be worth making a fuss about.'

Pygmalion went on to break all box-office records and, as Lawrence Langner wrote, 'won the hearts of audiences and the plaudits of critics all over the world'. In the United States, where a censored version had to be shown to meet the Protection Code Administration's objections to 'comedy treatment of illicit sex', it was given two Academy Awards. Shaw happily described his Oscar for the year's best-written screenplay as 'an insult', by which he meant that *Pygmalion* should be advertised as an 'all British film made by British methods without interference by American script writers . . . a revolution in the presentation of drama on the film'. This served well in his propaganda war, and *Pygmalion* was soon being spoken of as having 'lifted movie-making from "illiteracy" to "literacy" '.

Against most odds, Pascal had carried Shaw to the top of the most powerful myth-making empire in the twentieth century. It was 'a tremendous triumph'. He felt as if Pascal had opened an Aladdin's cave, and the effect was spectacular. 'You . . . persist in making plans for me on the assumption I am 35; but actually speaking I am a dead man; and a grasshopper is a burden,' he tried to complain. 'I discovered you ten years too late.' But as Charlotte saw, Pascal's extraordinary vitality had rejuvenated her husband so that he was 'twenty-five years younger'.

'I am Cagliostro to Shaw,' Pascal boasted, ' – I keep him alive fifteen years more.'

5

THREE PLAYS FOR HISTORIANS

'Does it matter?' My reply is that it does.
What I Really Wrote About the War (1931)

If it had been the love of money-making that kept him at work, as some neighbours at Ayot suspected, Shaw would have moved wholeheartedly into films. 'It would pay me better to turn my old plays into scenarios,' he wrote to Trebitsch who was growing increasingly dependent on his Shavian income. But 'I cannot do this'. He still had new work to do. In the late 1930s he composed a pleasant and an unpleasant play, began a 'Comedy of No Manners' and completed a variant ending to a Shakespearean romance.

Cymbeline Refinished was conceived at a Governors' meeting at the Stratford-upon-Avon Shakespeare Memorial Theatre. The business of improving on Shakespeare had been going on since Colly Cibber's popular adaptation of *Richard III* and the 'happy' version of *King Lear* by Nahum Tate. As a drama critic Shaw had often ridiculed the acting versions put on by Henry Irving and other actor-managers of the Victorian theatre which he now saw as precursors to the sentimentalities of Hollywood. But, by perpetrating 'a spurious fifth act to *Cymbeline*' was he not joining this optimistic band of saboteurs himself?

Shaw's battles were fought against the surrender of power from composers to performers. In principle he had little objection to a 'collaboration' between authors. Updating a post-Marlowe play into a post-Ibsen play was a type of translation.

It was while preparing Ellen Terry for her part in Irving's mutilated production at the Lyceum that he had become involved with the text of *Cymbeline*. His flights of invective against 'this silly old "Cymbeline"' were largely improvised to raise Ellen's spirits and get her over the difficulties of giving a convincing performance. But it had fixed the last act in his mind as a hopeless mess. Now, while preparing to tie the dangling ends into a Shavian knot, he found that Shakespeare's last act was full of verbal workmanship and theatrical entertainment.

Biographical criticism has treated *Cymbeline* as the dream-work of a man in the sunset of his life, too exhausted to invent new devices, filling it with echoes from *Othello, King Lear, As You Like It*. In this interpretation the contortions of the plot, grandiloquences of speech, emotional disorientation all become symptoms of Shakespeare's second childhood;

signposts in a world of fairy-tales which 'complete existence for the young, and replace it for the old'. But in the context of historical criticism Shakespeare's change of mood reflects a change in the country under a new monarch, King James I, a generous patron of Shakespeare's company, who claimed descent from the mythical King Arthur and encouraged the arts to draw their inspiration from ancient English history. The extraordinary last act, with its profusion of dénouements leading to the King's final speech, 'Publish we this peace to all our subjects', becomes in this historical context a commentary on King James's intricate policy of appeasement – with a flattering masque served up to appeal to the new Court's love of pageant. Later, in post-modernist criticism, *Cymbeline* was to be transformed into a post-Shakespearean romance that deconstructs the forms of Elizabethan tragedy.

What Shaw does is to replace Shakespeare's fairy-tale with his own, introduce a number of contemporary political comments, and continue the work of deconstruction with a parody of diplomatic realism. He makes short work of the 'ludicrous' battle sequences, jettisons the masque, banishes all apparitions, gods, soothsayers, and, condensing five scenes into one, straightens out Shakespeare's meanderings in little more than twenty minutes ('Are there more plots to unravel?' demands Cymbeline impatiently). He also uses the English victory over the Romans as a history lesson for Neville Chamberlain, advocating the preparedness of military training and rearmament. Finally, in the dismayed reactions of Guiderius and Arviragus to the discovery that they are the King's sons ('Not free to wed the woman of my choice . . . I abdicate and pass the throne to Polydore,' cries Guiderius, to which Arviragus objects, 'Do you, by heavens? Thank you for nothing, brother'), Shaw makes an approving reference to the abdication of Edward VIII which was announced while he was writing the play.

Cymbeline Refinished retains eighty-nine of Shakespeare's lines, but Shaw gives none of them to Imogen whom he converts, as if she were a posthumous gift for Ellen Terry, into the incipient New Woman. Though some beautiful lines are forfeited, there is more than one '*hilarious sensation*' in the best Shavian manner and fleeting moments of beauty, such as Imogen's plea to the smiling Iachimo (who is made cleverer at the expense of Posthumus) and his response to her:

IMOGEN   Oh, do not make me laugh.
  Laughter dissolves too many just resentments
  Pardons too many sins.
IACHIMO   And saves the world
  A many thousand murders.

Cymbeline, by William Shakespeare and Bernard Shaw opened at the Embassy Theatre for a three-week run on 16 November 1937, the day before Chamberlain began his policy of appeasement with Lord Halifax's visit to Hitler. The performance 'left the impression that the actors were saving themselves up for Shaw at the expense of Shakespeare,' wrote *The Times*. ' . . . [They] visibly thrilled to a brand new challenge when the fifth act began.' But the general public, worried by the news of the Japanese capture of Shanghai, General Franco's blockade of the Spanish coast, and the riots in Sudeten Czechoslovakia, were in no mind to enter fairyland. They wanted something that spoke to the problems of the present – which is what Shaw, in his next play, tried to give them.

*

Shaw's expedition to the League of Nations Palace in September 1928 had been made towards the end of its ascendant phase. In this age of early tanks and aeroplanes, poison gas, new guns and bombs, people looked to the League to quell their anxieties. 'I see again Mr Bernard Shaw stalking out of the dining-room of the Residence,' wrote the diplomatist Bruce Lockhart, 'an object of greater hero-worship and reverence to the throng of League visitors than any political delegate.'

Shaw was vividly aware of his starring role. 'Fortunately, the young ladies of the Secretariat, who have plenty of theatrical instinct, arrange the platform in such a way that the president, the speakers, and the bureau are packed low down before a broad tableau curtain which, being in three pieces, provides most effective dramatic entrances right and left of the centre,' he wrote.

'When a young lady secretary has a new dress, or for any other reason feels that she is looking her best, she waits until the speaker – possibly a Chinese gentleman carefully plodding through a paper written in his best French – has reduced half the public galleries to listless distraction and the other half to stertorous slumber. Then she suddenly, but gracefully, snatches the curtains apart and stands revealed, a captivating mannequin, whilst she pretends to look round with a pair of sparkling eyes for her principal on the bureau. The effect is electric: the audience wakes up and passes with a flash from listless desperation to tense fascination, to the great encouragement of the speaker, who, with his back to the vision beautiful, believes he has won over the meeting at last.'

Swarms of journalists circled through the whispering atmosphere, plunging after gobbets of scandal, as the politicians, like monsters from the past, grappled clumsily for personal advantage. Among these relics of what seemed like a species already extinct, G.B.S. saw sparks of hope. The smaller states had sent to Geneva their 'heaviest champions' to hold the fort for sane internationalism against the cabinets of big Powers seeking to reduce the League to impotence. In such a situation the Whitehall socialite 'soon suffers a Lake change,' Shaw noticed. 'In the atmosphere of Geneva patriotism perishes . . . In short, the League is a school for the new international statesmanship as against the old Foreign Office diplomacy.'

The social, economic and humanitarian work of the League was carried out by the International Labour Organization, whose offices occupied a newly designed building where Labour was glorified in stained glass and muscular statuary. 'Here the air is quite fresh: no flavor of Whitehall leather and prunella can be sniffed anywhere,' Shaw wrote. 'These neo-Carthusians are of a new order.' To his eyes they were genuine internationalists working at what he had regarded all his Fabian life as the realities of politics: improving labour conditions; fighting epidemic diseases; finding accommodation and work for displaced people; controlling the traffic in opium; establishing the rights of women; caring for children, protecting strangers, welcoming sojourners like Shaw himself, and generally forcing up the moral standards of the big Powers.

Shaw's Fabian Tract No. 226 put the question: 'What do all these people do besides pretending that the League can prevent war?' He gave as his answer that Geneva could justify its existence ten times over through this work of the International Labour Organization.

His play, *Geneva*, written mainly in the late 1930s, when the League was diminished by the Japanese invasion of Chinese Manchuria, the Italian invasion of Abyssinia and the German invasion of the demilitarized Rhineland, was a make-believe about what might have happened if the Geneva Idea had spread. He pretends that there is no veto to make the League sterile, that the Idea has blown a fresh moral climate into the political atmosphere. He converts the natural theatre of the League's Palace into a Platonic forum for international opinion, using none of the three institutions at its centre, but two of its satellites: the International Court at The Hague and the International Institute of Intellectual Co-operation in Paris.

Of all the functions of the League, the permanent Court of International Justice at The Hague was the most widely understood. 'The League is still too uncertain of its powers to call the offenders to account,' Shaw wrote in 1930. Six years later he gives his Judge in *Geneva* this certainty and makes the Hague Court the League's operative organ.

This Judge, who presides over the last act of the play, has been called forth by applications for warrants against the dictators of Europe issued in Act I from the office of the International Institute for Intellectual Co-operation. So little known was this organization that many of Shaw's audiences believed he invented it. In fact he had merely invented its usefulness.

The first chairman had been Henri Bergson, but it was not until Gilbert Murray took over the chairmanship in 1928 that Shaw began to grow interested in its possibilities. Murray himself had shied away from this 'beastly Intellectual Travail' which attracted what Arthur Koestler called the intellectual 'Call Girls' of the world to its conferences. 'It was rather like a Shaw play,' Murray decided after one of these bureaucratic comedies. Yet in spite of himself 'I find that I am getting interested in the wretched business, from having to explain and defend it!' By the end of 1933 Murray had come to see its meetings as 'a record – fragmentary indeed and imperfect – of the unseen process which creates and maintains human progress; a process which seldom gets into the front page of any popular newspaper, because it does not consist of explosions or spectacular triumphs; only of the steady growth, and amid much discouragement, of the activity that will save civilisation, if civilisation is to be saved'.

Gilbert Murray was godparent to Shaw's *Geneva*. In 1933 he published a study of Aristophanes which he dedicated to Shaw, 'lover of ideas and hater of cruelty, who has filled many lands with laughter and whose courage has never failed'. 'Thanks mainly to Gilbert Murray, I know as much as anyone need know of the ancient Greek drama,' Shaw later wrote. In *Geneva* he went back to the Old Comedy of Aristophanes, satirizing contemporary politicians to illustrate recurring historical processes. 'The play is a lampoon with Hitler and Mussolini unmistakably on the stage,' he told the theatrical producer H. K. Ayliff. Though still making fun of Murray's Institute, Shaw gives it something to do at last.

The first act opens in its invented Geneva office, a 'rotten little room' on the third floor of a 'tumbledown old house full of rats'. With her heels on the dingy table, sits a good-looking self-satisfied young English-woman smoking and reading an illustrated magazine. Her name is Begonia Brown. 'Nobody ever comes in here,' she says. But that May morning near the end of the 1930s she is astonished to be called on by five claimants in succession, 'each with a grievance which they expect her to remedy'. Begonia Brown refers all grievances to the International Court at The Hague.

As the play proceeds into and beyond the second act we are introduced to the Spirit of Geneva in the person of the League's Secretary: Shaw's portrait of the permanent British Secretary-General Sir Eric Drummond, to whom he grants the 'Lake change' he referred to in his Fabian Tract. Opposing him is the British Foreign Secretary, Sir Orpheus Midlander, 'a very well-dressed gentleman of fifty or thereabouts, genial in manner, quick-witted in conversation, altogether a pleasant and popular personality' – a damning Shavian description. He represents time present – 'Nothing wrong with the world: nothing whatever,' he tells the League of Nations Secretary in the manner of Tom Broadbent cheering up the disfrocked Irish priest Peter Keegan in *John Bull's Other Island*; and he prescribes 'a cup of tea' to cure despair rather as Broadbent recommends phosphorous pills to brighten up Keegan's view of the world. Sir Orpheus is opposed to change and believes that politics should be left to professional politicians ('we cant have literary people interfering in foreign affairs'). He is Shaw's portrait of Sir Austen Chamberlain (Secretary of State for Foreign Affairs between 1924 and 1929) whose naïve patriotism had been a standing joke at Geneva, 'so outrageous that only a man with a single eyeglass could have got away with it,' Shaw recalled in his Fabian Tract.

Begonia Brown's unprecedented action creates European chaos and a war, in consequence of which she grows so popular in Britain that the government is obliged to make her a Dame of the British Empire. Like Sir Orpheus she is a patriot, but she is far more pugnacious and parochial than the Foreign Secretary, treating all 'foreigners as her inferiors, especially when they differ in colour'. She represents the spirit of the past, and its aggressive resurgence into the present. 'If you want to know what real English public opinion is, keep your eye on me,' she tells the League's Secretary. 'I'm not a bit afraid of war . . .' Though everyone agrees she is a political ignoramus, 'she has courage, sincerity, good looks, and big publicity,' Sir Orpheus acknowledges, ' . . . Everything that our voters love.' She is also intensely ambitious and knows that 'victory in war is the key to fame and glory'. This Boadicea is to become 'the first female Prime Minister, too late for inclusion in the play,' Shaw was later to tell readers of *Everybody's Political What's What?* This is his prophetic warning against the backward-looking culture of a nation in decline that will raise from its legendary depths a Warrior Queen to relive its heroic days.

It is to gain the good opinion of the world that the three dictators present themselves at the international court. 'Where the spotlight is, there will the despots be gathered.' Signor Bardo Bombardone, 'a man of destiny' got up in the British première as a Roman emperor, has had previous reincarnations as Nero and Napoleon; Herr Battler with his 'resolutely dissatisfied expression' and attired as Lohengrin suggests Hitler's permanent place in German medieval romance; and the name General Flanco de Fortinbras connects the contemporary Spanish leader to the Prince of Norway who calls for 'Soldiers' music and the rites of war' over Hamlet's body at the end of Shakespeare's play.

'What an actor!' exclaims Battler in admiration of Bombardone. He is indeed a wonderfully bumptious presence, with a flight of words for every occasion, enunciating the doctrine of power, the praise of war, the belief in will and impulse that belong to Nietzsche. Bombardone is somewhat contemptuous of Flanco, a limited archetypal gentleman-soldier from the old school; but he feels wary of Battler whom he sees on a razor's edge between inspiration and the megalomania that is a recurrent theme in Shaw's later work.

Hitler had turned out to be 'a very difficult character to dramatize'. It was not easy for Shaw to get 'any credible account of the man'. He distrusted the newspaper stories he read and in 1936 and 1937 there was little else to go on. Some people he questioned, such as the German biographer Emil Ludwig, described Hitler as 'an illiterate semi-idiot'. However a book called *I Knew Hitler* (1938) by Kurt Ludecke, an early Nazi who had left the party and gone into exile, gave Shaw a picture he could recognize – that of a patient learner determined to rise above his obscurity.

In trying to explain the phenomenon of Hitler, Shaw involves everyone. His Battler has been born a nobody, grown up in a humiliated country and matched his life to Germany's history. This is no freakish homuncule accidentally visited upon an unfortunate world, but a terrible combination of us all, and it is we who have created him and called him forth. He bears witness to having been carried forward by 'a mighty movement in the history of the world.

'Impelled by it I have stretched out my hand and lifted my country from the gutter into which you and your allies were trampling it, and made it once more the terror of Europe, though the danger is in your own guilty souls and not in any malice of mine ... You must all come my way, because I march with the times, and march as pioneer ...'

But for those who expected him to prove the most ominous of the dictators, bringing extra intensity to the last act, Battler is a disappointment. Partly it may have been that Hitler was beyond Shaw's range: he had chosen a brief period when he played 'understudy' to Mussolini. Partly it may be that his interest in power had declined in old age: many of Battler's lines lack bite and he is given no confrontation with his chief accuser, the Jew, to match the confrontation between Warwick and Cauchon in *Saint Joan*. Partly, too, Shaw may have been worried by the consequences on Trebitsch of a horrifying stage presentation of protofascism ('I could not involve you in such a controversy,' he had written earlier, ' . . . you would run all the risks and I none').

Shaw tried to develop the character of Battler through the many revisions of *Geneva*. The first draft had been written between the second week of February and the first week of April 1936. 'I think I shall be able to turn Geneva into a presentable play after all,' Shaw wrote that May. A year later, now nearing his eighty-second birthday, he announced: 'Geneva is finished. So am I – very nearly.' Both statements were untrue. The world première, however, took place in Warsaw on 25 July 1938 while Germany was preparing to mobilize. The British première opened at Malvern on 1 August in a last-minute revised version that with further modifications was then transferred to London towards the end of November.

Shaw's alterations to *Geneva* were of three kinds: changes 'to cut it to the bone', changes to keep it up to date, and changes to appease Jewish feelings. None was perceived as being successful.

The fashionable length for a play in the 1930s was a little over two hours – 18,000 words. Shaw's plays were from a third to half as long again. 'I now overwrite to such an extent,' he had said at the end of 1933, 'that I have to cut the play down by a full third to pull it properly together and bring it within possible limits of time.' Yet they were still too long – and when he added a new penultimate act in 1945 the length of *Geneva* was extended to nearly three and a half hours.

'All plays with topical gags (and there is nothing else in Geneva) must have been altered almost from night to night in pantomimes and burlesques,' Shaw wrote to the producer, H. K. Ayliff. The most substantial of his topical changes was to be the 600-word scene he added in September 1939. 'The declaration of war is the making of Geneva which has always lacked a substantial climax,' he told the theatrical presenter Roy Limbert. In the last weeks of 1938 and during the first eight months of 1939 *Geneva* had scored a spectacular success, playing for 237 performances in London before going on tour. 'When do you sail?' Shaw asked Maurice Colbourne on 17 September 1939. 'I can let you have the new version by the end of the week.' But Colbourne, who with Barry Jones was to give it an adventurous tour through Canada and the United States, believed that 'Hitler worked too fast . . . the play was out of date before its ink was dry.' By the time *Geneva* opened at the Henry Miller Theater in New York on 30 January 1940, the League of Nations was moribund and Shaw's courtroom proceedings sounded 'extraordinarily futile'.

Yet one day something would have to take the place of the League of Nations. Though 'weak and slow and helpless and confused' as Gilbert Murray acknowledged, it had been a first tentative step towards Shaw's court of pure justice now being dismissed by critics as a midsummer night's dream. Shaw had wanted to use his audiences as juries who would evaluate this Platonic investigation into public morals and hear the case for open government where 'no walls can hide you, and no distance deaden your lightest whisper'; he wanted to show them the enormous pains that dictators will take to win public opinion – their opinion; he wanted them to attend another Shavian Judgment Day and see in the false apocalypse the falsity of despair.

But many critics disliked it. They had hoped to see a grand Shavian paradox with the tyrants tumbled from their thrones and the victims raised up into high places. Where audiences laughed, these critics felt uneasy. Shaw had admitted that his play 'flatters them [the dictators] enormously'. This embarrassed many Shavians. Reviewing the London production, Desmond MacCarthy objected: 'In this disputatious extravaganza, which Mr Shaw calls "A Play of the Moment", the case for the Jew ought of course to have been vigorously put. It was not. Nor was the case of the democrat . . . [Shaw] has been false to his mission in life. Until recent years one of the things I have admired most in him has been a spontaneous chivalry . . . Speaking for myself, it [*Geneva*] made me ask if it were possible that I had been a fool about Bernard Shaw all my writing life.'

Shaw's extra act is an attempt to give a technical answer to MacCarthy's objections without destroying the genre in which he was working. The act defines the 'Lake change' that has turned the League Secretary away from the philistine mainland towards the rich and strange figure of the Judge. It also separates everyone into their political and biological components by allowing them a few minutes' privacy in this public play. As political beings they have come to Geneva to air their grievances and push their interests. In this political aspect they are all their own worst enemies. But biologically their differences are life-enhancing. Begonia Brown pairs off with the Judge; the Jew dines with the Widow; and Sir Orpheus spends his evening with the Soviet Commissar. All this supports the Judge's statement in the last act that even the dictators themselves seem 'personally harmless human beings' though their political deeds call for 'nothing short of your immediate execution'.

Shaw believed that critics were reacting to his characters as if they were actual people rather than political abstractions. They had wanted him to take sides. The result was that Shaw's play was equally unpopular with pro- and anti-Nazis – the proper fate, perhaps, for an unpleasant play.

The question remains as to whether his use of Aristophanic comedy was appropriate in presenting part of history that would culminate in the killing of six million Jews in concentration camps. *Lysistrata* had been written to stop a war and *Geneva* was written in the hope of helping to prevent one. It is a piece of stage diplomacy, a variant to Neville Chamberlain's appeasement policy, by someone who remembered the horror and futility of the first war against Germany and refused to be drawn into popular confusion between reality and myth. All that a playwright can do, Shaw wrote, 'is to extract comedy and tragedy from the existing situation and wait and see what will become of it'. The tragedy is implicit in his play, the comedy broad and explicit. Battler protests to the Judge that the court is 'making fun of us', and one of the prosecutors gives Shaw's answer: 'God has ordained that when men are childish enough to fancy that they are gods they become what you call funny. We cannot help laughing at them.'

But it was not possible to laugh in the 1940s and *Geneva* was to become Shaw's 'most frequently disparaged play'. He disparaged it himself. 'What a horrible play!' he exclaimed. But 'I have to write plays like *Geneva*. It is not that I want to.' He believed that the effective way of exposing his dictators was not to falsify historical fact by allowing their accusers to dominate the court, but to let us see the authentic miming of their dramaturgical tricks, their bluster and defiance, mystical flights and neurotic fears, and the face-saving gestures that reveal the littleness of their brief authority.

'Authority is a sort of genius: either you have it or you have not,' Bombardone tells the court. The nature of authority is the theme of *Geneva*. 'Your objective is domination,' the Judge replies to the dictators. His own objective is to create a code of justice that serves the desire for harmony underlying the discord of our lives. The dictators' authority stands on Will, is violent, and artificially imposes order; the Judge's authority proceeds from the imagination, is settled, and stands on faith. When the future of the world is threatened by a science fiction disaster, the dictators are suddenly reduced from archetypes to stereotypes.

'A moment ago we were important persons: the fate of Europe seemed to depend on us. What are we now?' asks the Judge. Only he and the Secretary retain their stature. Only they, at the final curtain, can still tell truth from falsehood and know that the end of the world is not in fact at hand.

*

Shortly before the opening of *Geneva* in London, Shaw began his last pleasant play, *'In Good King Charles's Golden Days'*. 'It's about the time of Charles II,' Charlotte wrote. 'Such a lot of interesting people lived then & he is throwing them all in together to sink or swim. I am rather pleased about it.' Beatrice Webb also felt pleased. 'I read the first scene

– brilliant dialogue . . . ' she wrote on 11 January 1939. 'If he can bring in some sort of striking incident into the play and not limit himself to sparkling talk, it may turn out A.1.'

Written in the aftermath of *Pygmalion*'s cinema triumph, '*In Good King Charles's Golden Days*' was begun as an 'educational history film' for Gabriel Pascal. The cast were to be sumptuously clothed in seventeenth-century costumes 'regardless of expense, numbers and salaries'. By the time he completed it on 3 May 1939 it had turned into a Shavian Restoration comedy. Either because he now lacked the vitality or else because he had no interest left in the devices and excitements of dramatic action, the play lacks the 'striking incident' that Beatrice Webb believed characterized his best work. It is a conversation piece, diversified by moments of burlesque, recitation and vaudeville, and alive with anachronisms that anticipate the future. 'Playwrights have their just privileges,' wrote Maynard Keynes, celebrating 'the proleptic quality' of these anachronisms.

The two continuous scenes of the long first act are set in the cheerful library of a large house Shaw invents for Isaac Newton at Cambridge. Here, one golden day, Newton's calculations into the future and the past are creatively interrupted by a procession of unheralded visitors. Charles II (travelling incognito as Mr Rowley) and a big man dressed in leather with bright eyes and a powerful voice who turns out to be George Fox arrive together ('the spiritual powers before the temporal,' says Charles, ushering in Fox before him). They are pursued by Charles's brother James, an obtuse and bigoted Catholic; and three of the King's ladies, Nell Gwynn, Barbara Villiers, the jealous Duchess of Cleveland, and the 'baby-faced' Louise de Kéroualle, Duchess of Portsmouth, who has called on Isaac Newton for a love philtre. Finally the portrait painter Godfrey Kneller turns up in search of the King. All of them stay to lunch.

'You find yourself dining with all sorts,' Begonia Brown had remarked in the extra act to *Geneva*. There are several cross-references between the two plays. In *Charles*, whose education was completed 'at the Hague', the Geneva spirit resides. But Shaw has now turned from the riddle of authority to the mysterious process of learning. From the blends and clashes of this diverse group everyone learns something. 'You unsettle my mind,' Fox tells James, Duke of York. 'I find your company agreeable to me, but very unsettling,' he tells Nell Gwynn. Charles encourages this unsettling process: 'The settled mind stagnates, Pastor.' Fox's imagination acknowledges that 'Divine grace takes many strange forms' as he goes in to lunch arm in arm with 'the player woman' Nell Gwynn. 'You remind me that where my Master went I must follow.'

The meeting Shaw arranges in his play between Newton and Kneller had its origin in his own meeting with Einstein at the Savoy in 1930. Here he coupled Einstein's name with Newton's as great 'makers of universes' (as opposed to the 'makers of empires' who populate *Geneva*). 'Newton invented a straight line,' he said.

'... he invented the force which would make the straight line fit the straight lines of his universe – and bend them – and that was the force of gravitation ... the book of that universe ... was not a magical marvellous thing like a Bible. It was a matter-of-fact British thing like a Bradshaw ... Then an amazing thing happened. A young professor got up in the middle of Europe and [said]... "The world is not a British rectilinear world. It is a curvilinear world, and the heavenly bodies go in curves"... I reminded myself that Leonardo da Vinci, the artist, born twenty-one years before Copernicus, wrote down in his notebook ... "The earth is a moon of the sun." And later on the English artist, William Hogarth, a contemporary of Newton – their lives overlapped by thirty years – ... said "The line of nature is a curve". He anticipated our guest.'

When he came to write *Good King Charles*, Shaw found that Hogarth's life had overlapped with Newton's by only twenty-two years and could not be fitted into the year of his modern genesis 1680. So he fell back on Kneller, whose dates just fitted in, granting him a paraphrase of Hogarth's 'the line of beauty is a curve'. When the artist's 'different kind of understanding' joins issue with the scientist's, Newton suddenly wakes from his dream of a rectilinear universe and is endowed with the foresight of an Einstein. 'I have made Newton aware of something wrong with the perihelion of Mercury,' Shaw gleefully explained in his Preface. 'Not since Shakespeare made Hector of Troy quote Aristotle has the stage perpetrated a more staggering anachronism.'

'You presume to teach me my profession,' objects the arrogant Kneller in his first speech of the play. *Good King Charles* is a demonstration of how every professional can learn something from the amateur. The atmosphere, over which the King presides rather like the Waiter in *You Never Can Tell*, is largely created by Charles's mistresses – it is, for example, Louise de Kéroualle who sees that 'Mr Kneller and Mr Newton seem to mean exactly the same thing; only one calls it beauty and the other gravitation.'

Charles II's regular business on the stage had been to act the principal lover in historical romances. He would stride on as a gorgeously costumed walking gentleman and from time to time sit down so that Moll Davis and Sweet Nell could nest on his knee. Shaw transforms the Merry Monarch who lived so badly and died so well, who never said a foolish thing nor ever did a wise one, into a version of King Magnus from *The Apple Cart*, a man whose reputation has been warped by official histories.

Good King Charles is both the culmination of Shaw's work as a historical dramatist, which had begun in 1895 with the 'Fictitious Paragraph of History' about Napoleon he called *The Man of Destiny*, and a merging of the chronicle play into allegorical fable and extravaganza. The third scene, which takes the form of a short second act, reads like an epilogue to the play – but it does not resemble the Epilogue to *Saint Joan*; it is a companion piece to the Interlude from *The Apple Cart*.

In the 'late afternoon' the Shavian King comes to the untidy boudoir of his wife, Catherine of Braganza. He has left 'one of Nature's queens' and come home to his domestic queen, who is 'guiltless of sex appeal'.

They talk and the fifty-year-old Charles asks: 'can anything I can ever do make up to you for my unfaithfulness?' Shaw allows Catherine to answer: 'People think of nothing but that, as if that were the whole of life. What care I about your women? . . . You have never been really unfaithful to me.' Though this reads like a sentimental gloss on what Charlotte had once felt, it may approximate to her retrospective view, at the age of eighty, of G.B.S.'s flirtations. But Shaw has the honesty to hold some balance between the two women 'I was born to love'. Charles admits to one real unfaithfulness, with the beautiful childish Frances Theresa Stuart, whose portrait as Minerva by Sir Peter Lely he insisted should figure on the coinage of the realm. By making the woman who represents Stella Campbell no longer a Queen of Nature with an act to herself, but merely one of the Queen's Maids of Honour who does not actually have a part in *Good King Charles*, Shaw was making amends to Charlotte for *The Apple Cart* Interlude. 'I never touched her,' Charles tells his wife. 'But she had some magic that scattered my wits . . . I was furious when she ran away from me and married Richmond.' And Catherine admits: 'it was the only time I ever was jealous.'

But they had come through: 'we are grown-up now,' Charles hopes. The play exhibits Charles as 'the best of husbands', and the message he is sending to Charlotte is that theirs had been the best of marriages made on earth. The 'hopeless tenderness' that attaches the King to the Queen at the end of *The Apple Cart* unites the King and Queen throughout this second act of *Good King Charles*. There is only one fear that falls between them, and that is a fear of the other's death. 'Long live the King!' cries Catherine. 'May the Queen live for ever!' exclaims Charles.

And the curtain descends on them both.

6

TREBITSCH ÜBER ALLES

I am tired of the way in which the newspapers . . . continue to make it
appear that I am an admirer of dictatorship. All my work shows the truth
to be otherwise.

'G.B.S. Replies to the Man in the Street',
The Star (4 August 1938)

By the end of the 1920s Shaw had acquired the status of a German
classic. While 'Sudermann has long disappeared from the stage . . . while
even Hauptmann occupies a very limited space,' wrote Leon Feuchtwanger
in 1928, ' . . . Bernard Shaw since the war reigns supreme'.

Despite the record run of *Saint Joan* Shaw was alarmed by what he
began to learn of Reinhardt's production. Scenes had been scissored,
speeches superimposed, and Trebitsch had been a wide-eyed collaborator
in this 'monstrous misrepresentation'. When they met in 1927 Shaw
rather took to Reinhardt. 'He looked extraordinarily well and open-airy,
as if he had never been near a theatre in his life,' he wrote. 'I never saw
a man less spoilt by his profession.'

But *The Apple Cart* was an even greater travesty than *Saint Joan*.
Reinhardt had sandwiched his political comedy between episodes of
jazzed-up Bach and Chopin, and served it to German audiences as a racy
operetta. Boanerges, attired like a racegoer's bookie, appeared as a Jew;
Proteus was a 'bilious fool'; and the goddess Orinthia prostituted as an
'unscrupulous little kiosk-mamselle'. 'Why have you not challenged him
[Reinhardt], shot him, sabred him, buried him in unconsecrated ground,'
Shaw demanded of Trebitsch; ' . . . you must either quarrel with Reinhardt
or quarrel with me. Clearly you must quarrel with Reinhardt.'

Alas, it was almost impossible to quarrel with Trebitsch. He was as
sensitive as a child and full of innocent happiness. What neither he nor
Reinhardt realized at the time was that their versions of these plays fed
the atmosphere that, substituting one sort of pornography for another,
was lifting the Nazi regime into power. No wonder Hitler was to declare
that St Joan was portrayed 'much more faithfully by Shaw than by Schiller'
when the German version emphasized the mystical nature of power vested
in someone physically unimpressive yet gifted with the oratorical magic
of patriotic 'voices'. No wonder William Mackenzie King, Prime Minister of Canada, expressed the conviction that Hitler 'will one day rank
with Joan of Arc'. The lonely genius of power was again underscored by
Reinhardt's King Magnus in *The Apple Cart*. The King's 'strangely inno-

cent relations' with the flapper-cocotte Orinthia were presented as the sexual recreations of a Nietzschean Superman whose political inspiration rose clear above the poisoned well of anti-German Jewish democracy. What had been intended by Shaw as a warning against dreaming the old dreams became the inducement to a new nightmare, in short 'a pornographic Jew baiting farce,' he told Trebitsch. 'How can I ever expect a decent German to speak to me again? . . . Rheinhardt [sic] must find other authors to drag through the mud . . . I have been kinder with him than he deserves (merely for your sake) . . . I cannot afford another such disgrace, nor can you.'

A colleague of Reinhardt's, Robert Klein, directed *Too True to be Good*. Shaw was accused of nihilism and warned that the new Germany would no longer tolerate attacks on the family. When the play moved to Mannheim early in 1933, it was disrupted by Nazi shouts of 'Jew Shaw!' until the police came to restore order. 'Can it be possible that my vogue in Germany, of which I have been so proud, has been all a mistake?' Shaw had asked.

At the beginning of 1933, when Hitler became Chancellor, Shaw's reputation seemed to be on the turn. In March Reinhardt left Germany for Austria and that summer ceded his theatres via the government to the German people. By 1937 he was safely unemployed in the United States. 'In all he had introduced nine of Shaw's plays to Berlin, produced another five and added two others in Vienna for over 1,300 performances,' Professor Samuel Weiss notes, 'second only to Shakespeare in Reinhardt's repertory.'

Until Hitler entered Austria early in 1938, Trebitsch experienced the Nazi phenomenon chiefly as an economic setback. The new Germany did not want foreign playwrights: 'snobbish trifles', as Shaw and Pirandello were described. Trebitsch came from a wealthy family and was married to the widow of a Russian Grand Duke. Expensive habits were ingrained. During the 1930s he looked towards Shaw's films to buoy him up. But G.B.S. was oddly unhelpful. He refused to license a German film of *The Chocolate Soldier* (the musical version of *Arms and the Man*), he was downright discouraging about the Hollywood prospects of *Jitta's Atonement* and he accused Trebitsch of deception over his German-language film of *Pygmalion*. Rather than be a party to such bargains, he preferred to 'advance' Trebitsch money. 'Shall I lend you £500 (equivalent to £15,000 in 1997) on account pending some transaction between us for your translation rights?' he asked at the end of 1935. 'If so, send me a wire with the single word Yes, and I will remit.' But such sums were small in comparison with Trebitsch's dreams of a movie fortune.

Most years, right up to 1939, Trebitsch would come over to England

and every time Shaw would amaze him by picking up the conversation exactly where they had left it twelve months previously 'as though the earth had not, after all, travelled once around the sun since we had last been face to face with each other'. Trebitsch had come to know 'what English hospitality meant'. At Ayot it meant sessions round the piano while G.B.S. sang Tristan to Tina's Isolde, periods of tranquillity while he disappeared into 'his tent at the bottom of the garden', and when they all came together again there were 'the blessings of vegetarian cookery'. There were also regular walks in the 'hilly' countryside. Keeping up with Shaw's long joyful strides had put a terrible strain on the seams of Trebitsch's suits. With the passing years, as his own panting figure solidified and slowed, G.B.S. appeared to be sprinting into the future, his arms swinging, nostrils eagerly extended.

To mitigate the rigours of English hospitality, Shaw would book Trebitsch into a first-class London hotel. He also encouraged him to bring German friends to lunch at Whitehall Court – often refugees like Stefan Zweig – so that he could learn more of what was going on in Germany. It was difficult learning much from Trebitsch himself, though G.B.S. could pick up something from the fate of his translations. *The Black Girl* remained unpublished because 'it would have been banned by the German censorship' (it was eventually brought out in 1948). In 1934 *On the Rocks* 'was a very great success,' Trebitsch insisted, yet he had been obliged to give it the subtitle 'England, Arise!' which was taken as a summons to follow Germany's example. *The Simpleton*, which was banned in Austria, and in Germany did not transfer from Leipzig to Berlin, was the last of Shaw's plays 'I was to translate into German while still living in my native country,' Trebitsch recalled.

Joseph Goebbels attended the Berlin première of *The Millionairess* in December 1936, but the play had to be published without its 'Preface on Bosses' speculating on Hitler's Jewish ancestry and diagnosing Judophobia as 'one of those lesions which sometimes prove fatal'. Shaw's reputation in Nazi Germany was by now full of anomalies. Whatever he wrote for the British press was, to Trebitsch's bewilderment, carefully edited in the German newspapers. Hitler himself went to a revival of *Caesar and Cleopatra* in 1939, but *Geneva* was forbidden to be either published or performed that year and the actor who had played Battler at Warsaw's Teatr Polski was imprisoned after the annexation of Poland. The Nazi ideologist Alfred Rosenberg placed Shaw among the 'army of half-breed "artists"' opposing the 'revived racial spirit'; yet tributes were still paid to him in *Germania*, *Berliner Tageblatt*, and *Deutsche Allgemeine Zeitung* on his eightieth birthday. Even during the war, his work was protected from wholesale censorship and he was classified by Goebbels as a satirical, anti-plutocratic Irishman: a case on his own.

As the 1930s advanced, Shaw felt increasingly responsible for Trebitsch. Hitler's name is not mentioned in their correspondence until May 1933 when, condemning the Nazi Judenhetze, Shaw advised him to 'keep out of the mêlée as much as possible. If you are pressed as to why you translate me, who am a notorious Communist . . . you must say that you are not concerned with all that – that you have introduced me to Germany as a great artist . . . But you are not committed to my opinions.'

For much of this time Shaw treated Hitler as if he were a fellow-playwright under attack from foreign critics whose animosity was driving the Nazi national theatre crazy. Certainly the Nazis were mad on the Jewish question. 'It is idle to argue against this sort of insanity,' he wrote in 1933. 'Judophobia is as pathological as hydrophobia . . . The Nazis are suffering from an epidemic of a very malignant disease.' Setting aside the Jewish question, he took care to be 'scrupulously polite and just to Hitler (which nobody else in England is)'. He welcomed the incorporation of the German trade unions into a state-directed Labour Front, as well as the introduction of a compulsory labour service.

Shaw recognized the human instinct called nationalism that made people 'dissatisfied unless they think they are governed by themselves and not by foreigners'. He believed that the Treaty of Versailles, which placed Germany in an inferior position, was an affront to that instinct, and that Hitler had been hoisted to power by the force of national resentment. Such was the outcome of an abuse of victory. He had urged the Allies to dismantle the military frontiers imposed by the Treaty, and believed that the weak liberal parliamentarianism of Western democracies had produced a 'Four Power Funk' that was positively encouraging Nazi expansionism. He saw the best hope of peace in a rearmament programme by the Allies and a pact between Britain, France, the United States and Soviet Russia which would banish the communist taboo and hold a broad equilibrium until Germany and Italy inevitably split apart and Hitler's supremacy came to its natural end.

Every country, Shaw believed, was entitled to its civil wars without foreign interference. He looked on the Spanish Civil War as an internal class war with Franco standing for property, privilege and 'everything we are all taught to consider respectable'. But 'Spain must choose for itself,' he wrote: 'it is really not our business.' As Stanley Weintraub concluded: 'For Shaw, a victory for the wrong side in Spain was preferable to a general European war, which the internationalizing of the Civil War seemed to be making inevitable.'

'My slogan is "Africa for the Africans!"' Shaw wrote in 1938. His most extreme expression of this principle came in a letter to Beatrice Webb where he admitted 'the right of States to make eugenic experiments by weeding out any strains that they think undesirable'. This was written when, wishing himself to 'intervene' over Sidney Webb's stroke, he was obliged to stifle the impulse by 'an exercise of conscious reasoning'. He had called the Nazis 'a mentally bankrupt party', and described Hitler as a reincarnation of Torquemada, meaning that he was not uniquely beyond historical processes but part of a pattern in human behaviour that, at some time or another, had infected all nations. 'In every country you can find rabid people who have a phobia against Jews, Jesuits, Armenians, Negroes, Freemasons, Irishmen, or simply foreigners as such,' he had written in the *Jewish Chronicle* in 1932. ' . . . Political parties are not above exploiting these fears and jealousies.' When asked by a journalist in 1938 whether Hitler had solved the Jewish problem, he replied: 'He has created it.' But no single nation could tackle this problem with clean hands. G.B.S. persisted in reminding readers of unfortunate facts (such as England's treatment of the Irish or the Ku-Klux-Klan's lynchings of Negroes) in case the itch to intervene grew virtuously irresistible. But although making the miscalculation that Hitler 'shrinks from the massacre which the logic of his phobia demands', he recognized that by the late 1930s this had become a world problem.

In much that he wrote about Germany in the 1930s Shaw had Siegfried and Tina Trebitsch in the back of his mind. On 13 March 1938, the day after Hitler's troops entered Austria, their car had been commandeered by the Nazis and their chauffeur beaten up. Three days later, having obtained Czech passports, they left Vienna, travelling to Prague and some time later to Zurich.

'I dare not write a line frankly to anyone in Germany,' Shaw had explained. The day after Hitler announced Austria's annexation, he sent a card to Trebitsch in Vienna welcoming the 'glorious news' and suggesting that 'if Tina's health obliges you to travel, why not come to England, where we are having an extraordinarily fine spring?' This card was forwarded to Prague. It upset Trebitsch. He could not crack its code. 'And now you reproach me because I did not write letters pointing out that you are a Jew marked out for Nazi persecution,' Shaw explained.

Even after this escape, Shaw refused to take the terrible verbal revenge on Hitler that Trebitsch longed to translate. 'What good does it do?' he wrote. ' . . . I might do you a great deal of harm.' He immediately despatched almost £1,000 and advised Trebitsch to 'keep very quiet within reach of Zurich until the atmosphere is a little less electric'. After reading a report by the Berlin correspondent of the *Observer* stating that his translator was a Jew, he wrote to the paper describing him as 'an uncircumcized and baptized Lutheran German . . . married to a lady of unquestioned Christian authenticity' – a description puzzling to Trebitsch, who wanted to know what uncircumcised meant.

Though living in exile, the Trebitsches did not regard themselves as refugees. They were to pass little of the next year in Switzerland, but resided at rather grand hotels in Nice and Paris. From time to time their chauffeur and housekeeper would smuggle out some of their possessions. Otherwise they lived on what they had taken with them (including Tina's jewels) supplemented by what Shaw gave them (another £1,000 in April 1939).

'I am still very sceptical as to the likelihood of war,' Shaw wrote in March 1939. Raising Trebitsch's morale was a method of keeping up his own spirits. He based his predictions not on what he feared but on what he hoped would happen. Having urged the Allies to make a pact with Soviet Russia, he represented Germany's non-aggression pact with the USSR as the next best thing because now 'Hitler is under the powerful thumb of Stalin, whose interest in peace is overwhelming'. Everyone else seemed terrified. 'Why? Am I mad?' he asked in *The Times*. A week later Britain and Germany were at war.

Such optimism had become a necessary bond between Shaw and his German translator. At Whitehall Court that year they had both experienced what Trebitsch called 'the justifiable premonition that this would have to be my last visit for a long time'. Before parting, they took special care to ask whether they had not forgotten anything, since it might be years before they saw each other. But, Shaw affirmed: 'We shall both survive this bloody business.'

NINETEEN

UNCOMMON SENSE AND CARELESS TALK

History always repeats itself and yet never repeats itself.
Shaw to C. H. Norman (22 April 1940)

A young boy on holiday at Frinton-on-Sea saw them walking along the parade the day war was declared. They were arm in arm: he measuring his springy pace to hers and looking grave: she very slow and in tears. After the shocks of Shaw's illnesses this news of a second world war in Charlotte's lifetime produced a sort of nervous breakdown. She retreated miserably to her bed, while Frinton filled up with evacuee children carrying gas masks and paddling like ducks in the sea ('they are having the time of their lives'). G.B.S. strove to lift everyone's spirits with displays of bravado. ' "War is Over", Shaw Says,' announced the *New York Journal-American* in the first week of October; and the following week the *Daily Worker* carried more Shavian optimism across its front page: 'Cease Fire, Turn up the Lights.'

All over the country false alarms were carrying their single note of warning through the air. 'I absolutely refused to budge,' Shaw wrote to Blanche Patch; ' . . . there are no safe places in Frinton and the beds are very comfortable, besides being respectable places to die in.'

It seemed that everyone had reluctantly acquiesced to this war. Public libraries and schools were commandeered, petrol was rationed, mortgage rates raised. All were exhorted to make sacrifices – the *Daily Telegraph* gave up its book reviews. A National Service Bill came into force conscripting men between eighteen and forty-one. Up and down the streets paraded army officers, their boots and belts aggressively polished. The King opened Parliament wearing a splendid naval uniform.

Shaw studied the papers and listened to the news bulletins on the wireless which were becoming a focal point of the day in every home. Unlike the last war, everything was unnaturally dark and quiet. 'The psychology of September 1939 was terribly different from that of August 1914,' wrote Leonard Woolf. During the 1930s one political crisis had piled upon another until people now waited for the catastrophe with feelings of helplessness. 'Yet the catastrophe we braced ourself to face did not happen,' recorded Cecil Beaton in his diary. On 10 December Sir

Henry Channon, a Parliamentary Private Secretary in the Foreign Office, noted that 'the war is 100 days old, and a damned bore it is . . .' As these months of what Churchill called the 'pretended war' lengthened into 1940, London began to fill with 'pathetic couples having last flings together', crowds of bony youths, airmen on leave, debutantes, tarts, all jostling to the jazz bands of the night-clubs, gazing at the *tableaux vivants* at the Windmill Theatre.

Could the war itself have been a false alarm? 'There is still half a chance of a negotiation,' Shaw wrote to Kingsley Martin, editor of the *New Statesman*. He saw Neville Chamberlain as having been bullied by British Imperialists, without the ghost of a mandate from the people, into challenging Hitler with an unconvincing ultimatum when Britain was unprepared for war. He described the British guarantee to Poland as 'thoughtless' because it had nerved the Polish army to put up a desperate resistance to the German invasion, leading to the loss of many thousands of lives on both sides – while Britain, without 'a soldier within hundreds of miles of her frontiers nor a sailor in the Baltic', could not use her bombers for fear of starting a series of retaliatory raids.

When, early in October, Hitler extended peace feelers to Britain and France, Shaw responded with an article 'Uncommon Sense about the War' in the *New Statesman*. This proposed setting up truce negotiations (accompanied by a suspension of hostilities) to which Britain would go 'with quite as big a bundle of demands as Herr Hitler' to find out whether another world war was truly unavoidable. That much was owed to those who had known the heartbreak of the last war.

There was little enthusiasm for war in the country. 'Everyone I speak to seems utterly bewildered and downcast,' Beatrice Webb wrote in her diary. Harold Nicolson, then a National Labour Member of Parliament, shared this apprehension. Like Leonard and Virginia Woolf, he privately supplied himself and his wife Vita Sackville-West with the means of committing suicide, but kept up a brave face in public. 'I would rather go down fighting and suffering than creep out after a month or two at the cost of losing our pride.'

G.B.S. felt no such pride. 'I am an Irishman and you an Englishman,' he reminded Maynard Keynes. ' . . . bear with me. I am sometimes useful.' On this occasion, however, Keynes was convinced that Shaw's uncommon sense might do harm 'both to the chances of success in peace and the prospects of success in war', and he recommended that his article for the *New Statesman* be forwarded to the Censor. When Kingsley Martin consulted the Foreign Office, he found to his surprise that Lord Halifax, the Foreign Secretary, was 'strongly in favour of publication'. The Cabinet, some of whom wanted to 'cease fighting Hitler and join Germany against

Stalin', was evidently curious to see what this debate between 'responsible writers' would reveal about public opinion. The correspondence columns of the *New Statesman* prolonged the debate for two months. Shaw still hoped that the defence of freedom might be left to the German people themselves. Surely they must wake up soon from the spell of Hitler's eloquence. Keynes, too, though he quarrelled with Shaw's mischievous tone and tactics, did not yet 'rule out the ideal peace. It may fall within our grasp', he wrote in the *New Statesman*, 'in ways we cannot yet foresee. And then we could indeed cease fire . . .'

*

. . . and turn up the lights. At the beginning of the war the Home Secretary had decided to close all 'places of amusement' – art galleries, cinemas, concert halls, museums, theatres. Only churches and public houses were exempt. Shaw, who believed that the arts and learned professions must be defended against any presumption that they were 'an immoral luxury', advised the Royal Academy of Dramatic Art to follow the example of the Windmill Theatre and stay open every day, backing up his advice with a cheque for £1,000 (equivalent to £27,000 in 1997). In letters to *The Times* and *Daily Telegraph* he recalled that during the Great War the theatres had been overflowing with soldiers on leave desperately needing recreation after their miseries in the trenches. 'Are there to be no theatres for them this time?' he asked. 'We have hundreds of thousands of evacuated children to be kept out of mischief and traffic dangers. Are there to be no pictures for them?'

These war years, which began and ended with productions of *Saint Joan*, were to witness an extraordinary refuelling of Shaw's popularity. At the end of 1939 the curtain went up on *Major Barbara* at the Westminster Theatre, and the following summer *The Devil's Disciple*, with Robert Donat appearing as Dick Dudgeon, came in after a successful tour to the Piccadilly Theatre. During 1942 *The Doctor's Dilemma*, with Vivien Leigh playing Jennifer Dubedat and John Gielgud replacing Cyril Cusack as Louis Dubedat, ran for 474 performances at the Haymarket Theatre. Outstanding among the four London revivals the next year was a luxurious production of *Heartbreak House* at the Cambridge Theatre, with costumes by Cecil Beaton and starring Edith Evans and Deborah Kerr, which ran for 236 performances. But the topmost year was 1944 when no fewer than nine of Shaw's plays were put on in London, including the Old Vic Company's production of *Arms and the Man* with Laurence Olivier, Ralph Richardson, Sybil Thorndike and Margaret Leighton – all players lured back to the stage after making their names on the screen. 'The London stage is transformed out of knowledge,' wrote the theatrical manager

Ashley Dukes. ' . . . We laugh at the Balkans with a good conscience, and the shafts of wit aimed at heroism fall lightly at the feet of the returning warriors.'

'Another "success" would ruin me,' Shaw cried out. On incomes of over £30,000, after the deduction of income tax at ten shillings in the pound, every two pounds of gross income yielded one pound of net income, on which nineteen shillings of surtax was payable – giving the Shavian total of one pound and nineteen shillings taxation on one pound of net income. Nevertheless he let his reputation boom, with occasional reminders to the press that he was paying handsomely for everyone's fun. A touring Bernard Shaw Company took seven of his plays round the country in 1942 and 1943; and half a dozen of them were also regularly performed by the Travelling Repertory Theatre which went to villages and munitions factories, mining towns and blitzed towns, and established 'Plays in the Parks' in support of the Lord Mayor's War Relief Fund. 'They were a delight to do because they filled the theatre with laughter,' remembered Basil Langton, actor-manager of the Travelling Repertory Theatre, 'required little scenery or lighting, and provided wonderful acting parts for every member of the company.' It was his illuminating unconventionality, Beatrice Webb believed, that had relit this interest in his work. Revivals of his comedies, romances, fables, fantasias were appearing everywhere to meet the needs of a new public educated by the wireless. But 'I have written nothing for the stage since Charles,' Shaw told Beatrice in 1941, 'and will perhaps not write for it again.'

*

Meanwhile he poured forth journalism – over 250 broadsides, contributions to symposiums, answers to questionnaires. In his fashion he sought to fill the role Carlyle had occupied in the nineteenth century as keeper of the public conscience. But the world was larger, more uncertain, fragmented. 'One has to gather any major news nowadays by means of hints and allusions,' wrote George Orwell in 1940. Shaw used these hints and allusions as best he could, resenting his exclusion from more central sources of information. 'It was indeed a wonder to note how carefully the old man watched the news and kept up with events,' observed the Labour Member of Parliament Emrys Hughes.

One of the new war posters warned the populace that 'Careless Talk Costs Lives'. But the most careless talk of all, to Shaw's mind, came from Cabinet Ministers. Britain needed a speaker who was the mouthpiece of a nation, giving precise replies to Hitler and Stalin, because, as Sir Henry Channon was to write from the Ministry of Information in March 1940, 'we are being defeated all along the diplomatic line'. Shaw recommended a different set of guidelines on 'how to talk intelligently about the war' and disentangle the mesh of enemy-impregnated words – appeasement, communism, fascism, Hitlerism and National Socialism. 'We must not let Adolf give Socialism a bad name,' he rallied Beatrice Webb. In the Shavian dictionary appeasement on a grand scale was to be read as our war aim (rather than a defeatist term carrying 'accidental associations with unpopular bygones at Munich'); and he defined Hitlerism as a government founded on the idolatry of one person laying claim to the world on behalf of Germans as the Chosen Race. Such personal autocracy had no special connection with either fascism (which was the imposition of State-assisted privatization), or democracy (government in the interests of everybody and not a privileged class) or communism. 'If you are a Communist then the word requires a new definition,' Lord Alfred Douglas was to press him. But Shaw's definition was catholic, noncombatant, free from party political commitment, and unaffected by the abuse of power or the fall of empires. 'Communism has a hundred doors; and they do not all open and close at the same moment,' he wrote. 'Everywhere already we have communism in roads, bridges, street lighting, water supply, police protection, military, naval and air services . . . Civilization could not exist for a fortnight except on a basis of Communism.'

During 1941 he began a campaign to outlaw the reciprocal bombing of cities, calling on Britain to initiate this agreement with the German Government, since no military advantage could be won by a method of warfare that stiffened the resistance of the attacked and gratified passions among the attackers 'which civilised nations should not gratify'. Both sides were depending for victory on famine by blockade, he characteristically added, so any reduction in the number of civilian mouths to feed would be a tactical gain.

More serious, from the Government's view, was Shaw's conciliatory policy towards the Soviet Union. He represented Stalin's invasion of Finland as inevitable once the Finnish Government had allowed the country to be used by the United States and Western Allies. 'No Power can tolerate a frontier from which a town such as Leningrad could be shelled.' He asked his readers to imagine what England would do if threatened from the West. 'Ireland is the British Finland,' he wrote. 'Rather than allow Ireland to be occupied or invaded or even threatened by a foreign Power . . . England would be strategically obliged to reoccupy Ireland . . . That is exactly the Russo-Finnish situation.'

By the early summer of 1940, when the war had settled into its routine and Churchill's Cabinet replaced Chamberlain's, Shaw was invited to broadcast on the Overseas Service of the British Broadcasting Corporation. Though he believed he could get the better of William Joyce –

the notorious 'Lord Haw-Haw' who broadcast Nazi propaganda into Britain – 'I should scare the wits out of the official home front,' he warned. 'Better let this sleeping dog lie.' But the BBC persisted. It wanted someone whose vivacity and insight would stir foreign listeners as J. B. Priestley's broadcasts had inspired audiences in Britain. At the beginning of June Shaw sent in his script. He portrayed the British as 'champion fighters for humanity' and gave, as the Big Idea that 'we must risk our lives for', the need to defeat anti-Semitism. A year before Germany invaded Soviet Russia and eighteen months before the United States came into the war, he inserted one passage that sounded peculiarly Shavian in its prophetic unorthodoxy. 'The friendship of Russia is vitally important to us just now. Russia and America may soon have the fate of the world in their hands; that is why I am always so civil to Russia.'

The Ministry of Information immediately vetoed this broadcast. 'Shaw's main theme is that the only thing Hitler has done wrong is to persecute the Jews,' explained Harold Nicolson, then Parliamentary Secretary to the Ministry of Information and later to be appointed a Governor of the BBC. 'As the Minister [Duff Cooper] remarks, millions of Americans and some other people [believe] that this is the only thing he has done right.' The Controller of Overseas Programmes, Sir Stephen Tallents, tried to reverse this decision. 'The value, especially in America, of a broadcast talk by Shaw endorsing the war against Germany and Italy would be very high,' he explained. ' . . . Australia, too, urged me some months ago to secure a talk by him.' In an attempt to free Shaw from a total ban at the microphone, Tallents informed the Ministry of Information that Shaw had 'responded with entire good temper and generosity' to the cancellation of his talk, and had been 'willing to alter the text at any points which had been felt to give difficulty'. But Duff Cooper was adamant: 'I won't have that man on the air.'

'I shall have to confine myself to articles in The Daily Worker,' Shaw wrote. But when, at the beginning of 1941, this English Communist Party newspaper was banned for twenty months, another wartime outlet closed. Not wishing to embarrass Kingsley Martin at the New Statesman, he gave much of his war journalism to Forward, a socialist weekly edited in Glasgow by Keir Hardie's son-in-law Emrys Hughes. Here he warned the public against any government alliance with the Axis to destroy Russian Socialism because one day we would have to sit down with Stalin – and preferably Roosevelt also – to settle the ceasefire.

*

By 1939 Shaw gave Gabriel Pascal the go-ahead to film *Major Barbara*. The invasion of Holland and Belgium had put a stop to Pascal's plans for

European financing, and Shaw agreed to let his syndicate use £12,774 of his royalties from the *Pygmalion* film until it could raise in Britain the full £125,000 (equivalent to over £3 million in 1997) Pascal reckoned was needed.

The sixteen new film sequences Shaw supplied to help modernize his play were almost his only dramatic writing during these war years. One reason for making this film was Wendy Hiller's desire to play the title role. Shaw vetoed Pascal's choice of Leslie Howard for Cusins ('quite out of the question') and suggested 'a young actor named [Alec] Guinness' who had recently come to lunch at Whitehall Court. But eventually the part went to Rex Harrison, and Undershaft was played by Robert Morley.

'My film future depends on you,' Shaw appealed to Pascal. 'Ought I have your life insured?' But wars were little deterrent to Pascal. Towards the end of the 1930s *Time* magazine had placed him, along with Hitler and the Pope, among the ten most famous men in the world. With Shaw's help he had become a naturalized British subject, bought a large Tudor house in Buckinghamshire and, so G.B.S. hoped, 'shifted the artistic center of gravity of the film industry from Hollywood to Middlesex'.

On 26 May 1940, as the British prepared to evacuate Dunkirk, the location shooting of *Major Barbara* began on the Dartington Hall Estate in South Devon, later moving to Tower Bridge for some Salvation Army scenes and round Sheffield for distant views of Undershaft's factory. Three weeks after the shooting started at Denham Studio on 17 June, the Nazi bombing of Britain began. Pascal was to count 125 bombs that fell in the vicinity of Denham while they were making the picture. Technical equipment was destroyed, transportation often made impossible by land mines and railway disruptions, and when they did get to London to take exterior shots they would find everything in rubble the next day before their shooting was completed. Everyone agreed with Wendy Hiller that 'without Pascal's courage and almost demoniac energy the film would never have beaten all the difficulties of wartime production'.

The cast and crew bedded down 'as close to the studio as possible: dressing rooms, pubs, the homes of friends'. Whenever air-raid warnings interrupted a scene they would go to ground in a concrete shelter under the sound studio. Here Robert Morley filled the dim light with fantastic tales of Pascal's adventures culminating in a luxurious private shelter nearby, lined by tiger skins and crowded with '*lovvly vimmen*', where they imagined him to be taking his ease.

In fact Pascal never went to a shelter but would hold his infatuated scenario editor, Marjorie Deans, on the lawn in extended discussion of the script as the bombers raced overhead. 'Pascal bullied everyone,' Robert Morley remembered. Each morning his shouts of 'You are ruining my picture – you are crucifying me!' would greet the actors and at the end of the day the empty sets still rang to his cries. During the course of the film he sacked almost everyone and then, with a kiss and a grin, made it up again.

What ruined Pascal, in the opinion of Alexander Korda, was his mania to be a director. For he was determined to direct as well as produce *Major Barbara*. 'I was sadly missing the helpful direction of "Puffin" Asquith which I had on *Pygmalion*,' wrote Wendy Hiller. 'Pascal was no director.' He had, however, two directorial assistants: Harold French who rehearsed the actors with their lines; and David Lean, who was in charge of the shooting. When Pascal ordered impossible camera angles, Lean and the crew would turn over the camera with no film in it to keep him happy and these were referred to as 'Gaby's takes'.

On his eighty-fourth birthday G.B.S. was invited to the Albert Hall to watch the shooting of the Salvation Army revival meeting. 'Everyone wanted to be in that,' wrote the theatre historian Joe Mitchenson who was one of 500 extras assembled for the scene. Getting over-excited Shaw plunged into the sound equipment, spreading silent but expensive chaos, and played with the camera mounted on a trolley with a boom. Raising himself into its chair he began pulling handles and pressing buttons, lifting and swivelling and tilting himself until he almost crashed to the floor. After that he sheepishly climbed down and tried to behave better. But when the large band began to play, he darted down the main aisle and dived in among the chorus, voice uplifted, arms flailing. Next day he sent Pascal his 'apologies for interfering on Friday. I tried to keep quiet; but suddenly felt twenty years younger, and couldn't.'

Originally scheduled for ten weeks, the film eventually took six months to shoot, while the costs rose to almost £300,000 (equivalent to £7 million in 1997). Flushed with modified triumph, Pascal accompanied Katharine Hepburn to the grand opening in Nassau on 20 March 1941 'under the aegis of the Duke and Duchess of Windsor'. But *Major Barbara* was not to be the film of his or Shaw's dreams. 'They cut the last third of the film all to pieces,' he told Gilbert Murray. 'I saw the finished film once only – I wept with disappointment,' wrote Wendy Hiller. But Gilbert Murray was 'moved and thrilled' by parts of it, Beatrice Webb found its 'expression of the brutal power of mass murder in modern war' dramatically topical, and the general public relished the performance by Robert Newton as the 'rough customer' Bill Walker, the burlesque playing of Robert Morley's Undershaft and Wendy Hiller's achievement in catching Barbara's idealism yet making it so humorously attractive. Seldom had a film sought such sustained intellectual engagement with its audience. The final vision of Perivale St Andrews looked forward to the socialist-inspired plans for post-war reconstruction. 'The house was packed . . . and you could not have had a more responsive audience,' H. G. Wells wrote. 'They laughed at all the right places. Mostly young people in uniform they were . . . We shall rise again sooner than Marx did and for a better reason.'

Some of the best acting came from G.B.S. in a three-minute 'visual prologue' made for American audiences. By now reluctantly convinced that the only way of gaining peace was simply to defeat Hitler and Mussolini, and that 'a single handed victory would not be so good for us as an Anglo-American one', Shaw recorded a preface that was seen by many Americans as a rallying call for them to come and fight. The British argument was simple, he told one United States correspondent: 'there is a very dangerous madman loose in Europe who must, we think, be captured and disabled. If we are right, he is as dangerous to you as to us; so we ask you to join the hunt.'

Made a few days after the exchange of US destroyers for the lease of naval bases in Newfoundland and the Caribbean, Shaw's prologue announces his own contribution to the deal: 'I am sending you my old plays, just as you are sending us your old destroyers.' The Battle of Britain had reached its peak the previous month and one hundred and three German planes were shot down over London three days after Shaw made his recording. 'I am within forty minutes' drive of the center of London, and at any moment a bomb may crash through this roof and blow me to atoms,' he told the United States. An air-raid warning sounded while he was speaking and Pascal charged forwards – then stopped as G.B.S. imperturbably went on ('We'll keep it in the picture') against the grunting of the enemy planes. For this was a valedictory to which he had summoned his unseen audiences. When he was a little boy, he continued, the Dublin newspapers reported how America had abolished black slavery. When he grew up 'I determined to devote my life as far as I could to the abolition of white slavery' – the sort of slavery to economic dictatorship that had erupted in this war.

Then he lifted one hand, trembling slightly, to his forehead and held it there in a salute. 'When my mere bodily stuff is gone, I should like to imagine that you are still working with me . . . at that particular job . . . farewell!'

2

WIFE AND WIDOWER

Think of us always as we were.
Shaw to Lillah McCarthy (24 October 1942)

After Dunkirk and the Battle of Britain '[we] are snapping our fingers at Hitler and his threat of invasion,' Shaw notified Trebitsch. They carried on normally: from Wednesday noon to Saturday afternoon at Whitehall Court then at Ayot from Saturday afternoon to Wednesday morning, sleeping through the all-night air-raids in both places. 'My wife does not give a damn for bombs,' G.B.S. wrote to Alfred Douglas, 'but dreads shelters and prefers death to getting up and dressing.'

So it was business as usual until, one Saturday afternoon early in September 1940, arriving at Ayot a day before the German Blitzkrieg opened on London, Charlotte fell heavily on the gravel. For the rest of that month she was unable to walk and could go upstairs only backwards, with G.B.S. precariously at the helm. 'I have accidents,' she wrote to Nancy Astor, ' – but they seem to do me good.' This accident, G.B.S. added, had given them 'an excuse for skulking down here instead of coming up to town for half the week in our regular routine'.

By the time Charlotte recovered it seemed foolish to go back to London at all. Ayot had a small squeaky siren that importantly echoed all the alarms from the capital thirty miles away, and they could see the flashes in the sky and hear the thunder of the guns, like far-off celebrations. Stray raiders would occasionally float overhead and release a bomb near enough to shiver the house, and Charlotte 'is infuriated by the big bangs, which she takes as personal insults,' Shaw told Nancy Astor. In London one bomb destroyed almost 90,000 unbound sets of sheets of his collected edition ('plus their dustwrappers,' his bibliographer notes) and threw up enough insurance money for him to pay off his supertax. Another bomb whistled past Blanche Patch's bedroom ceiling, spilling her onto the floor and shattering a house nearby. Feeling rather 'out of sorts', she hurried down to join Shaw and Charlotte at Ayot.

In the middle of November came a 'full dress bombardment' with high-explosives crashing onto the roads and fields around them and the rattle of shrapnel on the roof. Shaw seemed chiefly worried by the effect all this was beginning to have on Charlotte. 'All through the war his nerve remained steady,' Miss Patch conceded, 'and often in the late evening when we heard the wail of the Alert siren, and the planes were droning overhead, he would sit down at the piano and play and sing the old Italian operas . . . Charlotte liked to lie in her room upstairs and listen to him.'

The mingling of these arias with the noise of the siren was peculiarly trying for Miss Patch. The fact was that of the three of them she alone wasn't going deaf ('a great point in her favor at the telephone,' Shaw admitted). But at least the old man wasn't under her feet so much as in Whitehall Court. After breakfast he would stalk down to his 'toolshed' at the end of the garden. Here he arranged himself with all the innocent technology of his work deployed around him – a thermometer and paste pot, some paper clips and scissors, red ink, alarm clock and portable Remington typewriter ('Could that typewriter type a play?' he had asked the demonstrator when buying it. 'Of course it could,' she indignantly replied. 'It could type anything'). But he only used two fingers and of course he couldn't touch-type like Miss Patch. 'He loved his red ink, paste pot and paper clips,' she observed; ' . . . the alarm clock was set each day to remind him when it was time for lunch. He never took any notice of it.'

His principal work during the war was *Everybody's Political What's What?* 'I find myself in a world in which everyone knows the XYZ of politics, philosophy, religion, science and art, and nobody knows the ABC of them,' he wrote to Upton Sinclair. He wanted to survey the natural laws governing political action and itemize those subjects which every member of a responsible democracy should understand before voting or becoming eligible for public work. Like much of his later political writings, *Everybody's Political What's What?* was to enquire after egalitarianism in the future while turning away from contemporary heartbreak and helplessness.

He would work at this book until lunch – to which he was summoned by the clanging of a loud handbell from the house. Then he slept for an hour in the early afternoon and would afterwards 'go about the lanes and woods with a secateur and a little saw and clear up overgrown paths' until the blackout came down. In spite of the world's miseries, these spring and summer months were 'altogether wonderful', and he did not find his old age or this 'cottage life' unhappy – at least not unbearably so as his youth had been. 'G.B.S. is like a lion,' Charlotte wrote to Nancy Astor. ' . . . he has taken to lopping & pruning trees. I wish you could see him when he comes in from the woods – dripping & smiling.'

Nancy Astor had offered the Shaws a home at Cliveden but 'it must remain a lovely dream for us,' Charlotte thought – 'I wish it could come true, but it cant.' By August however she felt so much better that they decided to go for three weeks' holiday there. Both of them were nervous: 'we are like people coming out of a dark cellar,' Charlotte warned Nancy.

And Shaw wrote: 'If I attempt to talk my teeth fall out . . . you must hide me in a corner.' What he had never accepted was that people might value him without all his self-dramatizing. 'He *is* older but he is incredible for eighty-five,' wrote Nancy Astor's thirty-year-old niece Joyce Grenfell who was also staying at Cliveden. ' . . . When he isn't putting on his act . . . then he is a charmer and what he has to say is worth hearing . . . Mrs Shaw is very deaf, which means that conversation takes time and must be executed *fortissimo.*'

They returned to Ayot, 'our little prison'. Shaw had hoped to finish *Everybody's Political What's What?* by the end of 1941, but the book hung fire. 'I am too old to know whether I can still write or not,' he confessed to Wells. He tried to start another play but themes and stories eluded him: 'I seem to have dried up at last: I am absolutely barren.'

He had found some pleasure however in preparing a *Graduates' Keepsake & Counsellor* for Diploma Students at the Royal Academy of Dramatic Art. A land mine had exploded at the RADA building in Gower Street in 1941 completely destroying the students' theatre that backed on to Malet Street. Shaw had immediately gone up to see the extent of the damage, picking his way through the splintered door, past the blown out windows to the debris of the Principal's office. Workmen were roughly shuttering up the windows with wooden boards and through a slit between these planks the actor Laurence Irving saw a shaft of sunlight through scintillating dust pierce the gloom and focus on G.B.S. huddled in a chair. 'The cocksure mobile features of the old champion of the RADA were pinched and aged; the challenging and mocking eyes were lustreless and evasive in undisguised dejection.'

After his eightieth birthday G.B.S. had finally given up platform speaking and five years later he retired from all committee work, including the Council of the Shakespeare Memorial Theatre, the British Broadcasting Corporation's Advisory Committee on Spoken English and the RADA Council. He could now work on his political textbook with fewer diversions and, whenever this became troublesome, he would renew his experiments (like the experiments of a literary alchemist) to discover an alphabet capable of spelling the English language.

One day was like another at Ayot. Miss Patch knitted for the soldiers, made soft dolls for the Red Cross and typed up Shaw's shorthand for the printer. But each day grew shorter and 'the darkness is hard to bear'. Charlotte longed to be back in Whitehall Court, but Shaw feared the effect of more bombing on her – his newspaper campaign against reprisal raids on cities was largely prompted by this fear. Perhaps 'a bomb could be the easiest way to end,' she had speculated in a letter to Beatrice Webb.

This was a gruelling winter for Charlotte. The rheumatic attacks grew more severe, and she seemed to be shrinking into infirmity. 'Her spine has collapsed to such an extent that she cannot stand without hurting herself unbearably by a one-sided stoop,' Shaw wrote to Nancy Astor in April 1942. When summing up their condition – 'very old and muddled . . . always late or wrong or both' – G.B.S. liked to add their ages together. By the spring of 1942 they were one hundred and seventy. While she was 'bowed and crippled, furrowed and wrinkled', he still stood strikingly erect yet was so insubstantial he appeared like Coleridge's 'a man all light, a seraph man'. In his prime his weight had been almost eleven stone; by 1941 it was barely nine stone. 'I am losing weight so fast that I shall presently have totally disappeared,' he wrote to Beatrice Webb. 'I look when stripped like a native in a famine picture, an imperfectly concealed skeleton.'

There were still moments when he felt nearly 'equal to anything'. And Charlotte, fitted with a reinforced corset designed by her osteopath, was 'getting through'. Could the two of them visit Cliveden again? Shaw explained the predicament to Nancy. 'A change would be good for her [Charlotte] one way, and in another possibly kill her.' Nancy urged them on and that July they decided to risk it, G.B.S. having first made arrangements for their cremation in case 'we die on your hands'.

While at Cliveden they were both medically examined by the Canadian military staff billeted there. 'I was passed sound in wind and limb,' Shaw wrote to Beatrice Webb. But after four years of torment Charlotte was found to have been suffering from osteitis deformans or Paget's disease. This inexorable breaking down of the bone structure had probably been caused by an accident in her youth and 'the prognosis was terrible,' Shaw told Wells, 'ending with double pneumonia'.

They returned to Ayot, and dug in for another winter. The weeks flew past 'like Hurricanes and Spitfires' to the cries of the siren, the distant crackle of gunfire and bumping rhythm of the air-raids. Shaw's almost transparent figure flickered between his workshed and the wireless. He could not quell his beating spirit of enquiry. 'The war is interesting all the same, diabolical, senseless, useless as it now seems,' he wrote to Sidney Webb. ' . . . I am rather curious to see how it will end.' But for Charlotte, horribly hunchbacked, unable to walk without help, unable to reach the garden, her body held in an armoured corset, there was nothing to desire except an easeful death. As the disease progressed her bones felt as if they were cracking and splintering whenever she moved or breathed too deeply. 'The difficulty with which she crawls about is heartbreaking,' Shaw wrote.

They were approaching their forty-fifth wedding anniversary. Many onlookers of the Shavian phenomenon imagined Charlotte to be a prisoner of wedlock. Accompanying her husband to his first nights, publishing *Selected Passages* from his works, nursing him through illnesses, keeping obscurely in the background, she seemed to have given up her life to his career. 'He [Shaw] is too clever to be really in love with Lottie, who is nearly clever but not quite,' Charlotte's cousin Edith Somerville had written. 'However it may be better than it seems.'

And it had been better, this childless partnership of a middle-aged couple. They had arranged their lives like characters from a previous century. Charlotte 'had decided views on etiquette,' noticed one of their neighbours, Captain Ames, and she led a life 'rather like that of a Queen Consort,' Lady Rhondda thought. ' . . . she had a number of the attributes of a Queen.'

'My wife is a woman of strong mentality,' Shaw answered one questioner, 'and expresses strong opinions to me twelve or thirteen times a day.' Many of her strongest opinions, such as her view that they should not have children, had been expressions of her anxieties. 'Sometimes I have been sorry that I was not more insistent on the point,' Shaw later conceded.

Not everyone thought her charming. Sean O'Casey was disgusted by the sight of her leaning determinedly forward, covering a huge pile of food in thick sauce and swallowing it down with sluggish energy – Johnsonian eating habits that some saw as a compensatory substitute for sex. Others ridiculed her quest, in the wake of her guru James Porter Mills, to locate the Great Architect in the works of Ouspensky and others. When Mills died in the 1920s, his teaching had been taken up by Charlotte's friend, the former actress Lena Ashwell. 'I am working to achieve a wireless set which will respond to the music of the spheres,' she wrote in Shotover style, pursuing Mills's merging of Eastern religions with Western technology. Such mystical tunings-in seemed eventually to invade Shaw's own work as he progressed from the *Pygmalion* romance between an East End flower girl and a West End gentleman to the surreal marriage of East and West in *The Simpleton of the Unexpected Isles*.

Charlotte had always admired the egalitarian vision of her husband's socialism. But it was as 'a dreamer of wonderful dreams' that he had become a great man to her. Perhaps something of her own intuitions quietly permeated those dreams. In any event 'something quite indestructible' had grown up between them. 'Finally a marriage consolidates itself until the two lose all sense of separateness, and the married life becomes one life,' they wrote to a friend, echoing the works of Pra and Prola at the end of *The Simpleton*.

Blanche Patch had one day come across G.B.S. sitting with his arms round Charlotte singing an impromptu version of 'O Mr Porter' – and quietly stole away. Barry Jackson, calling round unexpectedly, found them sitting side by side on a sofa looking through a large picture book – themselves the picture of a happy marriage. To Lawrence Langner, Charlotte appeared like 'a kindly mother whose grown son was distinguishing himself before an appreciative audience'. Her family, which had starred Granville Barker and T. E. Lawrence as sons apparent, was mostly played by the servants at Ayot. They saw his tenderness, her solicitude. Each morning he would go to her bedroom for a talk before breakfast, and she would insist on arranging the pillows for his siesta between their lunch and tea together. In the late afternoon, when he liked to stride outdoors after air and exercise, she would wait anxiously for him until he presented himself 'to show that nothing has happened to me'. In the evenings he sometimes played for her the songs his mother had sung in Dublin; and they would read together books she had chosen, such as Gerald Heard's *Pain, Sex and Time*. Heard's attempt to combine science and religion 'lighted up the whole pile of little personal discoveries,' she wrote, 'and made them glow with new lights'.

Shaw's anxieties rose to the surface as financial problems. Charlotte's anxieties were generally exercised over her servants at Ayot. It was as if she felt that human life could not be sustained without a housekeeper and cook, gardener and two maids. 'There is not much joy in life for her,' Shaw admitted to Sidney Webb. Beatrice, too, was finding prolonged living a painful experience. 'You can't cure old age,' she had reflected when considering Charlotte's condition as well as her own. But of course there was a cure. Once Sidney was dead she could easily kill herself. 'It will suit the public interest,' she reasoned. But on 30 April 1943, after a few days in a coma, it was Beatrice who died. 'I used to take it as a matter of course that if Beatrice died you would come and live with us,' Shaw wrote to Sidney; 'for I never counted on our living to this ridiculous age and being incapable of taking care of ourselves or anyone else.'

Shaw kept Beatrice's death secret from Charlotte. Such protection was not difficult. Her handwriting had grown so illegible she seldom wrote to anyone these days. 'Like an old witch', she seemed to have shrunk to half her size, yet was still not reconciled to her condition and would not stay in bed. She longed to escape her 'little prison' at Ayot and, after much hesitation, Shaw agreed to move her back in the summer of 1943 to Whitehall Court. If this plan worked, he could give the staff at Ayot a holiday and engage a professional nurse in London. The doctors had warned him that the journey would be risky. She was driven up on his eighty-seventh birthday. It was 'quite an adventure,' he told Wells; 'but it came off successfully and she is happier here.'

In the past Shaw's trick for distracting Charlotte from her illnesses had been to fall ill himself. 'If Charlotte were dying, I know an infallible way to restore her to health,' he had told St John Ervine. 'I should simply go to bed and say I was dying.' But now her condition was complicated by distressing hallucinations, and his sustained health became vital to whatever peace of mind she could grasp. He consulted friends for the names of new doctors and psychotherapists who might banish the spectres which filled her imagination and added to her terrors. 'She saw crowds of strangers in the room, and kept asking me to remonstrate with the managers and housekeeper here for allowing them to come up and intrude,' he wrote to Almroth Wright. 'She also spoke to me of imaginary kittens and little dogs in my lap. She was, however, perfectly reasonable on every point except the actual existence of these phantoms.'

The cumulative strain of these weeks in London grew terrible. Then, helping her to get up from dinner on the evening of Friday 10 September, Shaw noticed what seemed an extraordinary change coming over Charlotte. She appeared calmer and did not complain as usual when he took her through to the drawing-room. A miracle was rising before his eyes. He thought he saw the furrows and wrinkles on her forehead smooth away. She smiled easily at him and he heard her speaking again with her happiest voice. She seemed to look forty years younger, like the woman he had known at the time of their marriage when his own life seemed to be fading. He told her she was beautiful and that the illness was leaving her. 'She talked to me insistently and joyously, and, though it was almost all unintelligible, she heard and understood what I said to her, and was delighted by my assurances that she was getting well, that all our troubles were over.'

He settled her in for the night earlier than usual. Next morning he was woken by the nurse with the news that Charlotte had been found lying at the foot of her bed clutching her alarm clock and with her face bleeding. He helped to get her back into bed and immediately engaged a night nurse. In spite of this fall, she was still smiling and happy; and the mysterious process by which she appeared to be discarding her years went on: 'I had never known her so young.' He realized she was dying, and kept with her every minute while she went on 'babbling to me like a happy child,' he wrote to Mrs Higgs. ' . . . you may be sure I said everything to please her.'

Again he settled her in early for the night and slept well himself. At a quarter past eight on Sunday morning the night nurse came to his bedroom and told him he had been a widower for almost six hours. He went to her room and looking down at the body, saw that Charlotte's face was that of a young girl – like the portrait painted of her by Sartorio in Rome before he had known her. 'I have never seen anything so beautiful.'

She appeared so very much alive that he could not stop himself from going into her room again and again that day, and the next day, continuing to speak softly to her. 'Once, I thought that her eyes opened slightly while I was talking to her' and he took out his microscope glass and held it to her lips. 'I could not believe she was dead.'

All sorts of associations – an echo from Cordelia at the end of *King Lear*, a reversal of Wilde's ending for *The Picture of Dorian Gray* – mingled in this strange experience. He felt the need to tell everyone about her marvellous rejuvenation. 'It was a blessedly happy ending,' he wrote to Granville-Barker, breaking almost twenty years of silence. ' . . . You will not, I know, mind my writing this to you.' It was like a fairy story in which two fears magically cancel each other and finally allow Shaw's search for love to be fulfilled. 'I did not know I could be so moved,' he wrote to Wells. This vivid trance lasted nearly two days. Then the jaw dropped open and she was gone.

'No flowers; no black clothes; no service,' she had requested. Shaw arranged for a private cremation as he had for his mother and his sister. There was cheerful weather for the cremation. Nancy Astor and Blanche Patch accompanied him to Golders Green. The ceremony lasted only a few minutes. Handel, the composer Charlotte loved most, provided the music: 'But Thou didst not leave His soul in hell' from *Messiah* for the committal: 'Ombra ma fù' from *Serse* for the voluntary. 'Who could ask for more?' At the end 'Shaw lifted up his arms and softly sang the words as if to Charlotte whose coffin was just in front of him,' Blanche Patch noticed. Then, as the anthem neared its close, the coffin moved out and Shaw continued standing there, still singing, his arms outstretched.

3

SOME LATE APPEARANCES

I still regard myself as Charlotte's property. I really could not ask her to
mix our ashes with those of a third party.
                    Shaw to Nancy Astor (11 August 1944)

Shaw kept the news of Charlotte's death out of the newspapers until after her cremation. Once the news broke he was overwhelmed with letters and had to acknowledge them collectively in a notice to *The Times* assuring everyone that 'a very happy ending to a very long life has left him awaiting his own turn in perfect serenity'.

He took care to barricade himself against the possibility of grief. 'I do not grieve,' he insisted; 'but then neither do I forget.' Yet the armour that had shone so brightly for so long was suddenly pierced. 'He missed her far more than he had ever imagined he could miss anybody,' observed St John Ervine.

He fought this enemy, grief, with every Shavian contrivance. As a widower he was free to return to his bachelor life, eat when he was hungry, dress as he fancied, work without consulting anyone but himself and 'go to bed when I like' – which usually meant after midnight. His mother had never gone to bed before midnight 'and I won't either'. People thought he was lonely: but he was simply indulging the talent for solitude. As he had replaced emotion with money as his mother's motive for leaving him in Dublin, so now he covered his emotional deprivation with obsessional talk of death duties. Charlotte's death had been a great loss, he agreed, a great financial loss.

The method by which he strove to reverse his feelings, outwit them, transmute them into something else – at any rate keep them under control – sounded oddly callous. He would boast that his health was improving markedly since Charlotte's death 'set me free'. Even so he could not always prevent himself from crying even in the street. Over the next two or three years he 'seemed extraordinarily "caved in",' a local bookseller near Ayot noticed. ' . . . He looked very sad. I did not think he was capable of such emotional feeling, but he showed it quite obviously.'

*

There is a rumour that after forty years of marriage a widower must be in want of a second attachment. On several occasions Shaw had protested that he was not naturally a marrying man. But was he not protesting a little too much? People were already reflecting on the possibility of a sequel. Such a possibility played on the minds of both Lady Astor and Miss Patch as they drove back from Golders Green.

Indeed Lady Astor was hardly out of the crematorium before, to Miss Patch's disgust, she invited G.B.S. to Cliveden. Miss Patch knew her game. Standing with G.B.S. over Charlotte's body only three days before, Miss Patch had asked him whether he wished to invite anyone else to Golders Green 'and his reply was that he and I would go together'. Why then had Lady Astor 'insisted on coming with us' if she wasn't trying to supplant Miss Patch as G.B.S.'s closest female friend? Lady Astor was 'invariably kind to me,' she admitted, but these acts of kindness – proposals that she must be looked after by a nurse or given a new suit of clothes – were curiously condescending. She did not see herself needing charity. Her needs were more ambitious. When G.B.S. presented her with certain likenesses of himself – in short, his Max Beerbohm caricatures – or handed her Charlotte's £100 fur coat, it was surely obvious that these were not charitable provisions but tokens of a special attachment. She had been with him now for quarter of a century, sharing what he most prized: his work. And it was his work, she was pleased to note, that he cited when fending off Lady Astor's advances. 'I am full of unfinished jobs, some of them unbegun; and I must take my own advice and not attempt to combine them with visits to Cliveden.'

Even in her tweed suit, sweater and pearls, Miss Patch barely cast a shadow. Her Picasso-esque features, framed by a face 'like two profiles stuck together', were formidable. 'Piercing blue eyes,' one dismayed visitor noted, 'a nose like a knife blade, lipless mouth.'

Towards the end of 1943 Shaw left Whitehall Court and settled himself at Ayot. Miss Patch stayed uneasily in London while Lady Astor gave notice of whirlwind swoops on G.B.S. 'Don't come down here yet,' he pleaded at the beginning of 1944. But Lady Astor believed that Charlotte had implicitly bequeathed her this duty. So she persisted, dealing out offers of excursions to Cornwall and holidays at Sandwich. 'I shall never see these places again,' Shaw answered. 'The garden and plantation here are my world now'.

Though she sometimes got through his defences, Lady Astor found the encircling routine at Ayot difficult to penetrate. 'If I am uprooted I shall probably die immediately,' he threatened her. 'That is how I feel about it.' Besides there had been enough changes at Ayot in the year following Charlotte's death.

Early in June 1944 sinister robot planes began flying over the south of England. These were the Germans' mysterious new secret weapons, pilot-less rockets nicknamed 'doodlebugs' that suddenly cut out, descended silently and hit the ground with shattering explosions. One of these 'buzzer bombs', as Blanche Patch called them, fell near Charing Cross and had blown in the study windows of Shaw's flat, broken the grandfather clock in the hall and covered everything with debris. As the bombardment went on, she began to feel 'decidedly shaky'. Over 200,000 houses, mostly in the London area, had been made uninhabitable by the end of the month. 'The pilotless bombs have driven everyone out of London, including Blanche, who has returned to Ayot,' Shaw wrote to Nancy Astor.

Two months after Miss Patch arrived at Ayot, Henry and Clara Higgs, the gardener and housekeeper who had been with Shaw forty-two years, gave in their notice. They had put off going as long as they could. Higgs could not bear to leave his garden until he had seen it through one more summer; it had been a matter of pride to him that Shaw felt so attached to this garden – he liked to find out things about it, such as whether the large red poppies' seeds were poisonous. 'We must get a packet and send them off to Hitler,' he said after being told they were.

Higgs's place in the garden was to be taken in 1946 by his pupil Fred Drury. As a lad of nineteen, Drury had come to work as assistant gardener in 1934, then been called up six years later, and eventually returned to Ayot after the war, not wishing 'to work for anyone else'. Mrs Higgs's place in the kitchen was immediately filled by Alice Laden, a capable, grey-haired, pink-complexioned widow who had nursed Charlotte through her last weeks at Whitehall Court.

'I want you to come and look after me till *I* die,' Shaw told her. It was a tall order but Mrs Laden had felt lonely after losing her husband in the war – and besides, she reckoned that she knew how to handle G.B.S. 'I could sense his moods,' she said. ' . . . I had a way with him.' Shaw had sent his Rolls to fetch her and her cat Bunch and waited with Mrs Higgs who had volunteered to stay on for a fortnight to train her. But after two devastating days, Mrs Higgs fled, driven out with her husband 'before a terrible New Woman, of a species unknown to them, from the house where they had been supreme indoors and out . . . [to] fend for themselves in a world in which they are museum pieces'.

When the day came to shake hands and say goodbye, Higgs could see the old man was upset. 'They went away in a handsome cab, beautifully dressed, with the dog on its lead, greatly excited,' Shaw wrote to Nancy Astor. 'I kissed her goodbye, and waved after them until the car disappeared round the corner . . . when I went to the shelter to write, I found that my pen wobbled a little in my hand.'

Shaw made no secret of finding Mrs Laden a good-looking woman and she was soon speaking of him as 'a vur-r-r-ee good man'. Before long whispers began to breeze through the village that he was allowing her the intimacy of trimming his beard and buying his elastic braces ('without them my dignity would disappear altogether,' he apologized to Blanche Patch). Where would it end? 'I shall probably have to marry Mrs Laden,' he confided to Nancy Astor.

Both Lady Astor and Miss Patch felt qualms over this new regime. Since Higgs had left there was no other man on the premises – only Mrs Laden, Miss Patch and the Irish parlourmaid Margaret Cashin. It was a delicate situation. But before many weeks passed Mrs Laden had calmed Lady Astor's and Miss Patch's turbulent suspicions. They were particularly thankful that she knew her place. She never allowed G.B.S. into the kitchen. 'Your job is to write plays and mine is to keep house,' she instructed him. ' . . . You mind your business and I'll mind mine.' Some people were terrified of G.B.S. but she didn't appear frightened of him at all – indeed he seemed a little afraid of her. If he wanted anything he had to ask her for it through the kitchen hatch or leave a note for her on the hall table. 'I am a rank Tory and I heartily disagree with all Socialist views,' she told him. He seemed delighted. Her strong Aberdonian accent was wonderfully effective when discouraging callers on the telephone and at the front door. 'If I didn't have Mrs Laden I'd have an Alsatian watchdog,' Shaw told visitors. In the village she was referred to as 'the Dragon' and, accepting this as a compliment, bought herself a brooch in the form of a green dragon telling G.B.S. he was 'St George to my Dragon'.

In these days of food rationing Mrs Laden's job was not easy. Shaw never allowed her to buy black market goods and he wanted the calories in each dish to be calculated – though she often found him eating sweets, or with a chunk of iced cake in his hand, between meals. 'Sugar I stole,' he had written of his childhood. When he was past ninety, Mrs Laden would come across him in the evening spooning sugar into his mouth from a bowl. For the most part he lived off soups, eggs, milk, honey, cheese, fruit, cream, biscuits and lemon juice. Mrs Laden's husband had been a vegetarian and she had gone through a course of training in vegetarian cookery. Even Miss Patch melted somewhat at the new fare. 'After Mrs Higgs's two or three dishes over and over again, Mrs Laden's meals are the masterpieces of a beribboned chef,' Shaw told Nancy Astor.

As his secretary Miss Patch sometimes opened proposals of marriage from complete strangers, and G.B.S. would forward one or two of them to Nancy Astor with a note: 'You see, I am still in demand.' Would he really be silly enough to marry again? 'Second marriages are the quietest and happiest,' he wrote and Miss Patch agreed. Hadn't Lloyd George married his secretary Frances Stevenson in 1943? But Miss Patch worried that her employer might suddenly attach himself to the wrong person while Lady Astor felt convinced that any second marriage would be disastrous. There was no telling, they agreed, where his vanity might lead him. According to Shavian economics he was growing increasingly attractive to women as his life-expectancy shortened. 'I am rather a catch now,' he explained to Molly Tompkins, 'having only a few years at most to live (quite probably a few days).'

Old flames such as Molly caused Miss Patch and Lady Astor most apprehension. Having gone to Rome, Molly had like Sweetie in *Too True to be Good* led the life of a flamboyant aristocrat until, tired and lonely, she suddenly attempted to kill herself. Shaw had been apprised of her story by Cecil Lewis who still saw her occasionally in Italy. The Wall Street crash forced Molly to give up the palazzo on the Isolino San Giovanni and during the 1930s Shaw paid for the education in England of her son Peter. 'You may send me Peter's bills until I am broke,' he wrote to the headmaster of Ferndale, a private school in Surrey.

Molly had meanwhile turned to playwriting and sent Shaw a melodrama in which, as at the end of *Tosca*, the heroine leaps from a parapet and is drowned in the lake – only to be revived by G.B.S. who changed the plot into a farce like *Jitta's Atonement*. When Laurence mislaid this tragicomedy, Molly took up another career, arriving in London for a one-woman exhibition of her paintings at the Leicester Galleries. 'How terrifying!' Shaw greeted her. 'What on earth am I to do with you?' He bought one of her pictures, 'The Road to Stresa' which he still called The Road to Baveno. 'I found him his old self,' Molly wrote, 'if anything more dear and charming than ever.' After divorcing Laurence, she rented a studio in Chelsea at the end of 1937. 'You mustn't come near us,' Shaw commanded her. 'Why are you so terrified?' she asked, and he replied that he did not want her to see him at eighty-two 'and shatter your memories'. So leaving him her love and 'many more things' she did 'not know how to say but will always have with me', she took off for Rome again and eventually sailed into New York as the Japanese attacked Pearl Harbor.

Now surely, like the love-goddess Maya who was conceived from her and came to life on the *Unexpected Isles*, she must vanish. And so she did until Shaw summoned her up after Charlotte's death. 'Let me have a line occasionally. We can write more freely now that Charlotte can never read our letters.' So she wrote to him freely, proposing a last adventure. She would cross the Atlantic and come to him. They would make up for lost time. 'I am too old for such shocks,' he was to answer her. She was an atom bomb exploding in a havoc of romantic ridicule. 'I am ashamed of you for being afraid,' she replied. Besides, she only wanted a short visit. 'You must cast me off like a laddered stocking,' he pleaded. But she seemed unable to do this. 'When I can't write to you I am always a little lost.' So they continued playing on each other's emotions, conjuring up their phantom island and the endless road to Baveno. 'Have you not yet discovered that the only roads that remain beautiful are those that never led anywhere?' he had once asked her. 'For you never come to the end of them.'

*

Early in 1945 Blanche Patch decided to brave the bombs and move into a private apartment at the Onslow Court Hotel, a respectable address in Queen's Gate soon to be made notorious by John Haig's acid bath murders.

There were several reasons for her retreat. Very few people were privileged to be intimate with G.B.S. or could understand how such intimacy was enhanced by a judicious distance. She was also better placed to drop in for 'a chit-chat' with Shaw's solicitor and accountant. All the same, Miss Patch felt 'down in the dumps'. It was strange, she reflected, 'how indifferent he is to what makes me suffer'.

Putting aside their jealousies, Miss Patch, Mrs Laden and Lady Astor were beginning to form a wary alliance against three mysterious men Shaw had recently imported into his life to cope with the extra work created by 'Charlotte's death and the near prospect of my own'.

The first of these new men was John Wardrop, a twenty-year-old Scottish journalist who had arrived on 17 December 1939 at Whitehall Court from Edinburgh, crumpled, unshaven, 'like the hero in fiction ... with something around a shilling in my pocket and a picture in my heart'. Wardrop had no friends in London, and no plans other than that of attaching himself to G.B.S. He wanted to interview him, write articles about him, become his friend. He introduced himself to Gabriel Pascal, Hesketh Pearson and J. Arthur Rank as Shaw's prospective literary agent and sought to make his attachment indefinably closer after tracking down Erica Cotterill, then living under an assumed name in a North Devon farmhouse. 'Be kind to her,' Shaw advised: 'she is a nonpareil.'

Wardrop was difficult to employ, being 'too good for one level and not schooled enough for the other'. He dreamed of editing Shaw's correspondence, advising on the productions of his plays, representing him on the sets of his films. By 1942 however he was working less exaltedly as Shaw's editorial assistant and proof-reader on *Everybody's Political What's What?*

While waiting for his Shavian future to flower, Wardrop had begun living with Eleanor O'Connell, a capable woman fifteen years older than himself, at a house in Park Village West next to the one occupied by Lucinda Elizabeth Shaw during her last years. G.B.S. had gone round to their house after Charlotte's death and invited them to visit Whitehall Court. To Miss Patch's annoyance he showed them round Charlotte's bedroom and gave Wardrop a key to the apartment so that he could work there in the evenings cataloguing Charlotte's books. Desiring more, Wardrop gained Shaw's permission to carry off various papers from the study files 'for greater safety'. This was almost the last straw for Miss Patch. 'We had some really good rows over the Wardrops when Charlotte died,' she told Hesketh Pearson.

Wardrop sought the posthumous appointment as Shaw's official biographer. He saw the original 'shilling in my pocket' spinning into a magical fortune. 'You are to have my house and everything in it, including my Rolls Royce car, which you are already driving in your dreams,' Shaw was to tell him. ' . . . happy as the dream is, I must wake you up.'

Then, just as Miss Patch felt she had checked Wardrop's trespass into her territory, Shaw 'inflicts the Jew on me,' she complained.

757

The Jew was Dr Fritz Loewenstein. He too had been circling round G.B.S. before Charlotte's death, soliciting his help as early as 1936 in the compilation of a bibliography. Unfortunately Shaw was 'a man who had no understanding of or respect for the responsibilities of scholarship'. Loewenstein had left Germany in 1933 with little more than a doctorate from the University of Würzburg for a thesis on Japanese prints and after the declaration of war was briefly interned as an enemy alien on the Isle of Man. 'I am a Jewish refugee,' he wrote to Shaw in 1942, ' . . . and I am 41 years of age. I am married and have three children. I am as poor as a church mouse and make at present my living as a motor mechanic-trainee.' From his home in north-west London he set out to create a Shaw Society, backdating its foundation to Shaw's eighty-fifth birthday. By means of lectures and exhibitions, bulletins and publications such as Loewenstein's own bibliography, this Shaw Society was to work 'for the creation of a new Civilisation based on Shavian principles'.

Loewenstein's invention appalled Shaw. 'Do not, I beg you, let me see your handwriting, much less yourself,' he advised Loewenstein early in 1943. ' . . . Occupy yourself with your Society as much as you please, but not with G. Bernard Shaw.'

The Shaw Society became the power base for all Loewenstein's throbbing plans. By the beginning of 1944 Shaw was calling him 'a man to be avoided beyond any other fellow creature'. But Loewenstein was not easy to discourage. He weathered a storm of Shavian abuse and still trudged onwards. By the summer of 1944 he had advanced as far as Harpenden, three miles west of Ayot St Lawrence, where his wife was obliged to manage a lodging house in lieu of rent. Buoyed up with the title of 'official bibliographer and remembrancer', Loewenstein put himself entirely at Shaw's disposal.

'I've now reached the stage when I can only sit back and smile at the Shaw–Wardrop–Loewenstein struggles,' Miss Patch had written that summer. But there was bitterness in her smile. Everything was happening very differently from what she had imagined.

Loewenstein was an altogether different 'hero in fiction' from Wardrop – a Wellsian, almost Chaplinesque figure, middle-aged, bowler-hatted, with a homely moustache and forceful expression. While Wardrop was assuming 'not only the position of my literary agent but of my son and heir,' Shaw noted, Loewenstein 'is resolved to be the oldest and dearest friend I have in the world'. His own job specifications were more modest. He looked for a superior 'errand boy' in Wardrop and a 'first rate office boy' in Loewenstein. Whenever Wardrop was given some menial task he looked 'amazed' and became 'infuriated'. But no task was too menial for

Loewenstein who 'positively likes sorting papers and doing things that would drive you mad,' Shaw told Blanche Patch.

By the end of 1944 Wardrop accidentally secured an advantage after Loewenstein's wife hurried her family back to London. 'I am freed from the daily visits of Loewenstein, the Jew,' Miss Patch exulted. But no sooner had she herself returned to London than Loewenstein reappeared in Hertfordshire. Released from his wife and family he was free for five days a week to walk the two and a half miles to Ayot from his room near the Wheathampstead rubbish dump. Shaw hoped that Loewenstein could 'come to a co-operative understanding with W[ardrop]'. But in the second week of February 1945, reacting to information given by Miss Patch, Wardrop 'burst in on me,' Shaw wrote from Ayot, 'with a suit case, frantic about Loewenstein, and announcing that he had come to sleep here and live with me to protect his property (ME) against the Jew'. Shaw packed him back to London and drafted a note intended to resolve the crisis. Wardrop had 'proved impossible,' he decided. ' . . . The slightest encouragement turned his head . . . A rebuff prostrated him to the verge of suicide.' Loewenstein had 'captured the tidying-up job by sheer fitness for it'.

As Shaw approached his nineties this 'scramble for the rights to be regarded as the only friend of an old celebrity who had no friends' was providing what one visitor to Ayot was to call 'a fantastic ending . . . almost as sardonic as the last days of Swift'. These friends jostled round, taking measurements, calculating odds, advancing terms while G.B.S. looked on quizzically at his own obsequies.

The three women had now largely combined their operations. Mrs Laden reported what she saw at Ayot to Miss Patch who embellished the news for Lady Astor who then blazed her way down to Ayot and confronted G.B.S. with her accusations. Loewenstein, who was now being employed to prepare the Shaw archive for posthumous presentation to the British Museum and London School of Economics, as well as to take on various daily chores sorting out priceless 'old rubbish', hastened to prostrate himself before Lady Astor. 'My Lady . . . Future Shaw-Historians (including the present writer) will be most grateful for your Ladyship's intercession. I beg to remain, your Ladyship's obedient servant, F. E. Loewenstein.'

Lady Astor did not relish this falsification of her motives. After twenty-five years in the House of Commons, she had recently been pressured into announcing her retirement from politics. But she was finding this 'one of the hardest things I have ever done in my life'. At the age of sixty-six she was still teeming with energy. Yet she was without occupation. Seeking to regain a sense of 'positive authority', she entered aggressively into the domestic politics of Ayot. 'I don't like the company you are keeping,' she warned Shaw. ' . . . Charlotte would rise in her grave. Mercifully I am not in my grave . . . I must take active steps.'

Besides seeking cover from Lady Astor's heavy artillery, Loewenstein also had to dodge the crossfire from Mrs Laden who, being a war widow, 'has a particular antipathy to Germans,' noticed Miss Patch whose own antipathy favoured the Jews. When Mrs Laden spotted Loewenstein roaming from room to room, peering into drawers, rustling wastepaper baskets, ferreting for relics in the store cupboards, when she caught him listening at the telephone or hovering behind her in the hall so as to butt in after she opened the door to visitors, her ire was kindled and she breathed out her dragon's flames. 'I dont know when I gave a man such a dressing down,' she wrote to Miss Patch. ' . . . I will not have it when I am in charge of Mr Shaw's house.'

This was a valuable letter and Miss Patch made several copies of it. She had taken advice from Shaw's solicitor, and 'I dont think there is anything to be done about ousting the German as long as GBS is pleased with him,' she concluded. 'My one hope is that he will one day get such a drenching on his walk from Wheathampstead . . . that he will pass out.'

But then, late in 1945, Miss Patch was provoked into uncharacteristically dramatic action after the third of Shaw's 'peculiar friends', Stephen Winsten, stepped forward. Winsten was to fashion a career out of being Shaw's neighbour at Ayot. He was like a man 'who comes out one morning to find a meteorite in his back garden,' Brian Inglis wrote, 'and who turns out to be good at organising coach trips for the public to see it'. In their imaginations the Winstens lived through famous people, soliciting politenesses which, in the abundant retelling, swelled into exotic compliments. Shaw enjoyed playing with their cat Fuzzia (a tortoiseshell rival to Mrs Laden's bright orange cat Bunch), sitting for Clare Winsten (who was a sculptress and painter) and chatting to her husband (who had been imprisoned as a youthful pacifist in the Great War). Now that Apsley Cherry-Garrard had left Larmar Park, the Winstens were 'the only people in the village I can talk to or can talk to me'.

Of 'GBS's triplets – War, Win and Loew', it was really quite difficult for the three women to agree which 'parasite' was the most dislikeable. Mrs Laden 'detested' Wardrop, but Miss Patch generally remained loyal to 'the non-stop smoking German Jew' Loewenstein as the most poisonous of them all, though when Lady Astor described him as 'a sweet, little spring lamb' in comparison to the 'Polish Jew' Winsten, she could not help laughing and spreading the amusement from her hide-out at the Onslow Court Hotel.

Stephen Winsten was set on being Shaw's Boswell, and since 'many people had been pressing me to share my unique experience with them', he brought out what his publishers were to call three 'outstanding examples of Boswellian art'. After the first of these, *Days With Bernard Shaw*, was presented to G.B.S., 'he blushed like an adolescent; he loved it,' Winsten recorded. 'Whenever I called on him I would find the book beside him.' Alerted by Loewenstein to many concealed breaches of copyright, Shaw eventually picked it up and looked inside. 'In hardly any passage in the book as far as I have had time to examine it,' he wrote in the *Times Literary Supplement*, 'had Mr Winsten's art not improved on bare fact and occurrence by adding the charm of his own style to the haphazard crudity of nature.' Winsten admitted to being 'mightily amused' by his friend's letter. Shaw had been 'eager to help,' he explained, and had written it to provoke sales – indeed he even offered to draft 'a crushing answer', but afterwards 'he was most apologetic'.

Unlike Loewenstein, who deferentially referred to Shaw as 'the Master', the Winstens traded in superiority, especially Clare who described Lady Astor as 'an American chorus girl . . . grossly ignorant of how to speak to an English lady and a distinguished artist'. Shaw too was something of a disappointment to her. It was true that he extravagantly praised her work, came to use her drawings rather than Topolski's to illustrate his books, paid for her statue of St Joan in his garden, contributed £2,000 for the education of her son at university and provided a job as theatre designer for one of her daughters. But she could not abide his lack of generosity – for it could only have been meanness that prevented Shaw from purchasing her portrait of him. 'I will not buy the portrait quite simply because I dont want it,' he had told her.

Shaw's Trust Fund of £2,000 for Christopher Winsten's education came on top of a grant-in-aid for another £2,000 to John Wardrop: while Miss Patch's salary had remained static over twelve years. The injustice overwhelmed her. 'I have seen the wicked in great power,' she burst out to Shaw, quoting Psalm 34 Verse 35, 'and spreading like a great bay tree.'

After financing his old Fabian colleague Hubert Bland's son through Cambridge and the medical profession, Shaw had got in the habit 'of spending some of my spare money in that way,' he explained. There had been school fees for the son of his friend Frederick Evans, the bookseller and photographer; and then Peter Tompkins and now Christopher Winsten. 'They were all more or less Pygmalion experiments,' he told Miss Patch. Admittedly the case of John Wardrop was rather different. 'He was willing to matriculate and qualify for the bar . . . The result remains to be seen. Meanwhile he is offstage.'

But Blanche Patch was not appeased. She kept her grievance hot. 'While lacking all the things required from a secretary,' she wrote, 'he

[Loewenstein] possesses the racial knack of knowing how to extract money. In the past 18 months he has had about £745 from you in addition to his percentages, payments from newspapers for news of you and subscriptions from members of the Shaw Society.' During this time she had been issuing licences, checking royalties, vetting United States plays in production, all of which had 'grown to such an extent that it might be said I am expected to manage a play-leasing bureau . . . It is a feeling of resentment that you should look on me simply as a shorthand-typist.'

'My dear Blanche,' Shaw replied. 'You have given me a jolt at last.' In all their years together she had never seen anything in his socialism. Yet what more vivid illustration could there be of the curse of property, the absurd distortion of worth based on pay differentials and the disabling effects of inheritance than this unhappy scramble swirling round him since Charlotte's death? He had stopped raising Blanche Patch's salary, 'which has nothing to do with your merits,' he explained, once she 'had enough for comfortably ladylike life, with a pension that would leave you rather more after my death'. Recently he had analysed her financial position with an accountant to ensure it was fair and generous. 'For emergencies and luxuries you always could depend on me for a grant-in-aid . . . If you are pressed for money you have only to suggest a grant. Will that satisfy you? If not, what will?'

But how could it satisfy her? She could not say why it did not, nor what would make all the difference in the world. 'Dear, long-suffering G.B.S.,' she answered. 'I dont really want more money having quite enough for my modest needs – and, anyhow, you have always been generous in paying for things that dont come under my normal duties.' Money was a shorthand for something that could never be spelt out. She knew that G.B.S. would pay her salary or pension whether she continued working for him or not. She also knew that he gave those jobs which had plagued her to Loewenstein so as to 'leave you free as possible'. But free for what?

Hardly had Shaw recovered from Miss Patch's earthquake than Mrs Laden dropped a bomb on him over breakfast one summer morning by handing in her notice. For two years she had been living at Ayot like someone in solitary confinement. 'You have only to lift your little finger,' Shaw said, 'and I would double your salary.' But she told him off pretty smartly for that. 'When I want a rise I will ask for it.' She also refused his offer of a television set. But when Lady Astor gave her tickets for the Covent Garden ballet she became herself again, 'utterly repudiating the possibility of leaving me on any terms'. She needed occasional treats in London (spinning up in the Rolls), and also a motor scooter to take her to the shops and cinemas beyond Ayot – then she found out that her salary had been doubled after all.

Money seemed to mean different things for each of them. 'Money is power. Money is security. Money is freedom,' declares the heroine of *The Millionairess*. For Shaw the love of good economy was the root of all virtue. Equality of income was equality of truth. In a bad economy money was theft and made barren our lives. His parents had married for money; Miss Patch's fellow-resident at the Onslow Court Hotel was shortly to be murdered for money. Money was simply exchange value for some, and for others the freedom not to exchange what they valued. 'Are you fond of money?' the young doctor Harry Trench asks Blanche Sartorius in *Widowers' Houses*. Around Ayot the women seemed less acutely fond of it than the men – other people's money meant almost more to Miss Patch than her own.

It was a relief to Miss Patch and Mrs Laden when in 1949 the Winstens decided to live in Oxford. Shaw was to miss their company in the last year of his life but, as Clare Winsten made quite plain, it was really his own fault. He could have bought their bungalow for them or another place in the village. But all he did was to write on their behalf to the landlord, Lord Brocket. It was simply not enough. Indeed it was less than he had done for Loewenstein, she believed, and he was a mere employee rather than a fellow-artist.

Loewenstein's empire expanded through a proliferation of Shaw Societies round the world. His bibliography expanded too over numberless cards of dense, semi-illegible notes which, in their swelling shopping-bag, would eventually achieve the status of a master-parody of scholarship. But it was as an assistant secretary rather than the flower of scholarship that Loewenstein strengthened his position at Ayot. In 1946 Shaw printed a card announcing that since he had 'no time for any except the most urgent private correspondence', he must 'refer you to the Founder of the Shaw Society, Dr F. E. Loewenstein' who is 'better informed on many points than Mr Shaw himself, and will be pleased to be of assistance'.

Loewenstein's pamphlets and papers, thickened with pedantic superfluities, added a little to the salary Shaw gave him but were principally investments in the future. He looked for pre-eminence in the posthumous phase of Shaw's copyright kingdom where he would be crowned Curator of Shaw's Corner and reign there as his representative on earth. To this end he sought a privileged place in wills Shaw made in the late 1940s. But all G.B.S. finally guaranteed him was an introduction to the Public Trustee (who as the sole executor would appoint the tenant at Ayot), the naming of him as his bibliographer and a recommendation that he be employed or consulted whenever this might prove 'desirable'.

Fearing that too much was left uncertain in this legacy, Loewenstein at last pressed Shaw to borrow money so that he could buy a house in St Albans. G.B.S. refused to do this, but in 1949 guaranteed him a bank overdraft of £3,500 (equivalent to £67,000 in 1997) on the strength of which Loewenstein bought the house and renamed it 'Torca Cottage'. In the event of Shaw's death, he had balanced his risks between foreclosure at the bank and expulsion from Ayot. But still the risk was great and he attempted to add tenure to the prospect of tenancy by drafting a document guaranteeing him £500 a year for several years after Shaw's death. This document Shaw apparently tore up, while raising Loewenstein's salary to £500 a year for three years. 'He will have to take an overdose if he goes on pursuing you,' volunteered Lady Astor.

Lady Astor now looked on Ayot as her new constituency. 'Keep off, Keep off, Keep off, Keep off,' Shaw cautioned her. But whenever she was fuelled with fresh evidence of Loewenstein's 'disgraceful behaviour', she would take off for another devastating raid. All the village heard the rumours of her tirades. 'If you will not let me manage my work and my housekeeping in my own way you must not come at all,' Shaw eventually retaliated. This letter brought Lady Astor down again at once, and almost weeping she showed Mrs Laden what G.B.S. had sent her.

'You need looking after far more than I do; and nobody knew this better than Charlotte, except perhaps your unfortunate secretaries. You must upset your own household, not mine . . . As the keeper of a mental patient you are DISCHARGED.'

Though he had signed off 'Quite unchanged nevertheless G.B.S.' this marked the final battle in Nancy Astor's blazing campaign.

Miss Patch campaigned more discreetly. Realizing that Loewenstein's long-term aim was to be appointed Custodian of the Shavian shrine, she set about sabotaging his chances with those who might advise the Public Trustee after Shaw's death. What she wanted was recognition as the First Lady in Shaw's life at the end. Instead she was to be granted another sort of privilege when, in his ninety-third year, G.B.S. gave her the use of his letters (and Charlotte's too if she wanted them) for a volume commemorating their thirty years together. Through the dry leaves of this ghosted memoir, she would finally come to share his life.

4

FATAL ATTACHMENTS

Films, you know, are a strange business. You can get in, but you can't
get out.

Shaw to S. N. Behrman

For over two years following his film of *Major Barbara*, Pascal would
regularly 'go see Bernashaw'. He liked to motor across from his rambling
Tudor house at Chalfont St Peter and extravagantly 'talk cast'. He fancied
Marlene Dietrich in *The Millionairess*, or perhaps Greer Garson 'my
nearly wife' in *Candida*; he also dreamed of fixing up Clark Gable and
Cary Grant together in *The Devil's Disciple*, and actually persuaded Ginger
Rogers to appear in *Arms and the Man* – provided a few dance numbers
were added and the action moved from Bulgaria into Canada. 'Do not
argue with her,' Shaw responded; 'just throw her out of the window and
tell her not to come back.' The favourite of all Pascal's schemes was a
Saint Joan for which he had signed up Greta Garbo. Unfortunately the
idea took a fantastic turn after he tried to raise money from General de
Gaulle: 'instead of Garbo,' Pascal reported to Shaw, 'de Gaulle wanted to
play the Saint himself.' If the heroine had been the Blessed Virgin,
commented G.B.S., 'they would probably have suggested Miss Mae West'.

'We never met,' regretted Mae West, 'but I would have been happy to
entertain the gentleman.'

The speed with which absolutely nothing happened was often breathtaking. By the autumn of 1943 an agreement for three Shaw films had
been signed with Arthur Rank. 'We make *Caesar and Cleopatra*,' Pascal
announced. This sounded like the perfect vehicle for a superspectacle to
top *Ben Hur* and *The Ten Commandments*. Rank assumed total responsibility for the cost, gambling on drawing in large audiences from a war-
weary public after Hitler had finally been defeated. At the eleventh hour
Pascal was in his seventh heaven. 'But I pity poor Rank,' Shaw told him.
'The film will cost a million.'

'John Gielgud is Caesar. Vivien Leigh is Cleopatra,' Pascal declared as
he stepped off a boat at New York. 'Wonderful, no?' John Gielgud certainly
thought it wasn't wonderful. 'I do not like filming, and should be terrified
of risking giving an indifferent performance . . . So I must reluctantly say
no to the film, and hope that you will let me do the *play* some time not
so far distant.' What this meant was that Gielgud had no confidence in
Pascal as a director. Six months later, in what critics were to call 'an

utterly negative and phantom Caesar', Pascal cast Claude Rains who had taken the lead in *The Invisible Man* and *Phantom of the Opera*.

His other choice, Vivien Leigh, was best known to film audiences as Scarlett O'Hara in *Gone With the Wind*, but had recently filled the Haymarket Theatre for over a year in a revival of *The Doctor's Dilemma*. She longed to play Shaw's Cleopatra but was bound by an exclusive contract with David O. Selznick, until Pascal leased her with £50,000 of Rank's money.

The shooting began on 12 June 1944, six days after D-Day. On 29 June Shaw visited the set at Denham Studios. Never had there been so splendiferous a sight as Pascal's Egypt. The interior of the Memphis Palace with its pseudo-granite columns each weighing two tons, its carvings of men with wings, hawks' heads, black marble cats, was to cover 28,000 square feet; while the palace steps and quayside were immense exterior sets constructed for the thousands of extras he had hired. All their costumes, the hieroglyphs and statues were copied from originals – even the formation of the stars behind the mighty Sphinx was designed by an astronomer. It was impossible not to be impressed. 'When I look back on my work as a young man with my colleagues in the theatre, it seems to me we were like children playing with wretched makeshift toys,' Shaw said. 'Here you have the whole world to play with!'

Pascal had indeed created a wonderful toyshop for G.B.S. to play in. Placing a Roman helmet on his head, he posed for photographs. Then, as he left the studios accompanied by Miss Patch, a voice called out from the ranks 'Hail Caesar!' And all the soldiers stood to attention as the old man and his secretary passed by.

From the start exotic jealousies blossomed on the imported sand and choked the production. Most dramatic was Vivien Leigh's unexpected pregnancy. 'Everyone is *very, very* cross & keeps asking me how I suppose they are going to make me look like the 16 year old Cleopatra,' she wrote in mid-August. ' . . . I think it is a very good thing really because they'll just have to hurry up with the film.'

Yet everything conspired towards delay. No sooner had Pascal rearranged the schedules to shoot Vivien Leigh's scenes first, than she suffered a miscarriage after running up and down the palace beating a slave. Blaming him for not employing a double, she tried to get Pascal replaced. Amid the jungle of intrigues, his accent grew more heavily impenetrable. 'I was surrounded by saboteurs,' he later grumbled.

There was also the war. Four days after filming began the Germans launched their V2 rocket attacks. 'I am having the same gay start on the picture as I had with Major Barbara during the blitz,' Pascal wrote to Shaw. One flying bomb exploding in a field nearby damaged the Pharos set, another destroyed the dressmaking workrooms and a third almost killed some members of the production unit. Senior centurions changed from their armour into civilian suits and went off for Home Guard drill. Teenage girls were suddenly collected by their mothers from the palace pool and taken to work in factories in the north of England. Supply depots closed; telephone lines came down: and then there was the weather. For weeks, and then months, the cast waited on the gigantic location-sets of ancient Alexandria for the sun to shine. 'We had to clear away great slushes of snow,' Stanley Holloway remembered, 'and even then our breath was coming out in clouds . . .'

Exploiting Rank's belief that British films had been handicapped by 'a faintly claustrophobic indoor quality', Pascal persuaded him to move the location to Egypt itself. The enormous papier-mâché Sphinx was divided into sections, crated and sent down to the docks with all the other properties and costumes, and reassembled in the desert. As the British army reached the Rhine, Pascal came to Cairo. At Beni Ussef he waited for a tremendous sandstorm to subside so that he could produce a more filmic flurry of sand with the miraculous use of two aero-engines operated by the Royal Air Force. Two hundred and fifty horses had been placed at his disposal by the Egyptian Government which also supplied him with over 1,000 troops. Ephemerally dressed in the costumes brought out from England, they were charmed by the papier-mâché shields which, coated with a delicious sauce of fish glue, were quickly consumed, leaving the army defenceless.

Shaw continued to advise on all things: Caesar's smile, Cleopatra's accent, Britannus's eyebrows. 'In Heaven's name, no Egyptian music,' he appealed. Listening to the BBC's Third Programme he had kept his knowledge of twentieth-century music up-to-date, admiring Prokofiev and Sibelius, and praising Debussy, Schönberg, Scriabin and Stravinsky. 'Radio music has changed the world in England,' he was to write. Among British composers he was 'very much struck' by the originality of Benjamin Britten who 'had the forgotten quality of elegance'. The score for *Pygmalion* had been written by Arthur Honegger, that for *Major Barbara* by William Walton whom Shaw advised to add 'the effect of a single trombone sounding G flat quite quietly after the others have stopped. Undershaft pretending to play it. It ought to have the effect of a question mark.' But neither Walton nor Britten nor even Prokofiev were available for *Caesar and Cleopatra*. 'Write your Blissfullest,' Shaw urged. But Arthur Bliss took one look at Pascal and withdrew. Eventually Pascal contracted Georges Auric, a member of Les Six, who had written scores for René Clair's *A nous la Liberté*, Jean Cocteau's *L'Eternel Retour* and most recently Michael Balcon's *Dead of the Night*. Shaw came to a recording session by the National Symphony Orchestra. When the Roman soldiers raised their swords and Caesar's galley sailed from Egypt at the end, Auric's music, he said, 'is almost Handelian'.

The end of the film coincided with Japan's formal capitulation and the end of the Second World War. During these fifteen months Pascal, still looking very much himself, would go regularly to Ayot.

'Have you killed Ftatateeta yet?' G.B.S. asked one day.

'Killed her yesterday,' said Pascal, with satisfaction.

'How did you manage her death-scream?'

'Like this,' said Pascal and began to scream at the top of his voice.

'Too high,' said Shaw. 'Lower. Like this.'

Then he too started to scream in a deeper register, and the two of them stood in the garden counter-screaming.

On 13 December 1945, exactly ten years after the signing of the *Pygmalion* agreement, *Caesar and Cleopatra* had its première at the Odeon, Marble Arch. Queen Mary attended, and there was the most chaotic traffic jam since VJ Day – so impenetrable that Pascal arrived too late to be presented. It was 'a good picture, in my opinion,' said Blanche Patch. But many critics disagreed, and although the American notices were more favourable when it was shown in the United States the following year, *Caesar and Cleopatra* was to gain legendary fame as 'the biggest financial failure in the history of British cinema'. The Rank Organization had estimated a budget of £550,000, but when the shooting went on for nine months longer than expected costs rose to £1.5 million (equivalent to around £31 million in 1997).

'It is a triumph of technicolour and statuary, and makes quite an enjoyable illustrated chapter of Roman history,' Shaw concluded; 'but as drama it is nothing.' Unlike *Antony and Cleopatra*, it was never intended to be a love story; and unlike *Henry V*, also being made at Denham and starring Vivien Leigh's husband Laurence Olivier, it was not a patriotic adventure story. It was the 'educational history film' Shaw had once hoped to make with *Good King Charles*. But Caesar's education of Cleopatra and the development of his character vanish innocuously in a 'poor imitation of Cecil B. de Mille'. Shaw hated Hollywood with a sincere hatred, and Pascal had offered up the sincerest form of flattery.

Whenever Pascal began speaking of new productions – *The Doctor's Dilemma* for Alexander Korda, *The Shewing-up of Blanco Posnet* for Mary Pickford – his face would glow translucently, his smile crack open and all past tribulations fall away. He raced around Europe trying to raise money, find studios, sell his dreams. But the film world had lost confidence in him – what could be more ludicrous than his idea of a *Pygmalion* musical by Alan Jay Lerner and Frederick Loewe?

Their adventures had been fun, but Shaw was too old for any more. He urged Pascal to find 'new friendships and new interests and activities', and to 'live in your generation, not in mine'. Yet this was now curiously difficult. 'Somehow, whenever I try to be unfaithful to you and do any other picture than yours,' Pascal explained, 'I have no luck.' His marriage was failing; he was suffering from cancer; and it seemed there was 'an invisible conspiracy against me'. Each week he returned to Ayot. 'If you will not take care of your interests and think of your prospects when I am dead, I must do it for you,' Shaw wrote on 3 July 1950. 'Don't force me to break with you for your own sake.'

Had Charlotte still been living it might have ended differently. 'She liked me and sold all my ideas to him,' Pascal remembered. Without Charlotte, G.B.S. had withdrawn into deeper isolation. 'I have in me the makings of a first rate hermit,' he acknowledged.

'Don't leave me in a vacuum,' Pascal had pleaded. But though Shaw refused to give the English language rights of his films to anyone else, 'I do not want to see you,' he wrote. 'I do not want to see ANYBODY ... Keep away, Gabriel. Keep away EVERYBODY.'

5

THE STORY CONTINUES

Only in dreams my prime returns.

Epigraph to *Buoyant Billions*

In *Everybody's Political What's What?* Shaw tried to provide a basis for post-war social reconstruction. He had received his political education in the last two decades of the nineteenth century when government intervention, though setting limits to individual liberties, had brought great improvement to most people's lives. The problems of poverty and unemployment, homelessness, education and health would not be met, he believed, by a trickling down of money from the riches of privatization and profit-taking, but by investment in public services and leadership that encouraged pursuit of the common good. 'Parliament kills everyone except careerists,' he wrote. Politics for Shaw was simply the complicated business of 'organizing human society so as to secure the utmost possible welfare for everybody through a just sharing of the burden of service and the benefit of leisure'.

Everybody's Political What's What? is a ragged patchwork of autobiography, sociology, history and political economy, a rambling narrative of almost 200,000 words that repeats ideas that he had given better elsewhere and then repeats itself. The book had kept Shaw company over the war years, helping to guard his solitude. He moves across its pages like a solitary wanderer through the abstract scenery of economics from the false prosperity of *laissez-faire* to the imaginary riches of Social Credit.

Yet this summary of a life's teaching was a prodigious achievement for a man who at the time of its publication was in his eighty-ninth year. When he warns us that in a commercialized world everything is bought and sold; reminds us that no State may be accounted civilized that has poor people among its citizens; instructs us that democracy must find a use for every person and not put him off with a dole: when he attacks fundamentalists as the enemies of religion and advises us to canonize our modern literature, we can feel again a prophet of change conjuring his powers of transcendental reasonableness. His book is most eloquent as simple rhetoric:

'Socialism is not charity nor loving-kindness, nor sympathy with the poor, nor popular philanthropy . . . but the economist's hatred of waste and disorder, the aesthete's hatred of ugliness and dirt, the lawyer's hatred of injustice, the doctor's hatred of disease, the saint's hatred of the seven deadly sins.'

It was not as the adherent to a party line that Shaw had permeated the minds of more than one generation, but as a dreamer whose dream 'burned like a poem,' Edmund Wilson remembered, ' . . . stirring new intellectual appetites, exciting our sense of moral issues, sharpening the focus of our sight on the social relations of our world'. Within a year the book had sold 85,000 hardback copies in Britain. 'When it is finished I shall be finished too,' he had predicted in a letter to Lillah McCarthy. Yet in the prefaces he would add to *Geneva* and *Good King Charles* during 1945, and then in the articles and letters he issued from his garden shed at a production rate of almost seventy a year over the next five years, he precipitated G.B.S. into the atomic age.

'Do not tell me that war profits nobody: I know better,' he had written in *Everybody's Political What's What?* ' . . . I have never written a line to start a war . . . I feel the losses on both sides . . . I loathe war.' He welcomed the defeat of Hitler and Mussolini, 'but I don't intend to celebrate at all,' he told the *New York Journal-American*. 'The war won't be over on VE-Day.' On 6 August 1945 the United States exploded an atom bomb on Hiroshima. 'The war came to an end when the first atomic bomb was dropped,' Shaw stated in the *News Chronicle*. 'It is very doubtful if we have the right ever to drop another.' Another was dropped on Nagasaki three days later for experimental purposes, and even before Japan formally surrendered, G.B.S. had started Shavianizing the bomb.

It had had 'its momentary success,' he wrote, and now we could see that the institution of world war was reduced to absurdity. 'The wars that threaten us in the future are not those of London or Berlin or Washington or Tokyo,' he believed. 'They are civil wars . . . to say nothing of wars of religion . . . fundamentalists and atheists, Moslems and Hindus, Shintos and Buddhists.' He tried to move the debate from atomic warfare to atomic welfare. 'Atomic disintegration will some day make heat cheaper than can coal-burning,' he predicted. But, like the sorcerer's apprentice, 'we may still practise our magic without knowing how to stop it, thus fulfilling the prophecy of Prospero'. Occasionally G.B.S. warmed his frail spirit in this atomic conflagration which would 'end all our difficulties'.

Ever since a war crimes commission had been set up late in 1943, he had declared his opposition to putting the civil and military leaders of Nazi Germany on trial for crimes against humanity. For after the raining down of 200,000 tons of bombs on German cities and the dropping of a second atom bomb on Japan, where could we find the spotless men and women to act as judges? When the verdicts and sentences of the first Nuremberg tribunals were announced in the autumn of 1946, he gave his reaction to the press.

'We are all self righteous enough to enjoy reading denunciations of the condemned men as . . . hideous freaks of German nature who deserve all they suffered and are about to suffer, and a bit more . . . Instead of a row of countenances stamped from birth as murderous villains for exhibition in wax effigy in a chamber of horrors, what confront me are nothing but perfectly commonplace middle-class gentlemen who differ in no respects from any common jury or row of pewholders in the nearest church . . . it is as clear as daylight that if they had been left in their natural places they would have been no worse than an equal number of Bayswater ratepayers . . . Disfranchise them by all means. Disqualify them for the posts and powers they proved so tragically unfit for. I should let them loose as nobodies . . . I believe they will be quite harmless and negligible. Why make martyrs of them?'

In the opinion of Mrs Laden, Shaw 'could not bring himself to believe in the German concentration camps like Dachau and Belsen'. When he branded Hitler a 'rascal' or described the camps as if there were bad cases of overcrowding, his vocabulary became disablingly inadequate. 'It is sometimes better not to think at all than to think intensely and think wrong,' he wrote in the Preface to *Geneva*. Some thinkers were convinced that the hanging of war criminals was a final solution to war crimes. 'Ought we not rather to hang ourselves'? Shaw enquired. We were all potential criminals, he believed, and the solution lay in renewing ourselves through another morality.

Shaw had supported William Beveridge's report on social insurance, which led to the welfare state, as a modest instalment of socialism, and had prophesied Churchill's defeat at the general election of 1945. The red-hot socialist who once delighted William Morris with his cascading oratory, who, thin as a whipping post, had marched with Annie Besant to Trafalgar Square on Bloody Sunday, made speeches at street corners with Keir Hardie, met Engels and known Eleanor Marx was a legend to many younger socialists in the late 1940s. But he was also an ubiquitous nuisance. He, who accused Churchill of being 'a century out of date', was himself 'an obsolete Old Pioneer' in the words of a future Labour Party leader Michael Foot. 'One of the foremost educators of the past,' Foot wrote, he had become a 'blind seer' confusing his disciples just when many of his 'early dreams have started to be translated into fact'.

The last political initiative of his life was the Coupled Vote. Nearly twenty years after women had been granted the vote, the British people were 'misrepresented at Westminster' by 24 women and 616 men. Shaw's remedy was to make the electoral unit 'not a man *or* a woman but a man *and* a woman'. He called it the Coupled Vote. Having placed this democratic reform in the *Manchester Guardian* and his extended Preface to *Good King Charles*, Shaw handed over his plan to Lady Rhondda's Six Point Group. 'It is the right organ for it,' he wrote, ' . . . for I want it to come from the Women's organizations and not from a man.' At the end of 1948 the campaign was launched under the headline 'Revolutionary Political Idea' on the front page of *Wife and Citizen*. But the Six Point Group quickly ran out of money and the Coupled Vote receded into the history of Shavian might-have-beens.

*

A week after his eighty-ninth birthday, Shaw began writing plays again. His playwriting was an elixir, he sometimes felt, similar in its exotic effects to his mother's spirit communications on the ouija board. In any event, it gave him 'moments of inexplicable happiness' and he was taken 'out of the realm of logic into that of magic and miracle'.

Buoyant Billions was a play he had started while sailing to Honolulu in February 1936, briefly picked up again in August 1937, now retrieved and would continue to revise until the middle of July 1947. In a short preface he asked readers to forgive a 'trivial comedy which is the best I can do in my dotage . . . At least it will not rub into you the miseries and sins of the recent wars, nor even of the next one.' On the contrary, it is a romance spun around the theme of avoiding warfare. After his educational history play celebrating the use of good manners he had characteristically come up with 'A Comedy of No Manners'. But the manners he was dispensing with were verbal conventions that confused meaning and confined people to their social compartments. The characters in *Buoyant Billions* 'are simply frank, which is the extremity of no manners,' Shaw explained.

In the first act a father and son confront each other. 'We resist changes until the changes break us,' says the son. But Mr Smith does not resist his son. He pays his fare to go round the world investigating the beneficial use of atomic fusion. By the second act Junius Smith has reached the Panama Canal, on the tropical shore of which he comes across a young woman, 'Babzy' Buoyant, who charms the Punch-and-Judy-like snakes and alligators with her saxophone. They argue, but are so irresistibly attracted to each other that Babzy runs off into the third act and the safety of her father's Belgrave Square house in London. Junius pursues her and they both turn up in its curious drawing-room in time to contribute to a symphonic discourse on death and its duties which is being conducted by the family solicitor. Shaw manipulates everyone's views to illustrate his belief that 'differences of creed must be tolerated, analysed, discussed, and as far as possible reconciled'. In the short fourth act, the billionaire Old Bill Buoyant gives his blessing to the marriage of Babzy and Junius, and this human fusion quickens their faculties in the surprise and wonder of a happy ending.

'My fans must not expect from me more than a few crumbs dropped from the literary loaves I distributed in my prime,' Shaw wrote in the preface to his next play *Farfetched Fables*, 'plus a few speculations, as to what may happen in the next million light years . . .'

This 'batch of childish fables', written between July and August 1948, is a post-atomic fantasy in five conversation pieces and one monologue. Here the young man does not pursue the attractive young woman who is refusing to bring children into the modern world, but goes off to invent a peculiarly lethal gas. Having sold his terrible invention he retires to a safe place, the Isle of Wight, where unfortunately the first gas bomb is exploded. From here, we see the dark ages return and human beings change into a breed of super-gorillas. Time moves on bringing with it the discovery that humans need not after all eat grass but can live on air and water. They evolve into a race of supermen, superwomen and superhermaphrodites, and eventually thought struggles free from the body. In the sixth and final fable a schoolroom of sixth-form children, throwbacks to the twentieth century, are visited by a disembodied mind. Impelled by intellectual curiosity it has used the power of evolution, 'which can go backwards as well as forwards', to appear before them as a feathered youth named Raphael and experience what is called the word made flesh. The lesson for audiences as well as sixth-formers is that regardless of consequences the pursuit of knowledge and power will go on into the infinity of time.

Farfetched Fables is a toy version of *Back to Methuselah* and 'suitable only for little groups of amateurs,' he wrote. For its first presentation he handed the play to the Shaw Society which, led by Ellen Pollock, directed by Esmé Percy and with futuristic designs by Feliks Topolski, gave it thirty performances at the Watergate Theatre in the autumn of 1950. It was to be posthumously published in Shaw's standard edition together with *Buoyant Billions* and *Shakes versus Shav*, a ten-minute play for puppets which he wrote during four January days in 1949.

Puppets had some Shavian advantages over human material. They could preserve an unvarying facial expression and sustain treatment impossible for mere living actors. 'When I first saw them in my boyhood,' Shaw wrote, 'nothing delighted me more than when all the puppets went up in a balloon and presently dropped from the skies with an appalling crash on the floor.' He gave his own puppets some glorious acrobatics – Shakes and Shav sparring and knocking each other down, while their champions Rob Roy and Macbeth dance and spin until Rob Roy cuts off Macbeth's head with a claymore and Macbeth marches off, head under arm, to the tune of the British Grenadiers. This marks the culmination of what the critic Sally Peters was to call 'Shaw's unending duel with the ghost of Shakespeare'. In this playlet the 'real Shakespeare' is someone who 'might have been myself'.

Shakes is the darker face of Shav, a vengeful protagonist who introduces himself with excerpts from the soliloquies of his villainous Richard III and Macbeth. Their intertextual battle has Macbeth quoting Macduff from whose third son, Shaw had told his biographers Hesketh Pearson and Archibald Henderson, 'I am supposed to be descended'. It is a duel between the contradictory impulses Shaw had struggled all his life to reconcile. But Shaw is also one of Shakespeare's heirs and so after their jousting comes a plea for peace. *A light appears between them*, the stage directions tell us. Then the candle is puffed out and darkness embraces them both.

Shakes versus Shav had been commissioned by England's 'chief puppet master' Waldo Lanchester who sent G.B.S. 'figures of two puppets, Shakespeare & myself, with a request that I should supply one of my famous dramas for them'. It was then performed at Lanchester's Malvern Marion-ette Theatre during the 1949 Malvern Festival.

*

Nowhere were Shaw's plays more enthusiastically welcomed than in German-speaking countries where most theatres had been closed down by Goebbels in 1944 as part of the 'total war' effort. Between 1945 and 1970 in the Soviet and Allied sectors of Berlin there were to be forty-nine productions of twenty-four of his plays – more than Chekhov or Ibsen, Gorki or Strindberg, Pirandello or Eugene O'Neill.

All this should have benefited Trebitsch. During the war he had appealed desperately for money from the luxurious Dolder Hotel in Zurich. But Shaw's replies were often delayed or misdirected since Treb-itsch could not bring himself to reveal where he and his wife were living. In his seventies Trebitsch did not know how to live otherwise than as a rich man. 'I have not forgotten you and Tina in the least; you are very much in my mind at times,' Shaw wrote in 1945. But he was anxious to avoid seeing them after the war. It was too late. He was too old. 'We must make up our minds not to meet again,' he urged.

But Trebitsch had already made up his mind to fly over and pay his condolences over Charlotte's death. He remembered Charlotte vividly: her devotion to 'long walks', her exploits as a 'brilliant cyclist', how she 'loved sport and enjoyed riding' like her sister who was 'one of the best-known women riders to hounds in the British Isles'. Trebitsch gloried in these memories and was eager to bring G.B.S. the comfort of them.

Shaw looked forward to his visit with dread. But Trebitsch knew his duty. He came in the spring of 1946 and was in excellent spirits. It was six years since they had last met. 'You dont know what it is to be 90,' Shaw had warned him and it was true that Trebitsch, who was not quite eighty, did not know. He was surprised to see his old friend failing in a strange way. 'He was impatient, was afraid of falling asleep when he leaned back in his chair, and . . . of showing this understandable weakness even in front of a familiar visitor as I was.' Other failings such as his inability to 'walk more than a mile, very unsteadily and leaning on a stick' were not without their advantages.

On no account, Shaw insisted, could Trebitsch afford another senti-mental journey to England. Trebitsch however had some important business to discuss: a scheme for aiding G.B.S. with his income tax by taking over the burden of his income. 'I shall not see you starve if I can help it,' G.B.S. assured him. With this small encouragement Trebitsch was back again in the Dorchester Hotel in the spring of 1947 and hurrying down all smiles to Ayot St Lawrence. It was a lesson to Shaw of how unwise he had been to offer any encouragement at all. He would never do so again. 'I am no longer the Shaw you knew,' he had cautioned. But like the ageing Falstaff, Trebitsch was ever-confident of some special favours from his old companion. He simply could not believe Shaw's 'heartless' words and responded to them like a rejected lover with spells of recovery in expensive spas. Exasperation rose in G.B.S. What else could he do except run out a string of terrible blowings-up and dressings-down? 'Damn it, man, do you imagine that I am a pretty girl of 17 and you a blithering idiot of 18 . . . Can you not bear the thought of my having any friend in the world except yourself? Pull yourself together . . . I dont want to shake hands with you nor to contemplate your wrinkles.'

This bombardment halted Trebitsch at the Dorchester Hotel during his annual pilgrimage to England in the spring of 1948. He still sweated to see his friend for one last farewell, or perhaps two, or better still three. 'What do you suppose I care about last meetings at my age?' Shaw had demanded. 'I never see anyone now without being conscious that it is probably our last meeting . . . When the cat leaves the room it may never see me alive again.'

For Trebitsch, however, Shaw was still 'the last, greatest and strangest hero of my life'. He could not wait another year. In the early autumn of 1948 he slipped back into England and down to Ayot for what was to be their final meeting, leaving 'after a farewell that was kept light and airy'.

But their old business relationship had been broken up by the war and when Shaw advised Trebitsch not to 'speak or write to anyone over 40' he was trying to break his translator's dependence on royalties that must further diminish 'after my death, which is imminent'. But like Gabriel Pascal and Molly Tompkins, Trebitsch was lost without G.B.S. Shaw had been like a father to them all and they could not detach themselves. Trebitsch felt 'alone upon this earth, except for the one man whom I still had: Bernard Shaw'.

'If imaginary riches make you happy, by all means imagine them; but they will never materialize,' Shaw wrote after the production of *Buoyant Billions* which he had made Trebitsch translate as *Zu Viel Geld* ('Too Much Money'). It was a sad ending to almost fifty years of a relationship which Trebitsch counted as 'the greatest event of my life'.

6

A VERY LATE CONCLUSION

Well, goodbye, goodbye, goodbye, goodbye – all of you.
BBC television talk by Shaw on his ninetieth birthday

'Mr Bernard Shaw becomes a nonagenarian to-day,' announced *The Times* on 26 July 1946. He was threatened by a bristling programme of celebrations. 'I am doing what I can to escape,' he pleaded. ' . . . If I can survive it I can survive anything.' Congratulations and gifts converged on him from all around the world. There were tributes from Churchill and de Valera, salutations from the Labour Party and Trades Union Congress, sweets from local schoolchildren, greetings from anyone who had seen a play or read a preface. For a fortnight huge numbers of these messages and gifts went on avalanching into Ayot where Shaw desperately marshalled Loewenstein and Winsten to destroy the happy returns as if they were high explosives.

A policeman had been stationed outside his house earlier that month to repulse enthusiasts. 'I am fighting off all photographers and newsreelers,' Shaw insisted. But a few wriggled through his defences. 'I hope I shall interview you again on your 100th birthday,' said a young journalist. 'I don't see why not,' Shaw answered; 'you look healthy enough to me.'

'Mr Shaw is so vast a subject,' concluded *The Times*, 'that none will envy the ultimate biographer.' He had been asked by Oxford University Press to choose the five hundredth title in their World's Classics series from among his own work and he chose his masterpiece of wishful thinking, *Back to Methuselah*, using the chance to revise the play and its preface and attach a postscript. Besides this new volume and the million Penguin paperbacks, there was also a symposium, *G.B.S. 90*, in the bookshops, compiled by Stephen Winsten and containing memories from old friends such as H. G. Wells and Sidney Webb, Gilbert Murray and Max Beerbohm, together with surveys of his plays and music criticism, examinations of his ideas on phonetics, economics and education by C. E. M. Joad, J. D. Bernal and others, and statements of literary goodwill from J. B. Priestley, Maynard Keynes, Aldous Huxley.

On stage the Arts Theatre was playing *Don Juan in Hell*; on radio the BBC produced *The Man of Destiny* and later broadcast a Shaw Festival for its new Third Programme; in the evening Shaw appeared on television complaining that his popularity 'shews that I am getting old and feeble and nobody is afraid of me any longer'.

At the prompting of the Irish Trade Unionist James Larkin, he had been offered the Honorary Freedom of Dublin and replied in his letter of acceptance: 'Dublin alone has the right to affirm that in spite of my incessantly controversial past and present I have not disgraced her.' A little later in the year he accepted the Honorary Freedom of the Borough of St Pancras on whose vestry and borough council he had worked, and used the occasion to argue for the virtues of a local government system independent of central party political control.

'I need no publicity: I have already much more than my fair share of it,' Shaw wrote to the Liberal peer Lord Samuel a few days later. Public attention had once been his compensation for meagre family affection. Now it had expanded, he sometimes felt, into a substitute for political achievement. He would have traded all this publicity for an Act of Parliament legalizing the Coupled Vote, and he took more pleasure from legislation in the Dáil to municipalize his Carlow estate than anything else that happened that year.

'I wish you were not too far off to be within my reach,' he had written earlier in the year to Sidney Webb. Their old colleague Sydney Olivier had died within a few months of Beatrice and Charlotte, leaving Webb and Shaw the last two Fabian musketeers. 'So let us hold on as long as we can,' G.B.S. exhorted his friend. 'Everywhere I gained something,' Webb had written of their peripatetic work together. On 13 October 1947, in his eighty-ninth year, he died at Passfield Corner. 'I hope we have been a pair of decent useful chaps as men go,' G.B.S. wrote to him in his last letter; 'but we have had too short a lifetime to qualify for real high politics.'

In 1949 Shaw brought out a revised and expanded version of the autobiographical miscellany *Shaw Gives Himself Away* which the Gregynog Press had published in a limited edition ten years earlier. 'I have changed the title to SIXTEEN SELF SKETCHES,' he wrote to his American publisher, 'because a title must be easy to speak, easy to spell, and unmistakeable to pronounce.' The new title gives helpful evidence of Shaw's innumeracy since, as Brigid Brophy first noticed, the book contains seventeen self sketches. In his ninety-fifth year he completed what was to be the last of his ephemeral works for publication. *Bernard Shaw's Rhyming Picture Guide to Ayot* is a series of doggerel verses accompanying some endearingly awful photographs of the village.

Actors and authors liked coming down to see him occasionally in the belief that G.B.S. occasionally liked seeing them. 'Especially actresses,' the actress Lilli Palmer added. But when she asked him after an hour if he would like her to 'stay a little longer, Mr Shaw,' he answered truthfully: 'No. I'm always glad when people go.' 'Keep the old skeleton out of sight and touch as much as you can,' he wrote to the American showgirl Frances Day who wanted to see him. ' . . . Only in dreams is he young. Do not disturb them.'

Burlesques were less disturbing to him than gallantries. In his young nineties he performed a garden pantomime with Danny Kaye and, his eyes sparkling, sang a duet from *Aladdin* with Gertrude Lawrence.

> 'Come, little girl, for a sail with me
> Round and round the moon.
> No one to see us behind the Clouds
> Oh, what a place to spoon.'

'My voice is no penny whistle now!' he remarked to Kingsley Martin after bursting out with an aria from Verdi outside his house. 'I had not expected the strong Irish brogue,' wrote James Lees-Milne. 'This peasant origin makes him all the more impressive . . . When he smiles his face softens and becomes engaging.' To a journalist from the *Palestine Post* he looked like 'a very old and rather dangerous bird . . .

'Shaw is shockingly thin now. The famous beard has shortened . . . His skin is like parchment. The whole figure seems more like an echo of itself . . . [But] you see the eyes of a youth. Blue, radiating, quick and alert, they are the real Bernard Shaw . . . the great firebrand . . . who has gradually become an object of admiration and love, first in the world and then in his country.'

Many of his visitors felt like invaders in the separate world he inhabited. He 'looked more alone than any man I have ever seen,' wrote the American drama critic John Mason Brown. 'I can always tell myself stories,' he explained, 'and so am never lonely.'

Occasionally he would listen to other people's stories. Not long after Charlotte's death he had received the first instalment of a remarkable story-in-letters by Margaret Wheeler, a thirty-five-year-old housewife from Workington in Cumberland. 'I wanted an intelligent man to discuss things with,' she later explained, 'so I deliberately picked him up.' Her only chance, she reckoned, was to choose something close to his heart. So she wrote to him about phonetic alphabets. It was a sprat to catch a whale. 'I should like to give you my thanks now, anyway,' she ended her letter, 'for the enjoyment of reading and the stimulus of thought you have given to me many and many a time.'

'Not at all a bad beginning this of yours . . . Keep at it,' Shaw answered. He was referring to her alphabet. But in her next letter she began unburdening herself of an obsession. 'My problem is concerned with my little daughter, whom I believe to have been swopped by accident in the Nottingham nursing home where she was born, for another child born at the same time . . . I have been endeavouring to persuade the other parents to join with me in scientific tests . . . and they have refused . . . on the grounds that they are fond of the child they have and don't wish to give her up.'

Margaret Wheeler was a strong-willed, independent-minded, working-class woman, full of energy and argument, and 'in the grip of a passion to know about things'. In short, she was a species of genuine Shavian. 'Altogether a very difficult case,' he summed up, 'for which there is no harmless solution possible.' But she was determined to find a solution. He warned her 'not to prove your case legally and publicly', reminded her that 'unsuitable arrangements sometimes last longest', suggested the possibility of a 'reciprocal adoption' only if both sets of parents agreed it was best for the children, and counselled her to be 'content with the establishment of a private understanding between the two families'.

It was all sensible advice though 'my letters will not help you,' he promised. But they were soon doing her 'no end of good' and she felt justified in having appealed to him. 'I am serene in my confidence that you will not do anything against the interests of the two children whose future you have helped me to consider,' she assured him.

She did not want his money. She did not want to marry him – with five children and a husband she was sufficiently married already. 'I am perfectly happy just writing to you,' she told him. 'I cannot go on writing for ever,' he protested, 'and really should not indulge in this correspondence at all.' Yet he was interested by her curious situation. Orphans, foundlings, outcasts, changelings had always fascinated him. 'The serial keeps up its interest,' he admitted. 'I am still interested,' he added two years later.

This was partly because Margaret Wheeler was a natural writer. He recommended her to take it up professionally. 'I don't care a damn about seeing myself in print,' she replied. ' . . . I like having you around to practise on.' Writing to Shaw was like talking to someone over a garden wall. 'I should never have written to you in the first instance had I not felt completely safe with you.'

They exchanged photographs. He let her know she was 'an attractively intelligent woman . . . able to get round bank managers, solicitors, literary celebrities . . . You are what experienced men call a dangerous woman . . . I have been a dangerous man myself.' But looking at his photograph she could not see that he was dangerous at all. 'I'm not in the least frightened,' she boasted. She laughed so much at what he wrote and was so immensely bucked up that she 'felt like charging everybody else sixpence to look at me'.

So they both kept up their teasing and scolding, covering every subject from marriage and food rationing to hospital procedures and the control of floods. Over six years this correspondence unfolded into the story of a woman's life isolated and over-burdened with housework in post-war northern England. Writing to Shaw she could put the awful problem of the jactitated children to the back of her mind and relieve for a time 'the very strong feeling I carry around with me of being utterly completely and absolutely alone'.

'As long as I live I must write,' Shaw had said. His letters to 'Dear Mrs Wheeler, not to say Margaret or Maggie or Meg' became part of this process of living, lightening a little the solitude of these last years.

*

These last years were framed by two controversial wills. The net value of Charlotte's estate amounted to £150,976 13s. 9d. (equivalent to £3.25 million in 1997) out of which £49,702 9s. 5d. was to be paid in death duties. Apart from a number of small annuities for the servants, there was also a legacy of £1,000 to Sidney Webb and £20,000 to Charlotte's niece. By selling some of his own investments Shaw had paid these legacies almost immediately. He was appointed joint executor with the National Provincial Bank and given a life interest in Charlotte's estate. But since this would simply have raised his own supertax, he relinquished his role as beneficiary and strengthened Charlotte's residuary estate.

After Shaw's death, Charlotte's money was to be left in trust to an Irish bank for the development of Irish culture. The National City Bank was directed to use the residual £94,000 to make grants to institutions having as their objects 'the bringing of the masterpieces of fine art within the reach of the Irish people', the teaching of 'self control, elocution, oratory, and deportment, the arts of personal contact, of social inter-course', and the establishment of a 'Chair or Readership' at an Irish university to give instruction in those subjects.

What incensed potential beneficiaries were the reasons Charlotte advanced for these charitable endeavours. She had observed how 'the most highly instructed and capable persons' were derided by reason of 'their awkward manners . . . by vulgarities of speech and other defects as easily corrigible by teaching and training as simple illiteracy', and how the lack of this teaching and training 'produces not only much social friction but grave pathological results'.

The will had been partly worded by Sidney Webb, but the blame was loaded on to G.B.S. People lamented that the good intentions of a sweetly nurtured, gently connected Irish lady should have been interfered with by a 'counterfeit Irishman' with a 'bad temper'. G.B.S. was pictured as a wizard changing her gift into an insult. The *New Yorker* concluded: 'anybody who thinks the Irish can be taught self-control is a crazy optimist, and anybody who thinks they need to be taught elocution is just plain crazy.'

Shaw's last will, which he completed shortly before his ninety-fourth birthday, has connections with Charlotte's over its disposal of papers, its complementary annuities to servants (with a clause respecting inflation) and a charitable trust challenging England to mind its language. It is an extraordinarily public-spirited document giving works of art by Augustus John, Rodin, Strobl, Sargent, Troubetskoy to public galleries and theatres in Britain, Ireland and the United States, his furniture to the National Trust, papers of sociological interest to the British Library of Political Science at the London School of Economics, and an enormous collection of literary papers to the British Museum 'where all the would-be biographers can find it and do their worst or their best'.

The most original feature of this will was its disposal of his royalties over the then posthumous fifty-year copyright period. During the first twenty-one years following his death, he directed that these earnings should be used for the creation and promotion of a new phonetic alphabet containing at least forty letters 'one symbol for each sound'. Over the following twenty-nine years his copyright income was to be shared equally by three residuary legatees: the National Gallery of Ireland 'to which I owe much of the only real education I ever got as a boy in Eire'; the Royal Academy of Dramatic Art (on whose Council he had served thirty years and on which he forced the admission of women) representing the theatre where he had derived his livelihood; and the British Museum 'in acknowledgement of the incalculable value to me of my daily resort to the Reading Room of that Institution at the beginning of my career'.

By appointing the Public Trustee as his executor and making him responsible for challenging English orthography, Shaw hoped to give his proposal additional authority. He knew that people 'just laugh at spelling reformers as silly cranks'. So he attempted to exhibit a phonetic alphabet as native good sense while making traditional spelling sound foreign and absurd. 'Let people spell as they speak without any nonsense about bad or good or right or wrong spelling and speech,' he urged. He would wrinkle his face into the most terrible shapes when pronouncing the word 'though' with six letters instead of two. But when an enthusiastic convert suggested that 'ghoti' would have been a reasonable way to spell 'fish' under the old system (*gh* as in 'tough', *o* as in 'women' and *ti* as in 'nation') the subject seemed almost engulfed in the ridicule from which Shaw was determined to preserve it.

'The fact that English is spelt conventionally and not phonetically makes the art of recording speech almost impossible,' he had complained in his notes to *Captain Brassbound's Conversion*. When he came to *Pygmalion*, a romance advertising the science of phonetics, he abandoned his attempt to represent Eliza Doolittle's broad cockney with transliterated 'nu speling' which looked illiterate and was 'unintelligible outside London'. 'It cannot be done with our alphabet,' he stated in 1936.

This failure was one of the 'everyday workshop grievances' with which he ventilated his alphabetical campaign. From his years policing pronunciation for the British Broadcasting Corporation he knew that his battles with the 'mob of spelling cranks' would be hard and long. 'The only danger I can foresee in the establishment of an English alphabet is the danger of civil war,' he wrote. But after forty years he had concluded that 'no British Government will ever be stirred to action in the matter until the economies of a phonetically spelt scientific and scholarly Pidgin are calculated and stated in terms of time, labour and money'. Providing this economic argument was Shaw's unique contribution to the spelling reform debate. If he could demonstrate a large financial saving, large enough perhaps to pay for a third world war, what government could resist?

Between Charlotte's death and his own he returned to this windmill and charged with heroic persistence. 'I am a citizen desirous of bequeathing my property to the public for public good,' he announced in a public letter which was printed in 1944 as a leaflet and sent to twenty-two government departments as well as to colleges, trusts, societies and 'all other stones I could think of to turn'.

There was gathering interest after the war in adult literacy, initial teaching alphabets for children and the reform of language. This interest was to reach its conclusion in 1975 with the Bullock Report, *A Language for Life*. But already by the late 1940s it seemed that a change in English lettering was more likely than changes in coinage, the measurements of weights or distances or temperatures. Shaw's circular unleashed an extraordinary response.

Unharnessed languages rushed in at him from everywhere and he beat them off with blue printed postcards, statements for debates in Parliament, letters to *Tit-Bits* and *The Times*, and an ultimate brochure launched at all members of the House of Commons and the House of Lords, at the entire Dáil and sixty Irish senators. But still they came at him, the champions of Basic English and Simplified Spelling, knights of Interglossa and

Esperanto, Novial and Volapük, ancient lords of Visible Speech, irascible young linguists, strange panoptic conjugators, calligraphers, mathematical symbolists, firers of pistics, shorthanders, Pidgin fanciers. 'It is clear that if I wait for a solution before making my will I shall die intestate as far as the alphabet is concerned,' he told the educationist James Pitman.

That a man of letters might want to improve his implements so as to lessen the disparity in speed between written and spoken language, between thought and its communication on to paper, is not unreasonable. Shaw took many sensible precautions. He defined a limited experiment to place a new alphabet into free competition with the old (as Arabic numerals had competed successfully with Roman numerals), 'until one of the two proves the fitter to survive'. Neither was he deaf to the many regional accents in Britain, nor did he claim that one was better or any ideal: he simply relied on what was generally intelligible. He never contemplated designing the new alphabet himself or appropriating the reform personally. Yet in spite of all this surrounding sense, the scheme remains illusory.

This was partly because he omitted from his will the familiar virtues of alphabetical reform such as its educational benefits for infants and the environmental saving of trees. He believed that a good phonetic script would make English easier for foreigners and improve its chances of emerging by natural selection from international Babel to become the lingua franca of the world: 'the language with the best spelling and the least grammar will win,' he predicted. But this too is omitted from the will. He argued that any operation for rescuing the handicapped language should be led by economists. He put his trust in James Pitman, who was not only a Member of Parliament but also the grandson of the inventor of the phonographic system of shorthand. 'You are, I should say, by far the best equipped adventurer in the field,' he wrote to Pitman. ' . . . You have no enemies and a great phonetic name.'

Under the eccentric rationality of Shaw's proposals, the American writer Jacques Barzun was to detect a symbolic motive. 'His expressed purpose was not his real purpose,' Barzun wrote; 'he did not want to save ink and paper, help the child and favor the foreigner. What did he want to do? Simply to get rid of the past, to give a part of mankind a fresh start by isolating it from its own history and from the ancestral bad habits of the other nations.'

In old age a peculiar passion enters his crusade and ties it to his family name. 'All round me I hear the corruption of our language,' he writes, 'produced by the absurd device of spelling the first sound in my name with the two letters sh.' This impurity weighs on him like a defect in the blood. In the will his desire is expressed as an equation involving labour, cost and time: the mental labour to which he had been so ecstatically if regretfully addicted; the cost into which he had transferred much emotional profit and loss; and the time that was running out. 'Saving time is of no significance,' protested Hesketh Pearson. But at ninety it may be. Shaw calculated that phonetic spelling would 'add years' to a writer's life.

He had shed a good deal that belonged to his past before he came to sign his will. He gave the surviving holographs of his novels to the National Library of Ireland. Then there was his property. 'I own the freehold of a ten roomed house in the village of Ayot St Lawrence in Herts,' he had written to the secretary of the National Trust shortly after Charlotte's death. ' . . . Has such a trifle any use or interest for the National Trust?' A member of the Trust, James Lees-Milne, came down one dismal day in early 1944, glanced at the exterior of this 'ugly, dark red-brick villa', glanced through its 'far from beautiful' rooms with their pinched fireplaces, flaking walls, and decided that the National Trust was positively interested. Shaw transferred many of his possessions from Whitehall Court to add zest to what he called 'the birthplace'. The rooms brimmed with memorabilia and mementoes. Here is the Bechstein piano on which he played to Charlotte; the weighing-scales that registered his decreasing weight; his fountain pen, gold propelling pencil, mittens, cameras, steel-rimmed spectacles and the typewriter that could type plays. Here are the colour-coded postcards on Capital Punishment, Vegetarian Diet, Temperance and the Forty-Letter British Alfabet. Here too is a Staffordshire figure of Shakespeare picked up cheap at the seaside, an ancient exercise bicycle bought in France, a filing cabinet with its drawers marked 'Ayot', 'Russia', 'Keys and Contraptions', together with his admission card to the Reading Room of the British Museum for 1880 and his membership of the Cyclist Touring Club renewed in 1950. There are his books, the framed parchment scrolls of his honorary freedoms of Dublin and St Pancras; his Hollywood Oscar and Nobel Prize for Literature as well as a medal from the Irish Academy of Letters and the master key to the Malvern Festival. In the meagre writing-hut stand a wicker chair, narrow bed, flap table, telephone, thermometer, toothbrush. Everywhere, from the brass door-knocker inwards, are images of G.B.S., and pictures of those he knew: the Sartorio portrait of Charlotte; photographs of the two heralds of his career, William Morris and Sidney Webb; his special friends and loves, Archer and Barker, Ellen and Stella; his sparring partners Chesterton and Wells; fellow-playwrights and compatriots, Ibsen and Barrie, Sean O'Casey, W. B. Yeats, Lady Gregory; and others he admired such as Lenin, Gene Tunney, Gandhi, Lawrence of Arabia, Einstein and Uncle Joe Stalin.

Early in 1949, he notified the managing director of Whitehall Court that he wanted to be transferred to a smaller flat in the building. He had last come up to Whitehall Court at the end of 1946 'and it is unlikely that I shall ever see London again,' he wrote. ' . . . all I need is a study for Miss Patch to work in, a lavatory, and perhaps a bedroom . . . in an emergency.' He finally gave up number 130 Whitehall Court in May 1949 and became the absentee tenant of number 116, a two-roomed furnished flat downstairs which at ten guineas a month was half the cost.

He was impatient to sell 'every stick and stone' not needed at Ayot. There were 1,100 books at Whitehall Court and he was determined to make them 'more saleable by every trick in my power'. Into eight of the more valuable volumes he inserted reminiscences. The Cranwell Edition of T. E. Lawrence's *Seven Pillars of Wisdom* went for £460, a facsimile set of four folios of Shakespeare's plays for £163. Apsley Cherry-Garrard bought the Ashendene Press edition of Dante's *Tutte le Opere* for £115, and Gertrude Lawrence snapped up Malory's *Le Morte Darthur* (illustrated by Beardsley) for only £58. Except for Wilde's *The Importance of Being Earnest* (which went for £125), the authors' presentation copies fetched tiny prices: £7 10s. 0d. for Yeats's *Trembling of the Veil*, £6 10s. 0d. for Virginia Woolf's *A Room of One's Own*; £6 for O'Casey's *Juno and the Paycock*. 'I am out for money: HARD,' Shaw told Sydney Cockerell; 'for the rest of the year my name is Harpagon.' His books raised £2,649 15s. 0d. (equivalent to £50,000 in 1997), which he used to offset the Capital Levy which the Labour Government introduced in 1948 to avoid national bankruptcy.

*

In the *New Statesman* in May 1950, Shaw published a defence of the 'Play of Ideas', responding to Terence Rattigan and making a final analysis of his own dramaturgy.

'Wherever there is a queue waiting for the doors of a theatre to open you may see some vagabond artist trying to entertain it in one way or another . . . I myself have done the same on Clapham Common, and collected sixteen shillings in my hat at the end for the Socialist cause. I have stopped on the Thames Embankment; set my back to the river wall; and had a crowd listening to me in no time . . . I, the roofless pavement orator, ended in the largest halls in the country with overcrowds that filled two streets . . . it illustrates the development of the theatre from the pavement to the tribune and the cathedral, and the promotion of its outcasts to palaces . . .

I was going back atavistically to Aristotle, to the tribune stage, to the circus, to the didactic Mysteries, to the word music of Shakespear, to the forms of my idol Mozart, and to the stage business of the great players whom I had actually seen acting, from Barry Sullivan, Salvini, and Ristori to Coquelin and Chaliapin . . . I know my business both historically and by practice.'

In one July week that year, Shaw wrote five small scenes of a 'little comedy', calling it *Why She Would Not*. The reason why the good-looking Serafina White will not marry the improving young man is that 'I am afraid of you,' she tells him. He is incredulous: 'I coerce nobody,' he protests: 'I only point out the way.' The play is a Christian allegory. In the first scene the man appears as a chivalrous 'newcomer', in the second he is revealed as 'a carpenter of sorts', in the third he acts an apparently 'unemployable walking gentleman', in the fourth he becomes 'a very smart city man' dealing in real estate, and in the fifth he is finally 'a wonder', admired but alone. Shaw's hero is like a miniature of Los in Blake's Symbolic poems: the voice of eternal prophecy, the spectre of reasoning, the creator of alphabets, divorced from the Female Principle and hammering out the future in his creator's shade. His Shavian name is Henry Bossborn, a good surname to adopt for a writer once unsure of his legitimacy who had won natural authority through the power of language. His solitude is the solitude G.B.S. had regained seven years after Charlotte's death.

Shaw's nature was rooted in solitude, but it was ringed with crowds of people, as if he lived in the eye of a perpetual storm. *The Times*, which now recorded his birthdays in its Court Circular, described his ninety-fourth birthday, three days after he completed *Why She Would Not*, as restful.

'Restful!!! Restful, with the telephone and the door bell ringing all day! With the postmen staggering under bushels of letters and telegrams! With immense birthday cakes . . . falling on me like millstones! With the lane blocked by cameramen, televisors, photographers, newsreelers, interviewers, all refusing to take No for an answer. And I with a hard day's work to finish in time for the village post. Heaven forgive *The Times*. I cannot.'

Mrs Laden would have refused 'the King of England' had he driven up without an appointment. But she could not stop people climbing the trees and peering down, or prevent photographers breaking through the hedges and setting up their cameras on the lawn, or silence the persistent telephone calls. 'I don't want to speak to anybody,' Shaw cried out, 'alive or dead.'

He had always been fastidious and could not bear people detecting signs of his infirmities – the egg stain on his tie, the weak bladder. But nothing was hidden from Mrs Laden. She had noticed pools in the lavatory and observed how the old man would empty the chamber pot under his bed each morning. Suspecting he was suffering from renal trouble or perhaps a failure of the prostate gland, she collected a specimen of his urine, saw that it contained blood, and sent to the doctor. He advised immediate treatment. But she knew it was hopeless. He did not want to speak about such things.

Apart from these secrets, he was not unhappy. 'Life is worth my while: if it were not I should end it.' Death did not frighten him. 'I sleep well, always in the hope that I may not wake again.'

By the beginning of September he was busy making bonfires in the garden. One of the neighbours rang up to complain about the smoke and Mrs Laden roared 'with the ferocity of a lioness' down the telephone. 'Your phone call to Mrs Laden reached her in a moment when a terrible misfortune had just overtaken her,' Shaw wrote to pacify him. 'Our pet cat had died in the night; and she was overwhelmed with grief. Forgive her if she vented any of it on you.'

The death of Bunch, her orange cat, at last persuaded Mrs Laden to go on holiday up to Scotland. 'It was the first holiday I'd taken for years,' she remembered. 'I was entitled to at least two weeks a year, but I usually felt that something would happen to him if I wasn't there.' Margaret Cashin Smith, the recently married Irish parlourmaid, bicycled back to look after him. Everything was prepared. All seemed well. Mrs Laden coached G.B.S. on the things he must not do in her absence, and left at the end of the week.

'I can hardly walk through my garden without a tumble or two,' Shaw had written in his preface to *Buoyant Billions*. On Sunday 10 September, once it had stopped raining in the late afternoon, he walked in the garden with his secateurs. 'Pruning with the secateurs was his chief interest,' the gardener Fred Drury had reckoned. But this time, while cutting a projecting branch, he slipped, fell on the path, and began blowing the whistle he carried for emergencies. 'I ran out into the garden and found him on the ground,' the Irish parlourmaid remembered. 'I had him sitting on my knees for fifteen minutes. "Put me down and go and fetch someone," he said, but I wouldn't put him on the wet grass and blew and blew at the whistle till my husband, who happened to be near, came and helped Mr Shaw into the house.'

His doctor arrived and sent for a radiologist who was driven to the house by Shaw's chauffeur Fred Day. A portable X-ray machine revealed that Shaw's left thigh was fractured, and his leg was put in a splint. The doctor sedated him for the night and later arranged for an ambulance to take him next morning to the Luton and Dunstable Hospital. He also telephoned Mrs Laden who flew back the following day.

'He was in great pain, but most stoical,' said one of the doctors at the hospital. At 5.15 on the Monday afternoon, he was operated on, the surgeon joining the broken surfaces of the neck of his thigh bone.

As soon as the newspapers heard of the accident 'all hell broke loose'. So many telephone calls came in from all parts of the world that the hospital had to employ an extra switchboard operator. The corridors and waiting-room seethed with reporters. Photographers offered the management £1,000 (equivalent to £18,500 in 1997) for a picture of Shaw in bed surrounded with the flowers sent by Winston Churchill, and when this did not succeed they put ladders against the outside wall in an attempt to climb into his room. Mrs Laden, arriving with fruit and pyjamas and an electrically heated bed-warmer, felt quite scared as they all pressed round her.

The hospital management set aside its boardroom for regular bulletins. Journalists filled the local accommodation and 'a few of the reporters were found room in a jail cell at the police station'. Their stories were remorselessly cheerful. They quoted the hospital staff as being 'amazed' at Shaw's 'grand colour', his 'lively and talkative' behaviour and other signs of his rapid recovery: 'G.B.S. Gets Out of Bed – and Stands,' miraculously announced one newspaper. When two nurses did lift him for a few seconds he cautioned them to tell no one or else 'they will say I've walked a mile'.

It quickly became apparent to surgeons and doctors at the hospital that Shaw was suffering from long-standing kidney and bladder trouble. They took temporary measures to relieve the condition and then, on 21 September, operated on him again. Though his fractured thigh was mending well, he was described as being only 'fairly satisfactory in the circumstances' and his doctor remembered that shortly after this second operation he became 'quite unmanageable'. He now had a silver catheter attached to his bladder which had to be cleaned each week and which he was told he must use for the rest of his life. He pestered Mrs Laden to let him come home. Eleanor O'Connell, who visited the hospital on 2 October, observed that he looked 'so fragile and strangely enough not a bit peaceful', and also that his voice was 'hoarse and tremulous'. She had to lean her elbows on the bed and put her head on the pillow next to his head. She asked him how he was.

'Everyone asks me that, and its so silly when all I want is to die, but this damned vitality of mine won't let me.'

She asked him whether he was looking forward to dying.

'Oh so much, so much (tremulously like a child) if *only* I could die . . . I'm in HELL (loudly) here, they wash me all the time . . . when I'm asleep they wake me, and when I'm awake they ask why I'm not asleep. Each time they pounce on me they tell me it will be just the same as last time and then I find they have added a new torture . . . (beating feebly against his thigh). Ah if only I could walk I would get up at once and go.'

According to the orthopaedic surgeon, Shaw 'might have lived till a hundred' had he stayed in hospital, allowed them to feed him up with butcher's meat, and enjoyed another visit or two to the operating theatre. In his preface to *The Doctor's Dilemma* he had written: 'in surgery all operations are recorded as successful if the patient can be got out of the hospital or nursing home alive.' The last hospital bulletin recorded his 'satisfactory progress'. And it was true that he was still alive, though such a shadow of G.B.S. he seemed a ghost. 'He died in effect the day he fell in his garden,' said the village postmistress Jisbella Lyth. ' . . . He died in his garden, like my husband, just as he had always told me he wanted to do.'

After twenty-four days in hospital, the ambulance drove him back to Ayot where, hidden from the crowd behind a white canvas screen held by his gardener and chauffeur, he was carried into the dining-room which Mrs Laden had fitted up as a bedroom.

Two nurses looked after him day and night. 'He is very well, thank you,' Mrs Laden brusquely informed a journalist from the *Manchester Guardian*. But in fact she could see that he was not at all himself. His face had fallen in, he was pale and quiet, a vacant thing, ghastly. Everyone saw it. 'It was pitiful to see him the last time I cut his hair,' said the man who had been his regular barber for almost twenty years. ' . . . he couldn't have had less flesh on him. Formerly he enjoyed having his hair cut, but that last time he was completely miserable. I don't know how I got through it. He was a changed man – just like a child. I hope I never have an experience like that again.'

Passing his room one morning Mrs Laden heard him ask the nurse not to prolong his life as he was a very old man. So she went in at once to upbraid him.

'You're much more than an old man, you are a national institution.'

'What's the good of trying to repair an ancient monument?' he asked.

Then she burst out: 'I wish it was I that was dying and not you.'

In the kitchen she set to preparing some 'vur-r-r-ee special' soups with something secretly added to buck him up. But he did not want to eat or drink. He wanted to make what haste he could and be gone. 'His mental worry about his kidney trouble killed him as much as the illness itself,' Mrs Laden could tell.

Blanche Patch went on with her secretarial work as best she might, coming down and reading some of his post to him, holding his wrist as she got a signature out of him. One of the first signatures he wrote on getting back to Ayot was on a large cheque to be divided among the hospital telephonists, porters and nurses whose duties had been so stretched by their newsworthy patient. 'I don't think I shall ever write anything more,' he said.

They had placed his narrow bed facing a long window so that he could see the lawn. Wearing a light saffron nightgown with wide sleeves he looked 'a Blake-like figure,' thought Esmé Percy visiting him there. 'He took my hand and pressed it against his heart . . . He just said, "Good luck, good-bye," and then a brief but heart-rending pause, and "Now get along with you".'

Visitors came to cheer him on, then to make their farewells. Loewenstein hovered near the bedroom and eventually took up his vigil in the next room. Nancy Astor came and went bringing many flowers. 'I don't want visitors. They tire me too much,' Shaw had said to Eleanor O'Connell. But a few people, mostly women, were briefly welcome. Sean O'Casey's beautiful wife Eileen came to see him and stroked his aching head. It was wonderful, he told her. She felt he was 'back again as a small child wanting a mother's comfort'. He asked her to kiss him.

For much of the last week he slept. Then his temperature rose rapidly, and in the early hours of 1 November, shortly before going into a coma, he spoke his last words: 'I am going to die.'

Mrs Laden asked the rector of Ayot to read the twenty-third Psalm over him as he lay on his bed, and the rector agreed for 'the man was surely no atheist'. Shaw had summed up his religious beliefs the week before when speaking to his one-time secretary, Judy Musters: 'I believe in life everlasting; but not for the individual.' For twenty-six hours he remained unconscious. Then, early on 2 November, Mrs Laden walked out through the morning mist and told the reporters waiting with their blinding flash bulbs at the gate that, shortly before five o'clock, G.B.S. had died.

*

'Life goes on as usual at Shaw's Corner,' the *Daily Herald* reported that morning. Outside Fred Drury was brushing up the dead leaves. The windows of the house stood open. Inside the nurses began packing and Lady Astor arrived. So did Pascal, flying in from New York with a suitcase full of vitamins, then bursting into tears, and stating that he would film the life of G.B.S. 'I shall write it myself,' he declared before driving off.

Death suited G.B.S. He hadn't appeared so well for a long time. 'When he was dead he looked wonderful . . . with a sort of whimsical smile on his face,' said Mrs Laden. Lady Astor went out later that morning and invited some twenty reporters into the house. 'I think you ought to see him, he looks so lovely.' At noon the rector conducted a short service at the bedside and seven women from the village came to pay their last respects. In the afternoon Shaw's body was driven to the Chapel of Rest at Welwyn. On Lady Astor's instructions a death mask was made.

Next day an outpouring of memories and obituaries began on the wireless, the television sets, and in the newspapers. The Indian Cabinet adjourned; theatre audiences in Australia rose for two minutes' silence; the Swedish National Theatre delivered a statement to the British Ambassador in praise of Shaw's creative life; and on Broadway and in Times Square the lights were briefly blacked out. 'There was a singular sense of loss,' recorded St John Ervine. Shaw himself would have preferred to be remembered 'as Sonny than as the ghastly old skeleton of a celebrity I now am'. But there was hardly anyone alive who knew him as Sonny – certainly not the presidents and prime ministers whose fine opinions were being blazed round the world. On the other hand it was strange that such a dry, unsentimental phenomenon as G.B.S. could have touched ordinary people unless something of Sonny had lived on. 'I sobbed my socks off,' said the housewife from Workington. 'It was a great loss to me,' said the village postmistress at Ayot.

Shaw had wanted the funeral service at Golders Green to be private, but some 500 people haphazardly gathered in the Garden of Remembrance. 'We'll never see his like again,' platitudinized a cockney woman. 'Madam, we must never underrate posterity,' an Irishman corrected her. A representative of the women's movement who unfurled a green, purple and white striped flag proclaiming G.B.S. 'one of our best friends during our fight for the vote' was hustled off by police.

The music was relayed to those outside: the hymn at the beginning of Humperdinck's *Hansel and Gretel* overture, the *Libera me* from Verdi's *Requiem*, extracts from Elgar's *The Music Makers* and the Nimrod section from his *Enigma Variations*. Sydney Cockerell read the final passage of Mr Valiant for Truth from *The Pilgrim's Progress*. So he passed over.

Charlotte had directed in her will that her ashes 'shall be taken to Ireland and scattered on Irish ground', but after the war started Shaw proposed that their ashes be mixed inseparably and distributed round the garden at Ayot. 'It pleased her, and she agreed.'

Charlotte's ashes had been waiting in a bronze casket at the Golders Green columbarium, and his were placed in a smaller casket which fitted on top of hers in the niche. Early in the morning of 23 November, the two caskets were taken down to Ayot. The Public Trustee emptied his ashes into hers at the dining-room sideboard, and stirred them together. Then, with his two deputies, Charlotte's executor from the bank, the local doctor, a news agency reporter representing the public, and Mrs Laden, he went into the garden. The doctor shook the aluminium sprinkler and a grey cloud drifted into the air and was carried to the ground by the falling rain. He led them past the flower beds, emptying the ashes along the path and round the revolving hut at the end – where G.B.S. had recently paraded with a famous actress and, waving her goodbye, asked:

'Well, did I give a good performance?'

APPENDIX

Well, now as to practical matters . . . Ive used my knowledge of the world
to invest my money in ways that other men have overlooked; and whatever
else I may be, I'm a safe man from the money point of view.

Mrs Warren's Profession

Shaw's will, when it was published in March 1951, turned out to be a most unpopular
document. 'Had he deliberately set out to ensure that the least possible profit should
accrue to future generations from his wealth,' commented *The Economist*, 'it is hard to
see how he could have done better.' Several newspapers carried a similar incredulous
headline: 'Left a fortune for reform of alphabet.'

The gross value of his estate amounted to £367,233 (equivalent to £6.2 million in
1997). It was an extraordinary sum for a writer: Thomas Hardy had left £91,000 in 1928;
G. K. Chesterton £28,000 in 1936; J. M. Barrie £173,500 in 1937; H. G. Wells £60,000
in 1946. In due course an assessment of his copyrights would have to be added to Shaw's
estate, and the total fortune had every chance of rising to a glittering £500,000. But
apparently it had been fool's gold, an old fool's gold, and was posthumously reverting to
base metal.

The British public had been living through more than a decade of austerity which only
now was coming to an end with the final lifting of food rationing and the long-awaited
opening of the Festival of Britain. Britain had borrowed over $2,500,000,000 in Marshall
aid from the United States, more than any other European country. By the beginning of
1951 her overseas trade enabled her to dispense with further borrowing, yet she appeared
to have traded away part of her sovereignty. The cultural, educational and intellectual
practices in which Shaw had sought to invest his residual copyright income were to be
eroded by the need to make Britain's academies, galleries and museums part of an
expanding entertainment industry. With its thirty acres of pleasure gardens and fun fairs
in Battersea, the Festival of Britain would retrospectively look more like a theme park for
tourists than a commemoration of the Great Exhibition that in 1851 had converted its
profits into funds for scholarships.

A Shaw Memorial Fund was set up in 1951 to subsidize young authors, dramatists
and musicians, encourage the 'worthy presentation' of Shaw's own plays at festivals, and
maintain the fabric of Shaw's Corner which he had given to the National Trust without
an endowment. But the public did not see why it should have to pay for all this when
there was so much of Shaw's own money apparently going to waste. The fact that Clement
Attlee, the Prime Minister, was associating himself with the fund, and that it was to have
the support of the Labour Government, made the venture all the more untimely. That
October the General Election swept Attlee from office and returned the Conservatives to
power. Within a few days all the Festival of Britain structures except the Concert Hall
were dismantled.

On 23 November, the new Chancellor of the Exchequer R. A. Butler (who that year
was elected President of the Royal Society of Literature and later created Baron Butler of
Saffron Walden) launched the appeal as 'a world tribute to Shaw's memory'. The target
was £250,000 and the total eventually reached £416: 'a complete failure and a disastrous
flop,' lamented Archibald Henderson.

Yet Shaw's finances were not quite what the public perceived them to be. The net value
of his estate was £301,585 (equivalent to £5.1 million in 1997) on which £180,571
became immediately due in death duties. Nor was this all. Once the copyrights had been

valued, seventy per cent of this notional amount would have to be paid in additional death duties. Besides this, there were more than a dozen annuities in Shaw's will, mostly bequests to those who had worked for him at Ayot and in London, which had to be met each year. Since his royalties were bringing in less than £50,000 a year, and might soon decrease (his earliest plays shortly coming out of copyright in the United States), there seemed a likelihood that the alfabet trusts, which were confined to twenty-one years from his death so as to avoid the legal taint of perpetuity, would be largely washed out. Towards the end of 1951 public attention turned to what *The Star* called 'The "Tangled Will" of Mrs Shaw'.

*

Charlotte Shaw had bequeathed £94,000 to Ireland for educational purposes. She wanted the money to be used for three objects: bringing masterpieces of fine art, including music and painting, within the reach of all classes of Irish people; teaching Irish people the secrets of self-control, elocution, oratory and deportment; and the endowment of a Chair or Readership at an Irish university for instruction in these matters of fine art and social intercourse. Her wishes were considered so unusual that the National Provincial Bank, as trustee of her estate, brought the matter before the Chancery Division of the High Court in London to determine whether under English law they constituted a valid charitable trust.

The English bank questioned the will, and an Irish bank defended it. The Attorney-General supported it and was himself supported by the Public Trustee on behalf of Bernard Shaw's estate. But lawyers representing Charlotte's next-of-kin challenged the trusts as being void by reason of remoteness and uncertainty.

A murmur of approval went round the court when the judge described Charlotte's will as 'a very interesting document revealing a mind of a very high quality and a lady with every wish to do right'. It was at Chancery because 'the lady seems to have got tangled up in a web of her own verbosity and it makes it very difficult to untangle her'. No one recognized the unconscious pun relating to Sidney Webb who had helped to draft the will. The document seemed oddly lacking in the good manners it sought to promote. There was laughter when Sir Charles Russell, a King's Counsel instructed by the National City Bank (an Irish bank appointed as the ultimate trustee under Charlotte's will), replied: 'Quite frankly, my lord, we are prepared to accept these insults.'

Charlotte had bequeathed her niece Cecily Colthurst £20,000 which was paid to her in 1944. But if the court declared a partial intestacy and Charlotte's wishes were blocked, then Mrs Colthurst would inherit the extra £94,000. Here was a case that needed to be presented with delicacy if it were not to appear grasping. But Pascoe Hayward KC, representing Mrs Colthurst, was not delicate. While Sir Charles Russell politely referred to Charlotte as a 'serious-minded lady dealing with a serious subject', Mr Pascoe Hayward called her a 'cranky' person whose fortune was in danger of being lamentably 'frittered away' by a lot of other 'cranky people'. It would be open to her trustees, he protested, to encourage social intercourse by giving 'a series of cocktail parties'. Were he himself a trustee, he persisted, he would instil self-control by building plenty of good strong nourishing prisons and seeing 'that people who do not control themselves go there'. These trusts were 'doomed to failure,' he concluded. There was no precedent for them. But refusing to test the validity of the trusts by presupposing perverse ways of applying them, Mr Justice Vaisey (otherwise Sir Harry Vaisey) decided that under English law Charlotte had kept herself within the necessary limits 'by a rather narrow margin'.

So the money passed out of England into Ireland. 'How the people of Ireland will react to such intensive treatment as Mrs Shaw appears to envisage,' Mr Justice Vaisey remarked, 'I ought not to speculate.' But a ripple of delirious speculation was already passing over the twenty-six counties of the Republic. Before long almost a hundred applications had been prepared by universities, cultural groups, local authorities and some enterprising individuals demanding art galleries, gramophone records, endowments for lectures, subsidies for theatres. '£94,000 sounds a lot of money,' parried an official at the National City Bank in Dublin, 'and many of the applicants seem to have dreams of building palaces.' £94,000 *was* a lot of money in 1952, equivalent to little over £1.4 million in the late 1990s. But the bands got no new instruments, and no foundations for new libraries were laid. After a year, cultural life in Ireland seemed unchanged; and after two years it was still further unchanged. 'Where is the £94,000?' the *News Chronicle* demanded.

The first results of Charlotte's bequest were witnessed in the summer of 1954 at a hostel in Termonfeckin, County Louth, where forty students assembled for a week of instruction by artists, linguists, and the director of a mannequin agency. The successful applicant had been Forás Éireann, an *omnium gatherum* of native 'sons of the soil' formed in 1949 to plant village halls in rural communities. Forás Éireann 'hopes to be able to lend itself further to the purposes of the bequest,' reported the *Irish Independent*.

In the 1990s Forás Éireann continues to distribute Charlotte's money as part of its policy for developing rural Ireland in accordance with 'Christian and national ways of life'. No Chair or Readership has been established at any Irish university. After more than forty years of capitalist expansion and inflation Charlotte's money would have risen to some two million pounds if it had been well invested. 'Each year we spend, roughly, about £2,500 to £3,000 under the heading of Art,' writes the Trust organizer at Forás Éireann, 'and this is used to support smaller ventures throughout the twenty-six counties.' It is a curiously small sum.

'It is the policy of the Bank,' writes the Bank of Ireland, 'for confidentiality reasons, not to reveal any details about the financial aspect of the Trust.'

*

On 15 March 1956 a spectacular musical adaptation of Shaw's phonetic romance *Pygmalion* opened at the Mark Hellinger Theater on Broadway. *My Fair Lady* contained fifteen numbers composed by Frederick Loewe with lyrics by Alan J. Lerner, and it was directed by Moss Hart. Yet the production was in many ways a very English affair. Stanley Holloway played the undeserving dustman Doolittle in a broad style that derived from the old music-hall tradition ('With a Little Bit of Luck', 'Get me to the Church on Time'). He incorporated the same ironic cheerfulness he had earlier brought to the grave-digger in *Hamlet*. Stella Campbell's part as the flower girl was taken by the twenty-one-year-old Julie Andrews. Known mostly as a pantomime performer in Britain, she had won a devoted American following in *The Boy Friend* and was to complete her conquest of New York by singing and dancing Eliza's new role ('Wouldn't it be Loverly', 'I could have danced all Night'). Rex Harrison brought off a histrionic triumph by turning his lack of singing voice into the half-rasping, half-caressing baritone patter of Henry Higgins's 'I'm an Ordinary Man' and 'Why Can't the English'. Cecil Beaton's rich costumes, which ranged from a street crowd of raffish cockney buskers to the wheel hats and feathered parasols of Mrs Higgins's fashionable tea-party and the mock-stately black, white and grey pageant of the 'Ascot Gavotte', were to be taken up by New York *couturiers* and judged to be more effective than the posters of the British Tourist Board. *My Fair Lady* seemed one of those rare theatrical collaborations in which everyone, working on top form, came harmoniously together. Like the comic operas of Gilbert and Sullivan, like *The Merry Widow, Oklahoma!, Annie Get Your Gun* and *Me and My Girl* (which also derives from Shaw's *Pygmalion*), this new musical exerted a lasting attraction. Moss Hart's production was to run on Broadway for 2,717 performances over six and a half years, by which time $55,000,000 had already been made from performances round the world, plus another $10,000,000 from recordings and film rights, breaking all financial records.

Even at the previews in New Haven it was obvious that *My Fair Lady* was destined to be a vast success. This prospect, together with a rise in the international performances of Shaw's plays, suddenly brought his six-year-old will into new focus.

*

The Official Trustee Act introduced by the Liberal Government in 1906 had created an official whose advantage over private and commercial trustees was to lie in the certainty that trust funds which he administered would never be embezzled, lost in speculation, or misdirected. Shaw had appointed the Public Trustee as his executor in a will he made in 1913 and in all subsequent wills. 'I was a strong advocate of a Public Trustee long before 1906,' he wrote.

Referring to Shaw's last will, the Public Trustee Wyndham Hirst (later Sir Wyndham Hirst) had stated in 1951 that his 'primary duty' was to satisfy all legatees and annuitants. Research into the proposed new alfabet was to remain 'a secondary matter' and could be considered 'only if anything is left over'. Owing to the 'very material increases in death duties', there did not appear much danger of serious money being left over. 'It may be several months, or even years, before we can submit all the valuations necessary for a final assessment,' an official in his department hazarded. For five and a half years the Public Trustee sat negotiating with the Estate Duty Office. Then, in the spring of 1956, he agreed on the figure of £433,500. It was a handsome amount, indeed unprecedented, bringing the net value of Shaw's estate nicely beyond £700,000 (equivalent to £9.5 million in 1997) and raising the final death duties to a magnificent pinnacle of £524,000 (£7.1 million in 1997). More than half this sum was due at once and might possibly be swelled by a generous accretion of interest. Nevertheless, it would still not be a substantial enough obstacle to keep the fearful alfabet long entombed. As the alfabet's custodian, there was only one judicious course of action open to the Public Trustee, and that was to bring the whole matter to Chancery where it would be placed under the scrutiny of the High Court. On 26 March 1956, eleven days after the successful opening of *My Fair Lady* on Broadway, *The Times* announced in London that the British Museum was to challenge the validity of these alphabet trusts.

It was not easy for interested members of the public to find their way to the case when it opened in January 1957. On the Warned List it had appeared somewhat eccentrically as *Public Trustee v. Day and Others*, Fred Day being Shaw's chauffeur whose annuity (with that of his wife) was to be reviewed during the first morning. Several wandering Shavians were mistakenly conducted to the more glamorous business of Diana Dors, the blonde bombshell who was petitioning for divorce in a court nearby. Extricating themselves from the crowd, they finally settled into the more reposeful atmosphere of the Lord Chancellor's Court and, during the afternoon, heard the legal distinction between 'benevolent' and 'philanthropic' begin to drift backwards and forwards.

'The Lord Chancellor's Court is Gothic in more than architecture,' observed the *Manchester Guardian*.

'Mr Justice Harman's face in repose – elongated and narrow-eyed, with the light falling on it from above – might at times have been that of a medieval king in effigy. The lethargy that sometimes overtook the spectators as precedents were unrolled might have put them in mind of something very old and long lasting – the case of Jarndyce v. Jarndyce, say – rather than the quick by-play of the court scenes in "The Devil's Disciple".'

Shaw had believed that the need for alphabetical reform arose from the fact that there were more sounds in the English language than there were letters in its Latin alphabet. Some letters were therefore used to signify more than one sound and the language was choked with illogical two-letter combinations, such as *sh*, *th* and *ng*. This notorious orthography was partly responsible for the number of semi-literates in Britain and had retarded the spread of English as an international language. English usage was overloaded with unnecessary grammar and tedious penwork.

All this Shaw had argued in his lifetime. But he advanced the economic case for a reform in his will. 'Write up in letters of gold around your office,' he had written to James Pitman in 1947, '*England Knows Nothing of Phonetics, Hates Education, But Will Do Anything For Money.*' Having found no public department or learned society to nominate as the executant of his easy alfabet, he had been obliged to create two private trusts. The first was designed to find out, by means of statistical inquiry, how much time could be saved by people who spoke the English language and wrote it using the proposed alfabet, thereby showing the extent of time and labour wasted by the use of the present alphabet, and then, if possible, to make a calculation of this waste in terms of loss of money. The second trust was to transliterate *Androcles and the Lion* into the phonetic alfabet, assuming a given pronunciation of English, to publish and advertise this transliteration in a special bi-alphabetic edition with the existing alphabet on one side and the proposed alfabet on the other, and so by the dissemination of copies in public libraries and by the general debate this would give rise to, persuade the English-speaking world to adopt it.

The legal machinery used by the Chancery Division of the High Court of Justice to test the validity of Shaw's trusts was the Preamble to a Statute of Queen Elizabeth I. Of the five categories of charity there enumerated, two appeared *prima facie* applicable to this case: education and public utility.

There were four parties represented in court. The Attorney-General was in it *parens patriae*, as the official protector of charities. His counsel, Mr E. Milner Holland QC (later Sir Edward Milner Holland) contended that the trusts were legal charities and could not be invalidated for unenforceability or uncertainty since the Charity Commissioners might modify them if necessary to see that the testator's wishes were carried out in spirit even if they could not be carried out to the letter. The Public Trustee was in it as Shaw's executor. Though unable to conceal his personal opinion that these alfabetical matters were a lot of poppycock, he argued through his counsel, Mr Robert Lazarus, that even if the trusts were not charitable, he should be allowed to carry out the provisions of Shaw's bequest. The British Museum and the Royal Academy of Dramatic Art were in it as ultimate residuary legatees and had instructed Sir Charles Russell QC – the same Charles Russell who had successfully fought for Charlotte's Irish trust over five years earlier – to contest the validity of these alfabetical trusts. The third residuary legatee, the National Gallery of Ireland, had engaged Mr K. Elphinstone, *not* to contest the validity of the trusts. 'Is that in order to put the Court in a greater difficulty by having no help from you, or what?' enquired Mr Justice Harman. To which Mr Elphinstone replied that the Governor and Guardians of the National Gallery of Ireland 'did not want to put forward any argument to defeat the intention of a very distinguished fellow-Irishman in a matter very dear to his heart'. He did not explain that, Irish charity laws being stricter than English, his participation might imperil the contestants' claim.

The residuary legatees were in a very favourable position, for even if they lost the case all Shaw's royalties after 1971 would still automatically become theirs. But if they won it the royalties would go to them immediately. 'They may be likened to a schoolboy who has a half-share in a bottle of pop, half of which gets spilt when the bottle is opened, and who proceeds to drink all that is left because *his* half-share was at the bottom,' wrote Barbara Smoker, a founder member of the Phonetic Alphabet Association. 'Not content with having the comparatively safe bottom half of the Shaw residue, the British Museum and the Royal Academy of Dramatic Art have also been claiming in the Chancery Court whatever can be salvaged of the top half – which will be so much more now than seemed likely a year ago.'

There were seldom more than thirty members of the public in court – mainly a scattering of intellectual-looking old gentlemen, some middle-aged women in astrakhan collars and brown hats, a few young Indian and Scandinavian students of British justice. There was also the thirty-four-year-old Barbara Smoker.

Barbara Smoker occupied two attic rooms on Catford Hill. She was a freethinker, ate very little meat, and bought her clothes mainly at jumble sales. Barbara Smoker had no job, but made a meagre living by winning competitions – literary competitions and competitions on the backs of tins and packets for slogans, jingles, ditties – with a little journalism besides.

Barbara Smoker never had a job but she was always busy. On Thursdays, for example, she could be heard on her soap box at Tower Hill contradicting what the Methodist minister Donald Soper (later Baron Soper) had been saying on Wednesdays. She was a passionate campaigner, coherent, courageous, iconoclastic, unconquerable in her crusade against the Big Lie of religion. For forty years she was to persist, without a job, working round the clock as Chairman of the Voluntary Euthanasia Society, President of the National Secular Society, a champion of the Family Squatting Movement, a force within the Radical Alternatives to Prison Committee.

She had come to the Chancery Court in her dual role as secretary of the Phonetic Alphabet Association and assistant secretary of the Shaw Society. It had not been easy. When Shaw's solicitors informed her they were allowed to divulge no information whatever, not even the date of the hearing, she took to telephoning the Public Trustee; and when she found he was never in his office, she wrote him letters which though acknowledged were never answered. Finally she had gone to the court itself, made friends with an official there, and arranged to speak to him each day until the case opened.

The setting and proceedings promised 'little scope for cut-and-thrust comedy,' regretted the *Manchester Guardian*. But amid their blue bags and pink ribbons, their interminable briefs, learned counsel essayed quite a few comic recitatives. When Charles Russell cited a precedent involving a man who left a legacy to a horse and dog which the court found was not charitable, Mr Justice Harman objected that there was no horse or dog in Shaw's will. 'No, My Lord, but I submit there is some analogy between a pet animal and a pet hobby.' To which his Lordship conceded: 'I suppose they might both be called hobby-horses.'

Sir Charles Russell was an impressive advocate on behalf of the British Museum and Royal Academy of Dramatic Art, and his speeches, enriched with many gnarled precedents and crackling Latin tags, made very pretty hearing. Listening to him from the public gallery, it took Barbara Smoker several minutes to realize that no one without prior knowledge of phonetics, and the allied subjects of typography and shorthand, could possibly understand that his mellifluous statements were mostly rubbish. It appeared that she was the one person in court who had this purifying knowledge – indeed she was bursting with it. Except for an affidavit from Daniel Jones, the Professor Emeritus of Phonetics at the University of London, and despite some expert advice from Shaw's old colleague James Pitman (whose heart quite frankly was in simplified spelling rather than alphabet reform), the Attorney-General's case sounded pitifully unprepared. Incredible as it seemed, he knew nothing of Jesperson and Zamenhof or even the difference between inflected and agglutinated language! When Barbara Smoker heard Charles Russell claim that the alfabet trusts would require a change of law because they were analogous to political trusts, when she saw this contention go unchallenged, knowing herself that nothing more would be involved than had been needed for the teaching of shorthand as a supplementary means of writing or the invention of Morse Code, she could bear it no longer. *My Lord!*

But 'there was nothing I could do there and then unless I wanted to risk being sent out of the court'. When the case was adjourned for the day, however, and before it was resumed next morning, she was on to the Attorney-General's counsel, and he could not throw her off. Though she was 'a mere nobody', Mr E. Milner Holland QC had little option but to receive her evidence.

He had no sense of the avalanche he had set in motion. From the public gallery she descended to the body of the court and into the thick of the fight. At the end of each day she had amassed thousands of potent words ready to slip into Mr E. Milner Holland's briefcase. She filled his bag with facts – facts about David's *Neuhand*, Kunowski's *Sprechspur*, the Ridge-Beedle design system, the Erhard Roman Augmented and Dewey's work on the relative frequency of English speech sounds. She gave him evidence to study in the evenings on the educational use of phonetic lettering in more than sixty West German schools, and explained why the word 'though' in two letters supported his case while the word 'enough' in four did not. Sometimes, quite often in fact, when especially horrified by the court's ignorance she could not restrain herself from sending over sheaves of writings to him in court. She was disappointed to find that it was considered bad form for barristers to refer to notes, let alone read out well-prepared arguments. It seemed that everything must appear to flow in a spontaneous stream of inspiration. She also discovered that it was impossible for any self-respecting barrister to correct himself. But she wrote on and was pleased to see that by the end of the week, when Mr E. Milner Holland QC opened his tremendously bulging briefcase and she looked into its jaws, most of the material to be digested there was from herself.

Public Trustee v. Day and Others spread itself over nine days with a three-day adjournment. This was Barbara Smoker's first experience of Chancery. Visiting Mr E. Milner Holland QC in his chambers she was horrified to find him catching up with his other cases. Each night she had been typing out her notes, while he had been merely using his train journeys for the Shaw case.

The hearing ended with Sir Charles Russell quoting a line from *Androcles and the Lion* – 'Did um get an awful thorn into um's tootsum wootsum?' – and querying whether a phonetic transliteration of this speech would really be charitable. Mr Justice Harman reserved his judgment for four weeks.

*

When making his will Shaw had discovered that his solicitor, unable to credit the alphabet trusts, had drafted the clauses as if they were ingenious devices for tax avoidance. He was therefore obliged to take up the pen and redraft some of these passages himself. His lucidity baffled the lawyers, while the legal repetitions and prolixities of the skilled equity draughtsman looked in their baroque magnificence like gibberish to the ordinary reader. It was 'a marriage of incompatibles,' admitted Mr Justice Harman when delivering his reserved judgment on 20 February 1957. The 'delicate testamentary machinery devised by the conveyancer could but suffer when subjected to the *cacœthes scribendi* [urge to write] of the author,' he regretted, 'even though the latter's language if it stood alone, might be a literary masterpiece'. The long and complicated document had been made when Shaw was in his ninety-fourth year but it 'was rather youthful exuberance than the hesitations of old age that marred its symmetry,' his Lordship remarked.

Mr Justice Harman did not sound hostile to G.B.S. He described him as 'an indefatigable reformer' who had acted as 'a kind of "itching powder" to the British public, to the English speaking peoples and indeed to an even wider audience'. English orthography and pronunciation, he continued, were obvious targets for the reformer.

'It was as difficult for the native to defend the one as it was for the foreigner to compass the other. The evidence showed that for many years Shaw had been interested in the subject. Perhaps his best known excursion in the field is *Pygmalion* ... It was indeed a curious reflection that this same work, tagged with versicles which I suppose Shaw would have detested, and tricked out with music, which he would have eschewed ... was now charming huge audiences on the other side of the Atlantic and had given birth to the present proceedings.'

Mr Justice Harman confessed to some reluctance in preventing a man disposing of his own money as he thought fit. Nevertheless this was what he was going to do. He was 'not at liberty' to confer a halo of charity on the trusts because they appeared merely 'to tend to the increase of public knowledge'. In the end it was excruciatingly simple. The trusts were for an object rather than a person and an object could not complain to Chancery which therefore was not able to control the trust and so would not allow it to continue. Consequently the will created neither a valid charitable trust, his Lordship concluded, nor a valid unenforceable trust. Both trusts therefore being void, the three residuary legatees were entitled to come into their inheritance at once – as soon as all legal expenses had been settled.

This summing-up pleased the lawyers. Mr Justice Harman, they reminded themselves, was himself an Irishman. They congratulated him on a brilliant pastiche of Shaw's style that 'will hold its place in any company in any age,' stated Lord Birkett. Two years later Mr Justice Harman was created Lord Justice Harman, and in 1961 his judgment found a place in *The Law as Literature: An Anthology of Great Writing in and About the Law* published by the Bodley Head which not long afterwards took over from Constable as Shaw's own publishers.

'If nothing happens, or the bequest fails through any cause,' Shaw had written to James Pitman in the summer of 1944, 'I have provided alternative destinations for the money which will prevent its being "left in the air" in any case.

'I cannot guard against litigation over my definition of a British alphabet; but as I attach much more importance to advertisement of the need for the alphabet than to the success of my attempt to provide it my ghost will be perfectly satisfied if the lawyers and litigants keep the subject in the headlines for the twenty years perpetuity limit.'

The two stalwarts in this business of keeping Shaw's alfabet in the headlines were Barbara Smoker and the half-Irish publisher and educationist James Pitman. One from Catford, the other in Chelsea, they formed an odd but admirable team. Pitman, then in his young fifties, was an engagingly eclectic character who had been an international athlete, director of the Bank of England and for the last dozen years Conservative Member of Parliament for Bath. 'He was not very quick on the uptake,' Barbara Smoker severely noted, and he wrote 'in the most appalling Pitman shorthand I had ever seen'. He would end each day in chaos, but all was smoothed back into order next morning by his paragon of a secretary, Miss Blisset.

Spelling reform circulated in Pitman's blood: it was his love, and eventually his infatuation. It was amazing to him that the judge had found his way to such a consummate misinterpretation of Shaw's intentions. It was equally amazing that the Attorney-General had no wish to appeal. As soon as the judgment had been given, Pitman called a press conference under his own name and that of his fellow adventurer Barbara Smoker. The costs of the Chancery case were estimated at between £6,000 and £10,000 and an appeal would require over £3,000 more. Apparently undeterred by the fate of the Shaw Memorial Fund six years earlier, Pitman suggested opening a public subscription, to be managed by the Shaw Society, which would facilitate the appeal or alternatively assist the implementation of Shaw's wishes privately. In confidence Pitman told the Shaw Society that if the subscription failed he would put up the money himself.

The press conference became front-page news when Pitman was rebuked by the Attorney-General Sir Reginald Manningham-Buller (then nicknamed Sir Reginald Bullying-Manner, and later created Viscount Dilhorne). This vexing business was beginning to plague the Attorney-General. He wished it would go away. Instead he was obliged to issue a statement reminding the press that James Pitman was not a party to the case. Naturally he would appeal if there were grounds for doing so. But, of course, there weren't. On 7 May the two of them clashed again and their irritated exchanges occupied twelve columns of Hansard's official report, further appeasing Shaw's ghost.

James Pitman and Barbara Smoker disagreed on many things. They disagreed on the conduct of the case in Chancery, on the legitimate grounds for an appeal, and on the conflicting merits of simplified spelling versus phonetic reform. But they campaigned together in Shavian style. While he kept matters boiling in the House of Commons, bending some ears and boxing others, she composed press statements from her lair in the Shaw Society which were quoted in news bulletins and reproduced in *The Times*. She did more: throwing out many thousands of words, loaded with research findings, in lectures, articles, and unanswered correspondence to the Attorney-General. 'But I do not kid myself that it does very much good,' she admitted.

Barbara Smoker and James Pitman could not reach the Attorney-General but they did force some action out of the Public Trustee who, on the last day allowed, lodged an appeal. His case was the same as it had been in the Chancery Court, namely that the trusts might be valid even if not charitable, and that Shaw's wishes should be implemented. Knowing by now that this was a futile position in law, and influenced perhaps by his Dickensian name of Mr Baulkwill, many Shavians believed that the Public Trustee had secretly been supporting the British Museum. On appeal this case had become a pretence behind which negotiations for an out-of-court settlement could take place. 'Efforts are being made to reach agreement, I understand, between certain beneficiaries under the will and the Public Trustee, who is Shaw's executor, and the Attorney-General,' reported the *Daily Telegraph* on 29 October 1957.

When *Public Trustee v. Day and Others* came up before the Court of Appeal on 19 December, the court approved the terms of this agreement. 'My only regret,' said the Master of the Rolls, Lord Justice Romer (who was assisted by Lord Justice Ormerod), 'is that we are deprived of hearing what might have been very interesting arguments.' Counsel for the Public Trustee agreed: 'From a lawyer's point of view it is rather a pity.' Counsel for the Attorney-General, for the Trustees of the British Museum and Royal Academy of Dramatic Art, for the Governors and Guardians of the National Gallery of Ireland all joined in the laughter.

*

The terms of this compromise were made public by Mr Baulkwill immediately the appeals had been dismissed. A sum of £8,300 (equivalent to £112,000 in 1997) had been entrusted to him by the residuary legatees and he was allocating £500 of this amount as the prize in a competition for the new phonetic alfabet. The closing date was to be 1 January 1959, and he had appointed a committee of assessors to help him with the task of finding a winner: Peter MacCarthy, Head of the Department of Phonetics at the University of Leeds, Alan Dodson, chief typographer at the Stationery Office (who later resigned on going to live in South Africa), and James Pitman. The copyright of the new alfabet would be vested in the Public Trustee who would encourage the English-speaking world to use it. 'It will take any intelligent person only 24 hours to learn it with slow progress,' James Pitman predicted.

With an army of 50,000 transliterated copies of *Androcles*, Pitman believed the new model alfabet would prove invincible. But to Barbara Smoker's mind £8,300 was 'a paltry sum' which might possibly fund a bi-alphabetic *Androcles* but could never promote the vital statistical survey into phonetic economy. 'The three residuary legatees may confidently expect to share more than a hundred times the alphabet allocation,' she complained; 'so they have hardly strained the quality of mercy in favour of a cause which their benefactor had at heart.'

She too had this cause at heart. But she could not carry her complaints too far without appearing churlish to James Pitman. It was he who had negotiated the £8,300 and without him the poor alfabet might have received nothing at all. Alternatively it might have won the appeal. Once more they disagreed, once again they sank these disagreements in their adjoining passion. They wanted to free the association between ideas and signs from common conventions. For the subject held a compelling beauty for them. They knew the public was deaf to these harmonious symbols and their reverberating possibilities. Nevertheless, like the person who invented zero in the numerical system and gave rise to dreams of riches, they shared a common purpose of lifting this alphabetic burden from the human mind. In their differing styles, they dreamed of replacing man's antiquated utensils and unearthing the clue to a mystery: why was it that spoken communication had always been comparatively rapid, easy and delightful, and written communication cumbrous and wearisome? Was there a deficiency in the optic nerve, a superiority in the aural nerve? This was a fundamental question on which the continuation of our literary tradition might depend. 'Why do we use a long series of arbitrary marks to represent what the voice utters at a single effort,' Sir Isaac Pitman had asked in his *Introduction to Phonography*. 'Why, in short, are not our *written signs* as simple as *spoken sounds*?' Shaw had reminded James Pitman of his grandfather's words when inviting him to keep a friendly eye on the progress of his will. To carry through the alphabetical clauses in this will, 'which generously and ingeniously sought to achieve for the language he so greatly loved the dearly cherished hopes of an exceptional man', was now James Pitman's sacramental mission.

My Fair Lady began its record-breaking run at London's Drury Lane Theatre in the spring of 1958. By the autumn James Pitman had inserted a two-page advertisement of the proposed alfabet into the programme sponsored by the silversmiths Mappin & Webb. Many of Shaw's ideas 'were so novel and penetrating that they were rejected by his contemporaries,' he wrote, ' – and this particular idea was so novel, and so demanding in its need to think freshly, that very few people have yet understood it'. He requested members of the audience to 'keep a space in your bookshelf' for the bi-alphabetic *Androcles*. Designs for the new alfabet were coming in from all parts of the world, and when eventually it was established we could look forward to savings in paper, ink, machine-time, storage and transport 'of £3,000,000 or $10,000,000 *a day*'.

By the end of 1958, 467 valid entries for the contest had been received by the Public Trustee. More than half of them came from the United Kingdom, but there were 60 from the United States, 40 from Canada, 11 from India, 10 from Germany, 6 from Ireland and several from Africa, South America and Eastern Europe. 'We were astonished by the merit and quantity of the work produced,' remarked James Pitman a year later. It had taken him and Peter MacCarthy the whole of 1959 to find a winner and even then they had failed to do so, coming up instead with four 'semi-winners'. Dr S. L. Pugmire, a psychiatrist working with mentally handicapped children at the Whittingham Hospital near Preston, had produced a geometric design; Mr Kingsley Read, the author of *Quickscript*, who had designed everything from pavilions for trade fairs to suits of armour for pageants, submitted a cursive system; and there were script or 'current' alfabets from Mrs Pauline Bassett from Nova Scotia and Mr J. F. Magrath, an insurance broker, who had worked out his design on daily train journeys between London and Kent. All of them received cheques for £125 and the Public Trustee announced that the four winning alphabets would be co-ordinated to produce a final design for use in implementing Shaw's wishes. 'We are launching a ship,' declared Mr Baulkwill, 'and we don't know where it's going.'

It did not look to Barbara Smoker as if this vessel would get far beyond the launching slip. She regretted Shaw's failure to tie up his trusts with infant literacy. Had he nominated Enid Blyton's *Noddy* instead of his own *Androcles* the Chancery Court decision would have 'undoubtedly gone the other way'. She also deplored the absence of any expert calligrapher or educational psychologist among the assessors, and pointed out that any fusion between the four winning designs was impossible. James Pitman however felt exuberant. The final alfabet was an improved version of Kingsley Read's aesthetically pleasing forty-eight letter 'sound-writing' system. It contained little reference to the other three versions but was 'better than most other alphabets,' conceded Barbara Smoker who was to be employed as specialist editor on the new *Androcles*.

In February 1961 *The Times* announced that this special edition of *Androcles* 'is likely to be on the bookstalls by early autumn'. By December the Public Trustee, now Sir Reginald Baulkwill, forecast publication early in the New Year. On 26 February 1962 the *Daily Mail* unveiled a scoop:

'The secret publishers of the weird, phonetic version of *Androcles and the Lion* which George Bernard Shaw provided for in his will, have been unmasked.

And it turns out that this is another scoop for Sir Allen Lane and his Penguins, who published *Lady Chatterley's Lover*, the money-spinner of 1961.'

The delay had been largely caused by contradictory instructions from Pitman, Penguin, the expert Phonetician and the Public Trustee. Eventually Barbara Smoker 'walked out in a huff' leaving Hans Schmoller, the publisher's master typographer, floundering among the hieroglyphics of 'the world's strangest type-face'.

Androcles and the Lion, An Old Fable Renovated by Bernard Shaw with a Parallel Text in Shaw's Alphabet to be Read in Conjunction Showing its Economies in Writing and Reading was finally published on 22 November 1962. The Public Trustee's issue comprised 13,000 copies of which 12,680 were presented free to libraries, 1,900 within the United Kingdom, 1,230 around the Commonwealth, 8,690 to the United States, 710 to Canada and throughout South America and 150 to 'National Libraries of the World'. Approximately 34,000 copies of an ordinary issue costing 3s. 6d. were on sale to the public, an indeterminate number being exported to the United States from the second English impression. Within each copy a white Guide Card was inserted on which two keys to the alphabet (one arranged phonetically for writers, the other graphically for readers) were duplicated from the last pages of the book. There were also some 'Suggestions for Writing' supplied by Kingsley Read, some 'Notes on the Spelling' from Peter MacCarthy and a Foreword by the new Public Trustee C. R. Sopwith (Sir Reginald Baulkwill having retired to Devon). The book was dedicated to James Pitman (now Sir James Pitman KBE).

It was a kind of triumph. The poetry lay in its algebra and arithmetic, and the mysterious dream encoded by these symbols and ciphers. In a disarming Introduction James Pitman sought to advise readers on the choreography of its use. 'Open the book and hold it upside down in front of a mirror,' he instructed. ' . . . Keep the back of the book pressed against your lips, and advance towards the mirror until you are able to see individual characters clearly enough to be able to copy them.' Before long, he promised, users would be able to speed up such exercises and for those who attained gymnastic facility 'reading may be 50–75 per cent, and writing 80–100 per cent faster, and even 200–300 per cent, by using simple abbreviations'. He urged owners of this wonderful book to make their friends buy copies so that they could all correspond with one another in the new script. The following year he offered to form circles of five or six of these correspondents who, 'drawn together in friendship by Shaw's alphabet, will all circulate their own letters to which each in turn will add'. But these dancing circles never joined and multiplied as he hoped. He was disappointed too by the conservatism of the Ministry of Education which was offered Shaw's alfabet in principle, in draft and upon completion, and turned it down at all three stages. But Shaw's trusts did assist in the temporary success of Pitman's Initial Teaching Alphabet for children, and encouraged him to go on and on battering at the walls of prejudice until his death in 1985.

Barbara Smoker still campaigns. From time to time, when not producing strings of verse with which to tie up the deity, conducting gay and lesbian weddings, speaking from the public gallery of the House of Commons against the Vietnam War or, with her Free Speech banner, being molested by crowds of Muslims calling for the death of Salman Rushdie, she has returned to her alphabetic high ground to see if the walls have yet come tumbling down. 'History is certainly on the side of a new alphabet,' she believes. ' . . . It is absurd that in the twentieth century we should still be using what is basically the ancient Phoenician alphabet, with its cumbersome letters and its bad phonetics . . . If Shaw's dream comes true – a dream shared by men of vision for nearly five centuries – who knows what miracles of human progress it may bring in its wake?'

The interest in Shaw's Alphabet rose with the renovated *Androcles* and then waned. There were few funds left for the clinical survey. Peter MacCarthy handed this over to one of his students, Gordon Walsh, who went off to conduct his investigations from the University of Ife in Nigeria. The first part of his paper was completed in September 1967. But since 'Shavian is not available in Nigeria,' Gordon Walsh concluded, it was 'necessary for tests to be conducted in Britain'. A year later *The Times* announced that the report was finished and that there would 'shortly be an exploratory meeting' to discuss whether it should be published. In January 1970 *The Scotsman* revealed that the results would soon be made known. When questioned about the findings in March 1970, the Public Trustee, Mr Brian Davies (Sir Charles Sopwith, as he now was, having gone to the Inland Revenue), replied: 'It's not very urgent, and I'm very busy.' Though he had forecast early publication, there was no more money left (equivalent to nothing in 1997). So the impression of a full report was conveyed, and an appearance of publication given sometime in the 1970s. The conclusions 'hardly caused a ripple of public interest,' Barbara Smoker vaguely recalled. In any event, as Peter MacCarthy made plain, all that had been attempted was the technical discharge of the Public Trustee's obligations. Sometimes he wondered if it had all been a Shavian joke.

*

Public interest quickly veered off from the letters to the figures, following the trail of money to the three residuary legatees. There had been rumours that Shaw's bequest to the British Museum was enabling the Government to cut back its normal subsidy. When reminded by James Pitman that Shaw's bequest to the Trustees of the British Museum had been 'in acknowledgement of the incalculable value to me of my daily resort to the Reading Room of that institution', Sir Edward Boyle, Financial Secretary to the Treasury, revealed that over the two years money had been coming in from Shaw's royalties £163,924 had been received by the museum, and up to £85,000 was owing to it in repayments of tax levied on the income of the estate prior to the settlement of the court action (the total equivalent to over £3 million in 1997). The terms of the bequest were legally 'unrestricted' in the sense that the trustees of the museum were free to do what they liked with this money and all further income over the next forty years. But since the income would virtually cease after the year 2000, when the main copyrights lapsed,* a capital fund had been set up. And so that 'no act of discourtesy was done to the dead,' explained Sir Edward Boyle, the trustees of the British Museum had decided that income from this capital sum 'should in due course be used primarily for the benefit of the library'.

Two years later the museum's assistant secretary reported that most of the money received had been invested by a firm of merchant bankers 'on the best terms the market will offer'. In answer to a question from the Fabian Member of Parliament John Parker, the Under-Secretary of State at the Department of Education and Science, Jennie Lee (later Baroness Lee of Asheridge), stated that £646,417 4s. 3d. (equivalent to over £7 million in 1997) had come to the British Museum as its share in Bernard Shaw's estate by the end of 1965.

'Sir David Wilson and the trustees are to be congratulated on the funds they have raised to improve the display of the collections,' wrote Lord Annan in 1991. During the previous fifteen years the royalty income of the Shaw Estate had settled down to between £275,000 and £500,000 a year. 'I conclude that in the fullness of time the whole library department of the Museum will benefit,' a *Sunday Times* journalist had predicted. But when the library department separated from the Museum in 1973, no reference was officially made to a Shaw capital fund to be used 'primarily for the benefit of the library'.

Donations from the Shaw Fund towards heritage purchases by the British Museum Manuscripts Department and the British Library between 1960 and 1990 amounted to approximately £400,000 – or a little over £13,000 a year on average. Such donations were given as 'a matter of grace' on the part of the British Museum Trustees, and since the British Library executive was never shown the accounts of the Trust it could not know how small a proportion of the Shaw Fund's expenditure it received – less than one tenth of its growing income. So the very 'act of discourtesy . . . to the dead' that Sir Edward Boyle assured the House of Commons in 1959 would not be committed actually was committed. In an attempt to clarify matters, the Shadow Minister for the Arts, Mark Fisher, asked some questions similar to those put by James Pitman and John Parker in

*After the extension of copyright throughout Europe to seventy posthumous years, Shaw's writings will now remain protected until the beginning of 2021.

the House of Commons in 1959 and 1965: what in effect was the total sum that had accrued to the British Museum by the end of 1990 and what was properly due to the British Library? But the Minister with responsibility for Arts and Libraries, Tim Renton, answered that this was 'not a subject on which I have any specific responsibility'. On the advice of the Director of the British Museum, Sir David Wilson, the Trustees had decided not to disclose the figure to anyone because they were 'the Trustees' private monies' and public disclosure would enable Treasury officials to take the Shaw income into account when determining the British Museum's annual grant. The annual amounts from the Shaw bequest were audited by the Comptroller and Auditor-General, but expenditure was not scrutinized by the Public Accounts Committee or the Treasury.

It was open for Sir David Wilson and his trustees to transfer this problem on to the shoulders of the British Library, along with the money Shaw had plainly intended to be used for library purposes. But short of such an act of integrity, the British Museum's secrecy was pragmatic in view of what happened to another of Shaw's residuary legatees, the Royal Academy of Dramatic Art.

*

Shaw had been fond of RADA. He gave lectures to its students, served as a member of its Council from 1911 to 1941 (coming to 102 of its 141 meetings in that period), and contributed £5,000 towards its new building in Gower Street in the 1920s (equivalent to £123,000 in 1997). His bequest was to change the status of the Academy. By the mid-1960s it had acquired the status of an independent charity and accumulated capital of £750,000 (equivalent to around £8.5 million in 1997). The Shaw bequest was producing a yearly income exceeding £30,000 (around £340,000 in 1997). This fortune, which transformed RADA from an orphan to an heiress, was to produce a watershed in the Academy's affairs as it moved from the amateur world towards modern marketing.

Early in 1990, though still based in Gower Street (which it leased from the University of London), the Academy purchased the freehold of a building nearby at 18 Chenies Street. The cost was £5,250,000. It was financed by a government grant of £500,000, a donation of £1,000,000 from British Telecom, and the sale of investments worth £3,750,000 from the RADA share portfolio. This was supplemented late in 1991 by a grant of £500,000 from the Foundation for Sport and the Arts for conversion costs, and another in 1996 of £22,752,283 from the Arts Council of England's lottery board towards an ambitious Centenary Project for rebuilding the extension at Gower Street and Chenies Street.

Would RADA have survived without Shaw's money? The chairman, Sir Richard Attenborough, believed it must have closed. During the Thatcher decade there was no choice for arts organizations but to expel the dilettante and measure efficiency by profit. But some of the dangers of implementing arts-marketing without the introduction of new tax laws had been spelt out a quarter of a century earlier when James Pitman argued in Parliament in favour of special arrangements for legacies to public and charitable institutions wholly or partly supported by government funds. If the Exchequer contribution to such institutions was consequently reduced, he explained, the purpose of the testator would be rendered void to the detriment of the public's future interests.

In the case of Shaw's estate, the Exchequer had already imposed death duties of more than £500,000 in the 1950s. Shaw's intention was not to benefit to any greater extent the generality of taxpayers but to favour two special sections of the public: those who would be using 'the Reading Room of the British Museum and those would-be actors, actresses and producers who would be thus receiving better training themselves for a part in the dramatic arts'. The Financial Secretary to the Treasury, Sir Edward Boyle (later Baron Boyle of Handsworth), had assured the House of Commons in December 1959 that the Treasury objected strongly to the principle that trustees should use trust funds 'in a way which would merely reduce their demand on public funds, either to maintain an existing service or to start a new one.

'The Treasury even in times of great stringency in our national and economic affairs has never sought to argue that the cost of a service should be reduced by a contribution from other resources available to the Trustees, or that public funds should not be provided to improve a service merely because the Trustees could afford to do it themselves . . . I do not think there has been a convenient occasion for stating the principle, which I think is an important one, that in deciding the expenditure on Vote-borne departments we do not say that the Treasury contribution should be automatically reduced simply because some other source may become available.'

Between principle and practice, private and public money, swirled many confusing cross-currents. In 1967 the Treasury cancelled its grant to RADA. This lesson was not lost on its co-residuary legatee, the British Museum. Until the mid-1960s the Trustees had been happy to make known what money was accruing to the museum from Shaw's royalties and to explain how it was primarily to be used. But over the next thirty years, as the cumulative under-funding of national arts institutions grew worse, secrecy and guile seemed to be forced upon those trying to represent the best interests of these institutions. Every one of them was in competition with every other one for sponsorship and grants, even complementary bodies such as the British Museum and British Library. It was not difficult in such embattled circumstances to overlook the wishes of the dead.

What were Shaw's wishes? When he referred to the British Museum in his letters, the context shows that he had in mind the library or manuscripts department of the museum (later the British Library Reference Division). 'Why do you not get a reader's ticket at the British Museum,' he asks his Polish translator Floryan Sobieniowski. 'I spent every day of my life there for several years.' His debt to that great institution 'contracted in the early days when I read and worked for many years in its Reading Room,' he explained to Edy Craig, 'is inestimable, and gives it a right to anything of mine that is of sufficient public interest to be worthy of its acceptance.' What he described in his will as 'such letters and documents as might be worth preserving in a public collection such as that of the British Museum', including the drafts of eighteen plays, were handed to the manuscripts department by the Public Trustee and now form the centre of its large Shaw Collection.

'There are people in this country who are watching very closely the interests of Bernard Shaw . . . to see that the purpose for which [he] left his money will be fulfilled,' Emrys Hughes had told Parliament at the end of the 1950s. But as such people died, the knowledge of these interests and that purpose faded. This was what James Pitman had warned the House of Commons might happen. 'Let it not be said in the world of literature and throughout the whole English-speaking world,' he exhorted his fellow Members of Parliament, 'that a great Irishman and genius of the English language who sought to help English literature and English drama found honourable respect for the terms of his will only in Ireland.'

*

Compared with its English counterparts the National Gallery of Ireland had what the *Sunday Times* described in the early 1960s as a 'delightful' policy 'which is to invest not in shares but in pictures'. No tablets were then placed under pictures bought by the gallery showing the source of the purchase money, and there was no list of the works bought from the Shaw Fund. Gradually rumours began circulating in Dublin pubs that Shaw's money had been spent on a number of marvellous fakes and forgeries. Barbara Smoker, arriving from London in the 1960s and asking to see some pictures bought from the Shaw bequest, was shown a couple of religious works by Murillo and a Crucifix by Giovanni di Paolo (a rare and highly valued work) which considerably offended her. Twenty years later, when challenged to put on an exhibition of selected works bought from the Shaw Fund over a quarter of a century so as to celebrate the old patronage and invite new business sponsorship, the director of the gallery regretfully declined because 'it will not be within our resources to mount the Shaw show'. The gallery's resources were shortly afterwards reported in the *Sunday Press*. According to figures supplied to the Comptroller and Auditor General, £164,714 had been received by the gallery from the Shaw bequest in the twelve months ending on 31 March 1990, and the total in investments and at the bank was £751,173.

The 'delightful policy' of buying pictures had long been modified by the Governors and Guardians of the gallery. Increasingly money from the Shaw Fund was spent on the insurance of paintings and, in the 1980s, on the conversion and refurbishment of an extension to the gallery at 90 Merrion Square, as well as on the purchase of other sites in Clare Street and Clare Lane. The last work bought by the gallery was a modest picture by William Ashford called 'A bowl of flowers' in 1985. Nothing was purchased in the following twelve years.

The gallery's stewardship of the Shaw bequest during much of the time it has been receiving Shaw's royalties has been set out by one of the Keepers, Dr Michael Wynne.

'As monies come in from the royalties we endeavour to allow the substantial sum to be accumulated, and from this we buy significant works of art and designate that they have been purchased from the George Bernard Shaw Fund. Occasionally some of the works bought from the fund are relatively minor. This situation arises when towards the end of the financial year we have spent all the government grant for acquisitions and are anxious to seize the opportunity of acquiring something that is important for the collection.'

What was important for the collection was the strengthening of various schools of painting. This has meant that the Shaw Fund purchases were not artistically integral and could not be made to 'form an exhibition of a worthiness due to our great benefactor,' Dr Wynne explains (though a very interesting exhibition of this sort was shown in 1987 from purchases made by Sir Michael Levey on his retirement as Director of the National Gallery in London). By the year 2000, Dr Wynne believes, it may be appropriate to publish a brochure with illustrations in colour and a comprehensive list of Shaw acquisitions. 'In the meantime the best tribute which we can pay is to make sure that the purchases made through the Shaw Fund are correctly labelled, and have the descriptions of them published through books like your own.' In 1991 Dr Wynne compiled a list of these purchases from the gallery records.

Paintings, watercolours and drawings

1384 DOMENICO TINTORETTO *Venice, Queen of the Adriatic* (1959)
1385 DOMENICO GHIRLANDAIO (?) *Portrait of Clarice Orsini* (1959)
1645 LOUIS LE NAIN *Adoration of the Shepherds* (1961)
1646 JEAN NATTIER *Carlotta Frederika Sparre, Countess Fersen* (1961)
3315 MAURICE QUENTIN DE LA TOUR *Louis August Thibault-Dunois* (1961)
1719 MURILLO *The Holy Family* (1962)
1720 MURILLO *St Mary Magdalen* (1962)
1721 EL MUDO *Abraham welcoming the three angels* (1962)
1722 COURBET *Dr Adolphe Marlet* (1962)
1723 BOUCHER *A young girl in a park* (1962)
1737 JACK B. YEATS *The double jockey act* (1963)
1766 JACK B. YEATS *About to write a letter* (1964)
1768 GIOVANNI DI PAOLO *Crucifix* (1964)
1769 JACK B. YEATS *Grief* (1965)
1770 JACQUES IVERNY *The Annunciation* (1965)
1790 NATHANIEL HONE THE ELDER *The Conjuror* (1966)
1812 CIGOLI *The Siege* (1967)
1822 MARQUET *Porquerolles* (1967)

1824 ROSLIN *Le Marquis de Vaudreuil* (1967)
1835–58 VARIOUS SCHOOLS *Twenty-four icons (The Allen Collection)* (1968)
1867 ETIENNE DE LA TOUR *The Image of Saint Alexis* (1968)
1859 WALTER OSBORNE *Portrait of a gentleman* (1968)
1860 THOMAS HICKEY *Colonel William Kirkpatrick* (1968)
1928 GOYA *El Sueño* (1969)
4025 VALENCIAN SCHOOL *Landscape with canopy and a legionary* (1971)
4026 VALENCIAN SCHOOL *Landscape with an angel bearing a martyr's crown* (1971)
1982 VOUET *The four seasons* (1971)
4050 EVA GONZALES *Two children playing on sand dunes* (1972)
4052 THOMAS ROBERTS *A landscape* (1972)
7515–33 FRANCIS PLACE *Twenty-three drawings* (1972)
4055 BARON GÉRARD *Marie-Julie Bonaparte, Queen of Spain with her two daughters Zenaïde and Charlotte* (1972)
4060 JACQUES-LOUIS DAVID *The funeral of Patroclus* (1973)
4074 NATHANIEL GROGAN *A view towards Cork, on the river Lee* (1973)
4089 SOGLIANI *The Virgin and Child with St John the Baptist* (1974)
4137 WILLIAM ASHFORD *A view of Dublin from Marino* (1976)
4138 WILLIAM ASHFORD *A view of Dublin from Chapelizod* (1976)
4170 FRENCH SCHOOL *Large apse* (1976)
4171 FRENCH SCHOOL *Small apse* (1976)
4186 JUAN FERNANDEZ *A still life with citrons, a knife etc* (1976)
4303 NATHANIEL GROGAN *A harbour in County Cork* (1978)
4304 PHILIP HUSSEY *An interior with members of a family* (1978)
4313 FRAGONARD *Venus and Cupid* (1978)
4315 PROVOOST *Triptych: Virgin and Child with saints* (1979)
4326 REYNOLDS *The Right Honourable John Hely-Hutchinson* (1979)
4339 WHEATLEY *The Marquess and Marchioness of Antrim* (1980)
4355 VAN DONGEN *Stella in a flowered hat* (1981)
4361 SIGNAC *Lady on a terrace, Saint Tropez* (1982)
4367 HENRY BROOKE *The continence of Scipio* (1982)
4459 CAMILLE PISSARRO *A bouquet of flowers in a vase* (1983)
4463–66 THOMAS ROBERTS *Lucan House and three views in the demesne* (1983)
4468 ITALIAN SCHOOL *A young man of the Branconio family (c. 1610)* (1983)
4485 SOUTINE *Man walking the stairs* (1984)
4490 NOLDE *Two women in a garden* (1984)
4508 WILLIAM ASHFORD *A bowl of flowers* (1985)

Sculptures

8011 RENOIR *Pendule: hymne à la vie* (1966)
8028/29 ATTR. BRUSTOLON *A pair of jardinières* (1967)
8030 DUQUESNOY *Cardinal Guido Bentivoglio* (1967)
8031 ATTR. JUAN ALONSO VILLABRILLE Y RON *Elias overthrowing the false prophets of Baal* (1967)
8050 COURBET *Madame Buchon* (1968)
8051 ATTR. CAFFIERI *Bust of a lady* (1968)
8052 THOMAS KIRK *Judge Charles Burton* (1968)
8081 DIETZ *Chronos eating one of his children* (1970)
8246 RICHIER *The Virgin* (1978)
8247 RICHIER *St John the Evangelist* (1978)
8049 GHIBERTI WORKSHOP *Virgin and Child* (1968)
8303 LAWRENCE MACDONALD *Eurydice* (1984)

The outstanding features of the gallery's collection have been a small but spectacularly good choice of seventeenth-century French paintings (among which are an excellent Claude and Poussin), special attention to religious art which has resulted in a fine holding of Italian baroque pictures, and some creditable examples of Irish art. The list of works bought from the Shaw Fund shows how the gallery has complemented these areas with a number of art-historically interesting pictures. To the Claude and Poussin, for example, it has added a composition by a comparatively rare painter Louis Le Nain, a late and beautiful Vouet (whose reputation following an exhibition in Paris early in 1991 has been rising) and a fascinating work showing the extraordinary effects of light by Etienne de la Tour, son of the more famous Georges de la Tour. Additions to the eighteenth-century collection include an excellent portrait by the Swedish painter (of the French school) Roslin and, merging into the nineteenth century, an early and uncommon baroque studio work, David's *Funeral of Patroclus*. A more characteristic example of David's school is represented by the portrait of Marie-Julie Bonaparte by his pupil Baron Gérard.

The Italian baroque section at the gallery, which has works by artists such as Castiglione, Lorenzo Lippi, Felice Ficherelli and Carlo Dolci who are little represented in the United Kingdom and were bought earlier in the century when religious pictures were not greatly valued elsewhere, has been enriched by a unique battle scene from Tasso by Cigoli, a major seventeenth-century Florentine painter. Unable to afford a Simone Martini, the gallery bought instead *The Annunciation* painted in 1410 by Jacques Iverny. It cost £250,000 in 1965 and was valued at considerably more than ten times that sum twenty-five years later. The gallery also picked up a wrongly attributed painting of a sleeping girl, a subtle exploration of virtually one colour, later confirmed as a Goya.

The plan appears to have been to buy Renaissance and Baroque sculpture in the 1960s and 1970s when, as compared with Old Master paintings, this sculpture was inexpensive. The two works by Richier, the sixteenth-century French Renaissance sculptor, are remarkable purchases, the Duquesnoy's Cardinal Guido Bentivoglio is the bust of a distinguished art patron (who discovered Claude Lorrain) by a comparatively unknown and wonderful sculptor.

The Irish school has been reinforced with some beautiful eighteenth- and early nineteenth-century landscapes, notably two beautiful paintings by Nathaniel Grogan, three pictures by the idiosyncratic Jack Yeats and Nathaniel Hone's satire on Reynolds as an eclectic artist, a masterpiece which provides a commentary on eighteenth-century art theory and, possibly better than any other single work, sums up the feeling of these Shaw Fund purchases.

Perhaps there is the odd picture from which Shaw himself would have recoiled (though his art criticism does not reveal him as being irredeemably hostile to religious paintings). He would see, however, that the collection he had got to know as a boy as he wandered through the gallery rooms catching sight of a larger imaginative world and dreaming of being an artist himself, has been remarkably enhanced through his bequest.

*

There are two further threads in the financial tapestry of Shaw's estate. When his sea-going uncle, the Rabelaisian doctor Walter John Gurly, had died at the end of the nineteenth century, G.B.S. found himself the owner of 'his cursed property and debts' in Carlow. He had little power to control or direct the management of these Irish properties, and instead of title deeds had received a bundle of mortgages and a packet of worthless pawn tickets. The principal site was known as the Old Assembly Rooms in the centre of Carlow. It was a fair-sized building, measuring some ninety feet in depth and commanding a fifty-foot frontage described by the *Carlow Nationalist* as being 'inspiringly designed in the style of the classic revival of the eighteenth century, characteristic of Irish Public buildings of that date'. For many years it functioned as some class of a country club and was used for public entertainments, though according to Shaw's uncle it would have made a better observatory as you 'could watch the movements of the heavenly bodies through the holes in the roof'.

In 1915 Shaw received a petition inviting him to present this property to the town of Carlow for use as a Technical School. As the consideration for this deal he was promised that his 'honoured name will be revered in perpetuity'. There was a good deal to be said for complying with this request. 'Unfortunately the place is leased and subleased,' he replied. ' . . . Lately I had all but succeeded in buying out the lessor when he fell into the Barrow and was drowned; and I have not yet succeeded in discovering who his successor is.' It took Shaw until the autumn of 1919 finally to disencumber the Assembly Rooms and sign the deed transferring them to Carlow 'in consideration of the place being used for public purposes and (if possible) the old front of the building being retained for the sake of its decorative effect'. The property was later turned into a Vocational School and after Shaw's death, its façade still intact, has become the County Library Headquarters.

The remaining seventeen parcels of Gurly property (including a burial ground called 'The Graves') Shaw retained for another twenty-five years. To assist matters he employed a local man, Major Fitzmaurice, as his business agent. 'Many people who dont know me (and perhaps some who do),' he told Fitzmaurice, 'imagine that I am a difficult man to deal with because my writings rub them up the wrong way.'

Actually most of his tenants soon came to realize that he was peculiarly soft-hearted. Sometimes he would receive bills from Carlow shopkeepers due from his tenants who had pledged his credit by guaranteeing payment from him in London. 'I wonder would Mrs Aylward take £50 to leave the country and settle in China,' he wrote of one tenant who regularly calculated at the end of each quarter that he owed her money. His correspondence with Major Fitzmaurice shows him making the roofs good, guarding against vandalism, replacing cisterns, clearing gutters. 'My attempts to repair houses on my estate have generally begun by the collapse of the whole edifice,' he admitted. By his eighty-eighth year he decided that 'if I could live another 88 years I would knock down every house on the property and replace it with a new one, with a garage and a modern kitchen, with all the latest labor saving contrivances and conditioned air, to teach the Carlovians to want such things'.

In his published writings G.B.S. represented himself as a conventional absentee landlord. 'There is no alternative open to me,' he wrote. 'I am strongly in favor of this little estate of mine being municipalized.' With this in mind he wrote asking the Taoiseach Éamon de Valera in May 1945 to introduce into the Dáil a new law enabling local authorities to accept, hold and administer gifts of property provided they adopt a 'Civic Improvement Scheme'. To his delight, this Local Authorities (Acceptance of Gifts) Bill was quickly drafted and passed that summer. 'Splendid!' Shaw congratulated de Valera. 'It would have taken thirty years in this unhappy country.' On 13 August 1945 all Shaw's Carlow property was passed to the Urban District Council. According to the Act, civic improvement included anything that tended to 'improve the amenities' of the area or was 'conducive to the welfare of the inhabitants'. A condition of all gifts, and their income, was that they could not be absorbed into general assets for the relief of rates since, drawing on his experience on the St Pancras Vestry, Shaw believed that a reduction in rates merely assisted landlords 'on whom the rates finally fall, without benefiting the country or improving the town'.

'I am far too good a Socialist to believe that Socialism can be established by private enterprise,' Shaw had written to Major Fitzmaurice. Yet by his own private enterprise he had established a modest instalment of socialism in Ireland. For nearly twenty-five years the Carlow Urban District Council made financial help available from its Shaw Fund for cultural and artistic purposes. But subsequent legislation in Ireland, including the Local Government (Planning and Development) Act 1963, the Housing Act 1966, and the Arts Act 1973, all of which enabled local councils to subsidize a widening range of endeavours out of the rates, brought about a Gilbertian situation in which the Shaw Fund could not be used for any identifiable civic improvement without being in breach of its rates relief condition. For another twenty-five years, while lawyers brooded on this predicament, the funds were frozen at the bank except for one strange payment each December to erect a Christmas Crib at the courthouse. Tiring of this stalemate, the Carlovians eventually came up with a brainwave, and invited the British ambassador to open their own Shaw-funded Shaw Festival in 1991 with its programme of lectures, workshops in the Old Assembly Rooms, school prizes, musical events (including a selection from *My Fair Lady*), the renaming of the Town Park after G.B.S. and a spirited production of *How He Lied to Her Husband*.

The last financial thread was spun from Shaw's Nobel Prize for Literature. 'I cannot persuade myself to accept the money,' he had written in November 1926 to the Royal Swedish Academy. Four months later, on 27 March 1927, he signed a Trust Deed creating an Anglo-Swedish Literary Foundation for the translation into English of classical Swedish literature. To this he donated all his prize money which amounted to 118,165 Swedish kronor then worth approximately £6,500 (equivalent to £167,000 in 1997).

The objects of the Anglo-Swedish Literary Foundation were defined in the Trust Deed as 'the encouragement of cultural intercourse between Sweden and the British Islands through the promotion and diffusion of knowledge and appreciation of the literature and art of Sweden in the British Islands'. The first patron of the Foundation was the King of Sweden and its trustees still include the Swedish ambassador. Though some grants were made to facilitate productions of Strindberg's plays and to support Swedish music in Britain, most of the money has been spent on the translation of Swedish books. There were translations of Swedish Nobel Prize winners Pär Lagerkvist, Eyvind Johnson and Harry Martinson, novels by Hjalmar Bergman (considered by many critics to be the greatest Swedish prose writer of the twentieth century), Strindberg's plays, anthologies of Swedish poetry and short stories, and some non-fiction including a vivid description of nineteenth-century England by Erik Gustaf Geijer, Ingvar Andersson's history of Sweden (for many years the only history of Sweden available in English), and biographies of Carl Linnaeus by Knut Hagberg and of the Swedish composer Franz Berwald by Robert Layton.

After the Second World War the Foundation reconstructed the Swedish section in the library of University College, London, enabling it to become a lending centre for Swedish books, and made donations of books to libraries round Britain that had been depleted in the war. 'The Foundation's funds are not advertised,' wrote the Swedish cultural attaché. By 1974 its unadvertised balance at the bank appears to have dwindled alarmingly to £1,157 plus a few pence. But with a deft redefinition of its objects (replacing 'the literature and art of Sweden' with the words 'Swedish culture') the trustees were able to replenish the capital with money from the sale of the Swedish Institute's office in London.

From the early 1980s the Foundation has widened its ancillary activities by supporting the newly formed Swedish-English Literary Translators' Association and its journal, *Swedish Book Review*; by assisting a translator-in-residence scheme; and enabling Swedish writers to visit Britain, English translators to visit Sweden. In the autumn of 1991 this contribution to Anglo-Swedish relations from the man who was 'dead against prizes' was recognized by the creation of a three-yearly Bernard Shaw Prize, for a translation from Swedish to English, presented at the Swedish Embassy in London.

*

'Please do not ask Mr Bernard Shaw for money,' reads a blue-green stereotyped postcard G.B.S. had drafted in 1935. ' . . . He can write for you: he cannot finance you.' During the last years of his life he fended off an increasing number of appellants with variously coloured cards. All his income, he would explain, 'except enough to meet his permanent engagements is confiscated by the Exchequer and redistributed to those with smaller tax-free incomes or applied to general purposes from which everyone benefits'. He did not complain of this system, 'having advocated it for half a century, and nationalized all his landed property', but his correspondents could not have his income in cash from himself as well as in services from their country. 'It is useless to ask him for money: he has none to spare,' reads a rose-coloured card drafted in 1949. Then, having demonstrated that 'No other reply to appeals is possible', he would secrete a cheque into his envelopes for the Actors' Orphanage, Royal Literary Fund, the Society for the Protection of Birds, the Lord Mayor's National Flood Distress Fund, the King Edward Memorial Hospital, Travellers' Aid Society, Chaim Weizmann's Zionist Appeal, the Shakespeare Memorial Theatre at Stratford-upon-Avon, the National Theatre in London and, as bail money or pension money, for eyeglass or boots, to an always-lengthening list of individuals. 'On your life, don't tell anybody,' he warned the actor Esmé Percy to whom he had made a gift of £100.

In his biography published in 1956, St John Ervine described Shaw's testament as being 'one of the most public-spirited documents in the whole history of bequests'. Forty years after his death the author of *Socialism for Millionaires* (1901) was at last becoming recognized, in the words of Dan H. Laurence, as probably 'the most charitable professional man of his generation'.

INDEX

Cotterill 417, 419; and Shaw's affair with Stella Campbell 418–19, 425–7, 429, 442–3; influenced by James Porter Mills 427–8; takes Shaw to France 430, 433; joins Mills and wife in America 443

1914–43

in Devon with Shaw 447, 448; and outbreak of war 448; concern for Trebitsch 448; like a 'fat white Persian cat' 460; aggravates Beatrice Webb 460–1; with Shaw at Ayot (1917) 461; in Ireland 463, 464; supports Casement 470; loathes *Heartbreak House* 489; and 'Bloomsbury' 489–90; and Blanche Patch 492, 495; engages Fred Day 496; motoring with Shaw 497; meets Langner 509–10; further visits to Ireland 512, 513. 514; finds *Jitta's Atonement* 'brutally realistic' 516; finds ideas for plays 'for the Genius' 341, 523; reads Lawrence's *Seven Pillars* 534–5; their subsequent relationship 535–7; and the Shaw-Stella Campbell love letters 545, 546; and Molly Tompkins 547, 550–1, 552–3, 554; gets on better with Beatrice Webb 552; and move to Whitehall Court 562; and Lady Astor 563, 564; Bennett on 565; at Malvern 576; friendship with Elgar 579; on the Riviera 580; carries Shaw off to Geneva 580; disapproves of Frank Harris 581, 582; and Jane Wells's death 602–4; at Hardy's funeral 600, 601; with Tunney at Brioni 605; entrusts Shaw to Lady Astor on Russian trip 619, 620, 629; amused at Shaw's 'Little Talk on America' 660; on *Too True to be Good* 634, 639; on S. African trip with Shaw 640, 641, 642; injured in car crash 644, 646; on world cruise (1932–33) 648, 649; in love with China 654, 655; in United States 661–2; worried over Shaw's Metropolitan Opera House speech 663; returns to Ayot 666; in New Zealand with Shaw 667, 668–9; 'the most unconventional of persons' 670; 'one of the best' 676; approves of Casson 684; at the opening night of *On the Rocks* 685; illness 695; and Shaw's illness 697; uneasy about Pearson 700; her lunch guests 711; enjoys film of *Pygmalion* 715, and pleased about '*In Good King Charles's Golden Days*' 725; in the Second World War 735, 744–6; crippled by arthritis 746–7; relationship with Shaw 747–8; disgusts O'Casey 748; last year 749–50; death 750–1; her will 781–2, 792, 795; Shaw to 51, 54, 420

Shaw, Charlotte Jane ('Aunt Shah') 2

Shaw, Elinor Agnes ('Yuppy') (sister) 7, 9, 14, 25, 27, 29, 31, 35, 36, 218, 255

Shaw, Frances (*née* Carr) (grandmother) 2

Shaw, Frances (aunt) 2

Shaw, George Bernard:

1856–82

ancestry, aunts and uncles 1–4; and father *see* Shaw, George Carr; and mother *see* Shaw, Lucinda Elizabeth; and Lee *see* Lee, George John Vandeleur; birth 7; childhood 7–11, 15–16; rejection of 'George' 14, 27; religious education and views 16, 17, 22–3; formal education 19–21, 24; friendship with McNulty 21–2; self-education 22, 23–4, 25, 49; and Shelley 23; musical training 25, 31–2, 49; as office boy 27, 32–3; and 'The Calypso Infatuation' 33; early works 33, 34; theatre- going in Dublin 34–5; leaves Ireland 35–7; 'unoccupied' in London 38; ghosts Lee's *Hornet* criticisms 38–40; early works (*Passion*

Play, My Dear Dorothea, Immaturity – see Works) 43–6; 'conquered' by Ellen Terry 196; corresponds with Elinor Huddart 64; with Edison Telephone Company 47–8; re-enters literary world 48; writes *The Irrational Knot* 49 (*see Works*); joins societies 75; meets Webb (*q.v.*) 101; further self-education at the British Museum 51, 54, 58–9; becomes vegetarian 51–3; starts *Love Among the Artists* 54 (*see Works*); gets smallpox 54–6; physical appearance 56–7; teaches himself shorthand 58; 'a complete outsider' 59–60; early friendships 60–62, 63; relations with women 63–5

1882–9

affair with Alice Lockett 65–8; influenced by Henry George 76; writes *Cashel Byron's Profession* 68 (*see Works*); takes up boxing 62–3; writes *An Unsocial Socialist* 69 (*see Works*); novels published 72–3; political interests 72, 74–7; meets William Archer (*q.v.*) 79; joins Fabian Society (*q.v.*) 78; meets Annie Besant (*q.v.*) 98–9; elected to Fabian executive 101; 'slips into paid journalism' 79; contributes to *Pall Mall Gazette* (*q.v.*) 116–21; attends Hampstead Historic Society 104; contributes to *Our Corner* 82; and Jaegerism 93–4, 95; begins affair with Jenny Patterson (*q.v.*) 93; infiltration of Avelings, 89–91, and Blands 91–2; becomes art critic of *The World* (*q.v.*) 82; and Grace Black 88–9; writes 'Don Giovanni Explains' 87; delivers 66 public lectures 110–12; moves to Fitzroy Square 109; in 'Bloody Sunday' (1887) demonstrations 105–6; as music critic ('Corno di Bassetto') for *The Star* (*q.v.*) 121, 124,131–5; drives himself too hard 122–3; and horrors of Surrey 123–4; first trip abroad 124; sees Janet Achurch (*q.v.*) for first time 145–6; works on *The Cassone* 157–8; and Grace Gilchrist 124–5; 'rather in love' 125–6; Sunday husbandship at Salts 126–7; with May Morris (*q.v.*) 127–31; as editor of *Fabian Essays in Socialism* (*q.v.*) 107

1890–8

as music critic ('G.B.S.') for *The World* 135, 136–40; attempts holiday with Webb 124; meets Florence Farr (*q.v.*) 140–1; and Beatrice Webb (*q.v.*) 152; and Grein's 'Independent Theatre' 158–9; sits to Bertha Newcombe and their relationship 239–42; and staging of *Widowers' Houses* 159–60 (*see Works*); brings out *The Quintessence of Ibsenism* 113 (*see Works*); and Fabian strategy 154–5; writes *The Philanderer* 162–3, and *Mrs Warren's Profession* 164 (*see Works*); begins *Arms and the Man* 168 (*see Works*); turns to Elizabeth Robins 177–8; and London School of Economics 229–30; begins *Candida* 178 (*see Works*); agrees to write for *Saturday Review* (*q.v.*) 184–6; his appearance 185; starts war against censorship 188–90; meets Wells 327–8; writes *Man of Destiny* for Ellen Terry (*q.v.*) 196; antagonism towards Irving (*q.v.*) 199ff.; lack of success with *You Never Can Tell* 192 (*see Works*); takes up bicycling 152–3; further involvement with Janet Achurch 211–16; first sees Lillah McCarthy (*q.v.*) 339; meets Charlotte Payne-Townshend 243; and subsequent 'courtship' *see under* Shaw, Charlotte; writes *The Devil's Disciple* 221 (*see Works*); sits for portrait 221; accepts Grant Richards as publisher 224–5; elected member of St Pancras Vestry Committee 224, 231–8; works on *Plays*